Dominica prima aduentus

Sermo. Ciues comynge.
Siwa hora est. Ro. 13.
Þe tokon as by leue
þat epistils of apos
tlis. ten gospelis of cit
for he grat hem alle in hem. þ
crist may not erre. þ alle þe gos
pelis ben ȝou gret þingus. of iope
of þe blisse of heuene. þ alȝt þe
holy goost fern y eche word of
holy writ. neueles crist grat
in ȝoule more plenteuoslý þ
intellý. þ þis meueþ some men
to tresou in englýsh ȝoulis prite
lis. for some men may lecture
wrýte herbý. What god meueþ
bý ȝoul. Þus epistle of ȝoul
tellýþ holp þat men shulden
býge þer tyme. for al þt godri
ne þ reþ tyme. as liȝt þ opre ȝt
tus of knýue. neueles bý tyme
of man. tyme is loþ to come
to heuene. þ not only bý tyme
of adam. but bý sinne of þche
man. þat wole not i tertuof
crist býge þe tyme þat crist
ȝýueþ. for to wýnne þe blisse of
heuene þ þis marchaundise
schulde eche man do spenallý
for þis cause. for þe dayes for
lý me leu þuele. and maken
monye for tyme to leese þer
tyme. ȝoul bý gýnneþ to sture
þus. to take heed to godus tyme
þ to leese not þis tyme. leenyn
ge to diuerue blisse. Breþren
we schulen be wýtýnge. þat
our is nolw us to rýse fro sleepe
for nolw is oure helpe neer. þan
þ was whanne we bý leueþon
þche man contrýteþ kyndelý to
haue blisse. þat god haþ ordey
ned to man kýnde to resoun me
but monýe men contrýen he self

for ȝei coueýston comunlý to haue
þis blis. but þer lust þ fleshlý
wit letton hem to wýnne þis
blis þ bringon resou a sleepe þ
make men to contrýue hem self
for eche man schulde furst coueý
te his lecture þ ele his þuel þ so
a man schulde more þýlle blise.
þen aný sensible lýf here þ þis
takuþ ȝoul as bý leue. Who me
be bidduþ men rýse fro sleep. þ
ȝoul meueþ bý þis sleep. Þ þuue
þat fleshis lý non þ nue. for rýȝt
as man whon he sleepuþ. Wantuþ
wit to kepe hým. þ is ner deed
þen a beest. so it is of synful me
for what deere cuere he doþ. být
lettuþ þanne to diuerue blisse.
þ dispoluþ hým to þe reýne of
helle. þat is worse þan beþis deþ
þ for men schullen rise on morwe.
þ do þer werkis aftur resoun. þ
men han nolw lustul resoun tý
me. to regard of cole ȝadýrs. þer
fore seýþ ȝoule here. þat our is
nolw to rýse from sleep. an our
is a lustul tyme. þ sunne of cýt
unswelle is up. Þe secounde
word þat ȝoul seiþ. sturep to þe
wýt of þe formere word. Whonne
be seiþ. þat nolw is oure helpe mo
re nýȝ. þan whoune we bý leueþ.
þ it is knolwen bý kyndelý stýle.
þat þo þingus þat mouen kýn
delý. mouen faftere tolward þe
eude. þ it is alsó knolwen bý stý
le. þat as tyme paffuþ to meu
so it comeþ nýȝ domeldaý. Whou
ne men schulen haue fullý þer
helpe. for alȝt crist be fullý men
nýs helpe þ ȝet he makiþ not bet
þe i man but as resou of tyme
afluþ. þ herfore to þe daý of dom
schal not al cristus chirche be in
ful helpe. ne sleepe in blisse wiþ

ENGLISH WYCLIFFITE SERMONS

Volume I

Edited by

ANNE HUDSON

CLARENDON PRESS · OXFORD
1983

Oxford University Press, Walton Street, Oxford OX2 6DP

London Glasgow New York Toronto
Delhi Bombay Calcutta Madras Karachi
Kuala Lumpur Singapore Hong Kong Tokyo
Nairobi Dar es Salaam Cape Town
Melbourne Auckland
and associates in
Beirut Berlin Ibadan Mexico City Nicosia

OXFORD is a trade mark of Oxford University Press

Published in the United States
by Oxford University Press, New York

© Oxford University Press 1983

British Library Cataloguing in Publication Data

English Wycliffite sermons.- (Oxford English texts)
Vol. 1
1. Lollards-Sermons
I. Hudson, Anne
252'.04   BX4900
ISBN   0-19-812704-9

Set by Macmillan India Ltd
Printed in Great Britain
at the University Press, Oxford
by Eric Buckley
Printer to the University

PREFACE

In my continuing work on these sermons I have incurred many debts, more than I can here acknowledge, more indeed than I can now remember. First I wish to thank the authorities of the various collections whose manuscripts form the basis of the edition and its apparatus: the British Library, Cambridge University Library, the Bodleian Library Oxford, Christ's College Cambridge, Corpus Christi College Cambridge, Magdalene College Cambridge, Pembroke College Cambridge, Peterhouse Cambridge, Sidney Sussex College Cambridge, St. John's College Cambridge, Trinity College Cambridge, Hertford College Oxford, New College Oxford, Lambeth Palace Library, the Essex Record Office, the Leicestershire County Record Office, and Wisbech Town Library. I am also grateful to Mr Robert Taylor for allowing me to consult his manuscript at Princeton and to print material from it. To the assistants in these libraries, and to those in other libraries here and abroad where I have worked, I am deeply indebted for help; in particular, I am glad to acknowledge the patience of the staff in Duke Humfrey's Library in the Bodleian over many years. Those years would have been very much longer without the generous grant given by the University of Oxford for the purchase of microfilms and photostats of many of the manuscripts here; these made it possible, along with sabbatical leave and other financial aid granted by the University and by Lady Margaret Hall, to produce this edition within a reasonable time. I am also grateful to the British Academy and to the Waldorf Astor Research Foundation for grants towards a visit to the United States, during which I was able to see Wycliffite manuscripts there and, most importantly, Mr Taylor's text. I acknowledge the permission of the relevant authorities to reproduce the plates in the present volume.

Amongst individual scholars who have helped me I should like to mention first Dr Neil Ker and Dr Ian Doyle; both have been unfailingly helpful and generous of their time and knowledge.

My debt to Dr Doyle's advice about palaeographical matters will be evident in chapter II; but the deductions that are drawn from his information in chapters IV and VI are mine and any misinterpretations are entirely my responsibility. My debts to other scholars will be more apparent in the final volume of this edition, but I should now like to thank for their help, encouragement, and information the late Professor J. A. W. Bennett, Dr Michael Benskin, the Hon. Mrs Margaret Buxton, Professor Henry Chadwick, Professor Eric Dobson, Mr Alan Fletcher, the late Dr S. L. Fristedt, Professor C. Lindberg, Mr Malcolm Parkes, Miss Jean Preston, Professor Richard and Mrs Mary Rouse, Dr Kathleen Scott, Miss Helen Spencer, Dr Christina von Nolcken, and Professor Michael Wilks. To Professor Norman Davis I owe encouragement and guidance, from the beginning of my work on this edition until its final stages; to him I am very greatly indebted. When the full scale and complexity of the task emerged, Dr Pamela Gradon agreed to collaborate with me in the work; she will edit the sermons of the *Sanctorale* that will appear in volume II, and will be involved in the final volume of commentary. Her willingness to become engaged in a daunting task so unselfishly, and to discuss many minor details, has helped me immensely. I am grateful also to all those at the Oxford University Press who have been concerned in the handling of a difficult typescript.

An edition of this kind involves a very great deal of tedious checking: I have endeavoured to make it accurate, but I remain fully aware that errors there will remain, errors of commission, but perhaps even more errors of omission. These I regret and deplore, but would ask the critic to remember that, even if much study is not a weariness of the flesh, much checking certainly is.

October 1979   ANNE HUDSON

CONTENTS

PLATES

Introduction

BIBLIOGRAPHY, ABBREVIATIONS AND METHODS OF CITATION

Bibliography

The following is intended to be a guide to the material covered in the present volume; a full bibliography will appear in vol. iv.

Manuscripts

The manuscripts of the sermons here edited and their sigla are:

A   Bodley 788
B   Cambridge University Library Ii. 1. 40
C   Bodleian Laud Misc. 314
D   British Library Additional 40672
E   Bodleian Douce 321
F   Bodleian Additional A. 105
G   British Library Royal 18 B. ix
H   St. John's College Cambridge C. 8
I   British Library Cotton Claudius D. viii
J   Robert Taylor Esq., Princeton
K   Trinity College Cambridge B. 2. 17
L   British Library Additional 40671
M   Trinity College Cambridge B. 4. 20
N   Sidney Sussex College, Cambridge 74
O   Trinity College Cambridge B. 14. 38
P   British Library Harley 1730
Q   New College Oxford 95
R   Corpus Christi College, Cambridge 336
S   St. John's College Cambridge G. 22
T   Pembroke College Cambridge 237
V   British Library Harley 2396
W   Magdalene College Cambridge, Pepys 2616

X   Lambeth Palace 1149
Y   Christ's College Cambridge 7
Z   Bodleian Don. c. 13
α   Leicestershire County Record Office, Leicester Town Hall 3
β   Leicestershire County Record Office, Wyggeston Hospital
    10 D. 34/6
δ   Wisbech Town Museum Library 8
Eˢ Essex County Record Office D/DPr 554
Hᵗ Hertford College Oxford 4
Pᵗ Peterhouse Cambridge 69

Manuscripts of the derivatives (see chapter III) and their sigla are:

Ad Cambridge University Library Additional 5338
Bd Bodley 806
By Bodley 95
Gg Cambridge University Library Gg. 6. 16
Lb Lambeth Palace 392
Ry Manchester, John Rylands Eng. 109
Tr Trinity College Dublin 241

Printed Books (abbreviated titles are shown in brackets)

(i) Works by Wyclif

J. Loserth, revision of W. W. Shirley's *Catalogue of the Extant Latin Works of John Wyclif* (London, [1925]).
The majority of Wyclif's Latin writings were edited by various scholars for the Wyclif Society between 1883 and 1921; references and quotations are from these editions except for the following works:
De Officio Pastoralis, ed. G. V. Lechler (Leipzig, 1863).
Trialogus, ed. G. V. Lechler (Oxford, 1869).

(ii) Works by Wyclif's Followers

E. W. Talbert and S. H. Thomson, 'Wyclyf and his followers', in *A Manual of the Writings in Middle English 1050–1500*, ii, ed. J. Burke Severs (Hamden, Conn., 1970), 354–77 and 517–33.
A. Hudson, 'Contributions to a Bibliography of Wycliffite Writings', *Notes and Queries* ccxviii (1973), 443–53.

The Holy Bible . . . made from the Latin Vulgate by John Wycliffe and his Followers, ed. J. Forshall and F. Madden (Oxford, 1850), 4 vols. (*WB*)

Select English Works of John Wyclif, ed. T. Arnold (Oxford, 1869–71), 3 vols. (Arnold)

The English Works of Wyclif hitherto unprinted, ed. F. D. Matthew (EETS 74, 1880, revd. ed. 1902). (Matthew)

Selections from English Wycliffite Writings, ed. A. Hudson (Cambridge, 1978). (*Selections*)

(iii) Other

Missale ad Usum . . . Sarum, ed. F. H. Dickinson (Burntisland, 1861–83), 2 vols. (Dickinson)

The Sarum Missal, ed. J. W. Legg (Oxford, 1916). (Legg)

C. Brown and R. H. Robbins, *The Index of Middle English Verse* (New York, 1943). (IMEV)

A. B. Emden, *A Biographical Register of the University of Oxford to A. D. 1500* (Oxford, 1957–9), 3 vols. (Emden *Oxford*)

F. Madan, H. H. E. Craster et al., *A Summary Catalogue of Western Manuscripts in the Bodleian Library at Oxford* (Oxford, 1895–1953). (SC)

Abbreviations Other Than Those Given Above

EETS: Early English Text Society; volumes in the Original
  Series are given by number with no prefix, those in the Extra
  Series are prefixed ES, those in the Supplementary Series SS.
EV: the Early Version of the Wycliffite Bible.
LV: the Later Version of the Wycliffite Bible.
MED: *Middle English Dictionary* (Ann Arbor, 1952–).
OED: *Oxford English Dictionary* (Oxford, reissued 1933).
Vulg.: *Biblia Vulgata.*

Methods of Citation

Quotations   All quotations from the sermon cycle here edited are, unless otherwise stated, in the orthography of the base text used. In unprinted material and in quotation from older editions modern punctuation and capitalization have been supplied; abbreviations are expanded without notice.

References   In references to manuscript material, the numeration provided in the manuscript has been used even when this is incorrect; where more than one numbering is found in the manuscript the most correct (normally the most recent) is used. To avoid the easy confusion of ^{r} and ^{v}, only verso is marked save where a recto-to-verso turnover is in question. References to printed works are given by page or column number according to the usage of the book in question, followed in the case of editions by an oblique stroke and a line number; line numbers that have been supplied ignore all headings. The opening line number only is given unless some particular point requires the provision of the closing line number as well. Biblical references are in all cases to the Vulgate text; in almost all instances save in the Psalms and in some books of the Apocrypha, the numeration of chapters and verses is identical to that of the Authorized Version.

PLAN OF THE PRESENT EDITION

The sermons were first printed by Thomas Arnold in the first two volumes of his *Select English Works of John Wyclif* (Oxford, 1869–71) from MS Bodley 788; Arnold knew of a further nineteen manuscripts, but he admitted that his examination of many of them was hurried and he did not systematically collate any of them. The notes to his edition fail to explain many obscurities in the texts. Since Arnold, only a handful of the sermons have again been printed; the few studies that have appeared have been hampered by the absence of a critical edition. The purpose of the present edition is to produce a new text of the sermons, with full collation of all the manuscripts now known, and to study the context in which they were written and the light they shed upon the Lollard movement.

The edition will appear in four volumes. The first three will consist largely of the text with variants; in the first are the sermons on the Sunday gospels and epistles, in the second will be the sermons on the Sanctorale, and in the third those on the ferial gospels. The present volume contains an account of the sermon cycle as a whole and of all the manuscripts in which it occurs; it also deals with editorial procedure and certain other matters which apply to all the volumes of the text. Each of the three volumes of text will contain an examination of the textual relations of the manuscripts in the sermons that are edited in it; for reasons that will emerge, one general statement is impossible. Rather more arbitrarily other general questions will be divided between the introductions to the three volumes; this is partly to avoid excessive length in the first volume, and partly to handle with as little disruption to the reader as possible the problem of line references to prose in an edition that will not all appear simultaneously. Obvious questions of authorship, date and purpose of the sermons are therefore postponed from the present volume. The fourth volume will be divided into two main sections: the first a discussion of those questions, mainly of Lollard teaching, that recur repeatedly through all the parts of the cycle; the second a commentary on the individual sermons, their sources, and their difficulties, but excluding matters that have been covered in the first section.

References to the sermons within this edition will be by number in a sequence running throughout the gospel sermons in the three volumes, and in a second sequence whose numbers will be prefixed by E for the Sunday epistle sermons. Arnold used the same system, but unfortunately his copy text led him to make an error over sermon no. 104 in his edition; in the present edition, therefore, the numbers from 104 to 196 inclusive relate to sermons numbered one higher in Arnold (105 to 197), and Arnold's sermon 104 is 197 here; thereafter the numbers again agree. Where references in the present introduction are to texts to appear in the second and third volumes they will be made to Arnold by volume, page, and line numbers (ignoring all headings); there are relatively few of these, and a note will be given in volume iii to supply the references for the present edition. Quotation from such sermons will, however, be in the spelling of the base text here and not in that of Arnold's edition. A table is given on pp. 214–22 showing the complete collection of sermon numbers and occasions; this table is designed to be used in conjunction with the discussion in the introduction to avoid repetitive explanations.

I

The Sermon Cycle and its Organization

The material to be printed in the present edition consists of 294 sermons, providing a complete homiliary for the ecclesiastical year.[1] That these sermons make up a single entity can be seen from internal cross-references between them; that they form an independent group can be shown from their preservation in the manuscripts, where they occur without intermingling with other sermons. The basis for all the sermons are the gospel and epistle readings of the Sarum use[2]: each sermon is headed by the Latin incipit of the lection, gospel or epistle as appropriate and most include within them a full English translation of that lection. Despite digression and elaboration, the lection's meaning dominates the major part of most of the sermons. There can, therefore, be no question of any intention that the sermons should form a 'repertory of preaching material' on which a preacher could draw at random to fit his inclination. Each sermon is indissolubly tied to the occasion on which the biblical passage would have been read. This is confirmed by the liturgical occasion that is

---

[1] The discussion here supersedes the preliminary examination of the problem published in *Medium AEvum* xl (1971), 142–56. In view of the complexity of the argument here, footnotes have been kept to a minimum; in particular references to the Sarum Missal have been curtailed since the arrangement of material in the editions makes information easy to trace.

[2] For details of this see J. W. Legg, *The Sarum Missal* (Oxford, 1916) and F. H. Dickinson, *Missale ad Usum . . . Sarum* (Burntisland, 1861–83); the first of these utilized manuscripts earlier than the sermons here in question, the second printed editions of a later date. Since, however, in most points the sermons agree with both texts, their evidence is taken as a sufficient indication of the norm of Sarum usage. In an attempt to find parallels to the few departures from this norm a brief investigation was undertaken of those Sarum missals from the fourteenth and fifteenth centuries now in the Bodleian Library, and also of lists of gospels and epistles; no significant coincidence with these departures has been found. That the sermons cannot be based on either the York, Hereford, or Lincoln rites can be seen from the divergence of the gospel texts for feria 4 and feria 6 in the first week of Advent here (respectively Mark 1: 1–8 and Matt. 3: 1–6) from that in all three other rites for the same occasions (respectively Matt. 3. 1–6 and Luke 3. 7–18); for a chart showing further differences see *Missale ad Usum . . . Eboracensis*, ed. W. G. Henderson (Surtees Society lix-lx (1874), ii. x).

specified along with the text in the heading of each sermon.[3] Similarly the sermons are arranged into schemes dictated not by a biblical order of their texts but by incidence of their occasions within the liturgy.

The 31 manuscripts in which the sermons, in whole or in part, are preserved can be divided into three groups according to their arrangement of the sermons for the Temporale. Because this division is basic to an understanding of the descriptions of the manuscripts, the normal editorial order has been reversed to give an account of it before the descriptions. For the sake of brevity sermon numbers are often used in the ensuing account; reference should be made to the tables on pp. 214–22 for the expansion of these.

A. Overall arrangement

Three differing schemes are found in the manuscripts for the ordering of the sermons. The differences between them concern the Temporale sermons, but in the ensuing account the Sanctorale sermons are also included.

Scheme 1: the 294 sermons are divided into five sets which are kept separate. These are:

Set 1: 54 sermons on the Sunday gospel pericopes. Taking the normal order of the liturgical year,[4] the following are provided: 4 Sundays in Advent, Sunday within the octave of the Epiphany, octave of the Epiphany, 5 Sundays after the octave of the Epiphany, Septuagesima, Sexagesima, Quinquagesima Sundays, 5 Sundays in Lent, Palm Sunday, Easter Day, 5 Sundays after Easter, Sunday within the octave of Ascension, Pentecost, Trinity Sunday, and 25 Sundays after Trinity.[5] The only non-dominical occasion covered here is the octave of the

---

[3] Some manuscripts lack some headings, either because of abbreviation or because their rubrication was never completed (see pp. 126–30); the majority of manuscripts, however, make it clear that the original had these headings.

[4] The unusual opening of the year that appears to be original is discussed below, pp. 35–39.

[5] The Latin sermons provided by Wyclif for the Sunday gospels (*Sermones* i) cover all of these occasions, and are likewise based on the Sarum lections. Wyclif included in this set three further sermons for feasts within the Christmas season, nos. v–vii for Sunday within the octave of Christmas, the Circumcision, and the Epiphany, all of which are found in set 3 here (the first having the same lection as no. 94), and three for occasions not in the liturgical calendar (nos. lviii–lx for the dedication of a church, the Sunday after, and the octave of the dedication day), the first two of which are found at the end of set 4 here.

Epiphany. The material provided is for a theoretical ecclesiastical year, with the maximum number of lections for the periods after the octave of the Epiphany and after Trinity; though variation in the incidence of Easter makes possible a greater number of Sundays in the Trinity season, the Sarum missal did not provide further lections for these. Since the material agrees exactly with the Sarum provision in these seasons, it should be taken as determined by that pattern and not used for speculation about the date at which the sermons were composed.[6]

Set 2: 31 sermons for the Commons of the Saints. The following are provided: 1 for a vigil of an apostle, 2 for commons of an apostle, 1 for common of an evangelist, 5 for commons of a martyr, 1 for common of a martyr also a bishop, 11 for commons of many martyrs, 4 for commons of a confessor also a bishop, 1 for common of a confessor also a doctor, 1 for common of a confessor also an abbot, 2 for commons of many confessors, 1 for common of a virgin also a martyr, 1 for common of a virgin not a martyr.[7] All of these occasions, with their lections, are found in the Sarum use, and the occasions are usually covered in the same sequence. A few occasions in the Sarum missal are omitted here, and the order of readings within a category is not invariably identical.[8]

The first sentence of the opening sermon of set 2 alludes to the next set,[9] and no manuscript is found to preserve either the Commune Sanctorum or the Proprium Sanctorum sermons without the other. But since there is a difference in content between them, and a query arises about their ordering, the two sets have been numbered separately here.[10]

[6] See Legg, p. 196. With an Advent opening to the liturgical year, a sequence of five Sundays after the octave of the Epiphany would imply a late date for Easter (22 April or later), and consequently make it impossible for there to be twenty-five Sundays after Trinity before the beginning of the next Advent. The same point applies to the provision in sets 4 and 5.

[7] The coverage coincides with that by Wyclif in Sermones ii, nos. xxix–lix, save that Wyclif has no equivalent to the English sermons nos. 55, 77, and 78 and that conversely the English has no equivalent to Wyclif's nos. xxxi, liii, liv. The divergence seems fortuitous.

[8] Thus the eleven sermons for commons of many martyrs in the present collection omit, apparently at random, three of the lections provided in the Sarum rite; the five sermons for the commons of one martyr use all the lections but reverse the order of two as found in both Legg's and Dickinson's editions and in Wyclif's Latin (nos. 60–1 here).

[9] Arnold i. 165/1, for which see below p. 28.

[10] Legg, Dickinson, and all the missal manuscripts examined contain the Proprium before the Commune material; Wyclif in his Latin sermons follows that order (Sermones ii. nos. i–xxviii, xxix–lix respectively). For evidence that here set 2 must have been intended to precede set 3 see below p. 28.

Set 3: 37 sermons for the Proper of the Saints. The following are provided: the vigil, feast and octave of St. Andrew, Christmas Eve and Day, St. Stephen, St. John the Evangelist, Holy Innocents, sixth day after Christmas, New Year's Day, vigil and feast of the Epiphany, Conversion of St. Paul, Candlemas day, feast of St. Peter's Chair, St. Matthias, the Annunciation, St. Philip and St. James, vigil, feast, and octave of St. John the Baptist with, before the last, vigil of St. Peter and St. Paul, translation of St. Martin, octave of St. Peter and St. Paul, Seven Brothers, St. James, vigil and feast of Assumption, St. Bartholomew, beheading of St. John the Baptist, Nativity of the Virgin Mary, Exaltation of the Cross, vigil and feast of St. Matthew, Michaelmas day, vigil and feast of All Saints. There is also a directive at the appropriate place, between the feast of the Seven Brothers and the vigil of the Assumption, to find a sermon on the gospel for the feast of Mary Magdalen amongst set 4 (no. 231); this appears in all manuscripts containing set 3.[11] One manuscript, H, also has a directive (f. 160) to find a sermon suitable to the feast of St. Thomas the apostle amongst set 1 (part of no. 47); more surprisingly, another manuscript, G, has a similar directive (f. 14ᵛ) for a sermon for the feast of St. Thomas à Becket to be found amongst set 2 (no. 78). With the exception of this last, only surviving in one manuscript (though cf. p. 26 below), and of the feasts of St. Martin's translation and the Seven Brothers, all the occasions where a person is specified concern biblical figures.[12] This reduction in the Sanctorale is in line with Lollard views on the honour due to saints, though it is slightly less drastic than the reduction found in Wyclif's own Latin sermons.[13]

[11] α actually has a copy of the sermon itself at this point, ff. 86–7, despite the absence of set 4 from this manuscript.
[12] Some biblical saints for which the Sarum rite provided specific material are, however, omitted here, for instance St. Mark, St. Luke, and St. Barnabas.
[13] Wyclif provided sermons for the feasts of St. Mark and St. Sylvester (nos. xii and vi) and, within the Proprium Sanctorum, for those of Thomas à Becket and Mary Magdalen (nos. v and xviii) where the same text is used as is provided in the English cross-references. Wyclif, however, omitted any sermon for the vigils or octaves of Andrew, John the Baptist, and Peter and Paul, for the vigils of Matthew or All Saints, and for the feasts of the Epiphany (found in his *Sermones* i), Assumption, or Seven Brethren. For Lollard views on saints see J. F. Davis, 'Lollards, reformers and St. Thomas of Canterbury', *University of Birmingham Historical Journal* ix (1963), 1–15.

Set 4: 120 sermons on the ferial gospels throughout the year.[14] The following are provided: sermons for the Wednesday and Friday of the four weeks of Advent and for Saturday in the Advent ember week, for Wednesday and Friday in the first four weeks after the octave of the Epiphany, for Wednesday of the fifth week after that octave, for Wednesday and Friday after Septuagesima and Sexagesima, for Ash Wednesday, (a directive to set 1 indicates the sermon for the lesson on the day following,) for each day save Sunday throughout Lent to Easter Eve (though those for Tuesday and Wednesday in Holy Week are very brief), for each day in the week following Easter, for Wednesday and Friday in the four weeks thereafter, for the Rogation day on Monday before the Ascension, for the vigil and feast of Ascension,[15] for the Friday before Pentecost and for the vigil, for each day in the week following Pentecost, for Corpus Christi Day, for Wednesday in the weeks following the first to the twenty-fourth Sundays after Trinity, with the exception of the eighteenth,[16] for Wednesday, Friday and Saturday in ember week in September. There then follow seven sermons for various occasions: for the dedication day of a church and the Sunday following, for the mass *Salus Populi*, for a mass for peace, two for masses for the dead, and one for a mass for a wedding.[17] The lections used follow exactly those of the Sarum rite, and, as far as the end of the liturgical year, cover all the occasions for which that rite prescribes specific gospels. The last seven, which are missing in one manuscript, G, that contains this set, use lections found in the rite but collected from various parts of the normal Sarum missal.[18]

[14] The number of 120 is that preserved in the system witnessed imperfectly in nine of the seventeen manuscripts having this set (see below pp. 130–34). It numbers separately the brief passages for the Tuesday and Wednesday in Holy Week and includes the sermon for Ascension day. In order to keep the numbering of the gospel sermons as close as possible to Arnold's, the first two of these have not been included in the main numbering used here.

[15] For the error of A with regard to the Ascension day sermon, an error unfortunately followed by Arnold, see below pp. 39–40.

[16] For the positioning of the Ember week sermons see pp. 40–3.

[17] Wyclif is not known to have written any set of ferial sermons, and the vast majority of this set is unparalleled in his writing. The *Sermones Quadraginta*, however, have sermons for six occasions (*Sermones* iv nos. ii, vi, viii, ix, x, lxiv equivalent to English nos. 237, 144, 181, 195, 200, and 201 respectively), and two, those for Ascension Day and Corpus Christi Day are found concluding Wyclif's Sanctorale sermons (*Sermones* ii nos. lx and lxi corresponding to English nos. 197 and 206).

[18] No. 233 and 234 usually at the end of the Temporale (Legg, p. 203, first only, Dickinson, cols. 553, 555), 235–9 from among the votive masses (Legg, pp. 393, 395, 432 twice, and 416 respectively, Dickinson cols. *742,*783,*865,*866, and*838).

Set 5: 55 sermons on the Sunday epistles throughout the year. The following are found: sermons for the four Sundays in Advent, for Christmas Day and the sixth day after Christmas, for the Sunday within and the five Sundays after the octave of the Epiphany, for Septuagesima, Sexagesima and Quinquagesima Sundays, for the six Sundays in Lent, for Easter Day and the five Sundays following, for the Sunday after the Ascension, for Pentecost and Trinity Sunday and for the 25 Sundays after Trinity. Two non-dominical occasions are covered, Christmas Day and the sixth day after it.[19] Again, as with set 1, the material is for the theoretical year with the maximum number of Sundays after the Epiphany and Trinity that are provided with separate lessons in the Sarum rite. It should be noted that the coverage does not entirely coincide with that of set 1, and that the discrepancy is found where each set trespasses outside the dominical limits. Set 5 has sermons for Christmas Day and the sixth day thereafter, whilst set 1 has a sermon for the octave of the Epiphany. Manuscripts of the Sarum rite normally include these occasions, and others of the Christmas season, within the order for the Temporale;[20] but, since they are fixed by exact calendar date as well as by liturgical incidence, they might equally well be included in the Proprium Sanctorum where calendar date determines position. The writer of these sermons has divided the various feasts of the Christmas season somewhat illogically between Temporale and Sanctorale, and differs in his practice between sets 1 and 5. As will be seen below (pp. 22–6), further modifications were introduced by some of the scribes.

This scheme of five separate sets is found in whole or in part in twenty manuscripts, though the ordering does not always follow the sequence of sets from 1 to 5 as they have been described above. As will be seen, the distinctive factor is the separation of sets 1 and 5. Nine manuscripts, ABDMTYαβδ, contain both sets as separate items. But, if either set 1 or set 5 appears in a manuscript alone, that manuscript cannot have been intended to conform to schemes 2 or 3. Seven manuscripts, CFKLNSP^t, have set 1, in whole or in part, without set 5; four, OPE^{s}H^t, have set 5,

---

[19] The occasions are those found in Wyclif's Latin sermons (*Sermones* iii), except that they have no equivalent to the English E5 for Christmas Day, whilst providing four other sermons for the Christmas season (nos. v–vii and x).

[20] See Legg, pp. 25–40, Dickinson, cols. 45–90.

again in whole or in part, without set 1 [21]. This scheme is then the commonest exemplified.

There are three manuscripts which, since they cannot be shown to belong to either of the following two schemes, may be mentioned here. R and W do not contain either sets 1 or 5, though they do have the other three sets; they cannot therefore belong to scheme 3, but are indeterminate with regard to schemes 1 and 2. Q contains basically only set 4, though into this are introduced seven sermons from set 3 and one from set 1; the same conclusion as in the cases of R and W follows. This is, however, an unrealistic way of formulating the situation, since there is no evidence that R or W ever contained, or was intended to contain, sets 1 or 5, and there is positive evidence that Q never did. [22] However, in so far as all three present copies of set 4 in isolation from any other set, they can be held to support, albeit only partially, the group of twenty manuscripts under scheme 1.

The table below shows the coverage of the 23 manuscripts in scheme 1; it does *not* show the ordering of the sets, which will be discussed below.

i.	Containing all of sets 1–5	ADTβ
ii.	Containing sets 1–4	KL
iii.	Containing sets 1–3 and 5	M$\alpha\delta$
iv.	Containing sets 2–4	RW
v.	Containing sets 1 and 5	BY
vi.	Containing set 1 only	CFNSP^t
vii.	Containing set 4 only	Q (with additions)
viii.	Containing set 5 only	OPE^{s}H^t

It will be noted that, as mentioned above, set 2 never appears without set 3, nor the obverse, a linking that seems logical. There are, however, some less obvious constraints. With the exception of Q, set 4 never appears in this scheme without sets 2 and 3, to which it is not linked by colophon in any manuscript. Equally with the exception of Q, the only sets that occur alone are 1 and 5; even if sets 2 and 3 are counted as a single unit, as the numbering

---

[21] Though E^s and H^t are very fragmentary, each shows the transition of one epistle sermon to another that makes certain their place in scheme 1; how much of that scheme they originally contained is, of course, indeterminable. The same information is available for the more extensive P^t, though here the gospel sermons of set 1 are in question.
[22] See the description of Q below pp. 75–6.

of the sermons in some manuscripts would suggest,[23] these do not occur without some other set. Q is not entirely isolated here, in fact, since the incorporation of seven sermons from outside set 4 reveals knowledge of other material.[24]

Scheme 2: the sermons are divided into four groups. These are:
   Set 5 plus set 1: the two sets as described above are brought together into a single dominical cycle. For each Sunday the epistle sermon is placed before the gospel sermon, according to the order of the two readings in the Mass. In the Christmas season where, as noted above, there is discrepancy in the coverage between the two sets, there is some variation in ordering between the manuscripts that exemplify this scheme; this variation will be discussed below, pp. 22–6.
   Set 2: sermons as above.
   Set 3: sermons as above.
   Set 4: sermons as above.
This scheme, though not necessarily in this order, is found in five manuscripts, EIJXZ. All five of these manuscripts contain, or did contain before loss of leaves, all 294 sermons.

Scheme 3: the sermons are divided into three groups. These are:
   Set 5 plus set 1 plus set 4: the three sets as described above are brought together into a complete Temporale cycle. The weekday sermons are inserted after the Sunday epistle and gospel sermons (in that order) for each week as appropriate. Again, difficulties arose in the Christmas season that will be discussed below. The seven final sermons of set 4 that are not liturgically fixed were omitted in one manuscript having this scheme, but are included in another at the end of the Temporale.
   Set 2: sermons as above.
   Set 3: sermons as above.
   This scheme is found, in whole or in part and not necessarily in this order in three manuscripts, GHV. In G and H it is complete, or was so before loss of leaves, save that G omits the seven final sermons in set 4. In V only a section of the Temporale cycle survives, from the second Sunday in Advent to the fourth week

[23] See pp. 130–34.
[24] See pp. 24–6.

after the octave of the Epiphany; V does not contain either set 2 or set 3.[25]

It is obvious that schemes 2 and 3 necessitate the inclusion of more than one set. With the exception of V, having scheme 3, it might appear that these latter two schemes would only be found where the full corpus of sermons was known to the scribe. As will be seen from the account of it (pp. 81–2), V is defective as it now stands at the beginning, and would in its unmutilated state almost certainly have opened with the epistle sermon for the first Sunday in Advent. But it is unlikely that anything has been lost at

Manuscript	Sets 1	2	3	4	5	
A	×	×	×	×	×	
B	×				×	
C	×					
D	×	×	×	×	×	
E	×	×	×	×	×	
F	×					
G	×	×	×	×	×	(set 4 minus 7)
H	×	×	×	×	×	
I	×	×	×	×	×	
J	×	×	×	×	×	
K	×	×	×	×		
L	×	×	×	×		
M	×	×	×		×	
N	×					
O					×	
P					×	
Q	y–1		y–7	×		
R		×	×			
S	×					
T	×	×	×	×	×	
V	y–9			y–14	y–10	
W		×	×	×		
X	×	×	×	×	×	
Y	×				×	
Z	×	×	×	×	×	
α	×	×	×		×	
β	×	×	×	×	×	
δ	×	×	×		×	
E^s					×	
H^t					×	
P^t	×					
Totals (including V, but excluding Q from sets 1 and 3)	24	18	18	17	21	

[25] See pp. 81–2; the format is too small for it to be likely that the manuscript ever contained all 294 sermons.

the end of the manuscript. There is therefore no evidence that sets 2 or 3 were available to the scribe of V. But V's idiosyncrasies are so numerous (see p. 165) that little weight should be given to its evidence in this discussion. From the other seven manuscripts having schemes 2 or 3, it seems reasonable to argue that these schemes were only used when it was intended to present a complete collection of the sermons.

The survival of the sermons may be shown by the table opposite; *x* shows the presence of the set complete, or presumed to have been complete before loss of leaves, *y* the inclusion of an individual sermon or group from the set with the number present following.

B. Internal evidence about the original organization of the sermons

Cross references within the sermons provide some evidence to answer the question as to which of these three schemes was that originally intended. There are two passages that imply that sets 5, 1, and 4 were intended as separate sets, thus necessitating the originality of scheme 1; these are:

41/101 But, as þe sixþe sermoun seiþ, scribis and pharisees seyden þat mansleyng was forfendut but neiþur yre ne yuel word;

a clear reference to sermon 6/51 'And so þe false pharisees tauȝten men þat *Godes lawe forfendith not but manslawtre or oþur sensible wrong*'.

E32/51 And, as it is seide in þe nexte sermoun, of þis loue ben many gabbyngis.

a reference back to the previous epistle sermon E31/58 ff where various kinds of false love are discussed.

There are no divergencies between the manuscripts in either of these in the crucial words, save with Z who changed *sixþe sermoun* in the first to *gospel*, and *sermoun* in the second to *epistle*.[26] The numbering in the first, and the allusion to the previous sermon in the second, will not work if either scheme 2 or scheme 3 had been original. In scheme 2 sermon 6 (as numbered here) would have been at least sermon 12, because of the intrusion of the epistle

---

26 The nature of Z's text is described pp. 98–9; it is extremely unlikely that Z here presents the original reading; it is rather an intelligent emendation.

sermons before each gospel sermon; E32 would have been immediately preceded by gospel sermon 1 (as here numbered) which contains nothing relevant. In scheme 3 sermon 6 would have had an even later number because of the intrusion of the ferial gospel sermons as well as those on the Sunday epistles, whilst E32 would have been immediately preceded by a ferial gospel sermon from set 4.

There is a third reference which excludes scheme 3 but is inconclusive concerning schemes 1 and 2:

6/1 Hit is seyde in þe nexste gospel whate nettis prestys schulden haue,

referring back to sermon 5 where the nets used by Peter and the apostles on the sea of Gennesaret are explained. Since all manuscripts have *gospel* rather than *sermoun*, this allusion would still be appropriate in scheme 2 where 5 would be the last gospel sermon; it would not be suitable in scheme 3 where 211 would be the previous gospel sermon.

Evidence to support the view that scheme 1 was that originally intended comes from the numbering systems found in various of the manuscripts. These systems work only within each set, so that in the three sets 1, 4, and 5 involved in the present discussion, there are three separate systems; there is no trace of any consecutive numbering of either all dominical sermons or of all Temporale sermons. Not all the manuscripts preserve these numbering systems, even in part, and it is not possible to prove that they were part of the original text. The manuscripts that show the numbering systems are largely those of scheme 1: for set 1 ABCDLMβ have the system regularly or sporadically, for set 4 ADKLQβ, and for set 5 ADPYβ. But traces of the system for each set are found in manuscripts from the other schemes: for set 1 in J, for set 4 in JZG, and for set 5 in I. The numbers, since they are attached merely to the word *sermo*, not specifying gospel or epistle, are incorrect in the first and last cases, and in G in set 4 where this is incorporated into scheme 3. In these three manuscripts at these places the numbers must have been transmitted as fossils, and must go back to an exemplar in which the relevant set was preserved alone without intercalation. It seems reasonable to conclude that at least some of the scheme 2 and 3 manuscripts derive from an antecedent arranged as scheme 1. X of scheme 2 and G of scheme 3 also show the numbering systems in sets 2 and 3. From this it would seem justifiable to deduce that the earliest stage of the organization that can be traced is that which followed the arrangement of scheme 1.

This conclusion is to some extent further supported by evidence that the surviving manuscripts of schemes 2 and 3 were not in each case all descended from a single hyparchetype in which the intercalation had been carried out, but are the result of several independent intercalating efforts. It will be seen in chapter 5 that the groups EIJXZ of scheme 2 and GHV of scheme 3 do not form genetic families in their textual errors; the work of collation for this edition was undertaken on the expectation that they would, and the manuscripts of each scheme therefore were collated immediately one after another, but the expectation was totally frustrated. Apart from the evidence of textual minutiae which will be considered later along with other questions of manuscript affiliations, discrepancy of detail between the manuscripts of each group in the ordering of certain sermons makes it unlikely that each group had a single hyparchetype. The evidence is as follows:

(A) Scheme 2: manuscripts involved EIJXZ

The divergencies are concentrated in the period between 4 Advent and 1 Lent, save in J where the trouble continued to 5 Lent. Since E lacks most of the sermons because of a loss of quires, its position is not precisely ascertainable. But each of the other four manuscripts has individual errors of arrangement not shared by the others. The reason why it is this period that caused most trouble will be discussed more fully below, pp. 22–6, since it affects a manuscript of scheme 1. Here a purely schematic demonstration will be given of the independence of each of the four manuscripts IJXZ.

    (a) I has an error of sequence: it has

        E5–E6–30–E7–31–E8

    This is wrong because the epistle sermon should always precede the gospel sermon for the same day; hence the correct order would be

        E5–E6–E7–30–31.[27]

---

[27] The epistle lection of E7, Isaiah 60. 1–6, is that appointed in the Sarum rite for both the feast of the Epiphany itself and for the Sunday within the octave of the feast. Some of the manuscripts, OPTαδJZH, give the occasion of the sermon as the feast, the rest, ABDYβIXGV, for the Sunday. The discrepancy does not affect the fact that E7 should precede 30.

(*b*) J has a long error that can be divided into two parts: it has
28–E5–E6–29–E7
J omitted entirely E4 and displaced 29; the correct order
would be 28–E4–29–E5–E6–E7
There then follows the sequence
E7–30–E8–31–E9–32–, where E9 is the sermon for the
second Sunday after the octave of the Epiphany, but 32 the
gospel sermon for the *first*; this wrong positioning continues
through to the fourth Sunday in Lent, with the gospel
coming one Sunday too late, then 43 is completely omitted
and the sequence put right with E20–44; sermon 43 is added
at the end of the dominical cycle in another hand.

(*c*) X has two sequences not found elsewhere and both
incorrect:
E6–94–E7
Though the intrusion of 94 is a reasonable attempt to iron
out one of the divergencies in coverage between sets 5 and 1,
this sermon is not found in any of the manuscripts having
scheme 1 in set 1; the numbering scheme of set 1 does not
allow for its presence there. X in fact has two copies of 94,
one here and another in the correct place in set 3.

X also omits 31 from its proper place in set 5 plus set 1,
and includes it instead in set 4. Whilst Q also incorporates 31
in its unique arrangement, no manuscript having set 1 in
scheme 1 omits it; again, the numbering system of set 1, so
far as thàt is evidence of originality, necessitates the presence
of 31.[28]

(*d*) Z got into a bad muddle which has only partially been corrected. As it was originally written the sequence in Z was:
E5–30–E6–31–E7–32–E8–, and thereafter to Quinquagesima having the gospel sermon before the epistle
sermon for the same day; then E15–E16–40 to correct the
sequence. From sermon 32 onwards a medieval hand,
possibly that of the main scribe, corrected the sequence by
putting letters by the beginning of each sermon to show the
order, but this still leaves uncorrected the wrong position of
30.

(*e*) E is only available from the Sexagesima gospel sermon on

---

[28] For the oddities of X here see pp. 24–6.

(no. 38). It does *not* share the divergent errors of either J or Z from there on.

(B) Scheme 3: manuscripts involved GHV

Taking first the two complete manuscripts, G and H, each has one oddity of order not shared by the other:

(*a*) G has 36–139–140–E13–37–141. G alters the heading of 140, calling it for feria 6 after the fifth octave of the Epiphany (as does X of scheme 2); but this is an error, the correct assignment being for feria 4 after Septuagesima. H does not make this mistake.

(*b*) H has 96–E7 here ascribed to Epiphany–97–30. Leaving aside the propriety of introducing 96 and 97 into this area from set 3 (see below pp. 22–6), the order in G is 96–97–E7–30, with E7 assigned to the Sunday in the octave of Epiphany. Liturgically, either assignment is possible. Two explanations of the divergence between G and H are possible: that both descend from a common scheme 3 exemplar but one has altered both heading and order, or that G and H descend independently from two exemplars of set 5 in scheme 1 with different headings and that the difference of order results from two independent intercalation. In the light of (*a*) above, the second explanation seems more probable.

V is more difficult to assess. It does not contain the occasions covered by (*a*) above. In (*b*) it does not agree with either G or H, in that it does not intrude any sermons from set 3; like G, it assigns E7 to the Sunday. V has an independent error in the assignment of 128: properly this is for the Friday of ember week, the week following the third Sunday in Advent, but V heads it as Wednesday. Whilst this shows that V cannot be the ancestor of G or H (an impossibility amply reinforced by textual evidence), it could be an error of V himself working from G or H or from an exemplar of either. Though the extreme carelessness of V makes it perhaps unlikely that V himself would have troubled to extract the set 5, 1 and 4 sermons from the confusion with set 3 in the Christmas season found in both G and H, it is obviously possible that the scribe of an antecedent to V could have done so. But equally it is possible that V derives from yet a third effort at intercalation.

If then the five manuscripts of scheme 2 and the three of

scheme 3 can be thought to descend, provably in most instances, from a series of independent labours of intercalation, it might seem reasonable to conclude that the five separate sets, scheme 1, was the original format. However, the process of rearrangement was demonstrably not all in one direction; it was not always from five separate sets to a more complex ordering within four or three sets. The first piece of evidence for the reverse process was mentioned by Arnold. Arnold used as his base manuscript A, MS Bodley 788, which has scheme 1. But, as Arnold perceived, there is clear indication that A was copied, in part at least, from an exemplar that had scheme 2. In set 1 A began his copy of sermon 42 on f. 32^v and continued on f. 33; but when he turned over to f. 33^v he transferred from 42/103 to the epistle for the following Sunday E19/4, copying as far as line 21 before realizing his mistake; he then reverted to the gospel sermon, and the erroneous material has been crossed through in ordinary and in red ink. Since there is no verbal similarity between the two passages that could account for the error, the scribe in turning over the leaf was presumably distracted and either turned over also the leaf of his exemplar or returned to the wrong column of it. If his exemplar were of scheme 2,[29] such a mistake could lead him on to the epistle sermon for the next Sunday, that is to E19. This seems the only way to explain the error. It is not, however, necessary to add with Arnold that this shows that scheme 2 was the original arrangement intended. It will be shown below (p. 162) that A was not such an excellent manuscript as Arnold supposed.[30]

The second piece of evidence is of much greater complication. Ideally it should be discussed separately later, but since it bears upon the question of the original scheme it must be examined here. An account of the oddity will be given, and its implications for the present question then explained.

If scheme 1 is accepted as the original arrangement, sermons for the Christmas season are awkwardly distributed between three of the sets. The table below shows the coverage, arranged

[29] An exemplar of set 3 is less likely, since there sermon 42 would have been followed by 159–64; the scribe would have had to turn over several folios of his exemplar to come to the copy of E19. In scheme 2, whatever the size or format of the lost exemplar, E19 could have hardly been more than a side distant from 42/103.

[30] Arnold i. xiii and xvii; even more clearly E's value is not nearly so great as Arnold considered.

under the sets in which the sermons occur, but with gaps across the page to show where the different sets would interlock in an actual year:

Set 5	Set 1	Set 3
		89 Christmas Eve
E5 Christmas Day		90 Christmas Day
		91 St. Stephen
		92 St. John
		93 Innocents day
E6 Sixth day after		94 Sixth day after
Christmas		Christmas
		95 Circumcision
		96 Eve of
		Epiphany
E7 Epiphany *or*		97 Epiphany
Sunday within octave	30 Sunday within	
of Epiphany[31]	octave of	
	Epiphany	
	31 Octave of Epiphany	
E8 1 Sunday after	32 1 Sunday after	
octave of Epiphany	octave of Epiphany	

Thereafter sets 5 and 1 revert to their normal provision of only Sunday sermons; the next set 3 sermon is for the feast of the Conversion of St. Paul (25 January). It is obvious that the division between the three sets at this point is almost entirely arbitrary: both sets 5 and 1 include sermons for occasions that would not necessarily fall on a Sunday (E5 and E6, 31), whilst the gospels for the same days as E5 and E6 are found in set 3. As has already been seen (pp. 19–21), the lack of symmetry between sets 5 and 1 caused difficulties for those wishing to intercalate the two sets.

All of the occasions involved above, up to and including the Epiphany and the octave of the Epiphany, are feasts fixed by the ordinary calendar to a firm date; they therefore belong logically with set 3, the only set where this operates, as opposed to sets 1, 4 and 5 which are only fixed to the liturgical calendar and not to precise dates, or to set 2 where no date, liturgical or ordinary, is prescribed for the sermons. On the other hand, the feasts from Christmas Eve to the Epiphany are also placed within the

---

[31] See above, n. 27, for the alternative assignments of this lection.

liturgical calendar; it is hardly surprising to find Christmas incorporated into a liturgical sequence when that already includes feasts such as Easter, Pentecost, and so on. Having introduced Christmas, it is an easy step to add the other feasts of that season. Liturgical manuscripts often incorporate all of the occasions concerned here into the Temporale.[32] It should further be noticed that set 4 has a long gap over the Christmas season: it jumps in its provision from 131, feria 6 in 4 Advent, to 132, feria 4 in week 1 after the octave of the Epiphany, a period that could not have been less than two and a half weeks.

Given the arbitrariness of the assignment in the three sets, it is not surprising to find adjustments made in some manuscripts. Four manuscripts incorporated sermons from set 3 into a Temporale sequence: these are G and H of scheme 3, X of scheme 2, and Q, having only set 4 and thus indeterminate between schemes 2 and 1. Because of the point made at the end of the last paragraph, it seems reasonable to look for the origin of this incorporation in manuscripts of scheme 3; without such additions, the Christmas season would look, as it does in V, very scantily provided with sermons compared with the rest of the year.[33] The four manuscripts, however, do not have the same sequence of sermons. Schematically their contents can be set out as follows:

G	129	130	89	E5	90	91	92	93	E6	94
H	129	130	89	E5	90	91	92	93	E6	94
X in 5 + 1				E5					E6	94
X in 4	129	130	89		90	91	92	93		94
Q	129	130	89			91	92	93		

G	95	96	97	E7	30	31	E8	32	131	132
H	95	96	E7	97	30	31	E8	32	131	132
X in 5 + 1				E7	30		E8	32		
X in 4	95	96	97			31			131	132
Q	95	96	97			31			131	132

[32] As in Legg, pp. 25–40, Dickinson cols. 45–90. One of the sermon manuscripts, T, has a table of lessons preceding the sermons; this incorporates all of the occasions here mentioned into the Temporale, adding epistles for those occasions here uncovered, and further lections for the various masses on Christmas Day. The table of lessons found in various manuscripts of the Wycliffite Bible, printed FM iv. 683–90, does the same.

[33] Thus, for the two and a half weeks mentioned at the end of the last paragraph, V has only five sermons; this may be compared with the minimum provision of four sermons a week in the rest of the Advent and Epiphany seasons.

G's copy of E6 actually comes at the end of the manuscript, ff. 194ᵛ–195ᵛ, but a note shows that it was intended to come in the position shown above. The discrepancy between G and H in the relative order of E7 and 97 has already been remarked (p. 21).

The sequence of sermons as presented by G is quite comprehensible. A note in set 3 in G, however, suggests that the scribe was aware that sermons 89–97 might be expected there: after sermon 88 a marginal note in the original hand reads (f. 161ᵛ) 'þou schalt fynde þe gospels of Cristmasse woke in þe temperal'. G regularly numbered the sermons of set 3, and there is consequently a gap of nine numbers in his sequence; he did not incorporate the numbers into the new context. H, apart from the transposition of E7 and 97, is identical with G and equally comprehensible; H does not have either the directive in set 3 or the numbering of that series.

X's two sequences, on the other hand, are illogical and awkward. They are, moreover, only intelligible as attempts to sort out an arrangement such as is found in G or H. Most significant in this regard is the error of placing 31 in set 4: this shows that the exemplar must have had sets 5, 1, and 4 mixed into a single sequence. If X were working from an exemplar in which the Christmas season sermons had been incorporated in to sets 5 plus 1 as in scheme 2, there would be no way in which this stray from set 1 could get into set 4 if the sermons were subsequently re-sorted. But in disentangling the material it seems that X must have had two exemplars: one of scheme 3 which provided the festival sermons in the same sequence as sets 5, 1 and 4; and a second of set 5 alone. This second explains why X correctly placed E5 and E6, notwithstanding the fact that they are not for Sundays. That he did *not* have an exemplar containing set 1 alone according to scheme 1 explains why he was not similarly able to place 31, and why he incorrectly kept 94 in his set 5–plus–set–1 sequence. It would seem that X himself was baffled about the correct placing of sermon 94: when he copied it in set 4 he wrote the nonsensical heading (p. 345) 'Sexta die a Natiuitate. Þis gospel wiþ his epistle is writen bifore among þe Sunday gospels.' Oddly, the same note appears in G immediately before sermon 94, where it is even more incomprehensible. In G this note was crossed through and a note substituted at the foot of the page, but by the original scribe, 'þe pistel þat longiþ to þis gospel is writun in þe eende of þe book' (it is added on ff. 194ᵛ–195ᵛ). [34]It would seem that X's note and G's cancelled note must derive from their use, possibly independently, of an exemplar or exemplars of set 3 from which a smaller number of Christmas season sermons had been extracted than is their own practice; in such an exemplar such a note in this position might be appropriate. Like G, X usually numbered the sermons of set 3 and consequently has a gap of nine numbers. But there seems no way of completely explaining X's two sequences. If 94 were brought into the dominical cycle of set 5–plus–1 because of the existence of E6 there, an epistle sermon for the same occasion, and equally if 31 were demoted to set 4 because there was not an epistle sermon for that occasion in the dominical cycle, then why was 90, the gospel for Christmas Day, not added immediately after E5, the epistle sermon for the same day? Logically, 90 and 94 should be treated in the same way.

Q's sequence seems, when first encountered, even more incomprehensible. Here in a manuscript essentially having only set 4 are seven sermons from set 3 and one from set 1. But, when Q's sequence is arranged under those of G, H and X, the explanation seems, if not complete, at least easier. Q is nearest to set 4 as that appears in X, including the misplacement of 31. The differences from X are the absences of 90 and 94. Since there seems no reason why Q should independently have omitted these two sermons, it is necessary to assume that his exemplar was not X but another manuscript which had been engaged on an exercise similar to that of X, but had left a slightly different set of anomalies. That Q goes back to a scheme 3 archetype is also suggested by a directive that has been erased. On f. 15 after 93 is a note in the scribe's hand now partially erased 'de sancto Thome martyre Euangelium homo quidam no' Luc. 19'. The only other manuscript that has any directive concerning the feast of Thomas a Becket is G; G's note amplifies Q's and occurs at the same place 'Homo quidam nobilis Luc. 19 Seche þis gospel in þe comoun sanctorum among bischops and confessours'. The sermon on this text is number 78 in set 2.

If these arguments are accepted, it follows that at least three manuscripts were copied from exemplars that had schemes of

---

[34] For the error see above p. 25.

greater complication than that which they themselves reveal. A, itself of scheme 1, was copied from an exemplar of scheme 2. Q, itself indeterminate between 2 and 1, must have been descended from an exemplar of scheme 3 (or possibly from one of scheme 2 itself descended from scheme 3). X, of scheme 2, must derive from an exemplar of scheme 3 plus, for set 5 only, one of scheme 1. Moreover, both A and possibly X were themselves making the changes of scheme–so much is evident from the tracks they have left behind them. It is important to notice that, though it has been the mistakes that have been discussed here, for the vast majority of the time the scribes were completely successful in imposing an arrangement other than that of the exemplar before them. Were it not for A's mistake on turning one leaf, his activity would never have emerged.

It would appear therefore that different schemes were known to a number of the scribes, and that these schemes might be utilized not automatically according to the nature of the exemplar, but consciously according to the will of the scribe or his supervisor. One pattern, that of scheme 1, seems to have been the original intention. Given, however, the substantial agreement between the manuscripts respectively of schemes 2 and 3, but the evidence that this agreement is not the result of derivation in each case from a single-archetype, the other two patterns must have had an authority and must have been available from an early date.[35]

C. The evidence for the ordering of the sets

If scheme 1 was the original intention, the question still remains of the ordering of the five sets. Within the sermons there is a small number of cross references; these are not sufficient for a complete ordering, but they are, so far as they go, self-consistent. Many of the cross references are within a single set, and so are of no help.[36]

[35] It is obviously likely that the choice of scheme was dictated by the use to which the manuscript was to be put, or by the decision of the 'patron' for whom the manuscript was being made. But there is no direct evidence on this question. Few of the manuscripts have any sign of medieval ownership (see the descriptions below), none has indication of the person, or group, for whom it was made. Though there is evidence in marginal annotation, and in the derivatives considered below, that the sermons were read and used, no indications have yet been found to determine whether they were ever preached, as was clearly intended, regularly through the year.

[36] See Arnold i. 215/17, 262/23, 277/20, 313/24, 351/22; ii. 191/26, 201/13.

Equally references from one set to another that do not include indication of sequence are unhelpful.[37] The following, however, appear to give clear information:

(a) that set 1 was intended to stand first:

Arnold ii. 13/1 (no. 129) þes wordis [Luke 7: 17–28] ben expounned in þe firste part of þe sermouns,

a reference to sermon 28 where the same story of the Baptist's enquiries of Christ is told from Matthew 11. The reference in sermon 129 is found in all manuscripts, whether or not they also contain set 1.

(b) that set 2 must precede set 3:

Arnold i. 165/1 (no. 55) as comun þing is betture and byforn oþre þingus so þis gospel þat is rad in comun sanctorum schulde men knowe somwhat.

This is somewhat enigmatic, but seems to have no meaning at all unless *comun þing* refers to the common of the saints, *oþre þingus* to the proper. Unfortunately there is no other direct evidence settling the order of sets 2 and 3.

(c) that set 2 must precede set 4:

Arnold ii. 171/1 (no. 207) þis gospel is telde bifore and expounnyd to literal witt;

the sermon is based on Matthew 5: 17–19, and the reference back is to sermon 80 on Matthew 5: 13–19 in set 2.

(d) that set 3 must precede set 4:

Arnold ii. 53/6 (no. 149) and to þe þrid part of þis gospel of Cristis modir and his briþeren it is teld also bifore hou þis gospel vndirstondiþ; seek þe þridde Sunday of Lentene and in propre *sanctorum in die vii fratrum*.

This set 4 sermon is referring back to sermon 42 in set 1 and to sermon 110 in set 3.[38]

Since the interpretation put upon the obscure allusion under

---

[37] See Arnold ii. 163/37, 168/8.

[38] The set 4 sermon, no. 149, should cover Matt. 12: 38–50 but in fact only translates and expounds as far as the end of verse 42. Sermon 110 has as its lection Matt. 12: 46–50. Sermon 42 in set 1 has the parallel passage from Luke 11: 14–28 as its text. It is not clear why Arnold omitted the second half of this sentence, since his base text A preserves it (with the additional words at the end *more of þis*). Q and H omit *seek . . . fratrum*; Q also omits *bifore*; only the latter is significant for order, and Q's reliability, as will emerge in vol. iii, is not great.

(*b*) is compatible with the sum of the evidence in (*c*) and (*d*), it may reasonably be accepted.

(*e*) that set 5 must come after set 1:

E55/59 and þus may prestis of Cristis sect teche þe puple on Sundayes boþe bi þe gospel and þe pistele.

This seems to be a concluding remark that could only be appropriate at the close of the two sets. In schemes 2 or 3 the sentence is oddly placed at the end of the last epistle sermon but before the final Sunday gospel sermon. Yet only Z omitted the sentence as inappropriate; IJXGH, the other manuscripts available at that point, include it. Unfortunately, there is no further internal evidence for the position of set 5. The sentence above seems to make most sense if set 5 immediately followed set 1, but there is no further confirmation of this; no manuscript contains set 5 immediately after set 1.

The internal evidence thus points to scheme 1 as the original design and, within that scheme, to an ordering of sets 1–2–3–4 with set 5 coming after set 1 but of uncertain relation to the other three. The sequence of gospel sermons so established is to some extent confirmed by evidence from the headings of the sets in some manuscripts. As well as the numbering of individual sermons already mentioned (p. 18), some manuscripts number the sets; the manuscripts that show knowledge of this are ADEGIJKLMQZ$\beta\delta$. The number usually appears in the rubric at the beginning or end of the set, but in K it is also used as a running title at the head of each opening. Interestingly in view of the doubts about the position of set 5 shown above, this set is never provided with a number. Set 1 only has a number expressed in K, as *prima pars euangeliorum* but this prior position is implicitly acknowledged by the other, much more widely evidenced numbers. Set 2 is described in ADEGIJKLM$\beta\delta$ as *þe secunde part* or *secunda pars*; set 4 in ADIJKLZβ as *þe pridde part* or *tertia pars* (Q had a numbering of this set but the actual number has been cropped). This implies that the *Commune Sanctorum* sermons and the *Proprium Sanctorum* sermons were regarded as a single sequence, and this is borne out by the fact that the individual sermons are numbered through these two sets in one list.[39] Whilst these headings confirm the original intention of a

[39] The numbering of the sermons, from 1–68, is preserved fairly regularly in seven manuscripts, ADMβJXG (see p. 131 below).

sequence 1–2–3–4 (using the numbering of the sets adopted here), two points should be noted. In the first place, the numbers in the headings are found even where the sequence of sets in the actual manuscript is other than that which they would seem to require. Thus, for instance, L has the numbering for sets 2 and 4, but in L as it stands set 4 is placed before set 2; similarly I has the same numbering but has the sets in the unalterable order 4–3–2. In a sense this suggests that the numbering, if not original, is at any rate ancient in the tradition, and has been handed down as a fossil in the headings. But it also shows that the scribes, or (as will be suggested below) in some cases the rubricator or binder, did not regard them as necessarily to be observed. In the second place, similarly, the implication that the *Commune* and *Proprium Sanctorum* sermons belonged together in that order is one that a number of scribes, who separated them, did not draw.[40]

Turning to the external evidence, the present state of the manuscripts may be deceptive. In any case, as a glance at the table below on p. 33 will show, the sequence of sets in the surviving manuscripts is far from unanimous. Since the situation is confused and confusing, the possible explanations must be considered in detail. At the one extreme, the sequence from one set to another may be unalterable: this is most easily demonstrable when the transition occurs on the same side of the leaf, on the recto and verso of the same leaf, or within the same quire provided that the quire is uniform with its neighbours and has not been tampered with. Even if an item is interposed between two sets, the sequence may be unalterable if these conditions are met at both ends of the intruding text. Thus in A the transitions from set 2 to set 3 and from set 4 to set 5 are in each case on the same side of a leaf; between sets 1 and 2 are two items other than the sets here, and between set 3 and set 4 another, but, since the transitions at the beginning and end of these are on the same side of the relevant leaves, the sequences 1–2 and 3–4 must have been intended by the scribe. The entire cycle in A, therefore, of sets 1–2–3–4–5 is unalterable. At the other extreme, if the first of two sets ends a quire and the second begins a new quire, the scribe may not have intended the sequence as it now stands in the bound manuscript. Indeed, he may not have had any thought about the ordering of the two sets in relation to each other, or even have considered the question of binding them into a single volume. T stands at this extreme: whilst the sequence of set 1 followed by set 4 cannot be altered, set 5, the pair of sets 1 and 4, set 3 and finally set 2 are in four groups of quires, each self-contained. Gaps at the end of quires, compression of the hand at the end of others, and the addition of an extra leaf at the end of the final quire, all point to the contrivance of this separation. The ordering of T, therefore, may owe nothing to the intention of the scribe, but merely reflect a decision after his work was complete. In between these two extremes, best shown by the examples of A and T, lie cases where the evidence is more confused.

First, quire signatures may suggest that the manuscript as it now stands has been displaced from the original scribe's understanding of the order that he was to follow. A fairly certain example of this is α; α's present arrangement is of the form sets 5–3–2–1. The middle element 3–2 cannot be altered since the transition occurs in the middle of f. 99^v. But sets 5 and 1 are in independent groups of quires; set 5 takes seven quires (1–6^8, 7^{10}, and the signature g is still visible on f. 52 in the seventh quire), whilst at the beginning of set 1, on the first leaf of the present quire 20, the signature h is visible, the appropriate signature if this group of quires had originally been intended to follow set 5. As will be seen, the order set 5–set 1 is found in a number of other manuscripts (even if they cannot all be shown to have been designed in that sequence), whilst an order set 3–set 2–set 1 is unparalleled. It seems most likely that α, as envisaged by the scribe, was to be in the order 5–1, 3–2, though whether this second group was always intended to follow the first or was an addition made to suit subsequent circumstances is less certain.[41] Unfortunately, the preservation of quire signatures is often not sufficient for deductions of this sort to be made.[42]

Secondly, the order might be determined by the main scribe

[41] See below pp. 88–9 for Dr Ker's suggestion that the manuscript, despite first appearances that two scribes were involved, was written by a single hand in the order set 5, set 1, sets 3–2.

[42] A case in point is X. One scribe wrote the first and last items, respectively sets 5 plus 1 and set 4, each in groups of quires separable from the intervening material; another scribe was responsible for the rest. No quire signatures remain, so it is impossible to know whether the first scribe intended the division of his work as it now stands. See further below pp. 84–5.

but after he had written the whole text. This is a possibility that
arises in the case of β. β as it now stands has the same order of sets
as A; the sequence of 1–2–3 cannot be changed because of the
run-on on the same leaves; quire signatures make it likely that,
despite loss of quires at the actual transition, set 3 must have been
intended to precede set 4. Set 5 starts a new quire, and this quire
is signed a, suggesting that this section was regarded as a separate
unit. But the scribe added the relevant catchwords to the last
verso of the preceding quire, thus fixing the order. The possibility
that this might have been an addition after the writing of the
entire manuscript arises from the fact that if set 5 were transposed
from its present position to initial position in the manuscript the
order of all the items, five sets and additional texts would be
identical with D;[43] β is textually more closely related to D than to
A.[44] Whether or not this was actually what happened in this
instance, the possibility reveals another point at which the fixing
of the order could occur.

Yet a further point is that when the rubrication was begun. In a
number of the manuscripts this was clearly done by someone
other than the scribe(s), and, even when the scribe was
responsible, he may have filled in the rubricated headings after
finishing the copying (see description of the manuscripts for
details in each case). There is some evidence to suggest that the
headings may in some instances derive from a manuscript other
than that which supplied the text proper.[45] There are, therefore,
many ways in which the rubrication might impose an order on a
manuscript that had not been intended during the work hitherto.
Many of the numbers for the sets mentioned above (p. 29) are in
the hand of the rubricator. But, as has been said, these numbers
are in any case difficult to interpret since they appear to have
carried no obligation about the positioning of the set to which
they are attached. The most obvious way in which a rubricator
could impose order at one point was the size of capital which he
chose to attach to the beginning of one set, and the scope of
ornamentation which he added to the leaf. Thus the prior
position of set 5 in D, an item which fills a separable group of

[43] β departs from the order of A in one regard, placing *De Ecclesia et membris eius* before set
5, whereas A places it after set 5; the order cannot be altered in either manuscript.
[44] See below pp. 132–3, 161; the relationship between D and β is much closer in set 4.
[45] See below pp. 127–30, 134.

quires, is fixed by the fact that the ornamentation around the first page of that set is more extensive than anywhere else in the manuscript.[46]

There are then three stages at which the order of the present manuscripts could become fixed: when the scribe was at work, while the rubricator and ornamenter was handling the manuscript, and when the quires were eventually bound. Obviously, the effect of the last could be disturbed by subsequent rebinding; but there seems to be no instance amongst the present manuscripts where this can be shown to have occurred.

In the following table of the present state of the manuscripts, those manuscripts that contain only one set, CFNOPQSE^{s}H^{i}P^t, and V, which contains nothing beyond a partial copy of scheme 3 (sets 5 plus 1 plus 4), are omitted; they can offer no evidence on this question. The numbers refer to the sets, and are arranged in the sequence shown by each manuscript; a dash between the numbers shows a sequence that cannot be altered because of transition of a single leaf; an asterisk shows prior position of a set, not otherwise fixed, by ornamentation.

A	1–2–3–4–5	α	5 3–2 1
B	*5 1	β	1–2–3–4 5
D	*5 1–2–3 4	δ	5 1–2–3
K	*1 2–3–4	E	5 plus 1 3 2 4
L	4 1–2–3	I	5 plus 1–4–3–2
M	5 1–2( )3	J	5 plus 1 2–3–4
R	2 3–4	X	*5 plus 1 2 3 4
T	5 1–4 3 2	Z	5 plus 1–3–4–2
W	*4 3–2	G	5 plus 4–2–3
Y	5–1	H	5 plus 1 plus 4–3–2

[Note: M has lost leaves at the end of set 2 and the beginning of set 3 in such a way that it is impossible to tell whether the transition from one to the other was at the end of a quire or not. In β set 5 is attached to set 4 by catchwords, as described.]

From the table there can be seen to be a fair amount of support for the sequence 1–2–3–4, or for some part of this where manuscripts either do not have all four sets or have some

[46] The elaboration of the decoration similarly fixes in prior position the sets now standing at the beginning of BKWδX; in all of these this cannot be shown to have been determined before the rubricator and decorator began work. M and E are defective at the beginning; in L the rubrication and ornamentation was never completed.

transitions that cannot be proved original. Accepting only necessary sequences, the following have all or part (sometimes only one link) of the sequence 1–2–3–4: ADKLMR βδJG. To this can be added, if present actual order rather than necessary order is accepted, X. But there are some contradictions to this pattern that cannot be explained as misapprehension on the part of rubricator or binder. Thus the following sequences are imposed by transitions on the same leaf: 4–3–2 in whole or in part shown by WαH, also witnessed in part though not imposed by such transition in E; 3–4–2 shown in Z; 1–4 established in T. As will be seen when the relationship of the manuscripts is discussed in chapter V, the texts that come together in these minority groups do not form genetic families. The position of set 5 seems regularly to be either first or last, the latter only occurring in manuscripts that possess all five sets. The fact that set 5 covers epistles, rather than gospels, makes it something of an anomaly amongst the sermons; from the occasions covered, however, it obviously belongs with set 1. Liturgically, it would make better sense to put the epistle sermons before those on the gospels, as is done in schemes 2 and 3. On the other hand, the final sentence in the epistle set suggests (see above p. 29) that it was intended to follow the Sunday gospel sermons. The prior position of the Sunday sermons seems reasonable, both from the greater usualness of dominical preaching and from the manuscript evidence; only L of all the manuscripts that contain either set 1 or set 5 or both does not have either of these first, as the manuscript is now bound.[47] This leaves a choice for the original order of 5–1–2–3–4, well evidenced by the manuscripts, or 1–5–2–3–4 for which there is no manuscript evidence but some internal support. A possible hypothesis that would explain this contradiction would be to suppose that the author composed set 1 before set 5, and hence included the final sentence of set 5 commenting on the availability of sermons on both gospels and epistles for each Sunday; but, in order to keep together all the sermons on the gospels, either he or another placed set 5 before set 1. The final position of set 5 in A and β, manuscripts that are not otherwise related, could

---

[47] Although L lacks quire signatures, and all ornament, it is perhaps unlikely that set 4 was ever intended to stand anywhere other than it now does. The first scribe wrote slightly under half set 4, then a second scribe took over and the whole of the rest is in his hand. But for a manuscript where, as it now stands, a scribe's work is divided, see above n. 42.

be explained by subsequent and possibly independent
rearrangement, preserving the collection of gospel sermons as a
whole. For reasons that will be explained in chapter V, D has been
chosen as the base text for the present edition. However, in the
light of the preceding discussion it seemed legitimate to depart
from its order and place set 1 before set 5; though this sequence of
1 then 5 is not witnessed in any manuscript, it seems to be
required by the final sentence of the last sermon in set 5.

As has been said, questions of 'original order' do not seem to
have counted for much in the arrangement of the manuscripts.
Thus, to take only sets 2, 3 and 4 in the five manuscripts of scheme
2, four differing arrangements are found and only two possible
permutations are unwitnessed (2–4–3, 4–2–3). It will emerge in
chapter V that textual relationships shift from one set to another;
each set clearly had its own textual history. This implies that
often a scribe must have had a different exemplar for each set that
he came to copy. The sets might therefore come to him without
any indication of where they should go in a complete collection.
Equally, a scribe might have to depart from the order he thought
or knew to be superior because of the lack of an exemplar at the
moment when it was needed.[48] Within the sets, however, apart
from the eccentricities of the Christmas season already discussed,
the order was immutable and the presence of a sequence of
sermons invariable. There is no trace of the insertion of odd
sermons from another source into the sets, as is the case with some
of the manuscripts of Myrc's sermons.[49] Equally, with almost no
exception, there is no trace of the casual copying of one or a small
group of these sermons in manuscripts of other texts.[50] The sets
are autonomous, and exclusive.

D. The opening of the year in set 1

As far as its occasions are concerned, the ordering of the sermons
within set 2 follows exactly that of the Sarum use; this use, in its
turn, is an arbitrary arrangement, as of necessity it must be in the

[48] The situation here is not, of course, that of *pecia* copying, for which see most recently
G. Pollard 'The pecia system in the medieval universities', in *Medieval Scribes, Manuscripts and
Libraries, Essays presented to N. R. Ker*, ed. M. B. Parkes and A. G. Watson (London, 1978),
pp. 145–61.
[49] For the comparison with Myrc see further below pp. 45–6, 190.
[50] For the few apparent exceptions see below, chapter iii.

case of prescriptions for types of saint rather than individual saints. The order of set 3 likewise follows Sarum; both are organized to start in November with those saints whose calendar fixed feasts would fall within the season of Advent. In the Temporale material the Sarum rite opened, as did all western medieval liturgies, with the first Sunday in Advent. This Advent opening is found in all manuscripts of the present sermons in set 4. It is also found in all manuscripts of set 5, save for one where its absence is dependent upon the oddity to be discussed here. Though some manuscripts of sets 4 or 5 lack sermons at the beginning of the sets, enough of the following material remains to establish this Advent opening in all except for the fragments E^s and H^t. But in set 1 more divergence is found. The majority of manuscripts open, not at 1 Advent, but at the first Sunday *after* Trinity; this is found in ABCDKLMT$\beta\delta$. Of the remaining manuscripts of scheme 1, F, Y, and α have the liturgically more expected opening at 1 Advent, whilst N has an otherwise unparalleled opening at Pentecost. The opening of S is not determinable since the group of these sermons that the manuscript contains runs from the middle of 33 (2 Sunday after octave of Epiphany) to the middle of 54 (Trinity Sunday); there are no numbers attached to the sermons that would allow one to assess whether 54 was to be the last. The fragment P^t probably followed the 1 Trinity opening, though the composition of the four-leaf fragment is somewhat problematic and so certainty is impossible. The two complete manuscripts of scheme 3, G and H, both open their temporale cycle at 1 Advent; whilst V is defective at the beginning, there is no evidence to suggest that it differed from the other two. In scheme 2 the majority of manuscripts, I, J, X, and Z open the dominical cycle at 1 Advent. But E started at 1 Trinity, and consequently was obliged to rearrange set 5 to bring it into line with this opening. That E differed from the other four manuscripts is not now immediately evident from the beginning of the manuscript, because of loss of leaves, nor from any sequence from 25 Trinity to 1 Advent again because quires have been lost at the relevant point; it is only ascertainable from the end of the combined sets 5 plus 1 where, after the Trinity Sunday gospel sermon, the original scribe provided an explicit. It seems certain that, whatever the position with regard to set 1, set 5 originally had the normal 1 Advent opening. This is evident from the concluding observation in E55 already quoted (p. 29) concerning the completion of the material for Sunday preaching. It is thus reasonable to conclude that E's rearrangement of set 5 is secondary, and was dependent upon his decision, or that of his exemplar, to follow in the dominical cycle the 1 Trinity opening of set 1.

If it is to be claimed that the liturgically abnormal 1 Trinity opening for set 1 is original, it is primarily manuscripts of scheme 1 that must support it. Obviously it is more likely that the abnormal opening should be modified to the normal by the scribes than that the reverse should happen. On the other hand, a 1 Trinity opening takes set 1 out of line with sets 3, 4, and 5. Yet there is plain evidence that the 1 Trinity opening was original. The best evidence is the back reference (quoted above p. 17) in sermon 41 of set 1 'as þe sixþe sermoun seiþ', a reference that will only work with the 1 Trinity opening; with a 1 Advent opening the *sixþe* sermon would here be number 31 which has nothing appropriate. The word *sixþe* is found in all manuscripts having the sermon, even FYα of scheme 1, IJX of scheme 2 and GH of scheme 3 in all of which the number is inappropriate because of their modified arrangement; only Z substituted *gospel* for *sixþe sermoun*. Similarly the numbering system for the set 1 sermons (above p. 18), where this is found, will only work from 1 Trinity; there is no trace of a rival system beginning with 1 Advent. Seven of the scribes who used the numbering system in set 1 have scheme 1 and anyway open with 1 Trinity; they are ABCDLMβ.[51] But the eighth is J, using scheme 2 and opening at 1 Advent; the numbers in J, therefore, are meaningless in terms of J's own copy (his copy of sermon 32, marked by him *sermo 32*, is actually sermon 15 in his ordering).[52] As has been said, this numbering cannot be proved to be part of the original design, but it clearly goes back some way in the tradition.

It would appear then that the three apparently normal manuscripts of scheme 1, F, Y, and α, are here incorrect. As will be seen in chapter 5, the three do not in other features appear to form a genetic group, and it seems likely, though this is not

---

[51] K numbers only the first sermon, and is therefore excluded from consideration since it cannot be held to support any 'system'.

[52] Taking sets 5 and 1 together; if the numbers are held to refer to set 1 sermons only, *sermo 32* is actually sermon 7.

formally provable, that the rearrangement was in each case
independent. None of the manuscripts number set 1. This cannot
be regarded as significant in α, since no other set is there
numbered; F only contains set 1, so that no deduction can be
drawn. The absence may be significant in Y, since the scribe does
number all the epistle sermons; he may thus have suppressed the
numbers in set 1 as inappropriate to his rearrangement. It is
tempting to conjecture that some or all of these three manuscripts
may have derived their Advent opening for set 1 from their use of
an exemplar of scheme 2 (one following the dominant pattern of
IJXZ), from which they extracted just the gospel sermons.[53]
There is, however, no formal proof of this. Textually (see below
pp. 171–9) none of the manuscripts is closely allied with any of
the scheme 2 or 3 texts; equally, however, the affinities of all three
are hard to trace at all.

It has been mentioned that N has an opening different from all
other manuscripts at Pentecost. As will be described below (p.
115), after each set 1 sermon N has a continuation on the epistle
for the same day; these continuations are completely other than
the sermons of set 5, and are not edited here. But the material of
the continuations makes it plain that these were organized for a
Pentecost opening.[54] N is therefore not unique by accident of
preservation, but its uniqueness owes nothing to any tradition in
the descent of the set 1 homilies.

Everything then points to the originality of the 1 Trinity
opening. Why this time should have been chosen is utterly
obscure. It is not that found in Wyclif's Latin sermons for the
Sunday gospels, nor does it appear in any complete cycle of

[53] The skill with which scribes extracted or combined the sets has been remarked above,
p. 27. The extraction of Sunday gospel sermons from a scheme 2 exemplar would have
posed no problems (unless the exemplar had the muddle at the Christmas season
witnessed in X), and consequently might have left no trace in the extant copies; extraction
from an exemplar of scheme 3 would have been more difficult (e.g. no. 31 might have been
rejected as belonging to set 4, where indeed it was placed by Q).

[54] The Whit Sunday epistle sermon introduces, logically enough, the gifts of the Holy
Spirit, and teaching on these continues through the ensuing three sermons (for Trinity
Sunday, 1 and 2 after Trinity); an opening on 1 Trinity is thus ruled out. An Advent
opening is impossible for similar reasons: the epistle continuation of the sermon for 18
Trinity opens a consideration of the Ten Commandments, teaching on which absorbs the
preacher's attention through to the sermon for 1 Sunday after octave of Epiphany, and, to
emphasize the continuance, that for 1 Advent announces continued discussion of oaths, a
topic that had been begun the previous week.

sermons listed by Schneyer.[55] Whether the peculiarity should be used in attempts to date the sermons will be considered in a later volume along with the other evidence. It may be here noted that this removes, though for set 1 only, the problem of using all the sermons in a single year: whilst with an Advent opening no year could contain five Sundays after the octave of Epiphany, necessitating a late Easter, plus twenty-five Sundays after Trinity, a number only reached with an early Easter, a 1 Trinity opening divides the sermons between two liturgical years (the first having an early Easter and long Trinity season, the second a late Easter and the five Epiphany Sundays). But, as has been said (p. 10), it is far more likely that the provision reflects not actuality but the normal Sarum theoretical material. The fact that in sets 4 and 5 no opening other than 1 Advent can be suggested as original makes it unlikely that any other explanation is correct.

E. Anomalies of organization

(i) The sermon for Ascension Day in A

Arnold printed the sermons from A, and followed its ordering without question; he seems to have worked straight through the manuscript, not looking ahead as he went. A preserves two copies of the sermon for Ascension day. The first is found in set 3, f. 105^{r-v}, after that for the feast of St. Philip and St. James and before that for the vigil of St. John the Baptist. Arnold accordingly printed the sermon in set 3 and numbered it, in his continuous sequence, as 104. In the second volume of his edition, published two years later than the first, Arnold noted that a sermon identical with 104 appeared 'in all the MSS.' in the appropriate liturgical place in set 4.[56] A has here (f. 173^{r-v}) a second copy of the sermon. Arnold did not acknowledge that it was not the second that should have been omitted but the first, since the feast is only liturgically fixed and varies in calendar date; it has no

[55] J. B. Schneyer, 'Repertorium der lateinischen Sermones des Mittelalters . . . 1150–1350', *Beiträge zur Geschichte der Philosophie und Theologie des Mittelalters* xliii (1969–   ). Of other Middle English sermon cycles Myrc, the *Speculum Sacerdotale* and the Northern Homily Cycle (for references see below nn. 69–70) all begin with the Advent season; the sermons in MS Royal 18 B. xxiii are not organized into a coherent sequence, and are a conglomeration of sermons of varied origins. For other cases see below ch. iii.
[56] Arnold ii. 158; Arnold's comments here and i. 295 footnote show that he had misunderstood the correct position of the Ascension Day sermon.

place in the Proprium Sanctorum where calendar date determines
position. It is evident that the original text did not make Arnold's
mistake, nor did it contain two copies of the sermon. No other
manuscript contains the sermon in set 3, and conversely all
manuscripts of set 4 preserve it. The numbering system of set 4
includes the sermon for Ascension Day as number 78, and the
remainder of the sequence will not work without it. Arnold did
not print the numbers in A in any part of his edition, so the oddity
of his inclusion of the sermon in set 3 is not so readily apparent as
it would otherwise have been. In fact, A has the number 78
attached to both of its copies of the sermon; in set 3 it is obviously
out of place, since it comes between sermons 49 and 50, both
numbered (though mistakenly as 58 in the latter case) in A.[57]
Arnold's error over the placing of this sermon was unfortunate
since it results in a discrepancy between some of the sermon
numbers in the present edition and in his.

Why A should have included the sermon in set 3 seems
impossible to explain. If A were disentangling an exemplar
having scheme 3 (rather than scheme 2 as was argued above), he
would have had to reassign the sermon for Ascension. But by the
time he had got as far as that season he must have been
completely used to consigning the weekday sermons to set 4.
There is no reason why set 3 should have been involved in such an
operation, except possibly at the Christmas season if that
exemplar had the arrangement then that is found in G and H.
But whilst it is certain that A was using a scheme other than 1 for
the production of set 1, it is not provable that he was similarly
disentangling the sermons of set 5, let alone those of set 4.[58]
Whilst most of the other anomalies in ordering can be explained,
usually on liturgical grounds, this seems completely baffling.

(ii) The autumn ember days

In the ecclesiastical year four sets of ember days are prescribed:
all are on Wednesday, Friday and Saturday, and they fall after
(a) the first Sunday in Lent, (b) after Pentecost, (c) after Holy

[57] There is slight evidence from textual details that the two copies in A do not derive from
the same exemplar; this would suggest that the mistake of including the sermon in set 3
arose at a stage before A itself.
[58] This implies that A's exemplar for set 5 was other than that for set 1; for other evidence
pointing to shifts in exemplar see pp. 155, 172–5.

Rood day on 14 September, (*d*) after St. Lucy's day on 13 December. If in the last two cases the governing feast falls on a Wednesday, the ember days are postponed to begin on the following Wednesday.[59] The sermons of set 4 show special provision for the last two of these sets; the first two are covered here by the provision of a sermon for each day in Lent and for each day in the week after Pentecost, and consequently needed no special attention. The last, the ember days in the Advent season, explains why in the third week of Advent there is a sermon for the Saturday; there is no Wednesday sermon in this week in most manuscripts, but a directive points to a sermon on the relevant text in set 3 for the feast of the Annunciation, on which occasion the same gospel was read (G has the actual sermon in both places).[60] The necessary three sermons for the three Ember days are thus provided.

The Lent and Pentecost ember days are fixed only by the liturgical year and, even had the cycle not provided so generously for those seasons, no difficulty could have arisen about the placing of them in set 4. But the Trinity and Advent season days are fixed by occasions determined by calendar. With the Advent days this would not actually affect their incidence in relation to the third Sunday in Advent. The earliest that the Wednesday ember day could fall would be 14 December, in which case Christmas day would fall on a Sunday and the third Sunday in Advent would be 11 December; the latest it could fall would be 20 December when St. Lucy's day was on a Wednesday, in which case Christmas Day would be on a Monday and the third Sunday in Advent would be 17 December. It is therefore not surprising that the rubrics in the manuscripts do not always mention ember days for this particular sequence: they are just *feria 4*, *feria 6* and *sabbato* after 3 Advent, with no explanation of the last.[61] More variation is possible for the incidence of the ember days following Holy Rood day in relation to the liturgical calendar. In calendar date the ember days might begin between 15 September and 21 September. But because of the varying date of Easter and the ensuing variation of all seasons up to the beginning of the next

---

59 For this, and for the ensuing computations, see the charts in C. R. Cheney, *Handbook of Dates* (London, 1945), 84–153.

60 G ff. 6v–7 in the Temporale, ff. 164v–5 in set 3.

61 In fact only G and V give any indication that ember days are in question.

Advent, these dates could fall in any liturgical week from that
after the 12th Sunday after Trinity to that after the 17th Sunday
after Trinity inclusive. The first is uncommon (occurring only if
Easter fell on 25 April), but the other five weeks are common.

In the majority of manuscripts having set 4 the Trinity ember
days were placed at the end of the set, immediately before the
sermons for the seven non-liturgical, occasional feasts. But a
week's gap was left in the normal Trinity ferial provision, to
avoid the waste of having two sermons for the same day. The
same principle is found in liturgical manuscripts, where one week
lacks any provision of gospel or epistle for feria 4. If the gap did
not correspond with the actual incidence of the ember days in a
given year, the lessons (and here the sermons) were moved one
week back or forwards to fit and give complete coverage, and the
ember material put in as appropriate. The gap in manuscripts of
the Sarum use was normally in the week following the 17th
Sunday after Trinity, the latest that the ember days could
occur.[62] But in the majority of manuscripts of the set 4 sermons
the gap is left in the week following the 18th Sunday after Trinity;
the gospel that should occur for feria 4 in that week, Matt. 13: 31–
35, is moved back and appears as for feria 4 after 17th Sunday
after Trinity. G and H actually include the ember day sermons
within their scheme 3 Temporale, instead of putting them at the
end of set 4, and they too have them after the 18th Sunday after
Trinity.[63] Four manuscripts, KTEZ, leave no gap at all;
consequently they have each of the ferial gospel sermons from the
week after 17 Trinity to the end of the season assigned to a week
one ahead of the liturgy.[64] The sole manuscript to agree with the
Sarum liturgy is R.

To say that R is right, and dismiss all the others as mistakes, is
to evade the problem. The error of KTEZ is perfectly
comprehensible: they continued numbering the weeks
mechanically, and their agreement in the error could be
purely coincidental. But why should eleven manuscripts,

[62] See Legg, p. 189, Dickinson, cols. 513–14; the gap is also left, or the ember days placed,
here in all manuscripts of the Sarum rite checked (see above n. 2), in T's table of lessons,
and in the table printed in FM iv. 689.

[63] G keeps the correct number 111 for the first ember day sermon (no. 230 in the
complete cycle).

[64] Because of this error they only provide for feriae in the weeks up to that after 23 Sunday
after Trinity.

ADLQWβIJXGH, all erroneously have the sermon on Matt. 13: 31–5 on feria 4 after 17 Trinity and then (with the exception of X which lacks leaves at this point),[65] provide nothing for feria 4 after 18 Trinity, or in the case of G and H insert the ember sermons at this point? The key to this may lie in the fact that ember days could *not* fall after 18 Trinity. It may be that the displacement was done to make it evident that this set of sermons was intended not for a single, actual year, but as a permanently usable programme. In other words, the eleven manuscripts are 'correct' in the sense of being what the writer originally intended; R has officiously corrected in the light of his knowledge of the liturgy, a correction that would be in line with his learned but irrelevant side-notes.[66]

(iii) The opening of set 4

The majority of the sermons in this cycle open directly with the translation of the text, usually introduced by a few words or at most a couple of sentences to make clear the speaker and context. The first of the sermons in set 4, as this appears in the majority of the manuscripts has an opening paragraph of some length dealing with the value of scripture, and its position as the validator of all earthly law.[67] This preface, whose contents are commonplace in the sermons, has some parallel of form with the first sentence of set 2 and with the opening paragraph (E1/1–7) of the first sermon in set 5. The only difference lies in the greater length of the introduction to set 4. In two manuscripts of set 4, however, the preface is not accepted as part of the sermon proper (number 123). In L set 4 appears at the beginning of the manuscript; a heading to the set has been partially cut away, but the heading to the first sermon does not appear until half way down the first leaf, after Arnold ii. 2/13. The same position for the heading appears in G, but there the preface is less conveniently accommodated. In G the first ferial sermon appears as the third sermon in the manuscript, following those for the epistle and gospel on the first Sunday in Advent (E1 and 26). The preface to set 4 is tacked on to the end of the second sermon without any break, even of a line. The scribe apparently realized that some change of material had occurred, since he wrote in the margin against the line 'þe prolog of þe freris'. There is some disjunction of subject-matter in this placing, since sermon 26 concludes with a diatribe against letters of fraternity, which, though possibly alluded to towards the end of the preface (Arnold ii. 2/1–2), is not its main subject. Nor is the paragraph properly a prologue to the treatment of the friars in the sermons, a subject that has already been introduced even in G's scheme. It seems likely that G must have been working from a copy that, like L, had the paragraph as a separate item and that G, not knowing what to do with it, tacked it on to the preceding sermon rather than, as would have been more sensible, inserting it after the heading for 123. It remains unclear whether L's treatment of the paragraph perpetuates the original arrangement. Such treatment is sensible: the paragraph does represent a prologue to the entire set, rather than to an individual sermon.[68] On the other hand, there is no evidence for similar treatment in any manuscript of the parallel, if briefer, prologues to sets 2 and 5.

F. Homogeneity of the sermon-cycle

The fact that the 294 sermons here edited belong together as a single sermon-cycle should have emerged from the preceding discussion. Though not all manuscripts contain all 294 sermons, those that have a selection of the whole are based upon a comprehensible liturgical pattern for that selection. A significant number of the manuscripts, eleven, contain the whole cycle, or can be assumed to have contained it before the loss of leaves or quires; a further five manuscripts lack only one fifth of it. The existence of three schemes of arrangement, and of other variants, few of which are peculiar to a single manuscript, confirms the idea that we have here to deal with a single preaching tool. The ramifications that have been described suggest that this programme of material was available for copying, along with certain plans for presentation, but that the adoption of a plan was left to individual choice. If a comparison is made with other English

[68] Similar prefatory remarks to sets of sermons are found in Wyclif's Latin sermons; there they appear within the first sermon of the Sanctorale (*Sermones* ii. 1/1–2/8) and of the epistles (*Sermones* iii. 1/4–8), but as a separate item before the Sunday gospel sermons (*Sermones i, Praefatio*). The discrepancy there is, however, logical since the last mentioned is an introduction to all the sermons, not just those for a particular series.

medieval collections of homilies, the striking features of the present assemblage are its organization and its size. Collections of sermons on the majority of the Sunday gospels through the year are not uncommon; equally, it is easy to mention collections, such as the *Speculum Sacerdotale* or that in British Library MS Royal 18 B. xxiii[69] where Sunday gospel sermons are interspersed with a number of sermons for festivals. The nearest analogies to the size of the present collection are the expanded versions of Myrc's homiliary and of the Northern Homily Cycle.[70] The first, however, with ninety items is much smaller, and, even within this smaller scope, differs from the present cycle in presenting more than one sermon on the same text and for the same occasion in some instances, whilst leaving uncovered entirely other occasions of equal importance. The expanded Northern Homily Cycle is a closer parallel, particularly in its inclusion of a large number of sermons for specified ferials. But though the size of the collection is more nearly comparable (though having only 117 items compared with the 294 here), the Northern cycle is far less systematic. The two manuscripts in which the cycle is preserved are arranged as a complete Temporale (i.e as scheme 3 here), but a glance shows the inconsistencies: thus in the period after the octave of the Epiphany there are Sunday sermons for only the first, second, fourth and fifth Sundays, whilst only four ferials are covered, the sixth after the first, second, and fourth Sundays and the fourth after the second Sunday. This sort of irregularity of provision is typical of the Northern Homily Cycle; it is not characteristic of the coverage in the present cycle.[71]

The present collection is also remarkable in that the sermons circulated almost without exception in large, liturgically comprehensible groups, the sets that an earlier section of this chapter described. Individual sermons are not found in isolation, either alone in a manuscript or incorporated into a different sermon

---

[69] See the editions of the first by E. H. Weatherly (EETS 200, 1936), and of the second by W. O. Ross (EETS 209, 1940).

[70] For the first see M. F. Wakelin, 'The Manuscripts of John Mirk's Festial', *Leeds Studies in English NS* i (1967), 93–118; the manuscripts of the expanded version are British Library Harley 2247 and Royal 18 B. xxv (see pp. 100–102). The second is being edited by S. Nevanlinna (*Mémoires de la Société Néophilologique de Helsinki* xxxviii (1972) and xli (1973)).

[71] For a list of the contents see Nevanlinna i. 17–23; the manuscripts are British Library Harley 4196 and Cotton Tiberius E. vii.

cycle. The sole exception to this is a copy of the last sermon of set 3 found at the end of Edinburgh University Library MS 93.[72] In a later chapter will be described certain derivatives from the sermons here edited; these in some instances do show an eclectic selection of material. But they are demonstrably derivatives, and are not for any length of time collatable versions of the texts here edited. They may show something of the influence that the sermon cycle attained, but they reveal nothing about its origins or its early dissemination. Equally the manuscripts of the present cycle do not intrude into the material sermons from other sources, either to duplicate or to extend the provision. The situation is utterly different from that which obtains with Myrc, where on the one hand odd sermons of Myrc's appear in manuscripts of material otherwise unconnected with Myrc, and on the other a lengthy sequence of Myrc sermons may be interrupted by an isolated example from a different background.[73]

Everything in the textual tradition that has so far been discussed points towards a common origin for all 294 sermons, and for their composition in fulfilment of a single coherent scheme. Whether one author was responsible for all 294 sermons is much less important than the clear indication that the plan for the sermons was thought out as a whole, and that the sermons were then composed to fit this plan. If the material here were an assemblage of sermons of diverse origins, then one would expect to find copies of individual sermons scattered over manuscripts, or incorporated into other cycles. Equally, it would appear that no part of the sermon cycle was allowed to circulate until the whole was complete. The implications of this for the dating of the cycle, as well as for its authorship, will be discussed in a later volume. But it may here be noted that the situation textually in the present cycle is utterly different from that revealed by a study of other Lollard works. In texts such as the Latin *Floretum/ Rosarium*, or the Wycliffite revisions of Rolle's Psalter commentary, or, most notoriously, in the Wycliffite Bible, there is evidence for 'publication' at various stages of revision.[74] With

---

[72] For this see pp. 98–9 below.

[73] See manuscripts Harley 2250, Harley 1288, Royal 18 B. xxiii, Douce 60, Hatton 96, Cambridge University Library Ff. 2. 38 as described by Wakelin (above n. 70).

[74] For the first see C. von Nolcken, *The Middle English Translation of the Rosarium Theologie* (Heidelberg, 1979), pp. 28–9; for the second D. Everett, 'The Middle English Prose Psalter of Richard Rolle of Hampole', *MLR* xvii (1922), 217–27, 337–50, xviii (1923),

the sermon cycle a complete and fixed body of material was prepared before 'publication' was allowed to begin; neither addition to, nor subtraction from that fixed body was allowed.

The question does, however, arise of whether, granted that the 294 sermons belong together as a unit, there are any other texts that should be added as intended by the original plan. The reason for this question is that there is a small group of texts other than the sermons that occur with considerable frequency in the same manuscripts as the sermons. It should be stressed that the evidence to answer this question is entirely that of manuscript location; there is no internal reference within the sermons to other works of a specificity sufficient to allow identification with any other text; conversely, with one possible exception, none of the works to be discussed refers to the sermons. But, given the evidence of planning that the sermon manuscripts have shown, their recurrent inclusion of certain works may indicate association.

There are seven manuscripts, BEFHLPV, and the three groups of fragments, E[s] H[t] P[t], that contain nothing but the sermons. Two manuscripts, O and Z, contain various orthodox writings; there is no overlap between those in O and those in Z. A number of Wycliffite texts are found in some of the manuscripts, but since these texts are only evidenced by one manuscript of the sermons, albeit in many cases also elsewhere, there is no reason to associate them with the sermons in original intention.[75] Two manuscripts, Q and R, contain a Lollard text, headed in the latter 'Pardoun', dealing with pardons, indulgences and their vendors; the text is of a kind familiar in Lollard literature, arguing against the orthodox position on a single issue. There is no similarity of structure with the sermon cycle, and insufficient reason to regard the text as part of it.

A more difficult case is that of an extra sermon provided in three manuscripts, M, T, and Y. The sermon is on John 10:1 *Qui non intrat per ostium*, and deals with simony and the way in which the 'four sects' are defiled by it; the vocabulary is full of Lollard

---

381–93; for the third most usefully H. Hargreaves in *The Cambridge History of the Bible* ii, ed. G. W. H. Lampe, (Cambridge, 1969), 387–415 and the same author's paper 'Popularising Biblical Scholarship: the Role of the Wycliffite *Glossed Gospels*' in *The Bible and Medieval Culture*, ed. W. Lourdaux and D. Verhelst (Louvain, 1979), pp. 171–89.
[75] For details of all of these see the descriptions of the relevant manuscripts below.

elements, and almost every phrase could be paralleled from other texts. The lection from John is the same as that used, with the introductory *Amen, amen dico vobis*, for feria 3 of the week following Pentecost (no. 201). In T this sermon is added immediately after no. 201 with the heading *Sermo de eodem*. Neither M nor Y contains set 4, and they have the sermon as a separate item: M includes it after set 5 with the correct indication of its occasion, Y has it also after set 5 but with the faulty rubric *Sermo in feria quarta Pentecostes ad processionem*. The only available internal information does not support the idea that this is an extra member of the sermon cycle: unlike the overwhelming majority of the sermons, this does not translate the whole of the lection in its course—only the opening words are directly translated, and a rough paraphrase given of selected phrases from the remainder. The polemical concern here is paramount, and a single issue dominates the whole. It seems likely that the text is not in origin a sermon but a tract (like that on pardons discussed above), which happened to open with a biblical text of obvious relevance. At some point the proximity of this text to the opening of a ferial sermon was noted, and the occasion wrongly added; because of this it was attracted into association with the cycle. But its claim to be considered a part of that cycle is weakened by the fact that two out of its three attesting manuscripts lack the set to which it should have belonged. It may therefore be rejected from the cycle.[76]

Two further texts, though included in each case by four manuscripts of the sermons, have few claims to be considered part of the cycle. The first of these is a short piece on the Eucharist, found in ADTβ, and in a single other manuscript, Trinity College Dublin 244; Matthew printed it from A with collation from the Trinity manuscript under the title *De Sacramento Altaris*.[77] Whilst the sentiments of this piece are those that can be found repeatedly in the sermons, its form is quite other than any of the sermons; it lacks any text or occasion. Its position in the four manuscripts is not constant, so that it cannot be regarded as an appendix to any item. The other tract is a much longer work, found in ADGβ, and elsewhere in Trinity College Dublin MS

---

[76] Since, however, it is brief and has not hitherto been printed, it will be edited as an appendix to set 4 in volume iii of the present edition.
[77] Matthew pp. 356–8.

245; it was printed by Arnold in volume iii of his edition under the title *The Church and her Members*.[78] The rubric in A describes it as *a tretice*, and this is correct; there is no text or occasion specified. Again there is no constant position in the four manuscripts in relation to the sermon cycle. The subject matter shares much with the cycle, and also with the second of the remaining texts to be discussed.

The most difficult cases are two texts that Arnold printed at the end of his second volume of the sermons. They are expositions of chapters 23 and 24 of Matthew, and have in some manuscripts the titles *Vae Octuplex* and *Of Mynystris in þe chirche*. The first is found in twelve manuscripts of the sermons, ACDGJMTXYZαβ and two others, St. John's College Cambridge G.25 and Trinity College Dublin 245; the second is in fourteen manuscripts of the sermons, ADGIJKMRTWXZαβ, and three others, the same two as the last plus BL Harley 1203. Both of these texts share with the sermons the translation of the entire biblical passages on which they are based, and the passages are to some extent in each spread through the whole. Both differ from the sermons in that no occasion is anywhere assigned for them. The second begins on the same text as sermon 73 in set 2, but whilst 73 (following the liturgy for its occasion) only deals with a few verses, this covers the entire chapter. But both have some claim to be regarded as sermons. Whilst there is not complete unanimity in the placing of these two long sermons, some possibly significant points emerge. *Vae Octuplex* does not have any very firm position: five manuscripts, ACDMY, place it after set 1 and a sixth, Z, places it after its combination of sets 5 plus 1. M seems to have felt that it belonged closely with set 1 since his rubric *Explicit prima pars euangeliorum* appears after *Vae Octuplex* rather than after no. 54, which immediately precedes it. In nine of the fourteen manuscripts in which it is attested *Of Mynystris* appears after set 3 (ADGIKMWXZ). Two scribes, those of A and G, regarded the work as part of set 3; this is evident from the fact that the explicit to that set appears after this text and not at the end of the sermons of set 3 proper. Similarly in K the running title *pars II* of sets 2 and 3 continues at the head of the leaves containing *Of Mynystris*. In T the work fills a unit of a quire plus single added leaf, and its position after set 4 may be the work of the binder only.

Both of these texts are related to works by Wyclif himself, and printed in his *Opera Minora*. The first two thirds of *Vae Octuplex* takes some of its ideas from chapters vii to xiii of the *Exposicio textus Matthei xxiii*, also called in some of the manuscripts *De Vae Octuplici*;[79] the last third, part of which deals with the Eucharist, is independent. Similarly, just over the first half of *Mynystris in þe chirche* uses some of the points from *Exposicio textus Matthei xxiv*; but the latter part goes on from the exposition of the biblical text for a much longer argument than is found in Wyclif's Latin text.[80] The dependence upon Wyclif is, in fact, irrelevant to whether the two English sermons belong to the present cycle; several sermons of the cycle draw ideas from Wyclif's Latin writings, both from his sermons and other compositions. But the similarity between these two works' development of their Latin source suggests that they should be taken as a pair. If one can be shown to belong with the sermon cycle, then the other should be accepted along with it.

From the internal subject matter, there is better evidence to connect the longer *Mynystris in þe chirche* with the cycle than is the case with *Vae Octuplex*. The longer text opens 'This gospel telluþ muche wysdam þat is hud to monye men, and specially for þis cause þat it is not al rad in þe chyrche. But siþen it is of euene auctorite wiþ oþre gospelis of Crist, and of hud sentence of God þat were profiȝtable to þe chyrche, somme men wolden seyn hit in her modyr language as þei cunnen'. This does not necessitate association with the cycle, but the second sentence seems at the least to imply knowledge of expositions of those gospels that are liturgically used.

Taking all the evidence together it would seem that there is reason to associate these two pieces very closely with the sermon cycle. The case is not overwhelming. But it would seem that if any texts are to be linked it must be these two. Consequently, they will be included in the present edition. *Of Mynystris in þe chirche* will be placed at the end of set 3, where the majority of scribes apparently felt it to belong; *Vae Octuplex*, which had a less fixed position, will follow it.

---

[79] *Opera Minora* 333–50; the text was edited from G in *Selections* no. 15, and the section independent of Wyclif begins there at line 228.

[80] *Opera Minora* 354–82; in Arnold's edition, ii. 393–423, the point at which the English text departs finally from the Latin is 409/5.

II

The Manuscripts

A description is given here of all 31 manuscripts in which the sermons of the cycle appear, even if (as is the case with two) they do not contain any of the texts in the present volume. Arnold knew 19 manuscripts, to which he allotted arbitrarily the sigla A–S; these sigla have been retained here and have been supplemented for the more recently discovered manuscripts by the sigla, equally arbitrarily assigned, of T, V–Z, α, β, and δ, and for the fragments of E^s, H^t, and P^t. The manuscripts are described in alphabetical order of sigel, with those with Greek sigla after the first sequence and the fragments last.

The descriptions are not intended as full codicological or palaeographical accounts of the manuscripts; such descriptions are beyond my competence and are not relevant to the present edition. Particular attention has been paid to three matters. First the accurate description of the contents of each manuscript, and secondly any signs that a manuscript may have of the way in which its order was planned; the reasons for these have been explained in the preceding chapter. Thirdly an account is given of the processes of correction visible in each manuscript; the significance of this will be explained in chapter IV. So far as is possible I have used as a model for the details (though not for the order in which they are given) the method described by Dr Neil Ker, *Medieval Manuscripts in British Libraries* i (Oxford, 1969), vii-xiii. For the characterization of the hands of the various scribes I am much indebted to Dr Ian Doyle and, particularly with α and β, to Dr Neil Ker.

The ownership of almost all of the manuscripts in the medieval period is unknown; I have given below the details that are available in each case. To trace the post-medieval history of 31 manuscripts would be a lengthy, and often unrewarding, search; the accounts below could doubtless be amplified.

A: MS Bodley 788   s. xv in.

260 parchment leaves, size 270 mm by 190 mm, written frame
193 mm by 182 mm. Collation: ii paper flyleaves, i stub, ii
parchment flyleaves, i⁶ (ff. v–x), 1–13⁸, 14⁸ plus 1 extra leaf after
8, 15–30⁸, 31⁸ lacks 6–8, ii parchment flyleaves, ii paper
flyleaves. In quire 22 leaves 3 and 6 are not conjugate but are
only stuck together; leaf 3 has been substituted for the original
leaf, and is written entirely by the corrector, a substitution,
judging by the compression of the hand, necessitated because the
original copyist had omitted some material. The remains of at
least two sets of medieval quire signatures are visible, but both
sets are confused and can never have been correct; catchwords
remain. The correct foliation is that in pencil, ff. i–x, 1–250.
Written in two columns.[1]

1. ff. v–x, calendar (not relating to provision of sermons that follow).
2. ff. 1–45ᵛ, Set 1 beginning at 1 Trinity; headed *Here bigynnen þe
   Sonedai gospelis expowned in partie.*
3. ff. 45ᵛ–48ᵛ,[*Vae Octuplex*] headed *Þe exposicioun of þe text of Matheu þe
   þre and twentiþe capitle of eiȝte siþis woo seid to þe scribis and pharisees
   ipocritis.*
4. ff. 48ᵛ–49, *De Sacramento altaris corporis domini*; text printed from this
   manuscript Matthew 357–8.
5. ff. 49–87, Set 2; headed *Here bigynneþ þe comoun sanctorum þe secunde
   part of þis book.*
6. ff. 87–119ᵛ, Set 3; at head of column *þe propre sainctorum* (sic).
7. ff. 119ᵛ–129, *Exposicioun of Matheu xxiiii⁰ c⁰ of mynystris in þe chirche
   sermo*; at end *here enden þe sermons on þe gospels of þe propre sanctorum.*
8. ff. 129–189, Set 4; headed, straight on from the previous item, *and
   bigynneþ þe þridde part þat is þe sermons on þe ferial gospels*; at end *Here
   enden þe ferial gospels of al þe ȝeer wiþ commemoraciouns.*
9. ff. 189–237, Set 5; headed, straight on from previous, *and bigynnen þe
   Sonedai pistlis.*
10. ff. 237–245ᵛ, [*De Ecclesia et membris suis*], headed *Here bigynneþ a
    tretice þat telliþ knowleche sumwhat of þe chirche and hir membris*; text
    printed from this manuscript Arnold iii. 338–65.
11. f. 246, two short devotional pieces.

Items 1 and 11 were not part of the original manuscript. Apart
from these two, the follow-on of items shows the manuscript must
have always had the present arrangement. The irregularity in
quire 14 does not coincide with a gap or the end of a set (f. 113).

[1] *Summary Catalogue* no. 2628.

Items 2–10 are all in a single text hand of the beginning of the fifteenth century. The whole manuscript has been carefully corrected by a hand very slightly different from the main scribe; these corrections are usually over a very effective erasure, and in short passages are not always easy to recognize. The whole of f. 172 is written by the corrector. The chief difference between the hands of the scribe and corrector is an extension of the cross bar of *e* in the latter. To judge by the letter forms, the corrector was also the rubricator. There are some original marginal notae and numbers, and a little later annotation of subject-matter, chiefly at the end of the manuscript. The initial of the Latin text is in blue with red flourishing; the initial on f.1 is slightly larger. The occasion and text reference are in red, followed by the Latin text in ordinary ink, underlined and touched in red; the translation of the biblical text is underlined throughout in red. The binding is post-medieval.

There are no signs of medieval ownership. The manuscript appears to have been acquired by the Bodleian Library some time between 1615 and 1620.

B: Cambridge University Library MS Ii. 1.40   s. xiv/xv

212 parchment leaves, size 222 mm by 150 mm, written frame 148 mm by 105 mm. Collation: iv paper flyleaves, i parchment flyleaf, $1-13^8$, 14^2 lacks 2, $15-27^8$, 28^6 lacks 3–5, i paper flyleaf. Medieval quire signatures a–e are visible on quires 1–5, s–x on quires 10–13. The manuscript is foliated from the second initial flyleaf onwards, but in the numbering 8–10, 116, 223–5 and 228 were not used. Catchwords remain. Written in two columns.[2]

1. ff. 11–115 (quires 1–14), Set 5 headed *Here suen þe Sondai pistlis þorouȝ þe ȝeer bigynnyng at Aduent.*
2. ff. 117–222 (quires 15–28), Set 1 beginning at 1 Trinity.
3. f. 222 ʳ⁻ᵛ, Latin note inc. *Augustinus dignitate sacerdotum sic loquitur o ueneranda sacerdotum dignitas . . .* expl. *intinguntur sanguine Christi poluantur sanguine peccati amen.*

The first two items are independent of each other and could be reordered, though the border around f. 11 is slightly more elaborate than that on f. 117.

---

[2] *A Catalogue of the Manuscripts preserved in the Library of the University of Cambridge* (Cambridge, 1856–67), iii. 369.

Two hands appear in the manuscript, the second beginning at f. 51; both are good text hands of the turn of the fourteenth and fifteenth centuries. There is some correction, usually over erasure, in both parts apparently by the original scribes. In item 1 there are a few marginal biblical references supplied by the scribe; otherwise there are virtually no marginalia. The initial of the English text at the start of item 1 and of the Latin text in item 2 is elaborately decorated and the ornamentation extended around the borders; the style of the borders, with the use of blue, red, gold, and white, is described by Dr Scott as c. 1395–1405 and probably not of metropolitan origin. Gold initials with blue and red backgrounds are found at some of the major festivals. Otherwise the initial of the Latin text is in blue with red flourishing, the occasion is in red, the Latin text and reference and the biblical translation throughout underlined in red. Blue paraph marks occur in the text to f. 50^v only (the end of hand 1). Scribble guides to the rubricator for the occasion are visible in the part written by hand 2 only, after f. 51. The binding is post-medieval. The hand of item 3 is medieval; it is probably not that of either of the two main scribes, though some attempt has been made to imitate the second.

There are no marks of medieval ownership. On f. 226^v in a sixteenth-century hand is the inscription 'iste liber pertinet ad me Thomam Treves'; an erased inscription on f. 155^v appears to have been the same. Below this name appear other names in a dif-ferent, though contemporary, hand; one is 'John ap Gryffythe'. On f. 227 is the name Sir James Clare, and the date 1628.

C: Bodleian Library MS Laud Misc. 314   s. xv[1]

158 parchment leaves, size 186 mm by 122 mm, written space 116 mm by 72 mm. Collation: i–iv^4 leaf 3 cut away, 1–19^8, i–iv leaf 3 cut away. Medieval quire signatures a–t appear on quires 1–19, but no catchwords remain. The manuscript is foliated i–iii, 1–155. The writing is in a single column[3].

1. ff. 1–143, Set 1 beginning at 1 Trinity.
2. ff. 143–152^v, [*Vae Octuplex*] headed *Exposicio textus Mathei xxiii capitulo Ue ve octiplici scribis phariseis et ypocritis imprecato*.

---

[3] *Bodleian Library Quarto Catalogues II Laudian Manuscripts*, H. O. Coxe revised R. W. Hunt (Oxford, 1973), pp. 246, 556.

There is no evidence that the manuscript was ever intended to contain more than it now does; any substantial addition would be unlikely given the already stout nature of the small volume.

The single hand is a 'good regular fere-textura . . . first half of the 15th century' (Doyle). The manuscript has been corrected throughout in a hand of different style from that of the original writing; these corrections are written informally in the margin, and may have been intended for more formal incorporation which was not done. The initial of the English text is in blue with red flourishing; the Sunday, text, and biblical reference stand in red immediately above the beginning of the sermon. The English translation of the biblical text is underlined in red throughout, and the start of each bit of translation is signalled by a blue paraph mark. The parchment is of very thick quality, though ff. 57ᵛ–64 are marked by having had something spilt on them; the binding is medieval.

On ff. 154ᵛ–155 appear in sixteenth-century hands the names of 'Robinsonus, Thomas Pepys, Hughe Casson rector [of] Harthill'. Before coming into the possession of Archbishop Laud, the manuscript belonged to John Leigh.

D: British Museum MS Additional 40672   s. xiv/xv

255 parchment leaves, size 355 mm by 243 mm, written frame 255 mm by 170 mm. Collation: ii paper flyleaves, 1–6⁸, 7⁶, 8–24⁸, 25⁶, 26–32⁸, 33⁴ lacks 4, ii paper flyleaves. Catchwords are still visible; quire signatures remain on quires 2–4 b–d, 6–7 f–g, 12 e, 18–19 l–m, 20–22 a–c, 27 g. The manuscript must originally have had even wider margins than now, since the pricking on some leaves has been cropped. Written in two columns.[4]

1. ff. 1–54ᵛ (end quire 7), Set 5. Text completed, with some compression and two more lines than usual, at foot of col. 2 of f. 54ᵛ *Expliciunt epistole dominicales per annum.*
2. ff. 102ᵛ, Set 1 beginning at 1 Trinity. At end *Expliciunt euuangelia dominicalia.*
3. ff. 102ᵛ–106ᵛ, [*Vae Octuplex*] headed *Exposicio textus mathei xxiiiⁱᵒ capitulo de ue octuplici scribis phariseis et ipocritis inprecato.*

---

[4] *British Museum Catalogue of Additions to the Manuscripts 1921–1925,* (London, 1950), pp. 117–18.

4. ff. 106^v–107, *De Sacramento contra fratres*; text printed Matthew 357–8, without notice of this manuscript.

5. ff. 107–150^v, Set 2; headed *Comune sanctorum incipit 2^a pars*; at end *Explicit comune sanctorum*.

6. ff. 150^v–185, Set 3; headed *Incipit comune (canc) sanctorum*.

7. ff. 185–196, [*Of mynystris in þe chirche*] headed *Egressus Iesus de templo Mathei 24 Exposicio textus*. Text ends 15 lines down col. 2 of f. 196^r, f. 196^v blank.

8. ff. 197–247^v (begins quire 26), Set 4; headed *3^a pars euangeliorum ferialium*; at end *Here enden þe gospelis*.

9. ff. 247^v–255, *De Ecclesia et membris eius*; text printed Arnold iii. 338–65.

Items 2–7, involving the sequence of sets 1–2–3 with the intervening material, cannot be altered; the explicit to item 8, in the hand of the main scribe of that part, implies that set 4 was designed to follow this sequence. Set 5 was written as a separate item, but its position was apparently determined before the opening initial was flourished.

Three hands can be distinguished: the first on ff. 1–32^v (end quire 4) and ff. 55–196, the second on ff. 33–54^v (quires 5–7), and the third on ff. 197–255 (quires 26–33). The appearance of the third hand varies considerably, from a very distinctive and mannered angular script to one more like hand 1. All are text hands with some modifications, of the end of the fourteenth, or possibly the beginning of the fifteenth, century. All parts of the manuscript have been carefully corrected by a number of contemporary hands, not those of any of the scribes. There are a few marginal references to biblical texts, all by the scribe of the accompanying text. There are almost no later marginalia. The ornamentation of the manuscript was done by two workers, one on ff. 1–54^v and 152^v–255 and the second on ff. 55–150^v. The difference is visible from the colour of the inks used and the style of ornament. Translation of the sermon's text is underlined in red throughout. Notes to the rubricator are sometimes still visible in the margins.

There is no trace of medieval ownership. At the foot of f. 1 appears the inscription *1566 Franciscus Comes Bedfordie*; an identical inscription appears at the top of f. 1 of L. These two manuscripts, together with J, were when Arnold used them part of the collection of the Grey family at Wrest Park in

Northamptonshire.[5] The Grey family had owned the three since at least 1697 when they were described as in their library by Bernard.[6] All three appear to have been purchased at the sale in 1687 of the Burghley library; the ownership of the manuscripts at the time of the sale is obscure, but the catalogue states that the library had been put together by William Cecil, Lord Burghley (c. 1520–98), chancellor of Elizabeth I.[7] Since Cecil outlived Francis Russell, second Earl of Bedford (c. 1527–85), it is evident that D and L must have passed from the latter to the former. Mr Laurence Witten, through whose hands J passed before it came to its present owner, suggested that Russell also owned J and that the upper margin of f. 5 that has been cut away contained his signature.[8] At the sale of the Wrest Park manuscripts in 1922 all three manuscripts were purchased by Quaritch, D and L going to the British Museum but J to the collection of Sir Leicester Harmsworth.[9]

E: Bodleian Library MS Douce 321   s. xiv/xv

252 parchment leaves, size 275 mm by 194 mm, written frame 225 mm by 145 mm. Collation: ii paper flyleaves, 1–7^8, 8^{10} lacks 1 (nothing lost), 9^8 lacks 4–5, 10–13^8, 14^8 lacks 1 (nothing lost), 15–26^8, 27^6, 28–30^8, 31^{10} lacks 5 and 7, 32^8, vii paper flyleaves. The contents show that quires have been lost at the beginning and after quire 2. Quire 31 was originally intended as a normal quire of 8, but for some reason the original fifth leaf was cut out and another leaf inserted; the stub of the old fifth leaf appears before the new fifth leaf, whose stub in turn appears before the

5 See Appendix to *Second Report of the Royal Commission on Historical Manuscripts* (London, 1871), pp. 4–9; D is no. 11, J no. 32, L no. 38.

6 *Catalogi librorum manuscriptorum Angliae et Hiberniae* (Oxford, 1697), ii. 391–2.

7 *Bibliotheca Illustris sive Catalogus Variorum Librorum* (London, 1687), p. 88 items 9–11; neither the descriptions nor the prices recorded in the British Library copy of the book are altogether clear, but it would appear that L was item 9 (fetching £7. 2s. 6d.), D item 10 and J item 11 (together fetching £10. 2s. 6d.). See W. Y. Fletcher, *English Book Collectors* (London, 1902), pp. 40–1.

8 Typewritten description and account of J kept with the manuscript in Mr. Taylor's Library. If the conjecture is right, the position of the signature on f. 5, rather than f. 1, must have been necessitated by the state of the first four folios, since (as will be described below p. 84) these leaves must have belonged to the rest of the manuscript from the medieval period.

9 Sotheby's sale 19 June 1922; J was item 641 (£78), L item 642 (£70), and D item 643 (£130).

sixth leaf; the two defective bifolia have both been stitched into the centre of the quire. Catchwords are still visible, but the only two remaining quire signatures are c on quire 11 and h on quire 16; all margins have been cropped. Parts of the manuscript have been affected by damp, and letters on some leaves have been retraced in darker ink; this, however, never leaves any doubt about the original reading. Written in two columns[10].

1. ff. 1–65^v (end quire 8), Set 5 plus set 1 in scheme 2 beginning at 1 Trinity. Begins incomplete 14/63–*ful men crie mekely*; gap from 21/41 *þat bitokeneþ galilee þat* to 38/57 *is vndisposid*. Set ends after 54 *Expliciunt tam epistole quam Euangelia Dominicalia secundum exposicionem Doctoris euuangelii.*
2. ff. 66–110^v (end quire 14), Set 3.
3. ff. 111–166^v (end quire 21), Set 2; headed *Incipit secunda pars comune sanctorum*; at end *Expliciunt Euangelia commune sanctorum.*
4. ff. 167–252^v, Set 4; headed *Hic incipiunt euangelia ferialia*; at end *Expliciunt euangelia ferialia.*

The four items could have been arranged in any order; the loss of quires at the beginning precludes any judgement of the ornamentation in scale.

The whole is in a single 'ungainly but well-formed and practised near text hand with some cursive touches' (Doyle). The original scribe corrected the text after it was written both in the margin and above the line, following marks in the margin that often remain. The rubricator also crossed through some words, following a guide in ordinary ink. Apart from some modern corrections to the biblical references at the head of the sermons, there are few later notes nor any corrections by anyone other than the scribe. The initial of the Latin text is in blue with red flourishing, the occasion in or underlined in red and the text and biblical reference in ordinary ink; the translation of the sermon's text is usually underlined in red; there are blue and red paraph marks.

There are no marks of medieval ownership. On ff. 255–8 (paper flyleaves) is an index to the sermons of the manuscript in an early eighteenth-century hand; the manuscript was obviously by then defective as it now stands. The manuscript came into the Bodleian Library from the collection of Francis Douce in 1834.

[10] *Summary Catalogue* no. 21895.

F: Bodleian Library MS Additional A. 105   s.xiv/xv

94 parchment leaves, size 230 mm by 150 mm, written frame 160 mm by 100 mm. Collation: i–iv⁴ leaves 2–4 cut out and 1 much mutilated, 1–11⁸, 12⁸ leaves 5–7 cut away. Medieval quire signatures a–k appear on quires 1–10. The foliation begins quire 1 with f. 2. Catchwords are regularly visible. Written in two columns.[11]

1. ff. 2–93 (leaf 4 quire 12), Set 1 beginning at 1 Advent.

There is no evidence that the manuscript was ever intended to contain more.

The single hand is an English text hand of the end of the fourteenth or early fifteenth century. The scribe himself corrected the manuscript, following marks that are still visible on many folios (e.g. ff. 29ᵛ, 30, 50ᵛ). There are a few later corrections or alterations (e.g. f. 41ᵛ). The initial of the Latin text is in blue with red flourishing; the occasion and biblical reference are in red, the opening text and the biblical translation is underlined in red save where the rubricator missed the original scribe's guide lines. Some capitals in the text are touched in red. The inner portion of all folios is badly puckered by stitching that was done too tightly or has shrunk. The binding is medieval.

On f. 93ᵛ there is a note, now partially illegible, in a fifteenth-century hand concerning excommunication and its meaning; there is no expression of Lollard condemnation for the practice. On f. 1ᵛ there appears the inscription, in a mid sixteenth-century hand 'peple of warwick men(?) M[r] hoys Richards merser William Risseton Thomas bradforth George tirvell Thomas attirby', and on f. 1, possibly in the same hand, 'The boke of antiquity speakyng agaynst all poperye'. The manuscript came into the Bodleian Library by purchase from Colonel J. S. North on 18 January 1871.

G: British Library MS Royal 18 B. ix   s. xv in.

196 parchment leaves, size 283 mm by 195 mm, written frame 205 mm by 141 mm. Collation: ii paper flyleaves, i parchment flyleaf, 1–24⁸, 25⁴, i parchment flyleaf, ii paper flyleaves. Medieval quire signatures a–z (omitting i, u, w) are visible on

---

[11] *Summary Catalogue* no. 29002.

quires 1–23; quire 24 is marked i. Catchwords remain. The manuscript is written in two columns.[12]

1. ff. 1–126, Set 5 plus set 1 plus set 4 in scheme 3 beginning at 1 Advent; omits the seven occasional sermons that in other manuscripts conclude set 4. Headed f. 1 *Here bigynneþ þe firste sonedai pistil of aduent*.
2. ff. 126–157ᵛ, Set 2; headed *Incipit 2ᵃ pars comune sanctorum Euangelia*; at end *Here is eendid þe comune sanctorum*.
3. ff. 157ᵛ–177, Set 3; headed, straight on from previous, *and now bigynneþ þe propre*.
4. ff. 177–185, [*Of mynystris in þe chirche*] headed *Exposicio euangelii Mathei 24⁰*; explicit *Here eenden þe gospels of propre sanctorum*.
5. ff. 185–191ᵛ, *Se now of þe chirche of Crist and of hir membris and of hir gouernaunce*; text as Arnold iii. 338–65.
6. ff. 191ᵛ–194ᵛ, [*Vae Octuplex*], headed *Ve vobis scribe et pharisei ipocrite Mathei xxiii*.
7. ff. 194ᵛ–195ᵛ, sermon E6 omitted in its proper place on f. 14ᵛ (see above p. 25).

The items can never have been intended to be in any order other than they now are.

The whole manuscript is written in a single text hand, with some influence of secretary script in individual letter forms, of the first quarter of the fifteenth century. The text has been carefully corrected throughout by the original scribe, and the note 'cor' appears at the foot of the verso of the last leaf in many quires. There are a few marginal headings and notes by the original scribe. An elaborate initial appears at the beginning of items 1, 2, and 3 in gold, with red and blue background, and with early fifteenth-century decoration in these three colours round the page involving spoon and kidney ornamentation. The normal initial for a sermon is that of the English text, in blue with red flourishing; the occasion and biblical reference are in red, the Latin text in ordinary ink underlined in red; the translation of the biblical text is underlined in red. The top and bottom of some of the leaves has been strengthened by the pasting over them of muslin. Binding is modern.

The manuscript is the only one in which clear marks of medieval ownership are preserved. On f. 196ᵛ appears a copy of the licence given by William Lynn, prior of the Dominican

[12] G. F. Warner and J. P. Gilson, *Catalogue of Western Manuscripts in the Old Royal and King's Collections* (London, 1921), ii. 291.

convent of Dunstable, to Thomas Dekyn of the same house to preach in the area of Cambridge, Thetford, and Norwich. Dekyn wrote his name, in varyingly complete and disguised forms, on ff. 114, 184ᵛ and 187ᵛ. On f. 196 appears the inscription 'Iste lyber constat Iohannes [*sic*] Dekyn'; also on f. 196ᵛ appears the name of 'frater Sigerus Byrd'. Dekyn, if he read the volume, appears to have left no trace in it of his reactions to its contents. The manuscript was in the royal collection by 1666, when it appears in the catalogue on f. 12ᵛ.

H: St. John's College, Cambridge, MS C. 8 s. xv[1]

207 parchment leaves, size 300 mm by 200 mm, written frame 216 mm by 138 mm. Collation: ii paper flyleaves, 1–11⁸, 12⁸ lacks 4–5, 13–18⁸, 19⁸ lacks 3–6, 20–22⁸, 23⁸ lacks 8, 24⁸, 25⁸ lacks 1, 26⁸ lacks 1; 27⁸, ii paper flyleaves. Medieval quire signatures c–m are visible on quires 2–11, o–p on 12–13, s on 16, x–y on 17–18, aa–bb on 21–2, dd–ff on 24–6, ii on 27. As this implies, a quire has been lost at the beginning, a second between 11 and 12 (after f. 88), three between 16 and 17 (after f. 126); nothing seems to be missing between 26 and 27; at least one quire is lost at the end. Catchwords are still visible. Written in two columns.[13]

1. ff. 1–155ᵛ, Set 5 plus set 1 plus set 4 in scheme 3, originally beginning at 1 Advent; begins incomplete f. 1, of which only the bottom inner quarter survives, the rest having been cut away, E3/26 *him in trewpe*; ends with the seven occasional sermons that conclude set 4. For the losses due to excision of leaves and quires see notes to text.
2. ff. 155ᵛ–177ᵛ, Set 3; ends incomplete due to loss of leaf 8 of quire 23 in sermon 123, Arnold i. 410/2 *in heuene bi blisse of þe le-*.
3. ff. 178–207ᵛ, Set 2; begins incomplete due to the same loss in sermon 55, Arnold i. 166/16 *in þis vyne and þus*; ends incomplete in sermon 82, Arnold i. 276/6 *whan Crist takeþ a soule*.

The surviving items cannot have been arranged in any other way, though it is possible that further items might have concluded the manuscript (cf the position of other texts in G).

The manuscript is written throughout by scribes using an anglicana formata of the early fifteenth century. How many

---

[13] M. R. James, *A Descriptive Catalogue of the Manuscripts in the Library of St. John's College, Cambridge* (Cambridge, 1913), pp. 75–6, no. 58.

scribes were at work seems uncertain: there are certainly changes of hand at the beginning of ff. 193 and 200, but in the early part it is difficult to pinpoint the shifts (if any). Correction has been made throughout the manuscript, following the marks in plummet that are still visible in many places; there is some indication that these plummet corrections were themselves checked before incorporation. The correction was largely incorporated by the scribe of the section in question, but corrections by another similar hand appear occasionally (e.g. ff. 40ᵛ, 88ᵛ); in the work of the final scribe a hand similar to that of the beginning of the manuscript appears as corrector on ff. 200ᵛ, 202, 207. The main initial throughout is that of the Latin text, in blue with red flourishing; the occasion and biblical reference are in red, the Latin text and the biblical translation throughout are underlined in red. Near the beginning of the manuscript a few letters are touched in red. The binding is post-medieval.

The only sign of medieval ownership is the name John Escryke in scribbling on ff. 178, 180; the hand is late fifteenth or early sixteenth-century. The name Thomas Mygers (?) appears on f. 145 in a sixteenth-century scribble. The bookplate records that the manuscript was given to St. John's College by Thomas Earl of Southampton in 1635 (his initials appear on f. 1), and that he had obtained it from the library of William Crashawe.[14]

I: British Library MS Cotton Claudius D. viii   s. xv in.

Two manuscripts of discrepant origin have been bound together; the following description refers to the second, ff. 109–310, only. 200 parchment leaves, size 325 mm by 215 mm, written frame 247 mm by 155 mm. Collation: 1–10⁸, 11⁶, 12–25⁸, 26⁴. The correct foliation is that in pencil at the foot of each recto. Catchwords remain, but no quire signatures or marks of pricking. Written in two columns.[15]

   1. ff. 109–191ᵛ, Set 5 plus set 1 in scheme 2 beginning at 1 Advent. Begins incomplete E5/5 *ben to speke*. (The later note that two folios

14 See P. J. Wallis, *William Crashawe, the Sheffield Puritan* (Newcastle-upon-Tyne 1963) and 'The Library of William Crashawe', *Transactions of the Cambridge Bibliographical Society* II. iii (1956), 213–28; for another Lollard manuscript owned by Crashawe see my paper 'A Lollard Quaternion', *RES* NS xxii (1971), 435–42.
15 *A Catalogue of the Manuscripts in the Cottonian Library* (London, 1802), p. 197.

are missing underestimates the loss; one quire of eight is more likely.)

2. ff. 192–246^v, Set 4; headed *Tercia pars euangeliorum ferialium*.

3. ff. 246^v–273^v, Set 3.

4. ff. 273^v–281, [*Of mynystris in þe chirche*], headed *Exposicio euangelii Egressus Iesus de templo Mt. 24⁰*.

5. ff. 281^v–310^v, Set 2; headed *Incipit 2^a pars Comune sanctorum*; ends incomplete in sermon 85, Arnold i. 291/8 *moche of charite*. It is uncertain whether a final leaf (which could have contained the remaining material of the set) is missing, or whether the scribe broke off his work at that point: *of charite* stands on the last line of col. 2 of f. 310^v, but the rest of the line is blank.

The items can never have been in any order other than that in which they now stand.

The whole is in a single idiosyncratic 'near text hand with many vestigial cursive traits' (Doyle) of the first quarter of the fifteenth century. Notes for correction were made by another hand, but these were never properly filled in; there is also some correction by the rubricator (e.g. f. 157^v). There is a considerable amount of marginal annotation. The most interesting is a series of comments on the material of the sermons in a fifteenth-century hand; the author was apparently familiar with Lollard doctrine (e.g. f. 231^v on sermon 196 'a noble lesson and a curious it passith comune loller' witt' and f. 241^v on sermon 224 'here is no lollardye') but was not a sympathizer with the movement (e.g. f. 126 against sermon 38 'a corious lessun as me semeth alwey wiþ a protestacion þat I loue no lollardye'), though he admitted the value of some of the material (e.g. f. 168 against E39 'meche good mater were the newe ordres left'). There are also some comments apparently in the hand of Charke. The capital of the Latin text of each sermon is in blue with red flourishing; the occasion, text, biblical reference and translation of the biblical text is underlined in red throughout.

There are no marks of medieval ownership. On f. 109 appears the name of William Charke, who also owned K.[16]

[16] For Charke's manuscripts see A. G. Watson, *The Manuscripts of Henry Savile of Banke* (London, 1969), pp. 52, 89, and the addenda slip in the British Library copy; Watson lists in addition to I British Library Cotton Vespasian D. vii, Cleopatra A. viii, Titus D. i, Royal 15 C. viii, and Trinity College Dublin A. 4. 21. Dr Doyle has added to this list British Library Titus D. xix, ff. 120–70 and Nero A. iii, ff. 90–129. MS Titus D. i is a copy of the Wycliffite *Thirty-Seven Conclusions* (see *Selections*, p. 198).

J: Robert Taylor MS, Princeton   s. xiv/xv

230 parchment leaves, size 297 mm by 193 mm, written frame
236 mm by 145 mm. Collation: 1^4, $2-6^8$, 7^8 lacks 8 cut out, 8–
10^8, 11^3 lacks 6 cut out, $12-13^8$, after which a leaf has been lost
(evident from loss of material, see below), $14-25^8$, 26^8 lacks 7 cut
out, $27-29^8$, 30^6. Catchwords are visible throughout but no quire
signatures; written in two columns. The first four leaves are in
diminishing degrees defective because of damage by damp and
mice.[17]

1. ff. 1^v-4^v, [*Vae Octuplex*] now defective at the beginning because of
   damage to f. 1 but sufficient remains to see that the text began at the
   head of f. 1^v.
2. ff. $5-8^v$, [commentary on the *Pater Noster*] headed *Here bygynneþ þe
   Pater Noster*, inc. *Siþ þe pater noster is þe beste prayere*, expl. *and ioie wiþ
   hym wiþouten ende Amen*; text printed Arnold iii. 98–110 from another
   manuscript.
3. ff. 8^v-98^v, Set 5 plus set 1 in scheme 2, beginning at 1 Advent;
   headed *Epistole dominicales per annum*. Sermon 43 was inadvertently
   omitted in its correct place (see above p. 20); it was added in a hand
   different from the rest of this item at the end of the year but now
   ends incomplete at 43/58 because of the loss of a leaf inserted after
   quire 13; a single leaf would have been sufficient for the completion
   of the sermon.
4. ff. $99-135$, Set 2 headed *Incipit 2^a pars Comune Sanctorum*.
5. ff. 135^v-164^v, Set 3.
6. ff. $165-223^v$, Set 4 headed *Tercia pars euangeliorum ferialium*.
7. ff. 223^v-230^v, [*Of mynystris in þe chirche*] headed *Exposicio euangelii
   Mt. 24 Egressus Iesus*; ends incomplete Arnold ii. 422/16 *makeþ hem*.

Item 1 is in a different hand from that at the start of item 2 and in a
separate quire; its position in relation to the rest of the manuscript
must, however, have been determined early (see below). Item 3
was intended to conclude with the end of a quire, but the
continuance of the hand with items 4–6 suggests that there was
never any intention that the two blocks (of 3 and 4–6) should
stand in any other order than the present one. Item 7 is in another
hand but must always have stood in its present position. On f. 1

[17] The manuscript is mentioned by J. V. Fleming, 'Medieval Manuscripts in the Taylor
Library', *The Princeton University Library Chronicle* xxxviii (1977), 118; the comments on the
content of the sermons should be ignored. I am indebted to Professor E. W. Talbert and
the late Professor S. Harrison Thomson for assistance when I was endeavouring to trace
this manuscript's whereabouts.

are some notes on the contents of the sermons by a medieval hand other than that of any of the scribes; the notes are not fully legible even with the help of ultra-violet light, but seem to refer to sermons in sets 3 and 4. By the time they were made item 1 must have been bound together with the rest of the manuscript.

At least five and possibly seven or more hands are distinguishable: i on ff. 1–4 and ff. 223^v col. 2–230^v; ii on ff. 5–14 col. 1; iii f. 14 col. 2–f. 16 col. 2 line 12; iv f. 16 col. 2 line 12–f. 25^v col. 2 line 20; v f. 25^v col. 2 line 21–f. 44^v; vi ff. 45–223^v col. 2 end set 4 excluding added sermon f. 98 col. 2–f. 98^v; vii f. 98 col. 2–f. 98^v. The identity of the two sections grouped here under i is not certain; hand vii is similar to hand i but possibly not the same. The most obscure section is that from ff. 5–25^v; here three hands are distinguished, but as the appearance of all of them varies considerably it is possible either that this is an under- or an over-estimate. The hands are all of *c.* 1400, varying from text hands in the cases of hands ii–iv, to 'a clumsy anglicana' (Doyle) of hand i. The main hand, hand vi, is an anglicana script. A number of correctors worked over the text, in some cases (e.g. f. 96 col. 1 sermon no. 24/1) a second corrector altering the work of a first; ff. 8^v–25^v are particularly heavily corrected. In items 3–6 the initial of the English text is in blue, sometimes with red flourishing; up to f. 45 the occasion, Latin text and biblical reference are usually in red with blue paraph marks, but thereafter these are usually in the scribe's ordinary ink touched with red; the translation of the biblical texts of the sermons are regularly underlined in red.

There are no marks of medieval ownership. For the history of the manuscript up to the Wrest Park sale in 1922 see above under D. J, item 641 in that sale, was bought by Quaritch but went into the collection of Sir Leicester Harmsworth. At the sale of the Harmsworth library on 16 October 1945[18] it was sold to a London dealer and eventually went to a bookseller in the United States, from whom it was purchased by Robert Taylor Esq. The manuscript is now in Mr Taylor's private library at Princeton.

K: Trinity College Cambridge MS B. 2. 17   s. xiv ex.

180 parchment leaves, size 290 mm by 195 mm, written frame 195 mm by 128 mm. Collation: vellum pastedown, ii paper

18 Harmsworth sale lot 2134.

flyleaves, ii paper stubs (conjugate with flyleaves), iv vellum stubs, 1^8, i paper stub (quire 2 follows straight on), $2-5^8$, 6^8 lacks 6–8, $7-22^8$, 23^8 lacks 8, i paper flyleaf, vellum pastedown. Medieval quire signatures +, a–d appear on quires 7–11. Catchwords are visible. Written in two columns.[19]

1. ff. $1-45^v$ (end quire 6), Set 1 beginning at 1 Trinity, headed *Incipit prima pars euangeliorum scilicet dominicalium.*

2. ff. 46–82v, Set 2, headed *Incipit secunda pars euangeliorum videlicet comune sanctorum.*

3. ff. 82^v-112^v, Set 3; marginal note *here bygynneþ þe propre sanctorum.*

4. ff. 112^v-121^v, [*Of mynystris in þe chirche*] headed *Textus Mathei de antichristo Egressus Iesus de templo.*

5. ff. 121^v-180^v, Set 4 preceded by a list of the sermons headed *Hec sunt capita sermonum 3^e partis*; the sermons begin on f. 122^v headed *Incipit tercia pars euangeliorum scilicet ferialium.* Text ends at the foot of col. 2 of f. 180^v with three extra lines written in the lower margin apparently by a different scribe.

From the quiring it is clear that set 1 could have been written separately and intended for another position, but its present position was certainly determined before the rubricator started work. The sequence of sets 2–3–4 is unalterably established.

The whole manuscript is in an anglicana formata hand of 'a distinctively 14th-century style' and Latin in a text hand (Doyle). It was corrected by the original scribe, in some instances following guides still visible (e.g. ff. 61, 130 where missing words were supplied by a corrector at the very bottom of the leaf and then written in below the relevant column by the main scribe). A very few corrections appear to be by another hand (e.g. ff. 177, 178^v). Towards the end of the manuscript another hand has entered some English translations of the Latin occasions (e.g. ff. 154^v, 161, 177). The first item begins with a large initial in red and blue with flourishing all around the page. Normally the initial of the Latin text is in blue with red flourishing and the occasion in red; the Latin text and the biblical translation throughout are underlined in red; the opening of each sermon is preceded by a blue paraph mark flourished in red; many capitals are touched in red. At the head of each opening is the heading Pars I, Pars II, Pars III, as applicable, in red and blue. Some sort of ornamental border seems to have been added to the lower margin of f. 123, but has now been largely removed by erasure; it was of later, and very different, style from the normal decoration found in these manuscripts. The binding probably dates from the sixteenth century, with remnants of clasps still visible, but the spine has been rebacked.

There are no indications of medieval ownership. The manuscript was given to Trinity College by Neville, the Master from 1593 to 1615. On f. 1 appears the name of William Charke, who also owned I.

L: British Library MS Additional 40671   s. xv[1]

157 parchment leaves, size 267 mm by 183 mm, written space 235 mm by 150 mm. Collation: ii papers flyleaves, 1[12], 2–3[8], 4[8] lacks 8 (nothing lost), 5–6[8], 7[4], 8–19[8], 20[8] lacks 7 and 8, ii paper flyleaves. No quire signatures are visible, but catchwords remain. Written in a single column.[20]

1. ff. 1–55 (end quire 7), Set 4 headed (partly cut away) *Pars* (no gap) *euangeliorum Ferialium*; ends *Explicit* ⌐*tercia*⌐ *pars euuangeliorum* (the addition is in the original hand). F. 55v blank.
2. ff. 56–97[v], Set 1 beginning at 1 Trinity; ends *Expliciunt euangelia omnium dominicarum tocius anni.*
3. ff. 97[v]–130[v], Set 2 headed *Incipit 2ᵃ pars Comune sanctorum.*
4. ff. 130[v]–156[v], Set 3; no heading but f. 131 is headed *Incipit sanctorum.*

The sequence 1–2–3 is established and cannot be altered. Set 4 was apparently made as a separate item, and its original position in relation to this sequence cannot be ascertained. The coloured initials have not been entered in any part of the manuscript, save ff. 97[v]–99, nor is there any flourishing.

There appear to be two hands, the first from ff. 1–21, the second from ff. 21[v]–156[v], but the point of change is not entirely clear and the appearance of both hands varies considerably. The first starts as 'an elegant anglicana with strong secretary features' but gradually more anglicana characteristics intrude, the second is an anglicana formata; both are early fifteenth-century hands (Doyle). There is very little correction, mostly by the original

---

[20] *British Museum Catalogue of Additions to the Manuscripts 1921–1925* (London, 1950), p. 116.

scribes, and almost no marginalia. The intended initials were those of the English text; the Latin text, biblical reference, and occasion have usually been underlined in red, as has the translation of the biblical text throughout. The binding is modern.

There are no signs of medieval ownership. The manuscript was no. 38 at Wrest Park; for the earlier post-medieval history see the description of D above.

M. Trinity College Cambridge MS B. 4. 20   s. xiv/xv

80 parchment leaves, size 340 mm by 220 mm, written space 275 mm by 172 mm in the first two items, 287 mm by 178 mm in the remainder. Collation: v paper flyleaves, ii paper stubs, 1^{10} lacks 1 and 2, 2^{8} lacks 8, 3^{8}, iv paper stubs (text goes straight on), 4–5^{8}, iv paper stubs (text goes straight on), 6–7^{8}, iv paper stubs (text goes straight on), 8^{8} lacks 4 and 5, 9^{8}, iv paper stubs (text goes straight on), 10^{8}, i parchment stub (text goes straight on), 11^{3} (probably originally a ́quire of 8 of which leaves 4–8 have been removed), i parchment stub, ii paper flyleaves, i parchment stub. Quire signatures, which cannot all be correct, appear: 1–2 marked b–c, 6 marked c, 9–11 marked d–f. From the content there is plainly a loss of quires between the present quires 8 and 9. Catchwords remain. Written throughout in a single column.[21]

1. ff.1–15, Set 5; begins incomplete E23/21 *bi þe which*; ends *Expiciunt* (sic) *Epistole Dominicales per annum.*
2. ff. 15^{r-v} sermon on John 10: 1 for feria III in Whitsun week, inc. *Crist seith þat may not lye.* For this sermon see above pp. 47–8 and T item 5, Y item 2.
3. ff. 16^{v}–47^{v}, Set 1 beginning at 1 Trinity; ends *Expliciunt euangelia omnium dominicarum tocius anni.*
4. ff. 47^{v}–50, [*Vae Octuplex*] headed *Exposicio textus Mathei de octiplici ve scribis et pharisees inprecato*; ends *Explicit prima pars euangeliorum.*
5. ff. 50–61^{v}, Set 2 headed *Incipit secunda pars Comune sanctorum*; ends incomplete at the end of quire 8 in sermon 72, Arnold i. 233/16 *two armes of þis cros and þanne mannus loue lokeþ frely.*
6. ff. 62–80^{v}, Set 3; begins incomplete in quire 9 at sermon 89, Arnold i. 314/26 *and prelatis boþe more and lesse.*

---

[21] M. R. James, *The Western Manuscripts in the Library of Trinity College, Cambridge* (Cambridge, 1900–4), i. 157–8, no. 134.

7. f. 80ᵛ, [*Of mynystris in þe chirche*] headed *Exposicio Euangelii Mathei vicesimo quarto Egressus Iesus de templo*; ends incomplete *þey schulden be most pore men and most* (Arnold ii. 394/35).

Item 3 begins quire 3 in a new hand. Items 1–2 form a separable block, which was plainly made separately. The sequences of items 3–5 and of items 6–7 cannot be disturbed, but because of loss of quires the relation of the first of these blocks to the second cannot be determined. The only sequence of sets necessarily established is that of set 1–set 2.

The second hand in the manuscript, ff. 16–80ᵛ, is a practised anglicana formata of the end of the fourteenth century; the first equally an anglicana formata but with several well assimilated secretary features. Dr Doyle suggests that the scribe of ff. 1–15ᵛ was working later, probably in the first or even second quarter of the fifteenth century, and endeavouring to conform to a lay-out previously established by the earlier scribe. The width of the written space and the use in it of a single column only makes the manuscript rather awkward to read, and this difficulty is greater in ff. 1–15ᵛ where the hand is considerably smaller than in the remainder. In ff. 1–15ᵛ there are a few corrections by the original scribe, together with some marginal biblical references; in the remainder there are a few side-notes by the scribe, but little sign of correction. A few biblical references in this latter part may have been supplied by the scribe of the opening section (e.g. ff. 25, 26ᵛ). Throughout the manuscript there are some annotations by various later hands; these become less frequent later. The two parts of the manuscript were decorated separately, though in similar styles. In part I the initial of the English sermons is in blue with red flourishing, the Latin text, reference, and occasion are in ordinary ink with a red paraph mark before them; the English translation of the biblical text throughout is underlined in red following guide marks left by the main scribe. The liturgical season is written in normal ink at the head of the page, save where it has been cropped. In part II the normal initial is again that of the English text, in blue with red flourishing; the initial of the first text in item 3 is in gold with ornamentation of late fourteenth-century type in blue, red, black, and gold. The Latin texts, sermon number, and biblical reference as far as f. 35ᵛ are usually at the head of each page, sometimes duplicated before the sermon; after f. 35^v the information is at the beginning of each sermon only. The translation of the biblical text throughout is underlined in red; here the scribe seems to have done the underlining as he went along. The binding is probably of the sixteenth century, with a newer spine.

There are no marks of medieval ownership. The donor of the manuscript to Trinity College is not known.

N: Sidney Sussex College Cambridge MS 74 s. xiv/xv

181 parchment leaves, size 255 mm by 165 mm, written frame 192 mm by 135 mm.[22] A large number of the original leaves have been lost or cut out, particularly at the beginning of the manuscript; the original state can be assessed to a large extent by means of the quire signatures, medieval foliation, and contents. The foliation is, however, demonstrably incorrect at times, and the contents are at best only a rough guide (for both points see below); the following collation must be regarded as tentative where so marked. Collation: ii paper stubs, ii paper flyleaves (making a quire of 4), i paper flyleaf with half an older flyleaf stuck over; 1^8 lacks 1–2, 4, 8, 2^6 lacks 1, 3^{12} lacks 1–2, 9–12, 4^{26} lacks 1, 3–5, 5^{12} lacks 3 and 9, 6^{12} lacks 1–2, 11–12, 7^8 lacks 5 and 7, 8^{10} lacks 2, 4–8, [1 leaf lost], 9–12^{10}, 13^8, 14^8 lacks 7, 15^8, 16^6, 17^{12}, 18–19^{14}, 20^{14} lacks 14, 21^8, 22^6; ii paper flyleaves and ii paper stubs (conjoint), 6 tabs of parchment used in an earlier binding. The most dubious parts of this are quires 3–4, covering the present ff. 17–22, 26, and 29. Ff. 17–20 are signed ciii–cvi, and there is stitching between ff. 20^v–21; the contents confirm the likelihood of a loss of two leaves before f. 17. There are two stubs after f. 22 that are conjoint with ff. 17–18. If the quire signatures are correct, then f. 26 should be conjoint with one of the two stubs that appear before ff. 17; but this is in fact not the case, and those two stubs appear to fold back towards the beginning of the manuscript in the binding. It thus seems better or conclude that f. 26 belongs to the next quire and that one of the numbers 23–25 was omitted. In fact a signature d is just visible on f. 26, though not the number. F. 29 is not conjoint with f. 26, but is the last leaf of the quire whose catchwords go on to f. 30. It seems probable

[22] M. R. James, *A Descriptive Catalogue of the Manuscripts in the Library of Sidney Sussex College, Cambridge* (Cambridge, 1895), pp. 52–3.

from content that three leaves have been lost between ff. 26 and 29, which necessitates the assumption of another misnumbering of the folios between them. The lost leaf between quires 8 and 9 is necessitated by the fact that the catchwords on f. 71ᵛ, the last leaf of the former, do not go on to f. 73; the matter lost would be expected to fill one leaf, as the numbering would imply. The lost leaf cannot have been conjoint with an outer leaf of either quires 8 or 9, since nothing is missing at the outer ends of these. As indicated the manuscript was foliated in the medieval period, apparently before any leaves had been lost; but the numbers 146, 163, and 177 appear twice. In default of any modern numeration, the medieval folio numbers are here used.

1. ff. 3–142ᵛ, Set 1 sermons used as prothemes to epistle sermons other than set 5 here; for the unique arrangement see below pp. 115–22. The opening is defective, but the sequence must have started with the set 1 sermon for Whitsunday, no. 53; f. 3 begins in the epistle sermon for that day *wyse men he seiþ*. F. 142ᵛ ends without rubric after the epistle sermon attached to no. 52, the gospel sermon for the Sunday within the octave of the Ascension. The gaps in N's text that arise from the extensive losses of leaves are indicated in the notes to the edition. All the set 1 sermons are present, or may be presumed to have been before mutilation of the manuscript, save no. 6 for which another sermon on the same text has been substituted; for reasons given below, pp. 117–119 it is possible that a similar substitution may have been made for no. 5, now absent through loss of leaves at the end of quire 2 and beginning of quire 3.

2. ff. 143–166ᵛ, [*þe Pater Noster of Richard Ermyte*]inc. *To his dere sustre in God Goddes hondemayden;* expl. *Nowe God for hys mercy graunte vs þis drede Amen.*²³

3. ff. 168–179, [sermon of Thomas Wimbledon] inc. *Redde racionem villi-cacionis tue. Luc' xvi°. My dere frendes ȝe schullen vndirstond þat Crist autor and doctour of treuþe;* expl. *blisse þat þey han in þe siȝte of God cui sit honor et gloria in secula seculorum Amen.*²⁴

4. ff. 181–189ᵛ, [treatise on the Ten Commandments] inc. *Hic incipiunt decem mandata Dei. Cristene childur in God seþen þe seruyse and þe wurcheþ of God is so nedful to vs;* expl. *and wiþ hise angelus wiþouten endyng to þat ioy he bringe ow þat bouȝte ȝow wiþ his blod Amen. Expliciunt decem mandata Dei.*

5. ff. 189ᵛ–191ᵛ, [On the *Ave Maria*]; text as Matthew 204–8 with variants from this manuscript.

---

²³ F. G. A. M. Aarts (The Hague, 1967), xv–xvi.
²⁴ See I. K. Knight, *Duquesne Studies, Philological Series* 9 (1967), pp. 15–16.

6. ff. 191ᵛ–207ᵛ, eight sermons not from the present cycle. The first, ff. 191ᵛ–192ᵛ, on Isaiah 9. 6, may have been added after the completion of the manuscript in a gap, since it is in a different hand and has not been rubricated as are the rest. For other manuscripts of the remaining sermons, and the relation of these to material in item 1 of N, see below pp. 115–22.

All the hands in the manuscript are of the late fourteenth or early fifteenth centuries, but it is difficult to be certain how many scribes were involved. Of item 3, ff. 168–178ᵛ are in a single hand, an anglicana formata style, not found elsewhere in the manuscript; the hand of the first sermon in item 6, ff. 191ᵛ–192ᵛ is likewise not found elsewhere but is of a more cursive type. There may be a change to a second scribe on f. 30, a third on ff. 194–204ᵛ (where the hand appears very similar to that of W and the second part of δ) and a fourth on ff. 204ᵛ–207ᵛ; but it seems possible that all of these are variations in the hand of a single scribe. In item 1 there is little sign of correction after the original writing, whether by the scribe or by others. The scribe provided some marginal references and a few Latin notes (e.g. ff. 54, 73). There is some marginal annotation in Latin by various hands of the fifteenth century, particularly near the beginning, drawing attention to the contents. In item 1 the initial of the Latin text is in blue with red flourishing; the Sunday title appears in ordinary ink usually ringed or underlined in red. The English translation of the biblical text is regularly underlined in ordinary ink; alternate red and blue paraph marks appear through the sermons. The decoration of items 2–6 is similar to that of item 1 and may well have been done at the same time. The binding is post-medieval.

There is no sign of medieval ownership. On f. 180ᵛ is a partially erased inscription of the sixteenth century with the name Henry ? Boyner. The manuscript was given to Sidney Sussex College by Samuel Ward, Lady Margaret Professor of Divinity, in 1643.

O: Trinity College Cambridge MS B. 14. 38   s.xiv ex.

179 parchment folios, size 182 mm by 120 mm, written frame 135 mm by 80 mm. Collation: i parchment pastedown, iii parchment flyleaves (i plus iii forming a quire of iv), 1–14⁸, 15⁸ lacks 3 cut away, 16–22⁸, 23⁴, i parchment stub, i paper flyleaf. Quire signatures are still partially present : a on quire 1, d on

quire 4, f–t on quires 6–19. Catchwords remain in items 1–3 Item 1 written in a single column.[25] The number 59 was missed in the foliation.

1. ff. 1–112ᵛ, Set 5.
2. ff. 112ᵛ–127, sermon of Thomas Wimbledon *Redde racionem villi-cacionis tue* inc. *My der frendis ȝe sȝulleþ vnderstonde þat Crist Iesu auctor and doctor of trewþe*; expl. *blys þat þey haue in þe syȝte of God to whom be honoure and glorie and to þe worldlis of worldlis and he vs graunt perof þis ioye parte Amen.*[26]
3. ff. 127ᵛ, [Richard Rolle's *Form of Living*] inc. *In euere synful man and womman þat is bounden in dedely synne*; expl. *grace of oure louerd Iesu Crist be wiþ vs euere Amen.*[27]
4. ff. 148ᵛ–150, [Commentary on the *Pater Noster*] inc. *[S]iþ þe pater noster is þe beste preiere*; expl. *who sȝal be dampned but such a quik fende*; text printed Arnold iii. 98–110 without knowledge of this manuscript; this manuscript ends incomplete at Arnold 100/36.[28]
5. ff. 150ᵛ–180, [version of pseudo-Bonaventura *Meditations on the Passion*] inc. *Hic incipit tractatus passionis Christi The tyme commynge and neghynge off þe reuthes and mercys of þe Lord;* expl. *For he vysited and maid redempcion off his pepill þat regned wiþ þe Fader and þe Holy Gost by all worldis þe which thrugh his marcifull grace brynge vs to his blysse Amen.*[29]

The items can never have been intended for any other order.

There are two hands, the first writing ff. 1–150, the second the final item, ff. 150ᵛ–180; the first hand is anglicana formata of the end of the fourteenth century. The text of item 1 has been corrected by the original scribe in the margins and between the lines; there seems to be no sign of correction by anyone else. There are a few side-notes by the original scribe recording obvious references and numbering points. Item 1 begins with an initial in gold with blue background; there is ornamentation all around the page of a rather rough kind in blue, red and gold. The

---

[25] M. R. James, *The Western Manuscripts in the Library of Trinity College, Cambridge* (Cambridge, 1900–1904), i. 437–8, no. 322.
[26] Ed. I. K. Knight, *Duquesne Studies, Philological Series* 9 (1967), pp. 16–17.
[27] Ed. H. E. Allen, *English Writings of Richard Rolle* (Oxford, 1931), 85–119 from another manuscript.
[28] The reason for the incompleteness of the copy here is unclear; no other manuscript stops at this point.
[29] The translation is not that of Nicholas Love and consequently is not mentioned by E. Salter, 'Nicholas Love's "Myrrour of the Blessed Lyf of Jesu Christ"', *Analecta Cartusiana* x (1974), 1–22; in a privately circulated list Professor Salter grouped this manuscript with six others as an independent southern translation of the Passion section.

main initial is always that of the English text. After f. 1 the next
five initials are in gold, but thereafter they are in red or blue; the
gold initials have brown flourishing, the others blue or red. The
Latin text and occasion are in red; the biblical reference for the
text is often absent. Alternate red and blue paraph marks are
found. Underlining of the translated biblical text in the body of
the sermons is usually missing; when present it is in red. The
binding is probably of the sixteenth century.

On f. iii verso is the name of G. Guggyn[30] in an early sixteenth-
century hand; there are no earlier marks of ownership. The
manuscript was given to Trinity College by Whitgift, Master
from 1567 to 1577 and archbishop of Canterbury from 1583 to
1604.

P: British Library MS Harley 1730.   s. xv in.

110 parchment leaves, size 220 mm by 145 mm, written frame
174 mm by 100 mm. Collation: iii paper flyleaves, 1[6], 2–14[8], v
paper flyleaves. Quires 1 and 14 are not part of the main
manuscript, nor do they belong to each other; both contain Latin
material. Quire 1 is foliated 1*–6*, and a new foliation begins
from 1 at the beginning of quire 2. Quires 2–13 are signed a–n;
catchwords are still visible. Written in single column.[31]

1. ff. 1–96[v] (end quire 13), Set 5. No heading in a medieval hand, but
    later annotator has added 'Wickliffs Postills'. Text ends incom-
    plete E52/27 *medeful þing* (catchwords *to stonde*); a further quire
    would have sufficed for the completion of the set.

There is no evidence that the manuscript ever contained
anything more than set 5; the size of the leaf would preclude the
likelihood of more than one further set.

The whole is in a single hand of the early fifteenth century of an
angular anglicana formata type. The scribe corrected the text
throughout, mostly by marginal additions; correction marks are
visible at the end of several quires. A mid sixteenth-century,
hand has been through the text annotating it in the margin with

---

30 Guggyn also owned Trinity College Cambridge MS B. 14.50, an extremely interesting
manuscript all of whose contents are Lollard; for further details of this manuscript see
JTS NS xxiii (1972), 77–8 and *Selections* p. 145.
31 *A Catalogue of the Harleian Manuscripts in the British Museum* (London, 1808–12), ii, 191.

English side-notes; the interest of the reader seems to have been particularly in the Lollard material, though his own attitude to this does not emerge. The set begins with a slightly larger initial than usual. The Sunday title is set in red at the head of each sermon; the Latin text and biblical reference are underlined in red. The first letter of the Latin text forms the chief initial and is in blue. The translation of the sermon text throughout is underlined in red. Blue paraph marks occur in the text.

There are no marks of medieval ownership.

Q: New College Oxford MS 95   s.xv[1]

148 parchment leaves, size 170 mm by 120 mm, written frame 131 mm by 78 mm. Collation: 1–12[8], 13–15[10], 16–17[8], 18[8] lacks 1–2. The last leaf of quire 16 is blank on the verso, and a new hand and text begin quire 17. Some catchwords but no quire signatures remain. Written in a single column.[32]

1. ff. 1–31, 33–121[v], Set 4 with additions in the Christmas season (see above p. 26); heading partially cut off, reading *(?) pars euangeliorum ferialium*; expl. *Heere enden þe ferial gospels Deo gracias*.
2. ff. 31–32[v] inserted between sermons nos. 143 and 144 at end of quire 3, untitled text beginning *[E]xamyne pardeneris and her bullis*; also found in R, p. 172.
3. f. 32[v], notes in Latin on heresy from canon law *Heretici canibus comparantur*.
4. ff. 121[v]–122 [Letter to Pope Urban VI], inc. *I haue ioye*; printed Arnold iii. 504–6 from MS Bodley 647.
5. ff. 122–122[v], tract on the Eucharist, inc. *I trow as*; the first seven lines and the last four and a half heavily erased.
6. ff. 122[v]–123 [Simonists and Apostates], inc. *þer ben two maner of heretikis*; printed from this manuscript Arnold iii. 211–12.
7. ff. 123–124, [Five Questions on Love], inc. *A special frend in God*; printed from this manuscript Arnold iii. 183–5.
8. ff. 124–127[v] [Of faith, hope and charity], inc. *Sicut enim corpus . . . For it is seide in holdynge of oure halyday*; printed from this manuscript Matthew 347–55.
9. ff. 127[v]–134, *þe seuen werkys of mercy bodyly . . . and gostly*; printed from this manuscript Arnold iii, 168–82.

---

[32] H. O. Coxe, *Catalogus Codicum MSS. qui in Collegiis Aulisque Oxoniensibus hodie adversantur* (Oxford, 1852), i. New College 34–5.

10. ff. 135–148ᵛ, [*Super Cantica sacra*], selected canticles only: 8 *Te Deum*, 11 *Benedicite*, 9 *Benedictus* (ends incomplete f. 142ᵛ at end of quire 17 . . . *ende to mankynde* (Arnold iii. 59/7)), 7 *Magnificat* (begins incomplete f. 143 owing to loss of first two leaves of quire 18 . . . *men sep hom ille* (Arnold iii. 50/29)), 10 *Nunc Dimittis*, 12 *Quicunque vult*; at end *Magister Johannes Wy*. Texts printed from other manuscripts Arnold iii. 48–81.

It is possible that item 10 was originally a separate unit, or at the beginning of the manuscript; there is no possibility of other rearrangement.

The variation of ink and script make certainty about the number of hands difficult to reach. It is possible that four are involved, hand 1 writing items 1 and 4–7, hand 2 adding items 2–3 in a gap (inexplicably) left by scribe 1, hand 3 writing items 8–9, and hand 4 writing item 10. But it seems possible to regard hands 1–3 as the same scribe writing at different times; hand 4 is rather more discrepant but even this could be the same scribe again at a different time and taking rather more trouble. Professor McIntosh has traced differences of language between hands 1, 3, and 4, but it is possible that this is the result of copying from different exemplars. Hand 1, that involved in the sermons here edited, is a neat but uneven near-text hand of the first half of the fifteenth century (Doyle). The original scribe corrected his work occasionally, and wrote a few marginal notae. Further notes in black and red ink were added in the seventeenth century, drawing attention to certain matters in the text. In item 1 the rubrication has not been completed, and becomes increasingly perfunctory as the series proceeds. On f. 1 the initial of the English text was filled in in blue; the remainder of the heading and the biblical translation throughout has been underlined in red. The intention in subsequent sermons was usually the same, but was only fitfully carried out.

An erased inscription on f. 148ᵛ records the gift of the book to dominus John Plumtre of Dalby (Leics.) by Henry Suanton in the fifteenth century.

R: Corpus Christi College Cambridge MS 336   s. xv¹

241 parchment leaves, size 220 mm by 152 mm, written frame 160 mm by 100 mm. Collation: i flyleaf, paper with parchment

stuck to it, $1-2^{12}$, 3^{14}, $4-5^{12}$, 6^8, 7^{12}, 8^{10} lacks 6–10 cut away, 9–20^{12}, 21^{10}, ii paper flyleaves. No medieval quire signatures remain, though catchwords and pricking on many leaves are still present. The manuscript is paginated on each recto and has the following mistakes: p. 175 is absent, pp. 181, 305, 391 are each followed by an unnumbered leaf. Written in single column.[33]

1. pp. 1–137, Set 2; at end *Explicit commune sanctorum*.
2. p. 138, originally blank, now with an eighteenth–century note from Bale on Wyclif.
3. pp. 139–171, [*Of mynystris in þe chirche*] headed *Exposicio euangelii Math. 24 Egressus Iesus de templo*; at end *Explicit exposicio istius euangelii secundum M. J.*
4. p. 172, text headed *Pardoun* inc. *Cristen men in þe bileue*; ends incomplete *þe comunynge of seyntys þat is to seie þat*; also found complete in Q, ff. 31–32ᵛ.
5. pp. 175–275, Set 3.
6. pp. 275–475, Set 4; at end *Expliciunt euangelia ferialia secundum M. J.*

From the quiring and pagination it is clear that, whilst items 3–4 and 5–6 must always have stood in those pairs, item 1 is separable and the relation of the two pairs to this and to each other could have been altered. Item 1 ends on the recto of the last leaf of quire 6, itself having an unusual number of leaves; item 4 ends incomplete on the verso of the last surviving leaf of quire 8.

The whole manuscript, apart from item 2, is in a single current hand of a rather untidy kind dating from the first half of the fifteenth century; its appearance varies somewhat in the course of the manuscript. There is some correction and annotation by the original scribe. There is also a good deal of annotation by another scribe of about the same date. Some of the annotation draws attention in Latin to notable material in the texts, but the majority give reference to homilies of patristic authors, usually by number. The function of these references seems to be to indicate other exegetical material on the same biblical text, not to show the source of the English homily. The appearance of the manuscript is plainer than most. The occasion appears in red before each homily; the initial of the Latin text is in red and the rest of the text, the reference, and the English translation of the

---

[33] M. R. James, *A Descriptive Catalogue of the Manuscripts in the Library of Corpus Christi College Cambridge* (Cambridge, 1911–12), ii. 166–7.

biblical text throughout are underlined in red. Some marks of punctuation and a few capitals are touched in red early in the manuscript. In set 4 the season appears in ordinary ink at the head of each opening. Some directions for rubricator are still visible. The manuscript has recently been rebound.

No signs remain of medieval ownership. On the parchment stuck to the verso of the opening flyleaf are some notes of the occasions of the sermons in a late sixteenth-century hand; on p. 1 pressmarks K 17 (deleted) and K 15 remain. M. R. James states that the source from which the manuscript came into Parker's possession is not known.

S: St. John's College Cambridge MS G. 22   s. xv[1]

112 parchment folios, size 209 mm by 137 mm, written frame 160 mm by 96 mm. Collation: iii paper flyleaves, 1–9[8], 10[6], 11[8], 12[8] lacks 7, 13[8], 14[8] lacks 4, 15[8] lacks 3–6, i paper flyleaf. Medieval quire signatures a–k appear on quires 1–10; catchwords are also visible on those quires but have usually been cropped thereafter. Written in a single column.[34]

1. ff. 1–78[v], a series of sermons (not Set 1) on the Sunday gospels from 1 Trinity to 25 Trinity; for these sermons see pp. 99–106 below.
2. ff. 79–112[v], Set 1; begins incomplete in the sermon for the second Sunday after the octave of Epiphany, no. 33/60 *sip qualite as colour*; ends incomplete in that for Trinity Sunday, no. 54/31 *conseyue it pis bapteem*; for the lacunae that result from losses of leaves see the notes to the texts.

The hands of the two items are different, and there seems no way of determining whether the two items were designed to go together. The first item ends at the bottom of the final leaf of quire 10; from the quire signature, it must have begun with the 1 Trinity sermon, whether or not anything originally followed that for 25 Trinity (see below p. 100).

The two items were written by two different scribes, the first perhaps a little earlier than the second. The second hand is an anglicana varying in formality of the fifteenth century, the first half and perhaps second quarter (Doyle). There is no correction

34 M. R. James, *A Descriptive Catalogue of the Manuscripts in the Library of St. John's College, Cambridge* (Cambridge, 1913), pp. 226, no. 190.

in item 2, and almost no medieval marginal annotation; a few notes appear in a seventeenth-century hand. In the first item the Sunday heading and biblical references appear in red; the initial Latin text is in blue with red flourishing; red paraph marks and touching of capitals appear. In the second item the rubrication has not been carried out; gaps were left for a coloured capital for the Latin text, and for the occasion to be inserted above; marginal notes for the rubricator are still often visible. The translation of the biblical text was not underlined, nor does there appear to be any guidance left by the scribe for this. The binding is post-medieval.

There is no indication of medieval ownership. On the front pastedown is an inscription recording the gift of the volume to St. John's College by [John] Gent, rector of Birdbrook in Essex; Gent was a member of the College in 1622, gaining his BA in 1625/6 and his MA in 1629. His family seems to have come from Steeple Bumpstead in Essex, a village notorious in the early sixteenth century for its Lollardy.[35]

T: Pembroke College Cambridge MS 237   s. xiv ex.

227 parchment leaves, size 293 mm by 208 mm, written frame 220 mm by 159 mm. Collation: iii paper flyleaves, i parchment flyleaf, a[4] (see below), 1–2[12], 3[10], 4[8], 5–8[12], 9[14], 10[12], 11[10], 12[8], 13[10], i stub, 14[8], 1 leaf (presumably conjugate with stub, but quire 14 is numbered as it stands ci–ciiij), 15[12], 16[10], 17[6], 1 leaf, 18–19[12] plus in quire 19 a half leaf after leaf 8 with a conjugate stub after leaf 4, 20[8], 21[10] leaf 10 cut away, i parchment flyleaf, iii paper flyleaves. Various sets of quire signatures appear in the manuscript, several of which appear to be meaningless; possibly significant, and not contradicted by other aspects of the manuscript, are a–d on quires 5–8, b on quire 19. Quire a is not foliated; after that the manuscript is foliated on the first leaf of each quire only. Written in two columns.[36]

    1. quire a, list of lessons beginning 1 Advent for Sundays, ferials, and festivals; the list does not correspond with the following sermons, most notably because the ferial epistles are included here.

[35] See C. Cross, *Church and People 1450–1660* (Edinburgh, 1976), pp. 40–2, 57.
[36] M. R. James, *A Descriptive Catalogue of the Manuscripts in the Library of Pembroke College, Cambridge* (Cambridge, 1905), 213–14; James points out that the manuscript is not found in the list made by Thomas James in 1600.

2. ff. 1–42^v (end quire 4), Set 5; headed *Epistole Dominicales.*
3. ff. 43–86, Set 1 beginning at 1 Trinity; ends *Expliciunt Ewangelia Dominicalia.*
4. ff. 86^v–144^v (end quire 13), Set 4. On f. 144^v the text is squashed, and an extra line allowed at the foot of column 2, to fit into the leaf.
5. ff. 130^v–131^v, sermon on John 10: 1 intruded after no. 201 on the same text, and headed *Sermo de eodem,* inc. *Crist seyþ þat may not lye.* For this sermon see above pp. 47–8 and M item 2, Y item 2.
6. ff. 145–153^v (quire 14 plus following leaf), [*Of mynystris in þe chirche*] headed *Egressus Iesus de templo.* On f. 153^v the text is spread out to fill the leaf.
7. ff. 154–182^v (quires 15–17 plus following leaf), Set 3. On f. 182^v text is compressed somewhat to fit into leaf.
8. ff. 183–217, Set 2, headed *Comine (sic) Sanctorum.*
9. f. 217, text headed *Contra illos qui dicunt accedentem sine subiecto esse post consecracionem in sacramento;* printed Matthew 357–8 without notice of this manuscript.
10. ff. 217–220, [*Sixteen Conditions of Charity*], inc. *Hyt ys seyd þat charite partiþ hyt one þe children of God,* . . . expl. *leue we þes frere lawes to rewe wiþ oure conscience and in kepyng of þis schal we serue blysse Amen.*
11. ff. 220–233, [*Vae Octuplex*] headed *Exposicio textus Mathei xxiii c^o de ve octiplici scribis phariseis et ypocritis imprecato.*

It is clear that items 8–11 must always have been in that order, and that items 3 and 4, that is sets 1 and 4, must have been intended to stand in that unusual sequence. But the relation of the latter block to sets 5, 3 and 2, and of these three last to each other, could have remained undetermined until the binding; the irregular size of the quires and the compression of items 4 and 7 to conclude with a quire suggest that the manuscript was never planned as a whole but as a series of pieces. The flourishing of the initial at the start of item 8 is of roughly the same elaboration as that at the start of item 2, though both are more extensive than that at the opening of items 3, 6 or 7.

The whole manuscript, including item 1, is written in an 'expert anglicana formata of the late 14th century' (Doyle) of somewhat varying appearance. It has been very heavily corrected throughout by insertion, deletion and marginal addition. Some of the correction seems to have been done by the original scribe at the time of writing, some apparently by him at a later time in a darker ink. Many corrections must have been made before the quires were sewn together, since they extend right into the central gutter (e.g. ff. 31ᵛ, 41ᵛ). There is some correction (e.g. f. 117) which may be by another hand, but because of the varying appearance of the main hand it is very difficult to be certain of this; a few corrections (e.g. f. 54ᵛ) are by a later hand. There are a number of marginal biblical references, notae and pointing hands, all probably by the original scribe; some other marginal notes (e.g. f. 53 on canon law, f. 54 on Rolle) are certainly by another. Throughout the manuscript the Latin text of each sermon stands at the head of the column in which the sermon starts; it is enclosed in a blue frame save where the decoration is missing. The occasion and biblical reference are in ordinary ink immediately above each sermon marked off by a blue or red paraph mark; alternate blue and red paraph marks also occur marking off sections in the sermons. The translation of the text of each sermon is underlined in ordinary ink throughout. All rubrication is missing from ff. 86ᵛ–116ᵛ.

The only mark of medieval ownership is the name 'Robert Harton' on the verso of the parchment flyleaf at the beginning; the date of the script would appear to be fifteenth-century. It is not clear when the manuscript came into the possession of Pembroke College.

V: British Library MS Harley 2396 s.xv¹

78 parchment leaves, size 210 mm by 132 mm, written frame varies, average 170 mm by 95 mm. Collation: iii paper flyleaves, i parchment flyleaf, i parchment stub, 1–9⁸,10²⁶ (sewn through quire), ii parchment flyleaves, ii paper flyleaves. There are no surviving quire signatures, but catchwords remain. The majority of leaves are ruled for a single column, but a few have two columns (e.g. ff. 15ᵛ, 45ᵛ, 58ᵛ) for no apparent reason.[37]

1. ff. 1–78ᵛ, set 5 plus set 1 plus set 4 in scheme 3. Begins incomplete at E2/79 *he was mynystre*; if, as seems likely, the manuscript originally began at 1 Advent, one quire would suffice for the material missing. The sequence continues to the end of no. 139, the Friday gospel for the week following the fourth Sunday after the octave of Epiphany. After this on f. 76 appears lines 1–4 of E12, the sermon that should follow. This is crossed through by the rubricator, and there follows no. 29, the gospel

---

[37] *A Catalogue of the Harleian Manuscripts in the British Museum* (London, 1808–12), ii. 383–4.

sermon for the Sunday 4 Advent, omitted in its correct place on f. 23^v, where a note in the original hand in red reads 'turne to þe ende of þe book'.

That this sermon ends less than a third of the way down f. 78^v suggests that no more was intended to follow. It seems possible that the intention was to divide the liturgical year into four parts, of which the surviving manuscript is the first.

There is very considerable variation in the appearance of the script. It is probably all in the same hand, though part of f. 69 could be by a second scribe. The same awkward, probably amateur, text hand is found in Gonville and Caius College Cambridge MS 179/212, containing a fragment of the LV version of the gospels. The scribe corrected the manuscript, thought a large number of impossible readings remain. The Sunday heading and biblical reference are in red; the main initial is that of the English text, in red; the Latin text is usually omitted. Translation of the biblical text is underlined in red. The binding is modern.

On the parchment flyleaf at the beginning is a small diagram that appears to be a part of a consanguinity table, perhaps in the hand of the scribe.[38] There are no marks of medieval ownership.

W: Magdalene College Cambridge MS Pepys 2616

s. xiv ex.

110 leaves, size 350 mm by 240 mm, written frame 270 mm by 167 mm. Collation: ii parchment flyleaves, 1^6, 2–6^{12}, 7^{12} lacks leaves 3–5, 8–9^{12}, 10^8, 11^2. No consecutive quire signatures remain. In quire 7 leaves 8–10, which would have been conjugate with the missing leaves 3–5, have been stuck together with strips of strengthening parchment; stitching is consequently visible both at the original centre of the quire (ff. 138^v–139), and between ff. 144^v–145 through the strip. The scribe regularly provided a catchword at the bottom of each verso in the first half of the quire, save for the central bifolium, as well as at the end of

---

[38] The inscription inside the frame reads 'attauus abauus proauus auus pater'; see the diagram reproduced by G. Ladner, 'Medieval and Modern Understanding of Symbolism: A Comparison', *Speculum* liv (1979), 243 and n. 102.

the quire. The manuscript is paginated from the beginning of quire 1. Written in two columns.[39]

1. pp. 1–108, set 4 headed *Hic incipiunt Euangelia Ferialia*; at end *Explciunt* (sic) *euangelia ferialia tocius anni*.
2. pp. 109–158, Set 3.
3. pp. 158–174 [*Of mynystris in þe chirche*] headed *Exposicio Euangelii Egressus Iesus de templo*.
4. pp. 174–215, Set 2 headed *Hic incipit comune sanctorum;* at end *Explicit comune sanctorum*. Sermons 65, 67–71, 73–5 inclusive and 83 were omitted from this set; the absence canot be due to loss of leaves from the present manuscript since it does not coincide in any case with the beginning of a new leaf.

Items 2–4 must always have been intended in this order. Item 1 ends half-way down the first column of the verso of leaf 8 of the fifth quire, the rest of the leaf being blank; its relation to the rest of the material need not have been determined before writing was complete. The ornamentation round the page at the start of item 1 is somewhat more elaborate than that at the start of item 2.

The whole manuscript is in a single hand, 'anglicana formata of a distinctly 14th-century style' (Doyle); the same hand appears as the second scribe of δ (see below) and is similar to that of ff. 194–204 of N. The scribe corrected his work after writing, and there are a few corrections by another hand (e.g. ff. 165, 167, 170); there is very little marginal annotation. On pp. 1 and 109 appear professional flourishing around the page in gold, red, blue, and white. M. R. James compared the decoration of Trinity Hall MS 17, the dedication copy made for Richard II of Dymmock's *Contra Hereses Lollardorum*. The resemblance between that lavish presentation copy and W's fairly modest decoration is, however, not close; a nearer parallel would be the ornamentation in Y of the present text. Apart from the two ornamented pages, the usual style is for the initial of the Latin text to be in blue with red flourishing; the occasion appears above this in red or in ordinary ink. The translation of the biblical text is underlined in red throughout. The binding is post-medieval.

There is no trace in the manuscript itself of medieval ownership. The first flyleaf consists of part of a document, described by James as an account-roll from Edward III's time; the document contains the names of places and people but these are scattered over a wide area, from Devon to Northamptonshire. Part of the same document was used for the strengthening strip in quire 7. There is no indication of how the manuscript came into the possession of Pepys.

X: Lambeth Palace MS 1149   s. xiv/xv

229 parchment leaves, measuring 260 mm by 175 mm, written frame 205 mm by 130 mm. Collation: ii paper flyleaves, $1–11^8$, 12^8 plus 1, $13–16^8$, 17^4, $18–21^8$, 22^4, 23^{16}, $24–28^8$, 29^8 lacks 4–7, ii paper flyleaves. Catchwords but no quire signatures are visible. The manuscript is paginated, and there are a number of errors in the pagination. Written in two columns.[40]

1. pp. 1–193 (recto of extra leaf after quire 12), Set 5 plus set 1 in scheme 2 beginning at 1 Advent; headed *Here ben wryte/and expownyd/þe pystlys and þe gospellis of þe Sundayes of þe 3er*; at end *Expliciunt epistole et ewangelia dominicalia per annum.*
2. pp. 195–266 (quire 13–leaf 4 verso quire 17) Set 2; headed *Euangelia comunia sanctorum.*
3. pp. 267–301 (quire 18–leaf 7 quire 20), Set 3; headed *Euangelia propria sanctorum.*
4. pp. 301–320 [*Of mynystris in þe chirche*] headed *Exposicio euangelii Mathei xxiiii Egressus Iesus de templo.*
5. pp. 320–326 (ends verso leaf 3 quire 22), [*Vae Octuplex*] headed *Ue uobis scribe et pharisei ipocrite Mathei xxiii.*
6. pp. 329–448 (quires 23–9), Set 4; headed *Here bygynnen þe feryal gospelis of al þe 3eer.* The loss of leaves 4–7 of quire 29 has resulted in the loss, partial or complete, of material between sermons 214 and 220; the text ends incomplete in sermon 223, since a final quire has been lost.

Items 3–4–5 must always have stood in this order, but the relation of items 1, 2, and 6 to this sequence and to each other is not fixed. The division of labour between the two scribes confirms particularly the possibility that items 1 and 6 need not necessarily have been intended to stand in their present position. The initial position of item 1 was, however, probably determined before the opening initial was done.

[40] M. R. James and C. Jenkins, *A Descriptive Catalogue of the Manuscripts in the Library of Lambeth Palace* (Cambridge, 1930–2), 824–5.

Two hands, both of the turn of the century, are involved; the first wrote items 1 and 6, pp. 1–193, 329–448; the second was responsible for the intervening section, pp. 195–326. The first is a neat text hand, the second a 'bastard anglicana'. The whole manuscript is carefully corrected, usually by the scribe of the section in question, and often over an erasure. There are a few corrections that appear to be in another hand, and also modifications to punctuation by erasure, and to spelling by subpunction and deletion (mostly of inflectional -n or -e), the responsibility for which cannot be determined. The manuscript has, apparently for a long time, been so tightly bound that cracking and tearing of the parchment has occurred, particularly at the upper edge by the binding; pieces of paper were stuck over some of these damaged portions, and these overwritten with the covered words (usually correctly). There are also some marginal catch titles by a later hand. The decoration of the manuscript was done in two parts: up to p. 329, and including the initial at the beginning of item 6, the capitals are in blue with red flourishing and the main initial that of the Latin text. After that the capitals are in red with mauve flourishing and are of the first word of the English text. The English translation of the biblical text is underlined in red throughout. The binding is of the late eighteenth century.

There are no marks of medieval ownership. The manuscript came into the Lambeth Palace library from the gift of Edward Jacob of Faversham in 1786, whose name is on the flyleaf; also on the flyleaf is 'Donum amici R. Halford gen.', presumably an owner before Jacob.

Y: Christ's College Cambridge MS 7   s. xiv/xv

146 parchment leaves, size 290 mm by 210 mm, written frame 196 mm by 138 mm. Collation: ii paper flyleaves, i parchment flyleaf, 1–17⁸, 18⁴, 19⁶, ii paper flyleaves. Medieval quire signatures a–t are visible throughout, as are catchwords. The manuscript is paginated pp. 1–289 on each leaf beginning at quire 1; folio numbers (used here) are found on the first leaf of each quire only. Written in two columns.[41]

---

[41] M. R. James, *A Descriptive Catalogue of the Western Manuscripts in the Library of Christ's College, Cambridge* (Cambridge, 1905), p. 8.

1. ff. 1–69ᵛ, Set 5; at end *Here eenden þe domynycal pistlis þorouȝ þe ȝeer.*
2. ff. 69ᵛ–70ᵛ, sermon on John 10: 1 headed *Sermo in feria quarta Pentecostes ad processionem*, inc. *Crist seiþ þat may not lie.* For this sermon see above pp. 47–8 and M item 2, T item 5.
3. ff. 70ᵛ–140ᵛ, Set 1 beginning at 1 Advent; expl. *Heere eenden þe dominical gospelis þorouȝ þe ȝeer.*
4. ff. 140ᵛ–145ᵛ, [*Vae Octuplex*] headed *And here bigynnen þe eiȝte woos sumwhat expowned*; at end *Heere eendiþ þe exposicioun of þe eiȝte woos.*

As is evident from the follow-on, the items can never have been intended for any other arrangement.

The whole is written in a single text hand of c. 1400, though its size and appearance vary somewhat. The text throughout has been carefully corrected by the original scribe; some of the corrections were, from the difference of ink-colour, made after the writing of the page in question. There are only a very few cases, for instance f. 98 (see 44/122), where another hand seems possibly to be involved. On ff. 1, 40ᵛ, 70ᵛ and 110ᵛ are elaborate capitals with border decoration of blue, with gold, red, green, and white; these are at the start of sets 5 and 1 and at the head of sermons for Trinity Sunday. The style is similar to that of B, though possibly a little later or more metropolitan (Doyle). Elsewhere the occasion, the text with reference, and in set 5 the sermon number, are given in red; the scribe himself obviously did these headings since, when a new quire begins with such a heading, the previous catchwords are also in red. In item 1 the Latin text is not given for E1–31 inclusive, and the initial of the English text is in blue red flourishing; elsewhere the Latin text is treated in the same way. The translation of the sermon text throughout is underlined in red. Some capitals are touched in yellow and, at the beginning of the manuscript, also in red. The binding is post-medieval.

There are no marks of medieval ownership. On flyleaf ii at the beginning is a deleted name 'Thomas Boys Esquire'; the manuscript was given to Christ's College by John Boys (BA 1623/4).[42] Following the end of the text on f. 145ᵛ and on the ensuing flyleaf recto are some notes of the sixteenth and seventeenth centuries in various hands on the contents of the sermons; antipapist and anticlerical views had attracted the annotators' notice.

[42] Dr Doyle tells me that Thomas Boys owned Durham Cosin K. II.9, a printed book.

Z: Bodleian Library MS Don. c. 13   s. xiv ex.

172 parchment leaves, size 300 mm by 215 mm, written frame 240 mm by 162 mm. Collation: ii modern card flyleaves (a letter stuck to the second), ii parchment flyleaves (ff. i–ii), ii stubs; 1–14^{12}, ii parchment flyleaves. Catchwords but no quire signatures survive. Written in two columns.[43]

A. ff. i–i^v fragment of liturgical manuscript.

1. ff 1–68^v, Set 5 plus set 1 in scheme 2 beginning at 1 Advent; at end *Expliciunt dominice tocius anni.*

2. ff. 68^v–69, [*Vae Octuplex*] headed *Exposicio textus Mathei xxiii^o c^o de ve octiplici scribis phariseis ipocritis inprecato.*

3. ff. 69^v–91, Set 3.

4. ff. 91–93, [*Of mynystris in þe chirche*] headed *Exposicio euangelii Mt. 24to.*

5. ff. 93–138, Set 4; headed *Tercia pars euangeliorum ferialium.*

6. ff. 138–162^v, Set 2.

7. ff. 162^v–166^v, six poems:

    (a) *Als þat a grete clerk*; IMEV 406

    (b) *I herd a harping on a hille*; IMEV 1320

    (c) *Habide gode men and hald ȝou stil*; IMEV 110

    (d) *Haile Iesu my creatour*; IMEV 1053

    (e) *Iesu my lefe Iesu my loue*; IMEV 1733

    (f) *Swete Iesu Crist to þe*; IMEV 3232

    (g) *Think man wharto þou ert wroȝt*; IMEV 3567

8. ff. 166^v–167, *Exposicio super orationem dominicam composita per Ricardum heremitam*, inc. *Pater noster . . . hec oracio priuilegiata est in duobus*, expl. *ineffragabilia et inuiolabilia esse confirmata in veritate Explicit*[44].

B. ff. 168–169^v fragment of liturgical manuscript.

From the follow-on of the items, the material can never have been in any other order.

The whole manuscript is written in hands of an anglicana formata style of *c.* 1400. There are certainly changes of hand for

---

[43] A typescript description of the manuscript is to be found in the Bodleian Library. The gift was briefly noted in *Friends of the Bodleian Sixth Annual Report 1930–31* (Oxford), pp. 15–16 with plates of ff. 1, 165^v; item 7 was more fully described by B. D. Brown, 'Religious Lyrics in MS. Don. c. 13', *Bodleian Quarterly Record* vii (Oxford, 1935), 1–7 with a plate of f. 166. The sermons in items 1–6 are here found in abbreviated form; for an account of the method of abbreviation see my paper 'The Expurgation of a Lollard Sermon-Cycle', *JTS* NS xxii (1971), 451–65.

[44] See H. E. Allen, *Writings ascribed to Richard Rolle . . . and Materials for his Biography* (New York and London, 1927), 155–7, and her note in *Times Literary Supplement* 17 March 1932, p. 202.

item 7 and again for item 8, but it is less clear whether earlier alterations in the appearance of the script (e.g. col. 2 f. 152^v) are due to change of scribe or change of pen. In items 1–6 the initials of the Latin texts are in red, the remainder of the text, the reference, the occasion, and the translation of the biblical text throughout underlined in red. There is some correction by the original scribe(s) probably immediately after the writing of the passage in question. There is some marginal annotation by another medieval hand, pointing out in Latin the topics under discussion and not frequently noting 'caue'. The manuscript retains the original boards and thongs, and there is a fragment of the red leather covering on the back board. The parchment flyleaves at the beginning and end come from a fourteenth-century Gradual and contain parts of the services for the first three Sundays in Advent.

The only marks of medieval ownership are on f. 168^v 'Mag. T. C.' and on f. 170 'Dominus J. Coldane', both in fifteenth-century hands. On f. 168^v in a sixteenth-century hand is the name John Savage. The manuscript was given to the Bodleian Library in 1931 by Dr. H. Watney through Miss M. Watney.[45]

α: Leicestershire County Record Office, Leicester Town Hall MS 3   s. xiv/xv

216 parchment leaves, size 240 mm by 165 mm, written space variable, average 185 mm by 126 mm. Collation: ii modern parchment flyleaves, 1–6^8, 7^{10}, 8–16^8, 17^{10} lacks 8 and 9, 18–22^{10}, 23–24^8, 25–26^6, ii modern parchment flyleaves. Quire signatures survive as g on quire 7, h on quire 20 and +o on quire 8. The correct foliation is that in pencil at the foot of the second column on each recto; it begins with quire 1. Catchwords remain on some quires. Written in two columns.

1. ff. 1–58^v (end quire 7), set 5; headed *Epistole dominicales per annum*; at end *Expliciunt epistole dominicales per annum*.
2. ff. 59–99^v, Set 3.
3. ff. 99^v–143, Set 2; at end *Here ende þe godspelles of comyn sanctorum*.

---

[45] The manuscript was sold by Sotheby's on 6 November 1899 for £40. 10s. 0d. to Quaritch; it had been in the possession of Sir F. A. T. C Constable Bt. of Burton Constable and Aston Hall, North Ferriby, Yorkshire, in the Tixall Library formed by Sir Walter Aston, first Lord Aston and an ambassador to Spain in the time of James I.

4. ff. 143–147, [*Vae Octuplex*] headed *Expositio textus Mathei 23 de octuplici ve scribis et phariseis imprecato.*

5. ff. 147–158ᵛ (end quire 19), [*Of mynystris in þe chirche*] headed *Egressus Iesus de templo.*

6. f. 158ᵛ, later Latin note on the interpretation of the text of the first set 1 gospel that follows.

7. ff. 159–216ᵛ (quires 20–26), Set 1 beginning at 1 Advent; at the end *Expliciunt euangelia dominicalia per annum Amen.*

Items 2–5 must always have been in their present order. Items 1 and 7 are on separate sets of quires and could be rearranged; judging by the quire signatures, and the hand (see below), item 7 was probably originally intended to follow item 1. The present order must, however, have been established before item 6 was written.

Apart from item 6, the whole manuscript is written in an anglicana formata of the turn of the fourteenth to fifteenth centuries possibly by one or possibly by two scribes; if two were involved, one wrote ff. 59–158ᵛ and the other ff. 1–58ᵛ and ff. 159–216ᵛ. Dr Ker suggests that only one scribe was at work, and that the material was written in the order ff. 1–58ᵛ, 159–216ᵛ, 59–158ᵛ. The whole manuscript has been corrected both by the original scribe(s) and by at least one other. There are a number of marginal notae and comments, including some, like that on the blank space on f. 158ᵛ, lengthy Latin passages; all are in medieval hands and some have been cropped in binding. On f. 216ᵛ appears a note, partially visible to the eye, but more fully legible in photograph or in ultra-violet light, *Ista euangelia dominicalia corriguntur per primum originale*; whilst the set has certainly been carefully corrected, the claim here cannot be substantiated, as will be seen in chapter V. The initial of the Latin text in all parts of the manuscript is in blue, flourished in red; the occasion is supplied in red in a hand other than that of the scribe; in set 1 from the beginning at no. 26 to 48 inclusive the occasion has not been filled in. The text in Latin and in its English translation throughout is underlined in red; it would seem that this was done by the main scribe as he went along. The binding is of the nineteenth century, but a portion of the mid sixteenth-century leather has been pasted to the new covers.[46]

46 See J. B. Oldham, *English Blind-Stamped Bindings* (Cambridge, 1952), p. 51, type HE. k(1) for the design on this. I owe this detail to Dr Doyle.

There is no mark of medieval ownership. A sixteenth-century hand on f. 36 scribbled a note signed *Robert Ormes*, and on f. 190ᵛ is a signature of the same date *Thomas Stought*. It appears that few additions were made to the Old Town Hall Library after 1669, so it is likely that the manuscript came into the collection before that date but its source is unknown.[47]

β: Leicestershire County Record Office, Wyggeston Hospital MS 10 D. 34/6   s. xiv/xv

279 parchment leaves, size 315 mm by 215 mm, written frame 239 mm by 150 mm. Collation: ii modern parchment flyleaves, 1^{12} lacks 1–2, 2^{12} lacks 5, 3^{12}, 4^{12} lacks 9, 5^{12} lacks 8, 6^{12} lacks 5, 7^{12} lacks 5–7 and 10, 8^{12}, 9^{12} lacks 1, 10^{12}, 11^{12} lacks 8, 12^{12} lacks 1–2, and 11–12, 13^{12}, 14^{12} lacks 12, 15^{12} lacks 12, 16^{12} lacks 1, 17^{12} lacks 4–5, 18–20^{12}, 21^{6}, 22^{12} (leaves 5–8 are misbound though the folios have now been correctly numbered), 23^{12} (leaves 5 and 8 are not conjugate but are single leaves whose stubs are visible before leaf 5 and after leaf 7), 24^{12}, 25^{12} lacks 11, 26^{12} lacks 2 and 8–12, 27^{1} (a single leaf from a later quire, not that immediately following quire 26). In quire 7 the remaining leaves are all bifolia; but material is missing after leaf 9 and catchwords added at the foot of leaf 9ᵛ by the scribe make it clear that a single leaf must have been inserted after this folio; the material missing at the centre of the quire would only have been sufficient for three leaves. In quire 20 leaves 5 and 8 are in a hand different from the rest of the manuscript and were substituted for the original leaves after the writing of the remainder of the quire. Medieval quire signatures b–k are visible on quires 2–10, a on quire 12, e–f on quires 14–15, h–m on quires 17–21, a–e on quires 22–26. The modern foliation in pencil at the lower outer edge of each recto omitted two folios after f. 33, and runs from ff. 1–277, with the two extra leaves as f. 33* and f. 33**. Written in two columns.

1. ff. 1–58, Set 1 beginning at 1 Trinity. Begins incomplete 2/77 *almes for we schal sue*; material is missing because of loss of leaves.
2. ff. 58–62ᵛ, [*Vae Octuplex*] headed *Exposicio textus Mathei xxiii capitulo de ve octiplici scribis phariseis et ipicritis imprecato.*

47 C. Deedes, J. E. Stocks and J. L. Stocks, *The Old Town Hall Library of Leicester* (Oxford, 1919), pp. xv–xix.

3. ff. 62ᵛ–63, *De sacramento contra fratres*; text printed Matthew 357–8 without notice of this manuscript.

4. ff. 63–109ᵛ, Set 2 headed *Comune sanctorum Incipit 2ᵃ pars*; material is missing because of loss of leaves.

5. ff. 109ᵛ–126 Set 3; material is missing because of loss of leaves; ends incomplete in sermon 100, Arnold i. 350/18 *is pouderid wiþ*.

6. ff. 127–133ᵛ, [*Of mynystris in þe chirche*]; begins incomplete Arnold ii. 407/1 *-feme prelatis*.

7. ff. 133ᵛ–212ᵛ, Set 4 headed *3ᵃ pars euangelorum ferialium*; at end *heere endene þe gospelis*; material missing because of loss of leaves.

8. ff. 212ᵛ–223ᵛ, headed *De ecclesia et membris eius*; text printed Arnold iii. 338–65 without knowledge of this manuscript.

9. ff. 224–277ᵛ, Set 5 headed *Epistole dominicales per annum*; ends incomplete E55/23 *wher dayes*; material missing because of loss of leaves.

The medieval quire signatures make it plain that two quires have been lost after f. 126ᵛ. Items 1–5 can never have been in any other order; the new start of the quire signatures comes within set 3. The position of item 9 is only determined by the catchwords on f. 223ᵛ, since it begins a new quire. No comparison of the ornamentation at the beginning of item 9 can be made with item 1, since the opening leaves of that have been lost. It should be noted, however, that items 1–8 correspond exactly to items 2–9 of D in order, and very closely in their headings; in both manuscripts the position of set 5 could have been determined after the entire job of copying had been completed.

With the exception of ff. 210 and 213, the whole manuscript is in a single hand of 'the larger size of English textura semi-quadrata' (Doyle) of the end of the fourteenth or beginning of the fifteenth century. The hand of the bifolium is a good attempt at an imitation of the main hand, but is distinguishable by its slightly thinner pen-strokes, and by the absence of the main scribe's distinctive 'marking-off' of biblical quotation for under-lining (hence these folios have no underlining). It would seem likely, from the slight compression of the hand on f. 210ᵛ but the cancelled fillers on f. 213ᵛ, that the original bifolium was removed because of errors; the substitution must have been done at an early stage since f. 210 has been supplied with a quire signature. The whole of the rest of the manuscript was carefully corrected by the original scribe, by the scribe of these insertions and perhaps by another; most of the corrections are marginal. There are few other marginal notes, but on f. 155ᵛ against Arnold ii. 61/ 11 (sermon 154) appears in a fifteenth-century hand 'here wyclef dide help of þis relesche and at þis tyme was he called flos mundi'. The initial of the English text is in blue with red flourishing; the Latin text, the occasion and sermon number, together with the translation of the biblical text throughout, are underlined in red. The scribe put in guide-marks for the biblical underlining in the form of an upward squiggle before and a downward squiggle after the words to be underlined. The modern rebinding is over medieval bevelled boards.

There are no marks of medieval ownership; on f. 2 is the name Chr[istopher] Bardsey in a late sixteenth-century hand. The date at which the manuscript came into the possession of the Wyggeston Hospital in Leicester is uncertain; to judge by the other manuscripts in the collection there is no necessity to assume that its origin was in Leicester.[48]

δ: Wisbech Town Museum Library MS 8   s. xiv ex.

101 parchment leaves, size 350 mm by 235 mm, written space 275 mm by 172 mm. Collation: i paper flyleaf, 1⁸ lacks 6–7, 2–4⁸, 5⁴ lacks 3–4, 6¹² lacks 11–12, 7¹² lacks 9, 8–11¹², i paper flyleaf. Quire signatures d–j appear on quires 6–11. The manuscript is foliated in modern pencil ff. 1–102, there being no f. 7. Written in two columns.

1. ff. 1–33ᵛ (end quire 5), Set 5 heading (probably only that for the first sermon) deleted.
2. f. 34, [Wyclif's *De Mendaciis Fratrum*] headed *Assit principio sancta Maria meo*, inc. *Pseudofratres publicant* . . .
3. f. 34, [Wyclif's *Descriptio Fratris*], follows on without break from preceding *Nota descripcioni pseudofratris. Pseudofrater degens in seculo*[49] . . .
4. ff. 34–63, Set 1 beginning at 1 Trinity; at end *Explicit euangelia dominicales per annum*.

---

[48] For instance 10 D. 34/16 was owned by John Geffrey, dean of the collegiate church of St. Mary at Stafford in the second half of the fifteenth century.
[49] For the two Wyclif pieces see *Polemical Works* II. 401–6 and 407–9 respectively; they are nos. 89 and 90 in Loserth's revision of Shirley's *Catalogue*. The Wisbech copy of no. 89 is the only known copy in England; a second copy of no. 90, also not mentioned by Loserth, is in Trinity College, Cambridge B. 14. 50, f. 20.

5. ff. 63–87^v, Set 2 headed *Incipit 2^a pars Commune sanctorum Euangelia*; at end *Explicit comune sanctorum.*

6. ff. 87^v–102^v, Set 3 headed *Incipit propre sanctorum*; ends incomplete in sermon 112, Arnold i. 377/14 *to þese apostels and leuyng to speke.*

In sets 5, 1 and 3 material is missing because of the excision of leaves, or on ff. 3 and 95 of parts of leaves; details are given in the text. The sequence of sets 1–2–3 cannot be disturbed; set 5 was made separately and could have been bound at either end of this sequence, but its prior position was determined before the decorator began work. There is no evidence as to whether the volume ever contained set 4; from its proportions it could easily have done so.

There are two hands in the manuscript, the first only in item 1, and the second in the remainder, English and Latin; both are 'anglicana formata', the second somewhat more old-fashioned in style than the first (Doyle). The second hand is that of W. The whole manuscript has been corrected, usually following guide marks that have been more or less efficiently removed. In the first item the corrector appears also to have been the rubricator. In the work of the second scribe the correction is considerably more frequent particularly in set 1; here correction is usually by the erasure of material, often lengthy passages, and rewriting; the corrector here was neither the scribe nor the rubricator. In both parts of the manuscript there are many marginal annotations in Latin, mostly translating brief words and phrases from the text. The style of decoration is the same throughout the manuscript, though the differing habits of the two scribes lead to variation in the amount the decorator supplied. F. 1 has a large blue initial for the Latin text, with flourishing in blue and red almost all round the page; for the rest of item 1 the initial of the Latin text is in blue flourished with red, the occasion in red, and the remainder of the Latin text and the translation of the biblical text throughout underlined in red, together with some touching of the punctuation in red. In the work of the second scribe the initial is that of the English text, in blue with red flourishing; the occasion is sometimes provided by the rubricator, sometimes only ruled through by him, as is the Latin text and reference; again the biblical text translation is underlined in red throughout. The modern binding incorporates part of the sixteenth-century leather with gold stamping.

There is no trace of medieval ownership. It is not known when the manuscript came into the possession of the Wisbech corporation, but most of the books in the library were collected before 1700. The nine medieval manuscripts were housed until 1878 in a room above the church porch, together with the printed books; more recently they have been housed in a room at the Town Museum.[50]

E^s: Essex Record Office MS D/DPr 554   s. xiv/xv

A single parchment leaf used as a pastedown; size (slightly cropped) 202 mm by 155 m; written frame 185 mm by 130 mm. Written in two columns.[51]

1. fragment of Set 5, from E16/8 *not þus* to E17/7 *ʒe in þis*.

The manuscript must have been of scheme 1, if indeed it contained more than set 5 only.

The hand is a book hand of the end of the fourteenth or early fifteenth century; there is no correction. The fragment contains the opening of only one sermon; here the occasion is written in red, and the initial of the Latin text is also in red with the remainder of the Latin text and reference in the scribe's ordinary ink. Guide marks at the beginning and end of the biblical translation left by the scribe were never acted upon by the rubricator. The style of the manuscript was similar to that of the majority of the sermon-cycle.

Between the two columns on the recto is the inscription in a late fifteenth or early sixteenth-century hand 'Thomas Brodewey(?) owys thys boke', but this may well refer to the book in which the leaf was used as a pastedown rather than to the original manuscript. The verso was stuck to the board.

H^t: Hertford College Oxford MS 4   s. xiv/xv

Ten fragments used as strengthening in the binding of a compilation of miscellaneous astronomical and medical tracts of

---

[50] See the notice by A. N. L. Munby in *The Wisbech Society Annual Report* 1953, pp. 10–12; the observation there that all the manuscripts come from the abbey of Bury St. Edmunds is incorrect, only one of them being accepted as from that source by N. R. Ker, *Medieval Libraries of Great Britain* (London, 2nd edition 1964), p. 22.

[51] I owe knowledge of this leaf to the generosity of Dr. Ian Doyle.

the fifteenth century. Five are single complete leaves, slightly cropped, used around the outside or in the centre of quires, with the original length of the leaf horizontal; the remaining five are separate half leaves. The parchment has been rubbed down with varying degrees of efficiency, but in no case is all the writing legible; all but one of the fragments allow of identification of the original text, but detail of the possibility of collation is given in the opening notes to the relevant sermons. The original leaf size must have been approximately 300 mm by 220 mm; the written frame approximately 223 mm by 152 mm. Written in two columns.[52]

1. ff. 2, 19, 42, 43, 50–51, 58, 59, 108, 125, 138–9, 195, 196, 209, fragments of Set 5. Of these f. 2 is illegible. The order of the fragments is (i) f. 195, lower half of leaf containing on verso part of E3, on recto part of E4; (ii) ff. 138–9, single leaf in middle of quire containing parts of E7–E8; (iii) f. 19, upper half of single leaf containing parts of E13–E14; (iv) ff. 196, 209, single leaf around outside of quire, containing part of E14 following on from last; (v) ff. 43, 58, single leaf around outside of quire, containing part of E14 following on from the last and part of E15; (vi) f. 42, upper half of leaf containing part of E16 and beginning of E17; (vii) ff. 108, 125, single leaf around outside of quire, containing part of E18; (viii) ff. 50–51, single leaf in middle of quire containing parts of E33–E34; (ix) f. 59, upper half of leaf containing part of E34 and beginning of E35.

The script of the fragments is a single text hand of *c.* 1400; there is some correction by the original scribe. The main initial of each sermon is that of the English text which is in blue; the Latin text and reference and the occasion are in red before each sermon, but are not always legible now. There are blue paraph marks, and the translation of the biblical text is underlined in red throughout. The layout of the manuscript was obviously that of the majority that are better preserved; the margins are of comparable width to those in D, but otherwise there is little to

---

52 A full description is given by M. B. Parkes, 'Manuscript Fragments of English Sermons attributed to John Wyclif', *Medium Ævum* xxiv (1955), 97–100; I am less optimistic than Mr Parkes about the legibility of some of the fragments, but have been able to identify the texts on fragments i and vi above which he states to be completely illegible. The volume in which the fragments were used is described by H. O. Coxe, *Catalogus Codicum MSS. qui in Collegiis Aulisque Oxoniensibus hodie adservantur* (Oxford, 1852), ii under St. Mary Magdalen Hall No. 2.

justify the claim made when the identity of the fragments was recognized that it is 'on the whole superior to other manuscripts of the same text at present in the Bodleian or the British Museum'.

On f. 2ᵛ is an erased inscription which Mr Parkes has interpreted as being the *ex libris* of John Chamber, fellow of Winchester College, admitted 1508–9. The folio was once used as the pastedown of an earlier binding. The fragments must therefore have been rubbed down and used as they at present appear by about this time.

Pᵗ: fragments in Peterhouse Cambridge MS 69   s. xv in.

Four parchment leaves, size 290 mm by 185 mm, written frame 230 mm by 145 mm,[53] bound in to the end of a late fourteenth-century copy of Robert de Cowton's Commentary on the *Sentences* in its abbreviated form.[54] The leaves seem to be the two outer bifolia of a quire of 10; leaves 1–2 and, separately, 3–4 run on, and there appears to be stitching between leaves 2ᵛ and 3. The gap in material between leaves 2 and 3 is roughly compatible with a loss of six leaves.[55]

1. ff. i–ivᵛ, fragments of Set 1 beginning at 1 Trinity. Leaves 1–2 contain 18/76 *of þis new sectis* to end, 19, 20, 21/1–68 *spiritual þinges bygynnen*. Leaves 3–4 contain 29/52 *þat þei knouen* to end; 30, 31/1–77 *obediense to Crist*. The writing on the verso of leaf 4 ends slightly less than half way down the second column; nothing further is visible to the naked eye or under ultra-violet light.

It would seem likely that work on the manuscript was for some reason abandoned at that point, since the intended rubrication and ornamentation has not been carried out. The reason for the abandonment seems not to have been disapproval of the content, since though the remainder of no. 31 is controversial, no. 30 had already been copied including its highly heterodox material on

[53] M. R. James, *A Descriptive Catalogue of the Manuscripts in the Library of Peterhouse* (Cambridge, 1899), pp. 87–8; James did no identify the contents of the fragments, and I was unaware of their existence when writing in *Medium Ævum* xl (1971).

[54] The commentary is no. 735 in F. Stegmüller, *Repertorium Commentariorum in Sententias Petri Lombardi* (Würzburg, 1947); for Cowton see Emden, *Oxford* i. 507.

[55] The missing material is 699 lines; judging by the surviving material six leaves should have contained 728 lines. It is perhaps possible that part of a column was left blank to begin no. 26, the sermon for 1 Advent, at the head of a column.

the Eucharist. Leaf 4 has a hole in the outer column, and has also been badly affected by damp; this latter has resulted in an offset of leaf 3 on the inner column so that little is legible on the recto.

The script is an anglicana formata of the early fifteenth century. Gaps were left for an initial for the English text; the Latin text, biblical reference, and occasion are filled in by the scribe. These, and the translation of the biblical text throughout, have been lightly underlined by the scribe as a guide for the rubricator. There is one correction in the scribe's own hand but otherwise there is no correction or marginal annotation.

There are no signs of ownership on the fragments. The main manuscript was already in the library of Peterhouse when the catalogue was made in 1418.[56] The manuscript now has a modern binding, but when M. R. James compiled his catalogue in 1899 he stated that the binding still showed traces of a chain mark. Since books have not been chained in Peterhouse since 1594, it would appear that the fragments must have been bound into the book since before that time.[57]

---

[56] James p. 21.   [57] James p. xxxi.

III

The Derivatives of the Sermon Cycle

The controversial nature of the subject-matter of this cycle is evident in almost every sermon within it; specifically Wycliffite tenets are discussed in many examples. If a manuscript of the sermons came into the hands of the ecclesiastical authorities during the period 1380 to 1520, no difficulty would have been found in identifying the contents as heretical. It is inherently likely, therefore, that many manuscripts were destroyed during this time. There are, however, cases where reaction during that period, whilst not altogether favourable, was less extreme, cases where the sermons were either expurgated or used, with more or less alteration, as the basis for less controversial preaching. Textually, at least in the present case, it is simple enough to distinguish these two types: the expurgations can be collated with the texts established here, since the principal change is omission and the linking of the remaining material is done with a minimum of verbal alteration; the derivatives, on the other hand, show more extreme rewriting and rearrangement and, most importantly, the incorporation of substantial new material. The motives behind the two methods, expurgation and derivation, may be very similar, and the outlook expressed by examples of either method may be closely alike. But for the editor the textual consideration is the determining factor: can the variants be economically handled within an apparatus whose primary interest concerns the original text and not these sophistications? In the present volume expurgation is most clearly seen in Z, a manuscript already described and one whose textual peculiarities are fully recorded in the apparatus. The position of Z with regard to Lollard views has been outlined in a paper published some years ago.[1] Because of the simplicity with which the alterations in this manuscript were made there are few

---

[1] A. Hudson, 'The Expurgation of a Lollard Sermon-Cycle', *Journal of Theological Studies* NS xxii (1971), 451–65.

problems in presenting Z's idiosyncrasies along with the present edition. It will be seen in the next volume that some rather simpler excisions were made by E and W in sermons of set 2; also in volume ii will be described the abbreviated version of sermon 122 found in Edinburgh University Library MS 93, ff. 22^v–25^v.[2]

The purpose of the present chapter is to give an account of the derivatives of the sermons in this volume that have so far been found. I have not undertaken an extensive search for these derivatives, and it is likely that, as further work is done on manuscripts containing fifteenth-century English sermons, more examples will be discovered. Four examples have so far come to light. As will be seen, the dependence ranges from the borrowing of complete sermons to quotation of only an odd sentence; recognition of borrowing is thus not always easy. The account that follows will attempt briefly to show two things: first, that the direction of the influence is from the sermons here edited to the other text, and secondly the nature of the material that has been borrowed. The first is necessary to justify the omission of these cases from consideration is establishing the texts here. The second may be of use in alerting scholars to the areas, some rather surprising, in which these sermons seem to have been influential, and where consequently further borrowing may be found.

A. Dependent set of sermons in three manuscripts

This is the most extensive example yet found of dependence upon the sermon cycle here edited: in its fullest form, the set uses 51 out of the 54 sermons of the present set 1 on the Sunday gospels and a further five sermons from sets 3 and 4.[3] This fullest form is only known in a single manuscript, Trinity College Dublin 241 (Tr), though that is now defective near the beginning from loss of leaves. As originally written the manuscript contained a set of Sunday gospel sermons throughout the liturgical year, beginning on the first Sunday after Trinity, followed by six occasional sermons, for All Saints' day, Ascension, Nativity, Circumcision,

---

2 My attention was drawn to this by Dr Anthony Warner. The rest of the contents of the manuscript are orthodox. The sermon has been abbreviated, but some unorthodox sentiments remain (for instance, Arnold i. 412/27–30).

3 There is a muddled reference to this derivative in Severs *Manual* ii. 523; see also Arnold i, p. iii.

Epiphany, and for a final unspecified day.[4] The sermons for the Sundays after Trinity are found also in two other manuscripts, St. John's College Cambridge G. 22, ff. 1–78^v, and Cambridge University Library Additional 5338 (Ad), ff. 1–67; the first of these two is S of the present edition. It will be recalled that S contains as its second item only sermons 33–54 of set 1, being incomplete at both beginning and end of this sequence. The quire signatures in the first item make it plain that the sermon on 1 Trinity was the first; the last sermon after Trinity ends on the verso of the last leaf of quire 10, and the fact that there are no catchwords may, since such remain at the end of the first nine quires, indicate that no more was intended to follow.[5] Ad has been extensively damaged at the beginning, so that the first legible material is on f. 4 where words may be identified with material in the sermon for 5 Trinity (equivalent to S, f. 13). Quire signatures later in the manuscript suggest, however, that as in the other manuscripts the sermon for 1 Trinity was the first. In Ad it can be demonstrated that there was no intention of continuing the set beyond the end of the Trinity season, as was done in Tr.[6] It should be noted that even in Tr a break occurs at the end of the Trinity season: a gap of a complete folio was left and 1 Advent starts a new quire.[7] This cannot, however, imply that the

---

[4] Old catalogue number C. 1. 22; the manuscript is parchment. It is listed in T. K. Abbott, *Catalogue of the Manuscripts in the Library of Trinity College, Dublin* (Dublin and London, 1900), p. 35 where it is said to be of Wyclif's Postills. As it stands, the material is misbound: f. 2 should stand first, since it contains the opening for a sermon for 1 Trinity, whilst f. 1 contains the beginning of a sermon for 5 Trinity. Judging by the length of the material in the other manuscripts, the original collation of this copy was 1^8 wants 2–7, 2^8 all now lost, 3^8 wants 4–5, 4–18^8. Quotations will be, as far as possible, from this manuscript.

[5] See above pp. 78–9 for a description of the manuscript. A letter in the Library's own copy of James's *Catalogue* from Sir Roger Mynors notes the identity of the sermons with the other two manuscripts here mentioned, and records the debt to the sermon cycle. The signature *a. 3* is visible on f. 3.

[6] A handwritten description of the manuscript is held in Cambridge University Library. It was formerly in the Phillipps collection as no. 11071 (see *Bibliotheca Phillippica*, Sotheby's Catalogue 1897), and was sold in the sale in May 1897 as lot 773. It is a paper manuscript; as far as f. 31 it has been interleaved with modern paper, but this interleaving is not counted in the foliation. The sermon for 25 Trinity ends on f. 67 line 5, after which the scribe wrote *Explicit*; the rest of the recto is blank. On the verso begins a set of sermons for 1 Advent through to the 5th Sunday after the octave of Epiphany, these are discussed below pp. 106–10.

[7] In Tr the sermon for 25 Trinity ends on f. 39^v column 1 line 8; the rest of f. 39^v and the whole of f. 40 is blank. The sermon for 1 Advent begins quire 8 on f. 41.

sequence has been rearranged, since the first of the occasional sermons follows straight on from the end of the sermon for Trinity Sunday (f. 114). Since the dependence of the sermons on those here edited is the same on both sides of this gap, the gap cannot be taken to represent anything of significance about the text.

This dependent collection uses primarily the sermons of set 1, but also four, nos. 122, 90, 95 and 97, from set 3 and one, no. 196, from set 4. The only sermon in the collection that is not in any way related to the present cycle is the last in Tr; no occasion is specified for this. The sermon also differs from all the others in the manuscript in not providing a complete translation of its announced text.[8] There is nothing within this sermon to suggest derivation from a Lollard source. The basis for the selection of the five occasional sermons is unclear: all are for important feasts, but they are not in a logical sequence nor are they the only important feasts to be found in set 3. It is possible that the maker of the collection used a manuscript which, like A, included the Ascension Day sermon erroneously in set 3; if that were the case then the compiler need have known only sets 1 and 3; textually, however, the derivatives are not close to A itself. It is not, however, possible that the compiler derived his knowledge only from a manuscript of set 1 with the peculiar dislocation of the Christmas season material described above (pp. 24–7); this will not account for his acquaintance with no. 122, the sermon for All Saints' Day. The opening of the liturgical year with the first Sunday after Trinity suggests that the compiler used a manuscript of set 1 that began there; the clear break that appears in all of these three texts at the end of the Trinity season does not, however, shed any light on the set 1 variation, since no such break is traceable in the tradition there.[9].

In the Sunday gospel sermons the only difference between the occasions covered in set 1 and in these derivative sermons is that the latter omit sermons for the Sunday within the octave of Epiphany and for the octave itself, thus ignoring nos. 30 and 31. The sermon for Palm Sunday, no. 45, on Matthew 27: 62–6 concerning the anxiety of the Jews for the safety of Christ's body in the tomb, is left out, its place being taken by a sermon on the

---

[8] Tr ff. 126–128ᵛ ends incomplete; the text is '[D]eus vester est et non cogonouistis eum etc. Iohannis viii'.

[9] See the discussion above pp. 35–9.

triumphal entry into Jerusalem, Matthew 21. 1–9, that draws on parts of no. 26, the sermon for 1 Advent that uses the same text.[10]

The existence of a relation between set 1 and the sermons in these three manuscripts is evident from an examination of any one of the latter. Proof that it is the sermons in the three that are the derivatives is simple. The compiler of these sermons almost invariably opens his homily with a translation of the lection for the day, instead of spreading out the translation through the entire sermon as is the case with many examples in set 1; after this translation he proceeds, with an introductory direct address to his listeners, to elucidate the story. In a number of cases the biblical translation corresponds exactly to that of the equivalent sermon in set 1;[11] in some cases the translation in the relevant set 1 sermon is much divided by intervening comments, or very freely rendered, and is not paralleled by the compilation here.[12] But the interesting cases are those where the compilation has the same translation as the set 1 sermon, but has within that translation some of the extra comments of the set 1 preacher that are not in the biblical passage. It is from these plain that the compiler has been careless in his borrowings, perhaps because his exemplar was not properly rubricated, and has not excluded all of the commentary.[13] Since in set 1 the preacher did not separate his sermons into two halves, translation and exegesis, the argument cannot be reversed. The same conclusion may be drawn from the fact that in the derivative, where this separation is aimed at, some material from the set 1 sermons is used twice. Thus in sermon 47 the compiler uses the biblical translation from

---

[10] The substituted gospel reading, though logical for the occasion, has no liturgical justification.

[11] Thus in the sermons derived from no. 38, lines 4–12, 16–25, and from no. 41, lines 2–8, 11–14 are taken without the material that breaks up the translation between the two sets of lines in each case but with the comment that intrudes in each block.

[12] Thus the translation of John 10: 11–16 is entirely independent of the version of no. 48; similarly those of Matt. 5: 20–4 and Matt. 7: 15–21 of nos. 6 and 8. A more varied treatment is found with the material derived from no. 39: lines 4–6 and 33–41, 44–49 are taken over, but between the first and second borrowings a new translation of Luke 18. 32–34 is supplied.

[13] Thus, for instance, the compiler took over from no. 28 lines 47–49, ' "When ȝe sawen Baptist in desert, what wente ȝe to see? sawen ȝe þanne a reed wawyng wiþ þe wynd?" Nay, suche men ben vnstable for louyng of muk, for Iohn was stable in þe loue of God', where the final sentence is commentary not text. Similar instances involve the borrowing of 13/11–34, 18/2–10, 47–57, 21/3–32, 32/3–14, 17–30, 35–40, 38/3–12, 16–27, all treated as if throughout biblical text.

lines 15–24, 29–31, 41–42, but the later exposition uses once more lines 17–23, 23–33 (with an independent passage before this), 34–35, 39–42.[14] In an attempt to avoid the double use of material a further awkwardness arose: in no. 26 the compiler had picked out first the translation, but then went back and utilized the intervening commentary which, in this version, jumps disconnectedly from one point to another.[15] All of these matters imply that the collection is the derivative. This is confirmed by the almost invariable use of blocks of exegesis, taken over in the same order as they appear in the set I sermons.[16]

Since this collection is the derivative, these manuscripts cannot help towards the establishment of the text of set I unless they can be shown to descend from a branch of the stemma that had fewer errors than the surviving manuscripts. This does not appear to be the case. The placing of this collection in the stemma is not possible, since it appears to share errors with a wide variety of manuscripts without any perceptible repetition or pattern.[17] Because of the nature of the borrowings, sometimes leaving gaps and sometimes repeating the same passage, it is impracticable to include variants from these three manuscripts; long passages can be (and have been) collated, but to include the variants and to explain their position would enormously increase the volume of the textual material.

The most frequent type of borrowing from the sermon cycle is of biblical translation, though, as had been said, when the cycle renders the text very freely the compiler supplied a new version. Occasionally, however, the reason for the compiler's rejection of

[14] Similar instances are borrowings from no.41/2–6, 15–17 commentary overlapping with text from 2–7, 11–24; 42/13–19, 47–50, 74–78 commentary overlapping with text from 3–19, 47–50, 75–81; 54/1–3, 3–23, 27–33, 35–48 commentary overlapping with text from 2–10, 27–29, 36–38, 41–2.

[15] Thus the commentary from no. 26/1–3, 6–9, 11–16, 18–21 is abruptly juxtaposed; similarly clumsy transitions arise in the versions of nos. 28 and 34.

[16] Thus in sermon 34 commentary derives in order from lines 1, 40–49, 52–53, 69–71, 87–95; in no. 39 from lines 1–4, 6–15, 18–32; in no. 44 from lines 1–4, 5–31, 34–40, 48–63, 63–84.

[17] The compilation has, of course, errors of its own, though whether these are peculiar to its own tradition or derive from a defective copy of the cycle now lost cannot be shown; an obvious case of haplography is in the borrowing (Tr f. 102) of no. 49/31–2 where the biblical clause 'and noo man schal take fro ȝow ȝowre ioye' (John 16: 22) is omitted. The readings of the compilation do not fall in with those of any single surviving manuscript; in some cases they appear to be close to C, but this is not invariably so and C has a number of errors not found in the compilation.

the biblical translation supplied by his source is less easy to explain: only personal preference seems to account for the substitution of 'Gederiþ first þe tares, and bindeþ hem in bindeles to brenne; and þe goode corn gederiþ into my berne' for the cycle 'Gedre ʒe furst þes tarys togydre, and byndeþ hem in knychys to brenne; but gedre ʒe þe goode corn to my berne'.[18] Beyond the use of biblical text, the amount of material taken from the cycle varies considerably. In some instances, for example those parallel to nos. 14, 15, 21, 24 or 48, nothing more is adopted. But the majority derive some exegetical comment from the cycle. A good idea of the extensive borrowing of material can be seen in the sermon for Trinity Sunday, derived from no. 54. In no. 54 the text was split up, but the compiler put the material together and filled in some gaps: he used for this lines 2–10, 27–29, 35–39, 41–42, 49, 52–53, 56–59, 62–65, 67–68, 72–74, and 98–100. He then went back and picked up much of the commentary, using lines 1–3, 3–23, 27–33, 35–48, 98–99, 109–113.[19] As can be seen, the compiler used the commentary in the sequence in which it occurred in the set 1 sermon. This is the usual method, though in the sermon derived from no. 41 a block of material taken from lines 25–59 was set after another block that derived from lines 60–87. With at least four sermons almost the entire material of the set 1 model was taken over: this is the case with the homilies derived from nos. 29, 34, 44, and 49.[20] Even when the borrowing was less extensive it usually consisted of not less than about two sentences; smaller units, the phrase or the clause, were rarely taken over without their context. It is also rare to find any reworking of borrowed material—exegetical ideas that could derive from the set 1 sermon but are expressed in different words, or ideas for moral teaching that are modified.[21] The compiler either took over his source verbatim or rejected it. The sermons of the compiler are

[18] No. 36/46–48, Tr f. 63ᵛ. See above n. 12 for similarly independent translations; they are not derived from either version of the Wycliffite Bible.

[19] The same was done in the sermon for All Saints' Day from no. 122.

[20] The material from no. 49 was divided between the two derivative sermons, that for its original Sunday, the third after Easter, and that for an earlier occasion, the 25 Sunday after Trinity. To the latter occasion (Tr ff. 38ᵛ–39) has been transferred the discussion of the four dowers of the body and soul from 49/45–97. This appears to be the only case apart from the Palm Sunday sermon where material was transferred from one occasion to another.

[21] One case where modification was made is in the exegesis of the parable of the Good Samaritan in no. 13/46–85, Tr ff. 11–12ᵛ.

consistently of greater length than those of the cycle here edited. Hence, even where almost the whole of the source material has been incorporated, quite a substantial amount of the preacher's own exegesis is found; whether this extra material is indeed the preacher's own, or whether it was adopted from yet another set of sermons, cannot be answered here.

It remains to consider the motivation behind the compiler's actions. Perhaps the strangest aspect (though it is one that recurs in another case) is the adoption of the biblical translation, even when that had to be laboriously pieced together from various parts of the original sermon. The existence of some independent translation in the compiler's work suggests that he had to hand a copy of the Vulgate, or another biblical translation. The compiler seems to have had sympathy with some of the Lollard causes, but not with all. Most noticeably he removed all questionable references to the Eucharist.[22] An instructive alteration occurs in the sermon dependent upon no. 47: having followed the exegesis fairly closely from lines 1–14, 23–36, 39–42, the compiler then altered the original concerning the power of the keys from 'And boste men not for þis priuylegie grauntyd to þe apostles, for hit is vndirstanden in as myche as syche apostles acorden wiþ þe keyis of þe chirche aboue' to 'Þus men seyen comunli wordes of Crist ben vndurstanden when þes keyes erren not from þe keyes aboue; and þes wordes weren seid to alle þe aposteles, and in persones of aposteles weren þei seid to prestes'.[23] In general the more extreme criticism of the higher clergy and of the private orders was removed, though the redactor retained, or added for himself, admonitions to the clergy to reform their worldliness and to teach the lay people more effectively.[24] On the other hand, one recurrent theme of the derivative sermons cuts

---

[22] The most striking case comes in sermon 46, where almost the whole of the original commentary was borrowed (lines 25–31, 36–58, 60–69, 78–88, 91–94), with the exception of nine lines (69–78) dealing with the dual nature of the sacrament, *kyndely breed* but *sacramentally verrey Godis body.*

[23] No. 47/42–45, Tr f. 98ʳ⁻ᵛ.

[24] See, for instance, S f. 6ᵛ (passage missing in Tr because of loss of folios at the beginning of the manuscript) 'And riȝt as in Cristis tyme þe phariseis and þe pristis of þe lawe were most pursueris to þe deþ of Crist bodili, riȝt so religious and pristis in þese daies be most pursueris to diȝstroiȝen Cristis lawe . . . þerfore it were good boþe lordis and comoun peple to be war of þe couetice of þese pharises . . . and drawe hem to trewe prechoures of Goddis lawe and meyntene hem aȝen þese banyoures of antecrist þat are euermore redi dai and nyȝt for to distroiȝe Crist and his lawe'.

straight across usual Lollard teaching: instead of the disparage-
ment of oral confession on grounds both doctrinal and practical,
the homilist repeatedly urges his hearers to take this duty
seriously.[25]

The precise placing of these sermons within the spectrum of
orthodox and heretical thought is the business of their future
editor and does not concern the present text. The preacher spoke
vehemently against 'þes stronge beggeres þat sellen þe gospel of
God boþe in here preching and begging', an allusion to the friars
that would seem to suggest that he himself was a secular.[26] He
apparently viewed with apprehension the wisdom of giving
advanced doctrinal teaching to simple men:[27] hence it is not
surprising that he discarded the more recondite theology found
in some set 1 sermons, whilst supplying more sensible discussion
of basic Christian morality. The revision that he made would
seem to have more to offer to the ordinary parish priest of the
fifteenth century than the original cycle: sympathy is shown
towards some of the reforming aims of the Lollards, but not
towards their more outspoken doctrinal views, and neither
preacher nor congregation would have needed the understanding of theology or of sect vocabulary[28] that the original sermons
often presuppose.

B. Derivative group of sermons in two manuscripts

The second case of a dependent group is of smaller extent and is
only known so far in two manuscripts.[29] The first of these is the
second part of MS Cambridge University Library Additional
5338, Ad of the last section. As has been explained, the first part of
the manuscript contains sermons for the Trinity season; after the

---

[25] For example S f. 20^{r–v}, Tr ff. 20, 25, 28^v, 35^v, 64^v, 82^v–83^v, 95^v–6.

[26] Tr f. 16^v.

[27] See Tr ff. 70^{r–v}, 79, 86^v–87; interesting is the comment in the sermon for 19 Trinity (Tr
f. 26^v) that if priests fail in the preaching of the gospel 'Crist seide þat stones shulden crie,
as seculer lordes shulden in defaute of prestes lerne and teche þe lawe of God in þer moder
tonge'.

[28] For elements in this see A. Hudson, 'A Lollard sect vocabulary?', *Philological
Essays . . . presented to Angus McIntosh*, ed. M. Benskin and M. L. Samuels (Edinburgh,
1981), pp. 15–30.

[29] I am indebted to Mr Alan Fletcher for drawing the Lambeth sermons to my attention;
these, with the additional material in Ad, are now being edited by Ms Ruth Evans of
Leeds University. Quotations here are given for Ad wherever this is available.

gap of two-thirds of a side, another hand on the verso continued with a sermon for 1 Advent. This set extends with sermons for each Sunday, plus one for the gospel on the octave of the Epiphany and an extra sermon for the first Sunday after the octave of Epiphany, up to and including the fifth Sunday after the octave of the Epiphany. There the set in Ad ends, two-thirds of the way down the verso; the size of the concluding *amen* suggests that the scribe had no intention of proceeding further. The second manuscript is Lambeth Palace 392, ff. 148–218ᵛ (Lb); this is the sixth part of a composite volume.[30] The first sermon is defective at the beginning, but is identifiable with that for the third Sunday in Advent in Ad (f. 73ᵛ). Thereafter the material in Lb agrees with that in Ad, but the set continues from the end of the Epiphany season with a Sunday sermon for each week up to and including Easter Sunday; it is not clear whether anything has been lost from the end of the manuscript.[31] All of the sermons are on the gospel pericopes, save that a second sermon is provided for Easter Sunday on the epistle. This, and the extra sermon for the first Sunday after the octave of Epiphany, owe nothing to the sermons here edited.[32] All the other sermons draw some material from the set 1 sermons of the present cycle. There seems to be no difference of relationship between those shared by Ad and Lb and those that survive only in Lb. Apart from one sermon, the amount of material borrowed is small, and is largely limited to the biblical translation of the gospel text. One sermon, however, that for the octave of the Epiphany, takes over virtually the whole of the present sermon no. 31.

[30] See M. R. James and C. Jenkins, *A Descriptive Catalogue of the Manuscripts in the Library of Lambeth Palace* (Cambridge, 1930–32), 540–2; the description there 'not Wycliffite' is understandable but conceals the debt to the present sermons. Part iii of the manuscript, ff. 59–111, contains a copy of the anti-Wycliffite anonymous (not Woodford as the catalogue states) Dominican tract *Pharetra Sacramenti*.

[31] The last surviving sermon ends at the foot of the verso of leaf 7 of the quire; the quires are normally eights, and the following half leaf may be the final leaf of the quire but the binding is too tight for certainty; this half leaf is blank.

[32] The extra sermon is Ad ff. 87–89ᵛ, Lb ff. 163ᵛ–166ᵛ, and occurs immediately after that using no. 32; the Easter epistle sermon survives only in Lb, ff. 213–215ᵛ and is found immediately before the gospel sermon for the same day that uses no. 46. In both manuscripts the sermon for the Sunday within the octave of the Epiphany (no. 30 here) is described as for the fifth Sunday in Advent (Ad f. 78, Lb f. 153), a crass mistake which cannot be explained from any of the surviving set 1 manuscripts.

Leaving for later consideration this one sermon, the method of handling the biblical translations here is very similar to that in the last derivative group. This collection again aims to give first a translation of the gospel text as a whole; the Latin words of the text on which the preacher plans to elaborate are then quoted again, and the exegesis follows.[33] As with the last group, in some cases the biblical translation is taken virtually completely from that here (as in those derived from nos. 35, 41, 43, and 46); in other cases where the sermon here has the translation broken up amongst the exegesis or modified to fit in with the sentence structure of the exegesis, the preacher provided a new translation (as in the sermons corresponding to nos. 36 and 44). In yet others the preacher adopted part of the translation and supplied the remainder (as in those corresponding to nos. 29, 33, 34, 37, 39, 40, and 42). The derivative nature of this compilation is again revealed by the fact that short phrases of commentary, introduced between translated words here, have been left behind in these versions. Thus, for instance, in the sermon for the 2nd Sunday after the octave of Epiphany the word *strangely* (no. 33/ 12, Ad f. 90, Lb f. 167) remains intruded into the gospel narrative; similarly, in that for Sexagesima Sunday the expanded wording of no. 38/18–20 remains (Lb f. 184ᵛ) '*þei seyinge wiþouteforþ see not* wyþinne in her soule *and þei herynge* þe wordys of þis parable *vndirstonde not* þe wit of hem'. Other evidence that reinforces this conclusion comes from oddities of translation: in the first sermon (Ad f. 67ᵛ) 'Lo thy kyng comyȝth tho þe milde or oonly sittyng on an asse' derives its corrupt *oonly* from no. 26/34 *hoomly*; in the third (Ad f. 73) the derivative copies the odd translation of *pauperes evangelizantur* (Matt. 11: 5) *pore men ben preysed* found in almost all manuscripts at no. 28/22. Apart from the biblical translation very little was borrowed from the sermons, and the few comments that were taken are of little interest and usually derive from material in close juxtaposition to the text in the original.[34] One modification deserves comment: in the sermon for Palm Sunday, speaking of the Jews who approached Pilate to express fears about the safety of Christ's

[33] The texts cited before the sermon do not always agree with those here because of the use of later words in the gospel on which the preacher intended to concentrate.

[34] For instance the explanation for Christ's appellation as a *lamb* (Ad f. 79ʳ⁻ᵛ, Lb f. 154ʳ⁻ᵛ) owes its material to no. 30/5–14.

body in the tomb, the preacher of the sermons edited here added (no. 45/26) 'þis pagyn pleyen þei þat huyden þe trewþe of Godis lawe', which survives in somewhat less vivid form as 'þus don þei þat now on daiis hydyn þe trouþe of Goddis lawe'.[35]

It is difficult to understand why sermon 31 should have been treated so differently by the redactor. Here the first sentence before the biblical story was slightly modified, but from the end of line 2 the redactor adopted the whole of the material in no. 31 and only added a brief prayer for grace at the end. As it stands in Ad and Lb the text sometimes fails to make sense, but this seems to be result of textual corruption arising from obvious causes such as haplography rather than from deliberate modification by the preacher.[36] The sermon contains fairly outspoken criticism of the claims of the prelacy to men's obedience, claims that they assert to be of higher priority than obedience to God; this criticism is not expurgated, but is, if anything, exphasized by some clarificatory added words.[37] It may be that the reason for the inclusion of this entire sermon lies in the fact that it provided material for an occasion not frequently covered in sermon cycles, whereas material for all the other occasions offered would be more easily come by. The validity of this suggestion can only be tested when further work has been done on the background of these sermons; it could be supported if the other sermons were found to contain borrowings from other known sermon collections.

Another puzzle about this derivative concerns the outlook of the preacher. The first three sermons, of which the major part only survives in Ad, show some sympathy with Lollard views: preaching should be 'wiþowtyn ony frere fablys or tales' (Ad f. 67ᵛ), 'antecrist and hys clerkys haue reryd anothir lawe, þe wyche is magnified more þan þis lawe of Crist, and thei hold yt betyr to rewle wiþ Cristis cherche' (Ad. f. 68), pilgrimages to 'stokks and stonys . . . to worschepe ther mawmettys' (Ad f. 74ᵛ, Lb f. 148ᵛ) are condemned. There is some trace of Lollard vocabulary in these early sermons: 'antecrist is now so heye þat onneþe dar ony trewe man apere; for men hat[y]þ now on dayes to here speke of

---

[35] Lb f. 209ᵛ.

[36] For instance the omission of 'and so riȝtwisnesse is al maner of makenesse' (no. 31/34–35). Lb is a much more careless copy than Ad, at least in this sermon.

[37] Thus line 80 *prelate* is expanded to *prelate or þy priour*; *any oþur lawe* of line 91 is specified as *ony sweche newe religiows lawe*.

Gods lawys' (A f. 70.ᵛ)[38] Later, however, there is much less to remind the reader of Lollard concerns. The question of confession is touched on several times, but there is no specific approbation of condemnation of oral shrift.[39] On one or two occasions the preacher seems to be approaching topics that excited the Wycliffites, but the topic remains unexplored: thus the preacher observes 'iche riȝtwis man schulde obeische to his souerayns in as moche as it acordiþ wiþ Goddis lawe and to obeische not to ony man in þe contrarie þerof,—noo, þou it were an aungil þat com doun fro heuene' (Lb ff. 204ᵛ–205), but the implications of this in relations with the clergy are not examined. There is consistently concern for the preaching of the gospel, but those hostile to such preaching are never defined in contemporary terms as would be the case in Lollard writings.[40]

The reasons for the borrowings then remain something of a mystery. As with the last example, the preacher must have had other tools available to obtain biblical translation; presumably his adoption of much translation from the present cycle arose from an appreciation of its idiomatic quality. Textually this derivative has nothing to offer to the editor of the present cycle. Its affinities with the surviving manuscripts cannot be precisely traced, but at no point does it provide readings that improve upon the extant manuscripts of the cycle, or help with any decisions about originality. Sermon 31 as a whole, and some biblical passages in other sermons, are collatable; but their addition here would only complicate the already heavy textual annotation without providing anything of value.

C. Bodley MS 806

The sermons in this manuscript cannot be described as derivatives in the same sense as was the case with the previous two examples. The material taken from the cycle here edited is much slighter in amount, and has been better integrated into the

---

[38] See above n. 28.

[39] For instance Ad f. 97ʳ⁻ᵛ, Lb ff. 171ᵛ–72, 202–6, 216–218ᵛ.

[40] Thus mention is made (Lb f. 197ᵛ) of 'glosers and flaterers þat glosyn þe people wyþ trifles and fablis and lesyngis', but it is not clear whether *glosers* has any meaning more precise than *flaterers*. A slightly more definite allusion to contemporary affairs is found in the sermon for Passion Sunday (Lb f. 207) 'But God forbede þat any man for þis stonynge lette to speake or to preche þe trouþe of Goddis . . . ne for deþ, ȝyf it come'.

preacher's own sermons. It seemed useful, however, to include this instance here to alert other scholars to the type of influence that the cycle had; it is to be suspected that many more such traces of dependence may be found.

Bodley MS 806 (Bd) contains a set of sermons largely on the Sunday gospels from the first Sunday in Advent to the 24th Sunday after Trinity;[41] the only sermons that break this pattern are one on the epistle substituted for the gospel sermon on Palm Sunday, and a sermon on the epistle for Easter Sunday added before that for the gospel on the same day; as in set 1 here a sermon on the gospel is provided for the octave of the Epiphany. The most obvious case of borrowing from the sermons here is in the homily provided for the Sunday within the octave of Epiphany (Bd f. 18^{r-v}) where is found 'And so Ion forþe in þe gospel, "*He þis is of whom I seyde 'aftir me comeþ a man þe whiche before me is maad', for he was* anon *my prioure; and furste I wiste hyme not.*" For, riȝt as Criste was a man þe firste time þat he was conceyued, so God made hym þanne prioure of al þis religioun, and he was abbot, as Poule seiþ. And ȝif al þat Ion wiste in soule þat Criste was borne, ȝut he koude not wiþ bodily yȝe knowe hyme fro anoþer man; *bot for to shewe hym in Israel "And perfore I baptise in watir*".' Here the material is taken straight from no. 30/23–31; there is alteration of first to third person in line 28 which makes the second direct speech abrupt; there is also corruption by the omission of the end of Paul's comment and by omission of 'and þis falliþ comunly' after 'fro anoþer man' which makes the ensuing *bot* inconsequential. The following exegesis of the descent of the Holy Spirit upon Christ incorporates a brief summary of the contentious discussion in no. 30: (Bd f. 19) 'and wyte ȝe wel þat þis culuere was a werrey foule as oþer ben; and hit bitokened þe Holy Goist, and in a maner it was þe Hooly Goist, as God seiþ in his lawe þat seuene oxen ben seuene ȝeer, for þey figurden seuene ȝere'. The preacher had obviously understood the somewhat recondite argument to make this summary, but he ignored the question to which no. 30 then goes on, the Eucharist.[42]

---

[41] SC 2688; the manuscript is parchment. The foliation is not wholly correct but for convenience has been followed here.

[42] For the issues see *Selections* no. 21B. That Bd's exemplar had the full discussion of the Eucharist is suggested by the side note in the scribe's hand '4to de consecracione dist' iiij', referring to canon law on the subject.

The other borrowings are less extensive. From the first sermon here four short passages were taken (Bd ff. 75ᵛ–8): 'Parable is to seye a worde of stori þat comprehendiþ in hymesilfe gostly vndirstondynge' (1/2–3), a commonplace whose position is the only proof of derivation; Dives 'was cloþed in purpore and bise (þat were preciouse cloþingis), and eche daye he was shynyngly fedde' (1/5–6, 8), where the parenthesis and the adverb are the main indications of source; the action of the dogs 'bytokeneþ þe seruauntes of lordes schulden counforte pore men' (1/13–14), and the request of Dives for a messanger to return to his brethren 'al þis preyed not Diues for charite [to] his breþeren, bot for he wiste þe moo come þere, more peyne schulde he haue' (1/52–56 conflated with 35–36), neither of which without the clearer reminiscences would be certain borrowings. From the next sermon here a more drastic summary was made of one passage (Bd f. 78): the explanation of the lord's great supper (2/13–18) is reduced to 'and so he mot nede make a greet soper, for boþe þe puple schal be greet and þe seruice schal be greet, for Crist schal be fulnesse of euerelastynge swetnesse'. Other parallels are likewise in isolation unconvincing. In the sermon for the octave of Epiphany one sentence reappears (f. 20) 'þis was grete mekenesse in Criste þe Lorde came to his seruant' (31/3–4); in the following sermon the observation (f. 22) 'þe children miȝten chese þat tyme where þey wolde weende wiþ þe fadir or wiþ þe moder', probably comes from 32/8–9,[43] but the preacher then launches into a thoroughly Wycliffite attack on the contemporary abuses of pilgrimages, a topic only briefly touched on in 32/13–14. Similarly the preacher of Bd expands from 48/63–66 'suche hirede men þat ben not heerdis þat louyn not þe flock, but to haue of heme þe dunge and þe mylke, and þe wolle and þe lomb and þe fleysch [and] þe skyn' (f. 61). All of these borrowings in Bd are taken into sermons for the same occasion as that in which they originally appear. But in at least one case the material was transferred. For Palm Sunday Bd has a sermon on the epistle; but one sentence from no. 45 for that day here was taken over into the sermon on the gospel for Quinquagesima Sunday: speaking of the view taken by prelates of the words of scripture, the preacher comments (f. 36ᵛ) '[they] seyn þat it is fals aftir þe lettre, but ȝif it

---

[43] Cf the brief phrase (f. 41ᵛ) 'and þis Crist dide to continue þe deuocioun of þis womman', possibly derived from 41/7–8.

be after here gloos taken and vnderstande', a probable reminiscence of 45/16–18.

This final instance emphasizes the difficulty of assessing
precisely the extent of the debt in this manuscript. The sentiment
is by no means uncommon in Lollard writings, and, were it not
for the more certain borrowings, could be dismissed as common
stock.[44] Other cases, where there is no similarity of wording or of
syntax but only a general similarity of exegesis or of polemic, are
even more problematic and are not here discussed. As has to
some extent emerged from the examples so far given, the sermons
in Bd show considerable sympathy with Lollard causes. The
subject of the Eucharist is largely avoided, but most other topics
are discussed. The sermon for 14 Trinity provides a summary of
repeated views on priestly absolution (f. 114ᵛ) 'for he [i.e. Christ]
oonly clensiþ man of synne, and prestes ben helpers wiþ
hyme; . . . and so bynde and vnbynde wiþ hyme whenne þei
haue þat power and þe keye of kunnyng, and elles þei neþer
byynden ne lowsyn but scateryn abrood'.[45] All associated
matters, pardons, indulgences, letters of fraternity, prayers for
the dead, images and pilgrimages, receive the usual Lollard
condemnation.[46] The identity of Antichrist is not discussed, and
neither is the papacy; but the venality of all orders in the church
below the pope is roundly castigated.[47] The church is repeatedly
defined as 'a gederynge togidere of riȝtwes lyuers'
(f. 126), 'þe congregacioun of trewe cristene men' (f. 120ᵛ), where
the reminiscence of Wyclif's *congregatio omnium predestinatorum* is
evident. The preacher outspokenly defends the necessity for all to
know the scriptures and the legitimacy of laymen teaching the
gospel; persecution of those who endeavour to promote these
aims is condemned.[48] Those who suffer persecution are,
moreover, precisely named: 'as it is ȝut þese dayes, of good puple
and of yuel fewe dar come to Iesu Criste, or to þe herynge of his
lore, for false cristen (worse þanne Iewes) demen suche folke wiþ
greet malice "Lollardes" or mysbyleuynge men' (f. 73ᵛ), and

---

[44] See, for instance, Arnold iii. 258/18, Matthew 376/9.

[45] See, also ff. 18, 42, 114ᵛ, 121ᵛ, 125ᵛ.   [46] For instance ff. 35ᵛ, 41, 61, 97.

[47] For instance f. 89ᵛ 'we may opynly knowe þat þis worlde is full of anticristis þat ben
aȝen trouþe boþe in þe chirche and in þe courtis, spiritual and temperal, in assises, in
counsels and parlementis, in chepyngus and tauernis . . . Who wole suffre now to here
Goddis worde þre dayes hungry? -ful fewe þre houres!'. Cf ff. 90ʳ⁻ᵛ, 97, 11, 121, 138.

[48] See ff. 10, 47ᵛ⁻8ᵛ, 65ᵛ, 78ᵛ, 80ᵛ, 85–6, 100ᵛ, 122ʳ⁻ᵛ, 133.

again 'for ȝif a man or a womman do wel, or speke wel, and gladly wolde plese God, þey ben contrarie to here dedis, and so þei scornen suche men and clepen hem "Lollardis" (f. 70ᵛ).⁴⁹ These persecutors, the preacher maintains, hold that 'it were almes . . . to brenne, to prisoun and to slee men þat seyne þe trowþe þat Crist hymsilfe was pursowed fore and hise hooly apostlis' (f. 70ᵛ).⁵⁰ But at no point is it plain that execution is the actual penalty for these views, thus suggesting that the sermons were written before the enactment of *De Heretico Comburendo* in 1401.

As some of the passages in the last paragraph indicate, many elements of Lollard sect vocabulary are used. Frequently the preacher castigates the modern pharisees, those who 'magnifien heme and here rewle aboue þe rewle of Iesu Crist' (f. 134), and 'haue wounden hemesilfe into mannes tradiciouns' (f. 80), whose 'ordre wantiþ grounde in þe lawe of Iesu Criste' (f. 134); they employ lawyers who deceive the common people who 'knowen not here cawtel[s] ne heere peyntid wordes' (f. 121ᵛ). Similarly these sermons share the contentious translation of *frater* in Pauline passages: just as E14/48 here renders 2 Cor. 11: 26 *periculis in falsis fratribus* as *in perelis in fals freris*, so Bd translates Gal. 2: 4 *propter subintroductos falsos fratres* as 'þe sly *vnderbrouȝte in fals freris* þat sotelly entreden to aspie oure fredam' (f. 92ᵛ), and 2 Thess. 3:6 *ab omni fratre ambulante inordinate* as *frome eche frere weendynge vnordinaly* (f. 91ᵛ).⁵¹ With such similarities of wording, and with the general sympathy of outlook, it is difficult to assess the size of the debt that the preacher of the sermons in Bodley 806 owed to the cycle here edited. For this latter, and particularly for the establishment of its text, Bd can offer nothing. But in its own right

---

⁴⁹ The name appears still to be one disliked by the sect itself; for the change of attitude towards the name see *Selections*, p. 185.

⁵⁰ Compare f. 134 where false priests and prelates are said to enter 'into wickide councel wiþ þe pharisees full of malice to take Cristes seruauntis in her wordes and wiþ þe power of þe kynge wiþ lesynges and false witnesse, namely ȝif þey speken þe treuþe'.

⁵¹ WB translates the word as *broper* or *britheren* in all three passages, with no variation or glosses noted. The version edited by A. C. Paues, *A Fourteenth Century English Biblical Version* (Cambridge, 1904) has *eferich broper pat walkep inordynatlyche* for the Thessalonians passage, but lacks the other two; the version in Parker 32 (ed. M. J. Powell, *The Pauline Epistles* (EETS ES 116, 1916)), has *broper* for 2 Thess. 3:6, *breperene* for Gal. 2:4 but *in perelys in false freris* for 2 Cor. 11: 26. It would not be right to regard the connection of the passages with the friars as conclusive proof of Wycliffite origin; compare *Piers Plowman* B xiii. 68–75 (ed. G. Kane and E. T. Donaldson (London, 1975)).

this set of sermons is perhaps the most interesting case examined in the present chapter.

D. N and its congeners

As has been described in the last chapter, and as has been known since E. W. Talbert's paper published in 1939,[52] N presents a collection of material unparalleled amongst the manuscripts of the sermon-cycle. The sermons of set 1 were used as the prothemes for sermons on the Sunday epistles; these sermons on the epistles bear no resemblance to anything in set 5. N as it stands is considerably defective because of the loss of many leaves, but the plan of the sequence is plain: the sermons began at Whit Sunday; each sermon was prefaced with a Latin text taken from the opening words of the relevant Sunday epistle (though the reference sometimes included the gospel book and chapter as well as that for the text announced), proceeded to the set 1 sermon, then, after a prayer, to an *iteracio thematis* with repetition of the Latin text, and concludes with the sermon on the epistle. There is only one place where N can be shown not to include the set 1 sermon: this is for the sixth Sunday after Trinity, where a different gospel sermon was substituted.[53] For reasons that will be explained, it is almost certain that N, when complete, also substituted another sermon for that edited here for the fifth Sunday after Trinity; but this cannot now be proved, since leaves are missing from N at the relevant point.[54] The epistle sermons introduced in N usually expound the prescribed text first, with varying fullness, and the preacher then continued to some aspect of basic pastoral teaching; there is often continuation of discussion of this from one epistle sermon to the next. This continuation, as has been pointed out (p. 38), makes it clear that the Whit Sunday opening was a deliberate choice and is not a chance of binding. N also contains, ff. 191ᵛ–207ᵛ, eight sermons,

---

52 E. W. Talbert, 'A Fifteenth-Century Lollard Sermon Cycle', *University of Texas Studies in English* (1939), 5–30; the comments on this manuscript in M. D. Lambert, *Medieval Heresy* (London, 1977), pp. 237, 246 are misleading. Talbert's dating of the sermons in N as 'at the earliest *ca.* 1412' (p. 15) is based on doubtful dating of the entire sermon cycle here edited; this matter will be discussed fully in a later volume.

53 N ff. 18–19.

54 By the medieval numbering of the manuscript (see above p. 71 for the defects of this) ff. 15 and 16 are missing; f. 14ᵛ ends with the heading *Dominica quinta post trinitatem*. See below for further points on this loss.

some not complete, that do not derive from any part of the present cycle.

Talbert made no attempt to investigate further the relations, if any, of N's additional material. Recently, however, important discoveries have been made of manuscripts that overlap with N.[55] A full account of the complexities of the relationships between the various manuscripts is not here relevant, but a summary must be made. In the first place, five of the sermons found in N ff. 194–204 appear in Cambridge University Library MS Gg. 6.16, ff. 8–26, (Gg) in the same order.[56] This, of itself, has no interest for the present cycle, since these sermons are in no way part of it. But the same five sermons appear, again in the same order, in a third manuscript, John Rylands Library Manchester Eng. 109, ff. 4–12 (Ry).[57] This last manuscript then continues with material found in N at an earlier stage, within the combined cycle of set 1 plus new epistle sermons. The overlap involves N's material (now incomplete because of loss of leaves) for the 5th to the 7th Sundays after Trinity. In Ry the two parts of the sermons are provided with separate headings, rather than with the marginal note *iteracio thematis* as in N, but since the second repeats the text of the first in each case, the linking is clear. The epistle sermon for the 7th Sunday after Trinity ends on f. 17 just over half way down the second column in mid sentence, for no

---

[55] The most important discovery, that of MS Bodley 95, was made by Miss Helen Spencer, that of the Manchester manuscript by Mr Alan Fletcher; to both of these I am very grateful. Miss Spencer plans a full discussion of the relations between the texts, and the account here, which primarily concerns matters that impinge upon the present sermon cycle, must be regarded as provisional.

[56] See *A Catalogue of the Manuscripts preserved in the Library of the University of Cambridge* (Cambridge, 1861–8), iii. 221; for material later in the same manuscript see A. J. Fletcher and S. Powell, 'The Origins of a Fifteenth-Century Sermon Collection: MSS Harley 2247 and Royal 18 B. xxv', *Leeds Studies in English* NS x (1978), 80–1.

[57] See M. R. James, *A Descriptive Catalogue of the Latin Manuscripts in the John Rylands Library at Manchester* (Manchester, 1921), i. 305–6; the folio numbers used here are those in pencil at the foot of each leaf. The main contents of the manuscript, ff. 37–120ᵛ, is a copy of the translation of Robert of Greatham's sermons known as *The Mirror*; see T. G. Duncan, 'Notes on the Language of the Hunterian MS of *The Mirror*', *Neuphilologische Mitteilungen* lxix (1968), 204–8. On f. 126ᵛ there is an inscription recording that the book was written in 1432 and belonged first to the abbey of Welbeck and then to 'domino Roberto Prestwold'. It is not, however, entirely clear that the manuscript as it now stands all belongs together; assessment of the quiring is impossible because leaves have been remounted and no quire signatures or catchwords remain in the main part. It cannot, therefore, be regarded as certain that the date 1432 gives a *terminus ad quem* for the section here of interest.

apparent reason. The remainder of the manuscript has nothing to do with the present question. Ry has for the gospel sermon for 7th Sunday after Trinity the sermon here no. 7; its textual affiliations will be discussed below. For the gospel sermon for 6th Sunday after Trinity it has the sermon substituted in N for no. 6. N is defective now at the point where the sermon on the gospel for 5th Sunday after Trinity should be; Ry has a sermon other than no. 5. The third manuscript that is relevant is Bodley 95 (By).[58] Basically By presents the epistle sermons that in N are tacked on to the set 1 gospel sermons. But it also has one of the sermons found at the end of N, and the new gospel sermons found in N for Trinity 6, and in Ry for Trinity 5 and Trinity 6.

The correspondences can be seen most clearly from the following table (p. 118). In this only general agreement is considered; detailed variation is found within each version. In the final column are noted other versions of some of the material. Since N is, for the present purposes, the main interest, its order is observed; square brackets indicate leaves now lost from N. Without going into the detailed textual relations of these manuscripts, it is obvious that, whilst N could have provided the material for By, Ry, and Gg, none of these three could have derived entirely in these contents from any other (save that Gg could derive from Ry). It should be noted that the scribe of ff. 194–204^v in N is probably not the same as the one involved in ff. 3–142^v, and that ff. 204^v–207^v are probably in yet another hand.

Many problems arise from this state of affairs, but only three seem relevant to an edition of the present sermon-cycle:

(i) Why did N substitute a different gospel sermon for no. 6, and probably for no. 5?

(ii) What is the relation of Ry to set 1 in sermon 7?

(iii) What is the relation of By to set 1, and particularly to N?

(i) As has been said, N lacks leaves where the gospel sermon for Trinity 5 should appear. But, as well as the agreement in the vicinity of this sermon among N and By and Ry, there is additional evidence within N itself that N originally had their gospel sermon for that occasion. On f. 204^{r-v} in N appears the

58 SC 1905, dated early fifteenth century; the manuscript is paper.

	N	By	Ry	Gg	other
	ff. 3–14^v epistle additions only	ff. 44–55^v			
gp. & ep.	[ff. 15–16^v] 17–18 204^{r-v}	ff. 55^v–60	ff. 12–14		Ross no. 44[59]
gp.	ff. 18–19	f. 60^{r-v}	f. 14^{r-v}		
ep.	ff. 19–20^v	ff. 60^v–62^v	ff. 14^v–15^v		Ross no. 45
gp.	ff. 20^v–21^v		f. 16^{r-v}		Set 1 no. 7
ep.	ff. 21^v–22^v [ff. 23–25^v]	ff. 62^v–65^v	ff. 16^v–17 ends incompl.		Ross no. 46
	ff. 26–105^v epistle additions only	ff. 66–107, 1–26^v			
	ff. 105^v–120^v				
	ff. 120^v–142^v epistle additions only	ff. 26^v–44			
	ff. 194–6		f. 4^{r-v} inc. incompl.	ff. 8–12	
	ff. 196–8		ff. 4^v–6	ff. 12–15^v	
	ff. 198–200		ff. 6–8	ff. 15^v–18^v	
	ff. 200–2		ff. 8–9^v	ff. 18^v–21^v	
	ff. 202–4	ff. 107–111	ff. 9^v–12	ff. 22–6	
	ff. 204^v–207^v ends incompl.				BL Additional 37677, f. 98^v ends incompl.

opening lines of this gospel sermon as far as Ross p. 289/33 *late out*; the scribe then broke off in mid sentence and wrote *alius sermo*; after a gap of a line another scribe added the final sermon of the manuscript. It seems reasonable to conclude that the incomplete-

[59] Ed. W. O. Ross, *Middle English Sermons . . . from British Museum MS Royal 18 B. xxiii* (EETS 209 (1940)). The question of the relation of the Ross material is not strictly relevant to the cycle here edited. But it may be noted that Ross (pp. xxv–xxvi) considered that his nos. 44–46 constituted a group separable from the rest of the manuscript in origin. Ross did not give a full quiring, and the present state of the manuscript is certainly hard to analyse; but it appears that these three sermons, ff. 150–156^v, are in a separate booklet. That the Royal manuscript derives from a text with the arrangement of N or Ry is shown by the words *vbi prius* at the start of nos. 45 and 46 (Ross p. 297/10 and p. 301/21), which points back to the first announcement of the text found in N and Ry but missing in Royal; the *vbi prius* in no. 44 (Ross p. 291/8) is in order since here the Royal manuscript also has the protheme section (Ross pp. 288/22–291/6). For further relations between Royal and N's epistle sermons see below p. 122.

ness of the material on f. 204^v resulted from the scribe's realization that this matter had been copied into the manuscript before, on the lost ff. 15–16.

A possible reason for the suppression of sermon 6 is easy enough to find: the text *Nisi habundauerit iusticia uestra plusquam scribarum et phariseorum* provided an irresistible invitation to a condemnation of the modern scribes and pharisees; lines 14–47 were omitted by the expurgating Z. It must, however, be said that there are many other places where N did not show himself so sensitive, and it will be seen below that the epistle additions shared between N and By contain equally outspoken criticism of the contemporary church. It is also difficult to see why sermon 5 was removed. The exposition of the miraculous draught of fishes is entirely uncontroversial, and was not expurgated in Z. The length of the substituted sermon is roughly the same. It is perhaps most likely that the antecedent set 1 manuscript used by N and its congeners had lost by inadvertence the sermons for 5 and 6 Trinity, and that the gap was therefore filled from another source.[60]

(ii) The copy of no. 7 in Ry could have been made from N itself. The two share peculiar readings at lines 4, 6, 20, 22, 33, 35–40, 44–52, 55–56, 58–59, 59–60, 62, 63, 71 and the conclusion after 75. Ry has further independent error, omitting 13 *to þe peple* . . . 14 *hem to* by haplography, and misreading N's *glutorie* as *glorye* in 57. There are only four cases where Ry agrees with a minority reading against N's participation in the majority version; all are cases where Ry's variation may bring it into line with others by coincidence.[61] How, if Ry was indeed copied from N, Ry came by its order of material on ff. 4–17 is more difficult to say, but it is a problem that does not directly affect the sermons here edited. Ry does not seem to have objected to Wycliffite material, though the most offensive lines of sermon 7, lines 44–52, are omitted in both N and Ry. Whether or not Ry was copied direct from N, there are no cases where Ry preserves a reading superior to N. There was thus no justification for including Ry's variants in the apparatus to no. 7.

---

60 The sermons in Ry and in the Royal manuscript printed by Ross lack any indication of the occasion for which they were intended; this is only deducible from the epistle text used.
61 The cases are at lines 15 A δ and Ry *fulfilled*, al. *fyllud*; 25 δ and Ry *departeth*, al. *partep*; 26 δ and Ry *departed*, al. *partyd*; 71 Tα and Ry *sentence*, al. *sentensis*. Despite the agreement of Ry and δ in three of these cases, it is clear that Ry cannot derive from δ since it does not share that manuscript's many peculiar readings (e.g. lines 32, 45, 56).

(iii) From what has been said so far, the relevance of the third question to the present edition is not clear. By, as has been described, provides a copy of the epistle additions to the sermons in N, and of the substituted gospel sermons described in (i) above for 5 and 6 Trinity. By reordered these epistle sermons to begin more normally at 1 Advent, proceded through the year to 25 Trinity, though omitted (not through loss of leaves in By) anything for the period Sexagesima Sunday to 3 Lent inclusive.[62] By therefore provides much of the material that has been lost from N because of the latter's mutilation, though where the two can be compared it is clear that By's versions have in some places been abbreviated and expurgated. This means that By can be of some assistance in the attempt to reconstruct N's original quiring, but that allowance must be made for the probability that N's text was in places much longer.[63]

It might be expected that By should show the original state of the epistle sermons before they were, as a secondary stage, incorporated into N. In fact this is not the case. In the first place By's conventional Advent opening is shown to be wrong by the fact that the preacher in the 1 Advent sermon that there stands first mentions that he has already dealt with the first two commandments, and will now proceed to the third on the question of oaths; the treatment of the commandments covers the sermons from 18 Trinity to 1 after octave of Epiphany, thus ruling out an opening in Advent.[64] The content of the epistle sermons shows that N's Whit Sunday opening was for that material correct (see p. 38). More importantly for the present edition, it can be shown that By's sermons were copied by someone who had the set 1 sermons in front of him. Each sermon in By begins, as in N, with an epistle text; this is followed by words, sometimes only part of a sentence, sometimes considerably more, concerning the gospel for the day; the call for

[62] The rearrangement accounts for the order of the folios in By in the table above. The sermon for Septuagesima ends on f. 26^v and that for 4 Lent follows immediately in the same hand.

[63] See pp. 70–1 for the problems of N's quiring. By confirms the loss of a single leaf between f. 71^v and f. 73, despite the oddity of quiring that this entails. By's tendency to abbreviate means that it is not a very helpful guide to the difficulties of quires 3–4; the account above has taken account of By's evidence.

[64] The back reference is in N f. 74^v, in By. f. 1^v. As has been explained (pp. 36–7) an opening at 1 Trinity is likewise impossible for the epistle sermons.

prayer then follows, with the rest of the material as in N. The words on the gospel in By derive from the set 1 sermons, as these appear in N. Thus for 3 Trinity By opens (f. 50^v) '*Sobrii estote et vigilate* II Petri. In this gospell tellythe Crist ii paraboles of conforte', which corresponds exactly to line 1 of no. 3; for 4 Trinity (f. 53) '*Spe enim salui facti sumus* ad Rom. octauo. This gospell meuythe men to mercy aȝayne the ypocrisye of the fals faryseus', the less obvious opening to no. 4. The most striking cases of quotation from set 1 in By are from sermons 24 and 45. In the first instance By (ff. 103^v–104) quotes, with some individual rephrasing but leaving a text that it is possible to collate readily with that here, lines 1–43, a passage now lacking in N because of loss of leaves. In the second By takes over (ff. 26^v–30) lines 1–19. It is furthermore evident that By's quotations from the set 1 sermons must come from reliance upon a text having the characteristics only found in N. This emerges from the words on the gospel for 4 Advent in By:

(f. 6) *Dominus prope est* Ad Phil. iiii^{to}. (This gospell telleþe of the mekenes of Iohn Baptist, and how muche he loued Crist. The Iewes send frome them dekenes and prestes to Iohn for to wete what etc. *vt in euangelio bene grundia* [sic] in the lawe. And þerfore holde we Cristus lawe and kepe we his relygyon and pray we here for . . .

The text of no. 29 essentially agrees with this up to 'for to wete what'; it has nothing corresponding to the rest. In all the manuscripts other than N the sermon concludes 'alle þese newe ordres þat ben presumed aȝeynes Crist'. N, however, goes on (f. 82^v) 'and vngrounded in his lawe. And þerfore holde we Cristus reule and kepe we his religyoun, and preie we herfore . . . '. N's *vngrounded in his lawe* is the source of By's impossible Latin *bene grundia*.

It emerges then that the apparently normal sermon set in By was derived by extraction from the superficially abnormal arrangement represented by N. Whether By was actually made from N itself is less easy to determine. In the epistle sermons found only in N and By, By has a number of errors not shared with N; these could suggest that By is a careless reworking of N. The smaller number of apparent errors in N not found in By might, on the contrary, indicate that By derives from N's exemplar; but many are of an obvious type that By could independently have corrected.[65] In the set 1 material that By reproduces it appears to be closely allied with N; unfortunately, its most extensive quotation, that from no. 24, cannot be compared with N because of the latter's loss of leaves.[66] In the present edition By's material has not been incorporated (though a collation of its extracts was made), since it cannot be shown to offer any information beyond what is available in N save where N is defective. N itself is idiosyncratic and its variants add much to the bulk of textual material; to supplement this by a derivative which also has oddities of its own would be perverse.

It is likely that further work on fifteenth-century sermon manuscripts may well reveal more parallels, sources, or derivatives of this group. As well as the overlap with sermons in MS Royal 18 B. xxiii, one other analogue may be mentioned. In the epistle sermons for 21 and 22 Trinity in N and By appears a comparison of the three estates of men to birds: the lords are compared to the nightingale, the labourers to the lark, and the clergy to the turtle. This comparison is found *verbatim* as an independent passage in MS Harley 2339.[67] The position of the epistle sermons in the range of Lollard or orthodox opinion is not easy to define. E. W. Talbert, who knew only N, suggested that there were only two passages in them that 'definitely show the author's Lollardy'; these two passages concern the worship of images and the attack made by the friars, called Caim's children, on preaching, apparently, though not declaredly, by the Lollards. [68] Certainly there is no unambiguously Lollard tenet on the Eucharist put forward, nor any outright condemnation of

---

[65] For By's errors see, for instance, f. 52 where By omits part of the translation of Isaiah 3:24 cited in his Latin (N f. 12 has a complete translation). Errors in N corrected by By mostly involve very simple modifications. A full edition of these sermons is the place for a definitive judgment about the relationship of the manuscript.

[66] By in no. 45 shares N's errors in line 7 *duden* (though By has further modification), al. *dredden, schulde not*, al. *schulde*; in no. 24 By shares with the group CKLMTY$\beta\delta$Z the omission of the biblical *bot slepiþ* in line 20.

[67] By ff. 97–8, 99^{r-v}; N has lost f. 60 where the first part must have started, but completes this and the second on f. 61^{r-v}, and has lost f. 63 where the third would have stood. See A. I. Doyle, 'A Treatise of the Three Estates', *Dominican Studies* iii (1950), 351–8. Where N can be compared with the Harley text the two are very close; By has several cases of careless haplography. Apart from the instances already mentioned, there are other parallels between the sermons printed by Ross and the epistle sermons in By and N; these include the first three sermons in Advent (N ff. 74–75^v, 77^v–78^v, 79^v–89^v, By ff. 1–2^v, 4^{r-v}, 4^v–6) which share passages with nos. 18, 20 and 21 respectively in Ross.

[68] Talbert p. 16 and n. 35.

the whole principle of 'private religion' in these epistle sermons. However, from some omissions in By, it may appear that some views in N were thought unduly outspoken: By removed much of N's condemnation of indulgences and letters of fraternity, and the more extreme observations on shrift.[69] By was not averse to fairly strong criticism of the clergy and contemporary abuses,[70] and included comments such as (f. 79) 'ther buþe other dyuerse lawes made by mannus witt þat letteþᵉ ofte tymes Goddes lawe to haue his cours; but sothely hit is but a bastard lawe, ymade by the fendus councell, but that hit be grounded in Goddus lawe whiche þat may neuer fayle'. Such sentiments, and the vocabulary in which it is couched, is familiar from the sermons here edited, and by the mid fifteenth century might be felt to be dangerously contentious. As a provisional characterization, that must be reviewed when these interesting sermons are properly edited, it seems that N's epistle additions were the work of a Lollard sympathizer, though not on the extreme wing of the movement. As with the first derivative here described, the twin sermons as they appear in N had much to offer a parish preacher, providing basic instruction as well as some tendentious material. They lack, however, the centrality of the cyle to the Lollard movement, and the coverage of Wycliffite views.

[69] N ff. 49, 80ᵛ, 83, 130, all omitted or so heavily edited as to be innocuous in By (ff. 88, 6, 7ᵛ, 35).

[70] For instance, that if the bishop lives a cursed life his blessing is not worth 'an old (N adds *bored*) bene' (N f. 92ᵛ, By f. 15); that sacraments celebrated by a symoniac are invalid (N f. 92ᵛ, By f. 15ᵛ); that the people are being deprived of God's word by the action of false preachers (N f. 101ᵛ, By f. 22ᵛ). It does not appear that the odd gap in By's coverage of the ecclesiastical year can be due to removal of incurably tendentious discussion: the sermons for Sexagesima to 3 Lent are preserved intact in N and are not particularly controversial.

IV

The Presentation of the Text in the Manuscripts

In the first chapter an account was given of the ramifications of arrangement found in the various manuscripts. The purpose of the present chapter is to consider the ways in which the scribes presented the texts, whichever arrangement they chose, and the evidence that this presentation was controlled. The most important section is that concerning the correction of the text, a question that obviously needs consideration before the relationship of the manuscripts can be assessed. Before that section a brief examination will be made of what might be described as the external aspects of presentation.

A. Layout of the manuscripts

At the simplest level there is considerable divergence between the manuscripts in appearance. The size of them is very varied, from the largest D, measuring overall 355 mm by 243 mm (13.7 by 9.5 inches) to the smallest, Q, measuring 170 mm by 120 mm[1] (6.4 by 4.7 inches). W and δ most nearly approximate to D, O and C to Q. In part, of course, the intended contents of the manuscript determined the proportions of the leaf used: Q, O and C contain only one set, whilst D contains all five, W three, and δ four sets respectively.[2] But there is no regular relationship between content and leaf-size: thus F containing only set 1 (and with no indication that it was ever intended to contain more) measures 230 mm by 150 mm (8.8 by 5.3 inches), whilst X, which possesses all five, is only 260 mm by 175 mm (10.3 by 7 inches), or α, possessing four sets, 240 mm by 165 mm (9.5 by 6.5 inches). In some cases the present size has been reached by substantial cropping of the margins, but this cannot alter the conclusion that no uniformity of size can

---

[1] Full details of all manuscripts are given in chapter II; only a few details will here be remarked.

[2] W is written in the same hand as items 2–6 of δ; there can, however, be no question that these two portions were originally part of the same manuscript, since material (sets 2 and 3) is repeated between the two.

ever have existed between manuscripts of similar contents. Equally there is variation between the use of a single column or two columns that is not dependent upon the extent of the content, nor upon the size of the leaf. The commonest format is of two columns, but ten of the manuscripts have only a single column. Of these, five are texts having only one set, a sixth is V that contained arrangement 3 for a short season of the liturgical year only, and a seventh is N, containing only one set of the present sermons but making considerable additions to these. The remaining three are R, having three sets, L and M having four each. Of these M is a peculiarly inconvenient text, since the over-all measurement of the leaf is 340 mm by 230 mm (13.4 by 9 inches), the size of the single column 275 mm by 172 mm (10.8 by 6.8 inches) in the first section, 287 mm by 178 mm (11.3 by 7 inches) in the second; the width of this single column, accompanied by the rather small hands, makes it hard to follow the script across the leaf (see plate 2). Again there is no regular relationship between the width of the written frame and the number of columns used; M's written frame is far in excess of F's (width 100 mm, 4.4 inches), but F is ruled in two columns.

It would appear then that the physical make-up of the manuscript and the design of the page were not subject to discernible regulations. All of the manuscripts are of parchment, but this may be a function of their early date rather than of a conscious decision on the part of those executing them.[3] The ruling is normally of a simple frame, columns where appropriate, and lines. No provision is made in the ruling for regular marginalia, though many of the manuscripts do contain marginal biblical references (see below pp. 137–8).[4]

Equally there is a lack of uniformity in the style of hand employed. A number of scribes used formal book hands, as is the case with ABDFGYβ (frontispiece); a hand influenced by secretary appears in M (plate 2); many manuscripts show hands

---

[3] The same material was used for the vast majority of manuscripts of the Wycliffite Bible and of other English Lollard texts. But the contrast with manuscripts of Wyclif's works copied in Hussite Bohemia is striking: there, even with copies dated before 1420, paper is the rule rather than the exception. Compare also the manuscripts of the derivatives in chapter III.

[4] See M. B. Parkes, 'The Influence of the Concepts of *Ordinatio* and *Compilatio* on the Development of the Book', *Medieval Learning and Literature, Essays presented to R. W. Hunt*, ed. J. J. G. Alexander and M. T, Gibson (Oxford, 1976), pp. 115–41.

of an anglicana type, more or less influenced by letters of book-hand derivation (plates 1, 3 and 4).[5] Leaving aside the three groups of fragments, and not including items now bound into the manuscripts which have no relation to the five sets here edited, nineteen of the manuscripts were probably written each in a single hand. But in the remaining eight there was no apparent attempt to match the different hands. Thus of the probable seven hands in J, the second is a rather ill-formed book hand, the sixth (which wrote the bulk of the five sets) is a fairly current anglicana. In all, some 47 hands are discernible in the 31 manuscripts, leaving out of account scribes whose work seems to have been limited to correction even if that correction did rarely include the supply of a complete leaf.[6] Within the sermons there appears to be only a single case of a scribe at work in more than one manuscript: the scribe of W seems to be the same as that of ff. 34–102^v of δ. The idiosyncratic hand of V has been found in a manuscript containing part of the Later Version of the Wycliffite Bible.[7]

B. Headings and ornamentation

None of the manuscripts has either illustration or historiated capital. There are, however, two recurrent forms of decoration. The first is the use of gold leaf for the background of the opening initial of the manuscript, and occasionally of those at other major occasions; a border, of varied scope but often extending around the entire page, is added to such initials using red, blue, white and sometimes green colouring. This type of decoration is found in BGWY; further details are given in the descriptions of the manuscripts. The second type is more common, consisting of flourishing of capitals with blue and red penwork; in most of the manuscripts in which this style is found the flourishing is more extensive at the opening of a set, but is found on the main initial for all sermons. It is found in ACDEFHIJKMTXZ$\alpha\beta\delta$ (frontis-

[5] I am heavily indebted to Dr Ian Doyle for characterizations of the hands; for the terms used see M. B. Parkes, *English Cursive Book Hands 1250–1500* (Oxford, 1969).
[6] For correction see below pp. 138–51.
[7] MS Gonville and Caius College Cambridge 179/212. In the course of work for this edition, I have looked at a large number of manuscripts of the Bible translation but have made no systematic search for the hands here. The styles of script and the layout of many of the manuscripts of the Bible translation are very similar to those here, but any summary must await the production of a full catalogue.

piece and plates 1–3), and after the opening initials in BGWY. Flourishing of this kind is common in manuscripts of the Wycliffite Bible, but also elsewhere in manuscripts of the late fourteenth or early fifteenth centuries. Absence of representational art in the manuscripts is probably the result of a conscious decision on the part of those responsible for their making: such distractions from the words of the sermons would be eschewed by men who sympathized with the views expressed in these.[8] It is improbable that the absence is merely the sign of less expensive production.[9]

As has been described in chapter 1, the sermons in the cycle are in each case associated with a particular liturgical occasion; each sermon is headed in such a way as to make this clear. The heading consists of three elements: the occasion, the opening words of the lection in Latin, and the biblical book and chapter reference for that lection. The majority of manuscripts regularly give all three parts of this heading. In a few instances a gap was left for the rubricated heading but this was never inserted: this is the case with S, where the scribe's informal scribble was not entered, in set 2 of L, and for the odd sermon in some other manuscripts where the rubricator missed an individual leaf. In O the book and chapter reference is normally not included, and in V the Latin lection's opening words are omitted. The order of these three elements is not regular, though the occasion is most frequently placed first (compare frontispiece and plates 1 and 4 with plate 2). In T the Latin lection opening was placed at the head of the column in which the sermon begins, thus giving this element visual preeminence over the other two which immediately precede the beginning of the sermon; a similar practice was followed in parts of M. In the large majority of manuscripts the headings are visually separated from the sermons by the use of red ink, by underlining in red, or by initial coloured paraph marks. Any departures from this norm are clearly attributable to

---

[8] Pictures would fall under the same condemnation as images, for which see *Selections* no. 16 and references there given.

[9] Many of the manuscripts must have been costly to produce in terms of parchment as well as labour. See H. E. Bell, 'The Price of Books in Medieval England', *The Library*, 4th Series xvii (1936), 312–32; also A. I. Doyle and M. B. Parkes, 'The production of copies of the *Canterbury Tales* and the *Confessio Amantis* in the early fifteenth century', in *Medieval Scribes, Manuscripts and Libraries, Essays presented to N. R. Ker*, ed. M. B. Parkes and A. G. Watson (London, 1978), p. 197 and n. 84.

oversight or, as in S, to the fact that the manuscript was not completed. In those manuscripts that number the sermons, this number is usually treated as part of the heading and distinguished in the same manner. Occasionally, as in some instances in D and P[10] (plate 4), the number appears in the margin and was not incorporated into the heading.

In some manuscripts it is plain that the main scribe filled in the headings in red as he went along; this is most easily provable in Y, where, if a new quire begins with a heading, this heading is also written in red in the catchwords at the end of the preceding quire. In other manuscripts, for instance often in D, the main scribe noted the material to be entered in red in an abbreviated form in small letters in the margin; the rubricator subsequently entered these. Sometimes it would appear that the note of the main scribe was merely a key to the rubricator who must have had another manuscript, or at least a list of headings, from which to obtain the full form of the heading. Thus in A just the sermon number was scribbled by the main scribe; so, for instance on f. 10^v his 'sermo 15' was expanded by the rubricator to 'þe fyftenþe Sondai gospel after Trinyte. Sermo 15'.[11]

Despite the overall uniformity of these headings, there is quite considerable variation in their details. The only possible variation in the biblical reference is in the use of words, roman or arabic numerals for the chapters. But the occasion and the Latin lection opening vary in the amplitude of their form. In the first case the heading may specify in the Temporale the season and the Sunday, or ferial, within that season, or it may rely upon a previous heading for the season and merely give the smaller limitation. Thus, for instance, for sermon 9 here G provides the information *Dominica ix post Trinitatem euangelium*, K *Dominica 9 post festum sancte Trinitatis*, whilst DCLMNTδ have simply *Dominica nona*. The language may be Latin, as in all of these, or English as in A *þe nynþe Sonda[i] gospel aftir Trinite Sonday*, followed substantially by BFY. Most of the manuscripts of arrangements 2 and 3 do not normally repeat identical inform-

---

[10] So D in set 1, ff. 55–102^v, has the number in the upper margin; P regularly has the number in the outer margin beyond the written frame.
[11] Similarly in F, for instance f. 47 the scribe left for the rubricator the somewhat enigmatic note '4 io 16', from which the latter supplied 'þe fourþe sunday aftir estyr' and the biblical reference 'ioon xvi'.

ation in their intercalated sermons, but allow the heading for the initial Sunday epistle sermon to carry over until another supervenes: thus JX have for this same sermon simply *Euangelium*, with the Sunday understood from E39 that immediately precedes, Z omits even this, leaving the reader to gather so much from the text. But G laboriously repeats all the information before each sermon. Most of the scribes have an individual pattern that they follow throughout a set, even if not throughout the entire manuscript, but this is not always the case; a glance at the headings of the sermons in this volume will show, by the incidence of square brackets, the variation found in D. To regularize, as has been done here, is perhaps to mislead about the importance that a scribe attached to the precise form of heading; it has been done to facilitate the reader's location of individual sermons. However, because of the amount and bulk of variation between the styles of heading in the various manuscripts, departure from D's reading has only been noted when this reflects a divergence in intent and not merely a difference of style.[12]

More interesting is the variation in the length of Latin text quoted before each sermon. To take one example: in sermon 11 here D reads, along with the majority of manuscripts, *Dixit Iesus ad quosdam qui in se confidebant tanquam iusti*, but Y and H only have the first four words, LαδI omit the last two words, and Aδ omit *in se*. Omission of medial words is relatively uncommon, but abbreviation of the heading as it appears in D is quite frequent. Conversely, some manuscripts appear frequently to preserve a longer text than is found in other manuscripts. This is particularly the case in M and T, and in sets 2 and 3, but not here in set 1, in L. Examples of this expansion can be seen in the variants to E2, E11, E26, E52, and others. It is difficult to be sure what was the original form used for the text. The obvious answer is that the longest form is the most authoritative, but this is not supported by the textual reliability of those manuscripts in which that form is most often found, nor by the fact that the longest form may be

---

12 Thus for no. 30 I's variant, and for E6 that of O and T are given, since the day that these minority manuscripts indicate is in each case different from that stated in D's heading. But divergence from D that consists merely in abbreviation or in difference of language (English as opposed to Latin) is not recorded; similarly ignored are variations in the method of calculating (e.g. after Easter or after the octave of Easter) which do not in effect vary the occasion.

witnessed, apparently at random, by varying manuscripts.[13] Yet, whilst it would obviously have been possible for a scribe to expand the shorter form of occasion heading to a fuller form without recourse to any manuscript beyond his immediate exemplar of the sermons from his own knowledge of the liturgical year, it is improbable that a scribe could in most instances correctly have expanded the biblical quotations without use of a reference work. This reference work need not have been another manuscript of the sermons; it is more likely to have been a list of lections.[14] Other evidence that scribes availed themselves of such secondary works, alongside their exemplar of the sermons, will be discussed below (pp. 131–4, 136–8).

As has been described, each sermon in most manuscripts has one ornamented or flourished initial. This initial is that of the first word of either the Latin lection or of the English sermon; in no manuscript is it that of the occasion. The manuscripts are almost equally divided between the Latin and the English. Normally a scribe settled upon one practice, though as in X or δ the existence of two scribes' work within the manuscript may result in variation. The responsibility was, of course, that of the scribe since he left the gap that the ornamentor then filled.

C. The numbering systems

Reference has already been made in the discussion of arrangements to the numbering systems found in all sets of sermons (see pp. 18, 36–8. These systems number sermons, not 'gospel' sermons as distinguished from 'epistle' sermons, and will only work according to arrangement 1. The system for set 1 runs from 1 to 54, that for set 4 from 1 to 120, and that for set 5 from 1 to 55; the Sanctorale sermons, here called sets 2 and 3, are numbered in a single sequence that runs from the Commune to the Proprium Sanctorum continuously from 1 to 68. It is not possible to prove that these systems are part of the original author's plan; in each set only a minority of the manuscripts attesting that set have any

---

[13] For the first point see chapter V below; for the second it may be noted that the extended form for E2 is found in T, that for E11 in TIJ, for E26 in MT and for E52 in T.
[14] T, the manuscript most frequently showing the extended quotations, has such a list of lections at the beginning of the manuscript; this, however, shows the opening words in a form often even more abbreviated than that found in D and the majority of sermons manuscripts, and cannot have provided T with his information.

trace of the system, but fifteen manuscripts at some point show knowledge of at least one of the systems. The manuscripts that nowhere have any numbering are EFHNORSTVWα; of these F, N, O, and S contain only one set, in the second case in unusual form and in the last uncompleted in its headings. Three manuscripts, D, A, and β, have the numbers in all five sets with reasonable regularity if not absolute completeness; a fourth, J, shows traces of them in all sets. Since each set is numbered separately, there were obvious difficulties in incorporating the numbers into sets 1 and 5 in scheme 2, and into sets 1, 4 and 5 in scheme 3. E of scheme 2, H and V of scheme 3 do not anywhere number their sermons; X of scheme 2 numbers only sets 2 and 3, Z of the same scheme only set 4. But despite the objection, traces of numbering systems remain in schemes 2 and 3: I of scheme 2 has isolated numbers in set 5, J of the same scheme more frequent numbers in set 1 and a couple in set 5; G of scheme 3 has some numbers in set 4.[15] The impossibility of these numbers in the manuscripts in question makes it likely that, if not original, the systems at any rate go back to an early stage in the textual history of the sermons.

The incidence of some trace of the numbering systems is as follows:

Set 1: in ABCDJKLMβ   (ADMβ)
Set 2: in ADGJMXβδ   (ADGMXβ)
Set 3: in ADGJMXβδ   (ADGMX)
Set 4: in ADGJKLQZβ   (ADLZβ)
Set 5: in ADIJPYβ   (DPYβ)

The sigla in brackets show those manuscripts in which the system was obviously intended to be complete, even if the odd sermon has not been provided with a number. In the case of D in set 5 only the first scribe and not the second used the system. K's use of the numbers in set 4 is exceptional in that, rather than being attached to the heading of each sermon, the numbers only appear in the list of the sermons prefixed to the set.

Any numbering system is prone to error, and there are isolated mistakes in individual manuscripts in all sets. In sets 4 and 5,

---

[15] I numbered E15, E22; J 32, 35, 37–42, 54 and E1 and E19 (this erroneously); G the directives after 177, 207–8, 210–11, 214–18, 220–30.

however, there are signs of more deep-seated problems. The simpler case is set 5. Here the trouble lies in the season between Epiphany and Easter. Sermon E7 is correctly numbered in DPYβ; thereafter Y continues correctly throughout, but D and β number E8 to E21 inclusive one number too high (as 9 to 22); P is correct for E8 to E15 inclusive, but joins the error of Dβ from E16 to E20 (with some independent eccentricities recorded in the variants), before returning to the correct number for E21; A, having numbered correctly E1 to E4, E6 and E8 and E9, then abandoned the numbering system though noting unhelpfully *sermo* beside E12, E15, E18, and E26, suggesting that his exemplar had a number which A felt to be wrong. It is difficult to explain this nexus of errors, especially since, as will be seen in chapter V, the manuscripts involved are not in other regards textually close. The reason for the starting point of the error may lie in the occasion for E7, whose lection could be used either for the Epiphany itself or for the Sunday within the octave of that feast;[16] it is perhaps possible that this led to that sermon being given two numbers. But whilst that would account for the advance of the numbers between E8 and E21 it will not explain the subsequent reversion to the original sequence.[17]

The muddle in set 4 is much greater, but is of a similar kind in that an apparent error begins in a few manuscripts and gradually gains more adherents. Here the trouble begins in the second week in Lent. The sermon for Tuesday in that week (no. 154 in the continuous sequence used in the table) is correctly numbered 32 in ADKLZβ; other manuscripts that, though lacking a number for that sermon, have shown sporadic and normally correct numbers up to that point are JQ. But the sermon for Wednesday of the same week is advanced by one to 34 in LQβ; thereafter through Lent these three manuscripts, whenever they have a number, show it one in advance of the correct number. D joins this mistake on the Friday of the same week, and A does the same on Friday of the third week in Lent; again the mistake in both manuscripts, once made, continues through Lent. Z regularly maintains the correct number, as does J on the occasions when he includes one; K has no numbers from the Thursday in the second

---

[16] See above p. 19.
[17] This reversion is clear for D in E24–6, 28–30, and for β in E26–31, 34, 44–6, 55.

week of Lent until after Easter.[18] In the final week of Lent no proper sermon is provided for Tuesday or Wednesday; Arnold (ii. 116–17) gave no numbers to the instructions given in place of sermons, and his omission has been followed here. Numbers are, however, found for these instructions in some manuscripts, taking the two as separate sermons. If the correct sequence were extended, the Passion week sermons should be numbered 55–60 inclusive; in fact the numbers found, in AD throughout the week and in GLQZβ for some days only, are those erroneously advanced by one, 56–61. The ensuing sermon for Monday after Easter is equally advanced in those manuscripts, ADLβ, that number it. But LZβ correctly numbered the Tuesday sermon as 62, though ADK have the erroneous 63. Thereafter the numbers in all manuscripts preserving them, ADGKLQZβ, have the incorrect advanced number wherever they record one (apart from odd eccentricities that are plainly incorrect). The explanation for this muddle is rather difficult to see. The point at which an error might easily have arisen is rather earlier: after sermon 22 for Ash Wednesday there is in all manuscripts save H a directive to find a sermon for the Thursday lection in set 1 (there sermon 34);[19] were the sermon for the Friday numbered 24, and all subsequent sermons one too high, the change would be readily explicable. But the mistake does not occur until nearly ten sermons later, and at a point where the sequence of daily sermons makes correctness easier than usual to check. Further, as well as the gradual accretion of manuscripts to the error, there is the strange reversion to correctness in three manuscripts for one single sermon.

It seems plain that these confusions in the numbering systems of sets 5 and 4 in various manuscripts must in each case go back to a single false exemplar; the agreements between manuscripts cannot be coincidental, since in neither case is there any obvious cause. Yet, as will be seen, within the texts of the sermons of each set, the manuscripts involved in the errors are not closely related,

18 In K's list 123–44 are correctly numbered 1–22; in the ensuing five numbers for 145–9 the second numeral has been erased, leaving just '2' for each; numbers 150–1 are wrongly numbered 29–30; no. 152 was omitted from the list as originally written and added at the head of the column without any number; 153–5 are correctly numbered. A gap then ensues from 156–81 inclusive.
19 The lection for the Thursday is Matt. 8: 5–13, the second half of that for 34, Matt. 8: 1–13.

in some instances not provenly related at all. It would seem that consideration must be given to the possibility that the numbering systems in those manuscript involved came to their scribes not as part of their exemplars for the texts, but as a separate list.[20] In other words, the stemma for the numbers would, if drawn, look quite different from the stemma for the remainder of the text.

D. Rubrication of the text

Each sermon contains a complete, or virtually complete, translation of the biblical lection whose opening words in Latin stand at its head. This translation is sometimes given at the beginning of the sermon (as in gospel sermons 5, 7, 9 etc. below), but is more often spread through the entire sermon with each section, or even each clause, being discussed immediately after the translation (as in almost every epistle sermon, and in gospel sermons 1, 2, 3 etc. below). Even when the translation is all grouped together, it is frequent to find the intrusion of odd words or clauses into it; some of these are for the sake of clarity where a section has been taken out of context (as no. 25/8), others to explain more fully or to emphasize a point (as in no. 10/5–7). In the vast majority of manuscripts the translation of the lection is underlined, at whatever point it may occur in the sermon; the words underlined are in the edited text italicized. There are three aspects of this that deserve comment. In the first place, the division of the translation and the intrusion of extra words into it make this underlining a task in which accuracy must have been hard to achieve. Yet the scribes regularly managed to exclude even the odd adverb, repeated pronoun or verb necessary to English syntax, as well as the introductory *þat* or *how* supplied as the direct speech of the Bible is turned into the indirect speech of the sermon. Examples of the exclusion of intruded words can be seen at E6/70, E7/66–68, E12/70, E13/19–20; for examples of the rubrication of words from the lection scattered through the sermon see E9, E12, E14 (and see plates 3 and 4). Secondly, if words from the lection are repeated in the exegesis, having already been translated once, they are not again underlined; this

---

[20] In set 5 D and β are not closely related, but they share the error described above in the numbering system of that set; this seems clear indication that the numbers came to one of the two scribes *apart* from the copy of the sermons.

Assupsit þe 12e disciplos. þi
þis gospel telliþ hou crist war
nyd his disciplis bifoꝛn of his pas
sion. to teche þat he oꝛdeyned it. &
suffride not aȝen his wille. but
chese foꝛ loue þat he hadde to man
to suffre þus. foꝛ þis man. þus tolde
his twelue disciplis. & seide þus to
hem. lo we steiȝen to ierslm. & alle
þingis þat ben wreten bi þe profete
of mannis sone schulu be endid. &c.

2. Trinity College Cambridge MS B.4.20, f. 8 (M)

3. Leicestershire County Record Office, Leicester Town Hall MS 3, f. 180v (α)

man þis eſt to deſtue þe body of ſyne: þat we
ſeuue not aſay to ſyne/ And þus þe body of
ſyne of man: is fleſſhelyneſſe of many ſeelte/
And þis body ſhulde be deſtued/ ⁊ ſloſt purpos
of ſpyrit gurþened/ And þus ſeiþ poul. þat he
þat is deed to ſyne: is iuſtefied fro ſyne/ þat
man is deed fro ſyne: þat is delyuend fro þt
ſyne/ And generaly man is deed to a þing. þt
is not gurþened to þat þing/ And þus it is a
grete grace. þat a man be deed to ſyne/ for þane
he mut be mixt to veįtu; ⁊ delyuend fro ſyne/
And þus ſeiþ poul. þat zif we ben deed wiþ
eſt we bileuen: þat we ſhulen lyue togideje wt
hym/ ffor zif þis old lif be deed? ⁊ ouje lif of
ſyne be deſtued/ lif of cleneſſe mut nedis dwelle/
And ſo men ſhulen be in blis wiþ eſt/ And we
ſhulen wite bi bileue. þat eſt riſynge azen fro
deed men: ſhal neuo moje aſay die in body/
And deþ ſhal not aſay be lord of hym. And þus
men ſhulde die fro ſyne/ and þus as eſt lyueþ
to god. ⁊ was eule moje deed to ſyne: ſo we
ſhulden fro þat we ben riſyn azen to lif of eſt.
fro ouje old lif: we ſhulden eule be deed to ſyne.
⁊ lyue to god in lif of veįtues/ and þus geſſe
zee zou deed to ſyne. ⁊ lyuynge to god bi mene
of iħu eſt ouje lord/ þat man is deed to ſyne:
þat wantiþ lif for to ſyne/ As ħe is deed to
þꝛ weſtneſſe. þat wantiþ wille to kepe it/ As
þat man lyueþ to ſyne: þat haþ ſtꝛengþe ⁊
wille to ſyne/ As þat man lyueþ to eſt: þt
woſe kepe his ſtꝛengþe to eſt/ Dñica viij

Humanū dico ppt infirmitate ꝛo 6.
Poul teciþ in þis epiſtle. hou men

þat is couſi to ſyus/
⁊ þꝛne he mut be iuſtified

4. British Library MS Harley 1730, f. 71 (P)

is reflected in the italicization (or absence of it) here, for instance E14/10 repeated at E14/21, 18/6–7 repeated 18/32–34, phrases from 20/3–23 taken up in the remainder of that sermon. Thirdly, the underlining is limited to the translation of the lection for the occasion; it does *not* extend to the translation of other biblical quotations incidentally introduced. Thus, for instance, the direct quotations used at E10/71, E15/28, 2/34, 3/47, 6/70 are not underlined in any manuscript. It is this last distinction that seems hard to parallel in other manuscripts of English sermons. It is not unusual to find biblical quotations marked off in some way from the surrounding exegesis, though, since in many sermons the lection's translation is given in a single block at the beginning, this presented fewer problems of accuracy than are presented by the present author's treatment. But the regular differentiation of treatment between lection and other quotation appears to be unusual in other manuscripts.[21] The care with which the lection's words are marked off obviously reflects Lollard concern for the precise words of scripture, and for the education of the laity and clergy in the discernment of authority.

The commonest form of underlining in the manuscripts is with red ink. In some, as for instance Y, the main scribe apparently worked with two pens (see above p. 86) and the underlining may have been done immediately after the writing of the relevant words. In others, for instance D, the scribe lightly underlined the words to be rubricated and the rubricator subsequently went over these. In yet others the scribe indicated the beginning and end of the quotation only: in A this was done by light underlining of the first and last words, whilst in β the scribe usually also marked off the beginning and end with two formations of dots. In other manuscripts there appear to be no guides to the rubricator, and it may be that the latter worked with a complete exemplar of the sermons before him.[22] Given the great complication of the

---

[21] No parallel is known to me outside the present manuscripts and those of the first derivative discussed in chapter III; most vernacular sermon manuscripts either do not mark off biblical quotation, or mark all quotations indiscriminately. The nearest analogy seems to be in manuscripts of scriptural commentary, either English or Latin, where the words of the book under discussion are often marked off by underlining or coloured paraph marks from the surrounding exegesis. This method can be seen in the manuscripts of the Lollard Glossed Gospels, Bodley 143 and 243, BL Additional 41175 and in Bodley 288 of the Wycliffite version of Rolle's Psalter commentary.

[22] Such is the case in B, H, and also M set 1.

task, it is not surprising that, when the rubrication was done by someone other than the scribe, there are odd places where the rubricator missed the signals left for him, or failed to follow his exemplar exactly. Actually such omissions are remarkably rare. The only manuscript which appears to be finished but in which the underlining of the lection has not regularly been done is O; S and P^t lack underlining, but there are other clear proofs that they were never completed, and the provision of rubricated headings in L has not been accomplished in part of the manuscript. The underlining in T is only in the scribe's ordinary ink, but this may have been all that was ever intended.

The rubrication of the text, together with the regularity of heading described above, gives the majority of the manuscripts a remarkable uniformity of appearance despite variation in their size and in their hands. The scribes must, given the difficulty of their task, have been convinced of the necessity of observing and maintaining the underlining in their exemplars. It is notable that this aspect is subject to meticulous correction in several of the manuscripts; the correction is most readily observable when underlining has been erased, but occasionally it is to be suspected where the underlining appears to be in ink of a slightly different shade from that normally found in the manuscript. Examples of erasure of underlining can be seen in D in E49/29–30 *in ryʒtwisnesse . . . trewþe* (wrongly underlining material repeated from 21),[23] or in 3/33–34, where the non-biblical intrusion had not been excluded; or in A in 16/9 and 18/4–5, again where intrusions had incorrectly been underlined. Erasure in D and in A is relatively common, but similar correction is found in many other manuscripts. In the original collation of the manuscripts variation in underlining was recorded, but it has not seemed practicable to print the variants so collected. Equally, since the intention of the scribes is so evident, occasional errors of underlining in D, the base text here, have been emended without notice.

E. Marginal references

Many of the manuscripts have been annotated, more or less systematically, by later readers; details of such annotation are

---

23 Similar erasure is evident in 4/41 *the . . . word*, 4/60–61 *furst . . . men*, 69 *to þer breþren*, 81–82 *for . . . spuyle*, 10/7–12 all the intrusions into the biblical text etc.

given in the descriptions of the manuscripts. Most are uninteresting, being largely concerned to note in Latin points dealt with in the text against which they appear; none throws any light on the origin or early history of the text.[24] The concern of the present section is with the marginal material that was entered by the original scribe of any manuscript, or by one of the correctors of that manuscript; corrections of the text itself will be considered in the next section. As with more recent annotators, the scribes themselves sometimes entered Latin words or numbers to draw attention to material in the text. These are not common, and usually are found only beside very clearly indicated matters (for instance *dubium* beside 43/54),[25] or beside very obvious lists (for instance in 49/50 ff).[26] Because of their infrequency, and the clear invitation offered by the text at those points where they occur, it seems likely that the presence of such comments is the result of individual enterprise by each scribe and is not derived from textual transmission.

A more difficult question is posed by the occasional marginal references that appear for biblical quotations incidently introduced into the sermons. A large number of such biblical quotations or references are not provided with any documentation in any manuscript (for instance E10/71, E15/28, 3/48, 6/70 lack any marginal note). Conversely, there are a very few places where a majority of the manuscripts do provide a precise reference. All the instances in the sets edited in this volume concern set 5: E3/88, E4/43, E21/42, E22/7, E39/8, E39/23, E39/29, E43/20 can be seen from the variants to be normally marked by the scribes. In all of these it would seem reasonable to suppose that the author, or at least the scribe of the hyparchetype, provided the reference, and that survival is the result of textual transmission. There are a couple of other instances, E13/55 and E47/29, where evidence for the reference is found in a smaller number of manuscripts, but where the same explanation probably holds. There do not appear to be any examples of comparable frequency in set 1. Beyond these, however, there are a number of references found

[24] The significance of the references in R (see p. 77) will be discussed in the editions of those sets, 2, 3, and 4, which the manuscript contains.

[25] Found in K, M, and Z; the *dubia* are numbered in δ.

[26] The *dowers* were numbered by the scribes of JMST, partially numbered by those of X and α, and named in Latin by the scribe of H; later numbering appears in I and N.

only in a single manuscript, or at most in two. The manuscripts most frequently involved are M (see plate 3) and T, less commonly N, δ, Z, and H.[27] It will emerge in the next chapter that none of these manuscripts is textually good, with the possible exception of H. It therefore seems highly unlikely that the references to which they in isolation witness have come down to them from the original; it is much more probable that they are the result of individual enterprise on the part of the scribe either of the extant manuscript or of his exemplar. If this is a correct inference, it follows that the initiator of each of the references must have used material outside his exemplar. Some of the references would have been relatively easy to supply, being either familiar biblical passages or having the name of the book already in the text; others appear to be less obvious.[28] Most of the references supply simply book and chapter, but M goes further in some instances by using the letter sub-divisions of chapters found in some manuscripts of the Bible and in lists of lessons.[29]

F. Correction

Because of the very great complexity of the correction procedures that can be seen within the manuscripts of the sermon cycle, and the problems with which these procedures face the editor, a fairly full description must here be given. Most of the points covered are matters of common sense, but they are sometimes ignored when editors describe a manuscript as 'corrected'. A classification will first be given of the types of correction, considered purely from a paleographical viewpoint; then the content of the corrections will be assessed. The conclusions drawn here affect the decisions on editorial method described in chapter VII.

Almost all of the manuscripts were corrected, many of them very heavily (see plates 1–4). The only one which shows no indication of correction is E^s; this is too short a fragment for any conclusions to be drawn from it. S, as the absence of headings

---

[27] See the variants to 2/34, 3/79, 14/50, 16/16, 17/67, 22/58, 69, 70, 23/43, 49, 54, 56, 73, 33/25, 37/5, 9, 21, 40/11, 92, 124, 41/17, 31, 32, 92, 101, 43/2, 38, 44/3, 99; E4/65, 68, E19/54, E24/49, 55, E25/31, 69, E30/144, E37/5, E40/86, E43/46, E44/93, 112, E47/38, 54.

[28] For instance the reference in M at 23/49 to Ecclus. 13 [: 15] or that in T at E25/69 to Josh. 10[:12–13].

[29] See for instance M at 23/49, 54, 56, 73; the same subdivision letters are found in the table of lessons prefixed to T.

shows, was never completed and correction as well as rubrication was probably intended; it was corrected slightly by the original scribe, almost certainly as he went along. P^t, like S, was never completed, and the only correction is one by the original scribe probably made immediately on writing.[30] In many of the manuscripts it can be demonstrated that the correction was done systematically and under supervision. The highest claim is made in α, where at the end of set 1 the corrector wrote 'Ista euangelia dominicalia corriguntur per primum originale'; textually this claim cannot be accepted if by *primum originale* the corrector meant the author's copy, since α, though sometimes alone preserving the right reading, is often faulty.[31] But the acknowledgement given to the importance of correctness in this remark is significant. In G and P many quires still show on their final verso a corrector's mark; in E, F, H (see plate 1) and K the correctors' guide instructions are frequently visible in the margins, along with the final entered corrections; in D on several occasions the first corrections have themselves been corrected. The elaborate process of correction was in some instances not concluded: in C, and sometimes in I, the correctors' guide marks remain but the alterations they require have not been formally made.

Since, as will be seen in the next chapter, textual affiliations may depend upon the responsibility for correction and the time at which it was made, it is important to consider the different types of alteration more closely. The following types may be distinguished:

(*a*) Correction within the line, where a word or rarely a phrase is cancelled, and immediately after it is written a word or phrase identical in syntactic function with that which has been cancelled. Examples of this type are from D in E39/14 *sectis* canc. *ordris*, E 39/77 *takun* canc. *temptid*, E45/31 *for* canc. *aʒeen*, or from K in 28/57 *sone* canc. *aungel*. It seems reasonable to suppose that the cancellation here was the work of the original scribe, realizing as soon as he had written that he had miscopied. In many cases, as with all those just mentioned, it is likely that the error was solely that of the extant scribe; many of them are simple instances

---

[30] At 19/11 where *wise* is inserted above the line by the original scribe.
[31] See below pp. 166–7, 177, 181–6.

of dittography, or of synonym substitution.[32] Occasionally, however, it may be suspected that the modification resulted from the scribe's access to a manuscript other than that which formed his main exemplar; this suspicion is aroused when the first reading and also the second are found unaltered in another text. Thus in H at E27/45 is found *telliþ* canc. *techiþ*, where I reads *tellep*, all other manuscripts *techeþ*, or in D at E29/74 *spirit* canc. *goost*, where ME have *spirite*, all others *goost*.[33] It may, of course, be that H and D first used the minority readings by coincidence and subsequently corrected back to their sole exemplar which had the majority forms. But in the light of similar corrections to be described below the possibility of conflation even in these, apparently simple, alterations must be borne in mind. It is an important part of the definition of this group that the cancelled words must be followed by words that are clearly alternatives to those removed;[34] a definition by grammatical function rather than by meaning seems preferable. That cancellation of this sort is often reinforced by ruling through the words by the rubricator does not invalidate the original scribe's responsibility, though it may make that more difficult for the modern editor to identify.

(*b*) Correction where the order of words as originally written is altered by the insertion of reversing marks, where letters or words are cancelled without any following substitution (e.g. frontispiece in column 1 and again in column 2), or where letters or words are erased. In none of these cases is it normally possible to determine the responsibility for the changes or the times at which they were made. They may have been done by the scribe immediately on writing, as in the category above, or they may be later alterations done by another and resulting from consultation with a manuscript other than the scribe's exemplar. The only cases where a decision can be made are those where a corrector's

---

[32] See for instance variants cited at 6/60 D, 33/41 D; E5/43 T, E8/23 D, E10/61 J, E15/108 D, E16/25 D, E17/23 β, E20/47 G, E24/58 D, E29/72 D, E30/63 D. The predominance of D here is due to the fact that the final reading in other manuscripts normally agrees with the base text and is not revealed by the variants (see below pp. 150–1.

[33] Similar instances are 11/16 αJ *gostly* canc. *grettly*, H *gostly and gretly*, al. *greetly*; 15/62 D *god heuene*, *heuene* canc., α *heuen* canc. *god*, CKLMTYβδEXZ *heuen*, al. *god*; 19/80 α *wot* canc. *marke*, I *woot*, al. *marke*; E3/61 P *folc* canc. *flok*, ABαδG *flok*, al. *folc*; E21/70 β *perfore* canc. *herfore*, αE *perfore*, al. *herfore*; E23/70 E *aboue* canc. *ouer*, M *abouen*, al. *ouer*; E30/112 β *lawe* canc. *lore*, I *lawe*, al. *lore*.

[34] Otherwise the cancellation may be of the type here assigned to b.

indication is still visible in the margin; in this event the alteration was obviously made after the section of the manuscript had passed from the scribe's hand, and the responsibility for the making of the correction presumably fell to the person incorporating corrections of other types into that particular manuscript; this latter person could be the scribe or another. This determines the time of those corrections, relative to the writing, but it does not indicate the source of the alterations, the scribe's original exemplar, or another text. Examples of this type of correction where no assignment of responsibility can be made are very common: for instance in X in 1/18 *so* canc. *solempnely*, K *so solemnely*, al. *solempnely*, and 1/45 *to* canc. *come*, CTY *com*, al. *to come*, in DX in 2/2 *þe blysse of* canc. *hefne*, FαIJ (*þc*) *blisse of heuene*, al. *heuene*, 2/21 *þe* canc. *best*, NαδIJZ *þe beste*, al. *best*. In all of these examples both uncorrected and corrected readings are attested in other manuscripts; conflation in the correction is therefore possible.[35] Simpler examples where this is not evident are from D 3/4 *toward*, *-ward* canc., 4/73 *of* canc. *godys*, E42/85 *prentyng* canc. *was*; in all of these instances the other manuscripts have the corrected reading.[36] Examples where a marginal indication of the need for deletion is found are relatively uncommon, presumably because it was more effective for the corrector to subpunct or cross through himself than to leave the task to another. An instance is in H at 13/81 *þese*, *-se* eras., BLMβ *þe*, al. *þese*. Because of the normal impossibility of assigning the responsibility for this type of change, it is usually indeterminable whether the text in its uncorrected form existed long enough for copies to have been made of it.

(*c*) Corrections where letters or words were erased and others substituted above the erasure. Where the erasure and the ensuant substitution are lengthy, it may be possible to judge whether the substitution is in the hand of the original scribe or not, but when

[35] See further examples for the manuscripts mentioned in the variants to 3/7 DX, 3/38 DX, 3/48 D, 3/53 C, 3/59 α, 3/66 D, 3/75 K, 4/19 α, 4/28 F, 4/58 D, 4/72 T, 4/76 α etc.; E1/50 δ, E1/70 J, E1/105 DX, E2/59 G, E2/91 PX, E2/95 X, E3/5 J, E3/12 J, E3/21 A, E3/48 J, E3/59 A, E3/75 J, etc.

[36] For reasons explained on p. 151 variants of this type are not normally recorded in the variants here. Further instances are 1/17 δ *an* canc. *aungell*; 1/53 δ *han in helle*, *in helle* canc., *þe* canc. *lyuyng*; 1/61 F *from* canc. *her*; 2/55 Y *he þat* marked for rev.; 2/97 Y *þese*, *-se* canc.; 3/4 α *per was a man* canc. *how*; E1/47 Y *þe of* marked for rev.; E1/62 Y *seie to* marked for rev.; E1/105 DX *men* canc. *ben*; E1/110 J *to* canc. *poul*; E2/15 δ *expressly more* marked for rev.; E2/44 β *and* canc. *þes*; E3/9 α *hatyde crist* marked for rev.; E3/83 β *a* canc. *prelat*; E3/90 α *þat* canc. *has*.

the change consists of only one or two letters this will inevitably be more difficult or impossible. The roughening of the parchment caused by the erasure, and the frequent difference in length between what was originally written and the correction tend to exaggerate the dissimilarity between the main hand and the alteration. Similarly fount and ink colour may be distorted because the correction is not made within a continuous spell of writing. These problems make it usually impossible to determine the time at which the alteration was made, unless the hand is clearly different from that of the main scribe's or a corrector's guide is still visible in the margin. Unlike the two previous types, it is frequently impossible with this type to identify the source of the trouble; the erasure is usually too effective for the original words to be read, and the erasure may often cover a large amount of surrounding material that did not require alteration. This can be seen most clearly in A and δ. In both of these frequent and lengthy passages were erased; in δ the hand of the corrector is clearly different from that of the main scribe at that point, but in A the corrector's hand is only distinguishable from that of the main scribe by a very few letter-forms. In both, from the compression of the material in the correction, the underlying trouble was plainly often haplography; but, since a passage was erased sufficiently to take with squashing the omitted and the correct material, what was left out in the first place is not clear. The editor, looking at the passage for opportunities for haplography or considering the variants of other manuscripts, may be able to make an informed guess; but it must remain even at best a guess.[37] The extent of the erasure and substitution in corrections of this kind is not, of course, significant textually; something was in the gap that the corrector was filling, and that material is irrecoverable. For this reason, corrections of this type, when they cover more than a single word or group of letters, are not

---

[37] Instances from A are 15/62 *we . . . vs*, where the difficulty was fairly certainly the omission *and riȝtwisnesse of hym* lacking in all manuscripts save B (and T by marginal addition); E15/137 *ȝong . . .* 141 *furste*, where the trouble may have been the omission in 138 found in GH; E41/2 *and . . .* 5 *placis*, where the cause seems obscure; E49/17 *sauereden . . .* 22 *myche*, in which there are opportunities for haplography. Amongst the numerous cases in δ are 1/68 *pis world . . .* 70 *askith* of obscure cause; 2/70 *and hyt . . .* 74 *his*, within which C also omitted material by obvious haplography; E37/13 *vnclennesse . . .* 15 *ryȝtwisnesse*, where both J and G omitted material; E38/11 *panne . . .* 12 *to do*, where there is an opportunity for haplography.

recorded in the variants save in the case of the base text, D. In collation such modifications were noted, but it did not seem on investigation that their evidence could be used as the basis of any argument. Extreme cases of this type of modification can be seen in A and β. In A a single complete leaf has been supplied in the corrector's hand, with excision of the original leaf of the quire; in β the same has happened with a bifolium.[38] In both it would appear that the cause of the substitution was omission of some material.

Of greater textual interest in the edition are the similar corrections in X, much briefer than those involved above. Here the erasure is only of a letter, group of letters, or at most couple of words, and the erasing was much less efficiently carried out so that it is often possible to read what was originally present. The substituted letters or words appear to be in the hand of the main scribe, though the time of the correction cannot be ascertained since the corrector's guides, if any existed, have disappeared in the cropping of the margins. The interest of these cases lies in the clear evidence they present of a close relation between X and D in sets 1 and 5. X's inefficiently erased original reading often agrees with that found in D (sometimes there corrected by other means). This is so frequent that the editor will often be safe in assuming that, even when the the erasure is no longer legible, it was, provided the extent is commensurate, of the reading as in D. Examples where the erased material is still legible are E22/37 X *perf*, *-f* eras., OT *per*, D and al. *perf*; E22/104 X *ȝyueþ*, *-þ* eras., DI *ȝyueþ*, al. *ȝyue*; E33/1 *schulden*, *-den* eras. and *-en* substituted, DBMδIJZ *shulden*, al. *shulen*;[39] examples where the erased reading is not legible but where it may be presumed to have been the same as D are 1/47 X gap, DBFIJH *hit*; 26/42 X *lawis*, *-is* on eras., D *lawe*, F *lawe*, *-s* eras., al. *lawes*; 26/69 X *boþe of* on eras. squashed, D *of*, al. *boþe of*.[40] To give in the variants all of X's modifications of this type would take disproportionate space; where the erasure is legible the change has normally been

---

[38] In A f. 172 covering parts of sermons 195–6; in β ff. 210 and 213 covering parts of sermons 234–7 and, in the second case, part of *De Ecclesia et membris eius*.

[39] For other cases see variants at 12/2, 21/48, 24/96; E1/41, E7/48, E11/87, E13/64–5, E21/23, E28/43, E34/38, E34/59, E36/39.

[40] Other instances are E1/58 *-wey* on eras., D *-what*; E1/98 gap eras. *to*, D ⌐*ofte*⌐ *to*; E4/87 *ȝaue*, *-aue* on eras., D *ȝiffe*; E5/42 *þe* on eras., D *þis*; E12/71 *al holy* on eras., D *hooly*; and similar cases at 1/43, 4/6, 6/42, 7/68, 13/16, 14/28, 15/64, 19/50, 21/5.

recorded, but where it is not it has usually been ignored. Other manuscripts have sporadic examples of the type that has here been illustrated from X, but, whilst the readings before and after change often agree with other extant manuscripts, there does not appear to be the regular alignment with one other text such as is found between X and D. They thus show the wealth of interrelationships between the manuscripts, but not any useful indication for any stemma.

(*d*) Correction made by marginal or interlinear insertion, with or without accompanying cancellation of material in the text as originally written. The correction may be of any extent, from a single letter to several lines. Here the original reading is normally ascertainable, and the source of the trouble identifiable. Occasionally the original reading has been erased rather than cancelled, and sometimes this type of correction may extend from the last type if the material originally omitted could not easily be accommodated in that way. Attribution of the correction is subject to the same difficulties as those in the last category: compression of hand, discontinuity producing distortion of script and a difference in the colour of the ink. Again indication of timing can only come from a clear discrepancy between corrector's hand and main scribe's hand, or from marginal guides. It is normally fair to say that the longer the insertion, the better the chance of correctly attributing the responsibility for the change. In many manuscripts this is the commonest form of correction;[41] only in A and δ did the corrector apparently prefer in the great majority of instances to erase and write over an erroneous reading.

These are the four main categories of correction. But a fifth group of a slightly different type must be mentioned: this is when a correction is then further altered. The alteration may, of course, be by any of the four methods described above, and the problems of attribution there encountered will be repeated. The manuscripts here where this 're-correction' is most frequent are D, less commonly T and H. The process can be seen most clearly in D. Thus in 18/41 the scribe originally wrote *lif*, a corrector added before this word above the line *his*, but this pronoun was subsequently erased (Z *his* canc. *lif*, al. *lif*); in 40/120 the original

---

41 Exemplification can be found on almost every page of variants.

reading was *þre*, to which a corrector added above the line *gret*, which was then erased (X *þre grete, grete* canc., EI *þre grete*, al. *þre*); in E45/82 the original reading was *þer*, *ȝit* was added in the margin to go before it, but then subpuncted (OTβδEJ *þer*, al. *ȝit þer*)[42].

Correction, whatever its scope, that affects the substantive readings of the text can be found in the variants below the text and does not require further exemplification here. A restriction upon its recording will be explained at the end of this section. Three kinds of modification may, however, be noted here since they do not appear in the variants. The first is the correction of the underlining of the biblical text that has been mentioned above (p. 136). The second is correction of punctuation. Correction may be by erasure or by addition or by modification. The first is usually easy enough to detect; the second and third can only be recognized if the ink of the alteration differs from that of the main scribe, though not even then with invariable certainty. All share the characteristics of the type *b* above, and the responsibility and timing cannot be determined. Fairly certain cases of subsequent modification, probably by someone other than the scribe, are to be seen in that part of J written by the second scribe (ff. 5–14 col. 1); here the ink colour of certain marks of punctuation is markedly different from that of the main hand, and some marks have obviously been squashed between words where originally no mark was intended. Almost all manuscripts have some changes of punctuation, but in most a decision of timing is less easy. Ideally an edition of these sermons should collate the punctuation, since it is plain that considerable care was taken over it by most scribes and that its incidence and nature is not normally casual. Because of the other complications of the text, this was not regularly done. A full study of the punctuation must be deferred to another place. The third type of correction is that of the language, where this is not substantively affected. This type is recorded in the variants for D, the base text, alone; otherwise, since linguistic variation is not recorded,

---

[42] See further in D E7/103 *loue we*, where *we* was added by a corrector and then cancelled (PZGH *loue we*, al. *loue*); E31/9 *þat* ⌐*þat*⌐, where the second was added by a corrector and then erased (OTYβδJXG *þat þat*, al. *þat*); 13/18–19 *þat . . . parable* all supplied by one corrector, within which *seyde . . . parable* is on the erasure of a shorter insertion by another corrector. T at 46/44 has *a* inserted by a corrector before *good*, but then erased; at E4/62 H has *in*[1] . . . 63 *preyer* in the lower margin supplied by a corrector but the word in it *of* before *special* is then cancelled.

corrections of this kind have had to be suppressed, though they were collected in the collation. The linguistic corrections do not appear in any manuscript to reflect an attempt to alter the dialect of the first scribe in any geographical sense. In many correction is fitful, and not perceptibly according to any principles. This is largely the case in the alterations in D, apart from a fairly consistent alteration of the first scribe's *ha* (for infinitive, plural present indicative and subjunctive) to *haue*.[43] The most regular alterations to the language appear in X, where a considerable amount of the text has been carefully modified. The corrector's objection seems primarily to have been to X's use of *-n* in verbal inflexions preceding a word beginning with a vowel or *h*; these final letters are regularly cancelled (thus in 11/43 *to kepen hit*, 11/49 *to dwellen among*, 11/59 *schulden ben of* the *-n* of *kepen, dwellen, ben,* but not of *schulden*, are subpuncted and crossed through). Linguistic correction stands out amongst the other types found by its restriction to individual manuscripts; there is no trace of any tendency towards coordination of correction.

This coordination of correction is, however, the most striking feature of the present manuscripts in the area of material alteration. The examples given above (pp. 139–40) have shown the way in which correction alters one reading, recorded unmodified in some manuscripts, to another, equally found as the original scribe's reading in others. Instances are extremely common, as may be seen from a glance at the variants on any page of this edition.[44] The most interesting cases are those where modification is found in both directions. Examples of this are 3/86 D *pe* canc. ⌐*pis*⌐ corr., α *pe, -e* canc. ⌐*-is*⌐ corr., JX *pe*, al. *pis*; 4/66 DδX *of* canc. *oper*, T ⌐*of*⌐ *opur*, FLMNIG *of opere*, al. *oper*; 9/5 D ⌐*pe*⌐, α *pe* canc., KLMTβI *om.*, al. *pe*; 9/23 DX *alle* canc. *kyngus*, α ⌐*alle*⌐ *kynges*, al. *kyngus*; 11/32 K *is* canc. *almy3ty*, H ⌐*is*⌐ *almi3ti*, J *is almy3ty*, al. *almy3ty*; E8/53 APJ *alle* canc. *his*, X ⌐*al*⌐ *his*, Dβ *his*, al. *al his*; E9/45 DX *be* canc., α ⌐*be*⌐, IJH *be*, al. *om.*; E13/35 X *pe* canc., T ⌐*pe*⌐, YβH *om.*, al. *pe*.[45] This nexus configuration of correction is very common. It is, further, to be suspected that, if one more

43 See 7/5, 14/64, 17/24, 20/84, 25/36 etc.
44 See variants to 1/3, 1/10, 1/47, 1/52, 2/2, 2/6, 2/14, 2/21, 2/39, 2/41, 2/56, 2/59, 2/67 etc.; E1/45, E1/50, E1/55, E1/58, E1/70, E1/98, E1/104, E1/125, E2/59, E2/91, E2/93, E2/108, E2/113 etc.
45 See further 11/52, 13/3, 15/43, 15/62, 16/80 etc., E5/55, E6/80, E15/16, E15/123, E16/45.

manuscript were found, many more such examples would become apparent—apparent in cases where now a correction leads to a reading not found in any manuscript unaltered, and in cases where now correction leads only in one direction and not in the reverse. It is noteworthy that all of the alterations in either direction amongst the examples of this nexus configuration just given do not in context materially alter the sense of the passage; the same is true of the bulk of one-way modification (see examples above pp. 139–40). This is typical. Yet the very insignificance of the modification materially is textually its most interesting feature. It seems in the highest degree improbable that the corrections in an individual manuscript can have been done spontaneously by the scribe or by another reading the text on its own, since the text as originally written makes perfectly good sense and even for stylistic reasons would not attract attention. The modifications must come from consultation of another manuscript where the corrected version was found. Equally it is plain that the man comparing the texts must have felt impelled to scrutinize both to the most minute particular, and to transfer any readings he found.

If a collection of these nexus corrections is made from a considerable run of sermons, some interesting points emerge about the participation of individual manuscripts in them.[46] Some manuscripts are found altering from one reading recorded unchanged elsewhere to another equally recorded unchanged elsewhere with considerable frequency; others rarely or never have such modifications. The distribution is by no means directly dependent upon the amount of correction of any sort in the manuscript. The heaviest concentrations of nexus corrections are found in X, α, and D (in descending order); these figures are for sets 1 and 5, and may be different for other sets. Of those having both sets the lowest are Z, M and I, and, though with very restricted coverage, V and E.[47] With only one set, L, N and O have few instances. Looking at those with a high concentration, two of them have clear evidence of very careful correction: D

[46] For this purpose scrutiny was made of all this type of correction from sermons 1–30 in set 1, E1–E30 in set 5; a similar collection was made from the first sixty sermons of set 4 as a check on the findings here.

[47] In set 4 the highest concentrations are in H, D, E, and X, the lowest again in I and V. E has very little in sets 1 and 5, though loss of folios diminishes the amount of evidence available.

from the fact that at least three correctors went through the whole course of these two sets, α from the claim made in the colophon at the end of set 1. It is noticeable that nexus correction is overwhelmingly more frequent in α's set 1 than in his set 5. Yet heavy correction does not necessarily imply frequency of nexus correction: T and J, in which correction in absolute terms is commonest, do not share in nexus correction nearly so frequently as X, α or D. At the lower end of the scale there is evidence that two of the manuscripts lie outside the mainstream of the tradition: Z, most obviously, by its expurgation and its translation of the text into a northern dialect, is an isolated case; I, it has been suggested by Dr Doyle, was written by an amateur. The only surprise is M, though it may well be that (as may be suspected also with L, to which M is genetically related) the manuscript as we have it had not been finally corrected.[48]

If the argument above is accepted that this type of correction must derive from comparison with another manuscript, it follows that almost all the extant texts must have been so compared. It should also be remembered that the primary exemplars (from which the original scribes in each case worked) and the secondary exemplars (from which the corrections were made) of the extant manuscripts may have been similarly corrected. The textual implications of this situation will be examined in the next chapter. Here it is worth looking at the practical questions. Leaving aside the manuscripts which appear to stand outside the main tradition, Z, V, and less clearly I and O, the sequence of events seems to be as follows. The scribe of a manuscript made a copy of an exemplar, possibly corrected, or by conflation of two exemplars. Then he or another compared that copy with a further exemplar. But the cross currents of correction make it plain that these secondary exemplars are unlikely to stand at the end of a branch of a stemma. The corrections are not centrifugal, as would be produced by such a situation, but centripetal. That the 'corrections' are often mutually contradictory does not contradict this. The fact that the corrections are often so trivial makes plain the force of attraction towards that centre. Editors often observe that an individual manuscript must have derived

---

[48] Both have a number of very obvious errors (see p. 164) which a corrector would have been expected to have put right. It may be that one layer of correction, where the text was read for sense, was made but that a second, where another exemplar was used, was not.

its text by a process of conflation. Here conflation is observable in the actual manuscripts surviving, and visually present in the corrections. What is striking is that this conflation is seen to be affecting the vast majority of the manuscripts, not just an isolated example.

The term 'correction' has been used hitherto in this section to denote any alteration made to the text as first written by the scribe (or in category *a* above by the scribe as he was writing). It does not imply that the text after alteration was necessarily nearer to the original than before. Consideration of the superiority or inferiority of the major alterations will be made in the next chapter. But it is plain from many of the examples given above that the vast majority of alterations fall into the category of indeterminable variant readings. The inclusion or omission of the definite article, of the conjunction *þat* at the beginning of an indirect statement, of a repeated preposition before a second dependent noun, and similar trivial alterations that form a large proportion of the host of modifications, can only very rarely allow for any judgement of 'originality'. The editor must make his choice of base text on other grounds, and then accept the trivia of that base text as they come. Consideration was, however, given to the question of whether any stratum of correction, particularly in the chosen base manuscript D, could be shown to lack authority, to derive, in other words, from isolated whim on the part of a reader rather than from the type of comparison that has been described. Obviously there are in all manuscripts individual modifications which take that text away from the reading of all the other manuscripts to an otherwise unrecorded variant. But these modifications are extremely rare, and in no manuscript do they appear to be attributable to one layer of 'correction'. The manuscript in which these isolative modifications are most frequent is T, but the same corrector is found making much more frequent alteration of the nexus type or of the kind that brings T's originally divergent reading back into line with the rest. The corrector then was sometimes misguidedly officious, but he was not in all his actions merely self-propelled. The editor, of course, does not have in most cases to make value judgements concerning the modifications made in the majority of manuscripts, given their indeterminate nature. But decisions do have to be made about the alterations in the base text, here D. As with T, it does not seem possible in D to detect any layer of modification as irresponsible; all three of the main correctors in sets 5 and 1 appear to have worked with an exemplar before them, and all incorporate alterations that may with fair certainty be taken as 'correct'. This being the case, those modifications made by the correctors where no judgement of originality can be made have also been accepted into the text, with only very few exceptions. Cases where D's corrections have not been accepted can be seen at 14/14, 17/10, 34/70, E17/33, E21/15; all save the last of these are of the type described above as nexus correction. Changes in D will be further considered when its relations to X is described in the next chapter.

It remains to explain, in the light of the foregoing analysis, the treatment of correction in the edition. Only the major decisions, and not the evidence on which they were taken, will be summarized in chapter VII. In the first place and affecting all manuscripts, no indication is given in the variants of the responsibility for the correction in question. The difficulties of assigning responsibility have been summarized in the four categories of correction described above. To attempt to indicate it in the variants would increase vastly their bulk, and would either mislead by unjustifiable certainty or confuse by a constant litter of question marks. In any case, since, whether the correction was done by the original scribe or by another, it can never be known whether the uncorrected text was ever available for copying before modification (or in a text corrected by several hands, between one modification and another), no textual argument can be based upon the information. In the descriptions of the manuscripts above an account has been given of the processes traceable in each. Such an overall view of each manuscript as a whole is more useful than judgements about a single variant. The remainder of the points may be set out as follows:

(i) D, the base text: all corrections, other than those to punctuation and to the underlining of the biblical text, have been recorded. Linguistic and substantive alteration is noted, including that where the modification stands above an erasure and the material erased is not legible.

(ii) all other collated manuscripts: corrections of punctuation, of the underlining of the biblical text, and of language are not included. 'Language' here is taken to refer to the modification of forms that do not affect function; thus, for instance, suppression of -*n* in verbal inflexions attributable to minor differences of date or dialect is not recorded, but suppression of -*þ* from 3 sg. pres. ind. is recorded since the effect is to change an indicative to a subjunctive. For reasons explained above under type *c*, the writing of material above an erasure, even when that erasure is very clear and the passage lengthy, is not normally recorded. The few exceptions (e.g. 41/56, E33/51) are cases which are discussed in chapter V, where a considerable textual problem is in question and where the point of erasure is clear. Because of the immense amount of correction found in the manuscripts, some reduction was necessary in the printed material. Where a correction is found isolatively in one manuscript, and that correction results in a text identical with that found in all other manuscripts, this correction is not noted; even lengthy, and in many instances obviously needed, corrections of this isolative sort are not recorded. This decision is open to criticism, but was taken as the only way to reduce the bulk of material without the charge of subjective judgement. If 'major' corrections of this type were included, invidious distinctions (that the discovery of another manuscript might well show to be false) would arise. Justification for the method can come from the arguments advanced above concerning the impossibility of ascertaining the timing of correction, and the consequent ignorance of whether the manuscript were ever in circulation uncorrected. Where, however, a correction, albeit found in only one manuscript, results in a reading *other* than that of the base text, that correction is recorded. Equally, if a correction to the reading of the base text is found in two or more manuscripts, the fact of correction is recorded, even though the uncorrected reading of those two is not evidenced in any manuscript. The reduction in the recording of isolative correction was made in order to accommodate in full the recording of nexus corrections. These, whether in one direction only or in both, have been set out completely. This choice was made because of the much greater textual interest of this latter type. As has been admitted, the discovery of one further manuscript would alter the decisions about exclusion; but immediate clarity (and considerations of cost) have to take precedence over such hypotheses.

V

The Textual Tradition

In this chapter will be considered the evidence for the relationships of the manuscripts to each other, using the traditional methods of textual criticism.[1] Only the two sets, 1 and 5, that are here edited will be discussed. It will become clear that a different tradition must be admitted for each of the two sets, and this textual independence of each set has been confirmed by work already done on sets 2–4; each volume of text will therefore have its own consideration of the relationships obtaining for those sermons contained in it. No mention will here be made, therefore, of manuscripts R or W, and Q since it contains one sermon here edited only (31) is largely ignored. For reasons that have been given above in chapter III, the derivative sets of sermons offer no help towards the assessment of the textual tradition of the present sermon cycle. In some instances it is possible to make a fairly certain analysis of the derivation of the dependent manuscript(s), but this sheds no light on the anterior history of the cycle. These derivatives are not used in the present chapter.

1. State of the texts

As can be seen from the table above p. 16, there are 24 witnesses to set 1 and 21 to set 5. This is, however, a misleading way to describe the situation, since a number of the witnesses to each set are, for reasons of accident or design, defective. Most seriously damaged are the three sets of fragments: E^s preserves only a part of two consecutive set 5 sermons; H^t, though more extensive physically, is largely illegible; P^t, with three complete and four fragmentary sermons from set 1, is the only one from this group to offer substantial evidence. Equally S and V, in each case

---

[1] For a bibliography of the subject see G. Kane, *Piers Plowman: the A Version* (London, 1960), pp. 53–4, supplemented by L. D. Reynolds and N. G. Wilson, *Scribes and Scholars* (Oxford, 2nd ed. 1974), pp. 247–50.

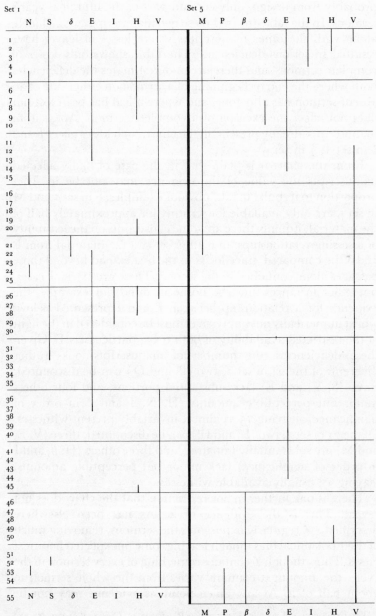

Lines show the sermons *entirely* lost in each manuscript. In addition in set 1 β lacks sermon 1, J lacks sermon 13 and in set 5 sermon E4.

probably from design, only contain part of the liturgical year's sermons. In the table (p. 153) these two manuscripts are included, along with the other manuscripts where losses of leaves have resulted in serious deficiencies. The table shows only losses of complete sermons, and therefore underestimates the deficiencies both where the end or beginning of a sermon on either side of an absent sermon has also gone, and where a leaf has been lost but does not effect the excision of a complete sermon. Apart from manuscripts already present on the chart, such losses affect β and J in set 1, J in set 5.

From the chart it is plain that in the case of badly affected manuscripts the value of the evidence may not be in strict proportion to its bulk: to take obvious examples, S in set 1 and M in set 5 are only available for scrutiny for approximately half of the material. Equally there are some constraints on the feasibility of assessing relationships: in neither set can the material from E and V be compared, since losses in the first extend beyond those passages alone contained in the second. These are extreme cases, but other instances must be borne in mind; for example, the evidence for a relationship between E and I presented below, whilst numerically not impressive, must be considered in the light of the restricted availability of both texts, particularly E. Given these deficiencies, the number of manuscripts looks rather different: of the 24 of set 1, two (P^t and Q) can be discounted, three (S, V, and E) lack substantial portions, and four others minor but perceptible amounts (H, N, I and δ in order of significance), leaving 15 as almost invariably present witnesses. Of the 21 of set 5, two (E^s and H^t) can be discounted, three (V, E, and M) are substantially impaired, and three others (H, β, and I in order of significance) lack minor but perceptible amounts, leaving 13 usually available witnesses.

There is one further major restriction that the chart does not reveal. This is the evidence of Z. As has been elsewhere described,[2] Z regularly expurgates the sermons, removing much of their polemical bias though leaving some unexpected heretical views. Thus, though Z contains something of every sermon in the cycle, the amount it contains varies from the whole sermon to about half of it. At any given point its evidence may not be

[2] 'The Expurgation of a Lollard Sermon-Cycle', *Journal of Theological Studies*, NS xxii (1971), 451–65.

available. Fortunately the changes that Z made were almost entirely effected by excision; only rarely did he reword a passage or link up the remaining material with phrases of his own. It is thus very rarely that any uncertainty exists about Z's agreement or disagreement with any variant readings within the material that Z offers. Since Z's expurgations are without trace in the other surviving manuscripts, there is obviously no question that Z was the ancestor of any of these. But his efforts reduce, perhaps by about a third, the evidence by which it might have been possible to place Z within any stemma.

It is obvious that those manuscripts which contain only one of the two sets edited in the present volume, C, F, N, and S of set 1, O and P of set 5, can only be used for half of the time, and the first group cannot be compared with the second. This restriction imposed the necessity of considering each set separately. It emerges, however, that the separation of each set is more extensive than is suggested merely by manuscript preservation. The material below will show a number of instances where a relationship reasonably established in one of the two sets is evidenced scantily if at all in the other. The most striking instance of this is with the group $M\beta$: this is witnessed by 23 common errors (plus others where the pair is found as part of a larger grouping) in set 5, but by only 1 in set 1. Yet in set 5 the area available for scrutiny is limited by the losses in each manuscript to 22 sermons, whilst in set 1 there is no such limitation. The only reasonable conclusion must be that, whilst M and β are genetically related in set 5, they are not in set 1. In other words, the textual tradition of the two sets is discrepant. This conclusion is confirmed by investigation of the other three sets, not here edited. For instance, in set 4, using only those manuscripts that contain all five sets, there is clear evidence for relationships between D and β on the one hand, and T and J on the other; neither of these pairings can be regarded as demonstrated by the present two sets.

Each set then must be considered separately. The work of collation for the present edition was begun on the assumption that textual affiliations would be likely to follow the lines of the three arrangements of the sermons described above in chapter I. Manuscripts of arrangement 1 were collated first, those of arrangement 2 next, and those of 3 finally; in each group collation proceeded in alphabetical order of the sigla. This procedure, it was intended, would facilitate the recognition of the genetic groups assumed to exist in the three major divisions, by bringing together without intervening sigla the smaller units EIJXZ and GHV. The assumptions on which this procedure was based proved, however, to be entirely false. Amongst all the variants to the text here edited, the group EIJXZ never appears alone as a family, whether the variant can be shown to be erroneous or not; only very rarely do all five manuscripts appear along with others in a larger group. The smaller group GHV is not unknown, but there is not a single instance amongst sets 1 and 5 where that group can be shown to exist in isolative error. The organizational divisions are not reflected in the internal textual relations. On the contrary, as will be seen, textual affiliations cut across these divisions: thus a close relationship in both sets exists between D and X, in set 5 between P and Z and again in set 5 between δ and J–in all three cases the first manuscript belongs to arrangement 1 and the second to arrangement 2. This realization prompted a closer investigation of the smaller groups, EIJXZ and GHV, whose results are analysed above in chapter I. Looking more rigorously at the oddities of arrangement in each of these manuscripts and at certain peculiarities in other manuscripts, it became clear that the work of reorganizing the five discrete sets into other schemes was done not once but several times. That being so, there is no reason to expect these smaller organizational groups to form genetic families within the text. Whilst it is reasonable to suppose that a pattern existed for each arrangement, this pattern was a schematic one; it might be imposed by an individual scribe upon material from an exemplar that had quite another pattern. In other words, any stemma for the arrangement would be quite different from any stemma for the text proper.

Exactly the same frustration of antecedent expectation emerges in the case of the other major organizational division affecting the present sets, that of the opening of the year in set 1. Again it was anticipated that the three manuscripts F, Y, and α, all having the liturgically normal but here unusual opening of set 1 at 1 Advent, would form a genetic group. In set 1, where alone F is available, the group FYα is never found in an isolative reading, whether erroneous or not. Of the possible pairings within this trio, only the pair Fα is found more than once in error in either set, and that only twice. Again it is necessary to conclude that the most obvious factor, the opening of the year, has no bearing on textual affiliations. Though, since all three manuscripts have a cycle without error, it is impossible to prove that the arrangement in each is the result of individual enterprise by each scribe without knowledge of the other, the lack of textual affiliations strongly suggests this.

If the discussion here must proceed without allowing the conclusions of chapter I to prejudge any issue, it must also derive caution from the questions discussed in chapter IV. In particular the heavy correction found in many of the manuscripts has both general and particular implications. In the first place, given the prevalence of correction in the surviving manuscripts, there is every reason to think that the surviving cases were copied from exemplars equally heavily corrected. Correction may derive from the rechecking of the exemplar originally used; equally it may come from comparison with an exemplar other than that copied. In the first case the stemma will not be affected; but in the second it will. Evidence has been cited in chapter IV to suggest that the second type was common as a method of correction, and that in some instances the correction was done by the scribe, as he was actually copying, by conflation of two texts. Conflation is thus likely to be widespread. Furthermore, it is inherently likely that many copies of the sermon cycle have been lost. From the very beginning of the attempts to suppress Wyclif and his followers, the authorities realized that books containing Lollard views must be confiscated and destroyed.[3] The earliest secular and ecclesiastical proclamations impose this duty on officials, and the search and destruction continued; a very large number of investigations during the fifteenth century mention that books have been confiscated, and the suspect was forced to promise that he would henceforward give up such books and inform the authorities where similar works could be found.[4] Little discern-

---

[3] For the early stages of legislation see H. G. Richardson, 'Heresy and the Lay Power under Richard II', *English Historical Review* li (1936), 1–28.

[4] For a survey of evidence see Margaret Aston, 'Lollardy and Literacy', *History* lxii(1977), 347–71. A typical promise is found in the model confession described in 'The Examination of Lollards', *Bulletin of the Institute of Historical Research* xlvi (1973), 145–59, here p. 156: 'Libros siue quaternos ac rotulos, hereses, errores siue erronea continentes, quos me scripsisse noui et quos penes me habeo, vel in aliorum manibus esse scio, ipsosque

ment would be required to realize the heretical nature of a manuscript containing any part of the present sermon cycle: Wycliffite views are shouted from every leaf. When copies of *Dives and Pauper* and *The Canterbury Tales* were confiscated on suspicion of their heretical content, it is inconceivable that manuscripts of this cycle should have escaped.[5] The decimation of the copies made in itself is bound to make any assessment of textual relationships difficult. When it is coupled with the extant evidence for correction and conflation, the problem is several times multiplied.

2. The identification of error

In the next sections an attempt will be made by traditional means to assess textual relationships. Some points must first be made, however, about the modifications of usual methods that are here necessary. The means available with a prose text are, obviously, more limited than those available for a verse text: there are no constraints of rhyme or metre, nor of alliteration. The style of the present sermons is not of a kind that ever allows the establishment of a reading as original because of its adherence to any rhetorical pattern. Because of the absence of such means of checking originality, the original dialect of the sermons is equally unascertainable. Whilst it may be reasonable, in view of the evidence of the vast majority of manuscripts, to think that the sermons were written in some form of east central Midlands dialect, this provides no assistance in the discernment of textual error.[6] In a few instances it may be feasible to isolate error by the elimination or modification of a word of Lollard sect vocabulary; but this is an area where little study has been made and where decisions are therefore hazardous.[7]

---

libros huiusmodi quos me recipere seu quos ab aliis recipi, scribi seu dictari scire me continget, vobis reuerendissimo patri seu deputatis vestris cum ad vestri seu deputatorum virorum presenciam cicius peruenire possem, absque dolo, fraude vel malo ingenio quocumque, liberabo'.

[5] See Aston, op. cit. p. 362.

[6] The language of the manuscripts is not, however, nearly so uniform as the observations of M. L. Samuels, 'Some Applications of Middle English Dialectology', *English Studies* xliv (1963), 4–5 might lead one to suppose.

[7] For some suggestions see 'A Lollard Sect Vocabulary?', *Philological essays . . . presented to Angus McIntosh*, ed. M. Benskin and M. L. Samuels (Edinburgh, 1979), pp. 15–30. A case where emendation of the base text has been made on this score is of *alþow* to *al* [ȝif]; *al ȝif* is

More positively, the usual ways of perceiving error through defective sense and defective syntax can be used. Equally the omission of material found in other manuscripts, and not demonstrably of derivative insertion there, may establish error. Dittography is less useful, since a scribe copying the erroneous text could often easily rectify the mistake. In readings where there is a choice between a rare or dialectal word and a common one, or between more complex syntax and a simpler construction, it is often reasonable, on the principle of *difficilior lectio*, to prefer the former. In all of these instances the identification of error is the more certain if it is possible to understand how the erroneous reading occurred, whether by mechanical or psychological cause.

One major cause of difficulty in the present case is the absence of any identifiable source for the sermons. In some instances Wyclif's Latin sermon for the same occasion has obviously provided hints for the English exegesis, but in no case is the English a sufficiently close translation for the source to provide any check upon the variant readings in the manuscripts.[8] The same is true of the other parallels that have been found between the English sermons and other Latin writings.[9] The one exception to this absence of source is, of course, the translation of the biblical lections upon which the sermons are based. Though the translations are often broken up into sentences or even phrases by intervening exegesis, and though changes are effected by transposition of direct into indirect speech and the reverse or by the introduction of explanatory words or phrases, it is clear from the care taken over the rubrication of the translation in most manuscripts (see above pp. 134–6) that great importance was attached within the tradition to the *ipsissima verba* of scripture.

---

a very common conjunction throughout these sermons, used in the majority of manuscripts to the complete exclusion of *alþow* but at the beginning of set 1 D has several instances of this unusual word (3/65, 4/8, 4/42, 6/8, 6/42, 6/50). Since the consensus of manuscripts even in these instances is in favour of *al ȝif* and since D thereafter regularly uses this conjunction, it seems reasonable to emend D's *alþow*.

[8] The relationship to Wyclif's Latin sermons, and the question of other sources, will be discussed in a later volume. For an example of fairly close dependence may be quoted as parallel to 1/52–56 *Sermones* i. 225/38 'Non autem hoc peciit iste dives propter caritatem quam habuit ad fratres suos viventes, sed quia puniretur gravius ex eorum dampnacione, ex hoc quod fuit consenciens eis in crimine.' But such proximity is rare.

[9] These will be quoted in the commentary to the sermons in the final volume.

This importance is evidenced also many times by the content of the sermons.[10] It therefore seems reasonable to assume that when one variant provides an accurate and literal rendering, whilst another offers a more rough and ready version, the former is to be preferred. But whilst the choice between an accurate and an inaccurate translation is not hard to make, legitimate doubt may exist about variants that are merely more or less literal. Whilst it seems impossible to trace in the sermons any systematic attempt to revise from a literal rendering to an idiomatic version such as is found in the modifications of the Wycliffite Bible, it must remain a matter of editorial judgment that the more literal variants are more probably original. In general, again by the principle of the *difficilior lectio*, this seems to be a justifiable position: it is more probable that an appositional absolute participle plus finite verb would be changed into two finite verbs linked by a conjunction, than that the reverse would happen. Thus at 41/4 *a womman of Chanaan wente owt of hire coostes, cryȝede vpon Crist* is more probably the original translation of *mulier Chananaea a finibus illis egressa clamavit* than the reading that adds *and* before *cryȝede*. But, given the undoubted changes that the author of the sermons introduced, it is hard to know how far to take this principle. There are a number of cases where doubt is legitimate; some of these will be discussed below pp. 181–8.

Furthermore, it is plain that the translation of scriptural passages is the area where any independent effort at correction by a scribe could most readily be made. The fact that the translation is rubricated would make it easy enough to pick out and check against a Vulgate. That it is not fanciful to suppose that a scribe might so verify the material is shown by the marginal biblical references examined above pp. 136–8, the evidence pointed plainly to the fact that many of these were not part of the original text of the sermons but were introduced by individual scribes at a later stage. The possibility of correction of the biblical translation at some stage in the transmission is also revealed by a number of very puzzling cases where the vast majority of manuscripts appear to be in error and the correct reading is found, if at all, in only one or a very small group of manuscripts; these single correct witnesses are not constant, but vary and are not infrequently

[10] See here for instance 30/50–52, E1/62–64, 83–84.

manuscripts otherwise unreliable. They will be discussed below pp. 181–8 when the quality of each manuscript has been described. At its lowest the hypothesis of correction of translation means that deviation of two manuscripts normally related, when this deviation is in translation, may not be significant of descent; the accuracy of one may be the result of correction not of an inherited right reading. For similar reasons little importance can be attached to the rubrics found in the manuscripts. The occurrence of, for instance, an erroneous ascription of occasion could easily be put right in a derivative manuscript, either by the scribe's own intelligence and knowledge of the liturgical year, or by the use of a service book or a list of gospels and epistles such as is found prefixed to T. The Latin texts are, as was argued above pp. 129–30, equally uninformative. The fact that Y, for example, never gives the Latin text in his opening rubric to each sermon of set 5 does not preclude the possibility that another manuscript which does include this information may in other respects, and without conflation from another sermon manuscript, be descended from it; the texts could derive from an independent reference book. Finally, the sermon numbers where they are found are an unreliable source of evidence for textual affiliations. The most notable instance is in set 5, where D and β share an erroneous numbering of sermons E8–E21. This might lead one to assume that the two manuscripts are genetically related. But whilst this may be true for a portion of set 4, it almost certainly is not for set 5; only one other certain isolative error links D with β in that set. The correct answer is more probably that the sermon numbers in the two manuscripts derive from a common exemplar, but that this exemplar was not the exemplar for the text but only for the numbers.

Also to be borne in mind in the present chapter are the observations made above (pp. 138–50) about correction. In particular, the usual impossibility of determining *when* a correction was made makes it hazardous to use the uncorrected form of a manuscript to argue textual affiliations, unless the uncorrected readings are in constant agreement with a specific other manuscript.

A note should be added about one particularly common form of variation, that between *schal* or *schulle(n)* on the one hand and *schulde(n)*. It would appear that any of these forms could be used for the expression of obligation; both are found in biblical translation as partial rendering of the Latin imperative. No decision of originality can be made between these forms if the context allows any implication of obligation. But it would seem that only *schal* or *schulle(n)* ought to be used to express simple futurity. It is only in clear cases in this sense that variation between these verbs has been used in the following discussion.[11]

3. Isolative error

It can be shown with reasonable certainty that in neither set 1 nor set 5 is any extant manuscript directly descended from any other extant manuscript. This can be shown from isolative errors in each surviving manuscript not carried over into any other. In the material that follows a small number of examples for each manuscript, and for each set where the manuscript contains both, are given in full together with a brief comment on the quality of the text presented; other instances are given by sermon and line reference in footnotes, selected where the manuscript is very corrupt, and these can be amplified by referring to the variants below the text. For ease of reference the manuscripts are given in alphabetical order of their sigla.[12]

A: 20/51 *hem*, al. *heuene*; 39/48 *heerynge*, al. *heryenge*; 45/57 *shewen*, al. *sewon*. E19/25 *gederide*, al. *gendreþ*, Vulg. *generans*; E39/38. om. *water of*; E50/22 *bigynnynge*, al. *biggyng*.[13] In set 1 A is a careful text, with few isolative errors; the copy of set 5 is markedly less good.

B: 21/14 *wormes*, al. *wordis*; 37/49 ȝ*yue*, al. *brynge*; 49/26 *peynte*, al. *prente*. E4/98 *ofte*, al. *eft*; E25/62 *suget*, al. *sugetis*, Vulg. *subditi*; E26/24

---

11 See F. T. Visser, *An Historical Syntax of the English Language* III. 1 (Leiden, 1969), §§ 1483–1561.

12 The reading of the majority of manuscripts, prefixed by 'al.' ('alia') is given in the spelling of D, or, when D has the aberrant reading, from the first available in the sequence ABCFKLMNOPQSTYαβδEIJXZGHV. The citation of 'al.' does not imply that in every instance all other manuscripts have this reading; independent errors by a manuscript or a minority of manuscripts are ignored. For reasons given above the full citation within the text does not use material from headings, though these are referred to in the following notes; equally, errors in biblical translation have not been admitted as the sole evidence. For reasons of space no explanation of the errors is included; it is hoped that reference to the text will confirm the justice of the decision.

13 See further 6/21, 7/22, 24/text, 24/84, 28/40, 33/69, 35/40, 37/100; E2/11, E3/12, E4/44, 85, E13/77, E15/6, E16/23, E18/text, 44, E21/1, E22/46, E24/23, E28/6, E30/144, E31/107, 109, E32/16, 62, E33/53, E34/56, E35/6, E36/47, E40/45, 88, E42/33, 82, 85, E45/74, E46/10, 21, 43, E47/87, E52/1, 27.

whilewis, al. *whylenesse*, Vulg. *vicissitudinis*.[14] B presents a fairly good copy, again with more errors in set 5 than in set 1.

C: 11/7 *thrise*, al. *twyes*, Vulg. *bis*; 24/51 *clepyng*, al. *clooping*; 28/50 *stole*, al. *stoon*.[15] C's copy of set 1 is not particularly reliable; part of the trouble seems to spring from the fact that C's dialect was more northerly than that of the exemplar or of the majority of the manuscripts surviving.

D: 8/36 *cristys*, al. *preestis*; 27/35 *bowht*, al. *brouȝt*; 39/29 *voys*, al. *voicis*. E15/41 *hem*, al. *him*; E35/2 *þis*, al. *þis lyf*; E43/53 *good*, al. *god*.[16] D's copy is very careful, and has been meticulously corrected by more than one person.

E: 41/76 *schapiþ*, al. *scharpeþ*; 44/55 *wordis*, al. *word*, Vulg. *sermonem*; 48/69 *enemyes*, al. *wolues*. E21/6 line om.; E23/74 *sone*, al. *word*, Vulg. *verbum*; E50/12 om. *wisdom*.[17] E's copy is much less good than Arnold suggested, though the accuracy in sets 1 and 5 is considerably greater than in set 4.[18]

F: 33/58 *a particle*, al. *apertly*; 35/17 *wynd*, al. *wyndus*, Vulg. *venti*; 51/91 *likyng*, al. *kyllyng*.[19] F is an accurate copy, most of the isolative mistakes being the result of a failure to observe the context of a word.

G: 30/13 *for*, al. *fordyde*; 32/80 *proued*, al. *prowde*; 40/65 *eir*, al. *eurþe*. E17/26 *comaundement*, al. *comaundementis*, Vulg. *praecepta*; E34/5 *suffrid*, al. *suffryng*; E47/19 *wake*, al. *walke*, Vulg. *ambuletis*.[20] G offers a good copy, with a certain number of isolative but few combinative errors; it has been carefully corrected by the single scribe.

H: 37/77 *and bygynne*, al. *bygynnyng*, Vulg. *incipiens*; 38/118 *put*, al. *prente*; 39/27 *turnement*, al. *turment*. E9/60 *so getynge of*, al. *sugete*; E16/36 *tribulacioun*, al. *tribulacionys*, Vulg. *tribulationibus*; E 47/50 *and crist*, al. *anticryst*.[21] H's copy of set 1 is better than that of set 5, but both are fairly accurate.

---

14 See further 9/66, 15/10, 28/52, 30/34, 31/35, 32/7, 33/22, 35/29, 38/30, 47/64, 48/20, 51/81, 52/5, 12, 68, 54/65; E3/105, E4/95, E7/1, E8/78, E10/44, E12/88, E14/124, E15/3, 26, E16/14, E17/rubric, E21/55, E22/60, E27/7, E29/32, E30/12, E32/49, E35/54, E49/61, E50/30, E54/51.

15 Selective examples only 9/40, 16/64, 17/text, 24/4, 24/47, 26/text, 27, 29/45, 68, 34/text, 60, 87, 35/15, 79, 39/12, 93, 44/108, 47/text, 51/89, 53/29, 52, 82, 54/9, 85.

16 See further 11/6, E4/87, E6/4.

17 See further 18/78, 19/17, 25, 20/text, 40/61, 41/38, 57, 43/92, 48/16, 49/72, 50/1, 51/12, 52/13, 53/78, 54/44; E16/15, E18/19, 81, E22/27, E23/55, E26/42, E27/text, E28/text, E29/19, 80, E30/30, 52, E45/28, E47/32, E48/12.

18 Arnold i. xiii and xviii.

19 See further 1/47, 4/17, 5/59, 6/15, 8/49, 9/62, 10/12, 11/58, 13/66, 22/text, 29/21, 34/2, 37/text, 92, 39/5, 42/41, 43/87, 49/77, 52/99, 105.

20 See further 2/41, 13/28, 14/44, 15/41, 28/66, 30/55, 32/23, 36/20, 37/text, 41/93, 42/text, 52/80, 54/70, 77; E9/74, E10/65, 73, E11/17, E15/90, 100, 115, E16/42, E19/72, 83, E21/55, E22/89, E31/112, E37/23, E40/49, E43/65, E44/15, 30, E47/19, 44.

21 See further 11/19, 24/30, 28/19, 47, 30/21, 36/24, 38/114, 48/42, 49/15, 52/70; E4/57, E5/22, E8/7, E9/42, E10/36, E14/89, E17/62, E19/92, E23/15, E24/text, E25/10, E27/67,

I: 9/69–70 line om.; 14/11 *foot*, al. *feet*, Vulg. *pedes*; 23/4 *feynynge wordis*, al. *fagyng wordys*. E12/33 *firste*, al. *fourpe*; E16/40 *wakinge*, al. *wakyngus*, Vulg. *vigiliis*; E28/67 *billes*, al. *bullis*.[22] I presents an idiosyncratic and very unreliable text, with many omissions and misapprehensions.

J: 4/61 *manere*, al. *mesure*, Vulg. *mensuram*; 31/88 *helpes*, al. *hepis*; 49/7 line om. E7/39 *tho*, al. *two*; E41/20–21 line om.; E47/89 *I*, al. *pei*.[23] J's copy is in general quite good, particularly in those parts copied by the main scribe.

K: 30/31 om. *pat he saw*, Vulg. *vidi*; 35/59 *disperid*, al. *distemprede*; 49/85 *auarous*, al. *a noyows*.[24] K's copy is extremely accurate for the first half of set 1; after about sermon 30 it becomes noticeably less good (see below pp. 172–3).

L: 16/38 *slowid*, al. *flowyde*; 33/25 *seruaunt*, al. *seruauntis*, Vulg. *eis*; 43/36 *flesche*, al. *frelte*.[25] L offers a reasonable copy, though with a fair number of minor errors.

M: 7/8 om. *of hem*, Vulg. *ex eis*; 18/34–35 line om.; 49/53 *suetnesse*, al. *swiftnesse*. E23/88 *witnessith*, al. *witnessude*, Vulg. *testificatus est*; E40/96–98 lines om.; E53/20 *cristis*, al. *poulis*.[26] M's copy has a number of bad cases of haplography, particularly in set 5 written by the first scribe.

N: 10/11 *place*, al. *paleys*; 18/32–45 lines om.; 29/60 *icome*, al. *to comen*, Vulg. *venturus*. N's copy, as would be expected from the way in which the set 1 sermons are used as prothemes to epistle sermons unrelated to those here, is an extremely individual one, with considerable omissions. At the beginning of the set there are numerous rewordings, often a very minor kind not affecting the overall sense; but these

E28/text, 50, 90, E30/87, E32/90, E41/47, E42/text, E43/45, E44/92, E45/23, E46/33, E53/78.

[22] Selective examples only 2/12, 22–4, 7/12, 11/53, 77, 14/39, 40, 21/2, 31, 37/38–9, 38/78, 88, 98, 110, 39/16, 26, 85, 44/40, 47/9, 11, 18, 54, 60, 52/6, 76, 79; E12/36, 74, 87, E15/18, 77, 102, 137, E22/4, 75, 88, 91, 97, E30/49, 75, 81, 96, 112, 141–2, E35/10, 24 (twice), 62–4, 80–2.

[23] See further 4/63, 5/34, 6/19, 7/58, 9/40, 26/76, 27/20, 29/67, 83, 88, 30/1, 37/72, 38/67, 39/87, 41/48, 50/59, 51/7; E4 homily om., E6/87, E7/8, E8/17, E10/43, 64, E21/56, E27/58, E28/22, E39/92, E42/30, E47/89, E49/46–7, E50/26, E53/70–1.

[24] See further 12/38, 22/text, 28/13–14, 71, 32/96, 34/89, 35/7, 41–2, 38/81, 41/116, 47/56, 48/28, 49/6, 66, 52/54, 53/36, 46, 54/24, 77.

[25] See further 1/13, 2/85, 4/3, 60, 5/15, 24, 14/23, 36, 15/16, 16/48, 17/text, 19/51, 73–4, 21/40–1, 22/53, 23/9–10, 73, 26/57, 75, 27/41, 54, 30/26, 30, 31/35, 34/34, 36/42, 37/54, 40/119, 41/19, 80, 104, 42/text, 44/93–4, 48/51, 55, 50/12, 25, 81, 110, 52/90, 53/47, 54, 54/39, 59, 61.

[26] Selective examples only 6/70, 79, 80, 9/35, 70, 20/28–30, 26/18, 49, 28/67, 43/11, 20, 71, 54/10, 12, 30; E25/14–16, 59, E29/33, 49, E32/22, 78, E33/37–8, 53, E34/9–10, 19, 43, E40/38, 75–76, 78, E47/9, 19, E51/76, 88, E54/3, 43.

become, fortunately for the editor of the present sermons, less frequent as the set progresses.[27]

O: E13/4 *game*, al. *gleyue*, Vulg. *bravium*; E16/40 *charite*, al. *chastite*; E30/17–18 line om.[28] O's copy of set 5 is rather careless, and has only roughly been corrected.

P: E9/58 *speke*, al. *kepe*; E23/74 *trewe*, al. *trewþe*, Vulg. *veritas*; E44/26 *fouretene*, al. *seuentene*.[29] P presents a very accurate copy of set 5, with few isolative errors or readings.

Q: only available in no. 31, 31/18 part line om., 31/85–86 line om. Q's copy of set 4, its main contents, is not good and this is reflected in the two omissions in its single set 1 sermon.

S: 42/79 *besynesse*, al. *besomes*; 44/55 *profete*, al. *prophetis*, Vulg. *prophetae*; 49/43 part line om.[30] S's text is quite good, particularly in view of the fact that correction had almost certainly not been done; the only alterations seem to be by the scribe immediately on writing.

T: 13/68 *preche*, al. *prikke*; 20/21 *foot*, al. *feet*, Vulg. *pedibus*; 27/59 *from panne*, al. *froþen*. E11/33 *he fulfilliþ*, al. *he haþ fulfullud*, Vulg. *implevit*; E27/93 *forme*, al. *folye*; E37/42 line om.[31] T made a considerable number of minor mistakes in his copy; the corrector worked over the text very thoroughly, but his alterations not infrequently take the readings out of line with the other manuscripts.

V: 27/29 *vertu*, al. *power*, Vulg. *potestate*; 28/35 *we weren*, al. *furst*; 32/75 part line om. E7/16 *mannes*, al. *maries*; E9/99 *sectis*, al. *staatis*; E11/35 *fredom*, al. *frend*. V is the most idiosyncratic of the manuscripts, with constant rewording of the text, misunderstanding of the sense, and careless omissions. Although there are some corrections, V entirely lacks the evidence of supervision so noticeable in other manuscripts. Because of the enormous increase in bulk that would result if its isolative readings were recorded in the variants, it was decided only to print V's divergences from the base text where these agreed with other manuscripts or where V's reading might be thought to cast light on the textual history of these.[32]

---

27 Selective examples of major departures only 3/7, 18, 23, 34, 45–6, 30/29–30, 63–4, 80–1, 86, 88, 32/14, 20, 48–57, 42/20, 29, 51/19, 84. A glance at any page of variants in those sermons where N is present will furnish numerous other examples.

28 Selective examples only E10/4, 12, 26, E28/38, 43–5, E31/3, 45–6, 81, 115, 120, 121, E39/55, 60, 74, 78, E49/16–17, 39, 65, 67, E50/3, 7, 17, 51–3.

29 See further E3/24, E11/5, E14/52, E18/text, E46/59, E47/1.

30 See further 34/5, 45, 35/37, 36/64, 37/17, 44, 91, 97, 38/68, 71, 81, 102, 108, 39/53, 67–8, 40/5, 54, 42/15, 25, 59, 84, 45/78, 46/42, 47/11, 24, 48/83, 49/64, 50/15, 53/39, 42.

31 Selective examples only 13/24, 50, 20/21, 31/54, 77, 37/37, 38/55, 42/29, 92, 43/73, 46/76, 47/54, 71, 50/72, 51/65, 91, 54/65; E15/119–20, 131, E17/16, 23, E30/38, E44/29, 52, E45/28, 83, E48/3, E53/50, 79, E55/33.

32 Selective examples of major divergences only are given. Because V's isolative readings

X: 7/34 *schullen*, al. *schulden*; E1/115 *closyd*, al. *clopud*; E50/36 *asoylyng*, al. *asaylyng*; E53/14 *hym*, al. *hem*. X in these two sets has almost no isolative errors, and very few isolative readings.[33] For a fuller discussion of its position see below pp. 167–71. In set 4 there are somewhat more isolative errors, though the text is still very good.

Y: 39/35 *al is*, al. *al ʒif*; 42/49 *armure*, al. *armys*, Vulg. *arma*; 53/53 *many*, al. *mysty*. E14/10 *visagis*, al. *visage*, Vulg. *faciem*; E21/4 *foold*, al. *flood*; E31/120 *heringe*, al. *beryng*.[34] Y in general offers a good text of both sets, with only a few minor errors.

Z: 29/73 *ynoghe*, al. *a pwong*; 41/73 and 42/29–30 lines om. by haplography; 54/55 *wilsomnes*, al. *wysdam*. E4/50 *nyʒt*, al. *nyʒ*; E31/3 *grettest of al*, al. *maxym*; E51/56 *assoile*, al. *assayle*.[35] The expurgated nature of Z's text makes it plain that no other manuscript can be descended from it.[36] Otherwise it presents a generally reliable text, with few scribal errors. Z is, however, written in a Yorkshire dialect, and has made considerable alterations to the vocabulary; these changes are not recorded in the variants.

α: 12/41 *suget*, al. *seghed*; 34/89 *groundid*, al. *grauntyde*; 53/37 *þe*, al. *ten*. E12/6 *entrayle*, al. *entraylis*, Vulg. *viscera*; E18/34 and 68 lines om.; E50/ 1 *wake*, al. *walke*, Vulg. *ambuletis*. α's copy of set 1 is considerably more accurate than that of set 5; in the latter there are a number of careless omissions and mechanical errors.[37] It will be remembered that the corrector of set 1 in this manuscript claimed that it had been checked

---

are not given in the variants details are here provided: 28/67 line om.; 30/43 om. *dowue*; 31/ 82 om. *fre*; 34/48 om. *seruaunt*; 61 om. *chyrche*; 35/40 part line om.; 96 *loueþ more*, al. *ioyeþ more*; E3/8 *worldly*, al. *lordly*; E5/31 om. *trespasede so moste mankynde*; E6/6 *not*, al. *owt*; E10/ 33 om. *liʒt²*; 59 *on his heed þat is þe vertu of his soule*, al. *vpon þe hyerste vertu of his soule*; E11/11 *wordis*, al. *rewle*; 50 om. *ʒif*.

[33] See also E4/17, E7/60, E55/21.

[34] See further 9/text, 67, 12/17, 19/54, 24/5, 28/text, 29/80, 32/8, 78, 34/72, 36/47, 37/72, 38/text, 11, 68, 85, 39/11, 40/30, 41/85, 99, 42/54, 46/82, 49/26, 50/1, 51/5, 53/text, 53, 54/ 83, 100; E2/70, E5/52, E6/14, E9/101, E11/87, E13/4, E14/4, 10, 35, 80, E16/20, E20/51, E21/74, E22/71, E24/text, E25/29, E28/61, E31/120, E32/18, E34/46, E35/34, E36/11, E40/41, E43/10, E45/14, 88, E48/4, 28, E50/54, E53/57.

[35] See further 2/50, 15/57, 24/51–2, 93, 27/82, 34/5, 36/33, 35, 37/73, 39/53–5, 42/92, 44/ 83, 46/42, 88, 49/22, 53/63, 54/87–8; E1/text, E2/35, E9/91, E10/71, E11/46, E13/21, E18/49, E29/2, E30/22, E34/48, E35/25.

[36] In a few cases doubt exists as to whether a divergent reading in Z is the result of inadvertent error or deliberate change. The examples given in the last footnote can reasonably be regarded as the former. An instance where uncertainty exists is E30/90 where Z reads *prelatis*, against other manuscripts *popis*; the change does not materially affect the criticism and may be a mistake.

[37] See further 3/3, 9/23, 10/11, 26/text, 33/44, 39/24, 75, 41/103, 42/43, 45/text, 48/65, 51/74, 52/94, 54/text; selective examples from set 5 E12/5, 23, 26, 34–5, 75, E14/101, 106– 7, E25/1, 66, E29/6, 29, 59, 74, E42/21–2, 36, 57, E45/36, E49/5, 25, 35, E51/17, 43, 69.

against the 'primum originale'. As will be seen below, in set 1 α's testimony is always worth attention.

β:10/29 *grawntid*, al. *growndyd*; 33/65 *bettur þing*, al. *beturyng*; 44/54 *writen*, al. *wyton*. E3/3 *seruyse*, al. *seruysis*, Vulg. *mysteriorum*; E13/23 *shal tile*, al. *chastise*; E31/81 part line om.[38] β has quite a number of minor isolative errors and peculiar readings; many of these oddities could readily be put right by an attentive scribe copying from β.

δ: 8/11 line om.; 29/65 *caklen*, al. *calculen*; 49/27 *traueled*, al. *traueylup*, Vulg. *parit*. E4/91 *laboreris*, al. *blabereris*; E17/43 *knewen*, al. *knowe*, Vulg. *ignorant*; E30/124 *firste*, al. *faste*.[39] In set 1 δ has a large number of divergencies from the tradition of the other manuscripts, many of them shared with N or representing a stage between the main body of texts and the reading in N; for these see below pp. 175–6. In set 5 the text is less eccentric, and most of the errors are minor.

Eˢ: E17/6 *taken*, al. *han takon*. The brevity of the fragment does not allow for an assessment of its reliability.

Hᵗ: E33/29 om. *al*, Vulg. *omnem*. Not sufficient is legible on the fragments to judge the quality of the manuscript from which they survive.

Pᵗ: 19/22 part line om.; 19/26 *sumtyme*, al. *smyton*; 30/95 om. *stryuen*.[40] In its uncorrected state the text appears to be of average reliability, so far as its brevity allows of an estimate.

The one case where descent of one extant manuscript from another could seriously be argued concerns D and X. As will be shown in the next section, the two manuscripts share a significant number of errors, four in set 1 and seven in set 5; in set 4 the relationship is much less well established. But within the two sets here edited the proximity of the two is much greater than the number of shared isolative errors would suggest. D and X share a considerable number of common corrections. In one case the text as originally written in both manuscripts was in error, and the subsequent correction in each was necessary: at 13/20–21 both scribes and written *and robbedon hym*, an insertion into the narrative at the beginning of the story of the Good Samaritan

[38] See further 8/50, 11/13, 13/60, 19/15, 33, 52, 22/27, 24/11, 83, 28/21, 33/14, 49, 55, 35/11, 38/32, 39/46, 56, 83, 84, 88, 41/9, 42/72, 43/79, 44/93, 52/94, 53/20, 32; E1/34, E4/3, 46, 135, E5/37, E6/16, E7/56, E9/1, 13, 32, 60, 63, 86, E10/text, E11/2, E15/53, 88, E16/14, E18/1, E21/46, 64, E24/text, 1, E27/28, 37, E28/text, 50, E30/text, E31/110, E34/20, E35/69, E37/13, E40/59, 61, E41/17, E43/12, E45/45, 62, 69, E55/6.

[39] Selective examples only from set 1 1/49, 6/33, 53, 61, 7/56, 35/27, 71, 37/24, 41/19, 63, 46/7, 72, 48/95, 50/33, 62, 53/89, 54/21; E12/43, E17/19, E23/51, E26/1, E35/8, 34, E37/text, 36, E39/79, 82, E42/42, 53, E45/text, 47, E51/52, E53/91.

[40] See further 20/7, 39, 30/4, 31/14, 61, 63.

justified by the drift of the subsequent events but not by the Vulgate or other manuscripts; the cancellation restores the original reading. Two less extensive cases occur in set 5.[41] But textually the most significant of these common corrections are the much larger number of trivial alterations, where the text both before and after correction was acceptable; it is hard to see such shared alterations as coincidental.[42] There are also a number of places where D as originally written was identical with X, though subsequently modifications were made to D.[43] In a number of cases the unmodified text was in error. The most obvious instance of this is at 22/3 where the biblically justified clause *whanne he bigan to rikene* was omitted from D and X, but subsequently added marginally to D alone. But, though the most obvious case, this is not the most convincing since a large number of other manuscripts also omitted that clause;[44] better evidence is a change at 25/55, where both manuscripts originally wrote *þat* to subordinate the following verb whereas a main verb was required; D cancelled the relative pronoun.[45] D, however, at some points has without correction the corrected reading of X. Again some of these cases involve readings where decisions of originality can be made: in four cases only the text as corrected in X will make acceptable sense.[46]

So far the evidence would point towards the derivation of D from X after some correction of the latter, followed by further correction common to both. It is plain, however, that X must then have undergone yet more alteration, since there are a number of corrections in X that are not shared with D, either as that was first written or as it was subsequently modified. Most of

---

[41] E17/33 DX *þing* canc., YδJG om., text *þing*; E39/69 DX ⌜þe⌝, X subsequently canc., ABPYαJ om., text *þe*.

[42] See variants to 2/6, 3/38, 4/66, 9/23, 12/51, 13/68, 15/42, 65, 68, 16/25, 36, 49, 70, 17/20, 78, 19/23, 42, 20/11, 57, 21/4, 19, 23/68, 24/31, 38, 26/85, 28/75, 29/71, 40/120, 45/25, 49/70, 50/114 twice; E1/41, 45, 105, E4/33, 49, 50, E5/61, E6/30, 32, 38, 79, E12/54, E14/27, E27/19, E30/115, 117, E31/31, E32/7, 16, 43, 56 twice, E45/83, E51/11, E52/39, E55/26.

[43] Examples where no decision about originality can be made are 3/48, 86, 4/13, 8/40, 23/87, 54/93; E1/116, E8/10, E11/86, E51/87.

[44] Namely CFKLMNTβIJXZGH.

[45] For similar instances see variants to 13/46, E4/105.

[46] For the four cases see variants to 15/17, 20/53, E15/32, E30/89; for instances where no decision can be made 15/42, 25/74, 45/71, E6/79, E7/41, 61, E42/37, E55/48, 60.

these are again readings of trivial import.[47] But in some the correction in X must be accepted as better representing the original text: 10/7 D *dayes*, X *dayes*, *-es* canc., text here *day*; 32/36 D *vndyrstonden*, X *vndurstonden*, altered to *-stoden*, text here *vndyrstoden*; 45/44 D *make*, X *ma⌐r⌐ke*, text here *marke*; E2/95 D *schulden*, X *schulden*, *-d-* canc., text here *schullen*; E11/89 D *þes*, X *þes -s* canc., text here *þe*; E15/37 D *to*, X *to ⌐come to⌐*, text here *to come to*; E15/41 D *hem*, X *hym* altered from *hem*, text here *hym*; E19/15 X ⌐*þat*⌐, D *om.*, text here *þat*; E33/51 D *giled*, X *gildrid*, *-drid* on eras., text here *gildred*; E50/55 D *herte*, X *hertis*, *-is* on eras., text here *hertis*.[48] In two instances, however, the alteration in X was erroneous: E22/37 D *perf*, X *perf*, *-f* eras., text *perf*; E34/59 D *delyueryng*, X *delyueryng* altered to *desyryng*, text here *delyueryng*; in both these cases the modification in X represents a sophistication of an originally correct, but unusual word.[49] If then D derived from X, the following stages seem imposed by the evidence so far: (i) writing of X, (ii) first correction of X, (iii) copying of D from X, (iv) correction of both D and X in the same way, (v) further and more extensive correction of X and independent correction of D. This is a very complicated sequence, particularly since the only corrector involved in these modifications in X appears to be the original scribe (though, as has been admitted, alterations by cancellation or erasure cannot be attributed); one would have to suppose that the original scribe went through his text at least three times after its first writing.[50]

The complication of that hypothesis would of itself lead one to favour instead the idea that D and X are independent copies of a common exemplar. This is favoured by a number of places where either D or X is independently involved in error with a group of other manuscripts. Since other texts share this error, it is unlikely that either D or X independently made the error in copying from the other. The cases are these:

[47] Cases are too numerous to list in full; see for instances variants to 1/43, 45, 16/35, 64, 65, 80, 21/5, 13, 46, 49, 72, 46/5, 22, 43; E15/80, 103, 105, 122, 143, E23/16, E33/1, E35/6, 41, E47/5 twice, 41.

[48] For the other manuscripts involved in some of these errors see the variants to the text at each point.

[49] For the first see OED *tharf* a.; for the second WB Rom. 8: 23 EV manuscript O *deliueryng tytil* rendering the same Vulg. participle *exspectantes*. D's reading is supported by δIJ, was that originally in X, and explains M's isolative *deseruyng*.

[50] See variants to 11/52, 26/7, 29/93, 36/80, 38/57, 109, 44/36, 45/90, 52/40; E1/98, E7/28 for instances where D and X have been corrected in opposite directions.

D in agreement in error: in all these D is emended in the text

1/47 DFIJH *hit kyndely*, al. *kyndely*; 16/42 DFI *þe*, al. *þis*; 17/3 DF *crist*, al. *iesu*, Vulg. *iesus*; 18/46 DNαδI *pharisees kepton*, al. *pharisee kepte*; 18/46 DFI *þer*, al. *þis*; 20/43 DABCLNTP^{t}I *terndyn*, al. *terreden*; 21/5 DAFαJG *com*, al. *schulde come*, Vulg. *adveniret*; 21/13 DFIJ *crist ofte*, H *of crist*, al. *eft crist*; 24/46 DFMI *hem*, al. *hym*; 26/80 DFT *in*, al. *and*; 28/63 DCNαδJH *þe*, al. *þi*, Vulg. *tuam*; 32/90 DLδ *byddyng*, al. *byndyng*; 33/27 DCFKTαIHV *and*, J *an⌜d⌝*, al. *an*; 36/45 DSI *to*, al. *two*; 37/27 DFTIJH *goo*, α ⌜*and*⌝ *go*, al. *and go*, Vulg. *et vos*; 52/101 DLMTI *drawon*, al. *drowon*; E23/43 DIG *or*, al. *and*; E50/30 DOαδEIJG *haþ*, al. *haue*; E51/40 DAB *þis erþe*, al. *þis eir*.

X in agreement in error:

23/10 ABCJX *techist*, al. *tellust*; 24/103 AFX *siþ*, al. *sych*; 26/9 CFKLMNTYβδXZ *mouing*, al. *moryng*; 29/83 AYXGV *clensen*, al. *syen*; 30/4 ABFKLMNTYαβδIJXZGHV *synnes*, al. *synne*, Vulg. *peccatum*; 36/23 SβXZ *tare*, Tδ *tare⌜s⌝*, al. *taris*; 51/104 FX *take*, IG *taken*, al. *tokne*; 52/67 ABCFKLNTYβδJXGH *profitiþ*, al. *profiȝte*; E22/10 OPTYαδEJXZ *hem*, al. *hym*; E25/71 BMOPTYαβδEJXZH *þat bryngiþ*, G ⌜*þat*⌝ *bryngiþ*, al. *brynguþ*; E51/17 ABMOPTYαEIXZH *þis*, al. *þe*, no demonstrative in Vulg.

In none of these cases is correction involved in either D or X; since the time at which correction occurred is indeterminable in any absolute way (though it may be determinable relatively), it seemed best to exclude such instances here. It is obvious that neither D nor X in the cases above are involved in any constant groupings of manuscripts; this observation does not, however, invalidate their evidence for the present question. Whether by conflation, coincident variation or divergent descent, D and X have a number of errors that they cannot have derived from the other, errors that are shared with other manuscripts.

This separation of D from X is confirmed by a number of cases where D has been corrected from a reading other than that of X. This state of affairs could, obviously, arise by an independent error of D in copying X; but since the error is not isolative, such an explanation seems unlikely. As examples of this may be cited: 38/7 D added by a corrector in the margin *and was defoulid*; the phrase was originally within the text in X but has been erased; it was omitted from CKLMNSTYαβIZG, but in agreement with the Vulgate included by ABFJH; E45/13 D *putt* altered by a corrector to *printe*, OαδEIJ *putte*, al. and text here *printe*; E47/5 D *not bounden*, altered by cancellation of *not* and supply of ⌜*not*⌝ after *bounden*, δEJH *not bounden*, al. and text here *bounden not*. Pointing towards the same conclusion are a large number of cases where no decision of originality can be made, but where D as originally written shared a reading with a minority of other manuscripts but not X;[51] again it seems unlikely that D's text was so frequently produced by independent variation which converged with variants in other manuscripts.

The most reasonable conclusion would appear to be that D and X are independent copies of a common exemplar in sets 1 and 5. Correction of each manuscript must also have involved the use of a common model, to explain the coincident correction of the two; but it was not in either case limited to this common model. Whether the common exemplar lay immediately behind the two extant manuscripts, or whether it was at a further remove, is hard to estimate. In favour of immediacy is the close similarity of language between D and X, extending to the same choice at any point between alternative graphs for what was probably the same phoneme.[52] Pointing towards a greater distance is the textual evidence of either D or X sharing common readings with divergent groups of manuscripts.

4. Group error

As well as establishing that no extant manuscript is copied from any other that survives, it is relatively easy to establish certain recurrent pairings that would suggest that the two manuscripts involved were descended, though often probably at some remove, from a common exemplar. It is difficult, since some pairs only occur within one set and others over both, to arrange these in order of certainty. The arrangement here divides the instances into three groups, the first where fairly convincing evidence of relationship exists, the second where some evidence is available, and the third where the pairings may be coincidental. In all instances cited the pair of manuscripts agree in error; the reading of *al.* is in the spelling of D and is that found in the printed text, save in the group DX where the spelling is that of A; isolative

---

[51] See for instance E15/142, E21/54, E22/63, E30/123, E31/135, E33/32, E45/82, E47/5, E53/18.

[52] For instance, between *i/y* for [I], and between *e/i/y/u* for unstressed *schwa*. The point is not that both manuscripts use the alternatives, but that at any given instances their choice is usually the same.

variation by other manuscripts not affecting the issue is not noted.

1. AB in both sets: 4/80 *maistris*, al. *maistur*; 7/67 *and*, al. *as*; 8/51 *children*, al. *child*; 9/80 *wickidnessis*, al. *wykkydnesse*; 10/15 *þe*, al. *þin*; 12/35 *stondinge*, al. *þat stooden*; 14/68 *preyeris*, al. *preyer*; 32/87 *ordeynede*, al. *ordeyne*, 34/67 A *trowist*, B *trowedist*, *-ed-* canc., al. *trowedust*; 38/59 *her*, al. *his*; 41/53 *shewiþ þat*, al. *þat*; 47/36 *wyne*, al. *wynd*; 53/text *Iohn 18*, al. *Iohannis 14*; 53/57 A om. *not*, B *not* canc., al. *not*; E15/149 *al 3if*, al. *3if alle*; E19/22 *seiþ*, al. *swiþ*; E23/66 *dampned*, al. *feendis*; E37/12 *goostli*, al. *grosseli*; E37/13 *in*, al. *and*, Vulg. *et*; E38/9 *his*, al. *þis*; E43/39 *euer*, al. *ouer*; E43/75 om. *þis*; E44/48 *fairnes*, al. *fames*, E45/5 *in*, al. *and*, Vulg. two parallel pairs; E45/68 *sowiþ*, al. *sowe*; E45/86 *don*, al. *goon*; E47/21 *lawes*, al. *lawe*; E47/80 *þei þat*, al. *þei*; E48/28 *from hem*, al. *hem fro*; E49/64 *euer holde*, al. *hoolde*; E50/11 om. *but*; E51/92 *pryntid*, al. *peyntid*, E52/29 *orisouns*, al. *resones*; E53/32 *assenten*, al. *assenteden*; E54/15 *speke*, al. *seke*; E55/52 *þat weren*, al. *weren*. Reinforced by some 70 cases where AB appear together as members of a larger erroneous group.[53]

The grouping seems to be satisfactorily established in both sets, and is supported by a large number of common readings. There is slight evidence from 34/61 and 53/51 that A derives from a corrected copy of their common exemplar, whilst B as originally written did not; any idea that A could itself derive from B is, however, ruled out by the evidence cited above.

2. CK in set 1 alone (C having no other set, K not containing set 5): 6/79 *sufferth*, al. *suffiseþ*; 33/39 *crist*, al. *god*; 38/31 *trowden*, al. *trowen*, Vulg. *credentes*; 38/89 *and erþe* transposed to after *fayle*; 39/17 *adam*, al. *abraham*; 40/63 *lightly*, al. *sewrly*; 40/80 *perseyue*, al. *perseyuede*; 41/62 *londes*, al. *lond*; 41/88 *sayden*, al. *seyin*; 44/105 *creature*, al. *trewþe*; 48/75 om. *doon*; 50/6 *hie*, al. *buye*; 51/11 *more*, al. *moste*; 51/74 *groundid*, al. *grownd*; 51/91 *ioye*, al. *ley3e*; 52/96 *goddis lawe*, al. *godys*; 53/3 C ⌐*men*⌐, K om., al. *men*; 54/87 om. *two*. With 45 cases where CK appear together in a larger erroneous group.

It will be noted that all of these examples except the first derive from sermons 33 to the end of set 1. Above it was pointed out (p. 164) that K's copy becomes noticeably less accurate after about sermon 30. It seems that K probably changed exemplar at about that point, and that the first instance of agreement with C just cited is coincidental. That a relationship between C and K exists

---

[53] These larger groups consist of three manuscripts up to the maximum number available at the point in question. The larger groups are of little significance.

from about sermon 30 on is supported by a number of shared readings, where no decision about originality is involved. The possibility that a shift of exemplar might occur within a set (as well as between sets) is confirmed much more strongly in set 4; there a number of pairings exist for the second half of the set alone, and there is a possibility that a major break in the textual tradition of the set occurred around its central point.[54] The present instance appears to be the only clear case in sets 1 or 5.

3. DX in both sets: 7/7 D *schulden*, X *schulden* altered to *schal*, al. *shal*; 25/ 55 DX *pat* canc. *is*, al. *is*; 32/12 *religious*, al. *religion*; E4/16 *ioye and þowt*, al. *þouȝt and ioie*; E17/text *rogamus et uos*, D *et* canc., X *et* eras., al. *rogamus uos*; E17/29 *mannys soulis*; al. *mannys soule*; E27/65 *refreyne . . . disseyueþ*, al. *refreyneþ . . . disseyueþ*; E30/45 *mannys*, al. *mennys*; E33/51 D *giled*, X *gildrid*, *-rid* on eras., al. *gildrid*; E39/88 *trewþe*, al. *trewe*, Vulg. *fidelis*. Reinforcing this are some 35 cases where DX appear together as part of a larger group.

The cases where X corrects the erroneous reading have been mentioned before. The evidence that has already been discussed makes this a convincing case.

4. EI in both sets: 42/text *Luc 2*, al. *Luc 11*; 48/100 *heerd*, al. *heed*; 50/99 om. *here*; 50/112 *and more*, al. *more*; 51/58 *ben seyde*, al. *he seyde*, Vulg. *locutus sum*; 51/98 *for we*, al. *we*; E20/7 *þe godis*, al. *godis*; E22/89 *and he*, al. *he*; E25/28 *ful*, al. *foul*; E27/30 E *siȝt as men may see of*, I *siȝt may men seen of*, al. *of*; E27/83 *rentis*, al. *rytis*; E29/25 *and men*, al. *men*, Vulg. no *et*; E50/65 *voys is*, al. *is uoys*. Reinforced by some 35 cases where EI appear together as members of a larger erroneous group.

In assessing the convincingness of this grouping it should be remembered that E has considerable gaps in its preservation of both sets. But, even allowing for that, the grouping is not certain. Both manuscripts have a considerable amount of isolative error, I in particular being an idiosyncratic and unreliable text. It may be that these cases should be treated as convergent and independent error.

5. IJ in both sets: 1/74–75 om. *felly for raueyne and summe schul be dampned more* (haplography); 2/65 *hemself*, al. *hymself*; 53/54 *him*, al. *hem*; 54/60 *ledeþ*, al. *leede*; 54/104 *hem*, al. *hym*; E8/34 J *laboryn*, I ⌜b⌝*labouren*, al.

---

[54] The question will be discussed fully in volume III; the break seems to come about the middle of the set, between 178 and 179 (this edition's numbering), and is evidenced in the relationships of D and β, T and J and the larger group TEJ.

blaboron; E9/21 *confessours*, al. *counselouris*; E11/66 *pes sectis*, al. *þis secte*; E11/80 *hym*, al. *hem*; E14/5 *story*, al. *scorn*; E30/143 I om. *god*, J ⌐*god*⌐ corr.; E31/38 om. *good*; E31/114, om. *lette*; E32/104 *here*, al. *heyȝere*; E32/107 om. *þe*, Vulg. *tibi*; E33/49 *tempteþ*, al. *temptide*; E34/3 *suffringe*, al. *suffryngis*, Vulg. *passiones*. Reinforced by 70 cases where IJ appear as members of a larger erroneous group.

Whilst I has short losses because of absence of leaves, it cannot be said that this group, particularly in set 1, is very convincing. Most of the errors are minor or easily made, and the apparent grouping may arise from convergence rather than from descent.

6. LM in set 1 alone (L does not contain set 5): 1/26 *seeþ*, al. *saw*, Vulg. *vidit*; 4/25 om. *to don*; 5/64 om. *and*; 6/34 *þus*, al. *þis*; 7/59 *parelous*, al. *likerous*; 9/26 *heye*, al. *grete*; 9/30 om. *here*; 10/13 *ne þe*, al. *ne þey*; 10/36 om. *and*, Vulg. *et*; 12/59 *lo*, al. *so*; 19/31 *trowe*, al. *trowþe*; 21/40 *man*, al. *mannis*; 21/78 *him*, al. *hem*; 23/88 *figuren*, al. *figuredon*; 34/52 *meneþ*, al. *mene*; 36/99 *lawe*, al. *wylle*; 38/23 *defouling*, al. *defowled*; 39/1 om. *byforn*; 44/38 *mankynde*, al. *kynde*; 45/32 *aȝen as pilat did*, al. *aȝen*; 46/55 part line om.; 47/77 *christe qui hanc sacratissimam carnem*, al. *criste*; 47/89 *hondis*, al. *hond*, Vulg. *manum meam*; 48/72 *strong*, al. *straunge*; 49/47 *oure*, al. *fowre*; 51/94 line om.; 52/37 *comeþ*, al. *come*. The group is reinforced by some 50 cases where LM appear together as members of a larger group.

The pairing seems a convincing one, with the instances of error spread throughout the set. L and M share certain other characteristics: layout in a single, over-wide column, a tendency towards a longer form of Latin text which they place at the head of the page, and the numbering of their sermons.

7. Mβ: in set 1 there is only a single instance 49/text om. *non*, reinforced by some 17 cases where they occur together as members of a larger group (though as 14 of these involve agreement of six manuscripts or more this may be of little significance). But in set 5 there are a large number of cases: E26/43 om. *and habundaunce*, Vulg. *et abundantiam*; E28/16 *fullich*, al. *folyly*; E29/54 om. *by*; E31/74 *mes*, al. *menes*; E31/92–93 line om.; E31/110 *his*, al. *to*; E32/10 om. *of þer lawis*; E32/59 *hymsilfe*, al. *hemsilf*; E33/70 M om. *conferme man in more good*, added β margin; E36/27 *shulden*, al. *shullen*; E37/28 *we*, al. *ȝee*, Vulg. second person; E38/36 *men*, al. *man*; E38/37 *þes*, al. *þus*; E40/1 *tellith*, al. *moeueþ*; E40/45 *werste*, al. *worse*; E40/104 *partith*, al. *departiþ*; E41/3 *of god as*, al. *as*; E42/69 *denyen*, al. *denyeden*; E42/72 *stone*, al. *stones*, Vulg. *in lapidibus*; E42/72 *to moyses*, al. *of moyses*; E43/13 *his*, al. *þis*; E43/31

anoied, al. *ayoudiþ*, Vulg. *evacuandam*; E43/39 om. *ouer*. Reinforced by some 11 cases where Mβ appear together as members of a larger erroneous group.

That the instances in set 5 are all between sermons 26 and 43 is not significant: M lacks 1–22 and β 46 to the end. It seems plain that the relationship between these two manuscripts only holds for set 5 and not for set 1. There is no evidence for any relation between L and β in set 1, nor for any group consisting of LMβ in that set. It seems plain that M changed exemplar between the sets, a likelihood made easier by the fact that the two sets are in different hands (though from the layout the two parts of the manuscript were probably always intended to belong together).

8. Nδ in set 1 alone (N contains this set only): 3/19 om. *frely*; 7/14 *þe*, al. *his*, Vulg. *suis*; 7/75 om. *crist*; 10/12 *falle*, al. *felle*; 10/61 N *goodes*, δ *godes* ⌐*þat arn brondis*⌐, al. *brondys*; 10/67 *to*, al. *and*; 12/6 *a doumpe*, al. *doump*; 12/65 *mater*, al. *maner*; 13/18 *and wytty*, al. *in witt*; 13/24 *and passed*, al. *passed*; 14/34 *assoyled*, al. *assoyle*; 14/38 *and þonkede*, al. *to þanke*; 14/65 add *and may do what so he wole and knowelache þat*; 16/73 N *nowe*, δ *nowe most*, al. *moste*; 16/81 N *nowe*, δ *nowe euen*, al. *euene*; 18/65 om. *alle*; 25/74 *mene*, al. *moo*; 26/37 *haþ*, al. *hadde*; 27/46 N *stablehed*, δ *stabled* canc. *be*, al. *sentence*; 27/68 *be ful bysy to*, al. *ful byssyly*; 31/42 *techyng*, al. *touchyng*; 31/102 *obeischeþ*, al. *obeschede*; 32/46 *religiouse*, al. *religioun*; 35/79 *oþer*, al. *erþly*; 36/18 *is*, al. *was*; 36/90 *queke*, al. *wickede*; 42/17 *desolatid or diffoundyd*, al. *desolatyd*; 42/25 *desolatid or defouled*, al. *desolate*; 45/7 N *duden*, δ *dereden* on eras. corr., al. *dredden*; 45/8 N *schulde not*, δ *schulde not*, *not* canc., al. *schulde*; 48/12 *ofte*, al. *eft*; 49/88 *foure*, al. *fowrþe*; 50/115 *comeþ*, al. *semeþ*; 52/77 *riʒtwisnesse*, al. *riʒt wylle*. Reinforced by 34 cases where the two appear as members of a larger erroneous group.

The instances at 10/61, 16/73, 27/46, suggest that N has further corrupted the already defective text that appears in δ. But, whilst it seems likely that N was indeed copied from a manuscript further removed from the original than δ's exemplar,[55] that model cannot have been δ itself in the light of the evidence above p. 167. But it is clear that these two manuscripts belong ultimately to the same branch of the stemma, and that this branch was one with many eccentricities. Had N alone survived of this pair, it would have been reasonable to treat it like V and

---

[55] For readings, not provably erroneous, where N seems to have altered the reading as it appeared in δ, see variants to 4/66, 10/53, 12/30, 16/9.

suppress its many individual readings; but δ is not so easily dismissed. In set 5 it presents a moderately good text; because of δ's support for many of N's readings in set 1, it seemed better to record the whole of both manuscripts evidence even at the expense of enlarging the bank of variants.

9. PZ in set 5 alone (P's sole content): E7/61 *figurid*, al. *figure*; E11/45 *maundementis*, al. *maundement*, Vulg. *mandatum*; E15/96 *to god*, al. *god*; E20/32 *graciouse*, al. *graciousere*; E21/53 *man*, al. *men*, Vulg. *hominum*; E22/14 om. *þis*; E27/95 *vnclennesse*, al. *vnkyndenesse*; E30/140 *world*, al. *worldis*, Vulg. *in secula seculorum*; E31/111 *and þis*, al. *in þis*, Vulg. *in hoc*; E45/72 *he þat*, al. *he*; Reinforced by a further 33 cases where they appear as members of a larger erroneous group.

The expurgation of the text in Z leaves only about two-thirds of the material from which errors might be discerned. Furthermore, as has been said above, both P and Z, for the portions the latter preserves, are both accurate copies. It seems likely, therefore, that this relatively small amount of evidence may be considered significant of a shared hyparchetype for these two texts.

10. δJ in set 5 alone. There seems no trace of any shared isolative errors in set 1,[56] though both manuscripts contain it. E5/33 om. *he*; E10/64 *god*, al. *good*; E12/28 om. *goode*; E12/49 om. *and*; E15/116 *sixtene*, al. *sexteþe*; E17/30 om. *þis*; E22/46 *vndisposyngis*, al. *disposyngis*; E23/83 om. *þe*; E25/58 *priuytee*, al. *prynte*; E35/69 om. *and*; E49/4 om. *vndirstonde*. Reinforced by some 58 cases where the two are together in a larger erroneous group.

It seems doubtful whether, despite the number of instances, this can be considered a valid pair. The instances are mostly small errors and, in view of the tendency of δ to minor alteration, they may well be coincidental.

It should be noted that this last pair is in conflict with the better evidence of group 5, IJ. The same difficulty afflicts the second category, in all of which there is incompatibility either with pairings set out above or with another in this group.

11. OT in set 5 alone (O's only item). E1/ text *hora est iam nos̈ de sompno surgere*, al. *scientes quia hora est*; E14/53 *and in*, al. *and*, Vulg. *et*; E17/54 *proude and coueytouse*, al. *pruyde and coueytise*; E18/64 O om. *opre men seyn*,

---

[56] In set 1 there are some eleven examples of errors shared between δJ in groups of less than seven manuscripts.

T added margin corr.; OT also agree in assigning E6 to the Sunday after Christmas rather than the sixth day after Christmas.

12. Oα in set 5 alone. E2/87 *louedist*, al. *louest*; E4/53 *cristus*, al. *cristene*; E4/82 *aftur*, al. *afer*; E15/40 *confermyþ*, al. *comformeþ*; E30/4 *whiche*, al. *while*.

13. TI in both sets: 4/50 *hem*, al. *hym*; 8/7 *after*, al. *afer*; E14/32 *ben of*, al. *ben*; E15/129 *schulden* twice, al. *schulen* twice, Vulg. *venerit . . . evacuabitur*; E23/14 *ouercome*, al. *ouurcomeþ*; E50/77 *anticristis*, al. *anticrist his*; E53/60 om. *owene*.

14. αI in both sets: 2/21 *his*, al. *is*; 10/35 *prayeres*, al. *preyȝer*, Vulg. *orationis*; 23/57 I *suwen*, α *sow⌐ne⌐*, al. *sownen*; 25/78 I *ben*, α *are*, al. *by*; E8/81 *helpes* canc. *lymes*, al. *lymes*; E22/75 *paire oper*, al. *opure*, E24/52–53 line om. (haplography); E30/128 haplography of *so he shal ende þis world*, added both margin; E46/41 *shuld*, al. *shullen* (future).

15. αJ in both sets: 4/76 J *and we*, α *and* canc. *we*, al. *we*; 7/39 om. *þis*; 9/34 J om. *and*, α ⌐*and*⌐, al. *and*; 17/54 *in dropesy*, al. *ydropisye*; 30/35 α *ysai* canc. ⌐*I sawe and*⌐, J *ysay and*, al. *I saw and*; E5/32 *stronge*, al. *strawnge*.

16. βI in both sets: 13/58 *for*, al. *fro*; 32/5–6 line om. by haplography, added in both in margin; 36/27 *doyng*, al. *dowyng*; E19/96 *þongis*, al. *þuoong*; E27/42 *for þat*, al. *forȝat*.

Whether any of the groups 11–16 can be considered significant seems doubtful. Five of these involve at least one of the manuscripts OTI all of which are, in varying degrees, idiosyncratic in their isolative readings. Since the recognition of a pair must depend upon cases where the two manuscripts stand apart in error from all other surviving manuscripts, supporting evidence from larger groups has not been cited.

Even less convincing are a large group of cases where agreement between two manuscripts is found; because they are probably random no detailed citation is given.

Agreeing in 5 errors: TH (2 in set 1, 3 in set 5); Tβ (2 in set 1, 3 in set 5).[57]

Agreeing in 4 errors: AI (1/3), BY (0/4), FJ (4/–), MT (2/2), Mα (2/2), Nβ (4/–).[58]

Agreeing in 3 errors: AG (0/3), Bδ (2/1), Bα (0/3), CN (3/–), CT (3/–), IH (2/1), LN (3/–), MH (0/3), MI (1/2), NT (3/–), OI (–/3), TG (0/

---

[57] TH at 10/63, 23/15, E11/84, E15/83, E25/27; Tβ at 11/48, 19/16, E2/73, E13/22, E33/39.

[58] AI at 24/44, E5/35, E16/20, E26/30; BY at E22/21, E39/50, E39/80, E42/56; FJ at 17/77, 29/21, 47/8, 51/23; MT at 10/45, 51/text, E35/48, E38/21–2; Mα at 4/72, 52/70, E27/39, E45/41; Nβ at 10/8, 10/20, 25/78, 37/46. The sign '–' means that one or both of the manuscripts are not available in that set, set 1 being put first.

3), TZ (2/1), Tδ (2/1), YI (2/1), YJ (3/0), αδ (2/1), δE (3/–), δI (2/1).
Agreeing in 2 errors: AL, Aδ, CH, CJ, Cβ, DG, Dβ, Fα, Fδ, GH, IZ,
MG, NI, Nα, OH, OJ, OP, OZ, Oβ, PT, TJ, Tα, YG, Yβ, Yδ, ZH,
αZ, αβ.
Agreeing in 1 error: some 77 pairs.

A number of points emerge from this evidence. It seems
reasonable to accept the first nine pairs above, with the
restrictions there noted, and with the possible exception of the
fifth, IJ. The large number of pairs that must probably be
regarded as random is noteworthy. Also worth observing within
these pairs is the frequency with which manuscripts that for other
reasons seem unreliable appear: I, N, O, T, and δ. Conversely
manuscripts that are generally accurate fail to appear within the
first nine pairs: for set 1 only F, for both sets G, H and Y. Such an
absence would not be remarkable, were it not that precisely these
manuscripts are most difficult to place in any larger groups.
Other manuscripts, of less reliability, that do not appear in any of
the numbered pairings or in a pairing occurring more than once
are V with both sets, S with only set 1, the fragments Eˢ, Hᵗ and Pᵗ
and Q, the last only available for one sermon.

Turning to the next stage, possible groups of three
manuscripts, a complete impasse is found. No single group of
three manuscripts is established with even fair probability. The
best attested are two groups each on the basis of four common
errors in set 1: CKβ at 33/19 pis, al. his, Vulg. personal pronoun;
37/112 CK ony nede, β ene neede, al. euenehed; 43/26 fed, al. fediþ; 43/
73 we, al. men; and CNδ at 4/89 blyndeth, al. byndeþ; 12/51 here, al.
hery; 49/64 hym, al. hem; 52/71 þilke, al. þicke. But whilst these may
reasonably be taken as supplementary evidence for the pairs CK
in the first case (with the restriction to the latter half of the set as
before), and Nδ in the second, they are poor proof of any larger
alignments: they are numerically ill-attested and mutually
exclusive. Similar conclusions emerge from those groups of three
even less frequently witnessed: DKH, LMδ and δIJ in three
instances,[59] ABY, ABα, AEI, AδJ, BZV, DFI, DFX, LMβ,
LMI, MTβ, OPZ,[60] in two instances, and the 131 different

[59] DXH at 47/97, E30/26, E30/115, all of which involve correction in at least one of the
three manuscripts; LMδ at 9/66, 25/76, 29/28; δIJ at E16/57, E23/77, E33/1.
[60] ABY at 2/73, 44/36; ABα at 37/51, E3/59; AEI at 48/29, E20/85; AδJ at E1/138, E28/
17; BZV at E4/1, E9/24; DFI at 16/42, 18/46; DFX at 10/7, 27/37; LMβ at 5/4, 48/53;
LMI at 6/63, 9/50; MTβ at 11/45, E38/26; OPZ at E1/78, E44/117.

groups of three manuscripts that are only attested once. It seems likely that all of these are random groupings, not significant of textual affiliations. Again, some back up pairings accepted above, AB, DX, LM, Mβ, PZ, but they do nothing more.

Exactly the same emerges when a search is made for larger groups. The group DδXG is found twice in set 5, that of ABEI twice in set 1 and of AδIJ twice in set 5;[61] otherwise 34 groups of four manuscripts appear once each in set 1, 39 in set 5. No recurrent group of five manuscripts is found in either set, though there are 34 in set 1 that appear once each, 25 in set 5. There are no recurrent larger groups of manuscripts.

It would appear, then, that the ordinary methods of textual criticism will not here serve. The incidence of shared error is so small that there is not sufficient evidence for even minor groupings, and such evidence as exists is conflicting. Groups are mutually exclusive and are, in any case, not proven. Admittedly, it is difficult given the losses of leaves from various manuscripts at differing points to bear in mind with any given group that the absence of a text may be due, not to original divergence, but to accident. But this, whilst it may be an important factor in larger grouping, has less relevance to groups of two or three manuscripts. There is not such an incompatibility of evidence, taking each set separately, that such small groups could not be established for the bulk of manuscripts. It is possible that another critic might be able to discern further common errors. The position adopted here is a fairly rigorous one: I have started from the assumption, often disputed by modern critical editors, that the medieval scribe is more likely to have understood his exemplar than the modern scholar, and that, therefore, the onus of proving an error lies on the editor. But, even if I have been too conservative in my assessment of error, it seems doubtful whether a more radical critic would come to different conclusions if he considered more evidence than I have. His number of random groups would be larger, but this would not help him towards the establishment of a stemma. He might admit more cases than I have in setting up pairs such as AB or Nδ; but this would get him no advantage. His plight would in all probability be the same as mine.

---

61 DδXG at E40/text, E53/25; ABEI at 45/97, 48/66; AδIJ at E10/55, E14/46.

Should recourse be made to other methods for the establishment of a stemma? The method that would accept as proof of relationship the evidence of common readings, rather than common errors, would not offer any assistance.[62] Leaving aside the question of principle as to whether this method is acceptable, it has yet to be shown that in practice it can work unless a close and small body of manuscripts, representing at worst almost the entire number ever produced, is concerned. In the present case such a method would result in a vast number of mutually incompatible groupings, and no help for the editor. The DX or AB alliances would be evidenced with much greater frequency; but, alongside these, would be found a large number of groupings of each individual manuscript which belied them. Since this method forbids any selection of *type* between groups, the only way to select is by mere numerical occurrence. Given the losses from individual manuscripts, number would be a most unsatisfactory guide. It would, furthermore, be difficult to operate once the possibility that a manuscript might change exemplar in the middle of a set had been admitted.

The ineluctible conclusion that emerges from all this is that no stemma can be drawn, and that only a few, very elementary, points can be made about manuscript relationships. Such a demonstration should not surprise. In view of the external hazards to which the text, once written and copied, was exposed, too many manuscripts have been lost.[63] Much more important, however, is the evidence that the extant manuscripts offer of extensive conflation and correction. As has been said, there is no reason to doubt that the exemplars of the extant texts were similarly affected. The evidence to be considered in the next section to some extent reflects this. There are also a number of cases where the amount of correction in the manuscripts points towards an obscurity in their exemplars—where correction had been effected rather awkwardly, or where the corrected and uncorrected readings existed side by side without indication of which was to be adopted. Examples of this may be seen in both sets: 11/16 αJ *gostly* canc., *grettly*, H *gostly and gretly*, al. *greetly*, where the two adverbs, both suitable in the context, may have

---

[62] See W. W. Greg, *The Calculus of Variants* (Oxford, 1927) and *The Play of Antichrist from the Chester Cycle* (Oxford, 1935).
[63] See further below pp. 189–202.

been written one over the other with no clear indication of which was to be adopted; 15/62 D *god heuene, heuene* canc., α *heuen* canc. *god*, ABFIJGH *god*, al. *heuene*, where the same may be suspected for the two nouns, though the Vulgate reading calls for *god*; 41/56 D *iacobus* on eras. corr., JXG *israels* on eras. corr., δ *iacob israeles*, ABCKLMNSTYαβZ *israelis*, where the alteration, whether right or not, may have been made obscurely; E11/1 J *tellip and* canc. *techyp*, I *tellep and techep*, δV *tellip*, al. *techep*, where again the roughly synonymous verbs may have been left without any indication of which was to be adopted.[64]

5. Errors in the common ancestor?

There is a relatively large number of places in both sets where the majority of manuscripts appear to be in error. Superficially this should provide evidence for the construction of a stemma; it does not here since there is no consistency in the manuscripts that attest the correct reading. A large number of the cases to be considered involve passages of biblical translation, and the difficulties that have been outlined in this regard should be remembered; in some instances it is very hard to decide whether the text was originally accurately and completely translated, and the inaccuracy or omission thus scribal, or whether the original writer was more cavalier than an individual later copyist. For this reason the treatment of these passages in the edited text is not entirely consistent. Similarly, possible errors not involving biblical translation considered below involve judgements about the syntactic regularity of the original writer, or his choice of vocabulary; again strict logical consistency has doubtless not been achieved. The cases are as follows:

2/26 DABCFKLTYαδIJXZG *seruauntes*, M *seruaunt*, Vulg. *servum*. It should be noted that a minority of manuscripts have the same error of plural for singular in relation to the same noun later in the sermon: line 66 F *seruauntis*, line 85 ACFLαZ *seruauntis*. In the Vulgate the noun is throughout singular, and this is followed in WB. In the course of the

---

[64] A manuscript like C shows how easily this could happen. A corrector has been through C marking in the margin or between the lines alterations to be made, but he neither cancelled nor erased the readings that were to be removed; these alterations are written faintly and were evidently intended as a guide to another who was to incorporate them properly; this was never done. In most instances it is absolutely plain which words have to be removed, but there are a few instances where reasonable doubt might exist.

allegorical interpretation of the parable in the sermon the *seruaunt* becomes plural (line 80), but the first two instances here are in anticipation of this. The text here at line 26 has been emended.

15/62 AB *and riȝtwysnesse of him*, T ⌜*and þe riȝtwesnesse þerof*⌝, DCFKLMYαβδEIJXZGH *om.*, Vulg. *et iusticia eius*. The difference in wording of T's addition may suggest that it derives not from an exemplar having the reading of AB but from comparison with the Vulgate text. The text here is emended.

21/23 DABCKLMNTαβPᵗEJXZGH *feuerys*, FYI *feuere*, Vulg. *febris* (WB *feuer*). The noun elsewhere in the sermon is variably treated: at line 4 all manuscripts have *feuerys*, but at line 51 all have *feuer*. In view of this, and of the common use of *feueres* in ME with singular force (see MED 1), the text has not been emended.

22/3-4 BY *whanne he hadde bigunne to rekene*, DAα added marginally by correctors, CFKLMNTβIJXZGH *om.*, Vulg. *cum coepisset rationem ponere*. The omission is not by homoeoteleuton. Though the clause is not essential for the sense of the story, the text here includes D's marginal addition.

25/14 CYβZH *in þe place þat*, DABFKLMNTαδIJXG *þat*, Vulg. *in loco*. The prepositional phrase is not essential to the understanding of the sentence. But its very insignificance makes it unlikely that the fuller reading should have been gained by checking with the Vulgate after the original writing. With some hesitation, therefore, the reading of CYβZH has been accepted.

28/22 DABCFKLMNYαβδJXZGV *poore men ben preysud*, for the verb H *be preched*, T *ben prechid*, *-chid* on eras. corr., Vulg. *evangelizantur* (WB *pore men ben takun to prechyng of þe gospel*). In set 4 the parallel passage from Luke 7 is translated, with all manuscripts having *prechid* save G, which has *preisid*.[65] The awkwardness of the WB translation makes it plain that no English verb was felt to be entirely suitable for the Latin; but the sense of the passage makes *preysud* inappropriate. The text here has been emended.

38/63-64 DABCFKLMNSTYαβδIJXZGH *and hit brynguþ in syche sowles fruyt to an hundertfoold*, E adds after *fruyt* the words *in pacience* translating Vulg. *in patientia*. It seems possible, however, that this is a scribal addition only since the end of the interpretation of the parable is very freely rendered by the homilist (38/48 ff, cf Luke 8: 14–15). The majority reading has been left.

40/4 DABCFKLMSTYαβEXZGH *aftyir his fastyng*, NδIJ *after his waschyng*. The phrase refers to the departure of Christ into the desert for the temptation. Since the homilist includes the clause *whan he hadde*

---

[65] See Arnold ii. 12/28: OED *preach* sense 4 shows that the necessary sense and use of the verb was available at the time.

fastyd fowrty dayȝes in the following line, the minority reading is most evidently good sense. But it is arguable that *fastyng* is the *difficilior lectio* and that the writer in that sentence was looking forward. For this reason the text here has not been emended.

41/4 BZ *lo*, A ⌐*lo*⌐, DCFKLMNSTYαβδEIJXGH om., Vulg. *ecce*. The text has been emended.

44/26 DBCFKLMNSTYβIJXZG *he was a Samaritan, siþ þat he hadde a fend*, αδ *and sepin*, H ⌐*and*⌐ *siþ*, AE *and* canc. *siþ*, Vulg. *et*. As so often the triviality of this instance makes the correction hard to explain. None of the versions is an exact translation of the Vulgate, and for that reason the majority reading has been allowed to stand.

44/65 α *bot I* ⌐*haue*⌐ *know*⌐*en*⌐ *hym and I kepe his worde*, DABCFKLMNSTYβδEIJXZGH om., Vulg. *sed scio eum et sermonem eius servo*. Though not a straightforward homoeoteleuton, the omission is comprehensible in the repetition of so many words between lines 62 and 67. α's correction can be similarly explained as the attraction of similar words in line 65. The text here has been emended to agree with α's uncorrected reading and the Vulgate.

47/100 H *þat ben not writen in þis boke but þe*⌐*se*⌐ *fewe bene writen for þis ende*, CKα *þat bene not wretyn in þis boke but þes few bene wretyn in þis boke for þis ende*, G⌐*þat ben writun in þis book*⌐ *but þese fewe ben writun in þis book for þis eende*, X ⌐*þat ben not wryten in þis boke*⌐ (corr.) *but þese fewe ben wryten in þis booc, in þis booc* canc., S *þat be not wreten in þis book for þis eende þat*, DABFLMNTYδEIJZ *but þese fewe ben wrytone in þis booc for þis eende þat*, Vulg. *quae non sunt scripta in libro hoc. Hæc autem scripta sunt ut* . . . Only H was in origin an accurate translation of the Vulgate text, though X by subsequent corrections came to this. The repetition of the verb makes the omission easy enough to explain, though it is less easy to see how the prepositional phrase *in þis booc* came to be transferred. It seems possible that at an early stage in the tradition the phrase *in þis boke* dropped out, and the two verbs were then compressed into one; subsequently a corrector added the phrase again but now in the wrong place. The text here has been emended to agreement with H and the Vulgate.

48/88 F *lesewe*, DABCKLMNSTYαβδEIXZGH *ledon*. F's reading is certainly the *difficilior lectio*, since the verb (see MED *leswen*) is not recorded after Wycliffite texts. In view of the isolation of F, however, the text here has not been emended.

49/14 KSY *a litel and ȝe schulen not se me and eft a litil and ȝe schulen se me*, α *a litil tyme shal com and ȝe shal not se me and efte he sais ȝe shal se me*, DABCFLMNTβδEIJXZGH *and eft ȝe schulle see me*, Vulg. *modicum et non videbitis me, et iterum modicum et videbitis me*. The repetitive nature of the speech makes the loss comprehensible, though as with 47/100 it is not a simple dropping out of a single group of words. The repetition of Christ's words by the disciples, here in lines 17–18, shows the correctness of the reading in KSY; but this may also have caused that correctness by secondary checking and not by origin. The text, however, has been emended to the reading of KSY. The difference between K and C here should be noted, as this is within the section where those manuscripts are closely related.

49/15 H *what is þis þat he seiþ a litil,* X *what is þis* ⌐*þat he seiþ to vs a*⌐ *lytul* (correction not by original scribe), DABCFKLMNSTYαβδEIJZG *what is þis lytul,* Vulg. *quid est hoc quod dicit Modicum?* Coming so closely after the last, this emphasizes the problem of these passages: none of the manuscripts that were there correct as compared with the Vulgate, is here right, but another pair has, in one case by modification, the accurate rendering. It seems more difficult here to be sure whether the more accurate version was intended, since the *he seiþ* produces an awkward sentence after the opening *þei seydon.* Because of this doubt the reading of the majority has not here been emended.

49/28 SH *for here our cometh but,* X ⌐*]* *hir our comeþ*⌐ *but,* DABCFKLMNTYαβδEIJZG *but,* Vulg. *quia venit hora eius.* X's correction appears to be in a later hand, but the spelling shows that it has been taken from a medieval manuscript.[66] The agreement of SH, two manuscripts that elsewhere show no affinities (though cf 47/100), is puzzling. The text has been emended.

E1/28–29 DABOTYβδJXG *so it is of synful men for what deede euere he doþ,* PαZ have *man;* there is no variation in the final *he doþ.* Since the *men* of the majority of manuscripts is contradicted by a singular *man* and by the forms of pronoun and verbs elsewhere in the second part of this sentence, it seems reasonable to emend here to *m[a]n.*

E10/52–53 DABPTβδIXZG *ʒif þin enemye hungreþ . . . and ʒif he þurste,* αH for the first verb have *hungre,* OJV for the second *þursteþ,* Y *priste, -þ* eras., Vulg. *esurierit . . . sitit.* The two conditions would appear to be parallel in sense, but since Middle English could express this type of condition by either indicative or subjunctive verb the variation in mood of the majority of manuscripts has not been emended.[67]

E14/52 α *wakynges in hungure and thriste in many,* G added by corrector, DABOPTYβδHᶦIJXZH om., Vulg. *in vigiliis multis in fame et siti in . . .* The omission is a simple case of homoeoteleuton, since the preceding word is *monye.* It would seem that the loss must have occurred very early in the tradition of the text. It has been emended here.

---

[66] The beginning is cut off in the cropping.
[67] See T. F. Mustanoja, *A Middle English Syntax* i (Helsinki, 1960), pp. 469–70. In WB an attempt was made by the EV translators to keep the variation of tense found in the Vulg. with the verbs *schal hungre . . . thirstith,* but in LV both verbs are present indicative *hungrith . . . thirstith.*

E15/5 DAYβδJXH ʒif he speke wiþ mannys tongis and aungel tongis, PZG have *mennus . . . aungels*, BOTαI *mannis . . . aungels*, Vulg. *hominum . . . angelorum*. (WB *tungis of men and of aungels*). The reading of the majority has not been emended since the forms *mannys* and *aungel* could be regarded as in effect adjectival, the first with the sense 'human'.[68]

E15/42–43 DABOPYαβδEIJXZGH *and þis is clepid benignite*, T *þe secounde condicion þat euere sueþ charite ys þat hyt is benygne to peple þat hyt dwelliþ wiþ benygnyte ys cliped gode fuyr of charite for men þat haueþ charite beþ brennynge in loue*. T's longer explanation of the second condition of charity is attractive in that it enumerates and brings out the quality in a manner comparable with the other conditions. On the other hand, it is difficult to see, if the majority reading is an error, how that error arose, and T is not a reliable text.[69] The reading of the majority has been allowed to stand.

E19/65 DABOPTYαβEIJXZH *þe sone of Abraham, þat was first born and fleschly pursuwede*, δG omit *and*. The verb *pursuwede* should not be linked with *born*, and the text has been emended.

E26/3–4 DABMOPTYαβδIJXZG *comyng doun fro God þat is Fadur of liʒt*, H reads for the last word *liʒtis*, Vulg. *luminum* (WB *liʒtis*). The text has not been emended. The singular is found in the exegesis at line 21 without variant.

E30/68–69 edited text *voysus ben prechyngis . . . þondryngus ben tellyng[is]*, DBTXH *prechyngis*, AMOPYαβδEIJZG *preching*, DBMOPTYαβEIX *tellyng*, AδJZGH *tellingis*. Only H is consistent in having a plural throughout, as seems to be required by the antecedents in each clause. The text has been emended to this.

E35/34 edited text *men shulden be temporat*, D *teporat*, -*t* altered from -*l*, AMOPTαβδIJXZG *temperaly*, BY *temperatli*, Vulg. *modesti* (WB *mylde*). The first examples of the adjective *temperate* given by OED date from the very end of the fourteenth century, and it was presumably the unfamiliarity of the word that gave rise to the corruption.

E39/41 DABOPTYαδIJXZG *we grucche not aʒenus God*, M for the pronoun has *ʒe*, Vulg. *murmuraveritis*. But, despite the agreement of M with the Vulgate here, it is unlikely that it is right; the remainder of the sentence also uses the first person pronoun, and M has no variant there. M's change is either by inadvertence, or by officious over-correction. The text is not emended.

E43/37 DABMOPTYαβδIJZH *God ʒaf Abraham þis biheste*, XG add by corrector ⌐by⌐ before *byheste*, Vulg. *Abrahae autem per repromissionem donavit Deus* (EV *bi aʒenbiheeste*, LV *of biheeste*). The fact that the accurate rendering of the Vulgate is only found by correction, and then only in

---

68 See some of the examples cited under MED *aungel* n. 1 b.f-g, and *man* n. 2b.
69 See above p. 165.

two manuscripts, leads to doubt as to whether it was in the original of the sermons. Because of this the text has not been emended.

E45/text DABMPYαβEIXZGH *Galatas 5*, T *Galatas 5 et 6*, J *Galatas 5* ⌜*et 6*⌝ added by a different hand, text actually is Galatians 5: 25–6: 10. In other cases where the lection spreads across a chapter division a larger number of manuscripts include both numbers.[70] Despite the bad evidence for both here, therefore, it cannot be assumed that the original merely gave the opening chapter of any lection. The text has consequently been emended.

E49/38–39 DABMOPTYαδJXZG *putte ʒe awey leesyngis . . . for we ben eche menbre*, I for the first noun has *lesinge*, E for the second *membris*, Vulg. *mendacium . . . membra* (WB *leesyng . . . membris*). None of the manuscripts is correct throughout. The text has not been emended, and it is assumed that *eche* attracted the following noun into the singular.

E50/text DABOPTYαδEIJXZG *uidete quomodo caute ambuletis*, M adds after *uidete itaque fratres*, Vulg. as M. The list of lessons prefixed to T has the first three words as these appear in the majority reading here, and the omitted words are not translated in the sermon; on the other hand, the manuscripts printed by Wickham Legg and Dickinson include them.[71] Because of the doubt the text has not been emended.

E51/94 DABOPTYαδEIJXGH *and alle þe dartis of þe feend*, MZ omit *and* and make the following words the subject of the sentence. The sentence is an awkward one, and there appears to be a disjunction within it. It is possible that the corruption is more deep-seated than any of the surviving readings now allow one to reconstruct. The text has been emended to agree with the reading of MZ, since this makes possible sense.

For the purposes of constructing a stemma these dubious cases are of little assistance; but they cast some light on the textual tradition. In all cases a very small number of manuscripts at best, only one or no manuscript at worst, preserves the reading that might be conjecturally proposed for the original. Further, there is no consistency about the manuscript(s) in which those original readings are found. It appears necessary to envisage either errors in the common ancestor of all manuscripts, with subsequent correction in a small minority, or convergent error of a remarkable extent. Given the amount and variety of the error, the first hypothesis is surely preferable. The question, however, arises of the authority of the 'corrections': since the majority of instances

---

[70] See E13, E14, and E53, but compare 52.
[71] T f. iii; Wickham Legg p. 191, Dickinson col. 519.

concern biblical translation, are the minority 'right' readings derived from the original of the sermons, or do they come from subsequent and unauthorized verification of the biblical translation against a Vulgate text? It seems impossible to give a firm answer to this question, or at any rate one that is equally certain for all instances. In favour of the first explanation are those cases where the 'correction' is of a text that, in context, is perfectly acceptable, where there is nothing in the majority reading that would alert a reader to corruption. In those set 1 instances (44/ 26, 44/65, 49/14) where α has the 'correct' reading, the claim that this manuscript has been corrected 'per primum originale' may be remembered; though, disconcertingly, the only instance where a modification of the text as first written is in question, that modification (44/65) has taken the text away from the close rendering that would be expected in the 'original'! In favour of the idea that the 'correction' was unauthorized subsequent meddling is the variety of manuscripts that witness these 'right' readings, and frequently their unreliability elsewhere. Looking at those 'corrections' accepted into the edited text for which the balance of probability seemed better, the manuscripts involved are not an impressive list: in set 1 H in four cases, B and Y in three, S and Z in two, and A, C, K, M, T, α, and β in one each; in set 5 α and Z in two, M, P, T, δ, G and H once each; this ignores cases where the 'right' reading appears only in a correction. T and δ, if no others, are often idiosyncratic texts, C, M and β often have stupid errors, whilst S is frequently in need of the correction that was never done.

Whatever is the true explanation of these problem cases, the variability of the 'correct' minority seems to point towards conflation within the tradition. They confirm the hypothesis already set forward from other evidence that, as well as the visible conflation evident from the corrections in the extant manuscripts, the antecedents to the surviving texts had equally modified the text as they inherited it. If this is right, then traditional methods of stemmatics will not work. The examples above fall into the category of 'major' errors, used for instance by Knott in his study of manuscripts of the A-version of *Piers Plowman*.[72] Even more evidently in that category, however, are

72 See T. A. Knott, 'An Essay toward the Critical Text of the A-Version of "Piers the Plowman", *Modern Philology* xii (1915), 389–421.

those rearrangements of the original order of the sermons found in the groups EIJXZ and GHV, or in the Advent opening of set 1 evidenced in FYα. Yet the one fact that emerges from the unsatisfactory morass of conflicting textual groupings, is that those organizational alliances do *not* hold within the text itself.

Finally, a word must be said about the type of error and scribal variation that is found. The reader of the sermons could be forgiven for expecting that scribal interference in them would be similar to that found in manuscripts of *Piers Plowman*.[73] The subject matter of the sermons shares many concerns with the alliterative poem; if anything, it deals with theological and political topics in an even more outspoken manner. Yet, unlike *Piers Plowman*, there is little sign that the scribes involved themselves in the text to the extent of either modifying the views that they did not sympathize with, or of exaggerating those criticisms that they felt to be valid. Z, a complete expurgation of the cycle, stands in isolation, apart from a few omissions in W and fewer in E, both of substantial sections whose views as repeated elsewhere are retained. Yet the sermons offer fewer inherent barriers to scribal meddling in the sense: no alliteration or metre that could restrain those of literary sensibility, no regular line division that would make it easy to check whether the entire text were present. Some substitution of synonyms there certainly is, though almost all of it is probably caused by a scribe's dialectal divergence from the main body of manuscripts. There is some apparently pointless alteration, particularly changes of *herfore* to *perfore* or the reverse. But otherwise the scribes' errors are apparently inadvertent, resulting from the mechanical problems of copying a long text or from a failure to take in more than the words immediately in question. Such a difference calls for explanation. It would seem that the scribes felt themselves obliged to copy without change, an obligation which is also reflected in the multifarious corrections. The situation that could have produced this obligation will be considered in the next chapter.

---

[73] See G. Kane, *Piers Plowman The A Version* (London, 1960), esp. pp. 125–45, G. Kane and E. T. Donaldson, *Piers Plowman The B Version* (London, 1975), pp. 128–213.

VI

The Production of the Sermon Cycle
and its Editing

i. The production of the manuscripts

The questions of the date and authorship of the sermons will be considered in a later volume; both involve the internal evidence of the content of the sermons as well as the external evidence of the manuscripts.[1] In this introduction, however, much has been said of the details of this external evidence. It may be reasonable to explain how the present editor would interpret this evidence as it relates to the production of the text. It should be said that this interpretation is based upon ten years' work with the manuscripts, but, with evidence of such complexity, it is quite possible that another ten years' work on the same manuscripts may produce another view, or at least a changed emphasis. Equally it must be stressed that the view put forward here is based upon the complete picture; individual details of evidence are open to many other explanations but these other explanations conflict with, or do not allow for, certain other individual details.

The first piece of evidence that must be accommodated in any overall view is that the majority of the manuscripts of the cycle are professional productions. The hands, whatever their individual styles, are practised examples; the layout is regular. Equally it is plain that in these texts the scribes knew that a rubricator and ornamenter would follow their own work; the style was determined before the scribe began work, and the scribe left heavily abbreviated instructions for the material that the rubricator was

---

[1] It should be said straightaway, however, that the textual situation offers no support whatsoever for a view that the sermons were composed over a long period of time, a view proposed by E. W. Talbert, 'The Date of the Composition of the English Wyclifite Collection of Sermons', *Speculum* xii (1937), 464–74, and developed further by M. W. Ransom, 'The Chronology of Wyclif's English Sermons', *Research Studies of the State College of Washington* xvi (1948), 67–114. If such a period were in question, a situation similar to that found in the Wycliffite Bible or *Floretum/Rosarium* manuscripts would be expected, with various different stages of the development of the text revealed. The invariable appearance of the sermons in sets makes it clear that 'publication' of them was simultaneous.

to insert. Though there is some evidence that each of the five sets might be regarded as a separate entity, within each set the work of copying is never interrupted by any gap or by any intrusion; if a change of scribe occurred within a set,[2] the second took up immediately where the first left off. There is nothing of the disjunction or irregularity that has recently led two critics to suggest that the copying of Chaucer and Gower manuscripts in London was done by independent scribes working freelance and without the discipline of a large scriptorium.[3] Equally most of the manuscripts of the present text must have been costly to produce.[4] The size of the leaf and the number of folios mean that the expense of parchment alone would have been considerable. The parchment is of good quality, and any minor tears have been carefully repaired. Though the majority of manuscripts has been rebound in modern times, there is no evidence that any of them circulated unbound, let alone in loose quires that have subsequently been roughly matched. The bindings of C, F, and Z are probably original: all are stoutly sewn, with heavy wooden boards covered with leather.

The physical appearance of the majority of manuscripts, then, differs drastically from many contemporary vernacular sermon texts. Many of these are unimpressive volumes, often at this date on paper, small and convenient for carrying in a pocket, written in a casual, often unprofessional hand.[5] The manuscripts of the present cycle would be easy to use as books for public reading. The headings are obvious, and the punctuation guides the reader to the sense. Certainly there are some exceptions to this picture. S and P[t] survive uncompleted, and as they stand are not impressive. N used the sermons for an idiosyncratic purpose, and

[2] Such is the case with D in set 5, with B in set 5, with H in set 2, more than once in J's combination of sets 5 and 1, with L in set 4.

[3] A. I. Doyle and M. B. Parkes, 'The production of copies of the *Canterbury Tales* and the *Confessio Amantis* in the early fifteenth century', in *Medieval Scribes, Manuscripts and Libraries, Essays presented to N. R. Ker*, ed. M. B. Parkes and A. G. Watson (London, 1978), 163–210.

[4] For the costs of medieval book production see Doyle and Parkes p. 197 n. 84 and the article there cited H. E. Bell, 'The Price of Books in Medieval England', *The Library*, 4th series xvii (1936), 312–36.

[5] Typical instances are MSS Bodley 95, CUL Gg. 6. 16, and Rylands Eng. 109 mentioned above pp. 115–22. The majority of manuscripts of Myrc's sermons and of the Northern Homily Cycle are equally unimpressive. (see p. 45 for references for these). Even Bodleian MS Holkham Misc. 40 of *The Mirror*, a more substantial volume, lacks the ordered regularity of the majority of the present text.

the form of the manuscript more nearly resembles the normal fifteenth-century casual sermon collection. Q is a pocket book, probably a private and amateur copy of one of the type of professional manuscripts that form the majority; here we can see, as it were through a dusty glass, the traces of those handsome books, but roughened and simplified. O, though from its contents the work of a man of milder views than Q, is not dissimilar physically. V is something of a puzzle: superficially disorganized, but with some signs of supervision. But these six merely serve to emphasise the professional quality of the remainder, and their remarkable uniformity.

Turning to the content of the manuscripts, certain other facts have to be fitted in to any explanation. First the fact that the sermons occur in comprehensible liturgical schemes, without intrusion into those schemes of any other material. Further items may appear in the manuscripts, but they are separated off; if the eccentric cases named in the last paragraph are excluded, only a very limited group of such other texts occur.[6] Conversely, individual sermons from the cycle are not found intruded into manuscripts of other sermons. Given that each sermon is (with the possible exception of E11–15 where the four sects are consecutively treated with some cross-reference) self-contained and could readily be used without knowledge of the rest, this isolation of the cycle is remarkable. Though an orthodox preacher, even if he came across the sermons, might recoil from their content, it is strange that isolated examples were not taken into the other surviving instances of Lollard sermon collections.[7] Secondly the existence of three arrangements, liturgically comprehensible and all apparently authorized, has to be accommodated. As has been argued, it would seem that the two secondary arrangements, witnessed by EIJXZ and GHV respectively, were not produced once and for all and then copied; rather they were schemes available to a scribe that might be imposed upon exemplars having other arrangements. Equally a secondary arrangement might be reordered into the primary

6 See above pp. 47–50; the only contents are Wycliffite, save for the additions to Z.
7 Such as that partially found in BL Additional 41321 and Bodleian Rawlinson c. 751. Equally, given that many Lollard manuscripts mix texts of different types, the sermons might have been expected in anthologies such as BL Additional 24202, Trinity College Dublin 244 and 245 or Bodley 647.

pattern, as was the case with A. Other minor variations likewise seem to have been offered as a pattern, which could be adopted or not at will. Within the rigid outer frame of the cycle that excluded all intrusions were certain authorized variations.

Looking at the individual sermon, other characteristics emerge. There is evidence that the heading might derive from an exemplar other than that used for the text, and that the sermon number, if provided, could come from an independent list. The biblical text in its English translation had to be rubricated, with all non-biblical words meticulously excluded, and with no rubrication for texts other than the lection that might be incidentally quoted, or for any repetition of parts of the lection.[8] Textually, the relationships between the manuscripts are extremely confused. Each manuscript has a fair amount of isolative error, but few combinations of erroneous manuscripts are constant, none involving more than a couple of texts. The evidence suggests that each set in any individual manuscript might have used a different exemplar; in some cases a change of exemplar seems to have occurred mid-way in the set. Changes of exemplar do not coincide with a change of scribe in the extant manuscripts.

Most evidently requiring explanation is the correction, both in its extent and in its relations. It is evident from statements within the cycle and from other observations in Lollard works that verbal accuracy was regarded as a matter of great importance.[9] Correction on the line, that can only have come from the scribe then at work, shows that there was pressure to copy these sermons carefully. It is therefore not very surprising to find alterations, made subsequently to substantive readings, that would affect the sense, or even to the more trivial details of the biblical translation. It is much more difficult to explain the constant modification to wording that could have no effect upon the meaning of the preacher's sentence. Even more difficult is it to account for the fact that many of these modifications are shared between several manuscripts, particularly in the nexus-corrections that have been described above. Many of the manuscripts have been worked over by more than one corrector; recorrection of trivia, the

---

[8] For these points see above chapter IV.
[9] See 19/80–82, 44/57–61, E1/83–84, E21/61–63, E41/46–47, E55/21 and especially E43/5–10.

addition and subsequent deletion of þe, is not uncommon. To make this type of alteration influence of a compelling kind must have been exerted upon the scribes or correctors. The sharing of correction, and the fact that the modifications bring the text into line with other manuscripts but out of line with yet others, must imply the availability of exemplars beyond those originally copied. Such influence and such availability of exemplars operated in the case of about twenty-five of the manuscripts here.

The explanation that most readily comes to mind for this state of affairs is that these twenty-five manuscripts are the products of a single scriptorium, and that this scriptorium must have possessed both the master copies and various derivative exemplars. The patterns for the various liturgical arrangements were there available, lists of headings and of sermon numbers. There were also reference books, at the very least a copy of the Vulgate. Work in the scriptorium must have been carefully overseen, particularly in regard to correction of the scribe's work. Yet certain, perhaps surprising, freedoms were allowed. The size of each manuscript and its layout were apparently not subject to strict control, even in relation to each other. Whilst the small size of α might result from a change of plan about its eventual content, with enlargement after its physical size was fixed, or conversely whilst the relatively large size of F compared with its possession of only one set might result from a curtailment of its originally intended contents, the awkwardness of M's layout and size cannot be explained away. Equally, such a hypothesis would be easier to accept were there more instances of a scribe at work on more than one manuscript. Only in W and δ does it seem that one of the main scribes of the manuscripts reappears. One relevant factor may well be that a large number of manuscripts has disappeared, by episcopal suppression as well as by the effects of time. Yet this to an extent exacerbates the problem. As has been said, for the extant manuscripts some 47 scribes must be postulated, or, if the six above (pp. 190–1) are ignored, 41; it would be stretching probability too far to suppose that all the lost manuscripts were written by just these 41. Any increase in the number of manuscripts proposed must allow for some increase in the number of scribes.

Before coming to look at the historical problems that such a hypothesis poses, it is worth comparing this situation with the position as far as it is known for other Wycliffite texts. The number of manuscripts surviving is in excess of those preserved for any of the texts apart from the Wycliffite Bible:[10] the nearest parallel is the number of manuscripts of English origin still surviving of the *Floretum/Rosarium*, with 27 in Latin, 1 in English, plus various known lost copies.[11] As far as numbers are concerned, the Bible translation is a case apart: despite its prohibition after 1407, it is provable that it was owned by orthodox men and it may well also have been copied by orthodox scribes.[12] The costly nature of many of the copies of the present sermon-cycle, with their professional script and decoration, is to be found in many copies of the Bible translation and in the *Floretum/Rosarium*;[13] it can also be seen in a few other Lollard vernacular manuscripts, for instance of the Glossed Gospels, of the revision of Rolle's Psalter commentary,[14] and Egerton 2820 of the variant version of *The Clergy may not own Property*. Outside these most of the Wycliffite vernacular manuscripts are less impressive productions, with little ornamentation and not designed for public reading. Until more work is done on many of the texts, it is difficult to compare the state of the sermons with them. But some points of similarity emerge. There is clear evidence in the Bible translation, the *Floretum/Rosarium*, the revised Psalter commentary, and the Glossed Gospels for extensive revision of the work, affecting the readings of the texts and in the second and last cases also its organization.[15] In all cases the revisers must have had access to a fairly extensive library of Latin theology. At least in the case of the Bible translation, the very greatest attention was paid to the minor details of the text. In that

---

[10] About 230; see C. Lindberg in *Studia Neophilologica* xlii (1970), 333–8; though some manuscripts are listed there twice, an equivalent number are not included at all.

[11] See C. von Nolcken, *The Middle English Translation of the Rosarium Theologie* (Heidelberg Middle English Texts 10, 1979), pp. 10–14.

[12] For instance Henry VI owned MS Bodley 277.

[13] For instance of the former BL Royal 1 C. viii, Royal 1 C. ix, Cambridge University Library Mm. 2. 15, Ll. 1. 13, and Dd. 1. 27; of the latter BL Harley 401, Bodley 55 and 448.

[14] Of the first text for instance Bodley 243 and BL Additional 41175, originally parts of the same manuscript, and York XVI. D. 2; of the second for instance MS Bodley 288 or Harvard University Library Richardson 36.

[15] For the *Floretum/Rosarium* see edition cited n. 11; for the Glossed Gospels the best statement is in the chapter by H. Hargreaves, 'The Wycliffite Versions' in *The Cambridge History of the Bible* ii, ed. G. W. H. Lampe (Cambridge, 1969), 407–9.

corrections in EV manuscripts are directed towards accuracy in rendering the biblical text, the case is not strictly comparable to the trivial correction and counter-correction in the Sermon manuscripts. But the account of the work given in the General Prologue, an account that can be verified in many of its stages from the Glossed Gospels and from the state of a manuscript such as Bodley 959, points towards an exercise of complex organization, and towards the existence of a centre at which such work could be done.[16] In the cases of at least the Bible translation, the *Floretum/Rosarium* and the Glossed Gospels, learning, organization, and a considerable amount of money must have been involved. In all of these aspects they resemble the sermon-cycle. This is, however, probably the most overtly Lollard of the texts. Without the General Prologue and a few glosses that are contained in a handful of manuscripts, the Wycliffite Bible translation would be hard to trace to Lollardy.[17] Much of the Glossed Gospels is neutral, though, once the connection with the Early Version is known, the Wycliffite leanings of some of the extra passages, particularly those from Grosseteste and John of Abbeville and especially the fuller versions of these that appear in the York text, become plain.[18] The most obvious evidence of the background to the *Floretum* is its inclusion of many long extracts from Wyclif's own works; but in the abbreviated *Rosarium* the majority of these have disappeared or been drastically abridged. The Lollardy of the present sermons is much more difficult to miss; though a few sermons contain nothing that even Arundel could have objected to,[19] the strong anti-clericalism of the majority would at the end of the fourteenth century have led any suspicious reader on until he came to the not infrequent instances of ideas distinctively Wycliffite.

The historical difficulties of the hypothesis proposed are, it must be admitted, formidable. If the copying of secular verna-

---

16 See the account of MS Bodley 959 given by C. Lindberg, *MS Bodley 959 Genesis-Baruch 3. 20 in the Earlier Version of the Wycliffite Bible*, (Stockholm Sudies in English vi (1959), viii (1961), x (1963), xiii (1965), xx (1969)).

17 To the list of manuscripts containing the *General Prologue* given in *Selections* p. 173 should be added MS Scheide 12 at Princeton, a complete copy prefixed to a complete LV Bible.

18 None of the York text has so far been printed. For some tendentious material even in the shorter version of the gloss see *Selections* no. 12.

19 For instances in set 1 nos. 1, 9, 12, 13, or 49.

cular texts even in the metropolis was so casually arranged, is it likely that unorthodox men should have organized such a large-scale undertaking? Certainly, the drive of a new religious ideal, an ideal that had many social and even political implications, might motivate some attempt at the dissemination of Wycliffite texts. But the organisation apparently involved here is more nearly similar to that of a monastic scriptorium in one of the larger houses; yet of all the possible locations for it, a monastery is the most unlikely, from the views repeatedly expressed in the sermons. Even if the work of copying were done on commission for a non-monastic patron, it seems unlikely that any house could countenance the dissemination of such heretical, and even seditious, texts. Moreover, any explanation that proposes a method of commission, whether from a scriptorium over which the Wycliffites had no control, or from a series of independent free-lance scribes, runs into problems with the centripetal corrections.

Until very recently it has been usual amongst historians to see the Lollard movement, even in the twenty years after Wyclif's death, as a scattered affair, lacking organization and deprived rapidly of any leaders of either academic pretensions or political influence.[20] McFarlane's work on the Lollard knights has altered that picture somewhat,[21] and Michael Wilks has argued that in the latter years of Richard II's reign Lollardy did indeed have friends at court.[22] Study of the texts that the Lollards themselves wrote has helped to redress the balance. Whatever the circumstances in which the manuscripts of the sermon cycle were written, whatever the libraries to which the compilers of the *Floretum/Rosarium* or the Glossed Gospels had access, these texts *were* produced and produced for, if not necessarily by, Wycliffites. Such productions must point towards a movement with money, learning, and organization. This new picture, moreover, makes

---

[20] See K. B. McFarlane, *John Wycliffe and the Begnnings of English Nonconformity* (London, 1952) and for the later period J. A. F. Thomson, *The Later Lollards, 1414–1520* (Oxford, 1965).

[21] K. B. McFarlane, *Lancastrian Kings and Lollard Knights* (Oxford, 1972), pp. 139–226; this section is based on lectures given in 1966 and posthumously published.

[22] M. Wilks, 'Royal priesthood: the origins of Lollardy', in *The Church in a Changing Society: CIHEC Conference 1977* (Uppsala, 1978), pp. 63–70; see also the same author's paper '*Reformatio Regni*: Wyclif and Hus as leaders of religious protest movements', *Studies in Church History* ix (1972), 109–30.

much better sense than the old of the fourteenth and fifteenth-century opposition to Lollardy: it explains the number and the comprehensiveness of the edicts against the movement, and the length and erudition of the texts that, from Wyclif's lifetime until the second half of the fifteenth century, were directed against it.

If the hypothesis of a single scriptorium were pursued, the most likely place to look for it would be in the household, or at least under the protection of one of the Lollard knights. The most convincing of these would probably be Sir Thomas Latimer, whose main estate was at Braybrooke in Northamptonshire, near the border with Leicestershire.[23] Latimer is known to have owned Lollard texts: in 1387 he was ordered to appear before the King in Council 'cum certis libris et quaternis in custodia sua existentibus de erronea et perversa doctrina fidei catholice ut dicitur'. Unfortunately no further details of the books, or of the results of Latimer's appearance, are known. The following year, however, Latimer acted in defence of a Lollard preacher cited by the bishop of Lincoln for his work at Chipping Wardon, another manor of his; he took the battle into the enemy camp by bringing an action against the bishop's summoner before the king's justices on assize.[24] Lollardy continued to flourish at Braybrooke. In 1407 Wyclif's works were to be found there, since it was one of the three places visited by two Czechs, Mikuláš Faulfiš and Jiří of Kněhnice, in their quest for Wyclif's writings; there they obtained a copy of *De Dominio Divino*.[25] The incumbent of Braybrooke from about 1401 was Robert Hook, a notorious Lollard, cited repeatedly until 1425 for his views and for disseminating them.[26] In the enquiries following the Oldcastle rebellion it emerged that men from Braybrooke had played a part in stirring up support in Northamptonshire and in Leicestershire. In particular one, Thomas Ile, was known as a *compositor ac asportator billarum* in Leicester and as a *factor billarum* in

---

23 For Latimer see McFarlane *Lollard Knights*. I have argued in *Journal of Ecclesiastical History* xxix (1978), 272–4 that two other Lollard knights, Sir William Neville and Sir John Montague, who assisted Nicholas Hereford when he was arrested as a heretic in 1387, may have provided him with the materials and the protection to write the Lollard *Opus Arduum*.
24 For these incidents see *Lollard Knights* pp. 193–5 and references there.
25 See Emden *Oxford*, p. 670 and *Notes and Queries* ccxviii (1973), 445; the manuscript in question is now Vienna 1294.
26 *Lollard Knights*, pp. 195–6.

Goscote.[27] The records for the early trials of his rector, Robert Hook, do not survive, but in his 1425 trial before Chichele a recapitulation is made of Hook's former citations and the judgments that were given.[28] From this it appears that Hook had been brought before bishop Repingdon of Lincoln in 1406 as a disseminator of heresy, had abjured and been given penance. In 1414 he had again been apprehended and brought before Chichele. Once more he had been accused of various heresies. More significantly for the present purpose, he was found to have held *scolas* and *conventiculas* in which he had propagated these heresies and in which he had used and handed out books. It was alleged against Hook 'libros diversos in lingua tam latina quam anglicana conscriptos in se multos errores et hereses continentes composuisti, scripsisti, et per alios scribi fecisti, ac scienter penes te habuisti, tenuisti et servasti.' From Hook's English recantation that followed his third trial in 1425 it would seem that his reading habits did not change after 1414, even if no mention is made of his instigation of the multiplication of such books.[29] For at least thirty-seven years it thus appears that Lollard books were available in Braybrooke. Moreover, it would seem that this availability was to some extent common knowledge: someone must have alerted the authorities in 1387, the two Czechs must have been directed there, probably from Oxford, in 1407, and in 1414 Braybrooke was known as a centre for the dissemination of heretical leaflets in Leicester and the county.

This is the area where documentation over a long period of time is easiest to find. But recent research has revealed a much more widespread support for Lollardy amongst the gentry and middle classes before the Oldcastle rebellion than historians have

---

[27] PRO KB9. 204/1 nos. 111, 130, and 141; in no. 134 the *rector ecclesie de Braybrok* is said to be *commune lollardus*, holding views against the catholic faith and against the dignity of the king. In no. 111 mention is made of Thomas Scot of Braybrook *scriveyn*; it is not clear whether he is to be identified with Thomas Ile, or whether Scot was a second writer in the village. For the Leicester group J. Crompton, 'Leicestershire Lollards', *Transactions of the Leicestershire Archaeological and Historical Society* xliv (1968–9), 11–44.

[28] See *The Register of Henry Chichele*, ed. E. F. Jacob (Oxford, 1938–47), iii. 105–12.

[29] Loc. cit. p. 111 'I have wittinglych hadde in myn warde and kepyng many divers bokes and tretees, the whiche contene many foule and horrible errours and heresies, . . . the which bokes and tretees were late founden with me by the kinges officers'. The four heresies listed as having been contained in the confiscated books reveal a Lollardy even more extreme than that in the present sermons (for instance, that goods should be held in common).

traditionally allowed.[30] It may well be, therefore, that the origin of these manuscripts should be sought elsewhere. A search through the ecclesiastical records between Wyclif's death in 1384 and the Oldcastle revolt, dates that seem to be the furthest limits during which the sermon-cycle could have been written, has produced no trace of any scriptorium as such, though ample evidence for the wide distribution of books that the authorities considered heretical, a fair number of individuals connected with the book-making trade and suspected of Lollardy, and a good system of Lollard schools.[31] This is not very surprising. The texts that I have been discussing show many signs of organization; to add to them an efficient system of concealment from ecclesiastical scrutiny is not to strain credibility much further. Short of the unlikely discovery of the daybook of the scriptorium it is hard to see how its existence can finally be proved.

Are there any alternatives to the explanation here offered? That the scribes were physically all together in one place does not seem to me essential, though it would certainly be the simplest way to explain the facts of the manuscripts. But it is possible that the scribes were supplied with an exemplar from a centre, and that they returned copy and exemplar there; the copy was then checked by a small group of men within the centre. But some sort of centre there must surely have been, to account for the cross-currents of correction and modification. Methods for the reproduction of manuscripts in the medieval university offer some parallels to the situation here, but do not furnish a complete explanation. The *pecia* system gave rise to comparable obscurity of textual descent, and, when properly supervised, would provide similar correction. But the surviving manuscripts of the sermons do not show the most significant traces of *pecia* origin: there are no numbers on the quires or in the margins that could be derived from that source, no gaps or compression of text within a set of sermons that would suggest copying from a succession of *pecia* as

---

[30] See the valuable detail collected by C. Kightly, *The Early Lollards: A Survey of Popular Lollard Activity in England, 1382-1428* (unpublished York D. Phil. thesis, 1975).

[31] References are too numerous to give here; Kightly's thesis sets out the details in full. The Close and Patent Rolls for the period amplify the ecclesiastical material from secular documents. For a succinct view by one writer of the period see *Eulogium Historiarum* (ed. F. S. Haydon, Rolls Series 1858-63), iii. 355 'Discipuli praefati Johannis [Wyclif] studuerunt in compilationibus sermonum et sermones fratrum congregaverunt, euntes per totam Angliam doctrinam hujus magistri prædicabant'.

they came to hand.[32] Similarly, the process of *pronunciatio*, a process familiar in Prague before and during the Hussite period, would explain some features. In this method a text was dictated to a group of assembled scribes; often the scribes were apparently amateurs, students obtaining their textbooks cheaply, but some cases are known where the writers were professionals. The attractions of this suggestion are again that the impossibility of establishing more than a very few rudimentary genetic groupings would be explained, and that the work could have been completed very much more quickly than in any system reliant upon the circulation of exemplars to be visually copied, so that concealment of the process of multiplication would be easier to effect. But it seems unlikely that *pronunciatio* was known in England.[33] Also the physical neatness and order of the surviving manuscripts of the sermons could hardly have been achieved if their texts were taken down from dictation. It is possible that, even if the extant manuscripts were produced by the conventional procedure, the multiple exemplars were made by *pronunciatio*. But, if they were, they must have been very carefully finished by visual methods. Both these methods of reproduction, by *pecia* and by *pronunciatio*, were devised for the provision of university text-books, though the second was used in Hussite Bohemia for the circulation of polemical works by Hus and of material originating in Wycliffite circles in England.[34] It is possible that the Lollards responsible for the multiplication of copies of the present sermon-cycle learnt something from the *pecia* method; but it is clear that, either from choice or from necessity, they did not adopt this method in its entirety.

[32] For a survey of the scholarly work done on the *pecia* system, and for pertinent comments upon the textual implications of this method, see most recently R. H. Rouse and M. A. Rouse, *Preachers, Florilegia and Sermons: Studies on the 'Manipulus florum' of Thomas of Ireland* (Toronto, 1979), pp. 170, 176–7 and references there given.

[33] For *pronunciatio* see *Journal of Theological Studies* NS xxv (1974), 137 and references there. G. Fink-Errera, 'Une institution du monde médiéval: la "pecia"', *Revue philosophique de Louvain* lx (1962), 232–3, suggests that *pronunciatio* was limited to universities in central Europe, and cites evidence for it from Prague, Vienna, Heidelberg and Erfurt.

[34] The most familiar case of a text so disseminated is Hus's *De Ecclesia*; Hus finished the work, and it was then dictated to 80 persons in the Bethlehem Chapel in Prague on 8 June 1413. Though none of the copies made then seems to survive, some extant manuscripts may derive directly from them; the genetic affinities of the extant manuscripts are untraceable (see S. Harrison Thomson, *Magistri Johannis Hus Tractatus de Ecclesia* (Cambridge, 1956), pp. xvi, xxii–xxix). For the circulation of the *Rosarium* and the *Opus Arduum* in Bohemia by this method see *Journal of Ecclesiastical History* xxix (1978), 259.

The acceptability of the explanation above does not turn upon the possibility that the scriptorium, or the centre, was at Braybrooke. Such a location would fit the prevailing dialect of the manuscripts reasonably.[35] But any place within the east central Midlands would equally be possible, provided that it could offer the finance and the protection that would be involved in such an undertaking. Looking at the other texts described above, the claims of Oxford to have been the location are strong: there would have been available the necessary books, scholars conversant in the academic techniques so evident in many of these Lollard works, and professional scribes. Less clearly could the work have been concealed there. But it may be that the idea that concealment would have been essential is wrong. To some extent this depends upon the date at which the work was done: the need for concealment probably increased as the fourteenth century wore on, and would seem to have been overwhelming after Arundel's 1407 Constitutions. The date *post quem* for the copying of the sermons is plainly that of their composition, a date that will be discussed in a later volume. Suffice it here to say that there seems every reason to look for a composition date before 1401 when the death penalty for heresy was introduced into England; a date at least ten years earlier seems probable. The copying could then have occurred in the last decade of the fourteenth century. The same reasons that have led to the hypothesis that all manuscripts were made in one geographical location point towards a relatively short temporal period for their making. Despite the different dates given above in chapter II for the manuscripts, dates being given to each on general palaeographical considerations and not in knowledge of the argument here advanced, it seems possible that all scribes could have been working within a few years around 1400. Leaving aside the six

---

[35] With the help of Dr Michael Benskin an analysis of the orthography of the various scribes is being made at the Edinburgh University Middle English dialect survey; the results will be published elsewhere. Though none of the manuscripts so far linguistically placed derives from the immediate vicinity of Braybrooke, it should be remembered that this localization identifies the origins of a scribe's orthography and not the place at which the scribe was actually writing the extant manuscript. Thus, for instance, scribes 2 and 3 of D wrote in an orthography localizable a long way east of that used by scribe 1, yet from other features of the manuscript it is evident that at least scribes 1 and 2 and probably all three must have been working in one place. As would be expected, the situation is further complicated by the textual transmission: the spelling habits of scribe 1 in set 1 are in certain features distinct from those he used in set 5.

manuscripts rejected from this centre for other reasons, the range
of dates is from 's. xiv ex' to 's. xv^1', with the majority 's. xiv/xv'.
It seems possible that the hands dated 's. xv^1' could have
belonged to younger men, but men already at work about 1400.

Such then is the interpretation of the manuscript evidence that
seems at present most plausible. More work on Wycliffite texts of
all kinds, English and Latin, may provide further evidence either
to support the view or to suggest another. Traditionally, the
Lollard movement has been studied from the documents set down
by its opponents, ecclesiastical or civil records, the tracts of men
such as Woodford, Gascoigne or Netter. These have been
interpreted with the hindsight that Lollardy apparently made
little impact on the established church or its practices in the
fifteenth century; the threat that men such as these must have felt
Wycliffism offered, in order to induce them to spend so much time
and energy in its refutation, has been forgotten. It should not
surprise that investigation of the Lollards' own writings, the case
for the defence as it were, should outline the defects in the
traditional view and should provide a rather different picture. In
coming to a balanced assessment of this case the present sermon-
cycle provides vital evidence.

ii. The editing of the sermon-cycle

The impossibility of constructing any stemma, or even of dividing
the manuscripts roughly into main families, leaves the editor
without any theoretical guide towards the choice of a base
manuscript. Of the thirty-one surviving manuscripts, only
twenty-five can be regarded as serious candidates for this choice
in any part of the cycle. The three sets of fragments are obviously
useless, V is a carelessly reworded version of only a part of three
sets, N converts the sermons to a new use and Z expurgates them.
Further S contains only about a half of one set, and would
therefore be a foolish choice even for that. For the sermons in the
present volume R, W and for the most part Q are not available.

This last point raises a question of some considerable difficulty.
Should a single manuscript be adopted as base text for all five sets
of sermons? Or should a choice be made for each set
independently? The convenience for the reader of the consistency
of orthography and linguistic forms that may come from a single

exemplar throughout is plain, though in many cases a change in the scribe within a single manuscript may to varying extents nullify this. If the textual evidence pointed towards the superiority of a manuscript that contained less than the full five sets, then it would have been tempting to use that manuscript for the material it presented. Within the two sets edited here, however, that does not appear to be the case. Of the manuscripts that contain only one of these sets, the only claim to superiority that could seriously be maintained is that of P for set 5; but even this does not appear to be sufficiently good to overcome its lack of the other four sets and its losses at the end of set 5. Three manuscripts, M, α and δ, contain both sets here but lack one of the other three. Of these δ is an idiosyncratic text, M rather careless. The claim at the end of α's set 1 that it had been corrected 'per primum originale' attracts the editor's attention to it; but, if a justified claim, the editor can only conclude that the correction was done with some lack of attention. Compared with the majority of the manuscripts also α's language is eccentric[36]. Certainly at any problem the editor would be well advised to give serious consideration to the reading offered by α, but he would be rash to use it as base text.

In favour of using as base manuscript one of the exemplars that contain all five sets is the evidence presented in chapter 1 that the 294 sermons were put together as a single unit. There is nothing in the organization or in the textual minutiae considered in the last chapter to suggest that the 294 sermons were of varied origins. The implications of the evidence here for date and authorship will be considered in the introduction to one of the later volumes. If one turns to manuscripts that present the whole of this cycle, there are ten, apart from the expurgated Z, that were originally complete: ADEGHIJTXβ. Of these, three have in the course of time been badly damaged, E, H and β; to choose any of these as base text would be to lose the advantage described of a single manuscript. From the details given in the last chapter it will be clear why I cannot be chosen as the basis for any edition. T falls under much the same condemnation: its text is

---

[36] The hand that wrote the two sets involved here used a more northerly dialect than any of the manuscripts other than Z, writing -*s* as the third person singular present indicative where all apart from Z normally have -*þ* (though C rarely has -*s*), and *are* as the present indicative of the verb 'to be', Z, *er*, all other manuscripts *be*(*n*) or *beþ*.

idiosyncratic, heavily corrected but often in the wrong direction, needing much alteration to get rid of its deficiencies. Of the remaining five, A, D, G, J and X, the weakest candidates are J and, less obviously, A. J has a number of cases of homoeoteleuton, and the scribes other than the main writer were haphazard. A's text of set 1 is generally good, but its text of set 5 is much less accurate; even less satisfactory is its text of set 4. There was no textual justification for using A as base text; anyone interested in it can find a reasonably accurate print of it in Arnold's edition.

This leaves the next difficult question. Of the three manuscripts still available for choice, D represents arrangement 1, X arrangement 2 and G arrangement 3. Use of any of these three as base manuscript could be justified on considerations of textual excellence within the individual sermons. It has, however, been argued that the original arrangement of the 294 sermons was according to scheme 1, and that either of the other schemes, whilst they may have been authorized, leave oddities of wording within the sermons that would disturb the reader. It would seem to follow that any edition should present the sermons according to scheme 1. Choice of either X or G as base manuscript would therefore force upon the editor the disentangling of their new arrangements, with X of sets 1 and 5, with G of sets 1, 4 and 5. The problem is easily resolved with regard to X. It has been shown above that X is closely related to D. In some regards X, because of its corrections not shared with D, presents the better text. But it has been damaged and has lost sermons 224–39 of set 4. If either D or X were used, D would be the better choice as base; the corrections in X can, when necessary, be incorporated.

The cases for D and G need to be set out in full. In favour of D is its completeness, lacking nothing of the 294 sermons either by deliberate omission or subsequent loss, its preservation of the original arrangement 1, and its relatively small number of isolative errors. Palaeographically it is early, its hands being dated at the end of the fourteenth century. Against D is the fact that several scribes worked on it, with the resulting changes in orthography that may inconvenience a reader interested solely in its subject matter.[37] In favour of G is its uniform scribe

[37] The differences do not reflect any considerable divergence of dialect; they consist mainly in variation between *sh/sch* and similar orthographic (even if locally assignable) points, though the first scribe has a rather higher number of *u* spellings for OE *y* than is found in any of the other hands.

throughout, with the linguistic homogeneity that this brings; the orthography of the scribe is regular and lacking in distracting idiosyncrasies. Palaeographically G is probably somewhat later than D, of the first quarter of the fifteenth century. G's text in sets 1 and 5 is careful; it is noticeably less accurate in set 4. G omitted the seven occasional sermons found in all other manuscripts at the end of set 4. The chief objection to G is its arrangement of sets 1, 4 and 5 in a complete Temporale cycle. Though G's individual sermon headings within this arrangement are full, the reordering that would be imposed on the editor would leave the edition as a misleading representation of the manuscript. The claims of the two manuscripts, D and G, seem nicely balanced. Finally, it was decided that the question of arrangement must decide the balance in favour of D. It may seem odd that G was used for the five sermons in *Selections from English Wycliffite Writings*;[38] but it was precisely because only a very small selection was there printed that G's ordering did not matter, and its uneccentric orthography was for an anthology greatly advantageous. For a complete edition of the entire cycle D seems the better choice.

Since no stemma can be constructed, the edition that follows cannot rely upon genetic considerations to govern the choice of material readings. The editor cannot either rely upon a diagram to justify his decisions, or even check the validity of one reading against that from a manuscript genetically far removed from it. The present edition is therefore, like those of *Piers Plowman* by Professors Kane and Donaldson, one in which a decision on correctness must be taken for each individual case. Unlike those editions, however, the treatment of the base text has been conservative. The readings of D have been allowed to stand unless it can be demonstrated with fair certainty that they are incorrect. It has been concluded, from the amount of correction to which D has been subjected, that considerable care was devoted to its text, and that if the editor rejects its readings this must be on arguments of considerable persuasiveness. At all times the balance of probability has been given to the manuscript, the onus of proof against it laid on the editor. As has been shown, D is, notwithstanding all the correction, not faultless; all the errors described in the last chapter have been corrected here. But in

---

[38] *Selections* nos. 10, 13, 15, 21B, and 23.

matters of indeterminacy D's readings, even if isolated in the tradition, have been allowed to stand. Most frequently such matters are the trivial details of the inclusion or exclusion of a definite or indefinite article, the repetition of pronoun or preposition before the second element in a parallel construction. That these were not 'trivial details' to the scribes of the manuscripts is evident from the care with which they were altered in many of them; but that very fact of alteration must lead the editor to respect the decision that the scribe of his base text has made. The corrections that have been made to D have also been accepted in every case save where it is provable that they are wrong. When an emendation has been made, either from the testimony of other manuscript(s) or conjecturally, the emendation has been adapted to the orthography of that scribe of D currently in question.

The details of the methods used in citing variants from other manuscripts will be set out in the next chapter. It was decided that, in the absence of a stemma, the most reasonable way to arrange the variants was according to the three arrangements of the cycle, and within that threefold division in alphabetical order of sigla. They are therefore cited in the order D (if the base text has been rejected) ABCFKLMNOPQRSTWY$\alpha\beta\delta$ E^{s}H^{t}P^{t}EIJXZGHV. In fact, of course, since no part of the cycle is evidenced in all 31 manuscripts, only parts of this sequence will appear, but they will always be in this order. It may be objected that this confuses the relationships that exist, for instance, between D and X, P and Z, δ and J, where the two manuscripts follow different arrangements. But in fact these pairings are best established by individual errors that the two manuscript alone share, and in these the two sigla will appear side by side. Even a cursory glance at the variants to the text will reveal how few groups, however small, recur with any frequency. The order of citation then becomes merely a matter of convenience. It seemed best to allow the primary division between the three arrangements every opportunity to be revealed in the variants, but beyond that to use an order where completeness is simplest to check. When a series of variants follows a lemma, an attempt to order them has been made. First come any corrections to or from the reading as found in the lemma (when these corrections are recorded, see below pp. 211–12, then the nearest relative to that corrected reading, or to the lemma. But in many instances no decision about proximity can be made between multiple variants; here the order has been determined by the position of the first manuscript that attests it on the list above.

VII

Editorial Practice

This section will summarize the treatment of the base text and variants in the present edition. For the reasons that have led to this treatment reference should be made to the foregoing chapters; they will not be repeated here.

i. The text

The edition of the sermons is based on D; the readings of D have been allowed to stand unless there is positive evidence that they are incorrect. Modern punctuation and capitalization has been substituted for that in the manuscript, modern paragraph division has been introduced and modern word division used. Marginal or interlinear additions to D are shown by half brackets, ⌐. . .⌐; responsibility for these is not noted if they were made by the original scribe, but otherwise they are designated in the variants *corr*. Other modifications in the manuscript are recorded in the footnotes. Emendations that consist in the addition to, or alteration of, what is written in the manuscript are shown by square brackets [. . .]. Emendations that consist in the suppression of words or letters in the manuscript are recorded in the variants. Italics are used to show the translation of the biblical lection of each sermon, underlined in red in D as in the majority of the manuscripts. Since the intention of the scribes was plainly the rigid exclusion from this underlining of any words intruded into the biblical translation, when this intention has not been fulfilled in D the italicization has been silently emended. As italicization is used to show material underlined in the manuscript, words that in normal modern punctuation would be italicized are usually enclosed in single quotation marks (e.g. 44/106). The headings of the sermon in D have, if they are abbreviated in the manuscript, been expanded to their most explicit form for ease of reference.

All abbreviations, whether in the Latin or the English text, have been silently expanded. The abbreviations in D are for the

most part standard, and they give rise to no doubts of
interpretation. Expansion of ꝑ to *per* or *par* follows the modern
spelling of the word in question unless the normal unabbreviated
spelling in the manuscript departs from this. *Iħu(s)* is expanded
Iesu(s); *āncrist* is transcribed *anticrist* (since the sense normally
favours *anti-* rather than *ante-*), though *antecrist* written out in full
by the scribe is so retained (e.g. 2/36). The only modification that
has been made to the language of D is the suppression of his
occasional use of ⟨o⟩ for the unstressed vowel, normally spelt ⟨e⟩;
thus at 19/78 *assento perto* is printed *assent[e] perto*, and the rejected
reading recorded in the variants.

The beginning of a new folio in the manuscript is marked by a
line | in the text, and by the details in the margin. The start of a
new column is not recorded.

ii. The variants

At the beginning of the variants for each sermon is given a list of
the manuscripts in which it is attested, with details of any
incomplete copies. This list is given in strict alphabetical order A-
ZαβδEˢHᵗPᵗ; any problems of legibility are there mentioned.
Thereafter the lemma given is always that of the edited text.
When the lemma is a long one only the first and last words are
given, with line number for the latter if necessary, separated by
three dots. A longer lemma will always precede a shorter one
within the longer. After the lemma is given first, if appropriate,
any details about the base text D. Then follow the departures
from this lemma. In a variant found in multiple texts, the sigla
are cited from the sequence DABCFKLMNOPQRSTWY
αβδEˢHᵗPᵗEIJXZGHV in that order. The spelling of the variant
is that of the first sigel cited following it. Absence of a sigel from a
variant or series of variants is to be taken to imply agreement of
that manuscript with the base text, subject to the presence of the
manuscript at that point indicated at the beginning of the
sermon. When a series of variants to a single lemma is in question,
an attempt is made to order these in a sequence from the closest to
the most distant; but in many cases no decision on proximity can
readily be made, and in such instances variants will be cited
according to their first witnessing manuscript in the sequence set
out in full above.

With the exceptions to be described, the variants aim to list all material deviation from the base text. The treatment of corrections will be described below. The exceptions to the full listing of material variation are these:

(i) isolative variation peculiar to V is not recorded unless such variation seems to cast light on variation in other manuscripts. Textually V is of negligible value, and the citation of full variants from it would disproportionately increase the bulk.

(ii) in the headings to each sermon only substantive variation is recorded, interpreted as a departure from the intention of the base text. Variation in the order in which the various pieces of information of the heading (occasion, biblical text, biblical reference, and sermon number) are given is not noted. Change of language for the occasion from Latin to English is not noted, nor alterations in the method of calculation (e.g. after the octave of a feast or after the feast itself) if these do not affect the occasion intended. Alterations, including abbreviation, of the biblical text are recorded.

(iii) cases of the omission of a capital, through failure of the rubricator, have not been noted unless these omissions have given rise to error in the surviving manuscripts.

(iv) variation in the rubrication of the biblical translation is not noted.

(v) the obvious dittography of words from one line to the next where this has not given rise to error is not recorded, nor is the use of single letters or small groups of letters as line fillers. The only exception to this absence is in the case of D.

(vi) erasures of words such as *pope* in no. 16 deriving from a later reader; modern corrections to the sermons, mostly in the biblical references at the head of each; modern fill-in additions, particularly in X, to overcome minor damage.

(vii) obvious errors of a single letter where this has not given rise to error in another surviving manuscript, and would be extremely unlikely to do so; an example of this would be α *chaundid* for *chaungid* at 27/46.

Linguistic variation is not recorded. 'Linguistic' has here been interpreted in its widest meaning, to cover orthographic, phonological, morphological and, in the case of Z only, lexical modification. The last two categories call for further comment. Variation is recorded in the case of mood alteration: thus, when the base manuscript has a form that can only be regarded as subjunctive, but other manuscripts have forms that can equally only be indicative, this is treated as material variation since sense may be affected, and the variation is recorded. On the other hand, variation between, for instance, *ben* and *are*, both as indicatives, is not noted. It is plain that in α and less frequently β the form *þo* functions as the definite article and not as a demonstrative; in those two manuscripts variation of *þe/þo* is not recorded. To minimize the amount of material in footnotes the lemma and variants have been kept as short as possible. Where the function of a word changes as a result of modification elsewhere in a clause but its form is not altered, both lemma and variants exclude this unchanged form. Thus, for instance, at 38/87 the change in FYH of the base text *may* to *many* alters the function of the following *dowte* from infinitive to plural present indicative, but since there is no change made to the form, the verb is not included in lemma or variant. Outside Z, lexical variation is minimal and has, with the exception of variation between *from* and *fro*, been recorded. The lexical variation in Z is extensive and is not recorded. In most instances it affects single words only. In one instance the construction of the sentence may be affected: Z regularly suppresses the verb *mot* substituting *bihoues* or *bihoued*, sometimes using these as impersonal verbs with consequent alteration of the original subject pronoun to an oblique form, but sometimes treating them as personal. These changes have not been noted. The division between linguistic and material variation is a difficult one to maintain, and it is doubtless true that inconsistencies here remain. In general a separate entry in the MED, or where this was not available the OED, has been taken as determining material variation.

The amount of correction in the manuscripts poses considerable problems for the editor. All corrections to the forms in D are recorded in the variants. For reasons explained above pp. 138–50, neither with D nor with any other manuscript is any attempt made to record the responsibility for this correction. The only exceptions to this are (i) additions in D apparently by the original scribe are not noted in the variants, (ii) in a very few cases where attribution of responsibility is a matter of major textual interest, and can with fair certainty be made, a suggestion is recorded. Correction affecting punctuation, capitalization, rubrication, or, outside D, language is never recorded. Correction affecting the readings of manuscripts other than D has been treated as follows:

(i) isolative correction that brings the single manuscript *into* agreement with the remainder is not recorded; thus E1/6 T originally omitted *þis* found in all other manuscripts, but it was added by the corrector; this modification is not noted.

(ii) isolative correction that takes the single manuscript *out of* agreement with all other manuscripts is recorded; thus E3/29 H as originally written had, like all the other manuscripts, *falshede*, but the suffix *-hede* was cancelled; this change is recorded.

(iii) isolative correction that takes one manuscript from a reading attested uncorrected in another manuscript to a different reading attested uncorrected in a third is recorded; thus E2/59 G has *and for*, with *and* cancelled whilst OδJ have *and for*, all other manuscripts *for*; G's change is noted.

(iv) all correction found in more than one manuscript is recorded, whether or not the correction brings those into line with the remainder.

In most manuscripts the reading to be rejected has been erased or cancelled quite plainly. But in C the correction is usually made in the margin, and occasionally between the lines, without any indication of the material it is meant to displace. Since it is usually quite clear what the intention was, C's corrections are treated like those in all other manuscripts. The same type of correction is found occasionally in I.

With few exceptions all marginalia have been ignored. The only material included is (i) any marginal notes in D by the original scribe; (ii) biblical references in any manuscript that were provided by the original scribe of that text or by one of the correctors. The extent of other medieval annotation has been indicated in the descriptions of the various manuscripts in chapter II. In no case does it appear that either medieval or modern annotation casts any light upon the state of the text or its origin.

The following conventions are used in the variants:

] a single square bracket to separate lemma from variant.
, comma to separate variants to the same lemma.
om. omitted.

rev. order of two words reversed.

marked for rev. words written in order stated but marked for reversal, e.g. 1/37 dampnyd man] man dampnyd *marked for rev.* A, intended to be read as 'dampnyd man'.

canc. cancelled, either by subpunction or crossing through.

eras. erased.

corr. corrected.

on eras. corr. written over an erasure by a corrector.

/ change of line.

// change of folio or column. These last two sometimes account for otherwise incomprehensible errors.

⌐. . .⌐ insertion above the line or in the margin.

[. . .] addition to, or alteration of, the base text.

TABLE OF THE 294 SERMONS
Set 1

40	40	1 Lent	Matt. 4: 1–11
41	41	2 Lent	Matt. 15: 21–8
42	42	3 Lent	Luke 11: 14–28
43	43	4 Lent	John 6: 1–14
44	44	Passion Sunday (5 Lent)	John 8: 46–59
45	45	Palm Sunday	Matt. 27: 62–6
46	46	Easter Sunday	Mark 16: 1–7
47	47	1 Sunday after Easter	John 20: 19–31
48	48	2 Sunday after Easter	John 10: 11–16
49	49	3 Sunday after Easter	John 16: 16–22
50	50	4 Sunday after Easter	John 16: 5–15
51	51	Sunday next before Ascension (5 after Easter)	John 16: 23–30
52	52	Sunday within octave of Ascension	John 15: 26–16: 4
53	53	Pentecost	John 14: 23–31
54	54	Trinity Sunday	John 3: 1–15

Set 2 Commune Sanctorum

55	1	Vigil of an Apostle	John 15: 1–7
56	2	Common of an Apostle	John 15: 12–16
57	3	Common of an Apostle	John 15: 17–25
58	4	Common of an Evangelist	Luke 10: 1–7
59	5	Common of a Martyr	John 12: 24–6
60	6	Common of a Martyr	Matt. 16: 24–8
61	7	Common of a Martyr	Luke 10: 16–20
62	8	Common of a Martyr	Luke 14: 26–33
63	9	Common of a Martyr	Matt. 10: 26–32
64	10	Common of a Martyr and Bishop	Matt. 9: 35–8, 10: 7–8, 16.
65	11	Common of many Martyrs	Luke 6: 20–3
66	12	Common of many Martyrs	Matt. 10: 23–6
67	13	Common of many Martyrs	Luke 21: 14–19
68	14	Common of many Martyrs	Luke 6: 17–23
69	15	Common of many Martyrs	Luke 21: 9–19
70	16	Common of many Martyrs	Luke 12: 1–9
71	17	Common of many Martyrs	Matt. 24: 3–13
72	18	Common of many Martyrs	Matt. 10: 34–42
73	19	Common of many Martyrs	Matt. 24: 1–13
74	20	Common of many Martyrs	Luke 11: 47–54
75	21	Common of many Martyrs	Mark 13: 1–13
76	22	Common of a Confessor and Bishop	Matt. 24: 42–7
77	23	Common of a Confessor and Bishop	Matt. 25: 14–23
78	24	Common of a Confessor and Bishop	Luke 19: 12–27
79	25	Common of a Confessor and Bishop	Mark 13: 33–7
80	26	Common of a Confessor and Doctor	Matt. 5: 13–19
81	27	Common of a Confessor and Abbot	Luke 11: 33–6
82	28	Common of many Confessors	Luke 12: 35–40
83	29	Common of many Confessors	Matt. 10: 5–8
84	30	Common of a Virgin and Martyr	Matt. 13: 44–52
85	31	Common of a Virgin not a Martyr	Matt. 25: 1–13

Set 3 Proprium Sanctorum

86	32	Vigil of St. Andrew (29 November)	John 1: 35–51
87	33	St. Andrew (30 November)	Matt. 4: 18–22
88	34	Octave of St. Andrew (7 December)	Mark 1: 14–18
89	35	Christmas Eve (24 December)	Matt. 1: 18–21
90	36	Christmas Day (25 December)	Luke 2: 1–14
91	37	St. Stephen (26 December)	Matt. 23: 34–9
92	38	St. John the Evangelist (27 December)	John 21: 19–24
93	39	Holy Innocents (28 December)	Matt. 2: 13–18
94	40	Sixth day after Christmas (30 December)	Luke 2: 33–40
95	41	New Year's Day (1 January)	Luke 2: 21
96	42	Vigil of Epiphany (5 January)	Matt. 2: 19–23
97	43	Epiphany (6 January)	Matt. 2: 1–12
98	44	Conversion of St. Paul (25 January)	Matt. 19: 27–9
99	45	Candlemas Day (2 February)	Luke 2: 22–32
100	46	St. Peter's Chair (22 February)	Matt. 16: 13–19
101	47	St. Matthias (24 February)	Matt. 11: 25–30
102	48	Annunciation (25 March)	Luke 1: 26–38
103	49	St. Philip and St. James (11 May)	John 14: 1–13
104	50	Vigil of St. John the Baptist (23 June)	Luke 1: 5–17
105	51	St. John the Baptist (24 June)	Luke 1: 57–68
106	52	Vigil of St. Peter and St. Paul (28 June)	John 21: 15–19
107	53	Octave of St. John the Baptist (30 June)	Luke 1: 18–25
108	54	Translation of St. Martin (5 July)	Luke 12: 32–4
109	55	Octave of St. Peter and St. Paul (6 July)	Matt. 14: 22–33
110	56	Seven Brothers (10 July)	Matt. 12: 46–50
111	57	St. James (25 July)	Matt. 20: 20–3
112	58	Vigil of the Assumption (14 August)	Luke 11: 27–8
113	59	Assumption (15 August)	Luke 10: 38–42
114	60	St. Bartholomew (24 August)	Luke 22: 24–30
115	61	Decollation of St. John the Baptist (29 August)	Mark 6: 17–29
116	62	Nativity of the Virgin Mary (8 September)	Matt. 1: 1–17
117	63	Exaltation of the Cross (14 September)	John 12: 31–6
118	64	Vigil of St. Matthew (20 September)	Luke 5: 27–32
119	65	St. Matthew (21 September)	Matt. 9: 9–13
120	66	Michaelmas Day (29 September)	Matt. 18: 1–10
121	67	Vigil of All Saints (30 October)	John 17: 11–26
122	68	All Saints (31 October)	Matt. 5: 1–12

Set 4 Ferial Gospels

123	1	Feria 4 in week 1 of Advent	Mark 1: 1–8
124	2	Feria 6 in week 1 of Advent	Matt. 3: 1–6
125	3	Feria 4 in week 2 of Advent	Matt. 11: 11–15
126	4	Feria 6 in week 2 of Advent	John 1: 15–18
127	5	Feria 6 in week 3 of Advent	Luke 1: 39–47
128	6	Sabbath in Advent Ember week	Luke 3: 1–6
129	7	Feria 4 in week 4 of Advent	Luke 7: 17–28
130	8	Feria 6 in week 4 of Advent	Mark 8: 15–26
131	9	Feria 4 in week 1 after octave of Epiphany	Matt. 4: 12–17
132	10	Feria 6 in week 1 after octave of Epiphany	Luke 4: 14–22
133	11	Feria 4 in week 2 after octave of Epiphany	Mark 6: 1–6
134	12	Feria 6 in week 2 after octave of Epiphany	Luke 4: 31–7
135	13	Feria 4 in week 3 after octave of Epiphany	Mark 3: 1–5
136	14	Feria 6 in week 3 after octave of Epiphany	Matt. 4: 23–5
137	15	Feria 4 in week 4 after octave of Epiphany	Luke 9: 57–62
138	16	Feria 6 in week 4 after octave of Epiphany	Mark 10: 13–16
139	17	Feria 4 in week 5 after octave of Epiphany	Matt. 21: 28–32
140	18	Feria 4 after Septuagesima	Mark 9: 29–36
141	19	Feria 6 after Septuagesima	Matt. 12: 30–7
142	20	Feria 4 after Sexagesima	Mark 4: 1–9
143	21	Feria 6 after Sexagesima	Luke 17: 20–37
144	22	Ash Wednesday	Matt. 6: 16–21
145	23	Feria 6 after Quinquagesima	Matt. 5: 43–6: 4
146	24	Sabbath after Quinquagesima	Mark 6: 47–56
147	25	Feria 2 in week 1 of Lent	Matt. 25: 31–46
148	26	Feria 3 in week 1 of Lent	Matt. 21: 10–17
149	27	Feria 4 in week 1 of Lent	Matt. 12: 38–50
150	28	Feria 5 in week 1 of Lent	John 8: 31–47
151	29	Feria 6 in week 1 of Lent	John 5: 1–15
152	30	Sabbath in week 1 of Lent	Matt. 17: 1–9
153	31	Feria 2 in week 2 of Lent	John 8: 21–9
154	32	Feria 3 in week 2 of Lent	Matt. 23: 1–12
155	33	Feria 4 in week 2 of Lent	Matt. 20: 17–28
156	34	Feria 5 in week 2 of Lent	John 5: 30–47
157	36[1]	Feria 6 in week 2 of Lent	Matt. 21: 33–46
158	37	Sabbath in week 2 of Lent	Luke 15: 11–32
159	38	Feria 2 in week 3 of Lent	Luke 4: 23–30
160	39	Feria 3 in week 3 of Lent	Matt. 18: 15–22
161	40	Feria 4 in week 3 of Lent	Matt. 15: 1–20
162	41	Feria 5 in week 3 of Lent	John 6: 27–35
163	42	Feria 6 in week 3 of Lent	John 4: 5–42
164	43	Sabbath in week 3 of Lent	John 8: 1–11
165	44	Feria 2 in week 4 of Lent	John 2: 13–25

[1] For the error in numbering that begins at this place, see pp. 180–1.

166	45	Feria 3 in week 4 of Lent	John 7: 14–31
167	46	Feria 4 in week 4 of Lent	John 9: 1–38
168	47	Feria 5 in week 4 of Lent	John 5: 17–29
169	48	Feria 6 in week 4 of Lent	John 11: 1–45
170	49	Sabbath in week 4 of Lent	John 8: 12–20
171	50	Feria 2 in week 5 of Lent	John 7: 32–39
172	51	Feria 3 in week 5 of Lent	John 7: 1–13
173	52	Feria 4 in week 5 of Lent	John 10: 22–38
174	53	Feria 5 in week 5 of Lent	John 7: 40–53
175	54	Feria 6 in week 5 of Lent	John 11: 47–54
176	55	Sabbath in week 5 of Lent	John 6: 54–72
177	56	Feria 2 in week 6 of Lent	John 12: 1–36
	57	[Feria 3 in week 6 of Lent][1]	
	58	[Feria 4 in week 6 of Lent][1]	
178	59	Maundy Thursday	John 13: 1–15
179	60	Good Friday	John 18: 1–19: 42
180	61	Vigil of Easter	Matt. 28: 1–7
181	62	Feria 2 in Easter week	Luke 24: 13–35
182	63	Feria 3 in Easter week	Luke 24: 36–47
183	64	Feria 4 in Easter week	John 21: 1–14
184	65	Feria 5 in Easter week	John 20: 11–18
185	66	Feria 6 in Easter week	Matt. 28: 16–20
186	67	Sabbath in Easter week	John 20: 1–9
187	68	Feria 4 in week 2 after Easter	Mark 16: 9–13
188	69	Feria 6 in week 2 after Easter	Matt. 28: 8–15
189	70	Feria 4 in week 3 after Easter	Luke 24: 1–12
190	71	Feria 6 in week 3 after Easter	Matt. 9:14–17
191	72	Feria 4 in week 4 after Easter	John 3: 25–36
192	73	Feria 6 in week 4 after Easter	John 12: 46–50
193	74	Feria 4 in week 5 after Easter	John 17: 11–15
194	75	Feria 6 in week 5 after Easter	John 13: 33–6
195	76	Feria 2 in Rogation week	Luke 11: 5–13
196	77	Vigil of Ascension Day	John 17: 1–11
197	78	Ascension Day	Mark 16: 14–20
198	79	Feria 6 before Pentecost	Luke 24: 49–53
199	80	Vigil of Pentecost	John 14: 15–21
200	81	Feria 2 in week after Pentecost	John 3: 16–21
201	82	Feria 3 in week after Pentecost	John 10: 1–10
202	83	Feria 4 in week after Pentecost	John 6: 44–52
203	84	Feria 5 in week after Pentecost	Luke 9: 1–6
204	85	Feria 6 in week after Pentecost	Luke 5: 17–26
205	86	Vigil of Trinity Sunday	Luke 4: 38–42
206	87	Feast of Corpus Christi	John 6: 55–8
207	88	Feria 4 in week after 1 Trinity	Matt. 5: 17–19

[1] For the brief paragraphs provided for these days see pp. 180.

208	89	Feria 4 in week after 2 Trinity	Mark 11: 27–33[1]
209	90	Feria 4 in week after 3 Trinity	Matt. 5: 25–30
210	91	Feria 4 in week after 4 Trinity	Matt. 17: 10–17
211	92	Feria 4 in week after 5 Trinity	Luke 8: 22–5
212	93	Feria 4 in week after 6 Trinity	Mark 10: 17–21
213	94	Feria 4 in week after 7 Trinity	Matt. 12: 1–7
214	95	Feria 4 in week after 8 Trinity	Mark 9: 37–47
215	96	Feria 4 in week after 9 Trinity	Luke 16: 10–15
216	97	Feria 4 in week after 10 Trinity	Luke 21: 34–6
217	98	Feria 4 in week after 11 Trinity	Luke 18: 1–8
218	99	Feria 4 in week after 12 Trinity	Matt. 11: 20–4
219	100	Feria 4 in week after 13 Trinity	Matt. 12: 14–21
220	101	Feria 4 in week after 14 Trinity	Luke 12: 13–24
221	102	Feria 4 in week after 15 Trinity	Luke 20: 1–8
222	103	Feria 4 in week after 16 Trinity	Mark 8: 22–6
223	104	Feria 4 in week after 18 Trinity[2]	Matt. 13: 31–5
224	105	Feria 4 in week after 19 Trinity	Matt. 13: 36–43
225	106	Feria 4 in week after 20 Trinity	Luke 14: 12–15
226	107	Feria 4 in week after 21 Trinity	Luke 6: 6–11
227	108	Feria 4 in week after 22 Trinity	Mark 11: 23–6
228	109	Feria 4 in week after 23 Trinity	Matt. 17: 23–6
229	110	Feria 4 in week after 24 Trinity	Matt. 21: 28–32
230	111	Feria 4 in Ember days in September	Mark 9: 16–28
231	112	Feria 6 in Ember days in September	Luke 7: 36–50
232	113	Sabbath in Ember days in September	Luke 13: 6–17
233	114	Dedicaton of a church	Luke 19: 1–10
234	115	Sunday within octave of Dedication	Luke 6: 47–8
235	116	*Missa de salus populi*	Mark 12: 41–4
236	117	*Missa de pace*	John 16: 32–3
237	118	*Missa pro defunctis*	John 11: 21–7
238	119	*Alia missa pro defunctis*	John 5: 24–9
239	120	*Missa pro sponsalibus*	Matt. 19: 3–6

---

[1] So in DAKQTβIX; RJZ have Matt. 21[: 23–7] which agrees with the Sarum Missal, but the two narratives are substantially the same. E misread *11* as *ii*; LG have *Mt. 11*; W omits the reference.

[2] For the mistake, found or implied in all manuscripts of set 4 save R, see pp. oo

Set 5 Sunday Epistle Sermons

I · SERMONS ON
THE SUNDAY GOSPELS

Dominica prima post festum sancte Trinnitatis.
Ewangelium. Sermo primus.

Homo quidam erat diues qui induebatur purpura et bisso.
Luce 16.

Crist telluth in this parable how richessus ben perilows, for liȝtly wole a riche man vsen hem in to myche lust. A parable is a word of story þat by þat huydyth a spiritual wit. The story tellith *per was a riche man* þat disusede hys richessys in pruyde and in glotenye, *for he was clopid in purpure and bys* (þat ben preciouse clopis, bothe reed and whit), and so he was an ypocrite þat schewed hym to þe world boþe austerne and clene, as worldly men don. And ouer this *eche day was he fed schynyngly*, bothe for schynyng of vessel and precious foode. *And tere was a poore man lyeng at hys ȝate þat was clepyd Lazarus, ful of sore buyles; and he wolde be fyllud with crummes þat fullen fro the riche mannys bord, but no man ȝaf hym hem* for auarice of þe lord. *But þe howndys* of þe lord *comen and lykkyden his buyles*; and þis syngnefieth compassioun of riche

5

10

MSS: D; ABCFGHIJKLMNTXYZαδ.

Dominica . . . ewangelium] *om.* LMZ   sermo 1] *om.* CFLMNTYαδIJXZGH
homo . . . bisso] *om.* LM, si diligamus inuicem deus in nobis manet N   qui . . . bisso]
om. ABTαδIH   qui] et K   purpura et bisso] *om.* YZ   Luce 16] *om.* CL, ion
þe sixteenþe chapitir Y, iohn iiii N   1 this] his C   richessus] richesse CαδZ
2 a riche man] ryche men δ   hem into myche] hem to myche in F   3 by . . .
huydyth] huydeþ wiþinne hym N   by þat] in hym T   huydyth] bidiþ L
spiritual] gostly N   þer] þat *canc.* þer B, þat þer Nδ   4 richessys] richesse
ACLNα, ryche δ   in 2] *om.* δH   5 ben] was L   6 bothe] of N   8 eche
. . . fed] he was fed euery day I   was he] *rev.* δ   he] *om.* N   fed schynyngly]
rev. H   10 hys] the M   clepyd] called αδZ   he] ⌐he⌐ α, *om.* TδH   wolde]
coueyted to δ   11 with] by ABCKLMTYG, of NδZ   fullen] fellen doun
FαIJH   bord] table T   12 hym hem] *rev.* N, hem to hym δ   lord 1] world
T   þe 2] *om.* δ   lord 2] lordes δ   13 syngnefieth] signyfied L   14
mennus] men T   seruauntis] seruaunt T   þat] þat þat C   þei] ȝet þei

mennus seruauntis þat tey han of pore men, but þei ben lettyd to
15 helpen hem.

And *hit is maad* by Godes wille *þat þis begere was deed, and was bore
by aungelys into Abrahmes bosom. þis ryche man was ded,* but not
solempnely to God, *and he was buriet in helle* in tokne þat he ssulde
euere dwelle þere. Abrahmys bosum ys clepyd a plase of rest þat
20 holy soules resteden inne byforn Cristes assencion. And here may
we se þat neiþer riche men ne pore, in þat tat þei ben syche, ben
blessyd in heuene, syth Abraham þe riche man tok Lazarus into
his bosum. But disus of richessys, and inpacience of pore men ben
dampned of Crist, and ellys not suche men; and þei ben not
25 preisud of Crist but by contrarie vertues. *This riche man lyfte vp his
eyen in his turmentis* of helle, *and saw Abraham afer and Lazarus in his
lappe, and he criede 'Fadur Abraham, ha⸢ue⸣ mercy on me, and send þe
lazar hyder, wetyng his fyngres ende in watur to colde my tonge, for I am
turmentid in this flawme.'* The maner of speche of holy writ is to
30 vndurstonde by names of body vertues of the soule þat dwellen
for a tyme in suche bodyes. And so, for this riche man was bostful
in speche and lykerous in fode, he was turmentid in vertu of his
tonge. And thus men in weye to blys, wan þei traueylen in sotyl
and medful werkys, þei swagen in a maner þe peyne of dampnyd
35 men, for they han slakyng of her peyne, in þat tat þei hopen to
haue fewer felowes in helle to be peyned with hem. *And Abraham
seyde to þe* riche dampnyd *man 'Sone, ha mynde how þow haddist lust in
þi lif and Lazar peyne;* and terfore by ryht iugement of God *he is now*

N   16 is maad] *on eras. corr.* D, was maad N   by] at N   17 aungelys] an *canc.*
aungell δ   but . . . god (18)] also N   18 solempnely] so *canc.* solempnely X, so
solempnely K   he¹] *om.* T   19 clepyd] called αZ   rest] restes δ   20 here
may we] we here may, we here *marked for rev.* α, here we may I   21 men] man
M   in] men in δ   þat tat] that Mδ   22 into] in⸢to⸣ α, in IJH   23
disus] mysvsyng δ   richessys] richesse CFNαδIJZH   24 ellys . . . þei] *om.*
N   not¹] mote M   suche] of suche H   and²] *om.* δ   ben not] *rev.*
N   25 of crist] *om.* N   contrarie] contrarious M   vertues] vertues ben men
brou3t to reste N   26 saw] seeþ LM   27 lappe] bosum N   he] *om.*
TIJH   haue] -ue *added corr.* D   on] of LN   þe lazar] lazarus δ, lazar
H   28 in] in þe C   colde] cole ZGH   my] wiþ my BN   29 to] *om.*
H   30 body] þe body C   32 speche and] *om.* N   in²] *om.* N, of α   in
vertu] in vertu *canc.*, ⸢inwardly⸣ T, in þe vertue δ   of] in T   33 thus] *om.*
N   men] men þat ben N   to] of Y   sotyl] meedful I, *om.* N   34 and]
om. N   medful] nedful N, sotyle I   35 tat] at X   36 fewer felowes] *on eras.*
corr. D   37 dampnyd man] man dampnyd *marked for rev.* A, *rev.* H   how] *om.*
Z   lust . . . lif (38)] *on eras. corr.* D   lust] *om.* T   38 þi] þis ABCKL-
MNTZ   and¹] ioye and T   lazar] lazarus δH   peyne] hade peyne

counfortyd and tow now art turmentyd, for he suffrede peyne paciently, and tow toke þi lustes synfully'. And summe men þenken, for this 40 dampnyde riche man clepith Abraham his fadur and Abraham clepith hym aȝen his sone, þat he was an Ebrew and Abraham was his fadur. *But Abraham answerud hym* by trewþe þat God telde hym *þat þere was a muche voide place stablid bytwixen hem, derk and vnordynel, þat lettuth dampnede men to come to hem,* ⌐al⌐ *ȝif þei wolden,* or 45 hem to comen to dampnede men, for thei desiren hyt not. And, ȝif somme seyntes coueyton kyndely to counforten her frendis, þei han strengure wille to conformen hem to Godys wille; and so men may neyther falle fro heuene to helle, ne fle fro helle to heuene at þer owne wille. *But þe riche man preyde Abraham to sende Lazar to his* 50 *fadur hows, for he hadde fyue breþuren and he wolde þat þei weren warnede* to amenden hem of here lyf – not for charite þat men dampnede in helle han to|lyuyng men or ellis to dampned men (for, as seyntes f.55ᵛ in heuene wanten enuye, so dampnede men faylen in charite), but he dredde hym of peyne þat he schulde haue by dampnyng of 55 hys breþren, for he assentude to hem in here wykkyde lyf. *But Abraham seyde to hym þat tey han Moyses and prophetes* in þere bokes þat tey wryten, *here þey hem* spedily and kepe þey Godes maundementes. *And þis* riche dampned *man seyde to Abraham 'Nay, fadur Abraham, but ȝif any of dede men wende to hem and warne hem, þei* 60 *schal do penaunce and fle þer dampnacion.' But Abraham seyde aȝen* þat 'ȝif þey here nowt Moyses and prophetes þat spoke by God, þey schul

---

δ   now] *om.* N   39 tow now] *rev.* α   now art] *rev.* ABYH, art N   40 and] þat L, *om.* T   þi] þes H   lustes] lust B   for] wonder for T   41 dampnyde riche] *rev.* T   clepith] clepid ANT, calde δ, calles αZ   42 clepith] clepede N, calde δ, calles αZ   aȝen] *om.* N   43 answerud] answeriþ BCFLMNTYδ, answeriþ, -þ *on eras. corr.* X   44 stablid] stablischid Y   derk . . . vnordynel (45)] and vnordinel derk I   and] *om.* δ   45 þat] and G   lettuth] lettid Aδ   to come] to *canc.* come X, com CTY   alȝif] al *added corr.* D, þouȝ δ   46 to¹] *om.* ABT   for] but þat δ   thei desiren hyt] desyren þey δ   47 somme] ⌐sum⌐ α *om.* N   coueyton] coueytide F   kyndely] hit kyndely DBFIJH   48 strengure] stranger C   conformen] conforme FTH, counforte δ   49 neyther] noȝt δ   50 lazar] abraham F   52 amenden] ⌐a⌐mende αH, mende J   lyf] lyf þat þey come noȝt to þe place of tourmentrye δ   men dampnede] *rev.* NαIJH   in helle han] han in helle H   53 ellis] *om.* G   men²] *om.* H   54 men] men in helle Z   faylen in] wonten Nδ   55 hym] *om.* Y   peyne] his peyne AB   by] þe more by N, of T   of²] in T   56 assentude] consentide Nδ   57 to hym] *om.* M   58 þat] *om.* Y   wryten] han writen N   þey²] thi M   59 maundementes] comandementis ABKYαδIJGH, comaundementes þat god to moyses tok N   riche dampned] *rev.* δ, riche N   seyde] onswerede and seide N   60 of] *om.* T   men wende] ⌐wende⌐ I   wende] wenten Nα   warne] warnede N   61 schal] schuld C   do] þenne do N   þer] *om.* M   62

not trowe to dede men', for þere wordus ben of lasse euydence. And
hit fallith not to God to maken a new lawe and newe miraclys for
65 yche man þat schal be dampned, as Crist wolde not come doun of
þe croos to conferme þe false Iewes.

In this gospel may prestes telle of false pruyde of ryche men,
and of lustful lyf of myhty men of þis world, and of longe peynes
of helle and of ioyful blisse in heuene, and þus lenkþe her
70 sarmoun as þe tyme askith. And marke we how þis gospel tellith
þat þis riche man was not dampned for extorcion or wrongys þat
he dude to hys ney3bore, but for he faylede in werkys of mercy.
And þus schulde we warne bothe o man and other how somme
schul be dampned more felly for raueyne, and summe schul be
75 dampned more softly for mysvsyng of Goddes goodes.

---

65 Matt. 27: 40–4; Mark 15: 29–32; Luke 23: 35–6, 39.

þat¹] but I   here] herden N   spoke] speke TδIJ   schul] shulden H   63
to] no M   þere . . . euydence] of lasse euydence ben dede mennes wordes
N   þere wordus] þei K   64 and] ne δ   67 in . . . askith (70)] *om.*
N   in . . . gospel] when þey sayden come adoun of þe cros we wul leue in þe and here
δ   telle] -n *canc.* D   false] þe false H   68 of¹] *om.* δ   lustful] lusty
δ   of⁴] *om.* δ   peynes] peyne δ   69 of²] *om.* ABKLMTY, of þe δ   in]
of δ   lenkþe] lengþe forþ δ   her] his δ   70 þe] *om.* T   askith] may dure
T   and marke] noteþ wel N   we . . . tellith] *om.* N   we] we wel T   71 or] ny
N   wrongys] wrong AB   72 ney3bore] nei3boris FN   he . . . goodes (75)]
his foule auerice þat he wolde not fulfille þe seuen werkus of bodily mercy and so þenne
muche mo⌐re⌐ peynfully schulen þei be dampned þat not onlyche of hire trewe geten
goodes wolen not helpen and releuen poure nedy men bote falsely bynymen hem and
taken of hem þo goodus þat þei schulden lyue by and þerfore prei we to god þat we so here
oure goodes spende boþe bodyly and gostely þat it be plesyng vnto hym and helpyng to
oure neighebores in heuen to hauen of hym rewarde and þat it be so etc. N   in] in þe
δ   73 schulde we] *rev.* α   o man] on M   somme] sum men AB   74
felly . . . more (75)] *om.* IJ   75 softly] sotilly H   goddes goodes] godis of god T,
goddes goodes þat god leueth hem δ   goodes] good IJ

Dominica secunda [post festum Trinitatis].
Euuangelium. Sermo 2.

Homo quidam fecit cenam magnam. Luce 14.

This gospel meueþ men by wyt of a parable to desyre spedly to
come to hefne. We schal vndirstande þat yche word of Godes
lawe ys soth algatys, ⌜al⌝ ʒif somme men vndurstanden hyt falsely,
for so þei vnderstonden God and ʒet þei makyn hym not false.
And so priue vndurstondyng of this holy gospel ys algate soth and 5
þe story bothe. The gospel tellyth þat *þere was a man* ⌜þat⌝ *made a
gret soper and clepude þerto many men.* Thys man ys Iesu Crist, bothe
God and man. And thys grete soper ys the grete mangery þat
seyntes in heuene schullen ete of Godes bord, and this schal
euurmore laste withowte werynes or noye, for þere sc[h]al 10
nothyng fayle þat seyntes wolle desire. And, for þis schal be þe
laste mete, hit ys wel clepyd a soper, for soper is þe laste mete þat
man takith in the day. And for foure causes hit is a gret soper: for
þe lord ys gret þat maketh ⌜þis⌝ soper, so þat no man but he may
make such a soper; also þe pepel ys gret and manye þat sittuth 15
atte ⌜þis⌝ soper; also the mete ys precious þat þey soupe with,

MSS: D; ABCFGIJKLMTXYZαδ; N *ends incompl.* 25 to alle suche; β *inc.* 77 almes

Dominica . . . euuangelium] *om.* Z   sermo 2] *om.* CFKNTYαδIJXZG   homo
. . . magnam] nolite mirari si odit vos mundus N   luce 14] iohn iii N   1 this] þe
NY   gospel] gospel of þis day N   meueþ] mony C, telliþ F   a]
om. LM   spedly] specyaly δ   2 hefne] þe blysse of *canc.* hefne DX, þe blisse
of heuene F, blisse of heuen αIJ, heuen blisse N   3 al ʒif] al *corr.* D, if
ABCLMTYαIJXG, al be hit N, þouʒ δ   hyt] hem LN   4 vnderstonden]
vnderstoden FNI   and ʒet] al þawe δ   þei makyn] made þei N   5 so] so
algate N   priue . . . of] *om.* N   this holy] þe N, þis TI   algate soth] soth Z,
trewe seþen crist þat is treuþe speke hit N   and 2] *om.* N   6 bothe . . . gospel] *om.*
N   þat made] and he *canc.* ⌜þat⌝ *corr.* made D, þat *on eras. corr.* made X, and he made
FαδJ, and made I   7 clepude] called αδZ   man ys] *twice, 2nd canc.*
D   bothe] þat is boþe AB   9 in] of N   10 euurmore] euer ABY   with-
owte] and wiþout M   werynes] irkyng ABCKLMTYZ, any yrkyng δ, irkyng
werynesse G   noye] wontyng N, anoye δ   11 wolle] schulen N   schal be]
rev. M   12 hit . . . mete] *om.* I   wel] *om.* N   clepyd] called αδZ   for
. . . soper (14)] *om.* N   13 man] oon δ   a gret] clepid a δ   14 þis] þe *canc.* þis
corr. D, þe X   so . . . soper (15)] *om.* T   but he] *om.* N   15 such a] also
siche δ, þis I   also] and also δ   16 atte þis] þis *corr.* D, at þe δG, atte X   18

siþthen Crist ys al maner of mete and drynk þat tey ben fed with;
also þe tyme of syttyng at þis soper ys withowten ende. Þis lord
clepith mony to þis soper; for þer is no man but ʒif he longe sum
20 wey after blis, for eche man longeth aftur goᵕoᵕde, and þe laste
goᵕoᵕde and best in whych only man schulde reste is blys. But þe
gospel seyth þat many ben clepude and fewe ben chosen, for alle
men þat God ʒyueth desyryng to blys ben clepud, but al only þese
ben chosen þat lasten in loue of God to þer ende day, for to alle
25 suche and only suche haþ God ordeyned blys.

*And he sende owth his seruaunt in ⌐h⌐owre of þis soper to sey to men
clepid herto to come, for now alle þynges ben redy.* Þe hour of this soper ys
tyme of þe incarnacion, for in þat tyme was heuene furst persud
and men set furst in heuene with Crist. This seruaunt sent owht is
30 þe manhode of Crist with his membres þat lyueden here with
hym, as Iohn Baptist ⌐and oþer apostlis⌐ and other trewe
seruauntes. Alle þingus weren redy, for þe godhede and manhed
of Crist was fro þat tyme redy to fede seyntes in heuene, and Crist,
as Powle seyth, is alle þingus in alle men þat schul be saued; and
f.56 35 riht so ⌐h⌐ys lawe is þe furste and þe laste and fully|ynow after
which schulde be none oþure lawe, for antecristes lawe clowtyd of

---

22 Matt. 20: 16, 22: 14; **34** Col. 3: 11.

---

also] *om.* N   þis¹] þe F   ys] also is N   þis² . . . mony (19)] mony clepeþ þis
lord N   19 clepith] calles αδZ   soper] blesside soper N   is] nys
ABT   but ʒif he] þat he ne Z   20 wey] -e *eras.* D, weyes N, what F   goode]
2nd o *corr.* D, good þat hym þinkeþ comforte inne N   21 goode] *2nd* o *corr.* D   and
best] *om.* F   best] þe *canc.* best DX, þe beste NαδIJZ   whych] -e *eras.* D, þe
wyche Tαδ   only] ony CN   man] a man F, *om.* δ   is] his αI, þat is
δ   þe . . . þat (22)] *om.* N   22 many]ᐟ many men A   clepude] called
αZ   and] but YI   chosen] chosen as þe gospel seiþ N   for . . . chosen (24)]
om. I   23 ʒyueth] ʒeth δ   blys] b *canc.*/blys D   clepud] callede αZ   24
in . . . day] to þer endyng day in þe loue of god N   loue] þe loue αδ   ende]
endᵕeᵕ, -ynge *canc.* J, ending ABFYδI   to²] *om.* G   25 and . . . suche] *om.*
LIJ   26 seruaunt] seruauntes DABCFKLTYαδIJXZG   howre]h-*corr.*
D   men . . . to (27)] hem þat were beden to þe soper þat þey schulde δ   27
clepid] called αZ   herto] here I, þerto Z   come] -n *eras.* D   hour] oure or
tyme δ   this] þe I   28 persud] perfyʒt T   29 set furst] fyrst sytte δ   30
lyueden here] *rev.* ABCKLMTYδXZ   31 and . . . apostlis] *corr.* D   32
manhed] þe *canc.* manhed D, þe manhed FδIJX   33 of] oft C   was] *om.*
M   fro] for ABCKLMTYδXZG   34 *margin* Cor' 5 T   þingus] þing
δI   men] the men M   35 hys] h-*corr.* DT   36 which] -e *eras.* D, þe whiche

monye is ful of errour and deseyueth manye men (as lawe of
Sarasenus and of þese newe ordres).

And, as þe gospel seyth, *alle* suche *men bygan togydure for to
excusen hem,* for alle þese men, and alle only syche þat tellen more   40
by such lawe þan by Godes lawe, excusen hem to come ⌈þe⌉ riht
weye to heuene. And, as þer is þre maner of sunne, so þre maner
of men excuseden hem fro þis soper. *The fyrste seyde þat he hadde
bowht a town and was nedit to go owht and sen hyt.* And this bytokneth
prowde men þat, for worldly lordschipe, wenden owt fro þe   45
weye of God and okupyen here wittes abowte worldly heynes.
And, for þe furste seyde þat tis was nedful, þerfore *he preyde þe
lordys messanger to han hym escused. The secunde seyde þat he hadde bowt
fyue ʒokkys of oxen and he wente to assayen hem, and þerfore he preyde hym
to hau⌈e⌉ hym excused.* These fyue ʒokkys bytoknen plente of   50
worldly goodes, for traueyl and foure profiʒtes þat comun of
oxen; and for þis bussynesse turneth rowndly in hymself, þerfore
hit ys wel seyde þat þer ben fyue ʒokkys; and, for suche worldly
men ben ʒokyd togydere with þe fend and þe world, þerfore þe
gospel clepith hem ʒockys. *þe þridde man seyde ⌈þat⌉ he hadde weddud*   55
a wyf and þerfore he myhte noht come. This þridde bytokneth men þat
ben ouurcomen with fleschly synne, as gloterie and lecherie; and
þese men, more beestly, excusyde hem not curteysly as þese two
furste deden, but seyden schortly ⌈þat⌉ þei myʒhte not come. þe
furste two ⌈men⌉ excuseden hem by this þat þei wolen be lordly to   60
destruye Godes enemyes, and þey wolen be riche to helpe pore

C   37 monye] mony men δ   errour] erroures δ   as] and as δ   of²] or
G   39 men] om. M   bygan] on eras. corr. D   for to] ⌈for⌉ to α, to IG   40
alle only] rev. δ   41 þe] to canc. ⌈þe⌉ corr. D, to canc. þe FY, om. G   42 as] om.
I   þer] on eras. corr. D   43 of] om. AM   excuseden] excusen G   seyde]
seyþ T   he] om. Y   hadde] haþ T   44 was nedit] it it neded hym δ   45
for] loueþ T   46 heynes] hyernesse or wurschypes δ   47 furste] fur canc./furste
D   þe²] þis Y   49 to] out to M   þerfore] tere canc. þerfore D   hym]
hem CT   50 haue] -e corr. D   these] þe Z   fyue] foure Z   51 foure] for
T   profiʒtes] poyntes canc. profiʒtes D   52 hymself] hemsilf AIJ   53 þer]
þai CZ   and] om. T   54 þe²] wiþ the M   þerfore] and þerfore δ   55
clepith] calles αδZ   þat] corr. DYαX, om. IJ   56 he myhte] myhte he marked for
rev. D, myʒte he, he canc. YX, myʒt ⌈he⌉ L, myʒte he G, myʒte he ACKZ, he ne myʒt
T   come]-n eras. D   58 more . . . hem] excusen hem more beestly þei F,
excused hemself more bestely δ   excusyde] excusen ABCKLMTYαIJZG   not]
and not αδ, not more G   þese] þe Z   59 furste] oþere δ   seyden] seien
ABCKLMTYαδXZ, þei seiden F   þat] corr. Dα, om. ABIJG   þei] om.
M   myʒhte] may ABCKLMTYαδXZG   come]-n eras. D   60 men] corr.
D   wolen] wolden CTYαδIJZ   lordly] worldli F   61 wolen] wolde

men; but þe þridde, þat hath his flesch as his wyf, maistur ouer his sowle, is an vncurteys fool and þerfore he answerede þus.

The seruaunt turnyd⌐e⌐ aȝeyn and tolde his lord þe answer of þese þre
65 *men,* for euury creature seith to Crist fully hymself. *But þe lord was wroth* wiþ þe excusacion of þese beden foolys, *and bad his seruaunt wenden owt into stretys of þe cite more and lesse, and bryngon into þis feste þese þre maner* of men: *pore feble men, pore blynde men and pore lame men* – these þre ben Godes prisoune⌐r⌐'s þat boþe God and man
70 helpen with almes. And hyt semeth þat þese and none oþure schal come to heuene: for who schal come to heuene but ȝif he be pore in spirith? who schal come to heuene but ⌐if⌐ he be feble in spirit and nede to haue mercy? who schal come to heuene but ȝif he be liȝtned of his blyndnesse? and who schal come to heuene
75 but he þat haltyth now hyȝe in vertues and now lowe in synnes? – certys none but þe lord of þis feste. And to syche bodyly pore men techiþ þis gospel men to do þer almes, for we schulle suwe Crist þat doth specially his grete almes to þese þre men; and of þese þre maner of men many comen to heuene.

80   But Godys seruauntes, boþe of men and aungeles, seyen aftur þis secunde maner of clepyng, '*Lord, hit is don as tow comaundest, and ȝet þere is a voyde place* for men þat schulde sowpe with þe.' For þis maner of clepyng of men to þe ioye of heuene fulleth not heuene of men þat God hath ordeyned to blys; and herfore þe lord of
85 heuene, in his þridde clepyng þat schal ben in tyme nyȝ þe day of

αδZ   be] be richesse be M   62 ouer] of A   63 is] he is αIJ   þus] þer þat
he nolde nat come T, hym so δ   64 turnyde] -e *corr.* D   65 euury] euerilk
Z   hymself] hemself IJ   66 þe] *om.* A, þis α   excusacion] excusaciouns F,
excusaciones, -es *canc.* C   beden foolys] foles þat were beden to þe soper
δ   seruaunt] seruauntis F   67 wenden] go α   stretys] þe *canc.* stretis Y, þe
stretes MδIJ   68 lame] halte δ   69 prisouners] *2nd* r *corr.* D, presouns
LMX   71 who] whoso M   72 who . . . spirit (73)] *margin corr.* C, *om.*
I   who] whoso M, fro who T   if] *corr.* D   73 nede] nedid ABY   who]
whoso M   74 liȝtned] liȝtid FαIJ   who] whoso M   to heuene] *om.*
M   75 he] þat he M   now[1]] *om.* L, now heyȝe now lowe now M   76 none]
om. δ   but] *om.* δ   and] *om.* δ   bodyly] *om.* δ   77 þis] in þis
δ   gospel] *om.* I   men] hou men δ   to do] schul do δ   almes] almesses
δ   crist] ⌐to⌐ crist I   78 men] maner of men δ   79 of] *om.* F   many]
may L   80 aungeles] of *canc.* aungelis A, of aungelus MI   81 þis] þo β   cle-
pyng] callinge αδZ   comaundest] comaundidist YδZ   82 schulde] schullen
IJZG   for[2]] and for δ   83 of[1]] *om.* LM   clepyng] callynge αδZ   84
blys] hys blysse δ   herfore] þerfor TδZ   85 clepyng] clepid L, callynge
αδZ   in[2]] in þe B   86 seruaunt] seruauntis ACFLαZ   weyes] þe wayes

doom, *byddeth his seruaunt gon owht into weyes and hegghes ant
constreyne men to entre 'þat myn hows be fyllud'*. For now in þe laste
dayes whan prestys ben turnede to auarice, stones schullen crie
and constreyne prestes þat maken hem a priuat religioun as an
hegh⌐e⌐ and oþer men þat sewen hem in þe brode weye to   90
helleward – þese stonys, þat ben myhty men in þe world,
schullen constreyne boþe prestes and puple for to entre into
heuene by holdyng of Godys lawe. For drede of takyng of here
goodes and punyschyng of here bodyes schal constreyne hem by
drede to kepe þis streyte wey to heuene. And so þe nombre of men   95
þat God hath ordeynud to blisse|mut nede be fulfyllut magrey   f.56v
antecrist. *But* Crist seith to his apostles þat *none of þe fyrst men þat
God clepyd⌐e⌐ to þe mete* and wolde not come *schal taste his soper* in þe
blys of heuene. For God hath ordeynud wyche men schal be
sauyd and wyche schal be dampnyd, and boþe þese noumbres   100
mut nede be fulfyllud. And lordus for here profiȝt mut nedus
helpe herto, and antecristis feynyng mut nedys be knowen. Here
may men towche of al maner of sunne and specially of false
prestis, traytours to God þat schulden trewly clepe men to blys,
and telle hem the weye of þe lawe of Crist, and make knowen to   105
þe peple þe cawtelis of antecrist.

αδZ   87 fyllud] fulfulde δG   88 whan] w *canc.* / whan D   auarice] couetyse
δ   89 hem] hym J   an] an an D, in a Z   90 heghe] -e *corr.* D   91 þese]
þe C   þat] *om.* δ   92 schullen] shuld α, þat schul δ   puple] oþer peple T, þe
peple δ   entre] -n *eras.* D   93 holdyng] boldyng C   94 schal] for suche
drede schal δ   by drede] *om.* δ, in drede I   95 þis] þe MYIJ   wey] -e *eras.*
D   heuene] heuenewarde δ   þe] þo Lβ   96 nede] nedely δ   fulfyllut]
fillid ABFLMαIJ   magrey antecrist] *om.* Z   97 antecrist] þe deule and anticriste
α   98 clepyde] -e *corr.* D, called αδZ   mete] soper δ   schal] shuld
αδI   taste] -n *canc.* D, not taaste BY   his] þis, þ- *eras.* T   100 wyche] whiche
men BCδI   101 nede] nedely δ   profiȝt] profites M   nedus] nedely
δ   102 herto] þerto BCTβδZ   antecristis] ypocritis Z   103 may men] *rev.*
F   towche] -n *canc.* D, teche δ   of¹] *om.* F   of sunne] *om.* M   104 clepe]
calle αδZ   blys] þe blysse of heuene δ   105 telle] -n *canc.* D   the] treuly þe
Z   crist] god α   knowen] konwen β   106 cawtelis] lawes *canc.* cautelis I, fals
lawis δ   antecrist] ypocritis Z

Dominica tercia [post festum Trinitatis. Euangelium.] Sermo 3.

Accesserunt ad Iesum publicani et peccatores. Luce 15.

In þis gospel tellith Crist two parables of counfort how his peple
schal be sauyd, al ȝif prestys gruchchen þeraȝeyn, boþe prelatis
and religious, for her pruyde and coueytyse. The story of þis
gospel tellith how *publicans and synful men weren comyng to Iesu* to
5 heren his lore, and he treted hem graciously as a good lord. *But
scribes and pharisees gruchchedon aȝen þis* and blasfemeden aȝen Crist,
and seyden he eet with ⌜hem⌝ vnlawfully. And þis dede may fygure
þyng þat fallyth now, siþ prelates as scribes and religious as
pharisees gruchchen aȝen trewe prestes, membris of Crist, þat
10 comunen with comunes as publicans and secler lordys as synful
men, and seyn hit fallyth not to hem to knowe Godes lawe, for þey
seyn hit ys so hyȝ, so sotyl and so holy þat al only scribes and
pharises schulden speke of þis lawe. And þese secler prelatys may
wel be clepyd scribes, for þei, boþe more and lasse, writen þe
15 money þat þey pylen of þe peple more bysily þan þey prenten in
ther sowles þe knowyng of Godys lawe. And þese religious beth
pharisees, for þei beþ deuyded fro comun maner of lyuyng by her

MSS: D; ABCFGIJKLMNTXYZαβδ.

Dominica . . . euangelium] *cut off* L, *om.* Z   sermo 3] *cut off* L, *om.* FKNTYαδ
IJXZG   accesserunt . . . peccatores] *partly cut off* L, erant appropinquantes ad
iesum T, sobrii estote et vigilate N   publicani et peccatores] publicani α, *om.*
δ   luce 15] *cut off* L, ii petri in fine N   1 tellith crist] *rev.* δ, techiþ crist X   his] þis
CM   2 al ȝif . . . coueytyse (3)] *om.* Z   al ȝif] þauȝe δ   prestys] þey
δ   þeraȝeyn] *om.* N   3 religious] religion α, relygyouse men δ   and[2] for I
coueytyse] here couetyse δ   of þis gospel] *om.* N   4 synful] pharyseus and
synneful δ   comyng] comen δ   to[1] -ward *canc.* D   iesu] *on eras. corr.*
D   5 as . . . lord] *om.* N   6 crist . . . hem (7)] *on eras. corr.* D   7 he eet] *om.*
N   he] þat *canc.* he DX, þat he αδG   and . . . weren (18)] *om.* Z   8 as[1]]
and FLM   religious] religiounsJ   as[2] men as δ   9 gruchchen] gruccheden
T   11 men] *om.* M   hit] þat hyt δ   fallyth] fal C   to[1]] *om.* δ   12
and[1]] *om.* G   13 speke] -n *canc* D   þese] þus N   14 clepyd] called α-
δ   þei boþe] boþe þe δ   lasse] þe lasse of hem δ   15 þat] þat þat Y   pylen
. . . peple] of þe pepul pilen N   prenten] preyen L, prentynge α   16 þe] þo
L   religious . . . pharisees (17)] pharisees religious ben M   17 deuyded]

roton rites as pharises weren. Thre causes ther been why þis
heuenly leche receyued frely þese synful men and eet wiþ hem.
Fyrst for he wolde conuerten hem to confusion of prowde prelatys   20
þat letteden þe fredam of Godes lawe to han his cours; by þis
schulde þey mekely knowen þat heynesse of state maketh not
euermore a man bettur to God. The secounde cause ys þat Crist
wolde ȝyue his prestys in tyme of grace lore and ensawmple to do
wisly so and to stonde for þe fredam of Godys lawe. The þridde   25
cause ys for Crist wolde schewe his general lordschipe and
sauyng, not only of Iewys but of heþen men in dyuerse statys.
Þese prelatys wolden fayn þat al Godys lawe were hangyng on
hem, for to spuyle þe peple; for þanne wolde þey telle þis lawe
and putte þerto false vndyrstondyng as þey myȝten ha⌈se⌉ more   30
wynnyng of þe peple.
   The fyrste parable stondyth in a question of Crist. He axet
whyche man of hem hadde an hundred schep to kepe and he were nedud
to sauen hem echone, *and he hadde lost on of hem ne wolde he not leue*
fowre skore and nyntene in a sykur *desert and go and seke þis loste schep tyl*   35
þat he fownde hit; and whanne he hadde fownden hyt wolde leyn hit on his
schuldres with ioye. And whan he come⌈þ⌉ hoom, he clepith togedyr his
⌈*frendes and* ⌉ *neyȝbores, and seyth to hem 'Be ȝe glad⌈e⌉ and þanke me, for*

departed δ   comun] þe comoun AB   18 weren] by hure comyn lyfyng by mony
veyne tradiciouns N   thre] and þre N, þes þre I   ther been] *on eras. corr.* D, þer
were and ben M, ben I   þis . . . leche (19)] crist δ   19 frely] *om.* Nδ   and]
so frely and dude δ   hem] hem frely N   20 fyrst . . . hem] *om.* N   con-
uerten] conforte α   to] to *canc.*// to D   prowde prelatys] þaim Z   21
letteden] lettis Z   to] for to δ   cours] curse α, crusse β, cors as hit schulde and be
knowen to þe pepul N   22 schulde þey] *rev.* δ, suld men Z   mekely knowen] *rev.*
N, knowen K   heynesse] worldly hyenesse N   23 euermore a man] a man
euermore ABMZ, a man δ   bettur] þe better δ   cause] *om.* N   24 ȝyue] -n
canc. D   to do] þat þei schulden do N   25 so] *om.* Z   to] *om.* β   for]
strongly for N   þe] *om.* NZ   godys lawe] þe lawe of god δ   26 schewe] -n
canc. D   his] is β   and] in K   27 sauyng not only] not onely sauyng L, hys
power of saluacyoun noȝt onely δ   of²] *om.* T   heþen] heuene I   28
þese . . . peple (31)] *om.* Z   hangyng] hengyde αδG, hangged ⌈hanggyn⌉ *corr.*
C   on] of α vpon δ   forto] to N   29 þey] *om.* M   30 hafe] -fe *corr.*
D   more] most δ   32 he] and he δ   axet] asketh hem δ   33 man] men
M   hadde] þat hadde F   schep] sche β, of schiep IJ   and] ȝef N   he]
om. T   nedud] bounden δ   34 to] þerwhit to N, *om.* Z   and . . . hem] *om.*
N   of hem] *om.* M   he not] *om.* M, he β   35 nyntene] neynte⌈ne⌉ α, nenty
M   sykur] *om.* M   go] -n *canc.* D   þis] his M   schep] *om.* T   36
fownde] fynd CFKLMNTYβδZ, hadde ifounde IG   whanne] when þat δ   hadde] haþ MN   wolde] he wolde G   leyn] put CFKLMNTYβδXZG   37
schuldres] shuldre Fα   whan] *om.* J   comeþ] -þ *corr.* D, come CLαI, com⌈et⌉ N,
com⌈ryng⌉ J   clepith] calles αδZ   his] *om.* I   38 frendes and] *corr.*

I haue fownden my schep þat was perisched.' Certys I seye to ȝow þat þus
40   schal ioye be in heuene vpon o synful man þat doth penaunce, ȝe more þan
vpon fowre ⌐score⌐ and neyntene ryȝtwyse þat han no nede of penaunce. This
man is Iesu Crist þat was of þe Iewys, and he was herty and wys,
and hadde in his kepyng þe aungeles confermede in heuene and
with hem mankynde. Neynty and neyne bytokne⌐þ⌐ þese
45   aungeles, for þese neyne ordres þat ben knyttid in Crist. And þis o
schep ys mankynde, þat acordeth more togydere þan þese neyne
ordres of aungeles. This o schep þat was lost perisched⌐e⌐ by
synne of Adam, as þe salm seyth. Heuene ys cleput desert by
many enchesones, for hit is selde visited of men þat slowly comen
50   þider, and hit is not tylud as is eurþe here with us, and hit is
florisched with gostly trees þat euurmore ben grene, for grenesse
f.57 |in vertues may neuer fayle in heuene. And this is a syker place, for
fendes tempte not men þere. Crist lefte þis aungel kynde
dwellyng in heuene, for Crist tok not aungel kynde but tok here
55   mannes kynde. And by hys grete vertu he suffrede peyne as oþure
men þre and þritty ȝer, and browte mankynde to heuene and bad
þe aungeles, his frendes, and man next hym in manhed reioyse
hem with hym, for he hadde sauyd mankynde þat was perischid.
And by þis aungeles in heuene, mankynde and fendes, schulden
60   be glad by resoun, for þe mo þat ben dampnyd þe more ys fendes
peyne. And þus more ioye is in heuene of þis o schep þan of neyne
ordres of angeles þat neden no penaunce, for þey synneden
neuere. This on schep þat ys mankynde synnede for þe more part

---

48 Ps. 118: 176.

D   and¹] and his N   seyth] say C   glade] -e corr. D   me] ȝe canc. me
DX, ȝe me FαIJ   39 þus] þis β   40 ioye be] rev. ABCY   be] -n canc.
D   vpon] vnon B   o] ⌐o⌐ IJ, om. C   that doth] doinge N   penaunce]
penaunce for his synne N   more] om. I   41 vpon] of C, on α   score] corr.
D   neyntene] neynte I   42 þe] om. Z   44 neynty] þe nynti Y   by-
tokneþ] -þ corr. D, bytokene N   þese] þe⌐se⌐ Y, þe T   45 þis . . . mankynde
(46)] mankynde is þis on schep N   þis] þis is I   46 ys] om. I   þat
. . . aungeles (47)] om. N   47 perischede] -e corr. D   48 synne] þe canc. synne D,
þe synne FαδIJX   as . . . seyth] om. N   cleput] called αδZ   49 is] ⌐is⌐ F, om.
M   selde] -n canc. D, sedun L   visited] vsed T   50 hit¹] om. I   is¹] ⌐is⌐
β, om. Y   is eurþe] rev. δ, is I   is²] it L   52 neuer] neuermore Nδ   a
syker] sikir ⌐a⌐ F   53 not men] men noght marked for rev. C, rev. ABFI   54
here . . . kynde (55)] monkynde here N   57 reioyse] -n eras. D   59 þis] -e eras.
D, þuse N   mankynde] and canc. mankynde α, and mankynde IJ   schulden]
schullen I   60 for] that for M   fendes] þe fendes δ Z   61 more . . . is] ⌐is⌐
more ioye, is canc. X, is more ioie ABCFKLMNTYβδZ   63 for] mo for M   64

and was qwyked by Crist, þat was one with his breþeren; ⌐and
he⌐, al [ʒif] he myhʒte not synne, suffrede peyne for his schep. 65
And more ioye is in heuene of hym and his membris þan of neyne
ordres of aungeles, for þei ben betture and lyueden more
medfully as trewe knytus of God.

The secunde parable of Crist standeth in this, that *a wis
womman þat hadde ten dragmes, ʒif sche hadde lost on, sche wolde liʒte her* 70
lanterne and turnen vp her hous to seke þis loste dragme. And whan sche
hadde fownden hit, sche wolde make ioye as hit was seyd byfore of hym
þat loste þe schep. This womman ys Iesu Crist, wysdom of the
fadur. Þese ten dragmes ben his resonable creatures, for þey ben
alle made to ymage and lyknesse of þe Trinnyte. The tenþe 75
dragme þat ·was lost ys mannus kynde; þe lanterne þat was
liʒtned ys þe manhode of Crist. Þe turnyng vp of þis hows ys
chaunghyng of states þat ben maad in þis world by manhede of
Crist, for þe aungel wolde not suffre Ion to knele and worchipe
hym, for his Lord was Ionys brother and þe aungeles weren his 80
seruauntes; and so many þyngys of þis world weren turnede
vpsodoun, siþ euery part of þis world was betured by Cristus
manhed. We may towche in this gospel what spedith men, and
what þing lettyth men ⌐for⌐ to be saued, for men mote nede do
penaunce in beryng of þis schep and haue liʒt of þis lanterne for te 85
fynde ⌐þis⌐ loste dragme.

79 Rev. 19: 10.
_____

qwyked] quykened NYδIZG   and he] *corr.* D   65 al ʒif] and *canc.* alþow D,
alþouʒ Fδ, and al ʒif J   synne] -n *canc.* D   schep] *on eras. corr.* D   66 and²] in
T   his] of *canc.* his D, of his CFαδIJX   67 betture] mykel bettur N   68
medfully] nedefully Z   69 of crist] *om.* δ   70 þat] *om.* M   dragmes]
besauntes NTδ   hadde²] *om.* M   liʒte] -n *canc.* D   71 þis] þat Y   dra-
gme] besaunt NTδ, light dragme M   and whan] *on eras. corr.* D   whan] *om.*
δ   72 was] is I   73 þe] þo L   74 dragmes] besauntys T, dragmez or
besauntez δ   resonable] ten resonable C   þey] *om.* δ   75 alle made]
maad alle *marked for rev.* K, *rev.* AB   76 dragme] besaunt δ   ys]
bytokeneþ N   mannus kynde] mankynde ABFLMTαIJZ   77 liʒtned] liʒtid
ABCKLMβXZG, lyʒt TαδIJ   vp] *om.* Tδ   þis] his LN, þe TI   78
manhede] þe monhede NI   79 ion] seynt ioon F, ion þe euangelyst δ   to] for to
Z   *margin* apoc. vlt. δ   80 þe] *om.* δ   81 þyngys] ymagis F   82 part]
partye δ   betured] made better δ   cristus manhed] þe manhed of crist δ
83 we] here men δ   towche] -n *canc.* D   in . . . gospel] *om.* δ   what] what
þing Nδ   spedith] helpeth δ   men] man M   84 for¹] *corr.* D   for to] to
NIJ   men²] man δ   nede] nedeli F   do] haue δ   85 for te] to
δ   86 þis] þe *canc.* ⌐þis⌐ *corr.* D, þe, -e *canc.* -⌐is⌐ *corr.* α, þe JX, wyth þis δ   dragme]
besaund T, ⌐lost⌐ besaunt δ

Dominica quarta [post festum Trinitatis. Euangelium.] Sermo 4.

Estote misericordes. Luce 6.

This gospel meueth men to mercy aȝen þe ypocrisye of þese false pharisees. And Crist byddith furst generally men *to be merciful* '*as ȝowre Fadur is merciful*', for whan a general word ys seyd by hymself hit schal be taken for þe moste famous. Ther beth many
5 fadres, as fadur of kynde and fadur of lore, but þe moste proper fadur ys he þat made men of noht, for he is fadur of mennys body and fadur of her sowles, and in vertu of hym worchen alle other fadres. And þis fadur schulde we suwe in alle oure werkys, for, al [ȝif] we may not ⌜at⌝teyne to þis fadur, nerþeles þo werkys be
10 nohȝtys þat ben noht ensaumplyd and wroht bi þis fadur. Þe mercy of þis fadur kan we not telle fully, for he ys þe moste worchere þat may ben in þis world; and he can not worche but ⌜ȝif⌝ he medle mercy, for he wrohte by mercy wan he made þis world, syt⌜h⌝e he dyde good to aungeles and made hem parfiȝt
15 and broȝte hem to heyȝer stat withowten here desert. And so whanne he doth good to ony creature, he makyth hit parfit of his pure grace. Siþ God almiȝty, al witty and al goodly, kan not

MSS: D; ABCFGIJKLMNTXYZαβδ.

Dominica . . . euangelium] *om.* Z   sermo 4] *om.* CFKNTYαβδIJXZG   estote mi-
sericordes] estote ergo misericordes T, spe enim salui facti sumus N   luce 6] luc 18 δ, *om.*
M, ad ro. viii N   1 þe] *om.* CNIJZ   þese] *om.* NIJZ   false] *om.* LM   2
and] ⌜and þe feyned clergy þat nowe regneth⌝ and T   3 word] lord L   4 hymself]
hytself δ   for] in δ   5 fadur¹] fadirs, -s *canc.* K, fadris L   and] *om.*
C   fadur²] *om.* N   lore] lore or techyng δ   6 made] maki⌜þ⌝Y, makiþ *on*
eras. corr. X, makiþ ABCKLMNTβδIZG   mennys] mannus MG   body] bodies
ABKNTαδZ   7 fadur] eke N   vertu] vertues δ   worchen . . . fadres] alle
oþere fadres wurchen δ   8 þis . . . werkys] in alle oure vertues schulden we sue þis
fader N   schulde] schullen I   suwe] -n *eras.* D.   al ȝif] alþow DδG, þouȝ
F   9 atteyne] en- *canc.* ⌜at⌝ *corr.* D   þo] þe CFLMNTαδIZ   werkys] dedis
ABCFKLMNTYαβδIJZ   10 nohȝtys] nouȝt N, nouȝt ⌜his⌝ α   noht] *om.*
F   wroht] tauȝt N   bi] in F   þis] his L   11 not] *om.* M   ys] was
and is M   12 he] *om.* β   13 ȝif] *corr.* D, *om.* X   by] wiþ Z   mercy²]
mery C   þis] þe LM   14 sythe] -n *canc.* ⌜h⌝ *corr.* D   sythe . . . grace (17)] *om.*
N   good] *om.* M, goode goode J   15 desert] deseruyng δ   17 pure] pore
F   siþ] seþen þenne þat N   almiȝty] al al *2nd canc.* miȝty D   al¹ . . .

worche but ȝif he worche by mercy, be we þanne merciful for
goodnesse of God. Þe leste mercy of men ys among clerkys, þat
wol⌐en⌐ not ȝyue goodus of grace but ȝif þei sullen hem. And   20
þerfore þis sinne is heresye byfor God, þe moste and þe fyrste þat
partiþ men fro God, for þey weyen her wynnyng more þan þer
God. And herfore al þat we doon schulde be doon in Godys
name, to worchipe of oure God and profiȝt of his cherche. Ȝe, ȝif
we be holden bothe to God and man by resoun of dette to don a   25
good dede, loke þat þis resoun be fyrst hid in owre þowt. And so
no man may excusen hym fro werkys of mercy, as no man may
wante werkys of a good wille| for þat werk ys þe furste and heyȝest   f.57v
in man. Furst schulde a man haue mercy of hymself, and mercy of
his moder þat is holy cherche, and þan hath he mercy of al þe   30
ende of his kyn.

The secounde word of Crist *forbedyth fool iugement*. And resoun
of þis stondeth herynne þat God may not iuge folily ony man;
and so, as oure wille haþ nede to be cloþid wiþ mercy, so oure
vndurstondyng hath nede to haue riȝt iugement. For many men   35
wenen to be merciful to ypocrites, and þei don harm to men to
whiche þey wenen do profiȝt. And many men wenen to iuge þer
breþren, and ȝet þei iugen falsely and cruelly of many. And yche
man schulde tempre such iugement aftyr God, for God in his
iugement may not faylen fro resoun.   40

goodly] *om.* N   goodly] godly TI   not] no L   18 ȝif . . . worche²] *om.*
N   ȝif] *om.* C   by] wiþ N   be] what so he doþ be N   for] of δ   19
goodnesse] þe godnes TJ, þe *canc.* goodenes α   god] oure god N   of²] among
I   20 wolen] -en *corr.* D   and] *om.* C   21 god] god almyȝthy N, *om.*
J   22 partiþ] departeth δ   for] ys *canc.* for D, is for αδIJ   wynnyng]
wynnyngis LδZ   more] and so more M   þer] *om.* N   23 herfore] *om.* δ,
þerfor Z   doon¹] doun herfore δ   schulde] schul β   be] we Y   godys]
god *canc.*/godys D   24 worchipe] þe wurschype δ   ȝe . . . þowt (26)] *om.*
N   24 ȝif] þouȝ þat δ   25 be holden bothe] biholden boþe YJ, ben boþe holdden
δ   man] to man αIJ   to don] *om.* LM   26 loke] ⌐miche more to god þan to
any man and so⌐loke T, and loke I   þowt] hert L   so] *om.* N   27 hym] hem
CZ   as] seþen N   may²] *om.* M   28 wante] mayntene C   werkys]
werke α   a] ⌐a⌐ A, *om.* T   heyȝest] þe *canc.* hiȝest F, þe heyest KNZ   29
man¹] a mon δ   schulde] schul C   of¹] on FNT   of²] on FN   30 þan]
om. M   hath he] *rev.* FNδI   of] on F   þe ende of his kyn] his ende kyn
ABCKLMTYβXZ, his kynne αJ, ende his kyn N, þe ende of his kynde I, hys euene
cristene δ   32 fool] fooli Fδ   33 herynne] þerinne L   iuge folily] *rev.*
ABCKLMNTYβIJXZG, fully iuge α   35 hath] haue G   36 þei] ȝet N   men]
hem δ   to⁴] *om.* δ   37 do] to done C   profiȝt] profyt to δ   men] *om.*
N   38 þei] þat þei I   cruelly] truely L   39 schulde] schul C   40 faylen]

The þridde word *biddyth cristen men be war of foly dampnyng vppe peyne of þer dampnacion.* And, al [ȝif] þis semeth no comun sinne among men, nerþeles alle maner of men synnen herinne, as prelatys þat dampne men in maner of þer cursyng and ofte
45 tymes þei wyten not how þei ben to God; and by reputacion þat schulde be taken of Godes lawe þes men don wel as God biddeþ hem do. Lordes iugen ofte tymes þat oþer men don amys, whan þey displeson hem in þer wrong wille, as we dampnen Clement with his fautours and þei dampnen vs, and o kyng dampnyth his
50 ⌜aduersary⌝ and he dampnyth hym aȝen, and comunes dampnon prowde men and oþur men to ben ypocrites. And comunly fool iugement ys a þing þat men knowen not, for þey ledon not þer wit aftyr Godes lawe, for þei presumen as þe fend to connen þat þei knowen not.

55   The fourthe and þe fiþe word *biddeth men forȝyuen, and ȝyue sum maner of goodys, and so schal God rewarden hem.* And not al only God, but seyntes in heuene schal rewarde men after þat þey han here don to hem; for þese fyue dedys alarged to alle men mute haue summe men seyntys in heuene, and þese seyntys schullen rewarde
60 men here in habundaunce of foure þingus. Furst þei schullen rewarde men *in a good mesure,* for seyntys in heuene don bettur to ⌜men⌝ þan þei duden to hem here in þis lif; and where men dyden scarsly good to þer breþren, seyntes fullen trewe men with alle maner of goodys. ⌜And⌝ þis fullyng ys not voydid but *sadly*
65 *replenyched* and at þe laste *hit is hepid* as myche as hit wole take. And sych metyng of corn, mele or oþer þyng wolde be preisud

falle T   41 word] wor⌜l⌝de C   cristen] *om.* M   vppe] o NZ   42 þer] hire N, þe I   al ȝif] alþow DFδ, al ȝif þat, ȝif þat *on eras. corr.* X   semeth] seme LNYα.   43 of] *om.* M   herinne] here M   as] and A   44 maner] a manere I   þer] *om.* LMT   45 not] it nat M   47 do] *om.* Z   lordes] but lordis J   48 þer] hire N   as . . . not (54)] *om.* N   dampnen] dampned α   49 o kyng] þe kyng ⌜is⌝ F   50 aduersary] *corr.* D   hym] hem TI   51 men²] *om.* AB   fool] foly ABFδ   52 iugement] iugementz IG   a] *om.* A   wit] wyttes δ   54 knowen] kunnen δ   55 and¹] in L   forȝyuen] to forȝeue δ   56 hem] him I   57 in] of I   men] hem δ   þat] *om.* N   han . . don (58)] here han don T   here don] *rev.* ABNαδIZG   58 to hem] in herthe to hem δ   for] *om.* T   alarged] arnlarged, -rn -*canc.* D   men] maner *canc.* men D, manere men F   haue] nedes haue N   haue . . . heuene (59)] mut seintis in heuene haue summe of hem δ;   59 men] *om.* LMNIZ   60 men here] *rev.* M   men] hem δ   here] in a gode mesure here L   61 a] *om.* BZ   mesure] manere J   62 men¹] *corr.* D   þan] þat α   hem] men I   in] on B   where] þeras δ   63 scarsly] scharply J   fullen] fulfille αJ   64 and] *corr.* D   voydid] voide ABCFKLMNTYαβδIJZG   65 hit is] þis is δ   wole] wold L   66 metyng] mesure Z   mele] ⌜of⌝ mele α, of mele ABCFKLMTYβX, ⌜or⌝ mele δ, or mele NIZ   or] oþer T   oþer] of *canc.* oþer

among men for largenesse of þe metere. And þis þyng men han
here in her bosim, but God fulleth þe substaunce. For certys, *in
such mesure as men mesuren* to þer breþren, *schal hit be mesurut to hem*
by iugement of God 3if þe mesur be good þei schal haue good   70
a3en, and 3if þe mesur be vniust þey schal haue peyne a3en.

And, for defawte in al þis comyth of ypocrisye of prelatys þat
schulden techen pleynly Godys lawe and not here erþely
wynnyngus, þerfore seith Crist in his parable þat *3if þe blynde lede
þe blynde þei fallen boþe in þe dy3k.* But for Crist schulde be oure   75
maystur, and we schulde not straunghe from hym, we schulden
leue þese ypocrites and suwe lore of þis goode maystur, siþen he
may not leue trewþe, ne faylen in techyng of trewthe. And þus
schulde *men ben parfi3t* and fle þe rote of falsehed. And þese
prelates han of þer maistur comunly þis maner þat *þei kan see a*   80
mote in þer brother y3e, but a beem in þer owne y3e þenke þey nõt on; for þer
wyt is set to spuyle and to acusen and not for to helpen hem ne
oþure men, and herfore þer coueytyse blendiþ hem þus. But by
lore of Crist men schulden seye to hem '*Ypocrite, cast furst þe beem*
owt of þin owne y3e, and þanne maistow pyke betur þe mote fro þi broþur'.   85
Here may we see þat sugetys schylden blame prelatys whan þey
sen opynly greet defawtys in hem, as defawte of Godus lawe in
kepyng and techyng; for þis is a beem by þe whyche þe fend
byndeþ his hows, and þei schulden knowe þis, as þei schulden fele
þe lore herof.   90

DδX, ⌐of⌐ oþur T, of oþere FLMNIG   67 among] of N   68 here] *om.*
T   fulleth] fully K, falliþ L   certys in] *om.* N   69 hit] *om.* F   hem] hym
C   70 iugement] good iugement I, þe iugement G   71 þe] þis β   vniust]
vnry3tful δ   a3en²] *om.* N, þerfore a3en δ   72 for] for *canc.* T, *om.* δ   in] of
Y   of¹] *om.* Mα   ypocrisye of prelatys] prelatus ypocrisye N, ypocrisie of curatis
Z   73 techen pleynly] *rev.* Nδ   godys] of *canc.* godys D   here] -n *canc.*
D   74 wynnyngus] wynnyng CβXG, þingys or wynnyngys T   þerfore] and
þerfore N, herfor αJ   in] þus in N   þat] *om.* N   75 þei fallen boþe] boþe
fallen ABCKLMNTYβIXZ, boþe þey fallen δ   in] into ZG   dy3k] lake
δ   76 straunghe] ⌐be¹ straunge T, be strange δ   we²] and *canc.* we α, and we
J   77 þese] *om.* Z   lore] þe lore Aδ   maystur] lored maister M   78
ne . . . trewthe] *om.* N   79 and² . . . prelates (80)] for ypocritis Z   80 maistur]
maistris AB   81 þer¹] hys T   brother] breþeren KLM   þey] *om.*
M   on] vpon N   82 wyt] wyttes δ   is] ben δ   helpen] amende
δ   83 herfore] þerfor Z   84 lore] þe lore δ   crist] god T   þe beem owt]
out þe bem δ   85 of] *om.* Y   maistow] þou maist I   betur] þe bettur
NTδ   broþur] broþer eye Tδ   86 we] men ABCKLMNTYαβδIJX-
ZG   blame] blake blame M   prelatys] curatis Z   87 of] in KI   88
þe¹] *om.* ABCFKLMNTYαβδIJZG   89 byndeþ] blyndeth CNδ   knowe . . .
schulden] *om.* J   þis] þese B   as] and F   schulden²] schulen C   fele] fle
YβδJ, know α   90 herof] þerof AB, of þis α

Dominica quinta [post festum Trinitatis].
Euangelium. Sermo 5.

Cum turbe irruerent ad Iesum. Luce 5.

f.58 The story of þis gospel telliþ good lore|how prelatys schulden
teche folk vndur hem. Þe story is pleyn how *Crist stod by þe ryuer of*
Ghenasereth, and fyscheres comon doun to wasche þerynne þer nettys. And
Crist wente vp into a boot þat was Symondys and preyde hym to meuen hyt a
5 *luytel fro þe londe; and he sat and taȝte þe peple out of þe bot. And whan*
Crist cesyd to speke, he seyde to Symount 'Lede þe boot into þe hiȝe see, and
lat owt ȝowre nettys to takyng of fysch.' And Symon answeryng seyde to
hym 'Comaunder, al þe nyȝt traueylynge toke we nowt, but in þi word schal
I lowce þe net.' And whanne þey hadde don þus, þei tokyn a plenteuows
10 *multitude of fysch, and þer net was broken. But þei beekneden to her*
felowes, þat weren in þe toþur boot, to comen and helpen hem. And þei
comen and fulleden boþe bootys of fysch, so þat wel ny were þey boþe
drenchyd. And whan Petur hadde seen þis wondur, he fel down to Iesus kne,
and seyde 'Lord, go fro me, for I am a synful man', (for Petur gessyd
15 hym not worthy to be wiþ Crist ne dwellen in his companye), *for*
wonder cam to hem alle in takyng of þese fysches. And so wondreden Iames
and Ioon, Ƹebedees sones, þat weren Symondys felowes. And Iesus seyde to
Symont 'Fro þis tyme schaltow be takynge men'; and þei setten her botys to
þe lond, and forsoken al þat þei hadden and seweden Crist.

20 Byfor we goo to spiritual vndurstondyng of þis gospel, we schal

MSS: D; ABCFGIJKLMTXYZαβδ; N *ends incompl.after occasion.*

Dominica . . . euangelium] *om.* Z   sermo 5] *om.* CFKTYαδIJXZG   cum] dum
δ   turbe] turba A   irruerent] irruerunt ACLG, irruerint β   ad iesum] *om.*
Kδ   1 prelatys] prelatis and prestis δ   2 folk] þe puple F   þe¹] *om.*
M   pleyn] pleyner δ   crist] iesu Y   þe²] *om.* LM   4 into] in
G   hym] hem LMβ   6 into] to L   þe²] *om.* Y   7 fysch] fysches
C   8 hym] hem I   þe] *om.* δ   toke we] *rev.* Fδ   9 þe] þi L   þey] *on*
eras. corr. D   þus] þis ABCKTYβδZ   a] *om.* M   10 but] and Y   11 þat]
and þer I   þe toþur] þe oþer T, anoþer δ   helpen] to helpe T   12 bootys]
þe botes CδZ   of] wiþ α   were þey] *rev.* δ   þey] *om.* T   boþe²] *om.*
I   13 fel] felde X   14 seyde] ⌜he⌝ sayde δ   a] *om.* G   petur] crist *canc.*
petur D   gessyd] held ABδZ   15 hym] hem L   to be] be A   16 þese]
þe C, þis T   19 seweden] foloweden δZ   crist] hym δ   20 byfor] fyrst or

wyte þat þe same Cristys disciple þat was furst clepyd Symon was
clepyd Petur aftur of Crist, for sadnesse of byleue þat he took of
Crist, whyche Crist ys a cornerstoon and growndeth al trewthe.
Ouer þis we schal vndurstande þat þe apostles weren clepyd of
Crist [in] manye degrees: furst þei weren clepyd and acceptud to   25
be Cristus disciples, and ȝet þei turneden aȝeyn, as Crist hymself
ordeyned, to lyuen in þe world. After þey weren clepyd to see
Cristes miracles and to be more homly wiþ hym þan þey weren
byfore, but ȝet þey turneden ⌈aȝen⌉ to þe world by tymes, and
lyueden worldly lyf to profiȝt of folc þat þey dwellyden with; and   30
on þis wyse Petur and Iames and Ioon wenten now to fysche. But
þe þridde clepyng and þe moste was þis, þat þe apostles forsoken
holly þe world and worldly þingus and turnede not aȝen to
worldly lyf, as, aftur þis miracle, Petur and his felowes seweden
Crist continuelly.   35

Hit is no nede to depen vs in this story more þan þe gospel
tellith, as hit is no nede to busyen ⌈vs⌉ to wyte what hiȝte Tobies
hownd; hold we us payed on þe mesure þat God hath ȝyuen vs
and dreme we noht aboute newe poyntis þat þe gospel leuyth, for
þis is synne of curiouste þat harmeth more þan profiȝteth. Þe   40
story of þis gospel telliþ vs gostly wit boþe of lyf of þ⌈e⌉ cherche
and medful werkys, and þis schilde we vndurstande, for hit is
more precious. Two fyschyngus þat Petur fyschude bytoknen two

21 Matt. 10: 2; Mark 3: 16, Luke 6: 14;   **22** Matt. 16: 18;   **23** Matt. 21: 42;
Mark 12: 10; Luke 20: 17; Acts 4: 11; Eph. 2: 20; 1 Pet. 2: 7.

δ   21 wyte] leue I   cristys disciple] dyscyple of crist δ   clepyd] called
αZ   22 clepyd] called αδZ   aftur] afterwarde δ   of[1] as M   of[3] om.
M   23 whyche] þe whike αJ   cornerstoon] coruen ston L, cornel stone
T   24 ouer] euer L   þat] om. β   clepyd] called αδZ   of . . . and (25)
twice β   25 in] and D   clepyd] callede αZ   26 hymself] him G   27
after] afturwarde δ   clepyd] called αδZ   see] om. β   29 aȝen] *corr.*
D   tymes] dyuerse tymes δ, tyme J   30 profiȝt] þe profyt δ   folc] þe folke
Cδ   31 and[1] om. ABI   32 clepyng] callynge αδZ   apostles] a *canc.*//
apostles D   33 holly] hoole C   þe] þo L   not] om. β   34 worldly] þe
worldli F   lyf] lyuyng δ   as] as þey duden byfore T, and δ   felowes] om.
J   35 continuelly] contynently J   36 depen] go deppere δ   this] om.
Z   37 as] and Y   vs] *corr.* D   to wyte] om. ABCKLMTYβZG   38
hold] but holde δ   payed] apaied AB   on] wiþ K, of Cα   39
aboute . . . poyntis] *on eras. corr.* D   40 is] ⌈is⌉ Kβ   synne] a synne AB, om.
T   profiȝteth] profit C, hyt profyteth δ   41 of þe] *on eras. corr.* D, and of þe
FδZ   42 and[1]] and of δ   for . . . precious (43)] om. M   43 more] most
δ   two[1]] þe two M, for to be vnderstonden þus þe two δ   fyschyngus] fyschynge

takyngus of men vnto Cristys religioun and fro þe fend to God. In
45 þis furste fyschynge was þe net broken to toknen þat many men
ben conuertyd, and aftyr breeken Cristys religioun. But at þe
secounde fyschyng aftyr þe resureccion, whan þe net was ful of
many grete fyschys, was not þe net broken, as þe gospel seyth, for
þat bytokneth þe seyntus þat God chesuth to heuene. And so þese
50 nettys þat fyscherus fysche wiþ bytoknen Godys lawe in whyche
vertuwes and trewþus ben knytted; and oþer propretes of nettis
tellen propretes of Godes lawe, as voide places bytwene knottys
bytoknen lif of kynde þat men han bysyde uertues; and fowre
cardynal vertuwes ben fygured by knyttyng of þe net. Þe net ys
55 brood in þe bygynnyng and aftur streyt in þe ende to teche þat
men, whan þei ben turnyd furst, lyuen a brod worldly lif but
afturward, whan þei ben depyd in Godis lawe, þei kepen hem
strei3tlier fro synnes. Þese fyscherys of God schulden waschen þer
nettys in þis ryuer, for Cristys prechowres schulden clenely tellen
60 Godys lawe and not medle wiþ mannys lawe þat is trobly watur;
for mannys lawe conteyneth scharpe stonys and trees, by whiche
þe net of God is broken and fysches wenden owt to þe world. And
þis bytokneth Genazareth þat is a wondurly ful burthe, for þe
f.58v byrthe by whyche a man|ys born of watur and of þe Holy Gost ys
65 muche more wondyrful þan mannys kyndly burþe. Summe nettis
ben rotune, and summe han hooles and summe ben vnclene for

---

47 John 21: 1–11.

F   two²] tweyne maner of δ   44 takyngus] takyng δ   vnto] into δ   in]
and L   45 broken] to broken M   to toknen] in tokenyng δ   toknen]
bitokene F   46 aftyr] afterwarde δ   48 not . . . net] þe nette was not δ, was not
J   49 bytokneth] bitoknede I   þe] om. AB   49 chesuth] chase α   þe-
se] þe δZ   50 fyscherus] þese fyschers δ   fysche] fyscheden δI   bytoknen]
bitokneden I   51 trewþus] truþe αδ   52 as] and ⌐as⌐ C, and A, as þe
δ   places] place Tδ, places of þe net α   knottys] nettys canc. knottys D   54
cardynal] cardinalis β   ben . . . by] bytokenen δ   fygured] fow canc. fygured
D   55 þe¹] þo L   streyt] hyt ys streyt δ   þe²] om. A   teche] -n canc.
D   56 þei] om. α   turnyd first] rev. K   lyuen] lede α   worldly] a
worldly M   57 afturward] aftir CZ   depyd] depere F, more deped δ   58
strei3tlier] streytli G   synnes] synne α   þese] þe Z   god] goddis
F   schulden] schul M   waschen] om. M   59 clenely tellen] rev.
Mα   clenely] cheuely A, cleerli F   60 wiþ] ⌐it⌐ wiþ T, it wiþ αIJZ, þerwyth
δ   trobly] trubled αI, as trowbly δ   61 for] and for L   conteyneth] hath in
hym many δ, conceyueþ I   trees] tren rotes δ   whiche] þe which M   62 to]
of L   63 is] on eras. corr. tokneth canc. D   wondurly ful] woundirful ABCF-
KLMTYαβδIJZG   þe] þo L   64 whyche] þe wyche T   of¹] ⌐of is⌐ of
C   and] om. LM   ys²] þat is LM   66 and¹] om. A   han] ben and han

defawte of waschyng; and þus on þre maners fayluth þe word of
prechyng. And mater of þis net and brekyng þerof ȝyuen men
gret mater to speke Godis word, for vertuwes and vices and
trewþes of þe gospel ben mater inow to preche to þe peple.   70

δ   summe²] ⌜sum⌝ αβ, om. J   67 waschyng] warisshing M   67 þe] ⌜men⌝ in
T   word] world CαI   68 and²] in T   69 godis] þerof canc. godis
D   word] words I   vertuwes] weitnys β   vices] ⌜vices⌝ α, wittis β, om.
J   70 ben] wil fynde a man δ   mater] materes LM   preche] teche and
preche T   to²] ⌜to⌝ Y, om. Cβ

Dominica sexta [post festum Trinitatis].
Euuangelium. Sermo 6.

Nisi habundauerit iusticia uestra plusquam scribarum
et phariseorum. Mathei 5.

Hit is ⌐seyde⌐ in þe nexste gospel whate nettis prestys schulden
haue for to drawe men fro see of þis world to þe druye lond of lif;
thys gospel tellith of þe de⌐ue⌐lus net in wiche he fyschyth and
draweþ men to helle. Cristus net is knyt wiþ riʒtwisnesse to God
5 aboue men, to creaturus byneþe men, to men and to aungeles on
oþer syde of men. And þis cleputh God fully riʒtwisnesse; and
feynud falsely riʒtwysnesse of ypocrites clepuþ Crist no
riʒtwysnesse, al [ʒif] ypocrites clepon hit so, but of scribes and
pharisees, þat is to seyne vnriʒtwisnesse, feynud, as hit were,
10 riʒtwisnesse of scribus and pharisees. And as Crist seith '*But ʒif*
⌐ʒ⌐*our riʒtwisnesse passe a poynt þe* feynud *riʒtwisnesse of scribes and of*
pharisees, ʒe schal neuer ⌐*come to*⌐ *heuene.*' We may vndirstande by
scribes and pharisees men of þe fendys chirche as we duden
byfore, so þat scribes ben clepud seculer prelates, and pharisees
15 ben clepud þes newe religious. Þese men maken hem a riʒtwis-

MSS : D; ABCFGIJKLMTXYZαβδ.

Dominica . . . euuangelium] om. Z   sermo 6] om. CFTYαδIJXZG   nisi] quia
nisi T   iusticia . . . phariseorum] om. δ   plusquam . . . phariseorum] om.
FTαI   scribarum . . . phariseorum] om.CKLMβJZ   scribarum et] om.
AB   mathei 5] om. F   1 seyde] corr. D   nettis] maner nettes þat δ   2
see] þe see ABCKLMTYαβδIJZG   to²] vnto αJ   þe] þo L, om. Z   lif] þis
lyf A   3 of] men of δ   deuelus] -ue-corr. D, fendes δ   wiche] þe wyche
Tδ   5 to men] om. T   on] in BT   6 oþer] þe toþer I   of] om.
M   þis] þus G   cleputh] calles αδZ   god fully] rev. L   7 feynud . . .
riʒtwysnesse (8)] ryʒtfulnesse falsely feyned is not calde ryʒtfulnesse of crist δ   falsely]
⌐and⌐ fals, -ly eras. T   clepuþ] calles αZ   no] not ABCKLMTYβIZG   8 al
ʒif] alþow DFδX   clepon] calle αδZ   so] not so I   of] om. δ   9
þat . . . pharisees (10)] om. T, feynen an ryʒtwysnesse as þauʒ hyt were ryʒtwysnesse
δ   vnriʒtwisnesse] ⌐vn⌐riʒtwisnesse I, rightwisnesse C, vnriʒtuesnesses L   feynud . . . were] twice, 2nd canc. D   10 seith] sayth to hys dyscyples δ   ʒif]
om. M   11 ʒour] ʒ-corr. D, oure LM   riʒtwisnesse¹] ryʒtnesse T   a] in a
K   of²] om. ABCFKLMTYβδIZG   12 ʒe] on eras. corr. DT, we LMZ   come
to] corr. D   we] men δ   13 scribes] þese scrybes δ   14 so . . . and (47)] om.
Z   clepud] called αδ   15 clepud] callede αδ   þes] þe δ   religious]

nesse by hemself, as þei maken hem a lawe of antecrist; and certys
þis lawe may neuer Crist confermen. And so, as Powle seith, þes
anticristes disciples heyen hem ouer Crist, boþe ouer his godhede
and ouer his manhed. For riʒtwisnesse generally is fulfullyng of
lawe; and so fulfillyng of Godys lawe is verrey riʒtwisnesse and   20
fulfullyng of mannus lawe ys antecristus riʒtwisnesse. And so þre
degrees ben in þe lawe of scribes. Þe furst and þe moste is in þe
popes welle and, as men of þe world seyn, þere is welle of
riʒtwisnesse, but þei goon ofte bysyde þe riʒt for þer roton ground.
Þei tristen on riʒt of mannys lawe and gon ofte bysyde þe soþe;   25
and ʒet þei excusen þis false lawe and seyn þat hit mut nede iuge
fals, for ellis hit faylede in his cours and riʒte of þe world were
fordon. But þei þenke not how Crist forsook to iuge by mannys
lawe, techyng þat ilke iugement whiche is not don by Godis lawe
is iugement of þe fend, and we witen not wer hit be riʒt. And þat   30
man is a fool þat iuget aftur any lawe, and whot not wheþur he
iuge by God or ellys by iugement of þe fend; and ʒif men
auyseden hem on þis resoun none schulde iuge by mannys lawe.
And þis false riʒte is more feynud in consistorie lawe and chapitre
lawe, for algatis þei supposen þat witnesse may not faylen, or ellys 35
þe iuge may not failen þat iuget aftur false witnesse; and of þis
rotone blasfemye comen manye false iugementys. Iuge we by riʒt
conscience þat God telliþ or spesefieth, and leue we mannys
iugement, and suffre we fewe wrongus þat fallen ⌈for⌉ mo
wrongus schulde be don for foly of mannys dom. Þe riʒte of þe   40

---

17 2 Thess. 2: 4; **28** Luke 12: 14; cf. Rom. 2: 1–5.

religioun I   hem] *om.* F   riʒtwisnesse] ryʒtfulnesse δ   16 as] and
δ   hem] *om.* δ   and] but δ   17 þis] þat δ   neuer crist] *rev.*
ABFKLMTYβδXG   18 hem] hemself α   19 and . . . manhed] *om.*
J   ouer his] *om.* I   riʒtwisnesse] ryʒtnesse M   fulfullyng] fullyllyng
C   20 lawe[1]] þe lawe M   21 mannus] a mannus A, riʒtwisnesse in ⌈mannes
power⌉ I   riʒtwisnesse] lawe *canc.* riʒtwisnesse D   23 welle[1]] wille BCFTαJG, whel
KYI, w⌈rh⌉il β, lawe δ   seyn] seen I   welle[2]] wille F, wel, e *altered from* i
J   24 þei . . . ofte] ofte þey gon M   ofte] of C   riʒt] -wisnesse *canc.*
D   þer] þe β   25 riʒt] þe ryʒt δ   of] on β   26 þis] þe C   seyn]
seythen C   þat] *om.* AB   hit] ⌈þey⌉ T   iuge] deme δ   27 ellis] *om.*
M   of] as F   28 fordon] vndone α   29 techyng] and so he techeth
C   whiche] þat ABCKLTYβδIXG, þat it M   don] *om.* G   30 we] ʒet we
δ   31 man] a man M   not] *om.* Y   he] his C   32 fend] deuel δ   33
auyseden] avysen δ   on] of α   34 þis] þus LM   is more] *rev.* T, is most
δ   feynud] *om.* J   consistorie] constorie T   chapitre] in chapitre AB-
FJ   35 or] for G   37 iuge] but iuge δ   38 mannys] menes C, mannys, a *on eras.*
of e *corr.* J   39 for] *corr.* D   40 schulde] shulen ABδ   þe[2]] *om.* BTδI   42

pharisees burioneþ to harm of þe chirche, not only among
hemself, þat holden alle þing wel doon þat is doon by þer ordre al
[ʒif] hit be a foly feynet by mannys wit; but howeuere þei may
gete good, by colour of þis feynyd ordre, þei clepon hit hiʒ
45 riʒtwisnesse for þe grownd is good and holy. Triste we to Cristys
religioun for þat is bettur þan þis newe; for ellis we comen not to
heuene, but schullen be dampnyd with ypocrites. And wit
of þese scribes is so muche set in worldly goodis, þat þei clepe not
riʒtwisnesse but ʒif hit be of worldly catel þat is geton by mannys
50 lawe, al [ʒif] Godis lawe dampne hit.

    And so þe false pharisees tauʒten men þat *Godes lawe forfendith*
f.59 *not|but manslawtre or oþur sensible wrong*, and not oþur priue wrong
þat is worse rote herof; and þis were blasfemye in God to leeue þe
worse and dampne þe betture. And herfore declareþ Crist þre
55 maner of wykkyd ire. *Þe fyrst maner of ire is wan a man is wrapthed*
withoute resoun, and sych is coupable aʒen God to be iuged to helle. For
þis vnkyndely venym aʒeyn þe stat of innocens is rote of malice
wiþowteforþ, þat in cas is lesse euyl; and for þis cause vsen men
whan þey drawe to þer deth to forʒyue men alle wrongus and axe
60 men mercy of her synne. *The secunde degre of þis ire is whan a man*
hath conceyued wrapthe, and brekith owht in scornful wordis of his fyrste
conceyued ire. Soþly ire may falle to men for to venge Godus
cawse, and so may men scorne oþur for þey folyly synne in God,
as Hely scornnede þe prestys of Baal. But boþe þese ben perilouse.
65 And herfore he þat scorneth þus *is coupable to fallen in counseyl,*

þing] þinges α   al ʒif] alþow DFδ, al ʒif, ʒif *on eras. corr.* X, al þouʒ if G   43 hit]
he *canc.* G   a] *om.* T   howeuere þei] how þey euere T, loken hou þey δ   44
good] worldli good, -is *eras.* F   clepon] calle αδ   hit] *om.* K   hiʒ] an hyeʒ
δ   45 is] is *canc.* αX, *om.* ABCKLMYβδIG   good] hiʒ G   triste] but trouste
δ   46 þis] þese BFY   for²] or δ   47 with] in helle wyth δ   and] for
Z   48 þese] þe Z   is] was Z   in] into α   clepe] cale αδ, callid
Z   not] no K   49 ʒif] *om.* M   be] ware Z   50 al ʒif] alþow
DFδX   dampne hit] dampnede BF, dampneþ β   51 þe] þese G   godes
. . . not (52)] noʒt forfe[n] did goddis lawe Z   forfendith] defendiþ A   52 or] and
δ   wrong²] wrongez δ   53 is] ben δ   rote] rotes δ   herof] þerof
Z   þe] *om.* FT, þese δ   54 þe] þere α   55 maner¹] maners CKLMTYI-
XZ   wykkyd] *om.* I   ire¹] ire or wrathe δ   ire²] wrathe δ   58 vsen
men] men vsen *marked for rev.* αJ, *rev.* ABδ   59 þer] þe I   to²] and trowen to dye
to δ   men] alle men I   wrongus] her wrongys T   60 men] ⌈men⌉ α, *om.* I,
hem C   ire] synne *canc.* ire D, wrathe δ   61 scornful] sternefully δ   wordis]
word T   fyrste] *om.* M   62 conceyued] conceyuyng δ   ire¹, ²] wrathe
δ   soþly] hyt is soth þat δ   for to] to β   63 may] many LMI   þey] her
FαJ   folyly synne] foli synne FαJ, synen folyly δ   64 as] *om.* F   þese] *om.*
Z   65 herfore] þerfore TZ   to fallen] *om.* T   66 his] þat hys δ, þis

where his foly schal be hardyd til þat he falle to more synne. *þe*
þridde degre of þis ire is whan a man spekith folily, as he þat sclawndriþ a
man, or repreueþ hym falsely and þat man, as Crist seith, *is cowpable of*
þe fuyr of helle, for his ire is turnyd to hate; and, as seyn Ioon seiþ,
alle syche ben mansleerus þat ben worþi to be dampnyd.   ⌐ 70

And so schulden men kepe charite, boþe in wille and in word,
and not only spare strokys as pharisees falsely seyden. And
herfore schulden irous men axe mekely forȝiuenesse, for ȝif þei
wanten charite al is euyl whateuer þei do. And þerfore *ȝif þow*
offre þi ȝifte to God, þat þe scribes preysen myche, *and þow þenke þat*   75
þi broþir for þi synne *haue any cause aȝeynes þe, leue þin offryng at þe*
auter and go furst to ben acordid wiþ hym. For meke offryng in
mannys herte is bettur þan offryng wiþowteforþ. And ȝif þi
broþur be fer fro þe, Godis lawe is so resonable þat hit suffiseþ
þat þow go owt of yre and be recounsiled in herte wiþ hym, and in   80
hool purpos to maken asseþ also sone as þow goodly maist. By þis
lore may we see how fer hit is fro þe scole of Crist for to chiden or
to plete or to fiȝte as men now doon.

---

70 1 John 3: 15.

I   þat] om. Z   to] in Mα, in ⌐to⌐ δ   67 þis] *om.* T   ire] wrathe
δ   folily] folye I   69 ire] wrath δ   70 ben¹] men M, men are α   71 so]
þerfor Z   schulden men] *rev.* δZ   kepe] kepe to δ   72 strokys] strikynge
Z   73 herfore] þerfor Z   74 al] as ⌐al⌐ I   whateuer . . . do] þat euere þei
don F, what is don Y, þat þey don δ, what þei don G   þerfore] herfor Fδ   75
myche] þus moche I   þenke] þenkist F   þat²] hou þat δ   76 þi¹] þei
L   haue any] haþ a ABCKTβδX, haiþ LMZ, haþ any I, haue a YG   cause]
⌐þing⌐ J   þe¹] *on eras. corr.* D   78 mannys] a mannes δ   79 fer] *om.*
M   so] *om.* M   suffiseþ] sufferth CK   80 þow . . . in²] *om.*
M   yre] me L, wrathe δ   and²] and þat þou be δ   81 asseþ] nys gre
δ   goodly] god⌐e⌐ly J, godly T   82 may we] *rev.* αJ   fro] *om.* L   þe] þe
canc. X, *om.* ABCKLMTYβIZG   for to] to Z   83 to¹] *om.* I   to²] *om.* I, for to
αJ   now doon] *rev.* F.

Dominica septima [post festum Trinitatis.
Euangelium.] Sermo 7.

Cum turba multa esset cum Iesu nec haberent quod manducarent. Marci 8.

For alle werkys of Crist ben good lore to cristen men to techen hem how þey schal lyue for to gete þe blisse of heuene, þerfore this gospel of Crist telluþ how he by boþe his kyndis dude a miracle of mercy in fedyng of þe nedy folc. *Whan myche peple was wiþ Iesu and*
5 *þei hadden not to ete, he clepyde his disciples togedre and seide 'I ha⌐ue⌐¹*
rewþe on þe peple, for þei han suwed me þre dayȝes and now þei han not for
to ete. And ȝif I lete hem go fastyng[e] hoom, þei schulen faylen in þe
weyȝe, for summe of hem come fro fer.' And his disciples seydon to hym
'Wherof myȝte a man fede þes folc here in þis wast place?' And Crist axede
10 *hem how manye louys ⌐þat⌐ þei hadden; and þey seyden seuene. And Crist*
comaunded þe peple to sytte doun on þe vrthe, and takyng þese seuen louys
and doyng þankkyngus to God, he brak hem and ȝaf to his disciples to putte
to þe peple. And þei ȝaue to þe peple þis bred. And þei hadden a fewe lytel
fysches, and hem he blessyde and made his disciples ȝyuen hem to þe peple.
15 *And þe peple eet and was fyllud. And ȝet þei gadreden seuene bereleþys of*

MSS: D; ABCFGIJKLMNTXYZαβδ.

Dominica . . . euangelium] *om.* Z   sermo 7] sermo 2 δ, *om.* CFKNTYαIJX-ZG   cum . . . manducarent] exhibete membra vestra seruire iusticie N   nec . . . manducarent] *om.* LMTαI   haberent] haberet ABβδ   quod manducarent] *om.* C, quod manducarunt β, quod manducaret δ   marci 8] mathei 8 ABLδIZ, m^r 8, m^r *altered from* m^t J, ad ro. vi cum turba multa N   1 for . . . kyndis (3)] þe gospel of þis day telleþ hou Crist N   for] *om.* F   2 schal] shulden F   for to] to δ   blisse] kyndam δ   þerfore] herfore δ   3 he] he *canc.* ⌐criste⌐ T, *om.* α   kyndis] kyndes boþe of hys godhed and of hys manhed δ   of mercy] of crist mercy M, *om.* N   4 þe] *om.* LMNδI   folc] folk and seith on þis wyse N   myche] many CKLMTYβδIZG   peple] folk N   5 þei] *om.* Y   to ete] mete I   clepyde] calde NαδZ   his . . . togedre] togedre his disciplis Y   haue] -ue *corr.* D   6 on] of CT   now] *om.* N   for to] to CNδ-I   7 I] *om.* Y   fastynge] fastyngo D   hoom] *om.* K   schulen] schulden D, schal, -den *canc.* X   8 of hem] *om.* M   9 myȝte a man] *twice* I   here] he L   10 þat] *corr.* D, *om.* NT   and²] *om.* C   11 comaunded] comaunde Z   þese] *om.* L   seuen] *on eras. corr.* D   12 þankkyngus] þankinge I   he] *om.* T   to²] *om.* C   13 to¹] to his disciples to putte *canc.* to D   to² . . . bred] þis breed to þe puple ABCKLMNTYβδIZG   14 hem¹] *om.* K   his] *om.* Nδ   ȝyuen] to ȝen N, to ȝeue δ   15 þe] his discip *canc.* þe D   fyllud] fulfillid Aδ   ȝet] *om.* NδI   gadreden] gederen C   bere-

relyf þat was left. And þere was of þe peple, hungry and longe fast-
y[n]g, *as it were fowre þowsande. And Crist lefte hem and leet hem gon
hoom.*

The gospel telliþ of two syche festis þat Crist made here in
eurþe. In þe fyrste weren fyue þowsande fed and ⌐in⌐ þe toþur   20
foure þowsande, and þis was þe secounde feste as seynte Mark
telluþ. And of greet wit weren þere two, as seyntes beren witnesse,
for two is þe furste noumbre þat comeþ aftur onhede; and þerfore
men clepon hyt|a nowmbre withowte fame, for hit is þe furste   f.59v
nowmbre þat parteþ from vnite. And certys, ȝif no mon hadde   25
partyd fro God by synne, hit hadde be no nede to make syche
festus, for ylche mon schulde redyly haue mete whanne hym
neded as bestys han ⌐gras in⌐ plenteuows pasture. And so by þis
bodily werke of mercy of Crist been we tawte to wiche men we
schulde do syche almys. For Crist techyþ in þe gospel of Luc þat   30
we schulden feeden syche men þat han gret nede; and, ȝif we
feden oþur men bysyde resoun of almes, þe fruyt of oure almes in
þat is aweye. And so curates þat ben bettur ocupyed abowte
spiritual needys schulden for þer feblenesse, fer fro stat of
innocens, take bodily almes to parforme þer office – ȝe, ȝif þei   35
been strong[e] in body in reward of oþer men. And þis title of
almes ys moste acordyng[e] to prestys. But in stat of innocense

---

20 Matt. 14: 15–21; Mark 6: 35–44; Luke 9: 12–17;   **30** Luke 11: 8.

---

lepys] ⌐grett⌐ berelepis C   16 relyf] ⌐þe⌐ relyfe α, þe relyfe Nδ   þat was] *om.*
T   and . . . it (17)] *on eras. corr.* D   17 fowre] *on eras. corr.* D   19
the . . . eurþe (20)] *om.* N   two syche] *rev.* AB, tuo sylke *marked for rev.* α   20 in¹]
and at *canc.* ⌐in⌐ α, and L   fyrste] firste feste þat crist made here in erþe N   fed
and in] *on eras. corr.* D   in ²] at α   in² . . . þowsande (21)] foure in þat oþer
N   þe²] *om.* β   22 of . . . two] þey weren boþe maad for gret wytt N   þere]
þes C   two] tweyn festes δ   witnesse] wittis A   23 þerfore] herfore ABC-
FKLMY/αβδIJZG   24 men . . . hyt] hit is cald N   clepon] cale αδZ   hyt]
om. C   a] *om.* N   withowte] wiþ, -outen *canc.* I   þe furste] *om.* M   25
nowmbre] *om.* N   parteþ] departeth δ   26 partyd] departed δ   fro] for
Y   27 ylche] vche a N   mon] *om.* T   redyly . . . whanne] haue had redy
þat N   redyly haue] *rev.* δ   haue] haue ⌐hadde⌐ T, haue hadde F   28
neded] ⌐hadde⌐ nedid T   gras in] *corr.* D, grace in A   29 werke] pasture *canc.*
werke D   been we] *rev.* Nδ   we²] þat we δ   30 syche] oure δ   *margin*
luc. 14 T   þe . . . luc] lukes gospel N   31 men] *om.* AB   þat] þe wuche
N   and] so fedde for to ben and N   32 bysyde] bi siche L   resoun] þe resoun
AB, bi resoun δ   33 curates . . . ben] þey þat ben curates N   34 schulden]
schullen X   stat] þe state FNαδJ   35 take] and take N   bodily almes] *rev.*
N   bodily] boldely C   ȝe . . . synne (40)] *om.* N   ȝe ȝif] al þauȝ δ   36
stronge] strongo D   in¹] of Z   oþer] þer L   37 acordynge] acordyngo

schulde þis almes ben aweye, for men schulden haue redily fruyt
þat þei hadden nede of; and þis feblenesse of body is fallen to men
40 for synne. Crist þat was boþe God and man hadde not þis
feblenesse, for he miȝte haue mete whanne and where he wolde.

But we schulle wyte þat Iesu Crist dide more miracle, and bad
hise disciples serue þe peple atte mete to techen vs þat we ben
ministres, and not autours of miracle. And þus he qwykede
45 Lazarus and made his apostles efte to lause hym, to teche þat he
forȝyueþ þe synne, and hise vikerus schewen hit to þe peple. But
þei assoylen on oþur weye, as prestis in þe olde lawe telden by
synes of þe olde lawe þat men weren clene of lepre. And ȝif þe
pope and his vikerus wolden studyen wel þis mater, þei schulden
50 leue to assoyle men so largely in þis forme. For oure byleue
techeth us þat no viker assoyleþ here but in as myche as Crist
assoyluþ hym furst whom he assoyluþ in vertw of Crist.

We schullen see moreouer þat þe folc þat Crist fedde here
weren fedde comunly and not by maner of þis world, for to
55 dampne riche mennys manerys þat feden hemself costly, and
ordeyne straunge and likorous mete and in greet multitude, and
excusen hem herby þat þe relyf goþ to pore men; for pore men
myȝten many mo be bettur fed wiþ comun metys, and so þis is a

D   38 haue redily] rev. T   39 þis] om. α J   40 hadde] he canc. had α, he
hadde FJ   41 whanne and where] where and when δ   and . . . wolde] he wolde
and where I   42 but] and I   we . . . iesu] om. N   iesu] oure iesu
AB   and] vs for to teche whenne þat he N   43 serue] for to serue N   þe] to
þe I   atte mete] om. N   vs] om. N   44 ministres] seruauntes N   au-
tours] makeres N, auctowrs or makers δ   miracle] miraclis CTδ, suche holy myracles
as crist þere schewede N   and . . . crist (52)] om. N   qwykede] qwykened
CYδZG   45 efte] ⌈eft⌉ T, om. I   to¹] for to δ   hym] or vnbynde hym δ, him
eft I   he] god canc. ⌈he⌉ α, god J   46 þe¹] om. T   to] om. Y   but
. . . crist (52)] om. Z   47 on oþur] anoþer T, on anoþer α   48 lepre] þe lepre
I   49 wolden] wolen δ   50 byleue] bileueþ F   51 assoyleþ] assoyle
C   52 hym] om. AB   whom] him whom AB   in] in þe B, first in L   53
see] om. C   moreouer] more lore in þis holy fest hou N   þe] þuse N   þat²]
weren nedy wuche þat N   here] om. N   54 weren] and he N   fedde
comunly] rev. T   comunly] hem comynly N   by . . . for to] wiþ gret coste as þis
world vseth to N   þis] þe Z   55 riche . . . multitude (56)] suche doyng as riche
men in hire festes ordeyne straunge metes and feden hem þat noun nede and leuen þe nedy
hungry N   mennys] mannis A   feden] fedden IG   hemself] hem
T   56 ordeyne] ordeynde I   straunge] stronge FLαJ, hem strange metes
δ   mete] om. δ, metes Z   and³] and þus þey N, of mete and δ   57 herby] of
glutorie and pruyde and seyen N   þe] þe canc. X, om. ABCFKLMYαβIJ   pore
men¹] þe poure N   for] bote mo N, but δ   men²] om. K   58 myȝten many
mo] myhten N, many mo myȝte δ   bettur fed] rev. FNδI, þe better fed
C   comun] oþur comune N   metys] om. J   and . . . howeuere (59)] þat
costen not so dere þat þe riche wasten and þus N   59 likerous] parelous

likerous pruyde, howeuere we gabbe to God. But go we nerre to
þe wit þat þe gospel techiþ us, and we schal see þat yche prest   60
schulde be vyker of Crist and taken of hym oyle of grace, and so in
a maner be Crist and feede þe peple gostly wiþ þe wordys of God,
for neythur Crist ne hise apostles hadden ay bodily foode to fede
folc þus. And Crist techyþ us in þis þat gostly foode is bettur þan
þis, and in tokne herof þis secunde feste was algatys lesse. But   65
goostly feste schulde encresen þat haþ fully ende in heuene. Þese
seuene louys beþ seuene bookys of þe Newe Testament, as fowre
gospelus and þerwiþ story of apostles, wisdam of bokys of Powle,
and apocalipce of Ioon. ⌐ Þes fewe lytel fyschis þat þey hadden to
companage ben pystelis of reule of Iames and Peter and Ion⌐ and   70
of Iudas. Þe seuene berelepes of relyf ben alle þe sentensis of
seyntes aftur, by whiche þei feeden trewe men by delyng of Godis
lawe; for many ben fedde wiþ relyf þat cowde not ete þis hool
mete. Þe multitude of iuste men ben þese fowre þowsande men
þat Crist graunteþ her owne wille to go to þe hows of heuene.   75

LM   we⌐] om. C   gabbe] galpen T   go . . . see (60)] more gostly ȝet þis
fest is vndurstonde hou N   nerre] neer BKLMTIJG   to²] om. δ   61
schulde] shal F, þorw grace schulde N   be . . . and (62)] om. N   and¹] ⌐and
fede þe puple gostly⌐ and T   62 þe²] holy lyfe and bodily help and whit þe
N   wordys] word N   63 neythur] om. N   ne] and N   hise] þe
Z   ay] not alwey suche N, euer more δ   foode] mete ABCKMNTYβδIXZG, me
L   to . . . þus (64)] þe folke for to fede N   64 folc] þe folk Z   crist . . . þat]
þerfore N   in] om. T   foode] mete Nδ   is] fedeth folk N, fedeth δ   þan
þis] om. N   65 feste was] rev. K   algatys] om. N   66 schulde] euer schulde
N   haþ . . . ende] endeth N   haþ fully] alefully α   þese] and þuse
N   67 beþ] bytokenen N   as] and AB, as þe Nδ   68 gospelus] of gospelys
M   þerwiþ] also þerwhit N   story] stories ABCFKLMNTYβδZG, stories, -es
corr. X   apostles] þe apostlis ABNδIZ   wisdam] as canc. wysdom α, as wysdom
J   of²] also of N   bokys] þe bokes α   69 and] and þe Nδ, and of G   of
Ioon] om. N   þes . . . Ion (70)] margin corr. D   70 companage] pytaunce
N   of¹] or N   reule] reules Nδ   and¹] and of Nβ   and²] of
BCKLMNTYβIXZG   71 of¹] om. FT   iudas] iude þat sweteden vs þe lawe
N   þe¹] þe⌐s⌐ δ   of relyf] þat afturward laften N   alle] om. β   þe²]
þese δ   sentensis] sentence Tα   72 aftur] þat comen aftur Nδ   by¹] þe
T   feeden] fedden NI   by delyng] declaryng N, bi dyuerse partis broken oute
Z   delyng] delynge canc. ⌐brekynge⌐ α, breking CKLMYβXG, ⌐expownyng or⌐
bregynge T   of] om. N   godis] cristes α   73 ben . . . relyf] after mete
N   ben] ⌐men⌐ ben X, men bene CKLMTβδIG   wiþ] wiþ canc. ⌐by⌐ α, by
ABCFKLMTYβIXZ   cowde] knowden β   ete] to eete β, om. M   74 þe]
þat holy men taughten and þe N   iuste men] hem þat seten ate mete N, þese ryȝtful
men δ   ben] bytokeneþ N   þese . . . þowsande] riȝtful N   75 crist
graunteþ] graunten N, graunteth δ   heuene] heuen whit god to be fedde and þus
may þis gospel today be remeuyd and þat we þis day fedde be whit godes holy word preie
we to hym þat fedde al þis pepul þat he wiþ myracle of his grace today fede vs alle þat we
mowe wynne to þat blisse þat euermore schal laste preie we to oure fadre wuche þat is in
heuen quilibet cum pater noster et aue maria N.

Dominica octaua [post festum Trinitatis.
Euangelium.] Sermo [8].

Attendite a falsis prophetis. Mathei 7.

This gospel byddith *cristen men to be war wiþ false prophetys þat comen in cloþyng of schep.* And þese wordys mowen ben aplied vnto false frerus, for soþly þis lore of Crist wolde he not ȝyuen in tyme of grace but ȝif syche men weren for to comen whyche þei schulde
5 fle. And so, be þei frerus, be þei oþur þat speken falsely in þer prechyng, oure goode maistur Crist bad þat we schulden be war wiþ hem. Þei ben prophetes in þat tat þei speken afer of þe day of doom, of blisse and of peynes. And þus seiþ Crist þat he sendiþ prophetes to men þat ben of false feyth and þei schullen
10 turmenten hem; and hit is no dowte þat ne syche men ben prophetys. And þei ben false prophetys ȝif þei lyuen þus þat þey schapen her lyf and her wordys boþe more for ypocrisye and wynnyng of þe peple þan for worschipe of God or helþe of her
f.60 sowle; ȝif þey|fynden nouelrye in þer false habites, and ȝet lyuen
15 as euyle as oþer comune men, who schulde dreden of hem þat ne þey ben false prophetys? Alle þer fownden signes þey schewen

---

8 Matt. 24: 11.

MSS: D; ABCFGIJKLMTXYZαβδ.

Dominica . . . euangelium] *om.* Z   sermo 8] sermo D, *om.* CFKTYαδIJX-
ZG   prophetis] prophetis qui F   1 to] *om.* LMδ   wiþ] of δ   2 in] to þe
in δ   and . . . soþly (3)] *om.* Z   mowen] may wel δ   vnto] to δ   3
soþly] soþe A   of . . . he] wold crist C, criste wolde α, wald not crist Z   wolde
he] wole ⌜he⌝ δ   not] *om.* δ   4 men] *om.* δ   for to] to δ   whyche] þe
whuche δ   5 be] . . . oþur] whateuer þai be Z   be²] ⌜or⌝ be αX, or be
ABCKLMTYβδIG   þat] þei LM   7 þei¹] ⌜for⌝ þey T   þat tat] þat
CTβ   afer] after TI   8 peynes] payne αδJ   þat] *om.* I.   10 þat] but þat
δ   ne] no M, *om.* δ   men] *om.* Z   11 prophetys¹ . . . ben] *om.* Z   ȝif]
ȝef þat δ   lyuen . . . þey] *om.* δ   þat] *om.* F   12 her²] *om.* C   and²]
⌜and⌝ α, *om.* F, ⌜or⌝ J   13 þe peple] worldely goode δ   for] *om.* LM   worschipe . . . or] *om.* δ   worschipe] þe wirschip CI   or] and CT   helþe] hele
αδZ   her] mennus δ   14 sowle] saules αδJZ   ȝif . . . nowht (23)] *om.*
Z   ȝif] and ȝef δ   in] and β   15 euyle] il C   comune men] men
comune *marked for rev.* D   ne þey] ne þey ne, *2nd* ne *canc.* J, *rev.* FLMαδ   16
fownden] newe founden δ   17 oþur] ⌜to⌝ oþer T, to other CYβ   þat] for

oþur men, þat þey schulden cryen her holynesse ouer oþer cristen
men. But, Lord, why schulde þei do þus siþ holynesse schulde be
pryue, and þei my3ten lyuen as holy lyf wiþowte syche sygnes?
Certus hit semuth no cause, but ⌐3if⌐ hit be ypocrisie þat þei   20
schewen to þe peple her holynesse as pharisees don, and so to be
more told by and ly3tlier to wynne go⌐o⌐dys; for, take awey þis
ende, and her sygnes seruen of nowht.

And, as Crist seyth, a good lore to knowen hem were to marke
þere fruytes þat specially comen of hem. Wel I wot þat þe chirche   25
profy3ted byfor þe frerys comen in, and syþen han be sowen
manye false loorus, boþe in þer religioun and preysyng of scribes,
as we seen of þe sacred hoost, of beggyng of Crist, of lettres of þer
breþurhede, and oþur worldly lyuyng. Þe knowyng of suche
signes scheweþ wel þer fruyt, how þey beþ charghows to þe peple   30
and false in þe⌐r⌐entent; for gret nowmbre and costly howsys and
greet dispenses of þis world, with rewlyng of worldly causes,
tellen what ende þey worchen fore. And herfore seyth Crist þat
þei be wiþinne wolues of raueyne. Wolues þey ben 3if þei louen more
catel þan mennys sowles, and oponen þer mowþus to heuene-   35
ward to feyne [pre]stys power, þat neyþur þei can grownden in
þe lawe of God, ne hit may not falle to God ⌐in⌐ hymself. And by
þis power þei spuyle þe peple of her godys, and not assoylen hem
frely for to saue þer sowlys. And *by þis fruyt may men knowen þe
falshed of* ⌐þes⌐ *woluys*; for we schal wyten as by byleue þat, wose   40

24 Matt. 23: 27-8.

δ   18 schulde¹ . . . þus] don þey þus δ   do þus] *rev.* Y   20 3if] *corr.*
D   21 don] deden δ   22 goodys] worldli goodis F   take] to take
TδJ   awey] from hem δ   þis] his M   23 and] þat ⌐is her wyn⌐ nynges and
δ   seruen] þat seruen F   24 and] bot Z   as] *om.* δ   knowen] kene
α   were] by were δ   marke] make ⌐marke⌐ C, ma⌐r⌐ke J, take kepe of Z   25
þere] þe CFβ   þat¹] of hem *canc.* þat D   wel . . . fore (33)] for þair feyned
halynes makis þaim dere to þe puple and þair entent vndir is ay false Z   26 byfor]
more befor α   þe] *om.* ABCKLMTYβI, þat δ   27 þer] *om.* L   preysyng]
prechyng C   28 of²] and of δ   beggyng] þe begginge ABF   þer] *om.*
LMδI   29 breþurhede] fraternyte F, fraternytees δ   30 þer] þe T   31 þer]
-r *corr.* D   32 dispenses] dispense α   of¹] and gret araye boþe in here chaumbres
and fyn cloþing δ   þis world] *om.* δ   33 what] openly what δ   worchen]
wrechen C   herfore] þerfore TαJ   seyth crist] *rev.* F   35 and . . . sowlys
(39)] *om.* Z   mowþus] mouþ ABCKLMTYαβδIJXG   36 prestys] cristys, cris-
on eras. corr. D   neyþur] *om.* M, neuer I   in] ne L, hit in T   37 ne] no
L   may] ne may M, many Y   not] *om.* α   in] *corr.* DT, *om.* AB   39 for
to] to M   þer] þe J   may men] *rev.* Z   40 þes] *corr.* Dα, þe⌐s⌐ δ, þe L, *om.*
JX   schal] *om.* LM   by] *om.* ABCFKLMTYαβδJZG   wose] whoso, -so
canc. α, who ABCKLMTYβXG, whoeuere I   41 louyþ] loue F   more . . .

louyþ more mannys good þan he loueth helþe of his sowle, he is
wolf and fendes child. And þis may men wel see by þese prestus
busynesse. And herfore seiþ Godes word þat *men gadren not of*
þornys grapes to glade men goostly wiþ, *ne gedren not fygus of brerus.*

45 For, as þese trees han not of kynde to brynge to men suche fruytes,
so suche children of þe feend feden not men goostly, neyþur wiþ
fygus of byleue, ne wiþ grapus of deuocion. But þey han more
busynesse to spuyle men fro þer worldly goodys, as boþe þornes
and brerus reuen fro schep þer wolle. *And þus yche good tre þat*

50 God haþ ordeynut to þe hows of heuene *bereþ here good fruyt, and*
euyl tre beruþ venym. For, ryȝt as Godis child may not do but good
þing, so children of þe feend may not do but harmeful þying; for
riht as feendys semen to do good, and hit turneþ at þe ende to
harm, so Godis children semen to don euyl but God turneþ hit to

55 þer good. And to þis wit seith þe word of Crist þat *a good tre may not*
beren euyl fruyt, ne an euyl tre good fruyt, for þey may not turnen as þe
wynd, for alle þyngus þat schulle come mote nede come as we
taken here. And *so ylche tre here in þis world þat makyth not þus good*
fruyt schal be fellut, and put to fuyr to brennen in helle wiþowten

60 ende. *And þus by fruyt* of prestes *schulle ȝe knowen whos þey ben,* and
herby be war of hem for condicions of here maystres.

And hit suffisuþ not to sey 'Lord, Lord!', but hit neduþ to lyue wel to a
mannys lyues ende. And so hit suffisyþ not to prestys to sey 'God
be wiþ ȝow', but þei mote sey wel in herte and wel in mouth, and

65 lyue wel, for ellys a man schal not be sauyd ne browt to lyknesse of
þe Trinnyte. Ne þis lore is not only constreynut vnto false frerus,

---

good] mannis good more I　　　mannys good] mennes goodes δ·　　　helþe] help C, hele
αZ, þe helþe I　　　42 wolf] a wolffe δ　　　fendes] a fendes δ　　　43 godes] cristes
Mδ　　　of] o α　　　44 gedren] men gederen δ　　　not] *om.* C　　　fygus of brerus]
of breres fygges δ　　　of] on I　　　45 to²] *om.* δ　　　fruytes] fruyte δ　　　46 not
men] *rev.* LMYI　　　47 wiþ] ⌐wiþ¹ α, *om.* J　　　48 men fro] men fro *marked for rev.* α, *rev.*
ABCFKLMTYβδIZG　　　49 reuen] renden F　　　50 god] *om.* β　　　51 beruþ] euyl
fruyt *canc.* beruþ D　　　child] children AB, clide L　　　52 children] þe chylderen
δ　　　53 þe] *om.* M　þer T　　　54 harm] ⌐þer¹ harm X, þer harm ABCKLMTY-
βδIZG　　　55 þer] oþer I　　　wit] word *canc.* wit D　　　þe . . . crist] cristis word
I　　　a] *om.* Z　　　57 þyngus] þing βδ　　　58 ylche] here *canc.* ylche D　　　not þus]
rev. L　　　59 fellut] fillid B, fellid down Fδ　　　and put] *om.* J　　　to¹] into
Y　　　fuyr] þe fier ABC　　　in helle] *om.* I　　　60 fruyt] frute, -s *canc.* α, þe fruytes
δ　　　of prestes] þat comen of prestes doynges δ　　　schulle ȝe] *rev.* δ　　　schulle]
schulde KαZG　　　whos] hem whos δ　　　61 herby] þerby δZ　　　of¹] wiþ
ABCKLMTYβIZ　　　condicions] þe condicions Z　　　62 hit¹] so it K　　　a] *om.*
αZ　　　64 sey] seen I　　　herte] here herte δ　　　65 lyue] also lyue δ　　　to] to þe
δ　　　66 only constreynut] *rev.* I　　　constreynut] construed CKαZ　　　vnto] to

but generally to prestys þat seyn þat þei han cure of mannys sowle,
for worchyng *by riȝt lyf endid* aftur Godus wille *makuth a man Godus
child and to come to þe blisse of heuene.*

ABδI   frerus] prophetis Z   67 generally] alswa Z   þat²] ⌐þat⌐ α, om.
CIZ   þei] þe Y   mannys] mannes, a *canc.* ⌐e⌐ *corr.* α, mennus ABFKLM-
TYJX   sowle] soulis ABLMαJ   68 aftur] bi LZ   makuth] and makiþ
L   69 to¹] to *canc.* X, *om.* ABCKLMTYβδIZG

Dominica nona [post festum Trinitatis. Euangelium.] Sermo 9.

Homo quidam erat diues et habebat villicum. Luce 16.

This gospel telliþ how men schulden maken hem frendes of worldly goodys for reward þat þey schulden haue aftyr in heuene.

f.60v Þe parable telluþ how *o man hadde a fermour,* as keper of a town,|þat *was famed to hym as he hadde wastyd his goodes* – but not al fully for he hadde spendut hem vnwarly, but þe lord hadde ⌐þe⌐ worschype. Þis lord clepud þis fermour, and seyde þus to hym, 'How here I þus of þe þat þow wastust my good? ʒyue a rekenyng of þi baylischipe, for þow may ⌐s⌐t no lengur ben in þis office.' And þis seruaunt seyde withynne to hymself, 'What schal I do, for my lord takyth fro me þis offis? Delue may I noʒt, and me schameþ for to begge, but I wot what I schal do þat, whanne I am remewyd fro þis offis, oþur tenauntys of þe lord schullen receyue me into þer howsus for goodys þat I schal doon hem whyle I am in þis offis.' And he gadrede togedre alle þe dettours of his lord, and axede þe furste how meche he owhte his lord. And he seyde he owhte hym an hundred bareles of oyle. And he seyde to hym, 'Take þi caucion, and syt sone and wrihte fyfty barelus'. And eft he seyde to anoþur, 'How myche owest þow?' And he seyde he owte an hundred skeppys of corn; þis mesure of corn is more þan a qwarter. *And he bad hym taken hise lettres,* by whiche he was bownden, *and write fowre skore. And þe lord preysude þe bayly of*

Line numbers: 5, 10, 15

MSS: D; ABCFGIJKLMTXYZαβδ; N *ends incompl. after occasion.*

Dominica . . . euangelium] *om.* Z   sermo 9] *om.* CFKNTYαδIJXZG   et] qui TZ   Luce 16] luk þe eiʒtenþe chapitir Y, *om.* C   2 for] for þe δZ   schulden] schull δ   aftyr] afterwarde δ   in] in þe blysse of δ   3 how] þat CKLMTYαβZ, hou þat δ   as] as a, a *eras.* α, a Tβ   þat] and *canc.* þat Y, and T   4 famed] ⌐de⌐famede α, defamyd ABCFKLMTYβδXZG   as] þat δ   he²] *om.* M   5 þe²] þe *canc.* α, *om.* KLMTβI   6 clepud] called αδZ   þis²] his YδG, þe α   7 wastust] wastid αβJ   good] goodes δI   rekenyng] rikynge T   mayst] myʒt T   8 þis¹] þine ⌐þis⌐ C, þin F, þi⌐s⌐ α   10 me schameþ] I schame Y   for to] to B   12 howsus] house C   goodys] goodenesse δ   þat] *om.* M   hem] to hem ALMδ   whyle] quhyle þat C   13 he] *om.* T   his] þis δ   14 his] þe δ   lord] lode C   hym] *om.* M   of] *om.* C   17 skeppys] schipes ⌐skeppys⌐ C, schippes α   of²] or δ   18 he¹] *om.* M   by . . . bownden (19)] of hys bonde δ   20 warly doon]

wykkudnesse for he hadde warly doon; for children of þis world ben more 20
war þan children of lyȝt in þer kynrede.

In þis parable schulden we whyten þat Crist is þis lord, þat is
kyng of kyngus and lord of lordys. Þis bayly of þis lord, or keper of
[h]is town, is eche man of þis world, seme he neuer so greet. For
emperour or kyng is tenaunt to þis lord and keper of his lytel town 25
to regard of Cristus grete lordschipe; for Crist is lord of heuene
and helle and of al þis eurþe, ȝe lord of þis world wiþ goodys of hit
opon and hyd. And no conquerour myhte ateyne to lordschipe of
al þis eurþe, for Alisawndre and Iulius leften myche for to
conqwere, and God wolde not þat þer lordschype were more here 30
in eurþe, techyng vs þat þe fend, ⌐prynce of þis world⌐, haþ not
but luytel lordschype of chyldren of pruyde, al ȝif he be now
partener wiþ Crist of mo seruauntys of þe feend þan schal come to
heuene. But Crist is cheef lord of þe feend and alle his lymes, and
þey mote nede seruen hym, oþur wel or euel, doyng[e] wel þat þei 35
schuldon do, or elles sufferynge peyne.

And, siþ Crist haþ lent vche man here al þat he haþ and wole
axe of þis streyte rekenyng how he despenduth hit, to eche man of
þis world may þis parable ben aplyed. And, whan men spenden
not warly Goddus goodes, þanne þei ben defamed to hym as þey 40
hadden wastid hem; but despendyng of alle goodys mote sowne
to Godys worchipe, for alle men schulden knowen ⌐þat⌐ alle þese
ben Godes goodes, and he wole þat þei ben spendyd þus to profiȝt
of his cherche. And so spekyng of þis loord is meuyng of mennus

rev. δ   22 schulden we] *rev.* AB, shuld men α   23 kyngus] alle *canc.* kyngus DX,
⌐alle⌐ kynges α   lordys] ⌐alle⌐ lordes α   lord²] world α   24 his] þis DIG,
⌐his⌐ α, *om.* J   town] ⌐lytil⌐ toun B, litil toun A, tounes C   seme] semeth C, be
δ   26 grete] heye LM   27 helle] of helle F   eurþe] world I   lord] and
is lord δ, lordis I   þis²] al þis ABFδ   wiþ] wiþ alle þe δ   of hit] þerof δ   28
opon] boþe opyn Fδ   lordschipe] ⌐þe⌐ lordschyp δ   29 eurþe] world M,
world *canc.* erþe J   iulius] iulyus cesar δ   for to] to AB   30 þat] *om.* I   here]
om. LM   31 in] on T   haþ not] not haþ *marked for rev.* D, haþ A   32 al ȝif] al
þauȝ δ   he] ⌐he⌐ K, *om.* G   33 mo] most δ   34 alle] of alle Yδ   and²]
⌐and⌐ α, *om.* J   35 seruen hym] *om.* M   or] oþer MYG   euel] ill
C   doynge] doyngo D   36 sufferynge] be suffrynge F   38 he despenduth]
dispend C, he haþ dispendid FIJ, he dispendid TG, he to, to *canc.* dispende⌐þ⌐
α   to . . . world (39)] *after* aplyed (39) δ   39 may] *om.* δ   ben] may be
δ   and] to whom god leueth godes and δ   spenden] dispenden ABCKLMTY-
αβδIJXZG   40 warly] worldely C   goddus] worldly J   goodes] good
F   41 wastid hem] *on eras. corr.* D   despendyng] spendyng F   42 godys
worchipe] wurschype of god δ   þat] *corr.* D   43 ben . . . goodes] goodis ben
goddis F   spendyd] dispendid MTδIZ   þus] ⌐þus⌐α, *om.* δZ   to] to þe
δ   44 of¹] to F   spekyng] meuyng of mennes speking δ   mennus] mannus

45 conscience; and þus God telluþ to men boþe more and lesse how
he knoweþ here traytorie wᴿhˡanne þei don amys, and how þei
beþ nedud to dye fro þis offys, and how þei ben nedyd to God to
reken for þis seruyse. And somme men han drede how þey schal
lyue aftur þis lyf, for after þeir deþ þei may not delue or do
50 medfully to þere sowle, and schamful þyng hit is to beggon, oþur
of men þat here lyuen or of seyntys in heuene, but as þei wyton
þat þei schulden helpen aftyr þat men han here d[e]seruyd while
þei lyuedon in þis lyf. And so þis fermer grauntude þre þingus þat
men schulden knowen here in þis lif: furst he grauntud þat aftur
55 þis lyf he my3te not worche medfully, aftur he grauntyde þat he
schulde schame to begge more þan he hadde deseruyd. And so
stronge beggerus here on lyue ben more vnschamful þan be
sowlys oþur in helle or purgatorie, þat wole not axe but þat þei
han deseruyd, for þei wyten þat hit were but veyn to axe more of
60 þer God.

But þis bayly wisly turnede hym to a good counseyl þat, while
he lyuede here in eurþe, he schulde make men his frendys wiþ
good of God þat he kepuþ, and þei schulden helpon hym whan he
is deed. And þus hit perteneþ to kyngus furst to do worschipe to
65 God, and siþ to do rihte to þer seruauntys and so to alle men
f.61 vndur hem.|And þis descharge mow baylies do wiþouten iniurie
to God, for summe men þenken þat þis bayly þat for3af fyfty
barelus of oyle and þerto twenty skeppys of corn dude wrong to
his lord, and so þe lord preisude hym not wel. But we schulle wyte
70 þat þis lord is God, and þis bayly lord of þis world; and so God

---

δ   45 more] to more δ   46 knoweþ] knewiþ F   whanne] -h -corr. D   and
. . . offys (47)] twice M   þei . . . nedud] hem nedeth δ   47 toˡ] for to
I   fro] for L   48 men] om. ABδ   50 medfully] medeful α   oþur of] rev.
LMI   51 men] man T   here lyuen] rev. I   lyuen] lyueþ T   or] om.
I   52 helpen] haue help C   han] haden C   deseruyd] doseruyd D   53
þei] þat þey δ   in] here in AB   so] ˹soˡ α, om. J   þre] two T   54 here]
om. I   þat] om. T   55 aftur] and after Fα, afturwarde δ   he²] hym
δ   57 here] þat lyuen here δ   vnschamful] ˹vn˺shameful αI, shameful
LM   be] om. δ   58 oþur] or ABLMβ, om. T, þat ben owþer δ, gon I   or] or
in ABCFLMTαδJZG, not into I   þat²] þat þat CM, at L   59 wyten] wot wele
αδJ   but] but canc. X, om. ABCFKLMTYβZG   61 þis . . . wisly] wisly þis bay-
lif M   wisly turnede] rev. AB   wisly . . . hym] turnede hym wiseli F   62
wiþ] of F   63 good] goode˹s˺ J, goodis ABTδ   of god] om. F.   þei] om.
β   schulden] schulen CYβ   whan] when þat δ   65 do] þe L   to²] of
L   þer] his Z   66 descharge] dischard B   wiþouten] wiþ LMδ   67
fyfty] þritty Y   68 skeppys] schipes ˹skeppys˺ C, shipes α   69 hym] hem
C   hym . . . andˡ (70)] om. I   70 is god] om. M   þis²] his C, þe δ   71
I

aproueþ wel forʒyuyng of mannys rente. And wiþ graunt of þe
cheef lord, baylyes may forʒyue þer dette. And so hit were a
medful þing to worldly lordys to forʒyue dette, and descharge
þere poore tenauntys of manye charges þat þei ben ynne. And so,
as þis myʒte falle in dede þat þis bayly was worldly wys, so   75
heuenely prudence myʒte falle to children of lyʒt; but þe furste
prudence falluþ more comunly þan þe secounde vnto men, for
pruyde and coueytise of goodys blendeþ men to don almes. And
herfore goodys of fortune ben clepyd by a feendys name 'þingus of
wykkydnesse', for þei ben ofte tyme vniustly delt. But counseyl   80
and byddyng of Crist, þat is chef lord of alle, is þat *men maken hem*
freendys here of suche goodis of wyckudnesse.

forʒyuyng] forgyfnes Z   72 forʒyue] *on eras. corr.* D   73 descharge] discharde α,
to descharge δ   77 more comunly] *rev.* I   þan . . . men] to men þen doth þe
secounde δ   78 goodys] worldli goodis F   men] many men F   79 herfore]
þerfor Z   clepyd] called αδZ   by] *om.* I   80 wykkydnesse] wickidnessis
AB   tyme] tyme *canc.* X, *om.* ABCFKLMTβδIZG   vniustly] vniustly or
vnryʒtly δ   81 byddyng] biding C   is¹] h- *eras.* D

Dominica decima [post festum Trinitatis.
Euangelium.] Sermo 10.

Cum appropinquaret Iesus Ierusalem. Luce 19.

This gospel telluþ generally what sorwe men schulden haue for
synne, siþ Crist þat my3te not do synne wepte so ofte for synne; for
we reden þat Crist wepte þries, and eche tyme he wepte for synne.
And so telluþ owre byleue in story of þe gospel þat *Iesus seynge*
5 *Ierusaleem wepte þeronne* for þe synne of hyt, *and seyde þat '3if þow
knewe þus synne, þow schuldest wepon as I do now; and certys in
þi⌐s⌐ day of þe þat schulde be comen in pees to þe,* 3if þow woldest
receyue þis day and pes of hit as þow schuldest. *For alle þese þyngus
þat þow schuldest kunnen ben now hydde fro þin ey3en, for day3es*
10 *schullen comen in þe* for synne þat þow schalt don in me; *and þine
enemyes schullen enuyrowne þe as a paleys al abowte, and parre þe in
Ierusalem* as scheep ben parrid in a folde. *And þei schal felle þe to þe
eurthe and þi children þat ben in þe; and þei schal not leue in þe ston lyenge
vpon a stoon þat ne þey schullen be remewyde* and þi wallys alle
15 destroy3ed. And þe cause of al þis schal be þin vnkynde

MSS: D; ABCFGHIJKLMNTXYZαβδ.

Dominica . . . euangelium] *cut off* M, *om.* Z
GH   cum . . . ierusalem] *cut off* M,
N   appropinquaret] appropinquasset αH
tatem ABFKTYδJZG, ierusalem vidit ciuitatem CLβ, *om.* H
C, I ad cor. xii N   1 telluþ . . . gospel (4)] today telleþ of cristes wepyng and of
veniaunce þat schulde falle for wyckedenesse of sunne N   2 do] ⌐do⌐ δH   3 þri-
es] for synne *canc.* þries D, *gap eras.* þries X, for synne þries I   4 in] in þe δG   þat]
om. N   5 þeronne] þer upon N   for . . . hyt] *om.* N   þe] *om.* Cαδ   of
hyt] þereof H   þat 3if] *rev.* I   þat] ⌐þat⌐ JZ, *om.* CTH   6 þus] þis Cβ   þow
schuldest] þou *eras.* schuldest ⌐þou⌐ T   7 þis] -s *corr.* D, þis þi, þi *canc.* H, *om.*
I   day] dayes DF, day, -es *canc.* X   3if] 3if þat I   8 for . . . schuldest (9)]
margin β, *om.* N   þyngus] þing J, *om.* β   9 kunnen] knowe NT   ey3en] ei3e
I   day3es . . . comen (10)] þer schul come dayes N   in¹] for N   for] in
N   synne] synnes I   11 enuyrowne] enuerne α   a] *om.* T   paleys]
place N   parre] barre, b- *altered from* p- X, þei schul parre N, þey schal barre N,
F   þe²] ⌐in⌐ þe δ   12 parrid] barrid, b- *altered from* p- X, barred δ, closid
F   a] þe δ   felle] felle, -e- *altered from* -a- T, falle Nδ   13 in² . . . lyenge]
lygging in þe a stone Nδ   in²] *om.* I   ston] ⌐a⌐ ston Kα, a ston LMT   14
vpon] vp T   a] *om.* CFKLMYαβJZGH   ne þey] *rev.* ABαIJ, ne þe LM   15
þe] þo N   þin] þe AB   16 vnknowyng] vn- *corr.* DG, knoyng, *gap before* β,

⌐vn⌐knowyng *þat þow wolt not knowe þe tyme þat God* by grace *haþ
visitut þe.'* Alle þese wordys weren schewyd in dede, and Iosephus
makyþ mynde of hem how Tytus and Vaspasian, þe secounde
and fowrtiþe ȝer aftur þat Crist was steyud to heuene, comen at
þe solempnyte of Pasc, and enseghedon Ierusaleem and de-   20
stroyeden men and wallys vtturly þat þei sownden þere. And þis
is o pryue synne wiþ whyche þe feend blendyþ men, þat þey
sorwe not more for synne þan þei doon for oþur harm, for þus
wille is mysturnyd and men faylen to serue God. And herfore
techyth Crist hyse apostles þat þei schulden not ben aferd for   25
perelys þat schulle come for to venge synne þat is doon; but þe
moste drede of alle schulde be to fallen in synne, for þat is worse
þan þe peyne þat God ordeynuþ to suwen herof. And þus in fowre
affeccionus þat ben growndyd in mannys wille stondiþ al mannys
synne þat he doþ aȝeynus God: for, ȝif sorwe and ioye of a man   30
and hope and drede weren rewlud wel, his wille were ordeynut
vnto God to seruen hym as hit schulde do.

    After þis telluth þe story how *Crist went[e] into þe temple, and caste
owht boþe sellerys and byggherys, and seyde to hem þat 'Hit is wryten "myn
hows schulde be an hows of preyȝer", but ȝe han maad hit a den of þeuys.'*   35
And for a long tyme aftur he was eche day techyng in þe temple. And in þis

---

34 Isa. 56: 7; Jer. 7: 11.

knowyng LM   þat¹] ⌐and⌐ þat H   þe] þi TH, *om.* Y   17 visitut] viset
CZ   and] as ABNδ   18 of hem] *om.* N   secounde] two Nδ   19
fowrtiþe] fourty ABFLMNαIJGH, þe fourtiþe C   comen] *om.* N   20 þe] *om.*
ABFKNTYαβJG   solempnyte of pasc] paskes solempnyte N   pasc] þe pasche
T   enseghedon] enseges N, ensegisen β   ierusaleem] in ierusalem
H   destroyeden] struyeden N   21 men] boþe men Nδ   wallys] vallis
L   vtturly] and alle þyng Nδ   22 wiþ . . . men] þat men ben blended wyth
N   wiþ] in F   whyche] þe wyche Tδ   23 sorwe] ne sorewen I   not] no
I   for² . . . harm] *om.* N   for³] and δ   þus] þis IJ   24 faylen] faⁿi⌐len
Yα   herfore] þerfore N   25 hyse] *om.* I   26 schulle] schulden N   for to]
to N   *margin* Luce. 21 TβZ   27 worse] w *canc.*/worse D   28 ordeynuþ]
ordeyned ACI, hath ordeyned NH, ordeyne Y   herof] þerof Z   in] þi
N   29 growndyd] grawntid β   mannys¹] mennis I, goddes N   mannys²]
mennes N   30 a] a *canc.* X, *om.* ABCKLMNTYαβδIJZGH   man] men
N   31 his] is I   32 vnto] to Nδ   hit] he Nδ   do] *om.* Nδ   33 þe¹]
þis T   how] forþe in þis same gospel N   crist] iesu AB   wente] wento
D   34 boþe] þis peple N   sellerys] bi *canc.* silleris K, bieris ABLNδ, þe beieres
I   byggherys] *first* y *altered from* u D, selleris ABLNδI   to] þus vnto N   þat]
om. N   35 schulde be] schal be calde N   preyȝer] prayeres αI   a] ⌐a⌐ T, *om.*
LMJ   36 and¹] ⌐and⌐ H, *om.* LM, ac T   for . . . aftur] *om.* N   aftur] *om.*
T   day] day efter Z   techyng . . . temple] in þe temple teching H   in¹]

dede þat Crist dede he techuþ his chyrche to bygynne for to
purgen his seyntuarye, þat ben prestys and clerkys þerof þat ben
⌐þe⌐ moste cause of synne, and siþ purgen oþur partys whanne þe
40   roote is destroy3ed. And þis telde Cristus wendyng into þe temple
aftur þese wordys, as 3if he wolde seyn in his worchyng 'Þe cause
of synne þat I haue teld is wyckydnesse of prestus and clerkys, and
f.61v herfore I bygynne at þe temple – not to destruy3en hem|in her
personys, but to take fro hem cause of her synne, and ordeyne þe
45   chyrche in temporal goodys as I haue ordeynyd hem to lyue.'
And hit is al on to sey þat þese goodys ben þus sacrude and 3yuen
to prestys þat no man may taken hem fro þese prestys, and to seye
þat antecryst haþ so weddyd þese goodys wiþ prestys þat non
may make ⌐þis⌐ dyuors, for prestis ben incorigible. But þis
50   diffamacion schulden prestys fle wiþ al þer my3t, and preyen þat
þei weren amendyd by þe ordynaunce of Crist, for reson schulde
techen heem þat þey ben worse þan frantykys, and so hadden
nede to be chastysud tyl þis passion were fro hem. For what man
wolde by resown, kepynge a man in franesye, 3yuen hym a swerd
55   or a knyf by wyche he wolde sleen hymself? Or who þat kepte a

aftyr in L   37 he techuþ] rev. N   bygynne . . . purgen (38)] clanse fyrste
N   for to] to H   38 his] her K   þat ben] and N   þerof] herof H   39
þe¹] corr. D   purgen] clanse N   whanne . . . destroy3ed (40)] om. N   þe²]
here δ   40 telde] meneþ N   wendyng] in hys wendyng þus N   41
aftur . . . wordys] om. N   þese] þis T   as] and G   3if] om. N, þau3
δ   his] om. NI, þis T   þe] om. N   42 þat . . . is] and N   þat] as
δ   of²] is in N   43 herfore] þerfore NZ   at] fyrst at N   hem in] ⌐hem in⌐
α, om. N   44 to] for to CNδZ, om. Y   cause] þe cause Nδ   synne] synnes
δ   and] and to N   and . . . obac (74)] om. Z   45 in] and MT   haue]
om. N   hem] for hem N   lyue] here beste lyueyng after myn owne reule þat I
myselfe haue ordeynede N   46 hit is al on] al one it is N   þese] þus T   47
to¹] so to N   no man] noun N   þese prestys] hem N   and] as N   to²]
om. T   48 haþ so] rev. N   wiþ] to L   prestys] þe prestis I   non] no mon
NTδI   49 þis¹] corr. DT   dyuors] dyuerse I   but] and wun not be amended
but N   þis² . . . my3t (50)] prestes schulden wyth al here my3te fle þis defamacyoun
N   þis diffamacion] þes defamaciouns AB   50 þat] wiþ al þer mi3t þat
I   51 þe . . . crist] cristes ordynaunce N   þe] þis I   reson . . . heem (52)]
om. N   schulde] schul β   52 ben] ben canc. ben D   and so] so and þei
δ   and] resoun schulde hem teche and N   so . . . nede (53)] om. N   had-
den] hadden þei, þei canc. F, þei canc. hadden Y, þei hadden ABIH   53 tyl] þey hadden
nede tyl N   fro] aweye N, awey fro δ   hem] om. N   54 kepynge . . . he
(55)] 3eue a woode mon knyfe or a swerde in hys honde if he he hade kepyng ouere hym if
he were in þe fransye and N   swerd] knyf H   55 knyf] swerd H   by] wiþ
L   sleen hymself] rev. N   who . . . hym (58)] 3if a mon louede anoþer and
wyste þat he were seke and wyste þe foode þat he couetede were but harme to hym he
schulde not 3eue hym þisse þyng but kepe hym þerfro yif þat he coueytede þe hele of þis

man in feuerys, and wiste wel how he schulde be rewlyd and þat
þis mete or þis wyn were contrarye to his helþe, wolde ȝyuen hym
at his wille þis foode þat schulde anoyȝen hym? So, siþ prestys
haue goodys of men, boþe of lordis and of comunys, and þei
disusen hem þus, þey myhten and schulden by charite wiþdrawe 60
þese brondys þat þus don harm to pᵣestys, and in mesur and
maner ȝyue þese goodis to prestys þat he hymself haþ ordeynyd
hym and hise to haue syche goodis. And þis may by charyte be
wiþdrawen by þe ȝyuerys þerof, syþ no man may do euele to men
and not do good to þe same men, but ȝif he be a qwyc feend, þat 65
we schulde not putte to seculerys. And to þis ende schulde clerkys
traueylen and procuren þat þis þyng were doon, boþe for loue of
Godis lawe, for loue of clerkys and of comunys. And ȝif þe fend by
enuye, þat is enemye to charyte seyþ þis þing may not be don by
þe lawe þat now is set, he seyth þat anticristes lawe sownden aȝen 70
Godys lawe is strengore þan charite, and anticrist strengor þan
Crist. For þis ende schulden clerkys wepe and preyȝe God þat his
ordenaunce were kept in his strenkþe and anticristys lawe put
obac.

mon N 56 and²] om. β 57 ór] and KLMTYβX were] schulde be
C helþe] hele C, bely T 58 at] al B þis] þat C anoyȝen] noye δH,
acloye F 59 haue] ʳshuldꜞ haue α goodys] good I of³] om. ABCFKL-
MNYαβδGH comunys] comuners C 60 disusen] dyceyue N þey] men
Nδ and] wel and N 61 þese] þe LM, þis T brondys] goodes N, godes
ʳþat arn brondisꜞ δ mesur] þe mesure β 62 maner] in maner αJGH þese]
þus MT, her Nδ he] crist Nδ ordeynyd]-yd on eras. corr. D 63 hym]
hem TH þis . . . þerof (64)] þusse mowe þey þat ȝaffen þese goodes wythdrawe
hem þus by charyte N by] wiþ H 64 wiþdrawen] wiþdrawyng F þe] þo
T, om. I ȝyuerys] gyuer αJ men] mon N 65 not] om. N men] mon
N 66 schulde¹] schul Nδ clerkys] secu canc. clerkys D 67 and] to
Nδ þat] om. M þis þyng] þes þyngis LM 68 for] and canc. for F, ʳandꜞ for
H, and for ABCNTδI of²] ʳofꜞ Mα, om. ABCLNβ 69 by enuye] be enemy
I seyþ] say CαJ þis] ʳþatꜞ þis T, þat þis Nβδ 70 þat²] om. Y 72
schulden] schul δ god] to god Tδ 73 kept] clene kepte N 74 obac] doun
and þat we bysye vs here aboute and lyue and ende in goddes lawe preye we to god at þis
tyme wiþ pater noster etc. N.

Dominica xi [post festum Trinitatis. Euangelium.]

Sermo 11.

Dixit Iesus ad quosdam qui in se confidebant tanquam iusti.
Luce ⌐1⌐8.

This gospel telluth in a parable how þat men schulden be meke,
and not iustifyen hemself and dispusen oþur men, for þis is a spice
of pruyde þat men clepon ypocrise. Þis parable tellyþ þat *two men
wenton* ⌐*in*⌐*to þe temple for to preye, þe ton was a pharisee, and þe toþer was
a publican. Þe pharisee stood* as a prowd man, *and preyde þese þingus by
hymself, 'God, I þanke þe for I am not as oþur m[e]n of þe world, robberys,
vniuste men, auoutrerys, as þis publican. I faste twyes in* þ⌐*e*⌐ *wyke, and
ȝiue typus of alle my goodes.' And þe publican stood afer and wolde not
lyften his yȝen to heuene, but he smot vpon hise brest* to fygure trewe
confession, *and seyde 'God, be helplyche to me þat am synful'.* But Cristis
iugement seiþ þat *þis publican wente hoom maad riȝtful fro þis pharisee,
for þe mekenesse þat he hadde; for eche þat þus heyȝeþ hymself schal be
mad low* be peyne, *and* ⌐*he*⌐ *þat mekyþ hym* by grace *schal ben heyȝed*
by mede of God.

Of þis gospel may we wyten ⌐how⌐ þe furste spice of pruyde þat
is ypocrisye enuenymuth greetly þe chyrche. And, for þis
ypocrisye is comunly among þese religiows, þerfore bad Crist his

MSS: D; ABCFGHIJKLMTXYZαβδ; N *inc.* 45 but þat þe.

Dominica . . . euangelium] *cut off* M, *om.* Z   sermo 11] *om.* CFKTYαδIJXZ-
GH   dixit . . . iusti] duo homines ascenderunt in templum T, duo . . . templo G, *cut
off* M   qui . . . iusti] *om.* YH   in se] *om.* Aδ   in] *om.* B   tanquam
iusti] *om.* LαδΙ   luce 18] 1 *corr.* D, luc 8 ABFI, *om.* C   1 a] *om.* Z   2 hemself]
hymsilf K   3 clepon] calle αδZ   4 into] in *corr.* D   was²] *om.* T   6
hymself] hemsilf F   oþur men] an-*canc and eras.* oþur man D   world] worlde ben
δ   7 vniuste] vnryȝtful δ   men] man C   þis] also þis H   twyes] thrise
C   in þe] a F   8 ȝiue] I ȝeue δ   wolde not] nolde G   9 his] ⌐vp⌐ hys T,
vp his CH   yȝen] eye J   to¹] vp to δ, vnto I   heuene] heueneward
T   vpon] hym vpon CK, on αIH   hise] þe C   10 helplyche] helpeful
H   synful] a synful L   cristis] crist in β   12 eche] ilkane Z   heyȝeþ]
seiþ *canc.* heyȝeþ D   hymself] silf Y   13 he] *corr.* D   mekyþ] makiþ β,
loweth δ   by] ⌐lowe⌐ bi A   15 þis] þe I   we] *om.* M   how] *corr.* D   16
greetly] gostly *canc.* grettly αJ, gostly and gretly H   17 þese] þes *canc.* αX, *om.*
ABCFKLMTYβδIZG   þerfore] þer L   bad] biddiþ AB   18 wiþ] of

desciples 'be war wiþ sowrdow of pharisees'. And Crist hymself
exponyþ þis, and seiþ hit is ypocrisie. Pharisees ben seyde as
departyde from oþer peple, and weren religious in Cristys tyme,   20
as saduces and essees. And alle þes þre ordres of men Crist
destruyde and sauyde þe personys, syþ boþe Powle and
Nychodeme weren pharisees as Godys lawe seyþ. And, siþ alle
Cristis dedys ben ensawmplys to trewe men, manye men þenkon
þat þese newe sectus schulden be destruyde and þe personys   25
sauyde, for þus ordeynude Crist, mayster beste of alle. And I
clepe sectis newe mannys ordres, þat on seweþ anoþur as he
schulde sewe Crist; and so eche secte smachchyþ many synnys,
but ȝif hit be þat secte whiche Crist hymself made, þat Godis lawe
clepyþ þe|secte of cristen men. For we schal byleue þat Crist may   30   f.62
not do synne in ȝeuyng of hys rewle to lede cristen men, and so þis
secte is best þat any man may haue siþ Crist, almyȝty, al witty
and al willeful, ordeynyd þis secte couenable for eche man; but
oþir newe sectis fownden by mannys wit mute nede smacche
synne for errowr of þe fyndere. And, riht as þer weren þre syche   35
sectis in Cristus tyme, so þer ben now monkys, chanouns and
frerus; and diuisiounes in þese þre ⌈seyen dyuysyonys in menus
wyl. Alle þes þre⌉ sectis mute nede smacchen errour, siþ þei
grownden a perpetuel rewle to alle men of þese ordres þat þe
gospel lefte by wisdam of Crist; and hit were wonderful þat þese   40
synful foolys schulden fynden a bettur rewle þan Crist hymself
foond. For who schulde make a rewle to men þat he knowiþ not,

---

18 Matt. 16: 6; Mark 8: 15; Luke 12: 1;   **22** Acts 23: 6, 26: 5;   **23** John 3: 1.

αδ   sowrdow] þe souredowe T   19 exponyþ] expouned H   seyde] calde
δ   20 and] and ⌈pharisees⌉ T, and þer Z   religious] religiouns Z   cristys
tyme] tyme of crist δ   21 alle] om. δ   22 margin Act' 23 H   23 godys] cristes
δ   24 ben ensawmplys] ensawmpliþ T   ensawmplys] ensaumple FL-
α   trewe] goode α   25 þese] newe ordres and Z   destruyde] stroyed
C   26 þus] þis αIJGH   mayster beste] rev. δ   and . . . hegghis (76)] om.
Z   27 clepe] cal αδ   mannys] mennes Tδ   ordres] ordre I   seweþ] sue
α   28 many] of oþur canc. many D   29 whiche] þat Fα, þe whuche δH   30
clepyþ] calles αδ   þe] om. ABH   31 do synne] synne H   32 best] ⌈þe⌉
best⌈e⌉X, þe beste ABCKLMTYβδIG   man] cristen man CT, om. M   al-
myȝty] is canc. almyȝty K, ⌈is⌉ almiȝti H, is almyȝty J   33 willeful] wilfully I   34
mute] mosten I   35 syche] om. Bδ   36 now] newe M   monkys] as monkis
F   chanouns] and chanones C   37 diuisiounes] dyuision C   in¹] of
α   seyen . . . þre (38)] margin corr. D   seyen] schewen T, semen δ   dyuy-
syonys] diuysion C   menus] mannes α   38 þes] þe C   39 grownden]
groundi⌈d⌉Y   men] me men M, þes men H   40 wonderful] wondur T   42

ne haþ noo maistrye of hem, ne techyng to kepon hit? But o complexioun and on elde axeþ o maner of lyuyng, and anoþur
45 anoþur – þat þes patrownys knewe not. And so only owre patrown Crist, þat is boþe God and man, chalangheþ as propre to hymself to grownde syche ordres; and herfore seynt Powle and Petur wiþ oþure apostles fledden to grownde syche ordres for drede of blasfemye. And so hit were more sufferable to dwellen
50 among Sarazenys or oþir paynyme sectis, as doon manye cristen men, þan to dwellen among sectis of þese newe religiou⌐s⌐. And þat þei seyn ⌐þat⌐ þei ben herberys bettur þan comun pastur, for eerbys of vertew þat growen in hem; – certes, makyng of eerberys in a comun pasture wolde destruye þe pasture and lyfe o[f] þe
55 comunys, boþe for dychyng and heggyng and deluyng of turuys. And, ȝif we marke alle syche eerberys in Englond þat be plantyd of newe in comune Cristis religioun, as þei spuylen þe remenaunt of temporal goodys, so (þat is more duyl) þei spuylen hem of vertewes: for alle cristen men schulden ben of o wille, and
60 variaunce in syche sectis makyþ variaunce in wille, and gendreþ discensioun and enuye among men. And herfore ordeynud Crist but þre partys of þe chyrche, eche to haue nede and helpyng of oþure; but certis hit is not þus of þis newe religiounes. Of þis

a] om. T   43 maistrye] maister C   44 axeþ] axe α   45 anoþur] ⌐anoþer⌐ T, om. Mβ, anoþer maner of complexyon and elde asketh anoþer manere of lyuynge δ   þat] but þat Nδ   þes] þe Nδ   patrownys] om. J   knewe] knowen LIG   owre . . . crist (46)] crist oure patroun N   46 chalangheþ] chalange C   propre] propre patron T   47 to . . . ordres] suche ordres to grounde N   and¹] om. LM   seynt] seyth N   and²] wyth N   48 petur] saynt petir CLM   wiþ] and N   fledden] felden Tβ, eschewede N-δ   49 so] om. A   hit . . . sufferable] om. N   50 or] and among T, more suffreable it were or N   paynyme] paynime⌐s⌐α, paynimes CFKLMTYδIJ   do- on . . . men (51)] oþer cristen men doun N, many cristen men don δ   51 þese] þis C   religious]-s corr. D, religiouns J   52 þat¹ . . . þat²] ȝette N   þat¹] om. δ, ȝit H   þat²] corr. D, þat canc. X, om. CKLMTYαβδJGH   comun] þe comen H   pastur] pastures Nαβl   53 eerbys] erbers, 2nd r canc. N, erberis I   growen] grewen C   makyng of] to make N   54 destruye] þis streye β   þe¹] þe corr. to þis α, þis ABCKLMTβIG, þi⌐s⌐Y   pasture²] pasturis F   of] on D   55 boþe] om. N   heggyng] for hegyng N   56 and] als CKLMNY-βδGH   marke] ma⌐r⌐ke H, make TαJ   eerberys] erbes N   57 comune cristis] rev. I   comune] om. N   cristis] þey wolle destruye cristis T   religioun] religiouns I   58 þat] om. CT, þey N   is] þ- eras. IJH, it is CTβ, doth as N   duyl] yuel F, reuthe δ   þei] is þey N   hem] hym N   59 of] om. K   60 variaunce¹] variaunte C   makyþ . . . . in] varyeth monnes N   wille] manes wille α   gendreþ] engendreth Nδ   61 discensioun] dyscencyons δ   ordeynud] ordenith C   62 eche] vche on Nδ   of²] at T   63 religiounes] religious ABCFLMNTYαβδIGH   64 hit . . . synne] after worse

trewþe may be maad sych a good resoun: hit is a greet synne of
two þingus to chese þe worse, whan a man as frely may haue þe   65
bettur as þe worse; but þese newe ordres ben worse þan þe secte of
Crist, and hit is more liȝt, more free and more parfiȝt þan any
oþer secte þat man may chese, and herfore hit is a synful errour to
chese syche sectis, siþ þe ordre of Crist wole betture ocupye at þe
fulle þan any sych secte fownden of men. And so, syþ þese   70
patrownes han no leue of God to make syche eerberys in his
comune pasture, lawe of þis cheef Lord schulde destruye þese
sectis, siþ Crist louiþ more his comunys þan þes newe eerberys.

And þus meueþ þe gospel þat þe þridde seruaunt of God schal
constreyne men to entren and sowpe wiþ hym in heuene, boþe   75
men in comune weyes and þese þat dwellen in hegghis. And þus
was Powle constreynyt to crepon ouȝt of þis hegghe and holde þe
secte of Crist, forsakynge þe secte of pharisees. And þis publican,
þat was a comun labore⌈r⌉, was betture þan þis pharisee, as þis
gospel seyth.   80

---

74 Luke 14: 23.

N   65 as . . . may] may as freely ABCKLMNTYαβδIJXGH   haue] chese α,
take δ   66 þe²] is þe N   67 hit] siþþe þe secte of crist T   parfiȝt] profit
L   68 may] here may N   herfore] þerfore CYαJGH   hit . . . errour] after
sectis N   69 þe . . . crist] cristes ordre N   at þe fulle] ⌈men⌉ at þe fulle T, a mon
Nδ   70 secte] sectis H   fownden of men] þat mon here hath founden
N   syþ] om. N   71 of god] om. T   his] þe δ   72 þis] þe I   schulde]
schul β   73 þes] he doth þese Nδ   75 sowpe] souple L   77 was powle] rev.
αJZH   crepon . . . and] om. Z   crepon] kepe I   þis] þe T   hegghe]
heggis δI   and . . . pharisees (78)] forsakyng þe pharysees secte to holde þe secte of
crist N   holde] helde β   78 forsakynge] and forsake T   secte²] sectis I, sete
M   pharisees] þes pharisees L   þis] þus þis AB, þe Z   79 laborer] -r corr.
D   þis¹] þe TZ   þis²] þe T   80 seyth] sayth and þerfore preye we to god so
to kepe hys lawe þat we leue oure sunneful lyfe and turne vs to þe goode and for grace
nedeful at þis tyme and alle oþere preye we god wyth oure pater noster N   H lower
margin Bede seiþ on þis gospel þat phariseis weren þat bi habite of religioun and signes of
riȝtwisnesse weren departid from oþere puple and ȝit werkis of truþe outward and true
loue inward þei wantiden. Þis seiþ Bede

Dominica xii [post festum Trinitatis. Euangelium.]
[Sermo] 12.

Exiens Iesus de finibus Tyri. Marci 7.

This gospel telluþ a miracle of Crist to make men to louen hym
and trowen in his power, how a def ⌐man¬ and doump was helyd
of Crist. *Iesus wente owt of þe cuntre of Tyrus, and he cam by Sydon to þe*
watur of Galilee; and he cam þorw a cuntre þat men callen Decapolios,
5 wyche contre contenyþ ten citees wiþinnen hym. *And men of þe*
cuntre broȝten to hym a deef man and doump man also, and preyȝedon
Crist to putte to hym his hoond, for þei conseyuedon þat by þis schulde
Crist fully helen hym. *And Crist took þis seke man asyde fro þis peple,*
and putte hise fyngrus into boþe hise eerus and, spyttyng, wiþ hise fyngur
10 *Crist towchid his tonge. And Crist, lokyng into heuene wiþ a deulful chere,*
f.62v *seyde to þis seke man 'Bee þi wyttys opened.' And anoon|weren hise eerys*
openyd for to here, and þe bond of his tonge ⌐was¬ openyd for to speke
riȝt. And Crist bad þese men to publische not þis myracle, but euer þe more
þat he bad þus, euer þe moo þei precheden, and euer þe more þei wondredon
15 *and seyden among þemself þat Crist hadde doon alle þing wyl, for deef he*
made to heere and doumbe men to speke.

MSS: D; ABCFGHIJKLMNTXYZαβδ.

Dominica . . . euangelium] *om.* Z   sermo 12] *om.* CFKNTYαδIJXZGH exiens
. . . tyri] *cut off* M, [f]iduciam habemus ad deum per Christum N   finibus] medio
α   tyri] *om.* H   marci 7] mathei 7 CFLZ, ii ad cor. 3 N   1 louen] low
β   2 and¹ . . . crist (3)] by helyng of a mon þat was boþe defe and doumpe to trowe in
his power thurghe þis myracle N   in] on T   man] *corr.* D   doump] a
doump DM, a *eras.* doumb X   3 he] *om.* N   4 he] *om.* KN   callen] clepen
ABCFKLMTYβIJXGH, called α   5 wyche] þe wyche TZ   contre] *twice*
M   ten . . . hym] wiþinne hym ten citees M   þe] *om.* β   6 to] vnto
N   doump] a doumpe Nδ   man²] *om.* BLNδ   also] *om.* N   7 crist] to
canc. crist G, to crist T, vnto crist N   to² . . . hoond] hys honde vnto hym N, hys
honde to hym δH   hoond] hoŋdis L   schulde crist] ⌐crist¬ schulde K, *rev.*
Nδ   8 crist took] takynge Nδ   þis²] þe CKLMNTYαβδIZGH   9 and¹]
hee Nδ   into] in αJ   11 weren] was C   12 for to¹] to K   was] *corr.*
D   for to²] to T   13 riȝt] ⌐a¬riȝt X, ariȝt ABCFKLMTYβδIG   þese] þus
T, þis I   to] *om.* N   14 þat] *om.* Tα   bad þus] *rev.* N   more]
ABCFKLMNTYαβδIJXZGH   þe²] *om.* T   15 þat] and sayden þat
N   þing] þingis ABCFKLMTYβZG, ⌐þese¬þingis H   deef . . . made]he made
deefe AB, he made þe dombe men I   deef]deef ⌐men¬XH, defe men CFKLMNTY-
βδZG   he] ben N   16 heere] speke I   doumbe] deef I   men] *om.*

Hit is seyd comunly þat holy writ haþ foure vnderstondyngus;
þe furste vndyrstondyng is pleyn by lettre of þe stori, þe secounde
vndyrstondyng is clepyd 'wit allegoric' whan men vnderstonden
by wit of þe lettre what þing schal fallen here byfore þe day of   20
doome; þe þridde vndyrstondyng ys clepud 'tropologic' and hit
techuþ how men schulden lyuen here in vertewes; þe fowrþe
vndirstondyng is clepud 'anogogic' and hit telluþ how hit schal
be wiþ men ⌜þat ben⌝ in heuene. We schulden knowe þis
secounde wit of þis gospel, for hit is byleue of cristen men in   25
eurþe.

We schulde byleue þat mankynde fel fro þe stat of innocence
for Adam⌜s⌝ synne and Eue, and Iesu, God and man, boȝte
mankynde fro þe feendys prisoun, as þis gospel telluþ. And so
owre Iesu wente fro þe lond of Tyrus, whan he wente fro þe   30
bosom of þe Fadyr of heuene; for Tyrus ys 'makyng', and God
made of nowht boþe aungelys and men and al þis broode world.
He cam by Sydon, þat is aungel kynde, whanne he grette owre
Lady by seruyse of aungel; and þis aungel Gabriel, wiþ alle oþur
þat stooden, heelden pees wiþ God and leften þe furste synne.   35
And Sydon is 'helþe' or 'leuyng such synne'. But owre Iesu wente
owht to þe watur of Galilee, for he took þe stat of man slyden from
innocens, for Galile is 'a whe⌜e⌝l whyrlyng' or 'passyng', and so
dyde mankynde aftur þat hit hadde synnyt. Crist cam þorw þe
cuntre þat had ten cytees, for he cam by alle men þat weren   40
seghed wiþ þe fend. And þuse men enseghede þus ben alle þes
cytees, and mankynde þus enseghed brynguþ to Iesu here kynde

Tδ   speke] here I   17 hit . . .þat] om. N   seyd comunly] rev. CKLT-
βδZGH, nat comunly seid M   writ] witt Y   haþ] hath comunly N   18 by]
after N   lettre] þe lettre BNH   of þe stori] om. N   19 clepyd] calde
NαδZ   wit] om. Nδ   allegoric] of allegorike CI, of allegorye F, allegorie
T   20 by] þe I   þe¹] om. δ   what] wha I   fallen] befalle MN-
Y   here] here of I   21 clepud] calde NαZ   23 vndirstondyng] om.
M   clepud] calde NαδZ   anogogic] vndurstondyng anagogik M   24 þat
ben] corr. D, om. β   schulden] schal δ   þis] þe I   25 þis] þe AB   of²] oft
C   27 schulde] sal Z   28 adams] -s corr. D   and¹] in L   boȝte] brought
CL, bouȝte aȝeyn N   30 iesu] lord iesu Mδ, lorde N   lond . . .þe²] om.
N   32 aungelys] aungel G   33 he¹] and he H   34 by] by þe δ   seruyse
of aungel] aungelis seruice H   aungel¹] an aungel N, aungelis I   þis] þus
I   35 þat stooden] stondinge AB, þat stonden δ   36 helþe] hele NαδZ   ie-
su] lord iesu ABMN   37 owht] om. N   to] of H   38 a] om. δ   wheel]
-e- corr. D, wel CT   whyrlyng] or whirlyng K   39 mankynde] mankinge Y   þat]
om. T   40 weren seghed] after fend N   41 seghed] ⌜en⌝segyd T, enseged CβJ,
bisegid IG, suget α   wiþ] be C, of T   þuse] þus Tα   43 deef] boþe def δ,

þat was deef ⌈and⌉ domp by þe synne of Adam, for þei leften to
here God and herdon þe fend, and troweden to þe feendys lore
45 and leften þe lore of God, and so weren ⌈þey⌉ deef to heren of God
what þei schulden do. Iesu took mankynde þat þus was seek, not
in eche persone but singulerly in one. And Crist putte hise fyngres
in eerys of þis doumpe man whanne he aplyed his vertew, sotelly
worchyng for to teche man how he wente fro God. And wiþ ⌈his⌉
50 spotle he towchyde his tong[e], whanne he ȝaf hym vertew to
hery God riȝtly. And so Crist hadde sorwe of þese two synnes of
man, and bad þat þe bond of his wit schulde ben openyd. But
Iesus bad þat þei schulde not preyson hym herfore by his
manhede; and for þis mekenesse þey preysoden hym more by his
55 godhede, and seydon soþ þat he made alle þingus wel, for he
made deef men to here and doumpe men to speke – for men deef
in Godis lore he made to here what God spaak in hem, boþe in
mawndementys and cownselis, and herby þei leernedon to speke.
And so þree miracles dude Crist togydre in sauyng of mannys
60 kynde: he made men deef by synne ⌈to⌉ here what God spaak in
hem, and men doumbe fro riȝt speche to spekon openly Godis
lawe, and so, bysyde þese vertewys to heren and to speke, God
mouyde mankynde to don as þei schulden. And so may men see
how myche þei ben to blame þat been dowmbe and deef in þis
65 maner of worchyng.

boþe doumpe N   and] corr. D   domp] deefe N   44 here] worchipe α   her-
don] worchipe⌈d⌉ α   fend] fende of helle N   to] om. T   45 þey] corr.
D   deef] doumbe LMNTβZ   of²] om. J   46 iesu] god T   þus was] rev.
I   48 in] into Z   eerys] þe eeres NαδZG   þis doumpe] þe defe N, þis defe
δ.   vertew] werkis K, vertues T   sotelly] ⌈to⌉ sotilly H   49 god] goo⌈d⌉
Y   his] corr. D   50 towchyde] tungede N   tonge] tongo D   vertew]
vertues C   to] of N   51 hery] -y on eras. corr. DJX, here CNδ, worchipe α, thank
and to loue Z   riȝtly] rightfully C   and . . . hadde] twice L   52 þe] he
N   wit] wittis H   53 herfore] þerfore LTZ, herof N   his] þis M   54
hym] hem C   55 þat] om. N   þingus] thing Cδ   56 men²] men/men
D   men³] suche men N   deef²] on eras. corr. D, deefid ABT, þat weren deefe Nδ,
om. αJ   57 to] hem to CN, om. I   58 and¹] twice G   cownselis] in counseylys
T, in canc. counseles α, in counseil I   and²] ⌈and⌉ αH, om. J   herby] þerby
I   leernedon] leriden H   59 so] lo LM   mannys kynde] mankynde
ABFLMNTIZGH   60 men deef] rev. N, men þat weren defe δ   to] om.
L   god] crist δ   61 openly godis lawe] goddes lawe openly N   63 may men]
rev. NαδJH   65 maner] mater Nδ   worchyng] wurchyng þat wolen not here
goddes worde and telle hyt to þe peple and þerfore preye we to god or we ferrer wende to
teche ȝowe and to here þe lawe of oure god so to lyue in vertues and sunne to wythstonde
þat hyt be wurschyp to hym þat wurschypede al monkuynde and þat hyt so be byseche we
etc pater at aue N

Dominica xiii [post festum Trinitatis. Euangelium.] Sermo [13].

Beati oculi qui uident que uos uidetis. Luce 10.

This gospel telluþ by a parable how eche man schulde louen his eemcristene and, for si3t prentyd in vs of þe manhede of Crist, ⌐Crist⌐ techeþ þis lore graciously. Þerfore bygynneþ ⌐Crist⌐, and seyþ on þis maner, *'Blessud ben þe ey3en þat seen þat 3e seen, for I sey3e to 3ow þat manye kyngus and prophetys wolden se þat 3e seen and sawen hem noht, and here wordys þat 3e heren and herden hem not.' And, lo, a wys man of lawe roos and temptude Crist and axede 'Maystur, what schal I do to haue þe blysse of heuene?'*; for he wiste wel by skyle þat hit was not inow to see þe manheede of Crist for to come to heuene,|for many þingus, as Scariot and beestys, syen Crist þat weren not able to haue blisse. *But Crist seyde to þis legistre 'What ys wryton in þe lawe? how redust þow?' And he answeryd and seyde þat þe lawe biddiþ þat a man schulde loue þe Lord his God of al his herte, and of al his sowle and of alle his strenkþis and of al his mynde, and his ney3ebore as hymself. And Crist seyde to hym þat he answerud ri3t; do* ⌐he⌐ *þis in dede, and he schal ly*[ue] *in blysse.*

But þis lawyer wolde iustfyen hymself, and þerfore he axede who was his ney3ebore. And Crist tolde hym a parable ⌐þat was sutil in witt, *for*

5

f.63

10

15

MSS: D; ABCFGHIKLMTXYZαβδ; N *ends* 58 my3ten.

Dominica . . . euangelium] *om.* Z   sermo 13] sermo D, *om.* CFKMNTYαδIXZ-GH   beati . . . uidetis] *cut off* M, facta est lex N   oculi] *om.* δG   que . . . uidetis] *om.* αH   luce 10] ad gal' iii luce x N, *om.* C   1 by . . . parable] *om.* N   by] *om.* δ   eche man schulde] men schulden N   his] her N   2 and . . . maner (4)] *om.* N   þe] *om.* A   3 crist¹] *canc.* X, *om.* ABCKLMTY-βδZG   3 and seyþ] *om.* I   4 ben] sayde crist be N   þe] þose *on eras. corr.* M   for] forsoþe F   5 þat¹] *om.* N   manye] may L   se . . . seen] haue seen þat 3e seen δ   sawen] sen CLMT, saw3em F   6 hem¹] *om.* N   and¹] ne L   and²] ne L   lo] lo, l- *altered from* s- A, so I   7 roos] rose up Cδ, aros T   9 for to] to T   10 scariot] bestis T   beestys] skarioth T   to] in heuene to N   11 blisse] þe blys I   þis] þe M   12 þe] *om.* T   biddiþ] was bidden Z   þat²] *om.* I   13 schulde] schal NZ   þe lord his] hys lord T   al²] *om.* T   of alle his] ⌐al his⌐ β   14 mynde] myndes M   15 to] vnto N   he²] he *canc.* H, þou Nδ, 3e β   þis] þis, i *altered from* u TY, þus I   he schal] þou schalt Nδ   lyue] haue lyf DF, haue *canc.* α, lyue *on eras. corr.* lyf *canc.* X   17 lawyer] man of lawe Z   he] *om.* β   18 hym] to him H   a] in a

Crist lokynge on hym seyde hym þis parable,[1] *how o man wente down fro*
20 *Ierusaleem into Iericho, and he fel into þeuys hondys þat spuyledon hym and*
fastnyde manye sorus vpon hym, and wenton and leften hym half qwyc. And
hit fel þat a preest passude þe same weyȝe, and he saw hym lye þus hurt, and
wente awey and helpude hym nowht. And a dekne, whan he was neyȝ þe
place and saw hym sych, passed awey. But a Samaritan, makyng his weye
25 *by þat place, cam bysyden hym and saw his stat and hadde mercy on hym.*
And he cam nyȝ and bond hise woundys, and helde in h[e]m boþe oyle and
wyn, and putte hym vpon his hors and browȝte hym into a stable of a town
and þere he dyde cure of hym. And anoþur day he took two pens, and ȝaf hem
to þe ostler and bad hym haue cure of hym, and seyde þus 'Whateuere þow
30 *ȝyue ouer, whanne I come aȝeyn, I schal paye þe.'* And whanne Crist
hadde seid þis parable *he axede of þis man of lawe whyche of þese þre*
men semyd hym to be neyȝebore vnto þis seke man þat þus fel into þe þeuys
hondys. And he seyde þat þe þridde man þat þus dude mercy vpon hym. And
Iesus seyde to þis legistre 'Go þow and do riht so'.

35   Þis man of lawe þat here is nemyd was neyþur cyuylyan ne
canonystre, but he was man of Godis lawe þat wolde lernen þe
weyȝe to heuene. And Crist supposuþ to þis wise man þat eche
man is to oþur a neyȝbore as nyȝ as he may, siþ þei ben boþe of o

---

δ   þat . . . parable (19)] *corr. margin* D   was sutil] *rev.* N   in witt] and
wytty Nδ   19 hym²] to hym FKNδZ   20 into¹] ⌐in⌐ to KT, to BNI   he fel]
he *canc.* felde X, felde ABKLMYβG, fel CNTδIZ;   into²] in ABCFKLMNTYαβ-
IZG;   þat] and N   spuyledon] dispuyliden ABCFKLMNTYαβδIXZ-
GH   hym] hem C   and²] and robbedon hym *canc.* and D, and robbeden *canc.*
and X, ⌐and robbiden him and⌐ δ, and robbeden him and I   21 fastnyde] ⌐þei⌐
festenede α, þai festened CFKLMNTYβδXG, fastiden AB   manye sorus] *after* hym δ
vpon] vp *canc.* on X, on ABCKLMNTYαβδIZGH   hym¹] hem C   half
qwyc] quyke half *marked for rev.* Cα   22 fel] byfel Nδ   passude] wente I   he]
om. Nδ   23 wente] he wente T   helpude] he halpe H   hym] *om.* Z   24
and] *om.* N   sych] ligge T, so α, seek IZ   passed] and passed Nδ   25 þat] þe
LTI   bysyden] by Nδ   26 he] *om.* Tβ   hem] hym DMα, hym, y *altered to* e
N, him, e *altered from* i H   boþe] *om.* N   oyle] wyn δ   27 wyn] oyle
δ   vpon] on CH   into] to N   a¹] *om.* ABCLMTβ   of . . . town] *om.* N,
of an im I   28 he¹] *om.* TI   and² . . . day] *twice, first canc.* D   anoþur] on
anoþer α   hem] ⌐hem⌐ H, *om.* α, him G   29 þe] þis F   30 ȝyue] ȝyuest
ABCFKLMTYαβIXZGH   come] am comen I   aȝeyn] *om.* K   31
whyche] wyhche D   þese] þere C   32 men] *om.* N   hym] *om.* N   vnto]
to Nδ   þis] þe LM   into] in F, vnto T   þe] þe *canc.* H, *om* ABCFKLMNTY-
βδZG   33 þat¹] *om.* IH   þe] þo þe β   þat . . . dude] þat dide/man þat
dide B   þus] *om.* ACKLMNTYαβδ ZGH   vpon] on AZH   34 to] vnto
I   and do] *om.* B, and do þou N   35 here is] *rev.* ABCKLMNTYαβδ-
IGH   nemyd] meued I   ne] ne no T, neþer G   36 man] a man
LNTδZH   of] in I   lernen] lere ZH   37 supposuþ] supposede α, meuyd
Z   38 is to oþur] to oþer is I   to . . . neyȝbore] neghebure to oþer N, a neȝbure

kynde. But of ney3boreschype of place or dwellyng or of worldly
frenchipe schulde men not rekken here; but we schulde wyte þat   40
alle men þat God ordeynuþ to blysse ben fulle breþren boþe of
fadur and of modyr, siþ God is þer fadur and his chyrche is þer
modyr. And so techiþ Crist in þis parable how eche schulde be to
oþur ney3ebore in good wille, boþe for we comen alle of Adam
and Eue, and specially for we cam goostly of Crist and his   45
chyrche, and þei ben owre nexte and moste fadyr and modyr. Þis
man þat cam down fro Ierusaleem to Iericho is owre furste eldrys
Adam and Eue, for þei comen fro 'sy3t of pees' to stat of 'slydyng
as þe mone'. Þese þeuys þat wowndeden hym ben þe fendys þat
tempteden hym; but þey leften lyf in hym, as God ordeynud hym   50
to blysse, but þei drowen fro þis man goodys of vertew and of
kynde and wowndedyn hym boþe in body and sowle, and
lettiden hym to lyue iust lyf. Þis prest þat furst passyd by
mankynde, and saw myschef þat hit was inne, weren patriarkys
boþe byfore þe lawe and in tyme þat God 3af lawe. Þe deekne þat   55
passyde by þis wey3e weren prophetys and oþur seyntys þat
weren byneþe þe furste seyntis, as deknys ben vndur prestis; and
boþe þei knewen þat þei my3te not help neyþur oþre men ne
hemself fro þe synne þat þei fellen ynne by temptyng of þe feend.
But þe þridde Samaritan þat was Iesu helpude mankynde, for he   60
was an alien as anentys his godhede, and he was keper of man by
boþe two kyndes þat he hadde; and he myhte not do synne, siþ he
was boþe God and man, and hadde not personel beyng of
mankynde as oþur men hadden, siþ he hadde a ful beyng byfore

to oþer δ   to] til α   boþe] om. δ   o] ⌈o⌉ T, om. β   39 or¹] or of
Nδι   or²] om. N   worldly] worldes ABCKLMNTβδIXZ   40 frenchipe]
hauyng H   men not] rev. IH, no mon Nδ   41 men] om. N   god ordeynuþ] god
ordeynid Tα, ordeynen N   blysse] þe blysse N   fulle] fully N   boþe] om.
Z   42 of] om. TIZH   þer¹] his I   his] -is on eras. of -oly corr. D, holy
Nδ   is²] om. N   þer²] þe I   43 þis] his CT   eche] eche man KMNδ,
ilkane Z   to oþur ney3ebore] nei3bore to oþer I   44 alle] om. δ   45 eue] of
eue BNIGH   46 þei] þese F   moste] owre canc. moste D, oure moost FX, most
tristi I   47 down] om. M   to] into Y   48 sy3t] þe si3t K, þe citee T   stat]
þe state NH   49 as] of ⌈as⌉ C, of G   þese] and þese Fα, þe I   hym] hem
CT   50 hym¹] hem T   hym²] hem T   52 sowle] in canc. saule α, in soule
LNδIZH   53 iust] a iust I, ryghtful Nδ   furst passyd] rev. ABMT   54
myschef] ⌈þe⌉ meschief H, þe myschef KNαδ   inne] brou3t inne N   55 boþe]
þat were N, þat weren boþe G   lawe²] þe canc. lawe G, þe lawe NTδIH   deekne]
dekynes C   56 þis] þe N   57 byneþe] be nene α   þe] þes ABCKLMTYαβ-
GH   58 knewen] knowen L   ne] neþer M   59 fro] for βI   60 samaritan]
was a samaritan I   helpude] helpig β   61 an] om. T   63 not] no

65 tyme þat he was man. He helde yn oyle to make wowndys softe
f.63v and to dispose man to ben hool, for he putte m[a]n in hope|to
come to heuene by feiþ of Crist; and he putte in wyn þerwiþ
whanne he spak scharpe wordis ⌐for⌐ to prikke men fro synne. He
putte mankynde vpon his hors whanne he made his owne
70 manheede to ben owre broþur and to beren owre synne, al ȝif he
owhte not for his synne. He browte mankynde to a stable whanne
he hilede men in þis chyrche, and þis is but a lytul stable to regard
of ⌐al⌐ þe chyrche. And he curede men in þis stable by sacramens
and heuenely ȝiftys. And on anoþur day aftur þe tyme þat he was
75 ded, whyche was þe tyme of grace and þe sunne was newe
sprongon vp, he ȝaf two pens to þis kepere, boþe of his godhed
and of his manhede, to fede mankynde tyl þe day of doom. And so
þe kepere of þis stable is alle þese men þat God haþ choson to
fedon his chyrche wiþ his lawe. And Cristis godhed wiþ his
80 manhede ben sufficient herfore, for þei ben wiþowten ende as
þese serklis of two pens. And, whateuere þat prelatis traueylen
vnto spede of Cristis chyrche, Crist wole at þe day of doom ȝelden
hem graciously, and so eche trew prelat þat helpuþ Crist to helon
his chyrche is trew neybore to þe chirche and doþ in part as Crist
85 dude.

LM   65 tyme] þe tyme δH   he²] and he δ   yn] þat Tβ   wowndys] þe
woundis F   66 to¹] om. T   man¹] men K   hool] holi F   man²] men
D   68 for to] for corr. D   prikke] preche T   fro] wiþ canc. fro DX   69
vpon] on IH   70 to²] to canc. X, om. CFKLMTYαβδIZG   al ȝif] and al ȝif T,
alþauȝ δ   71 to] into ABIH   72 hilede] i altered from e D, helide ABCNTδIGH,
herberid Z   men] man F   in] to I   þis²] þis chirche T   but] om.
G   to] as to Fα   73 þe] his I   he] om. T   sacramens] sacrament
I   74 on] vpon F   anoþur] oþer A   þe] þe canc. X, om. ABCFKLMTYαβ-
ZG   75 þe¹] ⌐þe⌐β, om. FH, in I   76 vp] canc. A   þis] þe⌐s⌐ α, þe Lδ-
Z   77 of¹] eke of δ   78 is] ben δ   men] chosen men H   80 as] as er
Z   81 þese] þe, -se eras. H, þe BLMβ   serklis] on eras. corr. D   þat] om.
L   traueylen] trauaileden I, of holi chyrche trauelen δ   82 vnto] to
δ   spede] -de on eras. corr. D, þe spede Lδ   cristis] holy δ   83 hem] it hem
G   84 part] parti α

Dominica xiiii [post festum Trinitatis.
Euangelium.] Sermo 14.

Dum iret Iesus in Ierusalem. Luce 17.

Crist wole teche by miracle in þis parable þat riȝt byleue is
grownd of mennys saluacioun. *Whan Iesus wente to Ierusaleem, he
wente þorw Samarie and Galilee. And whanne he wente into a castel, ten
meyselys comen aȝeynys hym; and þei stooden afer, and crieden on hym as
þei myȝten, and seyden 'Iesu, comaundor, haᵗueᵗ mercy on vs!' But whan*   5
Crist saw þese leprouse men, crienge þus and stondyng togedyr afer leste
þey blemyschedon oþur men, *he bad hem go and schewe hem to prestis,*
as God bad in þe olde lawe. *And as þei wenton þei weren helude of þer
lepre. And on of hem, whanne he saw þat he was þus helud* by miracle,
turnyde aȝen to Iesu, wiþ a greet voys preysyng God, and he fel down in his   10
*face byfore Cristus feet and þankede hym. And þis man þat þus cam aȝen
was a Samaritan. And Iesus spak and seyde þus of þis dede* þat was fallen,
*'Ne ben not ten made clene? [and] wher ben oþur neyne? þer is noon fownden
þat cam aȝen and þanky[de] God but þis alieen.' And Crist seyde vnto hym,
'Ris and goo wodyr þow wolt, for þi byleue haþ mad þe saf'.*   15

To þe wit of allegoric bytokneþ þis dede of Crist how he was
wendyng to heuene, þat ys clepyd Ierusaleem. And he passede by
Samarie and Galilee or he wente, to teche þat he wolde saue boþe

MSS: D; ABCFGHIJKLMNTXYZαβδ; E *inc.* 63 -ful men

Dominica . . . euangelium] *om.* Z   sermo 14] sermo 18 M, *om.* CFKNTYαδ-
IJXZGH   dum . . . ierusalem] spiritu ambulate et desideria carnis non perficietis
N   dum] cum ABαδJH   ierusalem] ierusalem transibat ABCFKLMTYβ-
JZG   luce 17] *om.* C, ad gal' v N   17] xiiii AB, 7 ᵗ17ᵗ I   1 wole . . .þat] in
þis gospel techeth cristen men hou N   miracle] þis myracle AB   2 mennys]
manus CMδI   whan] for when N   4 crieden] þey crieden J   5 haue] -ue
corr. D   on] vpon I   6 þese] þe LY, þes ten C   crienge þus] *rev.*
N   stondyng] stonden N   togedyr afer] *rev.* N   7 þey] þe L   blemy-
schedon] enblemesched N, suld blemysche Z   9 was þus] *rev.* I   10 a] *om.*
Z   fel] feld ABKX   11 feet] foot I   þus cam] *rev.* I   12 fallen] byfallen
NδZ   13 ne] *om.* G   not] þer not Nδ   and] *om.* DJXH, ᵗandᵗ α   oþur]
þe N, þe oþere δ   þer] and þer I   14 þankyde] þankyþ, -þ *on eras. of* -de *corr.* D,
þankede, -de *on eras. corr.* X, þankiþ ABKβIJZ   and²] but G   vnto] to
NδI   15 ris] ryse vp T   haþ] had L   16 þe] *om.* Y   allegoric] allegorie
CKLMNTYαβδJXZGH   was] ᵗwasᵗ K, *om.* B   17 clepyd] calde NαδZ, *om.*

heþene men and Iewys. For hit ys knowen of Samarye þat þei
20 weren not of Iewys kynde, but alyenys þat dwellyd þere fro þe
tyme of conquest of þat lond, and ten kynradys of Israelys sonys
weren euere put owt, as now be Iewys; and herfore þe Iewys
louedon not þe⌈s⌉[1] Samaritanys. And to repreef of Crist þei
clepuden hym a Samarytan, þat he grauntyde in a maner and
25 denyede þat he was lad by þe fend. Cristus wendyng into þe
casteel bytoknyþ his lytul chyrche þat ys armed wiþ vertewys as
þe castel is kept fro enemyes.

Ten leprowse men ben alle þe synful þat mekely axen
for3yuenesse of þer synne. Þei stoden furst fer fro Goddis folc, and
30 siþ þei wenten to Cristus prestis; and byfor þei comen to hem,
God assoylede hem of here synnys, for God seiþ in þe salm how
man in purpos to leuen his synne seyde þat he wolde schryuen
hym to God, and God for3af hym his synne. And so Crist taw3te
by þis dede þat assoylyng of men is nowht but 3if God assoyle
35 byfore, as God by hymself assoyled þese leprowse. And so prestys
assoylen as Godis vikerus acordyng to Godis assoylyng, and ellys
þei assoylen no more þan prestis of þe oolde lawe heluden men of
þer lepre – and þat my3te þei not doo. Þis alien þat caam a3en to
þanke God of his helþe bytokneþ trewe cristene men þat dwellen
40 in þis byleue. Þese neyne þat ben manye moo bytokne men owte
f.64 of byleue, þat trowen|þat hit is inow þat her preest assoyle hem,

---

24 John 8: 48; **31** Ps. 31: 5.

M   19 men] om. J   for . . . iewys (20)] om. M   for] and for N   of[1]]
to δ   þei] ⌈þei⌉ YH   20 of] om. N   iewys] þe iewes C   þere] om.
T   þe] om. Yδ   21 þat] þe Nδ   ten] þe ten T   israelys] þe israel
T   22 iewys[1]] þe iewes Nδ   herfore] þerfore Z   þe] þes TI   23
louedon] leueden L   þes] -s corr. D, þe CNδH, þus T   repreef] þe repreef
ABCFβ   24 clepuden] calden NαδZ   27 þe] a L   enemyes] enemies wiþ
armour T   28 ten] þe ten Nδ   þe] om. TH   þat] men þat Nδ   axen]
axeden, -den on eras. corr. X, axiden BFKLMTYαβδJZGH   29 synne] synnes
AB   stoden] stonden L   fer] om. N   30 þei[2]] þe F, þat þey Nδ   hem]
him I   31 synnys] synne I   32 þat] þat canc. þat α, þat þat, 2nd canc. J   33 and[2]]
dixi confiteor etc. and N   34 men] man H   is] was Nδ   assoyle] assoyled
Nδ   35 by] bi canc. B, om. AH   þese] þe I   leprowse] leprouse men
NZ   36 godis[1]] cristes δ   vikerus] werkis L   acordyng] when þey acorden
N   assoylyng] assoilinges A   37 heluden] leleden C   men] om. I   38 to
þanke] and þonkede Nδ   39 helþe] hele CNαδZ   trewe cristene] rev.
K   dwellen] dwelleden I   40 in] stable in N   þese] þus T, and þese I   þat
. . . moo] om. I   owte] þat ben out Nδ   41 byleue] þe byleue δ   preest]
prestis CNδIZ   42 and . . . iugement] om. Z   43 þus ben] rev. T   assoylud]

and specially þe hey3e preest, howeuere he erre in iugement, and
how þei lyuen byforn or aftur, þese men þat þus ben assoylud.
And a3eynes þis heresye schulden trewe preestes cry3e faste for by
þis synne is synne hyd, and assoylyng bow3t and sold as whoso   45
wolde byn an oxe or a cowh and myche more falsely. We
schulden comen a3en to Crist and confesse boþe hise kyndes, and
make couenaunt wiþ hym to leuen owre synne from hennysforþ,
and þenken how he bad þe womman 'goo and wille þow no more
do synne'. For þis couenaunt wiþ sorwe of synne and Godes grace   50
is ynow, al 3if men speke no more wiþ prestys; but speche wiþ
hem is nedful in þat þat þei teche men þis trewþe, and mennys
ordenaunce may not reuerse þis sentence. And þus we graunten
þat eche þing þat Petur boond or soylide in eurþe, or any viker of
Petre, in þat þat þey acordeden wiþ God is bownden or lowsyd in   55
heuene – and ellys not, for ellys þei ben false. And so ordenaunce
of men in byndyng and assoylyng brynguþ in manye errours, and
lettiþ trewe prechyng.

But Bede seiþ þat þese leprows men bytooknen eretykes of
manye colourys, þat schulden stonden afer fro men and turne to   60
Crist by riht feyþ, and knowe þat Crist by his word my3te haᴿueᴸ
mercy on hem, and afturᴿwardᴸ algatys þei schulde ben alyenys
fro pharisees. And so alle synful men schulden crie mekely wiþ
þes lepres þat Crist þat is boþe God and man schulde haᴿueᴸ
mercy on þer synne, for he is lord wiþowten ende, and þei han   65

---

49 John 8: 11.

assoilid rekkis not bot wenes it be ynoghe to þam Z   44 trewe] þese trewe N   for]
and G   by . . . synne² (45)] herby synne is Nδ   45 synne¹] *om.* CKLMTYαβ-
IJZGH   hyd] hyᴿrᴸed N   and²] or Nδ   whoso] whoso, -so *canc.* X, who
CKLMTYαβJZGH   46 an] *om.* Z   a] *om.* KYβZ   more] wors L   48
synne] synnes I   from] *om.* I   hennysforþ] henneforwarde δI, heþenforwarde
Nα, þethenfurth Z   49 he] crist AB   bad] had β   wille] wilne T, ne wille αJ,
om. C   þow] *om.* ABCKLMTYαβJXZGH   no . . . synne (50)] sunne no more
N, no more synne do, do *canc.* δ   50 do] to do BT, to βZ, *om.* F   margin io. 5. io. 8
Tδ, io. viii N   wiþ] kept wiþ AB   of] for H   51 is] þat is I   ynow] now
β   al 3if . . . prestys] *om.* Z   al 3if] al ᴿ3ifᴸ þou3, þou3 *canc.* F, alþawe
Nδ   52 hem] prestis Z   nedful] medeful N   in²] þat β   59 þat] þus þat M   60 haue]
-ue *corr.* D   62 on] of α   algatys . . . schulde] þey schulden algates Nδ   63
men] *om.* LM   schulden] *om.* E   64 þes] þis T   lepres] leprous
ABFKLMTYαβEIJZGH, leprose men Nδ   haue] -ue *corr.* D   65 on] of

euyle wraþþed hym; and so her synne ys so greet þat, but ȝif Crist
of his power and of his grace forȝyue þis synne, hit may neuer be
forȝyuen. And for þis þyng seiþ þe chyrche in þer preyer þat owre
God makiþ most his myȝt knowen in sparyng and in hauyng
70   mercy, for ȝif Crist dude not so no synful man myȝte be sauyd.
But we schulden vndyrstonden þat, as God is mercyful, so he is
riȝtful and hateþ men þat breken couenaunt; and þerfore holde
we couenaunt to God and deseyue we not owre self, for God may
not be deseyuyd howeuere prestys bygylen vs.

N   synne] synnes I   is] *eras.* E   lord] lord ⌐and⌐ is δ   and] and may do
what so he wole and knowelache þat N, and may do what he wul and knowelache þat
δ   68 seiþ . . . chyrche] þe churche saythe N   þer] hir F   preyer] preyeris
AB   69 knowen] in *canc.* knowen D, in knowinge I   in sparyng] *on eras. corr.*
D   in²] *om.* ABCNTYδH   70 mercy] of mercy H   myȝte] myȝt not
δ   71 schulden] schulen CNαβδZ   he is] *twice* Y   72 þerfore] herfore
N   73 owre] vs KMTYβEJXZGH   74 howeuere] hou G   prestys] þat
prestes N   vs] vs and þerfore preye we to god to whom we fyrst maden couenaunt
when we token oure bapteme to serue trewely to hym þat we þat couenaunte holden
thurghe helpe of hys grace þat he quyte vs to oure mede ioye þat euere schal laste and þat
it so be preye we vnto hym wiþ pater et aue N

Dominica xv [post festum Trinitatis. Euangelium.]
Sermo 15.

Nemo potest duobus dominis seruire. Mathei 6.

This gospel telluþ men how þei schal be bissy for blisse, and leue
oþur worldly bussynesse þat lettuþ men fro þis. Furst Crist seyþ
þis principle þat eche man schulde trowe þat *no mon may serue wel*
twey fulle *lordys, for oþur he schal hate þe toon and loue þe toþur, or*
susteyne cause of þe toon and dispuyse þe toþur, and þus algatis he seruyþ   5
amys. ȝif he serue hem togedre þe cause is more pleyn; and ȝif he
serue furst þe toon and siþ þe toþur, oþur he serueþ amys þe toon
or þe toþur. In alle þese resones we schal suppose þat þe gospel
spekyþ of suche lordys þat neyþur is wel seruaunt to oþur, as ben
God and þe feend; for, ȝif þer ben two lordys and þe toon serue   10
wel þe toþur, a man may serue wel to hem boþe as we seen alday.
But þe gospel vndyrstandyþ of syche cheef lordys þat han not
abouen hem anoþur chef lord. And so is þis world deuydut in two
maner of lordschipes, þat ben Goddis and þe fendys; for al ȝef þe
fend haᒋueᒃ no propre lordchype, neþeles he chalangheþ to haue   15
greet lordchype, and so magrey his he seruyþ ᒋtoᒃ God. And þis
seruyse is vnpropre as is þe feendis lordchipe, siþ he seruiþ not to
God to his owne mede but aȝeynes his wille he profiȝteþ to Cristes

MSS: D; ABCEFGHIJKLMTXYZαβδ.

Dominica . . . euangelium] *om.* MEZ   sermo 15] *om.* CFKMTYαδEIJXZG-
H   nemo . . . seruire] *cut off* M   mathei 6] *om.* M   1 telluþ] techiþ
ABKLMTYβδEIXZ   schal] shulden ABI   blisse] þe blysse of heuene δ   2
oþur] *om.* δ   furst] blysse δ   crist seyþ] *rev.* ABIJ   3 serue wel] *rev.*
ABI   4 fulle] ᒋfulleᒃ Y, *om.* δ   he schal¹] *rev.* ABCKLMYβEJZG   loue]
loue þe loue Y   5 cause] causis G   6 hem] hem boþe δE   7 furst þe toon]
þat on first I   oþur] ᒋoþerᒃ AG, or T   8 in] and B   9 wel] wilful T, *om.*
K   to] til α   10 þe¹] *om.* C   serue] serueth δI, loue B   11 wel¹] *om.*
L   þe] to þe H   serue wel] *rev.* δ   to] ᒋtoᒃ δ, *om.* H   seen] seyn, y *canc.* J,
seyn FG, *may canc.* sen Y, *may* seen H   12 of] *om.* I   cheef] cleef T   þat] at
C   13 hem] hym C   is þis] *rev.* δ   world] worᒋlᒃd L, worldely δ, word
C   14 þat] þan β   for] and K   al ȝef] alþauȝ δ   15 haue¹] -ue *corr.*
D   chalangheþ] chalange C   16 greet] *om.* L   his] hys hed T   þis] his
αH   17 is²] ᒋisᒃ X, *om.* FT, to δ   to] *om.* AB   18 his²] *om.* M   wille]

cherche. And þus for generalte of lordchipe of Crist, he seiþ 'who
20 is not wiþ hym is aȝeynes hym'.

And þus seiþ Crist wel þat *we may not serue God and richesse of þe world,* for þei ben contrariows; for, as we may not serue þe feend wiþ seruyse of God, so we may not serue þe world þat is þe feendis seruaunt. But in al þis speche we schal speke of riȝt seruyse and of
f.64v 25 vnpropre|seruyse þat þe feend mystakiþ, and þanne may we see how sych hed ser⌐u⌐ȝyse may not acorde to God and to þe world. For, ȝif a man trauele for goodys of þis world and haþ ryȝt entent for to worchype God, he seruyþ not þe world but hit seruyth hym; but hit is ful hard to haue sych riȝt entent, for to sych entent mut
30 be mesure of bussynesse and nowmbre of traueyle and wey⌐ȝ⌐te of mannys wille. And herfore forbedyþ Crist bussynesse of foode and helyng, for abowte þese two þingys schulde sonest men be bessy. And Crist spekiþ of byssynesse moste pryncipally in man, and so trewe men wyten wel þat eche man schulde casten al his
35 bussynesse in God, as seynte Petur byddyth. And þus seyth Crist þat *we schulde not be byssy to owre lyf, what we schulden ete, ne to owre body what we schulde be cloþud, for, siþ lyf is more þan mete and mannys body more þan cloþ,* as God ȝyueþ man þese two, so wole he ordeyne for hem. *Byholde ȝe þe fowlys of þe eyr, how þei sowe neþur ne repon, ne*
40 *gadre not into bernys, and ȝet God fedyþ hem; and, siþ ȝe be more worþ þan þey,* God wole take more heed to ȝow. For, as ȝe byssy ȝow not of þe body, so schulde ȝe not bussy ȝow of helyng þerof. *For what*

---

19 Matt. 12: 30; Luke 11: 23; **35** 1 Pet. 5: 7.

---

owne wylle δ   he profiȝteþ] to profit L   19 who] whoso E, wha þat Z   21
wel] *om.* L   god] to god FZ, wele god L   richesse] ritchessis FδJ   þe] þis
T   22 contrariows] contraries BCFLMTZ   23 seruyse] þe seruice H   so]
and *eras.* so G, and so JH   world] wold β   feendis] dules α   25
þanne . . . we] we þan may α   may we] *rev.* ABIG   26 acorde] serue ⌐acorde⌐
M   27 þis] þe, -e *canc.* -is corr. H, þe CT   haþ] haue E   ryȝt] *on eras.* corr. D,
þe right C   28 for to] to MH   god] to god C, *om.* M   þe] to þe B   29
haue] *om.* C   riȝt] *om.* LI   to²] *om.* A   30 weyȝte] wiȝte A   31 of] *orig.*
abowte, abo-*eras.* of *written over corr.* -wte *canc.* D   32 helyng] of hilyng E   sonest
men] *rev.* ABCKLMTYαβδEZG, man sonneste I, a man sunnest H   33 pryncipally]
principal ABCKMTYβEXZ   35 as] and T   36 ne] and F   37 schulde]
shuln H   cloþud] cloþid wiþ AE   38 more] is more E   as] for as
δ   man] *om.* M   þese] þus T   two] two ⌐to man⌐ M   wole he] *rev.*
M   wole] wolde δ   39 hem] hym T   þe¹] *om.* β   sowe neþur] *rev.* FE,
sawen not δ   ne¹] *om.* ABI   40 into] in⌐to⌐ þe C   siþ] seiþ J   worþ]
worþi BCαIJZH, wroþe L, *om.* δ   41 god] good β   wole] wolde G   ȝe] ⌐ȝe⌐
FM   ȝow²] now C   42 schulde] schullen I   not . . . ȝow] besie ȝow not
CI   of] abowte *canc.* of DX, for H   helyng] þe helynge I, þe *canc.* heliyng X,

*wolde hit profyte to a man to byssyen hym ⌐þus⌐ abowte þe body, syþ he may
not caste þerto a cubyte* ouer þat kynde ȝyueþ hym. And þus syþ God
by kynde of man ordeynuþ for mannys body, he wole ordeyne for   45
þe lasse how mannys body schulde be hylud. And, ȝif þow seyȝe
þat manye men by þis schulde sterue for defawt of mete, wel I wot
by my byleue þat no man schulde fayle of mete vnto harm of his
sowle, but ȝif his synne be cause þerof, and so þat hit be good and
iust þat he fayle þus of mete. And þus I rede þat God bad fowlus   50
and poore folc feden his prophete, and feeden hym as beste was to
profiȝt of his sowle. And *of cloþus what be ȝe bussye?* Loke ȝe lilyes of þe
*feld, how þei growen and ben cled, and þei traueyle not herabowte ne
spynnen* for þer clooþ, *and ȝet Salamon in al his glorie was not cled as oon
of þese ys,* for schap and colour of flour of lylye is not mad by   55
mannys craft. And so, *ȝif hey of þe feeld þat now ys and tomorwe is brent
is þus cled by Godis wyt, myche more wole he cloþe men* þat he telluþ
more by. And so lytelnesse of byleue makiþ men þus to be byssy,
for þei wyte not what maner of þyng is profiȝtable for mennys
sowlys. And so *be we not byssy what we schal ete or drynke, or wiþ what* 60
*þingis owre body schal be atyrud, for alle syche þingus seken heþen men
faste. And so seke we furst þe kyndam of God* [*and riȝtwisnesse of hym*],
and alle syche þingus schal be cast to vs.
 Aȝen þis lore synnen manye men of þe world, ȝee prestys and

---

50 1 Kgs. 17: 4–6, 9–14.

lyuynge Y   43 hit] *om.* M   a] ⌐a⌐ δ, *om.* ABFKLMTβEIZH   þus] *corr.*
DM   þe] ⌐þe⌐ T, þe *canc.* Y, his ABEI, *om.* CLMβZ   44 hym] to him Y   45 of
man] *om.* F   46 schulde] schal EZ   hylud] cloþid E   47 manye . . . þis] bi
þis men δ, bi þis many men E   men] man α   by . . . sterue] shuld sterue be þis
α   of mete] *om.* E   48 harm] harmynge ABFαIJG   50 iust] ryȝt δ   51
folc] men δ   feden] to fede H   prophete] prophete abacuc, abacuc *canc.* D,
prophetis δ   feeden] fe⌐d⌐den H, fedde ABFKMTYIZG, þei fede δ, þey fedden
E   hym] hem δ   52 profiȝt] þe profit H   of his] to M   of²] of his
M   cloþus] cloþing F   ȝe²] *om.* FβE   lilyes] ⌐þe⌐ lylyes A, þe lilies
BFLβδ   53 and¹] and hou þey E   herabowte] þereaboute ABδIZ   54
clooþ] clothes δ   al] al *canc.* E, *om.* F   55 schap] þe schap δ   and] of *canc.*
⌐and⌐ *corr.* C, of J   of²] *om.* J   flour of lylye] lely flours AB, lilie flour I   not]
no α   56 so] *om.* X   hey] þe hay ABF, þat heye δ   57 godis] mannes
Z   wole] wolde ABCYIG   men] man I   58 so lytelnesse] so⌐li⌐tilnesse L,
sotilnesse β   be] ⌐be⌐ α, *om.* L   byssy] wise I   59 profiȝtable] ⌐most⌐
profitable H   for²] to Tα   mennys] mannis ATαδEIJ, a mannys B   60
sowlys] soule ABCFKLMTYαδEIJZ   so] *om.* G   we²] ȝe F   ete] *twice*
H   or] and what we schal I   62 so] se F   we] ȝe δ   god] god heuene,
heuene *canc.* D, heuen *canc.* god α, heuen CKLMTYβδEXZ   and² . . . hym] *om.*
DCFKLMYαβδEIJXZGH, ⌐and þe riȝtwesnesse þerof⌐ and T   63 syche] þese
δ   to] til CKLMβZ, vnto I   vs] ȝow δ   64 aȝen] but aȝens I   manye]

65 clerkys and men of religioun, for þei bussyen hem for atyre and
for foode also þat profytuþ not to þer sowle, þat God here
forfenduþ. And, for brekyng of his heste brekiþ þe ten comawn-
demens – and alle men of þis world be ful ny3 to breke hyt, –
þerfore Crist and his apostles, and Baptist and oþur prophetis
70 kepten hem fer fro þis perel, leste þei slyden þerynne. And Crist
wiþ hise disciples wolden not be weddyt wiþ habytys ne manerys
of penaunce metys, leste þei weren to bussy for nowht. And,
howere we denyen þat we been to bussy here, nerþeles Godis
⌐lawe¬, þat is Crist, schal rekene wiþ vs, and iugen vs at þe day of
75 doom wheþur þis be soþ þat we seyn; and þanne worchipe of þe
world and curteys maner þat men axen schal not excusen vs, but
reson schal ben owre iuge.

many canc. αX, om. ABCKLMTYβδEIZ   þe] þis ⌐þe¬ corr. C, þis TE   65 for
atyre] for to atyren hem, hem canc. D, for atyre on eras. of longer corr. X   66 for] om.
αJG, aboute H   66 profytuþ] profet C   here forfenduþ] rev. ABI   67 his]
þis, þ -on eras. h- corr. α, þis ABCFKLMTYβδEXZGH   heste] heestis E   brekiþ]
þey breken δ   68 þis] þe IZ   ful] om. T   to] for canc. to DX   hyt] om.
M   69 þerfore] and þerfore T   his] om. T   70 fer] om. Z   slyden] suld
slide Z   71 manerys] manere AδI, wiþ maneris E   72 penaunce] penaunt
AKYαXZ, þe penaunt B, poynant C   to] om. K   for . . . bussy (73)] om.
L   73 we¹] om. H, þat we G   denyen] dynen C   godis lawe] -is lawe corr.
D   74 and iugen vs] ⌐and iuge¬ H, om. L   75 þis] hyt δ   þanne] om.
Z   þe] þis ABI

Dominica xvi [post festum Trinitatis.
Euangelium.] Sermo 16.

Ibat Iesus in ciuitatem que uocatur Naym. Luce 7.

This gospel telluþ of o miracle þat Crist dude of a deed body, þat
was þe secounde of þre þat Crist reisude|fro deþ to lyue. And so f.65
telluþ þe gospel þat *Iesu wente into a citee þat is clepyd Naym wiþ hise
disciples and oþur peple, and whan he cam ny3 þe 3ate of þe cytee, cam a cors
þat was boren to be beryed, þat was a child of a wydwe. And myche peple of* 5
þis citee caam wiþ þis wydwe and maden sorwe. *And whanne Crist saw
þis wydwe, he hadde mercy vpon hyre and bad hire wepe not, but went[e]
and towchide þe bere þat þey booren, and þise men þat boore þis beere stooden
stylle to see þe eende. And Cryst seyde to þe dede body 'Ʒong mon, I bydde
þe arys'. And þat 3ong man þat was deed sat vp and bygan to speke.* 10
*And Crist 3af hym to his modyr. And alle þe peple hadde drede, and
preysuden God, and seyden þat a gret prophete roos among hem and þat God
hadde visyted his peple* for þis myracle þat þei sawen.

The gospel telluþ of þre deede bodyes þat Crist reysude froo
deþ to lyue. Þe fyrste was þe personys dowtyr, þat he reysude 15
wiþynne in þe hows. Þe secownde was þiᵣsᵢ wydwe sone, þat he

---

15 Matt. 9: 18–19, 23–6; Mark 5: 22–4, 35–43; Luke 8: 41–2, 49–56.

MSS: D; ABCEFGHIJKLMNTXYZαδ; β *ends incompl.* 70 aftir crist.

Dominica . . . euangelium] *cut off* M, *om.* Z sermo 16] *om.* BFKMNTYαδ-
EIJXZGH ibat . . . naym] *om.* M, obsecro uos ne deficiatis N ibat] ibant
β que . . . naym] *om.* αH luce 7] luc 7 . . . luc 9 *(rubric)*δ, luc 16 H, ad
eph. 3 . . . luce 7 N 1 this . . . þat²] crist in þis gospel telleth of þe secounde body
N 2 þe] ᵣþeᵢLH þre] þe *canc.* þre D, þe þre FT crist] he N reisude]
areisede IJ to] vnto N and . . . þat¹(3)] *om.* N 3 telluþ . . . gospel] þe
gospel telliþ Tδ iesu] crist E into] vnto T is] was α clepyd] calde
NαδZ hise] hys owne N 4 oþur] wiþ oþer N 3ate] 3ates Nδ, water
I þe²] þat E cam] þer come Nαδ ᵣ6 þis¹] þe
AY 7 vpon] on NδH bad] he bad T wente] wento D, he wente AKNδJ,
he wente to I 8 þise] þe Z þis] þe ANδ 9 eende] wondre N, wonder and
þe ende δ 10 arys] ᵣaᵢrise G, rise CFδZ þat¹] þe I deed] so dede
δ 11 and²] *om.* A 12 þat¹] *om.* Z roos] was risen H 13 myracle]
miraclen T 15 deþ] dede CT þe²] a E personys] princes Nαδ þat
he] þe L 16 in] in *canc.* X, *om.* ABCKLMNTYβδZGH *margin* mt. 9, luc 7, io.

qwykede in þe ȝate. Þe þrydde was þe stynkynde careyne, þat he
qwykude in þe graue. And þis bytokneþ þre synnes þat God
forȝueþ in þis world. Þe fyrste bytokneþ ful concense for to don
a ȝeynes Godus wille but hit comeþ not owht in dede, as þe mayde
lay in þe hows. Þe secownde bytokneþ þe secownde synne whan a
man to wykkyd wille puttiþ a wickyd dede, but he comeþ not to
custoom as dyde Lazarus þat was beryud in a graue; and þis is þe
ȝonge man þat we speken of stoondyng in þe ȝate. Þe þridde
synne addiþ to þese two a long custoom to lye in synne, and þis is
Lazar þat lyþ stynkynde fowre dayes in his sepulcre.

Þis secownde is a wydwe sone for syche synnerus whanten God,
and so þey, faylyng of spowse of þe chyrche, may wel be clepud a
wydwe; but þei han sorwe of here synne and oþur neyȝeborwus
also. Crist byddiþ þe beere stonden whanne he sesuþ men of her
synne; and he towchyth þe body whanne he ȝyueþ hem
contricion; ⌐and⌐ he comawndeþ hit to rysen whanne he
comawndeþ meedful werkys. And þis man bygynneþ to speke
whan he þankyþ God in grace; and Crist ȝyueþ hym to hys
modur whanne he makyþ hym to helpon hys chyrche. And þus
wente Crist into Naym whanne he entryde newe to hys chyrche,
for Naym is as myche to seyn as 'flowyng' or 'mouyng'; for þe
chyrche fyrst flowyde wiþ synne, and syþ was meuyd to God by
bemys of þe Hooly Goost whan hit hadde grace to come to hym.

17 John 11: 1–46.

13 M, mt. 9 δ   þis] -s corr. D, þe MT, a E   17 qwykede] qwikened
CNαδEZG   in]wiþynne I   þe³]om. H   stynkynde]styngyng β   þat]
of lazar þat Nδ   18 qwykude]quykened NYαδEZG   þe]om. I   þis]þese
NI   bytokneþ]bytokenen NI   19 concense] consentyng Nδ, concience
I   for to]to E   20 godus wille]goddis wille, -dis wille canc. X, god
ABCKLMNTYβδEZG   owht]om. H   mayde]mayden δG   21 lay]⌐þat⌐
laye α, þat lay Nδ, lay ded H   22 to¹] to a Nδ   a] to a ABCKTYβδEXZ-
GH   he]it E   not]no L   23 is]was C   25 addiþ] h-eras. DX, addyd
T   to¹]or putteth to Nδ   þese]þe N, þis Y   a]om. N, ys a T   lye]lyue
F   26 lyþ . . . dayes]lieþ canc. foure daies lay stinkinge A, foure daies lay stynkynge
B, lieþ foure dayes styngynke EI   lyþ]lay α   stynkynde]styngynge β   se-
pulcre] graue A   27 þis] þe AFNαδEIJGH   whanten] wlaten H   28
faylyng] fallynge I   of¹] þe Fδ   spowse] þe spouse NH, spense C   may]
⌐and⌐ may M   clepud] calde NαδZ   a] om. I   29 synne and oþur] ⌐synne
and of her⌐ H   oþur] ⌐of⌐ oþere E, of oþere YδG, of here oþere I   30 þe] þis
Nδ   whanne] ⌐stille⌐ when α, stylle when Nδ   sesuþ]cesse α   31 he¹]om.
δ   hem] om. N   32 and] corr. D   he¹] ⌐he⌐ α, om. N   rysen] arise
AαIJG   34 þankyþ] þankid A   35 hym] hem I   to] to canc. X, om.
ABCFKLMNTYαβδEIJZGH   36 into]in T   newe] nowe N   to]in canc.
to DX, into NαδEGH, vnto C   37 to] for to BδE   38 flowyde] slowid

Wiþ Crist wenten his disciples and a greet rowte of folk, for   40
manye wheren helperus of God to bryngon his chyrche to riht
stat. Þe ȝate of þ[is] cytee is entre to religioun of Cristus chyrche,
in whyche ȝate been manye ȝong[e] men blynded and dede
gostly, for þei knowen not Cristus religiown, how hit passuþ alle
oþre. And so in þis ȝate ben two maner of dede men: to summe   45
lokiþ Crist and qwykuþ hem in grace and ȝyueþ hem power and
wille to come clene to his ordre, and wyte þat alle oþre ordres ben
charghows to men, as myche as þei adden to Cristes religioun, for
noon addicion is worþ but ȝif Godis lawe grownde hit. Summe
ben dede in þis ȝate þat Crist qwykenyþ not, but lasten in þere   50
olde errowrus to þer deþ day, and ben þese þat taken a lyf
vngrowndid clene in Godis lawe; and þese men lasten in þer
errour owt of þe bowndis of Godis lawe, and ben boren fro þe ȝate
to be beryut in helle. But þer is a pryue qwykyng þat God doþ ny
þe deþ þat we cannot telle of, but ȝif God wole schewon hit vs,   55
and þerfore foly iugement schulde be fled in þis mater. And þus
þese men þat beren þis beere to putte þis dede man in eurthe ben
men þat consenten and procuren to wyckydnesse. And so vpon
þes þre|synnys haþ God mercy here, but vpon þe furþe synne God   f.65v
cesuþ neuere to puny⌐s⌐che, for þei synnen to þer deþ and so aȝen   60
þe Holy Gost – þat God mut nede punysche wiþowten ende siþ
þis synne may haue noon ende in helle.
  In þis mater we schulde be war of perel of ypocrisye, for monye

L   meuyd] it moued Z   39 hym] god E   40 wiþ] and wiþ F   42 þe]
and þe αJH   þis] þe DFI   to] of K   of] to K   43 whyche] þe whuche
δ   ȝate] om. H   ȝonge] ȝongo D   blynded] blyndid, -id canc. G, blynde
ABCKLMTYβXZ, boþe blynde I   dede gostly] rev. N   45 so] om. K   in
. . . ben] ben þer in þis ȝate N   maner] maneres ABT   dede men] rev.
N   to] and F   summe] sum men F   46 qwykuþ] quykeneþ CNY-
αδEJZG   in] by δ   hem²] om. Kα   47 and . . . hit (49)] om.
Z   wyte] to wyte Nδ   ordres] om. E   48 as¹] in as E   as þei] om.
N   adden] haden C, handen L   49 is] it L   worþ] worthi C   summe] summe
men, men canc. DX, sum men ABCδI   50 qwykenyþ] aquykeþ AF, qwikeþ IH,
aquykeniþ J   51 errowrus] errour Nδ   and] as Z   52 clene] clene canc. B,
om. Aα   godis] cristis Nδ   53 bowndis] bondis ANYJH   þe²] godes lawe
canc. þe D, þis I   54 to¹ . . . helle] in helle to beryed N   qwykyng] quykenynge
ABCFKLMNYβδEIJZGH   god doþ] goþ H   ny] more ney I   55 wole]
wolde, -d- canc.α, wolde IJH   56 þerfore] for þis M   57 þese] ⌐þese⌐ Y, om.
T   þis beere] beȝere C   man] body N   58 men] body N   59 þes] þe
M   margin amos i M   haþ god] rev. AαI   60 neuere] nat M   puny-
sche] -s- corr. D, punysche it KZ   þei synnen] þer synne C   deþ] deth day
δ   61 þat] and þat Nδ   62 þis] om. LM   synne] om. Z   63
in . . . world (84)] om. Z   we schulde] rev. δ   schulde] shul⌐d⌐en F, shulen

feynen hem in statys and doon þe reuerse in her lyf. And ȝet þei
65 seyn þei beþ parfyter in þer lyf þan were þe furste clerkys ⌐of
Crist⌐. And þus enemyes to Cristys religioun chalanghen to ben of
his ordre, al ȝif þei doon euene ⌐þe⌐ reuerse to name þat þei
beren, as þe pope schulde be moste meke man, moste seruisable
and moste poore, as we ben tawte in seyn Petre þat was pope next
70 aftyr Crist. And now men seyn ⌐þat⌐ þe pope mot nede reuerse þis
ordenaunce and haue more power for to do þingus þat towchen
excellence. And þus byschopys, þat schulde be clerkys and poore
men as apostles weren, ben moste lordis of þis world and reuersen
apostles lif. Sum tyme monkys weren lewyde men, as seyntes in
75 Ierusaleem, and þanne þei kepton hemself fro synne, as seynt
Bernard beruþ witnesse. But now monkys ben turned vnto
lordys of þis world, moste ydel in Godus traueyle, and seyn þat
þei ben betture monkys þan were þe furste seyntys. And so frerys,
þat weren breþren in Crist and noȝt charghows to þe chyrche,
80 neþur in nowmbre, ne in cloþing, ne in mete, ne in howsyng, ben
euene turned aȝen fro þe fyrste lif of hem. And ȝet by þer
ypocrisye þei blynde þe chirche many gatis. And þus names of
offisys, and namus of vertewes also, ben chawnghed by ypocrisye,
and cursyd men rewlen þe world.

L   of¹] for C, of þe T   64 þe] þe canc. X, om. ABCKLMTYαβEIJGH   re-
uerse] reuerense C   lyf] lyuyng Nδ, lyfys T   and²] þat C   65 in þer lyf] in
here lyfe canc. αX, om. ABCKLMNTYβδEZGH   of crist] corr. D   66 to¹] of
AN   67 his] cristis T   al ȝif] alþoughe Nδ   euene] om. N   þe] corr. Dα,
om. TJH   reuerse] contrarie AI   name] þe name LNαδJGH   68 as þe
pope] a bisshop, bisshop modern corr. N   be] ⌐be⌐ TE   moste²] and most
IG   69 tawte] om. N   þat . . . pope] þe fyrst bisshop, bisshop modern corr.
N   70 crist] iesu crist N   þat] corr. DX   þe] þis I   mot] must
CI   72 þus] þese I   schulde] shulen F   73 apostles] þe apostles
αI   moste] nowe N, nowe most δ   þis] þis þis, 2nd canc. D   74 apostles] þe
apostles α   monkys weren] rev. AI   seyntes] seynt C   75 hemself] hem
E   76 vnto] to NYδI, into TH   77 seyn] ȝette þey sayn Nδ   79 chyrche]
puple δ   80 in²] ⌐in⌐ T, in canc. X, om. BKLMY   81 euene] nowe N, nowe euen
δ   82 ypocrisye] ypocrisinge I   þei] þe Y   chirche] churche by
N   gatis] weyes δ   83 offisys] office CT   also] ⌐also⌐ T, om. N   84
world] churche Nδ

Dominica xvii [post festum Trinitatis.
Euangelium] Sermo 17.

Cum intrasset Iesus domum cuiusdam principis phariseorum. Luce 14.

This gospel techeþ men how þei schal not by þer hyȝe statis
huyde þer synne and distorble þe ordenawnce þat Crist ⌈haþ⌉
made. *Þe story telliþ how [Iesu] entred into a pharisees hows on a
Satyrday to ete wiþ hym, and þei aspyeden hym* to take hym in defawte.
And a seek man in ydropisye was þere byfore Crist, and Iesu spak to wyse   5
men of þe lawe and to pharisees 'Wer hit be leueful to hele men in þe sabot?'
And þei weren stille, leste þat resoun wente aȝenes hem. *But Crist tok*
þis seke man and helyd hym þanne byfore hem. And Crist axede hem þis
demawnde þat 'Ȝif þer oxe or þer asse fel in þe dyche, wolden þei not drawen
hym owte anoon in þer sabat day?' And þei wisten wel þat þei schulden   10
byleue of þer owne lawe. *And þei myȝte not answeren hym* to denye
þat he axede. And vpon þis arguyde Crist þat myche more hit
were leueful to helpon in þe sabat a man put in more perel, siþ þis
werk is more spiritual and man is bettur þan a best.

MSS: D; ABCEFGHIJKLMNTXYZαδ; *β inc.* 64 hope here.

Dominica . . . euangelium] *om.* Z   sermo 17] *om.* BCFKNTYαδEIJXZGH
cum . . . phariseorum] fratres vocati estis N   cum] dum E   domum . . .
phariseorum] *om.* H   domum] in domum FTδIZG   cuiusdam . . . phari-
seorum] *om.* α   principis phariseorum] *om.* AFJ, pharisei δ   phariseorum] *om.*
BLMTYEIG, populorum C   luce 14] luce 10 L, mathei 22 C, ad eph' N   1
techeþ] telleth Cα, todaye techeth N   how . . . made (3)] curteysy boþe bodyly and
gostly and N   þer] *om.* Y   statis] staat ABCKLMTYαδEIJXZH, ⌈a⌉staat
G   2 distorble] destourbe δH   haþ] *corr.* D   3 þe . . . telliþ] sayth on þis
wyse N   how] when N   iesu] crist DF   entred] schulde entre N   into
. . . hows] *after* on . . . day N   on] vpon N   4 wiþ] brede wiþ N   hym²]
him *canc.* BαX, *om.* ACKLMNTYδEZG   5 ydropisye] þe dropesy TYαIJG-
H   þere] *om.* E   wyse] hym *canc.* wyse D, þe wise G   6 of] on α   to¹]
two T   pharisees] pharysee δ   wer] askede wer T   ʿbe] were ABCKLM-
NTYαδEIJZGH   men²] *om.* ABCKLMNTYαδEJZGH, it be F   sabot] sabot
day N   7 þat] ⌈þat⌉ E, at α, *om.* NH   wente] ȝede N   hem] hym C   8
hym] hem I   þanne . . . hem¹] bifore hem þan I   þanne] *om.* N   9 þat]
om. F   þer²] *om.* N   in] into NTδ   þe] a T   wolden . . . not] wolde
⌈he⌉ not Y   þei not] *rev.* N   10 hym] hem FαJG   owte] anoon out G, out vp,
vp *canc.* δ, vp NI   anoon] *canc.* Dδ, ⌈anon⌉ αH, *om.* ABIJG   in] on CN   þer
þe H   11 byleue] by bileue A, bi ſeue KG   of] in F, on LH, þat by Nδ, so
of E   not] *om.* Y   hym] to hym FI   12 axede] askede hem N   13 þe]
om. I   more] *om.* I   siþ] for Y   þis] þe I   14 werk] dede N   spi-

15　　And, for þe synne of þis men stoode in pruyde of þer statis, *Crist
telde hem a parable, techyng hem how þei schulden chese þe fyrste statis þat
God loued moste, þat was moste meke statis;* but þei chesen as
prowde men þe fyrste staatis to þe world. But Crist biddeþ in his
parable '*Whan þow art beden to þe feste, syt not in þe fyrste place, leste a
20　more worchipeful þan þow be bedon to þe same feste, and þe lord of þe feste
bidde þe ȝyf þis maan styde, and putte þe down owt of þi place, and þanne
schaltow bygynne wiþ schame for to hoolde þe laste place. And herfore,
whan þow art bedon, sit down in þe laste place, soo þat he þat haþ bedon þe
seye to þe* for þin mekenesse "*Frend, stey more vp.*" þanne schaltow
25　ha⌐ue⌐ worschipe and ioye byforn hem þat sytten at þe feste. For eche man
þat hyeþ hym* by presumpcion *schal be mekyd* by God, *and hee þat
mekiþ hym* in his sowle *schal ben hyȝed* by God.'

f.66　　Here we schal vndyrstonde|þat Crist spekiþ not here of worldly
feste, ne of place, for þanne his sentence were noht, siþ þanne
30　schulde strif be for plase, and onely one schulde doo Cristis
byddyng, and so Crist schulde ordeyne dissensioun wiþowte fruyt
among men. And herfore schulde we vndyrstande þat þis feeste ys
þe laste soper, þat schal ben in heuene of seyntis aftur þe day of
doom; and þe laste place at þis feste schulde be mannys
35　reputacioun, by whiche he schulde not presume to be in heuene
befor oþre, but reste mekely in þis þat he schal come to heuene.
Eche man schal hope for to come to blysse and, ȝif he lyue feblely
and make þis hope false, hymself is cause why his hoope is such;
for þis false hope ⌐þat⌐ summe men calle dispeyr schulde haue

ritual] gostly N　　man] a man αH　　a] suche a N　　15 men] ⌐two⌐ men
T　　statis] staat Y　　16 hem¹] *om.* LM　　hem²] him I　　chese] che
C　　17 loued] loueþ E　　þat] and þat N　　was] weren EZ　　moste²] þe
moste Nδ　　statis] state Nδ, staatis to þe world E　　þei] þe N　　18 staatis]
state⌐s⌐ is, is *canc.* α, is *eras.* J　　to] of B　　19 þe²] ⌐þe⌐ T, *om.*
Y　　20 þan] man *canc.* þan DαX, ⌐man þan⌐ δ　　be] art be N　　21 styde] place
N, place or stide δ　　owt] *om.* T　　þi] þe B　　22 schaltow] þou schalt
I　　for to] to H　　and] *om.* F　　herfore] þerfor Z　　23 sit] to a feste sitte AB,
to þe feest sitte E, sette þe δ　　24 þanne] and þan H　　25 haue]-ue *corr.* D, haue
more, more *canc.* C, haue more LIH　　and ioye] *om.* Z　　hem] men E　　26
hym] hymselfe here N, hymselfe δ　　schal] he *canc.* schal D, he shal αJ　　mekyd]
mekid lowȝ T　　27 in his sowle] his sowle *canc.* T　　by] in F　　28 here¹] crist as
N　　we schal] *rev.* T, we shuld α　　þat crist] *om.* N　　spekiþ] spak G　　not]
no L　　here²] *om.* E　　29 ne] no T　　of] worldely N　　his] þis M　　30
schulde strif] *rev.* AIH　　strif be] *rev.* FNδ　　onely one] vche one N, onely eche on
δ　　31 so] *om.* F　　crist schulde] *rev.* N　　34 at] of M　　feste] *om.* N　　36
befor] -n *canc.* D　　37 eche] for *canc.* ilke α, for eche IJG, and *canc.* eche H　　for to]
to Nδ1　　and ȝif] if þat N　　lyue] leue T　　38 þis] his LTYα　　hymself]
hemself I　　cause] þe cause Nδ　　39 þat] *corr.* D　　summe] *om.* N　　calle]

anoþir qualite, and hit schulde not be such whanne we witen þat 40
we schulden hope to come to heuene. Aftyr we make comparisoun bytwixen vs and oþre, and manye men for pruyde
hopen to passen oþre; and such presumpcion of hope is syttyng
here in hy3 place. We schulde reston in þis hope þat we schal
come to heuene, and leeue syche veyne comparisownys leste we 45
setten vs here to hy3e. And þis is þe laste place þat þe gospel
spekiþ of. And þus such false presumpcion of hey3nesse of stat,
and aftir þis presumpcion of hey3nesse in heuene, makiþ a man to
comen at þe laste to þe lowest place in þe world, þat is to seyn to
depe helle, þat is þe myddyl of þe world. 50

And so spekiþ þe gospel on two wey3es of þe laste plase: þe laste
place here stondiþ in meke reputacion, but þe laste place at þe
day of doom stondiþ in dampnacion. And so knitteþ Crist wel þe
helyng of þis ydropisye, for ydropisye is an euyl of false
greetnesse of mannys lymys and comeþ of vnkyndly watur 55
bytwyxe þe flesch and þe skyn, so pruyde of worldly goodis þat
ben vnstable as þe watyr makiþ a man in ydropisye and falsely
presumen of hymself; as monye men in greet astat and in richessys
of þis world þenken þat þei schulden þus in heuene be byforn
oþur men, for, as þei supposen now þey lyuen to God after þer 60
astat and so þei profi3ten more in þis world þan doon men vndir
hem, and aftyr þat þei profi3ten more, þei schullen ben hey3ere

clepen ABCFKLMTYEIJXGH   schulde] sch *canc/*. schulde D   40 anoþir]
oþere H   41 to¹] ⌐for⌐ to C, for to ABFKLMNTYδEIXZG   42 and²] ⌐and⌐ T,
om. N   43 to] for to E   presumpcion] comparisoun E   hope] pride
E   syttyng] s- *on eras. corr*. D   44 hy3] hyere δ   we¹] bot *canc*. we α, but we
JH   schulde] shulen FL   schal] schal, -den *canc*. a *altered from* u B, schuden
CδI   45 leeue] loue I   comparisownys] comparysoun Nδ   46 setten] sitten
LJ   þe²] þis N   47 spekiþ] telleþ I   presumpcion¹] presumpcions
I   of¹ . . . presumpcion (48)] *om*. M   48 a] *om*. N   49 þat] and þat
δ   þat . . . world] *margin* B, *after* plase (51) *marked for transposition* T   to³] ⌐to⌐ α, *om*.
CZ, to þe N   50 þe¹] *om*. FLMTJGH   myddyl] middes α   51 spekiþ . . . þe³]
on eras. corr. D   spekiþ] speke α   gospel] worlde N   on] of T   wey3es]
wyse N   þe²] ⌐þe⌐ TZ   plase] place ⌐here⌐ T   52 here . . . in] stondeþ here
in I   stondiþ in] is N   meke] moche I   53 knitteþ . . . wel] crist knyttiþ
wel KNH, knitteþ I   crist wel] *rev*. Cδ   54 ydropisye¹] in dropesy αJ   as]
ri3t as I   55 mannys] mennys ABCKLMNTYαδJZGH   comeþ] it comeþ
FI   vnkyndly] vnkuynde N, an vnkynde δ   56 þe¹] *om*. T   skyn] hide
α   of] and I   57 þe] *om* Y   ydropisye] þe dropesy TδI   falsely] so *canc*.
falsely α, so falsly JH   58 presumen] many men presumen F, to presume
E   hymself] hemsilf FH   monye] *om*. G   astat] state N   in²] ⌐in⌐
δ, *om*. BN   richessys] ryches ACFMNYαδIJGH   59 þenken] þei þenken
F   þus] be *canc*. þus α, be þus NδIJH   be] *om*. NδIH   60 men] *om*.
N   lyuen] *om*. G   after] euene aftir E   61 astat] staat ABLMNTδX-
H   doon] *om*. N   men] oþer *canc*. men α, oþere men FJH   62 hem] hem I

in heuene. And so þei seyn, as þei schullen hope to come to heuene, soo schulde þei hopen here to ben hey3ere in heuene. But
65 syche prowde men and presumtuouse of here astat schulden traueylen in vertewys þat þei bygyle not hemself. And þerfore techiþ þe wyse man þat, ay þe more þat þow be here, ay þe more meke schuldistow be in alle maner of mekenesse. And so, 3if þow be greet here, þow schuldest ⌐reste¬ in þe laste place, and suppose
70 mekely of þiself wiþowte syche comparisouns. For who is he þat may seye he seruyþ God aftyr his stat? And so statis here and state in heuene late or neuere acorden togydre, for fewe men here or noone serueþ God euene to þer stat. And so stat of men may be cause of þer dampnyng depe in helle, and for vneuene seruyse
75 here in statis may men be ful lowe in heuene. Þe lessoun of þis gospel is luytel knowen in þe chirche, for lordys stryuen wiþ hemself, and religiows among hemself, abowten heynesse of her state. And þe roote of ⌐al¬ þis is pruyde. And þei schulden wyte þat statis here ben harmful to men but 3if men aftir þer statis seruen
80 trewly to þer God, for falsenesse in statis makiþ men to be lowe or dampnyde.

---

67 Ecclus. 3: 20.

don, don *canc.* δ, hem doun N þei schullen] *rev.* E 63 and . . . heuene[1] (64)] *om.* N schullen] shulden A 64 schulde] shul αδ 65 astat] staat ABCKLMNTYαβIJZG, owne stat H 66 vertewys] goode vertues N hemself] hem hemsilf G þerfore] herfore E 67 man] men N þat[1]]*om.* B ay[1]] euere AMNδI more[1]] gretter and mare Z þow] ⌐þou¬ LM be] arte α here] hey3ere TI ay[2]] euer AYαIJGH, so muche Nδ þe[3]] *om.* Nδ *margin* ecc' iii N, ecclesiastici 3 in quanto magnus es humiliate in omnibus Z 68 meke] *om.* Nδ schuldistow] þou shuldist AαIJH be] be meke Nδ of] *om.* N mekenesse] godenesse L 69 reste] *corr.* D 70 of] on α þiself] þi liif Y syche] *om.* Nδ comparisouns] cumparisoun AFNδ-I who] what Z 71 he] *om.* β, þat he δ, her he H stat] astate δEI here] here in erþe T state] statis ABLNTδEIGH 72 or[1]] eþer G 73 noone] elles none Nδ euene] here I to] aftir C stat[1]] astate δEIG stat[2] stat⌐is¬ X, states ABCKLMNTYαβδEIZG be cause of] be *canc.* cause of, of *canc.* αX, cause ABCKLMTYβEIZG 74 dampnyng] dampnacioun B and] *om.* β 75 here] *om.* H statis] staat I heuene] helle T þis] *om.* β 76 knowen] -en *on eras. corr.* D, coud ABCKLMYβEIXZ, tolt by T þe] *om.* M 77 and . . . hemself[2]] *om.* I religiows] religiouns FJ, men of haly kirk Z among] *on eras. corr.* D of her] here of N 78 state] astaat I al] *corr.* D, al *canc.* X, *om.* CKLMNTYβδIJZG is pruyde] pride G, pride ⌐is sechyng of hey3e statis¬ T 79 to] ⌐vn¬to X, vnto ABCKLMTYαβEZGH but 3if] for fewe T statis[2]] state N, astatis I 80 to[1]] ⌐to¬ α, *om.* FJH 81 dampnyde] dampned in helle Z, dampned and þerfore preye we to god to meke vs so here þat we be brou3te to þat blysse þat euere more schal laste and þerto preye we to god wyth oure pater noster N

Dominica xviii [post festum Trinitatis.
Euangelium.] Sermo 18.

Accesserunt ad Iesum pharisei audientes. Mathei xxii.

This gospel telliþ how Crist destruyde sectis, techyng vs how we
schulden traueile suwyng[e] Crist in þis. Þe story of þe gospel seyþ
þat, *whan þe pharisees hadden herd þat Crist hadde stemned saduces,|on of* f.66v
þe pharisees þat was a doctour of lawe temptide Crist on þis wyse, and
axede hym þis questioun '*Mayster, which is a greet maundement in þe* 5
lawe?' And Iesu seyde to hym þus ' þow schalt loue þe Lord þi God of al þin
herte, in al þi sowle and in al þi mynde. Þis is þe furste and þe moste
maundement of alle.' And þis maundement is þre of þe furste table,
for þre of þe furste table techen for to loue God and contenyþ þre
partys, answeryng to þe Trinnite. Hit is seyd comunly þat in tyme 10
of Crist weren þre sectis of religioun, pharisees, saducees and
essees, but of þe two furste makyþ þis gospel mencion. Þe furste
was moste myȝty, and þerfore hit lastyde lengust for habundaunce of goodis, and long[e] rootyng in þe secte defenden þes
sectis and maken hard to destryen hem. But Crist destruyde þese 15

MSS: D; ABCEFGHIJKLMNTXYZαβδ; Pᵗ *inc.* 76 of þis new.

Dominica . . . euangelium] *om.* FZ   sermo 18] *om.* BFKNTYαδEIJXZG-
H   accesserunt . . . audientes] pharisei audientes quod iesus silentium imposuisset
saducees G, gracia dei data est vobis N   accesserunt] dcesserunt I   pharisei
audientes] *om.* H   audientes] *om.* MTα   mathei 22] *on* eras. corr. D, mathei
22 . . . 1 ad cor' N, *om.* L   1 gospel . . . þis (2)] day telleth N   how¹] hou þat
G   2 suwynge] suwyngo D, to folowe Z   þe²] þis BTI   seyþ] telleth δ, *om.*
N   3 þe] *om.* I   hadde] *om.* Nδ   stemned] stonyed BFYGH, stonʳyˡed C,
stoned K, stouned Tα, putte sylence to þe N, put sylence to δ   saduces] þe saducees
E, saduceis or put silence to þe saduceis H   4 a] *om.* H   of] of þe δH   5
hym] of hym E   a] þe δ   maundement] co-*canc.* D, comaundement NY   6
to hym] *om.* LM   þe lord þi] þi lord ABIH, þi lorde þi CKLNαδJ, þi lord god
T   7 in¹] and CT   and¹] *om.* BT   þe²] *om.* CαJH   8 þis] ʳin¹ þis T, þis
is þe fyrste N   maundement] comaundment Z   is] of N   þre] þe firste of þre
AB, on of þre I   of²] in I   9 for to] for *canc.* to X, to ABCKLMNTYβδ-
EIZGH, þe to J   10 tyme] þe tyme T   11 þre] þes þre C   religioun]
religious ABCKLMTYβEIXZG, relygyouse men Nδ   saducees] and saduceys
NTδ   12 but] weren þe thrydde but N   þe¹] þes C, *om.* ZH   two furste] *rev.*
I, twa of þe first Z   þis] þe NI   13 moste] þe most C   myȝty] myghty secte
Nδ   hit lastyde] lasteth hyt N   14 longe] longo D   defenden] defendede
NδZ   15 and] defended and δ   maken] makyng hit N, makynge T, maken hyt

sectis and sauyde þe persoones, as Powle and Nichodeme weren
maad by grace cristene men. And herfore seiþ þis gospel þat Crist
stemnide saducees, not þat he destruyde hem, siþ he louyde þer
personys; and so Crist destruyde þe errours of pharisees, as he
20 destruyde þe erroures of oþur two.

Summe men þenken licly þat þis doctour þat here temptyde
Crist dredde hym of his secte þat Crist schulde destruyen hit, ⌈or
ellis enfeblen hyt⌉ as he destruyde þe myddul secte; and þis is
more licly þan þat þis doctour dide þis for veyn glorye, or to ben
25 hoolden wys, or to lerne Godis lawe. He clepyd Crist reuerently
'maister', for hit ⌈is⌉ maner of ypocrites and of sophistrus to
phaghen, and to speke plesauntly to men but for an euyl entent.
But owre pharisees today doon wel werse, for þei putten obac
Godis lawe and magnifye þer ordres, and þus þei faylen in þe
30 furste maundement and so in alle oþre. And so manye men
trowen not ne supposon þat þei be men of holy chyrche, but
supposen þat þei ben lymes of þe fend. But he loueþ God of al his
herte þat loueþ hym of al his witt, and he loueþ God in al his lif
þat loueþ hym in alle his werkys, for cristene men lyuen in God
35 and ben meuyd to alle here werkis, for Crist is fourme of God, and
in Crist we lyuen, as Powle seiþ; and herfore we schulle not take
þe word of owre God in veyn. Þe þridde part of þis maundement,

---

36 Acts 17: 28.

δ, made Z   16 þe] þes E   weren . . . grace (17)] by grace were made
N   17 by . . . men] cristen men bi grace H   and] om. Cβ   herfore] þese þre
I, þerfor Z   þis gospel] crist in þis gosspel I,   þis] þe N, þus þe H   18
stemnide] stonyede FYG, stonnede K, stened T, stoned or stilled CH, putte sylence to
N   saducees] þe saduceys NδEH   19 þe] ⌈þe⌉ A, om. I   of] of þe
CNδE   20 þe] also þe N, ⌈þe⌉ Y, om. I   oþur] þe oþer AB, þese oþer N   21
men] om. Nδ   licly] ly3tly M   temptyde] þus temptid H   22 or . . . hyt
(23)] margin corr. D   or] on L   23 destruyde] enfeblede N, enfebIede or
dystruyede δ, destroie it as he destroyede I   24 licly] ly3tly M   þan] om.
I   þat] ⌈þat⌉ J, om. AME   þis²] om. A, þus NδI   ben hoolden] biholden
AL   25 lerne] lere H   clepyd] calde Nαδz   26 maister] om. N   is] corr.
D   maner] þe manere NδEI   to] for to N   27 to¹] om. BCFKLNTYZ-
G   plesauntly] plesyngly NY   but] ⌈bot⌉ Z, om. IJ   an] om. A   28
today] om. N   for] nowe for N   þei] þe E   obac . . . lawe (29)] goddes
lawe obacke N   ordres] ordre EZ   30 maundement] comaundement
Z   and² . . . fend (32)] om. Z   so²] om. A   31 men] om. H   32 þat]
om. E   þei] om. M   but . . . þing (45)] om. N   33 of] in E   in] of
I   34 in¹] of I   for . . . werkis (35)] margin Y, om. M   35 ben] ⌈goode men⌉
ben T   to] in him to H   here] his J   for] ⌈by crist⌉ for T   36 lyuen]
leuen T   powle] seynt poul J   herfore] þerfor Z   schulle] shuld α   37

answeryng to þe Holy Goost, byddiþ þe loue þi God in al þi
muynde, siþ he is muynde of þe Fadyr and of þe Sone and loue of
hem two. For vndyrstondyng in a man and acte of hym þat is his   40
lyf and reflexioun of lif, þat is muynde and wille of sowle,
bytookneþ to cristene men her God þat is þe Trinnite. And
herfore bydduþ Godes lawe haue mynde to holde þin haliday.
And þanne we loue þe Trinnite parfiȝtly as we schulden, wanne
we louen hit more þan any oþir þing. And, as manye men   45
þenkon, ȝif þis pharisee kept[e] þis, he schulde leue þ[is] straunge
secte as schulde þese newe religious.

   þe secounde maundement þat is seuene byddiþ þe loue þin neiȝebore as
þow louest þiself, and þat artow tawt by kynde. And in þese two
maundementes hanguþ alle þe lawe and þe prophetis. And whan þe   50
pharisees weren gadryd, Crist axede hem a questioun of þing þat þei
schulden byleue, what hem powte of þe kynde of Crist, and whose sone
Crist is. And þei seyden 'He is Dauydus sone'. And Crist replyed aȝen þis
how Dauid clepuþ hym his lord, siþ Crist is Dauyd sone and porere
man þan Dauyd was. Þe salm telliþ how Dauyd seyde of þe Fadyr   55
and of þe Sone ' Þe Lord þe Fadyr seyde to my Lord, sitte vpon my riȝt
syde as long[e] as I putte þine enemyes in helle a stool vndyr þine feet'. And
syþ þis dampnyng schal ben euere, God grauntyde here to Crist
þat|he schulde euere sitte in heuene on his Fadyr riȝt hand. For,   f.67v
ȝif Dauyd clepuþ hym Lord, how is poore Crist Dauyd sone? And þei   60

---

55 Ps. 109: 1.

---

word] word *on eras. corr.*/me *canc.* D, wordis, -is *canc.* β, name δE   38 answeryng]
⌜is⌝ answeringe T   byddiþ] ⌜and⌝ biddiþ T   39 of²] *om.* CKLMTYβXZ-
G   loue] þe loue C   of³] *om.* H   40 in] of E   þat . . . lyf (41)] *om.*
E   41 reflexioun] þe refleccioun B   lif] ⌜his⌝ *corr. eras.* lif D, his *canc.* lif
Z   sowle] þe soule δH   42 her] here I   43 holde] kepe E   44 þe] þis
ABCKLMTYβδEXZG   schulden] schulden do δ   45 þing] thynges
C   and . . .religious (47)] *om.* Z   46 þenkon] þanne konne I   þis¹] þe M,
þese Nα I   pharisee] pharisees DNαδI, farisees, -s *canc.* Y   kepte] kepton DN-
I   he] þey NI, *on eras. corr.* D   schulde] schulden DNI   leue] ⌜haue left⌝ M,
lowe β   þis²] þer DFI   straunge] stronge L, false N   47 as . . . religious]
and take to cristes relygyoun N   þese] alle þes E   religious] religiouns
BFJ   48 is] þis L, conteyneþ δ   þat is seuene] ⌜þat is seuene⌝ T, *om.*
N   seuene] þe seuenþe H, euen like to þis α   loue] þat þou loue N   as
. . . kynde (49)] *om.* N   50 alle] *om.* Z   þe²] *om.* KTδ, alle þe H   51 hem] of
hem K   of . . . byleue (52)] *om.* N   þing] þyngis L   52 hem . . . crist] say
ȝe of iesu N   53 crist is] is he N   53 he is] *om.* N   54 clepuþ] clepide ACLT,
calles α, calde NδZ   55 telliþ] sayth δ   seyde] sayth NδI   56 of] of *canc.*
X, *om.* ABCKLMNTαβδZGH   þe³] þi H   vpon] ⌜þou⌝ vpon K, on
H   57 longe] longo D   þine . . . helle] in helle þin enemyes I   enemyes] e/
enemyes D   58 grauntyde] grauntiþ YI   60 clepuþ] clepe CE, calle Nα, calleth

myʒte not here answere Crist, ne dyrst[e] not axen hym more fro þat day.
And her conuyctude Crist þese men of open vntrewþe in þer byleue,
and so mente pryuely þat þese sectis schulden be destruyde, siþ he
schal repreue þe world of ⌐þe⌐ synne of vntrewþe. And hit semeþ
65 to manye men þat alle þese sectis synnen þus, for þei loue not þer
God as þe gospel biddeþ here, for ʒif þei louedon wel God, þei
schulden kepe þis word of hym. Generally þese newe sectis louen
more þer owne ordre þan þei doon þe ordre of Crist whiche he ʒaf
his owne persone, and þanne þei louen her secte more þan þei
70 louen þe secte of Crist. Þis secte of Crist by þat is lesse þat þei
putten in þes newe sectis, siþ þei kepyng Cristis secte by þat
maden hys ⌐secte⌐ moore. And hit is on to loue a þing, and to
wylle þat þing good; but þei wolden þat al þis world were suget
⌐vn⌐to þer secte. And, Lord!, ʒif þat men wolden vndirstonden
75 what hit is to loue a þing, and whanne men loue þer God ouer
alle oþer þyng, þanne heresye of þese newe sectis and oþer errours
in þe world, schulden be more knowen vnto folc þan þei ben now
for ypocrisye. Þese ypocrites seyn þat her sectis, and alle þe dedys
þat þei doon, is growndyt vpon Crist as is Cristus religioun, and so
80 þei han none newe ordres bute newe customys þat þei mow leue.
And so schulde þei seye by resoun þat þer beþ not manye ordres
of freris, ne accepcions of persones, to helpen or to punysche men,

δZ   61 here . . . crist] onswere crist here I   dyrste] dyrsto D   not²] no
more IH, *om.* NE   more] *om.* I   fro] for F   62 her] *om.* L   conuyctude]
conuicte C, coueitude I   in] of G   63 so] so ⌐he⌐ H, he Nδ   pryuely] crist
priuely Z   þese] pharisees Z   destruyde] dampned L   64 þe²] *corr.*
D, *om.* NYE   of²] and N   and . . . lawe (85)] *om.* Z   65 þat] þat þat
E   alle] *om.* Nδ   þei] þi β   66 þe] þis N   here] *om.* Nδ   for]
herfore I   þei¹] ʒe I   god²] þer god E   þei²] þan *canc.* þei α, þan þey
JGH   68 more] *om.* G   owne] *om.* N, newe H   whiche] þe whuche
Nδ   he] *om* L   69 his] in his CYβ   þanne] ⌐þan⌐ α, *om.* J, þoughe
N   her . . . more] more her secte Nδ   secte] sectis CαJH   70 þis] þe I, and
so þe H   by] is lasse *canc.* by D   þat²] by þat þat T   71 kepyng] kepen
Nδ   72 maden] þey maken N, þei maden I   hys] cristis BN   secte] *corr.*
D   73 wylle] wilne CNβδH   þis] þe I   suget vn-] *on eras. corr.* D   74
vnto] to LNYδE   and] o FαJG   ʒif] leeue Nδ   þat] ⌐þat⌐ T, *om.*
KYG   75 what] þat N   hit is] is C   þer] *om.* N   god] good M   76
oþer þyng] *on eras. corr.* D, oþer þingis A, þyng E   heresye] heresies I   77
þe] þis E   schulden] schul δ   vnto] to
Nδ   78 ypocrisye] her ypocrisie F, ypocrisies I   seyn] seen
Pᵗ   her . . . and] *om.* E   her] alle here I   79 is¹] *on eras. corr.* D, bene
CKNEH   vpon] on H   as] and AB   80 none] now none T   þei²] me
T   81 schulde þei] *rev.* AI, þey schulden, *marked for rev.* J   þat] and þat I   82
accepcions] accepcyoun N   of persones] ⌐of persones⌐ α, *om.* J   83 ordre]

siþ eche man of Cristus religioun is of alle maner ordre. And so
lawe of apostatas, and oþur rewlys þat þei han fownden, schylde
be contrarye to hymself, as frerys dedus reuerse þis lawe.   85

ordres P^t   84 lawe] lawes N   schylde] shul β   85 hymself] hemsilf
ACFNαβδP^tEIJH   lawe] lawe and þerfore thruste we vnto one þat is goddes iesu
sone for he is sothfaste god and mon whos lawe may neuere more fayle and ȝif we bysyly
kepe þis lawe of heuene blysse we schul not fayle and ȝif we bysye vs in oþer reules and leue
cristes reule vnkepte we schul neuere come to blysse for al þat oþer reule may do preye we
þerfore vnto crist þat he vs reule thurghe hys grace to come to heuen to be wyth hym in
ioye and blysse þat euere schal laste and preye we bysyelye vnto hym þat he in vs duelle to
whyles we in þis worlde lyuen wyth pater noster etc. N

Dominica xix [post festum Trinitatis.
Euangelium.] Sermo 19.

Ascendens Iesus in nauiculam. Mathei 9.

This gospel telluþ of a miracle þat Crist dude byfor þe peple and
þerwiþ repreuyde þe scribys; and how he doþ awey synne. Þe
story telluþ how *Iesu steyȝ into a boot and cam to his cytee*; and hit is
seyd comunly þat he rowede to Galilee, and cam into Nazareth
5 þat was citee of his byrþe. *And þere þei browten hym a seek man by
palesye lyeng in a bed. And Iesu, seyng her byleue, seyde vnto þe seke man
'Haue tryst sone, for þi synnes be now forȝyue þe.'* And summe scribes
seyden wiþynnen hemself '*Iesu blasfemyþ in þis word.*' And whanne Crist
saw here þowtes ⌐wiþynne¬, *he seyde wharto þei þowten þus euyle in þer*
10 *hertys*; and by þis word he tawte hem þat he was God, for only
God may þis wyse wyte what a man þenkuþ wiþynne. Crist axede
hem '*Wheþur is hyt lyȝtur to seyn "þi synnes ben forȝyue þee"? or ellys to
seye "rys and goo"?*', as ȝif Crist wolde meue þis resoun: he þat haþ
power to do þe ton, haþ power to do ⌐hem¬ boþe. *And Iesus seyde
15 'For ȝe schullen wyte þat I haue power to forȝyue synne', he seyde to þe man
in palesye, 'Rys and tak þi bed anoon, and goo hol into þin hows'.* And he
roos and wente into his hows on þat maner þat Crist bad hym. *And þe
peple seyng þis þing dredden and glorifieden God þat ȝaf sych power to men*
as to Crist and his disciples.

MSS: D; ABCEFGIJKLMTXYZαβδPᵗ; N *inc.* 42 -selfe and to.

Dominica . . . euangelium] *om.* Z   sermo 19] sermo 9 β, *om.* BFKTYαδPᵗEIJXZ-
G   in] *om.* E   1 of] *om.* K   2 þerwiþ] *om.* Pᵗ   3 and² . . . byrþe (5)]
þis citee was capharnaum in þe cuntre of galilee þat was þe cuntre of cristis owen birþe
on eras. corr. M   4 into] to E   5 hym] to hym Cα   6 vnto] into C, to δ-
E   þe]þis ABCFKLMTYβδPᵗEXZG   7 for] *om.* A   8 hemself] hymsilf
β   þis] his C   word] world, -l- *canc.* α, world Pᵗ   whanne crist] crist when he
δ   9 wiþynne] *corr.* D   he] *om.* Y   þei þowten] thynke ȝhe Cβ, thoȝt þai
Z   þer] ȝowre Cβ   11 þis] ⌐on¬ þis J, in þis BG, þus α   wyse] ⌐wise¬
αPᵗJ   what] whan M   crist] and crist J   12 is hyt] *rev.* CFLTYδIG   to²
. . . go (13)] arise and go δ   13 as] and I   ȝif] þauȝ δ   haþ] *om.*
Pᵗ   14 hem] *corr.* D   hem boþe] *rev.* M   15 ȝe] he β   forȝyue] for
β   16 palesye]þe palisie βI   þi]þe Tβ   17 roos] aroos A   into] vnto T,
hool into E   18 þis] þe puple seenge þis β   19 crist] iesu ABCKLMTYβδPᵗ-

Þis story of Crist may bytokene þe lyf þat Crist lyuede here, so   20
þat þe takyng of his boot bytookne his manheede, or þe body of
his modyr, for mannys body is lyk a boot. In þis boot Crist wente
ouer þe watur of peynus of þis worᶜlᶦd, and wente not only ᶜinᶦto
heuene, þat is propre cyte of Crist, but into Nazareth in whyche
Crist dude þis miracle. But boþe men and aungelys offren to Crist   25
mannys kynde þat was smyton in palesye. For proprete of ᶜþisᶦ
euyl pallesye is a syknesse growndet in senwys of a man, þe
whyche ᶜsenewisᶦ ben vnstable to meuen a man a[s] þei schulden;
and moystnesse of þese senewys þat ben wlappude in moyste þing
is a cause of þis euyl, as philosophrus seyn. Schakyng in þe palesye   30
is vnstableᶜnesᶦ of byleue, for eche article of þe trowþe|schulde   f.67v
haue a senwe for to ledon hit, and alle þe articles schulde comen
of Crist þat is heed of hooly chirche. And, for þese þat offredon þis
man ben o persone wiþ hym, þerfore byddiþ þe gospel wel þat
Cristys sone schulde tristen in hym. And Crist for3yueþ hym furst   35
his synne of vntrewþe þat he was ynne, for vntrewþe is þe fyrste
synne þat comeþ ᶜvnᶦto man. And hit fel not to þis Lord to 3yue
but a myche 3ifte, syþ eche 3ifte þat man 3yueþ schulde answere
to þe 3yuer. But scribys þat knowe not Cristis godhede seyn þat
Crist blasfemyd in þis, for al only God may for3yue synnes. But   40
Crist techeþ þat he is God by þe werkys þat he doþ, for hyt is
yliche li3t to do myracles by hymself and to for3yue synne, for

EXZ   his] his to, *marked for rev.* α, to his β   20 þis] þe MI   bytokene] be
taken β   crist²] ᶜcristᶦ he α, he J, *om.* β   21 his¹] þis TδPᵗ   boot] booth
T   bytookne] bitokeneþ ABCFTYαPᵗIJG   22 mannys] a mannes αI-
J   lyk] siche L   in . . . boot²] *om.* Pᵗ   23 world] -l- *corr.* D   not]
out F, *om.* E   into] in *corr.* DX, to δE   24 into] to δ   nazareth] capharn'
M   whyche] þe wiche T   25 crist¹] he Z   þis] *om.* E   but] ᶜbutᶦα, *om.*
EJ   offren] offeriden E   crist²] god E, crist, -is *eras.* J, cristis I   26 mannys
kynde] mankynde AYαPᵗIJZG   smyton] sumtyme Pᵗ   palesye] þe palesie
EG   þis] *corr.* D   27 pallesye] of palasye δ   a¹] *om.* T   senwys] þe
synous αδG   man] mannis body I   28 senewis] *corr.* D   vnstable] vnstablid
I   as] aft D   29 senewys] synnes Pᵗ   wlappude] wrappid AMδIJ, whappid
F, shapid Pᵗ   moyste þing] moystyng β, moystryng Pᵗ, moystrþing T   moyste]
moost G   þing] þing, -is *canc.* Y, þyngis L   30 is] *om.* L   a] *om.* YE-
Z   þis] *om.* β   31 vnstablenes] -nes *corr.* D   of¹] in þe Pᵗ   þe] *om.*
BEI   trowþe] trowe LM, bileue I   32 for to] to Fδ   þe] þes ABI, þe alle þe
E   33 of¹] to L   hooly] *om.* β   offredon] offeren β   34 ben] weren
E   35 schulde] schul β   hym²] *om.* Y   37 vnto] vn *corr.* D, to δ, vnto a
PᵗI   to¹] vnto C   38 myche] greet A   þat] a Pᵗ   man] a mon
δ   39 knowe] knewen FKZ   seyn] sayden δPᵗZ   40 god] crist δE   41
þe] *om.* G   42 li3t] *om.* δ   to¹] for *canc.* to DX, do A   hymself] hemsilf
YαJG   synne] synnes ABCFKLMTYαβPᵗEIJZG, men her sunnes N   43 none]

none but God may do þese þingus. And herfore Crist helude
mankynde of his goostly palesye, and putte byleue in oþur men
45 þat Crist hadde power to do þus. And þus wente mankynde þat
God hadde ordeynot into blysse, from errour of þis olde synne
into þe hows of Cristis chyrche. But here men dowten of þe lettre wheþur prelatis may forȝyue
synne. And hit semyþ þat þei may, for prestis may assoyle of
50 synne; and hit is al on to forȝyue synne and to assoylen of þe same
synne. And hit semeþ þat prestys may not forȝyue synnes vnto
men, for þer is noo synne heere but ⌐ȝif⌐ hit be offence of God –
but no man may forȝyue þis but ȝif hit be God hymself. And so hit
semyþ þat owre prelatis may not here forȝyue synne. Soþ hit is
55 þat men may here forȝyue trespaas doon to hem, and remytte
mannys iniurye as myche as in hem is, but not remytten vttyrly
synne doon aȝenys God. Heere hit is nede to vnderstonde how
prestis assoyle men of synne, and how prestis forȝyue synne, for
boþe ben conceyuede wel and euyle. Prestis may assoyle of synne
60 ȝif þei accorden wiþ keyes of Crist; and ȝif þei discorde fro þe
keyes þei feynen ⌐hem⌐ falsely to assoylen. And so on two maneris
may men ben assoylud of her synne: furst pryncipally of God
whanne Godis iniurye is forȝyuen, and þe secounde ys assoylyng
by atturne þat prestis han and, ȝif þis assoylyng be trewe, þei kepe
65 þe bowndys þat God ȝaf hem. And þis assoylyng han prestis as

no man δ   herfore] þerfore NZ   crist] god E   45 hadde] haþ I   do]
om. Pᵗ   þus¹] þis I, om. Z   46 into] vnto ABCFKLMNYαβPᵗEJXZG, to
δ   þis] his ABCKLMNTYαβδPᵗEZG   47 into] in β, to I   48 but . . . men
(82)] om. Z   but] and E   þe] þee D   lettre] texte N   49 of] men canc.
of B, men of J   50 forȝyue] assoyle of on eras. corr. X, assoile of BCFKLMNTYδPᵗEG,
soyle of β, assoile men of, men canc. A, ⌐for⌐ȝiue I   assoylen of] forȝeue on eras. corr. of
canc. X, forȝyue ABCFKLMNTYβδPᵗEG   51 synne] om. E   þat] om.
B   prestys] prelatis L   synnes] synne FI   vnto] to Nδ   52 heere] om.
T   ȝif] corr. Dα   offence] offendit β   of] to on eras. of of J, to
FKLNYαδG   god] god himself δ   53 and] of his special grace and δ   54
may . . . here] on eras. corr. D, here may not Pᵗ   not] om. Y   55 þat] om.
E   men] om. Y   to] in L   hem] hemselfe N   56 mannys] mennes
NαG   as¹] at β   hem] hym Cα   57 heere] and here δ   vnderstonde
how] on eras. corr. D   58 how] om. L   59 euyle] eke euyle E   60 keyes] þe
keyes Nδ, þe keye I   and] om. β   fro] hem fro L   þe] þeʳˢ⌐ α, þes
ABCKMNYβδPᵗEIG   61 keyes] keyes of crist N   hem] corr. Dα   falsely]
fastly I   on . . . men (62)] men mowen on two maneres N   on] vpon
δ   maneris] manere J   62 may men] rev. A   synne] synnes AL-
M   furst] and first A   63 and] om. LNδG   þe] om. βG   ys assoylyng]
rev. C   64 atturne] autorite ⌐atorney⌐ C, autoryte N   þat] þaʳt trewe⌐
K   þis] here canc. ⌐þes⌐ δ, her N, om. I   65 þe] om. L   ȝaf] ȝeueth

vikerys of Godys wylle. And þer ly⌈e⌉n manye disseytus in sych
absolucion for, ȝif þis assoylyng be trewe, hit mut acorde wiþ
Cristys assoylyng; and so to sych assoylyng is nedful boþe wyt and
power. And so on two manerys may a man remytten or dymytten
trespaas þat is don to hym, and so remytte synne: furst remytte   70
wrong of God, þat ys propred vnto God, or ellys dymytte wrong
of his broþur in þat þat hit is maad aȝenys hym. And so remission
is complete þat perteyneþ only to God; or ellis remission
incomplete þat men schulden haue generally, for ellys Crist
wolde not teche men to preye on þis maner 'forȝyue vs, Lord,   75
owre dettis of synne, as we forȝyuen owre dettours'. Ȝif any man
wyle telle moore pleynly þis sentence by Godis lawe, I wole
mekely assent[e] þerto, ȝif þei grounden þat þei seyn; and ȝif any
man preue þis fals þat I haue seyd here now, or aȝenys Godis
lawe, I wole reuokon hit mekely. But wel I marke þat þis gospel   80
seiþ þat 'God ȝaf *sych* power to men', but þis gospel seiþ not þat
'God ȝaf *þis* power to men'.

---

75 Matt. 6: 12.

δ   as] and C   67 absolucion] absoluciouns, -s *canc.* Y, absoluciones Cαδ-
EG   ȝif] ⌈ȝyf⌉ T, *om.* F   acorde] nedis accorde G   68 so] *om.* AB   69
so] *om.* I   a] *om.* C   70 trespaas] trespassis G   71 wrong¹] wrongys T, þe
wrong I   þat . . . god] *om.* N   vnto] to δ   ellys] *om.* KPᵗ   wrong²]
wrongys T   72 þat þat] þat BPᵗ, þat at N   hit] þis L, *om.* YE   maad] *om.*
N   so] *om.* L   73 þat . . . incomplete (74)] *om.* L   þat] *om.* β   75
teche] touche I   76 owre¹] hur Pᵗ   dettis] dette I   synne] dedly synne
M   77 wyle] wold, -d *canc.* α, wolde AFNδPᵗIJG   moore . . . sentence] þis
sentence more pleynely Nδ   pleynly] pleynerly C   wole] wolde, -d- *canc.* α,
wolde NδPᵗ   78 mekely] *om* E   assente] assento D   grounden] wolen
grounde I   seyn] seynen β   and] or FN   79 man] *om.* N   preue] wole
proue I   þat . . . now] *after* or . . . lawe (80) ABCKLMNTYβδPᵗEIX, X *on eras.*
corr.   seyd . . . now] here sayd now CKβPᵗ   here now] *rev.* ALMNTYαδEIJ-
XG   80 marke] wot *canc.* marke α, woot I   þis] þe Y   81 ȝaf] ȝeueþ
Y   sych] *om.* E   to] vnto I   82 men] ⌈iche⌉ men T, men and þerfore preye
we iesu crist of helpe and grace to vnderstonde þe holy sentence of hys lawe to fulfulle it in
oure lyfe and so to come to heuene blysse etc. N

Dominica 20 [post festum Trinitatis. Euangelium.]
Sermo 20.

Loquebatur Iesus cum discipulis suis. Mathei 22.

This gospel telluþ in a parable what men schulde trowen of þes chirche from hennys to þe day of doom, as hit is towchyd sumwhat byfore. *Iesus spak wiþ his disciples in parablys and seyde þus.*

'*Þe rewme of heuene is maad lych vnto a man þat is a kyng, þat made*
5 *weddyngus to his sone and sente his seruauntes to clep[e] þese men þat weren*
f.68 *bedone to þe bruydale. And for þei\wolde not come, he sente oþre seruauntis, and seyde "Sey ʒe to men þat ben bedone 'Loo! I haue maad redy my mete, my bolys and my volatiles ben kilde and alle oþur þingus ben redy; come ʒe faste to þe feeste.'" But þei despuseden his byddyng; and summe wenten*
10 *into his town, and summe to his chaffaryng, and summe token þis kyngus seruauntys and punyschyden wiþ contek and kylden hem. And þe kyng, whanne he saw þis, was wroþ and sende hise hoostis and loste þese mensleerys and brende þer cytee; and seyde þanne to his seruauntis "Metys of þis brydale ben redy, but men clepude were not worþi; þerfore goo ʒe to*
15 *eendys of weyes and, whomeuere ʒe fynde, clepe ʒe to þe mete." And þese*

MSS: D; ABCEFGIJKLMNTXYZαβPᵗ; δ *expl. incompl.* 4 a man.

Dominica . . . euangelium] *om.* Z   sermo 20] *om.* BCFKNTYαβδPᵗEIJXZG   loquebatur . . . suis] simile factum ᵀest⁷ regnum celorum homini regi qui T, videte fratres quomodo caute ambuletis N   suis] *om.* ABCKLMαβPᵗEZ   mathei 22] mathei 20 E, ad eph' 5 . . . mathei 22 N   1 this] þe N   telluþ . . . byfore (3)] today seiþ on þis wyse N   in] *om.* Pᵗ   a] *om.* αJ   2 to] til I   3 sumwhat] sumdel δ   byfore] her bifore I   wiþ] to Nδ   4 maad] *om.* I   vnto] to Nδ, *om.*I   a²] made a β   5 to¹] vnto E   clepe] clepo D, cale αZ   6 þe] þis α   wolde] nolde T   7 seyde] seide þus N   sey ʒe] seiʒe I, say þou Pᵗ   men] þe men NPᵗ   bedone] *om.* Pᵗ   loo] loke I   8 alle] *om.* I   9 faste] *om.*N   his] þis, þ *on eras. corr.* X, þis CLMNTYαβPᵗEZ, þis kyngis K   10 into] to I   his¹] þis Cβ, þe *canc.* ᵀhis⁷α   to] into A   summe²] *om.* A   11 wiþ] hem *canc.* wiþ DαX, hem wiþ CMNβI   contek] cuncet L   12 whanne . . . wroþ] was wroth whenne he sawh þis N   wroþ] worþe J   13 mensleerys] mansleeris ABCFKNYαβPᵗEIJXZG   cytee] cites MZ   14 þis] þe E   men] þo þat weren F   clepude] callede α, þat ben clepid N, þat ware callid Z   were] bene CN   worþi] worþ β   to] into E   15 eendys] ᵀþe⁷ eendis X, þe eendis ABCKLMNTYβPᵗIZG   weyes] þe *canc.* weies B, þe wayes CKZ   whomeuere ʒe] wham ʒe euere M, wham sa euer ʒe Z   clepe] cale αZ   þe] *om.*

seruauntis wenton owht and gedryde men alle þat þei fownden, boþe goode
and euele, and þe bruydale was fulfyllud wiþ men syttyng at þe mete, al ȝif
þei weren not ⌐al⌐ fulle seruyde. *Þe kyng caam in to see hise gestis, and*
saw þere oon wiþowte bruyd cloþus, and seyde to hym "Freend, how
entredust þow hydere wiþowte bruyd cloþus?" And he was domp. Þanne þe   20
lord bad his seruauntis to byndon hym, boþe hondys and feet, and senden
hym into vttere derknesse; þere schal be wepyng and gnastyng of teeþ. For
manye ben clepude and fewe ben chosene.'

The kyngdam of heuene is þe chirche þat takiþ name of þe hed,
as þe gospel spekiþ comunly; and so þis rewme is lych a kyng, þat   25
is þe Fadyr in Trinnyte. And þis kyng made a mariage to Crist,
þat ys his Sone, and to þis cherche, þat is his spowse, and to
damyselys þerof. For as Salamon seyth fowre degrees ben in þis
chirche: summe ben qwenes, and summe ben lemmanys, and
somme damyselys, but oon is spowse þat conteneþ alle þese þre   30
and þat is al hooly chyrche. And þus þer ben manye chyrches,
and a new chirche wiþ Crist – ȝe, al þe chirche of men and
aungelis is newyd by þe incarnacion. Þes seruauntis of þis spowse
bydden men to þe feeste, whanne þei meue men to come to blisse
by þer iust lif. And þese seruauntis weren prophetis and apostles   35
of Godys two lawes; but þei weren cleput specially when Cristus
burþe was schewyd hem for, as hit was seid byfore, þanne alle
þingys weren maad redye. And manye men in boþe þese tymes
wolde not come þus to þis feeste. Aftyr þese seruauntis he sende

---

28 S. of S. 6: 7–8.

---

1   16 wenton] ȝeden N   17 fulfullyd] fulled NI   ȝif] *on eras. corr. D*   18
not] ⌐not⌐ IZ   al] *corr.* D, *om.* F   fulle] fully N   þe] and þe E   in]
om. L   see] -n *canc.* D, *om.* I   19 þere] *om.* E   bruyd] bruydale
N   and . . . cloþus (20)] *om.* N   20 entredust] enterest C   þanne] ⌐and⌐
þanne B, and þan A   21 seruauntis] seruaunt T   to] *om.* N   boþe] *om.*
LM   hondys] hond BT   feet] foot T   22 vttere] þe vtter BE, veterest
Pᵗ   derknesse] dernessis F   schal be wepyng] wepyng schal be N   gnas-
tyng] gnattyng LM   of] togidre of F   23 manye] many men α   clepude]
called αZ   24 name] þe name C   25 a] to a CZ   26 þe] *om.* TPᵗ   in] in
þe Z   27 þis] his I   to²] two T, to þe I   28 for . . . damyselys (30)] *om.*
M   for] *om.* TI   as] *om.* I   salamon] salon J   fowre] þer ben foure
N   ben] *om.* N   þis] þe NI   29 and¹] *om.* A   and²] *om.* I   30 somme]
sume ben, ben *canc.* β, somme ben NI   spowse] þe spouse N   31 chyrche]
chirche wiþ crist E   þer] þey N   32 al] and al T   33 incarnacion]
incarnacioun of crist E   þes] þe ABCFKLMNTYαPᵗEIJZG   34 þe] þis
NE   meue] sturen N   men²] *om.* T   blisse] heuen N   36 þei] *om.*
N   cleput] called αZ   37 was¹] whas T   38 in] and F   39 not] *om.*

40 oþre, as men þat nexst sewoden þe apostles; and bolys wiþ
volatiles weren slayne and mete was reedy to þis feeste. Þe bolys
bytoknen þe oolde fadris, as patriarkys and Dauyd, for þei dyden
batayles of God and ter[r]dyn his enemyes wiþ here hornys; and
ȝeet þei kepton ful byssyly þe grete mawndementis of God. Þe
45 volatiles, þat seruen seyntis at þe secunde cowrs of þis feeste, ben
seyntis of þe newe lawe þat wiþ þese maundementis kepton
Cristis counselys. And ȝet men forsooke to comen, notwiþston-
dyng sawmple of þese seyntys. And somme wenton aftyr
lordschipe of þis world, and summe aftyr chaffare of worldly
50 richessys. But summe slowen Cristis seruauntys, as emperoures of
Roome and prestes. Þe kyng of heuene was wroþ herfore, and
sende his hoostys to Ierusaleem, and slowe þe sleerys of Crist and
brente þer citee, as Iosephus telluþ; and þis dede, doon in
Ierusaleem þe two and fowrtyþe ȝeer aftur þe deþ of Crist,
55 bytokneþ þe veniaunce of God for sleyng of Cristus membrys.
And þus men þat stooden byhynde boþe in þe olde lawe and
newe weren vnworþi to fulfulle þe noumbre þat God ordeyned to
be sauyd.

And now in þese laste dayes God bad his seruauntis clepe men,
60 boþe goode and euele, into þe chyrche þat weren owte of þe riȝte
weye and wente by weyes of errour þat weren harde for to wende.

Pᵗ   come þus] rev. I   þus] þo T   þis] þe I   40 men] þos M   þe] om.
αJ   wiþ] on eras. corr. D, and K   42 þe] om. FPᵗE   43 terrdyn] terndyn D,
turneden ABCLNTPᵗI   his] here I   44 ȝeet] om. N   þei] ⌜þai⌝ α, om.
FNJ   ful . . . god] also þerwhit godes comaundement bysyly N   mawnde-
mentis] comaundementz I   45 seruen] serueden I   46 wiþ] om. Pᵗ   þese]
þis β   maundementis] comaundementes NI   kepton] kepis Z   47 men
forsooke] rev. N   forsooke] forsakis Z   notwiþstondyng] noȝt vndirstandand
Z   48 sawmple] þe saumple F, ensaumple N   þese] þis β   and . . .
world (49)] aftur lordchipe of þis world wenten somme N   49 lordschipe]
lordschippis Z   summe] sum men I   aftyr] to N   worldly] þis worldely
A   50 richessys] richesse ACNαPᵗEJG   summe] sum men C   slo-
wen] slow/wen D   51 heuene] hem A   herfore] þerfore CPᵗ   52 hoostys]
hoste β   to] out to AB   þe] þes, -s canc. α, þes ABFIJG   sleerys] clerkis
I   crist] cristus folk N   53 dede] om. C   doon] ⌜was⌝ don T, was canc. doon
X, was don FNPᵗ   54 þe¹] in G   fowrtyþe] fourty ACFLMNαJG, þe fourty
Pᵗ   þe² . . . crist] iesu cristes deth N   55 bytokneþ . . . membrys] om.
N   bytokneþ] ⌜ant⌝ bytokneþ T, and bitokeneþ FPᵗ   god] crist FT   sleyng]
sleyngis Pᵗ   56 stooden] stande canc. ⌜stoden⌝ α, stoonden AFJ   57 newe] in þe
canc. newe D, in þe newe, þe canc. X, in þe newe ABCKLMNEZG, in newe Yβ, ⌜in⌝ þe
newe α, þe new Pᵗ   fulfulle] fille A   þe] þat I   ordeyned] hade ordeyned N,
haþ ordeyned E   59 clepe] calle αZ   61 weyes] þe weyes L   errour] errours

And so, as Petre in his fyrste fyschyng took two maner|of f.68v
fyschys – summe dwellyden in þe net, and somme broke þe net
and wenten awey, – so here in þis chirche ben somme ordeynyde
to blisse and somme to peyne, al ȝif þey liuen iustly for a tyme. 65
And so men seyn comunly þat þer ben here two manerys of
chirches: holy chirche or chirche of God, þat on no maner may be
dampnyd; and þe chirche of þe feend, þat for a tyme is good and
lasteþ not, and þis was neuere holy chirche ne part þerof. But þe
kyng aftyr þis feeste cam in at þe day of doom, for God schewyþ 70
hym þanne to alle þat he knoweþ alle mennys lif. And þes þat
wolde not laste in grace were not cled in bryd cloþus; and alle
þese ben o man þat hadde no wit to answere God. But, for þis
man wiþ partis of hym profiȝtede to Cristes chirche and was of þe
same kynde wiþ Crist, Crist clepud hym 'frend', as he dide Iudas. 75
But alle þese men can not answeren how þei entredon into þe
chirche; for it was told hem openly þat þei ben traytours, but ȝif
þei lasten, and ben more to be dampnyd þan men þat neuere
entreden þus. And so alle syche men tooken peyne by iust
iugement of God, þat þer willes schulde be bownden and þer 80
profiȝtable werkis, and schulde be cast into helle, where men
schulde wepe and gnaste wiþ teþ. Wepyng schal be sensible sorwe
and gnastyng schal be wantyng of blisse; wherfore men schulle
moste gruchche syþ þei myton liȝtly ha⌐ue⌐ come to blysse, and

---

62 Luke 5: 6; **75** Matt. 26: 50.

AI   for to] to Pᵗ   62 so] *om.* Y   fyrste] *om.* N   maner] maners
C   63 in] stille in N   broke] breke *canc.* brasten α, brasten *on eras. corr.* X, borsten
ABCFKLMTβPᵗEI   þe net²] hit N   64 so] riȝt so N, and so TI   65 to¹]
vnto N   to²] ben ordeyned vnto N   al ȝif] ȝif *on eras. corr.* D, þeyg N   iustly]
iust lyf N   66 here] ⌐her⌐ T, *om.* βI   manerys] maner MαβPᵗEIJZ, *om.*
N   67 chirches] chirche⌐s⌐ M, chirche CKLYβPᵗ, þe chirche T   maner] mo
maner C   68 is] it is Y   69 and] in C   þerof] of holi chirche of god
N   70 aftyr] at N   cam] comeþ N   71 hym] *om.* Z   þat¹] for A, men as
N   knoweþ . . . lif] alle mennes lyf knoweþ N   mennys] mannis I   72
laste] liue M   bryd] bridis B, bruydal N, þe bridis I   74 partis] þe parties
I   to] sumwhat to N   75 clepud] clepiþ A, called αZ   iudas] to *canc.* iudas
α, to iudas JG   76 entredon] entren A   þe] þe *canc.* G, *om.* Tβ, cristis E   77
hem] to hem B   traytours] trec[. .] res Pᵗ   78 lasten] -st- *or ?* -ft- D, lastid
Z   ben] *om.* E   more] more worþi AB   79 þus] þus into chirche
T   tooken] tokenen T, takis Z   peyne] men I   80 god] criste α   81
where] þer as N   82 schulde] schulen N   wepyng] and wepyngis L   sorwe]
sowe B   83 wherfore] þerfore Z   men] þat men I   84 liȝtly haue] *rev.*

85 aftyr þis þei schal haue no wylle, neyþur to desyre ne worche
wel. And þus manye men ben clepude but fewe ben choson to
blisse.

C   haue] -ue *corr.* D   blysse] þe blis C   85 þei schal] *rev.* N   þei] *om.*
C   schal] ne *canc.* schal α, ne schal IJG   worche] ⌜to⌝ worche T, to wirche AYPᵗ,
wille to worche I   86 wel] *om.* I   men] *om.* C   clepude] called
αZ   but] and M   fewe] fewe men E   to blisse] *om.* F   87 blisse] þe blisse
and þerfore preie we to god of help oure lyues to amende þe while we tyme haue in þis
world to lyue in blysse wiþouten ende pater et aue N

Dominica 21 [post festum Trinitatis. Euangelium.]
Sermo 21.

Erat quidam regulus. Iohannis 4.

This gospel telliþ hou a kyng, þat somme men seyn was an heþen man, byleued in Crist and disseruyde to han a myracle of his sone. Þe story seith how *in Galilee was dwellyng a lytyl kyng in þe citee of Capharnaum þat hadde a sone ful syk of feuerys. And wan he herde telle þat Iesu [schulde] com[e] fro Iude to Galilee, he cam and mette hym on þe* 5 *weye, and preyde hym come down and helen his sone for he was in poynt of deþ. And Crist seyde to þis kyng* to amenden his byleue '3e byleue not in *Iesu but* ⌜*if*⌝ *3e seen sygnes and wondres'* – as þis man byleuede not in þe godhede of Crist, for, 3if he hadde, hee schulde ⌜haue⌝ trowyd þat Crist mi3te haue sauyd his sone 3if he hadde not bodyly come 10 to þe seek man and towchid hym. But þis kyng hadde more herte of helþe of his sone, þan he hadde to be helyd of vntrewþe þat he was inne. And þerfore he telde not herby, butte axede Crist [e]fte to helon his sone, and in þis forme of wordis in whiche he schewod his vntrewþe, '*Lord!*' *he seyde*, '*come down byfore þat my sone dye*'. But 15 Iesu, as a wis lord and merciful, helyd his sone in sych maner þat he my3te wyte þat he was boþe God and man. '*Go*', *he seyde*, '*þi*

MSS: D; ABCFGHIJKLMTXYZαβ; E *ends incompl.* 41 galilee þat, N *inc.* 12 þat he was, Pᵗ *ends incompl.* 68 þinges bygynnen.

Dominica . . . euangelium] *om.* Z   sermo 21] *om.* BCFKTYαPᵗEIJXZGH   1
þat] *on eras. corr.* D   men] *om.* C   seyn] sayden Pᵗ   was] þat was H   2
disseruyde] desiride I   a] ⌜a⌝ YαJ, to a G, *om.* FI   3 how] hou þat H   þe²]
om. CKLMYβPᵗZG   4 ful] *om.* F, wel H   of²] in α   feuerys] þe *canc.*
feuerys DX, þe feueris AFαI   he] *om.* Y   5 schulde come] com DAFαJG,
schulde com⌜e⌝ *on eras.* X   to] into E   and] *om.* J   on] vpon G   6
poynt] poyng H   7 þis] þe Y   in] *om.* B   8 if] *corr.* D   3e] *om.* Y   as]
and H   byleuede] byleueþ T   in] *om.* K   9 for 3if] for 3eue C   haue] *corr.*
D   10 3if] *on eras. corr.* D, al if B, 3if all α   hadde] nadde I   11 to] þere *canc.*
to D, doun to Z   þe] þis ABCKLMTYαβPᵗEJXZGH   herte] his herte Z   12
of¹] *on eras. corr.* D   helþe] hele αZ, þe heleþe β, help I   13 þerfore] herfore
KNI   herby] þerby FG   crist efte] crist ofte DFIJ, eft crist BCKLMTYβPᵗEX
(*on eras.*) Z, ⌜eft⌝ crist A, of crist H   14 wordis] wormes B   in whiche] *om.*
N   15 his] out his N   vntrewþe] vntrewe β   þat] *om.* PᵗEH   16 a] a
canc. α, *om.* ABCFLMYβPᵗIZH   helyd] he helide I   maner] a manere
PᵗI   17 wyte] verrayly wyten N   man] a man β   go he seyde] crist seide to

sone lyueþ.' And þerwiþ Crist tawte his sowle boþe of his manhede
and godhede, and ellys hadde not þis kyng trowyd; but þe gospel
20 seyth þat hee trowede and al his hows. And vpon þis trowþe *he*
wente hoomward and mette hys men vpon þe weye þat teeldon hym þat his
sone schulde lyue, for he is coueryt of his euel. *And he axede whanne his*
sone ferde bettere. Þei *seyden* ⸢þat⸣ ʒusturday þe seueneþe howr þe feuerys
forsoken þe child. And þe fadyr knew by his mynde þat hit was þe same owr
25 *þat Crist seyde 'þi sone lyueþ'; and herfore byleuyd he and al his hows on*
Iesu Crist. And þerfore Iesu seyde soþ þat he and men lych to hym
trowen not, but ʒif þei seen boþe syngnes and wondris. Hit was a
sygne of þe seeke child þat he dide werkis of an hol man; but hit
f.69 was ⸢a⸣ greet wondyr þat, by vertew|of þe word of Crist, a man so
30 fer schulde be hool, for so Crist schewyde þat he is vertew of
godhede þat is euerywhere, and þis vertew mut be God þat dide
þus þis miracle.

Þis story seiþ vs þis secownde wit þat God ʒyueþ to hooly writ,
þat þis luytyl kyng bytookneþ mannys wit by synne slydon fro
35 God, þat is but a lytul kyng in regard of his makere. And his sone
was seek on þe feuerus, as weren þese heþene folc and þere
affecciones þat comen of þer sowlys; but þei hadden a kyndly
wille to wyte þe trewþe and stonde þerinne. This kyng cam fro
Capharnaum, þat is 'feeld of fatnesse', for man fattid and alargid
40 wendiþ awey fro God. Þis mannis wit, whan he herde þat Iesu

---

hym go N   go] so α   þi] þis Y   18 crist] he E   manhede] godhede
NEH   19 godhede] of his *canc.* godhede D, his *canc.* godhede X, of his monhede NE,
manhed H   trowyd] byleued N   þe] þis N   20 seyth] telliþ T   trowede]
byleuede N   his] *om.* N   vpon] on N   21 þe] þis E   þat²] *om.* I   his
sone] he B   22 coueryt] cowerd C   23 ferde] fere Pᵗ   þei] and þei
AN   þat] *corr.* DT   feuerys forsoken] feuere forsoke FYI   24 forsoken]
leften N   þe child] hym N   owr] *om.* M   25 seyde] seiþ C   herfore]
þere T   on] in A   26 þerfore] herfore αJ   iesu²] *om.* Y   to] *om.* M, vnto
H   27 trowen] troweden FEZ, ne *eras.* trowen A, ne trowen I   seen] seyʒen
JZ   boþe syngnes] *rev.* I   boþe] *om.* MPᵗ   28 child] chide L   dide]
⸢was hol for he⸣ dyde T   hol] -y *eras.* D, old F   hit] *om.* Y   29 a¹] *om.*
I   greet wondyr] *rev.* M, grettere wondir H   vertew] þe vertu TI   þe
. . . crist] cristes word N   þe] þis G   a²] þat a N   30 for] and I   he is]
his β   is] was H   31 mut] nede mot N, mote nede H   god] good
I   dide þus] þus dide *marked for rev.* Y, *rev.* α, þus ⸢dede⸣ J   32 þus] *om.* N   33
þis¹] þe, -e *canc.* -is α, þe NEJZG, but þe I   vs] to vs Cβ, ⸢þ⸣ vs α, þus KPᵗZ   þis²]
þe NPᵗIG   þat] whiche E   ʒyueþ] haþ ʒyuen E   34 mannys] a mannis A,
mennes N   by . . . slydon] slyden by synne N   slydon] slydynge T   35 þat]
for þat H   36 on] of CNαZH   37 affecciones] affection C   38 wyte] knowe
N   this] þe N   39 feeld] a feld AIZG, felede α   alargid] largid Yβ-
EI   40 mannis] man LM   wit . . . þat¹ (41)] *om.* L   42 mette] and met C,

cam to heþene men (and þat bytokneþ Galilee þat is
'transmigracion') mette wiþ Iesu in pleyn weye, and lefte his
heþen possessioun, and preyde God to helon his folc þat weren
syke by gostly feuere. But Crist scharpede þes mennys byleue, for
feiþ is furst nedful to men; but vndirstandyng of man preide Crist   45
to come down by grace, byfor þat mannys affeccion dye abowten
erþly goodis. But, for men trowedon þe godhede of Crist, þei
weron hoole of þis feuere whan þei forsoken þis world and putten
her hope in heuenly godis. Þese seruauntis ben lowly vertewys of
þe sowle whyche, worching ioyfulli, tellen mannys witt and his   50
wille þat þis sone is hool of feuere. Þis feuere bytokneþ schakyng
of man by vnkyndely dystemprure of habundaunce of worldly
goodis, þat ben vnstable as þe watur; and herfore seiþ seyn Iame
þat he þat dowteþ in byleue is liȝk to flood of þe see þat wiþ þe
wynd is boren abowte. Þat þes seruauntis telde þis kyng þat in þe   55
seuenþe howr feuer forsooke þis child bytokneþ a greet witt, as
Robard of Lyncolne scheweþ. Furst hit bytookneþ þat þis feuere
goþ awey fro mannis kynde by seuene ȝiftys of þe Holy Goost, þat
ben vndirstanden by þese howris, and þis clerk dyuyduþ þe day
in two haluys by syxe howris so þat al þe day bytookneþ lyȝt of   60
grace þat man is inne. Þe fyrste syxe owres bytoknen ioye þat man
haþ of worldly þing; and þis is byfore spiritual ioye, as vttur man
is byfore spiritual. But in þe fyrste howr of þe secownde half leueþ
goostly feuer man, for whoeuere haþ worldly ioye, ȝif he haue

53 Jas. 1: 6.

he mette N   wiþ] *om.* N   43 heþen] heuene P^t   possessioun] possessiones N,
possioun β   god] to god H   44 scharpede] schappede I   þes] þus T   45
men] man M   man] men N   46 to] to *canc.* X, *om.* ABKLMNTYβP^t-
IZ   þat] *om.* AT   mannys] mennes N   48 world] *on eras. corr.* DT, lord
LMNP^tI   49 þese] þer C   ben] bi I   lowly] lowe, -ly *eras.* X, low, -ly *canc.*
-^r^e^1 α, low ABCKLMNTYβP^tIZH   50 þe] *om.* B   whyche] þe wuche
N   worching] þorwh ioyful wurchyng N   ioyfulli tellen] *on eras. corr.* D, tellen
N   mannys] mennes N   51 þat] hou þat N   þis^1] is C, his NP^t-
I   feuere^1] þe feueres I   bytokneþ] betokyn C   52 man] men T   vn-
kyndely] vnkynd C   dystemprure] temperure N   54 to] *om.* Y   flood] ^r^a^1
flood B, a flood AIZ, þe flood NY   þe^2] *om.* AT   55 þis] þe LMI   56 feuer]
þe *canc.* feuer α, þe feuere KNP^tIJH   57 scheweþ] sais α, telliþ H   hit] ^r^it^1 α, *om.*
I   bytookneþ] tokeneþ N   þis] *om.* I   58 mannis kynde] mankynde
FIZ   59 ben . . . howris] by þuse houres ben vndurstonden N   clerk] clerkis
α   dyuyduþ] departeþ N, diuydid T   þe] þis N   60 in two] into β   61
syxe] sixete β   ioye] þe yoie C, *om.* N   man haþ] men N, men han H   62
þing] þinges I   is] *om.* β   vttur] þe vtter I   64 feuer man] man feuer *marked*
for rev. D, feuere in man G   whoeuere] whosoeuere ABFNI, wha þat euer

65 grace on sum maner, ȝeet he tremblyþ in som feuere abowte
goodis of þis world. But anoon in þe seuenþe howr, þat is þe fyrste
of þe secownde haalf, whan wylle of worldly þing is left and
spiritual þingus bygynnen to be louede, þanne þis schakyng
passuþ fro man and gostly helþe comeþ to þe spiryt. And so
70 schadwes of liȝt of sunne fro þe seuenþe howr to þe nyȝt wexen
euere more and more; and þat bytookneþ goostly þat vanyte of
þis world semeþ ay moore and moore to mannys spirit tyl he
come to þe ende of þis lyf to þe lyf þat euere schal lasten. And so
þis man troweþ in God boþe wiþ vndurstondyng and wylle wiþ
75 alle þe meyne of his hows, whanne alle hise wyttes and hise
strengþes ben obeschynge to resoun whan þis feuere is þus passyd.
Of þis vndyrstondyng may men take moral wytt how men
schulle lyuen, and large þe mater as hem lykyþ.

Z   haþ] haue AZG   worldly] om. gaþ B   ȝif] þeiȝ N   haue] haþ
β   65 on] ouer B, of α   66 þis] þe A   þe fyrste of] om. Y   67 of¹] on
K   þing] þingis ABCKLMNTYαβPᵗIJXZGH   left] lost C   68 spiritual]
gostely N   bygynnen] bigunnen Z   þis . . . passuþ (69)] passeþ þis schakyng
N   þis] is C   69 man] a man N, men T   helþe] hele CαZ, help N-
G   comeþ] comyn C   so schadwes] rev. T   70 sunne] þe sonne NαI-
J   to] into AFαIJ   þe²] om. B   nyȝt] nynþe N   wexen euere] rev. AI,
waxen alwey N   72 semeþ] semeþ hem I   ay] om. N   and moore] and more
canc. X, om. ABKLMTYβZGH   to] til N   mannys] mennus F   73 þe¹] om.
β   ende . . . lyf] lyues ende M   þis] his IG   to²] til N, vn canc. to α, vnto
JG   þe²] om. A   euere] ay A   75 whanne] as whanne I   76
obeschynge] maad buxum N   to] vnto N   feuere] feueris H   77
of . . . lykyþ (78)] werfore preie we to þis leche þat al þing may hele wiþ word þat he vs
hele here in þis world of seknesses þat oure soulus ben inne þat we may lyfe in helful lyf in
heuen for euer whenne we heþen wende and þat it so be þorw his grace preie we hertely to
hym pater et aue N   of] and of Z   may men] rev. AI, may man H   men²]
man H   78 hem] him LM, ȝou I

Dominica xxii [post festum Trinitatis.
Euangelium.] Sermo 22.

Simile est regnum celorum homini regi qui uoluit racionem ponere.
Mathei 18.

This gospel telliþ by a parable how by ri3t iugement of God men
schulden be merciful. '*Þe kyndam of heuene*,' seyþ Crist, '*is ly3k to an
erþly kyng þat wolde rykene wiþ hise seruauntis. And* ⌐*whanne he bigan to*
rikene⌐, *on was offryd vnto hym þat owhte hym ten þowsande besauntis;*
and whanne he hadde not to payen of, þe lord bad þat he schulde be soold, his   5
wyf and his children and al þat he hadde, and þat þat he owhte þe lord
schulde algatis be payed. Þis seruaunt fel down, and preyde þe loord and sey-
de, "Haue paciense in me, and| *I schal qwyte þe al." Þe lord hadde mercy*   f.69v
on hym and for3af hym al his dette. Þis seruaunt wente owt, and fond on of
hise detowres þat owhte hym an hundret pens, and took hym and stranglede   10
hym and bad hym payen his dette. And þis seruaunt fel down, and preyde
hym of paciense and he schulde by tyme 3elden hym al þat he owhte hym.
But þis man wolde not, but wente owt and putte hym in prisoun, tyl he
hadde payed þe dette þat he owhte hym. And oþer seruauntis of þis ⌐*man*⌐,
whan þei saw þis dede, mornedon ful myche and tolden al þis to þe lord. And   15
þe lord clepude hym and seyde þus vnto hym "Wyckyde seruaunt! al þi dette

MSS; D; ABCFGHIJKLMNTXYZαβ.

Dominica . . . euangelium] *om.* Z   sermo 22] *om.* BCFKNTYαIJXZGH   simile
. . . ponere] oro ut caritas vestra magis habundet in scientia N   regi . . . ponere]
om. A   regi] *om.* G   qui . . . ponere] *om.* α   racionem ponere] *om.* BIH,
racionem ponere cum seruis suis F   mathei 18] mathei xvi F, mathei decimo nono K,
om. C, mathei 18 ad philip' primo capitulo N   1 by a parable] *om.* N   by²
. . . god] *om.* N   2 þe] crist seide to hise disciples þat þe N   seyþ crist] *om.* N, ⌐is
licned to man kyng⌐ siþ crist T   3 whanne . . . rikene (4)] *margin corr.* DAα, *om.*
CFKLMNTβIJXZGH   bigan] hadde bigunne ABα   4 vnto] to KN-
Y   hym²] to him Y   ten] two N   þowsande] þousandis I   5 to] for to
I   þat] *om.* ANT   6 and¹] *om.* N   þat þat] þat ⌐þat⌐ α, ⌐þat⌐ þat G, þat
FMNJ   þe lord] *om.* N   7 algatis be] *rev.* A, ⌐algatis⌐ be J, be N   fel] felde
BKY   8 haue] þus haue N   in] on β   al] *om.* L   þe²] and þe
C   11 down] adoun M   12 of] haue N   and . . . hym³] *margin*
Y   and]in hym N   he¹ . . . hym³] *om.* N   hym al] ⌐al⌐ M·   13 owt] *om.*
I   he] tyme þat he N   14 þis man] *corr.* D   15 whan] whenne þat
N   saw] seen C   ful myche] *om.* N   16 clepude] called αZ   vnto] to

I forȝaf þe, for þow preidust me; ne byhowued not þe to ⌐*haue*⌐ *mercy of þi seruaunt as I hadde mercy on þe?"" And þe lord was wroþ, and ȝaf hym to turmentowris tyl he hadde payed al þe dette þat he owhte hym. On þis*

20   *maner,' seiþ Crist, 'schal my Fadyr of heuene do to ȝow, but* ⌐*ȝif*⌐ *ȝe forȝyuen echone to hyse broþur of ȝowre free herte þe trespas þat he haþ doon to hym.'*

Þe kyngdom of heuene is hooly chirche of men þat now traueylen heere; and þis chirche bi his heed is lyk to a man kyng,

25   for Crist, hed of þis chirche is boþe God and man. Þis kyng wolde rykene wiþ hise seruauntis; for Crist haþ wille wiþowten ende to rykene wiþ men at þ⌐r⌐e tymes. Furst Crist rykenyþ wiþ men, whanne he techeþ hem by resoun how myche þei han had of hym, and how myche þei owen hym. Þe secownde tyme Crist

30   rykenuþ wiþ men, whanne in ⌐h⌐owre of mannys deþ he telliþ hem at what poynt ⌐þes⌐ men schullen euer iustly stonden. Þe þridde rykenyng is general þat schal be at þe day of doom, whanne þis iugement generally schal ben openly don in dede. As anemptys þe fyrste rykenyng Crist rykenuþ wiþ riche men of þis

35   world, and scheweþ hem how myche þei owen hym; and scheweþ by riȝtwisnesse of his lawe how þei and þeyres schulde be selde, and so maken asseþ by peyne of þingus þat þei parformedon not in dede. But menye syche men for a tyme han compunccion in herte, and preyȝe God of his grace to haue paciense in hem, and

40   þei schal in þis lif serue to Crist trewly. And so Crist forȝyueþ hem vpon þis condicioun. But þei wenden owt and sewe not Crist þere lord in mercy, but oppresson þer seruauntis þat owen ⌐hem⌐ but

Kβ   17 forȝaf] forȝeue I   not þe] *rev.* ABCKLMTYβIZGH   to] *om.*
N   haue] *corr.* D   of] on ABCKLMNTYαβIJXZGH   18 ȝaf . . . dette
(19)] til he hadde paied al his dette he ȝaf hym vnto turmentoures N   19 on] on
N   20 maner] wise N   seiþ crist] *om.* N   do] seiþ crist do N   ȝif] *corr.*
DH, *om.* G   21 echone] ech BH   22 to] to *canc.* FX, ⌐to⌐ K, *om.*
ABLMTYIZG   25 þis¹] hys TXH   26 to] *om.* β   27 rykenyþ] rekynnyd
β   28 techeþ . . . resoun] hem by resoun techeþ N   hem] men H   han
had] hadden M   29 crist] crist ⌐he⌐ M   30 men] man T   howre] h- *corr.* D,
þe houre AG   mannys] mennys, -e- *altered from* -a- X, mennys BKMNβIZG   31
hem] hem, -e- *altered from* -i- α, hym C, *om.* G   poynt] poyntis H   þes] *corr.*
D   euer] ouere β, euere more I   33 þis] þat þis C   openly] *om.* Z   don]
om. Z   34 þis] þe KI   35 scheweþ¹] schew C   36 riȝtwisnesse] ryȝtnesse
M   and þeyres] and þat huren is N, an heres I   schulde] schullen I   37 so]
om. N   by] so by sufferynge of N   peyne] peny Z   þingus] þinge α, þes
þingis H   38 in dede] *om.* N   39 god] g *canc.*/god D   his] ⌐his⌐ X, *om.*
F   and² . . . hem¹(42)] *om.* L   40 schal] wolen N   to] ⌐to⌐ α, *om.*
BN   to . . . trewly] treuly to crist I, god truli GH   hem] him I   41 vpon]
vp K   crist] to crist I   42 þer] *om.* N   hem] *corr.* D, *om.* J   43 þenkon]

a lytul dette, and putten hem in prisoun, and þenkon not on
Godis mercy. And oþre seruauntis of God, boþe in þis lif and þe
toþre, tellen to God þiṣ felnesse and preyen hym of veniaunce. No 45
dowte God is wroþ at þis, and at two rykenyngus wiþ man he
resounneþ þis cruel man and iugiþ hym iustly to peyne. And
þerfore Crist byddiþ by Luc alle men to be merciful, for þer fadyr
of heuene þat schal iugen hem is merciful.

But we schal vndirstonde by þis þat þis mercy þat Crist axeþ is no 50
þing aȝen resoun. And so by þis iuste mercy schulde men som
tyme forȝyuen, and som tyme schulde þei punysche—but euere
by resoun of mercy. Þe resoun of mercy stondiþ in þis: þat men
myȝten do cruelly þei don iustly for Godis sake to amendement of
men. And so men may mercyfully reproue men and punyschen 55
hem, and take of hem þer iuste dettis for beturyng of þese
detowres. On þis maner doþ God þat is ful of mercy, and seiþ þat
he reproueþ and chastisuþ his wantowne children þat he loueþ.
And þus Crist reprouede pharisees and ⌐punischede⌐ prestis wiþ
oþur peple, and punyschuþ mercifully alle dampnyd men in 60
helle; for hit stondiþ not wiþ his riȝte þat he punysche but
mercyfully. God ȝyueþ good of kynde by grace to þese men þat he
dampneþ; and, ȝif he punyschyde hem more, ȝeet he medlede
mercy. But heere men schulden be war þat alle þe goodis þat þei
han ben goodes of þer God, and þei nakyde seruauntis of God. 65
And þus schulde þei warly fle to take þer owne veniaunse, but
vengen iniurye of God and intenden amendement. Þus Crist,

---

48 Luke 6: 36; **58** Rev. 3: 19.

rek C   44 þe toþre] in þat oþer αI   þe] in þe ACNTGH   45 þis] þe
H   of] of his H   no] not β   46 man] men N   47 resounneþ] aresonet
NG   48 crist] he B   by luc] om. N   to] om. I   for . . . merciful
(49)] om. Z   þer] þe N   49 þat . . . merciful] is merciful wuche þat schal iugge
hem N   hem] hym I   51 so] om. N   schulde men] men shulen A, men
shulden FN, schulen men BI   som tyme] om. M   52 schulde þei] rev. M,
⌐shulden þai⌐ α, shulen þei FI, om. NJ   þei] men Z   53 þe . . . mercy] om.
L   þat] þat þat βZH   men] þey men N, ⌐þer⌐ men T   55 so] om.
A   mercyfully] merciful T   56 þese] þe N   57 seiþ] siþ F, syn
α   58 margin apoc. 3 c M   wantowne] vntoune N   59 punischede] corr.
D   60 punyschuþ] punysched CNαβ   mercifully] merciful β   alle] and
N   in] to N   61 punysche] poneschiþ G   62 ȝyueþ] ȝaf F   good]
goodis A   63 punyschyde] punysche CNTαH, punyschiþ FJG   medlede]
medliþ ABCFNαIJGH   64 mercy] mercy þerwiþ F   þat¹] for F   þe] þes
L   65 goodes] of godis C   þer god] om. M   nakyde] bote nakyd N   of
god] om. N   67 iniurye] þe iniurye N   intenden] intende ⌐of⌐ T, intent of

f.70 mekyst of alle,|suffryde his owne iniurye in two temptacionys of
þe fend, but in þe þridde he seyde 'Go, Sathan!', and repreuyde
70 hym scharply by auctorite of God. Þus Moyses, myldeste man of
alle, killide manye þowsande of his folc, for þei worschipoden a
calf as þei schulde worschipe God. And þus in owre werkis of
mercy liþ myche discrecion, for often tymes owre mercy axeþ to
venge and to punysche men, and ellys iustises of mennys lawe
75 schulde neuere punysch men to deþ; but ofte tymes þei don amys,
and þei wyten not whanne þey doon wel. And so religioun of
prestis schulden leue siche iugementis.

---

69 Matt. 4: 10;   **70** Exod. 32: 28.

KL, purpose to N   amendement] amenden hem N   68 in two] in tʳwˡo α, into
AβJ   69 þe¹] om. Y   he] temptacioun eras. he F, temptacioun he N   margin
mt. 4 M   70 hym] hem I   myldeste] myderst L, a ful mylde N   of alle] om.
N   71 þowsande] þousendes NH   margin exodi 32 M   72 schulde] om.
M   worschipe] worsche Y   73 tymes] tyme BNZ   mercy²] werkys canc.
mercy D   74 men] om. J   iustises] iustice α   mennys] mannis ABCKL-
MTYβIXZH   75 deþ] þe deeþ AN   77 iugementis] iugementes and þerfore
caste we vs to mercye ȝef we wolen mercy fynde of god and þat he graunte vs grace of (rest
lost) N

Dominica xxiii [post festum Trinitatis.
Euangelium.] Sermo 23.

Abeuntes pharisei. Mathei 22.

Þe storye of þis gospel telluþ how þe pharisees casten to desseyue
Crist by wordis of ypocrisye. And so *þe pharises, wendyng owht* fro þe
weye of trewþe, *maden a cownseil by hemself to take Iesu in speche*; and
fyrst þei spoken fagyng wordys, as ypocrytes don, but ȝeet *þei
senten here disciples* and come not hemself, leste þei weron conuycte   5
by wisdam of Crist. Þei senten to Crist two peples, *Iewys and
Herodyanes*, to witnesse aȝenys hym whateuere he hadde seyd,
oþur aȝen þe Iewes or aȝen þe emperour. '*Maister,*' þei seiden, '*we
wyte wel þat þow art sad, trewe, and þe weye þat lediþ to God þow techist in
trewþe, and þow takist noon hed of man* but boldly tellust þe soþe, *for*   10
þow reckist of noo man but puttist God byfore.' And aftyr þei axedon
þis questioun of Crist, þat he schulde tellen þat hym þowhte and
not by oþur mennys witt, *weþur hit were leueful to ȝyue taliage to þe
emperour.* Hem þowte þat Crist schulde nede sey ⌐oþur⌐ 'ȝe' or
'nay'; ȝif he seyde 'ȝe' he spak aȝen þe Iewys, for þei chalan-   15
ghedon of þer fadris to be sughet to noo man, and ȝif he seyde
'nay' he were aȝenus þe emperour; and so on eche syde hem

MSS: D; ABCFGHIJKLMTXYZαβ; N *ends incompl.* 25 god þat at is hisse by, δ *inc.* 81 and
houeuere.

Dominica . . . euangelium] *om.* Z   sermo 23] Sermo 22 C, *om.* BFKNTYαIJX-
ZGH   abeuntes pharisei] saluatorem expectamus dominum nostrum iesum cristum
N   pharisei] pharisey consilium inierunt TH   mathei 22] mathei 12 L, mathei
12 . . . ad eph' iii N   1 þe¹ . . . of] *om.* L   þis] þe N   telluþ] today telleþ
N   þe²] þes IH   casten] castiden CNβ   2 fro] of H   3 by] *om.*
K   in] in his N   4 spoken] speken X   fagyng wordys] fagyngly N, feynynge
wordis I   5 come] wolden not come N   6 by] wiþ B, by þe N   senten]
senden C   peples] disciplis K   8 oþur] or A   or] oþer YGH   9 trewe]
truþe α   þow²] and þou α   in . . . tellust (10)] *om.* L   10 noon] not
H   but . . . man (11)] *om.* KN   boldly] bodely ⌐boldely⌐ C, bo⌐l⌐dili
J   tellust . . . soþe] teches þe lore *canc.* ⌐tellist þe soþe⌐ α   tellust] techist ABCX,
þou tellist T, techiþ J   12 þis] þi C, a Z   þat²] þat at N, ⌐what⌐ þat B   13 leueful]
on eras. corr. D   14 hem] for hem N, or noȝt þaim Z, him G   nede] *on eras. corr.* D,
nedily N   oþur] *corr.* DαH, *om.* A   or] oþer T   15 seyde] hadde seid
N   chalanghedon] chalangen TH   16 fadris] fadur N   seyde] seie

þowte þat Crist was taken. But Crist schewyde furst þe purpos of
þese ypocrites. Whan Iesu knew þe wickidnesse ⌜of⌝ þes false
20 men, he clepud hem ypocrytes and *axede wharto þey temptydon hym*;
and eft Crist took a mene weye anoþur þan þei þowten on. *'Schewe
ȝe me' seyde Crist, 'þe mone of þe taliage.' And þei schewedon hym a peny.
And Crist axede ouer, 'Whose ymage is þis? and whose wrytyng aboue?'* Þei
seyden hit was þe emperours. And Crist ȝaf hem þis answer, general
25 and sotyl, '*ȝyue ȝe to þe emperour þat is his, and to God þat is his*'; by
whiche word hit semeþ þat Crist approuede þe emperour and
subieccion to hym, in þat þat he makiþ Godis pees, and seruyse
propre to God schulde be kept to hym. And so Cristys wordis
myȝte no man disproue.

30 Heere may men towche þe malis of ypocrisye for þer is no werse
synne, ne more general, ne more venemows, for hit is more euyl
þat hit þus contrarieþ to trewþe, siþ an ypocrite feyneþ hym
hooly, and he is a false fend. And herfore repreuede Crist
ypocrisye of ordres, for he wiste wel þat þey schulden after do
35 more harm in þe world. Furst suche ypocrytes lyon on hemself,
and seyn þei don for holynesse whateuere þat þei don; and so þei
venyme furst hemself and afturward oþur men. And hit is more
general þan manye oþre synnes, for eche stat of men is blemschyd
wiþ þis synne, but furst and moste religiows and clerkys. For þer is
40 no spedy cause why þey vson syche habytes, but to dyuyden hem
in holynesse from þe comun peple; syþ as meedful werkys myȝte
þei don in secler habytis and more pryuely, as Crist bydduþ vs
ben holy. And herfore Crist bidduþ to be war wiþ sowrdow of þe

---

42 Matt. 16: 6; 11; Mark 8: 15; Luke 12: 1.

MH   17 he] þanne he I   hem] þei α   18 þat] *om.* α   19 þese] þe
Nβ   þe wickidnesse . . . false] *on eras. corr.* D   of] *corr.* D   þes] þe C-
β   20 clepud] called αZ   to þey] *on eras. corr.* D   temptydon] tempid
C   21 eft] aftur N, *om.* T   took] to L   anoþur] and ane oþer C, and anoþer
βH   22 ȝe] he β, *om.* I   seyde] sayth C   hym] hem C   23 ouer] ane
oþer ⌜oon⌝ C   þis] *om.* N   þei] and þei DABFαIJG, and *canc.* þey X   25
þat¹] þat at N   is his¹] *rev.* αJ   to²] ȝeue ȝe to N   þat²] þat at N   by
. . . word (26)] *twice, 2nd canc.* D, be þe C   26 word] wordis β   approuede]
approueþ H   þe] here tributarie to þe T   27 þat þat] þat at C, ⌜þat⌝ þat α, þat
JG   29 disproue] reproue I   30 may men] *rev.* AIJG   malis] -lis *on eras. corr.*
D   31 more²] no more M   32 hit] it is LαJZG   contrarieþ] contrary
αJZG   to] þe MH   33 repreuede crist] *rev.* H   36 seyn] sythen
C   þei¹] þat þei IJGH   don¹] doen it G   37 hit] ȝit ⌜hit⌝ T   39 and¹]
om. I   40 to] *om.* FT   41 as] alle F   werkys] werk I   42 pryuely] priuey
C   43 and] ⌜and⌝ C, and *canc.* K   *margin mt.* 16 mr. 8 luc 12 M   to] vs

pharisees, siþ þer is no resoun to ypocrisye but to schewe mennys
synne, and to disseyuen on eche syde boþe þe ypocrites hemself   45
and oþre men þat dwellen wiþ hem.|And so her religioun serueþ   f.70v
to crye þat þei ben holy, and to make diuision bytwixen hem and
oþre men; and, syþ licnesse is cause of loue among men, sych
diuision is cause of hate and enuye. Godus lawe and kynde techen
þat eche beest loueþ bᵣeᵣest lic to hym. And so experiens techuþ   50
þat oon ordre loueþ his broþer more þan a straunge man, aȝen þe
rewle of charyte. And sych gadrynge of lompys by sencible sygnes
haþ not auctorite of Crist, but raþer reprouyng, for vpon Goode
Fryday Crist ordeyned hym to be cloþud þries aȝenys sych
weddyng wiþ cloþus of colour and schap. And, as Crist seiþ in   55
repref of syche sectis, 'kynrede of hordam sekiþ siche signes'.

Alle þe dedes þat þei doon sownen to ypocrisye, and aȝenys
noo men spak Crist scharplier. And, al ȝif frerys seyn þat þei
beggon for charite, whan þei han prechid for such beggyng, and
þat Crist beggude ᵣso and bad hem begge þusᵣ, nerþeles al þis   60
speche is powdret wiþ gabbyng. And, as ypocritys doon, þei
sekon her owne auauntaghe, and not þe worschipe of Crist, ne
profiȝt of his chirche; for ȝif þei diden, þei wolden sewe Cristes
rewle and leue chargyng of þe peple, boþe in nowmbre and
beggyng, and leuen her hiȝe howses þat þei propren vnto hem,   65
siþ Crist hadde no propre hows to reston ynne his hed. And, as
Macometis lawe takiþ myche of Cristis lawe, and medleþ oþur
lawes, and þere comeþ in þe venym, so doþ antecrist in þese newe

---

49 Ecclus. 13: 15;   56 Matt. 12: 39; 16: 4   66 Matt. 8: 20.

α   þe] om. AIH   44 mennys] men CFαIJG   45 on] men on G   þe] om.
I   47 bytwixen] byt/twixen D   48 licnesse] cause I   cause] liknesse
I   49 margin eccᵃ 13 c M   hate] enuye ABCKLMTYβIZH   enuye] hate
ABCKLMTYβIZH   50 loueþ] louest α   beest²] e corr. D, best GH, his I   hym]
hymselfe α, hym best I   51 straunge] strang L   52 and . . . men (83)] om.
Z   53 not] noon H   goode] þe good G   54 crist] god T   ordeyned]
ordeynniþ β   margin mt. 27d mr. 15c M   55 weddyng] weddyngis
FT   cloþus] clopinge I   56 margin mt. 12d. M   kynrede] kynredis
B   sekiþ] scechiþ T   57 alle] and al C   sownen] sowᵣneᵣ α, suwen
I   to] þe β   58 and] þan to pharisees and T   al ȝif] ȝif on eras. corr. of þow
D   60 so . . . þus] corr. D   begge þus] rev. G   61 gabbyng] gabbyngis
FL   as] alle L, so I   þei] om. I   63 profiȝt] to profite A   64 chargyng] þe
chargyng C   65 beggyng] in begyng CH   propren] apropren B   vn-
to] to K   hem] hemsilf H   66 hadde] nadde I   margin mr. 8d. luc 9g
M   67 medleþ] medlid B   68 lawes] lawis þerwiþ T   þe] ᵣþeᵣ A, om.

sectis. And so as þey bryngon in breþren by falshede of lesyngus,
70 so ben þer ordres growndide in falsheed on eche syde. And syche
men mute nede destorblen holy chirche.

And þus secler clerkis ben fulle of ypocrisye, boþe popes and
byschopes and clerkys vndyr hem. Crist forfendide to putte
miracles þat he hadde doon to þe manhede of hym, for errour in
75 byleue. But þe fend drediþ not to feyne absolucionys and
indulgenses, wiþ oþre ʒiftys þat God grauntyde neuere, to spuyle
men of here mone, and not for sowle helþe for þanne wolde þei
ʒyue freely þese ʒiftis, as Crist ʒaf hymself and bad oþre do. And
þus lowere clerkis trauelen by watyr and by londe for to haue
80 benefices and propre possessiounes, more þan þei don for help of
mennys sowles. And howeuere þei speke, þei lyuen alle in
ypocrisye. And þus whan men fiʒten, pledon or chiden, charite is
not þer eende, but pruyde and propre hauyng. And þus hit is of
seclers þat ben weddyde men. And so charite of men is blyndid by
85 ypocrisye, so þat no synne of þis world lettiþ now more charite;
and so ypocrisye is more general synne and more pryue synne to
bygyle men, and worse to destrye in comun peple. And al þis
figuredon pharisees aʒenys Iesu ⌐Crist⌐.

---

73 John 14: 10.

G   so] and *canc.* so DX   antecrist] ancristis β   69 so] *om.* A   as þey] *on*
eras. corr. D   in] *om.* C   70 so] and so I   þer] þes C   on] in A   71
destorblen] distrourblen H   72 and²] *om.* C   73 forfendide] forfendiþ
L   *margin* io. 14b. mr. 3b M   77 of here] for Y   helþe] hele ACα-
I   78 ʒyue freely] *rev.* I   *margin* mt. 10a M   79 trauelen] *om.* β   80
benefices] benifice Cα   help] -p *on eras. corr.* D, helth CKLMYβIXG   81
mennys] mannis ACMβIH   sowles] soule CKLTYβH   lyuen . . . in] han her
lyuyng and her delite in δ   82 þus] *om.* Y   83 is] ben I   85 lettiþ] lettid
δ   86 more¹] now more H   more²] most δ   87 men] moo *canc.* men D, ⌐mo⌐
men Tα, mo men BCKLMYβδXZGH   in] in ⌐þe⌐ A, in þe Cβ   þis] þes
I   88 figuredon] figuren LM   crist] *corr.* D

Dominica xxiiii [post festum Trinitatis. Euangelium.] Sermo 24.

Loquente Iesu ad turbas ecce princeps unus. Mathei 9.

This gospel tellyþ of þe furste dede body þat Crist reysude to lyue, and how Crist helude a womman as he wente þidre. Þe story telluþ þat, *as Crist spak to þe folc, a prince cam to hym and worschypude hym wiþ honowr, and seyde to hym 'Syre, my doȝter is now deed, but come and putte þin hand on here, and sche schal lyuen* by vertew of þe.' We   5
schullen vndirstonden þat in tyme of Crist weron princes of prestis, as princes of knytes, as Nychodeme was a prince, and byschopes of Ierusaleem weren clepyd princes of prestis. And þis man here þat was keper of a synagoge as now ben persownes, and þese men hadden comunly wyues and children, as prestis han   10
worse now for þei han owt of wedloc. *And Iesus roos vp, and sewede þis prince, and hise disciples*; for he was redy to do good. And *as he wente a syȝk womman by fluxe of blod þat lastyde twelue wyntur cam byhynde Iesu, and seyde| to hireself 'Ȝif I towche þe hem of þe coote of Iesu, I schal be saf*   f.71
for holynesse of hym.' *And Iesus turnede aȝen and lokyd on hire, and saw*   15
hire byleue and seyde þus to hire, 'Affye þe doȝter, þi byleue haþ mad þe saf.' *And þe womman was sauyd from þe same howr.* The gospel of Mathew telluþ furþer how *Crist cam to þe hows of þis prince þat þe wenche lay deed ynne. And whan Crist saw mynstrelys and folc makyng noyse, he bad hem go þenne 'for þe wenche is not deed ⌈bot slepiþ⌉'.*   20
And þei scornedon Crist, for þei wenden þat he hadde errut. And

MSS: D; ABCFGHIJKLMTXYZαβδ.

Dominica . . . evangelium] *om.* Z   sermo 24] *om.* BCFKTYαδIJXZGH   ad
. . . unus] *om.* δ   princeps unus] prynceps BCT, principes A, principes vnus β, *om.*
αI   mathei 9] *om.* C   1 to] fro deþ to Cβ   2 þidre] þiderwarde δ   þe]
and þe G   3 to²] til BLMT   4 now] new C   5 sche] *om.* Y   6 tyme] þat
time β   7 as¹] and *canc.* ⌈as⌉ C, and B   8 of¹] in I   clepyd] called
αδZ   9 keper] a keper Cδ   synagoge] synage J   10 men] *om.* G   11
worse now] *rev.* H   þei] þe M   sewede] seynde β   13 lastyde] hadde lasted
δ   wyntur] ȝeer G   14 þe²] *on eras. corr.* D   15 and³] *om.* G   16 and]
om. C   þus] *om.* B   affye þe doȝter] triste affie douȝter δ   þe²] þi G   saf]
safe or hole δ   17 sauyd] saaf I, mad hol δ   from] in T, *om.* δ   þe²] þat
C   the] þis L   18 to] into H   20 makyng] make I   bot slepiþ] *corr.* DG,
bot slepes *canc.* α, but slepid H, *om.* CKLMTYββδZ   21 þat] *om.* T   23 wenche²]

whan þe folc was cast owt, Crist wente into þe hows and took þe hoond of þe
wenche and seyde, 'Wenche, rys vp!' And þe wenche roos and dide werkis
of lif.

25   Hyt is seyd byforn how þis furste body reysude fro deþ to lyue
bytokneþ suche men þat goostly ben deede, for ful concense to
synne, but þei do not þe deede wiþowte; and þat is bytooknyd þat
þe wenche was in þe hows ȝit. Þis prince is mannys þowt, þat
kyndely haþ sorwe þat þe spiriȝt of hit is þus fylud wiþ synne; and
30   þus hit preyeþ to God þat þis dowȝtur be qwykyd. And whanne
Crist entreþ to þ[e] sowle of þis mayden and meuoþ wiþ his
worchyng hond þe spiriȝt of hit, þanne hit risuþ to lyf and
worchiþ by grace. And here men nooten how a lyggyng man þat
schulde ben areryd vp schulde bedon his hand, and þe reyser
35   ⌈schulde⌉ taken hit; and so by strenkþe of hem boþe schulde þe
man ryse. Eche man in synne lyȝþ at þe eurþe, and God helpuþ
manye men to risen vp to grace; and ȝif þei worchen wiþ God to
þis werk of lif, God wole make hem stoonde and counforten hem
to worche. Þis womman þat was helyd, as Crist wente to þis hows,
40   of þe fluxe of blood þat sche hadde twelue ȝeer, is euery persoone
of man combryd wiþ synne, wheþur hit be symple persone or
gaderyt of manye. And þese twelue ȝeer betooknen dowble age of
two kyndis of man by whiche he dwelluþ in synne. But man may
spendon al þat ⌈he⌉ haþ abowten oþur fysisyens and geten hym

---

25 *See Sermon* 16/19–21;   **44** Luke 8: 43.

---

to hir wenche δ   rys] aryse δ   24 lif] cristis I   25 byforn] byfore in anoþer
sermon δ   þis] þe Y, þis was þe I   body] dede body I   reysude] þat crist *canc.*
reiside F, þat crist reiside ABI, was reised M   26 bytokneþ] ⌈and it⌉ bitokneþ
I   goostly ben] *rev.* AI   27 þat is bytooknyd] it betokyneth C, ys bytokenid T,
þat bitokened H   þat²] ⌈by þat⌉ þat T   29 fylud] fillid, *first* I *canc.* J, fillid
ACFLH, foulid K, defouled δ   30 preyeþ] preied H   þis] his X   qwykyd]
quykened ABCFKLMTYαβδIJZGH   31 to] in *canc.* to DX, into CαδJH   þe]
þis D   his] þis δ   32 hond] and *canc.* ⌈hand⌉ H, and I   hit risuþ] riseþ I, is
resyd L   33 worchiþ] wurched δ   nooten] taken hede δ   34 areryd] areisid
AFJ, raysed αIZ, rered δ   bedon] bede forth δ   reyser] riser T   35
schulde¹] *corr.* D   strenkþe] strenge β   schulde] þe man] þe man schulde
δ   36 ryse] arise B   eche man] alle men H   in] þat ben in H   lyȝþ] ben
H   37 wiþ] to I   god] grace *canc.* god D   to³] wiþ I   38 þis] hys
T   werk] werkys T   wole] wolde I   stoonde] to *canc.* stoonde DX, to stonde
H   40 þe] *om.* H   41 man] men K   combryd] ⌈a⌉combred H   42
manye] ma *canc.*// manye D   þese] þis C   43 man¹] men I   man²] a man
δ   *margin* luc. 8 α   44 he] *corr.* D   oþur] *om.* I   hym] hem AI, *om.*

absolucion, – ȝee, after þe day of doom, – and manye in- 45
dulgenses wiþ lettres of fraternyte, þat heeton h[y]m to come to
heuene as sone as he is deed; and ȝet may þe fluxe of blood renne
wiþ al þis, and he may be deppere in synne wiþ alle þese
dispensis. And herfore mekenesse of Crist is a special medicyne,
þat a man þenke how he is in þe laste place, bedon of Crist to 50
sowpen in heuene wiþ hym. And þus þis clooþing of Crist ben
seyntes þat he cloþiþ, and þe laste of þis cloþing is þe laste place
þat men schulden reputen hem ynne by mekenes of herte; and,
doyng awey þ⌐u⌐s presumpcion, comen þei þus byhynde, and
Crist by sych mekenesse ȝyueþ hem grace to leue synne. And þis 55
is bettur þan medicynes þat fisisienes sullen. And syche men ben
counfortyde by wordis of Crist, for Crist heluþ none bodyly but
ȝif he hele hem of synne.

And þus eche story of myracles of Crist may be moralisyd to a
good witt. Ne hit is no perele to varien in suche wittis, so þat men 60
varye not fro trewþe ne fro good lore, for þe Holy Gost, auctour of
þese wordis, ordeynyth men to haue alle syche wittes; and he
ordeyneþ þis tixt to meuen hem herto. How scholde such sense
ben errour in man? But suche wordes axen good iugement, for
manye eretykes seyn þat þei han witt of God, and ȝet hit may ben 65
on of þe fendis eresyes.

Here men dowten comunly whanne men synnen deedly
wiþynne in þer sowle and don none euel dedys wiþowten in þer
body þat anoyen men. And men mouen ouer how reson may
assente to any synne of man, siþ eche ⌐synne⌐ is aȝenys resoun. 70

α   45 absolucion] absolucions AFYδIZGH   indulgenses] indulgence α   46
fraternyte] fraternytas δ, fraternytes H   heeton] bi *canc.* hotiþ F, ⌐byʔhoten Tβ,
bihotiþ ACKIZ   hym] hem DFMI   47 he] hee D   may] was
T   blood] bode C   renne] rennyʔnge⌐ T   48 deppere] departid I   49
herfore] þerfor Z   a] *om.* Z   50 þenke] þenketh δ   how] on hou δ   51
sowpen] spouse I   in . . . hym] wiþ him in heuene ABCKLMTYαβδIZG-
H   clooþing] clepyng C   ben . . . cloþing (52)] *om.* Z   52 cloþiþ] cloþid
Aαδ   of þis] *om.* δ   þe²] *om.* δ   53 schulden] schul δ   reputen] repute
altered to repente δ, repente C   54 þus] þis, -i- *canc.* -u- D, þes AB, þis TδH, ⌐þus⌐
α   presumpcion] presumpcions ABI   þei] ay Cα   56 bettur] þe betere
H   þat] ⌐þat⌐ TY, *om.* β   men] *om.* T   57 by] wiþ δH   58 hem] hym
CMδIJZH   59 to] by L   60 men] man C   61 varye] waien C   trew-
þe] þe treuþe A   62 þese] þis TI   ordeynyth] orden α   alle . . . wittes]
syche wittes alle *marked for rev.* D   63 ordeyneþ] ordende α   þis] his L   hem]
men αH   scholde] -o- *altered from* -u- D   64 ben] by L   man] men δ   65
witt] wittes C   hit] þai C   66 on] *om.* I   68 in¹] *om.* BT   sowle] soulis
M   þer] þe B   70 man] men I   synne²] *corr.* DMT, *om.* KLYβ   71

And ȝet somme men seyn þat hit is al on, resoun and mannys
spiriȝt; and so, ȝif mannys spiriȝt assente, resoun assentiþ, for
f.71v mannys spirit|haþ alle vertewes in man hangyng on hym, and hit
mut nedely do what anye of þese vertewes doþ. Here we schullen
75 conceyue þa[t] hit is not nedful heere to wyte which is deedly
synne and to wyte which is venyal; but eche synne schulde a man
fle, leste hit bee deedly to hym. But clerkis seyn comunly þat man
haþ two wittis: oon hanguþ on his body, and haþ monye partyes;
anoþur is abouen his body and dwelluþ wiþ his spiriȝt, whan
80 þe spiryt and þe body ben departid atwynne. And þis vertew in a
man is somtyme clepyd resoun. And so, as in þe furste synne Eue
temptede Adam and Adam synned not byforn he hadde assentyt,
so in eche synne in an hool man þe flesch temptiþ þe spiriȝt and
hit synneþ not byforn hit haue assentyd to lustis of þe flesch. And
85 so power of þe spiriȝt, þat somme men clepon resoun, assentiþ
aȝen resoun to fleschly lykyngus. And so þe spiriȝt is nedyd to
consente þus, but hit is not constreynot, siþ hit assentyþ frely.
And by þis may we see how argumentis gon awey by
equiuocacion of wordys þat men spekon, as a man haþ manye
90 wittes, boþe fleschly and spiritual, and so on monye manerys he
assentiþ to a þing. But somme foolis þer ben þat seyn þat a man
haþ no vertew of sowle, but ȝif hit be þe same sowle; and þis
errour brynguþ in oþre. And þus resoun of man is somtyme
clepyd trewþe, þat God causuþ wiþowten ende ȝif a man dyȝe.
95 And somtyme vertew of man þat goþ wiþ þe sowle is clepud
resoun of man to anoþur witt. By þis may m[e]n see somwhat how

men] *om.* L   hit] ȝit it I   mannys] mennus F   72 assente] assentiþ
H   resoun] ⌐to⌐ resoun δ   73 hangyng] hauyng L   on] in C   74
nedely] nedelingis A   we] men L   schullen] shuld αJ   75 not] *om.*
T   deedly...is (76)] *margin corr.* Cα   76 to] ⌐to⌐ X, *om.* AFT   wyte]
om. T   a] a *canc.* X, *om.* BCKLMTYβδZH   man] men δ   77 hit] in
C   hym] hem δ   man] a man Fαδ   78 on] in δI   79 anoþur] and
anoþer αδIJ   and] þat AF   80 þe¹] his H   þe²] his BKLMTYβδXZ-
G   atwynne] on two δ   81 clepyd] called αδZ   as] is I   82 temptede]
temperede I   83 so] and so I   temptiþ] temptid β   84 synneþ] ne synneþ
I   haue] hath CJG   assentyd] assentiþ A   85 clepon] calle αδZ   86
lykyngus] lykyng T   þe] þis B   87 assentyþ] assentide I   88 may we] *rev.*
I   89 equiuocacion] equiuocaciouns αδH   90 spiritual] spiritualy AT   on]
om. AL   manerys] manere I   91 a²] ⌐a⌐ α, *om.* IJ   92 ȝif] *om.* Y   93
brynguþ] bigynnes Z   man] men δ   somtyme clepyd] is clepid sumtyme C, is
sumtyme called αδ, somtyme callid Z   94 a] *om.* G   95 man] a man
C   clepud] called αδZ   96 man] a man C   may men] *rev.* δI   men] a

þei schulden answere to þe dowtis þat ben made and to oþre also. For we schulden byleue þat men may be dampnyde for synne in here sowle, ȝif þei worche not owhtward, for original synne and actual also. And þus may men be sauyd for þowtis in þer herte, al   100 ȝif þei do not owtward meritorie werkys. And þus may men don harm to oþre by þowtis of herte, and profiȝten also to hem ȝif þei ben fer from hem; and sych spiritual harmyng or profiȝt is myche moore þan bodily profiȝt.

man DF, a *eras.* men, -e- *altered from* -a- X, man α   97 schulden] schullen I   98 in] and L   99 ȝif] al ȝif LMI   100 may men] *rev.* I   þer] *om.* C   herte] hertis A   al ȝif] al þauȝ δ   101 outward . . . werkys] merytorye werkes vtwarde δ   owtward] outewardis β   may men] *rev.* αIJ   102 of] in H   herte] her *canc.* herte D, her herte BCKLMTYαβJXZG, here hertes δH   ȝif] al if F, þauȝ δZ   103 sych] siþ AFX   harmyng] harmyng, -is *canc.* Y, harmyus β   profiȝt] profityng M

Dominica xxv [post festum Trinitatis.
Euangelium.] Sermo 25.

Cum subleuasset oculos Iesus. Iohannis 6.

This gospel telluþ a miracle how Crist fedde þe folc, and þis miracle techiþ men boþe good feyþ and vertewus. Hit is seyd byfore how Crist fedde ⌐þe⌐ folc þus twyes; and of þe secounde feedyng hit is seyd byfore, and of þis furste fedyng schulde we
5 speke now. Þe gospel seiþ þus þat þis myracle was doon: *whan Iesus hadde cast vp his eyȝen, and saw þat myche folc was come to hym to here Godis word, he seyde to Philip wherof þei schulde bughge breed for to fede þis folc,* for he wiste þat þei hungredon. *Þis seyde Crist to Philip* ⌐*for*⌐ *to tempton hym, for he wiste ful wel what he hadde to do. Philip seyde*
10 *to Crist þat loues of two hundred pens ne suffysid not to hem, so þat echone myȝte taken a lytulwhat of breed. But anoþur disciple, Andrew, P*⌐*e*⌐*trys broþur, seyde þer was a child þere, þat hadde fyue barly louys and þerto two fyschis; but what wolde þis be among þus myche folc?* And Iesu baad hise apostles ⌐*to*⌐ *make þe men sytte down to þe mete, for þer was myche heyȝ [in*
15 *þe place]* þat þei myȝten sytton onne. *And þe men weren sette, as hit were fyue þowsynde. And Iesu took þanne þes louys and, whanne he hadde þankyd God, he delud hem to þe syttyng men, and also of þe fyschis as myche as þei wolden. And whanne þei weren fyllude, Crist seyde to his disciples, 'Gedre ȝe þe relef þat lefte, þat hit perische not'. And þei gadredon and*

MSS: D; ABCFGHIJKLMTXYZαβδ; N *inc.* 12 loues.

Dominica . . . euangelium] *om.* Z   sermo 25] *om.* BCFKTYαδIJXZGH   oculos
iesus] *rev.* αH   iesus] iesu et vidisset δ   iohannis 6] iohannis 16 I   2 hit] and
it I   seyd] *om.* M   3 þe¹] *corr.* D, *om.* CFKLMTYβδXZGH   folc þus] þus
folc *marked for rev.* Y, *rev.* C   4 hit is] *rev.* CKTβG   *margin* dominica 7 J   þis]
þe AG   schulde] schul δI   5 þat] *om.* I   7 þei schulde] *rev.* Y   9 for to]
for *corr.* D   tempton] temp C   for²] *om.* β   to²] ⌐to⌐ MY   philip] and
philip Aδ   10 loues] þe loues β   ne] *om.* Y   suffysid] suffisen H   ech-
one] echeon of hem δ   11 petrys] e *corr.* D   12 þer] þat þer H   a] *om.*
C   þere þat] *rev.* A   þerto two] þer two I   þerto] *om.* Nδ   13 wolde]
wolen I   be] do α   þus] so ABCFKLMNTYβδIZGH   14 to] *corr.*
Ð   þe¹] hise N   sytte] to sitte Nα   down] adown T   þe²] þe *canc.* X,
om. ABCKLMNTYβδZGH   in þe place þat] þat DABFKLMNTαδIJXG   15
þat] þat þat β   þei] men G   onne] vpon N   16 þes] *on eras. corr.*
D   whanne] *om.* Z   17 hem] hit N   fyschis] fysche Nδ   19 þe] *om.*

fulden twelue cophynus of relif of fyue barly louys, þat weron lefte of þis folc 20
þat eton. And þese men, whanne þei hadden seen þe sygne of þis myracle,
seyden among hemself þat þis is a verrey profete þat is to comen into þis
world,|as prophetis byfore hadde te⸍e⸍ld.   f.72
We schul suppose of þis myracle þat hit is dyuerse fro þe toþur,
for ellis Mark wolde not ha⸍fe⸍ teeld þese myracles so dyuersely   25
and in dyuerse places, for þe ton hadde þanne be false and hit
hadde ben superflu to þus haue teeld þis tale. And herfore we
schal suppose þat þese weren two myracles, þat weren done in þis
maneris as þe gospel telluþ. And we ⸍schal⸍ supposen ouer þat, as
Crist qwykyde þre men for a nootable cause, whoso cowde   30
vndyrstonden hit, so he maade þese two festis for a certeyn
resoun. And hit ys seyd comunly þat, as þe nowmbre of two is þe
furste þat comeþ from onheede of nowmbres, so þese two feestis
bytoknen þat men for þer synne ben fallen in þis neede to be fed
þus. For ʒif þat man hadde stonden in þe stat of innocens, he   35
schulde haue had no nede to be fed þus, for man schulde ha⸍fe⸍
felyd no peyne byfor þat he hadde synnyd, and so he schulde not
han hungred for defawt of mete. But, for he wente fyrst by synne
from onheede of God, þerfore he fel þus twyes in peyne for his
synne. And God telluþ suche trewþus on dyuerse manerys, now   40

25 Mark 6: 35-44, 8: 1-9; **30** *See* no. 16/14-26; **37** Gen. 3: 17.

Y   þat lefte] þat leueþ NTδ, þat ⸍is⸍ lefte X, þat is left MG, *om.* L   20 cophynus]
berelepys *canc.* cophynus D, ⸍lepus⸍ N   fyue] þe fyue H   þis] þuse NG   21
þat] at C   men] folk I   22 seyden] þei seiden H   þat¹] *om.* C   a] *om.*
LM, þe δ   profete]-phe- *written below* -f- *corr.* (*modern?*) D   to comen] ⸍to⸍ comen
H, come ABFY   23 byfore . . . teeld] tolde byfore N   hadde] han Cα   teeld]
e *corr.* D   24 of] *om.* N   þis] þis firste N   þat hit] *om.* N   hit] *om.*
M   25 wolde] wolde he I   hafe] fe *corr.* D   þese] þe δ   myracles]
miracle IH   26 and¹] *om.* Y   places] place C   hadde þanne] *rev.* CN-
I   be]-n *eras.* D   27 ben] be þanne T, þan ben H   to þus haue] þus to haue
Nδl   herfore] þerfore N   we schal] *rev.* N   28 in] on T   29 maneris]
maner⸍es⸍ α, manere FH   þe] þis αJ   schal] *corr.* D   30 qwykyde]
quykenyde BCLNδZG, qwikeneþ I   a] *om.* C   whoso] who⸍so⸍ H, who
CKLMTYβG   cowde vndyrstonden] vndurstod N   31 so] and *canc.* so αG, and
so TJ   two] *om.* H   32 hit . . . two] as þe noumbre of two comynly is seid
N   33 þese] þe A   34 for . . . ben] ben in þis nede N   in þis neede] for þer
synne N   to] þus to N   35 þus] *om.* N   þat] ⸍þat⸍ β, *om.* AB   man] a
canc. man D, a man Cα   innocens] þe innocensse β   36 haue] *om.* T   had]
om. CZ   be] haue be Nδ   hafe] fe *corr.* D   hafe...peyne (37)] no peyne
haue felte N   37 þat] *om.* TJ   he¹] ⸍he⸍ H, *om.* Y   39 he fel] *rev.* N   fel]
fledde I   his] *om.* I   40 manerys] manere F   41 and¹] *om.* α   þis]

for o cause and now for anoþur. And þus by þis resoun curatys of
puples, ȝif þei ben hoole in body, ben poore feble men: þey ben
poore ⌜men⌝ ȝif þei kepon her ordre, for þei schulden sewe Crist
in pouert nerre þan oþre comunys; and þei ben feble, for þei han
45 neede of sustenaunce þat þei schulde not haue had in þe staat of
innocens. And þei may not, as Crist, haue mete where þat þei
wolden; and þus for pouert and febulnesse þei taaken almes of
comunes.

Þese fyue louys ben fyue bookys of Moyses, þat beþ boþe
50 streyte and scharpe as seynt Petre seiþ. Þese two fyschis ben two
bookys of wysdam and of prophetis, þat ben sowuyl to þese fyue
louys. And þis o child þat haþ al þis mete is þe child born to vs,
þat Ysaye spekyþ of. Þis child makiþ his puple to sytte down in
mekenesse, þenkyng þat þei ben heyȝ whohis flour falliþ. But þe
55 goostly foode is purposyd of Crist for to be tooknyd by bodyly
foode. And fyue þowsynde of men fed wiþ þis mete weren alle þo in
whiche Godes grace was grene, for alle þese mute meken hem and
be fedde wiþ Godis word, for ellys may noo man come to heuene
blysse. And þus men þat ben falle down by þe pruyde of synne
60 schullen by mekenesse of þe centre be browt vnto heuene. For, as
lownesse of centre of þe world and þe eurþe is þe mooste lownesse
þat God may make, so mekenesse of Crist is þe moste þat may be.
And in þis mekenesse mut a man grownden his towr, ȝif hit
schulle teyne to heuene; for þe towr of þe gospel þat man schulde

53 Isa. 9: 6.

om. N   42 ȝif] al ȝif LMZ, þeyȝ Nδ   hoole] holy N   þey] ⌜and⌝ þey T   43
men] *corr.* D, *om.* T, feble men δ   45 sustenaunce] syche sustenaunce T   sch-
ulde] ne scholden I   not] *om.* N   þe] *om.* ABCKLMTβδIZGH   46
innocens] in noce L   and] as α   þat] *om.* ANYδIH   47 and²] of I   almes of comunes] mennes almes N   49 þese] þe L   þat] and N   50 two²] *om.*
Nδ   51 of prophetis] prophecie N   sowuyl] swete sufel N   fyue] *om.*
AB   52 o] *om.* I   haþ] had C   þis²] þe A   to] vnto I   53 his] þis
MI   to] to *canc.* X, *om.* ABCFKLMNTYβδGH   54 heyȝ] as hey N   falliþ]
sone falleþ N, faileþ I   55 is] þat *canc.* is DX   for to] to H   be tooknyd]
bytokne N, be bytokened δ   56 weren] þat *canc.* weren BT, þat were Y   57
whiche] þe whiche β   grene] ȝoue δ   58 may noo man] no man mai δ   heuene blysse] þe blisse of heuene F   59 þus] þese δ   ben] *om.* Y   þe] *om.*
ACNβ   pruyde] synne F, þridde H   of] *om.* N   synne] pryde F, fyue
KMTYβXZH, *om.* N   60 schullen] shuld α   vnto] into BCH, to T, vp
to δ   61 centre] þe centre ABCKLMNTYαβδIJXZGH   world...þe²] *om.*
C   and] in α   þe³] *om.* H   mooste lownesse] lowest N   62 so] and so β,
and so þe δ, and þe N   63 mut] must CN   a] *om.* T   64 schulle] *om.*

wyllen to rere is vndirstanden comunly hei3nesse of vertewys, of 65
whiche vertewys mekenesse is grownd, and charyte þe hey3est
part þat teyneþ ⌐vn⌐to heuene. Aftyr þis mete weren gedride
twelue cophynes, for hooly doctoures aftyr þese materis wheren
moore sutyl in wytt of hooly wryt, þan aftyrward been doctoures
in wytt of Godis lawe. For, siþ men stoonden in sophismys and 70
craft of worldly wynnyng, and loore of fowre doctoures is myche
leyd asleepe, nerþeles þis relif schulde feede folc now; for neiþur
þis hool mete, ne relif þerof, may rote or perysche siþ hit is trewþe
of God. And so þese twelue cophynes ben alle þe moo sentences
þat furst weren gederyde of wytt of hooly wryt; but þe seuene 75
leepys þat weren gaderyd aftyr weren fewor goode sentencys þat
weren taken of Godys lawe. And þis myracle of multiplyeng of
Godis lawe by so fewe prechowres among so fele folc was|more f.72v
myracle þan bodily wondyris. And þerfore hooly men þat
turneden to God glorifien hym and hoolden hym here kyng.   80

N   teyne] en *canc.* teyne DX, atyne CβI, reche αδ   65 wyllen] wylne δZ-
H   rere] rayse αZ   66 whiche] þuse N   vertewys] vertu B   mekenesse
is] *rev.* N   is] ⌐is⌐ AC   þe] is *canc.* ⌐þe⌐ α, is þe BG, *om.* M   67 teyneþ]
atenyth Cβ, reches α   vnto] vn *corr.* D, to Cδ   þis mete] þe mete δ, *om.*
N   68 cophynes] cofynes of relif FNJ   aftyr...sutyl (69)] were more sutel aftur
þes maretyres α   69 moore sutyl] wyttier and sueler N   wytt] holy wit
I   70 stoonden] han stonden δ   71 worldly] worldis LMTH   fowre] þe
foure δ   myche] *om.* F   72 asleepe] to slepe Nδ   73 þerof] herof Y   or]
ne K   74 so] also B   þese] alle *canc.* þes X, al þes AF   moo] mo⌐re⌐ T, many
Z, mene Nδ   sentences] sentense CαH   75 þe] *om.* G   76 aftyr] afturward
N, afterward in þe secunde fest δ   fewor] foure LMδ, fewe Z   sentencys]
sentence TαH   77 of ¹] in Nδ   78 by] are α, ben I   fele] miche CI, many α,
fewe Nβ   79 wondyris] w3ondes N   þerfore] herfore, h- *altered from* þ- X,
herfore BKLMNTYβδZGH   80 glorifien] gloryfye⌐d⌐ α   kyng] kyng ende F,
kyng amen I, king þer eenden þe dominical gospelis þorou3e þe 3eer Y, kynge expliciunt
euangelia dominicalia per annum amen. ista euangelia dominicalia corriguntur per
primum originalem α, king. amen. explicit. expliciunt epistole et ewangelia dominicales
per annum X, kynge. expliciunt dominice tocius anni Z, kyng prey we þerfore to god þat
is kyng of alle to bringen vs to his feste þat euermore schal laste þorwh heryng of his word
and lyfyng þeraftur and þat it so be etc. pater et aue N

Dominica prima Aduentus. [Euangelium.]
Sermo 26.

Cum appropinquasset Iesus Ierosolimis. Mathei 21.

This gospel telluþ of þe secounde aduent of Crist; and hit is no
drede hit techuþ vs vertewes, syþ alle þe deedis of Crist telle men
how þei schulden doo. Þis story telluþ how *Iesu cam* to his passioun
vnto Ierusaleem, to teche þat he ordeyned hymself for to suffre; for
5 he myhte ⌐haue⌐ fled þis passioun ⌐of hym⌐, ȝif he wolde hymself
not ha⌐ue⌐ suffryd þus. And so men seyn comunly þat þer ben þre
aduentis, bysyde ⌐þe⌐ comun aduent þat Crist comeþ to mannys
sowle. In þe furste aduent Crist cam to be man, and þis aduent
abyden seyntis of þe oolde lawe; and þis was no moryng but
10 lassyng of God, ȝe more lassyng þan to aungelis, as þe salm seiþ,
for God was maad eurþe whan he was maad man. Þe secounde
aduent is comynge to Cristis passioun, and of þis makiþ þis gospel
mynde today. Þe þridde aduent schal be whan Crist schal come
to iugement at þe day of doom to iuge boþe good and euyl. And in
15 alle þese þre aduentis Crist visitude euere his sugetis to amenden
hem and not to spuylen hem; and wolde God þat prelatys wolden
þenkon on ⌐þis⌐ now, þanne schulde þei not come in antecristis
name more to spuyle þer sugetis þan to amenden hem. Þe furste
aduent of Crist we byleuen as passyd, and þe þridde aduent

MSS: D; ABCFGJKLMNTXYZαβδ.

Dominica . . . euangelium] *om.* NαZ   sermo 26] *om.* CFKNTYαδJXZG   cum
. . . ierosolimis] abiciamus opera tenebrarum N   appropinquasset] appropinquaret T   ierosolimis] aduentus ierosolimis Cβ   mathei 21] mathei 22 C,
mathei 1α, ad ro' viii N   1 this] þe N   telluþ] today telleþ N   3 schulden]
schal G   þis] þe AN   4 vnto] to T   for to] to F   5 haue] *corr.* D   of
hym] *corr.* D, of hymsilf T, of hem J, *eras.* B, *om.* N   ȝif] and ȝef N   wolde] hadde
wold B   6 haue] -ue *corr.* D, to haue δ   þus] hit N, þis δ   7 þe] *corr.* D, þe
eras. X, *om.* BCKLMYβδJZG   8 be] bicom Z   9 seyntis] þe seyntes δ   of]
in J   moryng] -r-*on eras. corr.* D, moruynge, -r-*canc.* α, mouing FKLMNTYβδXZ,
mowyng C, mornyng J   10 as] and as G   11 god] he N   þe] and the
F   12 aduent] *om.* M   to] to *on eras. of* T, of Y   þis2 . . . mynde (13)]
mynde þis gospel F   þis2] þe ANTδG, þo α   13 be . . . schal2] *om.* M   14
and1] *om.* C   15 visitude] visit α   to amenden hem] hem to amende N   16
to] for to N   and1 . . . hem (18)] *om.* Z   þat] *om.* G   17 þis] *corr.*
D   þei not] *rev.* Y   18 name] lawe M   to2] for to J.   19 byleuen]

abyde we as to comen, but by þe secownde aduent we schulden 20
maken vs redy to suffren in owre body for þe name of Crist.
Crist cam to Betphage, þat is a lytul town in þe foot of Olyuete, a
myle fro Ierusaleem. And þis town was ȝyue to preestis for mete of
here mowþus, for Bethfage is 'hows of mowþ', or ellys 'hows of
etyng'. And by þis tawȝte Crist how he lyuede poore lyf and nedy 25
for þe loue of man, siþ he dwellyde in syche þropis; and he teelde
how prestis eten ⌈hym⌉ by enuye. *þanne he sente two disciples to*
Ierusaleem, þat was wallyd, and þerfore *Crist clepuþ hit a castel,* þat
was aȝen hooly chyrche. *Crist bad hise disciples to bryngon hym an asse*
and þe fole of þis asse, þat þei schulden fynden al reedy; and bad þat þei 30
schulden loosen hem and bryngon hem to Criȝst. And, ȝif any seyde owht to
hem, þei schulden seye '*þe Lord haþ nede of hem*', and he schulde leuen hem
anoon. *And þis was fyllyd, as Crist seyde by his prophete* longe aforn,
'*telle ȝe to Syon, þe doȝter of Ierusaleem* "*Loo, þi Kyng comeþ to þe, hoomly,*
syttyng ⌈vp⌉*on an asse and vpon þe asse foole*"', whiche asse was a 35
drawyng beest. *And hise disciples wenten and diden as Iesu comaundyde*
hem, for alle þese þingus mote nede be riȝt as Crist hadde
ordeynyt hem; and by þis myȝte þe disciples knowe þat þis Lord
was al wytty. *And hise disciples putteden here cloþus vpon þese two bestys,*
furst vpon þe fole, and siþ vpon þe asse, to techen vs þat heþene 40
men, þat weren wantowne as folys, schulde receyue Crist and his
lawe, and aftyr Iewes as asses, for þei schullen bere to þe eende of
þe world þe weyȝte of þe oolde lawe, as folte assis beren charghes,

---

33 Zach. 9: 9.

byleeuen *1st-e-canc.* D   as] hath δ   20 abyde we] *rev.* AYJ   as] þat is
ABJ   by] to AB   21 body] boy C   22 to] fro F   is] was T   24 of¹]
om. C   26 þe] *om.* ABCKLMTYαβδJZG   27 hym] *corr.* D   enuye] enymye
C   28 clepuþ] calleth δ, called αZ   29 to bryngon] *rev.* N   to] *om.*
Cδ   an] out of þis castel an N   30 þe . . . asse] hire fole N   þis] þe
J   þat] þe wuche N   fynden al reedy] al redy fynden N   31 criȝst] hym
N   any] any man J   seyde] seye J   32 þe] þat þe L   schulde] shal α,
anoun schulde N   33 anoon] *om.* N   fyllyd] ⌈ful⌉fild T, fulfillid δJ   by] to
C   his] þis T   aforn] bifore ABCKLMNTYαβδJXZG, aftir F   35 vpon]
vp *corr.* D, on CNYαδZ   þe] an B   whiche] þe whiche J   asse³] *om.*
T   36 iesu] crist F   37 mote] most F   as] a J   hadde] haþ Nδ   38
by . . . knowe] þe disciples myȝten knowe by þis N   myȝte] *om.* C   þe] his
J   knowe] knew C   39 vpon] vp Y, on α   two] *eras.* F   40 vpon¹] on
α   and] *om.* ABC   vpon²] on α   41 receyue] þorw grace resceyuen
N   42 lawe] lawe, -s *eras.* F, lawes ABCKLMNTαβδJXZG   iewes] þo iues
α   schullen] suld Z   to] fro N   þe] *om.* Tβ   43 weyȝte] whitte
N   folte] *om.* β   assis] asse C   charghes] charge C   44 whateuere]

whateuere be leyd on hem. *And hise disciples maaden Crist to sytten on*
45 *boþe þo bestys.* But þ⌐r⌐e maneer of folc comen owt of Ierusaleem
and diden worchype to Crist, for comunes louedon hym ri3t wel.
Myche puple þat was ryche spredden here cloþus in þe weye, and poorer
schreddon braunchis of trees and spredden ⌐hem⌐ *in þe weye; and oþre,* boþe
3ong[e] and oolde, *comyng byforn and byhynde, songon* ⌐þis songe⌐ in
50 worschipe of Iesu, Dauid sone ⌐⌐*We preyn make vs saf*; þis we seyen
to Dauid sone⌐, *blessyd be he þat is comen þus to vs in Godis naame.*'
Summe men seyn þat þese disciples þat weren sente to
f.73 Ierusaleem been herty prestis and worldly lordis þat schulden|be
boþe Cristys disciples, and brynge to Crist þis asse and her fole to
55 ry3de to heuenly Ierusaleem. And, as Ierusaleem was wallyt
a3enys Crist and hise apostles, so þese religiows today ben wallyd
a3en cristene men. But þis wal is mennys fyndyng, hepyd
wiþowten charyte; for hit is noo charyte to leue þe ordre þat Crist
3af, and to take þese stynkyng ordres, and tellen more pris by þis
60 reson 'þis synful patrown bad do þus, ⌐þerfore we schulden do
þus⌐' þanne by þis 'Crist bad alle men do þus, þerfore þei
schulden do þus.' He þat synneþ in þis feiþ synneþ a3en byleue,
a3en þe maundementis of þe fyrste table, and ⌐so⌐ a3en alle Godis
maundementis. And þus schulden cristen men brynge to Crist
65 boþe þis asse and her foole, þat ben bownden in Ierusaleem by
syche false religiows. And so þis asse and her fole ben comun to
þese pryuate ordres, but not to alle cristen men, al 3if þei ben

whatsoeuer ANJ, and whatsoeuer δ   on¹] vpon ABCFKLMTYαβJZG   45
boþe þo]þes boþe ABFKLMTYαβδJG, þir twa Z   þo]þuse N, *om.* C   þre]r *corr.*
D   46 to] *om.* M   comunes] comoun puple FδJ   hym] crist Nδ   ri3t]
om. N   47 puple] folk F   was] weren Y   poorer] pore⌐re⌐ α, pore, -re *canc.*
K, pore CβδZ   48 schreddon] men shradden δ, spradden N   of] of þe δ   and¹
. . . weye] *om.* N   hem] *corr.* D   49 3onge] 3ongo D, olde α   oolde]
3onge α   þis songe] *corr.* D   in worschipe] *om.* M   50 iesu] ⌐iesu⌐ B, *om.*
F   we . . . sone (51)] *lower margin corr.* D, *corr. margin* α   þis] þus M   51
blessyd] bissed C   be] is Y   he] ⌐he⌐ Aα   is comen þus] þus is comyn C, ys
to comyn þus T, is comen δ   53 herty prestis] archprestes α   be boþe] *rev.*
α   55 and . . . hem (90)] *om.* Z   57 mennys] manes CG   hepyd] helpid
L   58 hit] soþely it N   59 ordres] ordres wiþouten maundement of god
N   pris] prys þerby T   60 þis] ⌐and⌐ þis C, þat þis FαδJ   þer- . . . þus
(61)] *margin corr.* D   61 þis] *om.* N   crist] þat crist α   bad] þat bad
N   þerfore . . . þus (62)] *om.* N   þei] we FY   62 synneþ²] he syneþ
δJ   a3en] and a3enus J   63 maundementis] maundementis, co-*canc.* Y,
comaundementes FJ, maundement Nδ   godis maundementis] ten N   64
maundementis] maundementis, co-*canc.* Y, comaundementes FKαJ   65 her] þer
T   ben bownden] *rev.* N   66 syche] þuse N   religiows] religiouns
β   67 ordres] religiouns N   to] ⌐to⌐ A, *om.* Y   al 3if] all if þat α, þey3 N,

betture and han more nede. ʒet þese ʒeldis fownde of men helpon
alle þer breþren in nede [boþe] of temporal goodis, and laten hem
dwellen in Cristis ordre. But þese sectis of newe ordris helpe not   70
þus þer breþren, for b[e] þei olde, be þei ʒonge, be þei neuere at
sych meschef, þei wole not helpon hem wiþ goodys for to lyuen in
Cristys ordre, but raþur enprisowne hem or punyschen hem aʒen
Godis lawe. But, by þe rewle of charyte, þei schulden sille þer
hyʒe howses and alle þe mebles þat þei han, and helpe þer   75
breþren in neede, and lyue al afᵣterᵗ Cristis lawe. Þus Cryst ʒaf
boþe body and sowle for releuyng of hise enemyes. But how lasten
sych religious, oþur in mercy or in charite, þat wole not ʒyue þer
ydel goodys for ᵣþeᵗ releuyng of þer breþren? And þus hem
wanteþ heyʒeste loue [and] eche degree of charyte, for þei louen   80
moore þer ydel muc þan ᵣþey donᵗ þer breþren in God. Feyned
lettres of fraternyte wolen þei ʒyue to symple men; but to lordis
and to men þat þei seyn þei loue more wole þei not profre siche
lettres, leste þer falsehede be perseyued. For syche lettres or
chartres profyʒte not to men, but oþur to maken hem haue riʒt or   85
elles to defende her riʒt; siche lettres maken no riʒt, ʒe by mannys
lawe, and þis riʒt is not enpechid byfor þe day of doom. And ʒif
men schewen þanne þese lettres oþur to God or his lawe, þei
profiʒte noþing to hem, ne defenden hem aʒen God. And so þese
lettres ben superflew, as ben þese ordres þat maken hem.   90

and ʒif C   68 nede] mede N   ʒet] ʒef N   ʒeldis] ʒoldes A   fownde]
newe founden F   69 boþe of] of D, boþe in N   70 newe] þese newe Bα   71
be¹] by D   be²] ᵣor¹ be F, or canc. be J   72 sych] so muche Nδ J   wole] wold
C   73 but raþur] þen N   enprisowne] prisounne LM   74 þer] alle her F,
om. N   75 mebles] noeblis L   and²] to Y   76 al] om. J   after] -ter corr.
D   77 releuyng] reuelyng J   78 oþur] or ACKLMTYβδJXG, om. B   in¹]
om. C   or] eiþer F   in²] in canc. Y, om. KM   79 þe] corr. D, þe canc. J, om.
Nα   releuyng] helping ABCFKLMTYβδJG   80 and] in DFT   81 þey
don] corr. D   feyned] ᵣand¹ feyned T, and feynid CJ   82 to²] om. N   83
men] grete men N   þat] om. C   þei²] þat þei AMT   not] om. N   siche]
noun suche N   84 be] were FαJ, schulde be N   perseyued] knowen N   or]
of B, and T   85 profyʒte not] luytel or nouʒt profiten N   to¹] om. C   to²] om.
Nδ   haue] to canc. haue DX, to haue Y   riʒt] om. T   86 to] for to
C   her riʒt] riʒt her marked for rev. D   no] not β   ʒe . . . lawe (87)] neiþer
by on lawe ny by oþer N   ʒe] om. T   88 oþur] or N   his] to his ANαJ   90
superflew] so superflue K, in superflue β   as] and C   hem] hem and þerfore
truste we not in hem bote in cristes passyoun and in amendyng of oure lyfe and goode
dedes þat we do and preie we alwey faste to god to kepen vs fro suche false truste and sette
oure hope holly in hym and he wol graunte vs blisse and þat he so do preie we specialy to
hym pater et aue N; hem, there follows without division the first paragraph of sermon 124, that for
the Wednesday in 1 Advent G

Dominica ii Aduentus. [Euangelium.]
Sermo 27.

Erunt signa in sole. Luce 21.

This gospel telluþ derkly a prophesie of Crist, how hit schal be in
þis chirche byfore þe day of doom. Crist seyþ *þer schulle be signes in*
þe sonne and mone, and in þe sterrys of heuene, and in þe eurþe pressure of
folc by meuyng of heuene. For þese þre partyes of heuene, sonne and
5   mone and sterrys schul meue togedre boþe see and watyr, for þei
ben more redy to be meuyd by heuene þan oþur eurþe or eyr, for
þei ben bytwyxe þese two, neyþur to heuy ne to þinne, but large
in quantite, and disposud to take liȝt of þese þre bodyes of
heuene, *and to be confusyd and to make noyse.* And, siþ of þis see and
10   watur rysen wyndes, and blowen on londys, hit is no wondyr ȝif
owre eyr be chawnged in qualitees; and siþ chawngyng of owre
eyr makiþ chaungyng in mennys bodyes, hit is no wondyr ȝif
mennys bodyes ben chaunged by þis eyr. And so manerys þat
sewen þe chawngyng of mannys complexioun schullen be
15   chaunged in owre eurþe þat men dwellen inne. *And so men schullen*
waxen drye boþe by such eurþly eyr and by drede of oþur sygnes þat schullen
comen among men. And þanne men schullen fyȝten in eurþe, o
cuntre wiþ anoþur, for sych chawngyng in þe eyr schal make
chawngyng in mennys lif. And þus deede bodyes, caste in þe

MSS: D; ABCFGJKLMNTVXYZαβδ.

Dominica . . . euangelium] *om.* αZV   sermo 27] *om.* BCFKNTYαδXZGV   erunt . . . sole] *om.* V, spem habeamus N   sole] sole et luna KLMαδ   luce 21]
luce 21 . . . ad ro.15 N   1 derkly] today derkely N   hit] *om.* M   3 mone] in
þe mone T, þe *canc.* moone G   þe²] *om.* CZ   of heuene] *om.* δ   5 watyr]
watris AFYδJ   6 redy] *om.* T   to] for to C   oþur] eyþer J   eurþe] eyre
δ   or] eþer X   eyr] erþe δ   7 þese] *om.* N   ne] no L, ⌐nor⌐ δ   9 to
be confusyd] confused to be N   confusyd] counfoundid T   to² . . . noyse] noyse
for to make N   þis] þe β   10 londys] londys, -ys *canc.* X, lond CFKLNTYβδJ-
ZGV, lowde α   11 chawngyng] chaunging⌐is⌐ F   12 chaungyng] chaunging⌐is⌐
F   in] of TG   bodyes] *om.* Y   14 þe] *om.* N   chawngyng] chaunge
F   mannys] menes CNJXG   complexioun] complexiouns N   15 eurþe]
eyre CαZ   schullen] schuld C   16 by¹] in L   eurþly] eirely C   17 in]
on M   18 chawngyng] schame *canc.* chawngyng D, chaungingis F   in] of
C   þe] *om.* A   19 mennys] manus CF   þe] *om.* Z   20 in] *om.* AB, in þe

watyr or in|eurþe, chaungen þe eyr and al owre place þat we
dwellen inne oþur wyse þan hit schulde haue ben in þe stat of
innocens; for þanne owre place vndur þe moone schulde ha⌐ue⌐
be wiþowten such medelyng, for heuene worcheþ kyndely
dyuersely in diuerse materys.

And aftyr al þis schal men see Crist owre lord come from
heuene, and his aungelis wiþ hym to demen men þat dwellen
heere, *for þe vertewys of heuene* þat ben liȝtes schullen be chaunged
here, and al þe gouernayle of heuene schil be varied þus to men.
And þanne men schal se Crist, comyng down in a clowde wiþ greet power
and mageste to men þat can reede þes signes. And Crist counforteþ
hise children and biddeþ hem putte dreede awey, for *comyng of*
syche signes bytookneþ þat her blisse is nyȝ; and þerfore schulde þei
rere þer hedis and be glad of þese signes, and not hang þere heedis
down as men heuyed wiþ þe eurþe. For what man wolde not be
glad whanne he schulde gon owht of prisoun, and be b[r]owht to
blisse of heuene, and passen awey fro such peyne? *And Crist seyde*
to his disciplis þis symylitude in kynde 'See ȝe þe gardeyn of þe fyg[e] trees
and alle oþur trees of fruyt, whanne þei bryngon forþ fruyt of hem ȝe wyten
wel þat somer is nyȝ.' And somer is in somme contrees tyme to
gedre fruyt of þe eurþe. *'And so, whan ȝe see þese signes be maad, wyte*
ȝe þat ȝowre biggyng is nyȝ', for byggyng is clepid here fruyt þat
comeþ of þis byggyng. *And Crist seiþ soþly þat þe kynrede of his children*
schal not passen owht of þis world byfore þat alle ⌐þes⌐ þingus be done.
Heuene and erþe schal passe in chawngyng, but Cristis wordis schulle not
passe þus. Wel we wyten þe sonne stood and somtyme hit wente

25

30

35

40

45

CTYJ, into þe V   chaungen] chaungyng J   owre] oþer L   place] places
AαJ   22 place] places ABJ   haue] ue *corr.* D   23 wiþowten] wiþ
T   medelyng] medelyng⌐is⌐J   24 materys] maners C   25 come] comynge
GV   26 men] hym *canc.* men D   27 schullen] here schulen N   28 here] *om.*
N   29 crist] cristis C   greet] gr/greet D, gre C   30 counforteþ] counfortide
BJ   32 blisse] bisse Y   schulde þei] *rev.* JV   33 rere] reise Y   and[1]] vp
canc. and α, vp and C   þese] suche δ   heedis] heed Y   34 þe] *om.*
FKβJZGV   35 browht] bowht D   to] to þe AYJ, into þe δV   36 blisse of
heuene] heuen blisse N   37 gardeyn] gardeynes DX, gardin⌐s⌐ F   þe²] *om.*
ABCFKLMNTYαβδJZGV   fyge] fygo D   38 forþ . . . hem] of hem forþ fruyt
δ   of hem] *om.* N   39 somer²] in somer Nα, is somur δ   is²] is tyme N, *om.*
αδZ   tyme] ⌐tyme⌐ A, *om.* N, is tyme αZ   40 fruyt] þe fruyt N   þe] *om.*
α   þese] þos C   41 ȝowre biggyng] oure aȝenbiyng δ   is[1]] as δ   clepid
here] *rev.* C   clepid] called αδZ   here] he L, þair Z   42 byggyng] *on eras.*
corr. D   seiþ] sayd α   43 þat alle] *om.* N   þes] *corr.* D   be] alle *canc.* ben
δ, alle be N   44 erþe] eurþe, -u- *canc.* D   in chawngyng] and chaunge N   wor-
dis] word Nδ   45 wel] *om.* N   we] ȝe J   þe] þat þe CV, wel þe

aȝen, but þus may not sentence be chaunged of þe wordis of owre
Lord; but þere is more stablehede in wordis þat ben seyde of Crist
þan is in heuene or eurþe, siþ Crist is aboue þese two and comyng
in þese tweyen is not nedful.

50 But, for þat Crist haþ ordeynut hit, þeᵣsꞌ wordis of Crist may be
vndurstanden goostly, so þat þe sonne be Crist, God and man,
and þe mone be holy chyrche, and þe sterrys in heuene be seyntes
in þe world. Sygnes ben maade in hem, for þei meuen eurþly men
and chaungen as þe see temporal goodis, and for such chaungyng
55 chaungen men in wylle. And membris of þe feend ben drye fro
grace, and ben adredde for Crist and sentence of his chirche. For
vertewes of heuene schullen meue cristen men to vencuse þe
feendis lymes, and to feren hem, al ȝif þei for a tyme make greet
sownd, and stynken wiþ synne, and froþen wiþ lecherye, and þe
60 more fysches swolwen þe lesse; and cours of þiᵣsꞌ mone meueᵣþꞌ
worldly men, and wyndes of pruyde wawen þeᵣsꞌ floodes, so þat
hyt is perelows to schippes for to wandre, al ȝif þei ben boren vp
wiþ þe cros of Crist. But wel I wot þat men þat ben chosen of God
may floteren in þe see, but þei may not perysche, for alle þing mot
65 nede come þat God hymself haþ ordeynut. And þus sad byleue of
þis þridde aduent schulde styre men fro synne and drawen hem to
vertewus. For, ȝif þei schulden tomorwe answere to a iuge, and
wynne greete rentis or ellys leson hem, þei wolden ful byssyly
schape for þer answere; and meche more, ȝif þei schulde wynnen
70 or lese þer lif. Lord! siþ we ben certeyn of þe day of doom, þat hyt

N   46 sentence] þe sentence αG, stablehed N, stabled *canc.* be δ   þe] *om.*
C   47 but þere is] for N, for þere is V   stablehede] stabulnes NTZ, stable nede
LδJ   in] is in his N   þat . . . crist] *om.* N   48 is¹] ᵣitꞌ is C   in] ouþer in
N   eurþe] in *canc.* erþe J, ᵣinꞌ erþe F, in erþe LαV   is²] *om.* Y   49 in] of
δ   50 þat] *om.* N, ᵣþatꞌTδ   þes]s *corr.* D, gostely mowen þuse N   may] *om.*
N   51 goostly] *om.* N   þe] þis Nδ   god] boþe *canc.* god α, þat is boþe god
N   52 þe²] also þe N   in . . . seyntes] *om.* N   in] of δV   53 eurþly
men] men eurþly *marked for rev.* D, worldly men T   54 þe see] þei seen L   and²]
heere and N   such] *om.* T   55 chaungen] is men chaungen F   fro] for
β   56 adredde] aferd N, dredand Z   for¹] of YV, fro δ   his] þe δ   57
vencuse] ouercome NTV   þe] *om.* T   58 to . . . sownd (59)] ȝef þey make gret
sounde ȝet schal þey ben aferd N   59 sownd] soune ABYαJG   froþen] from
þanne T   60 cours] þe cours FV   þis] i *on eras. corr.*, s *corr.* D, þe Z   meueþ]
þ *corr.* D, meued N, *om.* F   61 wawen] weyfen N   þes] s *corr.* D   62 is] is to
C   to¹] *om.* N   63 þe] ᵣþeꞌ α, *om.* T   64 þe] þis BKLMNTYαδJZGV, þis
altered from þe β   þei . . . perysche] perische may þey not N   alle] *om.*
β   66 to] into N   67 to] *om.* M   68 leson] for to lesen N, to lese V   ful
byssyly] be ful bysy to Nδ   70 or . . . lif] hire oune lyf or lesen hit N, here lyf or lese

schal come to vs, and we wyte not how sone, and þere we schullen
haue iugement of heueneli lyf or ellys of deþ of helle þat euermore
schullen laste, how bissy schulde we be to maken vs reedy for þis!
Certis, defawte of byleue is cause of owre slowþe. And þus schulde
we fastenen in vs articles of trowþe, for þei wolen be lows in vs as   75
nayles in a tree, and þerfore hit is nedful to knokke and maken
hem faste. For hit is noo drede þat no man doþ synne, but 3if he
fayle in byleue vpon som maner. Somme wanten|byleue and   f.74
neuere hadden byleue, as paynymes and oþur men þat neuere
were turnede to Crist. Somme faylen in byleue, for þer byleue   80
slepuþ and oþur þinge wakyþ þat þei trowen moore. And þus
fayluþ eche man þat is ouercome wiþ synne, for lust wakiþ in hym
to whiche þe synne meueþ hym, and peyne and dreede of his
synne is leyd aslepe. And þus faylen in byleue þe moste part of
men. We schulden þenken freschly on þe day of doom, and how   85
no þing may þanne lette Cristys iugement, for trewþe and resoun
schullen fully go forþ þanne. And herfore seiþ þe gospel þat men
þanne nakyde fro charite schul be þanne doump, and not
schullen answere to Crist. And for þis cause prophetis of Godis
lawe clepen þe day of doom 'day of þe Lord', for in þat day no3t   90

---

90 eg. Isa. 2: 12, 13: 6; Ezek. 13: 5; Joel 1: 15.

δ   71 we² . . . laste (73)] of heuenely lyf or deth of helle schulen we alle haue
iuggement N   72 haue]om. G   -more]om. Y   75 fastenen]feste KβZ, make
siker N   trowþe] þe trouþe ABN   76 maken] to make BV   77 hit . . . þat]
dredles N   78 vpon] on NTV, vpon canc. ⌈in⌉ δ   maner] maner wyse
N   somme] sum men, men canc. F, summen, -n canc. Y, sum men ABMJG   and]
þat NV   79 hadden byleue] rev. N   as . . . crist (80)] om. Z   80
somme] sum men G   byleue²] bele C   81 þinge] þynge, -s eras. J, þing⌈is⌉ F,
þinges A   82 fayluþ] falleth C, faris Z   wiþ] be CKLMNTYαβδXZG   wa-
kiþ] wakyng L, is wakyng M   hym] hem, e altered to y δ, hem AJV   83 þe] þis
FY   meueþ hym] meueþ on eras. corr. hym meueþ, 2nd meueþ canc. D   hym] hem
ABδJ, hem to V   84 aslepe] to slepe δ, to slepe and wakeþ not N   byleue] trouþe
ABCKLMNTYαβδXZGV   moste] more ABCFKLMTYαβδXZG   85 on] of
δ   86 may þanne] rev. CM, may α, ne may J   þanne lette] rev. N   and] of
C   87 fully] þenne trewly N   þanne] om. NV   and] om. J   herfore]
þerfor αZV   men þanne] rev. α   88 þanne¹] þat ben þanne FV   be þanne]
rev. CYδV, be N   not schullen] rev. δV   89 schullen] om. N   crist] crist þat
schal deme hem N   for þis cause] om. N   of . . . lawe (90)] om. N   90
clepen] calle αδZ   þe¹] þis N   day²] þe daie AMαGV   no3t] om.

schal gon aȝenes hym. But þei clepon dayȝes byfore 'dayȝes of men', for þe fend and hise membris han now þer purpos, al ȝif þei schulle þanne bye þat ful deere.

N   91 gon . . . hym] þe lord vse his ryȝtwys dome N   gon] ⌜be⌝ δ   clepon] calle αδZ   92 al ȝif] ȝif on eras. corr. D   93 þanne . . . þat] bigge þat þan M   þanne] om. δV   bye] on eras. corr. D   þat] it AZ   deere] dere and þerfore aȝeyn þat day þat comeþ so sone make we vs redy in al þat we kunnen to haue oure endelas reward in þe blisse of heuen and þat we haue þat reward preie we to god pater et aue N

Dominica iii Aduentus. [Euangelium.]
Sermo [28].

Cum audisset Iohannes in vinculis. Mathei 11.

This gospel telluþ a story of Iohn Baptist, þat touchiþ alle þre aduentis of Crist but specially þe þridde, to whom seruen two byfore. Babtist was in prisoun wiþ Errowde Antipas, for he repreuyd his auowtre wiþ his broþur wif. And *Iohn, bownden in prisoun, herde of Cristis werkis,* and he made myche ioye and 5 preisude myche Crist, as oþur gospellys tellen and specially Iohnys gospel. Somme men in þe cuntre heelden Iohn more þan Crist, and Iohnys disciplys weren in þis errour; but ȝet þei trowedon þat þe greete prophete byhiȝte in þe lawe, þat þei clepedon Messyas, was more þan Iohn Baptyst. And herfore *sente* 10 *Baptist two of his disciples* for to speke wiþ Crist and purgen hem of þis errowr. And Iohn bad hem axe þus Crist on his byhalue *'Art þow he þat is to comen* and to saue manys kynde, þat þe lawe spekiþ of, *or we abyden anoþur?'* We schullen supposen þat Baptist was stable in his trowþe, and coueyted þat þe feiþ of Crist and loue of 15 Crist growede, and byfor þat he were deed, þat he trowede schulde come sone; for trewe men coueyten more þe honour of

---

7 John 1: 15, 26–7, 30–34.

MSS: D; ABCFGHJKLMNTVXYZαβδ. *In D the scribe erroneously copied the material of f. 74v, 44 a man . . . 96 crist, a second time on f. 75, and then crossed the second copy through; where the second, cancelled, copy corrects the first the variants are recorded as D².*

Dominica . . . euangelium] *om.* αZHV   sermo 28] sermo D, *om.* BCFKNTYαδJ-XZGHV   cum . . . vinculis] nolite ante tempus iudicare N, *om.* V   in] *om.* J   vinculis] vinculis opera christi Kδ   mathei 11] matheu 2 Y, mathei 21 . . . prima ad cor' 4 N   1 a . . . prisoun (3)] of aduent and of þe prisonyng of seynt Iohn N   2 crist] iesu crist H   two] þe twa Z   4 his¹] hym of his N, hym of δ   iohn] when iohn N   5 and¹] *om.* N   6 myche crist] *rev.* G   7 iohnys] io *canc.*/iohnys D   gospel] gospeles C, *om.* N   more] in þe *canc.* more D   9 þe¹] *om.* T   lawe] oolde lawe Y   10 clepedon] called αδZ   iohn] *om.* H   herfore] þerfore αZV   11 baptist] ihon baptist Z   for to] to G   purgen] to purge Z   of²] *om.* C   13 to comen] come H   and . . . of (14)] *om.* K   manys kynde] mankynde AFNYαJHV   15 loue] þe lofe βH   16 crist] hym J   and] *om.* αV   18 for] or H   19 þis¹] ⌐bi¬ þis

God þan þer owne honowr, for ellys þei weren vnresonable. And
þus caste Iohn þis weye to worschipe of Crist. And to þis entent of
20 Iohn spaak Crist and wroȝte in dede, 'Go ȝe and telleþ aȝen to Iohn
what ȝe han herd and seyn : ⌐blynde see⌐, crokyde gon, meyselis ⌐ben⌐
helude, deue heren, dede ryson, poore men ben pre[ch]ud of God; and blessyd
be he þat schal not be sclawndrut in me.' And on two manerys ben men
sclaundred in Crist. Somme men by worchyng putten errowrs in
25 hym, and þis maner of sclawndryng is algatis euyl, siþ þei fatlen
in heresye þat þus trowen of Crist; þese men ben suffryngly
sclawndred in Crist þat fallen fro byleue þat þei schulden haue of
Crist. On þe þridde maner we seyn þat men ben sclaundryd
whanne þei ben defamyd of any kynne þing, þat þei han hem
30 amys abowten any such þing; and þus manye hooly men weren
sclawndred of Crist. And so of þese seuene myraclis þe laste is ⌐þe⌐
moste. And alle þese seuene miracles techen how we schulden
loue Crist. For we, þat weren furst blynde by defawte of feiþ, seen
aftyr in owre sowle what we schulden trowe. And so furst crokyd
35 in medful werkys wandren aftyr in holynesse of liȝf. And so furst
leprows by heresye[s] of feiþ ben aftyr clansed of alle þese
heresyes. Deef men fro Godis word heren his lawe; and deede
men in sowle by costome of synne risen to spiritual lif of þer
sowle. Men þat weren pore byfore for þer hooly werkis ben seyde
40 goode lyuerys of hym þat may not erre. And hit semeþ þat Iohnys

J   crist] god H   20 spaak crist] rev. AV, seide crist N   ȝe] ȝe aȝeyn
N   telleþ] telle ȝe KV   aȝen] om. N   21 blynde see] corr. D   blynde]
blind men FYV   crokyde] crokid men YV, crokid men, men canc. F, and croked
Nδ   gon] good β   ben] corr. D   22 deue] deef men YV, and defe men
N   dede] dede men NV   men] om. B   prechud] preysud DABCFKLM-
NYαβδJXZGV, prechid, -chid on eras. corr. T   god] crist M   23 be] is
G   he] om. T   and] om. Z   ben men] rev. AFYJV   24 sclaundred
. . . crist] on eras. corr. D   errowrs] sclaundres and errours JG   25 of] om.
J   sclawndryng] sclawnder CαZ   fallen] faylen L   26 of] on α   þese]
þus T   suffryngly] soueraynly CNZ   27 schulden] schule N   of] in
G   on] and Y, and on JV   29 of] on C, wiþ M   kynne] om. N, maner of
δ   30 þing] þing⌐is⌐ F, þingis V   31 of¹] in FH   þe¹] and þe C   þe²]
corr. D   32 alle] by N, om. Z   miracles] om. N   techen] we ben tauȝt
N   33 blynde] bynde C   by] by þe J, for HV   defawte] faute B   feiþ]
bileue H   34 what] and what L, what þat N   35 wandren] wandreden F, walke
NV   aftyr in] after, -ward eras. F   in²] more euene in N   holynesse of] haly
Z   furst] þe first C   36 heresyes] heresye DN   37 men] om. T   heren]
heryng C   38 men] om. Y   to spiritual] spritualy to N   39 sowle] saules
Z   þat] þer N   hooly] gode H   40 hym] hem, -e- canc. -⌐i⌐- H, hem

disciples sayen somme of þese miracles, or ellis hem alle in feiþ
þat Crist ȝaf hem.

And whanne þei weren wente fro Crist he preysud Iohn Baptist,
techyng þat men schulde not preise|a man in his presence, ne in   f.74v
presence of hise, leste he were a faiour. Crist preysude Baptist,   45
axyng of hym þree þingus so þat þe puple were nedid to graunte
þat Iohn was hooly. '*Whan ȝe sayen Baptist in desert, what wenten ȝee
to see? sayen ȝe þanne a reed wawyng wiþ þe wynd?*' Nay, syche men ben
vnstable for louyng of muc; for Iohn was stable in þe loue of God,
and soo was he growndyt in þe stoon of riȝtwysnesse. '*Or what wente*   50
ȝe owt ⌐*to see*⌐, whanne ȝe wente to see Ioohn? *Wheþur ȝee wenten to
see a man clad in softe cloþus?* Nay, loo, men þat ben cloþut þus drawen hem
to kyngus hows, and ben tendyrley fed wiþ metis þat pleson þe
flesch.' For Iohn Baptist was contrarye to syche men in boþe þese,
siþ he dwelte in desert and was fed wiþowte foode þat was maad   55
by mannys crafte; and so þe world and hys flesch ouercam he
parfiȝtly, and hit is noo drede to vs þe feend hadde ⌐þan⌐ noon
hold in hym. '*But what wente ȝe owht to see? Certys, to see a prophete?*
ȝee! I sey to ȝow Iohn was moore þan a prophete', for Iohn hadde offis of
God to see Crist and waschen hym, and to schewen hym atte   60
eyȝe, þat is moore þan a prophetes offis. '*And he is of whom hyt is*
wryton þat þe Fadyr spekiþ to þe Sone "*Loo! I sende myn aungel, þat*
ys myn owne messager, tofor þi face, þat schal make reedy þ[i]
weyȝe tofor þe" ', for Iohn Baptist meuede men to trowen in Crist
manye gaatis.   65

A   41 hem] sawen hem N   42 hem] hym F·   43 iohn] to ihon Z   44
þat]þan C   men]a man N   in²]in þe C   45 leste]lest þat δ   were]be
saide Z   a] *om.* α   faiour] faitour Y, faytour or a faiour H   baptist] ion
baptist H   47 ȝe] þey H   48 þanne] ⌐þanne⌐ G, *om.* AFMY   wawyng]
wawyd H   49 of¹] *om.* H   muc] worldly *canc.* mok J, worldely mukke A-
B   iohn]he N   þe . . . god]godes loue N   50 soo]flecchide not þerfro and
N   was he] *rev.* JV   stoon] stole C   what . . . see¹ (51)] *after* ioohn (51)
N   51 ȝe¹]*on eras. corr.* D   owt]*om.* N   to see¹]*corr.* D, oute *canc.* to se α, out
to see Nδ   ȝe²]he β   to see²] ⌐to⌐ þe syȝth of δ   52 a] man *canc.* a D   a
man]men T   in]wiþ NTV   drawen]drewen B   53 to]in L   þe]hym
canc. D, to Z, to þe V   54 flesch]fleschis Z   syche]*om.* N   55 desert] desert
among þe wilde bestes N   56 by]wiþouten H   þe . . . parfiȝtly (57)] perfitely
he ouercome þe world and his flech N   ouercam he] he ouercom *marked for rev.* α, he
ouercom δJV   57 þe] þat þe JV   þan] *corr.* DFδ, *om.* NV   58 certys] a
prophete *canc.* certys D   59 ȝow] ȝow more δ   60 crist] criȝst, -ȝ- *canc.*
D   waschen] to wash FV   hym¹] *om.* T   to²] *om.* C, so N   61 a] *om.*
ABCFKLMNTYαβδJXZHV   he] þes N   is²] it is YV   hyt] *om.*
N   62 spekiþ] speke C   63 tofor] before CNTβδZG   þi²] D², þe
DCNαδJH   64 tofor] before CNβδZGV   þe] *om.* δ   for] þerfore

Here may men towche manye synnes þat reignen among men,
and specially synne of clerkys, þat lyuen in lustis of foode and in
lustis of atyr contrarye to Iohn Baptist. And þus, as þe gospel seiþ,
þei putten on Iohn þat he hadde a feend and was lad in desert by
70 þis spyri3t þat susteynud hym, and he lyued not mannys lif, ne 3af
ensaumple to sewe hym. And in Crist þei ben sclawndred, and
seyden he lyuede a lustful li3f, and was freend to synful men, and
þus schulde not men lyue. And þus þese newe religious fallen in
heresye of Iewys, for neiþur þei maken Baptist ne Iesu Crist þer
75 patroun, but cheesun hem a new patroun and ⌜a⌝ new religioun,
and seyn þat Bapti3st was to hard, and Cristus li3f was to large,
but þei han founden a good mene and vertuows to lyuon inne.
And þus boþe clerkys seclerus, and þese newe religious forsake
þe⌜s⌝ two wey3es and taken wey3e of þe feend; for þere is noon oþur
80 wey3e but Cristus weye and þe feendys, syþ no man may lyue in
vertewes but 3if þat he sewe Crist, and noo man may lyue in
synne but 3if he sewe in þat þe feend. Boþe þese eendys been to
blame, but more þese newe religious, for þese ypocri3tes leuen
Crist and Iohn Baptist his prophete, and chesun hem a new weye
85 þat mut ofte tymes be clowtid, and be dispensud wiþ by antecrist,
as þe feend techuþ hem. Þe seculeris ben lasse ypocrites, but þei

---

68 Matt. 11: 18–19; Luke 7: 33–4.

T   in] *om.* F   65 manye] by mony N, *om.* T   gaatis] weyes KNδX-
V   66 may men] *rev.* ACFMYJV   reignen] rennen G   among] now among
N   67 synne] ⌜þo⌝ synne α   lyuen in] *om.* M   lustis] lust β, delicate lustes
N   in²] ⌜in⌝ α, *om.* FT   68 lustis of] *om.* T   and] for G   as] al
M   69 iohn] ion baptist T   he] seyden *canc.* he D   in] into NH, in þe
V   70 þis] his J, a H   he] *om.* TG, þat he ZV   71 sewe] *om.* K   in] so in
J   ben] were α   and²] þat Z   72 he] þat *canc.* he α, þat he FV   73 not
men] *rev.* CFαJ   and . . . hem (86)] *om.* Z   74 iesu . . . patroun (75)] þer
patroun ne iesu crist M   crist] cri3st, 3 *canc.* D   75 cheesun] ⌜þei⌝ chesen F, þei
chesen AB   a²] *corr.* DX, *om.* A   76 and¹] þei AB   was¹] lyuede N   77
han founden] foonden G   han] seyen þey han N   vertuows] a *canc.* vertuows D,
a vertuous V, vertues ANTβ   78 clerkys seclerus] *rev.* FY   seclerus] and *canc.*
seculeres α, and seculers CβV   79 þes] s *corr.* D   wey3e] þe way CFαHV, a way
δ   for] and for H   þere . . . wey3e (80)] oþer wey is þer noun N   80 and]
or *canc.* ⌜and⌝ C, or N   feendys] fendes wey δ   81 þat] ⌜þat⌝ α, *om.* LMH-
V   and] but δ   noo man] non T   82 he sewe in þat] D², in þat he sewe D, in
þat he sueþ F, he in þat sue G, þat he sue in þat T, hee sue ⌜in þat⌝ H, he sewe N   83
religious] religionus H   for] and *canc.* for D, and for F   þese²] *om.* Nδ   85
mut] most α, *om.* N   tymes] tyme B   be¹] mot be N   be²] *om.*
V   dispensud] dispendid Y   wiþ] *om.* H   by] ⌜by⌝ T, *om.* αβ   86
techuþ hem] *rev.* N, techid hem J   hem] hym δ   þe² . . . ypocrites] lesse

lyuen al amys, siþ þei dwellen wiþ kyngus and lordis for to getun
hem benefices, and ⌐in⌐ þe mene tyme þei lyuen in lustis and leuen
þe stat þat þei schulden kepe. And þus blynde men lede þe blynde
and boþe fallen in þe lake. For þer is noon oþur wey3e, but owþur   90
wenden vpward aftyr Crist, or ellys to wende down aftyr þe feend
into þe deppuste lake of alle. 3e! þese þat seemen in hey3ere stat
suen Petre in his errour, and seyen 'Syre, God forbede'–þat þow
lyue þus in þi membris, for wytt and worschipe þat þow schuldest
haue. And, certys, alle suche ben sathanas, for þei wolen reuerse   95
Crist,|oþur addyng to Cristys lawe or ellys wiþdrawyng þat he   f.75
bad.

---

89 Matt. 15: 14; Luke 6: 39; **93** Matt. 16: 22–3; Mark 8: 32–3.

ypocritus ben þuse seculeres N   þe seculeris] þir seculere clerkis Z   ben . . . þei]
folowis no3t ihon þat Z   87 wiþ] al wyth δ   88 benefices] benefice C   in¹]
corr. D, om. Z   tyme] wyle H   þei] om. Nδ   89 men] om. K   90 boþe]
⌐so⌐ boþe F   in] into ZV   is] nys A   91 wenden] go FV   ellys . . .
down] dounward N   to] om. ZH   down] downward T   92 alle] hel
CKNTV, helle alle H   3e . . . bad (97)] om. Z   3e] or elles into þe blisse of
heuene N   þese] ofte þuse N   in] in þe A   stat] in stat δ, ⌐a⌐stat X   96
oþur] or ABCKLMNTYβδJXHV, and G   addyng] elles adde N   97 bad] bad
and þerfore god þat is aboue amende þuse defautus whenne his wille is and þerto preie we
alle specialy pater et aue N

Dominica iiii Aduentus. [Euangelium.]
Sermo 29.

Miserunt Iudei ab Ierosolimis. Iohannis primo.

This gospel telluþ of godheede and manhede of Crist, and of mekenesse of Baptist, how myche þat he louyde Crist. Þe Iewes senten fro Ierusaleem prestis and deeknys vnto Iohn for to wyte what he was, and how|he growndyd his newe liȝf. Þese Iewis semeden hiȝe
5 preestis of þe temple and pharisees. *And þese þat weren sente to Iohn weren of þe pharisees,* for þei weren lesse of staat and semedon of more religioun. *But Iohn confessyd vnto hem and denyȝede not* trewþe, *and so he confessyd furst þat he was not Criȝst,* for hyt was mooste perelows to be holde Crist, and þerfore he putte fyrst þe moste
10 perele from hym. And þus lowe preestis vndyr hiȝe preestis of þe temple and deknes, þat boþe cowden þe oolde testament, and weren more liȝk Iohn in maner of religioun, and betture schulden enquere of his newe ordre, leste þe toon erryde and supplauntyde þe toþur, weren sente to Iohn to axen of his stat. Þer was byhiȝt a
15 greet prophete in þe olde lawe, þat þey clepeden Crist, and þis myȝte Iohn haʳueˑ ben holden ȝif he wolde haue ben prowd. And

---

15 Deut. 18: 15.

MSS: D; ABCFGHJKLMNTVXYZαβδ; Pᵗ *inc.* 52 þat þei; β *erroneously copied a second time* pharisees 83 *to end* (*see* 36/23).

Dominica . . . euangelium] *om.* αZ   sermo 29] *om.* BCFKNTYαδXZGH-
V   miserunt . . . ierosolimis] *om.* V, dominus prope est N   ab ierosolimis] *om.*
H   ab] ad M   iohannis 1] iohannis 1 . . . ad philipenc' 4 N   1 this] þe
N   telluþ] today telleþ N   of¹] of þe δGV   godheede . . . of³] *om.*
N   and¹] and of þe δ   of²] of þe YH, þe V   2 baptist] seynt iohn baptist
and N   þat] þat *canc.* FJ   3 vnto] to FV   4 hiȝe] *om.* N   5 and¹] of
BN   6 þe] *om.* A, þese δ   and] but Y   7 trewþe] þe treuþe NHV   8
he¹] *om.* δ   9 to] for to N   he putte] *rev.* N   10 lowe] *om.* N   vndyr] þat
weren lowe vndur þe N   11 þat] also þat N   boþe cowden] *rev.* A   boþe]
om. N   cowden] knowenden β   testament] lawe H   12 betture] þat bettur
N   13 of . . . ordre] þinges þat þey wolden wyte N   his] þis BZ   erryde]
suld erre Z   supplauntyde] supplant Z   14 weren] þat *canc.* weren Y, þai *canc.*
were α, and þei þat weren V   to¹] vnto N   stat] astate δ   byhiȝt] *om.*
N   15 greet] gr *canc.*/greet D   in] byhyȝte in N   clepeden] called
αδZ   þis] þus N   16 haue¹] -ue *corr.* D   ben holden] beholdyn

here be we taw3te to boste not of þis þat we ben membris of holy
chyrche, and so sullen owre suffragies, for hit is ⌐hyd¬ from vs
wheþur we schulle be sauyd; and 3if we schulle not be sauyd we
be not membres þus, ne owre prey3ere for þis is not worþ to vsself. 20
And to gabbe þus in þis poynt is a greet synne, and to take
mennys goodis by such a false chaffare, for a worldly man wole
not selle but þat he wot is his. And God haþ ordenyd þis pryue
þing to ben vnknowen of vs, for we schulde not þus boste ne
disseyue owre ney3eborus. And þus to putten of Godes or- 25
denaunse were a greet synne.

    Þei axeden Iohn þe secownde tyme *wheþur he were Helye, and he
seyde he was not þis Helye* in persone. Þe Iewys hadden in þe olde
lawe þat Helye was rauyschud, and leueþ 3et in a plase, and schal
comen a3eyn byfore þe day of doom and fi3te wiþ anticrist; and 30
þus þei supposuden þat Baptist was he, specially for solitarie lif
and penaunce in etyng. And to þis entent denyede Iohn þat he was
Helye. But Crist seyde þat Iohn was Helye in figure, for, ri3t as
Helye figured þe furste aduent of Crist, so Iohn figurede þe þridde
aduent of hym, and, as som men seyn, þei boþe figureden þe day 35
of doom. And þus þere is no falsehede in Crist ne in Baptist. *Þei
axeden þe þridde tyme wheþur Iohn were þe prophete, and he seyde nay* to
þer vndyrstondyng, for name of prophete by hymself bytookneþ
þe moste famows prophete. Crist seiþ þat Iohn is a comun
prophete, and boþe þese weren soþe. And aftyr þese þre 40

---

29 2 Kgs. 2: 11; **30** Mal 4: 5.

J   haue²] haue *canc.* X, *om.* ABCFKLMYβJG   17 here] þerfore Z   be we]
we are *marked for rev.* α, *rev.* TGV   18 hyd] *corr.* DH   19 schulle¹] shulden
H   schulle²] shulden H   we³] ⌐neþer¬ we M   20 be not] be M, schal not be
T   not¹] no K   worþ] worþi BCαZV   vsself] ouresilf KNYα   21 to
gabbe þus] þus to gabbe FY, to þus gabbe H   is] it is F, it *canc.* ys J   22 a¹] ⌐a¬ Y,
om. NδGV   chaffare] chaffering GV   23 but] ⌐a þing¬ but F   þat] if F, þat
þat ZV   is] þat ⌐it¬ is F, þat ⌐is¬ H   25 ney3eborus] nei3bore GH   of] ⌐of¬
J, *om.* V   26 a] *om.* B   27 he¹] þat he N   were] was Z   28 he] *om.*
Y   not] *om.* Y   þis] þus N   þe olde] oure LMδ, hire NT   29 leueþ]
lyue Y   31 baptist] anticrist N   was he] *om.* M   specially] *om.* N   for]
for his F   lif] lyf namely N   32 and¹] in L   denyede iohn] *rev.* NV   33
seyde . . . iohn] *om.* M   þat] to δ, *om.* T   was] þat he was δ   figure]
figurede H   ri3t] *om.* N   34 of] oft C   35 aduent] *om.* L   hym] crist
Y   as] *om.* MTH   som men] summe βJ   þei boþe] þei δ, þat þei boþen H,
om. N   figureden] figuren ACKLMTYαβδJXG, *om.* N   36 and] þat C   is]
nys A   ne] no L   in²] *om.* H   37 were] was Z   þe²] a *canc.* ⌐þe¬ α, a
L   38 bytookneþ] betokyn C   39 moste] more ABCKLMNTYβδJX-
Z   þat] ⌐þat¬ Y, *om.* α   40 þese¹] *om.* Z   41 of] *om.* Y   42 hadden] *om.*

purgyngus þei axeden of Iohn *who he was, þat þei myȝten answere to*
men þat hadden sent hem. And Iohn seyde mekely vpon Ysaye þe prophete
þat he was a voys of cryere in desert, to bydde men make redy þe
weye of owre Lord; for, riȝt as a voys scheweþ þe word of mannys
45 þowt, so Iohn schewede þe word of þe Fadyr. And clerkys
knowen wel þat a voys or sownd is substancially þat þing þat
sowneþ. And, al ȝif Iohn myhte haue seyd þat he was cryinge,
neþeles he ches to speke more mekely, for among alle þingus voys
is a freel þing.

50   *And þese messagerus axeden Iohn warto he baptisede*, and browte in a
new ordre, siþ he was noon of þese þre. *But Iohn answerede hem þat*
he baptisede in watyr, and on myddys of hem stood þat þei knewe not, and
þat is þe greete prophete þat þei sowton aftyr, for he is boþe God
and man to saue mankynde. In þat þat he is God, he is euerywere
55 myddel, as he is þe myddel persone in þe hooly Trinnyte. And, in
þat þat he is man and heed of hooly chyrche, he is myddel of alle
f.76 men gederyd in his name.|In vertew of þis man cam Iohn þus and
baptisede in watyr, to make redy byfore Crist, as a rude werk goþ
byforn a sotel; to þis prophete seruyde Ion and dude hym alle
60 worschipe in þat þat he was God. And for he was þis man, *he is to*
comen aftyr Iohn, al ȝif he be Iones priowr, for he was not maad byfore
Iohn in tyme, neiþur by his manhede nei⌐þer⌐ by his godhede; for
Iohn was man byforn þat Crist was man. And as anemptys
godhede Crist was not maad. And þei traueylen in veyn þat
65 calculen þat Crist was conseyued byfor þe sowle of Iohn was
knyttud to þe body, for Iohn spekyþ of forþe⌐r⌐hede of manhede
of Crist byfore Iohn in grace and also in worþinesse.

---

42 Isa. 40: 3.

NYδ   43 cryere] a crier GHV   make] to make Y   redy þe weye] weye redy
T   44 of¹] to E   owre] þe H   a] *om.* BN, þe Y   word] world N   45
schewede] schewiþ C   46 sownd] soun AFYXH, a sound NG, a soune α   47
sowneþ] souned N   al ȝif] ȝif *on eras. corr.* D, ȝef N   48 alle] alle oþere
H   49 a] *om.* Y   freel] fre N   50 warto] and wherto δ   51 hem] hym C,
to hem H   52 on] in N, oon in H, in þe V   stood] stode *canc.* ⌐stondiþ⌐
α   knewe] knewen, *first* e *altered from* o T, knowen K   54 in] and in
β   euerywere] oueral where α   55 myddel] in myddul N   þe¹] *om.*
H   in¹] of ZV   þe²] *om.* K   and] *eras.* J   56 man] a man
T   myddel] myddis ZH   57 in¹] in *canc.*// in D   60 to comen] icome
N   61 al ȝif] as ȝef N   62 iohn] *om.* N   manhede] godhede H   neiþer]
-þer *on eras. corr.* D, ne⌐þer⌐ F, ne CLMNYαδZH   by²] *om.* N   godhede]
manhed H   63 man¹] a man M   þat] *om.* Z   and] *om.* G   64 godhede]
⌐þe⌐ godhed T, þe godheed BαδV, his godhede J   65 calculen] ca⌐l⌐kelyn H, caklen
δ, talken T   66 þe] his ABCKLMNTYαβδP'JXZGV   forþerhede] *2nd* r *corr.*
D   manhede] þe manhede JV   67 worþinesse] wordynesse J   68 herfore]

And herfore seiþ Iohn þat *he is not worþi to lowse þe þwong of Cristes scho*, and þis men vndyrstonden þus þat Baptist is not worþi to declare Cristes manhede. But as me þinkiþ hit is betture and 70 more sewynge þis gospel to seye þat Iohn grauntiþ hym not worþi to lowse þe ordre of Crist, by wyche Crist hadde ordeynet to be patrown of cristen men, for þis ordre is a þwong to bynde mennys wille togedre. And þus me þinkuþ þat frerus chyden in veyn: Prechowres seyn þat Crist hadde hyȝe schon as þei han, for ellis 75 wolde not Baptist mene þat Crist hadde þwongus of syche schone; Menowres seyn þat Crist wente barefoot, or ellis was schod as þei ben, for ellis Mawdeleyn schulde not haue fownde to þus haue wasche Cristes feet. But leuyng þis chidyng, we supposen of owre Iesu þat he took ful lytel hede of syche maner of wendyng, but he 80 charghed myche þe wille of his religioun and affeccion of hise disciples to be bownden fro worldly goodys. And þus frerus as pharisees syen þe gnatt and swolwen þe camele, for þei duren aboue Baptist fownden hem newe ordres of rewlys þat Crist charghede not but ȝif hit were to dampnen hem. And coueytise of 85 worldly goodis chargen þese ordres not, ȝif þei ben getone wiþ false menes, whyche trewþe of Crist haþ dampned. *But þis was doon in Betanye byȝonde þe watyr of Iordan* in þe loond of two kynredys. And so men seyn þat þer ben two Betanyes in þat lond, on bysyde Ierusaleem where Lazarus was reysut to lyf, and 90 anoþur byȝonde þe watyr *where Iohn* hadde mater *to baptise men*. For Bethanye sowneþ þese þre: hit is 'hows of obedience', and

---

78 Luke 7: 38; **83** Matt. 23: 24; **90** John 11:1.

wherfore F, þerfor αZV   is] *om.* Y   worþi] worþ A   þwong] þongis, -is *canc.*
H, þowngis C   69 cristes] his N   þus] þis C   70 to . . . manhede] cristus
monhed to declare N   me] sum men Z   71 þis] þe H   iohn] iohn baptist,
baptist *canc.* DX   72 wyche] þe whilke α   73 a] as a G, *om.* F   a þwong]
ynoghe Z   74 wille] willes AFY   and . . . dampned (87)] *om.* Z   and] þat
N   75 as . . . schone (76)] *om.* M   76 of] on YH   syche] his *on eras. corr.*/
che *canc.* H   77 menowres] and *canc.* menours F, and menouris Y   or] *om.*
Y   was] *om.* T, ⌈he⌉ was δ   78 for] or N   mawdeleyn . . . not] shulde not
þe magdelene F   fownde . . . þus] þus han founde to þus H   to þus] to *canc.* þus
⌈to⌉ J, þus to FNYδV   haue] *om.* F   80 of¹] to Nδ   of²] *om.*
HV   wendyng] wedding Y   83 syen] clensen AYXG, syȝen or clenson δ,
clensynge V   swolwen] swoledyn J   85 ȝif] ȝif *canc.* F, ȝit H   and] and so
H   86 ȝif] ⌈al⌉ ȝif H, al ȝif CFαβJV, þeigh N   ben getone] begyle þe peple
α   wiþ] by Pᵗ   87 trewþe] ⌈þe⌉ trewþe T, þe treuþe BNαV   haþ] *om.*
β¹   88 two] tho J   93 of¹] *om.* β¹   hows²] also hous N   ȝifte] ȝiftis

also 'hows of penaunce', and 'hows of Godis ȝifte', ⌐and⌐ alle þese names acorden to Iohn, but þei ben contrarye to alle þese newe
95 ordres þat ben presumed aȝeynes Crist.

T   and²] corr. DG, and canc. X, om. ABCKLMNTYβδPʹJZ   94 but . . . crist
(95)] om. Z   but] for F   95 crist] crist and vngrounded in his lawe and þerfore
holde we cristus reule and kepe we his religyoun and preie we herfore vnto god pater et
aue N

Dominica infra octavas Epiphanie. [Euangelium.]
Sermo [30].

Vidit Iohannes Iesum uenientem ad se. Iohannis primo.

This gospel telluþ a witnesse, how Baptist wytnessude of Crist boþe of his godhede and eke of his manhede. Þe story seiþ þus þat *Iohn saw Iesu comyng to hym, and seyde* þus of owre Lord, *'Loo, þe lomb of God; loo, hym þat takiþ awey þe synne of þis world'*, for he is boþe God and man. Crist is clepud Godis loomb for manye resownes of 5 þe lawe. In þe olde lawe weren þei wont to offren a loomb wiþowten wem, þe whiche schulde ben of oo ȝer, for þe synne of þe peple; þus Crist, þat was wiþowte wem and of oo ȝer in mannys elde, was offred in þe cros for þe synne of al þis world. And wher suche lambren þat weren offred fellen som tyme to þe 10 prest, þis loomb þat maade eende of oþur felde fully to Godes hond. And oþur lambren in a maner fordiden þe synne of|o f.76v cuntre, but þis loomb proprely fordyde þe synne of al þis world. And þus he was ende and figure of lambren of þe oolde lawe. And þus scheweþ Baptist by his dowble spekyng þe manhede of Crist 15 and his godhede; for only God myȝte þus fordo synne, siþ alle

MSS: D; ABCFGHIJKLMNTVXYZαβδPt; Pᵗ *largely illegible from* 72 beestis *onwards because of offset from opposite page;* β *has second copy of* 1–6 offer a (*see* 36/23).

Dominica . . . euangelium] sexto die a natiuitate domini euangelium I, sonday gospel V, *om.* αZ   sermo 30] sermo D, *om.* BCFKNTYαδPᵗIXZGHV   vidit . . . se] surge quia venit lumen tuum N, *om.* V   vidit] videns δ   uenientem] *om.* JH   ad se] *om.* BTJH, ad CK   iohannis primo] ysaie lx N   1 this] þe N   telluþ . . . þat (2)] today telleþ þat N   wytnessude] wittenest C, wytnessyþ J   2 eke] ᵣekeᵣ α, also FYZ, sumdel I, *om.* C   seiþ] telleþ F   3 comyng to·hym] -yng to hym *on eras. corr.* D   to] vnto N   4 god] godhed Pᵗ   hym] he Y   takiþ] doiþ YI   synne] synnes ABFKLMNTYαβδIJXZGHV   þis] þis *canc.* ᵣþeᵣ F, þe NYαδIJZH   for . . . boþe] as he þat is moste meke verray N   is] *om.* F   5 clepud] called αδZ   6 weren þei] *rev.* FYIHV, þei weren *marked for rev.* α, ᵣþeiᵣ weren þey, þey *canc.* J   7 þeᵣ] *om.* I   ofᵣ] *om.* K   for . . . ȝer (8)] *om.* N   þe²] *om.* β   8 þus] and þus δI   þat] *om.* I, ᵣþatᵣ H   of] so of T   oo] *om.* P   9 was] þe wuche bytoknede boþe god and man þat N   in] on N-α   synne] sinnes F   al] *om.* K   þis world] þe word N   10 wher] *om.* N   11 prest] prestis T   þat . . . hond (12)] fel to godes hond þat made fully ende of oþer N   of] fully of δ   fully] *om.* δ   12 o] þe K   13 fordyde] for G   þe] *om.* K   al] *om.* T   þis] þe F   14 lambren] þe lambren FI   oolde] elde I   15 þus] ᵣþusᵣ α, *om.* L   scheweþ baptist] *rev.*

oþre lambren hadden wemmes þat þei my3ten not hemself fordo. And so, al 3if prestis han power to relese synne as Cristes vikeres, nerþeles þei han þis power in as myche as þei acorden wiþ Crist; 20 so þat, 3if þeir keyes and Cristes wille be discordynge atwynne, þei feynen hem falsely to assoylen and þanne þei neiþur lowsen ne bynden, so þat in eche sich worchyng þe godhede of Crist mut furst worche. And herfore seiþ Baptist of Crist, '*þis is he þat I seyde of, aftyr me is comen a man þe wyche is maad byfore me, for he was* anon 25 *my priour.*' For, ri3t as Crist was a man þe furste tyme þat he was conceyuet, so God made hym þanne priour of al his religioun, and he was abbot, as Powle seiþ, of þe beste ordre þat may be. '*And furst I knew hym not; I wyste in sowle þat he was born, but I cowde not wiþ bodyly y3e knowen hym fro anoþur man, and þis* 30 *falliþ comunly. But, for to schewen hym in Israel, perfore I baptise þus in watyr.*' *And Iohn bar witnesse, and seyde þat he saw a spiri3t come down as a culuer from heuene,* and lefte oþre *and dwelte on hym.* '*But God þat sente me to waschen in watyr, he tawte me and seyde þus, "On whom þow seest þe Spiryt come doun and dwellyng vpon hym, þat is he þat baptiseþ* 35 *men in þe Holy Gost." And I saw and bere wytnesse þat þis is Godys kyndely Sone.*'

We schullen wyte þat þis dowue was a verrey fowle as oþer ben, and so hit was not þe þridde persone in Trinnite, taken in onhede of þis persone, as Godes Sone took his manhede. But, for 40 meekenesse of þe dowue, and moo goode propretes þat sche haþ, sche bytokneþ þe þridde persone. And þis persone is seyd of here,

---

27 Col. 1: 18.

α   dowble spekyng] spekyng dowble *marked for rev.* D   16 only] *om.* N   17 þei] *om.* H   18 and so] synne ⌐and⌐ so J   synne] synnes HV   19 þei²] þes C   wiþ] wiþ wiþ *2nd canc.* DA   20 so . . . bynden (22)] *om.* Z   þat 3if] *rev.* Nαδ, 3yf þat *marked for rev.* J   and] of C   discordynge] discordyn⌐ge⌐ αJ   atwynne] *om.* N   21 lowsen] soilen H   ne] þe B   22 in] *om.* PᵗG   sich] *om.* Z   mut] moste N   23 herfore] þerfor αZV   baptist] ion baptist N   24 comen] ⌐to⌐ comen A, to comen BNδ   is²] w-*canc.* -is, i *on eras. corr.* D   me²] *om.* N   anon] a man δ, *om.* Z   26 god] crist L   þanne] *om.* PᵗV   al] *om.* N, ⌐al⌐ V   27 of] for T   be] *om.* K   28 I¹] he Z   knew] know Pᵗ   29 cowde] knowde β   wiþ . . . y3e] bodly T   bodyly] body C   y3e] ei3en I   and . . . comunly (30)] *om.* N   þis] þus δ   30 israel] ierusalem L   baptise] baptisid α   31 þat he saw] he sawh N, *om.* K   32 a] ⌐a⌐T, *om.* β   culuer] doue δZ   34 dwellyng] dwelle C   vpon] ⌐vp⌐on δ, on V   baptiseþ] baptiside B   35 I saw] ysai *canc.* ⌐I sawe⌐ α, ysay J   and²] ⌐and⌐ Cα   37 a] *om.* PᵗI   oþer] þis oþer δ   38 so] *om.* Z   39 þis] þis *canc.* //þis D   40 þe] þis YαIG   41 here] hir BCYδX-

for Iohn seiþ þe Spiryt cam down and dwellyde longe vpon Crist; and þis Spirit was þis dowue, and so hit semeþ þat þis dowue was God. And so, al ȝif þe two persones may be meued in creatures, nerþeles þe Trinnyte may not be meued in his kynde; but hit 45 semeþ þat we may graunte þat þis dowue was þe Holy Gost, as we graunte þat þis persone was comynge down in þis dowue. And þus, as God seiþ in his lawe þat seuene oxen ben seuene ȝeer, and þat þe sacryd bred is verreyly Godes body, so hit semeþ þat he seiþ þat þiᴿsᴵ dowue is þe Holy Gost. But clerkys wyten þat þer 50 ben two manerys of seyng, þat ben personel seyng and habitudynel seyng; þis dowue myȝte not be God in his kynde but by som habitude hit singnefieþ God, and þus by auctorite of God hit is God. And ȝif þow seye þat eche þing by þis schulde be God, as eche Godis creature signifieþ his makere (as smoke kyndly 55 signifieþ fier), and þus semeþ Powle to speke whanne he seiþ þat Crist schal ben alle þingus in alle þingus to men þat vndyrstonden hym, for aftyr þe day of doom al þis world schal ben a book, and in eche part þerof schal be God wryten, as God schal ben in his kynde in eche part of þe world; and þus, siþ God is bytokned furst 60 and moste in eche þing, why may men not graunte þat God is eche þing?

In þis mote men vndirstonde diuersite in wordis and to what entent þes wordes ben vndirstondene. And þus by auctorite of þe lawe of God schulde men speke her wordis as Godis lawe|spekiþ, 65 f.77 and straunge not in speche from vndirstondyng of þe peple, and algates be war þat þe puple vndirstonde wel, and so vse comun speche in þer owne persone; and, ȝif þei spekon in Cristes persone wordis of his lawe, loke þat þei declaren hem for drede of pryue

48 Gen. 41: 18–27; Matt. 26: 26; Luke 22: 19; 1 Cor. 11: 24; **56** 1 Cor. 15: 28; Col. 3: 11.

G   42 for . . . crist] *om.* M   seiþ] said C, saw α   43 þis²] þe IV   þat] *om.* H   þis³] *om.* I   44 þe] þes CαPᵗ   48 þus] þis δ   as] *om.* T   49 verreyly] verray CNβδH   so] and so β   50 seiþ] say Pᵗ   þis] -s *corr.* D   wyten] witen wel FV   51 manerys] manerᴿisᴵ F, manere AN   seyng¹] seyngis ABFY   55 godis creature] good creature G, creature of god LV   kyndly] *om.* N   56 þat] *om.* J   57 in . . . þingus²] *om.* TβPᵗ   þingus²] thyng C   58 al] als C   a] ᴿaᴵ δ, *om.* N   59 in¹] *om.* NδPᵗ   be god] *rev.* αI   god wryten] *rev.* L   his] *om.* N   60 þe] þis K   þus] *om.* I   siþ] saiþ C   61 men not] *rev.* MαV   is] is in M   63 in¹] and L, and in G   mote men] *rev.* AFYIHV   diuersite . . . vndirstondene (64)] *om.* N   in²] of K   64 þe . . . god (65)] goddis lawe YIJV   65 schulde men] *rev.* AFYIV, schal men G   66 straunge] strawge βPᵗ, stronge α   in] *om.* T   67 be] be we Nδ   69 þat] ᴿwelᴵ F   hem] hem ᴿwelᴵ J, hem wel HV   70 errour]

70 errour. And scorne we þe argumentis þat fooles maken here þat
by þe same skyle schulde we speke þus, for God spekiþ þus in
wordus of his lawe; siche apis liknessis passen bestis foly, for þei
wolden brynge by þis þat eche man were God. And so ȝyue we
God leue to spekon as hym lykuþ, al ȝif we speke not ay so by þe
75 same auctorite. Þese wordus þat God spekiþ schulde we algatys
graunte, and declaren hem to trewe vndyrstondyng. And recke
we not of argumentis þat sophistres maken, þat we ben
redarguede grauntynge þat we denyen; for we graunte þe
sentence and not only þe wordys, for þe wordis passen awey
80 anoon whan we han spoken hem. And, as Aristotle seiþ,
contradiccion is not only in wordis, but boþe in wordis and
sentence of wordys; and by þis we seyn þat Crist in speche is not
contrarye to hymself, ne o part of his lawe contrarye to anoþur.
And þus, ȝif we graunten þat Crist ys alle þingus, hit seweþ not
85 here⌐of⌐ þat Crist is an asse, ne þat Crist is eche þing, or what þing
we wole nempnen, for God seiþ þe toon and he seiþ not þe toþur.
But we graunten þat Crist is boþe lomb and schep, for Godis lawe
graunteþ boþe þese two of hym; and so Crist is a lyoun and a
worm, and þus of manye þingus þat holy writ telluþ. And hit is
90 ynow to seye for dyuersite þat God haþ special sentence of one
and not so of anoþur. And þus þe comun vndyrstondyng
schulden we algatis holde, but ȝif Godes wordis tauȝten vs his
propre sence. And such strif in wordis is of no profiȝt, ne proueþ

---

74 1 Pet. 4: 11; **85** Isa. 53: 7; Acts 8: 32; **88** Rev. 5: 5; **89** Ps. 21: 7.

errour⌐s⌐ J, errours AYI   þe] þe⌐s⌐ J, þese V   argumentis] argument δ   71
schulde we] rev. FN, shulden M   72 apis liknessis] folis Z   liknessis] lickenes
AMNαδPᵗ   73 by] in bi CV   and so] bot Z   ȝyue] if G   74 ay] all, -ll
canc. ⌐y⌐ α, euer δ   so] ⌐so⌐ CH   þe] þis G   75 þese wordus] þis word
G   we] be LPᵗ   78 þat²] þat þing þat B, þat thing Z   79 and] but
Y   þe¹] om. α   80 whan] as N   as . . . seiþ] after wordis¹ N   as] om.
I   81 is] stant T   in²] om. Y   82 sentence] in canc. sentence α, in sentence
FNYδHV   83 contrarye²] contrarieþ BZ, is not contrarye α, is not contrarie, not canc.
H   84 ys] om. F   þingus] þing C   85 hereof] -of corr. DJ, þerof αZ   eche]
all F   or] om. NZ   þing] þat AI, om. B   86 we] þat we Cα   wole] wiln
H   nempnen] meue N   god] om. N   þe¹] to canc. ⌐þe⌐ C, to þe Nδ   he]
om. N   þe²] to C, to þe N, to þat δ   87 we] om. T   is boþe] rev. T   88
graunteþ . . . two] grauntiþ þes two boþe δ   a¹] ⌐a⌐ J, om. β, boþe a δ   lyoun]
leow β, lombe N   89 þus] of þus K   of] om. T   91 so] ⌐so⌐ G, om.
NIV   þe] om. NT   92 his] hire N, om. Z   93 sence] sentense PᵗZV   is]
ne is I   of] om. Z   94 word] corr. D   is] om. Pᵗ   wey] on eras. corr. D,

not þat Goddis ⌜word⌝ is ony wey false. In þis mater we han inow
stryuen in Latyn wiþ aduersaries of Godis lawe, þat seyn þat hit is   95
falsest of alle lawes in þis world þat euere God suffrede.

where I   in . . . suffrede (96)] *om.* Z   mater] manere I   inow stryuen] *rev.*
IV   95 stryuen] *om.* P^t   þat seyn] *om.* MJ   þat²] *om.* Nδ   hit] *om.*
J   96 þis] þe F   suffrede] suffrede and þerfore god graunte vs grace þe while we
here schal bene to stonde trewe in cristus lawe for þat is verray treuþe and oþer lawes
maad by man may ofte tymes faylle and þat we þerfore holden þe trewe lawe of crist preie
we alle specialy wiþ pater and aue N.

In Octaua Epiphanie. [Euangelium.]
Sermo 31.

Venit Iesus a Galilea. Mathei tercio.

This gospel telluþ how Crist taȝte Baptist, boþe by word and myracle, how he schulde be meke. Þe stoory telluþ þat *Iesu cam fro Galilee to Iordan to Iohn* Baptist *to be baptised of hym*; and þis was greet mekenesse þat þe Lord wolde come so fer to his seruaunt ⌐and⌐ to

5 take of hym bapteme. *And Iohn forfendede hym* for wondring of þe dede, *and seide þat 'I schal be baptisud of þe, and þow comest to me* to be þus baptisud?' *But Iesu answerude* to Iohn, *and seyde to hym* wisly, '*Suffre þis now, for þus hit falluþ to vs to fulfulle al riȝt.*' Hit is open riȝt þat þe lesse be suget to þe more, and hit is more pryue riȝt þat þe

10 euene obesche to þe euene; but moste pryue riȝt of alle stondeþ in þis, þat þe heyȝest of alle obesche to his seruaunt, as Crist, priour of vs alle, obesched to Baptist. And so was hit syttyng Crist to teche þis mekenesse. And here schulle we wyten as men in comun speche seyn somme wordys rehersede hem of oþre, and somme

15 wordes þei seyn in þer owne persone, and þis may be varyed aftyr

MSS: D; ABCFGHIJKLMNQTVXYZαβδ; Pᵗ ends 77 to crist, *and defects in text because of holes in parchment.*

In . . . epiphanie] þe gospel on vtas of twelfþe dai and it falliþ sumtyme on sondai A, þe sondai gospel on þe vtas of þe twelueþe dai B, dominica in octabas epiphanie K, heer bigynneþ þe gospel on þe sunday in vtas of twelfþe day Y, dominica infra octaua epiphanie J   sermo 31] *om.* BFKNQTYαδPᵗIXZGHV   venit . . . galilea] confitemini domino et inuocate nomen eius N, *om.* V   a] *om.* A   galilea] galilea in iordanem J   mathei 3] isaie xii . . . mathei iii N   1 this] þe N   2 myracle] bi *canc.* myracle A, ⌐bi⌐ miracle F, by miracle NQδIHV   telluþ] sais α   þat] hou KLTY, hou þat Nδ   4 his] þe N   and] *corr.* D, *om.* CYZ   and . . . bapteme (5)] *om.* N   to²] *om.* FKLMTαβδPᵗIJ   5 of . . . bapteme] bapteme of him F   6 and . . . þat] *on eras. corr.* D   þat . . . be¹] i owe of þee N   þat] *om.* YδGV   be baptisud] *rev.* T   of þe] to be N   to be þus] þus to be NV   7 to¹ . . . wisly] wysely and seid þus to iohn N   to²] þus to δ   8 þis now] now þis *marked for rev.* D, þis now *marked for rev.* F, þus now N   þus] *om.* A   falluþ] bifalliþ F   to vs] *om.* Pᵗ   to¹] *om.* FI   9 þat¹] *om.* N   suget] opyn suget L   þat²] þan M   þe³] his BCFKLMNTYαβδPᵗIXZGHV   10 moste . . . þis (11)] in þis stondeþ moste priuey riȝte of alle N   moste] ⌐þe⌐ most J, þe mooste V   12 vs alle] *rev.* I.   obesched] obesshe Pᵗ, obeish⌐ed⌐ H, to obeischide B   baptist] ion baptist YGV   was hit] *rev.* IV   crist] ⌐to⌐ crist J, to crist αIV   13 þis] vs I   schulle] schuld Q   14 rehersede] rehersyng CNYαβ-

þre manerys. Sum þing men seyn wytyng þat hit is soþ, afermynge þe sentence wiþowten any condicioun, as trewe men seyn þat God is in heuene. Som þinge men seyn purposynge to fulfullen hit, but vndyrstonden 'ȝif God wole ȝyuen hem grace'; as men seyn þat þei schullen holde Godes comaundementis. And þus techeþ Iamys þat whan we spekon of owre dedis þat we schilde do, we schulden vndyrstonden 'ȝif þat|God wole'. But ȝet on þe þridde maner we supposen þat hit schulde be þus, and neiþur we wyten hit, ne trowen ⌜hit⌝, and wiþ þis we vndyrstonden a condicion 'ȝif God wole'. And þus spak Baptist whanne he forfendyd Crist to be baptysud of hym, and herwiþ he held obedience. But ouer þis schul we wyte þat þer is greet dyuerste bytwixe seruyse of a þing and obedience þerof, for God obeschede to mannys voys and seruede not to hym. But in mannys persone þei rennen boþe togydere, for þe more obescheþ to þe lasse and eke seruiþ to hym, for þe more is eurþe and þe lasse is spiriȝt, and so he is boþe more and lasse to his seruaunt. And þus Crist fulfillede al maner of riȝtwisnesse, for riȝtwisnesse is comunly callyd alle maner of vertew, and so riȝtwisnesse is al maner of mekenesse. And þus Iohn suffrede Crist to take þis seruyse of hym. And ȝet he seyde soþ in wordis þat he spak, for Iohn was baptisud of Crist as he schulde, siþ he ⌜was⌝ baptisude of þe Holy

20

f.77v

25

30

35

---

21 Jas. 4: 15.

V   hem] hym Pᵗ   15 owne] om. I   þis] þus þis B   aftyr] in I   16
manerys] perso canc. manerys D   sum] for sum δJV   þing] þingis FTIJ   hit]
om. MPᵗ   18 þat . . . seyn²] om. Q   som] ⌜and⌝ sum J, and sum YI-
V   19 but] be canc. ⌜bot⌝ α, be K, wiþ good N   vndyrstonden] vndirstondynge
BCFKLMNQTYαβδPᵗIJZHV   wole] wold Pᵗ   hem] hym β   20 as] but as
M   þat] om. Nδ   schullen] shulden LM, wolen V, om. Z   holde] helde
H   21 þus] þis CT   22 schilde] schal BCFKLMNQTαβδPᵗIJH   schulden]
shulen H   vndyrstonden] mekely vndurstonde N   þat] om. H   wole] wold
Pᵗ   23 þat] om. NYα   24 neiþur] neuer C   ne] ne we FQZ, no we T, neiþer
we BCKLMNYβδPᵗIJXGH, neiþer ⌜we⌝ V   hit²] corr. D   wiþ þis] þus
N   vndyrstonden] vndurstoden N   25 a] wiþ N   ȝif] ȝef þat NV   26
herwiþ he held] here withheld he C   herwiþ] þerwiþ Z   he] om. NG   held]
holde I   27 schul we] rev. BCKLMNTYαβδPᵗIJZV   schul] schulde
A   greet] a grete α   28 a] om. T   þing] kyng C   þerof] and seruyse
þerof Nδ   obeschede] obeschiþ T   29 hym] hem, e altered from y J   30
obescheþ] obesche T, obeschid CTZ   31 eke] also YZ   seruiþ] serwid ⌜seruyþ⌝
C, seruide IZ   is²] om. Nδ   and²] om. N   32 þus] þere G   crist
fulfillede] rev. N   33 fulfillede] fillide B   is comunly] rev. H   comunly
callyd] rev. IV   comunly] om. J   34 vertew] vertues N   35 suffrede] offerid
L   take] haue B   þis] om. I   37 was] corr. D   38 vndepartede] vnpartid

Gost; and werkis of þe Trinnyte ben vndepartede ⌜wiþ⌝owtforþ.
And wiþ þis cam Crist to be baptised in watyr of Iohn as he
40 schulde for manye enchesounes, first to teche þis moste degre of
mekenesse, siþ for to halwe þe watyr of baptem, for vertew of
touchyng of Crist strechchede ful fer; þe þridde cause is to ȝyuen
vs ensaumple to take mekely baptem, siþ Crist was baptisud þus.

And herfore Ion lete Crist to be baptisud of hym, for Iohn was tauȝt
45 in his sowle þat hit was Godes wille. And here taken men wel þat,
ȝif a man avowe a þing and he wyte aftyr ⌜þat⌝ hit were bettur to
leuen hit, þanne he schal leuen hit and haue sorwe of his foly
byhest; but hym nediþ not go to Rome to parforme þis medful
dede. And here manye ben disseyuede in power of þere
50 souereynes, for þei wenen þat hem nedeþ to haue leue of hem to
do as þei schulden do. Þis lore schulde men take of ⌜þer⌝ prelatis
aboue, and not traueylen in veyn, ne dispende more þan þei
schulden. *And whan Iesu was þus baptised he wente anoon owht of þe*
watyr to techen vs þat in syche meenys we schulde not dwelle
55 more þan nede is. And to confermen al þis þing *heuenys weren*
openede to Crist, and he saw þe spiriȝt of God comynge down as a dowue
and comyng vpon Crist. And þis þing þat he saw wiþ his eyȝe was a
dowue, and þis þing þat he saw wiþ his sowle was God; and þus þe
spirit of God cam down in a dowue. *And þere was a voys comyng down*
60 *from heuene,* and seyde in þe persone of þe Fadur '*þis is my sone, ȝe,*
þat I kyndely loue, in whiche I plesyde to myself. And þerfore here ȝe
hym!' And so by auctorite of þe Fadyr of heuene, and eke by
auctorite of þe Holy Gost, and also by auctorite of Godes kyndly
Sone, was þe manhede of Crist here schewed wiþ his dedys.

BCKLMTYαβPᵗIJZ   wiþowtforþ] wiþ- *corr.* D   39 þis] þat I   40 to] ⌜for⌝
to TJ, for to CKLMNYαβδPᵗIZV   41 vertew] þe vertue ZV   42 touchyng]
techyng Nδ   strechchede] strechyþ J, and recchede N, reched Z   43 mekely]
meke F   44 herfore] þerfore JZV   ion lete] *rev.* δ   crist] to *canc.* crist
D   • to] *om.* NH   be] ⌜be⌝ Y, *om.* Pᵗ   46 avowe] vowe N   he] ȝif he
IV   wyte] weste P   aftyr] afturward NV   þat] *corr.* D   hit] hym
N   to] *om.* N   47 hit¹] *om.* M   he schal] *rev.* K   48 byhest] heste
N   go] to *canc.* go β, to go ABCFQTYαPᵗIHV, go renne δ   49 dede] werk
J   and . . . schulden (53)] *om.* Z   manye] many men, men *canc.* α, many men
PᵗIJG   50 for] ⌜for⌝ AY   51 þer] *corr.* D, *om.* N   52 traueylen] to traueile
G   53 þus] *om.* KTV   54 in] *om.* Q   not dwelle] dwelle no H   dwelle]
wille T   56 openede] open I   crist] hym T   57 eyȝe] eyne CαV   58
þis] *om.* T   59 comyng] sounyng N   60 þe¹] *om.* J   ȝe] *om.* MH   61
whiche] whom δ   I¹] it H   plesyde] plese Pᵗ   þerfore] herfore H   62
eke] also αIZ, *om.* K   by²] be þe, þe *canc.* α, be þe CQ   63 godes] cristis
Pᵗ   64 here schewed] schewde here *marked for rev.* α, shewid here H, schewid ⌜here⌝

By auctorite of Crist schulden cristene men trowen þat he is þe 65
beste man, þe wysist and þe beste willed þat may ben in þis world,
siþ he is boþe God and man. And herof wole hit sewe þat Cristes
owne ordre is betture þan any new ordre fownden of synful men,
for ellis had Crist fayled in power, in wit or in wille. And, for þis is
aȝenes byleue, þerfore þei faylen in feiþ þat trowen þat þese newe 70
religious passen Cristes religioun. And herfore he ordeyned his
ordre for to stonden in vertewes of mannys sowle and not in
sensible signes. And as þe hooly Trinnyte aprouede Crist here, so
hit approueþ þe ordre þat he made and putte hit in þese þre
þingus, in obedience to God, in pouert and chastite wel 75
vndyrstonden. Men may|vndyrstanden amys þis obedience to f.78
Crist, and trowen þat hit stondeþ in doyyng of eche þing þat þi
pryuat priour byddeþ þe do, – and certis þanne þow puttest hym
to ben vnsynful aboue Crist, – or ellis þat þow schuldest don his
wille aȝen Crist. Certis, Crist haþ no power to lyuen as þiⸯsⸯ prelat 80
doþ, but ȝif Crist hadde fredom to fallen in synne! And þus þis
priour were more fre þan Crist. Herfore schulle we trowen þat
eche obedience to man is as myche worþ as hit techeþ obedience
to God; and ȝif hit fayle herfro by vnobedience, men schulden
leeuen þis aⸯsⸯ venym contrarie to obedience. For eche verey 85
obedience is obedience to God, and men schulden more obesche
to God þan to any creature. And so vnobedience browt in by þese

---

I   65 by] and bi þe I, and so bi V   66 þe¹] and þe I   willed] willid man
δ   þis] þe A   67 he is] is he is M   and² . . . signes (73)] om. Z   wole]
wolde NPᵗ, om. Q   hit] y L   sewe] sueþ, -þ canc. H, sueþ Q   68 any] ony
oþer I   ordre] ordris H, om. N   69 in²] om. N   wit] wille I   in³] elles in
Nδ   wille] wyt I   for] for canc. δ   70 byleue] þe bileue I   þerfore] and
þerfor δJ, herfore I   þat²] om. H   71 religious] religiouns β   herfore]
þerfore αV   72 for to] to AH   mannys] mennus β   73 aprouede] approues,
-s canc. ⸯ-dⸯ α, approuys PᵗJ   crist] ⸯþe ordre ofⸯ crist J, þe ordre of crist δ   74
approueþ] approuyd TV   putte] putteþ N, puttide Y   hit] om. βI   75
chastite] ⸯinⸯ chastite J, in chastite V   76 men . . . awey (106)] om. Z   men]
man H   77 stondeþ] stond CN   doyyng] dowynge T   þi] om. Q   78
pryuat priour] rev. H   þanne] om. I   79 to] þanne to I   aboue] aboue of
β   80 aȝen] aboue H   certis] and canc. certis T, and certys J   þis] s corr. D,
þi FQδG   prelat] prelates, -s canc. α, prelatis C   81 to] for to N   þis] þi
QH   82 herfore] and herfore AB   schulle we] rev. FQHV, schal we, marked for
rev. J   schulle] shulde A   þat . . . obedience¹ (83)] on eras. corr. D   83 man] a
man Cβ   worþ] worþi βI   84 fayle] falle altered to faile F, fayle altered to falle J,
falle V   by] om. M   vnobedience] noȝ- canc. vn- on eras. corr. D, inobedience MI,
non obedience T, obedience H   85 leeuen] fle Y   as] -s corr. D   for . . . god
(86)] om. Q   86 schulden] shulen H   more . . . god (87)] obeische to god more
Nδ   87 so] om. K   þese] þis T   88 fuyluþ] defouleþ NV   hepis] hepiþ

newe ordres fuyluþ manye hepis of men by foly of here prelates.
Soþly, in þese newe ordres men schulden obesche to eche þing þat
techeþ more obedience to God þan don suche prelatis. And hit is
not byleue þat þei techen betture obedience to God þan doþ any
oþur lawe, or þingus þat spekon to þese ordres. And þis meuede
Powle and oþure apostles to holden hem to Cristis ordre, siþ þe
abbot is betture, þe rewle and þe knytis, and algatis hit is more
free to holde Godes comaundementis, for þis feyned obedience
letteþ ofte to serue Crist. And herfore men schulden lernen
obedience to aȝenstonden. Whan any creature of God biddeþ þe
do contrarie to þat þat þi prelat byddeþ þe do by expresse signes,
and God by his creature biddeþ þe do þe contrarye, þanne þow
schuldest aȝenstonden þi prelat in þis, and obesche to God in
what signe þat he vseþ. On þis maner Petre and oþre apostles
seyden þat men mute more obesche to God þan to man. And
Godis lawe seiþ þat God obeschede to mannys voys, for ⌜to⌝ eche
þing men schulden obesche in þat þat hit sowneþ to obedience of
God. And ȝif þis byleue were kept wel, þis newe obedience
schulde gon awey.

Q, helpes J   89 soþly . . . ordres (92)] om. N   92 oþur] suche δ   lawe]
lawis H   þingus] oþer þingis Q   spekon] þei speken H, spedon T   to] of
H   ordres] newe ordris I   meuede] moues αJ   93 þe] om. J   94 þe¹]
þan þe α   and¹ . . . is²] more lyȝter and N   and²] of α   95 feyned] feynyng
β   96 ofte] men ofte N, of C   herfore] þerfore NV   lernen] lere αH   98
contrarie] þe contrary CFV   þat¹] godes wille canc. þat D   þat þat] þat
YI   do] to do I   99 and . . . vseþ (101)] om. N   101 singe] signes B   102
mute] mosten NV   man] ony man LM   and] as I   103 obeschede]
obeischeþ Nδ, obeishe H, obeschide hym I   to²] corr. D   104 in] and
L   sowneþ] sowne Y   to] om. A   of] to ABG   105 ȝif] om. T   kept
wel] rev. HV   obedience] o/obedience D   106 awey] awey and þerfore
obeie we to god and be we of his couente and þe while schal we not faile of crist to be oure
abbot and þerfore preie we to hym speciali þat we so kepen his reule þat we may wone
whit hym in blisse whenne we heþen wende etc N

Dominica 1 post Octavam Epiphanie.
[Euangelium.] Sermo 32.

Cum factus esset Iesus. Luce 2.

This gospel telluþ a lore of Crist whanne he was twelue ȝer olde,
and þis lore is ful of miracles, as oþre dedis ben þat he dyde. Þe
story telluþ þat, *whan Iesu was maad of twelue ȝer old, he wente wiþ*
Ioseph and Marie vnto Ierusaleem, as þei hadden custoom at Pasc for to
make þis pilgrymage. And whanne þe dayȝes weren endyde of makyng of   5
þis pilgrymage, *his fadyr and his modur wenten hoom and Crist lefte*
alone in þe cyte. And his fadyr and his modyr wyste not þat Iesu was left
byhynde, for children hadden in free custom to chesen weþur þat
þei wolden wende wiþ fadyr or wiþ modyr; and þus Ioseph
wende þat Crist hadde comen wiþ his modyr, and owre Lady   10
supposede þat Crist hadde comen wiþ Ioseph. And among Iewes
was þis religiou[n] kept þat men schulde goo by hemself and
wymmen by hemself, for þei kepten hem fro lecherye in sych
pilgrimage; but now pilgrimage is mene for to do lecherye. And
al þis ordeynede owre Maister for to techen his chirche to   15
enforme þe prelatis aftyr general doyngis, for errour in hem is

MSS: D; ABCFGHIJKLMNTVXYZαβδ.

Dominica . . . euangelium] om. αZHV   sermo 32] om. BCFKLNTYαδIXZGH-
V   cum . . . iesus] nolite confirmari huic seculo N, om. V   factus esset] rev. J,
factis esset Y   iesus] iesus annorum duodecim Kα, iesus xii annorum H   luce 2]
ad ro. 12 . . . luc 12 N   1 this . . . and (2)] om. M   twelue] of
twelf H   olde] elde H   2 lore] lore today N, lord β   dedis . . . dyde]
gospelles ben N   3 whan] w/whan D   maad] ⌈maad⌉ Y, om. V   of] om.
Nδ   old] elde BFKMTIXZH   4 vnto] vn/G, into B   for to] to BN   5
pilgrymage] iourney on eras. of pilgrimage N   and . . . pilgrymage (6)] margin
βI   6 þis pilgrymage] iourney on eras. N   þis] om. δ   lefte alone] al only lafte
N   7 cyte] citees B   8 hadden] om. Y   free] fer Y   to] for to
C   þat] om. CδV   9 fadyr] þe canc. fadir H, þe fadur N, þe fadur I   wiþ²]
om. αV   modyr] þe modur N, here moder I   ioseph wende] rev. N   10 crist]
he H, iesu JV   12 iewes] þe iewes δV   12 religioun] religious DX   13
þei . . . fro] om. N   þei kepten] to kepe δ   14 pilgrimage¹] iourney þat myhte
falle among hem, iourney on eras. N, pilgrimagyng G   but . . . chirche (17)] om.
Z   pilgrimage²] þis iourney, iourney on eras. N   mene] a mene NV   for to]
to J   15 al] in al N   for to] to I   16 general] þo general α   doyngis]

more and more harmful to þe chirche. And whanne þei weren
mette togedre and wantedon þe child Iesu, *þei wenden þat he hadde*
ben in feleschipe wiþ som kyn of his frendis. And þei wenten aȝeyn to
20 sekon hym among hem, and *o day þei wenton aȝen and fownden hym*
not in þe weye. Þe þridde day þei sowten in þe citee and þey
fownden hym not. *And aftyr þe þridde day þei fownden hym in þe*
f.78v *temple,| syttyng among doctours, heryng and axynge hem.* No drede þat
ne Crist kepte good ordre in his doyng, furst heryng and aftyr
25 axyng wordys of þe lawe. *And alle þat herden hym hadden wondyr vpon*
his wisdom and hise answerys; and, seynge þe ȝoukþe of þe child, *þei*
hadden wondyr of his dedis. And his modyr seyde to hym 'Sone, why dedust
þow þus to vs? Loo! þi fadyr and I boþe sorwyng han sowt þe.' And Crist
seyde vnto hem, *'Warto han ȝe sowt me? Ne wiste ȝe not þat I muste be in*
30 ⌜*þe*⌝ *nedys of my Fadyr?* And here schulde prelatis lerne furst to
worschipe þere God and to seruen his chirche, byfor þat þei
bussyeden hem abowte worldly werkys. For eche man schulde
serue God, byfore þat he seruede oþur þing, for his furste entent
schulde be to worchype God whateuere he dide; and þis mut
35 nede be in Crist, for he dide alle þing as he schulde. *But þei*
vndyrstoden not þe word þanne þat Crist spak here to hem. And Crist wente
doun wiþ hem fro Ierusaleem *to Nazareþ, and he was suget vnto hem* in
þingus þat þei beden hym do. *And his modyr kepte alle þese wordis,*
beryng hem in her herte. And Iesu profiȝtede in wisdom, in age and in grace
40 *boþe to God and to man.* We schullen wyte þat owre Iesu, siþ he was

doinge AB   errour] errours FJ   in hem] *om.* M   17 weren] *om.* B   18
and] þei N, and þei δ   þe child] *om.* L   þe] þis FH   iesu] of iesu M, iesu
crist J   þei] and þei N   þat] *om.* N   19 in] in þe Y, in sum G   wiþ] of
I   kyn] *om.* αI   and] as of his kyn and α   to . . . hem (20)] and founden him
noȝt in þe weye I   to sekon hym] hym for to sechen N   20 hym[1]] hem
G   among hem] *om.* N   wenton . . . and] *om.* N   21 þe[2]] and þe I-
V   in[2]] hym in CαδV   22 þe[1]] þo αI   23 doctours] þe doctouris H-
V   heryng] *om.* G   and] hem and NV   hem] *om.* N   no] ⌜and⌝ no
J   24 ne] crist *canc.* ne D, *om.* I   25 wordys] hem wordis I   þe] *om.* T-
β   hadden wondyr] wondriden Y   wondyr] wurdure L   vpon] on H, of
NV   26 and[2]] *om.* δ   28 þow þus] þis G   þow] *om.* Y   29 vnto] to
KYIV   ne] *om.* KV   þat] þat þat M   30 þe] *corr.* D, *om.* GH   prelatis]
prestis Z   lerne] lere αZH   31 þere] *om.* HV   to] ⌜to⌝ T, *om.*
GV   32 bussyeden] bysy α   for] and for A   schulde] shul α   33 entent]
enten Y   34 god] his god F   þis] þus β   35 þing] þingis AFJH   36
vndyrstoden] vndyrstonden DCH, vndurstonden, *2nd n canc.* NX   þe . . . þanne]
þanne þe word I   þanne] *om.* NV   spak here] þenne spak N, spak δ   37
vnto] to IV   38 þingus] alle þingus NV   þat] *om.* LM   wordis] þingus *canc.*
wordis D   39 profiȝtede] profite B   in[3]] and in KTI   in[4]] *om.* B   40
to[2]] *om.* BMαV   schullen] suld Z   siþ he] siþ þat TJ, sayth δ   41 growyde]

þis manhede and suget to oþre men, and growyde in waxyng
[and] in elde, he profiȝtude in connyng wyche þat cam of his
wittes. But he hadde connyng of godhede and blessyde connyng
of man, by whiche he was in al his tyme ylyche wys and knew alle
þing.   45
    Here may holy chirche knowe boþe religioun of Crist and
partis of þis religioun, as obedience and mekenesse. For Crist was
suget to his lesse and seruede hem ful mekely, for Goddis lawe
tawte hym þat þei weren enspiryd more þan Crist was bodily.
And Godes rewle schulde suffice to men, al ȝif þei clowtede not   50
newe rewlus. For Crist tawte parfiȝtly a ful rewle for alle cristene
men; and hit is a fowl pruyde to clowten ⌐oure¬ erroures to his
wisdam, for oold cloþ clowted to newe makiþ more hole, as Crist
seiþ. And we ben certeyn of owre byleue þat Crist haþ mesured
his ordre in liȝtnesse and in fredom, more þan oþur men konne 55
schape. How schulde blynde fooles aftyr amende þis rewle þat
Crist haþ ȝyuen? And so God enformeþ men of þis pryuate ordres
þat þre þingus of here ordres ben ydele and noyows: furst þer
clowtyng of her rewle, and siþen þer obedience, and aftyr þer
obligacioun to þer abytis and oþre vses.   60
    Furst, Cristes rewle were fully sufficient to alle men, and more
free and more liȝt and of more auctorite. How myhte þe feend for
schame cumbre men wiþ sich clowtyng? Ȝif a man schulde
wenden aweye, hit were no nede to chargen hym wiþ þingus þat
weren not profiȝtable, ȝif he hadde ynow bysyde. And so, as God 65

---

53 Matt. 9: 16; Mark 2: 21.

growiþ A   42 and in] in DF, and ABLMNTYαβδXZGHV, an I   connyng]
knowyng K   wyche] þe wyche TV   43 connyng¹] knowyng K   connyng²]
knowyng K   44 his] þis Nβ   45 þing] þingis BIV   46 here . . . hem (104)]
om. Z   here] and here JV   religioun] ⌐þe¬ religioun αX, þe religioun ABCFKL-
βIJGV, religiouse Nδ   48 hem] hym I   for . . . ȝyuen (57)] om. N   49
enspiryd] in spirit ABCFKLMTYαβIJHV, more in spyryt δ   more] om. δ   50
clowtede] clouten I   52 fowl] ful β   oure] corr. D   53 clowted] cloutyng C,
þat is clowtid FH   more] ⌐it¬ more J   hole] oldere J   56 amende] ⌐a¬mende
δJ, mend CMTYβIXG   57 ȝyuen] ȝeuyn ⌐vs¬ J, ȝouen hem I   and] ⌐and þus
god enformed þis rule þat crist hath ȝouyn¬ and H   58 of . . . noyows] ben nuyouse
of hire ordres N   ordres] ordre MI   þer] þe CKV   59 clowtyng] cloþing
δ   þer²] boþe I   60 obligacioun] obligaciouns β   abytis] prelatis
H   vses] reulis C   61 furst] seþen N, for δ   were . . . sufficient] sufficeþ
fully N   fully] ⌐fulli¬ H, ful δ, om. V   and] om. N   62 and more liȝt] ⌐more
liȝt¬ G   of] om. L   63 wiþ] in G   ȝif] and ȝif A   65 not profiȝtable]

forfendeþ men ⌐for⌐ to adde to his lawe or for to drawe þerfro, for
hit is maad in ful mesure, riht so we schulden holden his rewle, by
whyche he techeþ alle cristene men, neiþur adde to ne drawe
⌐þer⌐fro leste we peyren Godes ordenaunce. And luytel errour in
70 þis byleue groweþ to more in long tyme, and þis feendis
blasfemye in God distorbleþ þe chirche more and more.

As anemptys obedience, hit is knowen þat Cristys obedience
kept clene were sufficient to alle men here on lyue. And oþur
obedience þat is clowted doþ harm manye wey3es, for hit
75 supposeþ þat þis prelat erruþ not in his comaundementis, but
f.79 |euermore biddeþ hise sugetis þe same þing þat God biddeþ. And
þus eche prelat schulde ben yliche wys and euene wiþ God. And
whanne þei ben made prelatis by synful menus, as ofte falliþ, God
schulde algatis 3iuen hem wit and confermen hem in grace, for 3if
80 þei myhten aftyr do synne, þei myhten be prowde in þer prelacye
and rewlen here sugetis amys a3en þe comaundementis of God.
And þanne were hit profi3table to wante siche blynde lederis, siþ
affiaunce in God and preyng of hise gouernayle my3te not fayle to
men, but 3if þei schal fayle furst. Lord! why ordeyned not God
85 suche ordres in þe olde lawe, ne in stat of innocens, but destruyde
newe þat wer maade? Wheþur God be not now as wys as he was
in þe olde lawe, and ordeyne now for his spouse as tendirly as he
dide þanne? And þus alle þese newe ordres beþ fulle of heresye.

And as anemptis þese newe habites, certeynly þei ben of þe
90 feend, but 3if þer be som nedful cawse by[n]dyng men þus to
hem; for ellis þei weren superflu3, and not of God but of þe feend,
siþ þei taryen mennys wittis and her kepyng from Godis werkis.

vnprofitable ABCKLMNTYαβIXGV   66 forfendeþ] forfendide I   for to¹] for
corr. D, to IG   to²] in L   for²] om. α   67 so] as beste is so N   we
schulden] scholde þey M   68 to] þerto FYV   ne] no T   69 þerfro] þer corr.
Dβ   peyren] ⌐a⌐payryn J, apayren FV   70 feendis] om. T   71 distorbleþ]
distourbeþ I   72 as] and canc. ⌐as⌐ C, and as V   73 kept clene] clenly kept J, kept
cleneli H   to . . . here] here to alle men I   75 erruþ] ne erriþ F   but] but//
but D   but euermore] twice Y   76 euermore] euere H   biddeþ²] biddiþ
hem M   78 prelatis] prestis Y   menus] mennes ⌐ordynaunce⌐ A, mennys
ordenaunce BN, menes ordynaunce, ordynaunce canc. δ, men α   ofte] ofte tyme N,
ofte tymes δ   80 prowde] proued G   81 here] om. G   comaundementis]
commaundement α   83 and] in H   preyng] preuynge ABCL, priuyng
FH   84 schal fayle] fayleden N   85 in²] in þe BFTHV   86 wheþur] for
α   now] now canc. X, om. ABFTG   87 ordeyne] ordeniþ CK, ordeynede
AB   89 þese] om. α   certeynly] certeyne Nδ   90 nedful] medeful TH   byn-
dyng] byddyng DLδ   men þus] rev. H   to hem] to vse hem δ   91

But hit is knowen þing to men þat þese habitis profiȝte not to
werkis of vertewys, but huyden þese ypocriȝtes, siþ þei may wiþ
suche habitis be qwike feendis in þis world. And ȝif þei profiȝten   95
by any cas, þei doþ harm ofture, as doþ synne, ⌐and crien to men
ypocrisie of suche ordris þat vsen hem⌐. And ȝif þese signes ben
false, þei maaken men false þat vson hem. And so algatis, siþ
vertewis myȝte be kepte wiþowten syche signes moore pryuely
and sicurly, þei ben browȝte in by þe feend, and specially to   100
chargen hem more þan counselis or maundementis of God. Eche
man mut haue som custom; but looke he wedde hym not þerwiþ,
ne bussye hym not þat hit be kept of manye men, for þei ben
dyuerse, and axen dyuerse customes aftyr þat God moueþ h[e]m.

---

for] or δ   93 knowen] know L   94 wiþ] in F   95 þis] þe H   96 cas]
cause α   doþ¹] om. G   harm] om. K   ofture] aftir CKHV   doþ²] þei
doþ I   and . . . hem (97)] margin corr. D   97 ypocrisie] ⌐by⌐ ypocrisye
T   þat] as H   vsen] suen Y   and . . . hem (98)] margin corr. CJ   98
vson] v/vson D   so] om. H   101 counselis] þe counseiles NV   maunde-
mentis] commaundementes, co- canc. α, ⌐co⌐maundementis F, comaundementis YIHV,
þe comaundementes N   102 he] he þat he HV   103 þat] at C   104 hem]
hym DAXG   margin plus de ista materia in euangelio 3 post festum sancte trinitatis
H, hem bote kepe we bysyly cristus hestus for þat is beste custome to vse for wiþ þat custom
schal we not fayle for to wynne þe blisse of heuene þat we may wynne to þat blisse preie we
alle to god etc. pater et aue N

Dominica ii [post octavam Epiphanie.
Euangelium.] Sermo 33.

Nupcie facte sunt in Chana Galilee. Iohannis 2.

This gospel telluþ of þe furste myracle þat Crist dide in presence
of his disciples. And þus telliþ þe story þat *weddyngus were maade in
a lytul dwellyng place in þe cuntre of Galilee. And Iesus modir was þere wiþ
Iesu and hise disciples* for, as men seyn comunly, Iohn þe Euangelist
5 was weddid here, and Crist was his cosyn and Cristis modir was
his aunte; and herfore þei weren homlyere in þis weddyng of
Iohn. Studye we not to what womman Iohn was weddid, ne axe
we not auctorite to proue þat Iohn was weddid now, for þat þat
þe gospel seiþ here is ynow to cristene feiþ. *And whan wyn fayled at
10 þis feeste, Iesu modir seyde to hym 'þ ei han noo wyn.'* And herby þis lady
mente on curteys maner as sche durste þat Iesu schulde helpe þis
feeste of wyn by his miracle. *But Iesu answerude* straungely '*What is
þat to me and to þe, womman?*', as ʒif he seyde 'I haue noʒt by my
manhede of þe for to do syche myracles, but þerto nediþ my
15 godhede; but aftirward schal tyme come whan I schal offre my
body þat I hadde of þe for sauyng of mannys kynde.' And herfore
notiþ Austyn how Iesu Crist clepuþ specially in þese two places
his modyr womman, and here he figured his speche in his

---

18 John 19: 26.

MSS : D; ABCFGHIJKLMNTVXYZαβδ; S *inc.* 60 siþ qualite

Dominica . . . euangelium] *om.* αZV   sermo 33] *om.* BCFKLNTYαδIJXZGH-
V   nupcie . . . galilee] *om.* V, benedicite et nolite maledicere N   in . . . galilee]
in I, *om.* J   iohannis 2] iohn ii . . . ad ro. xii N   1 this] þe N   telluþ] telleþ
today N, *om.* Y   in] in þe G   3 a] þe I   þe] þe *canc.* X, *om.* ABCF-
KLMNTYαβδIJZGHV   5 here] *om.* T   6 herfore] þerfore BTαZV   7
iohn¹] ⌜þis⌝ioon Aβ, þis ioon BCKLMTYαIJXGV   ne] no L, to ny N   8 not]
om. CK   þat þat] þat at N, þat AJ   9 þe] iesu *canc.* þe D   is] it is
H   cristene] cristen mennus T   feiþ] men M   fayled] falyed D   10
þis¹] þe αH   to] vnto N   noo] not YV   12 straungely] strongely α   13
þat] *om.* M   to¹ . . . womman] womman to þee and me N   me] þe Z   to²]
om. Y   þe] me Z   as] and F   haue] ne haue T   14 for to] to
HV   nediþ] me nediþ F, nedid β   16 mannys kynde] mankynde AFNYαIZGH-
V   and] *om.* F   17 clepuþ] clepid CKβ, called α, calleth δZ   þese] *om.*
J   18 womman] ⌜a⌝ woman αX, a woman CFKLMNTYβδIJZG   here]

passioun. And to þis entent seiþ Crist þat *his howr is not ʒet comen,* in whyche howr he schal be suffryng put his|body in werk. But *his* 20 f.79v *modir,* supposyng ay goode of hire sone, *seyde to þe ministrys to do whateuere he seyde. And þere weren at þe feeste sixe watir pottys sette, and echone of hem held a galown or more.* Þe Iewys hadden a custome to waschen hem ofte for towchyng or seyng of þing clene ynow, as seyn Mark meneþ in his gospel. *Iesu bad þe seruauntis fulle þe pottis* 25 *wiþ watur, and þei fylluden hem alle vp to þe mowþ. And Iesu seyde þanne 'Heeld ouʒt now, and ber þe persown.'* An architriclyn was he þat was clepyd to blesse þe feste, and pryncipal in þe hows þat was of þre stages, as ʒif hit were now a persoun of a cherche. *And þei baren to þis persown þe wyn þat Iesu hadde maad. And whanne he hadde tastyd* 30 *þerof and wiste not how hit cam, (but þe seruauntis wisten wel þat drowen þe watyr,) he clepude þe spowse of þe hows, and seyde to hym þus ' þese men þat festen oþur putten furst good wyn,* whan þer tast is fresch for to iugge þe goodnesse, and aftyr, *whan þei ben dronkon* and þer tast fayluþ, þanne he putteþ *worse wyn; but þow* dost euene þe 35 contrarie, for þow *hast kept good wyn into þis tyme.'* Þis was ⌈þe⌉ *bygynnyng of signes þat Iesu dide in Galilee, and schewide his glorie* by doyng of þis miracle, *and hise disciples trowedon in hym.*

Þis weddyng bytookneþ loue þat God hadde to his chirche, how he wolde bycome man and be newe weddit to it. And herfore 40 was Crist not bygamus, ne brak not his matrymonye, siþ þe same chirche his wif lasteþ euermore; but wiþ newe wenchis is Crist

25 Mark 7: 2–4.

herefore CK, *om.* N   ·19 seiþ crist] *om.* N   his] þis CKβ   comen] to come C   20 howr] hour *canc.* B, *om.* AN   schal] shulde ABCFKLMNTYαβIJXZGH- V   be] in N   put] but C   21 ay] euere KXG, euermore V   þe] þes I   to do] do ʒe B   22 seyde] seie B   sette] *om.* K   23 echone] ech ABCFKLMNTYαβIJXGHV   hem] *om.* L   to] ofte for to N   24 hem] *om.* Y   ofte] *om.* N   of] *om.* N   þing . . . ynow] ⌈vnklene⌉ þyng clene inow, clene inow *canc.* J   25 meneþ] moueth CKTH;   *margin* Mr. 7 J   ser- uauntis] seruaunt L   fulle] to fille δ   þe²] þo I   26 alle] *om.* I   vp] fulle vp H   þanne] *om.* N   27 heeld] heelde ʒe HV   ouʒt now] *rev.* H   now] newe G   ber] bere ʒe to HV   an] and DCFKTαIHV, an⌈d⌉J   he þat] þat ⌈person þat⌉ T   28 clepyd] called αδZ   pryncipal] þe principal I, principaly ACK   29 ʒif] *om.* CKI   a²] þe Z   30 þis] þe T   hadde¹] bad C   hadde²] *om.* K   31 and] he M   32 clepude] called αδZ   to hym þus] þus to him H   33 oþur] oþere men H   35 he] *om.* L   he putteþ] þai putte Z   dost] hast don H   euene] euer C   36 þow] *om.* F   into] vnto ABCFKLMNTYαβδIJXYGH   þe] *corr.* D, *om.* IJ   38 in] to F   39 bytookneþ] bitookeþ Y   loue] þe loufe CFKLMNTYαβδIJXZGHV   god] crist CK   40 how] and hou H   41 crist not] *rev.* CKδYJ   not²] *om.* M   matrymonye] weddyng *canc.* matrymonye D   42 his] is his FI, ys

now weddid and on newe maner he kepte his furste matrimonye;
as, ȝif a spouse of a wif were newe cled, herfore were not dyuorse
45 maad bytwyxen hem. A newe weddyng wiþ membris of þis grete
womman makiþ not dyuors, ne brynguþ in no bygamye; as, ȝif a
wyf growede and hadde manye partis þat sche hadde not byfore,
sche were not þerfore left. And þus Chana þat is 'gelousnesse',
and Galile þat is 'a turnyng whel', bytoknen þe loue of Crist þat
50 he hadde to counforten his spouse in þis weye, and bryngon hire
aftur to blisse in þe chambre of heuene.

Þe turnyng of þis watur into good wyn techuþ vs how Crist
maade his lawe moore sauery, as þe wyn was betture þan þe
watur byfore. And riht as o substaunce is furst watur and siþ wyn,
55 riht so o lawe is furst coold and siþen hoot; and herfore seiþ Crist
þat he cam not to fordo þe lawe, but to fulfille þe lawe and maken
hit more sauery. And drede we not þese philosophres to graunten
hem apertly þat þe same substaunce is furst watur and siþ wyn; ne
drede we not dyuynes þat askyn in þis cas what ⌜þing⌝ was maad
60 newe of Crist in þis myracle, siþ qwalite as colowr or sauowr of
wyn may not be by hitself, as Austyn seiþ. We schal wyte þat
myracle of Crist was wroht here, so þat, riht as watur þat first was
in þe erþe is drawen into þe vyne tre, and siþ into þe grapis, and
by tyme defyed tyl þat hit be wyn, so Crist dide þis chaungyng in
65 a lytul tyme. But moore myracle was of beturyng of his lawe, and
þe moste of alle of swift turnyng to hit. Þese sixe watyr pottys þat
f.80 helden þis colde watur|ben men of þe oolde lawe þat kepton

T   lasteþ] þat lasteþ J   but . . . wenchis] *twice, first canc.* D   43 now] new
CZ, now newe H   his furste] fyrst hys *marked for rev.* δ, first his Z   44 newe]
now α   not] no H   45 a] as L   46 not] no⌜t⌝ Y, no IH   dyuors] dyuerse
L   no] om. K   in no] not in T   48 sche] om. F   þat] om. T   is] is
clepid G   49 a] om. C   turnyng] turmentyng β   bytoknen] bitoknede I,
betokenyng J   þe] þis F   50 þis] his C   51 in] into αV   chambre of
heuene] heuenly chaumbre N   52 þe] and þe J   turnyng] turyng β   into]
vnto H   vs] om. A   53 sauery] sauerly C   þe¹] om. I   54 and] ⌜and⌝ α,
om. B   as] so as B   substaunce] subs/staunce D   is] om. β   55 siþen] siȝt
β   herfore] þerfor αZV   56 to fordo] for to do L   to¹] for to F   to²] for
to J, om. TH   þe lawe] om. CKβ   57 þese] to L   58 hem] to hem
LM   apertly] a particle F   wyn] þe wiyn β   ne] no L   59 not] no β,
om. I   þing] corr. D, þing canc. G, om. A   60 newe] om. M   or] of S   61
hitself] himsilf BCKLMNSTYαβδIJXZGHV, hemsilf F   62 myracle] þis myracle
KIV   was¹] om. Z   riht] water I   watur] riȝt I   þat] was I   was²]
om. I   63 þe¹] om. N   vyne] wyn LMN   siþ] om. M   þe²] om.
B   64 dide þis] in M   65 moore] om. S   of¹] om. M   beturyng] þe
beteringe I, bettur þing β   66 þe] om. I   moste] most miracle, miracle canc. α,
most miracle CK   of²] is canc. of α, is of K, ⌜is⌝ of V   swift] swilth S   to] of

Godis lawe, but þei weren sixe for, fro ȝer to ȝer þei kepton þis
lawe, þat was hard as stonys, and maade men coolde on oþur
maner þan þe newe lawe, for hit makiþ men liȝte and hetuþ hem   70
and cownforteþ hem, as wyn doþ mannes body. As philosophres
seyn þese mesures of þese vesselis ben þe olde cerymonyes, þat
weren bedon of God, and somme fownden of Iewis; and alle þese
weren fullyd of Crist. But to anoþur wit þis architriclyn was þe
manhede of Crist, for he made þis miracle by his godhede: he was   75
þe furste þat tastede þis wyn, and ȝaf hit þese propretes boþe in
hym and oþre. And doyng of þis myracle passuþ mennys
feestyng, for God putteþ hymself to be boþe mete and dryng to
men þat he fediþ; and he is þe beste. For worldly festyng is furst
sauery to man and siþen hit is byttur as wermod to hym, but   80
goostly foode aȝeynward furst is vnsauery and siþ hit is swete
whan men han defyed hit; for Godis lawe sauereþ wel whan hit is
defowlyd, as spicery ȝueþ smel whan hit is poʳuˈnyd, but drit
sterid more is more vnsauery. And þus þe ȝyuyng of þe lawe of
God was grownd and bygynnyng of cristene mennys religioun,   85
and þus þe disciples of Crist, alle þat he haþ ordeynot for to come
to heuene by rit byleue, trowen in hym by vertew of þis wyn. And
þus is Crist glorified in heuene and in erþe by strengþe of his lawe
þat he þus ȝaf.

K   þese] þeʳsˈ αH, þe C   sixe] sixte G   68 but . . . lawe (69)] om.
N   but] for I   sixe] sixte G   ȝerˈ] þe ȝeer H   ȝer²] þe ȝeer þat
H   69 hard] so hard H   men] hem A, om. B   71 hem] om. H   mannes]
mennus H   72 vesselis] pottes J   73 somme] sumtyme I   iewis] þe canc.
iewis G, ʳþeˈ iewis X, þe iewes CFKLMNSTYαβδJV, þese canc. iewis B, þes iewis
I   þese] om. Z   74 to] om. Y   75 by] of I   76 þis] þe B   propretes]
proprete Z   77 hym . . . putteþ (78)] om. Cβ   hym] hem F   oþre] in canc.
ooþere Y, in oþere KTαI   and²] om. BF   passuþ] passide AKG   mennys]
mannys ABFKLMNSTYαδJXZGHV   78 feestyng] fastyng NδJ   putteþ] put
K   79 worldly] wo adly S   festyng] fastyng J   80 man] men FTIH   byt-
tur] betture canc. byttur D   hym] hem H   81 furst is] rev. αδZ   82 han
defyed] defien A   83 defowlyd] diffied T   spicery] spices F   smel] ʳgoodˈ
smel J, good smel FH   hit is] þei ben myche F, þat it is N   pounyd] defylud canc.
poʳuˈnyd, u corr. D   drit . . . vnsauery (84)] drit ʳay þe more it isˈsterid þe more it is
vnsauery J, þe more þat dritte is stured it sauereþ wel þe wurse N   drit] donge α, filth
Z   84 more¹] more and more M, more ʳinneˈ δ   more²] þe more MV   85
grownd] groundid CKδI   and] in CKN   cristene . . . religioun] cristus
religioun and cristen monnes reule N   mennys] men CK   86 þe] al þe
I   of] of canc. of D   alle] om. F   87 heuene] blisse H   rit] þe riȝte
N   þis] his BCL   88 þus] on eras. corr. D   strengþe] þe strengþe S   89
ȝaf] ȝaue þat we may lyue aftur his lawe preie we alle to hym etc. pater et aue N

Dominica iii [post Octavam Epiphanie. Euangelium.] Sermo 34.

Cum descendisset Iesus de monte. Mathei 8.

This gospel telluþ of two myracles þat Crist dide and contenuþ myche wyt abowte þese two miracles. Þe story telluþ how *Iesu cam down of þe hul whanne he hadde ȝyuen his lawe to his disciples, and a myche puple sewode hym* for deuocion þat þei hadden in his lawe and eke in his wordis. *And lo, þere cam a meysel man and lowtyde hym, and seyde 'Lord, ȝif þow wolt þow maist hele me.' And Crist seyde he wolde, and bad hym be hool.* Hit is comunly supposyd þat þis leprows man trowyde þat Crist was boþe God and man, and so Crist myhte helun hym; but of his owne worþinesse affyede he not þus, and herfore he seyde þat ȝif Crist wolde he myhte helon hym of his lepre. And þan was Crist God, and God wolde þat prowde men and leprows heretykys wolden [wel] confesson þe feiþ, and þanne schulde þei ben hool. *And Crist stregghide owt his hond and towchide hym, and seyde 'I wole, make þe hool* and able ⌐þe⌐ þerto.' And þus doþ God to whom he ȝyueþ grace. *And anon was clensud þe lepre of þis man.* And þis hasty helyng bytokneþ þis myracle, and þat Crist towchede þis leprous techeþ vs now þat þe manhede of Crist was instrument to his godhede, for to do myracles þat he wolde weren done; and þat towcheng of leprows men was lefful to men þat þus wolden

MSS: D; ABCFGHIJKLMNSTVXYZαβδ.

Dominica . . . euangelium] *om.* SαZV   sermo 34] *om.* BCFKLNSTYαδIJXZGH-V   cum . . . monte] nolite esse prudentes sed cum omnibus hominibus pacem habentes N, *om.* V   cum] *om.* H   descendisset] ascendisset C   mathei 8] ad ro. xii . . . mt. 8 N   1 this . . . miracles (2)] *om.* N   2 abowte] aboue F   two] *om.* G   þe story] storie of þe gospel N   3 he] *om.* Y   disciples] discipl/ples D   and] *om.* F   a] ⌐a⌐ αG, *om.* YV   4 eke] alse αZ   5 his] *om.* S   lo] *om.* Z   hym] to him M, *om.* S   6 maist] myȝt NTδ, makist L   bad] *om.* F   9 of] *om.* N   owne] *om.* N   affyede] affermede N   þus] þis N   herfore] þerfore NαδIZV   10 þat ȝif] *rev.* TδV   þat] *om.* N   11 þan . . . crist] so moste he be N   god wolde] *rev.* Nα   12 wel] *om.* DF, ⌐wel⌐ H   þe] þis BCKLMNSTYαβδJZHV   13 hym] *om.* S   14 þe2] *corr.* D, *om.* α   15 grace] his grace I   was] ⌐he⌐ was J   16 hasty] hastili B   17 leprous] leprouse mon δV   now] how K, *om.* G   þe] *om.* T   18 to1] of N   weren] þat weren FJ   19 was] þat Y   lefful] lewfful, w *canc.*

helpe hem, but Crist myhte not be blemyschid by towchyng of þis 20
leprows. And so tawte Crist hise euerelastyng good wille, and
taw3te vs to parforme þe good wille þat we han. *And aftyr Crist bad
hym 'See þat þow telle no man! but goo and schewe hym to þe preest, and
offre þat 3ifte þat Moyses bad in wytnesse of such helpe.*' And so men
seyn on þre maneres may þis word ben vndyrstonden; furst þat 25
þis man schulde telle noo man herof, byforn he hadde offred þat
Crist bad hym do. Þe secounde cause and betture is þat Crist bad
þis|to techen vs to fle bost and þank of syche men to whiche we f.80v
doon good by maner of mercy; and þus we schulde not telle þis by
entent of mannys þank. Þe þridde weye seiþ þat Crist bad þis 30
negatif to fle sclawndryng of Godus lawe and man, and fle
boostyng of hymself and conceyuyng of euyl of God. And for þe
oolde lawe was þanne cesud, Crist bad fulle þis lawe as auctour
þerof; and þus whan a man scheweþ by his holy lif actif lif, þat is
two dowue briddis, or contemplatif lif, þat is a peyre of turtres, by 35
siche signes he scheweþ þat his synne is for3yuen and þat vnto
preestys þat wel vndyrstonden þis. And þus synful men schulden
counsele wiþ preestis and taken of hem medicyne to flee more
synne.

Þe secounde miracle techuþ how Crist heelude an heþene 40
man, for loue of centurio þat kepte Capharnaum, þat was heed
town of þe cuntre of Galilee. *Þis centurio teelde Crist þat ⌐h⌐is child lay
in his hows sy3k on þe palesye, and was euele turmentud.* But Luk telluþ
how þis knyht dide al þis by oolde men of þe Iewis, þat myche
preysedon þis knyht and seyden þat he was freend to hem, and 45

43 Luke 7: 1–5.

D   men²] me L   20 by] wiþ I   þis] þuse N   21 euerelastyng . . . wille]
good wille euerlastynge N   22 taw3te] so tauhte N   23 hym²] þee NH-
V   preest] prestis T   24 wytnesse] witnesse ge, ge *canc.* Y, witnessynge
V   helþe] hele NZ   25 word] world Mβ   26 man¹] *om.* S   herof]
þerof Z   byforn] bifore þat AHV   27 and] is G   betture] þe bettire
βH   is] *om.* G   þat . . . þis (28)] *twice, 2nd after turn-over, 2nd canc.* D   þat]
þis þat NV   28 þis¹] *om.* N, þus δ   to] *om.* K   to²] to *canc.* β, *om.* BCM-
STYαδIJZ   whiche] þe woch J   29 doon] han do H   by²] *om.* β   30
seiþ þat] siþ ⌐þat¹T   bad] *om.* S   31 sclawndryng] sclaundre ABFαI   man]
of man CK   and²] but LMNTβJH   fle] to fle CK, boþe fle F   32 hymself]
hemself Nδ   34 whan] w *eras.*/whan D   his] þis I   actif] actis L   35 of]
om. δ   turtres] turtelis I   36 siche] whiche I   synne] synnes I   is] ben
I   and] hym and N, to him and V   þat²] þanne S   37 wel] wil CH   38
medicyne] medicynes G   40 an] and S   42 his] h *corr.* D   lay] ⌐was¹
K   43 his] þe KV   on] in CFK, of αZ   luk] saynt luke Z   44 þis knyht]

bylde hem a synagoge. And Crist cam wiþ hem ny3 þis kny3tis hows,
and þis knyht seyde þus vnto Iesu Crist: '*Lord! I am not worþi þat
þow entre vndyr my roof, but sey only wiþ word and my seruaunt schal ben
hool.* For I am a man put in þis place by power of þe emperowr, hauyng
50 *vndur me knyhtis* for to do myn offis, and ⌜I⌝ *seye to oon "goo" and he
goþ, and I seye to anoþur "com" and he comeþ, and I seye to my seruaunt
"do þis" and he doþ hit'*. And by þis wolde þis knyht mene þat Crist
hadde no nede to entre into his hows to hele þis seeke man, siþ
Crist is God almyhty vnder no power. *And Iesu, herynge þese wordes,*
55 *wondride* in hise wittes, al 3if he wiste and ordeyned byfore þat þis
knyht schulde þus be trewe. And herfore *seyde Crist to þe folc þat
sewedon hym 'Soþly I seye to 3ow, I fond not so myche feiþ in al þe folc of
Israel*—neiþur preestis ne comunes.' Crist mente not of his
apostles, ne of his modyr, ne of his meyne, for þei weren taken
60 from Israel, as Crist was þere a strange lord. And herfore byhetuþ
Crist his chyrche þat schal be of heþene men þat *manye of þe eest*
and west schal come, and reste wiþ patriarkes in þe kyndom of heuene,
where children of þis rewme schal be put owht and caste into helle; þere
schal be wepyng, þat is sensible sorwe, *and gnastyng of teþ* þat is
65 moore, for hit is peyne of harm of blisse þat passiþ alle sensible
peyne. *And Iesu seyde eft to þis knyht 'Goo! and þi seruaunt schal ben hool.*
For, as þow trowedust by my grace, *be hit doon vnto þe.'* And þe child was
maad hool in þe same howr þat Crist spak þus.

We schulle wyte þat feiþ is a 3ifte of God, and soo God may not
70 3yuen hit to man but 3if he 3yue hit graciously. And þus alle
goodis þat men han ben 3iftis of God, and þus, whan God

crist M   þe] *om.* T   45 þat] *om.* β   hem] him S   46 hem[1]] him
S   þis] to þis AB, þe FYα   47 vnto] to BNδV   iesu] *om.* β   lord] *om.*
N   48 vndyr] lord vndur N, withinne S   wiþ] bi YV   49 am] *om.*
LMI   in] into N   place] palesie M   50 offis] officis Z   I] *corr.*
DJ   seye] seyde DATIJG   51 seye[1]] seyde DASTIJG   com] come þou
H   seye[2]] seyde DATIJG   52 and[2]] ⌜and⌝ α, *om.* FT, a S   wolde] *on eras.*
corr. D   mene] meneþ LM   54 almyhty] and almy3ti B   and] *om.*
A   55 he] 3he C   56 þus] ⌜þus⌝ J, *om.* F   be trewe] trowe AB-
Z   herfore] þerfor FαZV   þe] *om.* G   57 sewedon] folowiden YZ   al]
om. FV   58 neiþur] neþer in FNV, ne⌜þer⌝ in J   ne] ny in NV, nowþer
δ   crist] and crist M, but crist JV   60 þere] here A   a] *om.* S   herfore]
þerfore NZV   byhetuþ] behetid C   61 þat[1]] þat it α   schal] *om.* of[1]]
of þe S   þe] *om.* αIG, þese δ   62 west] of þe west N, þe west V   63 children]
þe children I   put] ta *canc.* put D   65 moore] more paynful T   peyne]
harme CK   harm] payne CK   of[2] and wantyng of CK   66 eft] oft
J   and[2] *om.* I   67 trowedust] trowedist, -ed- *canc.* B, trowist A   hit] *om.*
Y   vnto] to HV   69 3ifte] 3if Lβ   god[2]] good β   70 man] a man Cβ,
no man α   3if] *canc.* D, *om.* T   71 3iftis] graciouse 3iftes N   72 rewardeþ]

rewardeþ a good werk of man, he corowneþ his owne ȝifte and þis
is of grace; for alle þingus ben of grace þat men han of wille of
God. And Godis goodnesse is furste cause why he ȝyueþ men þes
goodis; and so hit may not be þat God do good to men, but ȝif he   75
do þese goodis freely by|his grace; and wiþ þis we schal graunte   f.81
þat men disseruen of God for in grace þei makon hem worþi to
haue þis good of God. But ⌈we⌉ schulle not vndirstonde þat eche
grace of God is a lompe of þingus þat may be by hymself, but
grace is a maner in man by whiche he is gracious to God; and   80
oþer grace on Goddis syde is good wille of God. And for such
grace in God men receyuen grace in hem. And chidyng of ydiotis,
as was Pelagius and oþre, þat conceyue not þat a þing may be but
ȝif hit may be by hymsilf as ben substaunces, is for to scornen and
leue to foles; for nyne kyndes of accidens han contrarye maner,   85
siþ eche of hem is a maner of substaunce of a þing and hit may not
be by hymself as heretykes dremen. And herfore leue we þis, and
lerne we of þis knyht to be meke in herte, in word and in dede, for
he grauntyde furst þat he was vndir mannys power, and ȝet by
power of man he myhte do manye þingus. Muche more schulde   90
we knowe þat we ben vndur Godis power, and þat we may do noo
þing but by power of God; and, ȝif we disuson þis power, woo
schal us ben herfore. And so þis roote of meekenesse schal geton
oþre vertewes to vs and grace of God to disserue meede of heuene
and goodis of glorie, as hit was in þis gentel knyht.   95

rewardid Y   man] a man H   ȝifte] ȝif L   þis] so þis N   73 grace¹] his
grace J   for . . . grace] *om.* SV   þingus] þing C   han] ⌈han⌉ α, *om.*
N   wille] þe wille IV   75 goodis] -is *on eras of* -nesse *corr.* D   do] dos
αδ   76 þese . . . freely] frely þes godis H   his] *om.* S   we] ⌈we⌉ he
G   77 of] ⌈good⌉ of T   for . . . dremen (87)] *om.* N   þei] þi β   78 we]
corr. D   79 be] not be I   by] *om.* Y   hymself] hemsilf Fδ   80 a] in a
Mα   81 on] in S   good] a good G   such] whiche I   82 hem] hym
T   and] but J   83 conceyue] conceyueden LMδ   84 may] *om.* A   sub-
staunces] substaunce α   is] ⌈is⌉ T, *om.* δ   for to . . . hymself (87)] *twice*
δ   85 leue] to *eras.* leuȩ J, to leue ABCKLMSYαβXZGV, for to leue I   ac-
cidens] accidentis, -tis *canc.* -s *corr.* D   86 siþ . . . hem] *twice* S   a¹] *om.* B   87
be] *om.* δ   hymself] hemself C, itself Z   and herfore] bote N   herfore]
herefore, h- *altered from* þ- J, þerfore ZV   þis] wel þis S   and²] mater and
N   88 lerne] lere H   of] anoþur of δ   in²] *om.* δ   in³] *om.* N   89
grauntyde] grauntiþ K, groundid α   he²] *om.* β   ȝet] *om.* β   91 do noo
þing] no þing do B   92 power of god] godes power N   of] *om.* A   and] *om.*
N   disuson] mysvsen FαHV, defusen L   þis] ȝis L   93 herfore] þerfore
ABCKLMNSTYαβδIJXZGV   and] *om.* I   94 to²] also to M   of²] in
N   95 goodis] goddis C   þis] þe ACY   knyht] k/knyht D, knyȝt preie we
þerfore vnto god þat he graunte vs mekenesse and grace to disserue here of hym mede in
heuen blisse for euer etc. pater et aue N

Dominica iiii [post Octavam Epiphanie.
Euangelium.] Sermo 35.

Ascendente Iesu in nauiculam. Mathei 8.

This gospel telluþ a miracle þat Crist dide in þe watur; and syche
myracles confermen þe feiþ of hooly chirche ful myche in rude
men, al ȝif þei ben harde. And so doyng of myracles in watur and
in lond bytookneþ þat Crist schewe[de] hise wondres to dyuerse
5 men; somme men receyueden hem not to hele of her sowle, for þei
weren vnstable as watur and fordiden sone Cristes prente, but
oþre men weren stable as lond þat helden þe preente þat Crist
putte in hem, and by þe grownd of sich feiþ þei wenton fully þe
weye to heuene. Þe story telluþ of Iesu þat *he steyȝede into a boot and*
10 *hise disciples suedon hym. And loo, þe watur meuede faste so þat þe boot was*
hyd wiþ wawes, for þe wynd and þe watur weren contrarye to hem. Crist
slepte in þis tyme in þe boot, as he hadde ordeynut. *Þe disciples*
comen and wakeden hym, and seyden þus to Crist 'Lord, saue vs, for we
peryschen!' And Crist seyde to hem 'What drede ȝe of lytul feiþ?' And
15 *Crist roos vp anoon, and comaundyde to þe wyndes and þe watyr, and þei*
weren restude anoon. And al þe puple wondride herof, and seyden among
hemself *'What is he þis? for þe wyndus and þe see obesche to hym.'*
Siþ alle þe dedis þat Crist dide techen men how þei schulden

MSS: D; ABCFGHIJKLMNSTVXYZαβδ.

Dominica . . . euangelium] *om.* SαZV   sermo 35] *om.* BCFKLNSTYαδIXZGH-
V   ascendente . . . nauiculam] plenitudo legis est dilectio N, *om.* V   ascen-
dente] ascendit H   mathei 8] ad ro. xiii . . . mt. viii N   1 this] þe N   a] of a
N   3 harde] hardid FJ   so] *om.* F   doyng] doyngis J   4 in] *om.*
ACKβ   bytookneþ] bitokenyde FY   schewede] scheweþ DH   to] vnto
N   5 men²] *om.* ACN   hem not] nouȝt hym I   hem] hym SαJ-
Z   hele] heelþe, -þ- *canc.* Y, heelþe FHV, þe heele J   sowle] soulis FH   for]
om. N   6 fordiden sone] somme forduden N   prente]-ente *on eras. corr.* D, priuite
I   7 crist] god K   8 fully] f/fully D   9 hes] *om.* I   10 suedon] foleweden
NZ   11 hyd] hilid H   wiþ] wiþ þe NTIH   wynd] went β   and] in
L   watur] wawes I   to] vnto N   12 in¹ . . . tyme] *twice* I   in² . . .
boot] *om.* IV   13 wakeden] wakeneden FαβIJZ, wakynde C   þus] þere
G   to] vnto N   14 hem] him S   drede] do Z   ȝe] he β   of lytul]
rev. I   15 to] *om.* Z   wyndes] wynd C, water N   þe²] to þe KS, *om.*
N   watyr] wyndes N   16 herof] þerof ZV   17 for] þat I   wyndus]
wynd F, see N   þe see] wyndes N   obesche] obeien YH   18 þe] þes

do, þis restyng of Crist in þis boot bytookneþ loore to be markyd.
We schulde by tymes reste and prey ȝe to God in sylence, and here   20
of hym heelful lore þat we schulden aftir teche þe puple. And þus
schulde techerus flee preysyng of ⌐þe¬ puple, as Crist dide; and þis
is a pryue synne among men þat prechen ⌐to¬ þe puple, and certys
hyt is a greet synne, siþ God schulde haue al hool þe þank. And
þus þe slepyng of Crist bytookneþ his verrey manhede, and makiþ   25
his myracle more, and to preyen hym hertlyere in nede. And þus
al only we dreeden for defawt of feiþ in vs, and Crist slepuþ not to
vs but for defawt of feiþ, for þe godhede may not slepe. And ȝeet
we spekon vnto hym 'rys! why slepustow Lord? and help vs in þis
neede.' And þus on two manerys fayluþ byleue in men. Furst   30
|whan men wantiþ byleue, as þese þat trowede not þat Crist was   f.81v
God, for, ȝif þei hadden trowed þis holly, þey schulden ha⌐ue¬
trowed þat Crist myȝte slepyng haue don þis myracle. And
myche more on þe secounde maner fayluþ byleue, whan hit
worcheþ not wel in dede, but is ydel as a slepyng man; and þanne   35
clerkis seyn hit is in habyte. And þus may no man do synne, but
ȝif his byleue fayle, oþur on o maner or on oþur. For, ȝif he hadde
freschly byleue how fowl his synne is, and how myche hit harmeþ
hym, he wolde not for al þis world do þis synne, but flen hit. And
herfore preidon disciples to alarghen hem byleeue, and Crist   40
seyde to Petre 'Wy dowtustow of lytul byleue?' And Crist seide to

---

29 Ps. 43: 23;   **41** Matt. 14: 31.

H   how] what G   schulden] schulen N   19 þis²] his L, þe IV   by-
tookneþ] bitokenede B   to] for to CK   21 þe] to þe NY   22 þe] corr.
D   and] for J   23 is] om. B   þat] to F   to] corr. D   24
schulde . . . hool] alone schulde N   haue . . . hool] al onely han δ   25 þe] om.
K   his] om. B   26 his] þis CY   to . . . nede] hertilyer in mede to preyen
hym N   preyen] preche Z   hym] om. S   hertlyere] hartely CSV   27
only] hooly S   defawt] þe defaute S   in . . . feiþ (28)] om. N   not] om.
δ   28 but] om. T   defawt] þe defaute FSJ   for] in vs canc. for D   29
spekon] spenken B   vnto] to I   rys] arise JV   30 on] in CK   fayluþ . . . men] men faileþ in bileue J   men] man α   31 men] hem BCKLMST-
YαβδXZGV, þei J   þat¹] om. T   32 holly] fulli F, om. N   haue] -ue corr.
D   33 þat] holly þat N   34 myche] a muche N   fayluþ] men failiþ and, and
canc. F, men faileþ in J   hit] he T   35 wel] om. G   a] ⌐a¬ H, om. CK-
N   þanne] om. N   36 hit] þat it Z   37 his] om. S   oþur¹] or B-
H   on¹] in ZV   on²] in Z, om. V   oþur²] a/oþur D, anoþer TZ   he
hadde] þei hadden S   38 freschly] fresch TV   byleue] in byleue N   his
synne is] is synne NT   39 hym] om. N   40 herfore] þerfore ZV   disciples]
þe disciples NH   hem] him A, ⌐to hem¬ her δ, her FT   byleeue] in beleue CKα,
feiþ H   41 dowtustow] doutid þou Z   and . . . trowe (42)] om. K   43

a man þat he schulde trowe, for alle þingus ben possible to men
þat byleuen. And schortly no kynne vertew was preysud moore of
Crist þan was riht byleue, for hit is grownd of alle oþre.
Ne dowte
45 we not how byleue may now be lesse and now be more, siþ þanne
partis of byleue my3ten gon awey and come newe, and þanne þer
weren dyuerse byleues for dyuersite of partis. Syche dowtis we
schulden sende to þe scole of Oxenforde, and we schulden wyte
wel by God þat dyuerse feiþus in a man, now on and now
50 ⌈an⌉oþur, makyn o feiþ in hym, −3e, 3if þe tyme be dyuerse þat
þis feiþ þus comeþ or goþ.
And þus may God encreson owre feiþ, and we by synne
enfeblen owre feiþ. And Crist slepuþ ofte to vs for sich·slepyng of
oure synne, for, whanne wyndes of mennys boost maken vs to
55 dredon of worldly harmes and flodis of tribulacioun comen to vs,
þei maken vs dreden and cryen on Crist to haue help for faylyng
in ⌈oure⌉ byleue. For we schulden trowe þat noo sych caas myhte
anoyen vs, but for synne; and 3if hit come for owre synne, hit is
iust and Godis wille. Why schulde we þus be distemprede for þing
60 þat is nede to come? Loue we God and do we his wille, and drede
we no kynne þing but hym. For defawte in owre byleue makiþ vs
to drede for syche þingus. For þese fowre mannys affecciounes,
dreede and sorwe, hope and ioye, chaungen a mannys wille aftyr
þat he haþ vertewes. And, 3if he be rooted in synne, þei chaungen
65 myche in a man, for he haþ drede of þing of nowht, and aftyr ioye

---

42 Mark 9: 22.

schortly] certenly α   kynne] kyns Fα, *om.* δ   preysud moore] *rev.* FYJH   44
is] was T   ne] and βV   45 now be¹] *rev.* I   now¹] *om.* S   be²] *om.*
FNHV   þanne] þanne ne S, þat ZH   47 byleues] beleue S   we schulden]
rev. N   48 to] vnto N   scole] scoles NI   49 a] *om.* C   50 anoþur] oþer
ALMSYβV   3e] and S   3if] þeigh NV   þe] þo αδ   52 may god] *rev.*
JV   and² . . . feiþ (53)] *margin* α, *om.* V   we] *om.* βJ   53 enfeblen] we
enfeblen J   slepuþ] spekiþ C   to] til α, wiþ H   vs] þu *canc.* vs D   54
whanne] þanne B   mennys] monnes NδIH   vs] *om.* Z   to dredon] in drede
L, drede Z, fered N   to] to *canc.* X, *om.* BCKMTYαβδJGV   55 harmes] harme
CK   56 þei] and N   dreden] to drede Z   and] of worldly harmes *canc.* and
D   to] for to I   faylyng] fallynge I   57 oure] caas] a cas
A   myhte] schulde TV   58 anoyen] noye H   synne] synnes N   and] of
B   59 þus be] *rev.* ABFLMSTYαβIXZGHV   distemprede] disperid K   60
nede] ne C, nedeful FH   to] for to C   61 we] *om.* KN   kynne] ⌈kynne⌉ T,
kyns FαJ, maner δ, *om.* ANHV   hym] oñly hym J   for] and so for þe J   in]
of Bα   62 to] *om.* BCKLMNSTYαβδZGV   for¹] for *canc.* δ, vs K   mannys
affecciounes] *rev.* S   mannys] menus CKδ, manere F   63 and¹] ⌈and⌉ α, *om.*
I   a] *om.* CG   64 3if] þis β   he] ⌈it⌉K   rooted] roote S   þei] þes
LM   chaungen] chargen I   65 a] þat N   of¹] for N   nowht] þing *canc.*

of worldly þingus, and also sorwe of los of þing þat were betture
hym to wante, and hope of þingus fer from his helþe, as is welfare
of þis world. And alle þese techen þat his wille is not ⌐set⌐ on
heuenly þingus, ne his byleue groundid in God for defaute of
good loue. For eche man schulde drede more los of Godis loue by   70
synne þan he schulde drede los of any worldly þingus; for, as
byleue techeþ vs, los of Godis loue were worse. Why schulde we
not drede þis more, siþ hit brynguþ more harm to vs, and hope
more help by charyte þan by ony mannis help? And þus cursuþ þe
prophete hym þat tristuþ þus in man.   75

     And here may men haue a myrour to iuge wer þei loue God,
⌐and wher þey ben in charite by þe ordre þat þey schulde haue. Ʒif
þey louen God⌐ wel, þei schulden more haue ioye of hym þan of
any erþly þing. And so of los ʒif hit come: ʒif þei leson þe loue of
God by þer synne þat þei schulde knowe, þei schulden ha[ue]   80
more sorwe þerof þan of los of oþur þing. And þis ioye wiþ þis los
wolde make men to flee synne. Siþ manye men wiþ diligence flen
los of worldly goodis, and kepon hem þat þei ben not dampnyd in
sych los by mannys lawe, and drede not so myche to leson goodis
of grace þat ben betture, hit is open þat charite is not ordynel in 85
|hem. And þus of goodis of kynde men dreden myche to leson   f.82
hem, as rewle of kynde techeþ vs and comun experience, and ʒif
þei comen to vs we ioye ful myche, as we wyton wel, but goodis of
grace we putten byhynde, and þat fordoþ owre charite. And ʒif
we feynen falsehede in þese two þingus, boþe God and owre   90

---

75 Jer. 17: 5.

nowht D   aftyr] ⌐aftir⌐ CT, efterward Z   67 hym] to him H   helþe] hele
Z   is welfare] rev. S   is] his CT   68 þis] hys T   set] corr. D   70
drede more] rev. BV   71 drede] om. δ   los] on losse L   72 los] þat losse
J   worse] more worse J   we not] rev. Nα   73 þis] hit TV   more
. . . vs] to vs more harme J   to] til S   74 more] of more J, ⌐in grete⌐ T   cur-
suþ] cursyd S   75 hym] hem J   76 may men] rev. αV, we may J   men] man
S, we L   77 and . . . god (78)] margin corr. D   and] or H   þey¹] þe
M   78 þei] þan þei J   more . . . ioye] haue more ioye JHV   haue ioye] rev.
Nδ I   of²] om. T   79 erþly] oþer Nδ   þing] þyngis LJV   los] his loss
A   leson] louen C, leeuen K   80 haue] ha D   los¹] any losse
J   oþur] worldly I, erþely H   þis¹] so þis I   82 siþ] and siþ LM   di-
ligence] gret dilygence N   flen] kepen hem fro N   83 goodis] þinges N   84
not] om. K   so . . . leson] to lesee so myche H   to] for to J   85 ben] om.
S   86 hem] him S   of¹]. om. TH   men] for men I   87 and¹] in
CL   and²] om. H   88 wel] ful wel I   89 and¹] ⌐and⌐ H, om. G   owre] or
S   90 feynen] formen N   þese] vs canc. þese D   god] gude C   91

bussynesse schulle be iuges aȝeynus vs. Lord! weþur traueyle we
more abowte goodis of þese twey þingus or abowte goodis of
grace, oure owne traueyle schal iugen vs. What preest bussieþ
hym more now for to sewe Crist in vertewes þan for to geton a
95 benefice, or for to gete worldly goodis? – and þis techeþ þat he
ioyeþ more of worldly goodis þan goodis of grace. Howeuere þat
we stryuen now, owre iuge schal dampne vs at þe laste. And by
þis same skyle hope and sorwe schulle iugen vs, for we casten
more owre bussynesse in hope of a worldly prow þan we doon in
100 hope of heuene or heuenly blisse þat we schulden haue. And þus
we dreden more of los of worldly goodis, þat we hopen þus, þan
we doon of goodis of blisse; and þis reuerseþ al owre lyf.

schulle] shulden H   iuges] oure iugis Kδ, oure iuge NV, iuge Y   traueyle we]
rev. FJH   92 goodis[1]] om. N   93 bussieþ] besiþ C   94 a benefice] benefices
Nδ   96 goodis[2]] ⌜of⌝ goodes δ, of gudis CFKMNαI   97 dampne] demen
NV   98 hope] soro α   sorwe] hope α   99 bussynesse] binesse H   a] om.
CKLTαβH   100 or] or of JHV   101 of[1]] om. α   of[2]] or F   þat] þan
S   we[2]] we canc. T   hopen] hepen Nα   102 goodis of blisse] goddis blis
MSH   þis] om. T   lyf] lyfe turne we þerfore oure loue to god and seche we aftur
heuenly mede þat we may at oure endyng day haue þe blisse þat euer schal laste etc. pater
et aue N

Dominica quinta [post Octavam Epiphanie.
Euangelium.] Sermo 36.

Simile est regnum celorum homini qui seminauit. Mathei 13.

Crist in þis parable telluþ þe stat of his chirche, and seyþ þat þe *kyndam of heuene is lyʒk to a man þat sew good seed in his feld.* Þe kyndam of heuene telluþ boþe togydre, Crist and his meyne, but Crist pryncipally; and herfore Crist is often clepyd þe kyndam of heuene, and þe chirche, þat is his wif, is o persone wiþ hym. And 5 þus þe kyngdam of heuene seyþ þis spowse and þis wif. But here ys þe kyngdam take for Iesu Crist, þat is boþe God and man, and ordeynuþ wel for his chirche. *þis man sew furst good seed in þe feeld* of þis chirche, for he prentide good feiþ in herte of hise seruauntis; and þis seed is Godis woord, as Crist hymself seiþ. Furst þis seed 10 growide clene and browte forþ good fruyt, but þe feend hadde enuye þat þis seed growide þus; *and þis man, þat is enemye* to Crist and his chirche, *caam and sew tarus whan men weren aslepe.* For, by þe dowyng of þe chirche and neclygence of prelatis, is mannys lawe medlud wiþ Godys lawe, and þese dowble mennys lawes, þe 15

MSS: D; ABCFGHIJKLMNSTXYZαβδ.

Dominica . . . euangelium] *om.* CαZ   sermo 36] sermo 3 J, *om.* BCFKLNSTYαδIX-
ZGH   simile . . . seminauit] verbum christi habitet in vobis N   est] factum est
BCKLSαβIZ   celorum . . . seminauit] *om.* M   homini . . . seminauit] *om.*
T   seminauit] seminant L, semin' C, se α, *om.* H   mathei 13] mathei xiii . . . ad
coloc. iii N   1 crist . . . parable] in þis parable crist J   in . . . telluþ] telliþ þis
parable Y, telleþ in þis parable I   þis] his S   his] þe B, þis Z   3
telluþ . . . togydre] is N   boþe togydre] *rev.* J   but] boþe togedur bote
N   4 crist pryncipally] crist *canc.* pryncipally ⌐crist⌐ X, *rev.* ABCFKLMNSTYαβδI-
JZGH   herfore] þerfor αZ   often clepyd] *rev.* H   often] ofte tymes F   cle-
pyd] called αδZ   5 þat is] *om.* N   his] *om.* ABG   o] *om.* K   6 seyþ] is
N   þis[1]] þe G   þis[2]] his ABYIG   7 þe] þis BCKLMNSYαβI   for] of
N   8 ordeynuþ] ordeynede BNZ   9 þis] þe H   prentide] puttide first A,
printide first BG   herte] þe herte FδG, þe hertes NJ, hertes α   10 þis[1]] þus
T   þis[2]] þe KH   12 enuye] grette enuy β   growide] grow, -id *eras.*
B   þat[2]] *om.* T   13 his] to his βI   tarus] tares among N   þe] *om.*
ATZGH   14 dowyng] doynge Sβ, doutyng M   and] and þe I   prelatis]
men of haly kirk Z   15 medlud] now medled N   godys lawe] þe lawe of god
N   dowble] *om.* Z   mennys] mannes AFLMSTYαδIJXZ   lawes] lawe

popis and þe emperowres, letten Godis lawe to growe, and gnare
þe chirche as taris gnaren corn and lettuþ hit to þryue. And þe
fend wente awey and cesude somwhat to tempte men, for he was
syker of þis tare þat hit schulde myche lette þe chirche. And þis is
20 þe cautel of þe feend: to wiþdrawen his malice, and schewe signes
as myraclis whan he haþ sowen euyl seed, as 3if God were wel
payed wiþ sowyng of sych seed; and, as wete somerus norischen
siche taris, so lustful lyf of men þat schulden florischen in vertewis
brynguþ in syche lawes bysyde wordis of byleue. And þis lettuþ
25 trewe men to telle Godis lawe, and lettuþ þe chirche to growe in
feiþ and oþre vertewis. And furst, whan þe chirche growede wiþ
þis tare, 3it hit was hyd longe aftur þe dowyng, but siþ was þis
tare schewyd and Godis lawe hid, for manye wete someris ben
come to þe chirche; and so mannys lawe groweþ and Godus lawe
30 is lettyd, and specially by lawis of þese newe ordres. But whan
malice of þese lawe⌐s⌐ was knowen to trewe men, þanne þei and
aungelis speke to God and preyden hym þat þei myhten gedren
awey þese tares, so þat Godis lawe myhte renne frely as hit furst
f.82v dyde. *But Crist denyeþ þis to hem* for harm þat myhte|come, for
35 good corn myhte be drawen vp byfore þat hit were ripe, as trewe
men in God myhten be sone cullyde 3if þei schewedon to myche
þis cause of clennesse of Godis lawe. But God haþ ordeynet his
seed to growe til hit be rype, as God haþ ordeyned his membris to
helpon a3eyn þe fendys lymes, as long[e] as hit is good þat þe
40 chirche profi3te heere by hem. And þus 3if sowyng of þe feend

NZ   þe . . . emperowres (16)] *om.* Z   16 þe] ⌐þe⌐ H, *om.* α   lawe] lawis
L   gnare] to profit Z   17 gnaren] gnawis Z   corn] þo corne αδ   18
was] is Nδ   19 þis¹] þe K   hit] is S   schulde] s/schulde D   myche] do
myche L   chirche] kyrk to growe α   20 his] þe I, *om.* G   schewe] schewide
G   21 as¹] and C   22 wiþ] wiþ þe H, of CKLMNSTYαβδIXZG   and]
⌐and⌐TH, *om.* S   23 taris] tar⌐s⌐Tδ, tare SβXZ   lyf] ⌐lif⌐MG   florischen]
after this β continues with the second copy of 29/83-30/6, margin against this notes + is forfendid to
þe 3ondur crosse +   24 wordis] werkis H   26 oþre] in oþer β   þe] þis
MI   27 þis tare] þis tar⌐s⌐δ, þes tares α   dowyng] doyng βI   þis²] þe G, *om.*
T   28 hid] is hidde β   29 lawe²] *om.* S   30 and . . . ordres] *om.* Z   by]
þe K, *om.* S   31 malice] malices M   of] *om.* G   þese] *on eras. corr.* D, þe K,
þis Z   lawes] -s *corr.* D, lawe Z   trewe men] *rev.* S, gode men Z   þei and] þe
I   32 hym] *om.* N   33 þese] þe G   þat] *om.* T   renne] reigne
Z   hit] *om.* S   34 denyeþ] denyed CSZ   þis] *om.* H   come] co *canc.*//
come D   35 byfore] byfore er δ   trewe] gode Z   36 god] crist δ   be
sone] *rev.* MY   sone cullyde] *rev.* Sδ   cullyde] dede Z   to . . . of¹ (37)] þe
Z   37 ordeynet] ordeyne Y   38 seed . . . his] *om,* N   hit] þat it I   as]
and F   39 a3eyn . . . good] *om.* Z   longe] longo D   40 profi3te] profyteþ
N   hem] hym β   þus] *om.* I   3if] þis LZ   sowyng] dowyng

tarieþ here Cristis chirche, and makiþ Cristis corn here ful þinne,
and makiþ þicke þe feendis lymes, nerþeles þis good corn groweþ
more medily to þe chirche for þei han moore lettyng. But wel is
hym þat may stoonde!

And herfore byddeþ Crist þat *men schullen suffre boþe þese t[w]o* 45
growe til þe tyme of repyng, and þanne schal he seye to þe reperis 'Gedre ȝe
furst þeᶜsᶦ tarys togydre, and byndeþ hem in knychᶜysᶦ to brenne; but gedre
ȝe þe goode corn to my berne.' Tyme of þis repyng is cleput þe day of
doom or ellis tyme nyh hit, and þese reperis ben goode aungelis,
þat gedren partis of Cristis chirche, and þese goode aungelis 50
schullen bynde Cristis enemyes in knycchenys, and aftyr þei
schulle brennen in helle by þe riȝtful doom of God, and trewe
seruauntis of Crist schullen be gedrede by goode aungelis and
come to heuene as Godis berne. And heere supposen somme men,
siþ hit is nyh doomes day, þat sone heraftyr schal be destruyet 55
boþe mannyś lawe and here makeris; and so, ȝif God wole, boþe
ypocrites and tyrauntis schullen be destruyed, as þe antipope wiþ
his cowrt and þese newe religiouse, and þan schal Godis lawe
reygne wiþ þe trewe partis of his chirche. For, as þis gospel telliþ,
þese taares schul be gedrid furst, but at þe day of doom Cristis 60
lymes schulle furst be counfortid. And so hit semuþ þat Crist
spekiþ here of tyme byfore þe day of dom. And þus he meueþ
manye men for to trete þis mater now; and preyȝe we alle
deuoutly þat God doo here as hym likuþ, and stonde we stif in
Godis lawe, and preyse we hit byfore þis taare.   65

J   feend] fendes N   41 tarieþ] þe *canc.* tarieþ D, tary Cα, tares N   here]
myche here K   makiþ] make CNα   here] ᶜherᶦ α, *om.* IJ   42 makiþ] make
N   þicke] riche L   þis] þe CKN   43 medily] medefulli ABFLMTYXZG-
H   44 hym] hem BFKLMNTYαβδXZG   45 herfore] þerfor αZ   schullen]
schulde N   two] to DSI, two ᶜto ᶦ δ, two to H   46 til] to N   repyng] ripyng,
-i- *canc.* -ᶜeᶫ FL   and] *om.* β   he seye] be said Z   47 furst] *om.* Y   þes]
-s *corr.* Dα, þe I   knychys] -ys *corr.*/chenys *canc.* D, knyttis T   48 ȝe] *om.*
β   to] into NYGH   tyme] þe tyme I   cleput] called αδZ   49 tyme] þe tyme
K   and] *om.* G   reperis] gode reperis I   goode] goddis J   50 partis]
part KI   cristis] goddis Y   52 þe] *om.* H   53 goode] godes N   54 as] as
to LM, þat is J   and . . . chirche (59)] *om.* Z   55 þat] and þat LM   56
lawe] lawes B   57 and] *om.* β   tyrauntis] tryuauntis AY, tyrauntes boþe
δ   þe] *om.* KSG   wiþ] and N   58 religiouse] religiones CFMβ, religiouse
wiþ al hire hire newe founden signes N   59 reygne] rene C   trewe] trewþe
L   his] þe H   þis] þo *canc.* ᶜþisᶦ α, þe TIZ   60 þese] hou þese F, þe N, þis
Z   day of] *om.* I   61 lymes] lyme α   furst be] *rev.* CKSH   62 he
meueþ] ben moeuid T   63 for to] to H   þis] of *canc.* þis D   64 hym] hem
T   likuþ] siketh S   65 þis] þe LNδ   taare] tarᶜsᶦ δ, taris I   66

Manye men musen of þe vndirstondyng of þis gospel and þenkon þat hit ys folye to spekon aȝenus anticrist, siþ trewþe of Godis lawe telluþ þat he schal vencusche cristene men for a tyme; and we may see þis atte yȝe. And þus telluþ þe gospel þat [God] wole þat tare growe tyl þe day of doom among good corn; but who schulde reuerse God and don aȝeynes his wille? Here schulle we suppose comun byleue and comun distinccions þat ben seyde in Latyn. And þanne me þinkuþ þat we schulden preye þat Godis wille be don, as hit is in heuene so here in erþe; and ouer þis we schulden stonde sad in byleue of God and lyuen in vertewys, as Godis lawe byddeþ vs, and assente not to synne of anticrist þat reigneþ now, but haue sorwe þerfore, siþ Crist hadde sorwe for synne and wepte neuere but þryes for synne, as Godis lawe techeþ vs, and resoun acordeþ herwiþ siþ synne is moste euel. And so we schilden more haue sorwe for synne þan ⌐for⌐ any oþer euel. And þus, ȝif we myhten lette synne, we schulden be Godis procuratours, al ȝif we dyen þerfore and profiȝten here no more. But lyue we wel, and God fayluþ not to counselen vs how we schullen do. And þus assente we not to synne, but profiȝte we as God biddiþ vs. And herby may we answere to þe feendis argument: suppose we þat anticrist schal vencusche trewe men for a tyme, but þis is in bodily victorie, and not in vencuschyng of trewþe, for þus he ven|cuscheþ no man but euere is ouercomen

manye . . . yȝe (69)] om. Z   men] om. KJ   of¹] on eras. corr. D   þe] ⌐þe⌐ δ, om. ABCKLMNSTYαβIXG   67 aȝenus] before S   68 telluþ þat] telliþ þat//he telliþ þat C   he] it α   schal] om. Y   69 and¹] as we wel here and N   þis] om. I   yȝe] yȝee D   god wole] wole DABNSTδEJXGH, crist canc. wil α, crist wole FLM   70 þat] þe N   tare] þe tare KH, þis tare J   þe] om. L   good] þe goode N   71 schulde] shul L   don] ⌐so⌐ do A, so do B   schulle we] schulde we, -u- altered to -a-, -de canc. X, schulde we G, we schulen FJH   72 comun¹] þat comune J   byleue . . . distinccions] distincciones in byleue N   and] þat δ   73 þinkuþ] thynk C   schulden] sch canc./schulden D   74 is] om. β   we] om. Y   76 byddeþ] techit CKLMNSTαβδJXZ-G   vs] as S   not] we not K   synne of] ⌐synne⌐ M   of . . . now (77)] om. Z   77 siþ] seþen þat N   crist] crist hymself J   78 wepte] he wepte J, as þe gospel seiþ he wepte N   neuere but] ⌐neuer bot⌐ α, enterly IH, om. N   for] oneli for F   as . . . vs (79)] as god techiþ vs in his lawe J, om. N   as] and I   79 herwiþ] þerwiþ FαIZG   80 more haue] rev. NSTδIJXG   þan] þat S   for²] corr. D, for canc. X, om. LMSαβδZ   82 dyen] dyed αZ   profiȝten] profited αZ   83 and] on eras. corr. D   fayluþ not] wole not fayle F   how] what I   84 schullen] shald, -d canc. α, schulden δ   85 god] he B   and . . . world (91)] om. Z   86 we] om. KN   87 is] om. T   in¹] ⌐in⌐ αH, om. K   not] om. T   88 vencuscheþ] wenchuse C   euere] eueremore H   is]

hymself. And þus trewe men schillen euere haue matere for to
fiȝte goostly boþe wiþ þe feend and his membris þat ben wickede 90
men of þis world. And so wiþ [þis] vndirstondyng fiȝte we wisly
wiþ þis world; but algatis looke ⌐þat⌐ we ben armed wiþ pacience
and charite, and þanne þe fiȝtyng of þe feend may no weye don vs
harm. And ȝif þis skyle schulde meue men to parforme Godis
wille, neuere schulde man fiȝte wiþ synne, for God wole þat 95
synne profiȝte. But what wyten we wher tyme be come þat God
wole þat þis tare be destruyed? And herfore worche we wisly, and
fiȝte we aȝeynes þe feend, siþ þis stondeþ wiþ Godis lawe and wiþ
fullyng of Godis wylle.

he is NT   89 schillen] shald, -d canc. α, shulden H   matere] maistrie G   for
to] to M   90 goostly] -ost- on eras. corr. D   þat] þe wuche N   wickede] queke
Nδ   91 þis¹] þe I   wiþ þis] wiþ DFJH, wiþ ⌐þis⌐ X   fitȝe we] we schulde
fiȝte J   we] om. Y   92 þis] þe C   algatis looke] rev. β   looke] luke we
CK   þat] om. I   we ben] þou be T   93 þe¹] om. K   fiȝtyng] fiȝte
S   94 and . . . wylle (99)] om. Z   skyle] om. α   schulde] schul C   meue]
not moue α   95 neuere] euere, n- eras. F   schulde man] rev. H   schulde]
schul C   man] men Tβ   96 be come] bycome T   be] om. S   god] he
N   97 þat] om. Fδ   herfore] perforne N   we] om. G   98 we] we wiseli
L   99 fullyng] fulfillynge α   godis] his Nδ   wylle] lawe LM, wille and þus
schulen we þorwh grace wynne þe loue of god and mede in heuen etc. pater et aue N

Dominica in Septuagesima. [Euangelium.]
Sermo 37.

Simile est regnum celorum homini patrifamilias. Mathei 20.

This gospel telluþ by a parable how God haþ ordeynot for his chirche fro þe bygynnyng of þe world as long[e] as hit dwelluþ here. *þe kyngdam of heuene*, seiþ Crist, *is liȝk to a good hosbonde þat wente furst erly to hire werk*⌐*men*⌐ *into his vyneȝerd*. Þis hosbonde is
5 God, and þis vyneȝerd is his chirche, and at þe bygynnyng of þis world he huyrede men to worche þerynne; for alle þese men þat comen to heuene worche wel in þis chyrche, and her huyre is a peny þat þei taken for day of here lyf, and þis peny is had of men by godhede and manhede of Crist. *And, aftyr þis acord maad, he sente*
10 *þese werkmen into his chirche. And þis hosbonde wente owht in þe þridde howr of his day, and say oþre stondyng ydel in þe chepyng* to ben huyrede. *And þis fader seyde to hem 'Go ȝe into my vyneȝerd, and þat þing þat is riȝt I schal ȝyue ȝow.'* Þese werkmen ben seyntis þat God hadde ordeynot for to trauelen in his chirche aftyr þe furste age; and þei
15 stoden ydel in þe weye to heueneward byfor þat God hadde meuyd hem to trauele in his chirche. God byhiȝte þat he schulde ȝyuen hem þat were riȝtful hem to haue, and þat is þe blisse of heuene þat falliþ to þis large lord; but, for hit is vncerteyn to hem

MSS: D; ABCFGHIJKLMNSTXYZαβ, δ *ends* 40 ne we sch-.

Dominica . . . euangelium] *om.* αZ   sermo 37] *om.* BCFKNSTYαδXZGH   simile . . . -familias] castigo corpus meum N   patrifamilias] patrifamilias qui J,
om. H   mathei 20] mathei xxvi F, mathei xii G, mathei xx . . . prima ad cor. ix
N   1 this . . . here (3)] *om.* N   by] *om.* α   2 longe] longo D   dwelluþ]
duellyd Sδ   3 seiþ crist] *rev.* I   is] as δ   to] vnto C   4 furst] forþ
H   erly] *om.* B   hire] -re *on eras. corr.* D   werkmen] -men *corr.* D   5
þis¹] his MG   *margin* isa. 5 prouer. 23 N   is] *om.* N   þis²] þe AI   6 he]
om. β   men¹] werkmen G   7 comen] camen F   worche] worschepe wel and
werchen S   in] and C   8 day] þe day KαJ, daies N, a day H   *margin* gen. 3
N   9 aftyr þis] *om.* F   maad] man S   10 þese] his CK, þe J   wente]
ȝede K   11 his] þis Fαδl, þe CKS   stondyng] stonden Sδ   þe] -s *eras.*
D   12 þing] *om.* NY   is] war CKLMSTYαβZ   riȝt] ryhtful
α   13 ȝow] to ȝou BN   hadde] haþ CKNSYI   15 stoden] stondyn, -n-*canc.* C,
stoonden S   byfor þat] tyl δ   þat] *om.* T   god] he J   16 god] and god
AG   byhiȝte] byhiȝte hem, hem *canc.* β, bihiȝte hem I   17 ȝyuen] ȝe S   18

wher þei schullen parforme þis traueyle, herfore he byhoteþ to
hem to ȝyuen hem þat were riȝtful. *And þei wenton forþ and wrowten*   20
wel werk of þis vyneȝerd. *And þus he dide in þe sixþe howr, and in þe*
nynþe howr also, for God huyrede laboreris aftir þat his chirche
hadde nede; and so he bood furst on howr, and siþ two, to huyre
seruauntis. *He wente forþ abowte þe elleueþþe howr, and foond oþre men*
*stondynge, and seyde to hem 'Why stonde ȝe here al day ydel fro traueyle*of*   25
þis vyneȝerd?' And þei seyden to hym for no man hadde huyred hem. And he
seyde vnto hem '[And] goo ȝee [in]to my vyneȝerd.' He made noon oþur
couenaunt wiþ hem, for two byfore weren ynowe. Þese fyue
howres bytooknen boþe þe elde of þe chirche fro þe bygynnyng
til þat Crist caam, and trewe men þat traueylede þerynne. For hit   30
is seyd comunly þat þe world haþ sixe eldis: þe furste was from
Adam to Noe, þe toþur fro Noe to Abraham, þe þridde fro
Abraham to Dauid, þe ferþe from tyme of Dauid to passyng into
Babiloyne, and þe fiþe fro þat tyme til þe natyuite of Crist; þe
sixþe age is vndurstonden fro þennys tyl þe day of doom. Þanne   35
schal þe liȝt of Crist goo down fro dwellyng in þis world, and
schynen in þe toþur world by mene of þe day of doom. And for
notablete of Crist he telluþ not huyryng for þis hour. And, for þis
tyme is to come and Godis|lawe is ful herof, he telluþ not of þis   f.83v
sixte huyryng but vndirstondiþ hit in oþre. Ne we schulde not   40
knowe now þe quantite of þis age þat lasteþ fro Cristis ascencion
vnto þe day of iugement.
Þe traueyle in þis vyneȝerd stondeþ in þese þre þingus: furst dig

þis] þe M   but] *om.* AM   19 herfore] þerfore LδZ   byhoteþ] bihiȝte
I   to hem] ⌐to⌐ hem α, hem BCK   21 werk] þe werke δ   *margin* ecclesiastes
12 N   sixþe] sixe B   22 for] *om.* H   his] þe H   23 bood] abode
CFKβIJH   and . . . two] and sithe two and sithe, sithe two *canc.* S   24 abowte]
om. δ   men] *om.* KM   25 seyde] he saide Z   traueyle] þe trauel F   26
þis] þe F   and . . . hem (27)] *om.* F   27 vnto] to N   and goo] goo
DFTIJH, ⌐and⌐ go α   into] to DCJX, ⌐in⌐ to αH   28 two] two oþere δ   29
elde] -lde *on eras. corr.* D, eldes α, olde J   30 þat¹] *om.* KN   traueylede] traueile
BCKNαJG   31 is seyd] seid F   eldis] h- *canc.* D, ageis J   was] elde *canc.* was
α, age was J, *om.* N   32 adam to] ⌐adam vnto⌐ M   to¹] vnto Nδ   þe toþur]
and þe secounde J   33 þe] and þe N   from] fro þe BFαIJG   to ²] to þe Bδ,
vnto FH   34 and] *om.* CKNδ   þe¹ . . . crist] cristus natiuite N   35 sixþe]
sixe B   tyl] vnto I   37 schynen] schynynge T   in . . . doom] bi mene of þe
day of dome in þe toþer world H   and . . . iugement (42)] *om.* N   38 huyryng . . . not (39)] *om.* I   huyryng] þe hiryng K   for¹] of αZ   39 is to] isto
canc. is to D   lawe] la// Y   ne] no L   þis] þe SδH   40 sixte] -te *on eras. corr.* D, six
C   ne we] *rev.* J   ne] no L   41 now] ⌐now⌐ TG   ascencion] tyme of hys
ascencioun T   42 þe] *om.* A   iugement] dom *canc.* iugement MG, dom iugement
L, dome T   43 in¹] of G   þese] *om.* K   furst] ⌐þe⌐ firste N   dig]

abowte þe vyne rootis and dong hem wel and hule hem þanne; þe
45 secounde traueyle in þis vyneȝerd is to kitte wisly þe braunchis;
and þe þridde traueyle herof where to arayle þese growynde
vynes. Som of þis perteneþ to God, and som is doon by mannus
traueyle. God hymself makiþ þese vynes and plaunteþ hem in his
ȝerd, for God makiþ trewe men, and ȝueþ hem wyt to brynge
50 good fruyt. And prechowres ben helperis of God and deluen
abowte byleue, but God ȝueþ þe growyng, al ȝif men planten
and watren, for þus dide Ieremye in þe oolde testament, and þus
also dide Powle in þe tyme of grace. And so þese laborerus han
nede to delue abowte þese rootis, leste euyl herbis growen þere
55 and bastard braunchis wiþowten byleue. Þei ben dongude wiþ
fyue wordis þat seynte Powle wolde teche þe peple, þe whiche
somme men vndirstonden heuene and helle and weyȝes to hem,
but þe furste word and þe fiþe is þe hooly Trinnyte. Whan þese
fyue sentences ben preched and declared on good maner, þanne
60 þese vynes ben dongude and wel hulyde wiþ eurþe. But wyse men
kytte þese braunches whanne þei wiþdrawe cursede men, þat ben
superflew in þe chirche, and letten hit brynge forþ wyn. And to
þis helpen myȝty men þat drawen fro clerkis worldly goodis, þat
þei han aȝeynes Godis lawe and doon harm to his chirche. But þei
65 þat martyren Godis seruauntis, be þei knytes, be þei preestis, þei
ben foxes þat ben abowte for to destruye þis vyneȝerd. Þe rayling
falleþ to prelatis and oþre vykerus of God, þat maken þe states of

---

66 S. of S. 2: 15.

---

dyggyng N   44 vyne rootis] rote of þe vyne I   dong] dugge S, þanne donge
I   and² . . . þanne] om. I   hem²] hym F   45 in] on G   is]
it C   to] for to FH   kitte] knytte β   46 and] om. Tβ   herof] þerof
Z   where] weren N   growynde] ground Nβ   47 perteneþ] perteyne
J   48 makiþ] make C   vynes] vertues Z   plaunteþ] plante C   49 wyt]
wyttes α   brynge] brynge forþ FαJ, ȝyue B, bere N   50 prechowres] trewe
prechours N   51 abowte] faste abouten N   byleue] ⌐bi⌐ bileue A, bi bileue
Bα   but . . . watren (52)] om. N   al ȝif] and eras. al ȝif D   52 watren]
water hem, hem canc. C, watren hem F   for] and α   ieremye] semye
C   53 dide poule] rev. J   þe] om. YH   so] ⌐so⌐ C, om. I   54 delue]
trauaile and deluen N   þese] þe CN   herbis] herkis L, wedes N   growen]
springen vp N   55 ben] are wele α   56 teche] telle J   þe²] om. YI   57
weyȝes] þe weies K   58 fiþe] firste N   is] is canc. is D   59 sentences] sentence
Cα   ben] are wele α   on] in N, vnto α   61 kytte] kynten β   wiþdrawe]
drawen Y   cursede] cusid L   62 superflew] superfiul Y   64 his] þe
K   65 þat] ⌐þat⌐ T, om. J   be²] or be S   66 þat ben] om. I   for to] for
canc. to X, to ABCFKLMNSTYαβIZG   rayling] ⌐a⌐raylyng X, arailyng BCKLMN-
STYβZG   67 oþre] to oþer N   þe] om. FG   states] state LMT   68 þe]

men to stonden in þe bowndys þat God haþ ordeynyd; and ȝif
wyndis or oþre wedris putten down þese statis to þe eurþe, by
vertew and strenkþe of prelatis schulden þese statis ben holden 70
vppe. And so eche cristene man schulde helpe to þis vyneȝerd, for
growyng of cool wortis and oþre weedis maken malecoly and
oþre synnes, and glade men not to wende to heuene, but maken
hem heuye to falle to helle.

And, whan euenyng was come, þe lord of þis vyneȝerd seyde to his 75
⌈*procutour*⌉ *and bad hym clepe þese werkmen, and ȝyuen hem here huyre ,*
bygynnyng at þe laste werkmen vnto þe furste laboreris. Þe lord of þis
vyneȝerd is þe godhede of Crist and þe procutour herof may be
clepud his manhede. Þis euenyng is þe day of doom, þat somtyme
is clepud mydnyȝt and somtyme cler day to dyuerse men 80
þerynne, as þe same tyme is clepud here day and here nyȝt, here
fayr tyme and hoot, and here fowl wedir and coold. Clepyng of
þese werkmen is clepyng to Godis doom, þat is þe laste trompe
þat seynt Powle spekiþ of. Crist schal bygynnen at men of þis laste
tyme, for men of þe laste age schal be more blessyd and be furst in 85
worþinesse þan men of oþre ages, siþ þe manhede of Crist is in þe
sixte age, and his modyr wiþ apostles schal passen oþre in blisse;
and so in oþre ages þe latere hadden more grace, siþ Crist is þe
emperour þat wendiþ euere alargyng. Þe seuenþe age is clepud of
men þat slepon in purgatorie, and þe eiȝtþe age of blessid men in 90
heuene, and in þese eiȝte ages enduþ al þis world.

---

84 1 Cor. 15: 52.

---

om. H   69 or] and *canc.* or α, and TG   oþre] *om.* N   þese] þe K   70
schulden] þat scholden I   þese . . . holden] holde þes statis I   71 man] men
B   72 of] *om.* K   cool wortis] il herbis Z   wortis] wordis Y, and wortis
J   oþre] *om.* Z   73 synnes] signes Y   wende] go S   74 hem] ⌈hem⌉ C,
men FαG, men hem, hem *canc.* J, *om.* Y   falle] wende N   75 þis] þe G   76
procutour] porter *canc.* procutour D, prouctours L, procatouse N   hym] hem
AL   clepe] calle αZ   77 bygynnyng] and *eras.* bigynnynge G, and· bygynne
H   þe¹] þis C   werkmen] werkman, -a- *canc.* -e- F, werkman I   þe²] ⌈þe⌉
H, *om.* S   þis] þe Z   78 þe¹] *om.* M   þe²] *om.* KH   herof] þerof
Z   79 clepud] cald NαZ   his] þe M   þis] þe Z   80 clepud] cald
NαZ   81 clepud] cald NαZ   here¹] heie C   here³] and here J   82
tyme] *om.* F   and²] *om.* S   clepyng¹] callyng NαZ   83 clepyng] callyng
NαZ   84 seynt] -t *corr.* D   men] þese laste *canc.* men D   85 þe] þis
ACFK   and be furst] more N   and] in C   furst] þe firste K   in] in þe
B   86 of¹] of þe β   þe¹] *om.* CKZ   87 sixte] sixe B   wiþ] wiþ þe
BNSαI, wiþ hise CLM   oþre] *om.* Y   88 þe¹] of N   89 emperour] same
emperour I   euere] eueremore H   alargyng] largynge α   clepud] cald
NαZ   of] *om.* Y   90 eiȝtþe] eiȝte IH   age] *om.* H   of] is of CK, is
Y   blessid] bessed S   in²] so in F, *om.* Z   91 eiȝt] eiȝtþe S   þis] þe

And so alle þe laboreris took ychone his peny. But men of þe furste howr
demeden þat þei schulden ha⌐ue⌐ moore þan men of þe elleuenþe hour,
f.84   *for þei traueyleden furst and lengore.* |*And þus þei grucchiden*
95   *aȝeynes þe hosbonde, and seyden to hym 'Þese comen in þe laste howr, and*
þow madest hem euene to vs þat baren þe charge and þe hete of þe day of
traueyle.' But he answerede to oon of hem, and seyde þus to hym 'Freend, I
do þe no wrong; for of a peny þow acordedist wiþ me. Tak þat is þin, and go
ful apayed. For I wole ȝyue þis laste as myche as I wole ȝyue þe. Wher hit
100   *is not lewful to me to do myn owne þing as I wole? Wher þin eyȝe be*
wykkyde for þat I am good?' þus schal þe laste be furste, and þe furste be
laste. For manye ben clepyde, but fewe of hem ben chosone. Þis grucchyng
of þe seyntis is noo stryuyng of hem but wondryng of sowle, as
seyn Gregory seiþ. And so þis demyng and grucchyng þat þis
105   gospel spekiþ of is wondryng in sowle, and þankyng of Godis
grace þat he ȝaf so myche ioye to men for so luytel traueyle, for
more ioyȝe þei myhte not haue but fully as myche as þei wolden.
And so schullen alle wyte wel þat God doþ no wrong to hem; but
þat he hiȝte hem graciously, he haþ ful ȝyuen hem. Ne non of
110   hem schulde grucchen aȝeynes go⌐o⌐ldnesse of þis iuste Fadir, for
he may ȝyuen of his owne more þan any man may disserue by
mannys riȝtwisnesse, or euenehed of any chaffare. And so God

N   92 þe¹] þe⌐s⌐, ⌐s⌐ eras. D, þes ABFLMNSYαIJXZG   ychone] eche
F   his] þis H   þe²] þis β   furste] laste F   93 þat] what T   haue]
-ue corr. D   94 lengore] largere L   95 to] þus to H   96 madest] has made
Z   þe²] om. H   of²] and of þe I, om. β   97 to oon of] om. S   98 wrong]
þing N   of] ⌐of⌐ α, om. N   acordedist] cordidist SY, cordist ABCTβIJ, acordist
FLMαH   wiþ] om. S   is þin] rev. N   and . . . apayed (99)] ful apayed and
go H   99 apayed] pai̇̇ed ANYαI   I² . . . ȝyue] to N   ȝyue²] ȝyue to H, to
Y, om. KM   100 is] om. I   not] om. M   to do] to do wiþ BF, do wiþ
A   þing] þingis J   eyȝe be] eye is FK, eien ben A   101 þat] om.
T   þus] and þus B   þe¹] be þe B   be¹] be þe FTIG, be þe, þe canc. Y, þe
B   þe²] om. T   be²] þe Bβ, om. K   102 laste] þe canc. last G, þe
laste T   for . . . chosone] om. K   manye] many men MSI   ben¹] om.
S   clepyde] called αZ   but] and CLMSTαβI   of hem] om. H   ben²]
om. Cβ   chosone] chosen of hem H   103 þe] þes ABCFKLMNSTYαβIJXZG-
H   noo] not ABCFKLMNSTYαβIJXZGH   of³] in ABCKLMNSTYαβIXZ-
G   sowle] soulis H   104 grucchyng] þis grucchyng BNY   þis²] þe
G   106 he] ȝe I   107 þei myhte] rev. SYαJH   as¹] so CK   108
schullen] schuld C   hem] men H   109 þat] þat þat BZ   hiȝte] bihiȝte B,
lighten C   ful] ful⌐li⌐ X, fully ABCFKLMNSTYαβIJZGH   ne] and C-
K   110 goodnesse] o corr. D, þe goodnesse FJH   iuste fadir] fadir iust marked for
rev. H, fadir iuste S   112 mannys riȝtwisnesse] þe riȝtwisnesse of mon N   or] and
F   euenehed] -ehed on eras. corr. D, ony nede CK, ene neede β   any] manus

seiþ to eche seynt þat he schulde taken his meede by grace, and
gon into þe blysse of heuene, where seyntes schullen euere
dwellen in pees.   115

CFKLMNSTYαβXZ, ony//nes, nes *canc.* G   113 eche] euery I   114 gon] so go
A   þe] *om.* Mαβ   115 in] in/ in D   pees] pees iesus graunte vs alle grace to
wynne þis peny and haue þis pees and þat it so be prai we alle per charite etc N

Dominica in Sexagesima. [Euangelium.]
Sermo 3[8].

Cum turba plurima conuenirent. Luce 8.

This gospel telluþ in a parable how þat holy chirche growyde by gracious sowyng of Crist and growyng of þis hooly seed; and in tyme of Sexagesyme men sowen bodyly seed. Þe story of þe gospel telluþ *whan myche puple was come to Crist, and þei hasteden of citees* to
5 heeren of hym Godis word, *he seyde by a similitude. He wente owht þat soweþ ay to sowen his seed in his lond.* But on fowre maneris fel þis seed vpon his lond: *som fel bysyde þe weyȝe,* ⌜*and was defoulid*⌝, *and fowlis of heuene eton hit; and som fel on a stoon, and whan hit was sprongon hit druyede vp for hit hadde noo moysture; som fel among þornes, and þornes*
10 *growyng strangledon hit; and som fel into good erþe, and þat sprong vp and maade an hundurtfoold fruyȝt. And Crist, sey*⌜*i*⌝*ng þese wordis, cryȝede and seyde to þe puple 'He þat haþ heres to heren, heere he* and vndirstonde þis wyt.' And euermoore, as seyntis seyn, whan God biddeþ men here þus, his sentence is precious and schulde be
15 markid wel of men.

And hise disciples axedon hym what mente þis parable. And Crist seyde vnto hem þat to hem was grawntid to knowe þe pryuyte of þe rewme of God, and to oþre men in parablis, þat þei seyng wiþowteforþ see not wiþynne in

MSS: D; ABCFGHIJKLMNSTXYZαβ; E *inc.* 57 is vndisposid; δ *inc.* 83 of hys.

Dominica . . . euangelium] *om.* αZ   sermo 38] *om.* BCFKLNSTYαIXZG-H   cum . . . conuenirent] libenter gloriabor in infirmitatibus meis N   plu-rima] multa *upper margin, text* plurima M, multa αI   conuenirent] conuenirent ad iesum F, conueniret Y, *om.* AβH   luce 8] luce 8 . . . ii ad cor. 11 N   1 telluþ] seyth S   in] *om.* CKJ   2 sowyng] sownynge Y, *om.* K   þis] his B   3 tyme] þe tyme SH   sexagesyme] sixe ages N   sowen] vsen to sowe N   seed] seedys S   þe²] þis NYJ   4 telluþ] *om.* α   myche] þer was myche H   was] *om.* H   and] *om.* BG   of] oute of Z   6 ay] ⌜ay⌝ α, *om.* LNI   in] on N   maneris] maner JG   þis] his A   7 his] þis G   and¹ . . . defoulid] *margin corr.* D, *erased* X, *om.* CKLMNSTYαβIZG   8 and¹] ⌜and⌝ αH, *om.* F, and was defoulid and I   on] vpon N   9 þornes¹] þe þornes NS   and þornes] ⌜and þornys⌝ H, *om.* S   10 into] in BH   erþe] lond N   þat] *om.* N   sprong] grew CK   11-foold] fool Y   seying] i *corr.* D, se⌜i⌝ynge H   12 haþ] *om.* F   13 vndirstonde] vndirstode X   14 his] is Z   15 markid] noted N   16 hym] him, -i- altered from -e- Fα   what] what þat N   17 vnto] þis parable *canc.* vnto D   hem¹] him F   18 and] and *canc.*

þer sowle, *and þei, heeryng þe* wordis of parable, *vndirstonde not þe*
wyt of hem. Crist seyde *þat þis is* vndyrstondyng of *þis parable: þe*   20
seed is Godis word þat fel to men on fowre maneris. Þis furste seed is
Godis word *þat fel in somme bysyde þe wey3e,* for somme ben
combred wiþ þe feend, and so d[e]fowled wiþ þe world þat þer
eurþe is not able to take þis seed and hulon hit. *And herfore comeþ þe*
feend and takiþ Godis *word fro þer hertis,* for he putteþ in her þowt   25
straunge þing fro þis sed, and so he takiþ fro þer wyt þe vertew of
Godis seed. And herfore hit is perilows to dwelle þus bysyde þe
wey3e, and be defowlyd wiþ þe feend and wiþ sentence þat he
wole teche. Þe feend takiþ fro men Godis word þat þei trowe not
in hit; and, for by sych trowþe men may sonnest be saf, þe feend   30   f.84ᵛ
purposeþ to taken awey Godis word *leste þat men trowen hit and so be*
saaf. Þe fendis mow dwellen in comune weye, where God wole
not sowen his seed, and pyke awey þe seed bysyde and aspyen
vnsowe places, and gedre þe seed þat is sowen; hee haþ no power
of þis seed, but power of þe man by synne. And þus men owte of   35
byleue, þat ben hardid in þer vntrewþe, maken a comun wey3e and
pleyn where feendis and beestis may freely goo; and on londis by
þis wey3e ben manye voyde places, for manye semen in byleue
but feiþ is voydet from hem. *Þe secounde* place of þis lond þat Godis
seed is sowen ynne *is stoony lond* wiþ broode stonys, vpon whiche   40
þe seed falluþ, and stonys ben harde and eurþe luytel. *And for a*
tyme þei take wiþ ioye þe wordis of God þat ben sowen, *but hem wanten*

and D   men] *om.* Y   see] seyen S   in²] *om.* N   19 þe¹] þo Nα   pa-
rable] þe parable ATY, þis parable I, parables, -s *canc.* α   vndirstonde] vndurstode
TIGH   20 wyt] wittis Z   hem] hym J   seyde] *om.* M   vndyr-
stondyng] þe vndirstondyng FαZH   þis²] þe H   21 þat] to N   on] of L, in
S   þis] þe KSα   22 in] *om.* CT   somme¹] sum maner H   somme²] sum
men KI   23 and . . . feend (25)] *om.* I   defowled] dofowled D, defouling
LM   þer] þe A   24 þis] þe S   herfore] þerfore Z   25 þowt] þou3tis
H   26 straunge] stronge Sα   þing] thinges αI   27 seed] word N
herfore] þerfore Z   þus] *om.* K   28 wiþ²] wiþ þe I   29 wole] wolde
N   feend] *om.* α   þei] *om.* T   not] no L   30 and] and//and D   by]
om. L   sych] *om.* Z   sonnest] sunnere B   31 purposeþ] supposeþ I   tro-
wen] trowden CK   hit] ⌐in⌐ it Z   32 þe fendis] þerby þerfore N   god] good
β   33 pyke] pile F   þe] his I   bysyde] *om.* α   34 places] place
ABLMNSTYβIXZG   gedre] gaderiþ FJH   sowen] fowen C, isowe to lette þat
hit springe not N   35 þis] his C   36 byleue] þe bileue β   ben] men
S   hardid] hardenyd Z   in] by CK   þer] *om.* I   maken] and maken
H   37 by] biside A   38 manye²] many men I   semen] synnes Z   39
feiþ . . . hem] fewe ben founden þerinne N   voydet] voyde CFKL   40 whiche]
þo whilk αH   41 þe] þis ABCFKLMNSTYαβIJXZGH   falluþ] failiþ
C   eurþe luytel] *rev.* J   42 þe] *om.* I   hem wanten rootis] rotes hem wonteþ

rootis of charite, and so þei turnen to þe world for couetyse of
worldly goodis. And þis seed wantiþ rootus of loue to stonden in
45 Godis lawe, for þei loue moore worldly goodis þan þe fruyt of
byleue; for þis seed of Godis word mut be rotyd in charite, so þat
neiþur pouert, ne peyne, ne manas maad of anticrist make men
falle fro Godis lawe for stabulnesse in þe roote. *The þridde lond* þat
takiþ þis seed *is ful of þornes* and euele wedys, and þese growen vp
50 wiþ þe corn and destruye good sed; for siche ben ȝyuen to worldly
lustys, and lustful þing lykuþ hem, as þingus þat pleson þe body,
as mete and drynk, ydelnesse and lecherye wiþ worldly godis þat
susteyne bodyly lustes. And þus hit faruþ, as Gregory seiþ, al ȝif
richessis lyȝken þe flesch, nerþelees þei ryuon þe sowle, and
55 maken hit bussy abowte veyne þingus; and þus þei pryckon and
wownden þe sowle as þornys doon harm to þe flesch. And þus þis
lond is vndisposid by þre enemyes of a man, ⌈þe⌉ whiche ben þe
feend, þe world and þe flesch wantohwne of a man; of þese spekon
Iohn and Iames and Crist here in his wordis, for þese þre letton
60 Godis word to bryng[e] forþ fruyt in mannys sowle. And þerfore,
ȝif þow coueyte in God þat his seed profiȝte to þe, chastise wel
þese þre enemyes þat letten Godis seed to growe, and þanne þow
hast good lond and wel disposed to take þis seed. And hit bmgnuþ
in syche sowles fruyt to an hundertfoold, siþ goodis of blisse þat
65 ben in heuene passen alle owre goodis here, as an hundert doon
oon; and þese in substaunce ben þis seed. And þis lore is

---

59 1 John 2: 16–17; Jas. 4: 4.

N   43 turnen] tornid I   44 seed] sect N   to] for to α   45 worldly]
erþely ABCKLMNSTYαβIXZG   þe] þei do α   46 þis] þe CK   47 pouert]
peyne Y   peyne] pouert Y, penye L   ne² . . . anticrist] *om.* Z   make] may
make T, makis Z   48 falle] to falle IH, false M   49 þis] þe S   50 destruye]
destrieþ T   good] goᵣoᵔ dis C, þe goode N   sed] corn and destrieþ gode sede
T   for] and for I   worldly] þe worldly N   51 lustful] lusty G   52
ydelnesse] ⌈and⌉ idilnesse G, and ydelnesse ABCFKLMNSTYαβIJXZ   53 susteyne]
lusteynyn S   and] as α   54 richessis] rychesse ACαZ   ryuon] prikken
N   55 pryckon] picken T   56 þe²] *om.* C   57 þe¹] *corr.* D, þe *canc.* X, *om.*
BCKLMNYαβEIZG   whiche ben] *om.* N   ben] is S   58 þe¹] and þe F, and
þe false N   þe² . . . man] monnes oune wantoune flech N   a] *om.* CKαE-
Z   of²] and of H   þese] þis CKI   59 and¹] *om.* B   his] her AB   60
word] wordes α   brynge] bryngo D   61 in] of BCKβZ   his] þis I, *om.*
S   profiȝte] is good profite S, profitiþ J   to] in BNα   62 to] for to S   63
þis] þese S   hit] *om.* M   64 in] into H, *om.* E   fruyt] fruyt in pacience
E   65 owre] oþer BLH   here] þat are here α, here in erþe J   66 oon] on ane
Z, *om.* β   þis¹] þe E   seed] seedis T   67 holy . . . hit] to make holy chirche

profi3table to holy chirche, and makeþ hit to growe, and reyseþ hit fro þe eurþe to þe hy3nesse of heuene.

Þis seed haþ monye propretes þat fallen to bodily seed: for hit is luytel in quantite, and þe vertew of hit is hyd, but Godis grace 70 mut qwykon hit as li3t of heuene qwykeþ oþur seed; and dew of grace, þat comeþ of God wiþ þe hete of charite, norschen þis goostly seed and maken hit growen vp to heuene. But, as þe gospel of Iohn seyþ, þe corn of whete falluþ into eurþe, and siþ hit dyeþ, and þanne hit groweþ manye foold to myche corn. Þis 75 whete corn is Cristes body þat bycam man here in eurþe, þat furst was deed, and siþ roos, and browte of hym manye partis. And þus growyde hooly chirche from oon to hire fulle nowmbre. But bestis and lymes of þe feend ben myche to blame for þis fruyt, for þey letten hit to growe manye wey3es by feendys cautelys; and 80 somme, byfore þat hit be rype, þei kutten and letten fruyt to come. And herfore haywardis schulden be war, and do þer offis in þe chirche, for ellys|þei ben traytowres to God in false kepyng of f.85 his feeld. And vertewys of a sowle and specially mannys pacience ben as marle or dong[e] to men, and maken hem bryngon forþ 85 such fruyt.

Abowte þis tyxt may men dowte how þis seed may waxe druye or faylen in any wyse, siþ hit is Cristis word, and Crist seiþ þat heuene and eurþe schul passe and fayle but not his word. But here we wyten how trewþe of God may not faylen in his substaunce, 90

---

74 John 12: 24; **88** Matt. 24: 35; Mark 13: 31; Luke 21: 33.

N   to²] om. AKT   reyseþ] riseþ J   68 hit] om. Y   hy3nesse] lithnesse
S   69 þat . . . seed²] þat to bodily seed fallen N   seed²] sedys S   70 þe] om.
H   of hit] þerof Y   71 mut] mych S   qwykeþ] quykeneþ AKLMSTY-
αβEIZGH, quikene C, quykenyd B, doþ N   oþur] oure G   73 growen] to grow
CKN   vp to] to K, vnto T   74 iohn] seynt iohun N   seyþ] telliþ
Y   falluþ] it falliþ J   eurþe] þe erth CKNSTαEIH   hit] ⌈it⌉ C, om.
N   75 groweþ] groweþ vp N   76 here in eurþe] in erþe here I   77
and . . . nowmbre (78)] om. N   78 to] til αZ, vnto J   but . . . fruyt (86)] om.
Z   but bestis] om. I   79 myche] myche more F   80 hit] om. Y   cau-
telys] sley3te N   81 be] is be F   kutten] kutten it K   letten] om.
S   fruyt] þe fruyt IH   82 come] come forþe EJ   herfore] þerfore SH, herof
α   84 and¹] pite pacience and oþer N   of . . . pacience] wuche þat fallen to
monne soule N   a] a canc. δ, þe B   85 or] as M   donge] dongo D, dunk
LM   hem] om. Y   bryngon] to bryng β   86 such] þis CKLMNSTYαβδE-
XG, myche F   87 may men] rev. J   may] many FYH   druye] and dry
C   88 faylen] false I   in] on L   89 and eurþe] om. CK   fayle] fayle and

siþ þat hit is kynde of God, þat nedely is ʒif owht be. But þe fruyt
þat hit schulde make may faylen in men by synne of hem.
And þus þis seed haþ monye names, and by manye resownys is
knowen; and by dyuersite of resownes may men asoylen þᵣeˡs
95 dowtys. But moreouer men dowten here, siþ God is sowere of þis
seed, and he is ful of wyt and myʒt, why soweþ hee hit in euel
lond. But here we schullen vndirstonden þat noo defawte may be
in God, but, as he ʒyeuþ reynes and wederus to goode men and to
ylle, so he offeruþ his seed boþe to lond good and euyl. And, al ʒif
100 fruyt þat hiᵣtˡ schulde haue perische ofte for mannys synne,
nerþeles substaunce of þis seed may not fayle, siþ hit is God. And
þus meueþ Anselm þat þer is no trewþe but oon, for eche trewþe
in hise grownd is þe furste trewþe of alle. And leue we to ʒonge
men scole-tretyng of þis matere. But ʒeet men dowten what
105 meueþ God to wiþdrawen his grace froo men, and to lette þis seed
for to growe, as he scheweþ hit in parablis. But here seiþ Powle
þat no man schulde blame God for his good dede, siþ he doþ by
his grace alle þingus þat he doþ, and wiþdraweþ neuere his grace,
but ʒif man vnable hymself; and þanne ᵣbyˡ riʒtwysnesse of God
110 nediþ þis synnere to be punyschid. But somme men seyn þat alle
þingus mote nede come by God; and so, what harmes comen in

---

106 Rom. 9: 18–23.

erthe also CK   not] so schal not N   91 þat¹] om. KTG   hit] om. S   92
by] for α   hem] men K   93 þis] om. CK   monye] na canc./mes and bi many
H   is] it is K   94 dyuersite] dyuersitees, -s canc. Y, diuersitees β   may men]
rev. TJ, a man may S   þes] þe S   95 men] þes men A   þis seed] þese seedys
ST   96 he] om. T   ful] om. G   hit] om. δ   97 schullen] shulden
H   98 reynes] reyn ABCKLMSTYαβδEIJXZG   and wederus] om. I   we-
derus] wedur boþe N   to²] om. KYI   99 ylle] yuel ABCFKLMNSTYαβδEIJX-
GH   offeruþ] offrid AL   boþe] om. E   lond good] loond good marked for rev.
F, good lond NEJH   good] g canc./good D   euyl] to yuel NEJ   100 fruyt]
þe fruyt I   hit] -i- on eras. -it corr. D   perische] perischid BC, perischiþ
LMTYβXG   mannys] menes C   101 substaunce] þe substaunse J   þis] þe
S   102 meueþ] meneþ EG   but . . . trewþe²] om. S   trewþe²] om.
M   103 and . . . matere (104)] om. Z   we] ʒe I   104 scole] ᵣofˡ corr. scole
D, of scole YJH, in scole CNTαδ   ʒeet] ʒif L   105 and] om. α   to²] om.
βI   þis] his N, is β   106 for to] to KNH   scheweþ hit] rev. KI   hit] om.
YE   in] in his E, om. S   here . . . powle] here seynt poule seiþ J, ᵣsiþˡ poule seiþ
F   107 siþ] and siþ G   108 alle . . . grace²] om. S   109 man] a man
H   by] corr. D, by canc. X, om. CKLMNSTYαβEJZG   riʒtwysnesse] ryʒt-
fulnesse δ   110 þis] þe S   synnere] synne CE, sonnere I   but . . . so (121)] om.
N   men] om. B   111 mote] mosten E   nede] om. K   comen] þat canc.
comen F, þat comyn CKZH   in] to δE, into H   112 vnto] to E   ow-

þis world profiȝten vnto þis world, owþur to make good þing
betture, or to make good þing onewe, or ellis to preyse God, and
to ioye for peyne þat is to men in helle. And so Crist telluþ in
parables his wyt for manye causis: furst for men vnworþie to 115
knowen hit ben blynde by derk speche, moreouer for men, þat
medfully traueylen for to knowe þis parable wyt, boþe schullen
traueylen more medfully, and bettur prente þer wyt þusgate.
And also in syche parables as myche philosophie is knowen as is
nedful for a man for to konnen in þis weye, and so, ȝif God 120
ordeyne þus, hit is beste þat hit be so.

þur] or M, *om*. E   to] for to E   þing] þinges IJ   113 or¹] oþer ABTYβδX-
G   þing] þingis J, *om*. A   onewe] continue α   ellis] *om*. T   to²] for to
K   114 for] ⌐or⌐ for T   men] comen H   so] ⌐so⌐ H, *om*. β   crist] *om*.
K   116 blynde] blynd ⌐did⌐ CH, blyndid ABFKLMSTαβEIJXZG   moreouer]
and moreouere J   117 þis . . . wyt] þe witt of þis parable J   þis] þese B   pa-
rable] parablis BH   wyt] by wyt I   schullen] *om*. I, sal þei Z   118 traueylen]
om. K   prente] put H   þusgate] þusgate in her soule H, þis maner E   119
and] *om*. I   in] ⌐in⌐ T, *om*. Z   as¹] is as δ   myche] *om*. I   is¹] *om*.
δ   is²] *om*. S   120 a] *om*. EI   for to] to B   konnen] knowe δ   121
ordeyne] ordeyneþ G   þat] þat it best þat M   so] and þerfore preie we alle to
god þat we by goode werkus mowen so ablen ourself to þe grace of god þat þe seed of godes
word mowen wel bringe forth fruyt of vertu in vs and þat hit so be etc. N

Dominica in Quinquagesima. [Euangelium.]
Sermo 3[9].

Assumpsit Iesus duodecim discipulos. Luce 18.

This gospel telliþ how Crist warnede hise disciples byforn of his passioun, to teche þat he ordeyned hit and suffrede not aȝeyn his wylle, but ches for loue þat he hadde to man to suffre þus and bygghe man. *Iesu took his twelue disciples, and seyde þus vnto hem*
5 *'Lo! we steyen to Ierusaleem, and alle þingus þat ben wryten by prophetis of mannys sone schullen ben endyde,* as þei nede muten.' Crist clepuþ hymself 'mannys sone' bleþliche for þis cause: fowre maneris þer ben of men þat ben browt into þis world, þe furste man was maad of eurþe, but Eue was maad of man, þe þridde man cam of hem
10 two by comun gendrure of men, but Crist worschipede wommanys kynde and cam by myracle of Marie. And so, whan þat Crist clepuþ hymself wommanys sone or his modur womman, he specifieþ his manhede. And so, ȝif prophetis and oþre men weren seyde soþly mannys sonys, nerþeles Crist was proprely sone of a
f.85v 15 persone of man|kynde, for he was a vyrgynes sone wiþowte man þat gat Crist of hyre. Þese ferfadres of whyche Crist cam, as Abraham, Dauyd and oþre, gendrede not Crist of Marie, for sche

---

12 John 2: 4; 19: 26.

MSS: D; ABCEFGHIJKLMNSTXYZαβδ.

Dominica . . . euangelium] *om.* αZ   sermo 39] sermo 34 D, *om.* BCFKLNSTYαδEI-
XZGH   assumpsit . . . discipulos] cum essem paruulus loquebar ut paruulus
N   duodecim discipulos] discipulos suos αδ, duodecim Y, *om.* M   luce 18] 1 ad
cor. N   1 byforn] *om.* LM   3 for] ful S, ⌐hit⌐ for δ   4 and] to hym and
I   vnto] to LH   5 to] vnto E   by prophetis] *om.* F   6 muten] most
I   clepuþ] calleþ NαδZ, clepide BC   7 bleþliche] gladly α   8 browt]
broght forth CKE   10 gendrure] gendringe T, engendrure I, gendre I   men]
man ABNIZ   11 cam] *om.* Y   and²] *om.* A, ⌐þat⌐ β   þat] *om.* CKLT-
Y   12 clepuþ] calleþ NαδZ, clepid C   hymself] hym K   wommanys]
⌐wo⌐mannus H, mannes K   13 and²] or *canc.* ⌐and⌐ C, or *canc.* and H   14 seyde
soþly] *rev.* AH, soþely *canc.* seyde soþely E, seid F   mannys] menus KYG   sonys]
son C   15 mankynde] mannes kynde M   man . . . hyre] getyng of any mon
N   man] ony man FJ   16 þat gat] to get Z   of] on α   ferfadres] foure
fadris I   17 abraham] adam CK   oþre] oþer moo N   not] *om.* L   18

kepte euere hire maydenhed. And so for worschipe of his modir
and of kynde of men and wymmen, Crist wolde clepon hym
mannys sone and specifyen his manhede. Sixe þingus telluþ Crist   20
to comene in his passioun. Furst *Crist schal be ȝyuen* to Pilate and
knytes to be slayn, and alle þese weren heþene men, and
fygureden þat þei schulden be turnyde; and ypocrisye of Iewys,
whan þei feyneden vnleueful to hem for to sle Iesu Crist, telluþ
þat þei schulden ben endured. Aftyr Crist was manye weyȝe   25
scorned, and aftyr he was turmentyd, and aftyr he was *spyt* vpon,
and aftyr þis turment he *was kyld*; and he *roos on þe þridde day*, as hit
was schewyd aftyr in deede. *But disciples of Iesu vndirstoden not þese*
sixe *þingus*, for, al ȝif þei herden þe voys[is], þei vndirstoden
þanne noone of þes, for hit was vnsemly to hem þat anye of þese   30
þingus schulde falle, and so þei supposedon þat Crist spak mystily
in þese wordes.

   And whan Crist cam nyȝ Ierycho, a blynd man sat by þe weye and
beggyde, for synne of þe puple þat wolde not helpon hym wiþowte
sych beggyng, al ȝif Godis lawe forfende syche beggerys for to be.   35
Whan þis blynde man herde þe puple passyng wiþ Crist in þe weye, he
axede what þat was. And þei seyden aȝeyn to hym þat Iesu Nazaren passede
þerby. And he cryede on hym and seyde '*Iesu, þat art Dauid sone, haue*
mercy vpon me!' And men þat wenten byfore Crist blameden hym, and
beedon hym holden his pees. But he cryede myche moore '*Dauid sone, haue*   40
mercy on me!' And Iesu bleþly dide mercy whan he was clepyd

so] ᴿsoᴸ T, þus J, *om.* Z   19 men] man SI   wymmen] woman SI, of wymmen
H   clepon] calle NαδZ   hym] hymself J   20 sixe] and sixe J   telluþ
crist] *rev.* δ   21 in] to S   schal] seiþ I schal I   and] and to, to *canc.* α, and to
NI   23 fygureden] figifuriden Y   24 vnleueful] leuefully α   for to] to
I   25 endured] endurid ᴿymade hardᴸ T   weyȝe] weies ABCFKLMNSYβδEI-
JXZGH   26 turmentyd] turnementid H   he² . . . vpon] put vppon a cros
I   vpon] on S   27 turment] turnement H   kyld] sleyn EZ   he²] aftur
he α   roos] aroos I   on] vpon Y   28 schewyd aftyr] *rev.* α   vndir-
stoden] vndirstonden DNδX   not] non α   þese] of þese FTYαEH, þis I   29
for] *om.* Z   al ȝif] ᴿalᴸ if FL   þei herden] he herde M   þe] *om.* β   voy-
sis] voys D   vndirstoden] vndirstonden S   30 þanne] þat S   noone] of noon
H   31 mystily] iustly C   32 in] to hem in I, *om.* G   33 ierycho] vnto ierycho
δ   by] aftur by δ   34 beggyde] byggede S   for] be α   wolde] elles
wolde N   wiþowte . . . beggyng (35)] *om.* N   35 beggyng] biggynge S   al
ȝif] al is Y   forfende] forfendide BCFKTYβEIG   beggerys] beggyng
CK   for to] to BFN   36 þis] þe T   þe¹] þis LE   crist] iesu Y   37
þat was] *rev.* B   nazaren] of nazareth AG   39 vpon] on ANEH   40 beedon
hym] seide S   his] þi S   moore] þe more Y   dauid] and seyde dauid
T   41 on] vpon Lβl   bleþly dide] *rev.* H   whan] and when C   clepyd]

Dauid sone, for hit was soþ by Godis hest, and Dauid was
wondirful meke and figurede Crist specially in manye þingus þat
fellen to hym. *And þus stood Iesu and maade þis man be browt to hym.*
45 *And wanne he cam ny3, Crist axede hym what he wolde þat Crist dide to
hym. And he seyde 'Loord, þat I see!' And Iesu seyde to hym þanne 'Looke
þow, þi byleue haþ maad þe saf.' And he say anoon and sewede Crist,
heryenge God. And alle þe puple, whan þei sawen þis, 3euon louyng vnto
God.*

50   Þe goostly sence of þis gospel meueþ men to vertewis, al 3if
fleschly disciples vndirstonde þis not. A vertuows man mot
suffren of his kynde sixe maner of suffryngus, as Crist dide here.
And þanne in such pacience is þis man ordeynot to goo to
heuenly Ierusalem, as Crist wente here in eurþe to bodily
55 Ierusalem. A man schulde furst be 3yuen to þese heþene feendes,
and þei furst scorne þis man, and tempten hym by his flesch; and
siþ þei putten hym on þe cros to chastisen his flesch, as Powle
dide, and siþ to dye to þis world, and siþ to ryse spiritually, for þus
men schulden slen here flesch and rise to God in þer goost. And 3if
60 þese wordis ben scornyde of fleschly men and worldly, nerþeles
hit schulde be þus by ⌈bi⌉leue þat men schulden haue. And þus
we schulden sewe Crist, suffrynge as he suffrede; and we schulden
wende by Ierycho and speke wiþ þis blynde man, and do werkys
of mercy to hym goostly as Crist dide. Iericho is 'þe mone' or
65 'smellyng' þat men schulden haue, for eche man in þis lif schulde
smelle Crist and sewon hym; and ri3t as þe moone is pryncipal

57 2 Cor. 12: 7.

cald NαδZ   42 dauid¹] dauid þus M, þus dauid δ   hest] bihight Z, biheest
G   and] *om.* I   dauid² . . . wondirful (43)] wonderly dauid was N   44 be]
to be CYE   to²] vnto N   45 þat] *om.* E   crist²] he Y   46 he] *om.*
β   looke] see Z   47 þi] for þi K   and sewede] suyng N   48 heryenge]
and herying NS, louynge αZ, her⌈i⌉ynge J, heerynge A   whan] w *canc.*/whan
D   þis] þis þei J   louyng] praysynge α   vnto] ⌈vn⌉ to T, to ACK   50
sence] sentence, -ten- *canc.* B, sence *altered from* sentence G, sentence LMNδ, wit
Z   51 vndirstonde] vndirstodyn CLYIG   þis not] *rev.* I   þis] it BL-
G   vertuows] vertues KL   52 his] ⌈his⌉ C, *om.* Y   maner] maners
δ   of²] *om.* K   suffryngus] suffryng δ   53 þis] þat T   goo] god S   54 as
. . . ierusalem (55)] *om.* Z   in] on Mδ   55 a] and a J   furst be] *rev.*
H   þese] þis L   56 furst] firste þei J   scorne] scornyd β   tempten]
temptid S   57 as] and S   59 schulden] scil *canc.*/schulden D   rise] reyse
β   goost] spirit Z   60 worldly] worldes δ   61 by] ⌈bi⌉ AT, by *eras.* B, *om.* M,
bi oure J   bileue] bi-*corr.* D   þus] þanne þus I   62 as] þat CK   64
hym] hem α   65 smellyng] þe smellynge I   66 ri3t] *om.* E   pryncipal] þe

planete aftyr þe sonne, so Cristis manhede is pry[n]cipal after his
godhede. And as fadres of þe oolde lawe smelliden Crist in þer
deedis; so myche more we schulde now smelle Crist in alle owre
deedis; and þanne we schulden sewe þis│mone, and ende sikerly   70 f.86
þis wey3e. And for þis smel is Crist clepyd 'plauntyng of roose in
Iericho', and his weye is smellyng of a ful feeld þat God hadde
blessyd. And þis smel hadde Iacob and oþre fadres þat trowedon
in Crist. Þis blynde man is mankynde, þat was blyndid wiþ synne,
and beggede boþe of God and man, for hit was nedid herto.   75
Eche man mot begge of God, and axe of hym his eche day breed,
and begge goostly werkis of mercy of his breþren, for þei ben
slowe to do þese werkis as þei ben holde to do by þe lawe of God.
And þese men sitten by þe wey3e þat ben temptyde of þe feend,
þat takiþ of hem Godis word, and makeþ hem pore in byleue.   80
Þese men heren þat Iesu passiþ by þis weye in manye membris,
and þei cry3en faste on hym to helpon hem in þis nede. But Iesu
byddeþ syche blynde men to be browt to hym in þer byleue, and
þei axen furst of Iesu to see wel in riht byleue. And men þat ben
worþi herto seen anoon in þer byleue, sewynge Crist ⌜and⌝ louyng 85
God, for þanne þei wyten how þei schulden lyue. But þese men
þat comen byfore blamen faste þis blynde man, and letten hym
for to cry3e and axen help þus of Crist. For manye comen not wyþ
Iesu in þer lore þat þei techen, but comen byfore hym and seyn
þat þei ben betture þan he, and sewen hym not in þer lyf but   90
holden a lyf þat þei han fownden. And þese men þat smellen

principal N   67 is . . . godhede (68)] om. S   pryncipal] prycipal D   68 of]
in canc. ⌜of⌝ α, in J   oolde lawe] rev. K   69 deedis] dede α   more] þe more
M   now . . . crist] smelle crist now H   alle] om. IJ   owre] oþer C   70
sikerly] sureli G   71 þis¹] in canc. þis X, in þis FH   and] om. AJ   clepyd]
ycald NαδZ   roose] rosen δ   72 hadde] haþ NδG   74 was . . . synne] by
synne was blynded N   blyndid] blynde δ   wiþ] bi ABCKLMSTYαβδEIJZ-
G   75 beggede] biggide S   man] of man I   nedid] nedeful α   herto]
þerto IZG   76 of²] om. E   hym] om. Y   day] day⌜s⌝ δ, daies AFKNSYI-
G   77 of mercy] om. E   his] here I   78 to do²] om. N   þe . . . god]
godes lawe N   of] be S   80 of] from EZ   pore] bare E   81 passiþ]
passid A   þis] þe canc. ⌜þis⌝ Cα, þe LH   82 on] vpon T   iesu . . . men (83)]
suche blynde men iesu byddeth δ   83 byddeþ] biddid β   men] om. S   to be]
be Y   84 axen] axide β   85 herto] þereto SIZ   anoon] om. I   sew-
ynge] anon suwynge I   and] corr. D   louyng] lowynge G   86 þanne] om.
N   schulden] shullen LZ   lyue] -n eras. D   87 comen] camen
F   blamen] blamede J   blynde] bynde C   hym] hem I   88 axen]
axide β   manye] manye men Y   89 in] and C   þer] om. G   seyn]
sayden δ   90 þat] om. BN   hym] hem N   91 smellen] sewen N   92 in²]

Crist in his lif and in his lawe þei clepon hem ypocrites, and maken hem ceson to spekon of Crist. But þese men þat saueren God by syche wordis spekon more, and preyen Crist to helpon

95 hem to þe tyme þat þei ben deede; and euere þese men smellen more of Iesu Crist þat is þis roose, for good þing counforteþ men, ȝe more whan hit is more defowlid. And þus þei seen and sewen Crist to heuenly Ierusalem, and louen hym in word and dede fro tyme þat þei han þis siȝt.

⌐in⌐ H, om. A   clepon] callen NαZ, calden δ   hem] om. E   93 maken . . . ceson] ben abouten to stoppen hem N   maken] maden δ   ceson] to ceesse Bβ   crist] god K   saueren] seueren C   94 god] crist H   spekon] þei speken J   95 to] into B, til α   þe] om. S   96 of] om. L   iesu] om. L   þis] þe T   counforteþ] comfort C   97 ȝe] þo α   whan . . . more²] twice Y   whan] þat Z   more²] ⌐more⌐ LG   98 to] vnto α   in] om. B   and dede] ⌐and dede⌐ Tα, and in dede δJ   fro] fro ⌐þe⌐ X, fro þe ABCFKLMNSTYβδEIJZH   99 siȝt] syȝhte þat we may wynne to þis syȝt and loue hym euer whitouten ende pray we specialy to god wiþ pater et aue N

Dominica 1 Quadragesime. [Euangelium.].
Sermo 40.

Ductus est Iesus in desertum. Mathei 4.

This gospel telluþ how Crist was temptyd þre tymes of þe feend, and how he ouercam þe feend to techen vs how we schulden doo. Þe story telluþ þat *Iesu was laad of þe Holy Gost into desert* sone aftyir his fastyng *to be temptyd of þe fend*. And, for þe feend temptiþ men whan he supposeþ þat þei be moste feble, þe feend supposede þis 5 of Crist *whan he hadde fastyd fowrty dayȝes*. And resouns of þe fend wher Crist was boþe God and man marride hym, so þat he wyste neuere wer þis were soþ or false; and þis coueyted he to wyte, for þanne he wolde ha[ue] lettyd men for to haue doo Crist þus to deþ, leste he sauede mankynde. Hit was not pleyn to þe fend þat 10 Crist was God for þis fastyng, for Moyses and Hely boþe fastyden fully fowrty dayes, and ȝeet neiþur of hem was God, as þe feend wyste wel. But Iesu by his maner of fastyng passide boþe Moyses and Hely, for Crist fastyde fowrty dayes, and neiþur eet ne dranc in þis tyme; and he was in qwyc age and lustide wel to eete, and 15 he was not ocupyed on oþur wyse as þese two weren. Moyses was

11 Exod. 34: 28; 1 Kgs. 19: 8.

MSS: D; ABCEFGHIJKLMNSTXYZαδ; β *om.* 24 furst . . . 99 þus *(leaf lost).*

Dominica 1 quadragesime] *om.* αZ   sermo 40] *om.* BCFKLNSTYαδEIXZG-H   ductus . . . desertum] ecce nunc tempus acceptabile N   desertum] desertum a sp, a sp *canc.* D, desertum a spiritu vt [/taret a [/abolo δ   mathei 4] mathei [δ, ad cor . . . mathei iiii N, *om.* KI   1 tymes] tyme M   3 þat] how S-G   sone] *om.* M   4 fastyng] *on eras. corr.* D, waschyng NδIJ   feend] *om.* Y   temptiþ] temptid L   5 supposeþ] supposide S   þat . . . be] hem N   þis] þus N   6 and] *om.* N   resouns] þe resones CK, resoun β   of] and doutynge of N   7 was] were YE   8 were] was A   coueyted] couet C   he] *om.* β   9 haue[1]] ha D   for to] to ABCKLMNSTYαβδEIZ   haue doo] haue *canc.* doo X, do ABCKLMNSTYαβEIZ, haue þus do δ   crist þus] *rev.* FTαG, crist δ   to[2]] to þe A   10 sauede] schulde saue NZ, hadde sauyd E   mankynde] manys kynde BCKLMSTβδX   pleyn] p *canc.* /pleyn D   11 crist] *om.* L   hely] -e *canc.* D   *margin* exo. 24 and 34, III regum 19 H   12 fully] ful I   ȝeet] *om.* E   neiþur] neuer βI, *om.* N   15 in[1]] not in N   lustide] lusteth δ, lastide I   to] ᴦto[1]H, for to E, *om.* N   16 as] and N   two] two oþere J, ᴦoþere[1] two H   moyses] for moises FJGH   17 and fed] counfortid N   þis]

in þe mount wiþ God and fed wiþ hym in al þis tyme; Hely was an
oold man and fed wiþ dreede of þe kyng. But Iesu was a ȝong
man, and fowrty dayes lyuede wiþ bestis, and suffred of God for
20 to hungren more þan any oþur dide. And so Crist passide boþe
þese two and Iohn Baptist wiþ hem, al ȝif he lyuede aftyr comun
lyf to ȝyuen ensaumple to his chirche; but Baptist lyuede more
comunly peyneful lif þan dide Crist.

Þe feend bygan to tempte Crist furst at pruyde and glotrye, for
25 hym þoȝte þat by þese two he schulde sonest ouercome Crist. Þis
f.86v tempter seyde|þus to Crist, 'Ȝif þow be Godis sone, sey þat þese stonys ben
maade louys.' For þe feend wyste wel þat þis myhte God liȝtly haue
doo, for Crist dide more wondur whan he maade þis world of
nowht, and whan he fedde so manye folc wiþ fyue loues and fewe
30 fyschis, as þe feend wiste wel aftyr but ȝeet þis was hyd from hym.
And here we wyten þat owre philarghes ben more foolys þan is þe
feend, for þe fend wot wel þat God may liȝtly make stoones louys,
but owre philosophris seyn as foolis þat þis þing may no weye be.
And so þe feend supposede of Crist ȝif he were God, he schulde do
35 þis boþe for schewyng of his myht and for to abaten his hongur. But
here answerede Crist to þe feend by auctorite of hooly writ and
seyde 'Hit is wryten þerynne þat not oonly in bred lyueþ man, but in eche
word þat comeþ of Godis mowþ', þat is ⌜his⌝ vertew to speke to men in
þer sowle, and þis passeþ erþly breed. And so þe fend faylede
40 fowle in þis temptacion of Crist. For, ȝif Crist wolde for pruyde do

---

22 Matt. 3: 4; Mark 1: 6; **37** Deut. 8: 3.

---

his MI   18 a] om. α   19 for to] to F   20 any] om. YE   oþur] oþer ⌜man⌝
T   and] om. M   boþe] ⌜boþe⌝ α, om. β   21 iohn . . . hem] passede baptist
also N   lyuede aftyr] rev. N, lyue aftir Y, lyuede J   comun] ⌜a⌝ comyne
δ   22 to ȝyuen] and ȝaue E   23 dide] om. Z   crist] hym N   27 wel] om.
N   þis . . . doo (28)] god myȝhte wel do þat N   þis] þes E   god liȝtly] rev.
I   god] he K   28 wondur] wondiur D, om. M   29 so] om. I   manye]
myche E   fewe] ⌜a⌝ fewe K, a fewe TJG   30 ȝeet . . . was] þis was ȝit
K   hyd] ȝit hide C, om. Y   hym] hym, -y- canc. -⌜e⌝- corr. F, om. M   31
and . . . be (33)] om. Z   we] om. ST   þat owre] þese G   philarghes]
philosepheres αG, philosouris J   is] om. I   32 stoones louys] loues stones ⌜stones
loues⌝ L, of canc. stones loues α, ⌜of⌝ stones loues δ   33 philosophris] philosoris
J   þis] þus IZ   35 for to] for A, also to N   36 answerede crist] rev.
N   37 not] mon not N   oonly] al onely CK   oonly in] in ooli (sic)
F   in¹ . . . man] lyueþ in bred N   man] a canc. man α, a man SH   eche]
euery G   38 of] out of I   his] corr. D   40 fowle] fouli L   crist²] þe crist
N   wolde] wolde haue E   for . . . myracle (41)] do þis miracle for pride
T   41 breed] breed ⌜of stoones⌝ A, breed of stoonys BZ   a] om. AY   com-

þis myracle and make þus breed, hee wolde in a comunte do þis
deede and not þus only in desert; and ȝif Crist myhte þus make
breed, he myhte þus maake boþe flesch and fysch, and þanne
Crist hadde no nede þus to hungren aȝeynes his wille. And so þe
feend was a fool whan he temptyde Crist þus. But Crist   45
answeryde wysly, and for to ȝyue men ensaumple to answere by
Godis lawe and to loue more hit þan eurþly þyng. A sophistre
wolde denye þis resoun þat þe feend maade to Crist, but he cowde
not teche þus þat Godis word is more to loue þan ony eurþly
mete, and so hit schulde not be left þerfore. And þus ȝif we can   50
answere couenably by Godis lawe, whan þat we be temptyde of
pruyde, of gloterye or oþur synne, we may wel ouercome þe feend
and eche þing þat temptuþ vs þus. For, ȝif we louen bettere Godis
word þan any mete þat we schulden ete, we schulde not leue
Godis word and chese þis mete aȝeynes resown.   55

Þe secounde temptacion in whiche þe feend temptide Crist was
doon on þis maner for to meue Crist to pruyde. *Þe feend took hym
into þe hooly cytee.* And, as men seyn comunly, þe feend bar hym
ouer Ierusaleem, as Crist were fleyng in þe eyr, *and putte hym aboue
þe pynnacle of þe temple,* þat somme men seyn weren þe aleyes; *and*   60
*seyde to Crist, ȝif he were Godis sone, þat he schulde maken hymself goo
down.* And herto aleghede þe feend to Crist þe salm þat he myȝte
sewrly do þis, '*for God bad hise aungelis of Crist to kepon hym in alle hise
weyȝes, leste he hurte his foot at þe ston*', and myche more Crist
schulde not hurte hym at þe eyr, ne in his fallyng at þe eurþe, ne   65
at no þing þat Crist mette. And here men passen foly of þe feend,

---

unte] cominalte AYα   do] haue do E   42 not] *om.* S   þus1] ⌜þus1 H, *om.*
δ   ȝif] *om.* Z   þus make] *rev.* EI   43 maake boþe] *rev.* L, make
K   flesch] fische YEH   fysch] fleische YEH   44 no nede] mouede
I   þus to hungren] to hungure ⌜þus1 L   and] a S   45 crist þus] crist crist
M   46 and] *om.* N   47 to] *om.* TG   more hit] *rev.* CKTI   þyng] þingys
T, thinges, -s *canc.* α, *om.* Y   a . . . þerfore (50)] *om.* Z   49 ony] onus LM, is an
N   50 mete] meche S   þerfore] þer þerfore S, herfore δ   and2] *om.*
α   51 þat] *om.* G   of] by δ, wiþ I   52 or] or of LMNJH, oþer of T, or ony
I   synne] synes CKS   53 and] in Z   þing] *om.* E   54 word] wordis
S   þat] þanne S   55 godis] þis goddis I   56 whiche] ⌜þe1 whiche E, þe
wuche NTH   57 for to] to δ   meue] tempte Y   58 into] in E, to
H   and] *om.* B   60 þe1] vpon þe F   þat] and H   men] ⌜men1 T, *om.*
CK   seyn] seiden I   weren . . . aleyes] wher þe aleies weren S   61 to crist]
om. N   maken] *om.* TZ   hymself] hemself E, *om.* Z   goo] do L, to go Y, *om.*
M   62 herto] *om.* Y   aleghede] aleggi/ G   63 sewrly . . . þis] do þus surely
N   sewrly] lightly CK   þis] þus SI   bad] had C   64 at] to
N   þe] a YH   65 hurte] -n *eras.* D   in . . . eurþe] at þe erþe in his

for he wolde alegghen hooly wryt in temptacion of Crist to
preuen hym þat hit wer syker; but anticrist deyneþ not to legghe
Godis lawe for his power, but seiþ þat ȝif men denyen hit þei schal
70 be cursyde, slayn and brend – but þus þe feend temptide not
Crist, al ȝif he were of more power þan ben þese anticristis
disciplis to tempte Crist or cristen men. But Crist answeryde by
hooly wryt, as þe feend alegghede hit to hym, and *seyde to þe feend*
þat hit was wryton þat noon schulde tempte þe Lord his God – but hit were
75 al oon to lepe down þus and to tempte God. And so, siþ Crist
chargede more Godis word þan any worschype or mete, myche
more he chargede þe synne þus for to tempte God. Lord! what
f.87 nede schulde Crist haue to lepe down þus|fro þis pynnacle, siþ he
myȝte on oþur maner sewrly come down by þe aleyes? And ȝif
80 men perseyuede not þe hyeng of Crist to þe pynnacle, ne beryng
of hym ouer þe cytee, (for mennys eyȝen as hit is seyd weren hyd
fro lokyng vpon Crist,) myche more men schulde not wyte how
Crist cam down to þe eurþe, for lesse hit is for to come doun from
an hiȝ place þan to come þidere. And þus faylede foly of þe fend
85 to tempte Crist þus to pruyde.

But here men dowton comunly what hit is to tempte God. And
hit is seyd comunly þat eche man temptuþ God þat chesuþ þe
worse weye, and leuiþ þe betture þat he schulde knowen; and so
no man may do synne, but ȝif he tempte God in a maner. For God
90 dide no wrong to man ȝif he dampnyde man for synne, were hit
neuere so liȝt synne, and ȝif his temptyng were neuere so strong.

fallyng E   his] *om.* G   eurþe] eir G   66 and . . . men (72)] *om.* Z   68
preuen] re- *eras.* D   deyneþ] *on eras. corr.* L, deneith STαδIJH   legghe] alegge
AG   69 godis . . . power] for hym godes lawe to schewe and preue his power by
N   seiþ] he seiþ A, seien G   þat] *om.* NTEIG   hit] his power N   70
þus þe] þis I   73 hit] ⌐hit⌐Tα, *om.* SYZ   74 was] ys TH   noon] no ⌐man⌐
T   þe] hys T   his] *om.* T   75 to²] *om.* T   so] *om.* Z   76 mete]
bodyly mete N   77 chargede] chardede S   for to] ⌐for⌐ to YH   78 haue]
haue hadde E   down þus] *rev.* CK, doun G   fro] of G   þis] þe ABC-
KLMNTYαδEIJXZ   79 sewrly . . . down] com doune surly, doune surly *marked for*
rev. α   þe] *om.* H   80 perseyuede] perseyue CK, preised N   of crist] *om.*
M   ne] ne þe G   81 of] *om.* M   mennys] mannes δI   as . . . hyd]
were hyd as it is sayde α   82 vpon] vp to N   men schulde] *rev.* J   83 down]
om. G   to¹] vppon I   þe] ⌐þe⌐ α, *om.* T   for to] for *canc.* to X, to
ABCKLMNSTYαδEIZGH   84 to] hyt is to δ   þus] þanne H   foly] þe folie
H   85 crist þus] þus ⌐crist⌐ G   þus . . . pruyde] to pride þus E   þus] *om.*
K   86 and] *om.* H   87 man] *om.* H   88 leuiþ] leue J   betture] betere
weye S   so] also Nδ   89 no] *om.* T   man] *om.* Y   synne] ⌐no⌐ synne T, no
synne H   tempte] temptide M   for] and so E   91 liȝt] litil FN   synne]
a synne αI   and] *om.* G   ȝif] *om.* E   temptyng] temptacioun E   ne-

And þus þenkon manye men þat, whoeuere entreþ a new
religioun þat was not furst ordeyned of Crist, he temptuþ God
and synneþ greetly. For two weyes ben put to hym: þe ton is
religioun of Crist, of whiche he schulde be sur by feiþ þat hit is þe   95
beste þat may be; and þe toþer is newe fownden of synful
seruauntis of Crist, þat men schulden wyton is not so good as
Cristes ordre more li3t. And so þis man tempteþ God þat chesuþ
ᵣþusꜚ þis newe ordre. And þis synne is comun now among men for
chesyng of stat. For whoeuere chesuþ hym a stat to lyuen ynne   100
and to serue God, but 3if he trowe þat þis stat be bettur to hym
and more syker, þat man in þis temptuþ God. And þis man mut
putten awey þe world, þe feend and his flesch, þat þei disseyuon
hym not in chesyng of sych stat.

Þe þridde temptyng of þe feend maad to Crist is þus teeld: *þe*   105
feend tok Crist into an hul þat was ful hy3, and schewyde hym alle þe
rewmes of þis world and þe ioye of hem, and seyde to Crist 'Alle þese schal I
3yue þe, 3if þow falle and lowte me.' And þanne seyde Iesus to þe feend 'Go
awey, Sathanas! for hit is wryton in Godis lawe "þe Lord þi God þow
schalt worschypon, and to hym one þow schalt serue þus".' And here men   110
marken how þat Crist was pacient in two temptyngus byfore, but
in þe þridde he my3te not suffre þat ne he spak scharply to þe
feend. And in þis ben we tawte to suffre meekely owre owne

---

109 Deut. 6: 13.

uere] *om.* J   so²] *om.* Y   *margin* gen. 4 T   92 and . . . stat (104)] *om.*
Z   whoeuere] whosoeuere δ, who so N, who J   entreþ] entre AI   a] in a
K   93 religioun] þe religioun E   95 hit] *om.* NSα   96 may] many
Y   and] al B   97 crist] anticrist J   is] it is MI   good] of god T   98
more] is more LM, is *canc.* more α, ᵣþat isꜚ more δ, for cristis ordre is more E   chesuþ]
tempteþ I   99 þis²] þus L   comun now] *rev.* J   comun] comyn N-
α   100 stat] statis FJGH   whoeuere] whosoeuer NδEI   a] *om.* Y   101
and ¹] *om.* N   to¹] *om.* αG   but 3if] bote N   to hym] *om.* E   102 and¹]
or N   þat man] þat man þat ᵣdoiþ þus¹ δ   þat] þan S   in . . . god] þat þus
tempteþ god cheseþ hym a state of gret synne N   þis . . . mut] þerfore moste men
N   man²] *om.* S   103 putten] be put I   awey] a/awey D   his] hire
N   104 hym] hem N, *om.* I   stat] astaat I, statis FGH   105 temptyng]
ᵣtemptacioun¹ E   of] *om.* I   maad . . . teeld] was þis as þe gospel telleþ
N   106 into] to I   hym] to hym N   þe] þes H   107 rewmes] reme
C   þis] þe *canc.* ᵣþis¹ α, þe KZ   ioye] ioyes H   to] þus to NH, *om.*
Y   þese] þis YE   schal I] *rev.* MTEI   108 lowte] worschipe M   109 is]
om. F   lawe] lawe þus LM   þe] þi Nδ   þi] *om.* β   110 schalt] schal
Y   one] *om.* T   111] marken] may marke I   how] ᵣhou¹ G, *om.*
E   crist] *om.* Y   two] þese two Y   temptyngus] temptaciones α   112
he¹] *om.* Y   ne he] *rev.* BMTIH   113 ben we] *rev.* αIJG   owne] *om.*

wrong, but aȝen wrong of God we schulden ben woode to
115 venghen hit, for þus dyden Crist and Moyses and oþre men þat
suweden hem. And þus in þre temptaciones owre lord Iesu
ouercam þe feend by þe wysdam of God and auctorite of hooly
wryt. And ȝif we marken wel þese þre, we may not be temptyd of
yuel spyrit, but ȝif we han lore to ouercomen hym, ȝyf we studyon
120 wel þis gospel. And aftyr þese þre victoryes þis grete *feend lefte
Crist, and goode aungelis comen to hym and seruyden to hym* as to þer
God. And somme men seyn þat þis feend was Sathanas, þe moste
of alle, þat siþ was bownden in helle a þowsynde ȝeer, as seyn⌐t⌐
Iohn seiþ. For, as men seyn comunly, whan a feend is þus
125 vencuschyd, he haþ no power to tempte þat man, and specially of
þat synne. And þus d[e]lyuerede Crist þis world of þis feend and
hise felowes, þat þei anoyȝedon lasse his cherche aftyr by a
þowsande ȝeer.

---

124 Rev. 20: 2.

K   114 wrong²] þe wronge S   woode] bolde α   115 and¹] to A   116
hem] crist N, hym J   temptaciones] temptyngis B   lord] *om.* KE   117 þe²]
om. KH   118 be] wele be α   119 spyrit] spiritis L   ȝif] *om.* CK   120
and] and trusten vs sad in godes lawe and N   þese] *om.* FSJ   þre] þre ⌐gret⌐, gret
eras. D, þre grete, grete *canc.* X, þre grete EI   grete] geet Y   121 to²] ⌐to⌐ N, *om.*
Kα   to³] two S   122 and] as A   þe] ⌐þe⌐ Z, *om.* K   123 a] and a
H   *margin* appoc. δ   as] and C   seynt] t *corr.* D   124 a] þe H   125
vencuschyd] ouercome TE   þat] þan K   man] *om.* E   126 delyuerede]
dolyuerede D   127 anoyȝedon] anoye Z   128 ȝeer] ȝer god ȝeue vs grace strong
to be to haue þe maystry ouer þe fend and þat it so be preie we alle to god etc. N

Dominica ii Quadragesime. [Euangelium.]
Sermo 41.

Egressus Iesus secessit in partes Tyri. Mathei 15.

This gospel telluþ a myracle of Crist to sture men to hope mercy,
al ȝif þei ben synful. Þe story telluþ how *Iesu|wente owt of Iudee and* 87v
fel in þe cuntres of Tyry and Sydon, þat weren cuntrees ocupyed wiþ
heþone men and nyȝ to Iudee, and hem visitede Crist. *And [lo] a*
womman of Chanaan wente owt of hire coostes, cryȝede vpon Crist and 5
seyde þus to hym 'Lord! haue mercy on me, Dauyþus sone! my dowter is
yuel traueylut of a feend.' And Crist, to contynewen deuocion of þis
womman, *answerid not furst a word to hyre.* And here may we lernen
to contynewen owr good werk, al ȝif God graunte not owre wylle
at þe bygynnyng, for God wole haue owre herte deuowt to hym 10
wiþowten eende heere and in heuene. *þe disciples comen to Crist and*
spoke þus to hym, 'Leue þis womman, for sche cryeþ aftur vs.' But Crist
answerede and seyde þus comunly 'I am not send but to þe perischede
schep of þe hows of Israel', wer þis womman be sych. And by þis *þis*
womman cam and lowtide Crist, and seyde 'Lord! help me.' And Crist 15
answeride and seyde 'Hit is not good to take ⌈þe⌉ breed þat fallup to
children, and ȝyuen hit to howndes to ete fro þese children.' *And þis*

MSS: D; ABCEFGHIJKLMNTXYZαβδ; S *om.* 61 sence . . . 117 mannys (*leaf lost*).

Dominica . . . evangelium] *om.* αZ   sermo 41] *om.* BCFKLNSTYαδEIXZG-
H   egressus . . . tyri] non enim vocauit nos deus in immundiciam N   secessit]
ceset F   tyri] tyri et sidonis FKSTEIJ, tyry ⌈et sidon⌉ δ, *om.* αH   mathei
15] mathei 15 . . . ad tess'4 N   1 this gospel] þe gospel of þis day N   to²
. . . mercy] to mercy and hope Nδ   mercy] of *canc.*mercy Cα, of mercy T   2
how] how þat E   owt] *om.* E   3 in] into, to *canc.* Y, into BCFKNTαδZH   þe]
*om.*α   and] and of N   þat] þe wuche N   4 visitede] visite Y   and²] *om.*
β   lo] ⌈lo⌉ A, *om.* DCFKLMNSTYαβδEIJXGH   5 cryȝede] and cryede
ABCKLTβIZG   6 þus to hym] to him þus B   to] vnto N   on] vpon
LαβE   dauyþus] da *canc.* /dauyþus D   7 traueylut] tourmentid E   con-
tynewen] conty⌈n⌉ue H, contune CF   8 lernen] lere BCLTαβδEZH   9 werk]
werkis LN   graunte] grawtid β, ne graunte J   owre] ⌈þe⌉ K   10 deuowt
. . . hym] to hym deuoutely desyryng euer N   11 heere] boþe here N   crist] iesu
crist Y   12 spoke] seiden H   to] vnto N   hym] crist S   13 perischede
schep] schep þat perischeden N   14 wer . . . sych (16)] *om.* N   be] is B   þis²]
þat E   þis³] ⌈þis⌉α, *om.* S   15 and² . . . seyde] twice N   16 þe] corr. D, *om.*
I   17 children¹] þe children BG   to¹] ⌈to⌉ Tα, *om.* LM   fro] it fro

womman answeride, knowynge Cristes speche, *and grauntide þat hit
were good*, (as ʒif sche wolde mene þus 'siþ þow clepust me an
20 hownd, and I suffre mekely, ʒif þow som mete of children to þis
hownd',) '*For whelpis eton of crommes þat fallen of lordis bordis.*' *And
Iesu answerude to hyre*, and wiste hire entent, *and seyde* '*O womman!
greet is þi feiþ. Be hit don to þe riht as þow wolt.*' *And hire dowtur was
helyd riht in þat howr.*

25   Here men dowton comunly wher Crist mysseyde þis womman,
or scornede hire, and put on hire þat sche was an hownd, or ellis
alle þese wordis of Crist schulde be taken axyngly. Here we
schullen byleue þat Crist dide algate euene as he schulde do. And
þus, ʒif Crist scornede here (þat I dar not seye), scornyng was
30 leueful as hooly writ proueþ. For Hely þe prophete bad preestis of
Baal þat þei schulden crye strongly, leste þer god slepte or spak
wiþ oþre men, þat he myhte not heren hem. And þus scorneþ
Powle spekyng to Corynthios, 'wher I dide lasse to ʒow þan oþre
apostles diden? But þat I took not of ʒow, forʒyue ʒe me þis
35 wrong!' And so often in Godis lawe is scornyng wel ment, as ʒif hit
were leueful doon on good maner. But hit is seyd comunly þat þre
þingus ben harde to men: to scorne men meedfully, or medfully
plede wiþ men, or ellis for to fiʒte wiþ men by þe weye of charyte.
But alle þese may be doon, as wyse men þenkon. But, for þei ben
40 perelowse, manye men supposen þat Crist vsede hem neuere, but
wente þe kyngus weyʒe. And so Crist axsede by maner of

---

30 1 Kgs. 18: 27;   **33** 2 Cor. 12: 13.

E   *margin* Io M   18 grauntide] grauntyng δ   19 were] was Z   good]
g/good D   þus] *om.* LM   clepust] callest NαZ, clepiþ L, caldest δ   20
som . . . þis] mete sumwhat of mete as to an N   21 of¹] of þe BαIG   of²] fro
Aδ   22 answerude] seide S   o] *om.* Z   23 riht] *om.* T   wolt] wille
Z   24 in] *om.* N   þat] þe same CKE   26 and] or *canc.* and α, or ANY-
I   an] an an, *second* an *canc.* D   27 þese] þeʳsꞌ α, þe G   of crist] *om.*
E   axyngly] *on eras. corr.* D   28 schullen] schulden G   byleue] wite bi bileue
K   þat] at L   29 þus] ʳþusꞌ H, *om.* I   crist] *eras.* L, ʳcristꞌ E   scornede]
scorꞌnꞌyde H, scoryde E   scornyng] al be hit scornyng N   was] were
N   30 proueþ] seiþ N   prophete] holy profeete Y   preestis] þe prestis
H   31 þei] ʳþeiꞌ δH   schulden] *om.* I   crye strongly] *rev.* A   *margin* 3
regum xviii T, 3 reg. 8 M   32 men] me L   *margin* 2 cor. xiii T   scorneþ]
scornede K   33 to¹] to þe G, of S   wher] as wher N   34 þis] þis, -s *corr.* T, þi
L, þat BZ   35 so] *om.* G   often] afte S   in] on L   as ʒif] as YZ   36
were] is Z   leueful] wel and leefful, and *canc.* S   doon] to *canc.* done A, to don
H   on] in C   37 or medfully] *om.* NS   38 for to] to H   men²] man
A   weye] lawe E   39 þese] þis ABTI   ben] *om.* LS   40 supposen]
supposeden δ   41 weyʒe] ʳhyeꞌ weye A   axsede] axinge A   42 mete] mente

qwestioun wher hyt were not good to take children mete and
ȝyuen hit to þe howndes, as who seiþ 'tel þow'. And þus heþone
men weren clepide howndes of Godis folc, for propretes of
howndis acordyng to heþene men. But þis womman mekely 45
grauntide þis questioun, and þus men clepid howndis may
become Godis children, as hit byfel of manye heþone men þat
weren conuertyde by Crist and maad cristene men. And þus Crist
preysede þis womman by hire grete feiþ, and wiþ þis bodily
myracle maade hire sowle hool, and figurede þat heþene folk 50
schulden be turnyde to hym, and of men þat weren furst howndis
schulden be maad by grace hise children. And so þe word of Crist
|þat he was not sent but to þe seke children of Iacobus hows was f.88
soþ to þis entent, þat Crist was sent to hele þese. For, what man
hit be þat Crist conuerteþ and saueþ hym in heuene, he is 55
Iacobus sone, for he supplaunteþ þe fend as Iacob dide Esau, and
he is mad a man þat seþ God by feiþ. And Crist is cleput þus boþe
Iacob and Israel, and oþre holy fadres þat figuredon Crist; and
þus men ben maad by grace of þe hows of Iacob.

But hit were to wyte þe moral sence of þese wordes, siþ þis 60
curnel is more swete þan sence of þe story. Tyrus and Sydon
weren of þe lond of byheste, nyȝ þe hil of Libani; but Israel
suffisede not to casten hem owt of þis lond, and so heþene folc
dwelton þere til Crist cam. And so þis paynym womman is þe
substaunce of mannys sowle, þat ys meued of God to preyȝe for 65

S   43 to þe] vnto þe X, vnto ABCLMNSTYβEI, to FKαδZGH, þe J   seiþ] say
CαδZ   tel þow] to þe N   44 clepide] cald NαδZ   propretes] propirte BNT,
profites α   45 acordyng] ⌐is⌐ acordinge F, accorden H   to] wiþ H   þis]
mekely þis Nδ   mekely grauntide] rev. I   mekely] om. Nδ   46 þis] to þis
S   þus] ⌐þus⌐ H, om. β   clepid] cald NαδZ   47 hit byfel] fel N   he-
þone] om. E   men] om. A   48 conuertyde . . . crist¹] by crist conuertid N   con-
uertyde] comfortid J   maad] crist made E   50 sowle] douȝter soule J   ho-
ol] om. Y   folk] on eras. corr. D, men K   51 men] þe men S   weren furst] rev.
N   52 þe . . . entent (54)] was cristus word soth to þis entent þat he was not sent bote
to þe seke children of iacobes hous as he seide vnto hure N   53 þat] seiþ canc. þat DX,
shewiþ ⌐þat⌐ A, schewiþ þat B   þe seke] seke CKαβ   iacobus] israel canc. iacobus
D   54 þis] þat J   þat] and CK   crist] he A   þese] þus canc. ⌐þes⌐ α, þus
T   for] þus may þou see for N   55 hit] þat it α   crist] om. I   saueþ] saue
B, haueþ S   hym . . . heuene] om. H   56 iacobus] on eras. corr. D, israelis
ABCKLMNSTYαβZ, israels on eras. corr. JXG, iacob israeles δ   supplaunteþ]
supplauntid N   57 by feiþ] om. E   cleput] cald NαδZ   58 crist] crist oure
sauyour N   59 ben] by β   60 but] om. N   þis] þese δ   61 sence] þe
sense E   62 lond] londes CK   byheste] ⌐be⌐ þe hest β   nyȝ] nye of T-
δ   israel] israelis Y   63 suffisede] suffered αδ   casten] cacchen N   heþene]
sythen δ   64 til] til þat AE   þe] om. T   65 mannys] mennis ACLMYβJX-

hire dowtur heele, for boþe vertewes of þis sowle and werkis þerof
ben drecchid of þe feend, and lyuen vnmedfully. And such a
sowle wendeþ owt of þe costes of Chanaan, for hit forsakiþ þe
paynyme lif þat hit was byfore inne. And hit sekiþ not only Crist
70 in þe hows but on þe weye, and crieþ on hym kenely, wonne by
contemplacion hit is deuowt in God. And in doyng of werkys hit
preyeþ to hym þat hyt do fully to plesaunce of God. And
interpretacion of Chanaan acordiþ, siþ Chanaan is 'chaungyng'
or 'chaunghed', and a sowle þat is furst heþene and þus turnyd to
75 Crist is chaunghed by myracle more þan ony body. And Crist
norscheþ and scharpeþ þe preyer of syche sowles tyl þat þei ben
worþi to haue grace of hym. And so þese sowles knowen þat þei
ben sy3ke schep of þe hows of Israel, þat han nede of
counfort. And þei seyn þat syche whelpus schulden ete trenchow-
80 res of lordis, and knowen how God haþ fed hise children, and so
do by hem. For hit is li3t to God to make of syche whelpus hole
schep of Iacobus hows, and þus conuerte þer sowles. And þus by
gretnesse of feiþ enformed wiþ charyte ben syche sowles maade
hool, and turnede vnto Godis children. And, ri3t as in Cristis
85 tyme and aftyr by hise apostles he turnede manye heþene men to
Cristis religioun, so now in tyme of anticrist ben cristene men
made heþene and reuerse Cristis lawe, his lore and his werkis. As
now men seyin þat þei schulden by lore of þer feiþ werren vpon
cristene men, and turnen hem to þe pope, and sle þer persones,
90 þer wyues and þer children, and reuen hem þeir goodis, and þus

Z   sowle] saulis Z   66 heele] helþ FαEH   boþe] bothe þe δ, by þe
N   þis] þe Z   67 of] þer canc. of D   a sowle] om. Z   68 owt] om.
T   hit] om. Y   69 byfore inne] rev. EH   70 on¹] vpon ABCFKLMNTY-
αβδIJXZGH   weye] hye wey N   crieþ . . . kenely] kenely cryeþ on hym
N   kenely] kendli J   72 hyt] he δ   to²] þe BFKG, om. H   73
acordiþ . . . chanaan²] om. Z   acordiþ] acordiþ herwiþ E   chaungyng]
chaungid A   74 chaunghed] chaunging A   is furst] rev. N   þus] seþen
N   75 body] bodi here K   76 scharpeþ] schapiþ E   þe] syche H   pre-
yer] praieris IH   tyl] to N   77 grace] om. E   hym] hym siche grace E   78
han] had α   79 þei] om. T   ete] om. M   trenchowres] tenchouris Y   80
lordis] lord ⌐bordis⌐ T   how] hou þat E   haþ] had L   81 do] wel doun
N   hem] hym C   of] om. δ   hole schep] rev. H   82 by] of I   83
wiþ] bi KI   84 vnto] to I   85 heþene] om. Y   to] vnto E   86 so] and so
H   in . . . ben] syn and errouris makis Z   87 made] om. Z   and¹ . . .
tyrauntrie (101)] as syn of ire and slayng of cristen men Z   reuerse] om. I   88
men seyin] rev.α   seyin] sayden CK   þat] om. E   vpon] vp K   89 þer]
om. N   90 þeir] hire N   91 cam] was E   of¹] be α, om. E   chastisement]

chastisen hem. But certis þis cam neuere of chastisement of Crist,
siþ Crist seiþ he cam not to lese lyues but sauen hem. And þerfore
þis is chastisement of þe felle fend and neuere chastisement of
Crist, þat vsede pacience and myracles. For Crist techeþ in his
lawe þat al þat we schulden wylle þat men dyden skilfully to vs, 95
we schulden do to hem. But what man wolde by skyle be þus
chastised of his broþur for mannys obedience, þat he dowteþ to
ben a fend? Crist axsyde not sych obedience to be don to hym.
But woso wolde wiþ good wylle obesche to hym wiþowte ȝifte,
Crist wolde taken hym to grace – but þese man taken to 100
tyrauntrie. But, as þe sixþe sermoun seiþ, scribis and pharisees
seyden þat mansleyng was forfendut, but neiþur yre ne yuel
word. But Crist diffiniþ þus þat whoso is wroþ to his broþur is
worþi of iugement to be dampned in helle; and whoso wiþ þis yre
spekiþ|wordis of scorn, he is worþi to be dampned by counseil of 105 f.88v
þe Trinnyte; and whoso wiþ þis wraþthe spekiþ foly wordis of
sclaundre, he is worþi to be punyched wiþ þe fuyr of helle. Myche
more, ȝif prestes now wiþowten cause of byleue slen manye
þowsynde men, þei ben worþi to be dampnede. Croserie ne
assoylyng feyned now of prelatis schal not at þe day of doom 110
reuerse Cristis sentence. And take we heed to þese þre þat Crist
chargeþ by ordre: wraþthe, and scornful speche, and foly speche

---

91 Luke 9: 56; **103** Matt. 5: 22.

chastyment AMδ, þe chastisement B   92 crist] he I   he] þat he E   *margin*
luc 9 M   not] neuere δ   lyues] mennus lyues E   sauen] to saue
CKNYαEI, to *canc.* saue G, for to saue F   þerfore] herfore A   93 chastisement¹]
chastyment Aδ, a chastisment C   felle] fool G   chastisement²] chastyment
Aδ   94 vsede pacience] *rev.* N   95 wylle] wilne YH   to] til α   96 to] til
α   97 for . . . fend (98)] *om.* N   dowteþ] dowtide β   98 axsyde] com-
pellede N   sych . . . hym] men to obeye to hym in suche wise N   99 woso] who
B   wolde] *om.* Y   obesche] obeye N   ȝifte] any ȝift N   100 hym] hem
ABKLMNTYαβI   grace] grace and graunten hem lyf at his wille N   to²] hem
canc. to a α, now δ   101 sixþe sermoun] gospel Z   sixþe] sexe C   *margin* mt.
5 Z   102 mansleyng] mansleerys *canc.* mansleyng D   neiþur] not T, neuer
β   yre] wraþþe FGH   103 word] wordis I   crist] *om.* N   diffiniþ]
devyniþ ⌐diffineþ⌐ J, diuiniþ TI, diffinyshed α   whoso] whosoeuer E   104 of
iugement] iugement G, *om.* L   to . . . helle] in helle to be dampned N   whoso]
who N   þis] his Lαδ, *om.* L   105 he . . . worþi] *twice* L   by] by þe
E   106 whoso] who BC   þis] þus C, his LNαI   foly] folily ABCFKLNTY-
αβδIJX, *om.* E   of] *om.* C   107 be] *om.* K   wiþ] in H   myche . . . and
(111)] *om.* Z   109 to be] þei ben Y   110 feyned] ⌐feyned⌐ M, *om.* T   111
and] *om.* β   to] of α   112 chargeþ] chargide I   speche¹] spekyng

of sclaundre. And to þese þre Crist schapeþ iugement, counseyl
and þe fuyr of helle. Hit is hard to be dampnyd by iugement of
115 Cristis manhede, but hit is hardere to be dampnyd bi counseil of
þe Trinnyte, but hit is hardest to be put by þese to þe fuyr of helle.
Lord! ȝif God punysche þus wylle and mannys wordis, muche
more schal he punysche wil, word and wyckyde dede.

δ   114 to . . . trin- (116)] *on eras.corr.* D   115 hit] *om.* I   bi] of
LM   116 trinnyte] hooli trinite G   hardest] hardere K   to²] two to LTI,
þre *canc.* to G   117 punysche] punyshiþ H   þus] þese δ   118 wil] wycked
⌈wille⌉ δ   word] wordis C, wor L, and worde αI   dede] dedis Z, dede þerfore
preie we to god to graunte vs myȝt witt and wille to kepen vs clene from þuse þre þe while
we in þe world schulen lyue etc. pater N

Dominica iii Quadragesime. [Euangelium.]
Sermo 42.

Erat Iesus eiciens demonium. Luce 11.

This gospel telluþ how Iesu by a myracle and wytty wordis enformeþ his chirche to fle fro synne and perele þerof. Þe story telluþ how *Iesu was castyng owt a feend of a man, and þis feend was dowmþ*, for he made þis man dowmp. *And whan he hadde cast owht þis feend, þis man dowmþ byforn spak, and þe peple wondrede herof* for 5 gretnesse of þe myracle. But þe enemyes of Crist as weren þe scribes and pharisees, whan þei myhte not denye þis dede for hit was open to þe puple, þei interpretiden hit amys and *seyden þat Crist dide suche wondres in þe power of a fend*, to whom he seruede bussyly; and þis fend was clepud of hem *Belsebub, a prynce of oþre.* 10 And þuse men þat defamedon Crist þus weren preestis or pharisees, *but oþre men* by lesse enuye *axsedon* of Crist *a signe of heuene* to conferme þat he dide þis by þe vertew of God. *But Crist, whanne he knew þer þowtes*, þat þei weren turnede þus from trewþe, by manye resownes prouede hem þat þei weren false in þowt and 15 word. And furst he seyde þus to hem '*Yche rewme deuydet in hymself schal be desolatyd, and hows schal fallen vpon hows.* And þus, *ʒif Sathanas be deuyded in hymself, as ʒe seyn, how schal his rewme stonde* stabully wiþowten ende? For siþ ʒe seyn þat I caste owt a feend by anoþur, nedis o feend mot be contrarye to anoþur.' Þe furste 20

MSS: D; ABCEFGHIJKLMNSTXYZαβδ.

Dominica . . . euangelium] *om.* αZ   sermo 42] *om.* BCFKLNSTYαδEIXZG-
H   erat . . . demonium] estote imitatores dei sicut filii karissimi N   demonium]
demonium et illud F, *om.* H   luce 11] luce ii (2) EI, luce 4 L, luce ix G, ad eph. 5
N   1 this] þe N   2 fro] *om.* AN   and] a β   perele] peryles δ   3
owt] *om.* N   of] out of N   þis] þe I   4 þis] þe E   5 herof] þerof
δZ   6 þe¹] þis EI   þe³] *om.* AYαI   7 and] and þe NEG   8 open] sa
open Z   þei] *om.* Nδ   þat crist] he T   9 þe] ⌐þe¬ H, *om.* E   10 clepud]
cald NαδZ   a] ⌐ai¬ α, *om.* E   11 men] *om.* CK   crist þus] *rev.* S   or] of
α   12 of²] fro N   13 þis] þus NT   þe] *om.* NTE   god] almyʒti god
N   14 knew] kewe C   15 resownes] resoun S   hem] to hem BZ   16
deuydet] deuyd Y   in] into E   hymself] hymsilf, -y- *canc.* -⌐e¬- *corr.* F, hymself,
-y- *altered from* -e- J   17 desolatyd] disolat YI, desolatid or diffoundyd N
δ   hows²] houses δ   18 in hymself] in hym in hymself C   his] þis I   19
stabully] stable E, *om.* I   20 anoþur¹] power of anoþer N   nedis . . . anoþur²]

word þat Crist took is soþ by opon resoun, for þe strenkþe of a
rewme comeþ of acord of þe partyes of hit. And ȝif on contrarieþ
anoþur, nedis þe strenkþe is enfebled; and ȝif þe partis muten
euere lasten, and on wyte anoþres state, þat rewme mot nede be
25 desolate, al ȝif þese partyes schullen lasten ay. For oon hows of a
more miȝty prince schal fallen vpon anoþur hows, and by fiȝtyng
among hem schal al þe rewme be febled; siþ þese partyes ful
acorded schulden helpe þis rewme and maken hit strong. And
riȝt as a ruynows hows falluþ on anoþur and brekiþ hit, so o
30 meyne of a rewme falleþ on anoþur and fe[b]luþ hit. And so
schulde hit be of þe feendys, ȝif o prynce contraryede anoþur.
And so, ȝif Sathanas prince of feendis be þus diuyded in hymself,
how schulde his rewme be strenkþed by dedis þat Crist doþ? But
myche more Cristis rewme þat is strengþed aȝenes þe feend
35 schilde haue anoþur prynce contrarye to Sathanas.
    Also ' *ȝif I caste owȝt a feend in vertew of Belsebub, ȝowre children,* þat
ben my postlis, *in whose name schulde þei casten owt fendis?* Certis, not
in my name, for þan I were a wyckide man. And siþ þei don
f.89 comunly þus in my name þat is|Iesu, *þei schal iuge ȝow* as false in
40 þis interpretacion. *But certus,* ȝif Crist caste owt þus þe fend⌈is⌉ in
special werk of God, *þe rewme of God,* þat is his chirche, *is comen
among hem.* And so þe heed of þis chyrche, contrarye to
Sat⌈h⌉anas, is comen among hem, in whose vertew þese dedis ben
done. And so by chasyng of þese fendis don by Crist in þis maner
45 myȝte þei wel wyten þat Crist was euene contrarye to þe fendis.

om. N   mot] muste BCK, bihoued Z   contrarye] contrarius S   22 acord]
an acord F   þe] *om.* K   on] ony LM   contrarieþ] contrarie to BZ,
contraryeth to δ, contrary Cα   23 þe¹] is þe N   strenkþe] strengere H   is]
om. KN   enfebled] feblid SH   24 wyte] wiþ Fδ   25 desolate] desolatid E,
desolatid or defouled Nδ   al ȝif] and ȝif S, as ȝif I   þese] þe E, hit so be þat þuse
N   schullen] schulden N   ay] euere E   26 anoþur hows] an hous of
anoþere H   27 al] *om.* I   28 þis] *om.* S   29 as] so as I   ruynows]
renenus C, rewmes N   hows] *om.* T   on] vpon α   and . . . anoþur (30)]
om. Z   o] ⌈oo⌉ H, *om.* LM   30 febluþ] felluþ D, enfebliþ A, brekiþ β   so] *om.*
S   31 hit] *om.* K   contraryede] contraryeth to δ, contrarieþ I   33 his] þis
S   by] by þe N   35 to] vnto N   36 in] in þe S   vertew of] *om.*
I   37 schulde] schulen NSα   38 þan] þ- *on eras. corr.* D   39 comunly þus] *rev.*
ABCKLMNSTαβEJZ, þus I, þis comynly Yδ   þat] for *eras.* þat D   40
interpretacion] ⌈in⌉terpretacion C, terpretacioun β   certus] *om.* S   þe] *om.*
δE   fendis] is *corr.* D   41 þe . . . god] *om.* F   his] þis M   42 hem] men
CK   contrarye] contrarieþ, -þ *canc.* Y, contraryeth S   43 sathanas] h *corr.*
D   vertew] vertues C, name α   44 so] *om.* SY   chasyng] chaungyng
T   þese] þe⌈rs⌉ δ, þe CN   in] on E   45 myȝte þei] *rev.* α   wel wyten] *rev.*

And þanne Crist was a spirit, þat was nedis boþe God and man.
Also '3if a strong man wel armed kepe his castel, alle ⌜þe⌝ þingus þat he
haþ þerynne ben surly kepte in pees. And 3if on strengore þan he
come on hym and vencusche hym, he wole taken awey hise armys in whyche
he affyede hym. And siþ þis is don to fendis, as 3e may se by þer   50
dedis, 3e mute graunte þat o prynce more strong þan þe fend is
comen.' Þis strong[e] man is þe feend, his armes ben hise cawtelus,
his castel ben hise lymes þat he dwelliþ ynne; þe strengore is Crist
þat comeþ vpon þe feend þat vencusched þe heed feend in hise
þre temptaciones, and ofte tymes he caste owht fendis of men.   55
Alle þe cautelus of þe feend took Crist awey, and kyndely
vertewis of men þat þe feend spulede Crist delte graciously a3en,
as þe gospel telluþ. And, as Matheu seiþ, Crist took awey þe
vesselus of men þus seghede wiþ feendus, whan he dide awey þer
synnes þat weren fulle of venym to 3iue men to drynkon, and þe   60
powerus of þe sowle Crist fulde wiþ vertewys.

Also þe generalte of lordschipe of Crist s[ch]eweþ þat þe
feendus ben contrarye to hym. For whoeuere is not wiþ Crist, he is
a3en hym, as whoeuere is not wiþ trewþe holdeþ wiþ falsehede;
and whoeuere gedreþ not wiþ Crist, scatereþ of his good. And siþ þe   65
feend is not wiþ Crist, he mut nede ben a3enes hym. And herfore
comaundide Crist þe feendes þat he caste owt þat þei schulde not
speke to wytnessen his godhede, for þese weren false witnesses to
proue such a trewþe. And here supposeþ Crist þat he is trewþe,

E   euene . . . was¹ (46)] om. N   þe] þes KE   46 and¹] om. β   nedis]
om. δ   47 wel armed] rev. δ   kepe] kepiþ Y, kepʳteˑ¹ H, kept CKN   alle]
and alle T   þe] corr. D, þo NE, þese S, om. AYδH   48 strengore] be strengere
S   49 vencusche] ouercome N   hym²] om. F   wole] wold, -d canc. Cα,
wolde NTδ   armys] armurs KNG, armure Y   50 he] om. S   affyede]
tristide E   52 stronge] strongo D   armes] armurs KN, harmes B
δ   cawtelus] castelis L   53 castel] castels -s canc. Y, castelis LNαEH   hise]
om. E   þat . . . ynne] in þe wuche he dwelleþ N   he] om. β   54 comeþ]
comen N   vencusched] ouercome NT   feend] om. Y   55 ofte] of
C   tymes] tyme KH   he] þorw his my3t he N   caste] castis αI   owht]
om. I   56 þe¹] om. K   cautelus] casteles CKLβ   took crist] rev.
H   took] to β   kyndely] kyndelide, -de canc. F, kyndiled C   57 of] in
F   þe] om. α   spulede] dispoilide FJ   58 þe¹] om. M   59 seghede]
segeth S   feendus] þe fendes I   whan] and whanne B   60 of venym] om.
M   to drynkon] drinke Y   þe] om. E   62 scheweþ] seweþ Dβ, shewed
α   63 whoeuere] whosoeuer αδZ, who/for whosoeuere S, so euer N   he] om.
Bα   64 whoeuere] whosoeuer NSαδZ   65 whoeuere] whosoeuer Nαδ-
Z   scatereþ] he scatereth δ   of] om. J   66 hym] criste α   herfore]
þerfore Z   67 þe] to þe E   68 wytnessen . . . false] om. S   his] of his
CK   þese] þey Mα   witnesses] witnes αδ   69 a] ʳaˑ¹ α, om. AYI   70

70 and þat þe feend is fadur of lesyngus, and þat his lordschipe haþ noon enemye but falsehede. And þanne is þe resoun pleyn by his general lordschipe, and by contraryete of þe feend þat was ofte schewed. And aftur þese fyue resownes Crist telluþ a scharp sentence of

75 malis of þe feend, and how þat hit is endyd. '*Whan an vnclene spiri3t is went owt from a man, he wandreþ by drye places and sekiþ hym reste, and whan he fyndeþ noon, he seiþ to hymself "I schal turnen a3en to þat hows þat I cam offe". And whan he comeþ to þat hows, he fyndeþ hit ydel, clensyd wiþ besomes and schynygly arayed. Þanne he goþ and takeþ*

80 *wiþ hym seuene oþre spirites worse þan hymself, and þei entred into þe man dwellon in hym. And þus þe laste of þis man ben werse þan he was aforn.*' Þis vnclene spirit is þe heed feend, and þis man enseghed by hym is þe kynrade of Iewes of whom Crist schulde come. And þerfore he assaileþ hyt; but patriarkes and hooly fadres fowten wel a3en

85 þe feend, þat hym þowte he hadde no3t þere a plesyng place to dwellon ynne. And so he wente to heþene folc þat weren wiþowte grace, and 3et hym lykede not wiþ hem for þer kyndely resoun. And þanne þe feend seyde to hymself þat hee wolde gon a3en to generacion of Crist and peruerten hit more. And in tyme þat

f.89v 90 prestes reignedon he entrede to aspyen|hit. And he fond hit ydel fro kepyng of Godis lawe, and ocupyed wiþ mannys lawe þat sownede vnto coueytise; and by þis þei swepton þe comunte of men, and maden hem bare and coolde as flores ben made, but howses of preestis weren worldly arayede, and þei kepton as

95 sacramentis monye of here fyndyngus. And by þese þe feend

þat¹] at C   þat²] þay ⌈þai3⌉ C   71 þe] *om.* I   72 by] be his, his *canc.* α, bi his
I   contraryete] contrarye⌈te⌉ δ, contrarie β, contrariouste N   ofte] of F   74
þese] þe Y   fyue] *om.* I   a] and β   75 hit] *om.* M   76 is] *om.*
S   from] of *canc.* ⌈fro⌉ α, of E   wandreþ] walkeþ N   77 noon] not
H   to²] in *canc.* to F, into Y   78 offe] out of K   hit] *om.* CY   79
besomes] besynesse S   and¹] of T   80 þan hymself] hym þan silf K, þan he
himself I   and] is and S   entred] entryng L, entur α, entriþ J   þe] þat
Nαl   81 dwellon] ⌈and⌉ dwellen G, and dwellen T, for to dwelle α, to duellen δ,
dwellyng H   laste] laste þingis H   aforn] bifore ABCKLMNSTY-
αβδEIJXZ   82 is] w *canc.* is B, was K   83 iewes] þe iewis A   whom] *om.*
I   and] ⌈and⌉ H, *om.* G   84 assaileþ] assailide ABE   fadres] men S   85
hym] he I   he] þat he δE   hadde] nadde I   place] dwellynge place
H   86 so] *om.* I   he] *om.* S   87 hym] he CK   88 to²] to ⌈þe⌉ J, to þe
BSαH   89 and¹] to B   in] in ⌈þe⌉ T, in þe CKβI   90 he²] *om.* Tα   91
kepyng of] *om.* I   wiþ] it wiþ I   92 sownede] sownes Z   vnto] into CKα, to
E   þei] *om.* T   swepton] schepton T   comunte] cominalte AY   93
flores] bare flores N, floures A   made] *om.* N   94 þei] ⌈þat⌉ þei H, þat þey
I   95 fyndyngus] fyndyng M   þese] þis LMαE   96 hem] him

þowte þat he schulde ouercomen hem. And he gederyde to hym
alle maner of feendis and dwelte wiþ þis puple, and made hem
worste men, for þei growedon euere in malice tyl þei hadden
kyllud Crist. And þus, seiþ Crist, schal be to þis worste kynrade,
siþ ende of mennys wykkidenesse was for to slee Crist. And so hit   100
is licly þat þe chirche faruþ now by sleyng of trewþe þat is in
Godis lawe, so þat men in erþe-clepude cristene men passen in
malice Iewes and Sarazenys. And roote of þis malice is coueytyse
of prestys, and leuyng of Godis lawe and hy3yng of mannys lawe;
by þis is þe comunte of þe puple maad pore and swept as þe   105
pawment from hulyng of stree, and cooldid in charyte, boþe
þei and preestes. But howses of prestes ben worldly arayede and þis
aray is hy3ed from partyng of comunes; and þis is wey3e of
anticrist and ende of þe laste yuel. And sone aftyr þes lyf schal
come þe day of doom; but byfore, 3if God wole, þe chirche schal   110
be mendyt. And þis is moste perelows harm þat þe chirche hadde
euere, for cautelys of anticrist disseyuen manye men.

*And whan Iesu seyde þese wordes, a womman of þe puple hy3ede hire
voys and seyde þus to Crist 'Blessyd be þe wombe þat bar þe into þis world,
and blessyd be þe tetis þat þow hast sowkyd.'* But Crist blessuþ more þe men   115
þat heren Godis word and kepon hit wiþowten lesyng, as owre Lady
dide; for þis by hymself makiþ a man blessud. And hit is ly3cly þat
þis womman vndirstod Cristis wordis, and herfore sche blesside
þe modir þat bar such a child.

I   gederyde] gidere A   97 þis] þe Z   98 worste] wurse Nl   þei¹
. . . malice] þer malice woxe euer more and more N   growedon] groundeden
δ   euere] more Y   tyl] til þat T   99 kyllud] sleyn EZ   be to þis] to
canc. þis be ⌈to⌉ C   to] do to T   þis] þe MTδ   kynrade] kynrades
δ   100 ende] þe eende YαE, ⌈þe wickid⌉ ende F, om. G   mennys] manus
CKSTαG   101 faruþ] fare M   þat²] om. K   102 clepude] called
NαδZ   cristene] cristis I   103 iewes] þe iewes E   and¹] or//and
E   roote] þe rote E   þis] om. T   malice] maleise J   104 godis] cristys
S   105 by] bis β   þe¹] om. Y   comunte] comynalte AY   þe²] þe canc.
X, om. ABKMSTYβδEZ   þe³] a H   106 cooldid] coold BG, so arn þei colde
N   107 preestes] þe prestis H   howses . . . prestes] þe prestus houses
N   ben] but K   and þis] twice Y   and²] bote N   108 hy3ed] heid, -e-
canc. A, hid BCKNTαδEZ   of] wiþ þe N   and . . . men (112)] om. Z   wey3e] þe
way CKMαJ   110 but] þat E   þe² . . . schal] schal þe chirche G   111
mendyt] amendid, a-eras. X, amendid FαδEIJG   and] in T   þis . . . moste]
moost þis is S   moste] þe moost AIH   112 disseyuen] is deceyuynge of
α   113 whan] whanne canc. F   114 þe¹] om. Mβ   115 tetis] pappis
δZ   blessuþ] blessid ABCFKNSTαβδEIJGH   þe²] þe⌈se⌉ H, þes
ABCKLMNSTYαβδEIJXZ   116 hit] hem L   lesyng] leosyng D, losynge
α   117 hymself] itself CKβ, hemselfe δ   118 herfore] þerfore Z   119 such a]
þe S   child] praie we to þis child go graunte vs of his grace etc. N

Dominica iiii Quadragesime. [Euangelium.]
Sermo 43.

Abiit Iesus trans mare. Iohannis 6.

This gospel telluþ þe furste feeste þat Crist maade to þe puple by multiplyyng of mete, as þ⌐r⌐e gospellis tellen. *Þe story telluþ þat Iesu wente ouer þe watyr of Galilee, þat is clepud Tyberyadis and monye oþre names for townes and cuntrees þat hit ȝede bytwyxen. And a*

5 *greet multitude sewede Crist herfore þat þei sayȝen þe signes þat Crist dide on syke men.* And Iesus, whan he cam ouur þis watur of Galilee, *he wente into an hyl and sat þere wiþ hise disciples. And Pasch was ful nyȝ, a greet feeste among Iewes. And whan Iesu caste vp hise eiȝen, and saw a ful greet multitude was comen to hym, he seyde vnto Philip 'Wherof schulle we*

10 *bugghe loues þat þese men ete?' And þis seyde Crist to tempte Philip, for he wiste what he was to do. And Philip seyde to Crist þat loues of two hundret pens suffisede not to hem, þat eche man take a luytelwhat. And on of Cristis disciples, Andrew, Petres broþur, seyde to Crist ' Þer was a child þat hadde fyue barly looues and two fysches, but what ben þese among so manye men?'*

15 *And Iesu seyde to hem to maken hem sytte down to þe mete, for þere was myche heyȝ in þe same place. And so þei sat to þe mete, as fyue þowsande men. And Iesu took þese fyue loues, and ȝaf þankyng to God, and delude*

---

2 Matt. 14: 13–21; Mark 6: 32–44; Luke 9: 10–17.

MSS: D; ABCEFGHIKLMNSTXYZαβδ; J *ends incompl.* 58 poynt.

Dominica . . . euangelium] *om.* αZ   sermo 43] *om.* BCFKLNSTYαδEIJXZ-
GH   abiit . . . mare] christus nos liberavit N   mare] mare galilei F-
αδGH   iohannis 6] iohannis vi . . . ad galat. iiii N, iohannis C   1 þe¹] of þe
N   2 þre] r *corr.* D   *margin* mt. 14, mr. 6, luc 9 M   3 clepud] cald
NαδZ   4 townes] contres ABCKLMNSTYαβδEIJZG   cuntrees] touns ABCKL-
MNSTYαβδEIJZG   ȝede] wente H   5 crist¹] him H   herfore] for
α   þe] þes CK   6 on] in Y, to I   þis] þe *canc.* ⌐þis⌐ α, þe Z   8 iewes] þe
iewes NSαEZH   caste] hadde caste H   and²] a S   ful] *om.* H   9 was
comen] cam H   to] vnto L   he] and he H   vnto] to H   10 ete] shal ete
L, may ete T, miȝten ete I   þis] þus δI   seyde crist] *rev.* E   crist] crist to
philip H   11 wiste . . . he] *om.* M   what] wel what I   he] *om.* CTδ-
I   to crist] *om.* M   12 suffisede] ne suffiȝeden I   take] toke KI   13 þat]
þere þat I   14 men] *om.* N   15 to maken] make L   sytte] to sytte
δIH   down] adowne CKβ   down . . . mete] to mete doun I   þe] ⌐þe⌐ α,
om. BH   16 same] *om.* N   sat] seten doun E   þe²] *om.* H   as] and *canc.*

among þese syttynge men, and also of þe fysches, as myche as þei wolden.
And whanne þei weren fullyde, Crist seyde to hise disciples, 'Gedre ȝe þat
ben laft, releues, þat þei perysche not.' And so þei gedreden, and fulden   20
twelue cophynes of relef of fyue barly loues and two fyschis þat weren lefte of
hem þat hadden eton. And þese men, whan þei hadden\seyn þe syngne þat   f.90
Crist hadde don, þei seyden þus of hym 'þis a verrey prophete þat is to
comen into þis world.'

Þis bodily foode by whiche Crist fedde þe folc bytokneþ gostly   25
fode, by whiche he fediþ mankynde. His passyng ouer þis watur
wiþ hise disciples is passyng ouer worldly perelis to take Godis
loore. Cristus syttyng in þis hul is rysyng to spiritual lyf, and
Cristes lookyng on þe puple is gostly mercy do to hem. And
steiyng into þe hul of Iesu wiþ hise disciples is takyng of goostly   30
lyȝf for to lerne Cristes lawe. Axsyng of Philip, þat was maad to
schewe þe myracle more, and for to haue betture in muynde, is
fullyng of Godes word in deede. Þese fyue loues þat Andrew
schewede ben hard lyf, þat men mote lyue byfore þei konnen
Cristus lore. And two fysches ben þenkyng of God and heuene.   35
Syttyng down in þe heyȝ is meeke þowt of mannys frelte. And so
Andrew vndurstod more þan Philip þat God, þat mult[i]plyede
mete as þe lawe telluþ by Helisee, myȝte liȝtly multiplye þis
mete, and so feden al þis puple; but wiþowten myracle myȝte not

---

38 2 Kgs. 4: 43.

as C, and S   17 þankyng] þankyngis KZ   18 among] hem among E, it among
I   þe] þes CKE   19 to] vnto δ   20 ben] is L   releues] relif
M   þei¹] it L   and²] þai C   21 weren lefte] leften Y   weren] was
L   22 þe] þis MI   þat crist] of crist þat he δ   23 don] þer doun I   of]
to J   to comen] comyn CKTδG   24 into] vnto T   25 þe] þis KSTYαI   26
he] god I   fediþ] fed CKβ   his] is *canc.* his C, is I   passyng] goynge
T   þis] þe, -e *canc.* -ʳisˀ α, þe TI   watur] water of galilee T   27 godis]
goodis, *2nd-o- canc.* D   28 þis] þe K   and] *om.* G   29 on] in I   do to] to
don, *marked for rev.* H, to do to BN, to do L, do F   31 for to] to I   lerne] lere
αZ   cristes] crist β   maad] s *canc.*/maad D   to²] for to CKLMNSTY-
αβδIXZH   32 þe] þis E   more] þe more A   for to] to G   haue] hold it
α   in] *om.* G   is] h- *eras.* D, his BCδI   33 fullyng] ʳfulˀfilling K, fulfillyng
FGH   þese] þe I   34 lyue] lede α   byfore] bifore þat I   konnen] come to
δE   35 two] *om.* Z   ben] er to be Z   þenkyng] thankyng C   of god]
ʳgod ofˀ K   of] on NYEI   and²] in *canc.* K, in CTδ   36 down] *om.*
I   in] on NYδ   meeke] heiȝ I   þowt] þenkyng E   of] on Y   man-
nys] mennus ABCKLMNSTYαβEIJXZH   frelte] flesche L   37 andrew
vndurstod] *rev.* N   multiplyede] multplyede D   38 mete] þe mete H   as
. . . helisee] *om.* N   *margin re.* 4g H   helisee] helise þe profete Yδ   myȝte . . . so (40)] was myȝhty for to N   39 feden] fedde T   al] *om.* N   but]

40 so myche puple be fed of Crist. And þese fyue þowsande of men
wiþowte wymmen and children ben þe nowmbre þat schal be
sauyd by þis spirytual foode, for fyue is a rownde nowmbre þat
turneþ wiþowten eende into hymself; and so not alle þat ben fed
þus schullen come to þe blisse of heuene. Þe twelue cophynes of
45 relif ben alle þe seyntis gloses þat ben gedered of Godis lawe to
feede þe puple afterward. And goostly loore haþ proprete to be
multiplyed in men, for of o lore comeþ anoþur, and al is þe same
trewþe. And by þis fode men þanken God, and seyn þat Crist is
þat greete prophete þat is to comen into þis world and fullen hit of
50 heuenely lore. For of oþre myracles of Crist þis myracle is on of þe
meste: þat so fewe disciples of hise fylledon þe world in so schort
tyme wiþ þe same gospel of Crist; and he hit was þat dide þis
myracle.

And here men meuon þre dowtis. Furst how Crist absentyde
55 hym fro Ierusaleem at þis pasc, siþ Baptist hertly repreuede
Herowde, and Crist was more hardy þan Iohn for to suffre
passioun for þe loue of mankynde. But here we trowen þat Iesu
Crist, siþ he is boþe God and man, dide alle hise dedis at poynt
deuys, and myhte no weyȝe ben amendyd. And þus he absentede
60 hym now to profiȝte more to his chirche, for his tyme was not
come to dyen at þe Pasc þat he hadde ordeynot. For, as men seyn
comunly, Crist muste passe þis secounde Pasch, and in þe þridde
Pasch dye gladly for mankynde. And so Crist suffrede more freely
þan Baptist or oþre martires, but he was more nedid by wisdam to
65 suffren as hymself hadde cast. And so, as Crist hymself hadde
ordeyned, Baptist schulde dye byfore, and so go to purgatorye,

þeygh þei hadden be mony mo bote N   40 and] om. E   þese] þis CI, so þese
G   42 for] fo M   43 into] to β   hymself] hitsilf H   fed] om. I   44
to] into N   þe¹ . . . heuene] heuene blis E   þe¹] om. I   45 relif] relyfes
ABLMNSTYEIJ   þe] þese S   46 þe] om. G   proprete] propre Cβ   be]
om. Y   47 of] om. Z   is] þis is δI   48 seyn] sythen δ   49 þat¹] þe BI,
a Y   world] w/world   and] þorw his vertu and his grace to N   fullen]
fulfille E, fillid T   hit] om.T   50 myracle] om. NI   is] was E   52 þis] þe
L   54 and] om. J   55 hertly . . . herowde (56)] reprouyde heroude hertly
EI   hertly repreuede] rev. α   56 more hardy] hardier H   hardy] herty and
hardy N   for to] to EG   57 þe] om. EJ   iesu] ⌜iesu⌝ αGH   58 crist] om.
δ   is] was X   59 no weyȝe] on no wise Nδ   no] bi no F   he] om.
S   61 come] nowe come δ   þe] þat F   62 comunly] comyn Y   muste]
mote EI   þis] þe T   63 pasch] om. I   freely] ⌜frely⌝ for mankynde E   64
oþre] om. B.   martires] apostelis I   but] duden bote N   65 hadde] om.
I   crist] om. F   66 go . . . purgatorye] eras. N   purgatorye] buriall (modern

and be taken owt by Crist. And þus Crist ȝaf ensaumple to vs to
flee deþ whanne he meueþ vs, as al his lyf was ensaumple to teche
men how þei schulde lyue.

The secounde dowte is axsed here, why Crist wolde not take þe   70
rewme of Iude þat was owyd to hym, siþ þe puple profrede hit
hym anon aftyr þis myracle þat Crist hadde fed þus þe folc. But
here men seyn as to þe furste þat hit were a maner of bigyng to haue
þe rewme for such a feeste, and of puple þat was so symple. Also,
al ȝif Crist was kyng, he wolde not þus reigne worldlily, ne hym   75
was owed no sych|rewme, siþ God wolde not þat hit were so. Also   f.90v
Crist ordeyned hymself to lyue wiþowte wrong of anye man, and
so he wolde not reigne þus wiþowte þe emperowres leue, þat men
schulden wyte þat his lyf no weye reuersude þe emperowr; and so
wytnesses þat acusodon hym in tyme of his deþ weren oponly   80
false. And þus, as owre Lord forsok to be looued of þe feendis, so
he forsok now to take þis rewme þus of þis puple.

The þridde dowte þat seweþ þese two is how Crist myȝte
disseruen in suffryng of his passioun, siþ he was nedud to suffre
þus. But here we wyton, as Crist was nedud to suffre and dyen as   85
he hadde ordeynot, so he was nedyt to haue blisse for þis willeful
passioun, siþ al þis passioun of Crist was more willeful þan oþur
myȝte be; and for so myche wilfulnesse was his passioun more
medful. And here þese blynde heretykes wanton wyt as ydiotes,
whan þei seyn þat Petur synnede not in smytyng of Malcus here,   90

corr.) K   67 ensaumple] an enswmple β   68 meueþ] meuede N, moruenyþ
β   as] and S   was ensaumple] rev. I   to] to vs to I   69 schulde] schal,
-a-altered from -u-, -de canc. X, shal ABCKLMNTβ   70 dowte] dede I   wolde]
scholde I   þe] þis CKβ   71 iude] iury α   puple] om. M   hit]ᵣitᵔ A, om.
Sβ   72 hym] to canc. hym N, to him LZ   crist] om. I   fed þus] rev.
N   þe] -e on eras. corr.D, þis S   but] by miracle of his myȝte N   73
here . . . seyn] men seyen here N   men] we CKβ   as] om. N   furste þat]
firste þat maner of buggyng N   a . . . bigyng] om. N   bigyng] beggyng
T   74 þe] þis E   of] of þe, þe canc. Y, of þe BE   so] ᵣsoᵔ C, om. T   75 al
ȝif] ȝif I   was] were Bδ   kyng] a king I   he] for he M   not] nouȝ
I   þus reigne] rev. TI   worldlily] worldely ABKNSTYαG   ne] no
L   76 wolde] om. C   not] om. I   77 hymself] hym I   78 so] om.
K   79 schulden] s/schulden D   wyte] no wey wite I   þat] of β   no] by
no N, om. I   weye] wyse δ, om. I   reuersude] reuerse β   80 wytnesses]
wittenesse CNαI   81 þus] so H, om. E   looued] preisid AFNH, preisid or loued
δ   þe] om. α   feendis] fende δ   82 now] om. T   þisᵔ] þe
ABCKLMNSTYαδIXZ   þis²] þe IH   85 asᵔ] þat as E, þat Z   suffre] -n eras.
D   86 heᵔ] om. Y   hadde] om. N   þis] his E   87 more] om.
K   willeful] medeful F   oþur] ᵣonyᵔ oþer A, ony oþer BCKδE   88 more]
þe more Nδ   90 þat] om. I   here] eere BTYαXGH   91 ensaumple]

but ȝaf ensaumple ⌜to⌝ preestis to fiȝte, and þus Crist lettud hym
to fiȝte more; for hadde Petre and oþre apostles fowten þus,
þanne þei hadden lettud þe passion of Iesu Crist and sauyng of
mankynde. But here þese blynde heretykes, þat ben vnable to
95 conceyue sutilte of holy writ, schulden furst lerne þer owne
wordis. Soþ hit is þat alle þingus mote nede come as God haþ
ordeyned, and so eche dede of Crist mut nede be doon as he dide
hyt. And þus, ȝif men schulde not sewe Crist her, fore he muste
neede suffre, noo cristene man schulde sewe Crist in noo þing þat
100 he dyde, for alle þe þingus þat Crist dide musten nedly comen as
þei cam. And so suche heretykes musten nede sewen anticrist and
be dampned wiþ hym for defawte of here byleue. And ȝif þei seyn
þat þis is false, þat alle þingus mute þus nedely come – Lord! how
dremýden þese foolys þanne þat, ȝif Petur hadde fowte forþ
105 þanne, Crist schulde not haue suffred deþ ne haue bowt mannys
kynde? Certes þese ydiotis kan not schewe how þis schulde sewen
of any trewþe, but ȝif þei supposen here þat þus hit muste nedis
be. And ȝif we schulden herfore lette to take ensawmple to sewe
Crist, we schulden lette euermore to sewe Crist and take his lore.
110 But, siþ Crist reprouede Petre, and seyde a cause general þat
'whoeuere smyteþ þus wiþ swerd, he schal perische by Godis

104 Matt. 26: 51; Mark 14: 47; Luke 22: 50; John 18: 10–11;	**110** Matt. 26: 52.

exsamplis H	to¹] *corr.* D, *om.* G	to preestis] *twice* I	lettud] letteth δ	92
hadde petre] ȝef petre hade N	and . . . þus] fouȝte þus and oþer aposteles N	apo-
stles] *om.* E	93 þanne] also N	þei hadden] *rev.* α	lettud] þanne lettyd
N	þe . . . crist] cristis *canc.* þe passion of iesu crist α, cristus passyoun N	iesu
crist] crist iesu *marked for rev.* Y, *rev.* CKH, crist AS	94 but . . . wordis (96)] *om.*
Z	95 sutilte] þe sutilite LE	lerne] lere αH	96 þingus] thynge α	mo-
te . . . come] moten come nede δ	97 ordeyned] ordeyned it C	mut] muste
A	98 her fore] herfore for K, for E	99 cristene] *om.* G	schulde] schulde
noȝt δ	100 þe] *om.* FNYαGH, þese I	musten] moten Fα	nedly] nedis
CKNE	101 and . . . lore (109)] *om.* Z	nede] nedely α	102 for] for þe
S	here] *om.* S	103 þingus] þing ACKLMNSTYαβEX	mute] moste
α	þus nedely] *rev.* H	þus] ⌜þus⌝ α, *om.* LδI	nedely come] *rev.*
T	come] þus δI	104 dremyden] dremen H	fowte] c/fowte D	105
crist . . . not] scholde nouȝt crist I	ne] to F	mannys kynde] mankynd
ANαδEIGH	107 of] *om.* S	supposen] supposeden CKS	muste] mut
ANαEIH	108 herfore lette] lette herfore *marked for rev.* K, lette herfore I	109
lette euermore] *rev.* E	euermore] to *canc.* euermore D	his] ensaumple *canc.* his
D, þis F	111 whoeuere] whosoeuer NαδZ	swerd] a swerd N	112 knowe]

word', hit is knowe þing þat Petre synnede in þis fiȝtyng; and
more schulden preestes fiȝte not for a cause of lasse valu.

wel knowen N   þis] his L   113 more] ⌜muche⌝ more δ, myche more
E   preestes] not prestis H   fiȝte not] feyȝten not *marked for rev.* δ, *rev.* FαEZ,
fiȝten H   a] *om.* CKNβ   valu] valewe bote we schulden bysyen vs to fyȝten
aȝeynes oure oune foule synnes to wynne vs wiþ oure fyȝhtynge þe blisse of heuen þat euer
schal laste and þat we haue grace þus to fyȝhte preie we to god almyȝthi etc. N

Dominica in Passione. [Euangelium.] Sermo 44.

Quis ex uobis arguet me de peccato. Iohannis 8.

This gospel techeþ byleue by hiȝe wordis þat Crist spac, and how
men schulden lyue þeraftur and trowen in Crist and sewen hym.
Furst axseþ Crist þat *who of hem schal reprouen hym of synne*; and he
wolde mene þat noon myhte. And so Crist myȝte not do synne,
5 for ȝif he myȝte ⌜haue⌝ synned, þe Iewes myȝten haue reproued
hym of synne, as þei enforsedon manye gatis; but þei traueyledon
in veyn. And here we vndirstonden repref for mater þat is trewe
for cause þerof, as false peny is no peny, so false repref is no repref,
for eche þing mut haue trewþe in þat þat hit haþ beyng. And in
10 þis word Crist wolde mene þat he was boþe God and man, for, ȝif
he hadde not be God, he myȝte haue synned as aungelus diden.
And hit were lyȝt for to synne in veyn glorie or in gabbyng, for
eche gabbyng is synne; and Crist gabbyde or he was God. And
f.91 aftyr þis byleue of Crist|proueþ he þat þei schulden trowen hym,
15 for, siþ he seiþ but trewþe to hem, as he may no gatis synnen, þei
schulden trowen vnto þat trewþe, siþ þat God knoweþ alle
trewþe. And herfore seiþ þe word of Crist þat, *ȝif he seye trewþe,
why trowen þei noȝt to hym?* But, as Crist soþly takeþ, *he þat is on Godes
syde he heruþ Godes wordis* or bodily or spiritually, siþ no man ⌜may⌝

MSS: D; ABCEFGHIJKLMNSTXYZαβδ.

Dominica . . . euangelium] þe fyfþe sondai gospel in lente AM, *om.* αZ   sermo 44]
om. BCFKLNSTYαδEIJXZGH   quis . . . peccato] sanguis christi emundabit
conscienciam nostram N   me . . . peccato] *om.* A   iohannis 8] iohannis
viii . . . ad hebre ix N   1 techeþ] telliþ BCKNβH   2 schulden] shulen
H   3 axseþ] axide Kβ   þat] ⌜þat⌝ GH   schal] schulde K   *margin* eccᵃ
17 M   4 so] ⌜so⌝ T, *om.* L   do synne] synne N   5 he] ȝe β   haue] *corr.*
D   6 enforsedon] enforseden hem L, enforsis Z   gatis] weyes Nα   þei
. . . veyn (7)] al in veyn þei traueyleden N   7 repref] reprooth S   trewe] treuþe
L   8 for] and for CKLM   þerof] of E   as] for als CK, as ⌜a⌝ δ, as a TE-
J   repref¹] proue α   9 for . . . beyng] *om.* N   þat þat] þat SE   12 for²]
and CKβ   13 gabbyde] oþer gabbide LM   or] or ellis BNZ, ⌜not⌝ for FJ, not for
δ, er S   14 he] here J   15 as] so as δ   no] *om.* M   gatis] gate H, wey
N   16 vnto] to K   trewþe] *om.* I   þat] *om.* FE   god] *om.* β   17 þat]
om. N   he] y N   seye] seiþ ABYJG   18 trowen] leue N   þei noȝt] *rev.*
H   þei] ȝe N   to] in L   hym] me N   he] *om.* FNIJG   19 wordis]
word KE   or¹] outher CKLNαδEZH   spiritually] goostly Y   may] *corr.*

be but ʒif he here trewþus or o tyme or oþur. And so þese hiʒe 20
prestys of Iewes *heren not þus Godis wordis, for þei be not on Godis half,*
and þanne þei ben wiþ þe feend. But þese Iewes conceyuedon
þese wordes how þei weron scharply seyde to hem, and þei
hadden no weye to answere ne to replye aʒeynes hym. And
herfore þei bygan to chyde and acuseden Crist wiþowten cause. 25
And two þingus þei putten on hym, furst þat *he was a Samaritan, siþ*
þat he hadde a fend þat was felow and help to hym. But Crist lefte
answere to þe furste, and þe secownde he denyʒede; and so he
grauntede in a maner þat he was a Samaritan, siþ he was kepere
of mankynde as he telluþ in a parable. Þat man is seyd to hauᵣeˡa 30
feend whom þe feend disseyueþ, as he is seyd to haue an heed þat
is hedid by þis heed, and so of oþre relatyues as clerkis knowen in
maner of speche.

And aftyr þis answere Crist telluþ how he doþ trewþe and þei
don falsehede aʒeyn, for *he doþ worschipe to his Fadur, and þei* 35
vnworschypon hym. He sekeþ not his ᵣouneˡ glorie, but his Fadur sekuþ and
iugeþ. And þis is þe maner of speche þat Crist vseþ ofte þat he by
his manhede doþ not such þing, whan he by þis kynde doþ not
pryncipally þis þing. For Crist seiþ to þis entent þat ᵣ h ˡis lore is
not his, ne þe word þat þei herde is not his but his Fadres. And on 40
þis maner semeþ Ambrose to graunte þat þe sacred ᵣbreedˡ is not
aftur breed but Godis body, for hit is not aftur principally breed,
but Godis body in maner as Austyn seiþ. But, siþ alle werkys of þe
Trinnyte may not be departede, alle þe þre persones sekon glorye

---

30 Luke 10: 30–37.

D   20 he] *om.* S   or¹] oþere FLαδZ, *om.* N   o] ᵣin¹ o H   21 iewes] þe
iewis JGH   heren] herden G   wordis] word Sα   on] of αH   22 þese] þus
þese δ   23 wordes] word S   24 hym] hem I   25 herfore] þerfore Z   acu-
seden] accuse α   26 siþ] and *canc.* siþ AE, ᵣand¹siþ H, and seþin αδ   27 and help]
om. S   crist] *om.* S   28 answere] an answer Z   he¹] *om.* β   29 a¹] alle
S   siþ]sythen þat δ   30 mankynde]mannes kynde α, a mankynde β   in]by
E   haue]e *corr.* D   32 þis] his L   33 maner]a *canc.* maner αG, þer manere
S   speche] spechis Y   35 falsehede] false N   aʒeyn] *om.* N   36
vnworschypon] vnworschipiden, -id -*canc.* Y, vnworshipiden AB   hym] *om.*
Y   sekeþ] spekiþ L   oune] *corr.* D, owne *canc.* X, *om.* CKLMSTYβδI-
Z   sekuþ] spekiþ L   37 speche] speke Y   vseþ] vsid Tα   by . . .
manhede (38)] *om.* Z   38 not¹] no I   þing] þyngis LMTJ   he] *om.*
I   þis] his YE   kynde] mankynde LM   39 þis¹] þus T   þing] þingis
T   for] *om.* S   to] *om.* β   his] h *corr.* D, for his S   40 þe] ᵣþeˡ T, *om.*
FG   þei] *on eras. corr.* D, ʒe ABN, he CLMTβEXZ   herde] here α, seide
I   42 for . . . body (43)] *om.* N, *margin corr.* α   is] *om.* S   aftur principally]
rev. L   43 maner] a maner β   but²] *om.* I   werkys] þe werkis KN-

of Crist. But þe manhede of Crist is herto an instrument. And, as þe ax heweþ not but þe wryȝte by his craft, riȝt so sekiþ not Crist his owne glorie. But Crist, to schewe boþe hise kyndes, dowbleþ þis *amen* and telluþ þat he seiþ soþly to hem þat *whoeuere kepuþ his word schal not taste deþ wiþowten ende*. For he by comun speche kepuþ a þing þat wiþowte leesyng kepuþ þis same þing. And þus, whoeuere kepuþ ony word of Crist, he schal neuere ha⌜ue⌝ þe deþ þat euure schal laste. But here þe Iewes knewe not þe maner of Cristes speche, and replyedon aȝen hym and seyden '*Now we wyton wel þat þow hast a feend* þat leduþ þe in þi deedis. *Abraham was deed, and ⌜oþure⌝ hooly prophetis, and þow seist "whoeuere kepuþ my word schal neuere dyȝe."* Lord! *were þow be moore þan owre fadur Abraham þat is deed, and prophetis also? Whom makestow þe?* Wher þow be more þan onye ⌜of⌝ þese seyntes?' Here may we see þe folye of þese Iewes, for þei kouden ⌜not knowe⌝ dyuersite of þese wordes 'who þat lyueþ þus he schal not taste þe long[e] deþ', and 'whoso lyueþ þus schal neuere taste deþ'.

But Iesu lefte þis folye and spak to þe purpos '*Ȝif I glorifye þus myself, my glorie is noȝt; but I haue a Fadur þat þus glorifieþ me. And ȝe seyn þat he is ȝowre God, but ȝe han not knowen hym; but I haue knowen hym. And ȝif I seyȝe nay, I schal be liȝk to ȝow a lyere.* [*But I knowe hym and I kepe his worde.*] *Abraham ȝowre fadur hadde ioye to se my day, and he*
f.91v *say hit and hadde ioye.*' But here þe Iewes|knewe not þe maner of riȝt speche of Crist, for þei knewe not how Crist clepude God singlerly his

αδ 44 not] no L þe] ⌜þe⌝ T, *om.* YEI glorye] þe glorie SδI 46 wryȝte] carponter TE by] wiþ Y sekiþ . . . crist] crist sekiþ not A 47 to schewe] scheweþ I, to schewe oþere δ boþe hise] his boþe *marked for rev.* α, *rev.* KZ 48 amen] amen amen α whoeuere] whosoeuer NαδZ 50 leesyng] ceessyng F kepuþ[2]] kepe C þis] þe ACKNSαδEIH þus] *om.* BCKLMNSTYβδEIXZ 51 whoeuere] whosoeuer NδZ ony] þus ony BCKLMNSTYβδEIXZ haue] ue *corr.* D þe] *om.* Tα 52 euure] euermore N 53 and[1]] and ⌜þey⌝ A, and þei B 54 wyton] writen β wel] *om.* I þat[1]] *om.* NE was] is N 55 oþure] another S prophetis] profete S whoeuere] þat whoeuere I, whasaeuer Z kepuþ] kepe I word] wordis E 56 be] *om.* M 57 prophetis] þe prophetis I 58 onye] any oþer Nδ of þese[1]] *om.* N seyntes] oþer seintis I þese[2]] þe⌜se⌝ H, þe J 59 kouden not knowe]-ouden not knowe *on eras. corr.* D not] *om.* S þese] þe S who þat] whasa Z 60 he] *om.* KNY not] neuere, n *-eras.* T longe] longo D whoso] who þat Y 61 schal] schal he B, he schal EH neuere] euer N deþ] þe ded α 62 þis] þe deeþ *canc.* þis D, þer M, þer is L þe] *om.* δ ȝif] ⌜and⌝ ȝif H 64 ȝowre] oure I haue knowen] knowe K 65 but . . . worde (66)] *om.* DABCFKLMNSTYβEIJXZGH knowe] ⌜haue⌝ know⌜en⌝ α 66 ȝowre] oure I ioye] grete ioie AB he] *om.* N 67 hadde] he hadde I knewe] kouden L, knowen β maner of riȝt] riȝte manere of I 68 of crist] *om.*

Fadur, for þanne by ri3t speche God was his Fadur in kynde. God
is owre alþere Fadur; but whoeuere of vs seiþ 'God is my Fadur',   70
he blasfemeþ in God. Þis man is my fadur 3if þat I haue proprete
in gendrure of hym byforn oþer men. And þus þese fooles
replyedon a3en þe wordus of Crist and *seyden* ' *þow has not 3et fi3fty
wyntur in age*, and 3et þow menest in þi speche þat *þow hast seen
Abraham.*' And for þer furste blyndnesse þat þei weren to blame   75
fore, Crist spak more derkly to hem þan hee dide byfore and
seyde '*Soþly, soþly,*' (to shewe his two kyndis,) '*byforn þat Abraham
schulde be I am.*' And herfore þei weren depud in worse synne of
dede *whan þei token vp stones* to stone Crist to depe. But *Iesu hidde
hym, and wente owt of þe temple*, as hit was ly3t to hym to huyden   80
hym among manye, for boþe he my3te stoppe þer sy3t and
schewen hym in dyuerse formys. And here he tawte hise disciples
in dede for to flee, but he tawte hem neuere for to fi3te bodily.
And such blessud cowardise makiþ Godis children, siþ Crist seiþ
þat in þer pacience þei schulden ha⌐ue¬ þer li3f in pees. But þe   85
feend techuþ hise children to ben hardye heere, and fi3te
wiþowten heuenly cause; and þus þei leson þer li3f for techyngus
þus contrarye leeden to contrarie eendis.

But we þat ben in byleue ouer þese blynde Iewys schilden
knowe þese wordis of Crist þat he seyde to hem 'byforn þat   90
Abraham schulde be I am'. But, as we wyton by owre byleue þat
þese wordys ben fulle of wyt, so we wyte þat in hem Crist schewede
his godhede; for we wyten wel þat þis word 'I am' bytokneþ þe
godhede. For godhede may not be chaunghed, neyþur fro 3ougþe
to eelde, ne fro worse to beture, for hit is euere on; and a   95

N   knewe] knowe Tβ   clepude] calde NαδZ   singlerly] singulere
α   70 is¹] was I   whoeuere] whoso N, whasaeuer Z   vs seiþ] *rev.*
K   god] ⌐þat¬god AT, þat god BCKLMNSYαβδEIJXZGH   71 þat] ⌐þat¬Yα,
om. NIJ   I] *om.* M   72 in] in þe H   þus] *om.* NH   þese] *om.* E   73
replyedon] replien G   73 3et] ri3t C, *om.* KIZ   74 wyntur] 3eer ABCKLMNS-
TYαβδEJXZ   in¹] of K, *om.* C   menest] mouyst S   75 for] þus for
EI   þer] þe AEI   77 soþly soþly] soþly SδI   soþly² . . . schewe] *on eras.
corr.* D   þat] *om.* ST   78 depud] drouned δ, *om.* E   79 to²] to þe N   82
dyuerse formys] oþer fourmes diuerse I   hise] ⌐to¬ his H, to his EI   83 dede]
drede Z   hem neuere] *rev.* K   for to²] to E   84 cowardise] cowardes
δ   85 schulden] shal ABZ   haue] ue *corr.* D   but . . . eendis (88)] *om.*
Z   87 þus] *om.* E   techyngus] techyng TH   89 ouer] aboue I   90 þese]
þe CY   byforn þat] þat *canc.* bifore E   þat²] *om.* T   91 as] *om.* C   92 in
hem crist] crist in hem M   hem] hym J   93 for . . . godhede¹ (94)] *om.*
L   þat] *om.* G   word] wode β   94 for] for ⌐þe¬T, for þe N   95 eelde]

þowsynde ȝeer ben to hym as ȝusturday; and schortly alle þinge
þat was or euere schal be heraftyr is present vnto hym, for
strechyng of his long[e] beyng. And herfore telluþ God to Moyses
þat 'he þat is ⌜is⌝ his name'. And þis is a memorial to God
100 wiþowten eende. But ouer þis we schulden wyte whan Abraham
schulde be. And certis, siþ þat God wyste, ȝe, byforn he made þis
world þat Abraham schulde be, þanne hit was soþ. And herfore
seyn clerkys þat euerich creature haþ beyng in his sawmple þat is
wiþowten eende. And so þat Abraham schulde be is trewþe
105 wiþowten eende. But ȝet byfore þis trewþe is God þat knoweþ hit.
And so þis word 'byfore' bytokneþ forþerhede of beynge, and not
forþerhede of tyme, siþ al þis was wiþowten eende. And so to
blaberyng in þis speche mennys voises be not sufficient, but som
glymeryng we han in owre sowle of þis trewþe, and bettur
110 knowen hit in owre herte þan we kan speke hit in voys. And
blessud be þe Hooly Goost þat sette syche wordis in his lawe, þat
alle men here in erþe kan vnneþe vndirstande hem; for I am
certeyn, ȝif þow be neuere so wys ne oold, vnneþe þow wost
afferrun þis schorte word of Crist whan he seiþ þat 'byfore þat
115 Abraham schulde be I am'. And heere tellen seyntes cause of þis
derknesse. Furst we schulde wel wyte þat auctour of þis gospel is
more wytty in hymself þan we alle kan conceyue. Also he wole
þat hyse prestis trauelen faste in his lawe, and kepon hem

99 Exod. 3: 13–14.

old α   fro] for β   96 ben to hym] to him ben H   97 was] -as *on eras. corr.*
D.   euere] *om.* E   vnto] to E   98 strechyng] fer rechyng Z   longe]
longo D   herfore] þerfore Z   to] bi G   99 is is] is SZ   is²] *corr.*
D   name] mane β   *margin* exo. 3 T   101 be] *om.* J   þat] *om.*
δI   ȝe] *om.* NZ   he] þat *canc.* he C, þat he FNTδGH   102 be] *om.*
J   herfore] þerfore FZGH   103 seyn clerkys] *rev.* J   sawmple] a saumple
FJG, exsample H   104 and . . . eende (105)] *om.* Z   is] his CTβ   105 ȝet]
ȝif S   trewþe] creature CK   is] it S   knowiþ] kowyt β   106 word]
world C   forþerhede] þe forþerhede J   107 forþerhede] of forþerhed δ   to]
om. E   108 blaberyng] blabere K, varying C   þis speche] þes spechis I   110
knowen . . . herte] knowing in oure herte of it, in . . . herte *and* of it *marked for rev.*
G   knowen hit] k⌜n⌝owynge α   þan] þat β   kan speke] haue speche to
tellen N, haue to speke δ   hit²] *om.* N   voys] oure voyce SI   111 sette] sente
G   112 kan . . . vndirstande] vnneþe kunne Nδ   for . . . chesoun (123) *om.*
N   113 ȝif þow be] be þou CK   ne] no β, *or* T   114 afferrun] -un *on eras. corr.* D,
after⌜me⌝Y, afferme ABIG, affere me M, oferroume Z, to affermed, -d *canc.* α   whan]
where F   þat byfore þat] er I   þat²] ⌜þat⌝ T, *om.* LδE   115 heere]
herfore K   116 derknesse] mysty saiyng Z   auctour] þe auctor
δ   117 we alle] *rev.* K   wole] wolde δ   118 hyse] þes C   trauelen]

medfully from|oþre ocupaciones, for noon of vs haþ mater to sey f.92
⌐þat⌐ he can al Godis lawe, and so he haþ no more to lerne 120
þerinne. Also we schulden trowe þat alle mennys wordis may not
come to þe wyt þat is in Godis wordis, for we wyten þat nowt in
hem is seyd wiþowte chesoun, but in eche Godis word is more wyt
þan we knowe.

traueld αδ   hem] hym M   120 þat] corr. D, þat canc. α, om. BCFKLMSTY-
βE   lerne] lere α   121 wordis] wyttis T   122 þe] om. β   wordis] ⌐lawe⌐
Y   þat . . . hem (123)] in hem þat nouth S   in . . . seyd (123)] is seide in
hem H   123 hem] hym FαJ   chesoun] enchesoun, en- canc. FG, enchesoun
K   godis word] word of god N   word] wordis C   124 knowe] knowen and
þerfore preie we to god in whom is al witte þat we reulen oure lyf here by wysdam of his
lore etc. N

Dominica [in Ramis] Palmarum. [Euangelium.]
Sermo 45.

Altera autem die que est post Parasceuen. Mathei 27.

We suffise not here to telle pleynly þis gospel, but þe eende þerof
makiþ mynde of owre byleue how, aftir þe tyme þat Crist hadde
suffred deþ, þe nexte day aftur, þat is þe holy Saturday, þese men
þat hadden kilt Crist gedredon togedre. For þe gospel telluþ þat
5 *princes of preestis and þe pharisees comen togydre to Pilate*; and þese two
folc, as hiʒe prestis of þe temple and þese religiows, diden Crist to
deþe. And herfore telluþ Mathew how þese two dredden more
þat þe name of Crist schulde growen among men, and so þer
defamyng schulde growe and þei schilden be destruyede. And
10 certis as þese two maner of folc diden Crist to deþe, so þei be now
cheueteynes to destruyen his lawe, for þei letten þat þei may þe
trewþe of þe gospel; and no wondur is, for þei in þeir lyuyng
reuersen þe lif of Crist and ben weddide to contrarie lif. And siþ
þe gospel telluþ dampnyng of suche men, and how þat men
15 schulden flen hem as heretikes and false prophetus, þei dredden
þat þer gyle by þis schulde be knowe. And herfore þei seyn þat
Godis lawe is false, but ʒif þei gloson hit after þat þei wolen; and

MSS: D; ABCEFGIJKLMNSTXYZαβδ.

Dominica . . . euangelium] *om.* αZ   sermo 45] *om.* BCFKLNSTYαδEIJXZG
altera . . . parasceuen] dominus noster iesus christus in gloria est dei patris N   aut-
em] *om.* α   die que] dies qui A   que . . . parasceuen] *om.* EI   que est] *om.*
Yδ, que β   que] qui B   mathei 27] mathei 28 α, mat 26 . . . ad philipens. 2
N   1 here . . . telle] to telle here E   to . . . pleynly] playnly to telle S   4
kilt] sleyn EZ   togedre] hem togidre F   5 þe] *om.* KTIJG   to] vnto
N   6 folc] folkys F   religiows] religiouns β   to] to þe N   7 how] þat
N   dredden] duden N   8 þat] þat þan S   schulde growen] growe
K   schulde] schulde not N, schulde not, not *canc.* δ   growen] grew
C   among . . . growe (9)] *om.* I   men] hem N   and] for N   so] ⌐so⌐G,
om. K   þer . . . growe (9)] schulden þei be defamyd of þer false lyuyng
N   9 growe] grewe C   þei schilden] so schulde þei N, so þey schulden
E   and . . . trowe (19)] *om.* Z   and] ac CK, in gret sclaundre to hem
N   10 maner] maneres δ   deþe] þe deþ A   11 to] for to α   þat]
⌐prestis⌐þat T   þe] ⌐noʒt telle⌐þe T   12 is] his β   13 lif⌐] liuyng L   14
þat] *om.* TI   16 schulde] sc *canc.*/schulde D   be] ⌐be⌐K, *om.* Y   17 ʒif] if þat

þus þer gloos schulde be trowed as byleue of cristen men, but þe
tixt of Godis lawe is perelows to trowe.

Þese two maner of folc comen togydre to Pilate on þe nexte Saturday   20
aftyr þei hadden kylt Crist, and seyden þus to hym '*Syre! we þenken
on þat þis gylour seyde whanne he was on lyue þat he schulde ryson aftur þree
dayӡes. And þerfore comaunde his sepulchre to be kept til þe þridde day, leste
hise disciples comen and stelon his body, and feynen to þe puple þat he is
rison fro deþ; and so þe laste errour schal be worse þan was þe formere.'*   25
And þis pagyn pleyen þei þat huyden þe trewþe of Godis lawe.
*And Pilate seyde to hem 'Ӡowself han þe kepyng. Go forþ and kepeþ hit as ӡe
can,* for þis is not myn offys.' And þus seyn þese two folc to princes
of þe world þat þese heretykes ben false men aӡeynes holy
religioun, and þei casten to destruye lordschipes and rewmes, and   30
þerfore comaunde hem to be deed or lette hem to speke. But
lordis seyn aӡen þat þei schulden knowe þe lawe þat hooly
chyrche haþ to punysche suche heretykes, and þerfore þei
schulden go forþ and punyschen hem by þer lawe. And by such
execucion of false prelatis and frerus is Godis lawe qwenchid and   35
anticristes arerud. But God wolde þat þese lordes passedon Pilate
in þis poynt and knewon þe trewþe of Godis lawe in þer modyr
tonge, and haue þese two folc suspecte for þer cursed lyuyng and
huydyng of Godys lawe fro knowyng of seculeris; for by þis cautel
of þe feend ben manye trewe men qwenchede, for þei wolen iuge   40
for heretykes alle þat spekon aӡeynes hem–ӡe, ӡif þei tellon Godys
lawe and schewe synnes of þese tᵣwˡo folc. *And þei wenton forþ and
kepton wiþ knytes þe sepulchre of Crist, markynge þe ston þat was put at*

δ   hit] þis J   wolen] wolden Nδ   19 is] þey seggen is MN   to] for to
E   21 aftyr] aftir þat Kα   kylt] sleyn EZ   seyden þus] *rev.* A   22 on¹]
how T   ryson] reyse β   23 and . . . comaunde] comaunde þerfore N   to
. . . day] to þe þridde day to be kept N   24 feynen] layne α, sai Z   is rison] reisen
S   25 was] *om.* N   formere] firste N   27 ӡowself] ӡow- *on eras. corr.* DX, ӡhe
ӡowreself CKβδEI, ᵣloˡ ӡouself M, ӡe selfe Z   han] haue ӡe NδI   þe] *om.*
E   go] go ӡe K   forþ] *om.* E   28 þis . . . offys] myn office is not þis
I   two] ᵣtwoˡ Y, *om.* I   folc] ᵣmaner ofˡ folc T   to] to þe FJ   29 þe] þis
BKNδJ   þat . . . folc (42)] *om.* Z   heretykes ben] ben heretykes ben
δ   heretykes] men K   men] heretikis K   30 destruye] -n *canc.* D   lord-
schipes] ᵣþeˡ lordshipis F   and²] of T   31 comaunde] comaundede δ   32
aӡen] aӡen as pilat did LM   33 þerfore] herfor αG   þei schulden] *rev.*
N   þei] ӡe L   35 execucion] excusacyoun δG   false] suche false
I   prelatis] freris E   frerus] prelatis E   lawe] ᵣlaweˡ KE   36
anticristes] anticrist J   37 þe trewþe of] *om.* Y   38 suspecte] in suspect I   39
þis] *om.* T   cautel] cautelis J   40 wolen] wolden Nδ   41 tellon] speken
E   42 synnes] þes synnes I   two] w *corr.* D   43 at] on E   44

f.92v þe dore [i]n siȝt of þe keperus to ma[r]ke þer diligen|ce. And þus
45 doon owre hyȝe preestis and oure newe religiows: þei dreedon
hem þat Godis lawe schal qwikon aftur þis, and herfore þei make
statutes stable as a stoon, and geton graunt of knytes to confermen
hem, and þese þei marken wel wiþ witnesse of lordis, leste þat
trewþe of Godis lawe hid in þe sepulchre berste owt to knowyng
50 of comun puple. O Crist! þi lawe is hyd ȝeet; whanne wolt þow
sende þin aungel to remeue þis stoon and schewe þi trewþe to þi
folc? Wel I wot þat knytes taken gold in þis caas to helpe þat þi
lawe be hyd and þin ordynaunce cese; but wel I woot þat hit schal
be knowen at þe day of doom or byfore, whan þe lykuþ, aȝen alle
55 þin enemyes.

Here schulden men marke þe passioun of Crist, and prenton in
þer herte somwhat to sewon hyt, for hit was moste wylful passioun
þat evure was, and mooste hard passioun þat euere man suffrede.
Hit was þus wilful and so moste medeful. And herfore tolde Crist
60 þe forme of his passioun to his twelue disciples, whanne he wente
to Ierusaleem; and herfore Crist, þat hudde hym byfore to come
to þe citee, cam now to suffre to schewon his free wylle; and
herfore he seiþ at his soper 'Heere wiþ desyr haue I coueytud to
ete þis Pasch wiþ ȝow', for desyr of his godhede and desyr of his
65 manhede meuede hym to ete þus and to suffren aftur. But al þis
was mene and figure of his laste soper þat he etuþ in heuene wiþ
men þat he haþ choson. And þus, siþ no contrariete was in Cristes
resoun to suffre þis passioun, and his wyt was moste clene, no þing

in . . . enemyes (55)] *om.* Z in] and DI, and in δ þe³] þes CKLMNSTαβδ-
JX keperus] keper A, knyȝtes K marke] make DαJ, maʳrᵀke X di-
ligence] diligences α 45 newe] newere β 46 hem] *om.* NI herfore] þerfore
F, here L 47 a] *om.* BSTYIJG geton] þei geten A 48 þese] þis
AI marken] maʳrᵀken Y, maken J witnesse] w *eras.*/witnesse D, witnessis
MSE þat . . . of (49)] þey trowen N þat] *om.* α 49 trewþe] þe truthe αδ,
trewe β berste] þat hit schulde not bersten N to] to þe N, *om.* K 50
comun] þe *canc.* comoun A, þe comyn BNY þi lawe is] ȝet is þi lawe N ȝeet]
om. MN 51 þis] þe ABEI þi¹] þe NδI 52 þat¹] *om.* M in] lo in
M þis] ᵀþisᵀ α, þi G, *om.* F caas] cause N þat²] *om.* T þi] þe
βIJ 53 þin] þen β cese] ceessid Lδ, cesses β wel I woot] I wot wel
J 56 men] we L in] it in K 57 þer] oure L herte] hertis
J sewon] shewen A moste] þe moste EI 58 was] ȝet was N 59 hit]
and it EI medeful] needful I herfore] þerfore N 61 herfore] þerfore
Z þat] *om.* EI 62 cam now] *rev.* N, and cam nou E to²] for to A to³]
and *canc.* ᵀtoᵀ α, and to Lδ 63 herfore] þerfor Z seiþ] said Z heere]
om. T haue I] *rev.* AFYαEIJZG 64 þis] in þis L desyr¹] þe desire G de-
syr²] *om.* I 66 and] in *on eras. of* and T, in N, a C etuþ] eth S 67

þat man dide was to hym more wilful. And siþ Crist suffrede þus
for synne of his breþren, þei schulden suffre þancfully for her 70
owne synne. Crist axsuþ not so greet peyne in hise breþren, but
þat þei han sorwe for þer synne and ⌐in⌐ purpos to forsakon hit.
And þis is cause why þat God wole han his passioun þus rehersed
for profiȝt of his breþren and not for his owne. Þis peyne of Cristes
passioun passyde alle oþre, for he was moste tendre man and in 75
his myddel age; and God leet by myracle Cristes wyttis suffre, for
ellis he myȝte by ioye haue had no sorwe. But alle circumstaunses
þat schulden make peyne hard weron in Cristes passioun to
maken hit more meedful: þe place was moste sollempne, and þe
day also, þe howr was mooste knowen to Iewes and to heþene 80
men, and þe despiȝt was most, for men þat moste schulden loue
Crist ordeyneden þis moste fowl deþ aȝen Cristis moste
kyndenesse. And we schal byleue þat Crist suffrede not in ⌐n⌐o
maner but for certeyn enchesoun; for he, boþe God and man þat
maade alle þing in nowmbre, schop his passioun to answere to 85
byggynge of mannys synne. And so seuene wordis þat Crist spak
on þe cros answeren wondurfully to alle synnes of men. And
schortly no þing þat Crist euere dide was doon but for greet cause
and profiȝt of men. Suche cawses schulde we studye and prenton
hem in owre muynde, for wyte ⌐we⌐ wel þat al þis was doon for 90
profiȝt of cristene men. And trowe we not þese heretikes, þat ben
fooles owt of byleue, þat seyn we may not sewe Crist and namely
in his passioun, for Crist was nedyt to suffren here al þat he

contrariete] contrariouste KN, contrarie G   69 to . . . wilful] more wilful to him
Y   þus] om. J   70 synne] loue N   þancfully] gladly N   71 crist] but
crist F   axsuþ] askid C   so] ⌐so⌐ X, so canc. Fδ, om. B, to C   in] corr. Dδ, om.
BCKLMNSTYαβEZ   73 is] om. Y   cause] þe cause CKδ, hys cause
T   wole] wolde ANδ   his] þis SI   rehersed] rehersiþ A   74 for²] om.
G   75 passyde] passiþ FNJ   77 haue] he δ   circumstaunses] circumstance
C, þe circumstauncis I   78 make] om. S   80 iewes] þe iewes EI   to²] to þe I,
om. L   81 despiȝt] spiȝt J   moste schulden] rev. BTβI   82 fowl] fool
M   moste²] ⌐is⌐ most C   83 kyndenesse] kyn/kenesse E   in] ne canc. in δ,
⌐ne⌐ in X, ne in CKLMNSTYβEI   no] n- corr. D, o I   84 enchesoun] chesoun
BCKLMNSTYβZ   for²] fo M   he] ⌐is⌐ he N, he ys TEJ   85 maade] om.
K   þing] þinges N   86 byggynge] -gynge on eras. corr. D, bygynnyng NEI,
beggyng β   mannys] monne N   so] to B   87 men] man I   88 crist
euere] rev. αI   euere] spak euere or S   90 muynde] herte L   wyte we] we
wite marked for rev. J, we witen M   we] corr. D, we canc. X, om. ABCLSTαβ   wel]
om. I   91 and . . . ordeyned (95)] om. Z   trowe] þus trowe A   we] om.
MIJG   92 byleue] ⌐þe⌐ byleue T   we] þat canc. we Fα, þat we CK, we ne
JG   not] om. G   93 his] þis Bβ   here] om. E   94 fonnede] foltid

suffrede. Certis þese fonnede heretykes schulden wel wyte þat alle
95 þinge mut nede come as God haþ ordeyned. And so sewe we Crist
afer in his blesside passioun, and gedre deuowt mynde of hym,
and kepe vs aftir fro synne.

E   95 þinge] þyngis LMNTαβδJ   as] þat B   so] ⸢so⸣ T, om. N   96 afer]
eftir CKβEI   in] om. CE   passioun] passid passioun J   97 and ... synne]
bysyly kepyng vs fro synne god graunte vs grace to kepen vs þus and euer to be trewe to
hym and þat it so be pater et aue N   vs ... synne] on eras. corr. D   aftir] aferre
AB, fer EI

In Die Pasche. [Euangelium.] Sermo 46.

Maria Magdalene. Marci ultimo.

This gospel telluþ how þese holy|wymen comen to byleue þat
Crist was ryson fro deþ. Somme men seyn þat here weren but two
Maries, þat was *Marie Maghdeleyn* and *Marie Iamys modur*, and þis
secounde Marie was boþe owre Ladyes sustur and *Salomeus*
dowtur; but somme men seyn þat þer weren þree. But hit is ynow 5
to vs to trowen þat þer weren two, and leue to knowyng of God ȝif
þer weren moo. *Þese two Maries bowt[e] hem at euen oynementis,* for
hit was leueful to worchen at euon on þe sabaotis. *And erly on þe*
Sonenday þei comen to þe sepulchre of Crist at þe sonne rysyng, and seyden
togydre 'Who schal turnen us þe stoon fro dore of þe sepulchre?' And þei 10
lokedon þerto and sayen hit turnyd awey; forsoþe hit was ful greet, and
passyde þese wymmenys power to remeuen hit fro þe dore by
castyng of þe pharisees, for þei seyden þat Cristis disciples wolden
comen and stelon his body. And so þis stoon was remeuyd by
seruyse of aungelus, for disciples of Crist dredden hem ȝet to 15
walken. *And þese wymmen comen into þe sepulchre of Crist, and þei*
sayȝen an aungel of God in forme of a ȝong man, syttynge on þe riȝt syde,
and hulyd wiþ a whyt stole. And þei wondredon of þe siȝt. But þe aungel

---

MSS: D; ABCEFGIJKLMSTXYZαβδ; N *ends incompl.* 57 as he haþ y; H *inc.* 87 euere
nedeful.

In . . . euangelium] *om.* αZ   sermo 46] *om.* BCFKLNSTYαδEIJXZG   maria
magdalene] magdalene L, expurgate vetus fermentum N   magdalene] magdalene et
maria salomee S, magdalene et maria iacobi JG   marci ultimo] ad cor' 5 mathei
vltimo N   marci] mathei ACFLNβEIG, m' K   ultimo] xvi BG   1 þese] þis
L, *om.* β   2 here] þer I   but two] two but *marked for rev.* D   3 þis] þe
S   5 men] men *canc.* X, *om.* BSTβδJ   þer] þai CKLSYEIX   6 to³] þe *canc.*
to C, to þe N   of] to FJ   7 þer] þey E   moo] any *canc.* mo α, any moo N,
more δ   maries] maydenes δ   bowte] bowto D   oynementis] onyment
E   8 hit . . . sabaotis] on þe sabote it was leueful for to wurchen at euene N   on]
in A   sabaotis] sabot FTαJG   þe²] ʳseeˀ þe T   9 þe¹ . . . crist] cristus
sepulcre N   rysyng] arisynge T   seyden] þei seiden K   10 togydre] *om.*
S   us] ʳtoˀ vs T, to vs AB, vp to vs K, vs vp, vp *canc.* E   dore] þe dore
BCFKNSTYαδEIJZ   11 lokedon] lokynge K   and¹] *om.* K   12 passyde]
hyt passid T   þese] þe M, *om.* I   14 remeuyd] meuyd N   by] bi þe
I   15 for] and for Z   disciples] þe disciples α   16 into] to T   þe] ʳþeˀ
M, *om.* α   18 stole] clooþ or stoole δ   of] on CKI   19 to] vnto N   for] *om.*

seyde to hem 'Wole ʒe not drede, for I knowe ʒoure purpos. *Ʒe sekon Iesu*
20 *of Nazareth þat was doon on þe cros, but he is ryson to lyue and is not now heere, for here is þe stude voyde where þei hadden put hym. But go ʒe, and seye ʒe to Cristis disciples and algatis to Petre þat Crist schal go byfor ʒow to þe cuntre of Galilee, and þere schille ʒe seen hym, as he seyde ʒow byfore,* and he may not lye.'
25 Eche word of þis gospel beruþ greet mysterye. Furst Crist aperude to þese hoolye wymmen for to graunten a pryuylegie vnto wommannys kynde, for hit is seyd comunly þat Crist aperude ten tymes from howr of his rysyng to his steyʒyng into heuene. Furst Crist aperude vnto Marie Maghdeleyn, and made
30 hire sterre of þe see to ʒyue lyʒt to men, and to putten hire fro dispeyr of hire furste synnes. We denye not þat ne Crist byfore þis aperude to his modur how þat he wolde, or in body or in sowle, for sche was euere sad in feiþ. Þe comyng of þese two Maries, þat was þe secounde schewyng þat Crist schewode hym alyue þat þe
35 gospel telluþ, ⌐techiþ⌐ how Crist wole schewon hym vnto manye statis, and how men schal be disposyde to haue þe siʒt of Crist. Þis erly comyng wiþ liʒt of þe sonne is redy comyng in grace for to serue Crist; and ʒet þe makyng redy on þe nyʒt byfore is doon of Crist, but not in such grace; þe musyng of þese wymmen as þei
40 wenton by þe weye bytookneþ bussy þoʒt how men schal come to serue Crist. But lore of goode aungelus openeþ to men þis lessoun, for þe stoon of vnbyleue is furst ful greet in synful men. Þis entryng to þe sepulchre is comyng to þe seruyse of Crist. Þis aungel þat techeþ men trewþe is good aungel of God, þat syttuþ

EI   20 of] a I   doon] crucified F   þe] ⌐þe⌐ α, *om*. Z   is¹] he is
Fδ   now] *om*. I   21 here] lo here δ   22 ʒe] ʒe *canc*. X, *om*. CKLMSTY-
αβZ   algatis] *om*. N   23 to] into YEJ   schille ʒe] *rev*. CFKI   he] ʒe
S   30w] ⌐to⌐ ʒow T, to ʒou Y   24 and . . . lye] *om*. N   25 greet] *om*.
S   27 vnto] to A   seyd comunly] *rev*. δ   crist] he CK   28 from] fro þe
δJZ, fro þat G   29 vnto] ⌐vn⌐to Y, to CKI   marie] *om*. Y   30 men] þe
semen S   to³] *om*. α   putten . . . fro] putte from hem T   fro] awey fro
K   31 hire] here T   furste] furmere Y   not] nou C   byfore . . .
aperude (32)] apperide bifore K, apperide bifore þis I   32 how] hou so N   or¹]
ouþer NδE, *om*. I   33 in] in þe Z   þese] þe K   34 alyue þat] al if Z   35
telluþ techiþ] techiþ ⌐telliþ⌐ J   techiþ] *corr*. D, and techeth δZ, *om*. E   how] hou
þat N   wole] wolde, -de added B, wolde NαδEIZ   vnto] to NI   36 schal]
shulde AZ   þis] and þis G   37 erly] erþly β   wiþ] with þe Sα   þe] þis
CK   grace] weye I   39 þese] þe⌐s⌐ J, þo C, þe K   40 bussy] þe bysy T, *om*.
CK   schal] suld Z   41 lore] þe lore α   42 vnbyleue] beleue S   furst]
om. Z   in] and β   43 to¹] into MEI   comyng] entrynge I   to²] into
I   þe²] þe *canc*. X, *om*. CKLMNSTYαβδEZ   44 men] þus men δ   good] þe

on þe riȝt syde to teche men þe weyȝe to heuene, and to sytten on 45
Cristes riȝt hond at þe day of doom. Þe whytnesse of þis stole is
clennesse of victorie þat suche men han of þer gostly enemyes;
and, as Gregory nooteþ, þe face of þis aungel semede as lyȝtyng
and hise cloþus whyte as snow, for Crist and hise aungelus ben
dreedfulle to wyckyde men and plesynge to goode men, ȝe to þe 50
day|of doom. Þis aungel counforteþ men and riȝtuþ þer purpos, f.93v
and telluþ hem how now Crist is syttyng in heuene, for his state
here in erþe is fully parformed. And offis of suche men is aftirward
enioyned hem þat þei schulden parte wiþ þer breþren goostly
werkis of mercy, not only wiþ comunes but also wiþ prelatis. Þe 55
goyng byforn of Crist into þe cuntre of Galilee is goyng byforn of
Crist to heuene, þere he schal schewon hym to men, as he haþ
hiȝt to hem ofte in þe gospel.

Her aftur þis wyt men may large þis gospel, and trete what
matere þat þei wenon schulde profiȝte to þe puple. But hit is 60
comunly teld of þe sacrament of þe auter, and how men schal
disposon hem now to take þis sacrament. And hit is seid comunly
þat, as þese hooly wymmen hadden left þer formere synne and
take þeir fresch deuocion, so men schulden come to þe chirche to
take þis hooly sacrament, and þus come wiþ þese wymmen wiþ 65
lyȝt of þe sonne. And þus men schulden cloþen hem wiþ þese þre
vertewys: byleue, hope and charite to receyue þis sacrament.
Byleue is furst nedful, and algatis of þis breed, how hit is Godis

gode MαδG, þe N   45 on] in B   to¹] for to δ   46 hond] syde α   at] on
Nα   þis] his B, þe SI   47 of²] on α, ouer δ   þer] om. I   48 þis] þe
B   as²] as canc. riȝt as S   lyȝtyng] liȝtnyng A, leityng BFKLMNTβδEJG,
leytyng ⌐leuenyng¬ C, leuenyng Z   49 cloþus] clopinge I   whyte] were white C,
alse white α   snow] þe snawe Z   50 to¹] vnto δ   to³] til N   52 hem]
om. E   now . . . is] ⌐now¬ crist is G, crist ⌐now¬ is now C, crist is now Kδ, þat crist is
β   53 in] on þis M   offis] officis, -ci- canc. β, officis T   aftirward] after
I   54 hem] ⌐to¬ hem J, to hem CKβ   schulden] schulen B   55 comunes . . .
wiþ²] om. LM   56 into] to A   goyng] þe goyng L   of³] om. F   57 to¹]
into KSδ, vnto N   hym] us him B   58 to] om. E   hem] men Sδ   ofte]
om. δ   59 men may] rev. BCKSTβδZ   þis²] þe CK, ⌐in¬ þis T   60 þat] om.
TI   wenon] supposen E   to] best to δ   61 schal] schulde SαδIZ   62
now to take] to take now BCKLMSTYαβδEXZ, now to take now J   seid comunly]
rev. S   63 formere] forme S   64 take] toke Z, om. S   fresch] freschely
δ   þe] om. FJ   to²] and E   65 þis hooly] om. I   þus] þis I   come]
comeþ I   wiþ¹] wiþ canc. T, om. αZ   þese] þis T   wymmen] holy canc.
wymmen Y, hooly wymmen AG   66 men schulden] rev. α   68 breed] b/breed
D   how] and how CK   69 kyndely] and kyndely DFI, and eras. kyndely

body by uertew of Cristis wordis. And so hit is kyndely breed, as
70 Powle seiþ, but hit is sacramentally verrey Godis body. And
herfore seiþ Austyn þat þat þing is breed þat þine ey3en tellon þe
and þat þow seest wiþ hem. For hit was not trowed byfore þe
feend was loosyd þat þis worþi sacrament was accident wiþowte
suget; and 3eet dwellon trewe men in þe oolde byleue, and laten
75 frerus fowle hemsylf in þer newe heresye. For we trowen þat þer is
betture þing þan Godis body, syþ þe holy Trinnyte is in eche
place. But owre byleue is set upon þis poynt: what is þis sacrede
host, and not what þing is þere. Þe secounde vertew þat schulde
cloþe trewe men is þe vertew of hope, þat is ful needful how men
80 schulden hope by þer lif here, and furst wiþ þe grace of God for to
come to heuene. And to þis entent men taken now þis sacrament,
so þat by takyng herof þer muynde be fresched in hem to þenkon
on kyndenesse of Crist, to maken hem clene in sowle. And herfore
seiþ Poule þat 'he þat wantuþ þis eende, etuþ and drynkuþ his
85 iugement', for he iugeþ not þe worþinesse of Godys body, ne
worschipeþ not his ordenaunce. Þe þridde uertew nedful for to
take þis sacrament is uertew of charite; for þat is euere nedful, siþ
no man comeþ to Cristes feeste but 3if he haue þis cloþing. And
þus, as Austyn declaruþ, fowre poyntes þat fallen to makyng of
90 breed techon us þis charite, and algatis to haue hit now, for ellys
we gregien owre synne in etyng of þis breed. And 3if we han þis
cloþing, takyng þis mete in figure, hit schal bryngon vs to heuene
þere to ete Godis body goostly wiþowten eende; and þat is
mennys blisse.

69 1 Cor. 10: 16; **84** 1 Cor. 11: 29.

AX   70 verrey] *om.* CK   71 þat þat] þat ⌐þat⌐ A, ⌐þat⌐ þat α, þat SEI   72
þat] *om.* K   seest] suest δ   not] ⌐neuer⌐ M   þe] þat I, þat þe J   75
frerus] þes freris J   76 betture] no better T   þan] þan ys T   77 place] place
þerof T   what] what þing I   þis²] þe KSI   79 ful] ⌐ful⌐ J, *om.* T   ne-
edful] medeful δE   80 by] of E   81 and] *om.* X   82 herof] þerof
YEZ   fresched] strecchid Y   hem] hym I   83 on] of CKMSTβδZ   in
sowle] *om.* LM   herfore] þerfor ZG   84 etuþ] e/etuþ D   85 ne] neþer
M   86 not] *om.* ABCG   nedful] is *canc.* nedeful J, is nedeful T   for to] ⌐for⌐
to J, to EI   87 sacrament] holy sacramet F   is¹] ⌐for þis sacrament⌐ ys
T   uertew] þe vertu S   88 comeþ] couetis Z   he] 3he C   89 as] *om.*
δ   to] *on eras. corr.* D, in CKLMSαβδEXZG   90 techon . . . breed (91)] *om.*
Z   91 gregien] agregge ⌐multiplien⌐ F, agreggen E   synne] synnes K   of]
om. I   breed] *eras.* ⌐sacrament⌐ *corr.* F   92 in figure] *eras.* ⌐bodili⌐ *corr., margin*
spirituallie *corr.* F   93 goostly] *om.* β   eende] eende ⌐to þat heuene crist bring vs
to after þat we heþen shall goo amen⌐ *corr.* F   94 mennys] mannys BCβE

Dominica in Albis. [Euangelium.] Sermo 47.

Cum esset sero die vna. Iohannis 20.

This gospel telluþ of þe fy⌜f⌝þe aperyng, þat was þe laste and late doon vpon Pasch day; and þis is teeld wiþ oþre to conferme byleue of þe chirche. As þe secownde aperyng was to þese hooly wymen, so þe furste aperyng was alone to Marie Maghdeleyn, as telluþ þe gospel of Iohn in þis same capitle. Þe þridde tyme Crist aperude to Petre, as seyn Luc telluþ in ende of his gospel; and þis was, as somme men seyn, whan Petre and Iohn comen fro þe sepulchre, and Petre wente by hymself wondryng and musynge. Þe fowrþe apperyng was maad to t⌜w⌝o disciples þat wente to Emaws and Crist sowpede wiþ hem; of þis telluþ þe ende of seyn Lukus gospel. Þe fyueþe|aperyng was þis þat owre gospel telluþ f.94 of, and þis was þe laste of fyue þat Crist schewyde on Pasch day; and on þat day seueny3t Cri3st aperude þe sixte tyme, and of þese two aperyngus telluþ þis gospel.

Þe story seiþ *whan hit was late þe furste day of þe wyke* þat cam nexste aftur þe Fryday þat God was doon to deþe onne; and þat

5 John 20: 11–18; **6** Luke 24: 34; **7** Luke 24: 12; **11** Luke 24: 13–34.

MSS: D; ABCEFGHIJKLMNSTXYZαδ; *β ends incompl.* 70 synne þat.

Dominica . . . euangelium] *om.* αZ sermo 47] *om.* BCFKLNSTYαδEIJXZGH cum . . . vna] fides nostra vincit mundum N esset sero] *rev.* H die vna] vna sabbatorum T, die vna sabbatorum α iohannis 20] iohannis 2 C, iohannis v N 1 this gospel] þe gospel today N fyfþe] f *corr.* D, firste BN 2 vpon] on Z pasch] þe paske αH, estre T 3 byleue] þe bileue E þe[1]] þis T to] of *canc.* to D, of to I þese] þe A, þis T hooly] *om.* I 4 so] *om.* I marie] *om.* SY 5 telluþ] *om.* J iohn] ion telliþ J' þis] þe AKIH þe[2]] *om.* L 6 to] vnto N ende] þe ende BFKMNSTYαδEIJZH 7 whan] what M, þat quanne S 8 wondryng] wandrynge FJ, musinge Y musynge] wondringe Y 9 fowrþe] foure β was maad] *om.* I to[1]] vnto Nδ, til α two] w *corr.* D 10 sowpede] wente *canc.* sowpede D of[1]] ⌜and⌝ of A, and of B 11 fyueþe] fiftenþe I aperyng] a//aperyng D þis] þus N telluþ] spekiþ EJ, *om.* S 12 þe] *om.* A of[2]] of þe δ fyue] fyueþ C on] on þe M, him on KE pasch] estre T 13 on] ⌜in⌝ F þese] þis TZ 14 two] *om.* Y aperyngus] peryngis K telluþ] spekiþ E þis] *om.* K, þe SYδ 15 seiþ] sais þus Z 16 þe] *om.* LM god] god *canc.* ⌜crist⌝ A, god crist, crist *canc.* Y, crist Z to] on *canc.* G deþe] þe deþ CK and] *om.* I 17 was in] was

was in þe Sonenday next aftyr þe sabaot, but hit was laate, *and þe*
disciples weren gedrede þere to counforton hem togydre; and, *for*
dreede þat þei hadden of Iewes þat weren here enemyes, *þer ʒates weren*
20 *faste schet* for drede of þe same folc. *Iesu cam,* not lettyng þat þe
ʒates weron schut þus, *and stood in þe myddis of his disciples, and seyde*
þus *vnto hem 'Pees be to ʒow!* For I am olyue, wole ʒe not dreeden þe
whyle ʒe han such a kepere.' *And hee schewyde to hem hise hondys and*
hys syde. And þe disciples hadden ioyʒe whan þei hadden seen þus þe Lord,
25 for sorwe of his deþ and dreede of þe Iewes weren clenely put
awey by siʒt of þis Lord. *And Crist seyde aʒen 'Pes be to ʒow!',* to
tellon hem þe folle pes þat þei schulden ha⌜ue⌝ þeraftyr boþe in
body and sowle for þer meedful pacience. And þei schulde not
grucche for þis schorte pursewyng, for Crist telluþ þat, *as his Fadur*
30 *sente hym, so he sendeþ hem* to suffre tribulaciones, and þei schulden
holden hem payede of such forme of seendyng. *And whan he hadde*
seyd þis, he blew in hem and seyde 'Take ʒe þe Holy Goost, for herby ʒe
schal be strong by power and by wyt þat ʒe schal haue by hym.'
Here we schal wyte þat Crist blew not by chyldhede vpon hise
35 apostles but by greet wyt, for herby Crist tawte þat þe Hooly Gost
comeþ boþe of þe Fadur and þe Sone, as wynd of erþe and watur.
And comyng forþ of þis Goost is not natiuite, but sutil inspyryng
of þese two persones; and herfore þei ben clepud o principle of þis
Goost. And hooly wryt graunteþ þat þe Sone sendiþ þis Goost.
40 And herfore Crist graunteþ þis pryuylegie to his disciples þat
hose synnes þat þei forʒyuen þei ben forʒyuen to hem, and whose synnes þat

on αδEI, was ⌜in⌝ Z, ⌜was⌝ T   laate] done late E   þe³] *om.* BCKLMSTY-
αδJZ   18 counforton] gadere I   19 ʒates] euem I   20 cam] com inne
N   þat] for þat F   þe²] þer CK, þus þe N   21 þus] *om.* N   þe] *om.* αJG-
H   myddis] medil CKLMTαβJX   22 vnto] to αE   wole] ne wil Z, nyle
H   not] *om.* ZH   þe] *om.* BCKαZ   24 hys] *om.* B   syde] sidys
S   seen þus] *rev.* δ, þus sey K   25 þe] *om.* A   clenely] clene CK   27
hem] hym S   schulden] schule K   haue] ue *corr.* D   þeraftyr] herafter
F   28 and¹] and in NαβδEIZ, *om.* H   schulde] schullen I   29 þis] þus
S   þat] ⌜þat⌝ T, *om.* NI   30 sente] sete β   schulden holden] holden
I   31 hem] *om.* G   payede of] apayed on T   of²] *om.* I   and] *om.*
I   32 þis] þiis *altered from* þus D, þus ABFNαδEIJG, þese SYH, þes ⌜wordes⌝
T   in] o- *canc.* ⌜i⌝n K, on ABNYE   seyde] seide ⌜þus⌝ F   holy] he holy
Y   ʒe schal] ʒe shal ʒe, *2nd* ʒe *eras.* F   33 by³] of α, in S   34 wyte] wel wyte
N   vpon] on N   35 for] and B   crist] we ben N   36 comeþ] come
FJ   þe¹] *om.* T   þe²] of *canc.* þe DYG, of þe H, of þe *canc.* Z, *om.* KLS-
Tβ   as] and as H, *om.* I   wynd] wyne αβ   erþe] þe erþe H, þe ayre
C   38 clepud] cald NαδZ   o] of K   39 þis] his I   40 crist graunteþ] *rev.*
N   crist] *om. gap* K   to] vnto Nδ   disciples] apostlys H   41 hose] w-

þei wiþhoolden þei ben holdon to hem. And boste men not for þis
priuylegie grauntyd to þe apostles, for hit is vndirstanden in as
myche as syche apostles acorden wiþ þe ⌜keyis of þe⌝ chirche
aboue. And herfore schulden syche bosterus be certeyn at þe   45
furste þat þei ben verrey vykerus of þe hooly apostles, and siþ God
enspyruþ hem and зyueþ hem wyt and power to bynden and to
lowsen, as Crist hymself doþ; or ellys hem wanteþ þis power, and
þanne þei schulde not boste þat þei han such power. And so þei
myзte not pleynliere schewen hem haue ⌜no⌝ such power þan for   50
to bargeyne herwiþ, and boosten hem to haue such, for þanne þei
ben none of hem to whom Crist зaf þis power. For зif þer weren
two popis, þe ton aзeynes þe toþur, and þe ton lowsede al þat þe
toþur bond, hyt were not for to dreme wheþur of hem dide soþly,
but wheþur þat more sewyde Godis doyng and resoun. And siþ   55
God may not folde from riзte and fro resoun, hit is knowen by
Godis lawe þat no pope assoyleþ, but in as myche as Crist
assoyleþ furst. And herfore seyn Petre and oþre Cristes apostles
assoylede not þus, ne зeuen syche indulgenses, for þei diden
neuere syche dedis but won God enspyrede hem. And so no þing   60
is falsere þan ypocritis to boste þus. And зif men looke to resoun
þei may wel see þat manye syche feynyngus ben of þe feendys
schole.|For ellys myзte a pope assoyle men boþe of peyne and   f.94v
blame, for þei kyllen þer euenecrist⌜en⌝, and euere while þei don
so; and зif þei ceson fro sych kyllyng, þer assoylyng schal cese. 65

eras. D   þat¹] om. NI   synnes] om. Y   þat²] ⌜þat⌝ T, om. Yδ   42
holdon] withholden CFMYαδEH   boste . . . not] auaunte na men þaim Z   for]
of H   43 þe] om. α   44 acorden] corden K   keyis of þe] margin corr.
D   45 schulden . . . bosterus] þai suld Z   syche] sc canc. syche D   at] of
G   46 þe] þe⌜s⌝ X, þese BCKNSTYαβδJZG   hooly] om. Z   siþ] siþ ⌜þat⌝
G, siþ þat BCKLMNSTYαβδEIX, þat Z   47 зyueþ] зyue B   hem²] om.
K   to²]om. GH   48 hem] him I, he α   and . . . huyde (84)]om. Z   49
þei¹ . . . not] shulde not þei H   þei schulde] rev. B   and] om. A   50 not]
⌜more⌝ T   haue] to canc. haue α, ⌜to⌝ haue T, to haue ACKβ   51 hem] om.
N   such] siche ⌜power⌝ J, siche power ABδI   þei] þer T   52 none] not
α   þis] his CK, suche H   53 þe²] þo L   þe³] þat þe J   54 for to] to
YI   dreme] deme T   soþly] more soþli I   55 þat . . . sewyde] sued more
CK   sewyde] schewide I   and¹] in T   and²] ⌜and⌝ G, om. H   56
folde] fayle K, foylde H   fro] om. ABY   57 crist] god E   58 oþre cristes]
oþer of cristus Nδ   cristes apostles] cristis apostlis marked for rev. S   59 syche] non
siche S   60 enspyrede] enspireþ I   61 ypocritis] ypocrisie H   62 þei may]
þenne may þei N   feynyngus] resouns I   þe] om. TG   63 boþe] om.
CKLMNSTYβ   of] fro N   64 blame] blamen T   kyllen] killiden
B   euenecristen] en corr. D   euere] euene CKLMNSTYβIX   don so] rev.
N   65 þer . . . cese] þenne ceseþ hire assoyllynge N   schal] om. β   66 men]

But what men wolden triste to sich assoylyng? Wel we wyton þat
God is moste Lord of alle oþre, and no mon may do synne but ȝif
he do synne aȝen hym, and no synne may be forȝyuen but ȝif God
ⸯfirstⸯ forȝyue hyt. And so hit is propre to God to forȝyue þus
70 offense. And ȝif a man forȝyue such synne, þat is by power of
vyker; and such power haþ he not, but ȝif God schewe hyt hym.
For ellys myhte he graunte pardon for long[e] aftyr þe day of dom
to men þat God wole haue dampnyde, for a new fownde preyȝer,
and hyȝen hit for mannys loue more þan þe Pater Noster: as men
75 ⸯseynⸯ þat a pope haþ grantyd two þowsande ȝeer to eche man,
þat is contriȝt and confessud of his synne, þat seiþ þis orisoun
'Domine Iesu Criste' bytwyxe þe sacryng of þe masse and þe
þrydde Agnus Dei. And þanne hyt were ydel to traueylon for any
pardoun, siþ a man myȝte at home geton hym fowrty þowsande
80 ȝeer by noon! And so þat man þat schal be dampnyd, þat is
confessud and contriȝt, and seiþ þus ofte þis preyȝer schulde haue
manye þowsynde ȝeer in helle aftur þe day of doom. Triste we to
þe oolde byleue þat Crist assoyluþ as he wole, and þis forme is hyd
to men as oþre trewþus þat God wole huyde.

85   *Thomas, on of þe twelue þat is clepud Didimus, was not wiþ þese ten
whan Iesu caam and dude þus. And oþre disciples tolden hym how þat þei
syen þe Lord.* But he seyde vnto hem *'But ȝif I see in his hondys pryckyng of
þe naylus, and putte my fyngur in þe place þat Crist was nayled inne, and
putte my hond in his syde* where he was persud wiþ þe spere, *I schal
90 neuere trowen þat owre Iesu is ryson.' And on þe Sonday next aftur weren*

man Cα   wolden] ȝef þei weren wise wolden N   assoylyng] assoilyngis
F   67 no mon] noun N   68 he] ȝhe C   do synne] synne ABFNH   no]
so *canc.* no α, so no δ   ȝif] *om.* SβH   69 first] *corr.* D   propre] proprid E,
apropred I   to¹] vnto N   þus] þis S   70 and] *om.* I   a] *om.*
H   power . . . vyker (71)] vikares power N   71 schewe] schewed T   hyt
hym] to hym C, it to hym K, hym T   72 myhte he] *rev.*   longe] longo D, long
tyme H   dom] do/dom D   75 seyn] *corr.* D   a] þe Y   76 þat²] and
I   77 criste] christe qui hanc sacratissimam carnem LM   of . . . masse] *om.*
N   þe³] *om.* α   78 hyt were] *rev.* BN   ydel] ydul þing N   to] for to δ,
om. G   for] ferre for N   79 at . . . hym] gete him at hoom BN, gete at hom Y,
gete *canc.* at hom gete hym G   þowsande] þousand þousand F   81 schulde] shal
FJGH   82 manye] þus many CK, may Y   þowsynde] þousandis H   triste]
and truste G   84 men] many men δ   trewþus] trewe ys T, treweþes is δ   85
clepud] called NαδZ   wiþ] *om.* S   86 þus] þis I   tolden] cam and teelden
T   87 vnto] to N   but ȝif] aȝeyn bote N   hondys] honde is
S   pryckyng] picching ABCKLMNSYαδEJ, pricchinge T, fitchyng Z   88 þe¹]
om. H   and²] *om.* B   89 hond] hondis LM   in] into α   persud]
perschid M, sperschid S, perischid T   90 neuere trowen] not *canc.* ⸯneuerⸯ trow α, not

þese disciples ynne, and Thomas wiþ hem. And Crist schewyde hym as
byfore, *for he cam whan þe ʒatis weren closyde and stood amyddis, and
seyde as he seyde byfore 'Pees be to ʒow!'* And aftur he seyde to Thomas,
þat he sente aftur to Ynde, *'Put in here þi fyngur and se myne hondys,
and put hydyr þin hond and put into my syde, and wole þow not ben* 95
vntreweful but trewe in byleue.' Thomas answerude and seyde to Crist *'My
Lord ⌐and ⌐ my God!'* And Iesu seyde to hym þanne *'For þow say me þus,
Thomas, þow byleuedust in me; but blessyd be þei þat sayen not þis and
trowen as þow dost.'* Monye oþre signes dude Crist in syʒt of hise disciples
[þat ben not wrytone, in þis booc], but þese fewe ben wrytone for þis eende 100
þat ʒe byleue þat Iesu is Godis sone, and þat ʒe for þis byleue haue blisse in
his name, Amen.

byleue N   iesu] lord *canc.* iesu Y, lord iesu FM   91 þese] þe B   thomas
. . . hem] whit hem was thomas N   92 byfore] he dyde byfore] T   closyde]
closend S   amyddis] in þe myddes δ   and²] ⌐hem⌐ and T, hem and N   93
seyde²] dede S   be] *om.* LM   to¹] vnto N   94 he] is J   aftur] eftirward
Z   to] in *eras.* to F, into H   ynde] iudee NJ   in] ⌐in⌐ α, *om.* I   95 hydyr]
om. M   and put²] *canc.* T, *om.* Nδ, and put it M   wole] wilt α, ne wil Z   not]
om. KZ   96 vntreweful] vntrowþeful δ   to] vnto TZ   97 and¹] *corr.* DX, *om.*
H   say me þus] þus seiʒ me H   98 byleuedust] bileuest CKδE, beledist S,
leuedest T, trowed Z   þei] þo A   not] *om.* S   þis] þus N   99 trowen]
trowiden BFLMSTYαδJZH   100 þat . . . booc] *om.* DABFLMNTYδEIJZ, ⌐þat
ben not wryten in þis boke⌐ X, ⌐þat ben writun in þis book⌐ G   but . . . wrytone] *om.*
S   for] in þis booc for DABCFKLMNSTYαδEIJZG, in þis booc *canc.* for X   101
ʒe] we K   byleue] trewly byleue N   is] *on eras. corr.* D, was EI   and] *om.*
E   blisse] þe blis T   in] for M   102 amen] *om.* BαδX, þat we holde þis trewe
byleue and also haue þis blisse praie we to god wiþ oure pater noster N.

Dominica ii post Pascha. [Euangelium.] Sermo 4 [8].

Ego sum pastor bonus. Iohannis 10.

Crist telluþ in þis gospel þe maneris of a good herde, so þat herby
we may wyten how owre herdis faylen now. And defawte of syche
herdys is moste perele in þe chyrche for, as ry3t offis of hem
schulde moste bringe men to heuene, so defawte in þis offis

5 draweþ men moste to helle. Crist telluþ of hymself how *he is a good
herde.* For he is þe beste herde þat mankynde may haue, for he is
good by hymself and may no wey3e defayle, for he is boþe God
and man, and God may no weye synne. And þus we han þe
mesure to knowen a good herde and an yuel, for þe more þat an

10 herde is ly3k to Crist he is þe betture, and þe more þat he
f.95 straungeþ from hym|he is þe worse in þis offys.

And eft whan Crist haþ 3yue þe mesure for to knowe goode
herdys he telluþ þe hyest proprete þat falluþ to a good herde: *a
good herde,* as Crist seiþ, *putteþ his ly3f for hise schep,* for more charite

15 may noon haue þan to putte his lyf for hys frendis, and, 3if he
worcheþ wysly, for to brynge þese schep to heuene, for þus þe
herde haþ moste peyne and þe schep moste profi3t. Þus may we

MSS: D; ABCEFGHIKLMNTXYZαδ; J *inc.* 97 3if þey bringen; S *lost* 5 -self -57 for; β *inc.*
46 bletyng shep.

Dominica . . . euangelium] *om.* αZ   sermo 48] sermo 40 D, *om.* BCFKLNSTYαδEI-
XZGH   ego . . . bonus] caritas paciens est N   iohannis 10] iohannis 20 CE,
iohannis (*gap*) K, 1 ad cor' 13 N   1 þis] his C, þe N   þe] þre I   maneris]
maner CN   herde] hurdeman δ   herby] þerbi CK   2 we may] *rev.*
CK   how] how þat T   3 offis] officis F   4 schulde] schal E   moste] *om.*
I   to] vnto α   defawte] þe faute G   in] of ABNG   5 men moste] *rev.*
BNSTδIZ   6 is¹] his L   mankynde] euer monkynde δ   7 good] gode L, god
NδZ   defayle] faile ABFTαEGH   8 god] ⌜god⌝ T, *om.* E   synne] do synne
H   we han] *rev.* N   9 to] to/to G   an¹] *om.* G   þe more] euer þe more liche
N   10 ly3k] *om.* N   he . . . betture] þe bettur he is and more comendable
N   þe²] þus þe E   11 straungeþ] is *canc.* straungiþ G, is strange Z, dis-
cordeþ N   he . . . worse] þe wurse he is N   þis] this, t- *added* M, his L,
om. N   12 eft] efter Z, ofte Nδ   whan] w/whan D   for to] to
EI   goode] *om.* N   13 þe] *om.* C   a²] for a E   14 putteþ] he putteþ
I   15 noon] non man, man *canc.* α, no man K   for] þer *canc.* for D   16
worcheþ] wurche NαZH   wysly] *om.* E   for²] *om.* α   17 þe] *om.*
B   may we] *rev.* ATYEI   may] m *canc.* /may D   18 is] his α   good] a

see who is good herde and who fayluþ in þis offys. For as Crist
putteþ wysly his owne lif for his schep, so anticrist putteþ prowdly
manye lyues for his fowle liȝf; as, ȝif þe feend ladde þe pope to   20
kylle manye þowsande men to hoolden his worldly state, he
sewede anticristus maner. And, siþ þis proprete of heerde
growndeþ charite in men, eche man schulde haue herof algatis
more – or lasse, as he is fer fro þis maner þat wole not ȝyuen his
worldly goodis to his schep or his breþren, whon þei han gret   25
nede herto, for syche ben worse þan mannys lyf. And þus semon
owre religiows to be exempte fro charyte, for, nede a man neuere
so myche to haue help of syche goodis, ȝe ȝif þei han stonys or
oþur iewelus þat harmen hem, þei wole not ȝyue suche goodys ne
valuȝ of hem to helpe þer breþren, ne ceson to anoyen hemself in   30
buyldyng of hiȝe howsys, ne to gedre suche veyne goodis ȝif hit do
harm to þer breþren. Syche auerowse men ben fer fro manerys of
a good herde. And so þese newe religiows þat þe feend haþ tillud
in, by colowr to helpe þe formere herdys, harmen hem manye
gatis, and letten þis offys in þe chirche, for trewe prechyng and   35
worldly goodys ben spuyled by such religiows. And herfore
techeþ Crist to fleen hem, for þei ben rauyschynge woluys:
somme wolen as brerus tere wolle of schep and maken hem coolde
in charyte, and somme wolen sturdily as þornes slee þe schep of
holy chirche. And þus is owre modyr schent for defawte of   40
mennys help. And more mede myȝte no mon haue þan to helpe

canc. good FG, a good NαδEI   who[2] ⌜who⌝ T, *om.* I   þis] his CαE   as] *om.*
G   19 putteþ] puttide E   anticrist . . . wolues (48)] hirdis suld put þair life for
sauyng of þair schepe Z   20 lyues] limes B   as] and C, so N   ladde] lede
N   21 manye] may Y   his] vp his N   worldly] owne Y   22 sewede]
seweþ N   maner] maneres ABFEIGH   þis] þe EI, is N   proprete] propre
M   heerde] an herde Tα, hurdes δEI   23 algatis . . . lasse (24)] or more or lesse
algate H   algatis] *om.* δ   24 as] and C   fer] ferþer G   his] þes
I   25 his[2] to his YEI   26 herto] þerto AFTαδEIGH   ben] goodis ben
ABT   27 religiows] religion α   28 syche] worldly I   goodis] good
B   ȝif] al ȝif ABEI   han] hadden K   29 harmen hem] þey haue E   þei]
but þei AEI   wole] wolde N   30 valuȝ] þe ualew EI   32 fer] ful fer
N   manerys] þe maneres α, þe manere I, manere H   33 religiows] maner
religiouȝs T, ordres E   tillud] tollid ABTYδEIGH   34 þe] þer ABFLMα-
EI   harmen] and now þei harmen N   35 gatis] weies AN   in] of
Nδ   for] to bodyly harm and gostly for N   *margin* mathei 7 TIH   38
somme] sum men M   wolen] wolden Nδ   wolle] þe wolle Nδ   of] of þe N,
fro δ   coolde] ful naked and cold N   39 in] wiþouten N   wolen] wolden
Nδ   sturdily . . . þornes] as sturdy þornes δ   þe] ⌜þe⌝ C, *om.* Kα   40
schent] *om.* N   defawte] faute Y   41 mennys] mannys BδIGH   to] for to

þis sory wydwe, for prynces of prestus and pharisees þat calluden
Crist a gylour han crochyd to hem þe chesyng of manye herdys in
þe chirche, and þei ben taȝte by anticrist to cheson hise herdys
45 and not Cristis. And þus fayluþ Cristus chyrche. Lord! siþ herdys
schulden passe þer schep as men passen bletynge schep, how
schulde Cristus chirche fare ȝif þese herdys weron turnede to
wolues? But Crist seiþ þat þus hyt faruþ among þe herdys of þe
chyrche, þat mony of hem *ben huyrude hynes and not herdys ouer þe*
50 *schep, for þe schep ben not þer owne* and so þei louen to luytel þe schep.
For, ȝif þei han þer temporal huyre, þei recke not how þer floc
fare. And þus doon alle þese curatowres þat tellen more by
worldly wynnyng þan by vertewys of þer sugetis, or sowle heele to
come to heuene. Syche be not herdys of schep but of donge and
55 wolle of hem, and þese schal not haue in heuene ioye of þe schep
þat þei kepon. *Syche hynes seen wolues comynge to flockes þat þey*
schuldon kepe, and þei fleen for drede of nowht. *And þese wolues*
rauyschen þese schep and scateron hem for þis eende þat þanne þei may
f.95v sonnere|perische. And þis meuede Powle to fownde noon ordre,
60 for Cristes ordre is ynow, and þanne schulden alle cristone men
be more surly in o floc. Lord! ȝif coowardyse of suche hynen be
þus dampnyd of Crist, how myche more schulden wolues be
dampnyde þat ben put to kepe Cristus schep? But Crist seyþ a
clene cause why *þis huyrede hyne fleþ þus: for he is an huyred hyne and þe*
65 *schep pertene not to hym*, but þe dong[e] of syche schep, and þis
dong[e] sufficeþ to hym howeuere þe schep faren. Somme ben

F   42 calluden] clepiden E, callen H   43 crochyd] chorochid M, crokid
H   in] of N   44 hise] her C, þuse N   45 fayluþ] falliþ δ   chyrche]
chirche by sleyȝt of þuse two folk N   47 cristus] þis E   48 þat] om. G   þus] om.
Z   faruþ] is Z   49 ouer] of αH   50 and] om. H   þei . . . schep] to
luytel þey louen þat flokke N   þe²] þes E, her H   51 þer¹] om. M   þer²] þe
FE   floc] folc L   52 curatowres] curatis G   53 wynnyng] wynnyngis
H   vertewys] vertu LM, vertuʳesꞋ β, þe vertues Nδ   54 of¹] of þe
N   but . . . hem (55)] bote pykares of þe wulle awey þat plukken þe schep and
drinken þe mylk and maken hem gloues of þe felle N   of²] of þe δ   55 wolle] of
wlle T   and þese] on eras. corr. D   in heuene] om. L   þe] þer ABF, þe canc. X,
om. CKLMNTYβEZ   56 hynes] herdis I   seen] been N   wolues] þe
woluys A   57 þei] þen þei α   58 þese] þe, -se eras. X, þe ABCKLMNTY-
αβδEI   þanne þei] þei canc. þanne þei B, þei þanne A, þai Z   59 sonnere] þe
sunner BEIH   meuede] moueþ I   ordre] ordres δE   61 surly] sure
Z   o] cristes N   lord] a canc. lord α, a lord EI   coowardyse] cowardes
δ   hynen] hynen ʳseruandisꞋ C, hyne N   62 schulden] sal Z   63
ben . . . kepe] kepares ben maad of N   64 þis] þese BNI   hyne¹] hynneʳsꞋ δ,
hynen ABNI   fleþ] flen NI   65 to] om. B   donge] dongo D   syche] om.
B   schep] om. α   66 donge] dongo D   sufficeþ] suffiþ C, suffiʳciꞋs

wolues wiþowteforþ, and somme ben wolues wiþinne, and þese
ben more perelowse, for homly enemyes ben þe worste. Yuele
wolues ben religiouse þat Crist seiþ in Mathew book ben woluys
rauyschyng, al ʒif þei comen in schep cloþus, for by þis ypocrisye   70
þei disseyuen sonnere þe schep. And, al ʒif þeire dwellyng be
wiþowte parisches of þese schep, and þei ben straunge and newe
browt in by þe feend, ʒet þei forʒeton not to comen and visite þese
schep; but comunly whan þei comen, þei comen moste ⌐for⌐ to
spuyle. And þus doon generally boþe frerys, monkus and   75
chanownes. But þei ben wolues wiþinne þat seyn þat þei han
cures of sowles, and rauyschen goodis of þes schep and feedon
hem not goostly, but raþere meuon hem to synne, and wake not
in herdis offis.

   But Crist seiþ *he is a good herde and knoweþ his schep and þei hym*, for   80
þe offys þat falluþ to herdys makiþ hym knowen among hem. '*As
my Fadur knew me and I aʒen knowe my Fadur, so*,' seiþ Crist, '*I putte
my liʒf to kepe* my schep aʒen wolues.' And as þis knowyng myʒte
not qwenche bytwixe Crist and his Fadur, so schulden þese
herdys waken vpon þer schep, and þei schulden knowen hym, not   85
by bodily feestis ne oþre synnys þat he doþ, but by þ⌐r⌐e offis of
herde þat Crist haþ lymyted to hym. Hit falluþ to a good herde to

---

69 Matt. 7: 15.

Z   hym] hem ABEI   howeuere] housoeuer Nδ   somme] somme men, men
canc. DX, sum men CN   68 þe] *om*. E   yuele] outefurth Z   69 wolues]
enemyes E   religiouse] þa Z   þat] bote N   book] gospel AB   ben] þe
wuche ben N   *margin* mt. 7 Z   woluys rauyschyng] *rev*. YEI, rauyshinge vulues
marked for rev. α   70 al ʒif . . . comen] *twice* S   schep] scheepis ACFMNT-
αδEIH   cloþus] cloþinge αδ   71 and . . . chanownes (76)] *om*. Z   and]
om. Bδ   al ʒif] ʒef N   72 parisches] parishens ACKH, parishe α   þese]
þe⌐s⌐F, þe Nα   straunge] strong LM   newe] late E   73 feend] techyng of þe
fend N   ʒet] bot ʒit α   þei] þei men I   to] for to CK   comen] come in
N   þese] þe AαH, þer C   75 doon] *om*. CK   frerys monkus] monkis freris
marked for rev. E, munkis freris H   monkus] and monkes Aα   76 þat¹] whanne
þey E, þat þei I   þat²] *om*. I   77 cures] cures, -s *eras*. X, cure ABCFKLMSTY-
αβδEIZGH   sowles] mennes soulis Y, mannus soules E   þes] þe Z   79 offis]
offis and he is ferre fra charite þat wil noʒt gif his warldly goodis to his scheep or to his
briþir when þai haue grete nede þerto (*cf*. 24–6) Z   80 hym] knowen hym N   81
hym] hem Iα   82 knew] knowiþ AFαGH   knowe] knew BCLδI   83 my
liʒf] myself S   to kepe] for H   84 qwenche] wenche C, be qwenchid I, cesse
Z   85 vpon] on N   þer] þe C   hym] hem E   86 ne] and E, neþir
F   oþre] by oþer N   synnys] signes BYGH   þat] wuche þat N   þre]
þr- *corr*. D, þe I   offis] offices ABFKLMNYEIH   87 herde¹] herdes, -s *canc*. α,
heerdis ABδEI   haþ] *om*. E, hymsef I   hym] hem ABE   88 ledon] lesewe

ledon hise schep in hoole pasturis, and whanne hise schep ben
hurte or scabbude to heelon hem and to greson hem, and whan
90 oþre yuele bestys assaylen hem þanne helpon hem. And herto
schulde he putte his liȝf to saue hise schep fro syche beestys. Þe
pasture is Godes lawe þat euermore is greene in trewþe, and
roton pasture ben oþere lawys and oþre fables wiþowte grownd.
And cowardise of suche herdys þat dar not defende Godis lawe
95 witnessuþ þat þei faylen in two offisus sewyng aftyr: for he þat
dar not for worldys dreede defende þe lawe of his God, how
schulde he defendon his schep for loue þat he haþ to hem? And ȝif
þei bryngon in newe lawys contrarye to Godis lawe, how schulde
þei not faylen aftur in oþre offisus þat þei schulden haue?
100 But Crist þat is heed of herdys seiþ þat *he haþ oþre schep þat be not
ȝet of þis floc, and hem mot he brynge togedre, and techen hem to knowen his
voys. And so schal þer ben o floc and on herde* ouer hem alle. Þese schep
ben heþene men or Iewes þat Crist wole conuerte, for alle þese
schal maken o floc, þe whiche floc is hooly chirche,—but fer fro
105 þis vndyrstondyng þat alle men schulle be conuertyde.

F   89 or] and I   to¹] he is bisy to E   to²] *om.* H   greson] greche
δ   and²] and also to defenden hem N   90 þanne . . . hem²] *om.* N, *on eras. corr.*
Aδ   helpon] he *canc.* helpe α, he helpiþ δE, þei helpen I, to helpe Z   herto]
herfore S   93 ben] -n *corr.* D   94 herdys] hertis H   þat] and þat
C   defende] feden C   95 faylen] fallen δ   offisus] office CTαE   96
worldys] worldly Nδ   his] *om.* β   97 he¹] *om.* G   loue] þe loue H   98
contrarye] þat ben contrarie E   lawe] lawis KS   99 offisus] offis CN-
αβ   100 þat¹] *om.* S   heed] heerd EI   not] *om.* T   101 ȝet] *om.*
F   of] on α   þis] his CMH   floc] fold N   hem¹ . . . brynge] he mote
bringge hem M   mot he] he moste N, must he δ   102 þer] þei C, *om.*
H   herde] sheepherde H   103 crist] he N   wole] wold CKNδ   þese]
þis I   104 schal maken] maken N   fro] be it fro C   105 conuertyde] turnyd
for he wul pyke out here and þere hem þat wolen be saued þoru trewe turnyng to hym fro
synful lyf þat ledeþ to helle þis wey to chese þat ledeþ to heuene god graunte vs grace þerto
pater et aue N

Dominica iii post Pascha. [Euangelium.]
Sermo 49.

Modicum et iam non videbitis me. ⌐Iohannis⌐ 16.

Here telluþ Crist to his chyrche how þer wylle schulde be
temperyd, for uarying of þer heed aftur his resureccion.
He seiþ
furst to hise apostles þat *þer is nyȝ a luytel tyme and þei schal not seen
hym*, for he schal be deed and buryed, for þese wordys of Crist
weron seyde þe nexste þeresday byforn his deþ. And aftur seyþ 5
Crist|to hise disciples þat *þer schulde sewe* a more *tyme, and þanne þei* f.96
schulden see Crist, and ofte tymes be counforted by hym; and þat
was fro rysyng of Crist to tyme þat he steyȝ to heuene. But, for
Crist haþ lymytud tyme þat he schulde come to his Fadur, Crist
seiþ þis tyme schal be luytul *for he goþ to his* ⌐*Fader*⌐; for boþe 10
Cristus lying in þe sepulchre, and his dwellyng here in erþe was
lytel tyme, as God lymytede to answere to his ascencion. *And
somme of disciples of Crist seyden togedere 'What is þis þat Crist seiþ to vs,
"a lytel [and ȝe schal not see me], and eft [a lytel and] ȝe schulle see me, for I
go to my Fadur"?' And þei seydon 'What is þis lytul? for we wyte neuere* 15
what hee meneþ.' And Iesu wyste þat hise disciples wolden axe hym of þis

MSS: D; ABCEFGHIJKLMNSTXYZαβδ; H *lower half of f. 102 cut away, lost are* 39 we
han . . . 49 of hyre, 62 -ne or . . . 72 þeraftur, 86 han what . . . 96 no kyn.

Dominica . . . euangelium] *om.* Z   sermo 49] *om.* BCFKLNSTYαδEIJXZ-
GH   modicum. . . me] deum timete N   et] ⌐et⌐ δ, eciam I, *om.* YG   non]
om. Mβ   me] *om.* S   iohannis 16] iohannis 18 J, prima petri 2 N   iohannis]
corr. D   1 here . . . apostles (3) crist telleþ in þis gospel N   telluþ crist] *rev.*
I   2 for] fra Z   3 a] *om.* J   and] þat L   schal] ne schullen I   4
for²] and E   5 þe] *om.* S   seyþ crist] *rev.* AFYH, crist said α, said crist Z   6
schulde] schal Nδ   sewe] *om.* K   þei schulden] *rev.* δ   7 schulden] schulen
N   and¹ . . . heuene (8)] in diuerse tymes fro þat he roos to tyme of his ascencioun to
counforte hise disciples wiþ þe syȝte of hym N   and¹ . . .hym] *om.* J   8 rysyng]
þe risyng LSδI   tyme] þe tyme ALαZ   þat] *om.* G   to²] into αEI   9
tyme] þe tyme   his] heuene to hys T   10 þis] þat þat T, þat þis EI   schal]
schulde CK   fader] *corr.* D   boþe] *om.* N   11 cristus] crist IJ   þe] his
N, *om.* T   and] and also G   dwellyng] beyng N   in erþe] *om.* N   12
his] *om.* JG   13 disciples of] *om.* N, þe disciples of δI   of crist] *om.* L   to-
gedere] þus togedur N   to] vnto δ   14 lytel¹] litil tyme shal com α   and¹
. . . me¹] *om.* DABCFLMNTβδEIJXZGH   eft] aftur Nδ, *om.* H   a lytel and]
om. DABCFLMNTβδEIJXZGH, he sais α   15 lytul] a litil L, þat he seiþ a litil H,

vncowþe þing. *And he seyde þus to hem of þis 'ʒe axsen among ʒow þat I seyde a lytel tyme schulde come, and þanne ʒe schal not see me, and siþ a lytul* but more *tyme and þanne ʒe schal see me.* Forsoþe, forsoþe, I seyʒe to
20 *ʒow þat ʒe schal boþe greete and wepe, but þe world þanne schal ioyen; and þanne ʒe schal be sorweful, but ʒowre sorwe schal turne to ioye.*' And þis was soþ of þe apostles aftur þe rysyng of Crist, for furst þei maden more sorwe, and siþ lesse, and siþ ioye; and worldly men contraryeden hem, þat furst hadden ioye and siþ sorwe, for þei
25 ioyedon of þe apostles sorwe, and sorwedon of apostles ioye.

And eft Crist telluþ a kyndely sawmple to prente þis word more in þer herte. '*A womman,*' seiþ Crist, '*whan sche traueyluþ wiþ chyld, haþ sorwe of hyre peyne* [*for hyre hour comeþ*], *but aftur, whan sche ys d*[*e*]*lyuerud, sche haþ ioye of hyre child, and forʒetuþ hire formere sorwe*
30 *for man is born into þe world. And þerfore ʒe han sorwe now, but eft I schal see ʒow, and ʒowre herte schal haue ioye; and noo man schal take fro ʒow ʒowre ioye.*' Þis womman to Cristus entent is owre modir hooly chirche, and euery part þerof þat is also hooly chirche. And, as long[e] as we lyuen here, we ben traueylyng of child to bryngon
35 owre sowle to surete fro bussy sorwe of þis world, and so to bringe forþ þe hoole man to blysse boþe in body and sowle. And whan we comen to þi⌐s⌐ state we þenkon not of owre formere sorwe to owre anoyʒe or owre mornyng, for ioye of þe ende þat seweþ. But

⌐þat he seiþ to vs a⌐ lytul X   we] *om.* H   neuere] not K   17 vncowþe] vn-
kowth ⌐vnknowen⌐ C, vnknowun ABKLMSTYαβEIJXZH, vnknowynge N   þing]
om. N   of . . . axsen] ʒe asken of þis N   18 schulde] schal KNTδ   schal]
schulden YEI   19 but] tyme bote Nα   more] a more J   forsoþe forsoþe]
forsoþe ⌐forsoþe⌐ Tα, forsoþe δ   20 þat] for N, and δ   greete] grente T, weyle F,
wepe α   wepe] grete α   world] w *canc.* /world D   21 ʒe schal] *rev.*
ACKG   to] vnto N, into δ   22 soþ] *om.* Z   þe¹] hye S   þe² . . . crist]
crist was rysen N   rysyng] reysinge s, arisynge T   for] *om.* L   23 and siþ²]
whenne þei hadden N   ioye] more *canc.* ioye D   and worldly . . . ioye (25)] *om.*
I   24 contraryeden] contrarien N   þat] and þat S   hadden] han N, maden
E   siþ] aftur N   25 þe] *om.* ABCFKLMSYβδJ   of²] of þe NTEZH   26
eft] ofte δ   sawmple] ensaumple, en- *canc.* α, ensaumple Sδι, exsample H   pren-
te] peynte B   word] witt Y   27 þer] *om.* LIG   a] and a G   tra-
ueyluþ] traueled δ   28 for . . . comeþ] *om.* DABCFKLMNTYαβδEIJZG, ⌐] hir our
comeþ⌐ (*later corr.*) X   aftur] aftirward E   29 delyuerud] dolyuerud D, delyuer
Z   forʒetuþ] for retiþ C   30 man] a man N   þe] þis CK   eft] *om.*
N   31 ʒow¹] ʒou eft N   fro . . . ioye (32)] ʒour ioye from ʒou I   fro] ⌐hit⌐
from T, hit fro N   32 ʒowre ioye] ʒoure ioye *canc.* T, *om.* N   33 part] party
ABαJ   34 longe] longo D   lyuen] bileuen I   to] for to M   35 to¹] in
α   36 þe] *om.* β   to] in I   sowle] in soule NTαEI   37 þis] *on eras. corr.*
D   state] ⌐a⌐state X   of] on CFNSαEIJ   owre] þis S   formere] forme
C   38 anoyʒe] noye Z, anoying CK   or] or to ABNα   þe] *om.* A   se-

we þenkon in owre herte þat, for þis peyne þat we han now, we
schal haue myche ioye whan we ben fulle maade in þe world.   40
And þat schal neuere be doon fully byfore þat we comen to blysse;
for we mornen tyl þat tyme, for we may li3tly perische fro li3f.
But þanne a man is fully maad whanne he is corowned in blysse, for
þanne he is certeyn to lyue euere in blisse wiþowten peyne.

Clerkis seyn ⌐þat⌐ whan man is bro3t þus to Godis chawmbre,   45
þanne is hee fully spowsed wiþ God, and dowyd boþe in body and
sowle. Of fowre dowerus of þe body Crist took ernes here in þis
world; for whan he cam owht of his modur he brac not þe cloystre
of hyre but, as þe sonne comeþ þorw þe glas, so Crist cam from his
modir wombe. And þis more3if is clepud of clerkys dower of   50
bodyly sutilyte; and ofte vsede Crist þis dower fro þe tyme þat he
was ryson. Þe secounde dower of þe body is clepud agilite, þat is
swiftnesse þerof to meuen how a man wole; and þis dower vsede
Crist whan he wente vpon þe watur, and specially at þat tyme þat
he stey3 into heuene. Þe þridde dower of þe body is in-   55
coruptibilite þat þe body|may not dye, ne be broke by noþing.   f.96v
And þis dower knew þe feend, whan he alegghede to Crist þat he
schulde not hurten his foot, 3if he lepte down fro þe temple; and
by uertew of þis dower þe knytes broke not Cristus þies, ne whan
he cam in at þe 3ates bordis brooke not his body. Þe ferþe dower   60
and þe laste ⌐i⌐s cleryng of mannys body, whan hit schyneþ bri3te

---

54 Matt. 14: 25–6; **55** Luke 24: 51; Acts 1: 9; **57** Matt. 4: 5–6; **59** John 19:
33; John 20: 19, 26.

weþ] sueþ herof H   40 haue] herafter haue N   we] ⌐we⌐ CT   42 tyl] to
E   43 a . . . whanne] om. S   in] wiþ E   blysse] ioy of heuene N   44 he
is] rev. N   euere] om. N   blisse] blisse euermore N   45 þat] corr. D,
om. CK   man] a canc. man α, am an AFNSYEIJG   bro3t þus] rev. CK   þus]
⌐þus⌐ Tβ   46 is hee] rev. ABKSαIJZG, he F   47 sowle] in soule ATEI   fow-
re] oure LM   dowerus] doweries β   þe] om. S   crist] here canc. crist G, here
crist F, of wiche crist C, þat criste α   took] take L   ernes] ernys ⌐erlys⌐ C, erlles
αZ   here] ⌐here⌐ δ, om. FKLMNSTYβEJ   þis] þe Nδ   48 whan] om.
N   owht] noht N   modur] modris wombe FSEI, modur as oþer men comen into
þis world by myracle was he boren of hure and N   brac] ne brak N   49 crist
cam] rev. Y   50 more3if] more morifie I   is] om. C   clepud] called
NαδZ   clerkys] chirchis β   dower] dower ⌐3ift⌐ C, dowery αG   51 bodyly]
þe bo⌐di⌐ H   ofte] eft K   þis] þe I   dower] dowery α   þe] ⌐þe⌐ Y, þat
A, om. G   52 dower] dowery αG   clepud] called αδZ   agilite] cleerte
⌐clepud⌐ I   53 swiftnesse] suetnesse M   a] þat I   dower] dowery α G   54
vpon] on Y   þat] þe CLTα, þis K   55 into] ⌐in⌐to CM   dower] dowery
α   57 þis] þuse Nδ   dower] dowery α, dowers Nδ   to] vnto N   58 foot]
feet H   59 dower] dowery α, powere I   60 at] om. S   bordis] þe bordis

in heuene as þe sonne or oþre sterrus. And þis dower took Crist to hym in tyme of his transfiguryng; and herfore seyde Petre þanne þat good was hem to be þere, for þis is þe hiest dower þat falluþ

65 vnto mannys body. And aftur þese fowre dowerus fallen fowre vnto þe sowle. Þe furste and þe moste dower answeruþ to þe laste of þe body, þat a sowle blessid in heuene haþ cleer knowyng of alle þinge þat is or was or euere schal be. And siþ man haþ dely3t to see a pley here in

70 erþe, or a lord, or þing of wonder, and þerwiþ feeduþ his soule, myche more þis clere sy3t of God and alle hise creatures schulden fully feedon þe blessyde sowle, and þeraftur blesse þe body. And herfore seiþ owre Iesu in þe gospel of seyn Iohn þat 'þis is li3f wiþowten eende: to knowe þe Fadur and his Sone'; for þanne

75 men knowen in þis myrour alle creatures þat may be, and þis clere sy3t is more ioyeful þan any tonge may telle here. Þe secounde dower of þe sowle is vertew to kepe ful knowyng, so þat knowyng of o þing contrarieþ not to anoþur. And, ri3t as body schal euere laste for acord of alle his partis, so mannys wyt schal

80 euere laste for lookyng in þe furste myrour; and so man for3etuþ not in heuene þyngus þat he somtyme knew. Þe þridde dower of þe sowle is redynes for to knowen alle þingus þat man wole, how ofte þat he wole þenkon on hem. For, 3if he traueylede in þis þo3t

---

63 Matt. 17: 4; Mark 9: 4; Luke 9: 33;   73 John 17: 3.

ABα   dower] dowery α   61 is] i corr. D   cleryng] clernesse N   62 sonne] mone Nδ   oþre] þe TZ   dower] dowery α   63 his] þis L   64 good] god I   was] were N   hem] hym CNδ, heuy I   hiest] hei3ere S   dower] dowery α   65 vnto] to N, þat vnto S   66 dowerus] doweryes α, om. K   vnto] ⌐vn¬to T, to KY   67 dower] dowery α   to] vnto G   68 þinge] þingis ABF   þat] in heuen and erþe and helle þat N   69 euere] om. K   man] a canc. man α, a man ANTYEIJ   in] on M   70 or² . . . wonder] or anoþer wondurful þing N   þing of] ⌐a¬ þing of Y, a þing of TδI, thinges of α, a K   and . . . soule] þe wuche his body is fed whit N   and] þat I   soule] on eras. DX, bodi ABCKLMTYEIJ   71 myche] ⌐and¬ myche E, in moche I   þis] þe CK   and] in C   schulden] schulen BG   72 fully] om. E   sowle] sowlis T   73 herfore] þerfore E   iesu] ⌐lord¬ iesu E, lord iesu MSI   margin iohannis Z   is] om. N   74 his] þe canc. ⌐his¬ α, þe KNSδ   76 any tonge] om. I   telle here] telle ⌐ere¬ here N   77 dower] dowery α, om. M   sowle] s/sowle D, bodi F   to . . knowyng] ful knowyng to kepe N   ful] om. E   78 knowyng] o knowyng H   contrarieþ not] contrary not CZ, is not contrarie N   to] ⌐to¬ T, om. SH   anoþur] knowyng of anoþere E   body] ⌐a¬ body JX, o bodi EG, þe body NαδH   79 wyt] wittis δ   schal euere] rev. I   81 he] we canc. ⌐þe¬ C   dower] dowery α   82 how] and how α   83 he¹] om.

ony þing aʒeynes his wylle, he were not fully in blisse, ne
wiþowten a noyows peyne. And neþeles we byleuon þat seyntes 85
han what þei wolen haue, and þei wolen non yuel þing.
And þus
men grownden manye blissus, but alle ben browte to þese fowre
þat we can rykenen in seyntis; as þe fowrþe dower of men in
blysse, answeryng to þe furste of þe body, is sutylte of mannys
sowle, þat hit takyþ alle kynne trewþe and herby is not 90
vndisposud to casten owht o trewþe by anoþur; but, as manye
blessyde bodyus ben togedere in o place, so manye blessyde
knowyngus ben togedere in o sowle. Surete of syche goodys may
not fayle to þese seyntes, siþ þei seen clerly in God how hit ys
neede al þis to be. And so þei wyton how þei han al þe ioye þat þei 95
wolen, siþ hem wanteþ no ⌜kyn⌝ þing þat þei schulden desyre for
to haue.

S,hue δ   on] vpon N   þis] his YZ   84 aʒeynes] aʒeyn aʒeyn N   85
a . . . peyne] peyne anoyous I   a noyows] auarous K   86 what] whatsoeuere
δ   yuel þing] þing þat is yuel AB   88 can rykenen] rikene T   seyntis] holy
seyntes   fowrþe] foure Nδ   dower] dowery Aα, doweres Nδ   men] man
AB   89 answeryng] answereþ I   90 hit] om. G   alle] of alle I   kynne]
kynnes N, maner αδ   is] it is NY   not] om. EI   91 vndisposud] disposid Y,
vnsupposid Z   o trewþe] vntreuþe, vn- eras. I   92 in] þere in L   94 þese]
om. K   95 þe] þis S   96 wolen] wolde Nδ   hem] þei S   kyn] corr. D,
kynnes Nα, manere δ   for to] to ACNYEH   97 haue] haue pray we to god þis
syʒte to haue þat we in heuen may see his face endelasly to wurchipen hym for his mercy
and his grace etc. pater et aue N

Dominica iiii post Pasche. [Euangelium.]
Sermo 50.

Vado ad eum qui me misit. Iohannis 16.

This gospel of Iohn telluþ hiȝ priuyte of þing þat is to comene
byforn þe day of doom. And, for Cristes ascension is nyȝ, þerfore
Crist telluþ a word of his ascensioun, þat hise apostles schulden
trowe. Crist, to whom alle þinge þat schal be is present, seiþ vpon
5 þe Þeresday þat he schulde dyen on þe morwe '*I go to hym þat haþ
sent me to þe erþe*', and þat is a myche offys to buye þe chyrche of
men. And 'For my steyȝeng is so opon, as hit is hyd byfore tymes,
noon of ȝow axseþ me wodyr þat I go; but ȝeet, for I haue spoke þese þingus
f.97 *vnto ȝow*, ȝe trowe not but|liȝtly þat þei ben soþe. And so *oon hid*
10 *sorwe haþ now fyllud ȝowre hertys*, for I haue teeld ȝow how ⌐þat⌐ I
schal suffre, how I schal be repreued, and how I schal dye, and
how I schal after ben absentyd fro ȝow, and how I schal dwellon
in heuene tyl I come to þe laste day to iuge þe world to ioye or to
peyne.' And þese wordys schulden make frendys to mornen
15 among hemself. '*But I sey ȝow trewþe: hit spedeþ to ȝow þat I goo. For,
ȝif I go not, þe Hooly Gost schal not come to ȝow, and ȝif I schal go, I schal*

MSS : D; ABCEFGHIJKLMNSTXYZαβδ.

Dominica . . . euangelium] *om.* Z   sermo 50] sermo 54 β, *om.* BCFKLNSTY-
αδEIJXZGH   vado . . . misit] voluntarie genuit nos N   me misit] *rev.*
ABCKLMSTYβδEJZG   iohannis 16] *om.* E, iacobi primo N   1 hiȝ] þe Y   of
þing] *om.* E   2 þe] *om.* M   3 crist telluþ] *rev.* N   þat . . . trowe (4)] *om.*
N   4 þinge] thinges α   seiþ] seide NTZ   vpon] on N   5 on] vpon
YαβZ   morwe] morne αZ   6 to¹] in *canc.* to F, into N   þe¹] *om.*
NT   þat]þis N   is]*om.* E   a] ⌐for⌐ a T   myche]hye N   buye]hie
CK   7 as] þat T, and E   tymes] tyme T   8 me] me *canc.* X, *om.*
CFKLMNSTYβEZG   wodyr] þ *canc.* wodyr D, wheþer α   þat] *om.*
SY   þese] þus T   9 not] nou LMNSTYαEJXZG   liȝtly] luytel
N   þei]*om.* M   oon hid]oonhed A, vnhid KαE   10 now]*om.* S   fyl-
lud] fulfulde δE   ȝow] to ȝou F   how] *om.* IG   þat] *corr.* D, *om.*
NTIG   11 schal¹ . . . 1¹] *om.* M   and¹] *om.* N   how²] hou þat
M   and²]*om.* H   12 how¹ . . . schal¹]*om.* N   I¹] aftir I H   after]
afturward N, *om.* SH   absentyd] ascendid I   I²] *om.* L   13 day] dome
N   to³] at þat day to N   14 schulden make] maken N   schulden] shulen
FIG   15 hemself] himself S   ȝow¹] to ȝow CFKYH   to] *om.* M   16

sendon hym to ʒow. And whanne he schal come, he schal reproue þe world of
synne and of riʒtwysnesse and also of iugement.'

But þis schal be vndirstonde þus: God schal repreue þis world
of *'synne of vntrewþe, for þei trowede not in me'*. And þis is þe furste   20
synne and moste vnkynde þat þei myʒten do to God. For, siþ
Crist cam to þis world, and bycaam our broþur to buyn vs and
algatis to profiʒte to mannys kynde, and he is s[o] opon trewþe
schewed þus vnto man, þis is a greet synne to trowe not heere to
Crist. For in synnyng in þis feiþ, vnkynde men ⌜vn⌝trowen to his   25
Fadur, and to Crist, and also to þe Hooly Goost, for þis hooly
Trynnyte wytnessuþ þis iorneye. And as byleue is furst vertew
and grownd of alle oþre, so vnbyleue is þe furste synne of alle
oþre. And þerfore synne take by hymself is take for þi⌜s⌝ moste
famows; of þis synne schal þe Gost repreue men of þis world.   30
Secoundely schal þis Goost *reproue men of riʒtwysnesse* þat þei
schulden haue to Crist and vnkyndely wanton hyt; for such a
messanger schulde be worschiped of alle men, and heryed for
such a messaghe, siþ hit was so profiʒtable. And so þe world schal
be dampned for wantyng of þis riʒtwisnesse, and specially *for such*   35
a persone goþ aʒeyn to his Fadyr; and þat scheweþ þat Crist is þe
secownde persone in Trinnyte, and so by his godhede euene wiþ
his Fadur, and by his manhede lesse but euene in kynde wiþ his
breþren, and þus riʒte wolde axse þat þis persone were
worschiped. Þe þrydde tyme schal þis Goost *repreue men of þis world*   40
for þei iugedon folily þat Crist was lad by a feend, and ʒet þe moste

I¹] *om.* F   ʒif²] *om.* Y   17 he¹] ʒe L   schal²] *om.* β   þe] þis
T   18 synne] synnes N   and¹] ⌜and⌝ Y, *om.* FT   of¹] *om.* β   and²]
⌜and⌝ Y, *om.* IG   19 þis schal] þus schal þis N   þus] *om.* N   þis²] þe
YH   20 of²] of þis werd of S   trowede] bileueden K   21 and] and also
N   to] ⌜to⌝ C, *om.* Y   22 crist] ⌜he⌝ S   to¹] in *canc.* to EX, into N   and¹]
⌜and⌝ K, *om.* CMYβZ   23 to²] of *canc.* ⌜to⌝ α, of δ   mannys kynde] mankynde
AFNYδEIJZGH   so] as, -s *on eras. corr.* D   25 vntrowen] vn- *added* DTE,
troweden L, ⌜bene vn⌝trowen N   his] þis I   26 and²] *om.* C   for] and for
H   27 þis] þe H   furst] ⌜þe⌝ first A, þe firste T   28 grownd] grounded
C   so] riʒt so E, and so I   vnbyleue is] *rev.* N   þe] *om.* NG   29 þis]-i- *on*
eras. corr., -s *corr.* D, þe MIGH   30 famows] famous synne α   gost] holy gost
δZ   31 secoundely] þe secounde tyme T   33 worschiped] wurschyp δ   her-
yed] þonkeþ N, preysid E   34 such a] his N   35 þis] *om.* K, suche H   36
þat¹] *om.* Y   38 his¹] þe H   by] *om* Y   his²] *om.* M   lesse] *om.*
M   euene in kynde] in kynde euen E   39 wolde] wole AB   40 tyme] *om.*
Y   þis¹] þe *canc.* ⌜þis⌝ α, þe MZ   men of] *om.* E   41 iugedon] iugen
FβZH   was] *om.* LM   by] wiþ I   a] þe M   ʒet] riʒt L   þe] *om.*

hy3e feend, prince of þis world, is now iughed to helle for he
temptede þus Crist and dude hym vnworschipe.

45 '3et', seiþ Crist, 'I haue monye þingus to sey to 3ow, but 3e may not beron
hem now; but þe Spiri3t of trewþe schal come to 3ow and teche 3ow alle
trewþe, and make 3ow stronge to bere trewþe to suffryng of deþ
þerfore.' Þis goode maister schal here bygynne for to teche þe
book of li3f, and he schal neuere eende to teche tyl þat hise
disciples comen to heuene, and þere schal þei clerly knowe eche
50 trewþe þat men can telle. 'He schal not speke of hymself wiþowten
any cause byfore, but alle þingus þat he schal here of þe Fadur and of
þe Sone schal he speken and telle 3ow, and 3e schal aftur teche his
chirche; and þingus þat herafter ben to comene schal þis Gost telle 3ow'.
For þe apostles knewon here al þat now is neede to knowe, for in
55 þis mesure ladde God hem, and meuede hem to do his dedis. He
chargede hem not wiþ ydel wyt þat herfore þei schulde be
f.97v prowde, but al þat nedide hem|to konnen, þei cowden þat redily.
'Þis Goost schal clarifye me, for he schal taken of myn and schewe 3ow þe
trewþe þat I am, and þat I haue.' And so, in knowing of þis
60 trewþe, þe apostles schullen wel knowe Crist, how by his
godheede he is euene wiþ his Fadur, and anemptis his manheede
he is euene in kynde wiþ his breþren, but in grace of onhede he
passeþ alle oþre men þat may be, siþ noo man may be God but he
and welle of grace as he is.

65 And heere Crist declareþ hymself, and seiþ ⌜þat⌝ alle þat his
Faadur haþ ben hyse; and herfore he seyde þat þe Goost schal take of his
and schewe to hise disciples, as ben þe apostles and oþre aftur.
And in þese hy3e wordis of wyt Crist techeþ how he wiþ his Fadur

E   42 to] vnto N   43 temptede þus] rev. N   dude] om. S   vnworschipe]
⌜vn⌝worschip G, worschipe I, vnwurchep þere he schulden haue wurchiped hym
N   44 seiþ . . . haue] y haue seiþ crist N   crist] crist to his disciplis Z   46
trewþe²] ⌜testimon of⌝ trewþe T   47 bygynne] bygynne here δ   for to] to
TEI   48 eende] haue ende H   þat] om. N   49 schal] s/schal D   schal
þei] rev. AYEIG   clerly] om. E   50 men] man BNH   51 any] om.
I   byfore] fore Y   þingus] þing IG   53 and] in β   herafter ben] rev. S,
þerafter ben I   54 for¹] om. Z   þe] þes E   knewon] knowen CKI-
G   now is] rev. H   55 ladde god] rev. CK, led crist α   do] om. CK   he]
and E, for he I   56 hem not] rev. α   herfore] þerfor Z, om. I   57 konnen]
know C   cowden] knewen CN   59 so] om. J   60 by] he by N   61 he]
om. N   his¹] þe AI   anemptis] auentist J   62 euene] comyn δ   63
passeþ] is canc. passeþ D   men] om. N   man] om. Y   god] good, 2nd o canc.
D   heere crist] rev. δ   65 heere] herfore AB   þat] corr. D   his . . . haþ
(66)] ben his fadris I   66 ben] is E   þat] om. I   67 as . . . aftur] om.
N   þe] om. FαIJH   68 wiþ] is with SI   69 is] is canc. S, om. I   70 not]

is þe same God in kynde, and brynguþ forþ þe Hooly Goost. For
ellys þe Faadur hadde þis Goost, and Crist hadde not þis same   70
Goost, and so not al þat þe Fadur haþ hadde Crist as verrey God.
But siþ þis word of Crist is soþ, hit scheweþ oponly þat Crist is
God; and of hym wiþ hise Fadur comeþ forþ þe Hooly Goost. Þis
Hooly Goost may not be maad but euere comeþ forþ of þese two,
as ȝif þe schynyng of þe sonne come forþ euere of liȝt and   75
briȝtnesse. But for þis sentence ys myche hyd fro wyt of þe
comune puple, þerfore schulden preestis schapon of þe wordys of
þis gospel waᴿtᴉ myte profiȝte to his puple aftur vndurstondyng of
hem.

And we schulden marke þis word of Crist, whan he seiþ to his   80
disciples but ȝif he goo from hem to heuene, he schal not sende to
hem þe Hooly Goost. And manye musen of þese wordys, siþ Crist
was euerywhere almyghty, and so he myȝte as wel in eurþe as in
heuene sendon hem þis Goost, 'Lord! what nedid Crist to steyȝe
and speᴿkeᴉ wiþ mowþ wiþ þis Goost?' Suche wordis schewe men   85
ful rude to conseyue þis matere, and þerfore hit were neede to
hem to knowe wyt of þes wordis. We schal trowe þat Cristus
disciplus louedon hym heere to worldly, and þei muston be
purged heere of þis loue by þe Hooly Goost; and þis þing myhte
beste be doon whan manhede of Crist was from hem. And þus for   90
rudnesse of apostles seiþ Crist þat hit spediþ þat he go from hem.
But he dwelliþ by his godheede and his vertew euere wiþ hem;
and herfore he seiþ anoþur tyme þat he is alle dayȝes wiþ hem

om. I   þis²] þe KSδI   71 and . . . goost (73)] *om.* N   72 hit] he T   74
euere] euereᴿmorᴉ H   forþ] *om.* S   75 þe²] *om.* J   come] comeþ
ABKLMNSYδEIGH   forþ] ᴿforþᴉ H, *om.* MT   liȝt] britnesse N   76
briȝtnesse] lyȝt N, of briȝtnesse H   myche hyd] *rev.* N   fro] fro þe N   þe]
om. Z   77 schulden preestis] preestis schulden, *marked for rev.* Y, prestus schulden N,
ᴿprestisᴉ schulde G   schapon] carpen N   of . . . wordys] *twice* L   þe] *om.*
N   78 his] þe N   vndurstondyng of hem] þe vndurstondyng of hem EZ, hire
vndurstondynge N   80 and] but G   þis word] þes wordis I   81 he¹] ȝhe C,
ȝe LM   he²] ȝe L   to hem] to *canc.* hem αX, hem KLMNSTYβIZG, hym C,
om. J   82 manye] many men AB   of] on N   84 sendon] haue sende
E   hem] hym C   þis] þe I   goost] holy *canc.* gost α, holy gost
EI   nedid] nediþ C   85 speke] -ke *corr.* D   wiþ þis goost] þis gost wyth
δ   þis] his I   86 rude] rudy δ   þerfore] herfor N   87 wyt] þe wit
EG   88 heere] *om.* N   to] ouer Z   worldly] fleishly AB   þei] ᴿþeiᴉ
βH   89 heere] *om.* E   þis þing] þes þingis ABI   90 manhede] ᴿþeᴉmanhed
J, þe manhed KMNδEI   91 rudnesse] rurdynesse δ   apostles] þe apostlis
E   seiþ crist] crist sais *marked for rev.* α, crist seiþ AEIJ   þat¹] *om.* N   92 his²]
bi his I   hem] hym, -y- *canc.* -ᴿeᴸ α, hym CL   93 and] vnto þe end of þis warld
and Z   herfore] þerfore N   he¹] *om.* I   *margin* mathei vltimo in fine

vnto þe eende of þis world, by godhede and vertew of his
95 manhede. And þus, whan Crist was went to heuene, hise apostles
weron cler in loue and lefton loue of erþly þingus and þowten
clenely on heuenly þingus. And of þis wyt taken somme men þat
hit falleþ not to Cristus vyker, ne to preestis of hooly chirche to
haue rentes here in eurþe; but Iesu schilde be þer rente, as he seiþ
100 ofte in þe olde lawe, and þer bodyly sustynaunce schulde þei haue
of Godis part, as of dymes and offryngus and oþre almes taken in
mesure, þe whyche by þer hooly ly3f þei ableden hem to take þus.
Lord! siþ þe body of Crist vndisposede þe postles to take þis
Goost, myche more schulde worldly lordschipe vnable men now
105 to take þis Goost. And siþ þei han now o goost, hit is li3kly by þer
dedis þat þei han a wyckyde goost þat leeduþ hem an yuel wey3e.
And in þis word may we see how religiows þat ben today drawen
more to þer abyte and to þer stynkynge ordenaunce þan Crist
f.98 wolde þat hise apostles|chargedon þanne presence of his body.
110 And herfore Crist sente his apostles alone, scaterynge into þe
world; and certis þei weren more able now þan whanne he sente
hem two and two, for now þei weren ripe by þe Hooly Goost more
sadly þan þei weren byfore. But owre freris, þat ben syke, ben
closude now in cloystre togydre, mo þan twelue Cristus apostles;
115 and þis semeþ by þe feendus cautel þat, 3if oon blecke not his

---

110 Mark 6: 7.

M   day3es] þe daies δ   94 vnto] into δ   þis] þe CIH   godhede] his
godheed E   vertew] by vertu N   his] þis αJ   95 was went] went Z   96
cler] clene δI   loue²] þe canc. loue G, þe loue ABαEI   erþly] worldli L   97
on] of, -f on eras. corr. X, of ABFKMSYαβEZ   and . . . ly3f (119)] om. Z   of
. . . men] summe men taken of þis witt N   somme men] men sumwhat I   98 to¹] om.
TY   to³] om. I   99 here] om. EI   as] and F   100 sustynaunce] st canc.
sustynaunce D   schulde þei] þei shulde marked for rev. α, þei shulden AEIJ-
G   102 ableden] able αG   þus] þis I   104 worldly lordschipe] lordely ⌐or⌐
wurschype δ   lordschipe] lordschipis M   men now] nowe men marked for rev. δ,
now men BCFKNSTYαβEXG, ben L, men M   105 siþ] siþ þat H   han now]
rev. Y   hit] and it CK, þat N   li3kly] lik N   þer] þe C   106 a wyckyde]
an euyle E   an yuel] a wickyd S, in an yuel T, ⌐to¹⌐ an yuel Y   107 þis word] þes
wordis AB   word] world CKI   may we] we may marked for rev. α, we may
ACFKEIJGH   how] þat E   drawen more] rev. IG   109 þat] om.
F   þanne] þan þe, þe canc. α, þe KNEI, om. C   110 sente] assente L   alone]
aboute N   into] in⌐to¹ α, in Y   111 world] word F   112 ripe] more ripe
I   more] and more EI   113 syke] ful seke N   ben²] and I   114 in]
altered from and DX   cloystre] cloystrede, -de canc. DX   togydre] cristus]
togedre S   mo] more G   cristus apostles] apostlis of crist S   cristus] ⌐of⌐
cristis B, of cristis AFδJGH   115 semeþ] comeþ Nδ   þe] om. E   feendus]

broþur, anoþur worse schulde fuylon hym. And herfore somme freeris han wyt to hoolden hem fer fro such a lompe, and auente hem in þe world; and þanne schulde þei haue good gost, for þus dude Crist wiþ his disciples, and hym þei schulden sewon in ly3f.

deueles N   cautel] sley3te N   116 fuylon] defoule B   hym] hem A   herfore] þerfore H   117 wyt] a wit I   auente] auaunce I   118 in] fro S   þanne . . . haue] þey schulden haue þanne M   schulde þei] rev. CK, schulden Y   good] a good G, godis C   þus] þis M   119 wiþ] ˹and˺ K   ly3f] lyfe þat we hym folewe and þei also as he haþ tau3t þat wyseste is preie we hertely vnto hym wiþ pater noster et aue N

Dominica proxima ante Ascencionem.
[Euangelium.] Sermo 51.

Amen amen dico uobis si quid pecieritis. Iohannis 16.

Crist telluþ in þis gospel how hise disciples schulden ben helpude
by vertew of here prey3er whan he was stey3ed into heuene. And
furst he seiþ a general word, and takeþ boþe hise kyndes to
wytnesse þat, 3if þei axson owht þe Fadur of heuene in hys name, he schal
5 3yuon hyt hem. But, as Crist seiþ, *vnto þat tyme hise disciples axsedon not
in his name*; and þerfore afturward *schulden þei axsen þat* ⌈þere⌉ *ioy3e
were ful* and þei schulden take. Al þe hardnesse of þis matere is to
konnen parfi3tly to axson in Cristus naame, for hee schal haue
þat axsuþ þus; but, siþ owre Iesu is trewþe and helþe of men þat
10 trowon in hym, þat mon axsuþ in Cristes name þat axseþ in
trewþe his sowle helþe. Crist ys moste lord of alle, and þerfore he
wole haue despyt but ⌈3if⌉ men axson hym a greet þing, for ellys
his lordschipe and þat axsyng acorde not to his name. And so, 3if
þow wole axson in Cristus name, axe þe blisse þat euere schal
15 laste. And siþ Crist is trewþe and resown, loke þat þin axsyng be
resonable, and þanne mayst þow be sur to haue þe þing þat þow
þus axsust. And herfore Crist in þis gospel bydduþ us to axsen

MSS: D; ABCEFGHIJKLMNTXYZαβδ; S *ends incompl.* 46 of here preiere.

Dominica . . . euangelium] *om.* Z   sermo 51] *om.* BCFKLNSTYαδEIJXZG-
H   amen . . . pecieritis] vir oblitus est qualis fuerit N   amen amen] amen
αZ   pecieritis] pecierit MT, *om.* H   iohannis 16] *om.* E, iac' primo N   2 was
stey3ed] steied I   into] to αH   3 seiþ] seide S   boþe] *om.* F   to] *om.*
T   4 axson] askeden I   þe] of þe FTH   5 hyt] *om.* Y   hem] to hem
TY   seiþ] *om.* Y   6 þerfore] herfor A   þere] *corr.* D   7 ful] fulfuld
N   al] al 3if J   hardnesse] hardinesse I   to] for to T   8 to] *om.* NYI   9
axsuþ þus] askyng whitouten any doute N, asking þat he askiþ þus δ   axsuþ] he axeth
S   helþe] heel Z, help I   10 trowon] trusten N   11 helþe] hele Nδ-
Z   moste] more CK   alle] alle thynge S   12 wole] wolde EI   haue]
om. Z   3if] *corr.* D   axson] askiden E   þing] þing of muche value and
muche pris N   13 his¹] *om.* G   acorde] acordiþ BTZG, acordiden
YEI   to] vnto BFNSYδIZGH   so] *om.* Z   14 wole] wilt AFNSTY-
αδEIJXGH   15 siþ] seþen þat NS   þat] *om.* αJ   16 mayst þow] *rev.*
T   mayst] -st *corr.* D, may N   sur] seker SH, fulle syker N   þe] *om.*
CKβ, þat NI   þing] askyng E   17 þus axsust] *rev.* AYIJ, askeste NZ, askis þus,

owre fulle ioy3e, and þanne schal we haue hit 3if þat we axson hit
in resoun; for no man haþ but half ioy3e, but 3if he be ful of blysse.
And þis greete Lord wolde not be axsud but þis blis or menus   20
þerto. And 3if man axse þis in resown þat he be worþi to haue hyt,
he schal haue wiþowte dowte, whan beste tyme were þat he
hadde hit. And he schal haue on beste maneer þe þing þat he
axsuþ þus.

And herfore þe seuene axsyngus þat Crist techeþ in þe Pater   25
Noster meuen þis forme of axsyng, and algatis to axson in
charyte. And þerfore men þat lyuon in werre ben vnable to haue
þer axsyng, but þei axson þer owne dampnyng in þe fyᵣfᵀþe
peticion; for þere þei axson þat God for3iue hem þer dettis þat þei
owen to hym, ri3t as þei for3iuen men þat ben dettowres vnto   30
hem. And here we schal vndurstonde þat eche man is detour to
God, and eche man oweþ to eche oþur to doon hym good in
charyte. And so faylyng to loue God of al þin herte and al þi
wylle, þou rennest in greet dette boþe a3enys God and man. And
so in þiᵣsᵀ fyueþe axsyng þese men þat werron now o dayes axson 35
hym as þei wolden mene 'for3iue vs, for we ben euene wiþ þe', or
ellys 'tak veniaunce in yre of vs, as we taken veniaunse of owre
breþren', – and þis is no good prey3ere, but more axsyng of Godis
veniaunse. And for þis cause monye men ben|vnherde in her   f.98v
prey3er, and turned into more yuel for þer vnskilful prey3er; and 40
suche men weren bettur to leue þan to prey3e on sych maner. For
manye men prey3en for veniaunse and for worldis prosperyte,
and in þe yre of God he 3yueþ hem þat þei axson; but hit were

marked for rev. α   herfore] þerfor αδ   þis] his SI   to] om. CKE   18 schal
we] rev. T   þat] om. I   19 in] wiþ Z   haþ] askes N   3if] om. F   20
wolde] wole A   not] om. B   or] or þat δ   menus] þat meueþ herto
N   21 þerto] herto H   man] a canc. man F, a man KH, men MT   þis] þus
A   he] om. S   22 wiþowte] it canc. wiþouten A, it wiþouten I   23 on] on þe
AαEIGH, it on þe FJ   þe] þat N, þis E, om. IG   25 techeþ . . . noster (26)] in þe
pater noster techeþ N   þe²] om. K   26 axsyng] axingis S   27 werre] wraþþe
K, were and robry Z   28 dampnyng] dampnacioun E, dampne T   fyfþe] f corr.
D, ferþe L   30 men] to men Nδ   vnto] to NE   32 oweþ] awe Z   to
eche] rev. H   eche²] om. Nδ   hym] hem α   33 so] ᵣsoᵀ β, om.
N   faylyng] in failyng Z   to loue] of loue to N   god] o god δ   al²] of al
BKE   35 þis] s corr. D   þese] om. Z   36 hym] hem hym C   for] ᵣforᵀ Y,
om. M   37 of¹] on N   of²] on N   38 godis] om. I   40 vnskilful]
vnkyndeful N   prey3er] askynge N   41 to¹] om. I   on] in I   42 for¹]
for þe N   for²] ᵣforᵀα, om. FEJ   worldis] worldeli CFKαEIJ   prosperyte]
profyte δ   43 þe] om. E   hem] hym C   þat] þat þat K   hit . . . bettur

bettur to hem to preye not þus, ne to haue þis þing. And þus men
45 of contrarye londys prey3en God in greete processiounes, and for
vnworþinesse of þer prey3er hem were bettur to sytten at home.
And for men wyton not for what þing þei schulden prey3e God in
syche casus, þerfore good li3f profi3teþ more, and þe Hooly Goost
axseþ þanne for hem. And whoeuere sture men to yuel li3f, 3if þei
50 ben frerus þat cryen hy3e, God heruþ hem not to goode, but
raþer takeþ veniaunce of hem. For Crist seiþ þat not eche man
þat seiþ to hym 'Lord! Lord!' schal comen into þe blisse of heuene,
but he þat eenduþ in ry3t lif, for he prey3eþ in þe name of þe
Trinnyte. And þus Zebedeus sonys prey3eden for goode but in
55 euyl maner. And so algatis ri3twys lyf ys þe beste in mannys
preyere, for such lif preyeþ betture to God þan hy3e voyses of
ypocrites.

And aftur seiþ Crist to hise apostles þat *þese þingus he seyde byfore
to hem in prouerbys* and mystily, *but now is come tyme whan he schal not
60 speke þus to hem in prouerbys, but apertly of his Fadur he schal tellen* hem
as beste is. *In þat day schal cristen men axse in Cristus name* vnto þer
blisse. *And now he seiþ vnto hem þat he schal preyen his Fadur of hem,* for
þei schal be mater to Crist and maken his rewme, wherfore he
preyeþ þat *Fadur loueþ* þes apostles, and oþur men þat suwon
65 hem, *for þei louedon Iesu Crist and trowedon þat he cam fro God,* 3he þat

---

51 Matt. 7: 21; **54** Matt. 20: 20.

---

(44)] bettur were hit N   44 to¹] vnto N   to preye not] nou3t to preie I   to³]
om. N   þis þing] þes þingis AEI   45 greete] *om.* J   processiounes]
procession T   46 to] to *canc.* αX, *om.* CKLMTβZ   48 casus] causis AKLαEI,
caas NG   li3f] lyuyng AFαEI   profi3teþ] profet C   49 axseþ] asken
N   whoeuere] whosoeuer NδZ   sture] stireþ BCFKLMNTYαβδEIJZG-
H   yuel] ille α, do yuel δ   3if] þeigh N, þof Z, al 3if E   þei . . . þat (50)] al
on god þai Z   50 hy3e] on hy3 K   51 takeþ] to take ABE, take I   of]
on ABFNαE, vpon T   þat not] not to, to *canc.* B, not C, not þat δ   52 to hym] ⌜to
hym⌝ αE   schal] sal not Z   comen] entre NG   into] ⌜in⌝to α, to
KEI   þe] *om.* H   heuene] hem E   53 prey3eþ] pray C   in²] as he
schulde in N   þe¹] *om.* KH   54 prey3eden] bede T   for . . . maner (55)]
bote in yuel maner for good N   goode] god I   in] in an G   55 ri3twys]
ryh⌜wise⌝α, ri3t AEIJ   56 preyeþ] pray C   voyses] voice Nα   58 seiþ crist]
crist sais, *marked for rev.* α, crist seiþ FEIJG   hise] *om.* E   þese . . . seyde] he said
þir thingis Z   he] ben EI   60 speke þus] *rev.* B   to] vnto A   61 in¹] and
L   cristen] cristem, *last minim subpuncted* D   vnto] to N   62 vnto] to
N   of] for *canc.* ⌜of⌝α, for KEIJG   63 schal be] be K   to] vnto
EI   wherfore] ⌜w⌝herfore YH   he] ⌜þat⌝ he N   64 þat¹] þat þe, þe *canc.* Y,
þat þe ABNTαδEH, þat his J, þe K   loueþ] loue ANTαδEJ   þes] his
K   suwon] suweden I   65 hem] hym Cδ   louedon] louen T   tro-

Crist by hys manheede cam of God in his godhede. *Crist cam fro þe*
Fadur and cam into þe world; and now, whon Crist haþ don his
message, *he forsakuþ aȝen þe world, and goþ* by manhede *to his Fadur*.
And Cristus *disciplus seydon to hym 'Loo! now þow spekist openly, and*
þow seist now *no prouerbe, and perfore we wyton wel þat þow knowest alle*   70
þingus. And hit is to þe no nede þat ony man axse þe owt, for þow wost
byfore þe axsyng what men schulden axse and what þing leue. *In*
þis we trowen þat þow cam fro God as his owne sone.' And þis byleue
is grownd to men to haue of God what þat hem nediþ, and to
wyte what is beste to hem, al ȝif hit displese to þe world. But as   75
men þat ben in feuerus desyre not þat were beste for hem, so men
heere in synne coueyte not beste þing for hem. For þe world seyde
þat þe apostles weron foolys and forsakon of God, and so hit
wolde seyȝ today of men þat lyuedon lyȝk to hem; for worldus
ioyȝe and erþly good plesuþ to hem wiþ menus þerto, and þei   80
sauere not heuenly good, ne riȝte sewynge aftur Crist. And þis
iugement now in þe world is opon wytnesse aȝenus men þat þei
be not hoole in sowle, but turnede amys to worldly þingus. For as
a mowþ of a syȝk man, distemperid fro good mete, meueþ hym
for to coueyte þing contrarye to his helþe, so hit is of mannys   85
sowle þat sauoreþ not Godis lawe. And as wantyng of appetyȝt is
a sygne deedly to man, so wantyng of Godis wyt is signe of his
secownde deþ. And iugement þat now reigneþ of worldly
prosperite is tookne of men þat þei ben foolys, and sauere not of
Godis lawe. For þe world seiþ comunly þat, ȝif a man haue   90

wedon] trowen I   66 in] be *canc.* ⌜in⌝ α, bi E   68 manhede] his *canc.* manhede α,
his manhed H   70 and] *om.* CK   we] now we Y   71 þingus] þing
C   and] at F   to . . . nede] no nede to þe δ   to þe] þee K   wost]
knowist G   72 þing] thinges αJ   in] and M   73 þis¹] þis þing Y   cam]
comest I   74 grownd] groundid CK   to men] *om.* α   to haue of] *twice*
β   þat] *om.* CKNαIZGH   75 what] what þat δ   displese] disple H   76
in] in þe CαδJ   beste] most beste αEI   for] to TδH   77 coueyte] þei
coueiten I   beste] þe beste I   þing] thynges α   78 þe] *om.* H   79
lyuedon] lyuen δ   hem] þe apostlis E   worldus] worldli FαH   80 and¹] is
⌜and⌝ β   good] goodis Y   plesuþ] plese C   to] *om.* I   81 good] good⌜is⌝
F, godis δ, þingis B   riȝte] riȝtly EIJ   82 þe] *om.* I   þei] *om.* Z   83
amys] a *canc.*/ amys D   in YH   as a] als he C, as þe H   84
distemperid] distempreþ I, departid N   meueþ] mowþ C   85 for to] to
E   þing] þingis ABFαIJ, þyngis þat ben E   his] ȝour I   helþe] hele
CNαδZ   86 godis] of goddis H   wantyng] a wantyng δ   of] *om.* E   87
a] *om.* Z   sygne deedly] dedly sygne N, dedly taken Z   man] men CK, a man
δ   so] so þat J   signe] a sygne α   88 now reigneþ] *rev.* KH   89
prosperite] wurchipes and worldly profyte N   tookne] to konne ⌜tokene⌝ I   of¹]
to F   sauere] saruen C   90 for] *om.* β   world] w *eras.*/world D   91

worldly blisse, and þe world leyȝe to hym in kyllyng of hise
f.99 enemyes,|þanne God loueþ hym and doþ myracles for his sake.
But Lord! where is owre byleue? – þat we schulden trowen in loue
of God þat hit stondeþ not in þis but raþer hate of God. And, as
95 Gregory seiþ, as a bole þat schal be kyld goþ in corn at his wylle,
and is not pyndut, ne traueylut wiþ oþure bestis, so a lyme of þe
feend is left fro þe grace of God to figuren his dampnacion, and
suffred to do myche harm here to largen his peyne afturward. We
schulden leue þese sensible signes, and taken ensawmple of hooly
100 men, as of Crist and hise apostles, how þei hadde not here þere
blisse. But here Crist ordeynede peynes and hate of þe world and
pursewyng to men þat he moste louede, to techon vs þat comen
after hem. And þus signes of pacience and pursewyng in þis eurþe
schulde be tokne of Godus loue and not signes of anticrist.

worldly] a worldly I   leyȝe] lyȝe IJG, like T, lyiþ LN, ioye C, ioieþ K, falle
α   kyllyng] likyng F   92 enemyes] enmye GH   god] þei seien god
N   93 in] and C, in þe Nδ   94 þat . . . god²] om. LM   stondeþ] stoodiþ
Y   þis] þuse N   raþer] raþer in H, titter in Z   hate] it is hate N   95 as]
om. B   goþ] and canc. gose α, and goiþ E   at his wylle] where he wole I   96
and is] om. N   pyndut] pynned BNI, pyned KE   a] as ⌈a⌉ T, þo α   þe] a
α   97 þe] om. EZG   figuren] figure of G   98 suffred] here is suffred
N   here] om. N   largen] alarge BM   afturward] afturward for mede
deserueth he noun so N   we] for we EI   99 leue] trow Z   þese] þis
L   100 of] om. I   hise] of canc. his α, of his AIJ   here . . . blisse (101)] her
blisse here ABY, here blis EJ   101 peynes] peyne N, hem peynes EIJ   hate
. . . world] worldes hate N   102 pursewyng] pursuyt N   103 hem] hym canc.
hem E, hym J, om. N   104 be tokne of] betokene K   tokne] take FX, taken IG,
tokenes N   of¹] on. eras. corr. D   loue] sone G   and . . . anticrist] om.
Z   anticrist] anticrist and þerfore preie we vnto god in pacience for to kepen oure
soules and for to suffre in þis world to wynne wiþ mede in anoþer and þat it so be pater
noster N

Dominica infra Octavam Ascencionis.

[Euangelium.] Sermo 52.

Cum uenerit Paraclitus. Iohannis 15 [et 16].

Crist telluþ hise disciplus of comyng of þe Cownfortour whiche is
þe Hooly Goost, and what lif þei schal aftur lede.
And eche man
schulde heere conne þis lore, for þanne he may be sowlus leeche,
and wyte by signes of his lyȝf wher his sowle be seek or hool. Lord!
siþ a fysisyan lerneþ diligently his signes in vryne, in pows and   5
oþre þingus, wheþur a mannys body be hool, how myche more
schulde he knowe syche signes þat tellon helþe of mannys sowle,
and how he haþ hym to God. Al ȝif suche þingus ben pryuye and
passen worldly wit ⌜of⌝ men, neþeles þe Hooly Gost telluþ men
somme of suche signes, and makiþ hem more certeyn þan men   10
can iuge of bodyly helþe. And, for we schulden kyndely desyre for
to knowe þe sowles state, þerfore þe Hooly Goost þat techuþ vs to
knowe þese signes is clepud a Cownfortour of man, passynge oþre
cownfortoures. And, as mannys sowle is bettur þan þe body, and
endeles good passeþ temporal good, so þis knowyng of þe sowle   15
passuþ oþre mennys kunnyng.

MSS: D; ABCEFGHIJKLMNTXYZαβδ.

Dominica . . . euangelium] *om.* Z   sermo 52] *om.* BCFKLNTYαδEIJXZGH   cum
. . . paraclitus] caritas operit multitudinem peccatorum N   paraclitus] paraclitus quem e F   iohannis 15 et 16] iohannis 15 DABFKLMTYαβEIXZGH,
iohannis 5 C, iohannis 16 δ, prima petri iiii N   1 of¹] *om.* J   comyng] þe
comynge T   whiche] þe which AFNδIJZGH   2 þei . . . lede] aftur þei schal
lede N   schal] shulden, -de-*canc.* H, schuld CZ   aftur lede] *rev.* B   3 schulde
heere] *rev.* I   heere conne] cun here, *marked for rev.* α, cunne here A, kunne
E   sowlus] his soulis H   4 his¹] *om.* E   seek] hool E   hool] seke
E   5 siþ] saiþ ⌜siþ⌝ C, seiþ β   lerneþ] lereþ H   in vryne] and veyne
B   in²] and CKJ, and in E   and] in T, and in E   6 þingus] signes
α   wheþur . . . hool] to knowe þe hele of monnes body N   how] but how
I   7 he] ⌜he⌝ TJ   signes] þinges I   þat] and L   helþe] hele
NZ   mannys] mennes Y, a mannus E   sowle] saules αI   8 hym] hem
Yα   al ȝif] ȝef al N   þingus] signes Bαδ   9 worldly] þe ⌜worldly⌝
α   wit of]-t of *on eras. corr.* D   men somme] sum men B   11 bodyly] worldly
I   helþe] hele NαZ, helpe C, *om.* J   for to] to EH   12 sowles state] staat of
soule I   sowles] lordis B   13 signes] þyngis E   clepud] called Nαδ-
Z   man] men ABYIJ   oþre] alle oþere J   14 þe] mannus E   and] so

Crist seiþ þus to hise disciples 'Whan þis Cownfortour schal come,
þat I schal sende ȝow of þe Fadur, Goost of trewþe, þat comeþ forþ of hym,
he schal bere wytnesse of me; and ȝe schal also bere wytnesse, for ȝe ben wiþ
20   me alwey fro þe bygynnyng of my prechyng.' But heere may Grekis be
meuyde to trowe þat þe Hooly Goost comeþ not forþ but of þe
Fadur, and not of Crist þat is his Sone; for þe ton seiþ Crist and in
þis gospel leueþ þe toþur. And hit semeþ to somme men, ȝif þis
were trewþe þat schulde be trowyd, God wolde liȝtly telle þis
25   trewþe, as he telluþ oþre þat we trowen; and ellys hit were
presumpcion to charge þe chirche wiþ þis trewþe, siþ neiþur
auctorite of God, ne reson techeþ þat hit is soþ, and al byleue
nedful to men is teld hem in þe lawe of God. Here me þinkuþ þat
Latynes synnedon somwhat in þis poynt, for manye oþre poyntes
30   were now more nedful to þe chirche, as hit were more nedful to
wyte wer al þis chirche hange in power of þe pope, as hit is seyd
comunly, and wʳhˡer men þat schal be sauede ben nedide here to
schryuon hem to preestis, and þus of monye decrees þat þe pope
haþ liȝtly ordeynot. But me þinkuþ þat hit is soþ þat þis Goost
35   comeþ boþe of þe Fadur and of þe Sone, and þese persones ben o
cause of hym. And me þinkuþ to noon entent schulde Crist seye
he sendiþ þis Gost, or þat þis Goost is his, but ȝif þis Gost come of
hym. And to þis þat Grekys seyn þat Crist leueþ þis word, certis so
f.99v doþ he manye oþre for certeyn|cause, and ȝeet we trowon hem.
40   As Crist seiþ ⌈þat⌉ his lore is not his, for hit is principally his
Fadris, and ȝeet we trowon þat hit is hys, but þe welle is in his

---

40 John 8: 28.

J   15 passeþ] passand Z   temporal] þis temperal I   16 mennys] mannis
ABLMTYαδEZ, manere J   kunnyng] knowynge T   17 crist] and canc. criste α,
and crist T   þus] om. T   þis] þe G   margin ioh. xv N   18 ȝow] to ȝou
Fδ   goost] þe gost N   20 fro] for F   22 seiþ] saueþ I   in] om.
KT   23 þis¹] þ- on eras. corr. D, his KLNTαβJZH, þe G   ȝif] þat ȝif E   24
were] ⌈were⌉ Yα   26 þe] þis I   27 auctorite] þis auctorite T   hit] þis canc. ⌈it⌉
α, þis ABYI   soþ] so E   al] as T   28 nedful] ys nedful T   me] men
δ   29 synnedon] semeden I   30 more nedful¹] rev. I   to¹ . . . nedful²] om.
Z   31 hange] hangiþ FδIJZ, henge CK   power] þe power Nδ   32 wher] h
corr. D   here . . . hem (33)] to schryue hem here E   33 þus of] rev.
I   decrees] degrees ABEIJZ   þe pope] men Z   34 þis] þe holy
K   goost] g eras./goost D   35 boþe] om. α   of²] om. I   36 to] ⌈þat⌉ to T,
þat to Z   37 he] þat he E   sendiþ] sende α   his] om. I   ȝif] ȝif þat
I   come] comeþ LM, cam H   38 seyn] s eras./seyn D   leueþ] leue
C   þis²] om. L   40 þat] corr. D, þat canc. αX, om. ABCKLMNTYβEZ   lore]
doctrine H   41 þat] om. K   welle] wille, corrector margin welle F, wille, -i- altered

Fadur, so we trowen þat þe wylle by whiche þe Fadur loueþ his
Sone comeþ of wyt þat is þe Sone, but principally of Godis power;
and in þis word Crist techeþ us to do algatis worschipe to God.
And þus þese Greekys may not proue þat we trowen false in þis   45
byleue, or þat Crist lefte þis trewþe wiþowte cause to tellon hit
þus, for by þis þat Crist seiþ þe Hooly Gost cam of his Fadur, and
leueþ þus þe comyng of hym, he stoppeþ þe pruyde of þe chirche
and techeþ men to worschipe God. But whanne he seiþ þat he
sendeþ þe Holy Goost to hise disciples, and alle þat his Fadur haþ   50
ben hys, he techeþ clerly þat þis Goost comeþ of hym, and oþur
wyse schulde Crist not speke.

And þus Latyns ben to blame, for þei leuon nedful trewþe and
deepon hem in oþur trewþe þat is now not so needful. And þus
seyn somme men þat þe byschop of Rome, þat þei clepon heed of   55
þe chirche, and þerto pope and Cristus vyker, doþ more harm to
þe chirche of Crist þan doþ vyker of Thomas in Ynde, or vyker of
Poul in Grece, or þe sowdan of Babylon. For þe roote of whiche
he cam, þat is dowyng of þe chirche and hiȝyng of þe emperour, is
not ful hooly grownd but enuenymed wiþ synne; but þis venym   60
furst was luytel and hyd by cautelus of þe feend, but now hit is
growon to myche and to hard to amende. Soþ hit is þat eche
apostle was obedient to eche oþur, as Petre obeschede vnto Powle
whan þat he repreuyde hym. And þus þenkon som men þat þei
schulden obesche to þe pope, but no more þan Crist byddiþ, ne   65
more þan to oþre preestis, but ȝif he teche betture Goddis wylle

50 John 16: 15.

from -e- X, wille CKTβl   42 fadur] fadris K   wylle] welle βE   whiche] þe
wyche T, whuche þat δ   his] þe *canc.* ⌜his⌝ α, þe AEI   43 þat is] of F   þe] in
þe N   44 word] worde ⌜wolde⌝ C   45 false] flas β   46 lefte] kept ⌜left⌝
J   47 þe] þat *canc.* þo α, þat þe EI   48 þe¹] *om.* α   he] and he L   49 to]
for to δ   but] *before this* D *repeats* 45 and þus . . . 46 tellon hit, *all canc.*   þat] *om.*
CKI   he²] god L   50 þe] þis BLMNTYαβδEIJXZH   to] til N   51
ben] is E   he] here he N   clerly] hit clerly N   and . . . persecucion (75)]
om. Z   52 crist not] *rev.* δEH   53 trewþe] treuþis J   54 now . . . needful]
not so nedeful now H   now not so] not nou so E   not so] worse K   so] *om.*
C   55 þe] *om.* E   clepon] callen Nαδ   56 þe chirche] holy chirche
T   cristus] goddis H   57 þe . . . crist] cristis chirche BCKLMNTY-
αβδEIJX   in] of in, *in canc.* H   vyker] elles viker N   58 of¹] in BK   59
he] it N   þe²] *om.* F   60 not] *om.* B   synne] synne to muche harm of þe
chirche N   61 furst was] *rev.* αE   cautelus] cantels G   now] *om.* K   62
soþ] so B   63 to eche] ⌜to⌝ilke to, 2nd *to canc.* α, to *eras.* eche to J, eche to FKNEI   vn-
to] to KTα, hym to M   64 whan þat] when ⌜þat⌝ α, whan ABTEI, and whanne þat
C   som men] summe E   65 crist] cristes N   ne] ⌜ne⌝ no H, ne no C, no
ABFTYαδEIJG   66 he] *om.* M   67 profiȝte] profitiþ ABCFKLNTYβδJX-

and more profi3te vnto men; and so of al his ordenaunce, but 3if
hit be growndud in Godis lawe, sette no more pris þerby þan by
lawe of þe emperour. Men schuldon sey muche in þis mater, and
70 oþre men schulden doon in dede. But men wolden holden hem
eretykys, as þe feendis lymes dydon Crist, and so þicke ben hise
membris þat whoso hooldeþ wiþ Cristus lawys, he schal be
schend manye weyes and algatis wiþ lesyngus.

And þys telluþ Crist byforn vnto hise apostles to makon hem
75 stronge, and armen hem a3enys such persecucion. 'þese þingus',
seiþ he, 'I spak to 3ow þat 3e be not sclaundride. He is sclawndred þat is
lettyd by word or by deede, so þat hyse ri3t wylle falle down fro
his wyt. And so 3if man be pursewed and suffre hit paciently, he is
not sclawndred, al 3if men synnen a3enys hym. Þe furste pursewt
80 a3enus Crist schal ben of false preestis, not al only lettynge þe
membris of Crist to rewle þe puple in chirches, as curatus
schuldon doo, but putte hem owht of chirches as cursede men or
eretykes. And herfore seiþ Crist 'þei schal make 3ow wiþowte
synagogus.' But 3eet schal more wodnesse comen aftur þis, for þei
85 procuren puple boþe more and lesse to kylle Cristus disciples for
hope of greet mede. And herfore seiþ Crist certeyn of þis matere
'þat howr is comen þat eche man þat killuþ þus goode men schal iugen hym
f.100 to do to God meedeful obedience.' And to þis ende|procuren freris
anticristus disciples þat wel ny hit is now þus among cristene men.
90 Somme men ben somnyde to Rome, and þere put in prison; and
somme ben cryede as heretikes among þe comun puple. And ouer

GH   vnto] to AαE   men] man H   of] om. Y   3if] om. G   68 hit]
he α   be] om. β   growndud] ground B   no] ne α   by] bi þe
CKH   70 wolden] schulden G, om. H   holden] ⌐holde⌐ α, om. M   71 þe]
om. G   þicke] þilke CNδ   ben] þat ben N   72 lawys] lawe ABCFKLMN-
TYαδEIJXGH   73 manye] in many J   lesyngus] lesyng K   74 þys] -y-
altered from -u- D, þus N   vnto] to NE   75 persecucion] persecuciouns
AFEI   76 seiþ he] rev. Y, om. M   he² . . . sclawndred] om. I   þat] þas
β   77 by¹] oþer be α   by²] in CK, om. I   ri3t wylle] ri3twisnesse
Nδ   78 man] a man ABδEI   suffre hit] sufferiþ K   79 synnen] seien N,
semen I   hym] hem I   pursewt] pursuyd T   80 al only] aloon H   let-
tynge] settinge G   þe] om. CKLMNTYαβδEJZ   81 curatus] curatis in chirches
C   82 chirches] holy cherches I   83 þei] þat þei Aα   make] do Z   3ow]
þu L   84 synagogus] þe synagogis Z   3eet] ⌐þer⌐ M   85 puple] ⌐þe⌐
peple X, þe puple ABCKLMNTYαβδEJZ, to þe peple I   86 seiþ crist] rev.
AEαJ   certeyn] certeynte N   88 to god] ⌐to⌐ god T, good N   and . . .
resoun (108)] om. Z   89 anticristus] as anticristis E, and anticrist β   now þus]
rev. AYJ, þusgate CK, nou M   90 somme] as sum αδ   men] om. CKLMN-
TYβEJ, men canc. αX   ben] han be N   somnyde] mouyd L   þere put] rev.
FαJ, putte E, oþir putt G   91 somme] sum men BI   þe] om. α   93 and] but

þis as men seyn frerys kyllen þer owne breþren, and procuren men of þe world to kylle men þat seyn hem trewþe. And o dreede lettuþ hem, þat þei stert[e] not to more wodnesse, for þei defenden þat hit is leueful and medeful preestis for to fiȝte in 95 cause þat þei feynon Godys. And so, ȝif þer part be strengore þan seculerys, þey may meue þese preestis to fiȝton aȝenus þese gentele men. And, as þei han robbyd hem of temporal goodis, so þei wolden pryuon hem of swerd as vnable, and seyȝe þat such fiȝtyng schulde beste falle to preestis. Þus hadde preestis þis swerd 100 byforn þat Crist cam, and þei dr[o]won so fer ouȝt of religioun of God tyl þat þey hadden kyllid Crist, heed of hooly chirche. Alle men schulden be war of cautelys of þe feend, for he sleepuþ not, castynge false weyȝes. And al þis doon feendis lymes *for þei knowe not þe Fadur and his Sone* by propurtes of hem. Þe feend blenduþ 105 hem so in worldly purpos þat þei knowe not strenkþe of God, ne wysdam of his byddyng, for feiþ fayleþ vnto hem þat þei loke not afer but þing þat is nyȝ þer yȝe as bestis wiþowte resoun. *Alle þese haþ Crist spokon to hise disciples, þat whan tyme comeþ of hem þei schulden þanne haue mynde þat he haþ seyd hem þese pereles to comene.* And þe 110 Hooly Goost meueþ euere somme men to studye Godis lawe and haue mynde of þis wyt. And so loue of Godis lawe and sad sauour þerinne is a tokne to men þat þei ben Godus children, but ȝet of þer eende þei ben vncerteyn.

F   94 sterte] sterto D, styre α, forten β   95 hit] ⌐hit¬ T, *om.* δ   preestis] to pristis H   for to] for *canc.* to T, to CKYEH   96 cause] causes δH   godys] goddis lawe CK   þan] þan þe αβ   97 þese²] ⌐þes¬α, þe I, *om.* K   98 gentele] gentile EI   99 wolden] wole A   pryuon] preue BCI, proue F   seyȝe] seþ I   100 to] vnto δ   þus] and *canc.* þus α, and þus JH   101 crist] *om.* K   and] and out of goddes religioun N   drowon] drawon DLMTI, growen H   ouȝt . . . god (102)] *om.* N   of¹] of þe α   102 þat] *om.* CKE   hadden] haue L   kyllid] sleyn E   alle] and alle G   103 cautelys] canteles C   104 al] *om.* E   þis] þes TαEH   knowe] kowen C   105 and] ne KN   his] þe NYI   hem] him YJ   feend] feendiþ F   106 so] ⌐so¬H, *om.* J   in] by F, in hure N   strenkþe] þe strenght CKNI   107 byddyng] bid⌐d¬ynge αH   108 afer] aftur NβJ   þing] þinges α   þat is] *om.* E   is] are α   þer] þe β   þese] þis AJ, þes þingis F   109 þei . . . þanne (110)] þan þei scholde I   schulden] shulen F   110 þanne . . . mynde] haue mynde þanne E, han þanne mynde H   hem] to hem δ   pereles] ben pereylys H   to comene] byfore N   þe] þis N   111 men] *om.* C   godis] euere goddis T   113 a] *om.* A   þei] *om.* δ   114 þei ben] *rev.* F   vncerteyn] vncerteyne and þerfore preie we to god þat he graunte vs grace treuly to louen his lawe and reule vs þerby etc. N

In Die Pentecosten. [Euangelium.] Sermo 53.

Si quis diligit me. Iohannis 14.

In þis gospel meueþ Crist hise children to loue, for charite is þe beste cloþ þat ony man may haue. And herfore seiþ Godis lawe þat loue is strong as deþ, for loue meueþ men to suffre deþ gladly in Godis cause. And where deþ is þe moste þing þat man dreeduþ
5 heere, þis loue passeþ kynde, and makeþ men to coueyte such deþ; and þys wylle is not harmful but gloriows to men, siþ by sych loue men brennen as colys, and turnen into Godis cloþis as aungelus of heuene. Furst seiþ Crist þus *ȝif any man loue hym he schal kepe his word,* for þat is þe same trewþe. And, siþ God is kynde
10 aȝen to men þat louen hym þus, Crist seiþ þat *his Fadur schal louen hym aȝen;* and ȝif his Fadur loue a man, two oþre persones louen hym. And al such loue of God mut nedys ben euermore, and þe manheede of Crist worcheþ þus by þis loue: hyt schal brynge wiþ Crist siche membres of hym to heuene, and so ⌐to¬ cler siȝt of þe
15 Hooly Trinnyte. *And so Crist wiþ hise membris schal make þere þer dwellyng wiþowton any ende,* by loue of þe Holy Goost; for seyntes in heuene may not passe þis eende, for þanne þei weron foolys chesyng a worse ende.

And, for Crist wole schewon oonhede to louen hym and to
20 kepon hise wordys, þerfore he seiþ eft *he þat loueþ hym not, he kepuþ*

---

2 S. of S. 8: 6.

MSS: D; ABCEFGHIJKLMTXYZαβδ; S *inc. incompl.* 39 herd.

In die . . . euangelium] *om.* Z   sermo 53] *om.* BCFKLTYαδEIJXZGH   me]
me sermones meum seruabit δ, me sermonem meum seruabit IJ   iohannis 14]
iohannis 18 AB, ion þe þritteenþe chapitir Y, iohannis E, *om.* C   1 meueþ crist] crist
moues, *marked for rev.* α, crist moueþ EIJ   3 *margin* cant. 8 M   for] *om.*
E   men] ⌐men¬ C, *om.* K   4 and] as I   where] þe wheþer Z   man]
⌐kynde¬ M   man dreeduþ] men dreden E   5 heere] *om.* IJ   to] *om.*
KTE   6 þys]-y- *altered from* -u- D   8 of] in Z   seiþ crist] crist sais, *marked for
rev.* α, crist seiþ EIJ   9 word] wordes δE   10 men] siche men E   hym] hem
αE   11 two] ⌐þe¬ two A   13 þis] his M   14 to 2] *corr.* D, to þe L   15
hooly] *om.* EZ   and so] *om.* E   so] *om.* L   þere þer] here IJ   16 by] for
þanne by E   for . . . weron (17)] *twice, 1st canc.* D   18 chesyng] to chese
α   19 and 1] ⌐and¬ Aα, *om.* IJ   wole] wolde Aδ   to 2] *om.* BI   20
wordys] word Y   he 1] 3e β   he 2] *om.* CK   21 wordes] word

not hise wordes. And herfore Crist, discreuyng a man þat loueþ
hym, seiþ þus aftur in þis same gospel 'He þat haþ my
maundementis and kepuþ hem in his liȝf, he is þat ylke þat loueþ
me wel'. Héere may we wyte|wer a mon loue God, for ȝif he loueþ   f.100v
God, he loueþ his lawe and wordis of þe gospel, for alle þei comen   25
to on. And, ȝif he loueþ not Godis lawe, he loueþ not his God.
And herfore eche man þat loueþ not þus Godus word þat he
wolde dye þerfore to defenden hit, he loueþ not his God as he
schulde louen hym; for hit is al on, to loue God and to louen his
word. And, as myche as tow louest God schuldistow louen his   30
word. But ⌐for¬ loue of þi God þow schuldest lese þi lyȝf, and so
þow schuldest lese þi lyȝf for defence of Cristus word. And in
cowardise of þis loue ben monye men smyttede, but knytes by þer
ordre schulden be redy in þis loue. But, for Crist haþ seyd þat men
schulden kepe his wordis, monye men myȝte muse what þing ben   35
þese wordys. But Crist seiþ þat alle þese wordys ben trewþus, as
ten trewþus of þe maundementis and alle ben wiþowten ende.
And so he þat kepuþ not þe wordys of Crist, he kepuþ not his o
word, *þe wyche þei han herd. And þis o word, þe whyche þei han herd, is not
Cristus but his owne Fadres*, for hit is Cristus persone, and Crist is not   40
Cristus sone but þe sone of þe Fadur. And þus may we see
worþinesse of Godis word. Wordis of God ben monye by
dyuersite of resoun, but alle þei rennen togydre in o myddyl
poynt; and so þei ben alle Godis word, þat is hymself.

---

22 John 14: 21.

T   herfore] þerfore BE   22 þis] þes, -e *canc.* ⌐-is¬ α, þe ABTEIJ   23
maundementis] comandementis ABYαEIJ, comaundement F   hem] ⌐hem¬ þai
C   24 may we] *rev.* αIJG, may β   we] men E   loue] lufes CTαδ   he] a
man L   loueþ] loueᶜþ¬ Y, loue BCαIZH   26 loueþ¹] loue TαZ   he²] and
β   27 herfore] þerfor αδ   þus] ⌐þus¬ G, *om.* βE   word] law α   28 he¹]
he ne IJ   his] *om.* Y   29 al on] a luf C   to²] *om.* IJ   30 schuldistow]
þou schuldist YαE   31 for] *corr.* D   þow schuldest] *rev.* H   and . . .
lyȝf (32)] *margin* FT, *om.* I   32 þow schuldest] *rev.* H   schuldest] shalt F
defence] defende β   word] lawe I   in] so *canc.* in αδ   33 men] *om.* Y   þer]
om. I   34 ordre] ordowre β   for] *om.* Y   haþ seyd] seiþ I   35 his]
þes M   wordis] word G   men] ⌐men¬ Mδ   þing] þingis J   36 þese¹]
his K   þat] *om.* β   wordys²] *om.* K   as] and C   37 ten] þe ten δ, þe
α   trewþus of] *eras.* δ   maundementis] comaundementis, co-*canc.* Y, comaundementis ABδEIJ   ben] þey ben E   38 wordys] wordᶜis¬Z, word E   39 þe wyche¹]
whiche H, þat E   þei han] he haþ H   o] *om.* B   þe whyche²] þat whyche,
þat *altered from* þe, whyche *canc.* X, þe whiche ⌐þat¬ J, which YIH, þat BCKLMST-
αβδEZ   þei²] ȝe S, *om.* β   40 owne] *om.* AB   fadres] fadir G   persone]
persones S   41 and] *om.* T   may we] *rev.* AYαEIJ   42 worþinesse] þe
worþynesse LδE   godis] cristis S   word] wordis δE   43 dyuersite] dyuersi//

45 And for þese wordis ben mysty and derk to þe puple, þerfore
ȝyueþ Crist hem a cownfort in þis mater, and seiþ þat *he haþ spoke
þese þingus vnto hem, dwellyng wiþ hem*, and þei ben ȝeet mysty; *but
þe Counfortour, þat is þe Hooly Goost, þe whiche þe Fadur schal sende in þe
name of Crist, schal techen hem alle þingus* þat beþ now hyd to hem.

50 And þus hit falluþ now vnto men to knowen rudly furst a þing
and generally as philosophres spekon, and after schulde þei
knowe more sotylly þe same þing. And þus Crist by his manheede
teelde furst mysty wordys, and siþ God by his fingur schewode
sutilte of hem. And ȝet þis Hooly Goost schal haue ordre of his

55 lore, for furst he schal meue mennys erys in sensible voyses, and
siþ he schal be slydon in and teche mennys þowtis in al þat Crist
haþ spoke byfore in general wordys; ne þei schal not cese anoon to
lerne more sutylly, but euere in þis lyȝf þei wexen more rype til
þat þei comen to heuene, and þere knowe al fully.

60 And for pes of mannys sowle disposiþ hym to lernen, þerfore
Crist byhoteþ hise children þis pees and seiþ þus '*Pees I leue to ȝow,
and my pees I ȝyue ȝow.*' Crist wyste þat hymself schulde sone passe
from hise children, for on þe Þuresday at nyht he seyde to hem
þese wordis and on þe morwe at noon he dyede for þer loue. And

65 herfore he byhyȝte hem þat he schulde leuon hem pees. But Crist
specifieþ þis general pees, whon he seiþ þat he ȝyueþ hem his
owne pees; and þis schal be furst wiþ pursewyng of body, but hit
schal growe aftur to mooste ful pees. And herfore seiþ Crist þat *not
as þe world ȝyueþ he ȝyueþ hem*, but on contrarye maner. Þe world

Z   resoun] ⌈þe⌉ resoun E   alle] as alle δ   in] into S   44 hymself]
hym⌈self⌉ I, hym J   45 þe] *om.* S   46 ȝyueþ . . . hem] crist ȝeueþ hem
Y   crist hem] *rev.* CK   a] *om.* S   in þis mater] *om.* K   haþ] þat haþ
I   47 þese] þus T   vnto] into T, to E   hem²] hym CFJ   ȝeet] riȝt
L   48 þe⁴] *om.* LM   49 crist] iesu crist H   schal] and shal L   hem²]
men I   50 hit] ⌈it⌉ T, *om.* S   now] *canc.?* D, *canc.* X, *om.* ABCKLMSTYαβEIZ-
GH   vnto] to αE   men] hem E   rudly] ky *canc.* rudly D, redili FLδ   a
þing] *om.* I   51 and²] *om.* E   52 sotylly] sotilier H   þe] to C   same]
saue C   53 mysty] mystili L, many Y   fingur] fyngyr ⌈figure⌉ Z, figure Sβδ   54
sutilte] þe sotylte δE, sutili L   hem] him IJ   his] þis ABC-
KLMSTYαβδEIJZH   55 for] so I   erys] h- *eras.* D, heris β   in] bi K, and
I   56 schal be] *om.* Z   in¹] *om.* M   mennys] mannys B   in²] and
TZ   57 ne þei] *rev.* A, ne M, ne þey ne E   not] not *canc.* B, *om.* A   58 lerne]
lere ZH   sutylly] sutilte Sβδ   wexen] waxen C   til þat] til Kδ, to
C   60 disposiþ] disposid S   hym] hem β   lernen] lere αH   61
byhoteþ] hetes α   þus] *om.* M   62 and my] *om.* M   ȝow] to ȝou
H   hymself] he self Z   63 seyde] sent Z   64 þese] þis C   morwe]
⌈fryday⌉ E   65 herfore] þerfore δ   66 general] generaly C   whon] wher
Z   67 be furst] first ⌈be⌉ β   hit] *om.* S   68 mooste] more H   69 but] *om.*

ʒyueþ þingus þat now ben lykynge, but by processe of tyme þei   70
wexen more bytture, and so þei turnen to peyne and sorwe þat
furst weren lykynge; and so pees of þis world is euermore
decresynge, but pees of God groweþ vnto ful pees. And by þese
wordis of wyt Crist cownforteþ hise children|and bydduþ hem þat   f.101
þer herte be not distorbled ne dreede. For, whoeuere trowe fully þis   75
sentence þat ys seyd and hopude fully þat he were of nowmbre of
þese children, he were an vntrew man, ʒif þat he dredde þus.
Apostles dredden hem of perelys þat were nyʒ, but þei fayledon
not of þis trewþe þat ne þei schulden haue a good eende, and
what þing þat felde to hem schulde falle to hem for þer betture.   80
And so as þe world is syker of þing nyʒ hit and in dowte of þing
fer, so in contrarye maner ben Cristus children sykure of þer fer
ende, but of þer nyʒ menys ben þei somtyme in dreede. And
grownd of þis sentence is cr⌐i⌐sten mennys byleue.

And herfore seyde Crist 'ʒe herdon how I seyde to ʒow "I go and I   85
come to ʒow" '. And he þat troweþ fully þese wytty wordys of Crist,
he schulde not dredon hym of þis seyde sentence, for Crist seiþ as
God to whom alle þinge is present 'I go and I come to ʒow' for
certeynte herof. And as Crist was serteyn of his deþ, and his
steyʒeng vp, and of his comyng aʒen at þe day of dom, so   90
schulden hise children be certeyn of þis forseyde sentence. And
ʒet Crist meueþ hise children to haue ioye of his goyng, and þis
was a poynt for whiche þei mornedon moste. And Crist seiþ þus
to hem to abate þer mornyng 'Certus, ʒif ʒe louedon me ʒe schuldon

M   on] on þe Z   70 þingus] þing δ   by] þe C   72 þis] al þis K   73
decresynge] discressynge αIGH   of] *om. β*   vnto] into Yα   75 distorbled]
distrobilid C   whoeuere] whosoeuere δZ   trowe] trowe⌐þ⌐ X, troweþ
ABCFKLMSTYαβδEIJZGH   76 hopude] hope⌐rd⌐ β, hope Bα, hopiþ AFKE-
IJ   of 1] of þe EZ, dere of S   77 were] *om.* Z   þat] *om.* S   78 apostles] þe
apostels δH   hem] *om.* J   fayledon] faliden E   79 of] hem of S   þis
trewþe] þes trewthes C   ne þei] *rev.* AαδE   80 þing] þingis J   þat] *om.*
ST   schulde] it shulde ABE   þer] þer, -r *eras.* X, þe ABCKLMSTY-
αβδEIJZ   81 þing1] þis þing C   nyʒ] þat is nyʒ F   hit] *om.* KLM   82
fer ende] frende C   fer2] *om.* I   83 þei] *om.* KIJ   somtyme] in some tyme
J   84 cristen] -i- *corr.* D   85 herfore] þerfor α   seyde crist] crist seyde,
marked for rev. J, crist seide I   seyde] seiþ Kα   I3] ⌐i⌐α, *om.* CMG   86 he] ʒe
β   87 he] *om.* K   hym] *om.* CK, hem Sα   seyde] for *canc.* seid A, forseyde
TE   seiþ] seyde E   88 is] are α, *om.* K   and] *om. β*   89 certeynte]
certeyn⌐t⌐e α, certeyn E   herof . . . serteyn] *om.* δ   crist] he E   serteyn]
sent *canc.* serteyn D   his1] þis T   his2] of *eras.* his F, of his αEZ   90 and] *om.*
I   91 schulden] shulen H   92 ʒet] ⌐ʒit⌐ β, *om.* K   his] þis Y   93 for] for

95 *haue ioye, for I go to my Fadur, siþ he is more þan I,* for þus by
manheede I schulde encreson in blysse.' And he þat ioyeþ not
herfore, he loueþ not Crist; and hit is teeld byfore how eche man
schulde louen hym. '*And now I seyde to ʒow byforn þat hit falle, þat
whan hyt is don ʒe trowen* in my wyt.' And so schulde þei trowe to
100 alle þinge þat he hadde seyd, for þus he is God þat can wel alle
þinge. And Crist, techynge hise children to marke betture hise
wordys, seiþ þat *he schal now speke but fewe þingus vnto hem.* But þei
schuldon haue moste enemyʒte here of þe heed fend, þat Crist
haþ ouercomen; þerfore he telluþ hem þat *prynce of þis world is come*
105 for to tempte Crist, *and he haþ nouʒt in hym.* And þus in þis
ouercomyng schulde þei not drede þe feend. '*But al þis is don þat þe
world knowe þat I loue þe Fadur;* and so schulde ʒe do, for alle þingus
þat I do schulden ben ensawmple to ʒow. And herfore *I do as my
Fadur comawndede me,* for wel I wot in þis may I not fayle.' And al
110 þis sentence of gospel of Iohn is fully pertenynge to comyng of þe
Hooly Goost, and so redyng of þis gospel was wel ordeynot for þis
day.

þe T   crist . . . þus] þus seiþ crist H   96 ioyeþ] ioye C   98 hym] *om.*
T   now] hou δ   seyde] sayʳdeˈ α, sei LM   99 and] *om.* E   100 þinge]
þinges IJ   god] þus god L   þat²] and L   101 þinge] þingis J   techynge]
in techand Z   betture] þe betere S   102 seiþ] seith now S   now speke] *rev.*
AY, speke S   103 schuldon] schulen C   104 þerfore] and þerfore ABδ   þat]
þat þe FH   105 for to] to T   and¹] *om.* β   hym] me LM   106 þei] men
I   þat] at E   107 knowe] schal knowe δ   109 comawndede] commawn-
deʳdˈ β, comaunde α   may I] *rev.* E   Iˈ²] ʳIˈ H, *om.* T   110 gospel]
þe gosþel ABCFKLMSTYαβEIJZGH, þis gospel δ   is] *om.* G   fully] ful
CK   comyng] þe comynge YE   112 day] day to be seid to þe peple YH

In festo sancte Trinnitatis. [Euangelium.]
Sermo 54.

Erat homo ex phariseis Nychodemus. Iohannis 3.

This gospel vndur a story telluþ of þe Trinnyte and boþe þese ben
harde, as comunly is Iohnes gospel. Þe story telluþ þat *þer was a*
man of þe pharisees þat hiȝte Nychodeme, and was prynce of þe Iewes. He
cam to Iesu on a nyȝt and seyde þus to hym 'Raby, we wyton wel þat þow art
comen fro God.' And 'raby' is as muche as 'mayster' in Englisch.   5
And Nychodeme tolde þe cause why he trowede þus: '*For no mon*
may make', he seyde, '*þese sygnes þat þow makist, but ȝif God be wiþ hym,*
and so he comeþ fro God.' *And Iesu answerede Nychodeme and seyde*
þus *to hym* 'By my dowble kynde *I seye to þe, but ȝif a mon be born aȝen*
he may not see Godus rewme.' And þese wordis weron wondurful to   10
Nychodeme, *and þerfore he axede 'Wher a man myȝte be bore|whon he*   f. 101v
were an oold man? wher he myȝte creepon into his modyr wombe for tyme
þat he was oold, *and be born aȝen?'* Þis Nychodeme cam by þe nyȝt
þat figurede his ignoraunce, but to þe literal wyt he dredde hym
for his breþren to comen apertly in þe day and speke wiþ Iesu   15
Crist; and boþe þese vndurstondyngus schop þe Holy Goost. And

MSS: D; ABCEFGHIJKLMTXYZαδ; N *ends incompl.* 51 enspireþ þuse; S *ends incompl.* 31
þis bapteem; β *lost* 17 burþe . . . 101 mote.

In . . . euangelium] *om.* Z   sermo 54] *om.* BCFKLNSTYαδEIJXZGH   erat
. . . nychodemus] septem lampades ardentes sunt septem spiritus dei N   nycho-
demus] nichodemus nomine FIJ, *om.* STYαEH   iohannis 3] iohannis 2 α, iohannis
13 I, *om.* E, apoc. iiii N   1 vndur . . . telluþ] telliþ vndir a story E   of] *om.*
L   trinnyte] holy trinite N   2 comunly is] *rev.* α   3 þe¹] *om.* ABZ   þat
. . . nychodeme] nychodeme bi name H   þat] and I   prynce] a *canc.* prince T,
a prince EH   þe²] *om.* YH   4 to²] vnto N   þow] *om.* K   5 as¹] a
β   as²] ⌐to saye⌐ as T, to seie as NαEH   in] on N   6 why] whi þat
N   þus] þys,.-y- *altered from* -u- X, þis ABCKLMSTYβEIJZH   7 may] *om.*
δ   he seyde] *om.* IJ   þese] þe I   8 he] ȝe β   comeþ] come
N   nychodeme] to nychodeme F   9 to¹] vnto N   kynde] kyng C   to²]
þus *canc.* to F, þus vnto N   be] *twice, 2nd canc.* D   10 and . . . nychodeme (11)]
nichodeme wondrede of þuse wordus N   wordis] *om.* M   11 þerfore] herfore
E   wher] byfore *canc.* wher D, ȝif S   bore] bore aȝen SE   12 were] was
BCKLMNTβδEIJZ, is S   oold] elde E   creepon] *om.* M   for . . . oold (13)]
om. N   tyme] þe tyme G   13 by] in ABCKLMSTYβδEXZ, on N   14 þat]
and þat E   to] *om.* Y   hym] *om.* MN   15 for] of K   apertly] openly

so þis goostly burþe þat Nychodeme mot furst haue bytookneþ þe
Fadur of heuene þat brynguþ forþ two oþre persones. And so
Nychodeme to luytel knew þis persone of God, and for þis
20 vnknowyng he axede þis questioun, for he seyde not þat Crist was
Godis kyndely sone, ne þat he was Godus word and so God
hymself. And so þis Nychodeme hadde neede to be cristned in
feiþ. And so Crist louede his persone, al ȝif he hatede hise ordre;
for Crist sauede his persone and destruyede his ordre. And þus
25 Crist louede Powle þat seiþ he was a pharisee, but þe more part of
pharisees weron false and heretikes.

And þis natiuyte schewoþ Crist in þese wordys 'Forsoþe, forsoþe I
seye to þe, but ȝif a man be born of watur and þe Hooly Goost, he may not
entren into Godys rewme.' And þus by þis baptym, þis watur and þis
30 Hooly Gost Crist telde hym þe Trinnyte, ȝif he cowde conseyuon
hit. Þis baptym seiþ þe Trinnyte, in whose name hit is maad; þis
watur is þe waschyng þat ran of Cristus herte; and so baptyme
and watur and þe Hooly Gost tellen Nichodeme þe Trinnyte,
and þerwiþ þe sacrament, for Crist is compendious in spekyng of
35 hise wordys. But Crist makeþ distinccion of two maner burþes
and seiþ þat 'þing born of flesch is flesch in his kynde, and þing þat is boren
of spiryt is sp⌐i⌐ryt on som maner. And þerfore wondre þow nowht þat I
seyde to þe ȝe moton be born aȝen, ⌐and⌐ by Goost maad childron of
hooly chyrche, and so in spiryȝt maad Godus children, and so hys

---

25 Phil. 3: 5;   32 John 19: 34; 1 John 5: 8.

N   16 and¹] to I   þese] om. K   17 mot] muste S, bihoued Z   18 forþ]
om. E   two oþre] rev. δ   19 to luytel knew] knew to litil αEIJ   þis²] his
N   20 vnknowyng] vnkunnynge α   21 godis kyndely] rev. AY, cristes kyndely
δ   22 so] om. LI   þis] ⌐þis⌐ Z, om. α   to . . . feiþ (23)] in feith to be cristned
N   23 feiþ] þe faith Z   hatede] hadde I   24 for . . . ordre] om. K   25
crist louede] rev. K, crist loueþ I   þat] and N   seiþ] seyde S, syn α   þe
more] more T, most C, þe moste K   26 weron] was BCFKLMNSTδEIJX-
G   and] om. YH   27 þis] þus þis E   schewoþ] shewid H   þese] his
α   forsoþe forsoþe] forsoþe ⌐forsoþe⌐ T, forsoþe δ   28 þe¹] ȝou canc. þe α, ȝou
N   a] om. A   be] ⌐be⌐ M, om. K   þe²] of þe NYδEH, om. T   29 þis²]
of þis α   þis³] þe A   30 hym] hem α   he] þei α   cowde] om. M   32
þe] om. FαH   of] out of H   so] om. N   33 and²] in T   gost
. . . nichodeme] on eras. corr. D   nichodeme . . . trinnyte] þe trinite vnto nichodeme N   34 þerwiþ] so H   for] of δ   35 but] for N   burþes] of birþis
ABIJ   36 þat¹] þat þat M   born] ⌐þat is⌐ boren T, þat is boren N   is
. . . kynde] in hys kynde is flesch T   his] om. E   is²] ⌐is⌐ KJ   37 of] of þe
E   is¹ . . . maner] on sum maner is spirit N   38 seyde] say C   moton]
mosten K, miȝten C   aȝen] a//aȝen D   and] corr. D   goost] þis gost E, god
L   39 chyrche] chirche of god N   so¹] be N, om. B   godus] gostis

spouse schal be ʒowre moodyr.' Þis gendrure of þis Goost is boþe   40
free and wylful, and herfore seiþ Crist to Nychodeme þat *þe Spiryʒt
breþeþ where he wole, and þow herust his voys,* by whiche he meueþ þe.'
And on þis maneer þe Spiriʒt of owre Lord haþ fullud þis world
wiþ wyt of owre feiþ, and þat þing þat holdeþ al haþ science of
voys. And herfore at Whissoneday, whan þis Goost apperude, was   45
a greet sown and tongus of fuyr to telle þat men schulden speke on
heyʒte to þer breþren, and þei schulden haue charyte, whiche seiþ
þe Hooly Goost. And, al ʒif we knowen þe voys of þis Goost, *neþeles
we wyton not whennys þat hyt comeþ, ne whodur þat hyt gooþ* to men þat
ben bysyden vs, for we knowen not þe ordenaunce of God, why he   50
enspyreþ þes men, and to what ende, or wheþur he schal saue þis
man or wendon awey from hym. And so ys eche man þat is born of
þis Spiryʒt vnknowon to oþre by manye hydde resownes; and so
eche man ys somwhat knowon and somwhat vnknowon for
wysdam of þis Spiryʒt.   55

*But Nichodeme answerede and seyde here to Iesu 'How may þese
þingus be doon?' And Crist seyde to hym 'In þe lond of Israel* ben
manye blynde maistres, *for þou art maister in Israel and ʒeet þow
vnknowest þis.* And so hit is no wondur ʒif þis lond be myslad for, ʒif
þe blynde leede þe blynde, þei fallen boþe into þe lake. And   60
neþeles I teche hem as myche as þei ben worþi. And so', seiþ Crist
|to Nichodeme, '*soþly, soþly I seyʒe to þe,* defawte is not in me in   f.102
teching of þis puple, but in vntrewþe hardnesse of hyt. *For þing þat
we knowon we tellon to hem. and þat þat we han seyn* in godhede *we*

---

54 2 Cor. 6: 8; **59** Matt. 15: 14; Luke 6: 39.

L   hys] schal godes N, þis Y   40 schal] *om.* N   be] be maad N   þis²] þe
holy Y, þis ⌐holi⌐ F   is] schal be E   41 seiþ crist] *rev.* AFYEJG, crist said
α   to] vnto N   42 breþeþ] brethis or blawis Z   voys] voycis
T   whiche] þe wyche T   43 fullud] fulfuld NE   44 haþ] *om.* E   45
herfore] þerfore T   at] on H   46 greet] *om.* M   sown] sound BE-
H   and] of E   47 heyʒte] heiʒe CKαδ, hede I   þei] so þei G   whiche]
þe which ABNαδEZ   seiþ] is α   48 þis] þe holy K   49 not] ⌐not⌐ α, *om.*
E   whennys] whene α   þat¹] *om.* B   hyt²] he B   50 knowen] witen
H   why he] whiche I   why] whi þat N   51 to] vnto δ   or] oþer α, and
Z   52 hym] hem α   ys] *om.* A   53 vnknowon] is vnknowun AB   re-
sownes] resoun A   54 somwhat²] sum δ   55 wysdam] wilsomnes Z   56 þese]
þis T   57 to] vnto δ   58 maister] a mayster LMH   ʒeet] *om.* E   59
vnknowest] v/vnknowest D, knowest not δI   þis¹] þese BMYδEIJZH   þis²] þe
Y   myslad] mysbed L   60 leede] ledeþ IJ   into] into, -to *eras.* X, in
FYαδIJ   lake] *on eras. corr.* D   61 as myche] *twice, 2nd canc.* D   þei] *om.*
L   63 þis] þe E   vntrewþe] vntrewe ACKLMTYαEIJXZGH, þe vntrewe F,
treuþe B   hardnesse] hardines α   þat] *om.* Y   64 hem] it E   þat þat]

65 *wytnesson; and ʒe take not owre witnesse* for ʒowre vnkynde
hardnesse, and þerfore ʒe knowe not þe gendrure of þe furste
persone. *ʒif I seyde to ʒow erþly þingus, and ʒe trowon hem not, how ʒif I
seyde to ʒow heuenly þingus schal ʒe trowon hem?*" Crist teelde heere of
bodily burþe, and ofte tymes of erþely trewþe, but þei trowedon
70 hym not for þer hard fool herte.

But neþeles Crist telluþ þis man knowyng of þe secownde
persone, and in article of byleue þat is hys ascencion. *'No man'*,
*seiþ Crist, 'steyeþ into heuene but he þat cam down from heuene, mannys
sone þat is in heuene.'* And in þese wordys myʒte Nichodeme
75 vndurstonden boþe þe godhede of Crist and þerto his manhede;
and so schulde he knowe wel þe secownde persone of God. By þat
þat Crist steyʒede þus, and þus is mannys sone, myʒte ⌈he⌉ knowe
his manheede byfore oþre manhedys; for, al ʒif oþre men
steyedon a luytel in þis eyr, neþeles no man steyeþ into heuene
80 þus but Crist. And so noon oþre man comeþ to heuene, but ʒif he
be Cristus membre and be drawon by þe Trinnyte into þis hyʒe
place. And þus seiþ Crist soþ þat no man steyeþ into heuene but
hymself alone. And siþ þer ben fowre manerys of brynging forþ of
man and þe furþe and þe laste appropred vnto Crist is þat man
85 comeþ clene of womman ⌈wiþoute man, Crist clepuþ hym wel
here a⌉ sone of mankynde. And þus by þese two wordys myʒte he
knowe Cristus manhede, and by oþre two wordys myʒte he

þat ⌈þat⌉ A, ⌈þat⌉ þat T, þat EIJ   godhede] godnesse I   65 and] for B   not]
om. B   owre witnesse] *om.* T   witnesse] witnessinge Y   ʒowre] oure
C   67 seyde] say CKLM   68 seyde] say CKLM   to ʒow] to *on eras. corr.* D,
to *canc.* ʒou X, ʒou LTYEZ, to B   schal] schulde δ   69 trewþe] treuþis BT-
H   trowedon] trowen δ   70 hym] h/hym D, hem, -e- *canc.* ⌈-y-⌉ α, hem EI-
J   not . . . fool] *on eras. corr.* D   hard fool] hard fool, *marked for rev.* B, hardful
CK, fole hard AYαδIJ, harde F   herte] hertis E, hard G   71 þis] ⌈to⌉ þis T, to þis
CK   knowyng] k/knowyng D   þe] þis α   72 and] *om.* L   in] *om.*
E   article] an article ACLMTYδE   byleue] þe feyth δ   þat] þat þat
Y   no] and *canc.* no H, and no AB   73 þat] *om.* IJ   74 and] *om.*
H   þese] þis M, þe Y   75 vndurstonden] vndurstode C   godhede
. . . manhede] manhede and þe godhed of crist T   his] þe Z   76 knowe wel]
rev. δ, knowe E   77 steyʒede] steieþ K   þus²] þys A   is] *om.* I, bi þis
G   myʒte . . . knowe] miʒti to shewe H   he] *corr.* D, be I   78 his] bi his
I   79 þis] þe K   steyeþ] stiʒede YH   80 ʒif] *om.* CK   81 þis] his
FXG   83 hymself] crist E   siþ] seiþ A   manerys] manere⌈s⌉ F, manere
AIJ   brynging] bryngingis Aα, bringiþ Y, bryngyngeþ, -þ *canc.* H   of²] a
C   84 þe²] *om.* FIJ   vnto] to α   85 comeþ] þat comeþ LTJH, come
E   wiþoute . . . a (86)] *lower margin straight on corr.* D   crist . . . mankynde
(86)] *margin* T, *om.* LM   clepuþ] calles αZ   wel here] here wil C, here E, wel
IJ   86 sone . . . and] *on eras. corr.* D   he] be F   87 manhede . . . cristus

knowe Cristus godhede: furst by þat þat he seiþ þat þis man cam
down byfore from heuene, and þis my3te neuer be but 3if Crist
were God or he were man; þe secownde word, þat scheweþ þe 90
godhede of þis persone, is þat Crist seiþ þat he is mannys sone, þat
is in heuene, 3e aftur þat he bycam man. For þus Crist is two
kyndes: godhede for euermore in heuene, drawyng to hym whom
hym lykuþ; and þus Crist techeþ wel inow to knowe þe secownde
persone boþe in godhede and in manhede, as myche as he schulde 95
þanne knowon hym.

But to telle þe þridde persone in poyntys of byleue telluþ Crist
to Nychodeme '*As Moyses hy3ede þe addyr in desert*, to hele þe puple
in lokyng on hym, *soo mot mannys sone ben hy3ed* on þe cros, *þat eche
man þat troweþ in hym perische not* in helle *but haue lyf wiþowten ende*', 100
þat is þe blisse of heuene. Here mote we knowe þe story of þe
oolde lawe, how þe puple was hurt by styngyng of addres, and
Moyses preyede God to tellon hem som medicyn. And God bad
hym takon an addre of bras, and hangon hym hy3e in a tree to þe
puple to lokon onne, and he þat lokyde on þis addre schulde ben 105
helud of his yuel. And al þis was figure of hangyng of Crist, for
Crist was in forme of addres of venym, but he hadde no venym in
hys owne persone, as þe addyr of bras hadde no venym in hym.
But as ri3t|lokyng on þis addre of bras sauede þe puple fro venym f.102v
of serpentis, so ri3t lokyng by ful byleue in Crist saueþ his puple 110
fro synne of þe feendis. And þe feend was þe furste addre þat
euere noyede man; and Crist was hangud in tree as þis addre
hangude in tree. But hit were to wytone ouer ⌐how⌐ þis story

---

101 Num. 21: 6–9.

(88)] *om.* Z   oþre] þe toþer CK, þes oþere E   two] *om.* CK   he] be F   88
furst] þe first CK   þat þat] ⌐þat⌐ þat α, þat AEIJ   þat³] ⌐þat⌐ E, *om.* I   92
crist is] *rev.* AYE   93 for euermore] for euermore/and euermore, and euermore *canc.*
D, for euermore ⌐and euermore⌐ TG, for euermore and euermore LMYαEX-
Z   95 in²] ⌐in⌐ Bα, *om.* CK   96 þanne] kunne δ   97 poyntys] poynte
Z   telluþ crist] criste tellis, *marked for rev.* α, crist telliþ AYEIJ   99 in] by
ABCFKLMTYαδEIJXZG   on hym] þeron E   on¹] of FY   mannys sone]
mansuesse α   on²] in ABCKLMTYαEIJZ   100 man] *om.* Y   troweþ]
leueþ E   101 þe¹] *om.* A   of] *on eras. corr.* D   we] men H   *margin* num.
ii Tδ   102 styngyng] stongyng LβZ   103 hem] him ABCKEIJGH   god²]
om. Y   104 hym¹] hem IJ   hym²] ⌐hym⌐ T, *om.* α   hy3e] *om.* I   in] on
AYδ   105 lokyde] lokiþ L   106 his] þis δ   yuel] sekenes α   107 addres]
addre G   109 on] of IZ   111 furste] *om.* Y   112 hangud] hynging C,
hangynge K   in] on δ   tree] þe tre KE, a tre I   þis] þe CK   113 in] on
⌐in⌐ þe C, in þe KE, on a Yδ, in a I   to . . . ouer] ouer to wite I   how] *corr.*

pertenyþ to þe Hooly Goost, siþ al þis was doon in Crist. But we
115 schal wel wyte þat eche of þese þre persones is in eche oþur, as
eche bytokneþ oþur. And siþ þat Crist seiþ þat no mon haþ more
loue þan for to putton his lyf for hise frendis, þis blessude hying of
Crist in þe cros is þat hyȝe charite þat God louede man inne, and
þis charite is þe Hooly Goost. And þus was Nychodeme taȝt þe
120 feiþ of þe Trinnyte, and in þis feiþ monye oþre articles. And þus is
þis gospel appropred to þis feeste. Þer be monye wytnessys and
resones to þe Trinnyte, but þis maner of lore is more plenteuows
and more profiȝtable to men, and herfore Crist seiþ hyt þus. And
þus eche man schulde rewlon al his lyȝf aftur þis hooly Trinnyte,
125 for ellys hit mot fayle. Loke furst þat he be grownded in stable
bygynnyng, and siþ þat he procede in graciows mene, and siþ þat
he ende in fulnesse of charite, and þanne his lyȝf is sawmpled
aftur þe Trinnyte.
Expliciunt euuangelia dominicalia.

---

116 John 15: 13.

D   114 to] ⌜vn⌝to MX, vnto CKLTYαβδJG   þe] þis δ   115 wel wyte] rev.
Z, al wel witen H, wite Y   eche¹] eche on δ, ilkan Z   as] and C   116 eche]
ilkan Z   117 þis] but þis IJ, þat H   hying] hanginge ABC   118 louede]
loueþ KE   119 was] ⌜was⌝ Lα   120 monye] and many C   121 þis¹] om.
E   appropred] proprid CK   þer] for þer E   wytnessys] wittenesse
CαβE   123 herfore] þerfore Y   þus] is þus B   124 þis] þe H   125 hit]
he ABαE   126 he] þe β   graciows] a graciouce E   127 sawmpled]
ensamplid KαδEJGH, sawmple β   129 expliciunt . . . dominicalia] om. ABC-
FYαβIJXZGH, amen K, expliciunt euangelia omnium dominicarum tocius anni LM,
explicit euangelia dominicales per annum δ, expliciunt tam epistole quam euangelia
dominicalia secundum exposicionem doctoris euangelii E

II · SERMONS ON
THE SUNDAY EPISTLES

Dominica prima Aduentus Domini. [Epistola.

Sermo 1.]

Scientes quia hora est. Romanos 13.

We takon as byleue þat epistlis of apostlis ben gospelis of Crist, for
he spac hem alle in hem, and Crist may not erre; and alle þe
gospelis spekon goode ⌐ti⌐þingus of ioye of þe blisse of heuene.
And, al ȝif þe Hooly Goost spekuþ eche word of hooly writ,
neþeles Crist spac in Poule more plenteuously and sutelly. And 5
þis meueþ somme men to tellon in Englisch Poulis pistelis, for
somme men may betture wyte herby what God meneþ by Poul.
This epistle of Poul telluþ how þat men schulden byge þer
tyme. For al ȝif God ȝiue frely tyme, as lyȝt and oþre ȝiftus of
kynde, neþeles by synne of man tyme is lost to come to heuene; 10
and not only by synne of Adam, but by synne of yche man þat
wole not in vertu of Crist byge þe tyme þat Crist ȝueþ for to
wynne þe blisse of heuene. And þis marchaundise schulde eche
man do specially for þis cause: for þe dayes for synne ben yuele,
and maken monye to leese þer tyme. Poul bygynneþ to sture þus 15
to take heed to Godus tyme, and to leese not þis tyme, leeuynge to
disserue blisse. Breþren, *we schulen be wytynge þat our is now us to ryse*

MSS: D; ABGJOPTXYZαβδ.

Sermo 1] *om.* DBOTαδXZG   scientes . . . est] *om.* Y   scientes quia] *om.*
O   scientes] dcientes Z   est] est iam nos de sompno surgere OT   ro. 13] ro.
3 Z, *om.* O   1 we] men T   epistlis] þe pistlis BT   apostlis] þe apostelis
T   ben gospelis] *om.* O   3 spekon] *om.* O   tiþingus] ti- *corr.* D, þingys
T   þe] *om.* β   4 al ȝif] ȝif O   spekuþ] speke α   5 in] *om.* O   6 þis]
þus O   7 men] *om.* β   8 this] þe Oδ   of poul] *om.* α   þat] *om.*
OδJ   9 al ȝif] ȝif β   10 lost] lest sinne O   11 synne[1]] synne þe, *marked for*
rev. α   12 vertu] þe vertu Z   þe] þer α   14 specially] special Y   for[3]] of
α   15 monye] many men α, *om.* δ   to[1]] for synne *canc.* to DX, for synne to
δ   sture] sey O   17 blisse] þe blis Z   schulen] schulde now T, suld

fro sleepe, for now is oure helpe neer þan it was whanne we byleuedon. Yche
man coueytuþ kyndely to haue blisse þat God haþ ordeyned to
20 mankynde to reston inne. But monye men contraryen hemself,
for þei coueyton comunly to haue þis blis, but þer lust and fleschly
wyt letton hem to wynne þis blis, and bryngon reson aslepe, and
make men to contrarye hemself. For yche man schulde furst
coueyte his beture and fle his yuel, and so a man schulde more
25 wylle blisse þen any sensible lif here. And þis takuþ Poul as byleue
whonne he bidduþ men rise fro slep. And Poul meneþ by þis sleep
synne þat foolis lyuon ynne; for, ry3t as man whon he slepuþ
wantiþ wyt to kepe hym and is ner deed þen a beest, so it is of
synful m[a]n, for what deede euere he doþ, hyt lettuþ þanne to
30 disserue blisse, and disposuþ hym to þe peyne of helle, þat is
worse þan bestis deþ. And for men schulden rise on morwe and do
þer werkis aftur resoun, and men han now luytul tyme to regard
of oolde fadris, þerfore seiþ Poule here þat our is now to rise from
slep; an our is a luytul tyme, and sunne of ri3twisnesse is vppe.
35 The secounde word þat Poul seiþ stureþ to þe wyt of þe formere
word, whonne he seiþ þat now is oure helþe more ny3 þan
whonne we byleuedon. It is knowon by kyndely skyle þat þo
þingus þat mouen kyndely mouen fastere toward þe ende. And it
is also knowon by skyle þat, as tyme passuþ to men, so it comeþ
40 ny3 domesday, whonne men schullen haue fully þer helþe; for, al
3if Crist be mennys helþe, 3et he makiþ not helþe in man but as
reson of tyme axsuþ. And herfore to þe day of doom schal not al
f.1v Cristus chirche be in ful helþe, ne slepe in blisse wiþ|hyre spouse.
To þis entent spekiþ Poul in þe persone of al hooly chirche þat
45 now, whon ⌐þe¬ tyme is passud to byleue þat þe incarnacion is to

Z   our] þe our BβZ   us] *om.* O   18 fro] of α   is oure helþe] oure helþe
is B   þan] þat O   yche] euery B   19 haþ ordeyned] ordeynede G   20
men] man Z   21 þer] þey O   lust and] lust and þeir, þeir *canc.* G, lustis and here
J, lust and her δ, witt and T, and her O   22 wyt] lust T   23 to] *om.* Y   25
wylle] wilne BPZ   26 fro] for J   þis] þis *canc.* Y   27 man] a man
APYδZG   28 deed] þe dede Z   29 man] men DABOTYβδJXG   euere]
þat euer Z   30 blisse] þe blis Z   hym] hym þanne B   þe] *om.* T   pey-
ne] paynes Z   31 bestis] a beestis PZ   schulden] schullen, *margin* -d- *corr.*
D   on] on þe T   32 tyme] resoun *canc.* tyme D   33 our] þe our Yβ-
Z   34 sunne] þe sunne B, so sunne T, summe β   35 formere] forþere O   37
it] and it G   38 toward] toward þe P   40 domesday] to domesdai δ   41
mennys] fully *canc.* mennys DX, mannis BαG   not] no β   42 of tyme] *om.*
O   herfore] þarfore Z   to] til Y   43 ne] and T   hyre] þer T   45
þe¹] ⌐þe¬ *corr.* DX, *om.* AαδG   þe²] in þe δ   incarnacioun] ⌐in¬carnacioun T,

come, but þat þe incarnacion is passud, as þe chirche se⌐e⌐þ
ascencion, it mot nedis now be neer to þe ful helþe of þe chirche
þan it was byfore tyme, whan þe chirche only byleuede. For now
þe chirche passuþ byleue of þe incarnacion of Crist, siþ it wot wel
in heuene þat Crist haþ longe be þere man. And þis schulde moue   50
cristene men to disserue hastly blisse, siþ þei be neer þe ende þat
þei coueyton kyndely.

And to þis wyt spekuþ Poul aftur, *þe nyȝt*, he seiþ, *haþ gon byfore*,
and certis þe day schal come nyȝ. *And þerfore caste we awey þe werkis of*
derknesses, and be we cloþude wiþ armys of lyȝt. Walke we honestly as in   55
day. Here men vndurstonden ofte by þis nyȝt þe nyȝt of synne.
For as aungelis were not confermede, but euere stoden in nyȝt of
grace, so mankynde, siþ it was maad, stoot sumwhat in nyȝt
of synne tyl þat Crist was maad man. And he is sunne of
riȝtwisnesse, and he may not falle to synne siþ he is riȝtwisnesse   60
hymself. And herfore seyon grete men þat Moyses in book of
Genesis was moued by God to seyȝe þus þat 'euon and morwon
was maad o day'. And by þis ordre of þese wordis God techuþ
how synne wente byfore. But be we war and trowe we not þat
God hymself made synne. But boþe in aungel and in man was a   65
maner of derknesse byfore þat God confermede hem; and þis
confermyng was by his Sone. And aftur þe furste tyme of þe world
Adam and Eue synnedon, and not in þe furste tyme in etyng of þe
forfendyd appul. But ȝet byfore God confermede hem þei hadden
a derknesse of euyn, and wantyng of Godus grace þat cam   70
whonne þei weron confermede. And þus, al ȝif Adam was
confermyd as sone as he was maad of God (for Godus ordynaunce

---

62 Gen. 1: 5, 8, 13, 19, 23, 31.

---

carnacioun δ   46 seeþ] *2nd* e *corr.* D, seiþ β   47 ascencion] be ascencioun B, þe
ascencion PY, now *canc.* ascension α   now] *om.* O   helþe] beleue α   50
longe be þere] longe þere be *marked for rev. to* longe be þere β, be þere long *marked for rev. to*.
long be þere δ, be þer longe Oα   þis] þus O   51 blisse] þe blis Z   52
þei . . . kyndely] kyndely þai couet Z   53 poul] p *canc.*/poul D   aftur] afore
O   he seiþ] *om.* α   haþ] was O   54 and¹] he says and α   nyȝ] nithe
α   þe²] *om.* P   55 derknesses] derkenesse⌐s⌐ J, derkenesse OαβδG, myrknes
Z   56 þis] þi þis δ   58 so] *om. after long eras.* X   it] ⌐þat⌐ it P, þat it
β   sumwhat] sum wey ABOPTYαβJXG, as weye Z   59 þat] *om.* α   60 he¹]
om. α   61 herfore] þerfore Z   in] in þe BαZ   63 þis] þe T   þese] þo
α   techuþ] tekeþ O   64 we²] *om.* O   66 of] *om.* O   67 aftur] *om.*
G   68 in¹] oneli in α   etyng] þe fyrste etynge α   69 byfore . . . hem] *om.*
α   byfore] bifore þat B   70 a] *eras.* J, *om.* Aδ   euyn] euwþe β   and]

was þanne vpon hym þat he schulde þanne come to blisse),
neþeles Adam was kyndely byfore þat he was confermed of God.
75 Þis day þat schal come aftur is vndurstonden þe day of doom. But
somme men þenkon more sutely þat þis day is day of ordre, bytwixe
þe kynde þat man hadde furst and grace þat he haþ of Crist. And
to þis wyt spekuþ Poul þat, siþ þis ordre is reuersud by grace of
Crist þat furst ys liȝt, and siþen schyneþ vpon kyndely euyn, we
80 schulden caston awey werkis þat ben of derknesse of synne, and
furst in þis goostly gendrure be cloþude wiþ armys of þe furste
lyȝt. And þis dyuysion in mannys kynde, and priorite in liȝt of
grace, ben tolde here bi wordis of Poul, whon he clepuþ 'werkis of
derknesses' but synglerly 'armys of lyȝt'. And þus in þis heuenly
85 gendrure schulde we wandren in day of grace and flee derknesse
of synne, for ellis we kepe not Cristus ordre. It is knowon to
experte men þat man schameþ kyndely to do monye synnys in
f.2 lyȝt, þat he wolde do in|derknesse, as ben lecherye and þefte and
monye oþre syche synnys þat man doþ in derknesse of nyȝt, and
90 schameþ of hem in lyȝt of day. And herfore Poule bydduþ men
walke honestly as in day, þat men schulde kepe hemself in grace
by goode werkis, and fle synne; for ydelnesse in goode werkis
stureþ monye men to synne. And herfore Poul bydduþ us
walke – and not stonde ne ligge in þis weye.
95 And ȝet Poule specifieþ more of sixe synnes þat men don.
Dwelle we not in ofte etyngis and drunkenesse[s] þat sueþ aftur. Monye
men han a maner to ete ofte for to drynke, and þis mete is an ale
spore to sture hem ⌈ofte⌉ to drynke; and suche ofte etyngus of men
ben clepude 'comessaciones', and ofte aftur suche etyngus sueþ
100 drunkenesse in men. But, for men in þis lif reuerson þe ordre of
God, þerfore in þis secounde ȝok Poule rykeneþ synnys þat
comen byfore. Suche men þat synnen þus liggen ofte to longe in
þer beddis, and so þei han vnchastnesse in þouȝt, in word and ⌈in⌉

and a B, in J   71 was] were B   74 was¹] *om.* O   77 haþ] hadde TZ   78
siþ] seyþ OPZ   79 siþen] *om.* α   euyn] y *on eras. corr.* D   80 schulden] sal
Z   werkis] þe werkis B   81 þe] þis δ   82 þis] þus A   83 bi] *on eras. corr.*
D   clepuþ] calles αZ   84 derknesses] derknes ABOαβJZ   86 kepe] kepten
P   it] and it Z   89 syche] *om.* Z   90 day] *om.* G   herfore] þerfore
αZ   91 kepe] *om.* α   93 herfore] þerfore Z   94 walke] -alke *on eras corr.*
D   96 drunkenesses] drunkenesse Dαδ, drunkenesse⌈s⌉ X   97 men han] man
haþ O   a] *om.* G   for to] or for to Z   98 hem] men Z   ofte] *corr.* D, *eras.*
X, *om.* ABOPYαβδJZG   to²] for to ABOPYαβδJXZG   102 men] *om.*
G   þus] þey T   to] *om.* O   103 þer] *om.* T   in³] *corr.* D, *om.*

dede. And herfore seiþ Poul aftur þat we schulde *not* reste *in beddis, ne in vnchastite* þat sueþ ofte aftur þis reste. For monye ben 105 temptude of fleschly synnes by suche cowchyngus in þer beddis; and, ȝif þei ryson and wakedon byfore, þei schulden flee such vnchastite. And herfore monye men vson wel to come not in bedde wiþ schetis, but be hulude aboue þe bed, and rison anon whonne þei ben temptude, and þis semeþ Poule to teche more 110 þan to rise at mydnyt. Þe þridde ȝoc þat Poule forfendiþ is *chydyng and enuye*, for þese foure sustris byfore bryngon in liȝtly þese two; for ydelnesse in þis lif makiþ men to stryue aftur, and for strif wiþ yuele wordis ben men growndude in long enuye. But medicyne for alle such synne is to *be cloþud in Iesu Crist*. And þat man is 115 cloþud in Crist þat haþ fresch muynde of his lif, and cloþuþ his wille to sue hym, leste his soule be coold in loue. And þis were a general medycyn to fle synnes and sue vertuwes, for no man may synne in þes but in defauȝte of cloþing of Crist.

And for þis alle cristene men han nede to knowe byleue of þe 120 gospel, and so to knowe þe lif of Crist, and þe wisdam of hise wordis. And so cristene men schulden wyte þat Poulus wordis passon oþre writyngus in two þingus: þei ben pure, sutel, and plenteuous to preche þe puple. Þe sutilte of Poulis wordis may make me and foolis schame, whennᵗeᵗ we konnen not vndur- 125 stonde sutilte of his schorte wordis. Þei ben also plenteuous, for eche trewþe þat Poul spekuþ is knyttud wiþ eche poynt of byleue; and so aftur speche of oon may come speche of anoþur, aftur þat it profiȝtuþ to þe hereris, as þe laste word of þis epistle bidduþ us be cloþud wiþ Iesu Crist. And, siþ þis is gostly cloþing, in whiche 130 mannys soule schulde be cloþud, alle þe vertues of Iesu Crist may sittyngly be broȝt hereinne. And, siþ alle vertuwes ben hise, alle vertuwes may heere|be tauȝt; and vices þat ben contrarye to f.2v

T   104 herfore] þerfore αZ   schulde] s *canc.*/schulde D   105 þis] suche
Y   ben] men *canc.*. ben DX   106 of] wiþ α   cowchyngus] couchyng
ABTYαβδJZG, touchyng P, twochingis O   beddis] biddis G   107 wakedon]
walkid OYβG   108 herfore] þerfore αZ   110 þis] þus OδG   111 to] *om.*
O   forfendiþ] defendes α   112 and] in α   114 but] for β   115 synne]
synnes BOα   cloþud] closyd X   116 crist] iesu *canc.* crist D, iesu crist
X   fresch] -esch *on eras. corr.* D   117 leste] þat Z   coold] noȝt calde
Z   118 synnes] synne A   119 synne] fle *canc.* synne, -n *eras.* D   of²] in
Z   120 byleue] bileue and trouth Z   125 schame] ᵗtoᵗ schame A, to shame BZ,
ᵗaᵗschame α   whenne] -e *corr.* D   126 sutilte] þe sotilte BZ   127 byleue] þe
trouth Z   128 so] *om.* G   speche¹] þe speche OJ   129 profiȝtuþ] profit
β   þe¹] *om.* T   130 be] to be δ   132 hereinne] þerinne O   134 vertues]

vertues may be declarude to fle hem, as men þat takon pryuate
135 sectis, or putte not Cristus secte aboue, (siþ þis cloþ by hitself
wolde suffise) faylon of þe cloþ of charite. And so it is to drede to
hem þat, in tyme of þe laste soper, þei schullon be doumbe for
defauȝte þat þei han in bride cloþ. Þei schulde not be cloþude in
wollen and lynnene, ne putte secte of Crist byneþe, but putte þis
140 lordis cloþ aboue, and charge hem not wiþ oþre cloþis, siþ Crist
byddiþ men of his suyt þat þei schulde not haue two cotis.

---

138 Matt. 22: 11; **141** Matt. 10: 10; Mark 6: 9; Luke 3: 11, 9: 3.

vertues, -es *canc.* A, vertu BOPTYαβδJZ declarude] clarid G as . . . cotis
(141)]*om.* Z 136 wolde] wole T faylon] and failen O, þei fayle α to[1]]*om.*
J 137 tyme] þo tyme α þei] þe Y 138 in[1]] no β bride] brod
O schulde] shulden AδJ 139 secte] þe secte BOTαJ 141 schulde] schul α

Dominica ij in Adventu. [Epistola.] Sermo 2.

Quecumque scripta sunt. Ad Romanos 15.

This epistle of Poul techeþ how men schulden cloþe þer soule in byleue and hope and charite, and þanne þei beþ cloþude in Crist. Poul bygynneþ at byleue, and seiþ þat *alle þingus þat ben wryton* in oþer of Godys lawis *ben wryton to oure lore,* for þo þingus ben byleue þat men schulden konne byfore oþre. We speke not of enke and 5 parchemyn, but of þe sentence þat God seiþ. And by þe seyng of þis Lord we ben sikere þat it is soþ; as, whon a symple mon seiþ a trewþe, we trowon it not for he seiþ it, siþ he may gabbe and monye þingus may be vnknowon to þis man; but Crist is man of gret witnesse þat may not fayle in noþur of þese. And so his speche 10 makiþ trewþe to be byleue to cristene men. Ʒif men taken more largely þes wordis þat Poule spekiþ heere for alle maner treuþis þat ben wryton in ony book, ʒet alle þese trewþus ben wryton in Godus lawe on som maner; as trewþus þat ben more nedfull ben wryton þere more expresly, and trewþus not so nedfulle ben hydd 15 þere in comun wordis. And siþ falshede, as Austyn seiþ, is trewe in a maner, al falshede or heresye is wryton in Godus lawe. And so monye traueylon in veyn to wyte how heretykis schulden be knowone. But schortly al þis falshede þat is vngrowndud in Godus lawe is heresye in a maner, and al heresye is such. And so 20 menye men wenon þat alle þese newe sectis browt in, siþ þei be

MSS: D; ABGJOPTXYZαβδ; V *inc.* 79 he was mynystre

Dominica . . . adventu] *om.* P   sermo 2] *om.* BOTαδJXZG   que- . . . sunt] *om.*
Y   sunt] sunt ad nostram doctrinam scripta sunt T   ad . . . 15] *om.* O   1
þer] þe B   soule] soules δ   2 and¹] *om.* A   3 byleue] þe bileue B   wry-
ton] -e *eras.* D   4 lawis] lawe T   wryton] -e *eras.* D   oure lore] *on eras. corr.*
D   þo] þe O   5 byfore] tofore B   6 þe²] *om.* O   7 þis] þe J   lord]
lore α   8 it²] not it O   and] in β   9 þis] hym *canc.* þis D   man²] a man
β   10 gret] a *eras.* gret D   11 to²] of *canc.* to D   ʒif] ʒit A   12 þat²] *om.*
O   13 wryton¹] -e *eras.* D   wryton²] -e *eras.* D   14 on] and on T   ned-
full] -e *eras.* D   15 þere more] *rev.* O   16 and . . . ordris (25)] *om.* Z   fals-
hede] a *eras.* falshede D   trewe] treuþe B   17 wryton] witun Y   18 monye]
manye ʳmenˡ T   19 þat is vngrowndud] schulde be knowen þat *canc.* þat is vn- *on eras.*
corr. D   21 wenon] knowen *canc.* wenon D   alle] *om.* G   newe sectis] *rev.*

not growndud in þis lawe, smacchen somwat of heresye; and
þerfore cristene men schulden þenk[e] schame to cloþe hem
aboue wiþ raggus, and foule þe worþi suyt of Crist, as don alle
25 þese newe ordris.

Poul telluþ aftur for what cause God haþ ordeynud þese þingus
be wryton: *þat we han hope by pacience, and by counfort of þe[r]s[1]*
wrytyngus. But Poul passuþ ouer þese two vertuwis, and preyeþ
aftur charite þat *God of pacience and of solace ȝyue ȝow to konne þe same*
30 *þing among ȝow eche to oþur by þe lore of Iesu Crist; þat ȝe ben of o wylle,*
and wiþ o mouþ worschipe God, þe whiche God is fadur of oure lord Iesu
Crist. Poul clepiþ God of pacience, and of solace þat comeþ aftur,
for Crist tauȝte men to suffre boþe in word and in dede, and putte
hem in hope þerfore to be solasud of God; for greet vertu is in þat
f.3 35 man þat castuþ|hym to suffre, and kepuþ venianse to God, and
hopuþ þat God for þis pacience wole counforte hym. And herfore
he is God of pacience and solace. And heronne monye þenkon to
luytul, þat fyȝton and pleton, and caston weyus how þey
schulden be venged here, as ȝif God knewe not þer wrongus. And
40 so Godus lawe vndurstonduþ by þis same þing vnyte, whanne
men mekely knowon o Lord, and putton alle wrongis in his wylle.
And men þat slepon in þis þing reston surly in pees. And þis vnyte
schulden men haue by þe lore of Iesu Crist, and þanne schulden
þei be of o wylle, and wiþ o mouþ herye God. Þes men han o
45 mouþ þat preyen God for pees and loue, and, whateuere þei
spekon or don, it sowneþ into pees and charyte. And þis lesson is
þinne today, for men spekon of werrys and stryues, and how þei
schulden vencusche þer enemyes, boþe religiouse and oþre. And
certis þei han monye mouþis þat ben amys set vpon, and suche
50 feendis wiþ þer vyseris maken men to fle pees. And þes men
worschipe not Crist, neþur in his godhede ne in his manhede, for
Crist þowte pes and loue, and suffrede þerfore [i]n his manhede;

---

35 Rom. 12: 19; Deut. 32: 35.

T   22 þis] gods α   23 þenke] þenko D   24 aboue wiþ raggus] wiþ raggys
aboue T   27 be] *om.* O   þes] -s *corr.* D, þe β   29 of[2] *om.* α   32 clepiþ]
calles αZ   33 in[2] *om.*T   34 greet] a gret B   35 castuþ] may caste O,
chasties Z   kepuþ] g *canc.* kepuþ D   36 herfore] þerfore αZ   37 he is] [r]is[1] he
G   solace] of solace BJZ   monye] many men αJ, may men O   38 weyus]
many weies G   39 schulden] may Z   venged here] *rev.* A   40 þis] þe
G   43 þanne] *om.* O   46 and[2] ... god (56)] *om.* Z   is] *om.* O   47
þinne] þanne O   and[2] *om.* OT   51 in[2] [r]in[1]J, in *canc.* Y, *om.* P   52 þowte]

and he þat reuersuþ Crist in þis is Sathanas aȝenys Cristus
chirche. And by þis onhede toold here men worschipon þe
Trinnyte; and by discord of monye mouþis þes foolis fiȝton   55
aȝenys God.

And for þis good of vnyte Poul spekiþ ⌐þus⌐ aftur *and herfore take*
ȝe togydere eche oþur in charite, *as Crist haþ takon ȝow into þe*
worschipe of God; for Crist haþ mad us Godus children and breþren
to hymself, and þis is þe moste worschipe þat may falle to ony   60
man. It ys holdon a greet worschipe to be a kyngus sone and his
eyr, but it is muche more worschipe to be Godus sone and his
broþur. And here þenkon monye men þat þese newe ordris take
not þer breþren by þi⌐rs⌐ forme þat Crist tok us; but þei brekon
charite, and makon þat discord of hem makuþ discord in good   65
loue for, no drede, liknesse of breþren causuþ loue among hem,
and vnliknesse is cause of discord and hate of hem. And, in tokne
of þis sentence, oon ordre loueþ betture his broþur þan a man of
anoþur ordre, al ȝif he be betture loued of God. And þus þei han
monye mowþus to preye and to preche wiþ, for somme preyon for   70
þer breþren, and accepton þer persone byfore God; somme
prechen for money, and somme for oþur worldis good. And so
onhede of mouþ schulde make acord in holy chyrche; but now
dyuersite of mowþus makiþ discord among men. But þis
dowblenesse was not in Crist, siþ he traueylude for onhede.   75

And herfore seiþ Poul aftir *certis I seye þat Iesu Crist was mynystre*
of circumcision for þe trewþe of God, to conferme byhestis þat weron maad
to fadris. Iesu, to gete þis onhede, tok on hym circumcision, and so
he was mynystre of þis kynrede to make onhede among fadris.
God byhyȝte to Abraham þat in his seed he schulde blesse al   80
maner of folc, boþe kynde of Iewis and heþene men. And for þis
onhede suffrede|Crist, and wrouȝte in soule by his godhede. And   f.3v

---

80 Gen. 22: 18.

touȝt O   in] on D   55 discord] þis discord Y   57 good] god OαδJ-
G   poul spekiþ] *rev.* ABOPTYαβδJZG   þus] *corr.* D, þis O   herfore]
þerfore αZ   take] takeþ J   58 ȝe] ȝow J   þe] *eras.* J, *om.* ATδ   59 for]
and *canc.* for G, and for OδJ   61 be] -n *canc.* D   62 muche] *om.* Tβ   63
and . . . onhede (75)] *om.* Z   þenkon . . . men] many men thinke α   64 þis] -i-
on eras. corr., -s *corr.* D, þe G   65 makuþ] make T   67 is] of is O   69 he] it
J   70 preyon] prechen Y   72 worldis] worldly BOTJG   good] goudis
OTJ   73 mouþ] money Tβ, many δ   76 herfore] þerfore αZ   79 þis] his
BαJ   81 of¹] *om.*G   of²] and O   83 is¹] *om.*O   87 in] in þe

þis is þe trewþe of God, for God is souereynly oon. And so Poul
seiþ þat *gentile folc schulden honoure God* wiþ o mouþ, siþ þis Fadur
85 haþ don hem *mercy*, and knyttid hem in broþurhede wiþ Crist.
And to þis aleggeþ Poul foure wrytyngis in Godus lawe. Dauid
seiþ in persone of Crist, 'Fadir, for þow louest acord, *perfore I schal
knowleche to þe in* dyuerse maner of *heþene men, and I schal synge to þi
name*'. For men þat ben of oo wyl syngon in God þis vnyte. *And eft*
90 *seiþ þe same* lawe of God '*Be ʒe heþene men glad*, for ʒe ben on *wiþ his
puple*.' And eft seiþ þis same lawe '*ʒee alle heþene men, herye ʒe þe
Lord, and alle puplis preyse ʒe hym*', for alle maner men of mannys
kynde schulden be oned in o Lord. *And Ysaye seiþ eftsone* '*þer schal
be a roote of Iesse, þat schal rise to rewle heþene men, and heþene men*
95 *schul[l]en hope in hym*.' Þis rote of Iesse is Iesu Crist, for he was hyd
byfore Iesse, and aftur he sprong to cristene puple, and maade o
chyrche of Iewis and heþene folc.

And to þis entent Poul preyeþ þat *he þat is God of hope fylle ʒow
wiþ al ioyʒe and pes in byleuyng, þat ʒe be plenteuous in hope and vertu of þe
100 Holy Goost.* And þis vertu is charite, siþ þis Goost is loue of God.
And þus preyon men now þat holy chirche be maad oon, and þes
sectis be alle left, but þe sect of Iesu Crist. For we han hope in God
þat we schullen alle comen to heuene, and wiþoute suche sectis
lyue alle in oo secte, and ychone haue ioye of oþur wiþowten
105 enuye or discord. And to þis ioye wolde dispose onehede in
Cristus sect, for Crist ordeynede þis oo secte to brynge to þis fulle
onhede. And no drede þe feend haþ castud þis dyuersite in sectis
for, ʒif hyt were good, it hadde grownd of þe scripture of God; but
þis spekuþ of onhede, and algatis of onhede in soule. Thre partis
110 ben in þe chyrche, prestus and lordis and comunys, and God haþ

---

87 Ps. 17: 50; Deut. 32: 43; **90** Ps. 116: 1; **91** Isa. 11: 10.

ABOYV   louest] louedist Oα   88 maner] maneres Oαβ   89 wyl] -le *eras.*
D   91 þis] þe BOV   ʒee alle] *rev.* BV   ʒe] *canc.* PX, *om.* TYαβJZ   92
lord] lord of alle Z   alle¹] alle þe T   men] of men PT   mannys kynde]
mankynde AV   93 oned] -ed *on eras. corr./de canc.* D, oonheed ABPTYβJV   95
schullen] schulden DB, schulden, -d- *canc.* X   is] of β   iesu crist] *rev.* G   96
byfore] tofore B   he] *om.*α   o . . . folc (97)] ⌈of ⌉ heþen folk and of iewes o
chirche T   97 heþene] of heþen α   98 fylle] and vertu of þe holy gost *canc.* fylle
D   100 is¹] of J   101 preyon men] *rev.* B   and² . . . soule (109)] *om.*
Z   102 left] -e *eras.* D   sect] -e *eras.* D   103 schullen] shulden A   to]
canc. J   105 onehede] onhede *canc.* onehede D   106 sect] -e *eras.* D   or-
deynede] *om.* O   108 hadde] haþ G   grownd] growede α   of¹] of *eras.* in J,
in V   þe] *om.* ABOαδG   110 chyrche] kirk of crist Z   and¹] *om.*

ordeyned alle þese þre to helpe yche oþur to gendre loue, and
noon of hem to be superflu, but do þer offys þat God haþ
ordeyned. But þis dyuersete of þes sectis is comon in wiþouȝte
cause, and þus it makuþ discord of men for wantyng of good offys.

BTδJXGV   112 to] om. β   do] ⌈to⌉ eras. do D, to do OαδJGV   113
but . . . offys (114)] om. Z   þis] þ⌈u⌉s, -u- above -i- eras. J, þus Oαδ, þe V   in] and
α   114 good] -od on eras. corr. D

Dominica iij in aduentu. [Epistola.] Sermo 3.

Sic nos existimet homo. Prima Corintheos 4.

Poul telluþ in þis epistle how men schullon mekely fle worldus
stryuys, and byddiþ furst by oure lif þat *man* haue matere *to gesse
us as mynystris of God and dispensouris of his seruysis.* And al ȝif eche
cristene man schulde be founde trewe in þis, ȝet prestus boþe
5 more and lesse schulden ben here more trewe; and synne of
faylyng of preestis in þis seruyse is more foul. As, ȝif þe pope and
his byschopis schamen to be Cristus seruauntis, and in þer maner
of lyuyng þei schewon an emperours lif and lordly to þe world, siþ
þat Crist hatide þis, þei ȝyue noo matere to gesse hem to be
10 mynystris of Crist; and so þei faylon in þe furste word of þis byleue
þat Poul techeþ. Lord! what good doþ þis gabbyng þat þe pope
f.4 wole be clepid 'moste blessud fadur' here, and byschop 'moste
reuerent man', siþ þer lif discorduþ from Crist? Þei schewon in
takyng of þis name þat þei ben on þe feendis syde, children of þe
15 fadur of lesyngis. For, ȝif he seye aftur Gregori þat he is 'seruant of
Godus seruauntis', ȝet his lif reuersiþ þis name, for he fayluþ to
suwe Crist, siþ he is not dispensour of seruysis þat God haþ bedon,
but he partuþ þe lordschipe þat þe emperour haþ ȝouen. And so

MSS: D; ABGJOPTVXYZαβ; H *inc.* 26 him in trewþe, 39 iust be- . . . 46 -ment *lost*, 46 -
ment . . . 59 þe lest *only c.* 5 *letters left on each line, variants recorded but losses not,* 59 þe
lest . . . 66 knowyng *lost,* 66 þerof . . . 79 was I *only c.* 7 *letters left on each line, variants
recorded but losses not,* 79 -now . . . 85 þei wyte *lost;* δ 70 staf for . . . 89 -wis and iugementis
lost; Hᵗ *part of text from c. 70 but almost all illegible.*

Sermo 3] *om.* BOTαδJXZGV   sic . . . homo] *om.* YV   nos] vos α   exis-
timet] existimeþ J   homo] homo vt ministros Christi T   prima . . . 4] *om.*
O   prima] *om.* Y   4] *om.* P, iij c' V   1 schullon] shulden AOαβδJZG-
V   mekely fle] *rev.* O   worldus] worldly BδJGV   2 lif] lifes O   man]
men TZV   gesse] hope Z   3 mynystris] mystris Y   seruysis] seruyse
β   5 ben here] here *be marked for rev.* J, *rev.* ABOPTYαβXZ   6 and . . . neþeles
(30)] *om.* Z   7 and] ⌐and⌐ P, *om.* J   maner] þe maner δ   8 lordly] a lordly
B   9 þat] *om.* δ   10 mynystris] þe mynysteris BV   12 clepid moste] clepid
þe moost δ, clennest O   blessud] hooly A   byschop] þe *canc.* bischop J, þe
bischop O, bisshopis BαβV   13 man] men, -e- *altered from* -a- B, men αβV   14
on] of O   15 fadur] fadris δ   seye] seyþ OT   16 þis] þys, þ- *altered from* h- α,
his AδG   17 seruysis] seruice AOPTαβδJ, þe seruyce V   18 partuþ] departiþ

alle seruysis of þe chyrche þat Crist haþ lymytud to his preestis
ben turnede to þe contrarie syde, and so to seruyse of þe feend. So   20
þat, ʒif men takon heed to seruys of þe chyrche þat Crist haþ
lymytud, it is al turned vpsedoun, and ypocritis ben maade
rehetouris, so þat vnneþus is left ony seruys of Cristus chirche.
And so by þe seruyse of men ben þei chaungede into oþre kynde,
siþ þei ben anticristus mynystris and seruon in anoþur chirche.   25
For, as þe gospel of Iohn telliþ, Baptist held hym in trewþe and
preysude hym not in false name, as monye prelatis don today.
And suche ben þe feendus seruauntis and dispensours of his tresor,
þat is feyned falshede, as þe kyng of pruyde haþ tawt hem.

But neþeles, as Poul seiþ, *here,* in þis lif wole *men axe þat a man be*   30
fownde trewe among dispensours of an hows, for þis styward among
seruauntis may do muche harm to þe hows. And it semeþ to monye
men þat þe seruyse of Cristus hows is turned amys vpsedoun in
chaungyng into false mynystris, and for suche dispensours ben
ofte iuged of þe hows for þei wolden fare more lykyngly. Þerfore   35
seiþ Poul aftur *to me it is for þe leste þing þat I be iuged of ʒow, or ellis of*
mannys day. But I iuge not myself þat I serue trewly þe Lord, and
mynystre to hise seruauntis as he wole, *for, al ʒif I haue no conscience*
þat I do aʒenys Godus wille, ʒet it suweþ not herof *þat I am iust*
byfore God. But he þat iugeþ me, seiþ Poul, *he is Lord* of alle þingus (for   40
Lord seyd by hymself menyþ Lord of alle lordis). And þus men
schulde not be marrude for blynd iugement of men, for God mut
iuge alle men, oþur to good oþur to yuel. And herfore takuþ Poul
luytul hede to iugement þat man iugeþ, for he woot wel of byleue
þat, ʒif God iugeþ þus , þanne þis iugement mut ⌐nede⌐ stonde,   45
and ellis not, but Godis iugement. And þus þer ben two dayus:

---

26 John 1: 20; 5: 33.

GV   19 seruysis] seruise BOαβ   his] *om.* T   20 to²] to ⌐þe⌐ TY, to þe
AβδJGV   seruyse] seruises O   21 to] to þe, þe *canc.* A, to þe BV   22 al
turned] *rev* . B   23 vnneþus is] vnneþe þis T   24 so] *om.* O   seruyse] seruisis
PYV   oþre] þer P   27 today] to *canc.* today D, now today O   28 feendus]
deueles H   dispensours] dispensatours H   29 falshede] falshede, -hede *canc.*
H   30 as] and Z   31 dispensours] dispensatourus H, dispensoure α   of] as *canc.* of
D   þis] an yuel Z   32 and . . . mynystris (34)] *om.* Z   34 into] into *canc.*//
into D, of βV   for] *om.* G   35 ofte] of α   wolden] wole OV   36 aftur]
aftur þus O   37 þe] to þe BH   and] *om.* α   39 I¹] *om.* α   herof] þerof
αZ   40 he is] he is þe B, is þe V   41 lord²] ⌐oure⌐ lord O, ⌐þe⌐ lord B, þe lord
V   lordis] þinges O   men schulde] *rev.* AδG   42 for¹] by O   43
herfore] þerfore αZ   44 man] men α   45 þat] *om.* B   iugeþ] iuge αJ-

day of þe Lord, and mannys day. Day of þe Lord is day of doom,
whanne he schal iuge alle maner men. Day of man is þanne
heere, whonne man iugeþ by mannys lawe; and þis iugement mot
50 be reuersud, ȝif it owt reuerse reson. But at þe laste day of doom al
schal stonde to Godis iugement; and þus þis is day of þe Lord, for
al schal be þanne as he wole; and þis iugement schal not be
contraryed, for no þing may reuerse it.

And herfore seiþ Poul þus here *and so nule ȝee iuge byfore tyme, tyl*
55 *þat tyme þat þe Lord come, þe whiche schal liȝte þe hudde þingus of*
derknesses, and schal make knowe þe counselis of hertis. And þanne schal
f.4v *preysyng|be* doon in dede *to eche* good *man of God.* And ȝif at þe day
of doom þes two þingus schullen be opon, þe leste purpos þat man
haþ to do aȝenys Godus lawe, and þe leste counceyl of his herte
60 þat he haþ to do wel or yuele, what þing schulde be hud þanne to
God and al his folc? Bokis schullen be openede þanne , and men
schullen knowe þer owne dedis, boþe goode men and yuele. But
goode men schullen knowon alle þing, for þei schullen see in book
of lif alle þinge þat was or ys. And þis moueþ monye men to þenke
65 vpon Godus lawe boþe nyȝt and day, for þat disposuþ to knowe
what is Godus wille; and wiþowte knowyng herof schulde a man
do no þing. And þis moueþ monye men to flee mannys iugement,
boþe to be iuge and wytnesse, and to plede in þis marcat; for þis
maner of iugement sueþ to luytul Godus wylle. And, ȝif it sue ony
70 tyme, it falluþ as [a] blynd mon castuþ his staf. For, ȝif man haue
ryȝte to þing, þat ryȝte comeþ of God to hym, and God iugeþ þat
he is worþi to haue þis þing by his doom. But what iuge in mannys
ple kan knowe þis worþinesse? And herfore God forfenduþ þis
strif, for boþe þe iuge and his consentours doon heere aȝenys

---

47 Isa. 13: 6, 9 etc;   **61** Rev. 20: 12.

Z   nede] *corr.* D, *om.* ABOPYαβδJXZG   47 þe²] *om.* G   day⁴] þe day
ABV   48 men] of *canc.* men J, of men BTV   49 man] ⌐he¹ δ   50 of] *om.*
T   51 to] at H   þus] *om.* O   day] þe day BY   52 he] we O   54
herfore] þerfore αZV   þus] *om.* T   iuge] not iuge T   byfore] tofore
B   56 derknesses] derkenes αJZ   schal preysyng] *rev.* B   58 opon] opnyd
Z   59 to do] to *eras.* do A, don Bα   60 þat] *om.* J   to do] don Tα   be]
om. O   61 al] to al ZV   folc] folc *canc.* floc P, flok on *eras.* Z, flok ABαδG   63
men] *om.* α   þing] -us *canc.* D   see] know α   in] in þe ABV   65 vpon]
on YZV   godus] goodus, *2nd* o *canc.* D   66 knowyng] *om.* Z   herof] þerof
αZHV   schulde] schul α   67 þis] þus O   69 sue] sueþ GV   70 a] *om.*
DPYαβδX, þe BJZ   castuþ] caste α   man] a man OαJGV   71 þing] a þyng
JV   god²] *om.* O   73 worþinesse] witnesse O   and . . . on (87)] *om.*

iugement of God. And þus þer ben two wyckede lawys: lawe of 75
seculer iugis, but worse is þe lawe þat is maad of anticrist. And in
þese two pleus of men is myche synne aȝenys God. Poule
chargede not þese iugementis; but þe trewþe of hooly wryt, þat ys
wille of þe furste iuge, was ynow tyl domes day, to haue þe laste
iuge þanne in dede. And þus schulden stywardis of þe chyrche 80
iuge not nakydly by þer wille, but sykurly aftur Godis lawe in
þing þat þei ben certeyn of. And siþ popus and cardynalis white
not wher þis man be able to be prelat of Cristus chyrche, þei
takon ofte fool iugementis, and algatis ȝif lordschipe and
wynnyng be cause herof. For þei wyte neuere wher þei iugen 85
aȝenys þe iugement of God; and ȝif þei don, þei ben anticristus,
for Crist and God is al on. And herfore Crist ȝaf ensawmple to us
to fle such iugementis: 'O man,' seiþ Crist, 'wo made me iuge and
partere among ȝow?' And suche lawis and iugementis þat
anticrist haþ browt in, and put byhynde Godis lawe, marren to 90
muche Cristus chyrche. For anticristus lawis ben rewlis to þe
styward of þe chyrche, to make officeris þerynne and to deme
lewede men, anticrist chalangeþ here to be fully Godis felow; for
he seiþ, ȝif he iuge þus, his wille schulde be take for resoun. And
þis ys þe moste hyȝ poynt þat falluþ to God in his godhede. And 95
herfore boþe popis and kyngus schulden seke resoun aboue þer
wylle. For such blasfemye brynguþ men ofte aboue pruyde of
Lucifer; he seyde þat he schulde steyȝe vp and be lyk to þe hyerste
lord, but he chalangede not to be Godis felow, and euene wiþ
hym or passe hym. God brynge doun þis feendis pruyde, and 100
helpe þat Godis word renne! For I woot wel þat þis smoke schal

---

88 Luke 12: 14.

Z   forfenduþ] defen/ H   74 þe] om. OαG   75 iugement] þe canc. iugement
J, þe iugement BTV   two] here two β   76 þat . . . anticrist] þat antecrist haþ
maad Y   and] as O, om. G   in þese] rev. α   77 aȝenys] om. O   78
chargede] chargiþ YαJ   79 wille] þo wille αV   was] þat was α   80 iuge] om.
α   84 fool] foul G, foly V   85 herof] þerof αV   87 herfore] þerfore
ZV   herfore crist] rev. α   crist ȝaf] rev. H   88 iugementis] iugement
H   margin luk xij DAOYβ   seiþ] sayde α   89 partere] partyner BG, partye
H   and . . . byleue (107)] om. Z   iugementis] siche iugementis B, iugement
H   90 and] om. α   put] puttes α   92 to²] om. J   93 chalangeþ] calange
α   godis] cristis H   94 iuge] iugiþ AOδJG   schulde] schal α   96
herfore] þerfore αV   schulden] schullen T   97 wylle] willis B   pruyde] ⌐þe¬
pride A, þe pride B   98 þat] om. BO   and] aboue canc. and D   99 chalangede]
chalangeþ TJ, chalange α   and] but H   100 feendis] hye α   101 word]

be wastud, whonne it is hyerste. And so ȝif we takon heed to popus
f.5 and prelatis þat ben now, þey fay|lon foule in byleue, for it
strechchiþ not to domys day but restiþ in iugement of þer day;
105 but doomys day is poynt of byleue. And þus þei faylon as bestis in
þingus þat ben byfore hem now, for smoke of pruyde and
coueytyse lettiþ syt of þer byleue.

wordis J   103 prelatis] to prelatis BβH   104 to] til B   in] om. A   105
day] om. δ   is] þis is B   þus] þis O   faylon] fallen B   107 syt] þe siȝt BV

Dominica iiij in Adventu Domini. [Epistola.]
Sermo 4.

Gaudete in Domino semper. Philipenses 4.

This epistle of Poul telliþ fyue maneris þat man schulde haue wiþ
þre vertuwis of God, and wiþ þese schulde he lyue for to come to
blis of heuene. Þe furste maner þat God bidduþ is to be ioyeful
and glad. And herfore bygynneþ Poul and seiþ þus to cristene
men *ioye ʒe in þe Lord euermore, ʒet I seyʒe ioye ʒee*; and wiþowte þis   5
maner of lyf cristen man fayluþ algatis in byleue, in hope and
charite. Þe grownd of ioye þat man schilde haue schulde stonde
clenely in his God, and þis ioye schulde euermore be here in part,
and in heuene fully. For what man may haue þes þre, byleue,
hope and charite, but ʒif he þenke on Godus goodnesse, and by   10
þis haue ioye þerof? And þus he fayluþ in byleue þat wantiþ þis
ioye in God. And who hopiþ to come to blis, þat feiþ telliþ þat is
in heuene, but ʒif he ioye in þis hope þat he haþ of þis blisse? Or
who loueþ God by charite, but ʒif he ioye in Godis hyʒnesse? And
siþ eche man schulde haue þes þre, oþur in roote or in fruyt, eche   15
man schulde euere ioye in God þat is Lord of al. And ʒif þis ioye
or þis þowt slepe in man for a while, ʒet is schulde euere be and
qwykene his spiritis to Godward. For no þing schulde qwenche
þis ioye, but tribulacion of man; but wᵣhᵔere is þanne hope of
reward in hym þat þerfore ioyeþ not? A worldly man haþ myche   20

6 1 Cor. 13: 13.

MSS: D; ABGHOPTVXYZαβ; δ *inc.* 18 his; J *om.*; Hᵗ *part of beginning of text but illegible.*

Sermo 4] *om.* BOTαXZGHV   gaudete . . . semper] *om.* YV   semper] *om.*
OH   phil . . .4] *om.* O   1 maneris] maner β   man] a man AOG, men
BZV   2 lyue] lerne G   3 blis] þe blis BTYαV   god] *om.* β   4 herfore]
þerfore αZV   5 ʒet] and ʒit B   ioye] to ʒou ioye Y   6 man] *om.* α   in 2]
and in α, and H   7 charite] in charite OTαV   þe] þe þe, *2nd canc.* D   ioye]
þe ioye O   8 be] stonde H   part] parti BHV   10 on] of α   11 he]
ᵣhyᵔm α   12 to 1] to þe, þe *canc.* D, *om.* O   13 of] in H   or] o Z   15 þre]
om. G   16 ioye 2] þouʒt ABOPTYαβZGHV   17 þowt] ioie ABOPTYαβZ-
GHV   slepe] in man *canc.* slepe D, slepte X   man] a man O   19 man] a
man O, men G   is þanne] þan ᵣis ᵔZ   20 þerfore] herfore H   21 of 3] or of

ioye of hope of his victorie, of wynnyng of worldly goodis, or
fleschly lustis þat he coueytuþ. And siþ men schulde haue more
hope to haue euermore blisse in heuene, how schulde not a man
haue ioye in stabulnesse of þis hope? Certis defaute of heuenly
25 hope makiþ þis ioye in man to fayle. Lord! how traueyle men in
werre? – gladly, for hope of victorie; how traueylon men in
marchawndye? – for ioyful hope of worldly wynnyng; and how
ioyfully traueylon men þat ben lad here in fleschly loue? And siþ
þis hope schulde be more in þe blis þat man schulde haue, what
30 mon schulde not ⌐ay⌐ haue ioye? And þis ioye schulde be in God.
Of þis ioye schulde come anoþur: þat man schulde haue in
disseruyng of þis ioye. As we may se by forþere ensaumplis how
wilfully and ioyfully man traueyluþ for a worldly cause, as ben a
worldly victorie, worldly richessis or fleschly lust. And certis þis is
35 a ⌐veyn⌐ cause, schort, and bryngoþ no man to rest. And for þis
ioye of trauele for blis Poul biddoþ us ȝeet haue ioye.

Þe secounde maner þat man schulde haue *is sad maner, and
knowon to men.* And to moue men to þis maner Poul seiþ þat *þe Lord
is nyȝ.* Poul moueþ not here to ioye, as ioyen vnstable men and
40 gygelotis, but to sad ioyng in God, and suffre for hym wiþ glad chere,
f.5v   so þat it falliþ|not to men to wepe for suffryng for God, but þat alle
maner men myȝten knowe how hise knytus suffren gladly for
hym. And þus seiþ Matheu by Ysaye þat þe Holy Goost seiþ of
Crist, þat he schal not stryue ne crye, and no man in þe strete
45 schal here his voys. For, in al þe passion þat Crist suffrede, he
faylede not in sad chere; he criede not owt for his peyne; and so
suffredon hise aftur hym. And to moue men to þis glad chere,
Poul seiþ þat þe Lord is nyȝ. Cristene men takon as byleue þat

---

43 Matt. 12: 19; Isa. 42: 1–3.

B   22 fleschly] flesche α   23 a man] men T   24 þis] his H   28 lad] -a-
altered from -e- D   in] wiþ B   29 þe] *om.* AβδGH   30 ay] euer
αXV   haue] *om.* Z   33 ioyfully] how *canc.* ioyfully DX, hou ioyfully
BαβHV   man traueyluþ] men trauelen δ   a¹] *om.* αβ   cause] causes
α   a²] *eras.* A, *om.* BOV   34 worldly²] and *canc.* worldly A, and worldly
H   richessis] ricches BαZH   or] or or *2nd canc.* D, and α   lust] lustis
YαH   35 veyn] feynt *canc.* ⌐veyn⌐ *corr.* D   schort] and schort GV   38 moue]
mo β   þe] *om.* Y   39 to] men to H   ioyen] ioy of α   40 glad] good
H   41 men to] ⌐men⌐ P   þat²] *om.* P   42 suffren] suffrid OV   *margin*
mt. 12 DABOTYαβXZH   44 schal] schulde A   stryue ne crye] crie ne striue
T   strete] stretis H   45 þe] his O   46 he] he creyed not out in sad cheere he
β   47 glad] *om.* α   49 þat] *om.* Z   tyme] þe *canc.* tyme DX, þo tyme

Crist is lord and spouse of þe chirche, and þat tyme tyl þe day of
doom in nyʒ to regard. But wel we wytone þat a wyf, whan ⌜sche⌝   50
schal sone mete wiþ hire hosbonde, sche gladuþ hire herte and
her cher in hope to be cownfortud of hym. Whi schulde not
cristene soulis do so, whanne þei hopon þer spouse ys nyʒ?
The þridde tyme Poul bydduþ þat *we schulde not be bussy.* Þes
men ben bussy for nowt þat ben bussy for vanyte. And þerfore as   55
Petre bidduþ we schulden caston al oure bussynesse in God; for
no þing batuþ more mennys contenaunse fro þe plesyng to God
þan bussynesse abowte worldly þingus, for suche caston doun þer
hed fro God.

But Poul bidduþ þe fourþe tyme þat we schulden rere vp oure   60
hedys, and axe boldly of oure Lord in þe name of þe Trinnyte: *in
al maner preyʒer* in þe name of þe Fadur of heuene, *and in al maner
special preyer* in þe name of God þe Sone, *and in al maner of
þankyngus* in þe name of þe Hooly Goost. For God bidduþ us in
Lukis gospel þat byfore þe day of doom we schullen reyse vp oure   65
heedis, for oure ful byggyng is ny. And þus, what cristene man
haþ good herte, his axyng is knowe byfore God, siþ eche þing seiþ
to God trewly as þat þing is. And þus preyede Moyses wel wiþ a
good herte for his folc.

Þe fyueþe maner þat man schulde haue, for þes foure maneris   70
byfore schulden come to God *by his pees, þat schulde kepe oure willes
and vndurstondyngus,* and ʒyue us hertly lastyng in þese fyue
maneris to oure spouse. For no seruyse is crowned to blisse but ʒif
þis lastyng be þerwiþ. And þus seiþ Poul þat Godis *pees passuþ al
maner of wyt*; for he þat haþ his pees þus cryed, is sykur ynow of 75
alle hise enemyes. And al þis þing is doon by mene of Iesu, oure
alþere lord.

55 1 Pet. 5: 7; **65** Luke 21: 28; **68** Exod. 33: 13; Deut. 9: 26–9.

αβV   tyl] to O   þe²] to α   50 nyʒ] nyʒt Z   but wel we] *on eras. corr.* D,
but wel ⌜we⌝ X   wel we wytone] wel wyten we Tβ   þat] as H   whan] -a-
altered from -o- D   sche] *corr.* D   51 hosbonde] owne housebonde H   gla-
duþ] gaderiþ G   53 cristene] cristus Oα   54 poul bydduþ] *rev.* Y   bussy]
bisisy β   57 batuþ] abatis ZV, lettiþ H   to] of ZV   58 doun] adoun O   60
schulden] schal αZ   61 of¹] *om.* T   62 in²] *om.* A   63 god] *om.* Oδ   of²]
om. O   65 *margin* xxi c.Z   schullen] shulden AOG   67 his] *on eras. corr.* D,
her T   68 a] *om.* AZ   *margin* exodi xxxiii Z   70 man] a man Z   73 to²]
in Yδ   74 þus] þis O   75 þus cryed] þis tryed O   76 al] *om.* O   iesu]
iesu crist G   77 alþere] sauyour *canc.* alþere D   78 for to] to Z   79 seiþ]

Here it were for to speke of ioye þat men han in blis. And al ʒif
Poul þat was raauysched seiþ þat þis ioye is hud, so þat neiþur yʒe
80 haþ seyn hyt, ne eere haþ herd it, ne it haþ steyud vp into herte of
man in erþe, ʒet by glymeryng of Godis grace may men knowe þis
ioye afer. Austyn seiþ þat he is blessid þat haþ alle þinge þat he
wole, and he wole noon yuel þing; and þis ioye han men in
heuene. Þenk what staat were good to þe, and what þing þi wille
85 wolde coueyton, and þat þing han seyntis in heuene in þe beste
maner for hem. For ellys men were not fully medude, þat sugeton
here þer willis to Goddis, but ʒif he ʒ[au]e hem alle þer wille and
ladde þer resoun aftur his; for ellis þis wantyng were harmful and
man were not fully blissud. And þus men seyn þat two blissus ben:
90 blisse of þe sowle, and blisse of þe body. And of þe bodyly blisse ys
f.6 |furst for to speke, as blabereris may talke heere. It is seyd
comunly how Crist haþ dowyd his spouses body wiþ foure
doweris of þe body, and þerinne stonduþ myche ioye. The furste
dower is sutilte, þe secownde is agilite, þe þridde is clerte, and þe
95 fourþe is immortalite. Seyntis bodyes ben so sutyle, and so
schapon in þer partis, þat þei may perse oþre bodyes wiþowte
lettyng of þer wille. And þus cam Crist owt of his modyr, and
entrede eft to hise apostlis, al ʒif þe ʒatis weron schyt, for no þing
stood þanne aʒenys his wille. The secounde dower of þe body is
100 agilite or swiftnesse, so þat, as sone as þe blissude soule wole be
onywere in a place, as sone it moueþ þe body þidere by ablete of
þe body; and þe furste dower of þe body helpuþ to brynge in þis
dower. And ellis holy men in blis hadden not al þing þat þei
wolden, but som tyme þei myʒten ellis be taryed, and so morne

79 2 Cor. 12: 2; 1 Cor. 2: 9; 98 John 20: 19, 26.

say αZ   80 ne¹] noþer OGV   eere] om. G   ne²] neþer GV   herte] þe
canc. herte Y, þe herte BδP   81 men] man H   82 afer] aftur Oα   84 what
staat] þat O   85 wolde] wole A   þe] om. α   86 men] þai Z   87 here]
om. G   willis] wille BOG   ʒaue] ʒiffe, -iffe on eras. corr. D, ʒaf ABOYαδGH   88
ladde] lede T   89 fully] worþy be fully blissyd T   ben] þer are αβV   90
blisse¹] blissis δ   þe¹] om. BOδ   þe²] om. BOδV   þe³] eras. X, om.
AOPTYαδZG   91 for to] to Oα   blabereris] laboreris δ   talke] take
AβδH   94 is¹] of T   is²] om. α   þridde] þridde dowere ABPTYαβδXZ-
G   and] om. α   95 is] om. ABOPTYαβδZGV   so¹] om. G   96 may] om.
α   bodyes] boþe B   98 eft] ofte B   to] into HV   99 þanne] om.
H   þe] þis O   100 þat] om. Oαδ   wole] wolde AδG   101 onywere]
owwhere αH, ouþerwhare Z   a] any αV   þidere] þerto α   ablete] al'eꞌte
β   102 þe²] om. α   þe³] om. α   103 dower] t canc./dower D   104 ellis

for þing þat hem wantede. The þridde dower is clerte þat mut 105
nedis be medelud wiþ liȝt, so þat seyntis schynen in heuene as cler
as þei wolon coueyte, and no mon þat is þere in blis desiruþ more
clerte of his body. And þus was Crist clarified wiþ witnessis of
boþe his lawis. And þus seiþ Crist in þe gospel þat iuste men
schulen schyne as þe sonne in þe rewme of þer Fadyr. Who wolde 110
schame of foulnesse, but ȝif it were foulnesse of soule? – for þat
lettuþ aftur þis clannesse. The fourþe dower of þe body is clepud
immortalite, or vndedlynesse of man, for he may neuere wante
þis blis. And herfore seiþ Austyn wel þat þe moste part of seyntis
blis is surte þat þei han of þer ioye, þat þei may neuere wante þer 115
blis. And aftur þis haþ craft of God so medlud mannys partis
togydere þat noon contrarieþ to anoþur, ne fayluþ for
contrariouste; for, as soulis ben of o wille, so partis of bodyes
acorden in entent. But scorne we here þes heretikis þat seyn þat
no þing may befalle liȝtere þan þat eche seynt in heuene may be 120
deed, and dampnyd in helle, and eche body of dampnyde men
may be Cristis body in heuene; and þis vnstable byfallyng seen
seyntis in Godis wille. But trewe men trowon þat þis is fals, for al
Godus wille mut nedis be. And þanne blessude men schullen
clerly see þe opon resoun of Godis wille, and þanne þei schullen 125
scorne þese foolis þat wenon þat God may chaunge his wille. But
ȝet men dowton more in þis how þat seyntis schulon moue in
heuene, and what tyme schal be þanne, siþ blisse of seyntis schal
euere laste. But here men takon as byleue þat heuene and erþe
schal þonne stonde; and so þis day schal not be þanne by mouyng 130
of þe sonne and mone, but Crist schal be sonne to seyntis, in
whom þei schal be dowbully fed, boþe in soule and in body, as
fully as þei wolon coueyte. And þus, ȝif seyntis wolon moue in
heuene from o plase to anoþur, þey schullen moue riȝt as þei

108 Matt. 17: 4; Mark 9: 3; Luke 9: 33.

be] *rev.* O   taryed] trayed O   105 hem] -e- *altered from* -y- D, hym X, þei α   106
schynen] shyneden δ   107 wolon] wolden δ   108 his] *om.* H   witnessis]
witnesse ABαβδZH   110 schulen] sȝolde O   þe¹] *om.* δ   wolde] shulde
P   111 were] were of THV   soule] þe soule BV   112 aftur] aftre *corr. to* ofte
A, ofte V   þis] hys T   clannesse] clerenesse AB   113 neuere] reuere
Y   114 herfore] þerfor αZV   of . . . surte (115)] is surete of seyntis blisse
H   115 þer] *om.* T   117 to] *om.* OHV   ne . . . so (118)] *om.* O   120
liȝtere] liȝtlier Z   122 byfallyng] befaylynge α, bifallynt H   123 þat] *om.*
P   124 godus] at goddis Z   mut] must δ   schullen] shulden T   125
þanne] ⸢þanne⸣ β, *om.* Z   schullen] schulden G   126 chaunge] ch *canc.*/chaunge
D   131 mone] þe moone H   to] of Y   in whom] and whan α   133

135 wolon, and haue what þat þei wolon haue, boþe in tyme and in
stude. But trewe men þenkon ynow to wyte generalte of þis blisse,
al ȝif þei bussyon hem no deppore of þe willis of seyntis in heuene.
And somme men trowon þat God moueþ by þes tymes þanne in
f.6v |heuene, þat suwe not cowrs of þe sonne; but seyntis willis þat ben
140 in blis *secula seculorum*, þat ben alle oþre þan þes tymes. Of þis ioye
schulden men þenke euere, and ioyefully traueyle to gete þis; and
þanne men fullen þe byleue þat Poul bidduþ in þis epistle.

wolon¹] wolden B   wolon²] wilne H   135 þat] *om.* BαδZGH   haue²] *om.*
β   boþe ... stude (136)] *om.* β   in²] *om.* α   137 seyntis] þe seyntis
β   in] of B   138 and] bot Z   men] *om.* T   moueþ] meeneþ
BY   139 cowrs] þe cours THV   140 þat] þan Y   of] on TV   141
ioyefully] ioyful O

In Die Natalis Domini. [Epistola.] Sermo 5.

Puer natus est nobis. Ysay 9.

Aftir þe ioye þat Poul telluþ, we may seye on Cristemasseday þat
a luytul child ys born to us, for Iesu by oure byleue is born. And to þis
entent spak God, boþe in figure and in lettre, þat a child is born to
us in whom we schulden haue þis ioye. And so þre schorte wordis
ben to speke of Ysayes speche, so þat men may aftur ioye in oþur 5
seruyse of þis child.

Furst we takon of byleue þat, siþ oure furste eldris hadde
synned, þer moste asseþ be maad þerfore by þe ry3twisnesse of
God; for, as God is merciful, so he is ful of ri3twisnesse. But how
schulde he iuge al þe world but 3if he kepte here ri3twisnesse? For 10
þe Lord a3enys whom þis synne was doon is God almy3ty and al
ri3tful, siþ no synne may be doon, but 3if it be don a3enys God.
And euer þe more þe lord is, a3en whom þis synne is doon, euer
þe more is þe synne to take reward to þis lord. As it were a greet
synne to do a3enys þe kyngus byddyng, but þe synne is more 15
wiþowte mesure to do a3enys Godus byddyng. But God bad by
oure byleue Adam to ete not of þat appul. But he brac Godus
heste, and was not excusud þerinne, neþur by his owne foly, ne by
Eue, ne by þe serpent. And þus by ry3twisnes of God þis synne
muste algatis be punysched. And it is a li3t word to seye þat God 20
my⌐3⌐te of his power for3yue þis synne, wiþowton asseþ þat were
maad for þis trespas, for God my3te do þis 3if he wolde. But his
iustise wol not suffre þat ne eche trespas be punysched, oþur in

MSS: D; ABGHJOPTVXYZαβδ; I *inc.* 5 ben to speke.

Sermo 5] sermo 9 A, *om.* BOTαδJXZGHV puer . . . nobis] *om.* YV puer]
paruulus enim T ysay 9] *om.* OV 1 aftir] *on eras. corr.* D cristemasseday]
3ole day Z 3 boþe] bot α a] *om.* T 4 þre] þes α 5 to] for to
Z may] *om.* O 7 furst] for I of] as *canc.* of δ, as T 9 he is] *rev.*
I 10 þe] þis Y here] al her T 12 doon] *om.* I 13 þe¹] *om.*
O þis] þe TIH 14 þe¹] *om.* δ more] *on eras. corr.* D is þe synne] þe
synne is I 15 do] be B 16 bad] ⌐comandid⌐ δ 17 þat] þe β 18 heste]
hestis I, biddyng Z 19 by²] by þe OYGH synne] *om.* α 20 muste] mote
αβ 21 my3te] -3- *corr.* D þis] *om.* I 22 for¹] of Z trespas] synne
H god] ⌐he⌐ H þis²] þus J 3if] and B 23 iustise] ri3twisnesse

erþe oþur in helle. And God may not accepte a persone to forȝyue
25 synne wiþowton asseþ, for ellis he muste ȝyue fre leue to man and
aungel for to synne. And þanne synne were noo synne, and oure
God were no god. And þis is þe furste word þat we takon of
byleue.

The secounde word þat we takon is þat man þat schulde make
30 asseþ for synne of oure furste fadir mot nedis be God and man.
For, as mannys kynde trespasede, so moste mankynde make
asseþ; and herfore it were to strawnge þat aungel maade asseþ for
man, for neþur he myȝte ne he was þat persone þat synnede here.
But, siþ alle men ben o persone, þat persone makiþ asseþ ȝif ony
35 membre of þis persone make asseþ for al þis persone. And by þis
may we see þat, ȝif God made a man of nowt of newe to þe kynde
of Adam, ȝet he were holden to God as muche as he myȝte for
hymself; and so he myȝte not make asseþ for hym and Adams
synne. And þus siþ asseþ muste be maad for Adams synne, as it is
40 seyd, such a persone muste make þis asseþ þat were boþe God and
man; for worþinesse of þis persones deede were euene wiþ
vnworþinesse of þis synne.

The þridde word þat nedis mot suwe of þes two wordis of lore
is þat a child is born to man to make asseþ for mannys synne. And
f.7 45 þis child mot nedis be God, and|man ȝouon to man, and he mut
nedis bere his empire vpon hys schuldre and suffre for man. And
þis child is Iesu Crist þat we supposon was born today. And we
supposon þat þis child is only born to þo men þat suwon ⌐him⌐ in
maner of lyuyng, for he was born aȝenys oþre. Þes men þat ben
50 vniuste and prowde and rebelle aȝen God han þer iugement in

Z   wol] wolde AZG, wel H   ne] ⌐ne⌐ O, om. V   25 wiþowton] wiþ
J   fre] frely Y   to] om. δ   26 oure] om.α   27 no] noht, -ht canc. JH, not
T   29 word] w canc./word D   man] a canc. man V, a man AδG   þat3] ⌐þat⌐
V, om. δ   30 mot] bihoued Z   be] bi J   31 mannys kynde] mankynde
PαIZGV   moste] moot I   mankynde] mannis kynde AOYαβ   32 herfore]
þerfore ZV   to] om. V   strawnge] stronge α, strang J   for man] for man
canc. P   33 neþur he] he ⌐ne⌐Z   ne] neiþer YV   he2] om. δJ   þat1] om.
Z   34 asseþ] asseeþ ⌐for man ⌐ T, aseeþ for man PZ   ȝif . . . asseþ (35)] margin
OH   35 þis1] his I   make] makiþ AI   37 ȝet] ȝif β   38 adams] for
adams δ   39 muste] bihoues Z   40 a] om. G   muste] mot H, bihoues
Z   þis] ⌐þis⌐ Y, om. Z   asseþ] seeþ GH   41 for] þat α   þis] hys
T   42 vnworþinesse] þe vnworþines ZGV, worþinesse T   þis] þe on eras. corr. X,
þe ABOPTYαβδIJZGV   43 nedis mot] rev. YV, nedis muste P   wordis of lore]
wordis of loore on eras. corr. T, wordis byfore αδIJHV, byfore O   45 man2] men
B   he mut] mote O, he must JV   46 bere] be ⌐bere⌐ P   hys] om. δ   47
crist] om. G   48 þo] þe O, om. β   him] corr. D, om. β   51 nedis] om.

Crist, þat þei mote nedis be dampnede of hym, and algatis ȝif þei
ben vnkynde to þer deþ aȝenys his spirit. And þus, ȝif we
coueyton wel þat þis child be born to us, haue ⌜we⌝ ioye of þis
child, and suwe we hym in þes þre vertuwis, in riȝtwisnesse and
mekenesse, and pacience for oure God. For whoeuere contraryeþ 55
Crist in þese, vnto his deþ aȝen þe spirit, mut nedis be dampned
of þis child, as alle oþre schullen be sauyd. And þus þe ioye of þis
child þat was þus meke and ful of vertuwis schulde make men to
be lu⌜y⌝tul in malice, and þanne þei halden wel þis feeste. To hem
þat wolon fyȝte or chide I seyȝe þat þis child þat is born is prynce 60
of pees, and loueþ pees and dampneþ men contrarye to pees.
Studye we how Crist cam in ful tyme whan he schulde, and how
he cam in mekenesse, as his burþe techeþ us, and how he cam in
pacience fro his burþe vnto his deþ. And suwe we hym in þes þre,
for ioye þat we han of hym, for þis ioye in þis pacience brynguþ to 65
ioye þat ay schal laste.

Z   dampnede] demed G   52 we] men Y   53 we] corr. D   54 and²] in
I   55 god] goode, 2nd o and e canc. D, go⌜o⌝d P, goode Tβ, owne goode
V   whoeuere] whasaeuer Z   56 his] þe T   þe] hys αI   57 as] and
Z   58 vertuwis] vertu β   make] m⌜e⌝ke α   men] man A   59 luytul] -y-
corr. D   halden] -l- altered from -d- D, hadden β   þis] þe PZ   60 wolon] w
canc./wolon D   61 dampneþ] dampned AJ   contrarye] þat be canc. contrarye
DX, þat ben contrarie H   pees³] þe pees I   64 vnto] vn canc. to G, to
AOPTαδJZ   we] om. I   65 ioye¹] þe ioye H   þat] þa J   ioye²] om.
α   in] and TαV   66 ioye] þe ioye IV   ay] euere AOβIXGV

Sexta D[i]e a Natiuitate. [Epistola.] Sermo 6.

Q[u]anto tempore heres paruulus est. Galatas 4.

Poul tolliþ in þis epistle what fredom men schulden vse, and leue
seruys óf þe oolde lawe þat ledde men whonne þei weron
children. The furste word of Poul here is seyd to us in þis forme: *as
long tyme [as] an eyr is luytul, he dyuersuþ not fro a seruaunt* by sensible
5   dyuerste, *al ʒif he be lord of alle*. It semeþ þat Poul spekiþ here of
seruyse þat is bondage, and latiþ owt þe long tyme; and spekiþ
now of o part and now of anoþur, and spekuþ here specially of
alle mankynde þat schal be saued. Þis kynrede is an eyr of þe
blisse þat euere schal laste; and fro þe bygynnyng of þe world þer
10 is no dyuersite bytwene hym and þe seruaunt, siþ þe children of
Israel weron in gret bondage in Moyses tyme, siþ þei weron
tretude by Pharao in hard seruys fowre hundred ʒeer. And ʒet þis
kynrede þat is Cristus chyrche is lord of alle þingus of þis world,
for Crist, Godus sone and Lord of alle, puttude þis child ouer alle
15 his goodis. And, as a ʒong eyr of a man is for tyme of his
childhede, whon he is wiþynne age, not tretud as a lord, *but vndur
tutours and gouernours*, boþe in werkis, in foode and cloþ, tretud as
anoþur seruaunt *tyl þe tyme þat his fadir wole* þat he be tretud as
lord, so it was of þe chirche, þe whiche is kynrede of Crist. But
20 whon Crist was bycome man, þanne þis kynrede was take to

MSS: D; ABGHIJOPTVXYZαβδ.

Sexta . . . Natiuitate] dominica 1 post Natale O, dominica infra natiuite T, *om.*
G   die] de D   sermo 6] *om.* BOTαδIJXZGHV   quanto . . . est] *om.*
YV   quanto] qanto D   heres . . . est] *om.* H   est] *om.* A   gal. 4] gal. 6
H, *om.* O   1 þis] þe β   schulden] schollen I   2 seruys] þo seruyce
αH   þei] þe Y   3 as long tyme] *on eras. of shorter corr.* D, a longe tyme β   4 as]
om. D   6 þe] *om.* OV   7 anoþur] anoþer part αβ   8 man] maner, -er *eras.*
DX   saued] saf H   is] *om.* O   9 blisse] blisse of heuene OV   euere] ay
α   fro] fro, -ro *on eras.* D, for *canc.* ˹fro˺ A, for δJXG   12 tretude] tretyde, *2nd t over*
subpuncted d α, tredid J, drawen Z   seruys] seruises I   14 godus] is goddis
I   and] *om.* α   ouer] on Y   15 goodis] good B   a1] *om.* A   a2] *om.*
O   tyme] a tyme AG, ˹þe˺ tyme T, þe tyme PIZV   16 tretud] tretide, *2nd t over*
subpuncted d α, tredid J   as] of β   a] *om.* O   17 in2] and *eras.* in DV, and in
H   and2] and in O, and *on eras. of* in J, in G   cloþ] cloþid I   tretud] tretide,
2nd t after subpuncted d α, tredid J   18 tyme] tyme come T   as] as a BOα-
IV   19 þe2] *om.* BIV, of þe β   is] was B   but] *om.* A   20 þanne] *om.*

worschipe, and puttud fro þe seruys þat he kepte in þe oolde lawe.
And herfore seiþ Poul here *þat we* þat ben of þis kynrede *weron*
vndur þe elementis of þis world, seruyng as oþre bonde men. And it semeþ
þat Poul wolde sey3e þat þes elementis of þis world weron worldly
lawis, þat þe chyrche kepte|in tyme of þe oolde lawe. For ri3t as a   25   f.7v
myche bok is maad of lettris as elementis, so þe lore of þe chyrche
is maad of customys þat it kepuþ. And þus þis eyr lernede furst his
abece as a luytul child, and was holden þanne in drede to lerne þe
lore of Godus lawe.

    But *whan fulnesse of tyme cam* þat þe chyrche schulde be tretid   30
þus no more, *God sente his sone maad of womman, maad vndyr þis lawe,*
to bugge a3en þis eyr to fredom þat he hadde in innocence, al 3if he
were vndyr þe lawe for a tyme. Crist was maad as a creature, siþ
Crist was þis manhede, and so Crist was maad of Marie, as Poul
dreduþ not to graunte heere; and siþ eche part þat Crist hadde   35
was maad of God, as men wyton wel, what schulde moue men to
dreede to graunte þat Crist was al maad? But siþ Crist is of two
kyndis, fully God and ᴦfullyᴵ man, by his manhede was he maad,
and by his godhede not maad. And, for to knytte hise two lawis,
Crist made hymself vndur hem boþe. But in tyme of þe oolde   40
lawe men kepton monye partis of þe lawe þat men nede not now
to kepon, as cerymonyes and iugementis. But, for to schewe
onhede of lawe of God, oo lawe of þe ten comawndementis lastiþ
oon for euere more, þat men ben euere hooldon to kepe. And as
ful man in his kynde is maad of body and of soule, so þe fulle lawe   45
of God ys maad of þe oolde and þe newe. And soo men ben
holden now to kepe þe wit of þe oolde lawe, but as Godis goostly
chyldren to charge oonly þe moralte.

B   21 seruys] seruises I   22 herfore] þerfore αZV   þat²] *om.* H   þis] his
I   weron] þat weren H   23 þe] *om.* α   þis] þe I   and] þat α   24
wolde] wole AG   þes] þe I   þis] þe H   25 in tyme] in ty *canc.//* in tyme
D   tyme] þe tyme Tα   26 þe²] *om.* I   27 lernede] lerde αH, lerneþ
I   28 holden] þan holden I   þanne] *om.* IV   lerne] lere ZH   30 tyme]
þe *canc.* tyme DXH, þe tyme β   chyrche] child G   31 þis] þe H   32 eyr]
erþe O   fredom] þe *canc.* fredom DX, þe fredom IHV   he¹] it HV   in] *om.*
βδ   33 were] was Z   þe] *om.* J   as] *om.* αβ   36 men²] *om.* α   37 to]
at Z   38 fully²] ᴦfullyᴵ *added corr.* DX, fulli *canc.* J, *om.* Bδ   was he] *rev.*
δV   39 and²] ᴦandᴵ A, *om.* G   40 tyme] þe *canc.* tyme J, þo tyme α   41 nede]
nedyde α   43 of¹] of ᴦþeᴵ α, of þe ABGHV   þe] *om.* α   44 oon] *om.*
G   euere²] euer more α   to] for to B   45 ful] a ful T   of²] *om.*
TYI   46 of god] *om.* O   oolde] olde lawe PZ   þe newe] ᴦofᴵ þe newe δ, of þe
newe ABTαIJGHV   47 godis] *om.* Tα   49 in²] *om.* T   50 alle þe] in alle O,

Þes wordis þat Poul spekiþ here ben hy3e in trewþe and in wyt,
50 and alle þe men in þis world konne not blame þe ton of þes. But
wel I wot þat God grauntiþ to fewe men to knowe hem here; but
3et we schulden trowe þes wordis and worschipe hem, and
traueyle on hem to wyte what þes wordis menen, as men
schul[l]en wyte aftur in heuene. And for to haue mynde of þis
55 seynt þat men passe not fro his wyt, somme men wolon go ny3 hise
wordis by vndurstondyng þat God 3yueþ hem; for ellis my3ten
alle hise wordis be alyenyd, and al his wyt by anticrist. But þer
ben two maneris of sonys, kyndly sonys and sonys of grace. Crist is
kyndely sone of God, and his children ben sonys of grace. And þus
60 Crist, whonne he made hym man and made his chyrche to be his
broþur, he 3af a tytle to his chyldren *to make hem alle Godis sones by
grace. And for 3e ben þus Godis children, God sente þe spirit of his Sone,* þe
whiche spirit *crieþ in 3owre hertis,* and ⌜in⌝ 3owre persones *'abba
fadyr'.* And of þese wordis þat God seiþ here, by Poul whom God
65 haþ maad his whistle, it semeþ to monye trewe men þat þer
schulde be no secte but on, þat schulde be Cristus religioun, wiþ
oon abbot and oo reule. And þis wolde kyndely onehede and
loue, and is growndid in Godis lawe.

And þus þis chyrche þat is Godus sone *is not now seruaunt but sone.*
70 *And 3if he be þus Godus sone, he ys heyr by* Crist, *God* and man. By wyt
þat Poul spekuþ heere, it semeþ to monye breþren in God þat þe
chirche þat wandruþ heere ys maad þral by mannys lawe, siþ mo
be sprongon by anticrist þan weron in þe oolde lawe, þat ben now
lefte as God bydduþ. And so þe chyrche is now þral more þan in
f.8 75 tyme|of þe oolde lawe, siþ þes mannys lawis ben werse þan weron
Godis lawis þat now ben lefte; and anticrist is maad a tutour or a

al H   not] men not O   þe ton] oon TV   51 þat] *om.* αI   52 we] men
H   53 what] what þat B   54 schullen] schulden DB   aftur] afturworde
α   for to] to O   mynde . . . seynt (55)] þis seynt in mynde B   55 his] þis
TδJ   wolon] *om.* Bα   56 for . . . anticrist (57)] *om.* Z   57 by] be
Oβ   anticrist] anticristis, -is *canc.* DX, anticristis Oβ   58 maneris] maner
AαδIZGHV   sonys²] sone β   crist . . . grace (59)] *om.* α   59 children]
sones H   sonys] children H   þus] þis B   60 hym] *om.* O   61 hem alle]
⌜alle⌝ hem O   godis] god α   sones . . . godis (62)] *om.* Z   62 þe²] *om.*
I   63 in²] *corr.* D   64 and] *om.* PZ   65 þer . . . þus (69)] *om.* Z   66
wiþ] wiþoute O   68 and] and loue α   is growndid] is ground AG, hys grounde is
T   69 and] *om.* H   þis] þe H   70 be þus] *rev.* H   godus] god
α   by² . . . rewlis (92)] *om.* Z   72 mo] mo men, men *canc.* AG   74 þral
more] *rev.* H   75 tyme] þe tyme H   mannys] mens αIH   werse] werste
α   76 a tutour] tutour HV, autour BOβ   a²] *om.* BOV   77 þe²] *om.*

gouernowr of þe chyrche, more fool þan þe children þat schulden
be gouerned by Godus lawe. And, of alle synnes þat now ben, þis
is moste perelows and greuous þat leesuþ þe fredam þat Crist haþ
purchasid, and makiþ men þral to synne and to feend. And þus it   80
were a muche vertu to gete aȝen owre formere fredom, and trowe
no prelat in þis chyrche, but ȝif he grownde hym in Godus lawe.
And þus men schulden schake awey al þe lawe þat þe pope haþ
maad, and alle rewlis of þes newe ordris, but in as muche as þei
ben growndide in þe lawe þat God haþ ȝouon. But loke þis   85
growndyng disseyue þe nowt! – for yt may falle þat anticrist by
hyse newe lawis and hise byddyngus haue moo bussy seruauntis
to hym, þan ⌐haþ⌐ Crist by his lawe to serue hym for blisse of
heuene. And þis moueþ monye men to speke aȝenys foure newe
sectis; for yche man by hope of blisse schulde holde þe fredam þat 90
Crist haþ ȝouyn, and so he schulde meynteine þis rewle and
despuyse alle oþre rewlis.

B   78 þat] *om.* α   79 moste] þe *canc.* moste DX, þe most HV   leesuþ] losys
α   80 to¹] to þe I   to²] to þe, þe *canc.* X, to ⌐þe⌐ Y, to þe ABOTαβδIJHV   84
rewlis] þe rewles TIV   87 hise] be hys α   haue] haþ J   88 haþ] *corr.*
D   by] to H   blisse] þe blis TαV   89 foure] þe foure B, þes foure
TV   90 man] may O   91 so he] *om.* Y   þis] þe I

Dominica infra Octavam Epiphanie. [Epistola.]
Sermo 7.

Surge illuminare Ierusalem. Ysay 60.

Men expounen comunly þis prophecie of oure Iesu, þat Ysaye say
in spirit, how Crist schulde be lowtud sone aftur þat he was born
of þre kyngus of þe eest; and byleue þat Matheu telluþ techeþ wel
of þis tixt, to what wit it is spokon of þe prophete Ysay. Furst he
5   bygynneþ þus *rys and be þow liȝtned Ierusalem, for þi liȝt is comen, and*
glorie of þe Lord is sprongon vpon þe. Here trewe men vndurstonden
by Ierusalem, þat was heed citee in þe lond of Iude, hooly
chyrche þat wandruþ heere. For Ierusalem in dyuerse plasis
bytokneþ on dyuerse maner, now þe cite of þat cuntre, now þe
10 chyrche þat wandruþ heere, and now þe chirche þat is aboue;
and alle ben fygurede by þis cite. And Ierusalem by interpretacion bytokneþ 'a siȝt of pees'; but here men seen afer, and in
blisse verrey pees. Þis Ierusalem schulde ryse from synne, and be
liȝtned wiþ wyt and grace, siþ Crist, þat is þe furste liȝt, is maad
15 mon for þis ende. And Crist, þat is þe fadris wisdam, and so glorie
of þe Lord, is sprongon of þis kynrede and in hyt, siþ he is Maries
sone. And þus þis is a greet synne to leue to rise and opone oure
wyndowis, for þiᴿsᴸ spiritual liȝt is redy to schyne to alle men þat
wolon opone. Þat man reseyueþ in veyn þe grace of God, as Poul

---

3 Matt. 2: 1–5;   **12** Rev. 21: 2.

MSS: D; ABGHIJOPTVXYZαβ; δ *ends incomplete* 40 þus derke-; Hᵗ *inc.* 47 bi crist,
partially legible on original recto only.

Dominica . . . epiphanie] in die epiphanie OPTδJZH, in festo epiphanie α   sermo
7] *om.* ABOTαδIJXZGHV   surge . . . ierusalem] *om.* YV   ierusalem] *om.*
O   ysay 60] isaye þe fifty c. V, *om.* O   1 iesu] lord iesu TZ, lord iesu crist
V   say] seiþ B   2 þat] *om.* PT   3 þre] þe þre PTαδIJZ, þe V   4 þis] *om.*
J   5 liȝtned] lited OH   comen] command Z   6 sprongon] comen
G   vpon] on BH   7 heed] *om.* Z   8 wandruþ] wandryd J   9 maner]
maners AOH   12 a] þe H   siȝt] *on eras. corr.* D, sigh Z   and] *om.* Z   14
liȝtned] liȝtid H   wyt] lyght α   and] of Tαβ   þat is] is canc. A, þat is canc. B,
om. G   þe] *om.* OT   liȝt] verey lyȝt T   15 þe] *om.* I   so] þe O, so þo
α   16 siþ] sit *eras.* siþ D   17 and²] to I   18 wyndowis] wisdamys canc.

seiþ, þat takiþ of God monye ʒiftis, boþe of fortune and of kynde,   20
and wole not þanke God herfore. He is as vnkynde man, wiþowte
whom þe sonne schyneþ, and ʒet wole not opone his wyndowe to
take liʒt þat schulde saue hym. And here men seyn comunly þat
furst mannys foly is vnkynde; and, bycause of þis vnkyndenesse,
God ʒyueþ man no more his ʒiftus, siþ God approuiþ neuere   25
more þat vnkynde man schulde þus synne. But ʒit God makiþ of
synful man and vnkynde a good man; and al þe goodnesse of þis
comeþ of ⌈þe⌉ goodnesse of God. And bussy we not abowte
furþere cause, for God hymself is þe furste cause.

But þe prophete seiþ ouer þis *for loo! derknesse schal hule þe erþe*,   30
and picke myst schal hule|þe puplis. Here may we knowe two maner of   f.8v
men by þes wordis of Ysay. Somme men ben euermore derke, and
wanton grace to come to blis, as þe erþe is euere derk, and takiþ
not liʒt by clerte. And þis derknesse haþ wiþ hym Godis witt þat
þese men schulen be dampnyde. But somme men han for a tyme   35
myst, but ʒet þei ben a puple, as ben men of hooly chyrche, for
tyme þat þei ben in synne. And þes men by grace of God takon
liʒt þat persuþ hem, and disposuþ hem to heuene, and auoyduþ
her synne fro hem. And suche two maner of men weron in Iude
byfore Crist cam; and þus derknesse of synne hulede þe erþe til   40
Crist cam, and þicke mystis of synne hulede þe puplis þat schulde
be sauyde. But þis liʒt þat cam to men persude þis myst, and
made it cler; and so þis liʒt þat was maad man clerude þo men þat
he wolde saue. And for þis liʒt spekiþ þe prophete, and for þes
men þat schulen be sauyde, but *vpon þe schal þe Lord sprynge, and in*   45

wyndowis D   for þis] *on eras. corr.* D   21 herfore] þerfore αZV, þerof I   as] -s
on eras. corr. DA, an BOPδIJZH, as an V, *om.* α   man] a man T   wiþowte] opon
α   22 sonne] sunnen O   opone] openede G   25 ʒyueþ man] ʒif O   no]
om. T   26 vnkynde] an vnkynde B   man] *om.* H   schulde] s *eras.* /schulde
D   þus synne] neuere synne þus I   of] a T, *om.* I   27 a] man a I   28
þe] *corr.* D, þe *canc.* X, *om.* OPYβδJZGH   we] we vs ZV, vs δIJ   29 þe] *om.*
H   30 derknesse] þe derknesse T, dirkenes of þis α, þerkenesse J   31 schal hule]
om. O   þe] *om.* G   puplis] peple B   may we] *rev.* PIJZV   32 men²] *om.*
T   euermore] euer α   33 derk] þerk J   34 þis] ʒit O   35 schulen]
schulden TG, shullen, *2nd* l *altered from* d J   36 but] *om.* T   37 by] bi þe
B   grace of god] goddis grace Z   38 persuþ] pertys ZG   hem²] *om.*
α   auoyduþ] ⌈a⌉voidiþ Y, voydiþ O   39 two] tho J   weron] *om.*
O   iude] iury α   40 crist] þat crist ZHV   þus] þis OJ   hulede]
bihelede I   til] to αβZ   41 mystis] miste α   hulede] bihelede I   puplis]
peple⌈s⌉ X, puple OT   42 þis²] þe YI   43 so] *om.* T   þo] þe Bβ   44
saue] haue sauyd H   þe] þis I   45 þat] *om.* T   schulen] shulden PT-

þe schal glorie of hym be seen, for of kynrede of Iacob and in þat
kynrede was Crist boryn. And monye of hem weron sauyde by
Crist, and monye oþre of heþene men. And folc schul[l]en wandre in
þi liȝt, and kyngis in schynyng of þi burþe. For abowte tyme of Cristus
50   burþe þre kyngis camen owt of þe eest, and boþe þei and monye
oþre sawon þe liȝt of þis sterre. And muse we not whan þis sterre
aperyde furst in þe eest, and how long tyme þes þre kyngis weron
in comyng to Betleem; for sone aftur þat Crist was born þei
camen and þus worschipedon Crist for, as þe gospel beruþ
55   wytnesse, þei fownden þe child wiþ his modyr, and it is licly þat in
þe same stable þat Crist was born inne in Betleem; and so it mut
nedis be sone aftur þe tyme þat Crist was born.

And afturward þis prophete spekuþ to þe glorie and ioye of
Crist luft vp al abowte þin yȝen, and see alle þese ben gederude, and ben
60   comen to þe to do þe worschipe as þei schulden. And alle þese ben
figure to þe þat þyne sonys schulon come from fer, and þi dow⌐ȝ⌐tris
schulen ryse asyde, and monye cuntreyes schulen trowon in þe. þan
schaltow ⌐see⌐ and habownde, and þin herte schal wondre and be larged,
whanne þe multitude of þe see schal be turned to byleue of þe. And strenkþe
65   of heþene men schal come to þe and trow in þe. þe flowyng of camaylis
schal hule þe; men þat schulen ryde vpon dromedis; men of Madyan
and of Effa, alle men of Saba schulen come, þat God haþ ordeyned for
þis iorneye, bryngyng gold and encense, and tellyng heryeng to God. þis
lettre seemeþ somwhat mysty, and þerfore men tellon dyuerse
70   wittis of it. Som men seyn þat cameylis wateryng hylyde Crist in

---

55   Matt. 2: 11.

Z   vpon] on H   lord] hed O   46 schal] om. I   glorie of hym] on eras.
corr. D, ⌐hys⌐ glorye, gaþ foll. eras. X, his glorie ABOPYαβIJZGV   kynrede] oo
kynrede AB, þe kynrede P   48 of] om. βH   schullen] schulden DG, schullen, 2nd
l altered from d X, om. I   49 þi¹] om. H   in] of O   þi²] þe OβJ   tyme] þe
tyme ZV   51 oþre] om. O   þis¹] þe AT   52 tyme] om. α   þes] þe
α   53 in] ⌐in⌐ T, om. HV   sone aftur] rev. T   þat] om. TJ   54 þus] om.
Z   crist] him HV   55 his] þe T   56 inne] þenne β, om. αH   58 þis] on
eras. corr. D, þe G   ioye] þe ioye O   59 crist] iesu criste α   þese] om.
G   60 to þe] om. J   þe²] to þe α, þere X, om. I   61 figure] figurid
PZ   schulon] schulden, -d- canc. X, shulden ABG   dowȝtris] ȝ corr. D   62
schulen] shulde B   þan] and þen α   63 schaltow] þou schalt GV   see] corr.
D   wondre] w/wondre D, wandre G   larged] alargid B   64 of²] on, -n
altered from -f A, on Bα   and] om. O   strenkþe] þe strengþe ABOPTYαβH¹IJ-
XZGV   65 heþene] þe heþen T   66 men¹] and men P   ryde] om.
α   vpon] on αZ   men²] and men H⌐   67 god] om. O   for] ⌐to⌐ α   68
bryngyng] bringe G   tellyng] telle G   69 men tellon] tellon ⌐men⌐ J   71

his membris; for traueyle þat was doon in camaylis helpude to
hule cristene men; as Iohn Baptist and monye oþre weron hulede
by help of camaylis traueyle, and þei weron hastude to leue þer
drynk þat þei schulden take in þe watyr. But somme men
vndurstonden þees wordis to goostly vndurstondyng of hem. And 75
so men dowton heere ofte of what cuntrey þese þre kyngis weron;
and it is ynow here to wyte þat þei weron of þe eest,|wheþur þei f.9
weron of Saba or of Arabye, or of anoþur yle. And heere men
muson ydully how þese weron but þre kyngus, siþ þe hooly salm
seiþ þat kyngus of Tharsis and of þe yle schulon offre ʒiftis vnto 80
Crist, and þes mote nedis be two kyngis; 'þe kyngus of Arabie and
of Saba schulon lede ʒiftus to þis child', and þese ben oþre two
kyngus. And þus it semeþ þat foure kyngus camen to worschipe
þus þis child. But þis reson is to feble; forʒif we men þat arguen
þus þat Dauid spekiþ heere of þes kyngis, and þis were hard ⌜for⌝ 85
to teche. But ʒet þes þre kyngis myʒton wel haue monye names
by monye resonys, as þe kyng of Englond is kyng of Englond and
of more Bretayne. And so þese kyngis myʒton haue þes names, al
ʒif þei weron but þre or two. Or ellis hit myʒte han fallun þus þat
somme kyngis bysydon þes þre senten þer offryngis wiþ hem, and 90
so þes wordis ben algatis soþe. Or ellis it myʒte haue be þus þat
dyuerse kyngus dwelton at home, and maden þer offryngis to þis
child, and þei myʒton haue be tawt þere þat he was boþe God
and man. Monye suche wittis be not nedful to vs for to kunne
now. But do we worschipe to þis child wiþ gold, encense and wiþ 95
myrre; for we schulden byknowe his godhede, as gold is more þan
oþre metallys; and byknowe his wisdam, as gold schyneþ byfore

---

71 Matt. 3: 4; Mark 1: 6; **80** Ps. 71: 10.

for] fro T   traueyle] trauailis H   72 as] wiþ O   73 þei] þo B   þer] þe
PZ   74 men] om. T   77 ynow] not α   78 saba] arabi ABOPTYαβH¹IJ-
ZV   arabye] saba ABOPTYαβH¹IJZV   yle] ilede α   men] om. α   80
kyngus] þe kinges I   tharsis] taris H   yle] ilde α   vnto . . . ʒiftus (82)] om.
α   vnto] to ZV   81 þes] þes men A   þe] om. PZ   82 to] vnto
I   þis] þe YβV   oþre two] rev. B   83 it] om. I   84 þus] on eras. corr. D,
om. G   forʒif] for if αZ   85 þat] say þat α   kyngis] þre kynges I   for to]
for corr. to D, to V   86 wel] ʒit H   87 þe] om. H   88 of] of canc. X, om.
ABOPTYαβIJZG   89 but] om. T   þre or] two or H, om. O   two] þre
H   han fallun] falle B   90 offryngis] offeryng H   91 soþe] trewe
T   be] falle O   92 offryngis] offryng H   þis] þe Z   93 boþe] om.
G   94 monye] and many H   to vs] om. I   95 child] ch canc./child
D   encense] and encense B   96 schulden] shulen B   byknowe] knowe T, be

oþre. Þe secownde tyme we schuldon knowleche þat Crist is þe
furste prest of alle, and offre to hym deuocion, siþon he is boþe
100 God and man. Þe þridde tyme we schulden knowleche þat Crist
was deed for oure sake, and roos hool as he hadde ordeyned; and
so schullen we alle do at þe laste resureccion, oþur to blisse or to
peyne. And lyue we alle iust lif, and loue þis Lord op oure power,
and þanne he wole rewarde us in blisse aftur þes þre ȝiftus. And
105 here monye men þenkon þat men schulden liȝtly passe ouer þis,
and speke of þingus þat ben certeyne þat profiȝton to men þat
heron hem.

canc. know α   97 byknowe] be ⌜þis⌝ know α   his] þis T   98 schuldon] shulen
ABYβIJ   100 schulden] shulen APIJZV   crist] he H   101 hadde
ordeyned] ordende αI   102 schullen] schulde T   we alle] rev. B   103 iust
lif] iustlich O   loue] loue ⌜we⌝, we canc. D, loue we PZGH   op] opon AH, at
Z   105 monye] may T   106 to] more to O   107 heron] herem H

Dominica 1 post Octavam Epiphanie. [Epistola.]
Sermo [8].

Obsecro uos per misericordiam Dei. Romanos 12.

Poul telliþ here to gentile folc how þat þei schulden serue God,
and kepe hemself in charite, and serue togydere as o persone; for
whonne monye men acorden in oon and don o werk in Godis
name, þey don it more spedily, more strongly and by lesse blame.
Poul bygynneþ to preyȝe Romanys to kepe þe lore þat he techeþ,   5
for hee prechede not for money, ne for wynnyng of þis world. *I*
preye ȝow, seiþ Poul, *by Godis mercy, þat ȝe ȝyue ȝowre bodyes to God, a*
qwic oost and not deed, to serue God by his lawe. Þe secownde
tyme þe lif of ⌈ȝ⌉owre body schal be hooly aftur Crist. Þe þridde
tyme schal ȝowre body plese God by deuouȝt wille. And ȝif   10
ȝowre body be þus led to licnesse of þe Trinnyte, þanne be ȝe wel
disposude to serue God as ȝe schulden. And al ȝif alle cristene
men schulden marke þes wordis of seynt Poul, ȝeet lordus of þis
world schulden take more heed to hem; for þei camen of gentilite,
and þer staat schulde þus serue to God|to defende Cristis lawe   15 f.9v
and his ordenaunce, and late it not perysche for ydulnesse. And
þus schulde *þer seruyse* to God *be resonable,* and kepe þer staat. And
for suche men synnen ofte in nouelryes of þe world, þerfore
bydduþ Poul aftir *nyle ȝe be conformede to þis world, but be ȝe reformede*
in newenesse þat schal be maad *in ȝowre wyt.*   20

MSS: D; ABGHIJOPTVXYZαβ, H⁺ *ends incompl.*16 and², *most uncollatable.*

Dominica . . . epiphanie] dominica post epiphaniam O   sermo 8] sermo 9 Dβ, *om.*
BOTαIJXZGHV   obsecro . . . dei] *om.* YV   uos] vos fratres T   miseri-
cordiam] *om.* G   dei] *om.* JGH   ro. 12] *om.* O   1 god] to god IV   2
serue] serue god G   as] in H   4 it] ⌈it⌉ I, *om.* O   5 romanys] to romaynes
A   6 prechede] prechiþ J   money] none money J   wynnyng] no wynnynge
I   7 ȝow] how O   god] crist H   9 ȝowre] ȝ-*corr.* D   crist] cristis lawe
I   10 god] to *canc.*god D, to god XGH   by] wiþ a α   11 body] bodyes
α   12 ȝe] *on eras. corr.* D   and] *om.*G   al ȝif] ȝif O   alle] alle þese
G   13 men] ⌈men⌉ I, *om.* P   marke] make β   14 to hem] *om.* α   15 þus
serue] *rev.* H   to²] ⌈to⌉ H, *om.* OPTY   17 schulde] *om.* J   staat] astaat
I   18 nouelryes] suche *canc.* nouelryes D, nouelry α   19 conformede] confermed

Þer is no lord of þis world, neþir in more staat ne in lasse, þat ne
he schulde take þis lore of Poul, ȝif he wole serue God; for costly
metis and gaye garnementis, whan þei ben takone ouer mesure,
þei maken lordis bussye for hem, and spuylon wrongly þer pore
25 tenauntis; and þis mot nedis displese to God, siþ he is welle of
ryȝtwisnesse. Þes men þat lyuon þus ben conformede to þis world.
But man, be he neuere so greet, schulde coueyte to araye hys
soule wiþ Godis lawe and wiþ vertuwis, for þat is more precious.
And it falliþ ofte tymes þat preestis and freris, þat schulden here
30 teche, ben boþe false and vnkonnynge, and tellon but luytil by
Godis lore. And þis meneþ Poul heere whan he preyeþ vnto
Romanys þat þei schulden be reformed in newnesse of þer wittis.
And þus, of alle þe heretikis þat anticrist browte euere in, þes þat
blaboron vnto lordis, and seyon þat þei schulde not here, ne
35 konne, þe gospel of Crist, for clerkis schulden techon hem to lyue,
ben mooste perelous in þe chyrche, and moste to flee as anticrist.
Wiþ such lore of oure God schuldon lordis somwhat cloþe þer
sowlis, and be not to worldly, but þenke somwhat on þer sowlis;
for þis lif þat we lyuon here is boþe schort and ful of peyne, and is
40 ordeyned to be a mene to þe blisse þat euere schal laste.

And by wyt of Godis lawe *schulden men knowe* þis Trinnyte, *which
were þe good wille of God, wel plesyng and parfiȝt.* Þe wille of God mut
nedis be good lich to þe Fadyr of heuene. And so al þe
ordenaunce of Crist mut nedis be good, siþ he is God. Þe wille of
45 God to punysche men is good, siþ þat it is iust; but þis wille comeþ
not forþ, but by occasion of synne. Þe wille of God is wel plesynge,
as is þe secounde persone of God; for we redon þus of Crist þat 'in

---

47 Matt. 3: 17; 12: 18; 17: 5; Mark 1: 11; Luke 3: 22.

OV   21 is] nys AOI   of] in BYV   ne he] *rev.* AI   22 wole] wolde
I   serue] ⌐wel¬ serue X, wele serue ABOPYαβIJZGV   23 mesure] maner *canc.*
mesure D   24 wrongly] wrongfully BH   25 mot] muste P   to] *om.*
YIZV   26 þes] þen O   to] þus to I   29 preestis and freris] men of haly kirke
Z   30 boþe false] vntrewe Z   31 lore] lawe O   meneþ] moueþ
BαIGV   whan he preyeþ] to praye I   vnto] to HV   32 romanys] þe
romaynes IV   schulden] sal Z   þer] oþer O, alle I   33 and . . . anticrist
(36)] *om.* Z   of] *om.* O   þe] *om.* H   þat¹] þat euer OV   þes] *om.* O, þes
men IJ   34 blaboron] ⌐b¬labouren I, laboryn J   vnto] to αV   schulde not]
ne scholden I, schulden J   here ne konne] kunne ne heere A   35 schulden] ⌐þat¬
shulden P, þat shulden B   36 as] an O   37 lordis somwhat] *rev.* O   somwhat cloþe] *rev.* I   þer] of her H   38 but] and Z   on] in T   39 lyuon]
lede α   boþe schort] *rev.* T   43 good lich] godliche I   lich] licly BT-
β   44 good] god B   he] þat he IV   45 good] god B   þat] *om.*

hym it plesude wel to þe Fadur'. And þus men þat ben bussy to wyte what is þe wille of God ben wel payede of þis wille, and traueylon for to do þis wille. Þe þridde tyme, aftur þe Hooly 50 Goost, þis wille mot nedis be parfiȝt; for it is not schewid to man for fleschly lustis or worldly wynnyng, but for worschipe of God, and for profiȝt of his puple.

And for wyttis of monye men ben ocupyed for worldly þingis and lores þat profiȝte not to þe sowle, þerfore seiþ Poule aftur *I* 55 *seye forsoþe by þe grace þat is ȝouen to me* of God, and not for to plese ȝow, ne for coueytise of ȝowre goodis, but þis *I seyȝe to ȝow alle: to kunne no more þan is nede to kunne, but to konne to sobrenesse,* and to lerne vertuwes of Crist. Somme men ben here bussye for to kunne worldly wyt, as cautelis of mannys lawe, and craftus to wynne 60 myche money; and clerkis traueylon monye weyes veynly to haue kunnyngis. And|alle þes letton men to geten hem knowyng of f.10 God. And so Poul seiþ *to eche man þat he schulde konne his byleue, as God haþ partud byleue,* to some more, and to some lesse. And al ȝif byleue of God be grownd nedful for cristene men, ȝet acord in 65 charite mut nedis be ioyned wiþ þis trewþe; for fendis of helle han trewþe, but þei tremblon for defaute of loue.

And herfore seiþ Poul þus þat, *as we han monye lymes in oo body of dyuerse kyndis, and not eche lyme haþ þe same dede,* but eche is dyuerse from oþur, *so monye men* of oo byleue *ben oo body in Crist.* And þis 70 body is holy chyrche, þat is weddud wiþ Crist. And so eche membre of Crist schulde haue his propre deede, but alle þer dedis schulden come to þis: þat þei profiȝte to þe body of þe chyrche,

---

66 Jas. 2: 19.

PYZ   it] *om* T   47 is] it is H   48 it] is OTαJ   plesude wel] *rev.*
α   men] to men I   50 for to] to H   þis] his β   aftur] aftir þe wil of
Y   53 for] *om.* TZ   his] alle *canc.* his APJ, ⌐al⌐ his X, al his BOTYαIZG-
HV   54 wyttis] wytnes J   55 lores] lore β   I seye] ysaie O   57 ne] no
H   to²] *om.* B   58 no] ne O   nede] nedeful B   to³] þe β   to⁴] *om.*
α   59 lerne] lere αZ   for to] to O   60 worldly] here worldly T   61
myche] wiþ moche I, *om.* H   money] mone Z   veynly] ydeli and veynly
H   haue] gete H   62 kunnyngis] kunnyng B   men] man J   geten]
haue H   hem] *om.* H   knowyng] kunnyng HV   64 partud] partyd of
G   65 grownd] groundid IH   for] to PαZV   in] of O, and PZ   66
nedis be] *rev.* T   67 trewþe] þis trouþe B   68 herfore] þerfore αZV   þus]
aftir B   þat] *om.* OV   oo] *om.* T   69 kyndis] kynde T   haþ] þat haþ
β   70 oo¹] ⌐oon⌐ PJ, *om.* OTαZH   crist] o crist P   72 his] þis PαZ   74

and þanne þei profiȝton to eche membre and to worschipe of Iesu
75 Crist. And þus eche man schulde be war þat he be in such astaat
þat is aprouyd by Iesu Crist, and traueyle trewly in þis staat. Ȝif
þow be a prest of Crist, teche trewly Godus lawe; ȝif þow be a
worldly lord, defende þow Godus lawe by strenkþe; ȝif þow be a
l[a]bourer, kepe þow trewþe and trauele faste. And þus eche
80 man of Cristus chirche schulde helpon his broþur aftur his myȝt.
And ȝif he kowde monye helpis, *he schulde be monye lymes to hym.*
And þis lore bydduþ Poul þat is ful sutyl and nedful; and wolde
God þat þis byleue þat Poul techeþ in þis epistle were wel cowd
and wel kept of þes foure sectis of anticrist, þat ben newe comyn
85 into þe chyrche for to charge it and harme it.

and²] *om.* α   of] *om.* A   75 and . . . staat (76)] *om.* Z   astaat] staat
G   76 by] of YH   staat] astaat I   77 crist] iesu crist O   godus] bi
goddis G   ȝif] and ȝif H   78 þow¹] *om.* AIJ, þou þe B   godus] treuly goddis
P   by strenkþe] *om.* O   strenkþe] str *canc.*/strenkþe D   79 labourer]
lobourer D   81 lymes] helpes *canc.* lymes αI   82 þis] þus O   nedful] ful
nedful O, medful T   and³ . . . it² (85)] *om.* Z   83 þat¹] þas β   þis¹] *om.*
T   cowd] *om.* O, knowen H   84 wel] *om.* T   þes] þo αβG   sectis] seytis
I   newe] now BOV   85 into] in into B   it²] it more O

Dominica ij post Octavam Epiphanie. [Epistola.]
Sermo [9].

Habentes donaciones. Romanos 12.

Poul in þis epistle telliþ vnto Romayns how spiritual preestis schul[d]en passe seculeris, for prestis schulden be lif to qwikene þe comyntees. Furst techuþ Poul how þes preestis of ⌐þe⌐ puple schulde passon in ȝiftis of God þe comyns by þer good lif. And þus bidduþ Poul þat þey schulden *haue ȝiftus dyuerse* from oþre men, *by* 5 *grace þat God ȝyueþ hem.* Men may not grucche heere for þes wordis of Poul, for God mot sowe his grace dyuersely in men. And so men schulde not take þis staat, but ȝif þei passedon oþre in grace, and able þei hem in goode werkis; and þer grace schal be more.

Seuene and twenty ȝiftus of God telluþ Poule in suche preestis. 10 Somme of hem *han prophecye by reson of þer byleue*, as þes þat tellon of þe day of doom, and hard ende of mennys deedis þat discorden from Godus lawe; as men wyton by byleue þat deedis of men, þat ben done aȝenys þe biddyng of God, moton algatis haute an yuel ende, oþur suwyng anoon, or at þe laste in þe day of doom. And 15 þus monye tellon prophecies, boþe to good and to yuel. Also *þei han seruysis dyuerse in þer seruyng*, for prechyng and goostly werkis pertenon vnto siche men; and whonne þei doon straunge werkis þei passon to anoþur staat. As *somme men techon in þer lore*, as þes

MSS: D; ABGHIJOPTVXYZαβ.

Octavam epiphanie] epiphaniam O   sermo 9] sermo 10 Dβ, sermo 19 J, *om.*
BOTαIXZGHV   habentes donaciones] *om.* YV   donaciones] donaciones
secundum graciam T   ro. 12] ad ro. 22 I, romayns V, *om.* O   1 in . . . telliþ]
telliþ in þis epistle Y   þis] his I   telliþ] *om.* β   vnto] to αV   2
schulden¹] schulen DBOPYβXZ   lif] ⌐good⌐ lyf α   to] *om.* α   3 comyntees]
comens H   þes] þe A   þe] *corr.* D, *om.*β   5 shulden] sal Z   from] for
β   7 sowe] sue β   in] to A   8 ȝif] if þat B   9 more] þe more TI   11
by] for O   12 mennys] mannus β   deedis] synne H   13 lawe] lawes
I   þat¹] as α   of] *om.*Y   men þat ben done] þat men don Y, men þat
bynden β   15 laste in þe] *om.* AH   in þe] in *canc.* þe B, ⌐in⌐ T, at þe O   16
also] and also αHV   17 seruysis] seruise Bα   þer] *om.* Y   prechyng] þe
prechynge T   and] in Oα   18 vnto] to OGV   straunge] suche straunge
I   19 to] vnto H   men] men *canc.* X, *om.* ABPTYβIJZGHV   þes] sum I, *om.*

20 men þat prechon feiþ; and *summe styren men to goode,* as
counselouris by Godis lawe. And so þes men *þat ȝyuon almys in*
f.10v *symplenesse,* knowyng þat al is Godis|ȝifte ȝouon to hem to dele
forþ, ben in þe fyueþe degre; and þis ȝyuyng of double almys, þat
is pertynent to preestis, schulde be don in symplenesse, and
25 pruyde fled wiþ ypocrisye. Þe sixte seruyse takiþ he *þat is aboue in*
bussynesse, as ben curatis of þe puple, oþur hyere or lowere. And
alle þes prelatis schulden be bussy to kepe þe schep þat God haþ
ȝouen hem. And here þenken monye men þat, fro þis staat was
turnyd to pruyde, þei ben clepud prelatis and borun aboue by
30 wynd of pruyde; and þei be not aboue by God, but more foolis
þan þer sugettis, and þer bussynesse is turned to pruyde and to
robbyng of þer schep. In þe seuenþe seruyse is he *þat haþ mercy in*
gladnesse. Poul spekiþ not of þis prelat þat traueyluþ for symonye,
and takuþ money gladly for luytul traueyle þat he doþ; for þis
35 gladnesse is abowte his money, and not abowte seruys of God.
And in þis faylon cardynalis þat geton graces to monye men, and
absolucionys wiþ oþre feynede prauylegies. Al ȝif *loue wiþowte*
feynyng schulde be in alle cristene men, ȝeet þe preest neer Crist
schulde haue clene loue in God, and not loue more mennys
40 goodis þan þe profiȝt of þer soule, for þonne he feynede to loue
hem, and hatuþ hem and loueþ þer goodys. And þus þei schulden
hate yuel boþe in hem and oþre men, and speke wysly aȝen it, for to
make men clene þerfro; and in þis faylon flatereris, þat waschen
mennys heedis wiþ false oyle.
45   Aftur Poule techeþ algatis to preestis þat þei schulden *cleue to*
go[o]d, whon þei seen sentence of wynnyng, and sentence of Godis
lawe; þei schulden hoolde wiþ þe secounde siþ it is good on Godus

OG   20 men[1] *om.* Y   þat] *om.* I   summe] sum men OJ   21
counselouris] confessours IJ   22 godis] of goddis H   to hem] *om.* α   23
fyueþe] fyue J   of] is Z   24 schulde] and *canc.* shulde B, and suld ZV   25
wiþ] in B, and Z   26 and . . . schep (32)] *om.* Z   27 þes . . . schulden] þis
scholden prelatis I   schep] shipee H   28 hem] hem to kepe I   men] *om.*
H   29 clepud] called α   borun] ben borun G   31 þer[1] oþer α   and
þer] and þer and ȝare O   32 seruyse] seruisis β   33 þis prelat] þaim Z   34
he doþ] þai do Z   35 his] *om.* Z   seruys] þe seruise BIV   36 and[1] . . .
prauylegies (37)] *om.* Z   graces] grace Tα   to] for G   and[2] and also
H   37 feynede] many feyned H   38 feynyng] seruyng O   þe preest] prestis
Z   neer] nerere α   39 not loue]`rev.` T   40 þan] more þanne β   soule]
OαIZHV   he feynede] þai feyne Z   41 hem[1]] in hem I   and[3] *om.*
G   42 oþre] in oþer ABTGHV   men] `men` G, *om.* V   wysly] wylli
H   43 men] hem β   and] *om.*.G   flatereris] þes flatereris H   44 wiþ] in
I   45 þei] *om.* H   cleue] be *canc.* cleue DX, `be` clene α, be clene IJ, be cleuynge
H   46 good] god DOPTαβIJZV   seen] seiþ O, seyn J   wynnyng . . . of[2]]

syde. And in þis faylon ofte traueyloures in mannys lawe. And so
men schulden *loue* togydere *charite of breþerhede*.Charite haþ two
braunchis : loue of God and loue of man. Þat man þat loueþ a 50
man, loueþ charite of breþerhede; and for his propre or pryue
auauntage schulde not man lette to large þis loue. And þus men
schulden *come byfore in doyng worschipe eche to oþur*. He þat is hyere in
staat schulde be more meke þan þe lowere, and so in mekenesse of
his herte go byfore þe toþur in worschipyng. And þis my3te li3tly 55
be don aftur þe 3iftis þat God haþ grauntud; sensible honowrys
ben but luytule, and lesse to charge þan honouris of soule. And
þus cristene men schulden be *not slow in bussynesse*, to kepe onhede
in charite, but swift in þat þat sowneþ loue; and in þis faylon
monye men, þat wolen haue worschipe of þis world, and sugete 60
oþre men to hem for þe pruyde þat þei han in þer herte. And þus
men schulden by charite be brennyng in þer spirit, hauynge boþe
desyr and ioye to kyndle loue by mekenesse; and in þis faylon
monye men in tretees and acordis makyng. And þus men
schulden serue to þe Lord, and not to þe fadur of pruyde, ne to 65
þer flesch, ne to þe world, and lette to serue to þe Lord of heuene.
And þus men schulde *haue ioye in hope* þat þei han ⌐of⌐ reward in
blis; and þerfore bydduþ Poule to men þat þei schulden ioye
|euere in God. f.11

Poul bidduþ to cristene men þat þei schulden be *pacient in* 70
tribulacion þat falluþ to hem, for þer ben fewe men or noone þat
lyuon here þer fulle lif, þat ne þei han persecucion; and þus
pacience is nedful. And, for oure hope schulde be in God þat he
helpe us in þis weye, þerfore Poul techeþ aftur to *stonde bussyly in*
preyer. And, for men schulden be merciful, þerfore bydduþ Poul 75

om. T   47 good of] on T   48 and¹] *om.* G   in¹] on O   mannys]
mennus β   49 charite¹]in charite αHV   51 pryue]pryueþ O   52 not man]
rev. Z   man] a man Tα, men O   men schulden] *rev.* H   53 worschipe] of
worschipe T   hyere] heir I   54 meke] mekere TI   so] *om.* G   55
toþur] oþere Y   worschipyng] worschipe T   56 grauntud] 3ouen H   57
honouris] honour Z   soule] þe soule BαV   58 be not] *rev.* OV   kepe] speke
P   59 in¹] and Z   loue] ⌐to⌐ loue Z, to loue V   and] *om.* O   60 world]
lord β   sugete] so getynge of H   61 hem] hym J   þe] her H, *om.*
BOPYαβIJZGV   þer] *om.* Tα   62 þer] þe T   63 kyndle] kyndelich
O   in] ⌐in⌐ V, *om.* T   faylon] f/faylon D, fallen β   64 acordis] in acordes
α   men schulden] *rev.* H   65 þe²] *om.* H   ne] noþer O, and I   66 and]
þat α   lette] ⌐to⌐ lette T, tó lette PZ   to³] to *canc.* X, *om.* ABOPTYαIJ-
ZGHV   67 þus] *om.* α   in¹] and β   68 ioye euere] *rev.* Y   70 to] *om.*
T   schulden] *om.* α   72 þer fulle] *rev.* H   ne þei] *rev.* JV, ne α   73 for]
foure *canc.* for D   74 techeþ] telliþ G   75 bydduþ Poul] *rev.* BV   76
comynyng] comynge OPβIH, kunnynge B   fallon] shulden falle B   77 now²]

aftur þat men schulden *be comynyng in needis þat fallon to seyntis*
heere, helpyng hem now wiþ goodis, now wiþ preyer, and now
wiþ counseyl. And, as Poul bydduþ, no broþur schulde suffre, but
ʒif oþre suffre wiþ hym. And algatis men schulden do profiʒt to
80 þer broþur in medful lif; and þus men schulden bussyly sue
herboryng to þer neyʒebore, boþe ʒyue rest to body and soule, by
almes and by pacience. And þus bidduþ Poul aftur þat cristene
men schulden *blesse to oþre þat pursuwon hem* here, for þat restuþ
muche mennys sowlis. And so men schulden *blesse* þer breþeren
85 *and not curse* hem to wake hem, for suche cursyng comunly is
contrarye to hospitalite. And þus siþ alle goode cristene men
schulden be of oon herte to God, þei schulden *ioye wiþ* clene *ioyeris,*
and wepe wiþ men þat wepon heere. And so alle goode cristene men
schulden *fele onhede among hemself;* wheþur þei han ioye or peyne,
90 þei schulden haue ioye or sorwe in herte, and þenke þat oo body
of þe chyrche suffreþ by dyuerse membris.

And þus men þat lyuon in þis lif schulde *not smache hyʒe þingis,* to
caste hemself to be hyʒe and to harme þer emcristene. And in þis
synnen monye men and algatis þes foure newe sectis, for þey don
95 harm to þe chyrche for to hyʒe þer nouelrye. But alle men
schulden *assente to* meke statis and meke lyues, and hoolde hem
payede on þo staatis þat ben growndude in Cristus lawe. For as a
mete in a man þat is not defyed byfore makiþ monnys body to
gurle, so it is of þes newe staatis, þat Cristis lawe haþ not defyed.
100 Somme of þes wordis þat Poul seiþ here schulden trewe preestis
declare more, as it is profiʒt to þe puple, aftur þat God techeþ
hem.

---

78 1 Cor. 12: 26.

---

and now IJV   preyer] prayerys JV   78 counseyl] counseyles T   and] *om.*
THV   79 suffre] suffrede OV, wold suffre α, ⌜welyn⌝ suffre H   80 broþur]
breþeren HV   in] and Z   81 neyʒebore] neyʒboris BV   body] þe *canc.* bodi
J, þe body I   soule] to soule PZ, to þe soule I   82 by] *om.* TβV   83 restuþ
muche] ⌜miche⌝ restiþ B   84 mennys] mannus O, men Z   men schulden] *rev.* T,
men J   85 not] non J   to wake hem] ne warye hem α   86 to] in I   siþ]
seiþ β   89 fele] fle β   90 herte] here herte IJ   91 suffreþ] sufferid Z   93
to²] not *canc.* to D   and² . . . nouelrye (95)] *om.* Z   in þis] þus α   94
þes . . . newe] *on eras. corr.* D   95 nouelrye] nouelries Y   96 meke¹] make
Oβ   meke lyues] mekenesse H   meke²] make β   97 on] on, -n *altered from* -f
J, of IZ   þo] þe ABOPTYIJZ   for . . . hem (102)] *om.* Z   a] *om.*
BOJGV   98 monnys] ⌜a⌝ mannes Y, a mannus HV   101 aftur] and aftir
Y   god] crist Y

Dominica iii post octavam Epiphanie. [Epistola.]
Sermo 1[o].

Nolite esse prudentes. Romanos 12.

Poul telluþ in þis epistle how comynytes and alle men schulden
schape weyes for charite and oonhede to kepe heere. Furst Poul
bydduþ his breþren *to be not qweynte to hemself, and ʒelde to no mon
yuel for yuel.* It is seyd comunly þat þer ben þre lawis heere: lawe of
God, lawe of þe world, and lawe of þe feend of helle. Lawe of   5
God, þat Poul techeþ, is moste resonable and liʒt: to ʒelde men
good for yuel, for so doþ God þat may not fayle. Þe secounde lawe
of þe world is to ʒelde good for good, and yuel for yuel; for, as men
seyon, þus kynde techeþ men to do. Þe þridde lawe of þe feend is
to do yuel for good, as God seyde 'ʒe', and Eue doutide, but þe   10
feend seyde oponly 'nay'. Poul forfenduþ here þe myddul lawe
þat men schulden ʒelden yuel for yuel. And þus qweyntenesse to
a man is heere dispreysud of Poul, for þat worldly man is
qweynte,|boþe in werris and oþer lif, þat can ʒelde redyly an f.11v
yuel turn for anoþur. And þis lawe of þe world brynguþ in lawe of   15
þe feend. For it is takon for a rewle among worldly werryouris þat
þei schulden anoye þer enemyes on what maner þat þei may, and
it is holdon a riʒtwisnesse to do a wrong for anoþur. And ʒeet

---

10 Gen. 3: 1–6.

MSS: D; ABGHIJOPTVXYZαβ; δ *inc.* 34 and it is more resonable

Sermo 10] sermo 11 Dβ, *om.* ABOTαIJXZGHV
YV   prudentes] prudentes apud vosmetipsos T
epistola ro. 12 I, *om.* O   1 comynytes] comunes I
T   mon] o *altered from* a D   4 heere] *om.* O
helle] *om.* O   lawe³] þe lawe BV   7 for] and I
techeþ] *rev.* AIJ   men] *om.* I   10 for] for to H
forfendide T   12 ʒelden] *twice, 2nd canc.* D, ⌜not⌝ ʒeld J, not ʒelde V, *om.*
O   and] as O   qweyntenesse] queyntise APTHV
YV   14 oþer] in oþere βHV   ʒelde redyly] *rev.* OIJ, ʒelde ⌜redily⌝ T, ʒelde
V   15 turn] *om.* IJ   þis] þus I   brynguþ] redily bringiþ T   lawe²] þe
lawe BOPTYαβJXZHV, þis lawe G   16 worldly] *om.* Z   þat] *om.* H   17
schulden] sʒulle OTYαβJH   anoye] noye BZ

nolite . . . prudentes] *om.*
ro. 12] ro.13 β, ad ro. 24
2 heere] hyre J   3 his] vs
5 lawe¹] and law J   of
8 to] for to H   9 kynde
11 forfenduþ here] *rev.* IJ,
on] vpon H   18 a²] *om.*

Godis lawe bidduþ to ȝelde not an yuel for an yuel. And it is
20 certeyn of byleue þat þis yuel is ⌜a⌝ wrong; for yuel of peyne
schulde men ȝeelde by þe reule of charyte, siþ God ȝeelduþ peyne
to men aftur þat þei han disserued; and þis yuel of peyne is good,
siþ riȝtwisnesse doþ it þus. And þis, holdon comun lawe of men, is
turned into fendis lawe, for no lawe reuersuþ Godis lawe, but ȝif it
25 be þe feendis lawe. And as anemptis serpentis and oþre þingis þat
bryngon in peyne, þis bryngyng in of mannys peyne, þat by his
foly makuþ þis peyne, is noon yuel of iniurye, but riȝtwisnesse þat
God makuþ. But God forfenduþ here to do yuel of harm for yuyl
of harm.

30   And þus loue þat Poul bidduþ techuþ *to purueye good to men, not
only byfore God* to preyȝe God to make hem goode, *but byfore alle
maner of men* to forȝyue hem and disseruen to hem. And þis reule
þat Poul ȝyueþ is boþe liȝt and resonable, for it is more liȝt to men
to forȝyue yuel þan to take veniaunce; and it is more resonable,
35 for moore good comeþ to men þerfore. And by þis reule þat Poul
ȝyueþ here bateylus and stryuyngus in ple schulden be forsakone
of cristene men, as Godus lawe telliþ here. And so bidduþ God by
Poul þat, *ȝif it may be, þat is of ȝow, ȝee schul[d]en haue pees wiþ alle
men*, doyng good and suffryng wrong. But certis custom and mannys
40 lawe ben ful fer fro þis lore. Soþ it is þat monye men han of þer
owne synne myche malice, and þes wolon fyȝte wiþ men and slee
hem. But kepe þow pacience and mekenesse, and þanne þer yuel
turneþ þe to good by þe vertu of Godis lawe. But þis lawe, þat
Poul seiþ here, lettuþ not to chastise men, ne to take veniaunce of
45 hem by þe reulis of charite; but þis schulde euere be for þer goode,
and for loue þat men schulden haue to hem. And þus men

β   19 to ȝelde not] not to ȝelde BT   an²] anoþer I   and] *om.* α   20 a
wrong] ⌜a⌝ *corr.* wrong D, wrong ATI   21 ȝeelde] ȝeld gode J   þe] *om.*
Y   siþ] syþ þat O   22 to] to peyne to Y   men] man B   þei han] he haþ
B   23 it] *om.* T   þis] þis is, is *canc.* AH, þis is O, þus I   holdon] olde
I   comun] comynly P   24 fendis] þo fendes αIJV   reuersuþ] reseruiþ
O   25 as] ⌜as⌝ IJH   26 bryngyng] brynggiþ O   27 þis] hys αH   28
here . . . harm (29)] *on eras. corr.* D   of] for P   30 þus] þis B   32 and¹] and
to, to *canc.* α, and to HV   to hem] *on eras. corr.* D   34 to²] *om.* T   35 þerfore]
þerof OH   36 ple] puple H   37 cristene] cristis T   telliþ] techiþ T   38
of] oon of B   schulden] schullen DBβδH   39 but] for α   custom] customes
α,   costom⌜es⌝ V   and²] in α   40 monye] o *altered from* a D   42 hem]
men O   þow] ȝou O   þanne] *om.* α   43 turneþ] turnyd J, drawiþ
B   þe¹] *om.* I   þe²] *om.* T   þat] ⌜þat⌝ J, *om.* I   44 men] to men
T   ne] no β   of] on B   45 þe] *om.* H   euere be] *rev.* T, be euere *marked*

schulden by Godus lawe flee to comune wiþ heretykis. And þus
bidduþ Poul þat *we schulde not defende us as Godis derruste children, but
we schulden ȝyue stude to ȝre,* and reserue veniaunce to God oure
fadur. *For it is wryton* in Godus lawe how *God seiþ 'I have reserued*   50
veniaunce to me, and I schal ȝelde it, for it falluþ to my maieste, and I
mot do it wiþowte defaute'. *But ȝif þin enemye hungreþ, ȝyue þow hym*
mete; and ȝif he þurste, ȝif þow hym drynke. Þis mawndement is not of
bodyly foode, but of goostly foode of þe soule; for monye men han
not bodyly foode, and | enemyes wolden be worse herfore. But   55 f.12
mekenesse and pacience schulde eche mon haue redyly, and þes
woldon euere do good. And þerfore enemyes schulden be fed
wiþ þese. *For, ȝif þow do þis* to þin enemye, *þow schalt gedere colus of*
fuyr vpon þe hyerste vertu of his soule; and þat falliþ ofte to do hym
good and euermore to do þe good. *Nyle þow be ouercomen of yuel, but*   60
ouercome þow yuel in good. Þis yuel is synne of þin enemye; and
þanne it vencuscheþ þe ⌐by⌐ hyt, whanne it fowluþ þe þerwiþ,
and makiþ þe partener þerof; but þow ouercomest þis yuel in
good, whanne þow kepust þe þerfro, and by vertu of pacience
þow ȝyuest mater to do men good.   65
    And þis byleue þat Poul seiþ here is luytul vsud or trowed now.
And þerfore monye men in þe chyrche, as boþe þe poope and
cardynalis, ben smyttude foule wiþ heresye, and owte of cristene
mennys byleue. What charite or pacience schulde meue hem to
sende aftur men, and þanne do hem to deþ, for þei meyntene   70
Godus lawe? But Ysaye seiþ 'wo be to hem þat seyn þat good þing
is yuel, and yuel þing is good to hem', for þei ben contrarye to

---

50 Deut. 32: 35 **71** Isa. 5: 20.

for rev. δ   þer] *on eras. corr.* D, fer B   48 schulde] sal Z   not] we not
P   49 schulden] sal Z   yre] oþere I   52 defaute] fauȝtJ   hungreþ]
hungre αH   53 þurste] þriste, *final* -þ *eras.* Y, þursteþ OJV   þow] *om.*
B   mawndement] comaundement JV   of] *om.* J   54 þe] *om.* BGH   55
not] no H   wolden] wolen AδIJ   worse] þe worse BV   herfore] þerfore
αIZV   56 pacience] pacieence D   eche] euery B   haue redyly] *rev.*
T   þes] þus B   57 woldon] wolen AδIJ   þerfore] herfore H   be] euere
be IG   58 wiþ] euer wiþ A   þis] þus OαδIJV   59 and] *om.* δJ   þat]
⌐þat⌐ TH, *om.* α   60 þe] *om.* O, þis Z   61 good] god O, gode Z   þin] þine
canc. of þyne J   62 by] *corr.* D   63 partener] perseyuer J   64 good] god
δJ   kepust] keptyst J   vertu] vetu Y   65 þow] þat α   ȝyuest] ȝauest
G   66 seiþ] haþ I   67 and¹. . . lawe (71)] *om.* Z   men] *om.* O   þe²]
om. IJ   70 to] to þe BTV   þei] þe β   71 godus] cristis I   ysaye] ysai
quintose Z   þat²] *om.* JH   72 for] forþi δ   73 god] good, *2nd o canc.* D, gode

God. And so he is vencusched of yuel þat doþ yuel aȝeynes yuel; and
he vencuscheþ in good yuel þat doþ good aȝenys yuel. God ȝyue
75 grace to þe chyrche to lerne þis lesson þat Poul techuþ, for þis
schort lore of Poul wolde turne al cristenedom to Crist. And men
schulden boþe be pacient whanne mannys cause is towchid, and
do qwicly wiþ þer lippis by resoun of Godis cause; for þus dude
Crist Godis word and tawȝte hise children to do þus.

Z   is] *om.* G   and² . . . yuel¹ (74)] *om.* O, *added margin* P   74 vencuscheþ]
vencusid, *final* -d *canc.,* -s α, vencusshede BG   75 þe] cristis Z   lerne] lere
αZH   þis¹] þe I   77 mannys] mennes Z

Dominica iiij post [Octavam] Epiphanie: [Epistola.] Sermo 1[1].

Nemini quicquam debeatis. Romanos 13.

Poul techeþ here Romayns, and so alle cristene men, how þei schulden kepe charite þat God 3yueþ; and 3if þis vertu be wel kept of man tyl þat tyme þat he dye, oure byleue techeþ þanne þat þis cloþ brynguþ hym to blisse. Poule bidduþ at þe furste þis word of myche wyt *to no man owe 3e ony þing, but þat 3e loue togydere.* 5 Poul forfenduþ not dette of money, ne goode werkis of oþre vertuwis; but Poul wole þat alle þese dettis drawe to þis ende: to loue togydere. And so eche man by þis lawe is holdon ay to loue eche broþur. And so monye men in þis world ben byhynde of dette of loue; but God mot euere come byfore, to loue men þat 10 haton hym. Take hed to ocur and oþre synnes þat sowne not in charite, and counte not þis anoon for dette by Poulis rewle of byleue. And so þis word wel vndurstondon dampneþ alle errouris in þe chirche. And so þis o word of Poul axsuþ myche special declaryng. And excusyng of ypocritis, þat þei kepon þus charite, 15 schal be dampned by þe hierste iuge, whanne noo synne may asterte hym. Men of werre seyon comynly þat þei fy3ton for charite, for so schulden þer enemyes loue hem in such a caas; and þus seyn plederis|and pursuweris þat þei don þus al for loue. But f.12v

MSS: D; ABGHIJOPTVXYZαβδ.

Octavam] *om.* D sermo 11] sermo 12 Dβ, *om.* ABOTαδIJXZGHV nemini
. . . debeatis] *om.* YV debeatis] debeatis nisi ut inuicem diligatis TIJ, de bantis
β ro.13] ro. xij A, ro. J, *om.* O 1 techeþ] telliþ and *canc.* techyþ J, telleþ and
techeþ I, telliþ δV 2 god] *om.* β 3if] all *canc.* 3yf J, al 3if I þis] *om.*
I 3 þat¹] þe HV þanne] *om.* O 4 hym] hem Aδ 5 man] many
P 6 goode] of gode IJ of] or H oþre] gode α 7 wole] wolde
BV 8 ay to loue] to loue ay IH ay] euere O 9 broþur] oþir BV 11
and] or H sowne] sum men O 12 and] ʳandˊ β, *om.* A counte] acounte
AV anoon] now ABV, sone Z 13 so] *om.* Z word] ʳoˊ word BGH, oo
word AOαδIJ, wordis T vndurstondon] vndreston α dampneþ] dampnen
T errouris] þe errours OV 14 o] *om.* Oαβδ] 15 þus] þis I 16 by þe]
of þo αH may] ne may O 17 asterte] astir β werre] werris G 18 so]
so so, *2nd canc.* D a] *om.* B 19 þus al] al þys T, þis al V 20 mot] muste

20 þis excusacion mot be iuged by Crist hymself; and þis Lord is
charite, and knoweþ al resoun and al gabbyng.

And so eche man here in erþe schulde lyue so iustly to his
broþur, boþe in herte, in word and dede, þat it sownede al in
charite, For ȝif he passe þis rewle of Poul, he renneþ in dette
25 aȝenys his broþur. And Crist techeþ men to preyȝe hym þat he
forȝyue hem þis dette, but riȝt as þei forȝyuon here dettouris.
And þus men byddon aȝenys hemself þat faylon in mercy to þer
breþren, for charite is ⌜vn⌝iustly knyttud. Muse þow not how God
bidduþ þat þou schuldust loue eche man, siþ monye men ben
30 vnknowone of þee, and noon may loue but þat he knoweþ; God
techeþ to knowe generally, and to loue aftur þis knowyng. Do no
wrong to þi breþren, and þow fullust þis lore of Poul, *for whoeuere*
loueþ his neyȝebore haþ fulfullud þe lawe of God. Ȝif þou seyȝe þow
louest o man, and doost wrong to anoþur, þow gabbust to God
35 vpon þiself, and hatust þin furste frend. As, ȝif monye men baron
a weyȝte, and eche schulde helpe oþur þerto, he þat fayluþ to
helpe oon, mut nedys fayle aȝenys hem alle. And Poul telluþ
afturward how þis o word of loue comprehendiþ al þe lawe, as he
scheweþ by fyue lawis. For þis maundement of God þat bidduþ
40 *þow schalt not be a lechour*; þe secounde maundement þat bydduþ
þat *þow schalt not sle þi broþur*; þe þridde maundement þat bidduþ
þat *þow schalt not stele his goodis*; þe fourþe maundement þat
bidduþ þat *þow schalt not seye false witnesse*; þe fyueþe maundement
also *þow schalt not coueyte þi neyȝeborus good; and, ȝif þer be ony oþur*
45 *maundement, in þis word it is instorud, þow schalt loue þi neyȝebore as*

---

25 Matt. 6: 12; Luke 11: 4.

J   by] of Y   21 al¹] alle þe T   gabbyng] gabbingis BδJH   22 so¹] *om.*
α   23 in²] ⌜in⌝ B, and in IJ, *om.* PZH   and] in Tβ, and in V   it] is
Z   27 men] *om.* I   faylon] fallen I   to] aȝens T, agayne α   28 vniustly]
vn- *corr.* D, vn *canc.* iustely I, not iustly Y, iustli ABOPαβδJXZGHV   knyttud] kuttid
Y   29 men] *om.* PZ   30 vnknowone] vnknowynge I   31 to¹] for to
H   32 þow] þanne *canc.* þow D, ⌜þan⌝ þou H, þanne þou BOPTYαβδJXZ-
GV   fullust] fulfillist B   þis] þe T   whoeuere] whosoeuere OIJ, who
T   33 loueþ] leueþ I   neyȝebore] broþer G   haþ fulfullud] he fulfilliþ T,
haþ fillid G   seyȝe] seist OG   35 vpon] on H   þin] þe δ   36 a] *om.*
β   weyȝte] wᵉᵉyȝte X, wiȝt δ   37 telluþ] techis Z   38 as] and as
δJ   40 schalt] schuldist J   not be a] be no H   þat] *om.* IGV   41 þat¹]
om. BδZH   not . . . broþur] sle no man H   þat²] *om.* GV   42 þat¹] *om.* δ,
þat *canc.* J   43 þat] *om.* δJ   not seye] say no α   seye] bere T   44 also]
sais also þat α   45 maundement] maundementis PZ   schalt] schal β   þi] þe

þiself. As monye pens ben closude in o tresour comynly, so in þis o
word of God ben comunly oþre vndurstonden. He þat haþ þis o
lawe, and kepuþ it wel as he schulde, haþ fulfullud al þe lawe, as
Poul seiþ and Iamys boþe. And þis *loue of þi neyȝebore worchuþ no
synne* aȝenys hym; and *perfore fulnesse of þe lawe is loue,* ȝif it be wel   50
takon.

Þis schort tresor of word of loue schulde be takon owt, whanne
it is nede. For þis tresour may not fayle, ȝif it be groundud in þe
furste loue; for þat loue is wiþowton ende, and loue is þe more þat
it be vsud. Poule spekuþ not here of fleschly loue ne of worldli   55
loue, but of loue in God; for þes two loues ben more hate, and
schendon loue þat man schulde haue. For loue of God is ful of
resoun and holduþ no þing aȝenys resoun; for, ȝif it helde aȝenys
resoun, þanne it were aȝenys God. And þus clene loue puttuþ owt
alle synne. And in þis lore schulden men studye, and þis charite   60
schulde moue men to speke stabully herof.

And among alle men þat synnon aȝenys charite, þes foure
sectis þat newe ben comen wiþowton auctorite of Crist, semon
more stefly to synne aȝeyn þe lawe of charite. And heere is
somwhat to speke aȝenys þe furste of þes foure.| Þe furste ⌐hed⌐ of   65   f.13
þis secte is þe pope wiþ hise clerkis, and þer maner of lordly lif
aȝenys þe lore þat Crist tauȝte Petre. Þis aggregat of þes alle ben
þe furste secte newe comen in; and alle þes foure sectis ben
armede wiþ armure of ypocrisye. And somme clepon þis furste
heed anticrist, for his lif. Ȝif he sue his patroun as he feyneþ he   70
suweþ Crist, he suweþ more þe emperour þan oþur Crist or
seynte Petre; for þe world is his patroun, and þe fadur of prude

---

49 Jas. 2: 8.

β   46 pens] expens Z   o²] ⌐o⌐ A, *eras.* J, *om.* δ   47 oþre vndurstonden] *on
eras. corr.* D, vndirstonden oþere H   48 it] *om.* α   wel] *om.* H   lawe] lawes
T   49 no] not H   50 it be] it is δ, ȝe J   it] *om.* O   be] is GH, is wel
V   55 ne . . . two (56)] *on eras. corr.* D   56 of] ⌐of⌐ B, *om.* β   ben more] are
raþer α   57 man] man, -a- *altered from* -e- J, men AI   58 for . . . resoun
(59)] *om.* O   helde] -e- *altered from* -o- D, holde I, were H   59 puttuþ] partiþ
T   owt] aweye T   61 herof] þerof αZV   62 and . . . Poul (93)] *om.*
Z   and] for δ   63 comen] comen ⌐in⌐ A, comun in BOIHV   crist] iesu crist
B   65 þe furste] þe furste *canc.*//þe furste D, þe H   66 þis secte] þes sectis IJ, þis
firste secte H   is] ⌐is⌐ β, *om.* J   lordly] lordly *altered from* worldly Y, worldly
TIV   67 þat] of T   þis] ys T   68 alle þes] also I   69 armure] armes
AδIJ   somme] sum men ABOPYβδXGHV   70 he³] þat *canc.* he DX, þat he
αβV   71 þe] *om.* O   oþur] *om.* IV   72 þe¹] þe þe *2nd canc.* D   73 it] he

also. Furst it semeþ þat he synneþ in charite, þat Poul spekuþ of, for he disseyueþ mennys wyt by þis foule ypocrisy. 3if Petre in his
75 lif was passynge oþre apostlis, þat weron his felowis in pouerte and mekenesse and in trauele for þe chyrche, þanne he mut haue a successour contrarye to hym in alle þes þre. Certis a fend of helle schulde schame to disseyue men by such a skyle. And whanne men ben þus blyndude, he disseyueþ hem afturward of fredom
80 þat Crist haþ 3ouen, and makiþ hem þral by his lawis. Petre ne ony oþre apostle durste not seye þat he was so nedful, þat wiþowten his gouernayle moste þe chyrche nedis perische, and by þis blasfeme gabbyng sle monye þousynde men. He is not on Cristus syde, þat puttude his soule for his schep, but on
85 anticristus syde, þat puttiþ monye soulis for his pruyde. Þis man feduþ not Cristus schep as Crist bad þries ⌜to⌝ Petre, but spuyluþ hem, and sleþ hem, and leduþ hem in monye wronge weyus. 3if he louyde Cristus schep, he schulde lede hem by Cristus lawe, and wature hem and make hem reste by þe lesewis, and by þe
90 watres þat Crist haþ ordeyned for hys schep. Þis man þat þus hatuþ God, mot aftur nedys hate hymself, and alle his breþren þat he seiþ ben his schep, for his ri3t cure. It semeþ þat no man here in erþe reuersuþ more þis lore of Poul.

---

83 John 10: 11; 89 Ps. 22: 1–2.

I   74 mennys] mannus T   75 was] were Bα   apostlis] a/apostlis D   in] þa canc. in D   76 and¹] and ⌜in⌝ X, and in BOPTYαβδIJGV   mut] most IJ   77 alle] om. α   78 skyle] swyke α   80 hem] hym IJ   þral] þrallis H   81 ony] non IV   apostle] apostlis H   82 his] al canc. his D   83 blasfeme] blasfemye, -y- canc. H, blasfemye TV   sle] slees he α, he sleeþ I   84 puttude] puttiþ TH, putteþ ⌜not⌝ I, puttide ⌜no3t⌝ δ, puttes not α   85 puttiþ] puttiþ ⌜and sleth⌝ T   his] om. β   86 to] corr. D, om. ABOPYαβδIJXZGV   87 in] eras. X, om. OPTYβδIJGV   monye] may Y   88 lawe] lawes O   89 þe¹] om. I   lesewis] lawes O   þe²] þes D, þes, -s canc. X   90 ordeyned] ordeyne Y   91 hatuþ] hatide δ   aftur nedys] rev. BOY   hymself] him O   92 þat²] ⌜þat⌝ Bβ   93 in erþe] om. I

Dominica quinta [post Octavam Epiphanie].
[Epistola.] Sermo 1[2].

Induite uos sicut electi Dei. Colocenses 3.

For charite is þe moste vertu, and moste nedful to cristene men, þerfore Poul and oþre apostlus lernedon of Crist to sture þis most, and teche þis most to Cristus schep, for it contenyþ al good. Poul bidduþ furst þat *men schulden cloþen hem as chosone of God, hooly and loued of God, entraylus of mercy* to þer breþren. Ofte hooly writ 5 clepuþ mercy 'þe entraylus of mercy', for, as entraylis ben wiþinne, and clenson mete for mannys body, so þe habite of mercy schulde be stable wiþinne man, and algatis clense þe goostly mete for þe body of hooly chyrche. And þus spekuþ Lukis gospel, by Zacharie þe hooly prophete, þat oure God haþ 10 'entraylis of mercy', by whiche he visitude his puple. And siþ we schulden be Cristus children, and Cristus champyounys to fiȝte for hym, we schulden furst cloþen us in his suyt, and taken his armure for to fyȝte. And þus|seiþ Poul þe furste word þat we cloþe f.13v us as Godus chosone. Noo man may putte fro hym þat ne he 15 schulde be a choson of God, to fiȝte here wiþ goostly enemyes, and by victorie to gete blisse; and hoolynesse stonduþ in þis, for wiþ hoolynesse schulde men fiȝte. And al þis is a stronde of loue, þat strengore may no loue be. For where is welle of more loue

---

6 Rom. 9: 23; Phil. 2: 1; **10** Luke 1: 78; **13** Eph. 6: 11, 13.

MSS: D; ABGHIJOPTXYZαβδ.

Octavam] *om.* I   sermo 12] sermo 13 Dβ, sermo A, *om.* BOTαδIJXZGH   induite . . . dei] *om.* Y   sicut . . . dei] *om.* H   dei] *om.* A   coloc. 3] *om.*
O   1 moste²] þe *canc.* most J, þe moste I   nedful] medeful T   2 lernedon]
lerede αH   3 good] gode thynge α   4 hem] hemsilf Y   as] a O   cho-
sone] þe chosen H   5 loued] leuede α   6 as] þan as T   entraylis] entrayle
α   7 wiþinne] wiþynne men B   for] of PTZ, fro AαH   8 stable] a stable O,
stablid IJ   man] men T   9 mete] *om.* O   lukis] saynt luk Z   10 haþ]
wiþ I   11 visitude] haþ visitid B   12 cristus champyounys] chaumpions of Crist
T   13 furst cloþen us] cloþe vs first I   14 armure] armes ABδIJ   for to] to
T   seiþ] sey β   þe] in þe Y   15 ne he] *rev.* I   16 a] *om.* A   here
wiþ] her wiþ *marked for rev.* B, *rev.* AI   17 by] by þis T   to] *om.* I   18 men]

20 þan chesyng of God byfore þe world, for to brynge men to blisse,
and to alle menys nedful þerfore? Or where is more charite þan
God hymself to make us hooly, and droppe to us of his owne grace
wiþowton owre disseruyng byfore? Or where myȝte be schewid
more loue þan God to chese for his batayle siche men þat he makiþ
25 seyntis, and loueþ hem for his owne dedis? And þes þre knottis of
loue ben figured in þe Trinnyte. What men þat þus ben louede of
God schulden not be mercyful to oþre? And of þis mercy of men
schulden spryngon monye oþre goode braunchis.

Furst *men schulden be benygne*, for þei schulden brenne in charite.
30 Aftur men schulden be *meke*; for þis fuyr axuþ mekenesse, siþ it
may not kyndle ne growe, but ȝif mekenesse be þerwiþ. Þe þridde
vertu þat sprynguþ herof is *temprure* in oure deede, þat men
traueylon stabully for good ende whan þei schulden. Þe fourþe
vertu of þis mercy is *pacience* þat men schulden haue; siþ alle men
35 mote take of God alle þe goodis þat þei han, and so þei schulden
lerne pacience by suffryng of þe Lord aboue. Þe fyueþe vertu of
þis mercy is þat *men supporte togydere*; for what man is wiþowte
defaute and febulnesse in þis lif? And þus God haþ nedud us eche
man to supporte his broþur, for eche man nediþ to oþeris help,
40 and holde hym vppe þat he falle not. Þe sixte vertu of þis grownd
is to *frely ȝyue togydere* forȝyuyng of oure trespassis, for þus bidduþ
oure alþer Mayster. *Ȝif ony haue playnt aȝenys anoþur, as Crist haþ
forȝouen ȝow, so schulden ȝe forȝyuen ȝowre breþren;* and þis lore biddiþ
Crist in techyng of oure pater noster. And *ouer þese* sixe bidduþ
45 Poul þat *men schulden haue charite, for þat is bond of perfection* þat
knyttuþ togydere alle oþre vertuwis. Þe eiȝtþe tyme bidduþ Poul
þat *Cristis pees sprynge in mennys hertis*, for þis pees brynguþ
gladnesse and ioye *in o body* of þe chirche. And þus eche man

man I   19 þat] for G, and α   20 god] ⌜vs⌝ α   for to] to Z   23 or] for δ
schewid] *om.* α   24 to] *om.* O, for to δ   chese] chese vs T   his] þis
A   þat] as α   26 figured] figures α   þus ben] *rev.* α   27 not] not *canc.*
TX, nou *final* -ȝt *eras.* I, *om.* δJ   þis] his I   of²] *on eras. corr.* D   28 goode] *om.*
δJ   31 kyndle ne] kyndelich O, ⌜be⌝ kyndele ne I   32 sprynguþ] strecchiþ
I   herof] þerof αZ   deede] deedis Y   33 fourþe] firste I   34 þis] *om.*
Tδ   siþ . . . han (35)] *om.* α   35 þe] *om.* AδJH   36 lerne] lere
ZH   fyueþe] ferþe I   37 mercy] vertu I   supporte] schuld supporte
α   38 god haþ] *rev.* I   39 to²] *om.* T   40 hym] *om.* H   vppe] vpon
O   41 to] *om.* I   trespassis] trespas AαI   þus] þis BY   42 oure] o *canc.*/
oure D   anoþur] oþir YJH   43 schulden] shullen BI   ȝe] he δ   þis]
þus O   biddiþ] techis α   44 techyng] bydding α   þese] þe O   45
schulden] sal Z   þat¹] it α   46 alle] *om.* α   47 sprynge] be springinge
P   hertis] herte B   48 and¹] in mannys hertis *canc.* and D   o] ⌜oo⌝ G, *om.*

schulde *be kynde* and helpon his broþur, as he doþ hym, as eche
part of a body helpuþ anoþur to make þat body.   50

Þe tenþe tyme bidduþ Poul þat *Cristis word dwelle in us
plenteuously*; for it haþ vertu to kepe from yuel, and brynge in
good. And here monye men ben to blame þat vson wordis of
mannys lawe, and oþre þat be not medfule, and wordis of strif
wiþ oþre iapis; for word of Crist schulde putte þese|owt, as Petre   55   f.14
techiþ in his booc '3if ony man speke ou3t, speke he Godis
wordis', and certis þanne Cristis word dwelluþ in us
habundauntly. But a fool my3te seye here þat, siþ Crist is God
and man, eche word is Cristis word, and so veyn iangleris spekon
þis lore. Þerfore Poul knyttiþ ⌈after⌉ þat Cristis word dwelle in us   60
in al maner of wisdom, and þanne it is not superflu. Þe enleueþe
tyme Poul bidduþ þat *Cristis word be not ydle in us*; for euur þe more
þat it be vsud, ay þe betture it is, and more likuþ hym. And so
men schulden *teche* þer breþren, and *moneste hemselff* to kepe hem
hooly *in psalmys and ympnys and spiritual songis, syngynge in þer hertis
to God for grace* þat he haþ 3oue to men. Þe twelþe tyme bidduþ   65
Poul þat, *alle þinge þat we don in word or in dede, schulde we do it in
Cristis name*, for we schulden euere serue to hym, and he mot nedis
be oure Lord. And þerfore we schulden do nowt but þat we doren
auowe to þis Lord. And so *we schulden* ay *do þankyngis to God þe*   70
Fadur in þe name of Iesu Crist, þat is Lord of us alle, and hed of hooly
chirche. And soo no man schulde speke ne do in þe name of Iesu
Crist but trewþe, þat is skilful and bedon by þe lawe of God.

And here cristene men may see how þe secounde secte newe
browt in fayluþ in mercy and charite of oure Lord Iesu Crist.   75

---

56 1 Pet. 4: 11.

T   49 and] an α, *om.* δ J   his] oþur *canc.* his D   51 tyme] word I   us]
3ow T   52 brynge] beyng O, bringeþ T   53 of . . . oþre (54)] *om.* Z   54
mannys] mennys I   medfule] *altered from* nedfule D, nedful *altered from* medful X
nedeful ABOPYαβδIJZGH   55 word] þe word B, wordis O   þese] þis
AδIJH   56 godis] gode I   57 wordis] word H   þanne] *om.* O   word]
wordis I   60 þerfore] and þerfore G   knyttiþ] biddiþ T   after] *corr.*
D, þat after I   dwelle] d *canc.*/dwelle D, dwelleþ I   61 of] *om.* T   þanne]
om. T   not] non O   62 poul bidduþ] *rev.* I   þe] *om.* α   63 ay] euere
OXG   betture] more betere AI   64 moneste] monishe α   hemselff] *on eras.*
corr. D, hem β   65 psalmys] spalmys D   67 in²] ⌈in⌉ α, *om.* PIZ   it] it *canc.* H,
om. BOPTYαβδIJZG   68 to] *om.* B   69 schulden] schullen I   70 ay] euere
OXG   71 hooly] al holi BOPTYαXZG   73 bedon] be *canc.*/bedon D, leden
O   by] of T   74 and . . . ynne (90)] *om.* Z   here] herefore here
O   newe] now I   75 fayluþ] fallys α   in²] *om.* H   charite] in charite

Marke þei þe lordschipe þat þei han by title of þer holynesse, and
how lordis and þer pore tenauntis myȝton be releuede by þis
lordschipe; and so myche ben þei fer from mercy and charite. Þei
schulden by byddyng of þer patroun be not þus seculer lordis, but
80 þei dispuyson þis byddyng of God and drawon to a worldly
patroun. And þis is wantyng of loue to Iesu Crist and alle hise
seyntis, and wantyng of mercy to pore men dwellyng in rewmys
þat þei inhabiton. God schilde us from such preyȝer as þes
monkys byddon for men! for rotyng in þer heresye techuþ þat þer
85 biddyng is turned to synne. And þes þat loue not þus þer soulis
louen luytul þe bodyes of þer neyȝeboris, but louen yuele þer
owne bely þat þei feedon as þer god. How schulden rewmys haue
pees of God þat norischen suche double traytouris? For he is fer
from charite þat loueþ þus more his bely, þan he loueþ Godis
90 lawe, or þe chirche þat he dwelluþ ynne.

AI   76 þer] om. H   holynesse] bisinesse I   78 þei¹] om. P   fer] ferþer
A, þe ferre I   79 lordis] lord G   80 þis] þe TðJG   a] om. Tα   82
dwellyng] þat dwellen on eras corr. A   83 inhabiton] habiten I   84 rotyng] þaire
rotynge α   þer¹] om. H   85 to] into A   86 þer¹] þer pore A   87 bely]
helþe I   88 double] om. B   89 þus more] rev. H   his] charite canc. his
D   loueþ²] doiþ Y

Dominica in Septuagesima. [Epistola.] Sermo 1 [3].

Nescitis quod hii qui in stadio currunt. Prima Corintheos 9 et 10.

Þis epistle of Poul telliþ how þat men schulden lyue here, and be
Godis laboreris for to wynne þe blisse of heuene. Poul bygynneþ
on þis maner: *wyte ʒe not þat þei þat rennen in þe furlong* for þe pris,
certis þei rennon alle, but oon of hem takuþ þe gleyue. Renne ʒe on anoþur
maner, *þat ʒee alle take þe victorie.* It is knowon þing in cuntreyus   5
þat|men vson ofte þis gamon, þat two men holdone mooste swifte   f.14v
rennon a space for a pris; and he þat comeþ furst to his ende schal
haue þe gamon þat is set, wheþur it be spere or glouys, or oþur
þing þat is put. And so ʒif monye renne by tymes, ʒet oon takuþ
for onys þe prys. But oure rennyng in weyʒe to heuene dyuersuþ   10
muche fro þis rennyng: for monye þowsande rennen togydere,
and eche of hem comeþ to þe ende, and getuþ þe gamen þat is set,
for þat is þe large blisse of heuene. Þe secounde ensaumple of
champyonys is seyd of Poul in þes wordis: *eche þat stryueþ in fyʒtyng
abstyneþ hym from al* excesse, for he chargeþ not his body wiþ mete,   15
ne drynk, ne oþre þingis. And so schullon cristene men do þat
fyʒton heere for Godis cause. But þer is dyuersite in þes fiʒtyngis
and Godis fyʒt; for þer ende is algatus worse and þer traueyle
more vncerteyn, for *þei traueylon* for þis ende, *to take a brutel coroune*
heere. *But men traueylon in Godis cause to take a corone þat neuere may*   20
fayle. And Poule telluþ aftur to cristene men how he traueyluþ in

MSS: D; ABGHIJOPTXYZαβδ; Hᵗ *part of text but illegible.*

Sermo 13] sermo 14 Dβ, *om.* ABOTαδIJXZGH   nescitis . . . currunt] *om.* Y
quod] quid A   qui] *om.* δ   currunt] *om.* δJH   I cor. 9 et 10] *om.* O   I]
om. YH   et 10] *om.* ABTIH   ʒ of poul] *om.* α   of] *om.* B   schulden]
shulen PYβδJX   3 wyte ʒe] *on eras. corr.* D, wite ⌐ʒee⌐ P, wite OZ   þat¹] ⌐þat⌐ I,
om. OδJZ   þat²] *om.* β   4 gleyue] game O, gloue γ   on] *om.* δ   anoþur]
⌐an⌐oþere T, oþer PG   5 þing] *om.* Y   in] by O   8 set] sett ⌐vp⌐ T, sett þere
δ   spere] speris I   or²] *om.* β   9 monye] many men αI   10 in] in þe
BTH   11 þowsande] þousandis TZ   12 þe¹] *om.* H   15 abstyneþ] absteyne
T   excesse] excessis B   mete] *om.* P   16 ne²] and I   schullon] shulden
ABOPTαβIJZGH   þat] *om.* β   18 and¹] in β   fyʒt] fiʒting BH   ende]
endes T   is] ben T   worse] þe worse I   þer²] *om.* H   19 a] *om.*
A   20 to] and δ   neuere may] may not H   may] schal T   21

þis iorneye. *Certis, I renne not as in vncerteyn; I fyȝte so not as betynge þe eyr.* But I chastise my body by reson, *and brynge it into seruyse* to my sowle, *leste þat, whanne I preche to oþre, I myself be maad reprouable.*
25 And so þis rennyng and þis fiȝtyng is hastyly goyng of mannys soule to heuene by þe weye of vertuwis, and fiȝtyng wiþ enemyes þat letton þis.

And so God of blisse haþ ordeyned in tyme of his boþe lawys how men schulden haue sacramentis, to make hem able for þis
30 traueyle. And þerfore seiþ Poul here: *breþren, I wole not þat ȝe vnknowe þat alle owre fadris, þat wenton owt of Egipte, weron coueryd in day vndir þe clowde; and alle þei passedon þe Reede See, and alle þes weron wasschen by Moyses in þe clowde and in þe see.* Byleue techeþ cristene men þat signes of þe oolde lawe weron toknes of
35 owre signes now, as þei ben tokne of þe blisse of heuene. Þe clowde þat ladde hem in desert vpon dayus, as Godis lawe telluþ, figurede þe watur of Cristis syde, by whiche we ben baptisude now. Þe passyng þorw þe Reede See, and stondyng stable as ⌜a⌝ wal, figurede þe passion of Crist, by whiche we weron wasschede
40 from synne; and, as þe gospel of Iohn telluþ, Crist was deed byfore þat watur cam of þe clowde of his body to baptise men, as Poul spekuþ. Reednesse of þis see figurede þe blood of Cristus body; þe stable stondyng of þis see figurede þe stablenesse of Cristus godhede; and alle þingis þat felledon to hem figuredon
45 þingus in tyme of grace. And þus seiþ Poul soþly þat *alle þei eton þe same mete, and alle þei dronkon þe same drynk,* þat fedde *spiritually* þer sowle. Þer mete was þer byleue þat þei hadden of sadde þingus; and þer drynk was þer byleue þat þei hadden of moyste þingis; as Cristus body and his blood was mete and drynk to hem in figure,

---

32 Exod. 13: 21; 14: 22;   **37** John 19: 34; 1 John 5: 8;   **44** Exod. 16: 15; Deut. 8: 3.

traueyluþ] trauelid Z   22 in] *om.* Tβ   so not] *rev.* δ   23 chastise] shal tile
β   into] to I   to] into B, of αH   25 hastyly] hasty ZG   mannys]
mennes B   26 fiȝtyng] fiȝtyngis δ   28 haþ] has so α   his boþe] *rev.*
Z   29 hem] hym O   31 vnknowe] *final* -n *eras.* D   34 toknes] tokyn
α   35 ben tokne] bitokenen B   tokne] tokenes AδH   þe¹] þe *canc.* X, ⌜þe⌝ T,
om. YβH   36 desert] þe blisse of heuene *canc.* desert D   vpon] on Z   dayus]
day B   telluþ] techis α   37 figurede] figure β   by] by þe T   39 by] by
þe T   41 þat] þe T   of¹] out of YG   42 spekuþ] spekiþ of A, seiþ
BTI   reednesse] þe reednes B   þis] þe PIZ   43 þis] þe ZH   stab-
lenesse] stablehede I   44 felledon] felle αIZH   hem] hym B   45 þei] *om.*
G   46 þer] þe Bβ   47 þer¹] and her H   48 moyste] moᵣyᵗst T, most
OPβIJZ   49 was] *om.* β   50 dryng] oure drynke I   soule] saulis Z   51

|as ʒet þei be oure mete and dryng to fede oure soule in byleue of   50   f.15
hem. And þus in þis place and in oþre, þe figure haþ þe same
name þat haþ þe þing þat is figured; and þis speche is sutil and
trewe. And þus Poul spekiþ aftur þat *þei dronkon of þe spiritual
whanne þe stoon suwede hem; and þis stoon was Crist* in figure. Godis
lawe telluþ wel how þe children of Israel grucchedon, whonne   55
þei fayledon watur to drynke; and Moyses smoot þe stoon wiþ his
ʒerde, and watur cam owt of þe stoon, so þat þei and þer bestis
dronken. Þis dede teelde in figure how þe puple in tyme of Crist
wantide goostly watur to drynke. And Moyses was in double
figure: he figurede boþe goode men and Iewis. And, in figure of   60
wickede men, he smoot þis stoon wiþ his ʒerde, and þer cam owt
watur of lif, þat fullede men þat weron þursty. And þus seiþ Poul
here soþly to good entent þat [þe] stoon was Crist, for it figurede
in þis Crist. And wolde God þat heretykes in mater of þe sacred
oost kowden vndurstonde þis sutyl wordis and soþe, to þe entent   65
of þe Holy Goost! Þanne schulde þei not haue dreede to graunte
þat þis breed is Godis body.

Yt falluþ to telle a schort word how þe þridde newe secte, þat is
þe ordre of chanonys, fayluþ now in charite. Trewe men witon
wel þat in þe rennyng þat Poul telluþ, whan o man contrarieþ   70
anoþur in þe rennyng to his ende, ofte þe ton lettuþ þe toþur to
come sikurly to þis ende. And so it is of þes newe ordris þat
rennon bysyde Cristus ordre: þei letton in lif and byleue Cristus
secte to come to blis. And þerfore men schulden preyʒe for hem to
God by help of seynt Austyn, þat þei holden þe pleyn weyʒe by   75
euenesse of Godus lawe. Seynt Austyn was a seculer byschop, and
hadde prestis as hise felowis, and hadde goodis by title of almes;
and he dredde ful sore of hem, and wolde haue ʒouen hem to þe
puple, as Possydonye telluþ of hym. He was not weddud wiþ

55   Exod. 17: 1–7.

þis] ⌐o⌐T   in²] *om.* βH   52 þe] *om.* P   þis] þus þis α   54 *margin* Exo. 17
DPαβIZG, Exod. ij O   56 þei] hem TZ   57 bestis] besse α   58 teelde] ⌐is⌐
tolde α, telliþ H   61 þis] þe B   his] þis B   63 þe] *om.* D   64
and . . . goostly (86)] *om.* Z   wolde . . . kowden (65)] *eras.* X   mater] manere
I   65 soþe] so T   þe] *om.* I   66 þe] ⌐þe⌐ Y, *om.* O   not haue] *rev.*
J   69 þe] *om.* O   70 þe] *om.* β   þat² . . . rennyng (71)] *om.* I   telluþ]
techis α   71 his] þis TG   ofte] *om.* I   to come] ofte to come I   77 as]
alle β   goodis] good A   78 ful . . . hem¹] of hem ful sore A   þe] ⌐þe⌐O, *om.*

80 suche signes, neþur wiþ habite, ne wiþ cloystre, ne wiþ siche
veyne cerymonyes as newe ordris kepon today. But ȝif ony wolde
wende from hym, he ȝaf hym leue for betture lif; and men þat
weron of wickede lif he nedide to go fro hym. He puttude hem not
in prisoun, as heþene men putton þeuys. God graunte alle þes
85 foure sectis to holde þus fredom þat Crist ȝaf! Þanne schulde þei
not harme his chyrche, boþe bodyly and goostly.

β   80 neþur] ne αI   wiþ²] om. Y   82 wende] ⌈go⌉ α   hym²] hem
APβG   for] to O   83 nedide] nedide hem Y   hym] hem α   hem not]
rev. B   84 þeuys] her þeues T   alle] ⌈to⌉ alle T   85 þus] þus þe B, þis
αI   schulde] shul A   86 his] þis T

Dominica in Sexagesima. [Epistola.] Sermo 1 [4].

Libenter suffertis insipientes. Secunda Corintheos 11 [et] 12.

Poul techeþ in þis epistle, som tyme by maner of scornful speche,
how þat somme false apostlus disseyuon þe puple þat þei spekon
to, and he medeluþ þe grace of God and condicion of trewe apostlis.
He blameþ furst þis puple of Grece, for þei norischedon suche
false apostlis, and seiþ by a witty scorn *ȝe berun vp willefully vnwise*   5
men whon|þat ȝe ben wise men, as who seiþ 'in þis ȝe ben foolis'. *For ȝe*   f.15v
suffren ȝif ony man dryue ȝow to bondeschipe, ȝif ony man deuoure ȝoure
goodis, ȝif ony man take ȝoure goodis as ȝif þei weron grauntude to
hym by God; *ȝif ony man hyȝe his staat* ouer þat Crist hyede hise
apostlis; *ȝif ony man smyȝte ȝou in visage*, oþur of body or of soule.   10
And þus it falluþ by men today þat ben disseyuede by þes newe
ordris, for þei suffren hem gladly as ȝif þei weron wise men and
hooly, and as ȝif it were a wisdam to susteyne hem in þer foly; as
þe puple, boþe more and lasse, suffren þe foly of þes freris þat
bryngon in þer newe customys, as ȝif þei weron gospel of Crist.   15
And þis is þe moste bondage þat may falle to men in erþe, siþ for
suche cerymonyes men weron bonde in þe oolde lawe. And certis
þes cerymonyes of þes newe ordris comen not to þe cerymonyes of
God. And þus þes ordris deuouren þer goodis, and preyson þer

MSS: D; ABGHIJOPTXYZαβδ; Hᵗ 9 ȝif ony . . . 17 oolde lawe *missing, only* 17 and
certis . . . 54 bissines *collatable.*

Dominica . . . sexagesima] Dominica þe secunde sondai pistil in sexagesima G   sermo
14] sermo 15 D, sermo 5 β, *om.* ABOTαδIJXZGH   libenter . . . -pientes] *om.*
Y   insipientes] insipientes cum sitis ipsi sapientes T, *om.* α   II cor. 11 et 12]
corinth. 11 and 12 YH, 2 cor. xi⁰ G, *om.* O   et] *om.* D   1 techeþ] telliþ
BT   2 how] and ⌐how⌐ H   3 apostlis] a/apostlis D   4 þis] þe BO-
T   grece] greke P, grace ⌐grece⌐ I, grace TY   norischedon] norschiþ O, nurchen
T, norishe α   suche] sche Y   5 scorn] story IJ   vp] *om.* I   6 þat] ⌐þat⌐
Y, *om.* H   who] who so B   seiþ] say αZ   7 man¹] *om.* IG   8 goodis¹]
goddys T   ȝif¹ . . . god (9)] *om.* O   man] m *canc.*/man D   ȝoure goodis]
om. I   goodis²] goddis T   ȝif²] *om.* α   10 in] in þe BG   visage]
visagis Y   oþur] or TH   or] oþir Y   11 by¹] by by *2nd canc.* D   men]
many men α   þes . . . þei (23)] nouelries and new bigilyngis þat Z   12 ȝif] *om.*
AOαδIJ   13 ȝif] *om.* ATα   15 þer] þe I   ȝif] *om.* Tβ   gospel] gospelis
ABδJ   16 to men] *om.* G   17 þe] *om.* βH   19 ordris] newe *canc.* ordris Y,

20 ordris ouer Cristis ordre. And whonne þei takon þer children and
þer goodis, as þei weron herne. And þei smyton ofte seculer men
in faces of þer soulis, for þei takon byleue fro men and putton
heresyes þerfore, as ȝif þei smyton men in þer face, and maden
hem bollon vnkyndely.

25   And þus spekiþ Poul afturward *by vnnobley I speke, as we weron seke*
in þis part þat han take fredom of Crist. But neþeles, as Poul seiþ
who þat dar preise hym of go⌐o¬d, *I dar* preise me , seiþ Poul; *but þis
is foly* and no wisdam. Þei preyson hem, þat *þei beþ Hebrews*,
ordeyned of God to come to blisse; and Poul seiþ þat he is
30 ordeyned þus, and *an Hebrew* to þis entent. Þei booston þat *þey ben
Iacobus sones*, þat was a mon þat say God; and ȝet Poul seiþ soþly
þat *he is sone of Israel*. Þei seyn þat *þei ben Abrahamys kyn*, to whom
heuene is byhyȝt; but Poul seiþ he is on to whom blis is byhiȝt.
Þei seyn at þe fourþe tyme þat *þei ben Cristis mynystris*; but Poul,
35 þat kepte þe secte of Crist, seiþ þat *he is Cristis seruaunt* as þei. And
þus Poul *preysuþ hym ouer hem as lesse wys* to confounden hem; and
seiþ he passuþ a poynt ouer hem in trauelyng for Cristis lawe. For
he was *in monye trauelis* to teche Cristus lawe to þe puple, not for
his owne wynnyng, but to preche Crist to men. Poul was at þe
40 secounde tyme *oftere in prison* for Crist. Poul was at þe þridde tyme
in woundys ouer mesure for Crist. Poul was at þe fourþe tyme *ofte tyme
in monye deþis*; for he was *by fyue tymes beton* by ypocrisye *of Iewis*,
onys lesse þan fourty tymes, as ȝif þey hadden do mercy to hym. *He
was þries beton wiþ ȝerdis, and he was eft ones stonyd; he was þries in perele of*
f.16 45 *þe see, for he was nyȝt and day in þe depe see. He was ofte in perels of|weyes, in*
perelis of flodis, in perelis of þeuys, in perelis of hys owne kynrede, in

---

31 Gen. 35: 9.

newe ordris P   20 ordris] ordre⌐s¬ A, ordre BPYIGH   ouer] aboue
H   whonne] *om.* α   21 herne] here X   þei²] *om.* β   23 smyton] smote
α   men] þaim Z   þer] þe TZ   maden] maken H, gerris Z   24 bollon
vnkyndely] *rev.* H   25 I] þei G   26 han take] he takeþ O, we haue take
δ   fredom] þe fredom I   but . . . seiþ] *twice, 1st canc.* D   27 good] go⌐o¬d
DX, god BTI   28 hebrews] ebrewrewis Y   29 to come] *om.* A   30 and] þat
β   32 sone] þe sone B   ben] ben of TI   kyn] kynde T   33 but] ȝit
I   he] ⌐þat¬ he X, þat he ABOPTYαβδH'IJZG   blis] heuene T   34 at] *om.*
O, þat G   35 þe . . . crist] cristis secte I   secte] seete Y   36 þus] ⌐þus¬ Y,
om. G   as . . . hem (37)] *om.* O   37 for¹] of PZ   39 wynnyng] wynnyngis
H   men] þe men O, hem T   40 oftere] ofte YG   þe] *om.* β   41 tyme²] *om.*
Yα   42 by¹] *om.* H'I   44 he was¹] *om.* Y   eft] oftere þan I, eftesonys
J   ones] *om.* OJ   perele] perelis I   45 nyȝt] ⌐a¬ nyȝt B   day] ⌐a¬ day
B   perels] perel ABOPTYβδIJ   of] of // of *2nd eras.* D   in³] and

*perelis of hepene men, in perelis in cite, in perelis in wildernesse, in perelis in
þe see, in perelis in false freris –* and þis perele of alle þes eyʒte is þe
moste, as Austyn seiþ. And so, ʒif freris kepton hem clene, and
taken þis perele for Cristus sake, þei ben in þe moste perele, boþe   50
for prison and sleyng of freris. Bysyde alle þes eyʒte perelis *Poul
was in traueyle and myschef, in monye* [*wakyngus, in hungir and þurst, in
monye*] *fastyngus, in colde and nakidnesse; bysyde þo þat ben wipowte, þat
is hys eche day instaunce, byssynes of alle chyrchis.* For Poul seiþ þat *noon
is seek, but ʒif he be seek* wiþ hym in sorwe. *Who is sclaundrid* wiþ   55
synne, seiþ Poul, *and I am not brent* wiþ hym in schame?

    Ʒif it nediþ to haue glorie, I schal haue glorie in þes peynes of my
seeknes. And in al þis speche seiþ Poul þat *God woot þat he lyeþ* not.

    *þe styward of Damasc of þe folc of kyng Arethe kepte þe citee of
Damascenys to take Poul, and punysche; and by a wyndowe in a leep was he*   60
*late doun by þe wal; and so he ascapude þis mannys hondis. And ʒif it be
nede to glorie, certis it speduþ not* for hymself. For freris and þeuys ben
ofte peynede, but þat ys for þer owne folye. Poul seiþ þat he *schal
come to þe syʒtis and tellyngis of þe Lord;* for oure byleue techuþ us
þat, fro þe tyme of day of doom, men schullon see in Godis Sone   65
þingus þat bifore weron hyd, and God schal þanne telle men
reson why he ordeynede þes þingis. And in tokne of kalendis of þis
Poul telluþ of hymself þat *he knowiþ a man in Crist þat fourtene ʒeer
byfore was rauysched, wheþur in body or owte of body he woot neuere, but*

---

60 Acts 9: 23–5.

P   46 perelis¹] peril⌈s⌉ H, perel AOTδIJ   in¹] and in α   perelis²] perel
AδIJ   perelis³] perel AδIJ   hys] her   in³] and in I   47 in²] of
I   in⁴] of I   in⁶] and in I   48 in¹] and in BOPTYαβH'XZ   in²] of
ABIZ   of . . . seiþ (49)] as austen says is þo moste of al þes eyghte α   þes] oþre
canc. þes D, *om.* H   þe²] *om.* I   49 and¹ . . . freris (51)] *om.* Z   50 taken]
token I   þe] *om.* TY   51 prison] prisoun⌈rynge⌉J, prisonyng A   52 traueyle]
trauels P   and¹] and in H   wakyngus . . . monye (53)] *margin* G, *om.*
DABOPTYβδH'IJXZH   53 and] and in OT   wiþowte] oute I   54 hys] *om.*
Tδ   day] daies BYδ   byssynes] þe bisynesse H   þat] *om.* O   57 nediþ]
nede α   58 in] of I   speche] *om.* T   þat¹] *om.* BH   he lyeþ] y lye
B   59 þe²] alle þe O   folc] floc β   kyng] þe king BYI, kynd H   arethe]
of arethe I   60 poul] *om.* A   punysche] punysche hym Oα   61 late doun]
rev. T   þe] a H   ascapude] scapide AαδJG   þis] þus I   be nede] nedeþ
I   62 to] to to, *2nd canc.* D   speduþ] nediþ G   hymself] hym
I   for² . . . folye (63)] *om.* Z   freris] þeues P   þeuys] freris P   63
ofte] *om.* T   peynede] punyshid H   64 þe¹] þes T   syʒtis] siʒt I   oure]
ouþer β   65 þe] *om.* αH   day] þe day ATαδIG, þat day B   66 bifore weron]
rev. OH   þanne telle] *rev.* OI   67 in] *om.* β   69 or] oþer

70 *God woot.* For Poul knew þat fourtene ӡeer byfore he was turned to
Cristis secte, and in his fastyng of þre dayes he say monye
pryuytees of God. And þis is clepud þe þridde heuene, as seynt
Austyn declaruþ. Þe furste heuene is by bodily siӡt, as men seen
heere in lif; þe secounde is by ymaginacion, as men seen whon þei
75 slepon; þe þridde is by vndurstondyng, as seyntis seen þat ben in
blisse, and calendis of þis siӡt hadde Poul whonne he was
rauysched. But Poul and Iohn namen here hem not, to teche us to
flee veyn glorye. But Poul confessuþ his ignoraunce þat he not
wheþur he was rauysched in body, or ouӡt of body by his spiriӡt
80 takon fro his body. And heere men seen openly þat mannys
spiriӡt is þe man hymself; for Poul wiste þat he was rauysched,
but he wiste not wheþur in soule alone. And Poul telluþ aftur of
hymself þat *he knoweþ such a man, wheþur in body or owte of body he*
woot neuere, but God woot þat he was rauysched into paradys of God. *And*
85 þere *he herde pryuey wordis þat be not leueful to speke* heere. Monye
muson what wordis weron þes. And somme seyn þat þei wyton
wel, but it is not leueful to man to speke hem; and þus þei ben
f.16v stille. But somme|men wenon þat þes wordis weron ordenaunce
of men to blisse, and þes wordis schulde not be spoken for perel
90 þat myӡte come þerof.

For suche syӡtis schulde Poul haue glorie and no þing for hymself, but in
his *peynes* þat he haþ here and in hope to come to blisse for hem.
And ӡeet ӡif man wole þus glorie, hym nediþ to be not vnwys. And two
þingus ben nedfulle heere: *þat a man holde trewþe* and gabbe not,
95 and also þat he be not proud hymself, but schewe here hyӡnesse of
God. And þerfore seiþ Poul þat *he schal seyӡe trewþe, and þat he*
sparuþ to speke here, þat *no man gesse of hym ouer þis þat he seeþ in me,*

---

77 Rev. 1: 19.

I   woot] not O   but] for I   70 knew] knoweþ I   byfore] before þat α,
bifore ⌐þe writyng of þis epistyl⌐ J   71 his] þis TY   þre] þe thre αβ   72
clepud] callede αZ   73 by] *om.* IG   75 þridde] þridde heuene AB   77 here
hem not] hem not here BZ   us] *om.* Y   78 flee] fle here α   not] wot not
BαZG   80 seen] seien Y   mannys] þe mannus H   81 he] *om.* β   82
aftur] afterward T   85 he] ⌐he⌐ H, *om.* βG   monye] many men, men *canc.* A,
many men αδ   86 weron þes] *rev.* Z   somme] sum men αδ   þat] *om.*
α   87 to man] men I   to¹] no B   88 men] *om.* T   89 not] *om.*
H   91 schulde] schal α   and] in Z   for²] of T   92 his] þis O   haþ]
had α   and in] in I, anı G   93 þus] þis T   to be not] not to be OPIZ-
H   94 a] *om.* T   95 þat] so þat α   hymself] of himsilf AB   hyӡnesse]
mekenesse and heyӡnesse T   96 schal] *om.* Y   97 to speke here] here to speke

or heruþ ony þing of me. Poul wolde not þat men gessedon þat he
were hooly ouer þe soþe, for þis·ys maner of ypocritis þat hyȝen
falsly þer owne staat. And, *leste þat gretnesse* of Godus tellyng *hyȝe*   100
Poul aboue hymself, *God ȝaf hym a pricke of his flesch, an angel of þe*
feend to tempte ⌈*hym.* And herbi⌉ Poul wiste his owne frelte, and held
þe boundis of mekenesse, siþ an angel of Sathanas myȝte so liȝtly
buffate his soule. But ȝet *he preyȝede God þries þat þis* aungel *schulde*
wenden awey fro hym; but God seyde to hym aȝen, 'My grace is ynow to þe,   105
for vertu growiþ in seknesse'. And herfore seiþ Poul þat *he wole gladly*
haue glorie in his syknesses, þat Cristis vertu dwelle in hym.

     Here it is pertynent to speke of pruyde of þis fourþe sect, for
freris, al ȝif þei ben vngroundide, hyȝen hem aboue apostlis, and
seyn þer ordre is moste hooly of alle þe ordris þat euere God   110
ordeynede. And þus þei feynon blasfemy gabbyngus þat Crist
beggude as þei don. And on falshede of suche blasfemy⌈e⌉s is
hoolynesse of þes ordris feyned; but Crist slepte or knew hem
nowȝt, but for to ordeyne peyne for hem. And þus Poul telluþ a
good medicyn: to reste in ordenaunce of Crist, and take no part in   115
þis newenesse þat þes ordres han browt in. Wel we wyton þat þes
habitis and þes cloystres wiþ oþre signes ben browte in to blende
mennys yȝen in holynesse of þes ypocritis. Wel we wyton þat
Crist ordeynede fewe apostlis dwelle wiþ þe puple, and boþe in lif
and in word to teche hem by his lawe, and bad not lompis of   120
ypocritis lyue as doon þes newe ordris. And þus by lore þat Iohn
ȝyueþ trewe men schulde not dele wiþ hem, but ȝif þei hadden

---

122   2 John 10.

H   of] *om.* TH   þis] *om.* H   me] hym α   98 of] in T   me] hym
α   gessedon] gessede not O   þat²] þay O   99 þe] *om.* α   100 þat] þe
H   101 god . . . flesch] *om.* α   of² . . . tempte (102)] *on eras. corr.* D   102
to . . . herbi] and herbi *canc.* to tempte ⌈hym and herbi⌉ *corr.* D, and herby to tempte hym
I, ⌈was sente for⌉ to tempte hym and herby α, to tempt him and þerby Z, to tempten him
and H   his] herbi his H   103 boundis] bondis ABPTYδGH   mekenesse]
mekenesses A   an] ⌈an⌉T, *om.* βH   104 þis] his I   105 to hym aȝen] agayne
to hym αIZ   106 seknesse] sykenesses A   and . . . syknesses (107)] *om.*
α   wole] wolde AH   107 haue glorie] *rev.* I   his] *om.* Y   syknesses]
syknesse ABOβδIJZGH   108 here . . . hem (130)] *om.* Z   þis . . . sect] *on eras.*
corr. D   fourþe] foure AOTαIH   sect] sectis AOTαIH   109 apostlis] þes
apostelis T   110 þer] þe B, þat þaire α   þe] ⌈þe⌉ Yβ, þes α, *om.* O   112
blasfemyes] *2nd-e-corr.* D   113 þes] siche blasfe *canc.* þes D   þes ordris] þis ordre
Y   or] and β   hem] he α   114 for²] of α   117 and] in T   in] *om.*
β   118 yȝen] siȝt B   þat] *om.* O   119 dwelle] to *canc.* dwelle X, to dwelle
ABOTαδIJH   120 in] *om.* β   word] wordys T   121 doon] *om.* A   122

hope to turne hem to Cristus secte fro þer vanyte. For wel we
wyton þei byndon hem more to hoolynesse by þer signes; and wel
125 we wyton þei myȝten as myche holdon holynesse wiþ comune
signes. And þus þes ypocritus byndon hem wiþowte cause ouer
þer power. And siþ þei putton obac Cristus ordenaunce and
parformyng of his lawe, and wiþ þis falsehede spuylon þe puple,
boþe of vertuwis and worldly goodis, monye þenken þei ben
130 heretikes and foulon men þat mayntene hem.

dele] dwelle I   hadden] han T   123 hem] hym O   we] *om.* G   124
þei] we B   byndon] bidd *canc.* byndon D   125 þei] ⌐þat⌐ þei H   as myche
holdon] ⌐do⌐ as moche I   129 vertuwis] vertu P   and] and of T   monye]
many men αβ, as manye men G   þei] þat þei α

Dominica in Quinquagesima. [Epistola.]
Sermo 1 [5].

Si linguis hominum loquar. Prima Corintheos xiii.

Poul telluþ in þis capitle how men schulen knowe charite, and how men schulen|kepe charite; and þis lore is ful nedful to eche membre of hooly chirche. Furst Poul telluþ how nedful is charite byfore oþre, and bygynneþ at hierste werk þat man haþ in hooly chirche. Poul seiþ *ȝif he speke wiþ mannys tongis and aungel tongis, and he haue not charite, he is maad as bras sownyng and a symbal tynkyng.* It is knowen by byleue þat prechyng and oþur speche is þe hyȝerst dede of man, whan þat it is wel don. But, howeuere a man speke in dyuerse tongis of men, oþur Englisch or Frensch, Latyn or oþur langage, his voys is liȝk a sound of bras þat destruyeþ hymself, but ȝif he haue charite by which he disserueþ blisse; for suche men by long tyme waston hemself, and largen þer peyne. And on þe same maner, ȝif man speke in aungel tonge, wiþ cler voys or florischede wordis, speke he neuere so sutilly, ȝif he wante charite wiþ þis, he is as a tynkyng symbal, for he profiȝtuþ not to disserue his blis, but wastuþ hym to hys dampnyng. Aftur seiþ Poul þat *ȝif he haue prophecye, and knowe alle pryuetes, and haue alle*

MSS: D; ABEGHIJOPTXYZαβδ; Hᵗ *expl.* 35 be, *text uncollatable.*

Sermo 15] sermo 16 Dβ, sermo A, *om.* BOTαδEJXZGH   si . . . loquar] *om.*
Y   loquar] loquar et angelorum BT   I . . . xiii] *om.* O   I] *om.* YH   1
telluþ . . . capitle] in þis capitle telliþ H   capitle] epistle AαG   schulen]
shulden AOαIGH   2 men] þei Y   schulen] shulden AOTαβH, *om.* I   þis]
þus O   3 nedful] medeful B   is charite] *rev.* Y   4 bygynneþ] bigynnynge
PZ   at] at þe ABTαEIH   5 poul] and poul O   mannys] mennus
PZG   tongis¹] tunge B   aungel] aungels BOPTαIZG   6 haue] haþ
A   not] no I   he . . . sownyng] as bras he is maad sounnynge β (*corrected*
margin)   and] or Z   a] as TH, as a E   8 man¹] a man I, men H   whan
þat] wȝan wan O, whan Pα   wel don] *rev.* I   a] þat a I, *om.* O   9 or¹] oþer
T, *om.* I   latyn] or latyn G   10 sound] soun BOY   11 disserueþ] dysseyuyþ
OX   blisse] þe *eras.* blisse A, þe blysse OδIJ   12 hemself] himsilf H   13
man] a man I   in] wiþ αE   aungel] aungelis BYIH   tonge] tunges
α   14 or] and α   15 as] *om.* αδG   a] *om.* YJ   tynkyng symbal] *rev.*
H   16 his] his *canc.* A, ⌈his⌉ Y, *om.* Bα, him H   aftur] and aftur α   17 haue²]

maner of science, and ʒif he haue al byleue, so muche þat he translate hullis, and he haue not charite, he is noʒt to hooly chyrche. Þes foure, clepude
20 vertuwis of þe vndurstondyng of man, may be wiþowton charite, and þanne þei serue not to blis. Monye men may konne muche, and lyue yuele not þeraftur, as a man may worche wondris by þe worchyng of a feend. And so it is to nakud prof to preise men for such worchyng. And þus men may haue byleue vnformed by
25 charite; and such byleue profituþ not, siþ þe feend haþ such byleue. And þus men may haue profecye, and alle þes habitis in þer soule, and be schrewede worcheris wiþ yuel wille of þer soule. And þus seiþ Crist in þe gospel 'Syre, propheciedon we not in þi name, and castedon owt feendis fro men?' and ʒet he knowiþ hem
30 not to blis. Þe þridde tyme seiþ God in Poul þat *ʒif he dele alle his goodis into metis of pore men, and ʒyue his body so þat he brenne* (as somme men don in heresye), *and he haue not charite wiþ þis, it profiʒtuþ hym not to blis.*

And siþ þese werkis and þes growndus semon to make hooly
35 men, and eche mon wolde by kynde be blissid, it were aftur to wytone how men schulden knowe charite, sithen it is so nedful to men [to come] to þe blisse of heuene. And þerfore in þis secounde part of þis epistle telluþ Poul sixtene condicionis by whiche men mown knowe þis loue. The furste is þat *charite is pacient*, and so
40 meke þat he conformeþ his wille mekely to Godis wille; and þus he gnaweþ h[y]m not to deþe for no þing þat falluþ in þe world. But for good þing þat falliþ he haþ a brennyng loue to God, and

---

25 Jas. 2: 19; 28 Matt. 7: 22.

y haue β   18 of] *om.* H   al] *om.* I   19 he[1]] *om.* α   clepude] beþ cleped
O, callid Z   20 þe] *om.* H   vndurstondyng] vnderstondynges O   man] men
α   wiþowton] out of I   21 not to] to no α   may] *om.* B   22 þeraftur]
after I   a] *om.* G   23 to[1]] ⌐to⌐ Y, *om.* E   prof to] profte O, a preeft to
I   men] hem E   24 worchyng] worchyngys T   26 þus] siþ B   habitis]
hauyngis Z   27 be] bi H   28 we not] *rev.* α   29 castedon] casten
OαH   owt feendis] *rev.* I   fro] in þi name from A, of α   30 seiþ] sayde
α   in] bi B   alle] *on eras. corr.* D   31 into] vnto H   metis] mete
O   of] to G   he] hit T   32 men] *om.* PZ   not] no⌐t⌐ X, ne *canc.* not β,
no α   it] he A   33 hym] ⌐him⌐ H, *om.* A   34 and[1]] *om.* T   werkis] werk
I   36 it is so] *on eras. corr.* D   37 to come to] to D, to ⌐come to⌐ X   þe] *om.*
OPTαβδIJXZG   þis] *om.* β   38 telluþ poul] *rev.* G   39 knowe] kunne
T   is[1]] *om.* I   40 conformeþ] confermyþ Oα   41 gnaweþ] knawis
Z   hym] hem D, hym, y *altered from* e X, *om.* G   to] to þe BT   deþe] dye
Z   þe] þis E   42 and . . . benignite (43)] þe secounde condicion þat euere sueþ
charite ys þat hyt is benygne to peple þat hyt dwelliþ wiþ. benygnyte ys cliped gode fuyr of

þis is clepid *benignite* by speche þat Poul spekuþ here. The þridde
tyme telluþ Poul þat *charite haþ noon enuye*; and he spekuþ of
charite in name of man þat holdiþ it. And þus men mown wante   45
enuye, and repreue men in Cristus name for loue þat þei haue to
God, and for profiȝt to his chirche; for þus dude Crist ful scharply
and he myȝte not wante|þis loue.   f.17v

The fourþe condicion of þis loue is þat *it doþ not amys*; for, what
þing þat he doþ, hys laste entent is to do Godis wille, and so to   50
profiȝt of his chirche aftir þe lawe þat he haþ ȝouen. And þus alle
þese foure sectis semen to fayle in charite, for þei leuon Godis
lawe and worchen by here feynede fyndyngis; and so þei leuon
Godis worschipe and traueylon most for her owne wynnyng. The
fyueþe condicion of þis loue is þat *it bolneþ not by pruyde*; for he   55
þenkiþ mekely how he is a low seruaunt of God, and so ypocrisie
makiþ not þat he hyȝe hym ouer reson. The sixte maner of charite
is þat *it is not coueytous*. Vche man schulde coueyte blisse and
vertuose deedis to do þerfore; but Poul spekiþ of coueytyse þat is
contrarious to þis ende, as manye men languischen for pruyde to   60
haue a staat þat God wole not. And þus alle þese foure sectis
semen to faylon in þis poynt, for þei coueyton þat mannys wille
goo forþ and Godis wille be put obac; and so þei haue algatis
enuye and don amys as proude men, for þey coueyton her owne
worschipe and leuon þe worschipe of þer God. The seuenþe   65
condicion of þis loue is þat *it secheþ not his owne þingus*, but to
worschipe of God and to profiȝt of his chirche he entenduþ to don
his deedis aftur þe lawe þat God haþ ȝouen. ⌐And here it semyþ

charite. for men þat haueþ charite beþ brennynge in loue T   43 clepid] *on eras. corr.*
D, called αZ   44 telluþ poul] *rev.* T   of] in O   45 name of man] his name A,
þe name of þe man I   man] a *altered from* o D   men mown] many men
α   wante] a *altered from* o D   47 for¹] *om.* BP   to] of G   his] þe
H   48 þis loue] *om.* B   50 þing] *om.* G   to¹] for to H   do] ⌐do⌐ TJH, *om.*
I   godis] goodis, *2nd* o *subpuncted* D   51 of] to BOPTαβδEZH   þe] þat
E   and . . . wynnyng (54)] *om.* Z   53 lawe] *om.* β   55 it] *on eras. corr.*
D   by] to TI   56 a] *om.* α   58 man] a *altered from* o D   59 but] for
α   60 contrarious] contrarie EG   to þis ende] *om.* O   as . . . god (65)] *om.*
Z   manye] a *altered from* o D   61 god] ⌐god⌐ EH   wole] wolde B   62
semen] *2nd* e *altered from* o D   poynt] p/poynt D   mannys] a *altered from* o
D   63 forþ] bifore E   þei . . . algatis] algatis þey han E   64 þey] -ey *on eras.*
corr. D   her] euere þer T   65 of . . . god] *on eras. corr.* D   þer] *om.*
ABOPTYαβδEIJXGH   66 þis] *om.* δIJ   is] *om.* O   secheþ] sekenes, -n-
subpuncted α   to] *om.* β   67 worschipe] þe worschip I   to¹] *om.* G   pro-
fiȝt] þe profyt I   his] þe T   he] and he G, it E   68 and . . . ȝouyn (71)]

þat þes foure sectis faylen fouly in þis pᵣoᵧynt, for ech one sechiþ
70 þat his ordre and his reule be mayntenyd more þan þe comyn
ordre of Crist, or þe lawe þat he haþ ʒouynᵧ.

The eiʒtþe condicion of þis loue is þat *it is not stured vnto wrappe*
for, siþen he is pacient and trowiþ þat God mot haue ⌐hᵧys will,
he holduþ hym payed wiþ what þat falluþ, in þat þat it is Godus
75 wille. And þis fayluþ in þes foure sectis, for þei takon her owne
veniaunce bysyde þe lawe þat God haþ ʒouen, as ʒif þei weron
more hyʒe þen Crist. The nynþe condicion of þis loue ys þat *it
castuþ not yuel*, for it castuþ to worschipe God and menes þat ledon
herto. Lord! wher þes foure sectis casten to haue her owne wille
80 more bussyly þen þe wille of God? – and þenne þei ben alle yuele.
The tenþe condicion of þis loue is þat *it ioyeþ not on wickednesse*, but
haþ sorwe þat ony mon doþ aʒenys Godus wille. But ʒeet of þe
same þing haþ he boþe ioye and sorwe: he haþ sorwe of þe synne
by reson þat it vnlikuþ God, and he haþ ioye of þe same synne by
85 reson þat God punyscheþ it wel. And here it semeþ þat þes foure
sectis han ioye of her owne þing, and seyon þat God forbede þat
Cristus ordenaunce were fulfulled; and þus þei reuerson in deede
þe wille of God in monye maneris.

The elleuenþe condicion of þis loue is þat *it ioyeþ to trowþe*.
90 Trowþe is God and his lawe; and whenne þis lawe is wel kept,
þenne þis charite haþ ioye. And here þes foure ordris semen to
grucche muche aʒeynys þis trewþe, for þei magnyfyon her lawis,
and executon hem bussyly; but how þat Godus lawe is brokon þei

lower margin corr. D, *om.* Z   69 fouly] foule BTYαEH, *om.* I   one] ⌐oneᵧ E, *om.*
Tα   70 ordre] reule I   reule] ordre I   more] and more I   þe] *om.* α, to
I   72 vnto] to ABOPTYαβδEJZGH   73 siþen] he *canc.* seþ I   pacient] so
pacient E   hys] h- *corr.* D   74 payed] apaid OH   in þat] *om.* T   75
and . . . crist (77)] *om.* Z   þis] in þis α   in] *om.* α   76 lawe] wille α   77
more hyʒe] heiʒer I   crist] auntecrist I   78 not] noon T   worschipe] þe
worschip of I   god] of god OPTZ   menes] men O   ledon] bedeþ
O   79 herto] þerto TαEIGH   lord . . . yuele (80)] *om.* Z   wher] for
α   80 þe] þe *canc.* X, *om.* OPYαβ   þei ben] *rev.* α   81 it] *om.* O   on] of
BOPαδEIJZH   82 doþ] do δ   ʒeet] *om.* T   83 ioye] sorewe I   sorwe¹]
ioiʒe I   he haþ sorwe] ⌐he haþ sorweᵧ T, ⌐and he haþ sorweᵧ H   of] on
δ   84 by reson] by þe resoun E, because H   it] god punyscheþ it wel *canc.* it
D   vnlikuþ] lykiþ not to T, likeþ not H, myslikiþ E   of] on α   85
punyscheþ] punisshe BZ   and . . . maneris (88)] *om.* Z   here] herefore
O   þes] þe G   86 þat¹] ⌐þatᵧ T, *om.* BH   god] crist P   87 were] be
eras. were D   88 monye] mannus β   89 it] he I   to] of PαZ, in T   90
trowþe is] trowiþ his G   and¹] in Z   91 and . . . stonde (94)] *om.* Z   92
muche] *om.* β   lawis] owne lawis G   93 is] be PI   94 þat] *om.*

recchen to luytul, so þat her staat stonde. The twelþe condicion of
þis loue is þat *it suffreþ alle þingus*, for it ioyeþ of vche trewþe|in alse   95   f.18
myche as it likuþ God. Lord! why wole not þes foure sectis suffre
þat Godus word renne and þat Cristus ordenaunce stode hool? –
siþen yt were beste, as þei graunton. But certis þenne alle þes
foure sectis schulden leue her patrounis and her rewlis, and come
clenely to Cristus secte; and who schulde grucche aȝenys þis? The   100
þrettenþe condicion of þis loue is þat *it troweþ alle þingus*, for þing
and trowþe is al oon and so alle trowþis ben trowede of hit. And
þus it troweþ and assentuþ to alle maner trowþe and resoun. But
how fayluþ he not heere þat lettuþ þus Cristus ordenaunce, and
doþ harm to monye men, boþe to her body and to her soule? The   105
fourtenþe condicion of þis loue is þat *it hopuþ alle þingus*; for it
hopuþ þat ordeyned trewþe helpuþ to alle goode men, and þis
charite hopuþ to haue part of þis help. Here faylon þes newe
sectis, þat dredon hem þat þei schullen fayle from worldly fauour
and worldly wynnyng, and þat Godus lawe schal be kept clene;   110
and þus þei dispeyron in lif of þe fruyt of Godus lawe. The fiftenþe
condicion of þis loue is þat *it susteynet alle þingus*, for it helpuþ to
holde alle trowþe and abyduþ þe ende þerof, for aftur þe day of
doom schal be fruyt of alle trowþe. And þes þat ben vnpacient þat
Godus lawe riȝtede hem faylon in þis condicion, ᴦsiþ þey trystyn   115
to manus lawis. Þe sexteþe condicion¹ and þe laste þat folwiþ þis
charite is þat *it falluþ neuere awey*, nowþur in þis world ne in þe
toþur; for Godus loue may not falle, siþen God may not ceese to
ordeyne þes men to come to blisse, þe whiche he wole euere han
blisse. And þis loue þat is in God mot haue such charite in mon.   120

A   stonde] stode α   95 vche] alle I   96 god] to god PZ   lord . . . þis
(100)] *om.* Z   foure] newe foure H   97 stode] stonde BTIH   100 clenely]
clene δ, cleerli G   102 trowþis] troweris I   103 trowþe] ᴦofᴧ trowþe X, of treuþe
ABOPTYαβδEIJZH   resoun] of resoun Z   but . . . soule (105)] *om.*
Z   105 harm] haþ harm P   men] *om.* I   to³] to *canc.* X, *om.* BYβJ-
G   106 fourtenþe] fourteneᴦþeᴧ E, fourtene δ   it¹] he I   þingus] þing
H   for] for it hopuþ alle þingus *canc.* for D   it²] he β   107 ordeyned]
ordinat T   108 part] help *canc.* part D   help] helþe E   here . . . lawe
(111)] *om.* Z   109 schullen] shulde αI   110 schal] schulde Yαδ   clene]
clenly α   111 þe]*om.* H   112 alle] alle alle, *2nd canc.* D   for] but P   113
trowþe] truþis H   114 and . . . lawis (116)] *om.* Z   115 faylon] fallen
G   siþ . . . condicion (116)] *lower margin corr.* D   116 to] in I   manus]
mennis ABPYαβδIJH   sexteþe] sixtene δJ   and] of þese and T   117 awey
nowþur] *om.* T   118 falle] faylle, -y- *canc.* α, faile Aβl   119 þes] to T   þe
. . . blisse (120)] *om.* T   han] to haue G   120 blisse] blissed α   mon] men

Loke þou þese condicionis, wher þow haue hem alle in þe; and,
ȝif þow haue hem not, be abouȝte for to haue hem alle hoole, and
þenne þow hast wiþowton dowte þis loue þat mot brynge to
blisse. And of þis techuþ Poul þe excellence of charite, and þis is
125 þe þridde part of þis epistle, and makuþ ende of þis gloriouse lore.
Charite is wondurful good, as men mown see of wordis byfore;
and charite mot euere laste, owþur in lyue or in half lyue, for it is
not ful clene byfore þat men comen to blisse. *But wheþer þat*
profecies schulen be voydede, or þat [tu]ngis schulen ceese, or þat þis science
130 *schal be destruyed,* and alle þes þre mote nedis falle, þis *charite schal*
neuere fayle. For somwhat we knowon in certeyn, as ys beyng of oure
God, *and somwhat we prophecyon,* as þingis of þe laste day; *but*
whenne þat ⌐*schal*⌐ *come þat is parfiȝt, þis vnparfiȝt schal be auoydud.* And
so siþen at þe day of doom men schullen haue ful knowyng and
135 blisse, þe grees of konnyng and ioye here mot nedis passe, and þe
endyng mot come. And þus seiþ Poul of hymself, ⌐*and*⌐ so it is of
f. 18v alle þis chyrche, *whenne I was luytul I\spac as ȝong, I vndurstod as ȝong,*
I powȝte as ȝong, but whonne I was maad mon, I avoydede þes werkis of a
ȝong child; and so it is of alle men þat schullen come aftur to blis.
140 *We seen now by a myrour* in fer siȝt and vnpropur, but *we schulen se*
aftur in blisse þe furste trowþe *face to face.* Poul seiþ *he knoweþ now by*
⌐*a*⌐ *part* and not fully; and *þenne he schal knowe in blisse as he is knowon*
fully of God. And of þes wordis mowe men gydere þat *now þer*
dwellon þes þre vertuwis, byleue, hope and charite, but þe moste of þes is
145 *charite.*
And so, ȝif þis epistle of Poul were fully executed as it schulde,

H   122 haue hem¹] haue hem, hem *canc.* X, haue OPTYαβIJZG, hast AB   for
to] to BEH   123 mot] must H   to] þe *canc.* to β, ⌐þe⌐ to δJ, þe to TYαEI-
H   124 blisse] heuene E   of¹] aftur α   125 þis¹] þe H   126 of] *on eras.*
corr. D   byfore] here bifore I   127 mot] myȝte E   owþur] or H   or]
oþer OI   128 comen] comenen δ   wheþer þat] -þer þat *on eras. corr.*
D   þat²] *om.* O   129 schulen¹] schulden TI   voydede] void H   þat¹]
om. H   tungis] þingis DA   schulen²] schulden TI   þis] *om.* δ   130
schal¹] scholde I   falle] faile Aβ   131 fayle] falle T   ys] it is H, *om.*
O   132 þingis] þing is T   133 þat¹] it H   schal¹] *corr.* D   come] -þ *eras.*
D   þis] þis þat is ABG   auoydud] ⌐a⌐voydyd T, voidid BIG   134 and] of T,
in α   135 blisse] blesse δ   þe¹] þes H   ioye] þe ioie δ, ioyes I   136
endyng] ende E   come] nedis come IH   þus] *om.* T   and²] *corr.*
D   137 þis] his B, þe E   luytul] as litel I   ȝong¹] a ȝonge O   vndur-
stod] sauerid H   ȝong²] a ȝonge O   138 I¹ . . . ȝong] *margin* GH   ȝong]
a ȝonge OT   mon] a man BT   139 men] *om.* O   aftur] *om.* E   140 by]
in E   in] and in Y   142 in] fully *canc.* in D, fulli in δJ   143 mowe] many
T   þer] þer *eras.* X, *om.* ABOPTYαβδEIJZGH   144 hope] and hope
BOPTYαβEIZ   þe] *om.* ABOPTYαβδEIJZ   146 and . . . hem (161)] *om.*

þe rewme of Englond schulde be discharged of þes foure sectis
þat ben spokon of. And þenne myȝte þe rewme dispende monye
hundred þowsynde mark more þen it dispenduþ ⌜now⌝, ȝif alle
þese sectis weron auoydude. Marke what alle þes sectis dis-   150
pendon in oure rewme for a ȝeer, and ȝyue al þis to men in
charite. For ȝif þe⌜se⌝ four faylon in charite, oure rewme schulde
drawe from hem þis part. But rykene how muche þis comeþ to!
And bygynne þow to wyte of hem what þyng is þe sacrude hoost
wiþ reson of Godus byleue, and þat þei tellon not here to þe kyng but   155
þing þat þei wolon stonde by to suffre martirdom of men, and losse of
al þat þei han of our rewme. And þenne myȝte þe kyng wyte how he
schulde putte owȝt alle þese foure, and ouer þis he myȝte
more dispende by monye hundret þowsynd mark, and þe rewme
were more plenteuous to brynge forþ men to þe blisse of heuene.   160
And þus it falluþ kyngus to do by þe offis þat God haþ ȝouen hem.

Z   so] om. AY   fully] om. E   149 now] corr. D   ȝif alle] al ȝif
AB   150 sectis¹] new sectes α   marke] marke so O   dispendon] dispendid
β   152 þese] -se corr. D   153 hem] hym I   154 of hem] om. δ   þyng . . .
sacrude] on eras. corr. D   155 wiþ] bi I   here . . . kyng] on eras. corr. D   156
losse] lost O   157 of] in TE   þenne] om. β   þe] om. G   159 more] om.
O   hundret] an hundrid I   160 forþ] ⌜forþ⌝ GH, for β   þe] om.
OPYαβδJGH   161 þe] þer P

Dominica prima Quadragesime. [Epistola. Sermo 16.]

Hortamur uos. Secunda Corintheos 6.

Poul telluþ in þis epistle how alle cristene men schulden flee to take
in veyn Godus grace, and how þei schulden worche of þis. We
supposon of byleue þat vche good þing þat we han, be it staat, be
it konnyng, eche such þing is Godus grace, for God ȝyueþ it
5 graciously, for man schulde serue to hym by hit. And þus he
takuþ Godus grace in veyn, þat takuþ þis grace and leueþ his
seruyse. And þerfore bygynneþ Poul þus: *we moneste ȝow þat ȝe
take not þus in veyn þe grace of God;* and þuse wordis myȝten be
sayde to vche man in þis lif. And siþen defaute is not in God, but
10 al þe defauȝt is in his seruauntis, Poul meueþ ouer ⌐þis¬ word
a⌐noþer¬ word of greet wyt. Certis *God seiþ* to þuse men '*in
couenable tyme I haue herd þe, and in þe day of hele I haue helpud þe*'.
Furst men bydden to God her preyȝer þat he helpe hem in tyme
of nede; and ȝif þis be resonable, God helpuþ hem in couenable
15 tyme; and whon tyme comeþ þat God ȝyueþ hele, he helpuþ men
as he haþ hyȝt. And þese wordis of Ysaye ben general and in good

11 Isa. 49: 8.

MSS: D; ABEGHIJOPTXYZαβδ; Eˢ *inc.* 8 not þus; Hᵗ *inc.* 28 he haþ . . . *expl.* 39, *inc.*
47 . . . *expl.* 58, *almost all illegible and uncollatable.*

Sermo 16] sermo 17 Pβ, *om.* DABOTαδEIJXZGH   hortamur uos] *om.* Y   uos]
vos ne in uacuum ABPαδEIZ, uos ne in vacuum graciam dei recipiatis OT, uos in uacuum
βJ   2 cor. 6] 2 cor. P, cor. vi GH, cor. 16, *margin* 1 ad cor. 6 I, corynthyes þe sixte
chapitir Y, *om.* OE   2 worche] *om.* I   4 godus grace] goodis of grace H   5
man] a *altered from* o D   to] *om.* O   hym] god E   6 þis] his A   his] þys
OG   7 þerfore] herfore ABOPTYαβδEJXGH   bygynneþ poul] *rev.*
B   moneste] monyshe α   8 not þus] þis not O   in . . . god] þe grace of god
in veyn G   þuse wordis myȝten] þis word myȝt A   9 to] of PEˢZ   man] o
half altered to a D   and] but B   10 þe] *om.* AOT   ouer] euere I   þis
word anoþer] *on. eras. corr. into margin* D   11 anoþer word] and oþer wit *canc.* ⌐worde¬
I   12 couenable] commenable O, cownabil Z   þe²] þe *canc.* βX, *om.*
AOPTδEˢEIJZGH   hele] helþe ABOPTYαβδEˢEIJXGH   13 her] in ȝar O   he]
god O   14 nede] mede β   couenable] commenable O, cownable Z, resonable
B   15 ȝyueþ] ȝeue OTYβδJ   hele] helþe ABOPTYαβδEˢEIJXGH   he]
god E   men] hem O   16 haþ] *om.* Eˢ   hyȝt] ⌐bi¬ hiȝt X, bihiȝtABOPTY-

ordre, for furst God hereþ men and ȝyueþ menys, and siþen, w⌜h⌝enne neede is, he helpuþ. As furst God brynguþ m[o]n by ȝowþe, and siþen he ȝyueþ heele to mon as in tyme of monnys deþ; and aftur whonne he ȝyueþ hym blisse, þonne God helpuþ mon|at þe fulle, and helpuþ byfore to þis ende. And þus in age of f.19 holy chyrche God herde þis maydon in monye seyntis, and afturward in tyme of grace he helpude þis chyrche to come to heuene. And þerfore seiþ Poul þus: *Lo now is tyme acceptable, lo now is day of heele*, fro tyme þat Crist steyȝede to heuene. And so ȝe schulen lyue in þis tyme þat *ȝe ȝyue noon offence to ony, þat ȝoure seruyse be not blamed*, and þat God here not ȝoure preyȝer. *But in alle þingus ȝyue we us as mynystris of God*, in tyme of grace þat he haþ ȝouen. Now when hooly chyrche is eldere and haþ take more grace of God, he[o] schulde bussylior serue to hym, and more parfiȝtly by reson.

And þus telluþ Poul eyȝte and twenty condicionys þat he[o] schulde kepe now. Furst he[o] schulde haue *muche pacience*, for he[o] haþ lerned þis of Crist and of monye of his membris, and þus þis lore schulde be knowon betture. Aftur þe chyrche schulde more stabully suffre *tribulacionys*, for assaying of a þing schulde teche for to knowe þat þing. And so men schulden nowe be in *neede*, boþe suffryng and helpyng. And so seruauntis of Crist schulden be now *in angwisches, in woundis and in prysonys, in stryuyngus, in traueylis and in wakyngus, in fastyngus and in chastite, in science and in longe abydyng, in swetnesse, in þe Hooly Goost, in charite not falsely feyned, in word of trowþe, and in Godus vertu, by armes of*

αβδE^{s}EIJZGH 17 furst god] *rev.* O hereþ men] helpiþ, *margin d.h.* herieþ men J 18 whenne] h *corr.* D neede] nedys O mon] men DTGH 19 heele] helþe ABOPTYαβδE^{s}EIJXG, help ZH 20 ȝyueþ] ȝeue Y hym] hem AI 21 mon] hym O 23 helpude] helpiþ A þis] þe G, his H 24 þerfore] herfore E 25 is] *om.* H· day] *on. eras. corr.* D, ⌜a⌝ day X, a day BEIJGH, þe daie A heele] helþe ABOPTYαβδE^{s}EIJXGH tyme] þe tyme B steyȝede] is stied BTYβ to] up *canc.* to D, in to YE^s 26 schulen] shul⌜d⌝en H, shulden ABPTYαβδE^{s}EJXZG 27 and] and *canc.* lest J 28 þingus] þing I 30, 32, 33, 34 heo] hee *altered from* heo D 30 heo] siche βG bussylior] -lior *on eras. corr.* D, bisier G, more bisili H 32 telluþ poul] *rev.* O heo] suche G 33 heo] suche G, ⌜sc⌝he X 34 heo] such G lerned] lerid AδIJ 35 þis lore schulde] scholde his lore I 36 tribulacionys] tribulacioun H assaying] þe assaiyng B, assailyng G 37 for to] to EI nowe be] *rev.* I 39 angwisches] anguishe ABTH and] *om.* T 40 stryuyngus] stryues ABOPYαβδ E^{s}EIJXZ, striue T in^1] and αδH, and *canc.* in EX wakyngus] wakinge I in^3] and B, and in β fastyngus] fastynge H chastite] charite O 41 and] ⌜and⌝ Y, *om.* G in^3] of α 42 armes] armers G 43 good]

riȝtwisnesse on boþe sydes, in doyng good and suffryng wrong; and so
by glorie and vnnobley, as doon seyntis þat han lerned to take gladly
45 her reproues, by yuel loos and good loos to þe world and to seyntus in
heuene. For comunly men þat seruen God ben foolus to þe world,
and wyse to seyntis. As deseyuours and trewe men, for Godus
seruauntis schulen haue a nome of þe world þat þei disseyue men,
and ȝeet þei schulen hoolde trewly þe sentence of Godus lawe.
50 And þus þei schulden be as vnknowone and knowone men to God and
seyntis, for þei schulle not accepte personys, but telle trewly
Godus word, as þei were not knowone of men but as aungelis þat
comon from heuene. As were men dyyng and ȝeet lyuyng in grace of
God. Poul and oþre apostlus of Crist weron dyyng anemptus her
55 body, and ȝeet þei weron growyng and lyuyng anemptus þe vertu
of þer soule. Þei schullen serue as chastisude men, and not as men þat
weron deede, siþen þei schulden be qwic in soule, and take gladly
turmentyng, and wyte wel þat her spirit by þis ys strengþud in
God. As sorweful to worldly gomen, but euermore ioyng in God. And
60 here schulden mony men lerne to be sadde as aungelis ben. And
men schulden be as nedy for, as pore men of worldly goodis, but
þei schulden make monye men riche in vertuwis and in meedful
deedis. As hauynge not on worldly maner, and hauynge alle þingus
by title of grace. Eche of þese poyntis þat Poul telluþ may be
f.19v 65 alarged to|þe puple and declarud diffusly, aftir þat God moueþ
þe spekere.

godes α   wrong] wronges α   44 and] of I   vnnobley] bi vnnobley
E[s]   seyntis] se canc./seyntis D   lerned] lered αE[s]Z   45 her] canc. D, ⌐þer⌐T,
om. YH   loos[1]] om. T   48 þei] om. I   49 schulen] sȝolde OH   50
schulden] schullen TαI   and[3]] as δ   51 seyntis] to seintis I   schulle]
shulden BOPTYβδE[s]EIJXZG   52 of] to I   53 were men] men þat weren
BOPTYαβE[s]EIXZG, men ⌐þat⌐ weren AδJ, þei weren men H   54 anemptus] as
anentis TG   55 þei] om. E[s]Z   anemptus] as anentis G   þe vertu] þe vertues
ABOPYαβδIJXZGH, þer vertues T, uertues E   56 soule] soules Oα   schullen]
on. eras. corr. D, shulden AOTδIJZ   57 deede] dedid OPTYαδE[s]EJXGH   soule]
here soule I   gladly] in soule gladli δIJ   60 schulden] schullen I   men] om.
E   lerne] lere αZH   61 for] for canc. α, om. Z   63 on] in O, of T   65
and] and be T

Dominica ij Quadragesime. [Epistola.] Sermo 1 [7].

Rogamus uos et obsecramus. Prima ad Tessalonicenses 4.

Poul techuþ in þis epistle how cristone men schulden lyue togydere, and holde hem euene in Cristus lawe þat is tauȝt by his apostlis. And Poul bygynneþ wiþ þis preyȝer, for noon þar kepe þis, but ȝif he wole; and þus holdyng of Godis lawe schulde be wilful and medful. *We preyon ȝow and bysechen ȝow in þe Lord Iesu,* seiþ Poul, *þat, as ȝe han takon of us how ȝe moten wandre and plese to God, so wandre ȝe* in þis lif *þat ȝe habunde more* in vertuwis, as ȝe ben growyng in eelde. Poul preyȝeþ on two maneris, as Crist is of two kyndus: his manhed is signefied by comun preyer maad to mon; his bysechyng telluþ his godhede, þat is special preyer of man, as ȝif men preyȝedon namynge hooly þing, as who seiþ 'I byseche God by vertu of his passion þat he helpe me in my nede.' And þus ys loue of Crist axsud boþe by his manhede and by his godhede. And nede is knyttud by Poul herto, whonne he seiþ þat ȝe mote wandre þus ȝif ȝe wolon be sauede. And to þis takon men luytul heede of þes foure sectis þat we han teeld, for þei leuon Poulus lore, and feynon hem a new rewle þat is oþur bysyde Godus lawe, or contrarie þerto. For Crist seiþ 'who is not wiþ me, he is euene

5

10

15

18 Matt. 12: 30; Luke 9: 50.

MSS: D; ABEGHIJOPTXYZαβδ; Eˢ *expl. incompl.* 7 ȝe in þis; Hᵗ *expl. incompl., all illegible and uncollatable.*

Dominica . . . -gesime] þe firste sondai in lente B   sermo 17] sermo 18 DPβ, *om.* ABOTαδEˢEIJXZGH   rogamus . . . -cramus] *om.* Y   uos] et *canc.* uos D- X   et obsecramus] et obsecramus in domino iesu T, etc. H   prima . . . 4] *om.* O   prima] *om.* TH   1 techuþ] telliþ BYβEIH   2 euene] euer EˢZ, *om.* α   3 þar] dar δG   4 þus] *om.* β   schulde] sal Z   5 medful] *om.* Y   þe] oure I   6 han takon] taken Eˢ   7 habunde] w *canc.* habunde D   8 growyng] growyn T   of] ⌜of⌝ βX   9 to] of T   10 his¹] and his O   his²] þis I   11 þing] þingis B   who] who so B   seiþ] seie δZ   I byseche god] god I biseche E   12 by] þorow B, bi his H   13 his¹] *om.* G   by²] eke *canc.* by D   14 by poul herto] þerto bi poule I   herto] þerto Z   16 of . . . helle(25)] *om.* Z   sectis] newe sectis H   we] now T   teeld] of tolde α   17 lore] rewle and lore O   feynon] feyneden I   oþur] *om.* B   lawe] reule α   18 or] or ellis αE   euene] h- *canc.* euene Dβ, *om.*

aȝenys me.' And þus siþen þes newe rewlis letton þe rewle þat
20 Crist haþ ȝouen, þei ben rit contrarie þerto, and dyuydon fro
Cristis ordre; and þis dyuysion was som tyme clepud heresye of
wyse men. And so noon of þes wandruþ as cristene men moton
wandre, for siþ byfore þese foure camen in men wandredon þicke
and streyȝt to heuene, but for þe tyme siþen þei camen in haþ be
25 here hate and weye to helle.

But Poul seiþ to cristene men þat *þei wyton whate comaundementis
he haþ ȝouen hem by oure Lord Iesu Crist*, and þei schulden be not
suspect, for þei sounnen not to propre wynnyng but to worschipe
of God, and to sauyng of mannys soul[e]. And þerfore seiþ Poul
30 here þat *þis is þe wille of God, ȝowre holynesse*, and þat stonduþ in
seruyse of God as he bidduþ. And blessud be such a Lord þat
bidduþ but profiȝt of his seruaunt, not profiȝt of hymself, but
oneste and liȝt þing to do. And soo *men schulden abstene hem fro
lecherie*, for þat is foul; and so eche cristene *man schulde kunne kepe his
35 vessel in holynesse*. Þe vessel of mannys soule is his body þat holduþ
hit, and, whonne þis vessel is holy, þe soule þerynne mot nedis be
hooly. Somme men vndurstonden heere þat Poul spekiþ to
weddude men þat mote nedis haue wyues to kepon hem fro
lecherie; so þat eche such mon kunne kepe þis vessel in holynesse,
40 gendre and ȝyue dette whon it is tyme, and trete his wyf as his
f.20 felow. We|reproue not þis wyt, for God is large in his lore. And
þanne men kepon þis vessel *in honour, and not in passion of* fleschly
desyr, as heþene men þat knowe not God, ne how he wole be serued in
clennesse. And clerkis spekon þus of passionys þat ben lustus
45 bysyde reson.

And bysyde þis lecherie is a synne among þe puple, þat is
pruyde and worldly coueytise, þat fouluþ here monye men. Þer

P   19 siþen] seyen T   rewle] reulis δ   20 dyuydon] diuidide α   21 þis]
þus β   som tyme clepud] *rev*. BH, sum time callede α   23 siþ byfore] *rev*. T,
before α, seiþ *canc*. siþ bifore β   wandredon] wandren βEH   24 for] fro
BαδG   be here] *rev*. α   26 comaundementis] comaundement G   27
schulden] schulen δJ   be not] *rev*. OδIZH, ⌐not⌐ be E   28 to¹] *om*. OαδE-
IJ   29 to] *om*. T   soule] soulis DX   30 þis] ⌐þis⌐ H, *om*. δJ   ȝowre] as
he bydduþ *canc*. ȝowre D   and] *om*. G   þat²] in þat B   32 but¹] ⌐nouȝt⌐ but
P   of ¹] to PIZ   seruaunt] seruauntz I   33 þing] *subpuncted* DX, ⌐þyng⌐
TH, *om*. YδJG   34 for] *om*. PZ   35 mannys] a mannis ABβEX   his] þo
αE   37 to] he *canc*. to E, here to α, of G   39 such mon] man O   þis] his
EGH   42 fleschly] freschly T   43 knowe] knewen δ   he] *om*. E   wole] wolde
altered to wole δ, wolde AJ   44 passionys] þes passiouns PZ   45 reson] *om*.
Z   47 fouluþ] foleweþ I   48 monye] many men T   lyue] *om*.

ben ful monye here on lyue þat be not payed wiþ þer staat, but
gon by pruyde aboue þer breþren; and of þis comeþ fi3tyng and
strif. And monye men ben coueytouse, and bygylon þer breþren 50
in chaffaryng, and comen abowton hem monye weyus to bygylon
hem of þer goodis. And boþe þes two forfenduþ Poul and bydduþ
þat *noon go abouen* by pruyde, *ne þus go abowte his broþur, for God wole
venge of alle þes*. For þes ben pruyde and coueytise þat qwenchen
mekenesse and charite, *as Poul haþ seyd ofte byfore and wytnessud* by 55
Godus lawe. And þes two synnes ben ful comune and nedful to
warne folc of. For who wolde by good reson þat ony man seruyde
hym þus? And so God mot nedis venge hym of men þat brekon
þus hys heeste. And, *for God haþ not clepid us to vnclennesse but
hoolynes*, men þat seruon hym þus falsly moton nedis be puny- 60
schede for þer falsenesse. It ys foul to be a lechour, and foul to
dispuse þi broþur, and foul to bygyle hym in worldly goodis þat
ben drit.

 And þus, he þat dispuysuþ þis lore, *he dispuysuþ not al only man, but
God þat 3af his hooly spiri3t in his apostlis*, for his goodnesse and for 65
loue of his chyrche. And þus wonne men heron Godus word, þei
schulde not loke to þer broþur but to God and his wordis, and
worschipe hem for Godus sake. And wolde God þat men tokon
heed to speche of Poul in þis plase, to holde vertuwis and fle
heresyes, for boþe ben nedful to men. Þanne men schulden here 70
Godis word gladly, and dispuyse fablis, and erre not in þis sacrud
oost but graunte þat it is two þingis, boþe bred and Godus body,
but principally Godus body. Certis he þat dispuysuþ þe
prechour, whanne he prechuþ Godus wordus, dispuysiþ boþe
God and man, but moste to charge þe godhede. And þus men þat 75
dispuyson þis lore of þis hooly sacrament dispuyson God, and
seyn he is fals, and þis is a foul blasfemye.

O   payed] apaied G   wiþ] of P   49 aboue] aboute I   50 and²] þat
B   51 monye] in many I   to bygylon] and gyles Z   52 þes] *om.* O   53
noon] no man α   abouen] aboute Yβ   54 of] *om.* ATE   pruyde] proude
OT   coueytise] coueytouse O   57 folc] þe folk T, men αEH   58 so] þus
G   god mot nedis] mut nedis god B, moot god nedis G   59 heeste] heestis E,
biheste I   clepid] called αZ   60 hoolynes] to hoolynesse AEGH, ⌐in⌐ hoolynesse
T   61 it] but it B   62 dispuse] disple Y   broþur] briþeren H   hym]
hem H   in] of α   63 drit] but dryt O   64 dispuysuþ¹] dyspeysiþ not
O   þis] his AT   al] *om.* O   66 men] ⌐þei⌐ α   67 wordis] word
T   69 speche] -che *on eras corr.* D, speke Oβl   70 nedful] neful β   men
schulden] *rev.* α   71 þis] þe BOPTYαβδEIJZG, *om.* H   73 certis] and certis
ABJ   75 þe] *om.* T   76 þis¹] þe B   þis hooly] þe H   77 he] þat he AOG

Dominica iii Quadragesime. [Epistola.]
Sermo 1 [8].

Estote imitatores Dei. Ad Ephesios 5.

Poul bydduþ in þis epistle þat men schulden be Godis children,
and suwe Crist in maner of lif as derworþe children of hym. And
here men schulden take as byleue þat eche mon here olyue is
holdon for to suwe Crist vp peyne of dampnyng in helle. For, ȝif a
man wole be sauyd, he mot nedis be Godus child; and ȝif a man
be Godus child, þanne he suweþ God in maneris, and þis
childhede is þe derrurste þat may here falle to men. Somme men
ben here mennys children, þat þei louon for þer þewis; and þis
child|hede is dere ȝif it be growndud in vertuwis. Somme men ben
mennys children, for þei camen of þer kynde; and þis childhede is
betture, ȝif vertuwis ben castude þerto. But somme men ben
children of God, for þei lyuon parfiȝtly in vertuwis and louon
Godis lawe to þer ende; and þes ben þe derrerste children. And
herfore bidduþ Poul here þat *we schulen be folweris of God, as moste*
derworþe children. And blynde men stondon here a ȝeyn whon men
aleggen Cristus dedis and his lif and his wordis, and seyn 'lo! þis
heretik wolde ben euene wiþ Crist – but no mon may be so'. Here
þes foolis schulden wyte þat it is al dyuers to folwe Crist in maner
of lyuyng, and to be euene wiþ hym; eche man schulde desyre þe
furste, but no cristene man þe secounde. And so eche cristene

MSS: D; ABEGHIJOPTXYZαβδ; Hᵗ *inc.* 38 his lif, *not collatable* 78 for *to end.*

Sermo 18] þe ⌈xviii⌉ seuentenþe *canc.* sermoun Y, sermo 19 DPβ , sermo A, *om.*
BOTαδEIJXZGH   estote . . . dei] *om.* Y   estote] estote se T   dei] mei P, dei
sicut filii karissimi T, mei *canc.* dei E   ad eph. 5] effec' ij A, eph. E, *om.* O   1
schulden] schuld, d *canc.* α, schulen YβXZ   godis] gode β   2 crist] him Z   4
for to] to AEH   vp] vpon AGH, on Z   in] of Z   5 mot] most I   7 þe]
om. E   here falle] *rev.* ATδEIJGH   men¹] man IH   8 mennys] sum
mennus O, mannus EI   9 men] *om.* T   10 camen] come OTZGH   11
castude] caste H, chasid I   men] men *canc.* βX, *om.* APTYδJG   14 herfore]
þerfore αZGH   schulen] schulden TYαEIH   15 and] bot Z   16 aleggen]
leggen G   17 wolde] wole Yδ   euene] *om.* O   so] so euene O   *margin*
loke wel D   18 folwe] sue E   19 desyre] coueyte E   20 cristene¹] *om.*

man schulde take skyle of lif, of werkis and wordis of Crist, and
þeraftur suwe hym oþur nerre or furre. For, ȝif he reuerse Crist in
þis, he goþ streyȝt þe weyȝe to helle. And men may see by þis
skyle þat þis is excusyng in synne.

And þerfore seiþ Poule aftur þat *we schulden wandre in loue, but as*   25
Crist haþ loued us. Þer ben þre louys of man: fleschly loue, and
worldly loue, and þe þridde is heuenly loue; and by þis loue Crist
louede us, and by ensaumple of þis loue eche mon schulde loue his
broþur. And herfore seiþ Crist by Iohn 'a new maundement I
ȝyue ȝow, þat ȝe loue ȝow togydere, riȝt as I haue louyd ȝow'.   30
Crist ȝaf hymself for us, boþe offryng and oost vnto God, þat is his fadir,
into smellyng of swetnesse. It is knowon by byleue how mankynde
trespasude to God, and how by Godis riȝtwisnesse þat trespas
moste nedis be punysched, and how it myȝte not be punysched to
sauyng of mannys kynde, but ȝif Crist, boþe God and mon, hadde   35
offred hymself vpon þe tre; and þis offryng was sacrifise, maad to
God for oure goode. And herfore seiþ Crist by Iohn þat 'no mon
haþ more loue þan þis, to putte his lif for hyse breþren'. And þus
Crist is of most loue. We schulden suwe Crist afer in þis loue by
oure power, and offre oure body to þe Fadur of heuene for loue   40
and profiȝt of oure neyȝebore. And siþ eche man schulde serue
God, boþe by body and by soule, eche man schulde suwe here
Crist by trewe seruyse to God. And siþ þis martirdom of Crist was
so swete byfore God, Poul clepuþ it wittyly 'sich an offryng to
God into smellyng of swetnesse'; for dedis þat pleson to God   45
moten smelle wel byfore God. And here seyn monye men þat men

---

29 John 13: 34; **37** John 15: 13.

E   þe] schulde take ⌜þe⌝ T   21 skyle] ⌜sampul⌝ T   werkis] wordis AδEJ,
werk I   and¹] of O, ⌜and⌝ of α, and of EH   wordis] werkes AδEJ   22 oþur]
or TYαIH   furre] ferþer BOEIGH   23 men] ⌜so⌝ men H, so men α   25
þerfore] herfore E   26 þer . . . us (28)] om. I   þre louys] margin corr. nota þre
maneris loue of man D   louys] louyngis H   27 loue³] om. O   28
ensaumple] þe ensample H   loue²] om. O   29 herfore] þerfore ABYα   30
ȝow¹] to ȝou BYδH   ȝow²] om. BOH   31 and] an α   vnto] to I   þat]
for vs þat O   33 godis] gode I   riȝtwisnesse] riȝtfulnesse H   34 moste] mut
ABαEH   and . . . punysched²] om. α   35 mannys kynde] mankynde PEIZ-
GH   36 vpon] on H   þe] om. βE   sacrifise maad] rev. B   37 herfore]
þerfore αZG, here I   38 þis] þat O   hyse] om. I   39 of] om. T   we] and
we H   schulden] shulen δEJ   afer] aftir O   42 suwe here] rev. β   here]
om. B   44 so] om. E   clepuþ] calles αZ   it] om. OI   wittyly] witly
A   to] bifore A   46 seyn] seen I   47 cause] causis GH   48 fend] fend of

slayne in worldly cause ben but stynkynge martiris, and offryngis
to þe fend.

   And herof concluduþ Poul þat sixe synnes schulden be fled, as
50 ys *fornycacion, and al vnclennesse* of man, *or auarice*, synne of þe world
*be not nemyd in ʒow, as it semeþ hoolye men; or filþe or foly speche or
harlotrie, þat pertenyþ not to þing* of blisse. *But more vse ʒe ʒoure*
f.21 speche|clenely in *þankyng of God. For wyte ʒe þis and vndurstondeþ* as
byleue of cristene men *þat vche lechour or vnclene man or auerous man
55 þat serueþ to mawmetis haþ noon heritage in þe rewme of Crist,* þat is
boþe *God* and mon. Siþ eche mon makuþ þat his god þat he loueþ
mooste of alle, and an auerous mon loueþ more worldly goodis
þan he loueþ God, siþ he leeueþ riʒtwisnesse for loue of suche
worldly goodis, it is knowon þat he is fals and owt of riʒt byleue of
60 God; for he makiþ suche goodis his mawmete whiche moten nedis
be false goddis. And þus it is of oþre synnes þat men fa[l]lon ofte
inne. In þe furste fleschly synne ben monye spisis, as men
knowon; and Poul vndurstonduþ hem alle by vnclennesse, as
somme men seyn. Oþre men seyn wel ynow þat Poul telluþ þes
65 þre synnes fleschly synne, and synne of þe feend, and synne of þe
world, as alle synnes. For, al ʒif alle synnes ben vnclene, ʒeet þes
þre synnes of þe feend, pruyde, enuye and yre, þer sustir, maken
men more lik to þe feend; and by þis prente of þe feend þei ben
more foule byfore God.

70   Poul bidduþ here to trewe men þat *no mon bygyle hem* in byleue
by veyne wordis whiche þei spekon, þat þes be none synnes or lyʒte –
as lecherye is kyndely as þei seyn, and man schulde kyndely haue
loue of his owne excellense, siþ þat God haþ ʒouen it hym, and
God haþ ʒouen þis world to man to serue hym by help þerof.

helle δ   49 herof] þerfore Z, herfore H   sixe] siche sixe β   synnes] synne
β   50 al] *om.* B   man] a man H   51 nemyd] neuynde αZ   hoolye] in
holy AG, to holy Y   53 þankyng] þankyngʳisⁱ A   54 vche] ilke a α   or²
. . . man²] *om.* O   56 mon²] *om.* O   his] is O   57 auerous] a/auerous
D   59 he] it I   is²] *om.* O   60 for] *om.* O   goodis] gode α   maw-
mete] mawmetis AI   61 goddis] goodis δ   oþre] þer β   fallon] faylon
Dβ   ofte] ofte tyme T   64 seyn¹] s/seyn D, seen AG   oþre . . . seyn²] *om.*
O, *margin* T   seyn²] seen A   65 synne³] þe synne I   67 enuye] and enuye
EH   sustir] sustren IZ, aftur α   68 men] man APTYδJXZ, a man α, *om.*
I   more] *om.* G   to] *om.* E   and . . . feend²] *om.* α   prente] prute
O   þei] and þai α   70 poul] as poul β   here] *om.* Y   71 lyʒte] liʒte
synnes Z   72 man] a *altered from* o D, mankynde A, men I, no man G   schulde]
om. A   haue] haþ, -þ *on eras. corr.* A   73 loue] his loue H   þat] *om.*
TZ   haþ ʒouen] ʒeuiþ T   hym] to hym B   74 man] a *altered from* o

Syche veyn wordis þat excuson synne don myche harm among 75
men; as Adam and Eue weron bygylude by veyn speche of þe
serpent, and soo weron monye oþre aftur, vnbyleuynge trewþe of
Godus lawe. For, ȝif we taken heed to *yre of God*, oþur in þe oolde
lawe or in þe newe, it *cam by synne* þat was browt in by suche false
and gylynge wordis. *And perfore schulden ȝe not wille to be maad* 80
parteneris of hem, neþur spekyng þus ne trowyng, ne norschynge
such false speche. *For ȝe weron somtyme derknessis, but now ȝe ben liȝt*
in þe Lord. Men þat ben encombrud in synne ben maad derke and
blynde wiþ synne; but men þat ben in liȝt of grace knowen synne
as motis in sonne bemys. And þerfore *wandre ȝe as children of lyȝt* in 85
clennesse. *Þe fruyt of liȝt stonduþ* in þes þre: *in alle* maner of *goodnesse*
and rytwisnesse and trewþe. Þes þre wordis þat ben acordynge to þe
Hooly Trinnyte wolon make a man vertuous, and fleynge þre
maner of synnys.

D   77 oþre] *om.* Z   trewþe] to þe treuþe B   78 yre of god] goddis ire
I   yre] þe ire BT   oþur] or AδIJ   þe] *om.* AαδJ   79 or] oþer
O   80 gylynge] bygylynge OI   schulden] shulen β   wille] wilne BPZH,
om. I   to] *om.* I   maad] *om.* O   81 parteneris] perceyueris AI   ne¹]
nor B, *om.* β   trowyng] *om.* β   norschynge] norische E, murchinge I   82
speche] spechis T   derknessis] derknes BαH, in derknesse I   83 lord] worlde
α   encombrud] cumberid Z   in²] wiþ αEH   84 blynde] blyndid
H   wiþ] ⌈wiþ⌉ J, *om.* O, in αδ, by E   in] *om.* β   85 motis] mote
α   sonne] þe sunne ATG   and] *om.* I   86 stonduþ] *om.* O   87 and¹]
and in al manere of I   rytwisnesse] riȝtnesse I   þre] *om.* T   to] wiþ
H   þe] *om.* β   88 hooly] *om.* YE   þre] þe thre Z   89 maner] maners
A   of] *om.* E

Dominica iiij Quadragesime. [Epistola.]
Sermo [19].

Scriptum est quoniam Abraham. Galatas 4.

Poul telluþ in þis epistle of fredom of cristene men, how þei han
here ernes þerof, and fully fredom in heuene. And þus wole Poule
in tyme of grace þat cristene men be more free þan fadris weron in
þe oolde lawe, by fredom þat Crist haþ ȝouen. Poul seiþ þat *it is*
5 *wryton* in þe furste book of Godus lawe *þat Abraham hadde two sonys,*
Ismael and Ysaac; *Ismael was of his hondmaydon,* þe whiche was
f.21v clepud Agar, *and Ysaac of|his weddud wif,* þe whiche was clepud
Sara. *But þe furste þat was born of þe seruaunt was born bi þe flesch, þe*
topur born of þe free wif was born by byheste of God. Þe furste booc of
10 Godus lawe telluþ how Abraham in his myddul age gat Ysmael
his sone, whan he hadde kyndely strengþe; but whanne boþe he
and his wif weron passud þe tyme of childer getyng, God byhyȝte
hem Ysaac, and telde what schulde worþe of hym. And þes tuo
children of Abraham bytoknen two lawis of God, and two
15 children [þat] God haþ: þe furste child schal be dampned, and þe
secounde schal be sauyd. And so men seyn comunly þat hooly
writ haþ foure wittis: þe furste wit is of story, or euene as þe wordis
schulden toknen; þe secounde wit is allegoric, þat figureþ þing
þat men schulden trowe, as þes two sonys of Abraham figuren þes

5 Gen. 16: 15; 21: 1–13.

MSS: D; ABEGHIJOPTXYZαβδ; *for A's erroneous copy of 4–21 in set 1 see p.* 22

Sermo 19] sermo 20 Dβ, sermo 10 P, *om.* ABOTαδEIJXZGH   scriptum . . .
abraham] *om.* Y   quoniam] enim quoniam AT   abraham] abraham duos filios
habuit OTH   gal. 4] gal. 5 β, gal. x E, *om.* O   2 here] þer A, *om.* B   þerof]
here AB   in²] þerof *canc.* in D   wole poule] *rev.* I, wald paul Z   3 þan] a
altered from o D   5 godus lawe] holdy writte α   6 his] þe A   7 clepud¹]
called αZ   of] was of BG   weddud] weddid *canc.* ⌐fre⌐ *corr.* H, fre *on eras. of longer*
X, free BOPTYαβδEIJZ   clepud²] called αZ   8 of] by T   þe²] his
B   bi] of H   flesch] fleisches δ   þe⁴] *om.* I   9 free] *om.* E   by] bi þe
BG, bi *canc.* β   byheste] heest TδI, biheestis Z   11 strengþe] his strengþe
EH   boþe] *om.* TI   12 childer] child A   byhyȝte] hiȝte I   13 hem]
hym β   15 þat] *om.* D, ⌐þat⌐ X   schal] schild *canc.* schal D   and] *om.*
ATEI   17 story] þe storye ABOTEH   or] ⌐or⌐ E, *om.* T   18 schulden]

two þingis; þe þridde wit is tropologic, þat bytokneþ wit of   20
vertuwis; þe fourþe wit is anagogic, þat bytokneþ þing to hope in
blis. Poul swiþ here þe secounde wit, and he hadde auctorite
þerto. *þes two* sonys *ben two testamentis* in figure, as God spekuþ ofte.
Þe furste sone is þe oolde lawe: *þe furste* lawe *was in þe hul of Syna,
and gendreþ men into seruage, and þis is Agar* in figure (*Syna is an hul in*   25
Arabye þat is ioyned to Ierusalem here), and þe chirche þat is here
serueþ in þraldam *wiþ hyre children. But þat Ierusalem þat is aboue,*
þat is þe chirche þat haþ ouercomen, *sche is fre and sche is oure*
modir, for Crist oure hed is þere wiþ hire.
   Poul as a good doctour feyneþ no fable by mannys wit, but he   30
seiþ þat it is writon in þe lawe of oure byleue. And wolde God þat
þes prechouris woldon so do in oure dayes, til men cowden Godys
lawe, and lyuedon aftir þis bileue. And somme men han muche
counfort in þis trewþe þat is þus wryton, for þei wyton it may not
be fals, but mot nedis be fulfullid of God. And herfore þei ben   35
pacient and ioyefulle in þer turmentyng. And þus seiþ Poul to þe
Romaynys 'alle þingus þat ben wrytone', and algatis in Godus
lawe, 'þei ben writone to oure lore', and specially for þes two
endis: þat we kepe pacience and be in counfort of hooly wryt.
And þis byleue þat we trowon, þat Godus ordenaunce mot nedis   40
stonde and al oþur ordenaunce mot nedis be qwenched at þe
laste, counfortuþ monye cr[i]stene men to stonde by Godus
ordenaunce. For nedis þis ordenaunce mot be hooly and at þe
laste ouercome alle oþre; and he þat stonduþ for Godus lawe þus
in clene charite heere may be enporud and pursuwed in worldly   45
goodis and in his body, but he may not wante mede þat passuþ al

---

37 Rom. 15: 4.

schulen Y   toknen] bitokene BαH   21 þing] witt G   22 swiþ] -wiþ *on eras.*
corr. D, seiþ AB   and] for Z   23 god] crist E   24 is] was E   hul] mount
E   25 gendreþ] gederide A, gendride BαEZ   into] to O   26 ierusalem
. . . chir-] *on eras. corr.* D   27 þraldam] þral G   28 haþ] is I   30 a] *om.*
βIGH   he seiþ] it is seid I   31 þat¹] *om.* BPZ   32 þes] oure δ, *om.* Z   so
do] *rev.* ABOPTYαδEIJXZGH   cowden] knowe O, knoweden I, knewen
H   33 and . . . turmentyng (36)] *om.* Z   men] *om.* E   35 herfore] þerfore
α   36 ioyefulle] ioyinge I   turmentyng] torment I   37 alle] þat alle
E   and] *om.* I   38 lawe] lore O   for] to T   39 in] *om.* βG   coun-
fort] counfortid G   of] in G   40 and . . . riȝte (50)] *om.* Z   nedis] nedis
euer E   41 ordenaunce] ordinauncis B   42 confortuþ] hyt counfortiþ T   cri-
stene] crstene D   by godus] for cristes *canc.* by cristes α   43 ordenaunce²] ordy/
Y   44 for] in *canc.* ⌜for⌝ G, in I   45 enporud and pursuwed] enpouered and
pursuwed I, pursuyd and enporid E   47 and²] *om.* A   good is] godis beþ

þis harm and peyne. And siþ worldly good is but luytul, and þis lif is schort and peyneful, it were a wys chaung[e] to man to suffre þus for þe betture. And þus he is traytor and coward þat dar not

50 telle Godus riȝte for drede of los of wo[r]ldly|goodis, or for los of his body.

And for þis þraldam þat falluþ boþe to men of þe oolde lawe and to men þat schulen be dampnyde, *it is wryton* þus in Ysaye '*be glad þow* chirche of heþene men, þat now art *bareyne* of goostly
55 children, and bryngist but fewe children to heuene, for þe spouse of hooly chyrche is not ȝet ioyned to þe', by grace þat Crist schal ȝyue, whon he schal clepe heþene men. For tyme schal come þat þis chirche, þat is now bareyne of children of God, schal haue moo gostly children þan þe chirche of Iewis þat now haþ spouse. And
60 for ioye of þis byleue '*þow schuldust berste owt and crye.*' And þus Poul aleggeþ to Romaynes monye prophecies of þis. But Poul descenduþ to þis figure, and seiþ in þis tyme of grace *we ben children of byheste, as Ysaac* was Abrahammys sone. And so we ben children of þe free modyr, and schulden be tretude now as fre.
65 But riȝt as þe sone of Abraham þat was first born, *fleschly pursuwede hys goostly sone,* þat was born *spiritually, so it falluþ now* on dayus of men þat God haþ ordeyned to peyne, and men þat he haþ ordeyned to blis, and men of þe oolde lawe and of þe newe. *But what seiþ hooly writ? Caste owt þe handmayden and hire sone.* So we
70 schulde caste owt now cerymonyes of þe oolde lawe; for, as *þe child of þe handmayden was not eyr wiþ child of þe fre* wyf, so kepyng of þes cerymonyes schulde not laste wiþ þe blis of heuene. And in tyme of þis fredom, þat is nyȝ to þat fully fredom, schulde not þe chirche be bounden wiþ þat þraldam as it was furst, and specially

---

53 Isa. 54: 1; **61** Rom. 9: 6–13.

O þis²] his P　　48 schort] bot schort αEI　　chaunge] chaungh D, þing *canc.*
┌chayng┐ T　　50 for drede of] and noȝt for to lette for Z　　worldly] woldly
D　　goodis] good E　　or] or ellis E　　for²] of P, *om.* TZ　　51 his] *om.*
Z　　52 and] to tel goddis right and Z　　for] so for O　　þis] *om.*
Z　　þraldam] los Z　　53 schulen] scholden I　　54 now art] *rev.* B　　*margin*
Ys. 54 J　　56 is] is *canc.* /is D　　ȝet] ┌ȝet┐ T, *om.* α　　grace] þe grace
AOTYβδEIJXG　　57 clepe] calle αZ　　59 spouse] þe spouse H　　62 seiþ] seiþ
þat H　　64 tretude now] *rev.* O　　65 þe] *om.* I　　fleschly] and fleschly
DABOPTYαβEIJXZH　　66 now] *om.* I　　67 men²] of men E　　68 blis] blesse
O　　and¹] as Z　　of²] men *canc.* of D, of *canc.* X, ┌of┐, α, *om.* ABOPTYβδEJ-
Z　　69 writ] w *canc.* /writ D　　hand] bounde O　　71 hand] bonde
O　　child] þe child ABOYEIGH　　þe²] ┌þe┐ A, þe *canc.* X, *om.* βδJ　　72
not] *om.* G　　laste] last faste G　　þe] *om.* α　　73 to þat] þo E, þe tyme of
I　　fully] ful ABOPTYαβδEIJXZH　　75 it] þis T　　blisse] þe *canc.* blisse Y, þe

siþ it lettuþ to renne swiftly to blisse of heuene, as kyndely 75
mouyng is swift aȝenys his ende by help þerof.

And *so breþren* we schulden þenke þat *we be not children of Agar,
but* children *of þe fre* wif, *by whiche fredom Crist haþ maad us fre.* Lord!
fredam is myche coueytud, as men wyton kyndely, but more
schulde þis betture fredom be coueytud of cristene men. But it is 80
knowon þat anticrist haþ more þrallud now þe chirche þon it was
in þe oolde lawe, whon men myȝte not bere þat seruyse. And
anticrist makuþ now newe lawis, and grownduþ hem not on God
and mon; for mo cerymonyes be now browte in þan weron in þe
oolde lawe, and more taryon men to come to heuene, þan dydon 85
in þe oolde lawe tradicionys þat weron fowndone of scribis and
pharisees. And o rote of þis þraldam is lordshipe þat anticrist haþ,
for he chalangeþ to be ful lord, booþe goostly and temperal; and
so he tarieþ cristene men to serue Crist in his fredom, so þat
cristene men may seye, as þe poyete seiþ in his prouerbe, 'þe 90
frogg[e] seyde to þe harwe "Cursud be so monye lordis!" '. Now
cristene men ben cᴿhᴉullyd, now wiþ popis, and now wiþ
byschopis, now wiþ cardynalis of popis, and now wiþ prelatis
vndur byschopis; and now þei clowton her schon wiþ censuris, as
who schulde chulle a footbal. But certis Baptist was not worþi to 95
lo[o]wse þe þuoong of Cristus scho, and more an|ticrist haþ noo   f.22v
power to lette fredom þat Crist haþ browt. Crist ȝaf þis fredom to
men to come liȝtly to blisse of heuene; but anticrist chulluþ men
to ȝeelde hem to ȝyuen hym money. And so þis seruage is foul,
boþe for þis lord and his lawe; for it is foul to bere drit by þe 100
seruyse maad to fend, but euere þes ypocritis dredon þat Godis

95 Mark 1: 7; Luke 3: 16; John 1: 27.

blis BEI   as] and Z   77 þenke] wyte O   78 lord] for E   79 fredam] siþ
fredom A   kyndely] wel kyndely I   80 but . . . þus (106)] om. Z   81 now]
om. T   82 men] þei A   þat] þis α   83 grownduþ] groundid G   hem]
him A, hym *altered to* hem O   on] in O, of H   84 mo] many ᴿerᴉ T   85 more]
moo δ   heuene] þe blis of heuene E   87 o] oþer α   of] on α   88 he] om.
O   goostly] of goostli G   temperal] temperalich OTαδI   90 cristene] þe
cristen I   as] riȝt as B   his] his *canc.* X, om. ABOPTαβδIJ   91 frogge]
froggo D   now] for now I   92 chullyd] h *corr.* D, killid H   popis] þe popis
G   and] om. δE   93 popis] þe popes α   and] om. A   now²] om.
E   95 schulde chulle] schulleþ T, wolde choolle G   certis] om. E   96
loowse] -o- *corr.* D   þuoong] þongis βI   noo] no, -w *canc.* AE   97 fredom¹] þe
fredom AB   browt] bouȝt, bo- *on. eras. of.* bro- J, bouȝt BPYδEXGH   crist²]
and crist P   98 blisse] þe *canc.* blisse Y, þe blis BTI   99 hym] hem T   so] ᴿsoᴉ
T, om. Y   100 for¹] om. α   þis] his I   is] om. O   þe] om. αβE   101

lawe schulde be schewyd, and þei conuycte of falsehede, for God
and his lawe ben more strong. Þes ypocritis may for a tyme holde
men in þe feendys þraldam and feyne þat þei ʒyuon leeue to
105 synne, or gabbe on God þat is worse þat it is meedful to obesche
þus.

fend] þe fend BOPTαδEIJGH   euere] ouer I   102 falsehede] her falshed
G   104 men] om. α   þe] þese G, om. α   105 meedful] nedful
OG   obesche] obeie H

Dominica in Passione. [Epistola.] Sermo 2[o].

Christus assistens pontifex. Hebre 9.

Poul techeþ in þis epistle þe excellense þat Crist hadde ouer
byschopis of þe oolde lawe, al ȝif þei alle figuredon Crist; and þis
was pertynent to speke to Iewis þat knewon þe oolde lawe. Poul
bygynneþ and seiþ to hem þat *Crist was byschop* and nyȝ to God,
siþ he was boþe God and mon, and so was noon of þe oolde lawe.   5
And þus he passude in þre poyntis byschopus of þe oolde lawe.
Furst *he was byschop of godis of blis,* þe whiche godus ben hopud to
come; and þus seiþ Petre þat 'Crist is byschop of soulis', for he is
lord of hem. Byschopis of þe oolde lawe hadden bestis and dudon
som good, in þat þat þei figuredon Crist, and his passion, þat   10
bowte mankynde. Þe toþur excellense of Crist is þat his
tabernacle is betture þan weron alle þes tabernaclis þat weron in
þe oolde lawe, for Cristus tabernacle is þe word⌐le⌐. And Poul seiþ
þat *þis tabernacle is more large and more parfiȝt* þan was þe tabernacle
of Moyses, for þis was *not maad by man,* but maad of nowt by God   15
almyȝty; but Moyses tabernacle was maad and boron to greet
traueyle of prestis. Þe þridde excellense of Crist is þat his sacrifis
was betture, and maad more parfiȝtly þan sacrifise of oolde
byschopis. Bischopis of þe oolde lawe sacrifisedon *kydis blood, or
blod of geet or of caluys;* but Crist passude alle þuse figuris, *for Crist by*   20
his owne blood entrede onys into heuene. And þere *he fond euerelastynge*

8 1 Pet. 2: 25; **14** Exod. 25: 10 ff.

MSS: D; ABEGHIJOPTXYZαβδ

Sermo 20] sermo 21 Dβ, sermo 12 P, *om.* ABOTαδEIJXZGH   christus . . . ponti-
fex] *om.* Y   pontifex] pontifex futurorum bonorum T   hebre 9] *om.* O   1
poul . . . epistle] þis epistele telleþ I   techeþ] telleþ OTEH   þe] þat O   2
byschopis] oþere bisshopis H   þei alle] *rev.* G   and] as O   3 was] is
I   iewis] þe iewes TδH   6 of] in O   7 godis] þe godis EI   of²] *om.*
Y   8 is¹] was PZ   9 lawe] lawen H   hadden] kilden AB   and] þat
T   10 and] yn O   11 mankynde] mank/kynde D   þe toþur] þe oþer
O   12 weron¹] *om.* T   þes] þe Z, þo α   13 þe²] þis Y   wordle]-le *corr.*
D   16 and] *om.* I   17 sacrifis] sacrificis T   18 was] is *altered from* was A, is
B   parfiȝtly] perfite α   þan] bet *canc.* þan D   sacrifise] sacrifisi⌐s⌐ X,
sacrifisis BOTαβEIGH   oolde] þe olde BEIGH   19 þe] *om.* H   or] and
E   20 crist² . . . fond (21)] *om.* O   21 euerelastynge] lastynge O   22

byggyng þat noon oþur byschop my3te come to, and so he entride onys for euere to heuene, þe innere part of þis temple. But bischopis of þe oolde lawe weron nedide to entre 3eer by 3eer,
25 and 3et þei entrede not into heuene, but into a lytul holet, þat was þe west part of þe tabernacle; and, al 3if þis figurede heuene, 3et mannys blisse was not þerynne. But entryng of Crist to heuene, into a plase more hooly and large, was into þe same place where is blis wiþowton ende. And þus siþ Crist is God of heuene, and his
30 manhede in so ny3 God, oure bischop Crist in alle þese þingus mot nedis passe alle oþre byschopis; for, as þis lord may reche ferrere, so he is nerrere and graciousere. And, but by vertu of þis bischop, my3te neuere byschop do good to man. And þus
f.23 dignytes and pryuylegies þat ben now graun|tude by þe pope, but
35 3if Crist conferme hem furst, ben not worþ a fly3e foot. And so it semeþ to somme men þat bischopis of þe oolde lawe weron betture and more worþi þan ben þes emperouris bischopis, for þei seruydon and figuredon Crist by auctorite of God; but þes emperour byschopis now seruon and figuron anticrist, and þer
40 auctorite is takon of þe moste feend a3enys Crist. And þus þei seyn þat þe pope is heed viker of þis feend; but alle þe feendis and alle þe byschopis moten haue þer beyng of Crist, and moton serue to hym, oþer wel, or yuele a3en þer wylle; for oþur þei ben dampnede in helle wiþ þe hey3erste anticrist, or ellis þei ben
45 blissud in heuene by oure bischop Iesu Crist.

And afturward proueþ Poul by a prynciple of byleue þe sufficience of Cristis biggyng, by þat þat he is God and man. For, 3if Crist be verey man, he is a part of al mankynde, and so þis greete man haþ maad aseþ by Crist, for þat þat he synnede in
50 Adam. And þus seiþ Poul to his breþren þat, *3if blod of kydis or*

byggyng] bigynnyng I   he] sche I   23 innere] endre α   24 þe] *om.*
O   25 þei]*om.* B   entrede] entre αZ   26 þe¹] in þe PEZ   27 þerynne]
hereynne I   to] into BTYαδE   28 into¹] in G   large] more large I   is
blis] *rev.* Z   29 siþ] seiþ O   of] in T   30 god] to god Z   crist] god
O   alle] *om.* α   31 reche] teche A   32 ferrere] ferþer ABTEJGH, fer
I   so] as so O   graciousere] graciouse PZ   and²] *om.* H   33
and . . . crist (45)] *om.* Z   34 by] of α   35 ben] þey ben TGH   worþ]
worþy OPG   fly3e] flee βI   fly3e foot] *eras.* J   37 for] now *canc.* for D, ⌐now⌐
for T   38 þes] þe T   39 and figuron] in figure P   and²] and ⌐for þey seruide
and figuride crist by auctorite of god⌐ *corr.* T   40 þei] þe I   41 þis] þo
α   feendis] bisschopis I   and alle] *on. eras. corr.* D   and] *om.* β   42 þe] *om.*
TH   byschopis] fendis I   moten] *om.* I   44 þe] *om.* H   46 byleue] oure
beleue α   47 cristis] crist I   by þat] bi bileeue *canc.*/ bi G   þat þat] þat
OTI   god] boþe god IH   48 so] *om.* O   49 þat þat] þat EH   50 kydis

bolis, and poudur of a calf þat is scaterud, makiþ men hooly þat weron
fowlude as anemptis fleschly clensyng, how myche more Cristis blod þat
offerude hymself by þe Hooly Goost wiþowton wem to God þe Fadyr schal
clenson owt owre conscience fro deede werkis to serue lyuynge God. Þis
reson þat Poul makiþ ys ny3 byleue þat men moton haue. Þer ben   55
þre clensyngis, bodily, and goostly, and o clensyng of þes two, as
was clensyng of þe oolde lawe; for þis bodyly clensyng of þes
figuris of þe oolde lawe clensude not goostly but in figure, for oþur
clensyng were betture by watur. And so it figurede Cristis blood
and his herte þat was brend by loue. And þis halwyng þat laste   60
was figured mot nedis be betture þan his figure, as fuyr is betture
þan is smoke, and man is betture þan ⌜h⌝is ymage. And so, siþ
Crist is God and man, satisfaccion for þis synne þat he made þus
freely is betture þan ony oþur þat man or aungel my3te make. Þe
same man in nowmbre þat synnede by Adam oure furste fadyr,   65
þe same man in nowmbre maade asseþ by þe secounde Adam
Crist. And siþ he is more of vertu þan þe furste Adam my3te be,
and his peyne was myche more þan synful lust of þe furste Adam,
who schulde haue conscience here þat ne þis synne is clensud al
owt? And, siþ oure Iesu is verey God þat neuere may for3ete þis   70
mede, he is sufficient medycyne for alle synneris þat ben contrite;
for Crist ys euere and euerywere, and in alle suche soulis by grace,
and so he clensuþ more clenely þan ony body or figure may
clense. And herfore as Poul seiþ, *Crist is mediatur* of þe newe lawe,
for Crist haþ of boþe þes two, for he is God, auctour of þes boþe;   75
and knyttuþ þe ton wiþ þe toþur *þat by his deþ fallynge bytwixe, in*
byghgyng of þe furste trespassis þat weron doon in þe oolde lawe, þes men
take byheste a3en, þat ben clepude of aylastyng heritage. And al þis

---

67 1 Cor. 15: 22.

---

or bolis] bolis or kydis DAXH   or] or of E   51 a] *om.* Oβ   þat is] þus
α   scaterud] sacrid Y   makiþ] makyd α   52 as] *om.* IG   54 owt] *om.*
Z   56 of] is of B   59 by] in E   so] *om.* Y   60 by loue] byleue
T   laste was] *rev. δ*   61 þan] þan was E   fuyr] þe fyr I   62 is¹] hys αEJ,
om. OI   his] h *corr.* D, is *canc.* his A, ⌜h⌝ys T, is Z   ymage] ymage ys T   63
god] boþe god H   þus] þis O   64 ony] *om.* A   þat] *om.* β   68 and] iŋ
β   was] is T   myche] *om.* YZ   70 for3ete] forfete T   71 he is] his
H   72 euerywere] oueral where α, euer aywhare Z   73 so] *om.* Y   or] of
Oα   74 herfore] þerfore αZ, *om.* Y   poul seiþ] seiþ seynt poul E   mediatur]
a mediatour Yδ   75 god] good DG   auctour] and auctor E   76 knyttuþ]
knyt it B   in] and α   77 byghgyng] *1 st* y *altered from* u D, biyngis H   of] *om.*
I   þe¹] þes H   trespassis] -ssis *on eras. corr.* D, trespas Aα   78 aylastyng]

marchaundyse was don in Crist Iesu, oure alþer Lord. We takon
f.23v 80 here as byleue þat Iesu Crist þat chaffarude þus is eche|God þat
may be, and so þe same God þat maade man, and aftir bowte
man to blis þat he ordeynede byfore to man. But muse we not
wheþur alle þes men, and only þes, schulen be sauyde þat God
wolde haue maad here, stondyng in innocense wiþowte synne. It
85 is ynow to us to trowe þat as monye of þe same kynde schulen now
come to heuene as schulden haue come, ȝif no synne hadde be.
And more medycyn wiþ more blis falluþ now to man ⌐by
occasion of synne, þanne schulde haue fallen to man,¬ ȝif neuere
synne were don of man. And þus it is betture to mankynde, and to
90 profiȝt of þe world, þat man hadde synned, and þus were bowt,
þan ȝif man hadde neuere synned. And so men takon as byleue
þat alle þinge þat God haþ ordeyned mot nedis comen in his
tyme, aftir þat forme þat God haþ schapon.

euerlastynge OTE   and] om. I   al] om. α   79 crist iesu] rev. Y   80 god]
good I   81 þat maade] and α   aftir] afturward α   bowte] he bouȝte T,
brouȝt δ   82 we] om. α   83 wheþur] we for α   schulen] shulden
ATEI   þat god] om. B   84 wolde] wole AG   in] om. PTYαβδEIJZ-
H   85 schulen] shulden, -d- altered from -l- A, schulde EI   87 by . . . man (88)]
margin s. h. D, twice δ   90 hadde] om. A   92 in] to β   93 þat¹] þe BYH

Dominica in Ramis Palmarum. [Epistola.]
Sermo 2[1].

Hoc sentite in uobis. Philipenses 2.

Poul telliþ in þis epistel how þat men schulde suwe Crist, and
algatis in mekenesse þat is grownd of oþre vertuwis.
He bidduþ
þat ȝe schulden fele þat in ȝow þat is and was in Crist Iesu, not only þe
kynde of mekenesse but al þe flood by som part. Þe spryng of þis
mekenesse and þe welle was in Crist Iesu, and by takyng part   5
þerof alle Cristis children moten be meke. And so þis schewiþ
here more specially þan kynde of mekenesse, for it schewiþ al
mekenesse of men, wiþ grownd þat was in Crist. And so putte
þow awey false mekenesse, as is in ypocritis, and constreyned
mekenesse, as is in þeuys and prysoneris, and take þe vertu of   10
mekenesse þat haþ ground in Iesu Crist. And, haue þow neuere
so luytul þerof, þow mayt fele þat þat was in Iesu.

And it helpuþ myche to men to þenke how Crist was in forme of
God, for he is verey God in godhede. And þis godhede is forme of
godhede, for þat is a forme of þing of whom þat þing haþ a name,   15
as of manhede man is man, and of whitnesse a þing ys whit. And
so, siþ godhede may not falle to a þing byfore in kynde, þis
godhede mot nedis be God; and so o persone þat haþ þis forme.
And þus Poul seiþ in a maner þat Iesu Crist is verey God. And so
Crist feynede not by arbitracion of raueyne þat he was euene wiþ God, siþ   20

Sermo 21] sermo 22 Dβ, om. ABOTαδEIJXZG   hoc . . . uobis] om. Y   in] de
I   uobis] vobis quod in Christo Iesu T   philip. 2] om. O   1 in þis epistel]
om. A   2 grownd] gro canc./grownd D   he] and he δJ   3 þat³] om.
I   crist iesu] rev. AαE   4 flood] foold Y   þis] ⌐þis¬ E, om. O   5 and¹]
þat α   welle] wille β   in] om. Y   crist iesu] iesu crist, marked for rev. Y, rev. α,
⌐crist¬iesu G   part] om. I   6 cristis] cristene Bα   and . . . mekenesse (7)]
om. E   7 specially] spiritually I   þan kynde] þonkynge O   8 of] of of
D   10 is] om. B   11 mekenesse] on eras. corr. D   ground in] on eras. corr.
D   12 luytul] sutil β   þow] þat þou E   þat þat] þat Bα   13 and] om.
G   men] man E   how] how þat α   15 godhede] -hede lightly subpuncted D,
god⌐hed¬Y   a¹] al Y   16 man¹] om. I   of²] so T   a] of a T   ys] om.
B   18 so] om. Y   19 poul seiþ] rev. B   crist] om. AJ   23 þey] om.

he was þe same God. Þe furste aungel Lucifer feynede by false
arbitracion þat he was lich to God; and so don men þat synnen
here, for þei ben inobedient, as þey þei hadden no God aboue
hem. But for Crist mY̆ȝte not bugghe mon only by his godhede,
25 (for he muste make hym þat kynde þat synnede in oure furste
fadyr, so þat þe same þing make asseþ, whiche þing synnede of
man), þerfore seiþ Poul heere þat *Crist lessude hymself.* For,
whanne he made hymself man, he made hym a creature wiþoute
whiche creature is but veyn to regard of þe godhede. And þus seiþ
30 Poul þat *he tok* a special *forme of seruaunt*; and þis forme was þis
manhede þat is only in Iesu Crist. And so þis godhede and þis
manhede ben dyuerse kyndis but o persone. For, as þer is o
godhede þat is comun to þre personys, so þer is o persone þat is
f.24 comun to þes two|kyndis; and riȝt as o persone is diuerse fro
35 anoþur, al ȝif þei ben þis o kynde, so þes two kyndis ben dyuerse
but eche of hem is þis persone. And so men spekon now of Crist by
þe ton kynde and now by þe toþur, and graunton of þis same
persone dyuerse formes by þes two kyndis. But Poul grauntuþ not
here þat þis persone anyntischede hym, but he made hym lesse
40 and comun seruant whonne he made hym þus man. Þus Crist is
seruaunt of seruyng, but not seruaunt of synnyng, ne seruaunt of
bondage, al ȝif his kyn was such a seruaunt foure hondred ȝeer in
Egypte, as Godus lawe witnessuþ. And heere þenkon monye men
þat monye popis aftur Petre presumen falsely of hemself þat þei
45 ben euene wiþ Petre, and algatis ȝif þei feynon þat þei ben euene
wiþ Cristus manhede. Crist myȝte not by his manhede feynon þat
he were euene wiþ þe godhede. And so monye popis feynon hem
þat þei ben Cristus vikeris in erþe; and, siþ þei ben prowde

---

42 Gen. 15: 13.

ABOPTYαβδEJZG   þei[2]] eras. X   24 for] om. J   myȝte] om. δ   bug-
ghe] be α, om. δ   mon] om. δ   26 þe] om. A   þing[1]] kynde α   27 man] a
altered from o D   lessude] blesside I   28 whanne] a *altered from* o D   man] a
man T   hym] hymself E   a] om. β   30 was] þat was α   þis[2]] þe P, his
Y   31 þat] om. α   in] om. BTG   32 o[2]] om. G   33 þre] þes þre P, ⌐þe⌐
þre G   34 o] om. β   35 þis] þus TI   o] of o I   kyndis] endis T   36
and] om. EI   38 þes two] two J, diuerse I   39 anyntischede] amyntyschide
T   hym[1]] hem I   40 þus[1]] þis Z   þus[2]] om. E   41 but] om. O   42
a] om. E   *margin* Ge. 15 DAOPTYβZ   43 and . . . manhede[1] (46)] om.
Z   44 of] on α   46 not] om. β   47 were] was I   wiþ] to Z   and
. . . staat (49)] and þerfore na man suld feyne þat he war euen to cristis manhede
Z   48 vikeris] viker B   49 furþere] ferrer α   for] and Z   be] haue ybe

blasfemys, no mon is furþere fro þis staat. For Crist myȝte not be
God and man, but ȝif he hadde take þis mekenesse, how suweþ he 50
Crist in vertuwis þat is þus a prowd blasfeme?

And for to schewe þat Crist was no gylour, Poul seiþ þes two
wordis of Crist þat *he was maad into licnesse of men, and in habite foundon
as man.* Crist cam into þis comyn licnesse, for he was of þe same
kynde þat is eche man his broþur, and þis licnesse is in substancial 55
kynde. And he is founden in habite as man, for he tok þis syngler
manhede. Habite is takon in monye maneris, as Austyn declaruþ
wel, but here it is takon for þis mankynde þat Crist tok whonne he
was mon. And, for no þing in þe world is founden but ȝif it haue
verey beynge, þerfore þis habite of Crist ys verey man as oþre 60
ben. But, for as myche as Crist was byfore þat he hadde þis
habite, and in sixe and þritty owris he wantude þis bodily habite,
Poul spekiþ here sutilly þat 'he was fowndon in habite as man'.
But men trowon here as byleue þat Crist lefte neuere þis maad
spirit, and so he cesude neuere to be man, al ȝif he cessude to be a 65
body. Al þis saueriþ more to clerkis þan to comunte of men, and
þerfore men mote passe ouer þis spekyng to þe comun puple.

Crist mekede hymself, maad obedient to þe deþ, and not to eche
peyneful deþ but *to deþ of þe cros,* and þat ys moste abhomynable
deþ and moste peyneful of alle oþre. *And herfore* boþe *God hiȝede* 70
hym and ȝaf hym a name þat is ouer eche oþir mannys *name, þat in þe*
name of Iesu eche kne be foldud, of heuenly, of erþly and of hellis, for eche
wille of þes þre spiritis is obesschaunt to Crist. *And so eche tunge* mot
nedis *confesse þat* owre *lord Iesu Crist is in glorie of God þe Fadyr,* for, as
he is þe same God, so he haþ þe same glorie wiþ hym. 75

I   51 is þus] *rev.* AδJ   þus] þis O, *om.* I   blasfeme] b *eras.*/blasfeme
D   53 into] in ꝺY, to δ   men] man PZ   54 man] a *eras.* man D, a man
I   into] in E   55 man his] mannys B, man is his G   þis] þus I, *om.*
G   56 þis] his J   57 in] on Aα, *om.* OPTYβδJ   58 þis] *om.* T, his
G   mankynde] manhed G   59 for] for þat Z   þe] þis Z   ȝif] *om.* T   it]
he J   61 ben] men α   62 in] *om.* α   63 here sutilly] *rev.* A   as] a
I   64 maad] *om.* β   66 to¹] *om.* T   to²] *om.* T, to þe I   men] man
J   68 to²] *om.* T   69 deþ²] þe deþ I   and] *om.* EI   70 herfore] þerfore *canc.*
herfore β, þerfore αE   71 and ȝaf hym] *om.* I   ouer] aboue I   mannys] *om.*
I   þat²] *om.* δ   72 of³] and I   hellis] helly IG   73 wille] welle
I   74 lord] *om.* Y   glorie] þe glorie δE   75 haþ] is I

In die Pasche. [Epistola. Sermo 22.]

Expurgate uetus fermentum. Prima Corintheos 5.

Poul bidduþ in þis epistle þat men schulen clene forsake synne,

and algatis in þe|feeste of Pasc wonne þei han mynde of Cristus qwikyng. Poul bygynneþ and bidduþ cristene men þat *þei clense owt þe oolde sowrdow.* Poul telliþ to wyt of allegory what þe wendyng

5 of folc of Israel, whanne þei wenton owt of Egypte, figurede to wit of vertuwis; and so þre mysty wittis ben toknede in þis same story. It is knowon to trewe men by þe secounde booc of Godus lawe hou3 children of Israel wenton owt of Egypte, aftur ten myraclis þat God dude hem vpon Pharao and Egypcians, and made þes

10 children serue to hym. Þei wenton owt in gret hast, and flowr and salt þei tokon wiþ hem, and maaden þer breed wiþowten sowrdow; and þus þei eton þer pasc lomb. And þis maner þei kepton longe aftur, to haue mynde of Godis delyueryng. Poul seiþ to þis spiritual wyt 'clense 3e owt þe oolde sowrdow'. Sowrdow is

15 vndurstonden here synne þat men ben fowlude wiþ. And sorwdow whonne it is oold rotiþ and fowliþ oþur past; and so vndurstonde we by Poul by þis sowrdow oold synne. Þanne men clenson owt þis synne, whonne þei maken clene þer sowlis, þat no synne leue in hem to fowle men aftirward. Synne stonduþ in

20 monye þingis: in leuyng of þing þat man schulde do, in wrong doyng of þingis þat he schulde do to God, and schrewide custom

4ff. Exod. 12: 3–20.

MSS: D; ABEGIJOPTXYZαβδ; H *text only.*

Sermo 22] sermo Pβ, *om.* DABOPTαδEJXZGH   expurgate . . . fermentum] *om.* Y,
expurgate J   prima . . . 5] *om.* O   prima] *om.* YH   1 shulen] schuld, -d
canc. α, shulden ABTβEIG   2 mynde] *om.* J   3 qwikyng] quykenyng
ABEZG   þei] þey *canc.* þei D.   4 to] *om.* OαE   wyt] þe witt Aδ   of]
om. E   wendyng] wyndynge I   5 folc] þe folk AEIG   of[2]] *om.*
E   whanne] a *altered from* o D   6 þis] þe AδJ   7 *margin* Exo. 12 et infra
DOPTβXZ, Exodi xii Y   9 hem] for hem BY, *om.* J   and[2]] þat αE   10
serue] to serue αE   to] *om.* A   hym] him, i *altered from* e B, hem OPTYαδEJX-
Z   14 þis] *om.* PZ   sowrdow[2]] it α, *om.* β   15 fowlude] defoulid AE   17
þanne] þat A   19 men] hem BOY   20 of] *om.* G   man schulde] men
schulden BY   21 he schulde] men schulden BY, he shuld not α   to god] *om.*

in þese dwelluþ longe aftur his werk. Of þes þre schulde man clanse hym, as men clenson lond of wedis: þei plucken hem vp by þe rootis, þat þei growe not aftur in corn. Þus schulden men clense owt synne by lore and figure of Godis lawe, þat no 25 disposicion dwelle to drawe men to do synne.

And þerfore seiþ Poul aftur þat men schulden be in þer soule *as þei weron newe spryngyng, as þei be* now *perf.* Contricion is tokned by flour for propurte þat folwiþ it, and propurte of sorwe of herte þat folweþ man þat is contrite. Spryngyng of salt on þis flowr is 30 wisdam þat a man haþ to serue God in clennesse, fro þat he be delyuerid of synne. Poul seiþ þat men schulden be newe spryngyng and not newe spreynd, for þei schulden be lastynge in clennesse of þer good lif—as spryngyng may not be but spryngyng, but spreynd þing may be vnspreynd. Þe þridde word 35 þat Poul seiþ ȝyueþ cause of þes two byfore and seiþ *for certeyn þat owre pasc Crist is* now *sacrifi⌐s⌐ed.* For, riȝt as fadris maden þerf breed for to ete þer pasc lomb, so men eton þe sacred oost to ete Crist goostly, þat is to haue muynde of hym, how kyndely he suffrede for man. And such a fruytous muynde of Crist is gostly 40 mete to þe soule, and goostly etyng of Cristus body þat þe gospel of Iohn spekuþ of.

And here þenkon men by greet studye þat alle þes foure newe sectis, ȝif þei wolon clense hem clene of synne, moten leue alle þes newe customys þat þei han weddud bysydus Cristis lawe. For alle 45 þes customys ben disposyngis to synne aȝenys Cristus wille; and,

---

42 John 6: 53–6.

I   custom] custooms T   22 þese] *on eras. corr.* D   his] in þis T   23 lond] londys T   vp] *om.* I   24 rootis] rote EI   in] in þe T   25 lore] þe lore PZ   þat] and A   26 to do] to α   27 þerfore] herfore I   in þer soule] *om.* E   28 newe] now T   spryngyng] sprynge A, sprynkyllynge α   þerf] sterf O   tokned by] by ⌐tokenynge by⌐ O, tokenyd of T, bitokened bi δ   29 for] bi Ç   folwiþ] sueþ E   30 spryngyng] sprenge A, springe I, springyn J, sprynklelynge α   on] of Z   31 a] *om.* AE   32 of] fro BY   schulden] s/ schulden D   33 spryngyng] sprinkylynge α   34 of] and of A   spryngyng] sprynge A, sprinkyllynge α   be but] ⌐but⌐ Y   35 spryngyng] sprinkyllinge α   36 þat¹] as T   seiþ¹] takiþ E   þes] þe A   two] tuo wordes α   for] in I   þat²] *om.* α   37 sacrifised] s *added corr.* D, sacrified T   þerf] þer, -feras. X, þer OT   39 to] *om.* A   of] on I   42 iohn] ⌐ion⌐ E, *om.* O   43 and . . . ordris (95)] *om.* Z   men] many A, many men α   44 hem] þemselfe α   clene] *om.* A   45 newe] *om.* A   bysydus] to synne aȝein cristis wille biside I   cristis lawe] *on eras. of* lawe *corr.* D   46 disposyngis] vndisposyngis δJ   synne] synge A   wille] lawe T   47 man²] and man I,

as we han seyd byfore, of alle þes schulde a man purge hym. Man
f.25 schulde|be fresch in þat fredom þat Crist haþ ordeyned for his
chirche, and not turne to more þraldam þan Iacobus sonys
50 hadden in Egipte. 3if þow loue kyndenesse of Crist and
ordenaunce þat he haþ 3ouen, þow schuldust holde þat
ordenaunce and leue sowr ordenaunce of men. For we seen þat
clerkis louen 3onge men þat holdon þer weyes, how schulde not
Crist loue trewe men þat holdon his weye? But alle þes newe
55 sectis browt in han new opynyonys bysyde Crist; and no dreede
þei ben contrarie to Cristus weye þat he tawte, for he þat is not
wiþ Crist mot nedis ben a3enys hym. And þis crokyng by luytul
and luytul is now cropon fer from Cristus lawe, so þat men may
knowe it oponly; and þis is cause of muche malis.
60 Man may see by þre synnes how þes ordres faylon in oþre. Þe
furste synne of þe feend is pruyde; and herto helpen þes newe
sectis, as men may see in hem alle, by ypocrisye and boost. And
þus mouen þes newe staatis to boþe þes two pruydis: for þei
þenkon by þes ry3tis þat þei ben hoolyere þan oþre, and holyere
65 þan þei schulden be, to leeue hem as dydon apostlis; and certis
ellis þey ben foolis to traueyle so muche abou3te hem. Þe
secownde synne of þe world is synne of coueytise of men; but
wheþur þat þes newe ordris brynge not in þis coueytise? Traueyle
of monkis and chanonys, and of fowre ordris ⌐of¬ freris techeþ
70 pleynly þer coueytise þat þei han to strenkþe þer ordris. Þe feend
argueþ þus to hem: 'Þis is a feyr multitude, þat serueþ God wel in
þis ordre; and þus it were a greet almes to gete hem goodis to
meyntene hem, and to kepe hem in fayr. staat, and make hem
stronge to þus serue God.' Also þe feend moueþ by þer howsus
75 and by oþure goodis þat þei han to sture hem to coueytise a3enys
þe ordenaunse of Crist. As 3if þe feend arguede þus: 'O þis were a
fayr chirche, a fayr hows and an honeste, to men to serue God

57 Matt. 12: 30; Luke 11: 23.

om. β   48 fresch] fre αδIJ   haþ] hadde AδEJ, bad and hadde O   for] from
canc. for D   44 turne] turned α   to] it to I   þan] þat PδJ   51 he] om.
β   holde] loue G   54 weye] weyes I   57 hym] criste α   crokyng]
brekinge O   58 luytul] by litel O   fer] afer T   60 þes] þo α   faylon]
fallen B   63 newe] ⌐new¬ β, om. Y   þes two] two þes DG   64 holyere þan]
þan canc. ⌐holiowr þanne oþer¬ β   66 ellis] alle EI   68 newe] om. α   not in]
rev. δ   þis] om. I   traueyle] trauels G   69 chanonys] ⌐of¬ chanouns Y, of
chanouns B   of ²] ⌐of¬ β, om. δJ   of ³] corr. D   71 þus to hem] to hem þus
O   feyr] far Y   72 to²] and α   73 to] so to Tα   in fayr] rev. δ   74 to
þus] rev. αIG   75 oþure] þaire oþer αI   to coueytise] om. I   77 an] om.

ynne; who schulde not traueyle herfore?' But certis byleue techeþ
us þat boþe Crist and his apostlus were not mouede by þe soffimys
þat þe feend haþ now browt yn. But byleue techuþ us þat we han 80
not here a dwellyng cite; but þe cite þat is aboue we sekon by
ordre of Crist. And so what þat moueþ men to seke blis and leue
þis world, þat is a reson of Crist þat it falliþ to his ordre; and so
hard fare and pouert heere was coueytud of Crist and his apostlis.
And ȝet þe feend disseyueþ þes ordris by fleschly synnes monye 85
maneris. He stureþ hem to gedere heepis of men of dyuers
complexionys, and oon of hem moueþ anoþir to ete and drynke
more þan is good. And, for þe feend may moue a man to þe fowle
synne of Sodom, he may brynge in by luytul and luytul þe synne
of Sodom among þes hepis. And such knyttyng of enemyes 90
gendruþ boþe enuye and yre; so þat menye, ȝif þei myȝte auente
hem and do frely þat Crist bidduþ, and fle occasionys of synne as
dyden apostlis, and oþre men þat weron owte of þes religionys,
schulden synne lesse and profiȝte more. And þis is cause, as
somme men trowon, whi Crist and hise founde not þes ordris. 95

Poul seiþ in þis epistle on þis maner *ete we not in oure oolde synne,*
ne in synne of malis and wickudnesse, but in spiritual|swetnesse of clennesse f.25v
and of trewþe. Þis swetnesse schulde be growndut in vertuws lif þat
Crist tawte; for in al oþur ordenaunse is som sowrnesse of synne.
And þus alle þes newe ordris, þat crokon fro ordenaunce of Crist, 100
ȝyuon occasion to synne oþur pryue or apert. And ryȝt as a tre
þat is furst crokud harduþ by long tyme in his crokudnesse, so þes

---

81 Heb. 13: 14.

Tδ   to¹] *om.* δ   to²] *om.* O   78 who] and who G   herfore] herfore þus
O   79 þe] þese Aα   80 haþ now] *rev.* A   now browt yn] brouȝt ynne nou,
ynne nou *marked for rev.* E   81 a] *om.* β   82 ordre] þe ordre T   þat] *om.*
T   83 þis] þe TEI   his] þis I   84 coueytud] coueyteþ O   85 monye] in
many α   86 hem] men T   to gedere] to gete B   88 moue] foule I   þe²]
⌜þe⌝T, *om.* B, do αβ   89 he] and he EI   by] *om.* I   and luytul] and bi litil β,
om. G   91 so] and so A   menye] e *altered from* o D   myȝte auente] fiȝten
anente I, ⌜wolde⌝ auente J   92 do] so do T   þat] as α   occasionys]
occasioun E   93 religionys] religiouse AYEIJ   94 schulden] schulen G   95
founde] foundiden Bα   þes] *om.* EI   96 in¹] on I   epistle] manere
I   on] in I   maner] epistele I   in²] *om.* EI   97 ne in synne] *om.*
I   in¹] *om.* δ   spiritual] spiritual// spiritual D   98 vertuws] -s *added corr.* D,
vertues of G   89 oþur] oure A   100 þus] sa Z   þes newe ordris] *om.*
Z   ordenaunce] þe ordynaunce TαE   101 or] oþer I   102 harduþ]
hardenes Z, and hardiþ A   tyme] tymes G   þes . . . qwenchyde (106)] þai þat

fowre ordris by long tyme ben hardude more in þer malis. And
þus God ȝyue grace to hem to knowe þe fredom of Godus lawe,
105 and turne freschly to Cristus ordre, for þanne weron monye
synnes qwenchyde.

Dominica proxima post Pasche.[Epistola.]
[Sermo 23.]

Omne quod natum est ex Deo. Prima Iohannis 5.

Ion sturuþ here cristene men to flee synne þat comeþ of þe world, and þis synne is ful comyn in alle þre partis of þe chyrche. Furst cristene men schulden wyte þat alle men þat schulen haue blisse of heuene ben goostly borne of God and maad men of his ordre, siþ þat Crist mot be her fadyr and hooly chyrche be þer modyr. 5 And þis condicion settiþ Iohn þat mot nedis be fulfillid: *yche þing þat ys born of God ouercomeþ þe world* in al his tyme. For, ȝif he be ouorcomen of þe world for a luytul tyme þat he synneþ, neþeles he mot couere and ouercome þe world at þe laste; for ellys he was neuere born of Crist, ne suweþ his Fadyr in þis fiȝt. And Crist 10 wole haue none suche children but þat ben kynde and suwon hym. And þerfore Iohn telluþ a mene to men to ouercome þe world. *And þis* he seiþ *is þe victorie þat ouercomeþ þe world, oure byleue*; so þat noon ouurcomeþ þe world, ne þe feend, ne his flesch, but ȝif byleue be þat armour, by whiche he ouercomeþ þus. And 15 herfore declaruþ Poul to þe Ebreus þat seyntis ouercamen rewmys by byleue þat þei hadden, and maden monye oþre victories. And schortly þer is no mon ouercomen of his goostly enemye, but ȝif he be owte of byleue, oþur in o maner or oþur. And þus by som maner of speche byleue is boþe scheld of man, 20

16 Heb. 11: 33.

MSS: D; ABEGHIJOPTXYZαβδ; M *inc.* 21 bi þe which

Sermo 23] sermo β, *om.* DABOTαδEIJXZGH   omne . . . deo] *om.* Y   est] *om.*
β   ex deo] *om.* O, ex deo vincit mundum T   prima . . . 5] *om.* O   prima]
om. YH   1 ion] pon O   sturuþ here] stereþ I, telleþ here and stireþ O   3
cristene] crist δ, *om.* Y   schulen] schulden BTδIJ   blisse] þe *canc.* blis G, þe blis
TY   5 crist] iesu T   be²] ⌐be⌐ J, *om.* H   7 his] *om.* Z   9 couere and
ouercome] *on eras. corr.* D   11 þat] þat þat δJ   12 iohn telluþ] telliþ
⌐ioon⌐ G   13 þe¹] *om.* H   14 ouurcomeþ] ouercome TI   þe²] *om.* J   15
ȝif] *om.* O   byleue] he bileue H   be] by OH   þat] þe α   16 þe] *om.*
ABOPTYαβδEIJZ, þe *canc.* X   18 schortly] soth α   19 enemye] enemyes
M   oþur¹] or H   or] eiþer B, oþer I   oþur²] *in canc.* oþer Y, in oþer
ABOTαδEIJGH   20 of man] *om.* OI   21 whiche] þe which M   man

and swerd by whiche man fyȝtuþ, and victorie þat he makiþ. And
Iohn axsuþ by ensaumple *who is he*, breþren, *þat ouercomeþ þe world,
but þat man þat byleueþ þat Iesu is Godus sone?* Ȝif þow haue ful byleue
of Crist, how he lyuede here in erþe, and how he ouercam þe
25 world, þow ouercomest hyt as a kynde sone. For ȝif þow takust
heed⸢e⸣ how Crist dispysede it, and suwe hym here as þow
schuldust, þow most nedis ouercome it by byleue of þi Fadir.

And heere may men wyte oponly þat monye men ben in þis
world þat be not borne of God, ne byleeuon heere in Crist; for, ȝif
30 þis byleue were in hem, þei schulden suwe Crist in maner of lif.
But þei ben owte of byleue, as monye men of þe day of doom.
What man schulde byleue fully þat þe day of doom is anoon, and
þat God iugeþ men aftur þei han fowton in his cause, þat ne he
wolde byssyly enforse hym to suwe Crist for mede þerfore? Oþur
35 byleue of þes men slepuþ, or hem wantuþ riȝt byleue. As men, þat
louen þis world and reston in lustis þerof, lyuon as ȝif God sawe
not þis, and schulde not iugge for þis deede. Þus owre byleue of
f.26 |Cristus lif is nedful to alle cristene men. And herfore men
schuldon knowe þe gospel, for it telluþ þe byleue of Crist. And
40 þus it semeþ þat newe ordris ouercome not þis world bi bileue þat
þei han in Crist; for Crist lyuede not as þei lyuon now. Crist
purchasude not to hys apostlis rentis, ne howsis, ne worldly
goodis, but tauȝte hem boþe in comune [and] pryue to flee such
hauyngis of þe world. And þus þe falshede of þe fend disseyueþ
45 men of suche ordris, þat þei han þe world in comyn, but noon of
hem to hymself. Whan þei han þus þe world in comyn, eche of
hem assentiþ þerto, and þei ben algatys more strong to lette men
þat doon þeraȝeyn, oþur in word or in deede; and þus þe feendis
champion is strengore. Suche sofyms serue not byfore Crist, þe

. . . and²] he doth þe M   and²] in Tα   and³] *om.* EI   23 haue] hast
G   25 a] *om.* T   takust] take AOαδEIJZ   27 þow] þan þou α   nedis]
nede α   þi] þe MG   28 may men] *rev.* T   monye] *om.* J   men²] *om.*
I   29 byleeuon] bileuen not E   33 þei] þat þey OE   ne he] *rev.* MOTZ, ne
δJ   34 hym] *om.* T   þerfore] þerof, -of *canc.* -fore D   oþur . . . malys (56)]
om. Z   35 byleue¹] þe bileue M   hem] ellis hem E   37 schulde] ⸢ne⸣shulde
H   38 and] *om.* G   herfore] þerfore Pα   39 of] of of 2nd *canc.* D   40 it]
om. M   newe] þes newe M   ouercome not] han not ouercomen H   þis] þe
H   bi . . . þat] *on eras. corr.* D   42 to] *om.* O   rentis] certis I   ne¹]
neiþer I   howsis] hous P   43 and] or DIG, and in E   flee] hate suche/sy *canc.* flee
D   44 hauyngis] hauyng MEI   þe²] *om.* Oα   falshede] falsede hid
I   45 noon] not α   46 to] vnto M   whan] a *altered from* o D   þus þe
world] þe world þus EI   47 more] þe more M   48 in²] in *canc.* Y   49 suche]

laste iuge. And þus þes sophistres þat gabbon þat þei han nowt, 50
neþir in propur, ne in comyne, – and ʒeet men seen þat þei han
boþe plasis and howsus and oþre goodis, myche more plenteuously þan oþre poore men þat þei robbon, – þese false men mote
nedis be dampnede of Crist þat is þe furste trewþe, for þei dyuerse
not fro þeuys, but þat þei robbon more synfully to þis greet man of 55
hem þat is more strong in his malys.

þis ys he þat cam by watur and by blood, Iesu Crist. He cam not to þe
blisse of heuene by ypocrisye ne falshede, but by tribulacion and
by schedyng of his blood. And þus he was also maad Iesu, þat is
sauyour of þis world; and he was also maad Crist, to anoynte men 60
by welle of hys grace by vertu of his passion, and not by worldly lif
heere. For hee was heed of martiris and suffrede best mooste
peyne. On þis schuldon his sonys þenke, and suwe þer Fadyr in
þis maner. For, ʒif þei suwon a new fadyr, and leuen þe maner
þat Crist tawʒte, þei leeuon Crist and suwon anticrist, as false 65
men doon þat schulen be feendis. And þus Crist cam *not oonly in
watyr, but in watur and in blood*; for he suffrede not only tribulacion,
as monye men doon, but tribulacion and passion by mooste
feruour of charite. And by þis cause seiþ Poul þat God hyʒede
Crist, and ʒaf hym a name þat is ouer alle oþre namys, and 70
mooste of worschipe in þis world. And wytnesse of þis sentence is
sufficient boþe in heuene and erþe.

*þe Holy Goost is he þat wytnessuþ in hyʒe heuene þat Crist is
trewþe. For þer ben þre þat ʒyuon wytnesse in heuene, þe Fadur, þe Word*

69 Phil. 2: 9.

siþ siche P   not] of noght MI   50 þat¹] *om.* α   han] -n *added corr.* D   51
in²] ⌐in¹ P, *om.* YβδEJ   and] but T   seen] seien δ, seen alday I   52 plasis
and howsus] housis places H   myche] *om.* I   54 þe] *om.* E   55 fro þeuys] þus
E   þat] *om.* E   to] vnto M   57 þis] and þerfor men suld knawe þe gospel for
tellis þe bileue of Crist þis Z   by²] ⌐by¹ T, *om.* E   58 ne] and EZ   59 by]
om. OPδE   þus] *om.* O   also maad] maad also *marked for rev.* D, maad also H,
made BOPTYδJZG, also *eras.* made X   60 þis] þe M   he was also] also he was
B   also maad] maad also *marked for rev.* D, maad also O   anoynte] oynte
H   men] *om.* M   61 welle] wille MβEI   by²] and bi E   62 of] heere
canc. of D, heere of MEX   mooste] ⌐and¹ moost δ   63 on] vpon M   in] on
E   64 for . . . feendis (66)] *om.* Z   fadyr] manere I   66 feendis] dampned
AB   crist] *om.* M   67 in²] *om.* GH   only] *om.* I   68 as . . . tribu-
lacion] *om.* T   monye] oþer α   men] *om.* MβE   tribulacion] boþe
tribulacioun E   69 of] and T, loue of E   þat] *om.* B   70 a] *om.* H   ouer]
aboue *canc.* ouer E, ⌐abouen¹ M   71 þis sentence] þes sentencys T   72 boþe] but
OE   erþe] in erþe ABαδEIH   73 is he] *rev.* α   in hyʒe] *rev.* GH, in

75 *and þe Hooly Goost; and þes þre ben alle oon. And þer ben þre þat ȝyuon*
witnesse in erþe, þe soule, watur and blood; and þes þre ben alle oon, for
þei maken Cristus manhede. And so as þis special substaunce, þat
is godhede of Crist, is þre personys and o God, so þis comyn
substaunce is o persone of Crist. And þus whanne Crist cryȝede
80 on hyȝ, and þus sente owt þis mannys spyriȝt, and aftur he
schedde watur and blood, fro þe tyme þat he was deed, þes þre
þingus bytokne wel þat Crist was verey man and God. And in
tyme þat Crist was baptisud þe Fadur witnessude in voys, þe Sone
was schewid in manhede, and þe Hooly Goost in a dowue; and
85 þes þre ben sufficient wytnesse to teche owre byleue of Crist. For
ȝif we takon wytnesse of men to proue trewþe in cause of men, *witnesse*
of God þat is þre personys *is more* to proue þis byleue. *And þis is more*
f.26v *witnesse of God þat he witnessude þus|of hᵣi˥s Sone.* And so, siþ God is
euereywere, *whoso troweþ in Godus Sone, he haþ witnesse of God in hym,*
siþ he haþ þe Trinnyte.

---

79 Luke 23: 46; John 19: 34; **84** Matt. 3: 16–17.

α   74 trewþe] trewe P   word] sone E   75 þe] *om.* α   77] þei] þei/þei,
2nd *canc.* D   as] al δ IJ   78 godhede] þe godhed M   so] and so PZ   80
þus] *om.* M   82 bytokne] tokenen E   crist] he E   man and god] god and
man M   83 was baptisud] baptised O   þe²] *om.* δJ   86 ȝif] al ȝif
I   trewþe] þe truþe H   88 witnessude] witnessith M   so] *om.* EI-
Z   siþ] *om.* I   89 euereywere] ouer all where α

Dominica ii post Pascha. [Epistola.] Sermo 24.

Christus semel passus est pro nobis. Prima Petri 2.

Petre telluþ in þis epistle of þe passion of Crist, how myche it was in hymself, and ȝouen to ensaumple of cristene men. *Crist,* he seiþ, *haþ suffred for us, leuynge ensaumple to ȝow þat ȝe folwe þe steppus of hym;* and so his passion doþ good to men þat weron, and men þat ben, and to men þat schulen come aftur. But men mote dispose 5 hem to take profiȝt of þis passion. As men þat weron byfore þis passion token þis profiȝt by þer byleue, and men þat weron wiþ þis passion (as weron Petre and oþre apostlis) addydon to feyþ loue and sorwe; and þes men meneþ Petre here, whonne he seiþ Crist suffrede for us. Þe þridde men þat camen aftur ben þo þat 10 trowon þat Crist suffrede, and addydon loue to þis byleue, and suwen for Cristus sake his steppis. It is oftene seyed in Godus lawe þat, ȝif a man wole come to heuene, he mot nedys suwe Crist in feiþ, in hope and in charite. And herfore haþ God ordeyned so men þat noon may be excusud here, for eche man may suffre for 15 God, as eche man may trowe and loue. What man is so feble of power þat ne he mot nede suffre deeþ? – and so þis suffryng schulde be set in charite for Godus sake. And eche man haþ a

MSS: D: ABEGHIMOPTXYZαβδ; J *expl. incl.* 64 þing[1]

Sermo 24] sermo 50 β, *om.* ABMOTαδEIJXZGH   christus . . . nobis] *om.* Y   semel] *eras.* B, *om.* TJ   passus] *om.* Aδ   pro nobis] pro nobis vobis relinquens exemplum M, *om.* OGH   I pet. 2] *om.* O   I] *om.* H   2] þe þridde chapitir Y, 20 β   1 petre] poul β   2 to] vnto M   ensaumple] sample BMOPTY-αβEJ   of] to Y   3 to] vnto M   folwe] swe E   4 hym] hem I   to] vnto M   weron] ben E   men[2]] to men EH   5 ben] weren E   to] vnto M   schulen] scholden I   aftur] heraftir EI   6 profiȝt] ⌈þe⌉ profiȝt X, þe profit BMOPTYαβδEIJZ   þis] þ- *on eras of* h- D, his ATY   7 þis] *om.* O   8 weron] *om.* E   and] wiþ T   9 men] *om.* Mδ   meneþ] moueþ I   ˙seiþ] seyde T   10 camen] comeþ O   11 trowon] ⌈trouweden⌉ I, trowid Z   and[1]] *om.* O   addydon] adden ABMOPTYββδEJH   12 suwen] suweden I   oftene seyed] *rev.* H   13 to] vnto M   mot] muste M   nedys . . . crist] sue crist nedis H   suwe] su⌈ȝ⌉/we, ȝ *corr.* D   14 in[1]] *om.* ABPZ   in[2]] *om.* ABOPYαβδ-EIJZ   herfore] þerfore AOPTαδEIJXZH   haþ god] *rev.* ZGH   ordeyned] so ordeyned δ   so men] ech man M   15 be] *om.* M   man] -a- *altered from* -o- D   16 man[1]] -a- *altered from* -o- D   and] in E   17 ne he] *rev.* AMOα-

spirit wiþ wille and vndyrstondyng þerynne. And so God ȝyueþ
20 eche man power to come to blis of heuene, for God chargeþ
neuere man to do more þan he may do, for þis large Lord axsuþ of
man to be serued of his owne. But pruyde lettuþ man to suffre,
and moueþ hym to fyȝte and stryue; and þerfore suffrede Crist
contraryously to þis doyng. For man doþ as Adam dyde by
25 pruyde and inobedience; ⌐bot Crist suffreþ by mekenesse and
obedience⌐ to God. And here may men see now how þe fadyr of
pruyde moueþ hem to leeue þis meke pacience and to suwe Crist
in þis poynt; but he moueþ to do prowdly aȝenys Godis wille, as
Adam dyde. And þus it is now to dreede þat men þat suwe not
30 heere Cristus steppis maken þat Crist suffrede not for hem, for þei
take not of Cristus meryt; siþ a man mot dispose hymself to haue
wilfully part þerof. But no man may suffre euene wiþ Crist, and
þerfore bidduþ Petre suwe his steppis.

Þe greetnesse of Cristus suffryng is tawȝt by Petre on þis maner:
35 *Crist, he seiþ, dude no synne, ne gyle was fowndon in his mowþ.* And so
hys suffryng was more medful, siþ he suffrede not for his owne
synne, as þeuys whan þat þei ben hangude, or oþre traytorys
whanne þei ben kyllude suffre not so medfully as men þat seruede
not þis deþ. Crist was wiþowte synne, and so not gulty to suffre
40 peyne, but of his grace and his wille to bugghe men þat weron
cowpable. Petre declaruþ more þis suffryng by þat þat Crist was
so meke þat, *whanne he was cursud* of þe Iewis, *he cursude not aȝen,* but
suffrede mekely þer yuele wordis. And Crist, *whanne he suffrede* in
deede, *he manasude not aȝen,* but suffrede mekely his passion. And
45 by þis cause muche more þat he myȝte, ȝif he hadde wold, haue
f.27 |take greet veniaunce of hem.

Z   mot] muste M   19 so] om. β   20 eche] vnto ech M   man]-a- *altered
from* -o- D   power] om. M   to¹] for to M   blis] þo blisse αE   chargeþ]
chargide P   21 man] -a- *altered from* -o- D   for] and for δ   22 man¹] a man
I   to¹] for to M   man²] a man MI   23 and¹ .... stryue] om. O   suf-
frede] suffriþ A   24 doþ] dyde T   25 bot ... obedience (26)] *upper margin corr.*
D   crist] om. M   suffreþ] sufferid MαEIH   26 to] vnto M, done to
E   and ... þerof (32)] om. Z   27 meke] mekenesse and M   to²] so to T,
om. α   29 now] ⌐not⌐ *corr.* now D, not now H   31 mot] muste M, om. I   32
wilfully] wilful P   man] -a- *altered from* -o- D   may] om. M   34 on] vpon
M   35 ne] ne no B, nor M   36 medful] nedeful βδJ   owne] om. I   37
whan] -a- *altered from* -o- D   þat] om. BPYαδEIZGH   38 whanne] whan þat
A   39 þis] ⌐to⌐ þis E   synne] deþ *canc.* synne D   not gulty] vngilty
M   40 peyne] to payne α   his²] of his MEI   41 þat þat] þat O   crist]
he T   42 whanne] -a- *altered from* -o- D   þe] om. I   43 mekely ... suffrede
(44)] om. I   wordis] wille of wordis T   whanne] -a- *altered from* -o- D   45

Petre telluþ aftur of þe wilful peyne þat Crist suffrede for mankynde, by þat þat *Crist offerude hymself* to Pylate, *þat iugede hym vnriʒtfully.* For Matheu telluþ how Crist byfore telde al his passion, and how he cam to Ierusalem to suffre fully as he 50 suffrede; and so his suffryng was meedful, ⌐for it was so myche wylful⌐. For no mon hadde more desyr to dye þus þan Crist hadde, ne Adam hadde no more desyr to synne þan Crist hadde to suffre. And þus he spekuþ in þe gospel by hys godhede and his manhede 'By desyr haue I desyrud to ete þus þis Pasch wiþ ʒow'; 55 for etyng of þe Pasch lomb and sleyng þat was byfore of it was figure to þis lomb of God. And þus it cam of greet desyr, and Adam myʒte not wylle to synne by so greet desyr or lust. And Petre telluþ more of þis passion þat *Crist ʒaf hymself to þe man þat iuggede hym vniustly; þe whiche Crist,* for we myʒte not, *bar owre synnes* 60 *in his body;* and he bar hem *vpon þe tre,* as Adam synnede in a tre, *so þat we be deed fro synne and lyue* aftur *to ryʒtwisnesse.* Petre spekuþ heere by comyn speche þat þat man beruþ a þing, þat beruþ þe fruyt of þe þing, (as a man ⌐in⌐ berynge money beruþ þe þing þat is bowt þerwiþ). So Crist bar owre synne on þe cros, for hys 65 passion was pris þerof. And þus, as Crist was deed in þe cros, so schulden we be deed fro synne, þe whiche sprong of þe tre þat Adam synnede furst inne. And deþ of Crist in þis tre schulde teche us to dyʒe þus; but we schulden lyue spiritually · to riʒtwisnesse, þat is God, as Crist roos by goostly myracle and 70 wente to þe same riʒtwisnesse.

---

49 Matt. 26: 2, 11–12, 18, 21, 31–4; **55** Luke 22: 5.

by] mykil by Z   muche more] *om.* Z   þat] *om.* I   he¹] if *canc.* he δ   ʒif] ʒif þat H   46 of] on B   48 þat þat] þat Oβ   49 vnriʒtfully] vnryʒtlich OPYαδJXZGH, vnryghtwislich M, vntrewly I   *margin* Mt. 29 T   byfore telde] telde bifore *marked for rev.* β, *rev.* TI   al] of E, *om.* J   51 his] þis J   for . . . wylful (52)] *upper margin corr.* D   52 to . . . desyr (53)] *om.* α- I   54 to] for to M   and¹] *om.* O   and²] and by MTα   55 haue I] *rev.* OPIZGH, I M   *margin* luc 22 T   56 þe] þis EI   lomb] lomb *canc.*/lomb D   sleyng] þe sleynge Y   57 to] vnto M   58 wylle] wilne PZ   desyr] lust *canc.* desyr D   or] of ABTYδEJH, o O   59 þis] his I   passion] wilful passioun H   to] vnto M   60 we] alle we E   61 vpon] on MH   þe] a MI   62 deed] *om.* O   63 heere by] by by O   þat þat] þat δJ   man] a *canc.* man Y, a man O   þe] *om.* β   64 þe¹] a T   a] ⌐a⌐ β, *om.* M   in] *corr.* DX   in berynge] þat beris Z   money] of money EG   65 bowt] brouʒt PT   synne] synnes, -s *canc.* Y, synnys TEG   on] vpon M   66 in] on AOTαδ, vpon M   67 þe¹] *om.* B   of] on T   68 synnede furst] *rev.* H   69 dyʒe] do M   schulden] schulden//schulden 2nd *canc.* D   to²] vnto

And *by loue þat Crist hadde* heere *we ben helude* of oure synne. And, for Crist is þe beste herde þat þus kan qwikene and heele his schep, þerfore seiþ Petre aftur þat *mankynde was somtyme as errynge* 75 *scheep* wiþowton herde, *but þei ben turnede now by loue to þe herde and byschop of þer soulis.* Crist for his excellence telluþ but luytul by mannys body; but, for to feede mannys sowle and haue goostly cure þerof, þat falluþ to þis bischop. But buschopis now doon euene þe contrarye, for þei tenten neþur to body ne to sowle, but 80 to drit þat man haþ ; for, ȝif þei han money and oþre goodis, þei reckon but luytul of þes two.

M   71 riȝtwisnesse] myracle *canc.* riȝtwisnesse D   72 of] from BMOPTY-
αβδEIXZG   oure] *om.* I   and²] *om.* H   73 is] *om.* I   þus] crist *canc.* þus
D   qwikene] quike O   74 was somtyme] *rev.* H   75 scheep] as sheepe
H   turnede now] *rev.* I   to] vnto M   þe] þer T   76 for] bi I   77
but] *om.* δ   sowle] body *canc.* sowle D   haue] to haue E   78 to] vnto
M   þis] þe H   but . . . two (81)] *om.* Z   now doon] *rev.* Mβ   79 body]
þe bodi H   to²] to þe H, to *canc.* β, *om.* BMOPY   80 to] to þe M   ȝif þei
han] haue þei M   81 but] *om.* M

Dominica iii post Pascham. [Epistola.] Sermo 25.

Obsecro uos tanquam aduenas. Prima Petri 2.

Petre specifyeþ here mekenesse þat men schulden haue by
ensaumple of Crist, and how þei schulden be suget and obedyent
to alle men. Petre *preyeþ* to cristone men *to kepe hem* furst *from
fleschly lustis, as gestus and pylgrimes, for þes synnes fiȝton aȝenys þe soule.*
Fleschly d[e]syres mouen men to fiȝte and stryue wiþ þer   5
breþren. For men d[e]syren not þus money, but to meyntene þer
body in lust; for ȝif þey louedon more þer sowle, þei schulden
more traueyle þerfore. And here may men see þat men, and
algatis grete prelatis and lordis, faylon fowle in charite, and furst
in loue of hemself. For, siþ þat charite bygynneþ at þe loue of   10
mannys spirit, man schulde furst loue his spirit more þan goodis
þat|ben wiþowte. And þes goodys doon myche harm and luytul   f.27v
good to men þat han hem. Lord! what schulde reuerse mannys
loue to loue hem þus more þan his soule? Þe bussynesse þat man
haþ and traueyle to gete hym suche goodis techon þe greetnesse   15
of his loue ouer þe loue of hys soule; for necligence þat man haþ to
gete hym foode of his soule, and to do vertuous deedis, by whiche
his sowle schulde be norsched techeþ how man reckuþ to luytul of
hymself, for he forȝetuþ hys sowle. And neþeles Petre seiþ here
þat we ben gestis and pilgrimes to þis worldly lif here, for we   20

MSS: D; ABEGHIJMOPTXYZαβδ.

Sermo 25] sermo 15 P, sermo 5 β, *om.* ABOTαδEIJXZGH   obsecro . . . aduenas]
om. Y   tanquam] *om.* H   aduenas] aduenas et peregrinos MT, aduene G, *om.*
AH   I . . . 2] *om.* O   I] *om.* H   1 specifyeþ] spekes α   3 to²] vnto M,
first *canc.* to E, furst to O   furst] *om.* O   5 desyres] dosyres D, lustis I   and]
in α   6 desyren] dosyren D   to] for to M   þer] þe G   7 lust] lustis
T   8 here] herfore G   men² . . . lordis (9)] lordis and myȝty men
Z   men²] many men α   9 grete] *om.* I, heiȝe H   10 hemself] himsilf
H   þe] *om.* E   11 furst loue] *rev.* AOαδEJ   12 þat] þat//þat D   doon]
ben *eras.* doon D   13 þat] þat þat δ   what schulde] *om.* I   mannys] þus
mannys M   14 to] for to M   hem] him I   þus] *om.* M   þe . . . soule
(16)] *om.* M   þat . . . traueyle (15)] and þe trauel þat man haþ E   15 þe] *om.*
E   16 his] þis G   17 foode] such *canc.* foode D, siche foode AXG   of] to
M   to] for to BMOPTYαβδEJZGH   18 man] a *altered from* o D   19 hys]
þus his M   20 to] vnto M   worldly] *om.* E   23 of¹] fro E   pilgrimage]

schulden be traueylynge to heuene. And þus to make owre restyng
here in goodis þat ben so luytul worþ is an opon foly to us, and
lettuþ us of þis pilgri[m]age. And it is knowon of byleue þat
temporal goodus þat we han doon no good but luytul while þat
25 we wandren in þis pilgrymage. And þus men reuerson God, as
disciplis of anticrist; for goodis, þat he ȝaf for an ende, þei disuson
to þe contrarye. He lente þes goodis to spede þer weye to go to þe
blisse of heuene; and foul loue of þes goodis lettiþ hem to go þis
weyȝe. And þis falluþ in religious and in oþre men of þe world.
30 And aftur þis bidduþ Petre þat *men lyue a good lif among men þat*
þei lyuon wiþ, and ȝyue good ensaumple to hem, as Crist ȝaf to his
chyrche. And *so in þat þat þey spekon yuel byhynde ȝow*, as who spekuþ
of yuele doeris, þei haue ⌜no⌝ mater to speke þus, *but goode werkis* to
gnawe vpon. And *þus schulon þei glorifye God in day of þe laste doom*,
35 and haue sorwe þat þei duden þus, and preyse God in his
seruauntis. And þus whonne men þenkon on Crist, and of schort
tyme þat þey han here, *þei schulden be suget to alle maner of men*, not
for money but *for God*. And þus eche man may be suget to oþur,
siþ he is two kyndis—ȝe, man is suget to hymself, siþ his body
40 serueþ to his spyrit. But prelatis clepe now no subiection but in
ȝyuyng of worldly goodis; but men þenkon not to speke here to
suche ⌜rude⌝ and worldly prelatis.

But ȝeet men schulon kepe maner in þis subiection aftur
mannys staat, as *men schulen be suget to kyng as passyng byfore oþre*
45 *men*, for þus bidduþ Petre by dede of Crist; and so þei woldon þat
lordis weron. *And men schulden be suget to dukis, as to men sent fro þe*

---

31 John 13: 15.

pilgrinage D   and] *om.* G   is] *om.* O   24 luytul] ⌜a⌝ litil A, a litil
BMOPTYβδEIJZGH   25 men] *om.* I   26 goodis] þe godis M   for an] vnto
one M, to an O   27 þes] ⌜þem⌝ α   spede] spende TH   þer] in þer
T   weye] loue I   to⁴] vnto M   28 foul] ful EI   29 þis] þus
O   falluþ] failiþ Y   in¹] in þe M   30 þis] *om.* α   31 lyuon] leue
Z   ȝaf] did M   *margin* io. 13 Z   32 so] *om.* E   who] who so M   33
þei] and þei G   to¹] for to M   to²] forto M   34 vpon] on H   schulon]
schulde BMPTEIZ   day] þe day αE   35 þei] *om.* M   in] and B   36 of]
on þe MI   37 þey] *on eras. corr.* D   to] vnto M   38 þus] *om.* T   40 to]
vnto M, til α   spyrit] soule E   but . . . prelatis (42)] *om.* Z   now] *om.*
E   no] *om.* I   41 ȝyuyng] seruynge I   42 suche] *om.* α   rude] *corr.*
D   and] *om.* δJ   43 but ȝeet] and Z   schulon] shulden ABMPβδI, awe to
Z   maner] subiection *canc.* maner D   in] and M   þis] *om.* Z   44
mannys] mennes Z   schulen] shulden ABMPZ   to] vnto M   kyng] kyngis
E   as] *om.* O   45 for] and M   þus] þis O   dede] dedis M   46

kyng to veniaunce of yuele doeris, and to preysyng of goode men. For þis
schulden kyngis and þer mynystris do here for Cristus loue; for þe
hy3nesse of þer staat was 3ouen of God for þis ende. And þus
schulden popis be suget to kyngus, for þus weron boþe Crist and   50
Petre. *For þus is þe wille of God: þat men do wel* in subieccion, *and
make doumþ þe foly of men þat ben foolis* in Godis lawe. And þis þing
men schulden *do frely*, and not by constreynyng of mannys lawe;
but as þei hadde *not an hulyng of fredom of malice* of þis world, for
such fredom is luytul worþ, but fredom fro synne to serue God.   55
And þis kepyng of suche werkis wole make men fre *seruauntys of
God. Do 3e honour to alle men,* and specially to mannys spirit. And   f.28
drede 3e God in þis prynte; and do 3e alle 3oure werkis for God.
And *loue 3e breþerhede* by þe forme þat Crist haþ tawt. And þus, siþ
kyng is Godus viker, *drede 3e God* in þis viker; and *do 3e worschipe to* 60
þe kyng, for loue of God whos viker he is.

   Seruauntis, be 3e sugetis in al dreede, boþe goostly drede and
bodyly, *to lordis þat 3e han* here. For, as Poul techiþ, seruauntis
schulden serue to þes lordis as to God. And so by seruyse goostly
and bodyly schulde þei serue *not only to goode lordis and resonable* to 65
þer seruauntis, *but also vnto tyrauntis* þat destruye Cristus scole, as
duden boþe Erowde and Pilate. For certeyn *þis is grace in Iesu
Crist*, þat is *owre Lord*; for Crist was suget to þes tyrauntis, as God
obescheþ to mannys voys. Þis subiection is no synne, al 3if
tyrauntis synnen in takyng it; for, as suffryng is somtyme good   70
and doyng yuel brynguþ it in, soo subiection somtyme is good

---

69 Josh. 10: 12–14.

schulden] s3ulle O   suget] subgettis M   to¹] vnto M   48 þer] oþer
T   do] to O   here] *om.* E   cristus loue] þe loue of criste M   49 staat]
ᵣaˡstaat X, astate M   50 to] vnto M   þus] so M   51 þus is þe] *on eras. corr.*
D   þus] þis MOTI, ri3t þus H   53 men schulden] schulen men
Y   schulden] shul β   by constreynyng] constrayned α   55 worþ] worþry
β   but] wiþoute G   56 and þis] in E   of¹] frome M   wole] wiln
H   57 men] men//men D   to²] vnto M   58 þis] his A   prynte]
priuytee δJ   and] *om.* G   3e] 3oure T   alle] *om.* I   59 þe] *om.*
β   siþ] *om.* M   60 kyng] þe kyng BMYEH   61 loue] þe loue M-
EI   whos] who is β   62 sugetis] suget B   dreede] dredes α   drede] *om.*
δ   63 bodyly] bodly drede Tδ   64 to¹] vnto M   þes] þe α   as to god]
om. Z   to²] vnto M   goostly] bodily EH, boþe bodily I   65 bodyly] gostly
EIH   to¹] vnto M   66 vnto] to I   tyrauntis] tyrauntis *canc.* tryuauntis β,
tryuauntis PTYEXG, truiauntes I   cristus] cristene B   scole] stole α   67
duden boþe] *om.* E   68 tyrauntis] tryuauntis PY   69 to] vnto M   þis] þe
I   *margin* iosue 10 T   70 tyrauntis] tryuauntis PY   it] of it E   71

and men ben yuele in takyng of it. And þus ȝif men þenkon
sutelly kyngus and lordis schulden serue to men, al ȝif þei ben þer
bonde men, for þer bodyes schulden serue þer spiritis. And, siþ
75 bodyes ben worse in kynde þan onye spiritis þat mon haþ, and al
þe personalite of mon stonduþ in spirit of hym, why schulde not
men graunte þes wordis þat eche man schulde serue to eche man?
And wolde God þat þe pope knewe þis and oþre emperour
prelatis; þanne schulden þei be ensample of mekenesse, as was
80 Crist owre alþer Lord.

doyng yuel] he dos euel α   brynguþ] ⌐þat¬ bryngiþ G, þat bryngiþ BMOPTY-
αβδEJXZH   it in] rev. B   somtyme is] rev. MOαG   good] god I   72
of] om. Z   73 al ȝif] al þey O, al if þat δ   þer] om. I   74 spiritis] spirite
M   75 bodyes] þe bodies I   spiritis] spirit ABMOPTYαβδEIJZH   76
spirit] þe spirit ABMOPTYαβδEIJXZH   hym] man E   not men] rev. I   77
to] vnto M   78 and . . . lord (80)] om. Z   knewe] knowe β   80 alþer]
alle þer G   lord] maister M

Dominica iiii post Pascham. [Epistola.] Sermo 26.

Omne datum optimum. Iacobi primo.

Iames ȝueþ here a lore of cristene mennys religion, and ȝueþ as
a wys man a greet prynciple to þis lore. Eche þing ȝouen þe beste, seiþ
Iames, and eche ȝifte þat is parfiȝt is fro aboue, comyng doun fro God þat
is Fadur of liȝt. Þer ben þre þingis ȝouen to man, as worldly goodis,
and goodis of kynde; þe þridde þing is goodis of grace, þat ben   5
beste of alle þes þre. And þus seiþ Iames wittily þat al beste þing
þat is ȝouen is fro aboue, comynge fro God, as ben vertuwis and
grace. And so it is of alle oþre whiche ben parfiȝte ȝiftis. And here
þenkon monye men þat ȝyuyngis of popis be none ȝiftus. Þei seyn
þei graunton prauylegies and indulgensis wiþ oþre feynyngus;   10
but, siþ þei smacchen wynnyng of money, and þat is heuy and
drawiþ doun, and þei sownen not to charite and oþur reson þat is
in God, it semeþ þat þes ben falsely feynede of þe prynce of
derknesse; and þus þei spryngon fro byneþe fro þe fadyr of
lesyngis. And þus it semeþ to monye men þat þes fowre sectis þat   15
ofte ben spokone, siþ Godus lawe grownduþ hem not, ben not þus
fro abouen, but fro byneþe of þe feend. And þus men may knowe
wel Cristus religioun fro þis newe. For Cristus religioun desiruþ
heuenly þing and help of soule; but þes religious stonden mooste
in pruyde, falshede and coueytise.   20

MSS: D; ABEGHIJMOPTXYZαβδ.

Pascham] octavam pasche E   sermo 26] sermo A, om. BOTαδEIJXZGH   omne
. . . optimum] om. Y   optimum] optimum et omne donum perfectum MT   iac.
primo] om. O   1 as] vs δ   2 to] of E   ȝouen] ȝeueþ O   þe] om.
A   3 comyng] comyn O   doun fro god] fro god doun I   4 liȝt] liȝtis
H   to] vnto M   man] a altered from o D   5 þe] and þe B   7
ben . . . grace (8)] vertues and grace bene M   8 it is] rev. α   alle] om. E   and[2]
. . . men (23)] om. Z   9 ȝyuyngis] ȝyuynge AM   none] not H   ȝiftus]
profit A, perfit ⌐ȝiftis⌐ B   10 indulgensis] indulgence α   11 siþ] om.
T   wynnyng] wynnnyng D, wynnynges IH   12 to] vnto M   þat] þat
souneth M   14 fro[1]] inne frome M   15 to] vnto M   16 ofte ben] are oftare
α   spokone] spoken ⌐of⌐ A, spokyn of MαE   þus] þis O   17 fro byneþe] rev.
E   fro[2]] of O   men may] rev. H   knowe wel] rev. GH   18 þis] þes
A   19 þing] þingis MTI   help] helpe Mα   religious] religiones MOYαβδJ,
newe religiouse H   21 on] of AO, in M   22 fadyr] þe canc. fadir Y, þe fadir

Þe Fadur of liȝt is vnmouable fro trewþe and godnesse on alle
maneris; but fadyr of derknesse chaungeþ ofte, aftyr þat he hopuþ
more to noyȝe men. And þus seiþ Iamys þat *at God is not*

transmutacion ne|schadwyng of whylenesse, for he is euermore iɴ oon.
25 Þe feend varieþ in synful willis, and castuþ his schadwys by
monye weyes, and chaungeþ his wille by monye whiles; but noon
of þes is in God.

But for good religion mot be groundut in goode personys,
þerfore telluþ Iamys aftur how þes persones weren browt forþ. He
30 seiþ þat *God gendrude us wilfully,* and by his grace *wiþ his owne word
of trewþe,* boþe makyng us and byggyng us. And þes goodis of
mannys kynde mote nedis come of God fro aboue. And þus God
gendrude hys apostlus *to be bygynnyng of his chyrche*; for his chyrche
is a womman, a virgyne, and Cristus spouse, and a passyng
35 creature among alle þo þat God haþ maad. *Ȝe wyton, my moste deere
breþren,* how Crist haþ loued mankynde, and how he lyuede in þis
lif by cause þat ȝe schulden lyue so. And herfore *be eche man swift
for to here* Godus lawe; *but he schal be slow to speke,* but þat þat he
knowiþ is Godus word. And þus *he schal be slow to ire, for mannys ire
40 doþ not riȝte of God,* but worcheþ in þe feendus werkis. Wille of God
is bygynnyng of alle goode werkis of man; and ȝif he passe bysyde
þis wille, he doþ þe wille of þe feend.

*And herfore caste ȝe awey al vnclennesse and habundaunce of malis; and
take ȝe in mekenesse þe word of God prentud* in ȝow, *þe whiche word may
45 saue ȝoure soulis.* And þus dilauynesse of tonge ⌈in⌉ spekyng wordis
oþre þan Godis is passyng fro good religioun, þat God haþ ȝouen

BMH   þat] *om.* BMY   23 more to noyȝe] to noye OE, to more anoye δ, more to
anoye IH   men] vnto men M, men more O   þus] þis G   is] it β   not]
noᶫtꜞ P, no IG   24 schadwyng] schadowe G   whylenesse] whilewis B, wilynesse
IG   euermore] euer EZ   26 and] *om.* α   wille] willes α   whiles] willis
β   28 mot] moste M, mote nede T   30 þat god] *on eras. corr.* D   gendrude]
-ndide us *canc.* gendrude D, gendriþ AI   31 makyng] in makande Z   goodis]
good EI   32 mannys kynde] mankynde MδH, mennes kynde Y   nedis] *om.*
M   þus] þis P   33 be] *om.* β   his¹] þis O   34 and¹] *om.* E   35 þo]
om. O, þas Z   my] *om.* BY, sais Iames my Z   36 he] *om.* M   37 ȝe] we
M   schulden] shuln H   herfore] þerfor MαH   38 for to] to
MTEH   he schal] he B, *om.* E   be] be he E   to²] for to M   speke
. . . to (39)] *om.* O   40 not] no H   riȝte] ⌈þe⌉ ryȝt T, þe ryght M   wor-
cheþ] worschip I   in] to I   wille] þe will Mα   41 bygynnyng] þe
bygynnyng E   goode] þe good AMPTYαβδEJXZG   42 wille¹] wit E   43
herfore] þerfore MPZ   and habundaunce] *om.* Mβ   44 in¹] *on eras. corr.*
D   of god] *om.* P   45 tonge] tungis B   wordis] of wordis E   46 godis]

by hymself. And þus þes newe ordris eche one, whiche ben so leef
to lye, mote nedis be growndude in þe feend, þe whiche is fadur of
lesyngis. For ȝif God hadde þowt on hem, to make hem partis of
his chyrche, he wolde swiftly [h]a[ue] browt hem forþ by Crist   50
swiftuste of alle þingus. But, ȝif God ȝaue þes sectis, he ȝaf hem
alle in his woodnesse – as Godus lawe seiþ þat he ȝaf Saul kyng in
his wodnesse. Þus he ȝaf þes foure sectis for to turmente his
chyrche, for it faylede byfore in slowþe to do þe offis þat God bad.
And somme men hopon þat by þis cause alle þese sectis ben þus   55
wraþful whonne men speko[n] owt aȝenys hem, for þei dredon of
þer grownd.

52 1 Sam. 8: 7–18.

goude OI   good] cristes α, goddis Z   47 þes . . . eche one] þa Z   whiche]
˹þe˺ wyche T, þe whiche P, þat Z   48 to] for to M   þe²] om. EIG   49 on]
vpon M   hem¹] om. I   hem²] om. H   50 haue browt] abrowt D   51 swif-
tuste] swifterest A   but . . . grownd (57)] om. Z   52 alle] om. M   kyng] þe
kyng A   53 þus] and þus δJ   his²] þe E   54 chyrche] chyrge chyrg canc.
chyrche D   þe] om. E   offis] officis H   55 þus] so ABMOPTYαβδEIJ-
XGH   56 spekon] speko D   of] hem of M   57 þer] oþer J

[Dominica v post Pascham. Epistola. Sermo 27.]

Estote factores uerbi. Iacobi primo.

Iames techeþ in þis epistle how þe religion of Crist schulde be
clene kept of men wiþowton ordre of mannys fyndyng. And he
bygynneþ on þis maner: *be ȝee doerys of Godus word and not only
hereris, for þanne ȝe disseyuon ȝoureself* by medelyng of mannys ordre.

5 For alle þes foure newe ordris moten be lernyng al þer lif of þe
rewle þat þei han foundon, bysyde þe rewle þat Crist ȝaf; and by
þer rewlus þei ben tyede, as a bole by a stake, to dwelle at home in
þer cloystre, or to loue yuele þer owne ordre. Aȝenys þis spekuþ
Iamys heere wiþ oþre auctores of hooly wryt. And Poul seiþ to

10 Tymothe of þes veyne newe ordris þat þeᶠiˀ ben euermore
lernyng, and neuere comynge to fruyt þerof. It is knowon by

f.29 |Godus lawe þat heryng [and lernyng] of Godus word is schapon
of God for þis ende, to teche it and do it in deede. So, ȝif a man
hadde ful knowyng of þis word as Crist hadde, it were but ᶠfoly

15 andˀ veyn to here and lerne more of þis word. As ȝif a lond wolde
bere good corn wiþowte tylyng and donghyng þerof, it were but
ydel to traueyle þerfore, whonne it encresuþ not þe fruyt.

And herfore seiþ Iames heere þat þes men disseyuon hemself, as

9 2 Tim. 3: 7.

MSS: D; ABEGHIJMOPTXYZαβδ.

Dominica . . . pascham] *om.* D, dominica proxima ante ascensionem MβIXZ, dominica
xx ante ascensionem P, dominica vi . . . þe sixte sondai pistil aftir estir next bifore
ascencioun G   sermo 27] *om.* DABOTαδEIJXZGH   estote . . . uerbi] *om.*
Y   uerbi] verbi et non auditores MT, uerbi dei E   iac. 1] *om.* O   1 techeþ]
telleþ IGH   in] wel in E   þe] *om.* α   2 clene kept] *rev.* E   mannys]
mennys BYE   fyndyng] foundynge T   and] *om.* G   he] herfore he I   3
on] vpon M   godus] good I   4 hereris] þe herers M   5 for . . . ordre (8)]
om. Z   for] and M   foure newe] *rev.* B, ᶠfoureˀ newe H, newe E   7 rewlus]
rule B   þei] þat þey O   a¹] *om.* β   by] to BMYI   at] euere at I   8
þer¹] *om.* A   þis] þese BOPYαβEXGH, mannes ordre Z   9 auctores] autorites
ZG   10 of . . . ordris] *om.* Z   veyne newe] *rev.* E, veyn I   *margin* thy.
36 M   11 fruyt] þe fruyt BMI   12 and lernyng] *om.* DABMYβ   13 for] to
M   it¹] *om.* EI   do] to do BMEI   14 foly and] *on eras. corr.* D   15 and¹]
in *altered to* and A, and in T, in BOYβδIJXG   lerne] lere αδJ   16 wiþowte] wiþ
E   tylyng] dongyng H   donghyng] tillyng H   17 encresuþ] encresyde
α   18 herfore] þerfore MPαZ   þes] many M   hemself] hem J   19

doon monye traueyloris in scole. *For, ʒif a man be herere of* Godus
word and not doere, þis man schal be likned to man þat byholduþ þe face of 20
his ʒowþe in a myrour. And no drede þes wordis of Iames ben sutyl
and ful of wyt. And by techyng of God spekon somme men þus of
þes wordis, as tellon men of perspectif. Þer ben þre maneris of
bodyly siʒt: þe furste siʒt is euene siʒt, as man seeþ þing þat is
byfore hym; þe secounde siʒt is reflectid, whanne it is turned aʒen 25
by myrour; þe þridde siʒt is reflexud, whanne it comeþ by
dyuerse menys, and þei ben of dyuerse kyndis, as þe mone is seyn
aʒenes nyʒt. And þus men seen a peny in a dysch by heldyng in of
watur, and ellys not; and by þis siʒt may men see ful luytul þing
by fer space. Þe furste of þese þre siʒtus is moste cler and mooste 30
certeyn. We schulden wyte ouer þis for Iamys wordis þat þis man,
þat euere lerneþ and doþ not in deede Godis word, stondeþ
euermore in þe mene, and neuere comeþ to þe fruyt þerof. And
þus he faruþ as a man ⌐þat⌐ myʒte wel bettre se a þing wiþowte
myrour ⌐þan wiþ myrour⌐, and ʒeet he takuþ in veyn a myrour; 35
and þus he falluþ in monye errouris of place and quantite of þat
þing. And þus þes men þat euere lernon and leuon to do aftir þis
lore, ben as lokeris in a myrour of fisege þat þei hadden in ʒowþe.
For þis lore of Godus word schulde be a new lore and vnparfiʒt
syʒt, for þe ende in dede schulde come aftur þat schulde be euene 40
as þe furste siʒt. *And þus þis* man *þat* lokuþ *hym þus þowʒte on his*
sowle *for a tyme, but wente forþ* by curyouste *and forʒat sone* to worche

traueyloris] men *canc.* traueyloris DX   herere] heriere I   20 word] wordis
M   þis man] he M, þat man α, þis EI   to] vnto M   man²] ⌐a⌐man P, a man
BMOTδEIGH   þe] his δ   21 þes] þe G   sutyl] -tyl *on eras. corr.* D   22
men] *om.* T   23 þes] þe EIG   as] and I   tellon men] *rev.* Z   maneris]
maner AP   24 siʒt¹] siʒtis Z   man] a man OY   seeþ] seiþ, i *canc.* e *substituted*
H, seiþ β   26 myrour] a miroure α   27 þei] þes diuerse meenes M   of] on
A   28 nyʒt] þe nyght MI, siʒt Z   peny] peyne β   heldyng] ʒettyng
Z   29 watur] þe watir H   may] manye H   ful] but T   30 fer] feir
H   space] place EIG   of] siʒt as men may see of E, siʒt may men seen of
I   is] *om.* β   31 schulden] shulen AOYαδEIJGH   for] be α   32 lerneþ]
leres α   godis] godis godis *2nd canc.* D, cristis E   33 neuere] neuere ⌐more⌐ T,
neuere more P   neuere comeþ] *rev.* E   þe] *om.* Y   þerof] *om.* O   34
þus] þere I, *om.* E   35 myrour¹] a myrour B   þan . . . myrour²] *margin corr.* D,
om. MOβ   myrour²] a merour BI   36 of¹] in α   quantite] in quantite α,
qualite I   þat] *om.* E   37 euere] euere more T, neuere β   lernon] lere
α   38 a myrour] myrours, -s *canc.* E   fisege] þe visage M   in²] of α   39 be]
haue E   new] nowe M   vnparfiʒt] perfyte Mα   40 come] bicome
E   41 as] aftir EI   lokuþ] lokide BM   hym] *om.* M   42 wente] he *canc.*
wente Y, he wente BMOαEIZH   by] ⌐by⌐ a E   forʒat] for þat βI, lefte

þerfore. Þus don men þat stondon in science and worche not aftur
by þes science. And þus ben men of veyn religioun, as Iames
45 techeþ oponly, for worche we here in good lif, as ende of lore of
Godus word, and þanne we schulen se in heuene myche bettre
vsself and alle oþre þingus. On þe þridde maner of siȝt, wiþ
curyouste þat liþ þerynne, for we schulon se in Godus word alle
þe þingus þat God haþ maad, in a more cler kynde þan is þe
50 kynde þat þei han wiþowten. And clerkis clepon þis 'intuicion' in
cler siȝt in God and blisse; and þis þing þat we seen þere is in
substaunce God hymself, and in a maner þe same þing þat God
haþ maad wiþowteforþ. And þus seiþ Iohn in his gospel 'þat þing
þat is maad of God was lif in hym wiþowton ende', for it was
55 Godus kynde.

And þus seiþ Iames of Cristus religion þat *he þat lokuþ in* Godus
lawe, ⌐þat is lawe⌐ *of parfiȝt fredom, and dwelluþ parfiȝtly in þis lawe* by
al his lif, wiþowton medelyng of mannys lawe þat is derk, *and is not*
maad forȝetful herere, but makere of þe dede þat he haþ herd, *þis man*
60 *schal be blessud in his deede.* And þis is þe beste fruyt þat may folwe
mannys lif here. God þowte not only on þingus but made hem
f.29v wiþowton in þer|kynde; and so he wole not þat men konnen only,
but þat men do in deede þeraftur. And þus þe þridde gospel of
Iohn myȝte be teeld on Ȝol day. And of þis declaruþ Iames þat
65 *certis, ȝif ony man gesse þat he is a religious man, and ȝeet refreyne[þ] not*
his tonge, but disseyueþ his herte, ⌐*his*⌐ *is a veyn religioun.* On monye
maneris oure religious disseyuon hemself in vanyte. Furst þei
refreyne not þer mouþ in preyȝeris, but forȝeton to worche; as ȝif

---

53 John 1: 4; cf 1 John 1: 2.

E　　43 þerfore] þeraftir Bα　　　þus] and *canc.* þus β, and þus BM, þis O　　　and
. . . science (44)] *om.* α　　44 þus] þes ABMOPTYαβδEJXZGH　　45 techeþ]
telliþ *canc.* techiþ H, telleþ I　　oponly] vpynlich M　　47 of] *om.* E　　48 liþ]liȝt
β, liȝtneþ G　　þerynne] herinne J　　schulon] shulden Pα　　49 þe¹] *om.*
PIZG　　þingus] þinge I　　in] and B　　is . . . þat (50)] *om.* M　　þe²] *om.*
OαδEIJ　　50 clepon] calle αZ　　in] *om.* B, and OPTYαδEJZH　　51 blisse] bisse
O　　52 a] *om.* β　　54 is] *om.* O　　58 lawe] *om.* J　　not] *om.* O　　59
forȝetful] forgetil MIZ, for riȝtful E　　herere] here MTYαβEIJZH　　þe] *om.*
TEI　　60 blessud] *om.* I　　folwe] flowe Y, sue E　　61 on] vpon M　　made]
he made Z　　62 wole] wolde I　　64 ȝol] cristmasse TE　　of þis] þus E　　65
certis] *om.* M　　a] *om.* β　　religious] religion α　　refreyneþ] refreyne
DX　　66 but . . herte] *om.* M　　his³] *corr.* D, his *altered to* this A, þis BαEJ, he
MOδ　　on . . . swetnesse (77)] *om.* Z　　67 religious] religioun H　　68 mouþ]

preyeris weron þe beste þing by whiche men seruon and plesen
⌐to⌐ God. On þe toþur maner religious ben veyn, whanne þei   70
lernon þer owne rewlis and leuon þe rewle þat God ȝaf, and
ocupyon hem in þis lore, to seye and synge wiþowte book; as ȝif
þis plesude moost to God. On þe þridde maner þes ordris ben
veyn þat prechon iapis to begge betture, and to susteyne hem
cloystres and howsus, and oþre goodis þat þei coueyton. And   75
certis þes lompus faylon here, as mowon gras þat were vnteddid;
for þat gras mot nedis rote and fade in colour and swetnesse.

But Iames telluþ þat *clene religion, and religion wiþowten wem
anentis God þe Fadyr* of al, is religion þat lyueþ þus: *it visituþ moderles
children and wydewys in þer tribulacion, and kepuþ it wiþowte wem fro*   80
coueytise of þis world. Lord! siþ Iames and oþre apostlis ⌐knewe
not þes newe ordris and þes cloystres⌐, wiþ newe howsis and oþre
rytis þat þei han fowndon, what schulde moue to loue hem þus
and leeue religion þat God haþ ȝouen? It is blasfeme vnbyleue,
howeuere þat men spekon here. Þe apostlis weron tawt of þe Holy   85
Goost for to wandre in þe world, and teche men boþe by word
and deede, – for þat lore is best to men, – and not to gedere in
weete lompis, as doon owre newe ordris now. We schulden þenke,
as dydon apostlis, how men ben now wiþowton help of þer modyr
hooly chyrche, for prelatis and preestis ben turnyde amys fro þe   90
ordre þat Crist ȝaf. And siþ men ben þus wiþowton help of oure
modyr hooly chyrche, þei schulden visite more bussyly by þe
forme þat Crist haþ ȝouen. And for þis folye of nouelrye God mot

mouthes M   forȝeton] þei forgete α   69 þe] and *canc.* þe D, *om.* P   70
religious] þe religious P   71 lernon] lere H, seruiþ O   72 synge] to synge
T   73 þis] it E   to] *om.* T.   74 to²] *om.* PT   hem] þe M, here I   74
cloystres] in cloistris δ   howsus] house P   and² . . . coueyton] *twice, 2nd canc.*
D   76 mowon] moulid I   vnteddid] vnsprede α   77 fade] faile M   swet-
nesse] in swetnes TI   78 and religion] *om.* MPJ   wem] hem β   79 þe] *om.*
O   religioun] relioun B   80 it] *om.* E   81 coueytise] *om.* E   lord
. . . men (94)] *om.* Z   knewe . . . cloystres(82)] *margin corr.* D   83 rytis] rentis
EI   to loue hem] hem to loue I, hem to do E   to] for to M   84 religion] þe
religione MTE   god] criste M   ȝouen] formyd T   blasfeme] a blasfeme
ABOPTYαδJG, a blaspheme and oute of E, a blaspheme and I   vnbyleue] bileue
EI   85 þat] *om.* E   weron] *om.* α   86 men] hem EIG   by] in
BM   87 for] and for G   þat] *om.* A   88 owre] oþere H   schulden]
schullen TI   89 apostlis] þe apostles MPEI   ben now] *rev.* Y, ben E   help]
help nou E   90 turnyde] now tornid I   91 þus] þis Y, *om.* E   oure] *on eras
corr.* D, here I   92 by] by *canc.* by D, *om.* I   93 for] by T   þis] þe

nedis forsake men. And so þis chyrche is a wydwe, forsakon of
95 hyre spouse for hyre vnkyndenesse; and to counfort[e] men in þis
tribulacion were a greet almys deede.

94 Lam. 1: 1.

I   folye] forme T   nouelrye] nouestrie O   94 and so] bot Z, and seþ
I   þis] þer E, þe Z   a] now a Z   95 vnkyndenesse] vnclennesse
PZ   and] om. A   to] om. T   counforte] counforto D   men] it
Z   þis] om. Z

Dominica infra octavam Ascencionis. [Epistola.]
Sermo 28.

Estote prudentes. Prima Petri 4.

Petre ȝyueþ here anoþir forme to lerne þe lore of Cristis religion; but it is not contrarye to Iames, siþ God reuersuþ neuere hymself. *Mooste deere breþren*, seiþ Petre, *be ȝe war and wake ȝee in preyȝeris.* Petre puttuþ byfore prudence, and aftur stureþ men to preyȝeris. For monye religious may be blyndude in þer maner of preying; as 5 somme tellon more by newe preyȝer þat þe pope or oþre men haþ maad, þan þei don by þe Pater Noster maad specially of þe Trinnyte. And to conferme þis nouelrye þei alegghon of þe pope þat he made now late a preyȝer, þat he clepuþ 'Domine Iesu Criste', and|he grauntude to þis preyȝer at byddyng of þe kyng of 10 f.30 Fraunce, to eche mon þat is contrit, for o seyyng of þis preyer two þowsynde ȝer of indulgensis fro þe peyne of purgatorie. And so men nedon not to go to Rome to gete hem pleyne indulgense, siþ a man may gete here indulgense for monye þowsynde ȝeer aftur domes day, siþ he may gete in half a day an hundred þowsynde 15 ȝeer and more; but who wolde trauele þanne so folyly to þe court of Rome in perele for to gete hym indulgensis? For suche errourus

MSS: D; ABEGHIJMOPTXYZαβδ.

Dominica . . . ascensionis] here bygynneþ þe pistle on þe sixte sunday aftir eestir Y sermo 28] *om.* ABOTαδEIJXZGH estote prudentes] *om.* Y prudentes] prudentes et vigilate in oracionibus MT I pet. 4] *om.* O, prima petri x β, prima petri primo E, iac. 4 H 1 lerne] lere OαZ 2 is . . . contrarye] contrarieþ not I to] vnto M neuere] not BI 4 prudence] prudense or slenes Z and] *om.* I to] vnto M 5 religious] men Z blyndude] blynde M þer maner] *rev.* O 6 somme] somme men MOEZG by] bi a Z, bi her G preyȝer] prayers MGH þat . . . maad (7)] made of men Z pope] peple A 8 trinnyte] holy trinite AG and . . . mater (18)] *om.* Z to] so to B alegghon] aleggeden I, leggen H 9 now late] *rev.* O clepuþ] calles α 10 and] *om.* Y grauntude] grauntiþ BMYH to] vnto M, *eras.* I þis] þat α, his I at] at þe AMOPαδEIJGH 11 to] vnto M o] ones Mα 12 indulgensis] indulgence MTαI 13 to¹] for to M indulgense] indulgencis BOYIH 15 domes day] þe dai of dom H 16 wolde] schulde G trauele þanne] ┌þanne┐ trauele E folyly] *on. eras. corr.* D, fullich Mβ to] vnto M 17 for to] to I hym] hem AδJ indulgensis]

in þis mater bidduþ Petre furst to men þat þei schulon be war and
wyse, and flee errour spokon here; for it is no dreede to men þat ne
20 Crist, almy3ty and al witty, maade a preyer betture þan þis, þat
he wolde sonnere here. Lord! what mouede þe pope of Rome to
þus accepte mennys personys, þat he schulde for kyngus
byddyng, or for loue of his owne werk, graunte so myche pardon
here and not o day to þe Pater Noster? And algatis for God
25 bidduþ here by Petre aftur in þis epistle þat, 3if ony man speke
owt, he schal speke as Godus wordis. But Lord! where grauntiþ
God by his word so myche pardon for þis preyere? And certis men
schulen ellis trowe þat, 3if þe pope swere on a booc þat he
grauntuþ so myche pardon, for his graunt neuer þe more ne lesse;
30 for euene so as Crist grauntiþ is pardon or mede for mennys
preyer. And wolde God þe pope wolde ceese of syche grauntis, til
þat tyme þat he hadde tawt sufficiently þat God grauntuþ þis þat
he grauntiþ. Þerfore schuldon men be wyse here, and do good
aftur Cristus lawe; and by þis deede schulden þei prey3e betture
35 þon to wawe þer lippis, for werkis preyon ofte to God betture þan
mannys prey3er maad by mouþ. But neþeles men graunton here
þat prey3er of mouþ is good in mesure, as oþer þan þe Pater
Noster, whanne þei ben wysly takon. And þus seiþ Petre þat men
schulden wake whanne þei biddon þer prey3eris, and not slepe in
40 synne þanne whon þat þei preyon to God, but haue a wakynge
deuocion, for prey3er of soule is myche worþ.

---

22 Gal. 2: 6; **26** 1 Pet. 4: 11.

indulgence MT, indulcis G   18 bidduþ petre] rev. I   bidduþ] and þerfor biddis
Z   furst to men] om. E   to] vnto M   schulon] shulden ABMTδEIJ-
G   war] wise I   19 wyse] waar I   errour] errours BGH   men] trewe
men M   20 þis] swilke newe prayers Z   þat] and þat M   21 he] we
O   lord . . . grauntiþ (33)] om. Z   to þus] rev. α   22 mennys] mannes
YI   personys] prayers J   schulde] wolde J   23 graunte] g canc./graunte
D   24 here] herto M   algatis] also M   25 bidduþ] bidiþ Y   speke]
spekiþ B   26 grauntiþ] grauntid AMIH   27 word] wordis OδEIJ   28
schulen] shulden ABMαδEI   ellis trowe] not trow þis α   swere] swore
ABMPTY   on] vpon BMδ   29 his] þis B   neuer þe] neiþer ABMOPTY-
αβδEIJGH, neþer (-þer on eras.) þe X   30 mennys] mannys BMYαEI   31 þe] þat
þe BO   til] to AαE, vnto M   32 hadde] om. G   34 cristus] goddis I   þis
deede] þes dedis I   schulden þei] rev. M, schulden men E   betture] better þan
þei shulde M   35 to¹] om. B, for to M   ofte] ofte tyme T   to god betture]
beter to god ABOPTYαβδEIJZG, bettir vnto god M   þan] þat O   36 men] we
BY   38 wysly] bysilich O   seiþ] biddith M   39 whanne] -a- altered from -o-
D   40 þat] om. AMδIJZ   to] vnto M   a] om. Mβ   41 worþ] worþi

And þerfore seiþ Petre aftur þat, *byfore alle oþre þingis, men
schulden haue contynuel charite, for charite hyluþ multitude of synnes.* Ful
charite doþ awey synnes, al ȝif a man schryue hym neuere by
mouþ; and charite differruþ peyne, as ȝif God sawe not þis synne.   45
And þus seiþ Dauid þat 'þei ben blessude whos synnes ben þus
hydde'. Petre biddiþ aftur to his disciplis þat *þei schulen herbore eche
oþur wiþowton ony grucchyng,* siþ for þis ende God ȝyueþ howsus.
And here faylon þes newe ordris, for þei han large howsus and
fayre; and ȝeet vnneþe þei wolon herbore breþren of þer owne   50
ordre, and algatis þei gruchchen here ȝif þer gestis be costly, and
axson foode or oþur þing more þen men hemself han. And
heronne þenkon freris to luytul for, ȝif þei be neuere so yuele, ȝeet
þei chalangen to be herborud and fare as lordus wiþ pore men,
more þan euere Crist chalangede. Þei schulden þenke to flee wisly   55
boþe multi|tude and spensus, þat þei charge not þe chyrche more   f.30v
þan God wole þat þei do; and kepyng of þis rewle of Crist schulde
make freris to were awey. For *eche man,* seiþ Petre here, *as he haþ
takon grace of God* for to profiȝte to his broþur, *so schulde he mynistre
þis lent þing* – or ellis he is false traytour to God. And þus men   60
schulden *dispense Godus goodis aftur grace þat God ȝyueþ hem,* for man
haþ not þese for hymself, but to departe hem wiþ his neyȝebore.

And, for charite of man is schewid boþe in dede and word,
þerfore Petre spekuþ of word and bidduþ, *ȝif þat ony man speke, loke
þat his wordis be Godis wordis.* And wolde God þat þe pope knewe   65

---

46 Ps. 31: 1.

PZ   42 seiþ] s *canc.*/seiþ D   þat] *om.* I   43 hyluþ] -y- *altered from* -u- *corr.* D,
heelith MO   multitude] þe multitude MTE   ful . . . synnes (44)] *om.*
O   44 a] *eras.* X, *om.* ABOPTαβδEZH, he *canc.* Y   45 differruþ] referriþ G   46
þus¹] þis O   47 to] vnto M   schulen] shulden ABδJ   herbore] herfore
β   48 howsus] hous G   49 and . . . awey (58)] *om.* Z   large] fayre
TH   howsus] house α   50 fayre] large TH, faireþe I   þei wolon] *rev.*
B   herbore] herfore loue β   breþren] *om.* H   52 hemself han] *rev.*
Y   53 ȝif] þouȝ P.   54 chalangen] c/chalangen D   be] *om.* Y   55 þan]
a *altered from* o D   euere crist] *rev.* O   57 wole] wolde G   þat] at α   þis]
his I   58 seiþ petre] as petre sais Z   seiþ] as *canc.* seiþ δ, as seiþ ABMOPTY-
αβEXH   as] *om.* E   he] *om.* E   haþ takon] takeþ I   59 grace] þe grace
T   for to] to E   60 or] for OPZ   ellis] *om.* I   false] a fals T   61
dispense] dispende AEXZG   grace] *om.* Y   man] a *altered from* o D, a man
EI   62 þese] þis AI, þir goodis Z   but] *om.* O   to] ⌈to⌉ J, for to H, *om.*
E   neyȝebore] neyboris EI   63 dede] word IH   word] in word B, wordis E,
dede IH   64 ȝif þat] þ *canc.* ȝif þat P, þat ȝif TEZH   65 þat¹] *om.*
J   wordis²] *om.* G   and . . . fablis (86)] *om.* Z   þat²] *om.* H   66 þus

þis lore of Petre and kepte it wel; for þanne he schulde not þus
sende bullis of wordis þat he wot not be Godis. And here makon
men þes newe ordris to schame, and axson growndyng of þer
deedis; and certis þei may not proue by reson þat þei schulden
70 lyue on þis maner. And so þei ben nedut to seye þat þei ben
growndude by þe popis autorite, or by rewlis of charyte, or by
dremys of men or fablis. Hem schameþ for to seye þe furste, siþ
popis spekon monye wordis þe whiche be not Godus wordus; but
who schulde trowe to hem in þis? And siþ charite techeþ men to
75 not comune þus wiþ tryuauntis, but to fle hem in word and foode,
rewlus of charite teche not here for to mayntene þus þes men,
whos staat is not growndud by God. Ʒif men seyn þe þridde tyme,
þat dremes mouen to mayntene þes ordris, certis men schulde not
trowe þes dremes, for þei han browt in myche synne; and þerfore
80 þe wyse man bydduþ þat men schulde not rekke of dremes. Þe
fourþe tyme þes ordris blyndon men wiþ talis bysyde holy writ,
þat so monye myraclis han þei doon, and so manye seyntis of hem
ben canonysude. But þis speche þar no man trowe, but ʒif þei
teche þat it is Godus word; for it is ynow to men to trowe Godus
85 lawe, and oþre þingus þat þei perseyuen wiþ þer wittis, al ʒif þei
be not gylude wiþ fablis.

And Petre bidduþ aftur to his disciplis þat, *ʒif ony man mynystre,
þat* he mynystre *as of þe vertu þat God mynystreþ* in hym; and proue
he þis in good maner, betture þon ben þes foure falasis. And þus *in*
90 *alle* lyues and werkis of men *schulde God be worschipud* by þis mene,

sende] *rev.* E   þus] *om.* I   67 bullis] billes I   wot] knoweþ E   not be]
rev. I   not] *om.* α   be] by T   godis] goddis wordis B, goddis lawe
T   makon men] men axen M   68 growndyng] g/growndyng D, ground I, þe
groundyng H   of] þus of I   69 deedis] ordris T   71 þe] þes Mβ   rew-
lis] þe reulis PJ   72 fablis] be fables α   for to] to BE   73 þe . . . wordus]
om. T   þe whiche] þat E   74 þis] þus O   charite] þat charite M   to
not] *rev.* Tα   75 comune] come B   þus] *om.* H   tryuauntis] tyrauntis
OαI   but] *om.* I   76 here] herfore A   for to] to E   men] newe men
B   77 by] in Y   seyn] s *eras.*/seyn D   78 þes ordris] þis ordre α   schul-
de] wolden E   not] *om.* I   79 þes] to þese B   80 þe[1]] *om.* O   man] a
altered from o D, men O   dremes] suche dremes I   81 talis] *om.* M, fablis
T   82 han þei] *rev.* Y   manye] a *altered from* o D, many many β   of hem]
haue α   83 þar] þat O, dar EJ   man] a *altered from* o D   ʒif . . . þat (84)] *on*
eras. corr. D   ʒif] *om.* BTXG   þei teche] he be tauʒt BX(*on eras.*) G, þei taght M,
he tauʒt T   84 þat it] it þat *canc.* it A, it OαδEJ   it[2]] certis it M   to[1]] *om.*
δ   85 al ʒif] al I   86 gylude] bygilid α   87 man] a *altered from* o D   88
þat[1]] *om.* PZ   mynystre] mynystris Z   þe] *om.* Z   þat god] of god þat
δ   proue] proueþ I   89 þis] is I   in[1]] be α   betture . . . falasis] *om.*
Z   betture] ben *canc.* J   falasis] fables fallasis M   90 lyues] þes lyues J,

þat *Iesu Crist*, þat is *oure Lord*, moue men to worche þus. For, ʒif þis mene fayle to men, þei schulde not trow wordys þat ben teelde. For Crist moueþ somme by his lawe, and somme by resoun, for he is reson; and somme by lore of þer wittis, for he moueþ alle goode mennys wittis. And siþ Crist is boþe body and sowle, and ouer þes two þingis þe godhede, what þing þat Crist techiþ not þus schulde be left as suspecte.

95

lymes H   91 þat¹] *om.* MI   moue] þat moueth M   92 schulde] shul α   wordys] to *canc.* wordis E, to wordis H   93 somme¹] sum men IZ   by his] biis β   95 boþe] *om.* E   96 þing] *om.* H   þus] vs ⌐þus⌐ T

In Die Pentecostes. [Epistola.] Sermo 29.

Dum complerentur dies Pentecostes. Actus [2].

This story of apostlis deedis telluþ how þei weron disposude of God to receyue þe Hooly Gost, and medleþ monye notable wordys. Luc bygynneþ on þis maner: *whanne þe dayes of Pentecost weron fyllude, þat maaden fifty dayes in noumbre, alle þes enleuene* disciplis *weron togydere in þe same plase*; and þis plase was in Ierusalem, as it is licly by þe storye. No drede þes enleuene apostlis aftur þe resurection of Crist leddon deuou3t lif and hooly, and algatis aftur his ascencion; by þes ten dayes men seyon þe apostlis fastedon and preyedon. And þus þei camen into an hows on Wytsonday in Ierusalem. *And þer was maad hastyly fro heuene a sownd, as of a greet wynd comynge, and þis sownd fullyde al þe hows where þe apostlis weron sittynge. And þer apperudon to hem dyuersely partyde tongis as fyer; and þis fyer sat vpon hem alle* in forme of a tonge. *And þei weron alle fullude of þe Hooly Goost; and þei bygonnen to speke in langagis*, þat weron dyuerse in hemself, ri3t *as þe Hooly Goost 3af hem for to speke owt*. And so þre þingis weron seyne here, þe whiche alle bytoknedon þis myracle. Þe furste was sownd þat cam from heuene, þat fulfullude al þat hows; and þat bytokneþ þat apostlis hadden grace of God to speke his wordis. Þe secounde signe of þis

f.31 5

10

15

MSS: D; ABEGHIJMOPTXYZαβδ.

Sermo 29] *om.* ABMOPTαδEIJXZGH   dum . . . pentecostes] *om.* Y   dies] *canc.* G, *om.* O   pentecostes] *om.* AOGH   actus 2] *om.* O   2] primo DBPYαβδEIZH, 2 *on eras. of* 1 JX   1 apostlis] þe apostlis MαEIH   2 medleþ] mellid Z   3 whanne] a *altered from* o D   þe] þes M   4 fyllude] ful *canc.* fillid Y , fulfilled I   maaden] make α   enleuene] twelue α   5 in2] ⌜in⌝ G, *om.* IZ   6 no] and no δJ   enleuene] twelfe α   7 leddon] lyueden I   deuou3t lif and hooly] deuoutely and holily I   8 algatis] namely Z   his] ⌜his⌝ H, *om.* O.   þe] þat α, þat þe EI   10 in] into T   11 sownd1] soun BX   as] *om.* MβI   of] it were of δEJ   a] *om.* βG   þis] þe I   sownd2] soun BI   fullyde] fulfild T   12 þe] alle þe O   partyde] departyd T   13 as] of B   þis fyer] *om.*α   vpon] on G   þei] *om.* O   14 alle fullude] *rev.* αI   fullude] fulfillid T   of] wiþ I   in] alle in E   15 in] and β   16 hem] to hem H   for to] to H   þingis] signes P   17 alle] alle þei B   bytoknedon] betokyn α   sownd] soun B   18 þat1] and α   fullude] fillide PEZG   þat2] þe M   bytokneþ] betokynnid αEI   apostlis] þes apostelis P, þe apostlis TEIZH   19 his] alle *canc.* her E   20 þe] *om.*

myracle was of þe substaunce of fier, þat bytoknede þat þes 20
apostlis weron ful of charite to speke. Þe þridde signe of þis
myracle was of þes forme of fury tongis; and þat bytokneþ þat þes
apostlis hadden knowyng of monye langagis.

And þus seiþ Luk þat *in þe cite weron Iewis dwellynge of alle
nacionys, men of religion*; and þes Iewis cowdon dyuerse langagis of 25
contreyes þat þei hadden dwelt inne. For, aftur Cristus
resurection, and byfore his deþ also, Iewis weron scaterude in
monye londis and lernedon langagis of þes londis; and þus þei ben
clepude of þes nacionys, and camen to temple at þis feeste. And
whonne þis voys was maad to þe apostlis, þe multitude of þes Iewis camen; 30
and þei weron confusud in þer þowt, for ech of hem herde apostlis speke in þer
strange *tonge*, þat is spokon in þer contrey. And þis was a greet
wondur; *and herfore þei alle abaschedon, and wondredon, and seydon to-*
gydere 'Lo! ne be not alle þese þat spekon of þe contre of Galile? And how han
we herd, ech one his owne tonge, in whiche tonge *we weron borne*, fer awey 35
fro þis contrey?' And Luk rehersuþ sixten langagis þat þes
pylgrimes haddon at home. And þei wondredon how þes Galilees
kowdon speke þus alle þes langagis. And þe myracle was more
þat þei spakon Godus merueylis þus in so dyuerse tongis.

And here men dowton comunly wher þes apostlis spakon alle 40
on, or ech on of hem alle spac dyuerse langage fro oþur; so þat on
of hem kowde o langage, and anoþur cowde anoþur, but not þei
alle knewon eche langage. But here men þenkon by þe story þat
ech of hem knew alle þes langagis; and þus þei vndurstoden þes
men þat weron of so dyuerse contreyes. But difficulte is mouyd 45
ouer, wher eche of hem blaberude alle þes langagis. And it wolde
seme a greet wondyr þat o man spac at o tyme þus dyuerse

M   bytoknede] bitokeneþ B   þes] þe G   22 þes[1]] hys T   fury] fyre
MβEI   þat[1]] *om.* G   þes[2]] þe T   23 langagis] langagysch T   24 þe]
þis M   25 men] and men EI   and] *om.* M   26 contreyes] diuerse contrees
I   dwelt] ben I   28 lernedon] lered αH   langagis] ⌐manye⌐ langagys T,
many langagis PZ   ben clepude] are called αZ   29 temple] ⌐þe⌐ temple βδ, þe
temple ABMTαEIjZĠH   þis] þe I   feeste] festes α   30 þe[1]] *om.*
G   camen] and þei *canc.* camen D   31 apostlis] þe apostlis MTαEX-
G   speke] spekyng ABMOPTYαβδEIJXZ   32 strange] stronge B   tonge]
tungis H   is] þei M, was α   spokon] spokyn M   þer] þat β   contrey]
contrees δ   þis] þus O   33 herfore] þerfore TαZ   and wondredon] *om.*
M   35 ech one] eche H   owne] *om.* I   36 sixten] suche sixtene G   38
þus] *om.* I   more] þe more ME   39 þus] *om.* M   40 and] *om.* H   þes]
þe H   41 ech on] ech AEIXG   langage] langagis ABY   42 þei alle] *rev.*
H   43 knewon] koude M   þenkon] þeken Y   þe] þis I   44 knew]
koude P   vndurstoden] vnderstonden MTE   45 of so] *rev.* H, of α   46 alle]

langagis of men, siþ þat dyuerse langagis axson dyuerse for-
myngis of voyses, þe whiche myȝte not be togydere. But here men
þenkon by þe story þat þis myracle|myȝte be þus: þes apostlis
knewon dyuerse langagis, whonne þei weron spokone vnto hem,
but þei spakon alle o maner of voys to þes alyenys þat þei spakon
to – and þis was þer owne langage, þat hadde kyndely his forme.
But by þe same langage boþe þei and oþre conceyuedon
dyuersely, as þe same sownd of bellis moueþ men dyuersly: oon
þat þei spekon þus, anoþur þat þei spekon dyuerse. And it is liȝt
to God to moue men to dyuerse conseytis, al ȝif þe langage be þe
same. And þus þe myracle was þe more þat God mouede þus þes
ynwittis, al ȝif þe voyses weron oon þat þei herdon of þe apostlis.
And it is licly þat þes pylgrimes conseyuedon þe same langage þat
þei knewon mooste of alle, and þe wyt of þis langage. And so eche
mon hadde his owne myracle; and God mouede apostlis as he
wolde. And þis figurede oonnesse of herte; as þes men þat maden
þe towr weron toknede þat þei hadden by pruyde dyuerse hertis
by dyuerse langagis; and for þis God made þer langage chaunge.

Heere men may telle þe puple how men schulon dispose hem to
receyue þe Hooly Goost by þe gracious ȝifte of God. Þei schulon
faste and be deuout, as weron þe apostlis at þis tyme; and þanne
þei schulen fele sownd from heuene, þat schal moue hem to
goostly werkis. And algatis þat þei haue fier of charite to make
hem cleer, for fumys of temporal goodis letton monye to take þys
Spirit. And no men ben more vndisposude to take þis Spirit, þan

64 Gen. 11: 1–9.

---

om. I   48 formyngis] formyng P, sounynges I   49 voyses] voys Tα, versis
M   50 þes] þe I   51 knewon] knowe O   vnto] ⌐vn⌐to O, to H   52 of]
om. Z   53 þis] þus O   was] *om.* O   þer] *om.* M   hadde] þei had
M   his] þis I   54 by] *om.* Mβ   55 as . . . dyuersly] *margin* Y *om.*
M   as] and *canc.* as G, and as H   56 anoþur] and anoþer T   57 conseytis] y
altered from n D   58 þus²] *om.* G   þes] þe I, þaire Z   59 ynwittis] wittis in
α   voyses] voyce α   oon] al one E   þe] *om.* G   60 langage] langagis
B   61 of alle] able I   62 apostlis] þe apostlis TαI   63 þis] *om.*
Z   oonnesse] onhede I   þes] ȝif T, þa Z   64 towr] toure of babilone
Z   pruyde] sum pride T   65 for þis] þus BOPTYEXZ   langage] langagis
M   chaunge] to chaunge α   66 schulon] shulden ABMOTαβZGH, ⌐shulde⌐J,
om. I   67 þe²] *om.* O   schulon] shulden BMOYZH   68 weron] *om.*
E   þe] *om.* OαG   apostlis] apostlis weren E   at] as Y   69 þei schulen]
rev. Y   schulen] shulden ABOZ   sownd]s *canc.*/sownd D, soun B   71 cleer]
clere ⌐onhed⌐ J   fumys] fomys M, þe smoke Z   þys] y *on eras. corr.* D, his
Y   72 spirit¹] goodis *canc.* spirit D   73 fumes] smoke Z   distorblen]

ben suche men for þer enuye; and þer fumes distorblen þer eyr to
take þis Goost. And it is nedful to men to haue tongis as God
bidduþ, þat, ȝif ony of hem speke, þei speke Godus wordis and   75
not falshede, and not worldly, ne veyne wordis, þat ben fer fro
Godus lykyng. And þus þes þre condicions þat weron in apostlis
disposon men to receyue þe Hooly Goost, and contraries letton
men þerfro; for no drede defaute is in man and not in God, why
God liȝtneþ hym not.   80

---

distorben XH   eyr] iyȝen H   74 goost] spirit canc. goost D, spirite
ME   tongis] tokynnes α   75 þat ȝif] rev. AδIJ   þei speke] rev. E   þei]
þat þei α, he I   76 not 2] om. α   ne] om. δIJ   77 lykyng] dwellynge
T   þes] om. M   in] in þe BMY   79 for] fro H   defaute] þe canc. defaute
D, þe faute G   why] whi þat B   80 liȝtneþ] liȝtiþ H, lettiþ O, letniþ
β   hym] hem E

In die sancte Trinnitatis. [Epistola.] Sermo 30.

Uidi hostium apertum in celo. Apocalypsis 4.

This epistle of seyn Iohn telluþ monye statis of þe chyrche and medleþ lore of þe Trinnyte; wherfore þe chyrche reduþ it today. Þre sy3tis fallon to man. Þe furste is bodyly si3t, þat falluþ to a mannys y3en þe while he wakiþ; and þis is knowon. Þe toþur is
5 ymagynarie si3t, þat falluþ to man whonne he slepuþ; and in þis si3t ben monye degrees, somme hyere and somme lowere. Þe þridde si3t and þe hyerste is si3t of mynde of mannys soule, as spiritis seen wel in heuene in Godis word þingus þat schulen be. Þe secounde si3t hadde þis Iohn and þe vndurstondyng þerof; for
10 þe Trinnyte telde hym in huydyng and priuely alle þe grete staatis of þe chyrche, þat schulon come tyl þe day of doom. Iohn seiþ *he saw a dore open in heuene; and þe furste voys* of an aungel, *þat spac to hym as a trompe, bad hym þat he schulde come þidere, and he schulde schewe hym þingis þat moten be aftur* þis in þe chyrche. Þe dore in
f.32 15 heuene þat was opon bytokneþ|þe staat of hooly chirche. For oo staat þat comeþ byfore brynguþ in anoþur staat, as rest of man in þe ny3t disposuþ hym to traueyle o morwe. And so þe furste staat of hooly chyrche disposuþ it to þe toþur, and so þe laste rest in blis mot nedis come of oþre byfore; as prechyng þat apostlis
20 prechedon bro3te in aftyr martirdam, and staat of martiris whonne it was opon was an opon dore in heuene. But now synne

MSS: D; ABEGHIJMOPTXYZαβδ.

In . . . trinnitatis] *om.* P, epistola E   sermo 30] sermo o β, *om.* ABOTαδEIJ-XZGH   uidi . . . celo]*om.* Y   apertum in celo]*om.* OH, apertum PEZ   apoc. 4] *om.* O, apoc. x β   1 seyn] *om.* ABδIJ   3 furste] first si3t H   a] *om.* ABOαG   4 þe¹] *om.* Z   while] whiche Oα   þe toþur] þe oþer B   5 man] a man AδE   in] of α   7 si3t¹] *om.* A   þe] *om.* E   8 word] wordis B   þingus þat] *rev.* T   schulen] schulden B   9 þe²] in þe T   11 schulon] suld Z   tyl] to MαδE   12 open] opened B   an] *om.* ABPY, þe Z   13 a] *om.* α   bad] and bad Z   he²] *om.* β   14 moten] most α, schulde E   þis] þese BOPTYαβEJXZ, *om.* M   16 rest] *om.* Z   man] a man H   17 hym . . . disposuþ (18)] *om.* O   to] for to B   o] ⌜on⌝ X, on ⌜þe⌝ δ, on þe EZ, atte Mα, in þe H   18 rest] staat of holy cherche disposeþ it to þe toþer and so þe laste reste I   19 nedis come] *rev.* PZ   apostlis] þe apostelis OTZH   20 bro3te] b *eras.*/bro3te D   aftyr] *om.* AE   21 was¹] is T   was an opon] *om.*

of slow cowardis haþ closud þis dore for children drede; for, not
only for bodyly peyne, but for worldly godis and fauour of men,
men dreedon to meyntene trewþe of God and to telle it boldly.
And þus bodyly hardynesse haþ qwenched hardynesse of soule.　25
Þis siȝt of Iohn and þis voys weron ordeynede of þe Trinnyte, and
so Iohn dremyde not suche dremes as doon dronkone men and
lecherouse. But God prentyde figuris in Iohn, and tawte hem eft
by aungelis lore; and God medelude wordis of counfort þat Iohn
schulde not fayle in þis, siþ þis lore þat Iohn hadde here is needful　30
to þis fyȝtyng chyrche. Speche of þe aungel as a trompe is greet
auctorite of his word, þat it mot nedelyngis be so, siþ grete God
haþ ordeyned it. And so þis aungel counfortuþ Iohn to come to
hym and lerne þis lore.

　　And Iohn was anoon in spirit, and saw on þe secounde maner. A　35
man is teeld þanne in spirit whanne his spirit seeþ of God, and his
bodily werkis ceeson, and his owt wittis ben closude. *Iohn saw how
a seete was put in heuene,* as it were a trone, *and* a lord *sittynge þeronne,*
as it were Iesu Crist. *And he þat sat* vpon þis seete *was licly in colour to
þes two stonys: iaspis* is þe furste stoon, þe whiche stoon is grene of　40
colour, *and sardynys* þe secounde stoon, of reed colour as he
brennyde. And þe˹s˺ two tellon to men þat Crist oure lord is ful of
counfort, as grene colour makuþ men glad and brynguþ counfort
to þer yȝen; þe reede colour techeþ men how Crist counfortuþ
m[e]nnys charite, and makuþ hem boolde to be martiris, and schede　45
þer blood for his loue. *And þe reynbowe was abowte þe seete, lik to þe siȝt
of smaragdyn stoon.* Þis reynbowe tellude to Iohn þat þe
godhede abowte Crist tempreþ graciously þe veniaunce þat men
don aȝenys his chyrche, þat it fayle not for hard turment; and þis
counfort wiþ charite makiþ pursuede men to laste.　　　　　50

O　　　22 þis] þe G　　　drede] dredes Z　　　23 worldly] worldis B　　　24 to¹] for to
M　　　trewþe] þe trewþe T, ˹þe lawe˺ E　　　to²] *om.* AM　　　boldly] forth boldely
M, bodelich CαβIZH　　　25 hardynesse¹] h *eras.* /hardynesse D　　　26 þis¹] siþ DH,
þis *on eras.* X, þe α　　　of¹ . . . voys] and þis voys of Ion I　　　weron] was B　　　27
doon] *om.* M　　　28 lecherouse] lecchours ABMOPYβEIGH　　　in iohn] newe M,
noone β　　　hem] him G　　　eft] *om.* IJ, efter Z　　　29 god] *om.* Z　　　medelude]
medliþ AαδIJG　　　30 þis¹] þis lore E　　　needful] medeful Z　　　31 speche] speke
β　　　þe] *om.* TZ　　　a] *om.* H　　　33 it] it so H　　　34 lerne] lere αZH, to lurne
δ　　　36 of] *om.* G　　　38 þeronne] þerinne T　　　39 it] *om.* E　　　vpon] on
E　　　þis] þe Z　　　licly] liche ABOPTYαδEJGH　　　40 two] *om.* δIJ　　　of] in
MI　　　41 þe] is þe ME　　　he] it M　　　42 and] of E　　　þes] -s *added corr.*
DE　　　43 grene] a grene M　　　44 reede] þridde BO　　　45 mennys] mannys
DX　　　martiris] cristis martris δ　　　and²] to I　　　46 and] *om.* Z　　　þe¹] þes
O　　　lik] licly M　　　þe³] his δ　　　47 smaragdyn] a smaragdyn AME　　　tel-

And in compas abowte þis seete weron foure and twenty lasse seetis, and þes lesse setis weron luytule *tronys, and on hem saton foure and twenty elderne men*. Þis þing bytokneþ to Iohn þat in þe chyrche aboue in heuene is a noumbre of grete seyntis þat preyon God for þis

55 chyrche. *White clopis* of þes elderne men bytoknen clennesse þat þei ben inne; *and corounus of gold* þat þei han is goostly victorie þat þei han don. And þus, siþ Crist is in boþe his chyrchis, he haþ seyntis heere byneþe þat don in somme maner of figure, as don seyntis in heuene. So þes foure and twenty seetis ben foure and

60 twenty plasis heere; and þes elder men ben þo þat holden wisly Godus lawe, for, riȝt as foure tyme sixe makon þis noumbre, so

f.32v foure wittis of hooly wryt þat is parfiȝt maken þes elder men. |But þer konnyng is here ful þinne, as þis is clepud a þinne nowmbre. But þei han clennesse of lif, and þer victorie on som maner.

65 *Of þis trone comen forþ liȝtnyngis and voysis and þondres* boþe. Þis trone is Godus seete, þat ordeyneþ þes þre þingus to come heere; leyȝtyngis ben myraclis or holy lif, þat laston here for a while; voysus ben prechyngis of Godus wille of mede þat hise knyȝtis schulden haue; þondryngus ben tellyng[is] of gret peyne, þat men

70 schulon haue þat schulen be dampnyde. And þes þre comen of God, and by boþe hise chyrchis vndur hym; as mannys voys comeþ fro his herte, by his þrote and by his mowþ.

Seuene laumpis brennynge byfore þe trone ben seuene spiritis of God, as Iohn telluþ. Boþe Cristus chyrchis han seuene laumpis þat ben

75 brennynge byfore God. Þe furste seuene ben alle þes seyntis, þat ben in heuene and don Godus wille, and helpon mennys charite in erþe, and techon hem as laumpus brennynge. Þe secounde seuene ben alle þes seyntis þat don in erþe þis offys of laumpis, as

lude] telliþ AI   49 fayle] falle I   50 charite] þis charite OE   51 þis] þe Z   weron] was E   52 þes] þe I   lesse] *om.* E   54 god] g *eras.*/god D   þis]hys α   57 siþ]seiþ IZG   is]*om.* I   in]ᵈin¹δ, *om.* E   boþe] aboue E   his]*om.* O   chyrchis]chirche BE   59 so]and so H   60 plasis] pacis Y   þo] þes E   61 riȝt] *om.* E   tyme] tymes ABMOPTYαβδEIJ-G   þis] þe O   63 here] *om.* G   ful] wel þin *canc.* ful D   64 lif] crist E   65 liȝtnyngis] leityngis BPTYβδEIJGH   voysis] voyce α   66 ordeyneþ] ordeyned A   67 leyȝtyngis] liȝtyngis AMOTαH   or] of ATYδE-IJ   68 prechyngis] preching AMOPYαβδEIJZG   hise] þes Mβ   69 schulden] schullen, *2nd l altered from* d X, shulen ABMOPTYαδEIJZ   þondryngus] thundres αG   tellyngis] tellyng DBMOPTYαβEIX   71 by] be α   73 seuene²] þe seuen M, þo *canc.* seuen α   74 telluþ] seith M   chyrchis] chirche δ   75 byfore god] *om.* I   þes] þe Z   seyntis] siȝtis O   76 mennys] mannus M   77 hem] men OPαEIJZ   as] *om.* T   78 þes] þo I, þe

schulden be byschopis and grete prelatis; but þer laumpis ben
quenchede now. But God fayluþ not in neyþur of his chyrchis, to   80
ordeyne þes tuo vnyuersites to heete and to liȝtne comunes, boþe
by charite and wyt. And so þer wylle and vndurstondyng ben
fullide by þes tuo seuenes.

Iohn saw also *in compas of þis seete as it weere a see of glas þat were lyȝk
to cristal.* And þis bytokneþ þe chirche here, for it is in tribulacion,   85
as men ben ofte in þe see. But þei ben by craft of God sad to siȝt as
is glas; and þei ben of clene lif, as cristal is clene wiþowte motis,
for þe euerelastynge ordynaunce of God kepuþ his chirche here in
erþe þat it may be pursuwid wiþ flodis, but yt may not perische ne
synke. But popis and oþre þat seyon þes wordis schulden so lyue   90
and suwe Crist þat þei be partis of hooly chyrche; or ellis þes
wordis be not to hem.

Aftur *saw Iohn foure bestis in þe myddyl and compas of þis seete; and
þes bestis weron fulle of yȝen, boþe byfore and byhynde. Þe furste best was
liȝk to a lyon; þe secounde was liȝc to a calf; þe þridde hadde a face as a   95
mannys; and þe fourþe beest was lic to a fleyng egle.* As þes foure bestis
weron som tyme Mark and Luc, Matheu and Iohn, so þer ben
now oþre in þe chyrche lic to hem. As Mark telluþ of Cristus
rysynge, so þer be now wyse men þat tellon of þe laste rysynge.
And as Luc telde of sacrifice and of presthode of Crist, so þer be   100
now somme men þat tellon how folc schulden do þer sacrifise, and
how þat preestis schulden lyue to come to presthode in heuene.
And as Matheu telde wel of þe manhede of Crist, so somme men
tellon now to folc what lif þat Crist lyuede here. And as Iohn

Z	þis offys] þese officis B, þe offys M	79 but . . . now (80)] *om.* Z	80 his]
þes two M	81 þes tuo] boþe þes E	heete] hem I	and to] *om.* O, and ⌐to⌐
T, leyte *canc.* and β	boþe] *om.* H	82 and²] and be αEZ	þer] boþe her
E	wylle] ⌐charite⌐ J, *om.* I	and³] and her EH, *om.* I	vndurstondyng]
vndirstondinges I	83 tuo] *om.* α	seuenes] seuene G	84 þis] his
B	seete] cyte Z	a] *om.* T	85 and] *om.* P	þis] þat M	here] *om.*
δ	86 craft] þe craft I	87 is¹] *om.* Y, þe A	of] in I	as] a δ	cristal
is clene] is cristal H	89 yt] ⌐it⌐ X, *om.* M	90 popis] prelatis Z	91 hooly]
þis haly Z	þes] þe⌐s⌐ P, þe Z	93 aftur] and eftir M, after after I	þe] *om.*
MZ	myddyl] mydde αZ	and¹] of þe E, þe Z, and in H	94 boþe] *om.*
O	þe] and þe IH	95 to¹] vnto M	þe¹] and þe AδIJ	was] *om.*
A	to²] vnto M	as a] like to a E, as of a H	96 mannys] man αE-
H	foure] *om.* I	97 and¹] ⌐and⌐ β, *om.* B	matheu] and Mathew
I	þer] þey E	98 to] vnto M	cristus] crist E	99 so] and as luc telde of
sacrifise *canc.* so D, for OG	100 of²] *om.* α	101 now . . men] sum men now
α	now] *om.* B	102 preestis] p *eras.*/preestis D	lyue] do and life
Z	to²] to þe M	104 to folc] *om.* E	þat] *om.* BE	105 hyȝe] heȝy T,

105 fley3 hy3e aboue and telde þe godhede of Crist, ⌜so somme men
    telle now þe hy3e dyuynyte of Crist⌝. And þei ben fulle of y3en,
    boþe byfore and byhynde, for þei seen counfortis and perelis of
    tyme to come and tyme passud. *And ech one of þese foure bestus hadde*
f.33 *sixe wyngis| as* Ion seiþ, *and in viroun and wiþinne þei weren ful of eyen.*
110 Þe firste wynge was lawe of kynde, þe toþir was lawe of Moyses,
    þe þridde was lore of prophetis, þe feerþe was lawe of þe gospel,
    þe fyueþe was lore of oþere apostelis, and þe sixeþe was
    prophecye of Ion and story of Luke. By þes sixe partis of holy
    writt fleen alle þes foure beestes, boþe bifore and bihynde, and
115 now on þe ry3t syde, and now on þe left, now vp and now doun,
    aftir þat þe spiry3t moeueþ hem. For þei tellen now of þyngis to
    come, and now Goddis werkis þat ben passed; now of blisse of
    seyntis in heuene, and now of peyne of feendis in helle; now of
    hey3nesse of God aboue, and now of sorewe of men in erþe. And
120 þes foure weren ful of ey3en, for þei haue boþe out witt and
    innere.

    And Ion seiþ þat þes fowre beestes *hadden not reste day ne ny3t, but
    seiden 'hooli, hooli, hooly, þe* ⌜*Lord*⌝ *þat is God almy3ti, þat was and is and
    is to come'.* Þes foure beestis traueleden faste to worshipe of þe
125 Trynyte, for al þe trauele of þes seyntis was for worshipe of God.
    And þei seiden in word and dede þat God is oo kynde and þre
    persones; and so þei seyden þat þe same God is and was and ay
    shal be; and, as he made al þis world, so he shal ende þis world;
    and as God haþ power wiþinne, and resoun euene wiþ to þis

---

113 i.e. Rev. and Acts.

---

om. α   telde] telliþ E   þe] of þe H   so . . . crist (106)] *margin* D   106
telle] *om.* O   þe] in H   hy3e] he3y T   dyuynyte] digny *canc.* dyuynyte D,
dignite TG   108 hadde] has α   109 as] *2nd hand begins* D, and O   viroun]
verne α   110 of ¹] *om.* Y   111 lore] -ore *on eras. corr.* D, *om.* T   prophetis] þe
profetis M   þe²] and þe M   was²] *om.* PZ   112 was¹] *canc.* β, *om.*
BOPTYδIJZ   lore] lawe *canc.* lore β, lawe I   and] *om.* M   113 prophecye]
þe profecy M   story] þe stori BMYG   114 fleen] flyen MαE   alle] *om.*
O   and²] *om.* Y   115 left] left syde, syde *canc.* DX, lefte ⌜syde⌝ H, lefte syde
P   116 þat] *om.* T   117 goddis] of *canc.* goddis DX, of E   118 now²] and
nowe M   119 and¹] *om.* H   120 weren] ben ABMOPTYαβδEIJXZ-
G   out] outere δ   121 innere] inwit I, inne Z   122 þat] *om.* M   fowre]
om. α   not] no PZ   ne] and H   123 hooly] ⌜hooly⌝ β, *om.* I   þe] *om.*
δE   lord] *corr.* D, *om.* OδEIJ   and is] and is *canc.* J, *om.* O   124 faste] firste
δ   125 þe] *om.* Z   þes] þe Mβ   worshipe] þe wirship M   126 dede] in
dede E   and³] in M   127 ay] euer OTE   128 so . . . world²] *margin corr.*
αI   þis²] al þis B   129 as . . . inne] *on eras. corr.* D   wiþinne] *om.*

power, so he haþ euene likyng of hem; and alle þes þre þyngis ben   130
God. And þus aftir þis Trynyte man þenkiþ on power þat God
haþ ȝouen hym; and, aftir þe witt and resoun of God, he worchiþ
aftir þis power; and, aftir he haþ deuocioun of þes two þyngis, of
þe Fadir and þe Sone, and, ȝif alle his werkis ben þus ensaumplid,
þanne he sueþ wel þe Trynyte. But many men faylen in resoun, as   135
þes þat synnen aȝenus þe Sone, and many men in contynue
deuocioun, as þes þat synnen aȝens þe Goost, for þes ben þo þat
God shuttiþ out at domes day for defaute of oyle.

*And whan þes foure beestis hadden ȝouen glorye and honour and
blessynge to hym þat sittiþ vpon þe trone, lyuynge in worldis wiþouten ende,*   140
foure and twenti elder men fillen doun bifore hym þat sittiþ in trone, and
louteden hym þat is lyuyng bi alle tymes wiþouten ende. For as is ordre of
seyntis in blis, so shulde be of seyntis heere. For God biddiþ
Moyses werche by ensaumple shewid in þe hil; and as seyntis ben
in blis boþe wiþoute pride and stryf, so men shulden be in erþe   145
acordynge to trewþe of o God.

138 Matt. 25: 1–12; **143** Exod. 25–6.

E   wiþ] *eras.* X, *om.* MPTYβZG   to] ⌐to¬ δ, *om.* H   þis] his AT   130
haþ] *on eras. corr.* D, sȝal haue OE, shal δIJ   euene] *om.* M   alle] þus alle
I   132 haþ ȝouen] ȝeuiþ X   hym] to him PZ   þe] *om.* E   133 þis] his
BE   aftir²] afir Y   he] þat he E   haþ] doeþ B   of¹] in α   134 þe²]
of þe MαE   þus] so α   136 þes] þese men Y, done þes E, þa Z   men] *om.*
OαH   in] failen in δIJ   137 goost] holy goost MY   138 out] wiþoute
E   139 and²] et α   140 vpon] vp I   in] into H   worldis] world PZ,
woldis Y, þe worldis H   141 foure . . . ende (142)] *om.* I   elder] alder
O   fillen] felden ABOPTYβδG   in] on þe Y, in þe Mδ   142 þat] þat þat
B   lyuyng] lyfygynge O   is ordre] is ordre, *marked for rev.* B, ordre is AG, ⌐þer¬ is
ordre J, þer is ordre M, it is ordre E, his ordre I, ordre H   143 be] it be E   of] *om.*
β   god] ⌐god¬ J, *om.* I   144 werche] which A   *margin* exo. 26 T   145
boþe] *om.* IJ   men . . . erþe] scholden men in erþe be I   146 trewþe] þo truþe
α   o] ⌐o¬ J, *om.* APαZ.

Dominica prima post Trinitatem. Epistola.
[Sermo 31.]

Deus caritas est. Prima Iohannis 4.

Ion telliþ in þis epistle hou ⌜þat⌝ men shulden loue togidere, for
he þat wantiþ in þis loue wantiþ in lyf as a feend. First Ion takiþ
þis maxym as a principle of bileue: *most dere, God is charite*; and þus
of God comeþ al oure loue. Soþ it is þat God and man han summe
5 names comyne to hem, as ben þes comyn names, þe whiche tellen
noon vnparfy3t þyng. And, siþ loue is siche a name, loue mot
nedis acorde to God; and he is nedis welle of loue, and loueþ alle
þyngis in þis world. But, as he loueþ hymsilf moost, for he mot
nedis be best þyng, so he loueþ oþir men aftir þat þei ben good.
10 And þus aftir charite of God shulden men shape þer charite.
f.33v   And Ion declariþ þis sentense þus: *in þis þyng apperede God|dis*
charite in vs, þat he sente his on borun Sone into þe world, and made
hym man *þat we lyue bi þis Sone*. For, as alle þing is maad bi hym, so
he makiþ þyngis parfy3t. And so no man may come to blis bi
15 uertues but bi þis Sone, as no man may be saued, but bi suyng of
his lyf; for it mot nedis be a reule to eche man þat gooþ to heuene.
And for eche oþir man is a membre þat hongiþ on Crist, Crist seiþ
bi Ioon in his gospel þat no man styeþ into heuene, but mannus
Sone þat is in heuene. Knytte þou þe bi loue to Crist, or ellis þou
20 comest neuere to heuene. Siþ þe Fadir 3af Crist his Sone for vs, to

18 John 3: 13.

MSS: D; ABGHIJMOPTXYZαβδ.

Sermo 31] *om.* DABOTαδEIJXZGH   deus . . . est] *om.* Y   est] est et qui manet
in caritate T   I io. 4] *om.* OP, io. 4 ZH   I ion] pon O   þat] *corr.* DX, *om.*
AδIJH   shulden] shulen β   2 in¹] *om.* A   in²] *om.* A   a] ⌜a⌝ β, *om.* IJ,
þe H   takiþ] techeþ O   3 maxym] *om. (gap)* O, grettest of al Z   a] *om.*
αZ   4 al] *om.* I   han]-e *eras.* D   5 þe] *om.* B   6 noon]-on *on eras. corr.* D,
now OδIJ, now ⌜noun⌝ T, not α   siþ loue] *rev.* O, loue Z   name] name ⌜loue þes
komune names⌝ T   mot] moste M   7 nedis²] *om.* M   8 mot] moste G   9
þat] þat ⌜þat⌝ *2nd eras.* D, þat þat OTYβδJXG   10 shulden] shulen H   11
sentense] charite α   12 on] owne OH   þe] þis H   16 his] þis αβ   a] *om.*
Z   18 ioon in his] iones M   mannus] bi mannes Y   19 þe bi loue] þi beleue

bigge vs and saue vs, we moten nedis shewe hym sum loue bi his
ȝiftis þat he ȝeueþ vs. And þus to clepe oure werkis oure sone, we
shulden ȝyue þis sone to hym; for alle oure werkis shulde we do in
name of God, and to his worship. But as þis Lord is more þan we,
so moten his ȝiftis passe oure. *And þus is charite of God shewid, not as*   25
we hadden first *loued God, but þat he louede first vs, and sente his Sone helpe*
for oure synnes. We shulen vndirstonde heere þat God mot loue
kyndeli, and eche creature of God haþ kyndeli an appetyt to
sauyng of hymself, and to helping of oþir þyngis. And so þe synne
of a feend, þat is not Goddis creature, difformeþ hym and   30
contrarieþ hym fro þe firste ordynaunce of God; and þus þis is a
feendis manere þat anticrist quenchiþ loue, and for his owene
heyȝnesse haþ enuye þat oþere ben goode.

And þus seiþ Ion for mannus loue to telle hou þat it shal be,
moost deere, he seiþ, *ȝif God haþ loued vs, we shullen loue vsself togidere,*   35
for no creature of God may fayle algatis of þis loue. And þus we
shullen be parfite in loue, as oure Fadir of heuene is parfiȝt. For
ȝif man loue his owene good, and wiþ þat harme his broþer, þis
loue is no parfiȝt loue, but hate aȝenus charite. Loke þat eche loue
of þiself turne to profiȝt of þi neyȝhebore, for so doþ loue of þe   40
Trinite. And to þis enten[t] seiþ Poul þat charite sekiþ not his
owene þing, for charite loueþ comunyng and profityng, for so doþ
God. And þus, ȝif men haue clene loue, þei don non harm streytli
to þyng, but good aftir al þer power, oþer good profitable or
plesyng. And þus men in charite don good to boþe þes chirchis   45
and oþere þingis, for charite dooþ good and noon harme, but bi
occasioun of more good.

And þus werkis of þes popis shewen þat þei ben feendis
children, for o pope harmeþ anoþer for to gete hym propre good;
as many þousand markis of reumes ben dispendid for Vrbanus   50

37 Matt. 5: 48;   **41** 1 Cor. 13: 5.

α   20 to¹] in Mα   23 shulde we] *rev.* H   in] in þe I   24 god] hym *canc.*
god D   þis] þe δ   25 his] þes I   26 louede first] *rev.* αδZ   helpe] helþ
β   27 shulen] shulden PIZ   29 oþir] þer β   þe] *om.* O   30 a] þe
O   þat] ˹þat˺ H, *om.* β   31 contrarieþ] not *canc.* contrarieþ DX, not contrarieþ
δIJ   hym] *om.* H   32 anticrist] a man Z   33 haþ] haue Z   34 þat] *om.*
A   35 haþ] haue PTαE   shullen] shulden ABMPTYZ   37 shullen] shulden
ATYαδZH   38 man] a man AYαδ   good] god α, *om.* IJ   broþer] owne broþer
T   39 no] not ABTαH   41 entent] enten D   seiþ] spekiþ Tαl   42 and]
om. β   44 good¹] god *can.* ˹do˺ α   oþer] or BY   45 men] *om.* β   to
. . . good (46)] *om.* O   þes] his AH, þe Z   chirchis] chirges M   48

cause, and many þousand men slayn – but who shulde seie þat þis
were loue but moost harm? Heere is disseit of mennus soulis, in
feiþ, in hope and charite þat ben falsly feyned heere. And
whoeuere trowiþ to þis power þat is þus feyned of þe pope, he is
55 harmed in his soule more þan is bodili harm. And þus þes freris
and oþre ordris þat seien þat þei ge[n]dren charite, and maken
men to largen þer almes, feynen falsly aftir þer fadir. And þus,
whan þei maken freris, þei faylen in charite of God, for þei failen
f.34 of Goddis reule in multipliyng of felowis|þus – as þe feend þat
60 temptiþ men coueitiþ to haue feloushid in peyne, and a lecchour
seiþ to a womman þat he loueþ hire, and wile brynge forþ mo
creaturis of God to profy3t of holi chirche, and so a þeef þat getiþ
hym felowis to robbe trewe men of þer goodis. Alle suche failen in
charite, and ben ful of enuye; for faile in charite of on and faile in
65 charite of alle. For charite is an heueneli uertu, and dooþ not
good to o man, but 3if it do to alle men, and doþ neuere harm
strey3tli. And ri3t as man þat loueþ his beli doþ in þat harme to it,
so a frere þat loueþ a child to make hym frere harmeþ hym. And a
man, þat loueþ a womman to synne ⌐wiþ hire⌐, doþ hire harm, as
70 a feend þat temptiþ a man to haue hym euere his felou3 in helle
doþ hym harm a3enus charite, for hym failiþ ri3t purpos. For
charite dooþ neuere harm ry3tli, but euere good, for it mot nedis
come of God bi þe lawe þat he haþ 3ouen. An⌐d⌐ þanne it erriþ
not in doyng good ne in menes to do þis good. As, 3if God hadde
75 ordeyned þes foure sectis for to profite, þanne in takyng on of þes
shulde not man do harme to þe chirche; and 3if God ordeyned
noon of þes, þanne in mayntenyng of ony of hem, he doþ harm to
Cristis chirche – and þanne he failiþ in charite and loueþ neþer
God ne man.

80   And to þis entent spekiþ Ione þat man shulde kyndeli loue his

and . . . enuye (64)] om. Z   50 þousand] þousyndes T   dispendid] dispend O,
spendyde α   51 þousand] þousyndes of T   52 moost] þe moste M   53 in]
om. A, arid Mαβδ   and¹] in O   54 trowiþ] trowe T   to] in Y   þus] om.
M, þis O   55 is] his BO   56 þat²] om. M   gendren] gederen DIJX   57
largen] alarge I   59 of¹] in M   reule] rewlis O   þat] om. δ   60
coueitiþ] to coueyte T   62 of²] to ABOPTYαβIJ   63 trewe] om. M   suche]
suche men I   64 for faile] om. IJ   for] and sa wha þat Z   faile¹] þei faile M,
failis Z   and faile] failis Z   66 to¹] til α   it] he B   to²] til α   67
and . . . hym² (68)] om. Z   man] a canc. man Y, a man BMTαGH   beli] baly
O, helþ β   68 frere²] a frere BMTαG   a³] as a Z   69 wiþ hire] corr.
D   hire²] om. O   70 a¹] om. A, sa a Z   a²] om. A   euere] euermor
α   73 he] god α   and . . . entent (80)] om. Z   74 menes] mes Mβ   77

broþir; and for þis ende haþ God ordeyned þat man shulde
knowe his broþir heere. But *siȝte of God is not heere*, but oþir manere
of syȝte in heuene. But, *ȝif we louen vsself togidere, God dwelliþ þanne
in vs, and his charite is parfyȝt in vs*, and strecchiþ oure loue to alle
þyngis. And *bi þis may men knowe heere þat þei dwellen in God, and God* 85
in hem, þat he haþ ȝouen hem of his spiryȝt, to loue comunely as he
loueþ. *And we haue seen and beren witnesse þat þe Fadir sente his Sone to*
saue þis world, and to profite boþe to saued men and dampned. For
clerkis prouen heere bi resoun þat Cristis lif and his dedis don
good to alle creaturis bi perfeccioun þat he getiþ hem. For it is 90
knowun þat alle saued men haue good bi passioun of Crist, for
ellis þeᵣiⁱ shulden neuere haue comen to heuene, ne þer synne
haue be euere forȝeuen. Alle þat ben dampned in helle haue
greet good of Cristis passioun, for þei haue iust punyshyng, and
þat is good – ȝhe to hem; and, but ȝif Crist hadde dyed þus, þei 95
shulden haue synned more in þe world, and so þer harme shulde
haue be more, and þer peyne þat sueþ þis synne. Alle oþir partis
of þe world seruen in ordre to God and man. And, siþ þei haue
appetyt herto, and þis is performed bi Cristis passioun, eche oþir
part of þe world haþ good bi passion of Crist. And þus mennus 100
charite shulde strecche bi þe lawe þat Crist haþ ȝouen.

What man þat euere confessiþ þat Iesu is Goddis Sone, God dwelliþ in
hym, and he in God, bi þis parfyȝt confessioun. Þis confessioun
shulde be willeful in ryȝt lif, for ellis it is vncompleet, and
knowyng aȝenus his wille. And þus Ion was moeued of God to 105
seie þat he and his breþeren *hauē knowen and trowen to charite þat God*
haþ in hem. Ioon hadde knowyng aboue hope þat þis charite was
in hym, and he wot bi bileue þat þis charite mot saue|hym. *God is* f.34v

of¹] *om.* α   80 þis] þus O   spekiþ ione] and ion sais Z   81 and . . . broþir
(82)] *om.* O   and . . . haþ] *om.* β   83 ȝif] *om.* O   84 strecchiþ] strecchiþ,
-hiþ *corr./*þiþ *canc.* D   85 may] þat B   86 he¹] *om.* YH   to] and to
T   he²] god M   88 þis] þe AB   saued] damned α   dampned] to
dampned BMOI, sauede α   for] for as BY   89 cristis] crist is B   90 he] it
BY   91 haue] had O   passioun] þe passion Mα   92 ne . . . forȝeuen (93)]
om. Mβ   93 haue be euere] euer haue bene α   be euere] *rev.* Y, neuere be δ, bene
Z   euere forȝeuen] *rev.* H   alle] all men α   94 of] for T   96 þe] þis
Y   þer] þe O   97 haue] *om.* T   99 herto] þerto BYZ   oþir] *om.*
Y   100 passion] passiones, -es *canc.* D, þe passion MαH   101 þe] *om.* O   102
þat euere] *om.* I   104 ryȝt] riȝtful B   vncompleet] vncompleet ᵣþat is
vnfulfulledⁱ P, not compleet T   105 ion was] *rev.* I   106 knowen] knowynge
O   trowen] trowynge O   107 in] on O   knowyng] knowun A   108

charite, as Ioon haþ seide, *and he þat dwelliþ in charite dwelliþ in God,*
110 *and God in hym*, as in his Sone to take to blis.

In þis is parfiȝt charite wiþ vs : þat we haue trist in domes day. *For, as he
is* for his tyme in peyne and tribulacioun, *so we ben in þis world*, and
aftir þis mot nedis sue ioye; for, as þe riȝtwisnesse of Crist lettid
not his ioye to sue, so þe same ryȝtwisnesse wole not lette in his
115 membris. And al ȝif men wetyn not þis cleerli for þis tyme,
neþeles þei haue no drede þat ne þis shal sue in hem; for ellis þei
weren out of hope, and so out of charite. And of þis drede spekiþ
Ion and seiþ, *drede is not in charite, but parfyȝt charite sendiþ out* siche
drede, for drede haþ a greet *peyne. And so he þat drediþ* þus *is not parfyȝt*
120 *in charite*. For, as most peyne of man is of beryng of his synne, so
most seruyle drede is of punyshyng þerof; and þis drede mot be
aweye. Bi charite þat is parfyȝt, loue drede is in men wiþouten
siche seruyle drede; and þis holi drede dwelliþ eueremore in blisse
wiþ seyntis.

125   And *þus we shulden loue God, for he bifore haþ loued vs. And ȝif eny seie
þat he loueþ God, and hatiþ his broþer, he is a lyere*. And þus many men
seien þat þei ben in charite, and ȝit þei gabben vpon hemself, as
Ioon seiþ heere sharpli. And þus men may punyshe oþre bi entent
to do hem good, but not bi zele of ueniaunce, ne wiþouten
130 autorite of God. And þus þynken many men þat þis was a feendis
dede for to slee so many men, for a synful and a rotun offys þat þe
pope chalengiþ so folili, for þei boþe shulde be fayn to wante siche
a synful offys. *For he þat loueþ not his broþer whom he seeþ* heere at eye,
hou may he loue God whom he seeþ not þus? And so many leesyngis ben
135 maad on þe charitees of men, as many seien þei punyshe men for

and . . . hym²] *om.* Z   109 as] and A   he] ⌐as⌐ he A   110 god] *om.*
β   to²] his Mβ, *om.* T   111 in þis] and þis PZ   trist] criste Mβ   in²]
vpon M   112 his] as his Mβ   tyme] synne G   tribulacioun] in tribulacioun
IJH   113 þis] *om.* O   þe] *om.* B   114 his¹] þis I   lette] *om.* IJ   115
al ȝif] ȝif O   117 and¹ . . . charite] *om.* δ   118 but] for α   119 a] *om.*
BYG   120 of man is] is of man O   of²] in δ   beryng] betynge O, heringe
Y   121 of] o J   þerof] for synne M, *om.* β   122 aweye] alwey O   125
haþ] *om.* M   seie] seith M   126 many] *om.* M   127 þei²] þe B   vpon]
vp B, on TH   128 men may] many men I   129 hem] hym α   not] non *canc.*
⌐do⌐ I   zele] ȝerde M, yuel T   wiþouten] wiþ T   130 and . . . offys (133)]
om. Z   þis] it B   feendis] synfule α   131 dede] turne H   for to] to
H   so] ⌐so⌐ P, *om.* I   a rotun] aratoun O   a²] *om.* BMPYβIJ, a *eras.*
X   132 for] and for β   shulde] schullen B   133 a] *om.* H   þat] þat þat
O   134 þus] and not þus O   so] þus I   135 on] of B   charitees] charite
M   many] many men, men *canc.* D, many men δIJH   seien] seen β   þei]

loue of þer amendement, but þei holden not þe forme of punyshyng as Crist heeld. Prechyng and paciense shulde be menes to scumfite synne. *And þis maundement we haue of God þat, who þat loueþ God, loue he his broþer*; and þus ʒif we hatyn oure broþir, we hatyn God in oure broþir. Studie we Poul and Ioon to knowe 140 parfyʒt charite.

140 1 Cor. 13.

om. O, þat þei H   136 þer] *om.* A   amendement] mendement H   138
menes] mene I   þis] þus M   we haue] *rev.* α   who þat] who BTY   140
in] and α   poul] ion I   ioon] poul I

Dominica ij post Trinitatem. Epistola. [Sermo 32.]

Nolite mirari si odit vos mundus. Prima Iohannis 3.

Ion telliþ in þis epistele hou men shulden lyue þat suen Crist, and algatis hou þei shulden bisili kepe charitee. Þer ben two lyues heere: on of uerry cristen men; anoþir is of worldly men, whiche Ioon clepiþ heere þe world. Þe firste sectt holdiþ Cristis lawe
5 wiþoute contrariyng bi oþir lawe, and in þis ben many degrees, as preestis, lordis and laboreris. Worldli men ben suche men þat þe world haþ ouercomen, and boþe in lawis and customes þei ben reuled bi þe world. And þes two sectis ben myche medlid wiþ fals feynyng of ypocritis. For men þat ben not cristen men ben medlid
10 now wiþ cristen men, and þei haue lerned of þer lawis, of þer werkis and þer customes; and þe feend haþ tauȝt hem for to þenke þat þes ben betere þan lif aftir Cristis lawe.

To make algatis heuene mennus ende Ioon spekiþ to þe firste sectt, and biddiþ hem *wole not wondre ȝif þe world hate hem,* as Crist
f.35 15 biddiþ ofte tymes. And Crist to comfer|me men makiþ þis resoun to his disciplis, 'ȝif þe world hate ȝou, wete ȝee þat it hatede me ȝoure priour'. And 'it is ynowȝ to disciple þat he be as his maystir.' And now whan þes newe ordris ȝeuen hem þus to þe world, þei haten men speciali þat speken Goddis lawe aȝenus hem. And
20 wondre ȝee not herof, for þus hateden scribis and pharisees Crist. And Ioon confessiþ þe firste sectt and seiþ *we weten soþeli þat we*

---

16 John 15: 18; Matt. 10: 25.

MSS: D; ABGIJMOPTXYZαβδ; H *ends incompl.* 104 han nede.

Dominica ii] dominica β   sermo 32] *om.* DABOTαβδIJXZGH   si . . . mundus] *om.* OH   I io 3] *om.* O, io. 3 H   1 telliþ . . . epistele] in þis epistle tellith Mβ   shulden] schullen I   lyue] haue β   2 bisili kepe] *rev.* A   3 is] ⌜is⌝ Y, *om.* I   6 lordis] and lordis MPTYβZG   7 boþe in] *rev.* δ   customes] in *canc.* customes DX, in customes AδIJ   8 and] as A   wiþ] by M   10 men] *om.* J   lerned] lerid G   of þer lawis] *om.* Mβ   11 þer] of þer ABTαI   and2 . . . ende (13)] *om.* Z   hem] *om.* O   12 þan] þat B   13 heuene] heþene T   14 wole] wole ȝe, ȝe *canc.* Y, wole ⌜ȝe⌝ TJH, wole ȝe ABPZG   not] *om.* Z   hate] hatiþ BY   hem] ȝou AB   16 hate] hatiþ B   ȝee] ȝee wel, wel *canc.* DX, ȝe wel G   hatede] hatiþ A   17 disciple] þe disciple MαH   18 and . . . hem (19)] *om.* Z   newe] *om.* Y   20 herof]

ben translatid fro deeþ to lyf, for we louen men þat ben breþeren. Þes two
sectis ⌈ben⌉ dyuerse, algatis in þes two þyngis. Þe firste sectt haþ
þe Holi Goost, þat techiþ it and makiþ it lyue. Þe secounde sectt is
goostly deed, for it wantiþ qwekenyng of þis Spiri3t. Þe toþir   25
dyuersite is þis: þat men of þe firste sectt kepen hem in charite –
þe toþir sectt hatiþ þis. And herfore seiþ Ioon þus, 'we wetyn þat
we ben translatid fro deeþ to lyf, for we louen breþeren'. Eche
man vndir Crist, boþe cristen men and heþene, lyueden sum tyme
worldli lyf, til Crist hadde goostli baptisid hem; and heerfore seiþ   30
Ioon soþeli heere, 'we wetyn þat we ben translatid'. And þis
translacion is betere þan worldli translacioun of þe pope; for it
may falle ofte tymes þat men þat he translatiþ þus, ben more
deppere in goostli deeþ þan þei weren bifore þis. For spiritis of
men þat ben dampned haue more peyne bi þe synne þat þei   35
bigunnen to grounde heere, þan þei hadden bifore þis synne. As,
3if a dampned man was riche, and castid to gedere hym moche
good, and ordeynede whan he diede to gete hym worldli glorie bi
þis, þat spiry3t is more punyshid aftir þat þis errour groweþ. And
þus seiþ Bernard of summe heretikis þat men knowiþ not now þer   40
peyne, for þei weten not hou many men ben peruertid bi þer lore.
And heronne shulden þes sectis þenke, and stonde in lore of Iesu
Crist; for þer newe lore peruertiþ manye and makiþ hem ⌈more⌉
punyshid in helle. For, whan a spyri3t comeþ to helle þat synned
by errour þat þei tau3ten, who drediþ not þat ne þei haue peyne   45
bi newe comyng of siche felowes? And þis moeueþ many men to
holde þe boundis of Cristis lore, siþ þis lore is ynow3 and may not
erre – but oþir may. But Crist forbediþ not, but biddiþ his

a3enus *canc.* herof D, þerof T, *om.* M   þus] þis β   21 soþeli] soþliþ O   22 to]
vnto M   men] broþerhede men M   23 ben] *corr.* D   two] *om.* O   24
lyue] to lyue α   25 deed] deth M   qwekenyng] quickynge α   þe toþir] and
þe oþir B   27 herfore] þerfore IZ   ioon] saynt iohan α   28 fro] þus fro
δ   29 men] *om.* OZH   heþene] heþen men TH   30 worldli] a *canc.* worldly
Y, a worldli B   heerfore] þerfore Z   31 and . . . may (48)] *om.* Z   þis] so
þis δ   33 tymes] tyme H   34 deppere] deep AMOPTαβXG   35 þe] her
H   37 to gedere hym] hym to gedere *marked for rev.* D   to] *om.* Y   hym] *om.*
AO, his I   38 whan] him whanne IJ   diede] dredde I   39 more] mo *canc.* //
more D, þe more H   þis²] *om.* I   40 seiþ] *om.* O   summe] sum men
αβ   42 sectis] newe sectis H   lore] þe lore M   43 þer] þe I   more] *corr.*
DX, be more α   45 tau3ten] taken I   46 newe] þe newe BH   þis] þus
O   47 boundis] bondis BY   48 but²] *om.* Z   forbediþ not but] *om.*
Z   49 in figure] *om.* I   þei] ⌈þei⌉ H, *om.* α   gedere] gaderede B   51 he]

disciplis in figure þat þei gedere vp þe relef þat is left of Cristis
50 mete.

And to þis entent seiþ Ioon *he þat loueþ not dwelliþ in deeþ*. And, as
it is seide in þe nexte sermoun, of þis loue ben many gabbyngis.
For ypocritis seien þat þei louen, and don þus for charite; but þei
faylen in þer reule, and erren foule fro Cristis lawe. And þei ben
55 þes þat Ysaie discryueþ þat 'þei seien þat good is yuel'. And þus
seiþ Ioon aftir heere *eche man þat hatiþ his broþer is a mansleere*. And
here shulden þes sectis drede þat haue founden hem newe lawis,
and leeuen to profite and to teche aftir þe lawe þat Crist haþ
зouen; certis, þis is a greet hate, boþe of þe chirche and of hemsilf.
60 And, for perel of hardynge in synne, þei schulden dissoluen þes
sectis brouзt in; and eche of hem myзte at þe leeste saue hymself
bi Goddis lawe, and leeue alle þes newe sectis, and flee to þe clene
sectt of Crist. And axe he not leeue of þe pope to flee fro yuel to
f.35v Cristis lawe! For alle þes|foure newe sectis ben homycidis in many
65 persones. But Ioon seiþ aftir in þis epistele *зee wetiþ þat eche
homycide haþ not aylastynge lyf dwellynge in hym*. Lyf of heuene
bigynneþ heere bi þe comfort of Cristis lawe, and it lastiþ in þe
spiryзt aftir deeþ for eueremore – as Poul seiþ þat 'charite neuere
more falliþ adoun'. And þus shulden cristen men loke what lawe
70 souned to charite, and in so myche loue þis lawe, and forsake it in
alle oþir. And herfore ben sum men moeued to leeue þes foure
newe sectis; for alle þe lawis þat þei haue propre moten nedis
fayle aftir þis lyf.

And þus it is of worldis lawe þat techiþ heere to parte goodis.
75 But Ioon seiþ þat *in þis we haue knowe þe charite of God: þat he puttid*

---

49 John 6: 12;　**55** Isa. 5: 20;　**68** 1 Cor. 13: 8.

þat he I　　52 þe] *om.* β　　sermoun] epistle Z　　54 fro] in M　　55 þat³] *om.*
ABMPTαβδIJZ　　56 seiþ ioon] ⌐ion⌐ seiþ J, seiþ I　　eche] þat *canc.* eche DX,
⌐þat⌐ eche Y, þat eche ABδIJH　　is] here *canc.* is DX, here is δIJH, *om.* β　　and
. . . persones (65)] *om.* Z　　57 haue] haþ β　　58 crist] god α　　59 hemsilf]
hymsilfe Mβ　　61 and] and by þis myght M, and bi β　　myзte] *om.* M　　leeste]
laste OTYδH　　62 þe] *om.* TI　　clene] *om.* A　　64 þes] þes ne, ne *canc.*
D　　foure newe] *rev.* B　　ben] be *canc.* ben D　　65 but] and Z　　þis] hys
α　　66 aylastynge] euerlastynge OT　　67 þe¹] *om.* H　　lawe] lawes I　　68
deeþ] þe deþ AM　　þat] *om.* B　　neuere more falliþ] falliþ neuere more B　　69
adoun] downe αH　　þus] þis A　　shulden] *om.* I　　70 souned] sounnynge
O　　in²] for H　　71 and . . . goodis (74)] *om.* Z　　þes] þus þes T　　72
newe sectis] sectis newe comen in H　　newe] *om.* α　　þe] þes Mα　　74 heere]
hire M　　parte] departe T　　76 shullen] schulden, d *altered to* l T, shulden

his lyf for vs. And we shullen for breþeren putte oure lyues. He puttiþ his
life for his broþer þat traueliþ ⌜wiþ⌝ his kyndeli goodis, boþe of
bodi and of soule, for þe profy3t of his broþer. 3if man bi reulis of
þe world wastiþ his kyndeli goodis, and doþ harm to his
ney3hebores soule, al 3if he seye þat he doþ it for loue, he loueþ   80
not his broþer but hatiþ hym. Lord! wher þis pope Vrban hadde
Goddis charite dwellyng in hym, whan he stirede men to fy3te
and slee many þousynd men to uenge hym on þe toþir pope, and
of men þat holden wiþ hym? 3if þat Goddis lawe be trewe, þis was
an opun feendis turne! Ioon tau3te neuere þis charite, ne eny oþir   85
bi Goddis lawe, siþ God, þat reuersiþ not hymself, biddiþ þat
men shulde loue þer enemyes. But what loue may be colourid to
robbe pore men in a feendis cause, for to slee cristen men þat
trespasid not to be þus deed? Lord! wher þis was a good heerde,
þat puttid his lyf þus for his sheepe? Who wolde trowe heere to a   90
feend, and leeue þe lore þat Crist techiþ?

   But, for charite is shewid bi 3euyng of bodili almes, bi whiche
mannus bodi is susteyned, Ioon techiþ bi a lesse signe hou men
faylen in charitee. He seiþ *he þat haþ substaunce of þis world, and seeþ*
his broþer haue nede þerto, and closiþ his merci fro hym, hou dwelliþ charite   95
of God in hym? He þat wole not 3yue his broþer þes leeste goodis,
wole not 3eue hym more, neiþer traueile bi goodis of kynde, ne
lore to þe soule bi goodis of grace. Bi þes wordis yuele
vndurstondun may many trwauntis and stronge beggeris be
mayntened in Cristis chirche bi colour of almes of ypocritis. But   100
Ioon seiþ heere þre wordis þat shulden be chargid of cristene
men. He spekiþ not heere to alle men, but to riche men of þe
world: þat God haþ lent suche goodis þat þei shulden helpe wiseli
þer briþeren þat haue nede of hem. For hey3ere almes shulde be

---

87 Matt. 5: 44; **89** John 10: 11.

AMZ   lyues] lemes β   77 wiþ] *corr.* D, *om.* OδIJ   78 of¹] *om.* δIJ   pro-
fy3t] loue M   broþer] nei3bore G   man] a manT   79 wastiþ] waste
α   to] *om.* M   80 þat] *om.* Mδ   81 lord . . . techiþ (91)] *om.* Z   pope]
popis O   83 on] of M   84 of] on B   holden] helden B   lawe] ⌜lawe⌝H,
om. M   86 god þat] *rev.* I   87 shulde] schulle OPTYβ   88 pore] pure
M   a] *om.* T   89 was] were Oα   90 puttid] puttiþ H   93 mannus] his
canc. mannus D, a manse α   94 substaunce] þe substaunce BY   world] wold
Y   95 charite] þe *canc.* charite Y, þe charite B   97 wole] wolde ABMOPTY-
βZ   98 to] of Z   soule] *om.* M   goodis of grace] goudis grace O   99
vndurstondun] vnderstondiþ O   may] *om.* I   trwauntis] -wauntis *on eras. corr.* D,
tirauntis ABOα   100 ypocritis] ypocrisye T   103 helpe] kepe I   104

105 ȝouen of prestis and of parfitere men; and þus seyde Petir to þe
beggere 'gold and siluer is not to me, but þat þat Y haue þat Y
ȝeue þe'. 'Þus men shulde seye to stronge beggeris 'Y haue no
syche goodis to ȝyue þe, but Y haue lore bi Goddis lawe þat þou
shuldist not begge þus – and þat Y wole telle to þe. Take þou
110 Goddis grace ȝif þou wilt.' Þe secounde word þat Ion seiþ heere is
þat 'a man see his broþir'. And it semeþ to sum men þat þes men
of þes foure sectis ben not breþeren to cristen men, but of oþere
f. 36 straunge sectis. And þus þes freris þat beggyn þus ben|not oure
breþeren, but pharisees. And Ioon techiþ in his secounde epistele
115 to grete hem not, ne to deele wiþ hem, siþ þei brynge not þat lore
þat Crist ȝaf to his disciplis. For, as charite is not, but ȝif it be cleer
and general, so lore of Crist is not, but ȝif it be cleer, vnmedlid
wiþ errouris. But siþ siche ben oure breþeren in kynde, men may
bi loue seye þus to hem 'go þou and bicome my broþer, and teche
120 þat þou hast nede to þes; and þanne Y wole wiþ charite ȝeue þee
siche þyng as þee nediþ.' Þe þridde word þat Ioon spekiþ heere is
þat 'a man suffre nede', as ben hungri men and þursti, nakid men
and herborowles. But men parseyuen not þes þyngis of freris and
of stronge beggeris. And so þes wordis of Ioon stiren not wise men
125 to mayntene þus þes beggeris aȝen þe lawe þat Crist haþ ȝouen;
for þei ben not pacient, ne haue nede to þes goodis, but þei ben
harmed bi hem and bicomen Goddis traytores herbi. And þus
boþe þe beggere and þe ȝeuere ben ful vnkynde aȝenus Crist, for
þei susteynen blaspheme lieres aȝenus God and his lawe.

130 And þus seiþ Ioon aftirward *ȝee þat been my litil children, loue we
not* falsly *bi word or tunge, but loue we bi werk and treuþe.* And wolde

---

106 Acts 3: 6; **114** 2 John 10.

heyȝere] here IJ   105 of¹] by M   of²] oþer M   106 not] nane Z   þat
þat] þat BTY   þat³] *om.* Mα   107 þe] to þee Y, *om.* IJ   men shulde] *rev.*
M   108 Y] *om.* T   lore] lerned Z   109 to] *om.* α   110 ȝif] if þat
B   is] *om.* M   111 to sum men] *om.* Z   men² . . . sectis (112)] strang
beggers Z   112 þes] þe I   but . . . breþeren (114)] *om.* Z   of] to
M   113 straunge] stronge Bα   þus¹] *om.* T   þus²] *om.* IJ   114 his] þis
Tβ   epistele] chapitele I   115 to²] *om.* A   þat] *om.* I, þe Z   116 is] *om.*
O   ȝif] *om.* B   117 cleer] clene M   120 wiþ] by T   121 þyng] þingis
G   122 þat] *canc.* δ   þursti] þyrst O   men²] *om.* Mβ   123 not] none of
M   of freris and] *om.* Z   125 þat] of M   haþ] he hath M   ȝouen]
ordeyned *canc.* ȝouen D   126 to] of BY   127 hem] swilk goodis Z   bicomen]
ben comoun I   herbi] þer *canc.* ⌐her⌐ by α, þerby Z   and²] also δ   þus] þis
O   129 god] crist O   130 we] ȝe I   131 and²] *om.* P   133 were] we

God þat ypocritis vndirstoden wel þis word of Ioon; for þanne þer
beggyng were not þus fals bifore Crist þat is treuþe. For Crist
loueþ algatis treuþe and goode werkis, and hatiþ false wordis, for
he is Goddis word and treuþe; and þus þes wordis reuersyn hym.   135

Dominica iii post Trinitatem. Epistola. [Sermo 33.]

Humiliamini sub potenti manu Dei. Prima Petri vltimo.

Þis epistele of Petre techiþ men hou þei shulden wa⌈l⌉ke heere to
heuene; and first hem nediþ to be meke, for þat is ground of oþere
uertues, and proude men þat reisen þer heed moten algatis
spurne aȝenus God. And þerfore bigynneþ Petre þus and biddiþ
5　þat alle *men shulden be mekid undur þe myȝti hond of God*; and þis
biddyng is resounable. For, ȝif a chyld were ful sugett to a strong
maystir and witti, and his ȝerde were long and sharp, reysid
aboue þis childes hed, and his maystir myȝte not be lettid to
smyte þis child whaneuere he trespasid, a witti child wolde drede
10　þis maystir to trespase vndir siche an hond. But þus it is of alle
men undir þe large hond of God: men ben heere but ȝonge
children, and God shulde be maystir of hem alle; and Goddis
hond is long and strong, for it strecchiþ ouer al þis world, and he
mot nedis punyshe men whaneuere þei trespasen aȝenes hym.
15　And herfore seiþ þe prophe⌈te⌉ of God þat he haþ a wakynge
ȝeerde; and his hond is ȝit streyȝt to punyshe children þat sitten
vndir hym. And þis is a tokene of loue, þat þis maystir smytiþ þes
children whan þei trespasen aȝenus hym. And, ȝif þei ben
lastynge truauntis, and he leeueþ to chastise hem, it is tokene þat
20　he abidiþ to þe ende to bete hem sore. What man þat haþ þis
bileue shulde not be meke vndir þis hond? And no drede ⌈bi⌉ þis
mekenesse wole God take mannus hond, and heyȝe hym at þe

15　Jer. 1: 11.

MSS: D; ABGIJMOPTXYZαβδ; Hᵗ *inc.* 27 heuene, *little collatable.*

Sermo 33] sermo 32 β, φm. DABOTαδIJXZG　　　　manu] *om.* O　　　　I pet. vlt.] *om.*
O　　　vlt.] v A　　　1 men] *om.* I　　　shulden] schulen, -en *on eras. of* -den X, shulen
AOPTYαβG　　　walke] wake δIJ　　　to] to come to I, to come ⌈to⌉ J　　　4 spurne]
forȝiue I　　　bigynneþ petre] *rev.* M　　　5 shulden] shulen AOPTYαβZ　　　myȝti]
myȝt O　　　6 a²] *om.* J　　　8 þis] þe IJG　　　his] þis Y　　　9 whaneuere he] euer
when he α, whan he euere I　　　10 an] and O　　　11 ben heere] *rev.* I　　　but] *om.*
I　　　12 shulde be] is M　　　13 hond] ȝerde M　　　þis] þe I　　　15 herfore] þer for
α　　　17 þes] hys T　　　19 leeueþ] leue Z　　　tokene] a token APα　　　20 þis] þus
þis I　　　21 not] *eras.* Z　　　22 wole god] *rev.* I　　　wole] wolde APX　　　mannus]
þis mannis ABMOPTY αβδIJZG　　　23 ay] euere BMOTXG　　　petre biddiþ] *rev.*

day of dome vnto þe blisse þat ay shal laste. And þus Petre biddiþ
men be meke *þat God hey3e hem in þe tyme of þe laste uysityng,*
whan he shal rikene wiþ alle|his seruauntis. For God, þat may not 25 36v
lie seiþ 'he þat hey3eþ hym shal be lowid, and he þat lowiþ hym
shal be hey3ed', oþer to heuene or to helle; for þe peys of Goddis
ry3t mot nedis weye aftir mannus werkis.

And þus Goddis clerkis shulden heere *caste al þer bisynesse into
him, for he haþ cure of hem,* and for3etiþ not þat þei don. What man 30
shulde not take tent to siche a maistir for loue and drede? And þus
men ben to myche foolis þat lokyn fro God to worldliche þyngis,
for þei, as men out of bileue, seien þat God slepiþ or seeþ hem not.
And þus þei shulden wel gedere al þer bisynesse vnto hym, siþ he
sittiþ and seeþ here werkis, boþe of bodi and of soule; and God 35
chargiþ alle þer maneris, and þe leeste entent of hem. Who
shulde not drede to synne in presense of siche a Lord, siþ men
shamen comynli to trespase in presense of erþeli lord?

And, for þe feend tilliþ men bi many willis fro si3t of God,
þerfore seiþ Petre aftir *be 3ee sobre and wake 3ee; for 3oure aduersarie þe* 40
deuel cumpasiþ aboute as a roryng lyoun to seke what man he shal swolewe.
And no drede siche men þat ben not in kepyng of God, and waken
not in vertues to hym, but lyuen in lustis of þis world, þes ben þo
men þat þe feend swoleweþ to hym; for his bodi is his children,
and his defiyng is induryng. And herfore biddiþ Petre heere þat 45
men shulden a3enstonde þe feend, stronge in bileue þat Petre telliþ heere
and in hope of Cristis help. And þis shulden holi men *wite: þat þe*
same passioun of þe feend, bi whiche he temptiþ worldli men, *is*
maad to holi men in God; for þe feend temptide Crist, and assayede
wher he my3te ouercome hym. And þus þe feend þinkiþ hym sure 50

26 Luke 14: 11.

α   24 þat . . . hey3e] *on eras. corr.* D   þe¹] *om.* T   uysityng] visitacion
M   26 hey3eþ] hy3e O   hym¹] himsilf B   27 or] oþer I   28 mannus]
mennys AO   29 al] *om.* Hᵗ   into] to T   30 for3etiþ] he *canc.* for3etiþ
D   þat] what Oα   31 to] of G   32 ben] þat *canc.* ben D, þat ben δIJ   my-
che] muke O   33 þat] *om.* M   34 vnto] into T   35 of²] *om.* B   37
drede] þan drede M   to synne] *om.* Z   lord] lord to synne Z   siþ . . . lord
(38)] *om.* M   38 erþeli] an *canc.* erþely Y, an erþeli ABTαβJ   39 tilliþ] tisiþ B,
telliþ Tβ, tolleþ IJ   si3t] þe syght M   40 seiþ] seynt T   aftir] efterwarde M,
biddiþ after T, *om.* G   41 cumpasiþ] compasse α   a] *om.* YβG   he shal] *rev.*
B, he Y   42 siche] þat ne sich M   þat] as B   kepyng] þe kepyng M   43
of] to A   þes ben] þa er Z   þo] þir Z   45 defiyng] desyrynge OZ   in-
duryng] his *canc.* induring G, his enduryng AHᵗ   herfore] þerfore MZ   46
shulden] sal Z   a3enstonde] wiþstonde M   49 in] by T   temptide] tempteþ
IJ   assayede] assaieþ I   50 my3te] may I   sure] sikir *canc.* sure D   51

of synful men þat he haþ gil[dr]ed, and temptiþ sharpli hooli
men to lette hem of þer goode purpos.

And þus Petre preieþ to *God*, þat is autour *of alle grace, þat haþ
clepid men into his aylastynge glorie for suffryng lytil* here *for Crist, he*
55 *shal make fulli, he shal conferme and make sadde to hym bi glorie and
comaundyng into worldis of worldis, amen*. It is knowun to trewe men
þat þei may not ouercome þe feend but ȝif God ȝeue hem grace,
þat is firste flowyng and litil; and aftir þis grace is confermed, for
God holdiþ it in his place; and siþ his grace wexiþ sadde, þat it
60 may not falle awey. And þis ordre of þe Trynyte may men see in
bodili þyngis. Blessid be þe holi T[r]ynyte, þat þus bigynneþ bi
his grace, and contynueþ bi þe same grace, and makiþ ende bi þe
same grace, and makiþ man sad and parfyȝt. For, but ȝif he make
fulli man, ellis mannus werk is not worþ. Lord! siþ men trauelen
65 bisili to be confermed of þe pope of Rome in staat or beneficis
heere þat don ofte harme to hem, hou myche shulden men bisie
hemsilf to be confermed in grace of God? And þis is in mannus
power, more þan confermyng of þe pope; for man þar not trauele
more, but contynue uertuous lyf and clene, and God wole for þis
70 litil good conferme man in more good. And þus man þar ȝeue no
monye, ne trauele ferre in bodili trauele, but do he þis þyng good
and lyȝt, and God is redi to conferme.

gildred] giled D, gildrid, -drid *on eras. corr.* X, gedrid Z   temptiþ] temptid B   53
petre] *om.* M   autour] autorite A   alle] ⌈al⌉ P, *om.* Z   haþ] he *canc.* haþ B,
he haþ O   54 clepid] callede αZ   his] *om.* BTY   aylastynge] euerlastynge
BOTY, lastyng M   lytil here] *on eras. corr.* D, *rev.* αδIJ   here] he O   55
make¹] fulli *canc.* make D   and²] *om.* G   56 into] to I   worldis¹] þe worldis
AMT   57 ȝif] *om.* I   grace] his grace M   58 is¹] h-*eras.* D   and¹] a
δ   grace is] *rev.* O   59 his²] þis ABMPTYαβδIJZG   wexiþ] weyeth
MPβZ   60 trynyte] holy trinite AB   men] me O   61 trynyte] tynyte
D   þus] þis O   63 for] *om.* I   ȝif] god *canc.* ȝif D, god if δ, god ȝif, *marked for
rev.* J, *om.* TI   he] we *canc.* ⌈he⌉ T, he *canc.* J, god I   64 werk] werkis M   lord
. . . hem (66)] *om.* Z   65 or] of TG   beneficis] in benefice A, benefyse
MαI   66 don] *om.* α   harme] myche harm A   to hem] *om.* IJ   hou
. . . men] þerfore ilk man suld Z   67 hemsilf] himself Z   grace] þe grace
T   and . . . conferme (72)] *om.* Z   in²] *om.* T   mannus] a mannys M,
mennus β   68 þar] dar BOIJ   69 uertuous] vertues J   70 conferme . . .
good²] *om.* M, *margin* β   man¹] men I   þar] dar OIJ   71 ferre] forþer M,
for β

Dominica iiii post Trinitatem. Epistola.

[Sermo 34.]

Existimo quod non [sunt] condigne. Romanos 8.

In þis epistele techiþ Poule hou þat cristen men shulden laste in
þe seruyse of Ihesu Crist wiþoute grucchyng aȝenus hym. *Y gesse,*
seiþ Poul, *þat suffryngis of þis tyme ben not euene worþi to þe glori þat is to
come, þat shal be shewid in vs;* as who seie 'whoeuere suffriþ here
neuere so myche for Goddis sake, ȝit þis suffryng mot haue 5
reward þat shal passe al his trauele'. But who wole grucche
aȝenus God for þis trauele? – siþ þis is sooþ. Siþ God susteyneþ a
man, and moeueþ hym and helpiþ hym for to traue⌐le⌐ suche
trauele, hou shulde it not come of grace? And þus reward for þis
trauele mot nedis al come of grace. For, whan man traueliþ of his 10
owun myche more trauele þan is þis, ȝit men makyn asseeþ to
hym for reward in þis world; and, siþ reward of God in heuene is a
þousynd siþes betere þan þis, it is knowen þat ioye of heuene is not
euene worþi to þis trauele. For ȝif man suffre to þe deeþ on good
manere in Goddis cause, ȝit he haþ aylastynge lyf þat is betere 15
þan his ȝifte. For God of his grete lordship can not rewarde but
largeli, as an erþeli lord for litil rewardiþ men bi more mede. And
þus clerkis seien comynli þat a man disserueþ on two maneris:
couenabeli and euene worþili. On þe firste manere a man
disserueþ blis, for it is couenabel to God, worþi and iust boþe, þat 20

MSS D; ABGIJMOPTXYZαβδ; H¹ 1–41, 41 he mot . . . . 50 goddis so- *om.*, *ends incompl.*
61 was, *text partially collatable.*

Sermo 34] *om.* DABOPTαδIJXZG   quod] enim quod MT   sunt] *om.*
DδX   condigne] condigne passiones MT, *om.* O   ro. 8] *om.* O   1 hou . . .
poul (3)] *om.* I   shulden] schullen T   3 suffryngis] suffringe IJ   4 seie] seiþ
ATβ   who-] woso- OIZ   suffriþ] suffre AM   5 suffryng] suffrid G   6
his] þis BTY   wole] wolde ABMOPTYαβZ, schal I   7 a] *om.* T   9 trauele]
a traueile B   hou] and how A   and . . . grace (10)] *om.* M   for] of
T   10 of²] on A   11 myche more] moche//moche G   is þis] *rev.* A, þys hys
T   12 siþ] be α   reward] þe rewarde MαG   13 ioye] þe ioye M   14
worþi] worþ T   to¹] wiþ T   man] a man MPβZ   suffre] sufferid M   to
þe] *om.* T   on] in H¹   15 aylastynge] euerelastynge OT   16 his¹] al his AB,
is β   18 disserueþ] deseruyth blisse Mβ   19 and] an O   euene] *om.*
M   20 disserueþ] disserue β   couenabel] -i *eras.* D, couenably IJ   to] vnto

he of his grete grace reward[e] largeli his poere seruaunt. But man
disserueþ not blisse of God bi euene worþinesse, whateuere he do,
siþ God mot nedis of his lordship and his grace rewarde more
men. Þe glorie of heuene þat is to come is ȝit hid and shal be
25 shewid aftir to men in blis; and þis glorie is so myche þat men
shulden haue wille ⌜to trauele⌝ herfore. And bi þis skile weren
marrteris moeued to suffre ioyfulli al þer peyne, for no man
grucchiþ ne failiþ heere but for defaute in his bileue.

And siþ man is Goddis creature boþe bodili and goostli, man is
30 clepid bi hymsilf *creature* bifore oþere, and speciali þis man þat is
lastynge in hope of blis. And þerfore Poul clepiþ þis man
'abidynge of a creature', for þis *man abidiþ sadli shewyng of blis of*
Goddis children. For Ioon seiþ þat we ben now Goddis children, al
ȝif it be hid, but we wetyn wele at domes day, whan Crist shal
35 appere in his glorie, þat we shullen be like to hym. But þis is not
ȝit shewid to vs; and þe ground of al þis ioye is þat we ben Goddis
creaturis, and he haþ ordeyned of his grace vs to be Goddis sones.
And oþir resoun þat Poule telliþ is groundid on þis rote þat, fro
tyme þat man hadde synned, *man was suget to uanyte*, for he was
40 nedid to bere uanyte of his lif, boþe in peynys of his bodi and in
passiones of his soule; and bi þis he mot nedis suffere a
mescheuous deeþ for þis synne. What man shulde þanne grucche
to suffere willefulli for blis?—siþ ellis he mot nedis suffere more
peynefulli for lesse reward. Blessid be þat Lord þat *sugettid men* to
45 uanyte for þis cause, for *to haue hope* of blis! And þus suffere
willefulli for ryȝt.

Hope and solas in þis peyne is þat men trowen to come to blis
f.37v and ful heri|tage of Goddis sones for litil peyne þat þei sufferen
heere. And herfore seiþ Poul þus aftirward þat *þis creature shal be*
50 *delyuerid fro seruage of corrupcioun into fredom of glorie þat Goddis sones*

---

33 1 John 3: 2.

M   21 grete] *om.* Mα   rewarde] rewardiþ D   seruaunt] seruauntis
BTY   22 blisse] þe blis M   of god] *om.* I   26 herfore] þerfore BαZ   28
in] of AT   30 clepid] callede αZ   bi] *om.* M   31 clepiþ] calles αZ   32
a] *om.* OG   33 for] but M   now] *om.* I   35 shullen] sȝolde O   not ȝit]
rev. I   36 al] *om.* α   38 and oþir] an oþir, *medial* d *eras.* X, anoþir
ABPTYβZG   on] in A, vpon α, of IJ   39 tyme] þat tyme M, þe tyme Yα-
β   40 his¹] þis BY   in²] ⌜in⌝ B, *om.* α   41 passiones] passioun O   a] *om.*
AT, and *eras.* J, and BOPYβδIZ, in M   42 þis] hys T   43 willefulli] *om.*
M   blis siþ] *om.* I   44 peynefulli] paynful α   men] man B   45 haue]
om. T   46 willefulli] wilful Y   48 sones] glorie Z   49 þus] þis O   50

shul[l]en haue in blis. *And certis we wetyn þat eche man þat is creature*
ordeyned to blis *weiliþ and traueliþ peynefulli, til þat he parte fro þis
world*; for þus dide Crist oure alþer Lord, and so moten alle his
children do. And men þat hauen þer blisse heere moten nedis in
deeþ haue more peyne; and so þe wey þat Crist haþ ordeyned is   55
boþe þe ly3teste and þe beste. And *not al oneli oþir* children þat ben
ferþer fro knowyng of God, *but Poul hymself and oþir apostelis, þat
hadden þe firste fruy3tis of þe spiri3t, weileden heere wiþynne hemself,
delyueryng title of Goddis sones.* And so *þei abiden* in hope *biggyng a3en
of þer bodi*, bi Iesu Crist þat is oure Lord. Weel we wetyn þat man   60
was maad in staat þat he myte euere liue ynne, and wiþoute deeþ
and oþir mescheues be translatid into blisse of heuene. But bi
synne he was nedid to suffere peyne and bodili deeþ. But Crist
haþ bou3t hym a3en to staat þat he shulde first haue had. And
þus þes resones of þe apostele moeuen to suffre gladli for Crist.   65
And, as God rewardiþ man bi grace ouer þat he disserueþ, so
staat þat men han now in heuene is betere þan was staat of
innocense. And þis sentense shulde moeue men to be marteris of
loue of Crist.

into] and to þe A   glorie] þe glorye M   51 shullen] shulden DT   creature]
a creature M   52 ordeyned] or ordeynyd T   parte] parted T   54 blisse
heere] *rev.* I   55 more] ⌐þe⌐ more Y   56 þe ly3teste] li3ter A, þe li3ttereste
OJ   al] *om.* O   57 ferþer] ferrere OPTYαβZ   58 þe¹] ⌐on⌐ þe O, *om.*
Hᵗ   weileden] ABMOPTYαβðH'IJ   59 delyueryng] desyryng, *altered from*
delyueryng X, desirynge ABOPTYαβH'ZG, deseruyng M   60 crist] *om.* XG   61
euere liue] *rev.* A   62 and] or T   be] haue bene M   blisse] þe blisse AO, *om.*
M   of heuene] euen M   64 bou3t] brou3t ABT   65 apostele] apostlis
BT   to] men *canc.* to D, men to M   67 staat¹] þe state A, þat state Z   staat²]
þe state Z   68 of] for *on eras. of* J, for ABMPTYαδIXZG

Dominica v post Trinitatem. Epistola. [Sermo 35.]

Omnes vnanimes in oratione estote. Prima Petri 3.

Petre telliþ in þis epistle hou men shulden dispose hem to take ʒiftis of þe Holi Goost, and helpe of God in þis [lif]; and þis shulde be bi oonhed in vndirstondyng and wille, in whiche men shulden acorde to God, and þanne ben þei wel disposid. And herfore
5 biddiþ Petre þus þat *ʒee shulden be alle of o wille in ʒoure preyere*; and þus wille shulde be reulid bi resoun, and so vndirstondyng and wille shulden boþe sue God. And þus, as Poul techiþ, þer shulde be o bileue and o charite among alle men, and þanne myʒte þei preye strongere. But now men varien in bileue, as we seen in þe
10 sacrid oost; and men haue maad hem ⌜a bileue⌝ of þe popis and oþir statis, and oon seiþ oon, anoþir anoþir; and þus men uarien in bileue. Men uarien also in charite, for on loueþ þat his folc ouercome, anoþer þat his folk þat fiʒtiþ wiþ hem discumfyte hem and slee hem; and þis discord in charite and suyng discord in
15 preiere mot nedis be reproued of Crist, þat loueþ oonhede in þes þyngis. And to distrye þis heresie biddiþ Petre vs alle be of o wille, for ellis oure preyere mot be vnherd, but ʒif we haue goddis of Mannchees, on good god and an euel god, to heere þes contrarious preieris.

---

7 Eph. 4: 2–5.

MSS: D; ABGIJMOPTXYZαβδ; H¹ 1–9 varien, 9 in . . . 17 goddis of *om.*, *ends incompl.* 28 petre, *text partially collatable.*

Dominica . . . epistola] *om.* M   sermo 35] sermo 34 β, *om.* DABMOTαδIJXZ-G   omnes . . . estote] *om.* M   in . . . estote] *om.* O, estote α   in oratione] *om.* α   in] *om.* G   I pet. 3] *om.* O   1 shulden] shal APYβX   2 lif] *om.* D   þis²] þat M   3 be] *om.* I   bi] his A   4 herfore] þerfor Z   5 shulden] shulen AOPTYαδJXZ   be alle] *rev.* T   alle] ⌜alle⌝ H¹, *om.* M   ʒoure] oure O   and] *om.* B   6 þus] þys, y *altered from* u X, þis ABMOPTYαβδH¹IJZG   vndirstondyng] in vndirstonding A   8 þei preye] þer preier δ   9 strongere] strongliere A   10 a bileue] *corr.* D, able I   11 oþir] of oþer I   anoþir¹] and anoþer AMT, and anoþer sais αIZ   13 ouercome] ouercomeþ δ   anoþer] and oþer M   his] is O   folc] floc β   discumfyte] and discoumfitiþ δ   14 discord¹] discomfort T   16 and] *om.* δ-J   17 for] or M   goddis] g⌜o⌝oddis β   18 mannchees] -chees *on eras. corr.*

And Petre biddiþ aftir þis word to kepe ey3te uertues to blis. 20
First *we shulden be sufferyng togidere*, eche haue sorewe of oþeris
euel, and suffre iniurie of anoþir, suppose þat he worche a3en
hym. And þus cristen men *shulden be loueris of breþerhed*, not of
breþerhed of freris ne of breþerhed of gildis, but of broþerhed in
Crist and of holi chirche oure modir. For þes men|þat makyn þes 25 f.38
sectis trauelen a3enes Cristis breþerhed; for Crist trauelede many
weies for oonhede of þis breþerhed, and þes sectis trauelen faste to
dyuerse þis breþerhed; and so þei don a3enus Petre þat biddiþ to
loue o breþerhed. And þus men *shulden be merciful*, siþ eche shulde
be broþir to oþir of o fadir and o moodir. But now þei ben dyuerse 30
in kyndis: summe ben children of Satan, and summe children of
Belial, and summe ben children of God–but hou shulden þes
comyne togidere? Siche diuysioun of breþeren lettiþ loue in
cristendom. And þanne men shulden *be te[m]porat*, and alle sue
maneris of Crist, siþ Crist shulde be oure alþer fadir, whom we 35
shulden nedis sue. But now þes sectis uarien boþe in maneris and
in wille, and so hem wantiþ þis temperure þat Petre techiþ heere
cristen men. And þus alle men shulden *be meke*, siþ oure fadir and
modir ben meke; and God oure fadir haþ a 3erde to bete vs but 3if
we kepen mekenesse. And þus *we shulden not 3eelde yuel for euel*, for 40
þus doon feendis children; *and we shulden not 3eelde weriyng for*
weriyng, for þus doþ kynrede of Belial. *But we shulde blesse alle men*,
for þis vsen Goddis children, *for in þis ben we clepid, þat we haue*
Goddis blessyng bi heritage. Seyntis þat ben in heuene han fully

---

D   on] of o I   an] *om.* O   20 biddiþ] *om.* Z   þis word] þes wordes
I   to kepe] monestis vs to kepe Z   to²] of O   21 shulden] schullen
I   haue] haueand Z, to haue G   sorewe] so Z   oþeris] oþer αδ   23
shulden] shal M   24 freris] þer hede I   ne] *om.* I   of²] *om.* δ   bre-
þerhed²] *om.* I   of³] *om.* I   gildis] iewes O   of⁴] in M, of þe I   25
chirche] kirkis Z   for . . . breþerhed (26)] *om.* Z   26 a3enes] ⌈faste⌉ a3ens
T   27 þes sectis] wha þat Z   faste] *om.* Z   28 and . . . don] dos Z   29
eche] ilkane Z   shulde] shul β   30 o²] of o AMZ   31 kyndis] kynredis
BMOPTYαβδIJXZG   and] *om.* I   children²] beþ children O   32
and . . . ben] *on eras. corr.* D   33 comyne] come B   siche] siþe A   34 þanne]
þerfor Z   temporat] teporat, -t *altered from* -l D, temperaly AMOPTαβδIJXZG,
temperatli BY   sue] *om.* Y, siche δ   35 alþer] alle þer G   whom . . . uarien
(36)] *om.* Z   36 þes] þe I   boþe] here boþe I   37 þis] here þis M, þus
O   38 cristen] to cristen M   39 modir] oure modir Y   but 3if] wiþ but
I   41 þus] sa Z   feendis] ⌈þe⌉ fendis X, þe fendis ABMOPTYαβIZG   and]
also δ   3eelde] 3yue BMOPTYαβδIJZG   41, 42 weriyng] wrathyng M,
kursynge T   41 for weriyng] *om.* δ   42 þus] þis O   kynrede] þe kynrede
BMG, children Y   43 þis¹] þus Aδ   ben we] *rev.* BI   clepid] callede

45 Goddis blessyng, and þe title þat men haue bi aylastynge
ordynaunce of God passiþ al mannus title, þat man may haue to
worldli good. And þus þes seyntis ben eyris wiþ Crist bi title of
ordynaunce of God; and þis is propre heritage þat God haþ
ordeyned bi his lawe, and herfore men shulden loue þe firste heyr
50 Iesu Crist.

And aftir Petre ӡeueþ a reule to kepe Cristis religioun, and þis
reule mot nedis passe alle þes newe reulis of ordris. *He þat wole loue
lyf and see goode dayes* in blis, *constreyne he his tunge from yuel, and his
lippis þat þei speken not gyle; and bowe he awey fro yuel, and do he good
55 and seke he pees.* For man shulde seke pees wiþinne bitwixe God
and hymself; and man shulde *sue pees* wiþoute bitwixe hym and
his neyӡhebore, for bi þis reule men ben *maad iust, and God lokiþ*
graciously *on hem. And þe eren of God ben at preyeris of siche men; but þe
face of þe Lord is vpon men þat don yuel.* And þis reule of Dauyþ and
60 Petre is ynowӡ to alle men, and eche man shulde kepe þis reule bi
religioun of Crist. And herfore take þow noon newe ordre bifore
þis reule fayle to þe. And siþ þes foure newe sectis faylen in þis
reule of God, þei shulden leeue þis nouelrye þat makiþ hem turne
fro Goddis lawe. Alle þes foure newe sectis synnen in many
65 gabbyngis, boþe in gabbyng of dede, and in gabbyng of mouþe;
for þei spekyn gyle to þer breþeren and wiþdrawen fro hem iust
helpe. He þat studieþ more þis matere may see how þis gabbyng
gooþ.

And for surete of þis ordre seiþ Petre aftir as bileue þat no man
70 anoyeþ þis man in þat ⌜þat⌝ he sueþ wel Crist. Holde þis ordre for
it is best, and bryngiþ mannus soule streyӡt to heuene. And þus

---

59 Ps. 33: 16..

αZ   45 bi] beþ O   aylastynge] euerelastyng MOT   46 passiþ] it passith
M   mannus] mennys BYG, manere of mannis I   47 good] godis M   þes]
om. YI   wiþ] of T   48 is] *om.* MT   49 lawe] *om.* A   herfore] þerfor
Z   men] we A   51 and¹ . . . religioun] *om.* Z   þis] for þis P   52 þes] þe
O, *om.* Z   of ordris] *om.* Z   loue lyf] lyf J   54 þei speken] he speke
B   not] no O   awey] *om.* O   55 bitwixe] and bitwene G   58 preyeris]
⌜þe⌝ prayeres α, þe praieris AMO, siche preyeris T   siche men] men T, gode men
α   59 don] *om.* I   61 religioun] þe religion M   and . . . gooþ (68)] *om.*
Z   62 þes] *om.* δ   newe] *om.* Y   faylen . . . sectis (64)] *om.* I   64 foure
newe] *rev.* B   65 of¹] in α   in²] *om.* AI   66 to] wiþ α   þer] oþer
M   69 and] *on eras.* corr. D, *om.* δJ   seiþ] spekiþ T   aftir] *om.*
A   bileue] bi loue β   70 anoyeþ] anoye Z   þat²] corr. D, *om.* δJZ   þis²]
hys O   71 best] þe beste A   72 ӡee] he O   73 peyne] peynes M   74 is]

seiþ Petre bi bileue *who is he þat anoyeþ ʒou, ʒif ʒee ben goode sueris?*
Many men haue peyne heere in þer goodis and in þer bodi, and
many men ben dede for mayntenyng of ryʒtwisnesse; |but þis is   f.38v
non harme ne noye, but more winnyng of betere þyng. And   75
herfore seiþ Petre heere *ʒif ʒee sufferyn ouʒt for ryʒt,* ⌐and⌐ leeuen
not merite þat ʒee haue wunnen, *ʒee ben* þanne *blessid* of God. And
herfore Petre telliþ aftir þat *men shulde not drede þer manas,* for, ʒif
þei holden þis lawe of God, þei may bi no weie do hem harme.
And þerfore Petre biddiþ cristen men *be not turblid* bi þer manaas,   80
for þe feend moeueþ þes debletis to feere cristen men fro treuþe.
But Petre biddiþ aftir þat cristen men shulden *stable Iesu Crist in*
þer hertis. And blessid be þis reule and þis ordre þat alle cristen
men shulden hoolde!

nys I   76 herfore] þerfore MZ   and] *corr.* D   77 þat] þan O   wunnen]
wynnynge O   þanne] *om.* Z   78 petre telliþ] *rev.* I   79 hem] non I   80
þerfore] herfore BMY   petre biddiþ] *rev.* BP   cristen . . . biddiþ (82)] *om.*
I   manaas] manaces B   81 þes debletis] tyrauntis Z   feere] flaye Z   83
cristen men] *rev.* β, cristen Z   84 shulden] schullen T

Dominica vi [post Trinitatem]. Epistola.
[Sermo 36.]

Quicumque baptizati sumus. Romanos 6.

Poule telliþ in þis epistele how we shulden lyue bi loore of Crist, for Crist tauȝte til his deeþ hou men shulden holde his ordre; and Poule telliþ heere sutilli to what witt we shulden take þis. He bigynneþ and seiþ þus *whiche euere of vs be baptisid in Crist Iesu we ben*
5 *baptizid in his deeþ.* Bodili baptisyng is a fygure hou mannus soule shulde be baptisid fro synne, for witt of Crist wole not suffre to kepe þis figure but for greet witt. Bodili wasshyng of a child is not þe ende of baptisyng, but baptisyng is a tokene of wasshyng of þe soule fro synne, boþe original and actual, bi uertu takun of Cristis
10 deeþ. And þus *we ben biried wiþ hym bi baptem into* a manere of *deeþ*; and so Cristis resurreccioun was figure to vs hou we shulden lyue. And herfore seiþ Poule þus aftir þat, *as Crist was risen fro deeþ bi glorie of þe Fadir* of heuene, *so shulden we lyue* bi þis figure *in newenesse of* goostli *lif.* And so þis water þat we ben put ynne is tokene of
15 Cristis tribulacioun fro his bigynnyng to his deeþ, and techiþ how we shulde lyue heere. So þe baptysyng of vs in ⌈þis⌉ water bitokeneþ boþe biriyng of Crist, and hou we ben biried wiþ hym fro synne þat regneþ in þis world. Oure takyng vp of þis water bitokeneþ þe rysyng of Crist fro deeþ, and hou we shulden rise
20 goostli in clennesse of newe lyf. So, ryȝt as synne is rote of deeþ, so sholde we kepe vs fro synne aftir.

MSS: D; ABGIJMOPTXYZαβδ.

Sermo 36] þe foure and þritiþe sermoun Y, sermo 35 β, sermo A, *om.* DBM-OTαδIJXZG   sumus] *om.* O, sumus in cristo iesu bapptizati sumus T   ro. 6] ro.
7 M, ro. 5 β, *om.* O   telliþ] techith M   we] men δ   loore] þe lore
Mα   2 hou] howe þat M   4 crist iesu] *rev.* J   5 mannus soule] mennis soulis
A   7 of] *om.* J   is] *om.* J   8 baptisyng[2]] bodily baptisyng M   a] *om.*
Mβ   of[3]] for O, fro δ, *om.* J   þe[2]] *om.* T   10 we ben] er we Z   a] *om.*
Mβ   11 so] *om.* M   figure] figurid Y   12 þus aftir] *rev.* β   13 so] and so
A   14 þis] þus O   15 his[1]] þe I   how] *om.* I   16 we] *om.* M   þis]
corr. D   17 boþe] *om.* G   18 fro] for T   of] fro M   water] vater
δ   19 deeþ] þe deeþ β   20 newe] trewe δ   21 sholde we] *rev.* δJ   aftir]

For ȝif we be maad plantid to þe licknesse of Cristis deeþ, þanne we
shullen be also like to Cristis rysyng fro deeþ. Þe firste book of Goddis
lawe telliþ hou erþe is cursid in mannus werke, for erþe þat man
beriþ in his bodi crokide to synne til tyme of Crist. And for Cristis   25
body my⌈ȝ⌉te not synne, þerfore oure erþe was blessid in Crist;
and, ȝif we ben plauntid in Cristis body, þanne we shullen haue
þe fruyȝt þat sueþ. And þus we han in a manere an old man and a
newe man: oure olde man is ⌈þe⌉ flessheli man wiþ synne and
lustis þat suen hym, þe newe man is a spiryȝt purgid bi loue and   30
lyf taken of Crist. And þus seiþ Poul þat *oure oolde man is don on*
crosse on ⌈a⌉ *manere wiþ Crist, to distrye þe bodi of synne, þat we serue*
not aftir to synne. And þus þe bodi of synne of man is flesshelynes of
mannus freelte; and þis bodi shulde be distried and hooli purpos
of spiryȝt quekened. And þus seiþ Poul þat *he þat is deed to synne is*   35
iustified fro synne. Þat man is deed to synne þat is delyuerid fro þat
synne; and generali man|is deed to a þyng þat is not qwekened to   f.39
þat þyng. And þus it is a greet grace þat a man be deed to synne;
for þanne he mot be quekened to uertu þat is contrarie to synne,
and þanne he mot be iustified and delyuerid fro synne. And þus   40
seiþ Poul þat, *ȝif we ben deed wiþ Crist, we bileuen þat we shul lyue*
togidere wiþ hym. For ȝif þis oolde lyf be deed and oure lyf of synne
be distryed, lyf of clennesse mot nedes dwelle; and so men shullen
be in blisse wiþ Crist. And *we shullen wite* bi bileue *þat Crist, risyng*
aȝeen fro deede men, shal neuere more aftir die in body, *and deeþ shal not*   45
aftir be lord of hym. And þus men shulden dye fro synne. And þus,
as Crist *lyueþ to God* and was euere more *deed to synne,* so we

---

24 Gen. 3: 7;   **28** Eph. 4: 22; Col. 3: 9.

om. β   22 plantid] ⌈em⌉plantid X   we shullen] we shulen *altered from* we shulden
PT, we shulde MαβI, *rev.* O, shulde we A   23 also like] *rev.* I, also likyn
β   rysyng] *om.* M   fro] *om.* M   24 hou] þat M   25 beriþ] biries
Z   til] in I   tyme] þe tyme M   26 myȝte] -ȝ- *corr.* D   27 shullen]
shulden Mβ   29 þe] oure *canc.* ⌈þe⌉ *corr.* D   flessheli] fleisch δI   synne]
synnes Mβ   30 lustis] lust B   a] *om.* T   32 crosse] þe cros BMβ   a] ⌈a⌉
β, *om.* OPYδIJXZ   34 freelte] freleelte β   35 quekened] quikid β   is²] *om.*
G   36 to] fro PβZ   37 man] þat man A, a man I   þat] when he M   38
a¹] *om.* M   þat²] for M   39 mot be] mut nede be M, is Z   quekened] quik
BMOPTYαβZG, quyke, -nid *eras.* X   40 mot be] is Z   42 lyf be] be ⌈lif⌉
β   and] *on eras. corr.* D   43 mot] moste αδ   dwelle] dewlle β   shullen]
shulde AG   44 shullen] shulden AG   crist²] cristis M   45 deede] deeþ
O   aftir die] *rev.* β, die after, *marked for rev.* δ   aftir] *om.* M   46 aftir] *om.*
T   men shulden] men schulen B, *rev.* α   47 lyueþ] lyued A   euere] neuere

shullen, fro þat we be risen aȝen to lyf of Crist fro oure oolde lyf. We shulden euere *be deed to synne, and liue to God* in lyf of uertues.

50 *And þus gesse ȝee ȝou deed to synne and lyuynge to God bi mene of Iesu Crist oure Lord.* Þat man is deed to synne þat wantiþ lyf for to synne, as he is deed to ryȝtwisnesse þat wantiþ wille to kepe it; as þat man lyueþ to synne þat haþ strengþe and wille to synne, as þat man lyueþ to Crist þat wole kepe his strengþe to Crist.

T   48 shullen] schulden, -den *on eras.* X, shulden ABMOPTYαβZ   we] *om.*
MTβ   lyf[1]] þe liif M   we] and we A   shulden] sȝulle O   49 in] by
M   50 of] *om.* M   51 þat[2] . . . lyf] þat wantiþ lyue for synne to *all canc.* þat
wantiþ β   for to] for to do Z   as] and M   52 as] and M   53 strengþe
and wille] wille and strengþe T   as] so A   54 crist[2]] gode α

Dominica vii [post Trinitatem]. Epistola.
[Sermo 37.]

Humanum dico propter infirmitatem. Romanos 6.

Poul techiþ in þis epistele hou men shulden flee flesheli synnes,
and seiþ *he spekiþ mannus lore for sikenesse* of þer fleshe, as medicynes
shal be shapun aftir þat a sike man is disposid; as it is not
profitable to preche vnto rude men sutilte of þe Trynyte, or oþir
þat þei kunen not conseyue. And herfore biddiþ Crist in Mathew 5
þat his disciplis ȝyue not hooli þyng to houndis, ne scatere
margaritis among hoggis. Þes men in a maner ben houndis þat
ben þus hardid in synne þat, aftir þe tyme þat þei haue spewed,
þei turnen aȝen and etyn þer spewyng; siche men may tarie
seyntis, but hooli lore doþ hem no good. And þus special lore of 10
God and sad as ben precious stones is not sauerid of swynishe
men, for flesheli lustis þat þei haue. And þus biddiþ Poul grosseli
þat, *as þei haue ȝouen þer lymes to serue to vnclennesse and
wickidnesse for to mayntene wickidnesse, so þei shulden now ȝyue
þer lymes to serue to ryȝtwisnesse into holynesse,* þat is sadnesse of holi 15
lyf. *For whanne ȝee weren seruauntis of synne, ȝee weren free to
ryȝtwisnesse.* He is free to a þyng þat is not obleshid to þat þyng; as

---

5 Matt. 7: 6.

MSS: D; ABGIJMOPTXYZαβδ.

Post trinitatem] *om.* D   sermo 37] sermo 126 β, *om.* DABMOTαδIJXZG   hu-
manum] si humanum δ   propter infirmitatem] *om.* O   infirmitatem] infirmitatem carnis nostre T, infirmitatem carnis vestre M   ro. 6] *om.* O   1 techiþ]
telliþ Aα, spekith M   hou] here how A   synnes] synne α   2 spekiþ] kepyþ
O   medicynes] medicyne, -s *eras.* X, medecine ABMPTYαβIZG   3 a] *om.*
T   4 rude] roed M   oþir] of oþir G   5 *margin* Math. vii T   6 þyng]
þingis A   7 houndis] hoggis M   8 þus] þis O, sa Z   hardid] harded þus
O   þe] *om.* Y   9 þer] þe A   spewyng] castyng like houndis Z   10
seyntis] prechouris Z   special] precious M, special lore doþ hem no goude and þus
special O   11 and] *om.* Y   ben] *om.* G   12 grosseli] goostli AB, graciouȝsly
Tα, grecely I, gretely Z   13 to²] *om.* T   and wickidnesse] *om.* β   and] in
AB   14 for . . . wickidnesse²] *margin* G, *om.* J   so] *om.* β   þei] þes
I   now ȝyue] *rev.* T   now] *om.* OI   15 into] in *altered from* and D   16
of] to Bα   17 a] *om.* T   obleshid] obeischid BYG   as] and M   18

synful men ben free to ry3t, and iust men ben seruauntis to it; as,
ay þe more þat a man dooþ ry3t, ay þe more is he holdun þerto,
20 for God oblishiþ a man more þe beter þat he serueþ to God.
And herfore axiþ Poule aftir *what fruy3[t]* þe Romaynes *hadden
in þo þyngis in whiche þei shamen now,* siþ þat synne made hem
straunge fro ry3twisnesse, and it from hem. For God is more
holden to man, ay þe betere þat he serue hym. And þus seiþ Poule
25 þat *þe ende of synnes is* þe worste *deeþ* of alle oþere. And, siþ a þyng
f.39v shulde be preysid or di[s]prey|sid bi his eende, þes synnes shulden
algatis be fled þat ledyn a man to siche an eende. *But now,* whan
*3ee ben delyuerid fro synne and maad seruauntis to God, 3ee haue 3oure
fruy3t into holynesse, and 3oure ende aylastynge lyf.* And bi þis may men
30 see hou good it is to serue to God, for ay þe more þat man serueþ
to hym, ay þe more free he is; and ay þe lasse þat men ben holden
to God, ay þe more bonde þei ben. As, 3if a mannus holynesse
encreesce, he resseyueþ þe more goodnesse of God; and 3if a man
serue worse to God, God 3yueþ hym lesse of his grace. And þus he
35 þat haþ more grace of God is more endettid for more 3ifte. And
þus seiþ Poul soþely þat *þe hire of synne is deeþ*; and þus seiþ Austyn
þat a man serueþ God in sufferyng of peyne for his synne. *But grace
of God* þat a man haþ heere is endid bi *aylastynge lyf*; and so þis
grace þat God 3yueþ is þis lif wiþouten ende. But al þis is
40 groundid *in* grace of *oure lord Iesu Crist.*
And heere men douten comynli hou þat men seruen to God,
sum in doyng as þei shulden, and summe in suffryng as þei

ben²] *om.* Mβ   as] and M   19 ay¹] euere OT   þat] *om.* T   ay²] *om.*
M, euere OT   is he] *rev.* ABMYβδZ   20 oblishiþ] obeischiþ Y, oblisshe
α   more] þe mare Z   serueþ] serue T   21 axiþ] sais Z   fruy3t] fruy3
D   22 þo] two I   23 ry3twisnesse] ri3twisse Y   it] hidde it G   more
holden] *rev.* A   24 ay] euere OT   betere] more I   þat he] *twice*
I   serue] serueþ ABYαIZ   26 dispreysid] dipreysid D   his] þe M   27
to] *om.* G   whan] *om.* O   28 3ee] we Mβ   fro] of αI   29 and¹] in
A   aylastynge] into *canc.* aylastynge D, euerelastynge OT   lyf] blisse
M   and²] *om.* P   30 to²] *om.* ABMOPTαβIZ   ay] euere OT   þat] *om.*
α   man] a man ABTZ   31 to] to *canc.* B, *om.* AY   ay¹] euere OT   free]
frende α   he is] *rev.* I   ay²] euere OT   ben holden] serues Z   32 ay]
euere OT   as] and *altered to* as α, and AB, *om.* G   34 to] *om.* P   hym] *om.*
A   36 þus¹ . . . þat] *on eras. corr.* D   þus¹] *om.* O   seiþ¹] *om.* M   þat]
om. M   þe] ⌐T, *om.* B   synne] deeþ δ   deeþ] synne δ   37 god] to god
A   sufferyng of] seruyng M   38 a] ⌐a⌐Y, *om.* Mβ   aylastynge] euerlastynge
OT   39 þis¹] þe BOZ   40 groundid] ground I   grace] þe grace Mβ   41
men seruen] a man seruiþ β   to] *om.* P   42 sum] sum men, men *canc.* D,
summe   men   O   sum . . . and] *om.* T   and] *om.* AδJ-

shulden. Herof it semiþ to many men þat men þat ben dampned
in helle seruen as myche and as iustli as seyӡntis þat ben blessid in
heuene. But heere men seien þat bi dyuerse resones: þes two men   45
seruen to God, but iust men seruen medefulli, and dampned men
aӡenus þer wille; and so þer seruyses ben not euene, but of ful
dyuerse kyndis.

G   summe] sum men OG   44 as²] ay β   46 god] om. α   47 seruyses]
seruyce BT   ful] om. M

Dominica viii [post Trinitatem]. Epistola.
[Sermo 38.]

Debitores sumus non carni. Romanos 8.

Þe apostele telliþ in þis epistle hou boþe oure bodi and oure soule
shullen be shapped to serue to God aftir his wille and his lawe.
Poule bigynneþ on þis manere *we ben* dettouris to þe spiry3t, but
not dettouris to þe fleshe þat we lyue aftir þe fleshe. And heere men takun
5 comynli þat man is dettour to þre kyndis. First and moost to God
of heuene, þat is a spiry3t as Ion telliþ; and of þis dette and þis
spirit spekiþ Poul in þes wordis. And for þis spiri3t is betere þan
man, man shulde loue þis spiry3t more þan oyþer of his two
kyndis, to lyue as þis spiri3t wole. And so a man shulde bowe his
10 spiry3t to obeshe to þe spiri3t of God, and do what God wole þat
he do; and þanne he 3eldiþ þe firste dette. Aftirward man is in
dette to his owene spiry3t to do it good and, 3if he do harme to his
spiry3t, he renneþ in dette to hymsilf. And so man, þat reuliþ his
lif aftir þe lawe þat God haþ 3ouen hym, payeþ his dette boþe to
15 God and to his owene spiri3t, as God wole. Þe þridde tyme man
shulde be dettour to his fleshe þat is hymself; and þus seiþ Poul
þat neuere man hatide his owene fleshe. 3if he die for loue of Crist,
he trowiþ to profite to his fleshe; and 3if he fede his fleshe to
myche, he erriþ and weneþ to do it good; but 3it he fayliþ not fro
20 comyn loue, bi whiche he loueþ kyndeli his fleshe. But man

MSS: D; ABGIJMOPTXYZαδ; *β ends incompl.* 52 þe spirit of God.

Post trinitatem] *om.* D   sermo 38] *om.* DABMOTαβδIJXZG   debitores] fratres
debitores M   non carni] non carni vt M, *om.* O   romanos 8] romanos 6 β, *om.*
O   2 shullen] shulde ABMαβ   to[2]] *eras.* X, *om.* MOTIZG, oure AB   wille]
lawe T   lawe] wille T   4 dettouris] *om.* I   to] not to O   5 man] a man
T, men I   is] ben I   dettour] dettours I   þre] þe I   6 þis[2]] *of canc.* þis
D, *of* þis ATβ   *margin* io. 4 T   8 oyþer] oþir ABMOTαβδIJ   his] þese
BTYZ   9 þis] his AB, þe Z   a] *om.* T   bowe] loue T   10 what] what
þat αβ   11 man] a man I   12 his[2]] þis AB, his owne O   13 to] a3ens
Mαβ   and] *canc.* B, *om.* A   man] a man ABMαβ   15 god[1]] þo spirit of god
α, ⌐it⌐ β   to] *om.* P   16 hymself] his hymselfe M   17 neuere man hatide]
man hatede neuere I   die] deyde T   18 to[2]] of α   fede] fedde, *1st d canc.* T,
fedde I   19 erriþ] crieþ I   20 man] *om.* O   21 loueþ] loue O   for

shulde loue þe secounde spiry3t more þan he loueþ his fleshe, for
he shulde not loue his fleshe but to serue betir his soule. And þus
man þat passiþ þis loue hatiþ in a maner his fleshe.

And heerfore seiþ Poul‖heere þat *we ben not dettid to þe fleshe þat we*   f.40
lyue aftir þe fleshe, for þanne we maden þe seruaunt maystir; and,   25
a3enus þe lawe of God, we loueden more þat he loueþ lesse. And
whoeuere þus reuersiþ God, and chaungiþ in loue þe ordre of
kynde, God mot nedis reuerse hym, and resoun turneþ his loue to
hate. And to þis witt seiþ Poul aftir þat, *3if 3ee lyuen aftir 3oure fleshs,*
3ee shullen die anentis 3oure soule; for goostli deþ þat falliþ to man   30
is wantyng of grace to come to heuene. And herfore seiþ Poul aftir
⌈þat⌉, *3if 3e sleen bi 3oure spiry3t þe* synful *dedis of 3oure fleshs, þanne 3ee*
shullen goostli *lyue*.

And þus, for mannus wandryng is vnstable heere, Poul telliþ of
two wyndis bi whiche man is moeued heere, and þes wyndis   35
moten nedis lede man to contrarie endis. *Sum men ben ledde bi*
Goddis spiry3t, and þis comeþ fro aboue; and *þus ben Goddis sones* led
euene to þe blisse of heuene. Þe secounde spiry3t is flesheli, and so
it mot be erþeli, and come bineþe fro þe feend; and þis lediþ þe
feendis sones euene to þe peyne of helle; and þis wynd shulden   40
men flee. Loke bi what lore men lyuen, and þerbi mayst þou
knowe þes wyndis. And þis moeueþ many men hou þe wynd of
Goddis lawe shulde be cleer, for turblenesse in þis wynde mot
nede turble mannus lif. And þis wynd is spiry3t of seruyse and
makiþ man drede as seruaunt.   45

And herfore seiþ Poul aftir þat *3ee hauen not taken þe spiry3t of*
seruyse a3een in drede; but 3ee haue takun þe spiry3t of grace to take 3ow to
Goddis children. It is knowen to trewe men þat, bifore þat men
weren cristen, þei serued in drede of soule to þe feend and many
synnes. But, fro þat þei weren maad cristen men, and suen in lyf   50

. . . fleshe (22)] *om.* M, *margin* T   22 loue] *om.* O   to] for to I   betir his
soule] his soule beter I   24 heerfore] þerfore MZ   dettid] detty α, dettiþ δ,
dettours G   we²] þei I   25 maystir] þe maister I   26 a3enus] þan agaynes
Z   þat] þat þat T   loueþ] loued MTβ   27 whoeuere] whosoeuere
OZ   þus] *om.* I   29 to] *om.* T   30 anentis] efter anentis M   31 of] *om.*
I   33 goostli lyue] *rev.* α   36 man] a man A, men Mβ   contrarie] a contrarie
δ, contrarious I   endis] ende δ   men] me Y, *om.* I   37 þus] þes Mβ   38
flesheli] cletthly O   40 feendis] fende α   41 mayst þou] may P   44 mannus]
mennis AB   45 man] men B   drede] to drede Z   seruaunt] seruauntis
B   46 not taken] *rev.* O   47 haue] *om.* I   48 trewe] trowe δ   þat²] *om.*
Mβ   49 and] in M   many] ⌈to⌉ many J   50 þat] þat tyme þat Mβ, *om.*

þe scole of Crist, þei ben taken to Goddis sones, *and in hym crien
'fadir, fadir'. And þe spiriȝt of God þanne beriþ witnesse to mannus
spiryȝt, þat he is Goddis sone*; and þis is a fair title. *For, ȝif we þus ben
Goddis sones, we ben eiris* of God, *for we ben eiris of God and togidere eiris*
55 *of Crist.* It is knowun of bileue þat Crist is kyndeli Goddis sonne;
and, siþ Crist is man wiþ þis, Crist is also mannus broþir. And bi
medeful sufferyng of Crist man haþ title to come to blisse. For
noþyng lettiþ þat ne heritage is comen to many breþeren, but for
takyng þerof fro o broþir to anoþir, and make þe firste eire poere.
60 But þis is not in þe blisse of heuene, for Crist haþ fulli þe heritage
and, bi hym, alle his breþeren. And noon of hem haþ lesse
herfore, but oon helpiþ anoþir in ioye. And þus alle Goddis sones
ben eiris of God in sum manere, Crist as kyndeli Goddis sone, and
his breþeren as sones of grace.

Z   maad] *om.* A   suen] folowid Z   51 to] *om.* Z   goddis] god
α   53 þus ben] ben þus *marked for rev.* B, bene þus MO   54 for . . . god[2]] *om.*
MOPZ, *erased* T   55 goddis] god α   56 þis] *om.* O   bi] by by O   57
blisse] crist I   58 heritage] þe heritage A   comen] comune IZ   to] ynto
O   59 make] makiþ O   þe] *om.* Y   60 þis] *om.* O   þe[1]] *om.* B   63
as] is MG   goddis] god α   64 as] his M

Dominica ix post Trinitatem. Epistola. [Sermo 39.]

Non s[i]mus concupiscentes malorum. Prima Corintheos 10.

Poule telliþ in þis epistele hou men shulden flee fyue synnes, as it
was tauȝt in þe oolde lawe bi fyue figuris þat God made. Poul
biddiþ at þe firste þat *cristen men coueite not yuel þyngis* bi euel desiris,
for þis is rote of oþir synnes; for boþe Adam and Eue synneden bi
þis coueitise, for bi þer vnskilful desire þei coueiteden to ete of þe   5 f.40v
appul, and wenden þat þis hadde be good for hem, but þei
erreden in þis coueitise. Poul biddiþ aftirward þat a *man shal not be
maad a worshipere of false goddis* bi siche wickid coueitise, *as sum men
in þe oolde lawe maden a calf þer god.* And þus seiþ Poule aftir
þat sum men of þe olde lawe synneden fouli in þis synne, and þus   10
in many oþer synnes. *þe puple satt to ete and drynke, and þei risen aftir
to pleie*; for wantonnesse in siche wille þat is mysturned fro Goddis
wille bryngiþ in oþir synnes, and makiþ men out of bileue. And
þus alle þes newe ordris coueiten bi wrong desire straunge
patrounes, or oþir þyngis þat bryngen hem in wrong bileue. And   15
þus it semeþ þat many men of þes sectis ben heretikis, for þei
worshepen falsli þyngis aȝenus Goddis wille; as Poul clepiþ
auarous men þat louen to myche worldli goodis seruytouris to
maumetis, and þis is opun herisie. And þus may trewe men renne
bi many synnes þat now ben vsid.   20

---

4 Gen. 3: 1–7; 8 Exod. 32: 4; 11 Exod. 32: 6.

MSS: D; ABGIJMOPTXYZαδ ; *β begins incompl.* 63 faire men weren.

Sermo 39] *om.* DABMOTαδIJXZG   simus] sumus DBOδIXZG, scimus T, sitis
J   malorum]*om.*O   I cor. 10]*om.*O   1 shulden]shulen PTYJZ, schullen,
2nd l *altered from* d X   fyue] fro *canc.* fyue D   2 was] is T   4 eue] euene
O   bi]in α   *margin* gen. P   5 coueiteden] couet α   of]*om.* M   6
þat]*om.* M   þis] it A   8 sum]*om.* T   men]*om.* Y   9 in . . . men (10)]
om. I   *margin* Exo. 32 MOPTYαZ   aftir] afturworde α   10 men]*om.*
BMTY   11 risen] arisen B   aftir] efterwarde M   12 in]and T   13
wille] lawe M   and¹] þat M   and² . . . bileue (15)] *om.* I   14
alle . . . for (16)]*om.* Z   ordris] sectis *canc.* ordris D   15 patrounes] patronage
M   or] of M, and T   16 þat] to M   of] þat M   þei] men þat
Z   17 falsli] fals Oα   as] er heretikis as Z   clepiþ] calles αZ   18 to²] of
AZ   19 is]*om.* I   may]*om.* MZ   trewe . . . bi (20)] it is of Z   20

Þe þridde tyme biddiþ Poule þat *men shulden not do fornycacioun*,
neiþer bodili ne goostli, for God mot uenge for þes boþe. And þus
in þe oolde lawe God uengide fornicacioun *and killed foure and
twenti þousind in a day*, as Poule telliþ; but Poul leeueþ a þousynd of
25 þes, oþer for þes þousynd weren saued, or for oþir cause þat we
knowen not. But ay stondiþ þe treuþe of Goddis lawe in þe forme
þat Poule telliþ it; for, whoso killeþ foure men, he mot nedis kille
þree. Þe fourþe tyme biddiþ Poule þat *we tempten not Crist, as
summe of hem tempteden hym and þei perisheden bi eddris.* And þes men
30 tempten Crist þat loken as beestis to his cros, and wrappen
hemself in lustful lyf, and suen hym not in his peyne. And þus alle
þes foure sectis, þat forsaken Cristis reule, and maken hem a newe
reule to loke wher þat reule were beter, tempten Crist ful falseli;
and þus þei perishen bi þe olde eddre. And þis temptyng semeþ
35 more greuous þan was þe toþir temptyng in figure. For þe
children of Israel gruccheden for hem wantede water, but þes
newe ordris now, aftir more kyndenesse of Crist, hadden plente of
water of wisdom þat Crist ȝaf hem for to drynke. But þei
gruccheden aȝenus þis water, and drunken podul water of þe
40 canel; and resoun dampneþ more þis temptyng þan þe toþer in
desert. Þe fyueþe tyme biddiþ Poul þat *we grucche not aȝenus God*,
for worldli desir, ne flesheli, ne for peyne þat we sufferen; but be
we payed of Goddis sonde. For þe book of Moyses telliþ þat *many
men for siche grucchyng weren killid* bi God and his aungel, bifore þei
45 camen to lond of biheste. And, as hem wantid þe bihyȝt ende to
þe children of Israel, so þes gruccheris moten wanten blis þat God

---

23 Num. 25: 1, 9; 29 Exod. 17: 2; Num. 21: 6–9; 36 Exod. 17: 2–3; 43 Num.
14: 2, 29.

---

synnes] oþer synnes Z   22 mot] wole M, moot nedis I   for²] *om.* T   þes]
hem MZ   *margin* Num. 25 MOPTYαIZ   23 foure] thre α   24 in . . . telliþ]
as poule telleth on o day M   in] on Z   25 weren] was MZ   oþir] sume oiþer
M   26 ay] euer OT   27 poule] god I   killeþ] kille I   he] *om.*
Y   29 summe] sum men O   *margin* Exo. 17 et Num. 21 OPTYαIZ, Num. 21
M   bi] wiþ I   and] as O   30 tempten] temptede OαG   wrappen]
wlappen BMOPTYαZ   31 hym not] *rev.* I   his] ⌐him⌐ Y   32 þes . . . and]
om. Z   þes] þe Y   foure] *om.* B   maken] þat makis Z   a] *om.* Z   33
reule¹] reulis of lyuyng and forsakis cristis reule Z   wher] ȝif M   þat] þair
Z   ful] wel O   34 bi] ful *canc.* bi D   þe] *om.* OPZ   eddre] neddirs
Z   35 þan] þat I   36 hem] þei G   þes] nowe þes Mα, now Z   37
newe . . . now] men of newe reulis Z   now] *om.* Mα   plente] more plente
BI   38 water of] *om.* A   39 þe] *om.* Y   40 dampneþ more] *rev.* T   41
we] ȝe M   44 bi] of M   his] bi his G   aungel] angels MI   þei] þat þei δ   45
lond] þe *canc.* lond G, ⌐þe⌐ lond J, þe londe MPYδZ   hem] þai α   47

haþ bihyȝt to hise. And þus grucchen men today aȝenus þe ordynaunce of Crist, and shapun hem a newe reule, as ȝif þei leften Crist for a fool.

And þus in þes fyue fyguris may men licli suppose þat mo 50 perishiþ in tyme of grace bi þes fyue synnes þaᴵtᴵ reg|nen now, f.41 þan diden in þe olde lawe ᴦofᴵ þe children of Israel. And ȝit Poule seiþ heere þat *alle þes fillen in figure to hem*, for to teche þe chirche aftir to flee to synne as þei diden. And heerfore seiþ Poule aftir þat *þes ben wreten to oure snybbyng, into whom þe endis of þe worldis ben* 55 *comen*. It is knowun of bileue þat neyȝ þe ende of þe world þe feend temptiþ men faster þan he dide in þe bigynnyng, for þe shrewe is more enuyous, and drediþ hym of þe day of dome. And þerfore God haþ sent a gracious remedie to oure helpe, þat we haue a good lore of ensaumplis þat haue bifallen, boþe in þe olde 60 lawe and þe newe; and in þes shulden we studie, and leeue fablis and newe reulis, for þei helpen not but to flee hem. And þus ȝif we þenkyn wel of þe worldis þat weren bifore, hou strong and faire men weren þanne, and hou þe fruyȝtis weren þanne goode, and now is al turned vpsedoun, and ȝit we haue helpe of Crist bi his lyf 65 and his lymes, we shulden herfore leeue þis world and desire more þe blisse of heuene.

And herfore seiþ Poule heere þat *we ben þo ilke men in whom þe eendis of ᴦþeᴵ former worldis ben comen*. And þus þer welþe fayliþ, for siche þyngis moten nedis fayle in þer eende bi wey of kynde. And 70 herfore seiþ Poule aftir and *þerfore he þat gessiþ he stoonde, see he warli þat he falle not*. For boþe we ben now more feble and enemyes tempten vs more sutilli; and þerfore we shulden be more war, and sue Crist more bisili. And for it is nede here men to be temptid

hise] his children M   today] now Z   50 fyguris] figure M   licli] liȝtli
BY   mo] mo men Y   53 heere] *om.* α   fillen] fallen G   54 to²] ᴦtoᴵ Y,
om. IZ, fro α   55 wreten] weyten O   to] into I, til Z   endis] ende
α   þe²] *eras* Z, *om.* BPTY   worldis] worlde AOI   56 comen] bicomen
I   of¹] by O   þe²] þis OPYαXZG   57 men] man ABOPYδJ, *a canc.* man
T   58 of¹] more of I   59 þerfore] herfore I   a gracious] *om.* M   60 a]
ᴦaᴵY, *om.* MZ   þat . . . bifallen] byfalleþ O, has fallen Z   boþe] *om.* O   61
þe] in þe TIZ   in þes] þis M, in þis BOPTYαIXZG   studie] auoydie O   62
but . . . . hem] *om.* Z   ȝif] *om.* J   63 worldis] wordis T   65 al turned] *rev.*
G   ȝit] if G   66 his] by his Mβ   lymes] lyues Y   shulden] schullen
T   herfore] þerfore M   þis] þe I   desire] deserue M   68 and] *om.*
β   herfore] þerfore MZ   in] into M   69 eendis] ende B   þe] *corr.* D,
ᴦþeᴵ *canc.* X, *om.* ABPYαJ, þes I   former] *om.* M   71 þerfore] herfore
I   he²] hym M   he stoonde] to stonde δJ   72 boþe] nowe M   now]
om. M   73 tempten] temptid Z   more¹] now more A   74 sue . . . bisili]

75 many weyis, þerfore Poul telliþ what temptyng man shulde flee
on alle weies. Sum is *temptyng of man*, and sum is temptyng of þe
feend. He is takun in mannus temptyng whoos soule is temptid of
ony enemye, and oþer he aȝeenstondiþ þis temptyng, or ellis he
risiþ sone of his synne. And þus was Crist takun in temptyng, for
80 he hadde it boþe in bodi and soule; and þanne þis temptyng took
hym as a sugett to þis temptyng. But Poule biddiþ oþer
aȝeenstonde it, or ellis [sone] arise fro fallyng. Þe feendis
temptyng is þanne whan it is so hardid in man, þat it leueþ hym
neuere til þat he be brouȝt to helle. And so eche man þat is þus
85 temptid is a feend, as ben þei þat he gooþ to. And man shulde
trowe bi bileue þat noon may haue þis feendis temptyng, but ȝif
his synne or his folye brynge hym into þis temptyng. And herfore
seiþ Poul aftir *God is trewe, þat shal not suffre ȝou be temptid ouer þat þat*
ȝee may; but he shal make wiþ ȝoure temptyng fercomyng of grace, þat [ȝ]e
90 *may susteyne* ȝoure temptyng. And þanne þe victorie of suche
temptyng is medeful, as was in Crist; and so whos falliþ into þe
feendis temptyng his owene foli mot be in cause.

more bisily sue crist PTZ   nede] mede O   men] *om.* δ, to men I   75 poul
telliþ] *rev.* BY   what] þat *canc.* what D   man] men, e *altered from* a X, men
Tα   76 on] in A   weies] manere weyes I   77 temptid] takun *canc.* temptid
D   78 enemye] enuye O   aȝeenstondiþ] ȝenstondith M   þis] his M   he
risiþ sone] sone he risith Mβ   79 synne . . . in] om. δ   in] into M   80 he]
crist Y   soule] in soule δI   þanne] *om.* Mβ   þis] hys α   temptyng] *om.*
BY   81 sugett] seruaunt M   oþer] or þere I   82 sone] *om.* DOδIJ, *added on*
eras. X   arise] rise BOPTYαβIXZ   fallyng] knowing δ   83 so] *om.*
Bα   hardid] hardyned α   84 so] *om.* BY, þus M   þus] þis O   85 ben
þei] *rev.* Z   man] men O   86 þis] þe I   feendis] fende α   87 into þis] in
⌐to þis⌐Y   into] to Mβ, þer *canc.* to α   herfore] þerfore M   88 trewe] trewþe
DX   shal not suffre] suffris ȝow not α   ȝou] *om.* O, to α   be temptid] *om.*
B   þat þat] þat MPβIZ   89 shal] *om.* B   fercomyng] a ferre comyng A, for
comynge BMTY   ȝe] he DOI   90 þanne] *om.* δ   91 was] it was
B   whos] who so, so *canc.* X, who BOPTYαδJG, who þat IZ   þe] *om.*
BMPβZ   92 owene] ⌐owene⌐ T, *om.* J   in] *om.* Z

Dominica x post Trinitatem. Epistola. [Sermo 40.]

Scitis qu[oniam] cum gentes essetis. Prima Corintheos 12.

Poule moeueþ in þis epistele for former kyndenesse of Crist to be
kynde to hym aȝeen. For clerkis seien, and sooþ it is, þat boþe
God and kynde haten þat a man dwelle vnkynde aftir greet
kyndenesse þat he haþ takun; for sooþ it is þat alle synne turneþ
to vnkyndenesse to God. And þus Poul bryn|giþ to þes mennus   5 f.41v
mynde hou myche kyndenesse Crist haþ don hem. *Ȝee wetyn,* he
seiþ, *whan ȝee weren heþene, ȝee weren ledde to doumbe maumetis, goyng
as beestis from oon to anoþer, as ȝif ȝee hadden no soule of man.*
And siþ mannus God shulde be a þyng þat were þe fairest and þe
beste, in whiche shulde lye þe heleþe of men, and make mennus   10
soule like to hym, þe fouleste þyng þat falliþ to man, and most
perelus to his soule, is to haue a fals god, as hauen men þat
worshipen maumetis; for þei maken þer soule foul to greet perel
of þer soule. And þus it is a foul þyng to be led as a beere to a stake
bi vntrewþe of a feend, to loue ouȝt as it were god, þe whiche   15
þyng is not god; for alle suche ben false goddis.

   And þus seiþ Poule aftir þat *noon þat spekiþ ⌐in⌐ Goddis spiryȝt
puttiþ cursidnesse to Crist,* siþ al þe Trynyte approued hym, and
boþe his dedis and his wordis weren hooly and ful of resoun and
loue. And þus men seien comynli þat false men on þre maneris   20
putten cursednesse to Crist, and alle þes ben dampnable. First,

MSS: D; ABGHIJMOPTXYZαβδ.

Sermo 40] *om.* DABMOPTαβδIJXZGH   scitis . . . essetis] *om.* M   quoniam]
qui DδXG   cum] *om.* Z   essetis] essetis. de temptacione T, *om.* O   I cor.
12] cor. 12 H, *om.* O   1 moeueþ] tellith Mβ   in] ⌐men⌐ in T   2
to . . . aȝeen] aȝen to hym J   to] of I   3 dwelle] ⌐þat⌐ dwelle⌐þ⌐ δ   4
synne] synnes Mβ   5 to²] of α   þes] *om.* M   mennus] mannus M   6
mynde] myndis β   haþ] haue δ   hem] for hem M, to hem α   8 ȝif] *om.*
M   man] lif *canc.* man D   9 mannus] a mannis I   be] *om.* β   þe²] *om.*
β   10 lye] be I   heleþe] helpe M   men] man Mβ   mennus] mannys
B   11 soule] soule, -s *eras.* A, soulis Mβ   like] lyue M   hym] hem
I   man] a man Mβ, men I   12 his] mannus T   is] it is I   hauen men]
men han AMβ   13 maken] made α   14 þus] þis O   a¹] *om.* α   a²] *om.*
BH   16 suche] suche þinges I   17 in] wiþ *canc.* ⌐in⌐ D   18 approued]
approuyth MG   19 his²] *om.* T   and²] *om.* Mβ   20 men seien] *rev.*

whan men bi opun synne ben not kyndeli to Crist, as alle synful
men done for tyme þat þer wille is turned amys. Þe secounde
seyyng of cursidnesse þat false men puttyn vnto Crist is to seye
25 wiþ herte and word þat Crist was a fals prophete, and curse hym
bi vnbileue, as diden Iewis long tyme. Þe þridde cursyng and þe
werste þat false men putten to Crist is þat þei feynen þe name of
Crist, and his goodnesse wiþ his lawe; and ʒit þei falsen þis in
dede, and seien þat oþir lawe is beter. As men of þes foure sectis
30 þat puttyn bihynde Cristis lawe, and takun hem a newe patroun
and newe reule wiþoute Crist: þes men ben ypocritis þat Crist
hatiþ most of alle.

And þus seiþ Poul aftir, as treuþe suyng of his wordis, þat *noon*
may seye 'Lord Iesu' but in þe Hooli Goost. And Poul spekiþ heere of
35 seyyng þat is seiyng fulli formed, as is seiyng of trewe men in
herte, in word and in dede, þat seien ryʒtli to Goddis worshipe in
þe name of þe Trynyte. What men trowen we may þus seye 'Lord
Iesu is oure lord, and oure sauyour fro þe feend', but ʒif þe Holi
Goost teche hym? – for þanne he makiþ no departyng fro Cristis
40 godhed and his manhed. But whateuere Crist haþ ordeyned or
seid was don to his chirche at poynt deuys. And in þis cursyng
fallen þes sectis þat dispisen Cristis lawe; as ʒif his ordynaunce
faylede, but þer ordynaunce is myche betere. For what man
shulde chese anoþer lawe, but ʒif þat lawe were betere þan
45 Cristis? For he is fool of alle foolis þat þus chesiþ þe worse weye,
and leeueþ þe beter weye to heuene, more lyʒt and more redy.
For he puttiþ to Iesu Crist boþe cursyng and disseyʒt, whan he
seiþ bi his dede þat Crist hidde þe betere weye, and tauʒte þe

---

25 Matt. 27: 40–43.

BY   21 to] on M   þes] *om.* A   23 for] fro B   24 false] cursid
M   vnto] on Mβ, aʒeins I   25 word] mouþ T   curse] curside G   26
long] by longe OH   27 to] vpon A, on M, vnto I   29 seien] haldis Z   þat]
om. Z   is] *om.* Z   of . . . sectis] *om.* Z   sectis] newe *canc.* sectis D   30
þat] and T   cristis] goddis M   patroun . . . newe (31)] *om.* Z   31 newe] a
newe AMβ   33 of] *om.* Y   his] þe B   þat] þa β   34 lord] þe lord
G   in] *om.* Y   35 is seiyng[1]] hys saiynge ⌜is⌝ α   is[2]] *om.* Y   in] and
M   36 in[1]] *om.* I   and] *om.* A   37 men] man OαZH   we] he Z   38
lord and oure] *om.* M   and oure] *om.* A, our I   39 teche] techiþ H   hym]
hem AM   40 whateuere] what Z   or] and α   41 to his chirche] *om.*
Y   chirche] worchipe αβ   and . . . glosen(52)] *om.* Z   42 sectis] foure
sectis Y   43 what] whan O   45 cristis] cristis lawe Aα   fool] a fool
ABMαβI   chesiþ] techiþ A   worse] werste Mβ   46 þe] a ABOPYαβXG,
om. M   beter] *om.* M   48 tauʒte] *om.* I   þe[2]] *om.* M   49 vnparfitere]

vnparfitere weye, til þat God hadde sent þes sectis. And þes sectis
camen not fully out til ⌐þat⌐ Sathanas was vnbounden. Among　50
alle blasphemes þat euere sprungen, þis is þe mooste cursed; for
þei techen opunli in dede þat þus it is, houeuere men glosen. But,
al ȝif þes two kyndis of Crist ben dyuerse in hemself, ȝit þes two
ben o God and þer ben no mo goddis.

And þus men shulden in þer þouȝt þenken how dy|uysioun of　55　f.42
þyngis comeþ of þis oo God, þe whiche God is a spiryȝt. And
herfore seiþ Poule aftir þat *þer ben dyuysiones of grace, but* certis *it is*
þe same spiryȝt of whom camen alle þes gracis, as of o welle comen
many strondis. And þus of þis same spiryȝt moten come *dyuysiones*
of seruysis; for þis *o God* mot haue seruauntis aftir þe grace þat he　60
ȝeueþ, siþ þis Lord loueþ degrees in his seruauntis as it falliþ. And
þus in þe þridde tyme *þer ben dyuysiones of worchyngis, and ȝit it is þe*
same God þat worchiþ al in alle þyngis. Who shulde grucche for þes
dyuysiones, siþ þei ben þus ordeyned of God? as eche part of a
man mot haue þes þre dyuerse in ordre: as first he haþ an hid　65
power, and of þis power comen his willis, and of þis power and þis
wille comen worchyngis to mennus profyȝt. And þus, as it is in
man, so it is in hooli chirche; and ioye we of þis ordynaunce of
God, siþ it is boþe fayr and good.

And þus Poul declariþ aftir nyne degrees of mennus worchyn-　70
gis þat God haþ ordeyned in þe chirche, as þer ben þre ierachies,
for *eche* membre of hooli chirche haþ sum shewyng of þis
spiriȝt, boþe to *profyȝt* of it and to profyȝt of þe chirche. As to
summe bi ȝifte of God is ȝouen *þe word of wisdom*, for summe haue
sum knowyng heere of treuþis of þe heyȝe Trynyte. And *anoþir*　75
haþ word of witt aftir þis same spiryȝt; for summe men haue
knowyng of God, boþe of aungelis and of heuenes, and hou þis

50　Rev. 20: 7;　**56**　John 4: 24.

---

parfitere I, vnperfit G　　　weye] *om.* I　　　50 þat] *om.* A　　　51 alle] alle þe
O　　　þis] certis þis M　　　53 þes²] þei M　　　56 þe] *om.* A　　　57 herfore] þerfore
M　　　dyuysiones] dyuersioun B　　　58 camen] comes Z　　　welle] wille β　　　59
strondis] frendis β　　　þis] þe YI　　　61 falliþ] failliþ β　　　62 þus] *om.* M　　　63
god] spirit Z　　　al in] in *canc.* alle in T, *om.* G　　　64 as] and M　　　a] *om.*
Mβ　　　65 haþ] moot haue I　　　66 willis] wille α　　　þis³] of þis A　　　67
mennus] mannus H　　　as] ⌐as⌐ O, *om.* A　　　68 man] a man OTH　　　so] and so
A　　　71 in þe] to his M, to þe δ　　　73 to profyȝt²] ⌐to⌐ profyȝt T, profit β, *om.*
M　　　74 summe¹] sum men T　　　summe²] sum men I　　　75 sum . . . haue(76)]
om. M　　　and] *om.* H　　　76 þis] þe BIZ, þe *canc.* þis H　　　men] *om.* Aα　　　77

vnparfitere weye, til þat God hadde sent þes sectis. And þes sectis
camen not fully out til ⌐þat⌐ Sathanas was vnbounden. Among   50
alle blasphemes þat euere sprungen, þis is þe mooste cursed; for
þei techen opunli in dede þat þus it is, houeuere men glosen. But,
al ȝif þes two kyndis of Crist ben dyuerse in hemself, ȝit þes two
ben o God and þer ben no mo goddis.

And þus men shulden in þer þouȝt þenken how dy|uysioun of   55 f.42
þyngis comeþ of þis oo God, þe whiche God is a spiryȝt. And
herfore seiþ Poule aftir þat *þer ben dyuysiones of grace, but* certis *it is*
þe same spiryȝt of whom camen alle þes gracis, as of o welle comen
many strondis. And þus of þis same spiryȝt moten come *dyuysiones*
of seruysis; for þis *o God* mot haue seruauntis aftir þe grace þat he   60
ȝeueþ, siþ þis Lord loueþ degrees in his seruauntis as it falliþ. And
þus in þe þridde tyme *þer ben dyuysiones of worchyngis, and ȝit it is þe*
same God þat worchiþ al in alle þyngis. Who shulde grucche for þes
dyuysiones, siþ þei ben þus ordeyned of God? as eche part of a
man mot haue þes þre dyuerse in ordre: as first he haþ an hid   65
power, and of þis power comen his willis, and of þis power and þis
wille comen worchyngis to mennus profyȝt. And þus, as it is in
man, so it is in hooli chirche; and ioye we of þis ordynaunce of
God, siþ it is boþe fayr and good.

And þus Poul declariþ aftir nyne degrees of mennus worchyn-   70
gis þat God haþ ordeyned in þe chirche, as þer ben þre ierachies,
for *eche* membre of hooli chirche haþ sum shewyng of þis
spiriȝt, boþe to *profyȝt* of it and to profyȝt of þe chirche. As to
summe bi ȝifte of God is ȝouen *þe word of wisdom*, for summe haue
sum knowyng heere of treuþis of þe heyȝe Trynyte. And *anoþir*   75
haþ word of witt aftir þis same spiryȝt; for summe men haue
knowyng of God, boþe of aungelis and of heuenes, and hou þis

50 Rev. 20: 7;   56 John 4: 24.

parfitere I, vnperfit G   weye] *om.* I   50 þat] *om.* A   51 alle] alle þe
O   þis] certis þis M   53 þes²] þei M   56 þe] *om.* A   57 herfore] þerfore
M   dyuysiones] dyuersioun B   58 camen] comes Z   welle] wille β   59
strondis] frendis β   þis] þe YI   61 falliþ] failliþ β   62 þus] *om.* M   63
god] spirit Z   al in] in *canc.* alle in T, *om.* G   64 as] and M   a] *om.*
Mβ   65 haþ] moot haue I   66 willis] wille α   þis³] of þis A   67
mennus] mannus H   as] ⌐as⌐ O, *om.* A   68 man] a man OTH   so] and so
A   71 in þe] to his M, to þe δ   73 to profyȝt²] ⌐to⌐ profyȝt T, profit β, *om.*
M   74 summe¹] sum men T   summe²] sum men I   75 sum . . . haue(76)]
om. M   and] *om.* H   76 þis] þe BIZ, þe *canc.* þis H   men] *om.* Aα   77

world comeþ of God bi faiþ ordre þat he haþ ordeyned. *Oþir men
haue bileue* of hid þyngis and of heye; and alle þes þre comen of
80 God þat ȝyueþ þes to his chirche. *Summe haue grace of heleþis*, boþe
bodili and goostli, boþe to haue hem in hemsilf, and to ȝyue hem
⌈to⌉ oþir breþeren. And God is þat *ilke spiryȝt* of whom alle þes
gracis comen. *God ȝyueþ anoþir to worche uertues*, and speciali to
knowe Goddis uertu, and how God of his gracious uertu haþ
85 ȝouen men power to worche uertues, as in departyng of þe see,
and in stondyng of þe sunne, and in many oþir wondris þat God
haþ doon for mannus sake. And ȝit þe wisdom of God ȝyueþ for
profyȝt of his chirche *prophecie* to sum men, to sue good and flee
euel, as Ioon hadde in Apocalips, and sum men aftir hym haue
90 lesse. And þis secounde ierachie answeriþ to þe secounde persone.
To opere is ȝouen þe seueþe tyme *discrecioun to knowe spiritis*, and þis
is a greet ȝifte þat comeþ of þe Hooli Goost. For no drede siche
spiritis moeuen men to dyuerse werkis, and it is a good ȝifte of
God to knowe goode spiritis fro yuel; for goode spiritis moeuen
95 euere men to uertuous dedis, and yuel spiritis moeuen men to
yuel and to bigile men. Þis same Spiryȝt ȝeueþ to men *dyuerse
manere of langagis*, as þis Goost ȝaf apostelis witt and tungis on
Wittsunday. And at þe laste þis Goost ȝeueþ men *to vndirstonde
witt of wordis*, as þis Goost ȝeueþ many men witt to knowe what
100 holi writ meneþ. And alle þes þre ȝiftis of God ben proprid to þe
Hooli Goost. But ȝit siþ alle þes þre persones ben o God and o

---

85 Exod. 14: 21; 86 Josh. 10: 13; Isa. 38: 8; **97** Acts 2: 1–8.

and hou] *on eras. corr.* D   þis] þe A   78 ordre] *om.* M   79 of²] *om.*
α   þre] thre thinges α   80 þat] and he M   ȝyueþ] ȝyue B   summe]
sume men α   grace] graces A   81 boþe] *om.* Mβ   haue] *om.* T   hem¹]
þa heelis Z, *om.* H   82 to] *corr.* D   is þat] *rev.* T   83 anoþir] to anoþer
Z   to] for to I   85 as] and M   departyng] þe partyng M, depart þus
β   86 of] vp of I   in²] *om.* T   *margin* exo. 16, iosue 10, ysa. 38 T   87
for²] to A   88 sue] *om.* M   good] god A   89 in] in þo αG   men] *om.*
OT   haue] hadde O   90 þis] þe M   91 seueþe] seuene I   þis] þus
β   93 is] *om.* M   94 goode²] godis M   95 euere men] euermore α, men
euere I   uertuous] vertues β, goode werkis, werkis *canc.* Y   men²] *om.*
MOβ   to yuel and] *om.* O   96 and] *om.* α   to¹] for to M   men¹] yuel
men O   dyuerse . . . men(98)] *om.* M   97 manere] maners O   apostelis]
to apostelis T, þe apostlis Z   tungis] tonge I   98 men] to men ABY   to] wit to
H   99 þis] þe *on eras.* X, þe ABMOPTYαβδIJZGH   many] to many α   100
þre] *om.* A   to] til α   101 but ȝit] *on eras. corr.* D   ȝit] ⌈ȝit⌉ Y, *om.* Oαδ-

Spiry3t, noon of hem 3eueþ ony of þes, but 3if þei alle þre 3yuen hem. For *oo God doþ alle goodis; and he departiþ þes þyngis to men* aftir his power, witt and|wille; and þus he departiþ not amys, al 3if þe f.42v resoun be hid fro vs.

Dominica xi post Trinitatem. Epistola. [Sermo 41.]

Notum uobis facio euangelium. Prima Corintheos 15.

In þis epistele techiþ Poul bi many resones how his gospel is to be preisid of trewe men for fruyȝt of blis þat comeþ þerof. And euangelie is seid as 'good tidyng of blisse', and þus not oneli þes foure gospelis, but epistelis of Poul and of oþere apostelis ben
5 clepid euangeliis heere and in manye oþere placis; and þus ben men out of bileue þat denyen þat þes ben gospelis. And heerfore seiþ Poule heere *Y make knowe to ȝou þe gospel þat Y haue prechid to ȝou, þe whiche ȝee haue* medefulli *takun; in whiche gospel ȝee stonden* ȝit, *bi whiche,* ȝif God wole, *ȝee shullen be saued.* And þus may trewe
10 men see hou þis gospel is to be preysid bi many resones, bi þe fruyȝt þat spryngiþ to men of þis gospel. First bi autorite of God þat spak þis song in þis vessel, for precious licour in precious uessell shulden be preysid of hem þat takun it. Þis licour is wisdom of God, and seyn Poul is þis uessell; and he was raueshid
15 to þe þridde heuene and say þere wisdom of God. And þis licour shulde be takun more dereworþli þan oyle of toumbis, for it heliþ more mennus soulis þan siche oyle heliþ mennus bodies. And medeful takyng of þis witt is anoþer resoun to preyse it, and, siþ it areriþ mennus soulis and makiþ hem þus stonde in bileue, Poul
20 telliþ þe þridde resoun whi þat men shulden preise þis gospell. Þe fourþe resoun þat Poul ȝeueþ of þe preisyng of þis gospell is þat it

15 2 Cor. 12: 2.

MSS: D; ABGHIJMOPTXYZαδ; β *ends incompl.* 20 whi þat men shulden

Sermo 41] *om.* DABMOTαβδIJXZGH   euangelium] euangelium quod predicavi vobis M, *om.* OH   I. cor. 15] *om.* O, cor. 15 MH   1 his] þis T   be] *om.* Y   2 and] *om.* M   3 as] of god as Mβ, a δ, as a H   þus] *om.* T   þes] þe Z   4 of²] *om.* BMα   5 clepid] called αZ   þus] þes AB   ben men] þei ben H   6 of] *om.* O   bileue] þe bileeue B   ben] *om.* O   heerfore] þerfor Z   8 whiche²] þe which Mβ   9 shullen] shuld α   may] many α   10 þe] *om.* BO   11 of¹] by MI   12 in²] and BMPβZ, in a J   13 hem] hym M   14 and¹ . . . god (15)] *om.* I   þis] þe BOZ   15 to] vn *canc.* to D, vnto α, into H   wisdom] þe *canc.* wisdom X, þe wisdom AMαβ   16 dereworþli] derely Z   heliþ] helpiþ H   17 oyle] oþere β   19 areriþ] reiseth M, raisis vp Z, reriþ G   mennus] mannis I   hem] it I   20 þat] *om.* P   shulden] shulen A   þe . . . gospell (21)] *om.* J   21 of¹] to P   þe] ⌈þe⌉ Y, *om.*

is a ney3 mene to saue men in blisse of heuene. And Poule bosti‫þ‬
not heere of þis gospell for his persone, but bi resoun of his God, of
whom þis gospell sprong bi grace; and þis shulde moeue trewe
men to take þis gospell and leeue fablis. And Poul telli‫þ‬ aftir of   25
þis gospell hou men shulden laste þerinne, for ellis þer trauele
þeraboute were ydil and wiþoute fruy3t; for prechyng of Goddis
word and holdyng þerof in mannus mynde shulde be to gendre
bileue in men, and þerbi brynge forþ goode werkis.

    And Poul sei‫þ‬, but 3if þis sue, *þei haue bileued* heere *in ueyn*. As   30
clerkis seyen þat trauel is veyn, of whiche come‫þ‬ not þe goode
ende þat men shulden shappe to come þerof bi grace and
ordynaunse of God. And þus sei‫þ‬ Poul *for what resoun shulde Y haue
prechid þus to 3ou, and 3ee shulden haue holdun þis lore*, but for comyng
of þis eende? And, 3if þis ende come not, *3ee haue bileued* heere *in*   35
veyn. Y bitook first to 3ou loore þat Y haue takun of God, *þat Crist was deed
for oure synnes aftir* þe witnesse of *hooli writt*—and betere witnesse
may noon be, for þanne mot God witnesse it. Crist diede not for
his owene synne, as þeues dyen for here synne, but Crist oure
broþir þat my3te not synne diede for synne þat oþre hadden don.   40
And boþe ry3twisnesse of God, and grace and sauyng of men,
moeuede Crist to dye þus; and not oneli synne of men, for þanne
Crist hadde dyed for nou3t and ydilliche wiþouten cause. Y telde
3ou more|of bileue hou þat *Crist was aftir biried, and* hou *he roos on þe*   f.43
þridde day bi ⌈þe⌉ *wittnesse of holi writt*. And for þis bileue was wreten   45
in þe book of lyf and mennus soulis, and also in dede skynnes,
Poul clepi‫þ‬ it many scripturis.

    And Poule telli‫þ‬ of sixe degrees bi whiche Crist was seyen on
lyue, aftir tyme þat he was deed; and þis bileue shulde be trowid.
Poul telli‫þ‬ þat *Petre say3 hym, and aftir alle enleuene apostelis*. And,   50

---

50 Mark 16: 4, Luke 24: 34, John 20: 19.

A	22 a] *om.* G	blisse] þe blis M	23 bi] for *canc.* bi D	24 þis²] þus
O	trewe] *om.* Z	25 þis] þe T	aftir] *om.* M, here after I	of] in
T	27 þeraboute] hereaboute I		prechyng] þe preisinge I	30 þis] þei
H	31 þat] þe O	veyn] in veyne MZ	of whiche] þat α	not þe] noon
H	þe] to Oα, *om.* T	34 comyng] connynge O		35 come] comeþ
A	36 to 3ou] *om.* O	37 þe] *om.* B	38 mot god witnesse] god witnesith
M	40 hadden] han I	41 and³] of BYδ	43 nou3t and] nou3	ydil-
	liche] idil and α	telde] telle M	44 3ou] now O	hou¹] aftir *canc.* hou
D	þat] *om.* T	on] vpon G	45 þe] ⌈þe⌉ Y, *om.* AOH	46 and¹] in
α	in²] *om.* I	47 clepiþ] calles αZ, clepid H	many] *om.* Z	48 of] *om.*
BY	49 tyme] þe tyme AM	50 aftir] after him I	alle] al þe A	51 to]

aftir whan Crist styede to heuene, *mo þan fyf hundrid men sawen hym togidere,* for þei weren warned bifore heerof and þerfore mo camen to þis syȝt: *and summe of hem lyued to þis tyme* of Poul, *and summe of hem weren dede* bifore. *And aftirward was Crist seyen of Iames, and*
35 *aftirward of alle þe apostelis; and at þe laste of al was Crist seien to Poule.* And þus Poul, as ⌜a⌝ *chyld þat were mysborun,* distryȝede synne of þe synagoge, as summe children whan þei ben borun sleen þer modir þat beriþ hem. Þus Poul distryede þe synagoge whan he came to Cristis chirche.

60   Poul seiþ mekeli of hymsilf þat *he is þe leeste of apostelis, and þat he is not worþi* of hymsilf *for to be clepid apostele, for he pursuede Goddis chirche.* Heere we shullen vndirstonde þat Poul seiþ sooþ as he shulde, siþ noon shulde gabbe for ony cause. Poul seiþ þat he is leest of apostelis in his owene acountyng, for Poul was wundurly
65 meke, and hou he cam bi grace aftir oþere; and þus he seiþ he is not worþi to be clepid apostele wiþ oþere; and cause of þis vnworþynesse is þat he pursuede Goddis chirche. And heerfore seiþ Poule aftir, *bi grace of God Y am þat Y am*; and þus he is not euene worþi to be clepid a cristen man. But neþeles ⌜þe⌝ *grace of*
70 *God was not ydil in seynt Poule,* for it moeuede hym to profite to þe chirche, whiche he harmede bifore. And þus men may preyse God in þe ȝiftis þat he haþ ȝouen hem. But þenke we hou Poul trauelede for to gete worshipe to God; and sue we hym, in as myche as Poul þus suede Crist.

into Z   men] of men MTI   52 heerof] þerof AOZ   þerfore] herfore
M   54 aftirward] after AMI   was crist] *rev.* δ   was] *om.* α   of] to
Mα   55 of¹] to α   crist] *om.* O   to] of A   56 þus] *om.* B   as] *om.*
Z   a] *om.* MOPTYαIG   were] was M   57 þer] þe AI   58 þus] so þus
I   60 hymsilf] hym α   þe] ⌜þe⌝ T, *om.* ZH   apostelis] þe apostles
M   61 for to] to αH, for ⌜to⌝ δ   clepid] called αZ   goddis] cristis A   62
shullen] shulden AMαIH   63 þat] *om.* O   64 owene] *om.* I   acountyng]
countynge αIH   wundurly] wondurfully T   65 hou] knew hou BM   aftir]
of A   is] was α   66 clepid] called αZ   69 euene] *om.* T   clepid] called
αZ   þe] *corr.* D, *om.* BOPYδJZGH   71 men may] *rev.* M, many men
α   may preyse] praysede α   72 þe] þes M   hem] hym, e *above* y M, him
I   73 we] *om.* I   74 þus suede] *rev.* J   þus] *om.* H

Dominica xii post Trinitatem. Epistola.
[Sermo 42.]

Fiduciam talem habemus. 2 Corintheos 3.

Poul telliþ excellence of grace of þe newe lawe ouer grace of þe
olde lawe to come ly3tliere to heuene. And Poule bigynneþ þus :
we haue siche trist bi Crist, as bi þe beste mene *to God, þat we ben not
sufficient to þenke ou3t of vs as of vs, but oure sufficiense is* hoolli *of God.*
For, siþ mannus þenkyng among his werkis semeþ most in his   5
power, and 3it his þou3t mot come of God, more eche oþir werk of
man. It is knowun þyng to clerkis þat no creature may do ou3t,
but 3if God do first þat same þyng, and helpe þis creature to do it.
And, siþ we haue a betere procuratour in tyme of grace to preye
to God þan men hadden in þe oolde lawe, no wundir 3if þis be a   10
beter tyme. And þus shulde we putte of pride and hoolli triste in
Iesu Crist; for he þat may not þenke of hymself, may do nou3t of
hymsilf. But al oure sufficience is of God, bi þe mene of Iesu Crist;
and siþ Crist is boþe God and man, he is boþe iuge and
procuratour. And þes wordis ben bileue, siþ eche power is of God,   15
and so eche sufficiense of man|mot nedeli be 3ouen of God. And,   f.43ᵛ
3if þou grucche hera3een, þat a man doþ many euele werkis, and
God doþ al þat man doþ, and so God doþ many eueles—trewe
men grauntyn þis of God þat eche creature of þe world, wher þat
it be good or yuel, is maad of God, Lord of alle; but synne þat is no   20
creature, but defaute of man or aungel, is not maad of oure God,
siþ to do it is fayle to God. But, 3if synne were a creature, þat

MSS: D; ABGHIJMOPTXYZαδ; β *begins incompl.* 20 -ne þat is no creature.

Sermo 42] *om.* DABMOTαδIJXZGH   talem] enim talem M, *om.* O   habemus]
habemus per christum ad deum T   2 cor. 3] *om.* O, cor. 12 H   2 come ly3tliere]
rev. Y   3 bi²] *om.* I   4 as of vs] *om.* I   5 þenkyng] þekyng B   6 mot]
moste B   more] ⸢muche⸣ more T, myche more H, ⸢þan⸣ more α   8 þat] þe
I   9 procuratour] proctoure A   10 be . . . tyme (11)] tyme be betre I   11
shulde we] *rev.* MY   12 of] on T   13 þe] *om.* Y   15 procuratour] proctoure
A   16 nedeli] nede H   17 a] *om.* I   18 man] a canc. man D, a man
I   and] *om.* M   19 men] *om.* α   þe] god canc. þe D   21 but . . . crea-
ture (22)] *om.* α   defaute] a defaute A   is] it is O   god] lord god P, lord
Z   22 fayle] failyng M   23 hymself] it silf H   moste] mut M   of] bi

my3te be bi hymself, þanne synne moste nedis be maad of
God, and man my3te make þat it were synne.

25   And þis mediatour Crist *made apostelis*, and þer vikeris, *couenable
seruauntis of þe newe lawe*. And þis auaunsement is greet; for it is
holden a greet grace to be pope or oþir prelaat, but it is a
þousyndfold more grace to be a mynystre as Crist haþ ordeyned,
for þe wynnyng is more and þe seruyse more clene. For, siþ þe
30   newe testament is þe laste lawe of God, and bryngiþ men next to
heuene, þes mynystris bryngyn þus men bi grace þat God hymself
3eue[þ] and worchiþ þus wiþ þes mynystris. And þis is couenable
seruyse and hey3 þat prestis shulden haue. But 3if þei kepen not
wel þis offys, noon ben foulere traytoris þan þei ben. And greet
35   dyuersete is fro hem and fro prestis of þe oolde lawe, for prestis of
þe olde lawe diden figure of grace þat now is doon bi Crist. And
þerfore seyþ Poule heere þat preestis of þe newe lawe wirchen now
not bi lettere, but bi spiry3t þat God 3yueþ. And þis word
vndirstonden men þus þat prestis in þe newe lawe haue honest
40   seruyse and ly3t, and been not killeris of beestis, as weren prestis
in þe oolde lawe; but þe grace þat þei figureden is maad now of
God bi his preestis. And herfore seiþ Poul þat now prestis wirchen
not bi lettre, but bi spiry3t.

And heere anticristis truauntis spekyn a3en þe newe lawe, and
45   seyen þat literal witt of it shulde neuere be takun but goostly witt;
and þei feynen þis goostli witt aftir shrewed wille þat þei haue.
And þus þes foure sectis ben aboute to distrye literal witt of
Goddis lawe; and þis shulde be ⌜þe⌝ first and þe moste bi whiche
þe chirche shulde be reulid. And a3enus þis witt anticrist argueþ
50   many weyes: 'þat hooli writt is fals bi þis bi many partis of holi

H   25 couenable] comenable O   26 auaunsement] anhancement T   27
pope] a pape Z   it] *om.* M   a] *om.* M   28 as] of crist as H   29 þe²] *om.*
I   more²] is more M   30 laste] *om.* J   men] *om.* M   31 þus men] *rev.*
Mβ   þus] þes T   hymself] ⌜him⌝ Y   32 3eueþ] 3euef D   couenable] a
coueneable α   33 and hey3 þat] þat hie A, an hei3 þat I   kepen] kepten
I   34 þan] þat Y   þei ben] *rev.* BPZ   36 figure] figures α   37 þerfore]
herfore I   þe] ⌜þe⌝ X, *om.* β   38 þis] þus O   39 vndirstonden men] *rev.*
A   in] of AB   41 þe²] *om.* H   42 god] good δ   preestis] *om.*
J   now] *om.* I   43 not] now not I   lettre] lettris T   44 and¹] *on eras.*
corr. D   anticristis truauntis] wha þat Z   truauntis] tirauntis AOTI   46
and] *om.* Z   47 and . . . aboute] couetand Z   literal] þe literal M   48 þe¹]
corr. D, *om.* α   first] moste Mβ   moste] firste Mβ   49 a3enus . . . anticrist]
wha þat Z   þis] þus O   50 many weyes] *om.* Z   bi²] in T   holi writt] it

writt, and so þer is anoþer witt þan þis literal witt þat þou hast
ȝouen, and þis is a mysti witt, þe whiche Y wole chese to ȝyue'.
And þus fayliþ autorite of hooli writt bi anticrist. But Poul seyþ to
þis entent *þat lettre* in þe tyme of grace þat is takun of þe oolde
lawe, and holden þat it shulde euere laste, as it lasted for þat   55
tyme, *sleeþ* men goostli; for it lettiþ men of bileue þat þei ben now
nerr to blis þan þei weren in þe oolde lawe bi comyng of Crist in
tyme of grace. But leeue we þes heresyes, and bileue we þat many
þyngis were bedyn to fadris of þe olde lawe in fygure of þyngis in
tyme of grace; and þis figure shal be goostli knowen, for ellis   60
literal vndirstondyng wole slee mennus soulis bi vnbileue. *But*
spiritual vndirstondyng *quykeneþ* mennus soulis bi ryȝt bileue.
And, ȝif þou wilt knowe þe ground to iuge of þes vndur-
stondyngis, bigynne at cristen mennus|bileue, and trowe   f.44
þat Crist haþ now lyued heere, as it was fygurid in þe oolde lawe,   65
and abide it not as ȝit to come. And so eche word of þe newe lawe
þat souneþ to uertues of Crist and to charite of his chirche shulde
be takun aftir þe lettre. And heerfore been heretikis dampned, as
Austyn telliþ in his book, whiche denyeden literal witt of
vndirstondyng of Goddis lawe.   70

And þus seiþ Poul aftir þat, *ȝif seruyse of deeþ wretyn foulli bi lettris*
in stones was in glorie of Moyses, *so þat þe children of Israel myȝten not*
loke into his face, for þe glorie of his shynyng, þat was sone *uoydid* aftir,
hou not more spiritual seruyse of cristen preestis *shal be* in þis tyme *in*
glorie?–siþ þis glorie boþe is more and encresciþ vnto blis. And, ȝif   75

Z   51 so] sais Z   anoþer] oþer Y   þan . . . witt²] *margin* PT   þat] *om.*
O   þou hast] is Z   52 is] *om.* δ   y wole] he sais he wil Z   53 and þus] he
is aboutward Z   þus] *om.* α   fayliþ] to ger Z   autorite of] *om.* δ   bi]
om. Z   anticrist] autorite of anticrist δ, faile Z   54 lettre] þe letter Mαβ   þe¹]
om. BMOTαβδ   of] in A, *om.* M   þe²] *om.* H   55 lasted] ⌜hys⌝ lastyd
T   þat²] a B   56 lettiþ] lettide BY   57 nerr] þe neer Mβ, no nerre
α   þe] *om.* H   59 of¹] in A   60 shal] shulde δ   be goostli] *rev.* T, we
gostly I   knowen] knawyng Z   61 mennus] mannus δI   62 spiritual] bi
spiritual δ   quykeneþ] quykiþ Bβ   mennus] mannis I   soulis] soule
PY   63 and] *om.* T   þes vndurstondyngis] þs vndirstondyng H   65 fygurid]
figure δ   66 abide] bide ABOPTYIXZ   and²] an X   so] *om.* δ   þe]
þis A   67 chirche] chichire Y   68 heerfore] þerfore O   69 whiche] þe
whiche H   denyeden] denyen Mβ   of] and G   71 seruyse] seruyng
MOPTYαβIZG   foulli . . . stones (72)] in stones fouli bi letteris H   foul-
li] fulli BI   72 stones] stone Mβ   in²] *om.* YZ   of¹] to Mβ   þe] *om.*
α   73 into] in BM   þe] *om.* H   aftir] efterwarde M   74 not] my⌜rche⌝
H   cristen] cristis Mβ   tyme] *om.* M   in²] of T   75 þis] *om.*

men wolen vndirstonde þis resoun þat Poule makiþ heere, it were
nedeful for to wite hou þe face of Moyses shynede, whan he cam
doun out of Synay and ȝaf þe lawe wreten in stones, and so þe
puple durste not loke into Moyses face, þat was horned wiþ lyȝt.
80 And þus þer goostli eyen weryn hid whan þei lokeden to þis
Moyses; but he hidde his shynyng face, and þanne þe puple spak
to hym. And siþ Crist in þe newe lawe preentide it in his apostelis
hertis, myche more þer goostli seruyng shulde be in glorie þan
was Moyses; for preentyng in þer soulis was betere þan was
85 preentyng in þe stones, and þe shynyng of grace of Crist passed
bodily shynyng in Moyses face. And þis seruyse in Moyses lawe is
clepid 'seruyse of deeþ', for manye hadden deeþ of soule, and
deeþ of body sued ay þis seruyng. But seruyng in þe newe lawe
quekened sum men til þei camen to blis. And þus þis wrytyng in
90 lettris was foul to writyng in mennus soulis. Poule makiþ
aftirward anoþir skile þat, ȝif seruyse of dampnyng of many was in
worship and glori of Moyses, myche more seruyng of ryȝtwisnesse to
Cristis children shulde be in glorie. As whos seiþ siþ þis hid figure,
þat brouȝte men but fer fro blis, was in so myche glori and
95 worshipe to men þat hadden but litil bileue, myche more þe lawe
of Crist and seruyse þat his prestis don shulde be in more worshipe
and ioye, siþ it is neer þe staat of blis. But, as Moyses face was hid
þat teelde vntreweþe of Iewis to come, so þis hydyng figurede

---

77 Exod. 34: 29–35.

YI   encresciþ] ecresiþ Y, encresyng M   76 men] ⌈ȝe⌉ O   wolen] wolden
PTIZ   vndirstonde] vndirstoode Y   78 out] om. Mβ   stones] stoon
G   80 eyen] syhte α   weryn] ⌈was⌉ α   þis] om. G   81 þanne] om.
I   82 to] þan to I   preentide] printtiþ A, peyntide O   83 seruyng] shynyng
M   84 was moyses] rev. B   preentyng] peyntynge O   þer] þe M   was²]
were α   was³] prentyng canc. was D, om. Mβ   85 þe¹] om. M   grace] þe
grace OH   passed] passiþ A   86 in¹] of M   87 clepid] called αZ   ser-
uyse] seruyng BOYαIX, seruyces δ   for] and M   88 sued] sueþ A   ay]
euere T   but seruyng] om. O   89 quekened] quykeneþ ABMOPTYαβδIJXZ-
GH   camen] comen ABMTαβIZG   blis] heuene B   90 lettris] þir lettres
Z   to] into β   mennus] mannis I   91 aftirward] after T   92 glori] in
glorie I   seruyng] seruice AZ, suynge J   to] of α   93 shulde] -n canc. D,
schulen B   whos] who ABMOPTYαβδIJXZGH   seiþ] sey MOPTαβIZ-
H   hid] is hidde M   94 blis] þe blisse O   glori] wirship M   95
worshipe] glorye M   myche] þe myche T   96 seruyse] his seruice H   don]
shulden done M   in more] rev. B   97 and ioye] ⌈and glorie⌉ and ioye T   þe]
to PTYIZG   98 hydyng] bydynge O, comynge I   99 treccherous] trecchours

treccherous comyng of anticrist; for he is aboute bi many weyes to
hide and derke þe lawe of Crist, and bi his tradiciones fordo þe 100
fredoom þat Crist ȝaf.

AH   anticrist] þaim Z   for he is] þat er Z   bi] *om.* A   100 derke] to
derke Z   his] þair Z   fordo] for te ⌐fordo⌐ T, for ⌐to⌐ do, *marked for rev.* *to* to fordo
δ, to fordo Z   101 þat crist ȝaf] *om.* O

Dominica xiii post Trinitatem. Epistola.
[Sermo 43.]

Abrahe dicte sunt promissiones. Galatas 3.

Poul telliþ in þis epistele þe excellense of Crist and þis tyme ouer
þe tyme of þe oolde lawe, ȝhe ȝif men kepten wel þat lawe. Poul
notiþ first þis word þat *to Abraham weren seid bihestis and to þe seed of
hym. God seiþ not ⌈and⌉ to his seedis' as in many but as in oon—and to his
5 seed þat is Crist.* Poul notiþ, as trewe men shulden, eche uaryyng of
Goddis word, siþ no uariȝyng þerinne is wiþoute cause and witt.
And þus, whan God bihyȝte Abraham þat he shulde ȝyue þat
f.44v lond to|hym and to his seed, he seyde not pluralleche þat he
shulde ȝyue it 'to his seedis', but synguleerly 'to his seed', for
10 specialte þat was in Crist. And þat lond was but figure to þe heye
lond of blis, and þus Abraham hadde but figure to come aftir to
þe blis of heuene. And also whan God bihetiþ þat alle folk
shulden be blessid in his seed, he meneþ bi þis seed Iesu Crist þat
blessiþ in ioye alle manere of folk. And bi þis vndirstonden trewe
15 men þat Crist in ȝeuyng of his lawe dide alle þyngis wiþouten
defaute, boþe in worchyng and restyng, so þat no restyng ne
leeuyng was doon of Crist wiþoute cause. And siþ he lefte speche
of þes ordris, he wiste þat þei shulden harme his chirche. But in
þis men moten be war and take witnesse of quyc sygnes, for siche
20 leeuyngis ben not ynow but ȝif sensible harmes sue.

7 Gen. 12: 3, 13: 15, 15: 18.

MSS: D; ABGHIMOPTXYZαβδ; J ends incompl. 71 of hymsilf.

Sermo 43] *om.* DABMOTαβδIJXZGH   promissiones] *om.* OH   gal. 3] *om.*
O   1 and] in Z   þis²] of þis M   4 and to¹] into P, to δJ, and Z   in¹]
⌈in⌉to M   6 and] or T   7 þus] so M   whan] whan þat M   bihyȝte]
hight M   abraham] to abraham δ   þat²] hym *canc.* þat D   8 þat] to þat
I   9 it] *om.* H   10 þat²] *om.* A   was] þat was Mβ   but] fygu *canc.* but D,
by O, in T   heye] bi *canc.* hiȝt Y   11 þus] *om.* O   but] not but T   aftir]
aftirward β   12 þe] *om.* αβ   bihetiþ] bihight M   folk] floc β   13
shulden] sal Z   bi] in α   þis] his Mβ   seed²] *om.* I   14 of] *om.*
δ   16 restyng¹] in restyng BMαβ   so . . . restyng²] *om.* O   ne] ne no
O   17 leeuyng] lyuyng H   and . . . sue (20)] *om.* Z   18 ordris] wordis, w
canc. G   19 men moten] moten we Mβ, moten men I, men musten G   20

And Poul seiþ þat *þis biheste* þat God bihyʒt to Abraham was
*testament confermed of God, whiche biheste was aftir maad lawe bi foure
hundrid ʒeer and þritti.* Heere men moten knowe þe story and witti
maner of Poulis speche. It is knowun bi Goddis lawe hou God
byhyʒt to Abraham þat foure hundrid ʒeer and more shulde his   25
seed serue in Egypte, and þei shulden aftir go to þe lond of
biheeste; and hou in þe weye God ʒaf Moyses þe lawe wryten in
þe mount. And al þis lawe was in effect by biheste þat God bihyʒt
Abraham, siþ þis lawe was but a lore to brynge his seed to blisse of
heuene. And so seyþ Poul aftir þat makyng of þis into ⌜a⌝ lawe   30
⌜a⌝*uoydiþ not þe biheste* of God, but raþer confermeþ it. And so
gracious biheste of God was ground of ʒyuyng of þis blisse, and
not lawe þat God ʒaf Moyses, al ʒif it helpid aftir þerto. And þus
seiþ Poul soþeli þat, *ʒif heritage* of blis of heuene *were* groundid *of þe
oolde lawe, þanne it were not* groundid *of God bi gracious biheste* þat he   35
bihyʒt. But þis is knowen fals bi bileue, and so þis firste word is
sooþ þat *God ʒaf Abraham þis biheste.* And ʒif þou seye, *what seruede
þis lawe* siþ it groundede not þus blis? But *lawe was putt for
trespasouris,* þat wolden ellis haue be ouer wantoun but ʒif lawe
hadde þus chastisid hem; and so þis lawe was profitable. But þis   40
lawe hadde þre partis : þe firste part tauʒte men uertuis, þe
secounde part tauʒte iugementis, and þe þridde part tauʒte
figuris. Þe firste part mot euere laste, boþe in þe oolde lawe and þe
newe. Sum of þe secounde part may laste, þat techiþ iust
iugementis now; and ʒif it be to rigorous or inpertynent to oure   45
trespas, it shal ceesse on sutil manere, as Crist dide mercy to þe

---

24 Exod. 12: 40; **26** Exod. 20; **46** John 8: 3–11.

leeuyngis] lesyngis H   not] *om.* I   harmes] syngnes M, armes δ   *margin*
Gen. 15 DOPTYXZ, gen. 35 α, gen. 3 δ   22 whiche] þe which G   23 heere] and
here δ   men moten] *rev.* I, men may Z, men mosten G   26 to] into H   27
moyses] to moyses G   28 in effect] *on eras. corr.* D   by] ⌜bi⌝ G, *om.*
ABMOPTYαβδJZH   29 abraham] to abraham Y   was] nas O   his] þis
M, hy α   blisse] heuene *canc.* blisse D, þe blis MI   30 into] in α   a] *om.*
ABMI, þe β   31 auoydiþ] anoied Mβ   32 of²] and M   33 helpid] helpiþ
AH   34 soþeli] after soþli ABMαβ   of³] in H   þe] *om.* O   35
groundid] ground H   36 þis¹] þus β   is¹] *om.* δ   bi bileue] *on eras.corr.* D,
⌜be⌝bileue H, bileue ABMTαβδIJZ   37 abraham] to abraham I   biheste] ⌜by⌝
byheste XG   38 groundede] is groundid O   þus] þis Mα   for] *om.*
O   39 ouer] euer AB, *om.* Mβ   41 hadde] has α   part] *om.* M   men]
om. M   42 part¹] tauʒte *canc.* part D   iugementis] men iugement I, men
iuggementis O   43 figuris] men figures I   mot] most G   þe³] in þe
OTYαβIH   44 iust] ⌜iust⌝ Y, *om.* δ   45 to¹] *om.* αIZ   rigorous] rigous B,

womman þat was takun in auowtrye bi foorme þat þe gospel
telliþ. Þes figures or cerimonyes þat bitokneden comyng of Crist
moten nedis ceesse in tyme of grace, siþ Crist ende of hem is now
50 comen; and ellis we kepten as false Iewis a newe comyng of Crist
heraftir.

f.45 And to þis entent spekiþ Poul þat *lawe was putt for trespasouris|til
þe tyme þat Crist *cam*, þat was *seed* of Abraham, *to whiche* seed *God
bihyʒte* þat it shulde fully bigge mankynde, for Crist was maad a
55 mediatour bitwyxe God and mankynde. And *God puttid in Cristis
hond* lawe þat *he hadde ordeyned* bifore *bi aungelis*; and þus Crist
tauʒte þe olde lawe as lord þerof ouer pharisees. And of þis word
mediatour takiþ Poul wittily þat Crist is boþe God and man, for
ellis he myʒte not þus be mene. *A mediatour mot haue two partis* and
60 acorde in þe resoun wiþ hem boþe; and siþ þes partis ben God
and man, Crist mot nedis be þes two. *And siþ þer is but o God*, Crist
mot nedis be almyʒti. And so Crist may ʒeue þe newe lawe and
suspende sumwhat of þe oolde; and siþ he may not contrarie
hymsilf, his lawe may not contrarie his biheste. And herfore seiþ
65 Poul aftir þat *God forbede þat þe lawe be aʒenus Goddis bihestis*, for
þanne God reuersid hymsilf. Poul techiþ aftir how nedeful was
Crist þis mediatour, siþ þe oolde lawe brouʒte not man at þe fulle
to be ryʒtwis; for þanne o doyng of þis lawe shulde iustifie mannus
kynde, and þanne þis lawe shulde be ouer myche bi eueri part þat
70 sued aftir. And herfor seiþ Poul þus þat, *ʒif lawe were ʒouyn þat
myʒte quykene* of hymsilf, *sopli of lawe were ryʒt* groundid. As ʒif Poul
wolde seye þus: ouer þe oolde lawe þat was ʒouen mot come a
man to make aseeþ, and þis mote be boþe God and man. But *þis*

vigerous M   inpertynent] to inpertynent H   46 trespas] trespasseris H   on]
in I   *margin* Io. 8 T   47 bi foorme] byfore O   48 or] and AB   comyng]
þe comyng ABM, comyn α   49 moten] bihoued Z   50 and] or Z   of crist]
om. δ   52 to] so to G   til] to M   53 seed¹] þe seed M   whiche] þe
which MOβ   god] good D   54 it] he MH   a] *om.* M   55 and²] *om.*
B   puttid] put H   cristis] god cristes α   56 bi] bi ⌈his⌉ β, be his α, his
M   58 takiþ] techyþ Oβ   59 mot] most G   partis] partyes M   60 þe]
om. ABMOPTYαβIZ   and] *om.* H   þes] þe I   61 mot] must δH   þes]
þis, i *over* e *canc.*α, þis I   is] nys O   62 mot] must δH   nedis] *om.* T   63
oolde] olde lawe MTαβH   64 hymsilf . . . contrarie] *margin* H, *om.* J   biheste]
bihestis ABMβ   65 be] kepe O   bihestis] heestis ABYα, biheest G   66
nedeful] nedeful, n- *altered from* m- H, medeful Z   was crist] *rev.* I, was M   67
þis] oure T   68 mannus kynde] mankynde AB   69 part] party M   70 sued]
sueth M   71 quykene] quike α   lawe] þe lawe Mβ   were] *om.* O   72

lawe concludid wele *þat al mankynde was vndir synne*, and bi occasioun
yuele takun was synne aggreggid bi þis lawe. And þe blessid 75
eende of alle þis sorowe was conseyued in Iesu Crist, *þat biheeste*
maad to Abraham *shulde be ȝouen of bileue of hym*. So þat, ȝif men
bileuen in Crist and makyn a knotte of þis bileue, þanne þe
biheste þat God haþ bihyȝt to come into þe lond of lyf shal be
ȝouen bi vertu of Crist to alle men þat maken þis knotte. And 80
heere may men opunli see hou myche anticrist is to blame þat,
aftir þe free lawe of Crist, ȝyueþ anoþer contrarie lawe, for it
lettiþ kepyng of Cristis lawe and puttiþ men fro fredom of Crist.

seye] mene Mαβ   74 concludid] conclude Y, concludis αδH   occasioun] þis
occasioun G   75 aggreggid] gederid Z   þis] *om.* AB   76 alle] *om.*
B   conseyued] conteyned ABMOPTYαβZH, coueitid I   78 bileuen] bileueden
I   þis] his I   þanne þe] *on eras.corr.* D   79 into] to Mδ   81 anticrist is]
þai er Z   83 fredom] þe fredom G

Dominica xiiii post Trinitatem. Epistola.
[Sermo 44.]

Spiritu ambulate. Galatas 5.

In þis epistele techiþ Poul hou weyferyng men þat lyuen here
shulden go þe strey3t weye þat lediþ men to blisse of heuene. Poul
supposiþ at þis bigynnyng þat man haþ two partis, þe whiche ben
þe spiry3t and þe fleshe, and þei haue dyuerse lawis and dyuerse
5 weyis and endis, bi whiche þei leden men in þis lyf. And þus Poul
biddiþ *men wandre in spiry3t, and do not fulli desires of þe fleshe.* Þat
man wandriþ in spiry3t whos spiry3t is led bi þe Hooli Goost, and
heuy flesshe of man lediþ hym not doun þe weye to helle. And
Poul seiþ heere wisely þat men shulden not do fully þe desires of
10 þer flesshe; but sumwhat þei moten nedis do, as mete and drynke
and reste of man we moten nedeli take here; but loke þat þis be
reulid bi resoun, þat þe fleshe haue not þe maystrye. *For þe fleeshe
coueytiþ a3en þe spiry3t, and þe spiry3t a3en 3e fleshe.* And þis is soþ; – to
f.45v vndurstonde þe fleshs wiþ his strengþis | þat ben vnchastid bi þe
15 resoun of þe spiry3t, as it is led bi Goddis spiri3t, and to
vndurstonde mannus spiri3t bi þe resoun þat it is þus ledde. For
þis fleshs coueitiþ dounward, and þis spiri3t vpward; and þus þis
fleshs coueytiþ to drawe þis spiry3t aftir his desire, and þe spiri3t
coueytiþ a3en to drawe þis fleshs aftir his desire. But man þat þus
20 contrarieþ hymself mot nedis be vndisposid by synne; and so,
whan men ben led bi resoun, þei don not al þat þer fleshs wole.

MSS: D; ABGHIMOPTXYZαβδ; J *inc. incompl.* 9 poul seiþ here.

Sermo 44] *om.* DABMOTαδIXZGH   ambulate] ambulate et desideria carnis non
perficietis T   gal. 5] *om.* O, gal. 4 δ   1 hou] *om.* H   2 shulden] hou þei
shulden H   strey3t] ri3t I   blisse] þe blisse ABMOIGH   5 poul biddiþ] *rev.*
M   6 desires] þe desires H   þe] þe canc. X, *om.* MOPTYαβIZG   8 heuy] þe
heuy Y   not] *eras.* δZ, ⌐not⌐ H   9 desires] desyre α   10 þer] þe
MT   moten] bird α   11 nedeli] nedis α   þat] *om.* J   12 þe²] *om.*
δ   14 his] *om.* α   vnchastid] vnchastisid MOPTYαβδIJZGH   15 as] whan
M   to vndurstonde] by vndirstondinge I, vndirstonde G   16 þe] *om.*
AB   it] ⌐it⌐ M, *om.* G   þus ledde] *rev.* I   17 þis¹] þe OH   þis³] þe
AB   18 þis] þe AB   19 þis] þe ABIZH   þus] þis O   20 by] *on eras. corr.*
D   and] *om.* β   21 ben] *om.* I   led] rulid Y   not] ⌐not⌐ G, *om.* P   wole]

And, ʒif ʒee ben led bi spiryʒt, ʒee ben not vndir þe lawe, siþ oonli þei ben vndir þe lawe þat þe lawe biddiþ punyshe for þer synne; and þus whan a iust man is wrongli punyshed, his charite beriþ hym aboue þe lawe.   25

And for to make þis betere knowen Poul rikeneþ seuentene flesheli werkis and twelue werkis of þe spiriʒt, to flee þe firste and sue þe secounde. *Þe werkis of þe fleshs ben opun* to man, as ben fyue þat Poul telliþ first. As on is *fornycacioun,* as whan a man deliþ wiþ womman and neyþir is boundyn bi matrimonye; and þis   30 leccherie is knowun. *Vnclennesse* of þis synne stondiþ in vnclene shedyng of mannus seed, houeuere it be don, and flesheli men knowen hou. Þe þridde synne of þis kynde stondiþ in *vnchastite,* as ben vnclene kissyngis and vnclene touchyng of folc. Þe fourþe synne is generali þe comyn kynde of leccherye, on what maner   35 þat it be doon, and þis haþ many knowen partis. Þe fyueþe synne þat sueþ ⌜of⌝ þes is *seruyse of maumetis,* for wommen drawen ofte men to worshipe here false goddis; and bi þis synne was Salomon drawen vnto maumetrye. And in þis cercle of þes fyue turnen men bi leccherye. Þe sixeþe werk of leccherye is *uenefys,* þat is   40 þanne done whan men vsen experymentis to gete þis werk of leccherye; and þis is done on many maneris, as men knowun þat vsyn it. Þe seueþe synne aftir þis sixeþe is *enemyte* of contrarious partis, whan o part lettiþ þe lust þat is coueitid of anoþir; and þus regnen enemytees boþe bitwixe men and wymmen. Þe eyʒteþe   45 synne is *strif* þat spryngiþ of þes former synnes; for of leccherie comen stryues and chydyngis in wordis, boþe in men and in wymmen, aboute many manere goodis, as ben fames and oþir

---

38 1 Kgs. 11: 4–5.

wolde I   22 spiryʒt] þe spirit H   23 þe¹] *om.* Y   24 wrongli] wrongfully IG   25 aboue] vp *canc.* aboue D   26 seuentene] fouretene P   28 þe³] *canc.* X, *om.* Mα   29 as on is] *om.* H   whan a] whan BαJ, ⌜whan⌝ H, a I, *om.* T   30 womman] a *canc.* womman Y, a womman OδIZH   and¹] *om.* I   ney-þir] anoþer TIG   boundyn] *om.* G   bi] wiþ α   31 of] *om.* I   vnclene] *om.* M   33 hou] of I   as] -s *on eras. corr. of* -nd D, and OαδJ   34 kissyngis] cussynge O   touchyng] touchynges αZG   36 þat] ⌜þat⌝ Tα, *om.* O   37 wommen] womman A, why men O   ofte men] *rev.* I   39 vnto] into M, to I   þis] þe T   40 bi] to T   uenefys] venemous TJ   41 þanne done] pan, þ- *above* d *subpuncted* α   þis] þe G   42 on] in I   as . . . knowun] knawen to þaim Z   43 þe] þis M   þis] þe O   contrarious] contrarie O   44 part] partie I   45 boþe] *om.* I   46 þes] þe Y   47 chydyngis] chydyng MH   in¹] of M   in²] *om.* OPY, of H   in³] *om.* TβZH   48 fames]

goodis bi whiche leccherie is nurshid. Þe nynþe werk of þis synne
50 ben *enuyous wordis*, as sclaundris and oþir shrewid wordis þat
comen ofte of flesheli synne. And of þes comeþ þe tenþe synne þat
is *wraþþe* of man or of woman; for ofte aftir þes nyne synnes
comeþ wille to be uengid; and þis wille is ofte shewid bi shrewid
sygnes in þe face. Þe enleueþe synne þat comeþ of þis ben maner
55 of *stryues* þat suen aftir in wordis or in oþer cuntenaunce of folc for
to uenge hem. Þe twelfþe synne is *discenciones*, whan men or
wommen maken part for to uenge hemsilf more þan God uengiþ
hym; for God mot suffre mekeli and at þe laste take ful ueniaunce.

Þe þrittenþe synne of fleshs ben *sectis*, as we may now see of
f.46 60 foure sectis þat ben now brou3t yn aftir þe sect|of Cristis ordre;
and no drede þes newe sectis camen yn for defaute of loue, for
vnyte of Crist oure pàtroun and of his reule shulde distrie þes
sectis. Þe fourtenþe werk of fleshelynesse ben *enuyis* þat comen ofte
to syche sectis among hemsilf, and also to men þat spekyn a3ens
65 hem; and þus þes sectis wolden haue propre goodis þat is a3enus
charite, and þus þei quenchen good loue þat shulde be in holi
chirche. Þe fiftenþe werk þat sueþ aftir is *mansleyng*, þat comeþ
ofte boþe in þes newe ordris and bitwixe part and part. Þe
sixtenþe werk þat comeþ aftir ben *drunkenessis* bi feloushipis, for
70 þe feend stiriþ men to make hem glade þus out of mesure. Þe
seuentenþe synne ben *etyngis togidere*, as erly dyneris and late
soperis; for þeʳsˀ fallen to siche feloushipis and many
vnresounable wordis. Many siche werkis comen of þe fleshs þat
lettyn men fro þe reume of heuene. And so, 3if þou stodye wel, þes newe
75 sectis disturblyn reumes. And herfore þes paynym prynsis wolden
haue oonhede in bileue and oonhede in mennus hertis, for ellis þe

fairnes AB   50 as . . . wordis²] *om.* P, *margin* δ   as] and I   51 of¹] *om.*
β   synne¹] synnes α   52 of²] *om.* ABMOPTYαβδIJZG   womman]
wymmen α   ofte] *om.* I   nyne] ten T   54 sygnes] synnes I   in] of
B   þis] þis synne I   55 in² . . . cunte-] *on eras. corr.* D   oþer] *om.*
OIJGH   56 hem] hemsilf AB   57 part] partye MTG   hemsilf] hymsilf
J   þan] þa, -t *eras.* A   58 hym] hymsilf I   at þe] þanne atte I   59
fleshs] þe flessh MH   sectis . . . sectis (60)] *newe maner of doyngis* drawand fra Cristis
doyng Z   of foure] of oure M   63 enuyis] eneuyes MY   þat . . . sectis
(64)] of wickid doers bath Z   64 to¹] of *canc.* ʳtoˀ δ, of TG   65 and . . . chirche
(67)] *om.* Z   þes] *om.* T   is] *om.* O   66 þei] þes T   68 in] omange
Z   newe ordris] wickid doers Z   69 comeþ] sueþ T   ben] ys T   drunke-
nessis] drunkenesse BTβX   70 out] ʳwypˀou3t T   74 heuene] heuenes
H   and . . . feend (78)] *om.* Z   so] *om.* T   þou] þai α   75 paynym]
peynymes MT   76 for] or M   77 wol] wolʳdeˀ X, wolde ABOPTYαβδ, myght

comynte wol not stonde. And herfore haue men spoke so myche
of þes foure sectis of þe feend.

Poul telliþ aftir of twelue *fruyꝫtis*, þe whiche spryngyn *of þe
spiryꝫt*. Þe firste fruyꝫt is *charite*, and þat conteyneþ alle good, as
Poul shewiþ in anoþir plase bi sixtene condiciones þerof. Þe
secounde fruyꝫt of þe spiryꝫt is þat men haue *ioye* togidere: oon
ioyeþ of anoþeris welfare, whan þei acorden in Goddis lawe. And
þus þes foure newe sectis haue þer ioye in uariyng, and þat oon is
oppressid þat he myꝫte conquere Cristis sectt. Þe þridde fruyꝫt of
þe spiriꝫt is *pees* þat contrarieþ þes stryues; and þis pees shal be in
heuene where Cristis sectt shal be clene. Þe fourþe fruyꝫt of þis
spiriꝫt is *paciense* þat men shulden haue; for Crist bi souereyn
paciense groundid his sectt and fordide oþere. But as þe feend
haþ brouꝫt in sectis, so he haþ brouꝫ⌐t⌐ yn stryues; and, ꝫif a man
telle þis gospel, þei seyen þat he disturbliþ reumes, as þei
putteden vpon Crist þat he disturblede þe reume of Iude,
bigynnyng at Galilee to þe citee of Iherusaleem.

Þe fyueþe fruyꝫt and þe sixeþe ben *benygnite and goodnesse*.
Benygnyte is hete of loue, bi whiche a man wole make his broþir
hoot; and goodnesse is a beem of þis, bi whiche a man profitiþ to
his broþir in hauynge of worldli goodis bi good mesure for þe
soule. Þe seueþe fruyꝫt of þis spiriꝫt is *longlastynge* in uertues, for
þe drope persiþ þe stoon not bi ones but bi longlastyng. Þe
eyꝫteþe fruyꝫt is *bonernesse*, whan man dooþ and spekiþ good bi þe
forme of Goddis lawe, and not bi rancour and enuye. Þe nyneþe
fruyꝫt of þis spiriꝫt is þe *treuþe* þat men shulden kepe – not oonli in
bileue of God, but vpe þat profite to his broþir, as þat man were a

80

85

90

95

100

81 1 Cor. 13; **92** Luke 23: 5.

M   men] me O   78 of¹] aꝫens M   79 aftir] afterward I   þe¹] *om.*
I   80 þat] *om.* O   conteyneþ] continueþ I   81 shewiþ] shewid A   þer-
of] þat sueþ þerof H   82 togidere] to gadere O   83 in] to T   and . . . sectt
(85)] *om.* Z   84 newe] *om.* Y   and] whan α   86 pees²] parties I   87
sectt] folowers Z   89 fordide] forbedde MI   but . . . iherusaleem (93)] *om.*
Z   90 he] *om.* T   91 as] and B   92 putteden] putten H   vpon] on
H   þe] -s *eras.* D   reume] rewmes α   93 to] in δ, vnto H   *margin* Luc.
23. 7 M   95 is] his β   96 a¹] *om.* I   99 persiþ] perishiþH   ones] anes
fallyng Z   -lastyng] castynge O   100 is] of þis spirit is IZ   man] a man
Tδ   dooþ] spekiþ AB   and] or G   spekiþ] doiþ AB   101 lawe] *om.*
J   and¹] ⌐ne⌐ X, ne ABMPTYαβZG   102 of . . . spiriꝫt] *om.* Z   þe] *om.*
I   men] man B   not] but *canc.* not D   103 vpe] vpon O, ouer Z   pro-
fite] it profitiþ AB, þat profytith M, for to profit Z   þat²] *om.* M   a] ⌐a⌐ Y, *om.*

traytour boþe to God and to man þat saye a perel come to a puple
105 and hidde it and norshede it. Þe tenþe fruyȝt is *temperure* þat man
kepiþ ⌈in his⌉ lyuyng, boþe in noumbre and in spensis, and oþir
þyngis þat profyten to folc. And heere men þenken þat þes sectis
faylen in þis temperure, and þei disturbelen reumes bi þis defaute
f.46v þat þei mayntenen. Þe enle|uenþe and twelfþe fruyȝt ben
110 *contynense and chastite*. Contynence sufferiþ wiþinne stryf of
mannus flesheli lustis, but it kepiþ fro outward werkis; and
chastite kepiþ fro boþe. Þes twelue fruyȝtis ben ful rype in blis, as
Apocalips telliþ; and *lawe of God reuersiþ hem not*, siþ God loueþ
hem algatis. *And þes þat ben on Cristis side haue don on cros þer fleshs wiþ*
115 *synnes*; þanne is mannus fleshs don on cros, wiþ what vycis euere
þei ben, whan his fleshs is so punyshid þat it may not wandre in
hem.

---

113 Rev. 22: 2.

δ   104 to²] ⌈to⌉ P, *om.* ABI   a¹] *om.* O   a²] þe T   106 in his] ⌈in his⌉
corr./in canc. D   107 and . . . mayntenen (109)] *om.* Z   109 þei] þe B   þe
enleuenþe] *on eras. corr.* D   twelfþe] þe *canc.* twelfþe YX, þe twelfþe ABTδ-
GH   110 contynence] contynce Y   112 kepiþ] coueytiþ *canc.* ⌈kepiþ hym⌉
T   as] as þo α   *margin* apoc. vlt. T   114 cros] þe cros B   þer] þe
G   115 cros] þe cros B   vycis euere] euer vices þat G   euere] þat euer
Z   116 it] he δ   117 hem] hym OPZ

Dominica xv [post Trinitatem].
Epistola. [Sermo 45.]

Si spiritu uiuimus. Galatas 5[et 6].

Poul telliþ heere more speciali hou men shulen flee perelis of
synnes, and supposiþ his former wordis hou þat men shulen lyue
bi spiry3t; and biddiþ þat, *3if we lyuen bi spiri3t, wandre we* here *bi
spiry3t. And be we not made coueytouse of ueyn glory, stiryng to wrappe
togidere and hauyng enuye togidere.* And 3if þis maundement of God   5
were wel kept of eche persone, alle synnes weren exilid, boþe of
puplis and persones. Þe firste cautel of þe feend bi whiche he
disseyueþ men is to stire hem to ueyn glory, for in þis he hymself
was disseyued, and þus he castiþ many menes to coueyte siche
hey3nesse. Alle bataylis and stryues spryngen of þis cursid rote.   10
And þes men of þis ueyn glory lyuen not bi þe Holi Goost, but, 3if
þei lyuen spiritually, þat is bi þe wicked spiry3t; and þus lyuen
þes newe ordris bi couetyse of ueyn glory. And herfore printe we
mekenesse in stede of þis couetyse, and þanne we wandren sureli
bi þe weye þat Crist haþ tau3t.   15

And þus biddiþ Poule aftir *breþeren, 3if a man be bifore occupied in
ony trespas* to God or man, *3ee þat been spiritual enforme þis man in
spiry3t of softnesse.* And þis lore leuen þe popis, whan þe toon fy3tiþ

2 Gal. 5: 16.

MSS:D; ABEGHIJMOPTXYZαβδ.

Sermo 45] *om.* DABMOTαδEIJXZGH   si] *om.* A   uiuimus] viuimus spiritu et
ambulemus MT   gal. 5 et 6]gal. 5 ⌐et 6⌐J, gal. 5 DABMPYαβEIXZGH, gal. 4 δ, *om.*
O   1 heere] *om.* T   shulen] schulen, *altered from* -den H, shulden ABOPEI-
Z   2 synnes] synne AE   shulen] shulen, *altered from* -den G, shulden
ABMPEIZ   3 bi¹ . . . lyuen] *om.* P   þat 3if] þat if *marked for rev.* Y   bi³]
wiþ M   5 and¹] in AB   7 puplis] puple M   and] and of ABMEIH   per-
sones] alle oþer persones Z   8 hem] men MH   glory] ⌐to⌐ *eras.* glory D   he]
om. M   10 spryngen] *om.* O   11 þes] alle þes Mβ   3if . . . is (12)] *om.*
Z   12 þe] a Z   lyuen . . . ordris (13)] many lyues Z   13 couetyse]
coueitisis Yβ   of] and PαI   herfore] þerfor Z   printe] *altered from* putt D,
putte OαδEIJ   14 stede] studie Y   15 þe] þat M   haþ tau3t] tau3te
H   16 a] any MG   17 man¹] to man I   enforme] enformed O   18
softnesse] sothfastnesse I   lore . . . spiritis (30)] *om.* Z   þe¹] þes ABαδJG-

wiþ þe toþir wiþ þe moste blaspheme leesyngis þat euere sprunge
20 out of helle. But þei were occupied bifore many ȝeer in
blasphemye, and synneden aȝenes God and his chirche, and þis
made hem to synne more. For an aumblyng blynd hors, whan he
bigynneþ to stumble, he lastiþ in his stumblyng til he caste
hymself doun. And þus men of þes newe sectis, fro þe firste to þe
25 laste, procuren deþ tó trewe men, þat tellen hem euene Goddis
lawe. Lord! wher þei lyuen spirituali and techen men bi softe
spiryȝt? Certis þis is craft of þat spiriȝt þat cumpasiþ heere erþeli
men [to] loke hou he may tempte hem to putte hem fro Goddis
lawe. And ȝit blyndnesse of cristen men makiþ hem to sue þes
30 spiritis; and þis shulden spiritual men don, and þenke on þer
owene freelte, hou myche worþ it were to haue help *whan men ben
temptid* in hemself. And þus *oon shulde helpe anoþir* bi mekenesse and
pacience, whan he is temptid of þe feend to pride or ire or oþir
synne; and his broþir shulde bere hym vp aȝeen for tyme þat he is
35 temptid.

And þus men shulden bitwixe hemself *fulfille* loue þat is *Cristis
lawe. For, ȝif ony gesse þat he be ouȝt þe while he is nouȝt* but a shadewe,
þat man disseyueþ hymsilf. And in þes wordis þat Poul spekiþ may
men see hou God is substaunce of alle manere of creaturis, and so
f.47 40 þei ben nouȝt to God. Þe spiryȝt of man|is maad of God to ymage
and lickenesse of hym; and he may kyndeli turne fro God, and
þanne he is nouȝt bi synne. And so Poul techiþ aftir þat *eche shulde
proue his owene werk,* wher þat he haþ do þis werk aftir þe
comaundement of God, *and þanne he shal glorie of hymself and not of
45 bede men* ne worldli power. Fór tyme shal come þat *eche shal bere þe*

---

40 Gen. 1: 26–7.

H   toon] one EG   19 þe¹] *om.* O   leesyngis] lesynge O   20 out of] of
of O   many] bi many I   21 and²] in MI   22 an] ⌐an⌐ G, *om.* T   23
bigynneþ] gynneþ I   lastiþ] hastiþ H   his] þis β   stumblyng] stumble
O   caste] haue caste P   24 doun] adoun T   25 to] of *on eras.* X, of
ABMOPTYαβI   27 craft] a craft α   28 to¹] and DδEIJ   loke] lokeþ
E   to putte hem] *om.* T   29 of] in B   makiþ] make α   30 þis] þus
I   spiritual] þes spirituel H   31 worþ] worþi H   33 to] by M   or oþir]
oþere E   34 aȝeen] for *canc.* aȝeen D   tyme] þe tyme MH   36 loue] þe loue
I   cristis] goddes α   37 gesse] gesse hym T   be] is M, *om.* O   þe] *om.*
δG   while] whiche I   38 may] many I   39 hou] howe þat M   of²] *om.*
αH   and] *om.* A   40 ymage] þe ymage δ   41 hym] himself I   kyndeli]
vnkyndely Mα   42 bi]-i *altered by canc. from* -ut D   43 haþ] haue BαEZ   44
comaundement] mawndement T   45 bede men] hede men β, beden men I   ne]

charge þat God haþ bedyn hem do. But ȝit aftir þe lawe of Crist
eche man shulde helpe his broþer, oþir bodili or goostli, for þus is
eche man chargid of God. But as men helpen not þyng of nouȝt,
but ȝif þat þyng haue beyng first, so man helpiþ not his broþer
but ȝif he helpe hymself first. And heerfore biddiþ Poul heere þat   50
þis man þat is enformed shal comen wiþ his enformere in alle manere of
goodis, boþe bodili and goostli, for þat may oon do to anoþer. And
þus, ȝif freris disseyuen þe aȝenes bileue of Goddis lawe, ȝit helpe
hem goostli and wiþdrawe fro hem worldli goodis; for þus þou
dost hem myche good and drawest fro hem her synful lyf. And   55
God doþ good to many men, takynge fro hem worldli godis. And
among blyndnesses of þe world þis is oon newe brouȝt yn þat þes
newe sectis holden not þat a man doþ hem good, but ȝif he ȝyue
hem worldli goodis, al ȝif he do hem harm in þis. And heere men
spekyn to þes sectis þat þei bi lawe of charite taken goodis fro   60
seculeer men, and ȝyue hem not so myche aȝeen; whi shulden not
lordis loue hem þus? – siþ þei seyen þat þis is loue, and hem falliþ
bi Goddis lawe to be poere and lordis ryche. But Poul seiþ to þes
ypocritis þat *þei shulden not wille þus erre,* for, howeuere þes
ypocritis seyen, *God wole not* heere *be scorned.* For resoun of Goddis   65
lawe mot algatis be fulfillid, ⌐for⌐ oþer man shal liue bi Goddis
wille in doyng good, or sufferyng peyne.

And þus seiþ Poul aftir þat certis *what* werkis *a man sowe, þo*
werkis *shal he repe* in reward þat God mot ȝeue. *For he þat soweþ in*
his fleshs, lyuynge bi flesheli desires, *of his fleshs shal he repe* peyneful   70
corrupcioun. But he þat sowiþ in spiriȝt of his spiryȝt shal repe aylastynge

⌐ne⌐ of H   46 hem] hym, -y-*altered from* -e- P, hym MTZH   do] to do
AB   aftir] by M, *om.* O   47 oþir] or YH   þus is] þis O, þus δ   48
chargid] is charged Oδ   not] *om.* δ   50 ȝif] ȝif þat E   heerfore] þerfore
Z   52 goodis] goodnesse TY   53 freris] ypocrites Z   þe] *om.* O, ȝow
Z   bileue] þe byleue OI   54 fro] *om.* M   55 and²] as ABMOPTYαβδEIJ-
ZGH, ⌐as⌐ *on eras.* X   56 takynge] in takinge I   and . . . ryche (63)] *om.*
Z   57 blyndnesses] blyndenesse ABMPTYαβδIJGH, þe blyndenesse E   þis] þat
A   is] ⌐is⌐ Y, *om.* J   newe] newest AB, now P   58 holden] now holdun
P   not] *om.* Y   a man] man I   doþ] do G, þat doiþ H   good] no good
Y   ȝyue] do H   60 þei] ⌐siþ⌐ þey J, siþ þei ABMβ   61 hem not] not hem
marked for rev. DT, ⌐hem not⌐ β, not ABδ, hem O   62 lordis] þes lordis E   hem
þus] *rev.* EI   þei] þes O   seyen] seen β   þis] hit T   63 but] and
δ   64 erre] to erre EZ   þes] þe B   65 of] and MOPTYαβIZGH, and *on eras.*
corr. JX   66 mot] moten PT   for] *corr.* D, *om.* δEJG   oþer] euere I   bi]
in M   67 wille] law α   68 aftir] ⌐truly⌐ aftir H, trewly efter MOPTYαβZG,
⌐treuþe⌐ aftir X   what] sich M   a] as a M   sowe] sowiþ AB   69 he¹]
be O   soweþ] selliþ β   70 he] *om.* AE   71 he] *om.* O   in] in his

lyf. He sowiþ in fleshs or in spiry3t þat lyueþ aftir fleshs or spiry3t.
And þus stireþ Poul aftir þat *we do good and fayle not, for in his tyme
shulen we repe and not fayle* for euermore. Men þat God ordeyneþ to
75 blis, al 3if þei faylen ofte here, 3it sum manere þei holden onne
and doon sum good to hooli chirche. And herfore concludiþ
Poule þat *we do good, þe while we haue tyme, to alle manere of men, but
most to homeli men of bileue*. It is ofte seyd bifore þat Crist dide good
to al þis world, boþe to heuene and to helle, and biside to al þis
80 world. And so men þat shullen be saued ben laboreris in Cristis
werk, and profiten bi uertu of Crist to alle þis world, as Crist dide.
But þer is dyuersite in helpyng of men in þis lyf, for þes þat treuly
holden bileue and shullen be blessid for þer werk, ben homeli
men of Goddis hous, and holden wel cristen mennus bileue. But
f.47v 85 þes ypocritis þat feynen þat þei suen Crist and|þer patrounes,
and 3it þei suen þer goostli enemyes and goon contrariously to
Crist, men shulden not helpe þes so myche as trewe men in
Goddis cause.

E   shal] he shal PβZ   repe] he *canc.* repe D, he repe ABTα   aylastynge]
euerlastinge OT   72 he] he þat PZ   fleshs¹] spirit H   spiry3t¹] flesh
H   fleshs²] þe flesh H   spiry3t²] þe spirit H   74 shulen we] *rev.* M.
ordeyneþ] ordeyned A   75 al 3if] all α   76 concludiþ] seiþ I   77 þe] *om.*
IH   manere of] *om.* O   but] and M   78 to] *om.δ*   to homeli] *on eras.*
corr. DJ   ofte seyd] *rev.δ*   79 to¹] *om* M., til α   heuene] helle E   helle]
heuene E   and²] *om.* H   80 shullen] schulden BTI   81 uertu] vertues
I   82 þer] ⌐3it⌐ *corr. canc.* þer D, 3it þer ABMPYαIXZGH   lyf] world
E   þes . . . and (83)] som Z   83 bileue] þer *canc.* bileue DX, þis *canc.* bileue
E   þer] þe B   ben] as þa þat treuly haldis bileue and Z   homeli] hooly
T   84 and] þat Z   wel] wel alle H   85 þes] *om.* Z   and . . . patrounes]
om. Z   86 goon] don AB   87 þes] hem ABZ   88 cause] hous Y.

Dominica xvi [post Trinitatem]. Epistola.
[Sermo 46.]

Obsecro vos ne deficiatis. Ephesios 3.

Poul telde in þe nexte epistle hou eche membre of hooli chirche
shulde helpe to anoþir membre, as eche man shulde helpe to oþir;
and so þei shulden bere lyȝtliere and algatis betere come to
heuene. And þus Poul *preyeþ* Ephesianes *to fayle not in his peyneful
traueles.* For, siþ his trauelis ben goode to hem, and ⌈he⌉ tristiþ in 5
Iesu Crist þat he shal parfoorme þes peynis, and þus glorifie holi
chirche, þes folk weren to myche foolis ȝif þei faileden in þes
peynes—þat is to seye, ȝif þei fayleden to ioye of hem and helpe
hem. For Poulis tribulaciones *ben takun for goode of þes folk*; and þus
as Poule louede hem shulde þei loue hemself and hym. And þus 10
for lastynge in þi⌈s⌉ *peyne* boþe to Poul and to þes folk, *Poul bowede
ofte his knees to þe Fadir of Iesu Crist; and of þis fadirhed is named al oþer
in heuene and erþe.* Ȝif we spekyn of fadirhede, þat is trewe and not
fals feyned, þat mot haue o bygynnyng þat is fadirhede of þe firste
persone. Alle kyndeli fadirhede of erþe mot nedis come of þe 15
Trynyte, and so of þe firste fadirhede þat is welle of alle oþere.
Alle goostli fadirhede of God, þat þe Trynyte is fadir of men,
spryngiþ of þis fadirhede, bi whiche God faderiþ his Sone. And
þus, ȝif men clepyn soþeli oþir men to be þer fadir, þat fadirhede
mot nedis come of fadirhede of þe firste persone; as goode men 20
seyen heere þat þe Trynyte is þer fadir. But feyned fadirhed of þe

MSS: D; ABEGHIJMOPTXYZαδ; β *ends in text* vos ne de-

Sermo 46] *om.* DABMOTαδEIJXZGH   obsecro vos] peto M   ne deficiatis] *om.*
O, ne deficiatis in M, ne deficiatis in tribulationibus meis T   eph. 3] *om.* O   1
telde] telliþ OTH   þe] þis H   2 to ¹] *om.* E   membre] *om.* T   helpe²]
om. α   to²] ⌈to⌉ T, *om.* H   3 bere] helpe *canc.* bere D, *om.* T   lyȝtliere]
lyghter M   betere come] come þe better M   5 siþ] *om.* T   he] *corr.* D, *om.*
O   6 shal] shulde A   peynis] trauelis *canc.* peynis D   7 faileden] fayle
α   8 of hem] þaim Z   9 hem] of hem ABTδ   10 poule . . . hem] -le louede
hem *on eras. corr.* D   louede] loueþ A   hem] ⌈hem⌉ J, *om.* OδE   11 þis] -i⌈s⌉
corr. D, þe δEJ   12 þis] his OT   13 and¹] *om.* O   erþe] in erþe
BOαIG   trewe] truþe G   15 nedis] *om.* E   of²] to M   16 of¹] *om.*
BO   of²] to ABOPTαδEIJXZGH   17 alle] as OZ   god] þat E   19 to
be] to I   20 fadirhede] þe fadirhed BOTα   21 seyen] seen A   þer] þe

pope and newe fadirhede of þes abbotis, ʒif þat it be falsly feyned, is groundid in þe fadir of lesyngis.

And for loue of þis eende Poule preyeþ þus to God þat *he ʒyue to* 25 *þe folk, aftir þe richessis of his glorie, uertu for to be strengþid bi his spiriʒt into þe inward man, þat Crist dwelle bi bileue stableli in þer hertis.* And heere ben two trynytees: þe firste Trynyte vnmaad, and þe toþir trynyte maad, þat is feiþ, hope and charite; and to preye þus for þis Trynyte is betere preyere þan for worldly þyng. And bi þis 30 power of siche ʒiftis is God seyd riche wiþynne; and þis passiþ alle worldly richessis, for þis power may not fayle. And þus shulden men *be rotid and groundid in charite, for to take wiþ alle seyntis whiche is þe brede and lengþe and heyʒnesse and deepnesse* bi whiche God haþ siche names. And here many grete men vndirstonden bi þes foure 35 wordis dyuerseli. But sum men þenkiþ þat Poul meneþ þat God haþ þes foure names bi foure dyuerse resones þat shullen be knowen fulli in blis; so þat Goddis brede is shewid bi brede of God in creaturis, and Goddis lengþe is also shewid bi aylastynge of hem, and þe heyʒnesse of God is his excellense aboue creaturis, 40 and þe deepnesse of God is makyng of alle creaturis fro bodili þyngis þat ben made to þe laste goostli creature. Þis shullen we fulli knowen in heuene, but heere we blaberyn ⌈it⌉ as blynde f.48 men. And bi þis ʒee shullen knowe þe abouepas|syng charite of Crist þat passiþ alle kunnyng heere. And þus bi þes foure braunchis heere 45 men tellen of charite of Crist, for Crist loued boþe freendis and enemyes, and God þat is aboue his manhed and creaturis byneþen his manhed.

To þis Lord þat may do more plenteuousli þan we axen or we

I of] here of Z 22 pope] warld Z and . . . abbotis] om. Z þat] om.
G falsly] fasly H 23 is] yt ys T 24 preyeþ] prayses α 25 þe¹] þeʳsⁱ E,
þes ABMOPTYαZGH richessis] richesse ABαδIG hisⁱ] om. A for to] to
MOZG his²] þis T 26 bi] om. T 28 trynyte] om. E maad] is maade
M 29 for] om. MPZ þyng] þinges I 31 richessis] richesse ABM-
αδ 33 þe] ⌈þe⌉ T, om. J lengþe] þe length MYαδGH heyʒnesse] depnesse
H deepnesse] heiʒnesse H 34 many] may YE 35 meneþ] moueþ
I 36 bi foure] bifore J 37 is] be MPTZ shewid] myche schewid
AB 38 aylastynge] euerlastynge OT 39 of] om. H creaturis] men
T 40 þe] om. M 41 to] vnto H shullen] shuld αI 42 fulli knowen] rev.
α in] om. O it] corr. D, om. δEJ 43 and] and þus α þe] om.
E charite] of charite A 44 bi] ⌈bi⌉ M, om. P 45 loued] ⌈louyth⌉
M 47 byneþen] be nehe α 49 worchiþ] he worchiþ E be] bi

vndirstonden to axe, *aftir þe uertu þat worchiþ in vs, to hym b*[e] *glorie in þe chirche and in Crist Iesu bi alle kynredis of þe world of* alle *worldis.* Þes 50 wordis of Poul ben ful sutill, but it is ynow3 to vs to knowe sumwhat Cristis charite and þeraftir shape oure charite; for in blis shullen men kunne alle þes þyngis wiþoute trauele. And þerfore þe beste counsel were now to vs to practyse oure lyf in charite, and to a3eenstonde Cristis enemyes boþe for loue of Crist 55 and hem. And trowe we not to þes heretikis þat n[e] men may speke wel a3enes hem bi þe stronde of charite, for so dide Crist boþe God and man. Clense þee fro pryde and enuye, and cloþe þee in mekenesse and charite, and stond strongli a3ens Goddis enemyes; for þis is tokene of loue of God.   60

DAIJH   50 crist iesu] *rev.* M   bi] ben T   alle¹] alle þe T   þe²] *om.*
G   52 cristis] of cristis ABH   53 men] alle men I   kunne] knowe
O   56 we] we *canc.* X, *om.* MOPTYαIZ   þes] þe Y   ne] no D   57
speke wel] *rev.* αI   59 þee] 3e T   goddis] *om.* P

Dominica xvii post Trinitatem. Epistola.
[Sermo 47.]

Obsecro vos ⌜*ego*⌝ *uinctus in domino.* Ephesios 4.

Poul techiþ in þis epistele alle cristen men to kepe charite, for þis
is lore ful and ynow3 to eche man to come to heuene. Poul
bigynneþ and seiþ þus *Y bounden in þe Lord preye 3ow* to kepe þis
lore, for loue of God and of 3oure soule. Poul meneþ þat he was
5 bounden ⌜not⌝ for þefte ne for mansleyng, but for loue of God þat
he hadde to teche his lawe. And þus he was bounden in presoun
at Rome bi enemyes of Crist; and, siþ Crist is lord of alle, in þis
Lordis name was he bounden. And þis shulde moeue þes
Ephesees to take hede to Poulis wordis, for he chargiþ hem not by
10 money, ne biddiþ hem bi lordli maundementis, but preyeþ hem
for her soulis heleþe of þyng þat shulde be good for hem. Lord!
what loue hadde þis Poule to Crist and to cristen men, whan he
wrot þus in presoun to folk to turne hem to Crist; and whan he
my3te freli goo, he trauelede to hem in many perelis. Lord! hou
15 ferre is oure pope and his bisshopis fro Poulis lyf, whan þei
comaunden men to come to hem, al 3if God comaunde þe
contrarie; and þis is for worldli wynnyng and to shewe þer
lordshipe. Poul preieþ þes men mekeli and honestli, not for his
wynnyng, *þat þei walke worþili in þe clepyng þat þei ben clepid.* Þei ben

MSS: D; ABEGHIJMOPTXYZαδ.

Sermo 47] *om.* DABMOTαδEIJXZGH   vos] itaque vos M   ego] *corr.* D, *om.*
δEJH   uinctus] vinctis ABJ   in domino] *om.* OH   1 poul . . . epistele] in
þis epistle techith poule M   techiþ] telliþ ABTG   in . . . charite] *on eras. corr.*
D   men] *om.* Y   charite] *om.* P   þis] þat M   2 and] *om.* MPδI-
Z   to[1]] to tech M   3 preye] I preie δ   4 soule] soulis M   meneþ]
moueþ δ, meneþ not H   5 bounden not] not *canc.* bounden ⌜not⌝ D, not bounden
δEJH   for[2]] for *canc.* X, *om.* MOPαIZG   loue] þe loue ABMPTYZG, þe loue,
þe lo- *on eras.* X   7 and] *om.* A   8 was he] *rev.* δ   þis] þus O   9 ephesees]
offiseris M   poulis] poul E   10 biddiþ hem] *om.* M   bi] not *canc.* bi
D   maundementis] comaundementis M   11 of] for E   12 crist] god
E   13 wrot] wrou3te I   14 in] *om.* A   lord . . . lordshipe (18)] *om.*
Z   15 his] oure E   whan] and whanne G   16 comaunden] commaundede
O   18 for] *om.* A   19 walke] wake G   worþili] wysely M   þei[3]

clepid cristen men of Crist, Lord of alle lordis; and, ʒif þei takun   20
worþili þis name of þis Lord, þanne þei moten holde his lawe and
teche it and diffende it, for he is traytour to þis Lord þat fouliþ
falsly þis name. And þis preyng þat Poul preieþ is ferre fro
anticristis somenyng, for it conteyneþ fyue partis þat drawen to
oonhede and pees, and not to rebellioun ne lordshipe of anticrist.   25

Poul biddiþ hem at þe firste *to go wiþ alle mekenesse*. It is greet
mekenesse þat þe lesse obeshe to þe more; but it is more
mekenesse þat euene obeshe to his euene; but it is moost
mekenesse þat þe lord obeshe to his seruaunt; and þus cam Crist
to Baptist to be baptisid of hym. And þus shulden cristen men   30
kepe þes þre degrees of mekenesse, and speciali siþ men weten not   f.48v
what wit þat God haþ ʒouen þer breþeren to telle hem and to
counsele hem to þyng þat is Goddis wille. And heerfore Poul
biddiþ aftir þat þei go in *bonernesse*, þat is a uertu of mekenesse,
whan men don as þei ben counselid; for þes men ben tretable in   35
Goddis name as þei shulden. But cristen men shulden not trowe
to eche spiriʒt þat spekiþ to hem, for, ʒif it be aʒeen resoun and
soune to worldli heyʒnesse and not to profyʒt of mennus soulis,
þei shulden not do aftir it; for þat were feendis obediense and
vnobedyense to God. Þe þridde tyme preyeþ Poul þat þei go wiþ   40
paciense to God and suffre wrong of þer neyʒhebore, for bi siche
pacience may o man *supporte anoþir* and ouercome his pride and
ire, bi whiche þe feend temptiþ hym; and þis is a greet werk of
gostli merci to þi broþir. And bi siche pacience ben þe feend and
man ouercomen.   45

And aftir þes foure honest preiyngis biddiþ Poul þat *men be bisi*

29 Matt. 3: 14-15; **36** 1 John 4: 1.

. . . of ²(20)] *on eras. corr.* D   þei³ . . . clepid (20)] *om.* T   20 and] and þey ben
clepid cristen men T   21 þis¹] þo α   lawe] lawes AB   22 traytour] traytoour
D   fouliþ] defouliþ δ   23 falsly] or falseþ I   þis¹] his E   is . . . it (24)]
om. Z   25 pees] to pees T   anticrist] tyrauntis Z   26 greet] a
grete E   27 þat] *om.* M   28 þat² . . . mekenesse (29)] *om.* I   cuene¹] þe
euen ABOYEZ   his] þe BH   29 þat] of alle þat M   to] *om.* M   30
baptisid] baptist to be baptizid I   *margin* Mt 3 DMTH   31 þes] *om.* Z   32
wit þat] *on eras. corr.* D, þat E   þer] to þaire α   hem] *om.* AO   to²] *om.*
OαZ   33 heerfore] þerfor M   35 men¹] þey E   38 soune] souneth MO,
sowe Y   *margin* Io.4 T   of] to A   39 þat] it O   feendis] a fendes
α   40 vnobedyense] vnbediense J   god] criste M   41 to god] to god *canc.*
XG, *om.* MOPTYαZ   of] for E   neyʒhebore] neiʒboris ABG   44 gostli]
goost G   þi] þis O, be E   46 preiyngis] preieris E   47 knyttiþ] knytte

to kepe onhede of spiriȝt in bounde bi whiche God knyttiþ *pees*. And
wolde God þat þes foure sectis wolden trauele aboute þis
oonhede, for þanne shulde pees be in þe chirche wiþoute stryf of
50 doggis in a poke; anticryst haþ puttid dyuerse doggis in þe poke of
his obedyense, and þei grucchen aȝenus þis, for it is so vnkyndeli.
For alle men shulden be *oo body*, siþ þei shulden be oo chirche, and
þei shulden be *oo spiriȝt* as it was in þe former chirche. Luke seiþ
þat 'of þe multitude of men þat troweden þanne in Crist was o
55 herte and o soule'. And so shulde it ȝit be, siþ al þe chirche is *clepid
ȝit in oon hope of þer clepyng*; for alle cristen men ben clepid to þe
feeste of heueneli blis, but Crist seiþ þat 'fewe ben chosen', for
fewe holden oonhede of loue. And herfore haþ þe feend brouȝt in
dyuersite of þes newe ordris.

60   And herfore telliþ Poul oonhede in foure þyngis, þat shulde
moeue þes foure sectis to kepe oonhede in þer lyf. Þer is *oo Lord*,
seiþ Poul, and *oo bileue* to alle men, and *oo baptem* in þe ground; for
oo Crist baptisiþ þe soule, oo watir cam out of his herte, oo uertu
makiþ men clene; and þis is oonhede of þe Trynyte. Þe fourþe
65 oonhede þat Poule telliþ is *oo God* þat knyttiþ alle þes, for he is
Fadir of alle men and speciali of alle his children. And ȝit he is
aboue alle þyngis, and bi alle þyngis, and in vs alle. Blissid be þis God
þat þus drawiþ men to oonhede of hymself! And heere trowen
cristen men þat dyuersete of bileues þat ben in þe sacrid host
70 makiþ dyuersete in þe chirche, and þis mot nedis make aftir
dyuersete at þe day of doom, and make ᒥsumᒣ men be take to
heuene and sum men to go to helle. For Poul seiþ 'þere is o bileue'
þat alle cristen men shulden haue, and dyuersete in o part þerof

---

53 Acts 4: 32;   **57** Matt. 20: 16, 22: 14;   **63** John 19: 34.

B   48 þes . . . sectis] alle degrees of haly kirk Z   49 pees] onehed and pees
T   of] and noȝt fare as Z   50 anticryst . . . vnkyndeli (51)] *om.* Z   anti-
cryst] and crist H   þe] a δ   51 þis] þis obedience I   52 and] *om.* J   54
þat¹] ᒥþatᒣ Y, *om.* M   þe] *om.* Yα   *margin* Act. 5 T   55 herte] soule
I   soule] herte I   clepid] called αZ   56 clepying] callynge αZ   clepid]
called αZ   57 of] of þe M   58 herfore] þerfore OZ   59 of . . . ordris] in þe
kirk Z   þes] *om.* H   newe] ordris *canc.* newe D   61 þes . . . sectis] men
Z   63 cam] ᒥþatᒣ com α   65 oo] oᒥfᒣ H   66 alle his] his ᒥalleᒣ G   he is]
his O   67 þyngis²] þyng TH   and²] *om.* H   þis] *om.* I   68 hymself]
him G   69 þat ben in] of E   70 þe] holy E   mot] must δ   aftir
dyuersete] *rev.* α, dyuersite after, *marked for rev.* E   71 at] of G   sum] *corr.* D, *om.*
δEJ   be] to be MαEZ   72 sum men] summe EH   to¹] for to M, *om.*

makiþ dyuersete in al þe body. And wolde God þat lordis knewen
errour in þis vnyte, and constreyneden men in þe chirche to   75
acorde in þis bileue! As Crist seiþ, and seyntis aftir, þat þe hoost,
whan it is sacrid, is uerrili Cristis owene body in forme of breed, as
cristen men bileuen, and neyþer accident wiþoute sugett, ne
no[uȝ]t as heretikis seien. And errour in witt of holy writ haþ
brouȝt in þis heresye: þei seyen þat holi writt is|fals, and ȝeuen it   80 f.49
witt aftir hemsilf; and þus þis witnesse moeueþ hem not þat Crist
seiþ þus in hooli writt. But o newe sectt seiþ oon in þis and anoþir
sectt seiþ þe contrarie. But wolde God þat þe body of holi chirche
wolde forsake hem til þei acordeden! – siþ o sectt haþ o feiþ, and
anoþir haþ heere þe contrarie, but eche of þes false sectis   85
aȝeenseiþ bileue of Crist. And, ȝif þei seyen to plese þe puple þat
þis ost is Cristis body, þei seien preuyli þe contrarie, and
sclaundren þe pope and his court þat, al ȝif he seide sum tyme þat
þis oste was Cristis body, now þei haue tauȝt hym betere and
seyn þat it is werse þan ouȝt.   90

I   for] om. T   74 þe] om. T   75 errour] þe errour AB, errours E   76 as]
and α   77 is²] om. O   uerrili] verrey MIX   79 nouȝt] not DJ, nouȝt on eras.
X   of . . . heresye (80)] on eras. corr. D   80 þei] and canc. þei G, and þei δEJH,
þei þat AB   82 seiþ²] om. O   oon in] on I   anoþir] an anoþer O   83
sectt] om. H   þat] om. A   84 acordeden] accorden TδJH   o²] here o
M   85 haþ heere] rev. H   but . . . ouȝt (90)] om. Z   86 aȝeenseiþ]
agaynesay αIG   bileue] þe bileue BMTIGH   ȝif] ȝit α   plese] þe plese
E   þe] to M   87 preuyli] om. A   89 þei] I J   hym betere] spoken eras.
Y   hym] hem I   and seyn] om. I   90 ouȝt] nouhte αEH

Dominica xviii [post Trinitatem]. Epistola.
[Sermo 48.]

Gracias ago Deo meo. Prima Corinthios primo.

In þis epistele preysiþ Poul his disciplis, þat ȝit ben trewe and
stonden weel in Poulis lore, aȝenus þe wordis of false apostelis.
Poul seiþ *Y ȝeelde gracis to my God eueremore for ȝou alle, in þe grace þat
is ȝouen of God to ȝow* bi my trauele. Ioon seiþ 'Y haue no more
5 grace of alle my children þat Y haue getyn in Crist, þan þat Y
heere þes children walke ryȝtli in Goddis lawe'; for siche children
shullen bere wittnesse at domesday of apostelis trauele. And so
shullen dampned men bere witnesse hou þei were murþered in
body and soule in þis lyf bi euel prelatis; and þus þes fadris goon
10 wiþ þer sones to peyne of helle for eueremore. Poul ne eny oþir
apostele þankeden not þer sugettis for gold ne for worldli cause or
wynnyng, but for þei profiteden in Cristis lawe. And þus newe prelatis ȝyuen þer þankyng to men for loue of anticrist, where *apostelis
þankeden God in Iesu Crist* bi whom þei profiteden. And þus þes
15 prelatis suen apostelis as grehoundis suen an hare, for þei pursuen
trewe men for trewe techyng bi Goddis lawe; and siche suyng of
apostelis, siþ it is pursuyng of Crist, axiþ no mede of God but
peyne, siþ feendis children ben þerbi dampned.

Poul telliþ hou his puple *is maad riche in Iesu Crist in alle manere of*

---

4 3 John 4.

MSS: D; ABEGHIJMOPTXYZαδ.

Sermo 48] *om.* DABMOTαδEIJXZGH   meo] meo semper pro vobis T   1
cor. 1] *om.* O, cor. primo H   1 in . . . poul] poule prayseth in þis epistle
M   preysiþ] prayse α   ȝit ben] *rev.* α, bene M   3 Y] þat I PZ   god]
lord god T   þe] *om.* I   4 to] vnto M   no] *om.* Y   5 my] *om.* M   6
ryȝtli] ryȝtfully T   8 shullen] shullen, *2nd* l *altered from* d A, shuld α   men] *om.*
δ   9 prelatis] prelatis and curatis M, curatis Z   þus þes] *on eras. corr.* D   þes]
þeᶠseˡ H, þe δJG   10 peyne] þe peyne BH, þe *canc.* peyne Y   poul . . . dampned
(18)] *om.* Z   11 or] ne Mα, and I   12 for . . . profiteden] *on eras. corr.*
D   for] ˹for˺ JG, *om.* OδE   profiteden] profiten E   newe] nowe M   13
þankyng] þankyng, -is *canc.* G, þankyngis ABMδI   apostelis] þe apostelis
TY   15 suen[1]] suweden I   apostelis] þe aposteles αI   16 techyng]
prechinge Yα   bi] of αE   suyng] pursuyng ME   17 of[1]] to T   19 his]

word and kunnyng þat turnen hem to getyng of blis; for boþe þer   20
speche and þer kunnyng was so reulid bi Goddis lawe, þat þei
diden medefuli boþe bi þer speche and þer kunnyng. And þis
riches is myche more þan euere so myche hid money. Worldli
riches þat man gederiþ leeueþ aftir and drawiþ hym to helle; but
þes riches gooþ bifore to heuene, and moueþ trewe men to come   25
aftir. *And witnesse of Iesu Crist is confermed in siche men þat þei louen*
hym and his lawe. And hereynne stondiþ uerrey richesse. *And so*
no þyng fayliþ to hem in eny grace to putte hem fro heuene, *for þei*
abiden sureli þe shewyng of oure Lord Iesu Crist. For þei shulen be
knowen at domesday, bi clennesse and bi bride cloþis, þat þei ben   30
of Cristis sectt, and shulen be takun yn aftir his mustre. *And Crist*
shal conferme þes kny3tis wiþoute synne til þe eende, in þe day of þe
comyng of oure Lord Iesu Crist. And heere spekiþ Poul bi prophecie,
or ellis desiryng þat it be so.

þis PTα   of] *om*. BE   21 speche] bo *canc*. speche D   kunnyng] bygynnynge
O   22 þer²] by þer OT   23 is] was E   euere] euere, n-*eras*.   H, neuer
ABMOPTYαIXZG   hid] of hid YE   worldli] for worldli AB   24 riches]
richessis G   man gederiþ] men gederen H   aftir] after┌war┐T   hym] men
H   25 þes] -es *on eras*. corr. D   riches] richessis I   moueþ] makith many
M   26 witnesse] þis witnesse E   iesu crist] suche men I   siche men] iesu
crist I   27 and¹] in M   hereynne] þerinne Y   richesse] richessis H   28
hem fro] *rev*. AB, hem to Y   29 shewyng] schowynge knowynge O   be . . . -day
(30)] at domesday be knowe O   30 bride] bryhte α   31 cristis] crist E   his]
┌by┐hys T   mustre] my┌rny┐stre, *1ˢᵗ* -y- *altered from* -u- T, mynystre Oδ   32 til] to
I   þe¹] *om*. I

Dominica xix post Trinitatem. Epistola.
[Sermo 49.]

Renouamini spiritu mentis vestre. Ephesios 4.

Poul telliþ in þis epistele hou men shulden amende þer lyf, and
f.49v hou þat þei|shulen serue God boþe generali and speciali. And
Poul biddiþ þus first *be ȝee newid in spiriȝt of ȝoure mynde.*
And to vndirstonde þes wordis vndirstondyng of þre wordis is nedeful:
5 first what is a mannus mynde, aftir what is þe spiryȝt of þis
mynde, and aftir hou man shulde be newid aȝeen in spiriȝt of þis
mynde. No drede þis mynde of man is þe substaunce of his lif, þat
is, a spiriȝt like an aungel þat euere shal be in blis or peyne. And
bi resoun þat he may knowe hymsilf þis substaunce is clepid
10 mynde. And so þe secounde word of þe spiryȝt haþ many wittis,
but þis is oon: þat þe propre acte of þis spiryȝt, bi whiche he
saueriþ many þyngis, or heueneli þyngis or worldli þyngis, is
clepid a spiryȝt in þis place. And þus man is maad newe aȝeen in
þe spiryȝt of his mynde, whan his soule haþ good sauour of
15 heuenely þyngis as he shulde. For in tyme of grace of men, when
þei weren baptisid of Crist, or ellis bi grace confermed of hym, þei
sauereden þanne heueneli þyngis; and ȝif þei saueren þes aȝeen,
þei ben renewid in þis spiriȝt. And þis is a good preyere to bidde
for men þat þus haue fallen.
20 And þus biddiþ Poul aftir þat *men shulden cloþe þe newe man þat is*

MSS: D; ABEGIJMOPTXYZαδ.

Sermo 49] *om.* DABMOTαδEIJXZG   vestre] *om.* A   eph. 4] *om.* O   1
telliþ] seith M   shulden] schulen BTYX   2 þat] ⌜þat⌝ YJ, *om.* OαEI   þei]
þa Z   shulen] schulen/den *canc.* E, shulden AMαIG   3 þus] þis O   and]
eras. E   4 vndirstonde] *om.* δJ, vndirstondinge I   5 first] for I   a] ⌜a⌝ Y, *om.*
TE   aftir . . . mynde (6)] *om.* α   þe] *om.* Z   þis] mannus T   6 man] a
man Tδ   aȝeen in spiriȝt] in spirit aȝein I   7 mynde[1]] nynde O   þe] *om.*
TE   8 an] to an MPTαδZ   peyne] in peyne Tα   9 clepid] called
αZ   10 mynde] a mynde T   11 but] and E   is oon þat] is þat oon A, on þat
O   þis[2]] þe O   12 or[1]] oþir ABMPTYαδEIJZG   or[2]] oþer I   þyn-
gis[3]] *om.* M   13 clepid] called αZ   a] *om.* M   16 bi . . . þanne (17)] *om.*
O   confermed] conformid I   17 heueneli] uenely O   sauren] saueriden
A   18 renewid] renewlid PYEIZ   20 biddiþ poul] *rev.* M   21 trewþe] in

boren aftir God in ry3t, holynesse and trewþe. Poule clepiþ a newe man
þe substaunce of mannus soule, in as myche as it is newid to lyue
aftir Goddis ordeynaunce. And so þe good lyf of man is þe
cloþyng þat Poul biddiþ. But, for men may not haue þis cloþyng,
but 3if two þyngis worchen þerto, – þe grace of God is þe firste,   25
and þe toþir mannus werke – þerfore seiþ Poul aftir þat þis man is
maad of nou3t aftir ymage and licknesse of God. For þre þyngis of
his soule ben clene peyntid wiþ vertues, and þis is aftir þe
Trynyte, as Poul meueþ aftir bi þre wordis. In ry3twisnesse and
holynesse and trewþe shal al þis be don. Ry3twisnesse þat may   30
not foolde answeriþ to þe Fadir of heuene, and to þe\power of þe
soule þat Austyn clepiþ mannus mynde. Hoolynesse þat is so
stable answeriþ to þe secounde persone and to resoun of mannus
soule, þat is þe secounde þyng þerof; for no þyng is more
resounable þan to quemeli serue God. Þe þridde word þat is   35
trewþe answeriþ to þe þridde persone, for trewly shulde man loue
God euene wiþ þe knowyng of hym.

   And for þis þyng putte 3ee awey leesyngis, and speke 3ee treuþe eche wiþ
his ney3hebore, for we ben eche menbre to oþir. Alle þes þre seyde
uertues ben treuþis in a maner, siþ þei ben euenhed to Goddis   40
witt, and þat is treuþe as clerkis seyn. And herfore siþ God hatiþ
leesyngis most of alle oþir þyngis, we shulden putte awey
leesyngis and kepe treuþe in al oure lyf; and loue shulde moeue
men to þis treuþe, siþ eche man shulde be oþeris membre. Eche
man shulde come to blis and be membre of hooli chirche; and so   45
eche man shulde goostli do to oþir þe offys of eche membre. And
to þis witt seyen seyntis þat eche membre of hooli chirche is
transformed into Crist, for loue and werke þat he haþ.

   And þus as Poule biddiþ aftir *men shullen be wrooþ and not synne,*

---

treuþe E   clepiþ] callis αZ   a] þe AE   22 mannus] man M   newid]
newe G   23 lyf] lyf *canc.*/lyf D   24 cloþyng¹] cloþe MI   25 two] mo
α   26 mannus] is mannys M   man is] *om.* I   30 trewþe] in treuþe I   31
to²] so M   þe³] mannys M   32 clepiþ] clepid A, calles αZ   33 þe] þis
δ   to²] *om.*G   resoun] þe resoun O   35 þan] þat O   to] *om.*
I   quemeli] clenly α   serue] to serue OI   þridde] þrid/dde D   word]
þyng *canc.* word D   36 man] a man αδE   loue] serue E   38 leesyngis]
lesinge I   3ee²] *om.* E   39 eche] *om.* E   menbre] membris E   þre] *om.*
O   seyde] forseid G   40 treuþis] trewth M   41 herfore] þerfor
Z   siþ] seiþ, -e- *canc.* D   hatiþ] hath M   46 eche man shulde] s3olde eche
man O   goostli do] *rev.* I   and . . . membre (47)] *om.* J   48 into] vnto
T   for] by M   and] of O   49 as poule] *twice* E   as] *om.* P   shul-

f.50 50 for men|shulden hate mennus synne and loue þer kynde and þer
uertues. And þus was Crist wraþful, but *þe sunne fill not on his
wraþþe.* And þus shulden cristen men be wrooþ, and kepe þre
þyngis in þer wraþþe. First þat þer wraþþe shulde not longe laste;
and herfore biddiþ Poule þat *þe sunne goo not doun vpon þer wrappe,*
55 for þanne it were to longe lastynge. Þe secounde witt of Poulis
wordis biddiþ þat þe sunne of ry3twisnesse go not doun fro man bi
grace, for siche wraþþe þat he haþ. And so þe þridde witt of
Poulis wordis biddiþ þat man shulde not be wrooþ, but for þe
more ly3t of loue þat shulde shyne faste in his soule. And wele
60 were hym þat hadde þis lore þat Poul moeueþ in þes shorte
wordis! And, for as myche as a man haþ loue quenchid in his
soule, þe feend comeþ ⌜in⌝ in stede of loue and bryngiþ in synne
wiþ hym; þerfore seiþ Poul aftir *nele 3ee 3yue stede to þe deuel,* but
hoold 3oure loue euere hool, and þat shal hoolde þe feend out.
65 And heerfore biddiþ Poul aftur þat *he þat staale, stele he not now; but
more worche he wiþ his hondis þat þyng þat is good, þat he haue wherof to
3yue men þat suffren nede.* And þis lore þat Poul techiþ is vsid to litil
of freris and oþere, for þanne þes stronge men shulden trauele and
not þus begge and gabbe on Crist; and þanne þei shulden 3eue to
70 nedi men þat Crist haþ putte in his presoun.

len] shulden ABIZ   50 shulden] schullen I   synne] synnes α   þer²] oþere
Y   51 sunne] synne I   on] vpon B, doun vpon E   53 first] þe first
E   þer²] þe I   54 herfore] þerfore M   vpon] on I   þer] 3our
M   55 to] *om.* O   57 grace] ⌜3euyg⌝ grace T   siche] what Z   þat] as
I   58 man] men ME   59 faste] *om.* M   61 myche as] *om.* B   a] *canc.* Y,
om. MTEJ   62 in in] to *canc.* ⌜in⌝ *corr.* in D, in ⌜in⌝ þe δ, in OE, to him in I   synne
wiþ hym] wiþ hym synne T   63 aftir] *om.* M   64 euere] euere more δ   hool-
de] euer holde AB   out] euer *canc.* oute E   65 heerfore] þerfore MZ   aftur
. . . þat²] *on eras. corr.* D   staale] s3al stele O   67 þis] þus O   to] *om.*
Z   68 of] wiþ Z   freris . . . þes] *om.* Z   oþere] of oþer E   stronge]
þronge O   men] men þat Z   69 þus begge] *rev.* E, gang of beggyng Z   shul-
den] schullen T   70 in] on O

Dominica xx post Trinitatem. Epistola.
[Sermo 50.]

Uidete quomodo caute ambuletis. Ephesios 5.

Poul techiþ in þis epistele hou men shulden walke in þis lyf and knowe weyes to flee perelis, for many spyes ben maad to men. Poul biddiþ at þe bigynnyng to *see how men shullen warli walke*. For men ben trauelouris heere fro Iherusaleem into Iericho, and herfore it were nede to see first aspyes þat þe feend haþ leyd; for 5 blyndnesse in þis poynt makiþ men be taken in his gnaris, and þanne þei ben his presouneris, and lettid to serue freli Crist. And herfore seiþ Poule aftir þat men shulden *not walke as vnwise but as wise men*, bi wisdom þat God haþ ȝouen. And þis lore shulden prestis lerne, and speciali heyȝe prelatis, siþ þei shulden scure þe 10 wey to þe ooste þat comeþ aftir; but þei moten nedis kunne Goddis wisdom, for worldli wisdom wole make hem takun. And among alle synnes of þe feend bi þis synne he blyndiþ þes capeteynes: þat þei vsen not Cristis lawe, but mannus to gete hem worldli goodis; and bi þis blyndnesse of þes capeteynes þe feend 15 getiþ to helle many men.

And Poul biddiþ þat *we shulden bye aȝeen þe tyme, for þe dayes ben euele.* It is knowen bi bileue þat tyme was ȝouen of God to man for

4 Luke 10: 30.

MSS: D; ABEGIJMOPTXYZαδ.

Dominica . . . epistola] *om.* O   sermo 50] *om.* DABMOTαδEIJXZG   uidete . . . ambuletis] *om.* O   quomodo] itaque fratres quomodo M   ambuletis] *om.* M   eph. 5] *om.* O   1 techiþ] telliþ EZG   shulden] schullen, *2nd* l *on eras.* X, sȝulle OPTYI   walke] wake α   2 knowe] kowe Y   maad] to men *canc.* maad D   men] hem MY, man α   3 biddiþ] telleþ I   shullen] suld Z   warli] worþly O   4 men] many men A   5 herfore] þerfore MZ   aspyes] ˹þe˺ aspies T, þe aspyes M   6 be] to be ABOZ, to *canc.* be E   gnaris] grenys OE, k˹s˺nares α, gildris Z, gnare G   7 lettid] lettiþ O   8 as vnwise] ˹as˺ vnwise Z, as an vnwyse T, ˹vnwise˺ P   9 wisdòm] þe wisedome M   and] *on eras. corr.* D   þis lore] þus I   10 lerne] lere αZ   11 to] vnto M   þat] þe M   but] *om.* AB   12 wisdom²] *om.* E   takun] be taken Z   and . . . men (16)] *om.* Z   13 synnes] þe synes E   bi] wiþ E   synne] *om.* E   15 þis] þe M   þes] þe O   16 many] to many T   17 shulden] sal Z   bye] hyȝe O   þe¹] ˹þe˺ α, *om.* M   18 bi] of M   20 men] to men

to disserue þe blisse of heuene, and þis loste man bi his synne. And
20 þerfore it is nedeful now men to bie a ʒeen tyme; but þei weren not
riche herto, but bi uertu of Cristis passioun. And þerfore men
shulden putte þis passioun as þe ground of þis biggyng, and putte
to medicynes þat Crist ʒaf; and þus bye a ʒeen þis tyme and make
þis tyme, be it neuere so short, ynow to man to bye heuene. And
f.50v 25 þus men moten nedelyngis|putte þer peyneful lyf to þis tyme, for
bi þis peyne and loue drede, and wiþ wysdom þat Crist haþ tauʒt,
may men go sikir fro enemyes, and ellis þei ben cauʒt bi þe weye.
And þus sixe and þritty houris þat Crist lay in þe sepulcre
quykenen alle cristen mennus tyme bi þre partis of þe chirche, so
30 þat eche ha[ue] twelue houris, þe whiche maken o day to man; so
þat preestis haue twelue houris, and seculeer lordis twelue houris,
and þe comynes twelue houris. And þanne þei may come to
heuene, to kepe þe paþ þat Crist haþ tauʒt, so þat eche day of
cristen man be dispendid in peyne and sorewe, and hope of oure
35 maystir Crist, þat helpiþ his children fro þes enemyes. For certis
þes dayes ben ful euele bi asaylyng of þe feend.

   And heerfore biddiþ Poule aftir *perfore nyle ʒee be maad vnwar, but
vndirstondyng what is Goddis wille.* Þes men ben maad vnwar þat
reulen þer lyf bi mannus witt, and leeuen þe witt þat God haþ
40 ʒouen to passe þis paas fro oure enemyes. And þes men moten
nedis be takun and putt in þe feendis presoun. But þe wille of oure
duke forfendiþ þis, and he is hed of al þe chirche. And þus, ʒif eny
man be takun, his owene vnwitt is cause þerof. And þerfore Poul
biddiþ vndirstonde *what is þe goode wille of God*; and, al ʒif God be
45 hid fro men, ʒit studye þou ⌜w[e]l⌝ his lawe and þou shalt wete
what is his wille, boþe in oo þyng and in oþir.

   And þus Poul biddiþ aftir *nele ʒee be drunkyn bi wyne*, for siche
drunkun men ben vnable to studie aftir Godis wille, siþ *in wyn is
leccherie* bi whiche men wexen wood fro God; and goostli leccherie

EI   21 herto] þerto TIZ   bi] *om.* I   22 þe] *om.* I   þis²] *om.* I   big-
gyng] bigynnynge A   23 þis] þe I   24 to¹] a α   25 þus] here E   ne-
delyngis] nedelich O   26 bi] *om.* O   drede] *om.* J   wiþ] loue wiþ δ, *om.*
Z   27 and] or Z   28 þe] *om.* G   29 þre] þe EZ   30 haue] haþ
DOαδEIJG, haue, -ue *on eras.* X   maken] marken B   31 and . . . houris²] *om.*
T   32 and¹ . . . houris] *om.* O, *margin* P   33 so] as O   34 man] men
αE   in] to δ   35 his] þes AB   þes] þair Z   36 euele] of euyl M   bi]
for E   asaylyng] asoylyng X   43 man] men α   poul biddiþ] *rev.* I   45
wel] ⌜wyl⌝ *corr.* D   his] þis T   46 in²] *om.* I   47 biddiþ] sais α   bi] wiþ

of man mot nedis make hym fayle in witt. But men shulden *befillid*   50
of þe Hooly Goost, spekynge to hemself bi hym not in fooli but in
wisdom aftir þe profyȝt of þer soulis. And þes men þat ben fillid
þus spekyn to God and to hemself *in psalmes and ympnes and goostly*
songis, þat ben holden fooly to þe world, and þus þei *syngen in þer*
hert[*is*] *to God.* And þus pilgrymes, þat goon lyȝt and syngyn gladli   55
bi Cristis uoys and whistelen sweteli bi hope of blis, feren þus þer
goostli enemyes; for it is seid comynli þat a weygoere whan he is
uoyde syngiþ sure bifore þe þeef, and moneye makiþ hym drede
more. And þus bad Crist to his apostelis to bere nouȝt in þe weye
þat shulde lette hem for to wandre and do þer offys þat he bade.   60
And þus þe feend bi worldli lordshipis makiþ prestis today so
heuy þat he dryueþ hem doun to helle, as his sones þat swepten
his weye; and al þer song þat þei syngyn is of þe world and worldli
goodis, and into þis is prechyng turned and oþir preyeris maad to
God; and þis is uoys maad of þe feend bi whiche he cacchiþ on his   65
cart.

But cristen men shulden treweli ȝeelde þankyngis to God, and to þe
Fadir of heuene *euere*⌐*more*¬ *for alle þyngis in þe name of oure Lord Iesu*
Crist, þat is a mene to ȝyue alle þes to his children; and þis is a ful
greet grace. And þus, for men shulden be meke, Poul biddiþ hem   70
to *be sugett eche man to his broþir in þe* loue *drede of Crist.* Whan eche
man serueþ to oþir and|doþ hym good bi charite, þanne eche   f.51
man is þus sugett wiþoute loue of worldli worshipe. But, siþ þe
pope lettiþ þis lore, he koude not wite hou he shulde be sugett to
oþir men þat weren his sugetis; for he regned in Luciferis pryde   75

59   Matt. 10: 10; Mark 6: 8; Luke 9: 3.

α   50 shulden] schulle OT   fillid] fulfillid MT   51 bi . . . hemself (53)] *om.*
O   bi] in T   52 fillid] fulfild T   53 and²] in AB   54 songis] song
Y   fooly] faire M   55 hertis] herte DδJ, hertis, -is *on eras.* X   þus] þus þes
I   lyȝt] in lyȝt T   56 sweteli] swete I, swiftli δ   57 seid comynli] *rev.*
M   whan] while M   58 uoyde] sure I   sure] surely EJ, *om.* I   bifore]
bi A   hym] *om.* T, hem I   drede] to drede Y   60 þer] þe M   61
lordshipis] lordschip Tα   62 heuy] heuen α   63 þer] þe E   world and] *om.*
α   worldli] of worldly T   64 into] to T   is] *om.* I   65 is uoys] *rev.*
EI   maad] maad *canc.* X, *om.* MOPTIZG, is Y   cacchiþ] chasith M   67
þankyngis] þanckis E   to¹] vnto ME   68 eueremore] -more *corr.* D, euere
δJG   in] eueremore in I   þe] *om.* Y   69 þes] þes þyngis E   children]
dere children M   71 eche¹] as eche T   72 to] til α   73 worshipe] lordschip
T   but . . . awey (79)] *om.* Z   74 he¹] I α   wite] wel wite I   76 hou bi

and knewe not hou bi charite man shulde obeshe to his seruaunt. But, as Lucifer coueytid to haue ful euenhed wiþ God, so anticrist his viker wole be most in worldli worshipe; but whan he is hey3est as smoke, þanne he shal uanyshe awey.

charite] bi charite hou DI, how by charyte *on eras.* X   77 euenhed] onehede
M   wiþ] bi A   anticrist his] anticristis TI   78 wole] wolde T   hey3est]
he hi3est Y   79 he shal] shall he M

Dominica xxi post Trinitatem. Epistola.
[Sermo 51.]

Confortamini in Domino. Ephesios [6].

Poul techiþ in þis epistele to fyȝte wiþ oure goostli enemyes, and
hou we shulden be goostli armed and in what foorme fyȝte wiþ
hem. First Poule coumfortiþ Cristis knyȝtis to make hem hardi
for to fyȝte, and seiþ *be ȝee coumfortid in þe Lord and in power of his
uertu.* For þe capeteyn of oure batayle, þat is Crist boþe God and   5
man, haþ lordshipe of al þis world; siþ þat he is Lord of lordis,
what good knyȝt shulde drede hym to fyȝte in þe armes of þis
Lord? And bi þes same wordis of Poule it sueþ þat he is of more
power þan alle þe feendis þat ben in helle, or ouȝt þat may
reuerse hym. And, siþ he ouercam þe feend þat is heed of   10
contrarie batayle, he haþ uertu bi his manhed to ouercome alle
enemyes of his knyȝtis; and in þis knyȝtis of Cristis batayle
shulden be confortid for to fyȝte. And herfore biddiþ Poule aftir
to take oure armes in Goddis name. *Cloþe ȝou,* seiþ Poul, *wiþ
Goddis armer þat ȝee may stonde aȝenus þe feendis sautis. For þer is not*   15
fyȝtyng to ȝou aȝenus fleshs and blood of man, *but aȝenus pryncis and
potestatis, aȝenus gouernouris of þe world* þat is *in þes derknessis.* And
þus Cristis knyȝtis fyȝten not oneli aȝenes þe leeste feendis, ne
oneli aȝenus myddil feendis, but aȝenes þe heyȝeste feendis - and
Poul clepiþ þes *spiritual þyngis* bi kynde þat þei hadden of God.   20
But þes ben þyngis *of wickidnesse,* for þei heelden wiþ Lucifeer in
þe firste synne of alle þat was doon *in heueneli þyngis.*

MSS: D; ABEGHIJMOPTXYZαδ.

Dominica . . . epistola] *om.* O   sermo 51] sermo A, *om.* DBMOTαδEIJXZ-
GH   confortamini . . . domino] domino et in potencia virtutis eius T   eph. 6]
eph. 4 DAδEIXG, eph. 4 *canc.* ⌈6⌉ BH, *om.* O   1 techiþ] telliþ δG   4 power] þe
power M   6 þat] *om.* O   7 þis] his I   8 þes] þe δ   sueþ] semeþ
E   11 contrarie] þe *canc.* contrarie DYX, ⌈þe⌉ contrarie T, þe contrarye MOPαδEIJ-
GH   uertu] a vertu G   12 enemyes] þe ennemyes M   14 oure] ȝoure
δ   ȝou] þou α   wiþ] *on eras. corr.* D, *in canc.* B, *in* Y, *om.* MPαIZ   15 þer] here
J   not] no MOPαZ   16 fyȝtyng] fiȝten H   17 þe] þis ABMOPTYαEI-
XZH   derknessis] derkenes α   19 myddil] þe myddil YG   20 clepiþ þes] *on*
eras. corr. D   clepiþ] calles αZ   þes] *om.* OδEIJ, hem α   21 heelden] holden

Men shulden vndirstonde heere þat þei shulen fyȝte aȝenus fleshs and blood; but þis fyȝtyng is litil vnto þe fyȝtyng wiþ
25 feendis, for þey ben quyk enemyes and of myche power and sutill; and so Poule þenkiþ it but lytil to fyȝte þus wiþ fleshs and blood. Þat man is seyde to fyȝte wiþ fleeshs þat temperiþ it ın bodili foode; and þat man fyȝtiþ wiþ blood þat swagiþ lustis of leccherye, boþe ⌈in⌉ chastyng his spiritis and his blood þat
30 gouerneþ hem. And for as myche as feendis fillyn wiþ Lucifeer of many ordris, Poul clepiþ hem 'pryncis and potestatis' þat ben of þe myddil ordre. And feendis of þe loweste ordre ben clepid 'gouernouris of þis world', and þei worchen in derknesse þat heuene makiþ of þe nyȝt. And summe dremen of þes feendis þat
35 summe ben elues and summe gobelynes, and haue not but litil power to tempte men in harme of soule; but siþ we kunne not proue þis ne disproue þis spedili, holde we vs in þe boundis þat
f.51v God telliþ vs in|his lawe. But it is licli þat þes feendis haue power to make boþe wynd and reyn, þundir and lyȝttyng and oþir
40 wedrus; for whan þei moeuen partis of þis e[y]re and bryngyn hem neyȝ togidere, þes partis moten nedeli bi kynde make siche wedir as clerkis knowen. Þe þridde part of þes feendis is most heyȝ of alle oþre, as Lucifeer and his nexte spiritis þat assenteden most ⌈vn⌉ to hym; and þes ben þe felleste feendis þat cristen men fyȝten
45 wiþal. And þes feendis haue witt and power to moeue mennus hertis and oþere lymes, aftir þat þei gessen men be tempted to goostli synne. For, al ȝif þei knowen not þe þouȝt of mynde ne

TG   in] one I   23 shulden] schulen BPTYδEIXZGH   shulen] shuld
α   aȝenus] here aȝens MPZ   24 litil] but canc. litil D   þe] om. MT-
E   wiþ] aȝens M   26 it] om. OT   27 in] wiþ α   28 wiþ] in H   29
in] corr. D, om. MOPTYαδEIJXZGH   chastyng] chastisinge ABMOPTYαEIZ-
GH   and] in M   30 hem] hym I   31 clepiþ] calles αZ   of þe] of
E   32 ordre¹] ordires α   feendis] þe fendis I   ordre²] ordris ABMPXZ-
G   clepid] callid αZ   33 and] þat α   34 summe] sum men δI   þes] þe
O   35 summe¹] sum men G   ben] clepen G   summe²] om. I   go-
belynes] beþ gobelyns OTE, er gobelyns and thursis Z   haue] þei haue Z   36
tempte] tempe α   soule] here soule IH   38 vs in] on eras. corr. D   vs] canc. X,
om. ABMOPYαδEJZGH   it] certis it M   licli] liȝtly O   power] boþe
powere I   39 boþe] om. I   lyȝttyng] lyhtynnynge αG, leuenyng Z   40
wedrus] -rus on eras. corr. D, wedir ABMOPTYαδJZGH   þis] þe M   eyre] erþe
DAB   41 nedeli] nedis Oδ   42 wedir] weders A, wondir Y   knowen]
knowyþ wel O   part] partie δ   is] bene M   43 assenteden] assent
α   44 vnto] vn corr. D, to MOPTYαδEJXZGH, into I   45 witt and power]
power and witt, marked for rev. D, powere and witt αδJXGH   46 oþere] om.
I   aftir] oþer after I   þei] om.O   be] to be AδH   47 goostli] a canc.

purpos of it, neþele⌜s⌝ þei gessen ofte ney3 þe soþe, and þus
tempten men. Fy3tyng wiþ þes þre feendis is moost hard of alle
oþre, siþ Iob seiþ þer is no power vpon erþe so myche as is þis.   50
But 3it þes kny3tis haue cumfort þat Crist ouercam þe mooste
feend; and þis Lord wole not suffre feendis for to tempte his
kny3tis þat ne þei may ouercome hem, but 3if þer folye be first in
cause.

And *herfore* biddiþ Poule ⌜to⌝ vs to *take þe armer of God* and   55
rehersiþ sixe armeris, fyue to defende and þe sixte to assayle. Þe
armyng of þis goostli armer shuld be *to a3eenstonde in yuel day, and
stonde parfy3tli in alle* þes temptaciones. Þe firste armour of þe soule
is chast þenkyng þerof; and, for chastite of bodi makiþ ofte
mannus spiri3t to fayle not, þerfore biddiþ Crist to ⌜þe⌝ apostelis   60
þat *þer leendis be gird aboute.* And her men may see þat Poul meneþ
goostli armour not bodili, for ellis he woolde not telle first þe
girdill bifore he teelde clooþis to be gird. And for men shulden be
Cristis spouse, and hoolde to hym þe treuþe of weddyng, þerfore
Poule clepiþ heere þis firste uertu *treuþe* of spiri3t. And see we þat   65
Poul stireþ ofte heere *to stonde* in þis goostli batayle, for, 3if þe
feend haue ones man doun, he stiriþ hym ly3tli to foulere synnes;
and herfore mannus affeccioun, þat is þe foot of his soule, shulde
stonde staleworþli lest þe soule snaperide aftir; and herfore preyiþ
Dauyþ þus þat 'þe foot of pryde come not to hym, and þe hoond   70
of synful man moeue hym not to concense'. And þus Poul moeueþ
to stablete whan he biddiþ vs stoonde þus. He moeueþ aftir to
clene desire whan he biddiþ vs be þus gird, and aftirward to ry3t

---

gostli H, ⌜a⌝ gostly P, a goostli ABOTYαXG   þe] *om.* E   48 neþeles] -s *corr.*
D   49 tempten] þey tempten T, tempe α   50 is¹] nys O   vpon] vp A, on
M   51 3it] *om.* T, if G   52 wole] wolde δ   for to] to T   53 ne þei] *rev.*
α   3if] *om.* O   folye] synne ⌜fooly⌝ M   55 to¹] *corr.* D, *om.* δJX-
G   armer] armes Y   56 and] wiþ and δ   assayle] assoile Z   57
armyng] harmyng δ, armure I   þis] þo M   59 ofte] ofte tyme E   60 þe]
margin corr., above line ⌜his⌝ *eras.* D, his ABEXH, ⌜hise⌝ G, *om.* MOPTYαδJZ   61
aboute] aboue ABX   men may] *rev.* BMOPTYαδEIZH   62 not¹] and not
TYα   þe] *om.* P   63 teelde] telle H, tillid M   clooþis] þe cloþes E   74
hym] hem T   of] of þo α   65 clepiþ] calles αZ   þis] þe Y   66 heere]
om. O   67 ones man] *rev.* Z   man] a man Mα   ly3tli] li3tlier Aδ, *om.*
T   68 affeccioun] affecciouns OI   69 stonde] *om.* O   snaperide] swaperid
α, snapir Z   70 foot] food O   71 man] men O   hym not] *rev.* δ   con-
cense] consente AB, concience I   72 to¹] þe M   he² ... þus (73)] *om.*

entent whan he biddiþ vs stoonde in treuþe. And þes þre ben
75 nedeful to men þat fyȝten in slydir wey, cley and vnknowen. Þe
secounde goostli armure of soule clepiþ Poul *þe habirioun of
ryȝtwisnesse*, whan þat ryȝtwisnesse is cheyned to God and alle his
creaturis; and þis habirioun is þe beste to kepe þe soule fro þe
feendis sautis. Þe þridde armour is leg harneys, þat Poul biddiþ
80 *cloþe wiþ mennus feet in makynge redy of þe gospel of pees*. Þes feet been
affecciones þat prechouris of þe gospel shulden haue, not for to
wynne hem worldli goodus, ne to gete hem worldli fame, ne to
stire men to fyȝte, but to make pees wiþ God and man. And many
f.52 prechours|ben today þat faylen in alle þes þre poyntis, and so þei
85 shakyn not of þe poudir of þer feet fro þes þre.

Þe fourþe armere algatis to take is *þe sheld of bileue*, for *in þis may
trewe men quenche alle* ⌐*þe*⌐ *brennyng dartis of þe feend*. Mannus fleshs is
an euel enemy, but þe world is þe werse, and þe werste of alle þes
þre and þe felleste is þe feend; ⌐and⌐, for temptyng of þe feend is
90 hoot and moeueþ to many synnes, þerfore clepiþ Poul heere þes
temptaciones 'brennyng dartis'. But be þre corneris of þis sheeld
wel stablid in þe Trynyte, and oþir articlis of bileue sadli peyntid
wiþynne, and wiþ senewes of charite wiþouten holis wel
bounden, alle þe dartis of þe feend may not perishe siche a sheeld.
95 Þe fyueþe armour for þe hed is *an helm* of hope of blis. And ȝif
resoun and wille of man be wel wlappid in þis helm, no strook of
stones ne heuy þyng shal noye þis soule þat þus is armed. And
Poule clepiþ þis armour *an helm of heleþe*, þat is blis.

---

85 Matt. 10: 14; Luke 9: 5; Acts 13: 51.

O   aftir] vs *canc.* aftir D   73 aftirward] aftir H   74 þes] þe M   þre ben]
rev. I   75 wey cley] *rev.* G   cley] cleyi PX, cliþi α, claiþ ZH, and cley I   76
goostli] *om.* M   soule] þe soule E   clepiþ] calles αZ   77 whan . . . ryȝtwis-
nesse] *om.* O   whan] sen Z   alle] to alle T   78 þe soule] soulys T, ⌐a⌐ soule
J   þe³] *om.* PG   80 mennus] mennus, e *altered from* a H, mannis I   of¹] *om.*
EI   81 not for to] not for noȝt to I   82 goodus] good ABMPTYαδEJX-
Z   to¹] for to H   83 to²] *om.* M   85 shakyn] saken O   fro] for
E   86 to] is to O   is] *om.* O   87 trewe] alle trewe M   þe¹] *corr.* D, *om.*
ABMOPYαδEIJXZGH, þer T   88 an] and E   but . . . werse] *on eras. corr.* D,
but þe worse O   world] worde M   þe³] *om.* H   89 þe¹] *om.* T   and²]
corr. D, *om.* ABG   temptyng] þo temtynge α   90 clepiþ] calles αZ   91 but
be] and ȝif M, but þe δ   92 wel stablid] be stablid wel M   sadli] wele
α   peyntid] pryntid AB   93 wiþ] *om.* T   94 bounden] *om.* O   alle] and
alle DABOPTYαδEIJXGH   þe¹] *om.* A   perishe] perse BMPYαIZH   95
of¹] for T   96 no] ne H   97 ne] ne no H   heuy] of heuy MPZ   þus] þis

But, for he were a feble fyʒtere þat euere suffrid and neuere
smot, þerfore Poule clepiþ þe sixte armour *swerd of þe Hooli Goost*. 100
And þis armour is ful sha⌈r⌉þe siþ it persiþ more þan yrun swerd;
for it partiþ þe soule and spiryʒt, whan it makiþ man lyue to God
and leeue worldli affecciones, and þus dooþ no bodili swerd. And
þus þe tunge in mannus mouþ is a scaberk to þis swerd, and
shapun in forme of bodili swerd wiþoute boon or straunge paart. 105
And wiþ þis swerd was sum tyme wundir wrouʒt aʒenus spiritis.
But þis swerd failiþ now in prechynge of Goddis lawe, for prelatis
han scaberkis wiþoute swerdis, and oþere haue swerdis of leed, bi
whiche þei tellen worldli wordis wiþ fablis and gabbyngis on
God. And so no wondir ʒif þis swerd assayle not enemyes as it 110
dide.

O   98 clepiþ] calles αZ   an] þe B   99 but] and α   100 clepiþ] calles
αZ   swerd] is swerd I   þe²] *om*. T   101 and] of *canc*. and D   ful]
wondir M   persiþ] perischiþ AB   swerd] swerdis H   102 spiryʒt] þe spirit
MTYEIGH   lyue] to lyue MPZ, to *eras*. life O   103 þus] þis G   no] þo
α   104 in] of M   a] *om*. Z   106 wundir] wundirs M   107 prechynge
of] *om*. O, prechynge α   prelatis] many Z   108 swerdis¹] swerd M   oþere]
som Z   of] alle of M   109 gabbyngis] algatis gabbyngis T, gabbynge
α   on] in B

Dominica xxii post Trinitatem. Epistola.
[Sermo 52.]

Confidimus in Domino Iesu. Philippenses primo.

Poul techiþ in þis epistele hou prelatis shulden loue þer sugetis
and hou sugetis shulden loue aȝeen, and þus hou charite shulde
sprede. Poul wiþ his breþeren spekiþ þat *þei tristen in þe Lord Iesu,*
þat he, þat haþ bigunnen in hem a good werke to turne hem, *shal*
5 *parforme þis werk vnto þe day of Iesu Crist*; and þis shal be domes day
whan Crist shal haue ful uictorye. And þis werk þat Crist bigan bi
Poule and his oþir felowis passiþ al mannus ordynaunce – alle
byldyngis or worldli goodis; and þus shulden bisshopis edifye,
and not make hepis of dede stones. Poul is certeyn þat God bigan
10 þis goostli werke as he bad; and Poul is sekir þat God wole not
bigynne a werk but ȝif he parforme it. And herfore it is licli þat
newe sectis and mannus ordynaunce þat haue not þer ground in
God moten haue ende bifore domesday. And Poul seiþ þat he
shewiþ þus charite to hem, *as it is ryȝtful to hym to fele þis for hem alle,*
15 siþ a man shulde suppose or gesse good of anoþir whan he haþ
greet euydence of iust lyf þat he lyueþ. And for Poule haþ þes folc
f.52v as recommendid in alle his meritis, he haþ more euy|dense þat þei
shulen make a good eende.

And foure meritis he telliþ, þat passen sixe poyntis of freris
20 lettris bi whiche þei graunten men blisse in heuene, as ȝif anticrist

MSS: D; ABGHIJMOTXYZαδ; P *ends incompl.* 27 þing to stonde.

Dominica . . . epistola] *om.* MO   sermo 52] *om.* DABMOTαδIJXZGH   confidimus . . . iesu] *om.* MO   iesu] iesu quia qui cepit in vobis opus bonum
T   phil.I] *om.* MO   1 techiþ] teth M, telliþ OY   shulden] shulen A   3
þe] oure I   4 þat²] *om.* I   bigunnen] -unnen *on eras. of* -ynnynge *corr.* D,
bigynnyng δJG   5 parforme] refourme I   vnto] into MTα   þe] *om.*
H   6 ful] his I   7 his] by his M   mannus] mennys I   ordynaunce]
ordinantis M   8 byldyngis] beledynges α, biddinges I   or] of þe O, of
IJ   bisshopis] men of haly kirk Z ·   9 make] to make TH   poul . . .
domesday (13)] *om.* Z   10 werke] workis O   sekir] certeyn I   wole] wold
α   12 haue] hat O   ground] ende ⌈ground⌉ M   13 haue ende] nedis ende M,
ende P   14 þus] *on eras. corr.* D, his OαδJGH   þis] þus I   16 lyeuþ] loueþ
I   17 meritis] werkis *canc.* meritis D   more] þe more M   18 shulen] shulde
MαIH   19 þat . . . lettris (20)] *om.* Z   20 bi] in Z   þei . . . crist (21)] he has

passede Crist. Þe firste of Poulis suffragiis stondiþ in his *hertili*
preyere, þat he preyiþ for his children whiche he haþ getyn in
Crist. Þe secounde suffragie þat Poul telliþ is þat he haþ hem *in his*
bondis, for Poul was bounden and presouned for Crist and part of
þis peyne was ful medeful. Þe þridde suffragye þat Poul nemede is   25
defendyng of þe gospell; for þe gospell hadde enemyes in Poulis tyme
as it haþ now, and it is a medeful þyng to stonde wiseli aȝenus þes
enemyes. Þe fourþe help þat Poule weshiþ *is confermyng of þe gospel*
in prechyng and myraclis makyng, in resones and in oþere
trauelis; and part of þis semeþ more medeful þan suffragiis of þes   30
newe sectis. And marke þat Poul grauntiþ hem not part of þes
foure medeful dedis, but he seiþ þat he haþ hem in þes foure and
lat God parte.

And Poul dooþ not þis for money, ne to gete hym annuel rente,
but for pure charite *þat þei ben alle felowis of his ioye. For God is* 35
witnesse to me hou Y coueyte ȝou to blis in clene merci and no symonye,
and þat is *þe entraylis of Iesu Crist. And þis Y preye* not for ȝoure
goodis, but *þat ȝoure charite be more*, and bi double wey be *plenteuous*
more and more, as ȝe ben eldre boþe *in sciense and al witt*, for al þis
shulde turne to charite; *þat ȝee assaye betere* drynkis to cumforte   40
goostli ȝoure soulis; *þat ȝee be clene and wiþoute synne to domesday* þat
is Cristis; *and þat ȝee be fillid of fruyȝt of ryȝtwisnesse to heryyng and*
glorye of God. And Y preye God þat þis be don *bi* medlyng of *Iesu*
Crist. And wolde God oure prelatis now wolde lerne þis craft of
Poulis loue, and charge þer sugetis no more in erþeli goodis þat   45
drawen to helle.

þaim recommendid Z   as] al O   21 suffragiis] suffrage I   22 his] alle his
Y   whiche] þe whiche G   23 his] *om.* Z   24 presouned] pursued O   25
þis] þ- *altered from* h- D, hys TδJG   nemede] meuyde T   27 wiseli] *om.*
A   28 weshiþ] techis Z   29 and¹] in α, and in I   resones] orisouns
AB   in³] *om.* H   30 and . . . parte (33)] *om.* Z   medeful] meeful
G   32 he²] *om.* α   34 þis] þus T   to] *om.* O, for to I   hym] an
G   35 þat] þanne I   36 coueyte] coueitide δI   38 more] þe more
M   39 al¹] in *canc.* al, -le *eras.* DX, in alle M   40 to¹] in T   41 soulis] soule
A   and] *om.* Bα   42 is] bene ⌐is⌐ M   fillid] fulfild TG   and²] of
M   43 glorye] gloriynge I   god¹] ȝou *canc.* god D   Y] *om.* I   44
and . . . helle (46)] *om.* Z   oure] þat oure J   now wolde] *rev.* J   lerne] lere
α   craft] lawe T   45 loue] loore G   þer] he I

\

Dominica xxiii post Trinitatem. Epistola.
[Sermo 53.]

Imitatores mei estote. Philippenses 3 et 4.

In þis epistele techiþ Poul hou þat men shulden sue þer prelatis, and what þei shulden kunne and do to wynne hem þe blisse of heuene. Poul biddiþ at þe bigynnyng *to sue hym* in werkis and lyf, for he is certeyn þat he goþ þe ryȝte wey þat lediþ to heuene. And,
5 siþ prelatis lyuen today contrarieli to Poulis lyf, it is not good to sue hem, lest þei leden þer childryn to helle. And siþ þei contrarien þis bileue and may not soundly þus bidde þer children, men shulden not comyne wiþ siche prelatis, ne ȝeue hem worshipe ne worldli goodis. For Ioon biddiþ to greete hem
10 not, and resoun biddiþ wiþ charite to make hem not werse ne more heuy; for, ȝif enye men diden þus, þei token part of þer synne. And wolde God þat þis lore were wel knowen of worldli lordis! for þanne þei shulden seye to þes popis, þat reumes and men wolen obeshe to hem by forme þat men obesheden to Crist
15 and to Petre — and no more. And certis, ȝif þei chalengen more, þei ben opun anticristis. And þis answere shulden men ȝyue to
f.53 pre|latis and to oþir prestis. And it is opun, ȝif þis were holden, þe pope shulde not þus spuyle reumes, ne chaffare þus wiþ symonye wiþ beneficis þat ben in reumes; and þanne boþe prelatis and
20 prestis shulden holde hem paied wiþ Poulis reule, to take fode of

9 2 John 10; **20** 1 Tim. 6: 8.

MSS: D; ABGHIJMOTXYZαδ.

Dominica . . . epistola] *om.* O   sermo 53] *om.* DABMOTαδIJXZGH   imitatores . . . estote] *om.* O   mei] *om.* H   phil. 3 et 4] phil. 3 J (*but see* 74), phil. 3
AMTYZ, *om.* O   2 hem] to hem MOTαXZH   3 biddiþ] bygynniþ and biddiþ
T   at] in M, *om.* T   þe bigynnyng] *om.* T   in] *om.* I   and] of M   4
and . . . hymsilf (35)] *om.* Z   5 contrarieli] contrarie ABαδ, contrariously MOTYI-
GH   7 þis] cristis T   8 men] and men δ, *and eras.* men G   9 to . . . not
(10) ¹] hem not to grete O   11 enye] *om.* H   12 lore] *om.* T   14 wolen]
wolden AB   hem] hym X   obesheden] obeschen I   to²] vnto M   15
chalengen] scholden chalangen I   17 to] *om.* Yδ   18 þus¹] þis O   ne
. . . reumes (19)] *om.* M, *margin corr.* H   wiþ] *altered from* bi D, bi ABOYαδJ-
GH   19 prelatis and prestis] prestis and prelatis T   20 hem] *om.* O   poulis]

þe puple for goostli trauele þat þei don, and ȝit take not þis of þe folc but bi tytle of almes and loue. Mennus ⌐owen⌐ cowardyse is cause þat þei holden not þus Goddis lawe, but ben oppressid þus bi feendis and drawen bi þe brode wey to helle. Late witt wake [in] siche men to axe þer prelatis þat axen hem goodis, wher þei 25 shulden sue hem in þis and flee foul auarice. Ȝif þei seyen þe firste part, þei ben not prelatis of hem, siþ þes sheep shulden sue þer prelatis as cristen men suen Crist, and it is knowen bi bileue þat men shulden not þus be coueytous. Ȝif þei seyen þe secounde part, as cristen men moten nedis seye, and þei spuylen men of worldly 30 goodis bi symonye and oþir weyes, men shulden flee hem in þis and not assente for perel of synne; for, ȝif men assenteden heere to hem, þei shulden coueite worldli goodis and not ȝeue hem to be poere, siþ prelatis trauelyn þus for riches. And þus eche synne of þe feend is contrarie to hymsilf. 35

And herfore Poul biddiþ aftir *to kepe hem* wiseli *þat gon þus, as ȝee haue ȝoure forme,* and sue ȝee hem in so myche. For Crist and his apostelis and Cristis lawe þat is bileue techen þis lore: to sue goode prelatis and to flee fro euele prelatis. And Poul telliþ more speciali aftir of siche false prelatis : *many goon, whom Y haue ofte teld* 40 *ȝou, but now wepynge Y seye þat þei ben enemyes of Cristis cros;* for þei hatyn peyneful lyf, and louen lustis of þe world and of þer fleshs as beestis doon. And þus don foure sectis today. But, for þis lust mot nedeli haue habundaunce of worldli goodis to mayntene it among þe puple, þe feend haþ tauȝt a newe raueyne, more þan it 45 was in Poulis tyme, for sensuris to spuyle þe puple. And indulgensis þat now ben feyned weren not in Poulis tyme; and Poule myȝte wepe now herfore. Poul profecieþ þre þyngis of siche

cristis M   21 and ȝit take] *om.* I   take] þei take δ   þis] *om.* I   þe²] þis I,
om. MH   22 mennus] ⌐and⌐ mennus H, and mennys B   owen] *corr.* D   23
but] ben *canc.* but D   24 þe] ⌐þe⌐ H, *om.* O   wake] make O   25 in] and
DδXG   hem] *om.* M   26 shulden] shulen H   and] or M   27 þer] *om.*
M   28 suen] shulde sue M   30 seye] saue O   and] þat T   worldly] þer
worldely M   32 assenteden] assenten AB   33 coueite] not couet α   34 þus¹]
here þus T   riches] richessis I   36 herfore] here H, als Z   poul biddiþ] *rev.*
Y, he biddis Z   aftir] *om.* Z   37 ȝee] we I   39 goode] goddis I   fro
. . . prelatis²] men of il lyuyng Z   euele] þe euele I   more] efter mare Z   40
aftir] *om.* Z   siche . . . prelatis] il leuand men Z   whom] whilk Z   ofte]
om. O   teld] said α   41 þat] þat þat, *2nd canc.* D   42 þe] *on eras. of* þis *corr.*
D   þer] þe H   fleshs] fleisschis G   43 and . . . herfore (48)] *om.* Z   44
nedeli] nedis ABIGH   of] in M   it] þis G   45 raueyne] aueyn
O   þan] þat O   48 now] *om.* M   herfore] þerfore T   profecieþ]

false prelatis in his tyme: first þat *per eende is goostli deeþ*, for þei
50 moten nedis be deppest dampned. Þe secounde profecie of Poul is
þis : þat *per god is per beli*, for in glotenye and leccherie þei leden
þer lyf, as beestis doon. Þe þridde prophecie of Poule is þat *per
glorie is in per confusioun*, for *þei saueryn erþeli þyngis*, and litil or nouȝt
⌜of⌝ heueneli þyngis. Iuge men wher þes foure sectis þat ben
55 today ledyn þis lyf; and, ȝif þei doon, lerne þei of Poule to sue hem
not but to flee hem, for a mannes owene synne is ynowȝ, al ȝif he
gete not more to. And ȝif men grucchen aȝenus þes wordis, loke
þei ⌜þe⌝ bileue þat Poule telliþ heere, and grucche þei þanne
aȝenus God and aȝenus treuþe þat witnessiþ þis. Ȝif we in oure
60 owene persones taken þis lyf of þes sectis, woo is vs by peyne aftir
for þis dede and concense.

f.53v   But Poul seiþ þat *per lyuyng is in heuene* out|of þis erþe, boþe bi
þer þouȝt and þer wille. And þus shulden goode prelatis and
preestis seie treweli in þer lyf; and þanne myȝten þei sureli *abide
65 þer Sauyour and þer Lord Iesu Crist* at þe day of dome, for he is to siche
men sauyour to bodi and soule, and lord to blisse siche men. *Þis
Lord shal þanne reforme bodyes of his meke seruauntis* al ȝif þei been
now defoormed, and scorned of many worldli men; ȝit seyntis
hopen þanne þat þes *bodies*, þat now ben foule, shullen in blisse *be
70 like to þe body of Cristis clerenesse*. For men þat ben blessid in heuene
shullen haue foure doweris of þe body; and þis shal be *vp* ⌜þe⌝
worchyng of Crist þat was so medeful and so hooly *þat he myȝte make
sugett to hym* and his *alle* þyngis of þis world.

And aftirward spekiþ Poul to his breþeren wordis of cumfort,
75 and moeueþ hem to hoolde þe lore þat God haþ teeld to hem bi

---

prophecied, -d *altered from* -þ H   49 prelatis] profetis *canc.* prelatis D, gouernours
Z   tyme] *om. gap* O   50 moten] sal Z   deppest] depper T   51 þis] *om.*
MG   glotenye] gloterye MTαIZH   and] in α   52 is . . . glorie (53)] *om.*
O   is] is þis I   53 in þer] *om.* T   54 of] ⌜of⌝ H, *om.* ABMOδJG, in
T   iuge . . . concense (61)] *om.* Z   55 lerne] lere α   hem] him I   56
hem] hym I   a] *om.* O   57 not] hym ⌜no⌝ T   aȝenus] as Y   58 þe] *corr.*
D, ⌜þe⌝ T, *om.* MOYαδJXGH   telliþ] seiþ G   þanne] þat A   60 owene]
om. TI   by . . . aftir] *on eras. corr.* D   61 for] *om.* B   þis] suche T   dede
and concense] consense and dede T   concense] concience I   62 lyuyng]
bigynnynge I   boþe] *om.* Z   63 þer[2]] by þer OT   65 þer[1]] þe M   to]
om. O   66 men[1]] mennus O   sauyour] a saueour I   bodi] þe body
O   soule] to soule I   blisse] blesse Bδ   67 bodyes] body T   his] *om.*
I   69 now ben] *rev.* O   shullen] shulden A   70 of . . . body (71)] *om.*
J   71 shullen] schulden Y   vp] vpon MZ   þe[2]] *corr.* D, *om.* δJG   72
myȝte] of more myght M   73 his] to hyse TI   75 þe] *om.* J   lore] lord

Poule. *And so my mooste deere breþeren*, seiþ Poul, *and most desirid* of þyngis heere, *my ioye* in heuene *and my coroune, stoonde ʒee þus, moost dereworþe in þe Lord.* Þis biddyng þat Poul axiþ shulde make hym loued and vnsuspect, for he axiþ not worldli þyngis but goostli good for hym and hem. And Poule preyiþ aftir to two persones, þat weren two deuoʒt wymmen—þe ton was clepid *Euchodia*, þat was more stable in God, þe toþir was clepid *Synticen*, þat was more ʒong or freel, þat þei shulden *sauere þis same lore in þe Lordis* name as Poul haþ teld. And marke þou wel þat Poul preyeþ comynli þe firste persone, but he preyeþ speciali þe secounde—not for worldli goodis. And Poul hadde a man to felou þat was clepyd *German*, þat was *euene* wiþ hym in Goddis cause, boþe in prechyng and oþir help. Poule *preyeþ hym to helpe forþ* boþe *wymmen, and men þat haue trauelid wiþ Poul in þe gospel* of Crist, *wiþ Clement and oþere helperis of Poul whos names ben wretyn in þe book of lyf.* Poul hade helperis as men haue now, boþe of men and of wymmen, in good word and good dede to helpe apostelis boþe to preche, and herbore hem and wasshe here feet, for þer trauele was good and greet; and, but ʒif God hadde maad hem help, þei myʒte not haue parformed þis lore.

80

85

90

95

O   ⌐capitulum 4⌐ J   76 my] *om.* A   77 þus moost] *rev.* α   78 þe] oure
I   hym] hem, *altered from* him H   79 axiþ] axide T   80 good] goodis
H   hem] for hem αδ   persones] perso/sones D   81, 82 clepid] callede
αZ   83 or] and Aα   þis] þe IZ   84 þou] ʒe I   86 worldli] þe worldlich
O   man to] *om.* T   felou] his felowe H   clepyd] called αZ   89 haue]
haþ I   þe] *om.* O   91 of²] *om.* Yα   good] goddis δ   92 apostelis] þe
apostelis I   93 herbore] to herberewe IH

Dominica xxiiii [post Trinitatem]. Epistola.
[Sermo 54.]

Non cessamus pro vobis orantes. Colocenses primo.

In þis epistele telliþ Poul boþe his wille and his werk to profite to
Cristis chirche, þat it be þus tauȝt bi hym. Poule seiþ first to þis
puple þat *þei ceessen not for hem, preiyng and axyng þat þei ben fillid bi
knowyng of Goddis wille.* And no þyng is more nedeful to man heere
5 þan for to knowe what God wole þat he do for Goddis loue; for ȝif
man performe þis, he getiþ blis wiþoute drede. For siþ God is þe
moste Lord, and eche man shulde do his wille, it is most nedeful
þat his wille be comynli knowen; and God may neuere more fayle
in þyngis þat ben nedeful. Þerfore God telliþ certeynli what is his
10 wille of alle þyngis. Soþ it is þat alle þyngis þat kynde doþ, God
wole haue done, for God dooþ alle þes þyngis bi kynde, and God
f.54 doþ nouȝt but þat he wole do.|And so God wole make alle
creaturis þat ben maad. And, shortli for to seye, fille þou Goddis
comaundementis, and it is ynow to þee, for God wole axe no more
15 of þee. Leeue we to seke and argue þat God wole alle peyne for
synne, bi þis skele, þat it is iust and God makiþ alle siche peyne.
And summe seyen þat God wole synne be don, for ⌐þe¬ good þat
comeþ þerof; and þus þei seyen þat God wole alle þyng, boþe for
synnes and creaturis. But leeue we heere þis doute of scole; and

MSS: D; ABGHIJMOTXYZαδ; β *inc. incompl.* 3 preynge and

Dominica . . . epistola] *om.* MO   sermo 54] *om.* DABMOTαδIJXZGH   non
. . . orantes] *om.* O   orantes] orantes et postulantes MT   Col. 1] *om.* O   1
boþe] here boþe I   and his] *om.* α   to²] vnto M, of αIG   2 first] þus
M   3 preiyng] seying M   fillid] fulfild T   bi] wiþ H   4 heere] *om.*
α   5 for to] to MY   6 man] a *canc.* man Y, a man αI   performe] parformeþ
O   siþ] *om.* Y   7 moste] moist H   8 god] ⌐for¬ god H   more] *om.*
O   9 þerfore] and þerforα   10 of] in α   alle²] *om.* G   þyngis²] þing
J   11 done] hem don H   þes] ⌐þese¬ Y, *om.* ABOH, þos M   12 þat] þat þat
I   do] be do T   13 for to] to G   fille] fulfille T   15 seke] speke
AB   16 it] *om.* H   iust] most O   17 summe] sum men MαβIZ   synne]
þat synne αH, þat þat *canc.* synne J   þe] *corr.* D   18 þat] *om.* O   god] he
H   19 and¹] a α   scole] scoles H   21 axede] askis Z   god . . . so (23)]

lerne we what God wole þat we do, for þis is ful nedeful, siþ Poul 20
axede þis in his conuertyng. And no drede God wole þat alle men
holde wiþ þis lawe, and reuerse it in no manere; for ȝif þei don,
God wole punyshe. And so Goddis wille mot be fulfillid, for no
þyng may aȝeenstoonde it. And þus God wole þat we lyue not for
his profyȝt but for oure owene. And God wole no þyng but 25
honest; and alle honeste God wole haue don. And þus men wetyn
more synguleerli, bi good lyf and goode werkis, what þyng God
wole þat we do, whan we ben of betere lyf.

And herfore biddiþ Poul aftir to þes Grekis, þat þei be fillid in
knowyng of Goddis wille *in alle maner of wisdom*. It is a wisdom to 30
man to wite what God wole þat he do, and to do aftir þis
knowyng in his persone for Goddis sake. And it is myche to cristen
men to be fillid *in goostli vndirstondyng*; for eche creature of God
telliþ þat he wole þe beste, and what þyng God wole þat þei doo,
ȝif men vndirstonden it. And þanne *men goon worþili to God and* 35
plesyn to hym on alle maneris, boþe goostli and bodili; and þes
maneris ben *alle þyngis in eche good werk* þat men don. Þei shulden
make fruyȝt of reward, for al oure lyf shulde be ful of fruyȝt to
heleþe in blis of heuene. And bi þis shulden men *growe in þe*
kunnyng of God. It is but litil to men to knowe bi resoun Goddis 40
kunnyng, but ȝif þei turnen þis kunnyng of God to þer lyf and þer
goode dedis; for God is maystir practisour, and loueþ wel goode
dedis of men. And þus men shulden *be comfortid in eche vertu* þat þei
don *aftir þe power of Goddis cleernesse*, siþ þei shulden knowe as
bileue þat God seeþ cleerli alle þer uertuous dedis, and wille and 45
purpos þat þei haue, and castiþ to rewarde al þis. Who shulde not

---

20 Acts 9: 6.

om. α   22 þis] his, h- *on eras. of* þ- X, his ABMOYβIZG   it] not it I   in] on
MOTYβIXZH   23 wille] lawe Z   24 wole] wole not O   not] *om.*
O   25 no] not α   27 more] wele more M   bi] boþe δ   þyng] *om.*
Y   god] þat god H   29 herfore] þerfor M   fillid] fulfild T   30 in] and
α   31 to do] do YI   þis] his Y   32 to] more to β   33 fillid] fulfillid
TI   goostli vndirstondyng] *rev.* I   34 god] þat *canc.* god H, þat god T   þei]
he α   35 vndirstonden] vndirston H   god] heuene to god T   36 on] in
ABO   goostli] bodili ABT   bodili] goostli ABT   37 þei] þe M   38 to]
of H   39 þis] þis, -is *canc.* -⌐us⌐ T   þe] *om.* H   40 to¹] for M   bi] *om.*
Z   resoun] resoun of Z   41 þer²] to þer MIH   42 dedis] dede α   43
men²] þey T   comfortid] conformed M   44 shulden] schulen G   45 god
seeþ] god seeþ, *2nd* e *above* i *canc.* δ, god seiþ β, says α   þer] *om.* M   46 castiþ]

be cumfortid heere to contynue and worch⌐e⌐ Goddis seruyse?
And herfore seyþ Poul aftir þat þei shulden *lyue in alle paciense and
long abidyng wiþ ioye*, for trist þat þei shulde haue in God. For
50 bileue techiþ men þat God may not fayle on his syde for noun-
power or vnwitt, but al þe defaute is in men. And grace wiþ witt
of alle þes þyngis stondiþ in Iesu Crist oure Lord.

castid O   þis] þese G   48 herfore] þerfore M   aftir] *om.* M   shulden]
schulen G   alle] *om.* α   50 techiþ] tech M   god] *om.* T   noun- power]
none vnpowere α   51 vnwitt] vnwitti B   þe] *om.* ABY   wiþ] and O

Dominica xxv [post Trinitatem. Epistola.
Sermo 55.]

Ecce dies veniunt. Iheremias 23.

Þis lessoun of Ieremye telliþ whi þat Crist came in fleshs to
amende þes yuel herdis þat disseiueden Goddis puple. And þus
haþ þe chirche ordeyned þat þis be red in þis Sunday, to knytte
matere of þe Aduent to þis matere þat heere is seid. Ieremye
bigynneþ þus *loo! dayes comen, seiþ þe Lord, and Y shal rere vp Dauiþ,*   5
þat is a ryȝtful buriounnyng, and he shal regne kyng; and he shal be witty
and he shal make doom and ryȝtwisnesse in þe erþe. It is takun as bileue
þat Ieremye spekiþ heere of Crist, for he is ofte clepid Dauyþ
boþe bi fygure and witt|of word; for ⌐he⌐ is strong bi his hond, and   f.54v
figurid bi þe kyng Dauyd, for many propretes in Dauyd   10
answeren to þe manhed of Crist. And þus as Crist seide þat Ioon
was Helye, so Ieremye seide þat Crist was Dauyd. And alle þe
sophistris of anticrist kunnen not proue þat þis word is fals. For
sum þyng is seyd in fygure, and sum þyng by ⌐his⌐ owene kynde,
as Baptist is Helye, as Crist seiþ, and he is not Helye in persone;   15
and þus Crist and Baptist weren not contrarie in þer wordis, for
contrariouste in witt and not in nakid wordis shulde be takun.
Þus men shulden studie þe witt þat God spekiþ in hooli writt; for
no man may reproue God þat he shulde not speke þus, siþ he is
Lord of wordis and witt and of alle partis of þis world. But ȝit   20

---

11 Matt. 11: 14;   **16** John 1: 21.

MSS: D; ABGHIJMOTXYZαδ; β *ends incompl.* 23 wher dayes.

Dominica . . . trinitatem] dominica vltima post trinitatem M, dominica proxima ante
aduentum δZG, dominica xxv proxima ante aduentum J, dominica xx ante aduentum β,
om. O   sermo 55] *om.* DABMOTαδIJXZGH   ecce . . . veniunt] *om.* O   ve-
niunt] veniunt dicit dominus MTG   ier. 23] *om.* O   1 crist] iesu crist I   2
disseiueden] disseyuen ABMOδI   4 matere¹] þe mater M   þe] *om.* β   þis]
þe M   5 þus] *om.* M   Y] *margin, cut away* β   6 ryȝtful] riȝt A   bur-
iounnyng] bygynnynge O   be] *om.* β   witty] wys T   7 þe] *om.* T   8
for] and M   clepid] called αZ   10 þe] his *canc.* þe D   12 þe] *om.* H   13
for] *om.* M   14 by] in MI   his] *corr.* D   15 as¹] and I   as²] in figure as
α   18 men shulden] *rev.* α   studie] *on eras. corr.* D, take Oα   in] of in
δ   20 witt] of wit I   21 grucchiþ] grucchid A   þat] þat þes δ   dayis]

grucchiþ anticrist for God seiþ ⌐þat⌐ 'dayis comen': for he boostiþ
þat h⌐e⌐ can proue þat þer ben not many tymes, and hou shulden
þanne dayes come? wher dayes haue feet for to goo? But heere
men seyen to anticrist þat al þe tyme þat was bifore, and al þe tyme
25 þat is to comen, is present bifore God; and so many tymes ben oon
in oo tyme and anoþer in anoþer, and so many tymes passen
byfore oþere by many þousynd ȝeeris. And þus many dayes
comen as faste as ony tyme may come, for þei comen not bodili,
and þus hem nediþ not to haue feet; and ȝit many þyngis comen
30 bodili þat walkyn not bi þer feet, as þe smytyng of þe stoon
comeþ bodili but it walkiþ not. Þus oure Dauyd Iesu Crist is a iust
buriounnyng, for he makiþ al newe world and saueþ þe chirche
þat ellis were dampned. And þis Crist regnede kyng, boþe bi his
godhed and his manhed; for bi his godhed he is kyng of al þis
35 world, as bileue techiþ, and by his manhede he is kyng bi title of
staat of innocense whan it is ioyned wiþ his godhed. And what
trewe man may denye þis? And Crist is witti on many maneris,
and doþ many iugementis and þerto many ryȝtwisnessis. Blessid
be siche a patroun!

40 *In þo dayes shal Iuda be saued and Israel shal dwelle tristiliche*; for
men þat confessen Cristis lyf, hou he was boþe God and man, and
þes men þat seen God bi ⌐good⌐ bileue of Cristis persone ben
saued and dwellyn sureli in þe vertu of þis patroun. *And þis is þe*
name þat men shulen clepe hym 'þe Lord oure ryȝtful', þat is God.
45 *Herfore, loo, dayes comen, seiþ þe Lord, and þei shulen not seye ouer 'God*
lyueþ þat ledde ouȝt þe children of Israel fro Egypt'; but þei shulen seie a
more preysyng *'God lyueþ þat ledde out and brouȝte to þe seed of þe hous*
of Israel fro þe lond of þe norþ and fro alle oþer londis, to ⌐þe⌐ whiche Y
haue casten hem'. Þei shullen come aȝeen to Ierusalem and to þe
50 lond of biheste, *and þei shulen dwelle in þer lond*, seiþ God þat is

day is X   22 proue] not proue O   shulden] *om.* O   25 is¹] was aftur *canc.* is
α, was *canc.* ⌐is⌐ δ   to] *om.* M   oon] don A   26 in anoþer] *om.* O   and²]
tyme *canc.* and DZ, tyme *eras.* and X, tyme and I   27 þus] so Z   29 hem] *om.*
α   30 walkyn not] *rev.* I   31 þus] and þus M   is] as O   32 newe] a newe
ABMTYZGH   saueþ] *om.* O   33 þis] þus αIH   regnede] regniþ
T   34 his¹] by hys TδIH   godhed²] man *canc.* ⌐god⌐ hed D   36 staat] a *canc.*
state T, astaat I   of] *om.* M   whan] sen Z   his] þe T   38 and²] *om.*
H   ryȝtwisnessis] riȝtwisnesse OαI   41 þat] confe *canc.* þat D   was] is
Z   42 of] in ABMOTYαXZGH   44 shulen] shulden ABTαI   clepe] calle
αZ   lord oure] *rev.* I   45 seye ouer] ouerseen I   ouer] euere TG   46
shulen] sȝolde O   seie] soie A   48 þe²] *om.* O   þe whiche] *on eras.*
X   þe³] *corr.* D, *om.* MOYαδIJZGH   49 to¹] vnto M   50 and] þat

almyȝti. Heere Ieremye wolde mene þat boþe þes two presounyngis, þat Iewis weren flemed out of þer lond in Moyses tyme and Ieremyes, boþe þes figureden þe flemyng þat þe feend presoned mankynde in þe lond of synne; and þis lond was boþe Egypt and þe lond of þe norþ. But Crist brouȝte þes folc aȝen to heuene, þat is þer kyndeli lond. And it semyþ bi hooli writt þat Ieremye and oþer prophetis hadden þer witt of Iesu Crist, for ellis þer speche were to nakid. 55

And þus may prestis of Cristis sect teche þe puple on Sundayes boþe ⌜bi⌝ þe goospel and þe pistele, al ȝif false prophetis bigylen hem not; for false men of þes newe sectis, and speciali þe laste sectt, robbyn þe puple of þer goodis, and bigylen hem fro trewe lore. 60

Expliciunt epistole dominicales per annum.

M lond²] lord O god] þe lorde god M þat is] om. M 52 weren] þat weren AB þer] þe X 55 þe²] om. δH brouȝte] boȝt Z 57 for] or M 58 were] was H 59 and . . . lore (63)] om. Z may] many I puple] om. I 60 boþe bi] on eras. X bi] corr. D, om. OI þe¹] om. OH goospel] gospellis H 61 false] fale Y þes newe] þe M þe] of canc. þe Y, ⌜of⌝ þe H, þis α 63 lore] men M 64 expliciunt . . . annum] after gospel sermon expliciunt epistole et ewangelia dominicales per annum X, om. ABOTδIJ-ZGH